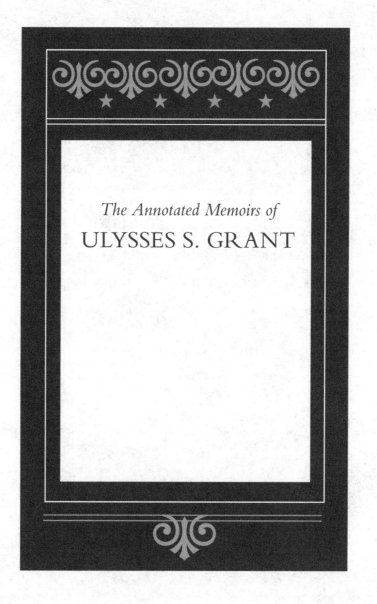

The Annotated Memoirs of

ULYSSES S. GRANT

The Annotated Memoirs of

ULYSSES S. GRANT

Edited with an Introduction by

ELIZABETH D. SAMET

LIVERIGHT PUBLISHING CORPORATION

A Division of W. W. Norton & Company

Independent Publishers Since 1923

New York   London

Frontispiece: Bust of Ulysses S. Grant, façade of former Union League Club, Brooklyn, New York. *Photograph by Elizabeth D. Samet.*

For information about permission to reproduce selections from this book, write to Permissions, Liveright Publishing Corporation, a division of W. W. Norton & Company, Inc., 500 Fifth Avenue, New York, NY 10110

For information about special discounts for bulk purchases, please contact W. W. Norton Special Sales at specialsales@wwnorton.com or 800-233-4830

Manufacturing by LSC Communications, Crawfordsville
Book design by Ellen Cipriano
Production manager: Anna Oler

Library of Congress Cataloging-in-Publication Data

Names: Grant, Ulysses S. (Ulysses Simpson), 1822–1885, author. | Samet, Elizabeth D., editor.
Title: The annotated memoirs of Ulysses S. Grant / edited with an Introduction by Elizabeth D. Samet. Other titles: Personal memoirs of Ulysses S. Grant. Description: First edition. | New York : Liveright Publishing Corporation, a division of W. W. Norton & Company, [2019] | Includes bibliographical references.
Identifiers: LCCN 2018029962 | ISBN 9781631492440 (hardcover)
Subjects: LCSH: Grant, Ulysses S. (Ulysses Simpson), 1822–1885. | Generals—United States—Biography. | Presidents—United States—Biography. | United States. Army—Biography. | United States—History—Civil War, 1861–1865—Campaigns. | United States—History—Civil War, 1861–1865—Personal narratives. | Mexican War, 1846–1848—Personal narratives.
Classification: LCC E672 .G756 2019 | DDC 973.8/2092 [B]—dc23
LC record available at https://lccn.loc.gov/2018029962

Liveright Publishing Corporation, 500 Fifth Avenue, New York, N.Y. 10110
www.wwnorton.com

W. W. Norton & Company Ltd., 15 Carlisle Street, London W1D 3BS

1 2 3 4 5 6 7 8 9 0

Yet to me he is a mystery, and I believe he is a mystery to himself.

—William T. Sherman on Ulysses S. Grant (1879), *The Century Magazine* (1897)

Gertrude Stein and Sherwood Anderson . . . found out that they both had had and continued to have Grant as their great american hero. They did not care so much about Lincoln either of them. They had always and still liked Grant. They even planned collaborating on a life of Grant. Gertrude Stein still likes to think about this possibility.

—Gertrude Stein, *The Autobiography of Alice B. Toklas* (1933)

Whether I shall turn out to be the hero of my own life, or whether that station will be held by anybody else, these pages must show.

—Charles Dickens, *David Copperfield* (1850)

**Grant Plinth, Soldiers and Sailors'
Monument, New York, New York.**
Photograph by Elizabeth D. Samet.

Contents

Text of *Personal Memoirs of U. S. Grant*

Volume I

Volume II

Editor's Note

When people ask me how I came to teach at West Point, I usually provide the short answer: "My father and Ulysses S. Grant." Were it not for my father's experience as a sergeant in the Army Air Corps during World War II, together with my accidental discovery while in graduate school of Grant's *Personal Memoirs*, I suspect the prospect of teaching literature to aspiring army officers would have held—to borrow Grant's own characterization of his feelings toward "military life" as he journeyed from Ohio to West Point for the first time—"no charms for me."

The long answer can be found in this book, for which I have unwittingly been preparing for years. During that time Grant has been my Virgil, his words a priceless guide to aspects of military culture as well as to the various social, political, and literary legacies of nineteenth-century America with which we continue to grapple today. I seek to share many of those illuminations in this edition of *Personal Memoirs of U. S. Grant*, which was first published in 1885–1886 by the firm of Charles L. Webster, in which Mark Twain was a partner. Here the reader will encounter Grant's words side by side with my annotations as well as with a wide-ranging selection of maps and other images of my choosing—and, in the case of some of the photographs, my making. Photography offered me another way to reckon with the interpretations of the Civil War that continue to texture the present moment. The notes and illustrations situate the memoirs in several contexts: military and historical, of course, but also literary, cultural, social, and political. This edition offers new insights into Grant's experience at West Point, where I have taught since 1997; presents previously unpublished archival material and images; and expands in both place and time the typical Civil War backdrop against which Grant's story is usually read.

Long recognized as a landmark military memoir, Grant's book has been edited primarily by historians, for whose expertise I am deeply grateful. The editors William S. McFeely and Mary Drake McFeely, James M. McPherson, and John F. Marszalek and his team at the Ulysses S. Grant Presidential Library at Mississippi State University have all illuminated vital aspects of the text and its author. Yet Grant's *Personal Memoirs* is also a significant work of American literature and a defiantly atypical narrative of war, if in certain respects a conventional expression of nineteenth-century attitudes. From my vantage point as a literary scholar I strive to do something new here by presenting the text as not merely an exemplary military memoir but an indispensable part of the robust tradition of American autobiography, which extends from the spiritual autobiographies of the colonial period to the confessional memoirs of the present day. Grant's book is a significant contribution to our national literature.

Thus while I strive to be scrupulous about historical and military matters, I am also invested in the complex linguistic and cultural tapestry of nineteenth-century America. It is not a particular event alone but the ways in which Grant and his contemporaries remember and choose to depict it that primarily engage me. Although, as I have suggested, much of Grant's thinking is clearly of its time, his book is utterly remarkable in its rejection of the deeply romantic, heavily sentimental mode of most nineteenth-century Civil War reminiscences. In order to illuminate this most radical aspect of the book, my notes often provide passages from other writers, which are meant to be read in parallel with Grant's text. Often these are contemporaneous recollections of identical, or comparable, events. But I have also drawn from different eras, cultures, and genres to illustrate the long tradition of war writing—fiction and poetry as well as nonfiction—and to place Grant's book along a continuum of written representations of war from antiquity onward.

One of the most noteworthy aspects of Grant's book is its style. Reviewing a volume of his letters in 1898, Henry James described the prose as having a "hard limpidity." Grant's correspondence sounded an "old American note," James explained. Its "austerity" conveyed "the sense of the 'hard' life and the plain speech."[1] *Personal Memoirs* is, as my introduction and notes

---

1. His "tone," James went on to say, "has something of the quality of that, when we meet its equivalent in an old, dry portrait or even an old angular piece of furniture, affects the historic, not to say the aesthetic, sense." Henry James, "American Letter," *Literature* 26 (April 16, 1898): 453.

demonstrate, a stylistic anomaly among nineteenth-century narratives of war, most of which run to the ornate. Grant's style is by no means unrelated to his understanding of the national cataclysm in which he found himself a leading participant. Yet many of the issues that seemed so clear to Grant in the summer of 1885, when he completed his book, have in the decades since been silted over by the pernicious nostalgia of Lost Cause revisionism, an alarmingly successful campaign to rewrite the history of the Civil War that began almost before the war ended and gathered momentum after Reconstruction through the industry of participants, historians, and organizations such as the indefatigable United Daughters of the Confederacy. As the eminent historian Eric Foner once neatly put it in a review of David W. Blight's pivotal *Race and Reunion: The Civil War in American Memory*, "the Confederacy lost the war on the battlefield but won the war over memory." Blight's book is the story of the degree to which "romance triumphed over reality, sentimental remembrance won over ideological memory" in the culture of postwar America.[2]

The ongoing national conversation about the meaning of the Civil War reveals the enduring influence of this revisionist campaign. Its mendacious rhetoric, polished and perfected over the years, has succeeded in masking uncomfortable truths by ignoring slavery and fetishizing states' rights and by giving moral authority to both sides of the conflict by placing a premium on physical courage, sacrifice, and a very particular concept of honor. Postwar rhetoric revised the South's own clearly stated motivation for secession—preserving the right to enslave human beings—while its obsessive focus on federal tyranny ignored the slave states' antebellum enthusiasm for federal power when, for example, it was enlisted to enforce the Fugitive Slave Law of 1850. The canonizing of Southern heroes, which intensified in the post-Reconstruction era, served to cloak with sentimental ritual the programmatic social and political injustice of Jim Crow. The battles being fought today in the media and on the streets of American cities and towns over Confederate commemoration are the reckoning for more than a century-long perversion of Civil War memory. There is no more fitting time to revisit the memoirs of the man Lincoln ultimately entrusted to win the war on the battlefield.

The revisionists also maligned Grant or used him to serve their reconciliationist program. His funeral, at which former federal and rebel generals

---

2. Eric Foner, "Selective Memory," review of *Race and Reunion: The Civil War in American Memory*, by David W. Blight, *New York Times*, March 4, 2001, BR. David W. Blight, *Race and Reunion: The Civil War in American Memory* (Cambridge, MA: Harvard University Press, Belknap, 2001), 4.

joined together to bear the coffin, became an important symbol of national reunion. Nevertheless, the absence of triumphant or vengeful sentiments in his prose—in contrast, for instance, to the vitriol of William T. Sherman—should not be mistaken for a tolerant, forgiving attitude toward his enemies' commitments. Grant himself was never confused about the fact that, as he wrote in the conclusion to his memoirs, "slavery" was the "cause" of the Civil War. Nor did he choose there to absolve those who rebelled to preserve it, many of them his friends and classmates. Their cause, he insisted, was "one of the worst for which a people ever fought, and one for which there was the least excuse." Resisting postwar cries for revenge, Grant refused to exult in the "downfall" of his enemies, yet he also refused to exalt the rebels, no matter how "long and valiantly" they battled and no matter "the sincerity" with which they suffered for their morally bankrupt enterprise.

Grant's reputation has been remarkably volatile over the years. At his death in 1885, Grant was almost certainly the world's most famous American. But after this heyday of celebrity his reputation fell precipitously until the 1950s, when the historians Lloyd Lewis and Bruce Catton initiated the process of rehabilitating Grant the drunken butcher. Lewis's biography of Grant's early life, *Captain Sam Grant*, remains a touchstone for contemporary biographers and historians. At Lewis's death, Catton carried out the former's planned trilogy with *Grant Moves South* and *Grant Takes Command*. Their endeavor was furthered by John Y. Simon's monumental edition of the *Papers of Ulysses S. Grant*, a project now helmed by John Marszalek at Mississippi State University. This series did not include *Personal Memoirs*, but Marszalek's 2017 scholarly edition has now remedied that omission. Brooks D. Simpson, William S. McFeely, Jean Edward Smith, Josiah Bunting, H. W. Brands, Joan Waugh, Ronald C. White, Edwina Campbell, Ron Chernow, and others have contributed to a growing catalogue of biographies and historical studies of various aspects of Grant's career. Most recently, Chernow, the biographer of Alexander Hamilton, George Washington, and John D. Rockefeller, has offered a sympathetic portrait that focuses on Grant's struggle with alcohol and recasts it in modern terms as a story of addiction and recovery as opposed to a tale of moral failing, as nineteenth-century Americans perceived alcoholism to be. On balance, these recent characterizations are overwhelmingly positive; even the most critical portrait among them, McFeely's Pulitzer Prize–winning biography, offers essential insights into Grant's particular gifts.

In November 1868, Grant the general was elected president without ever having made a campaign speech, and the same amalgamation of characteristics that led to his military successes contributed, as Catton argued decades ago, to eight years of political frustration. Grant was not a political innocent, but the climate was especially treacherous, and it is by no means clear that even Lincoln could have succeeded in winning the peace. Periodic successes and Grant's personal integrity notwithstanding, his administration was characterized by ephemeral progress and marred by corruption. Moreover, despite his own fairly consistent commitment to the rights of the newly emancipated and his breaking of the first Ku Klux Klan, governmental protections for African Americans in the South were short-lived, ending with his two-term presidency. A political deal that would come to be known as the Compromise of 1877 secured a Republican victory for Rutherford B. Hayes by sacrificing Reconstruction in exchange for the requisite Southern electoral votes in what had been a contested election.[3]

The recent wave of praise for Grant has also taken up his ambivalent administration. Chernow, for example, offers a laudatory evaluation of the presidency, which he deems grossly underrated, as a high-water mark for African American civil rights that would not be reached again for another hundred years. It is necessary to rescue Grant from the vilification of Southern apologists, but in our eagerness, it is also important to recollect the administration's shortcomings. Brooks Simpson assesses Grant's involvement in the politics of Reconstruction as follows: "Many Americans, sharing Grant's distaste for the methods and motives of professional politicians, looked to the hero of Appomattox to put an end to vicious partisanship and to bring peace to the land. Eventually, Grant accepted that responsibility." Nevertheless, Simpson concludes, "That, eight years later, he left the White

---

3. Despite the fact that Reconstruction technically ended in 1877, Foner notes that the retreat actually began after Grant's reelection. The corruption of his first administration had helped to undermine the Republican Reconstruction program by splintering the party. Although Grant did authorize the use of federal troops to protect black voting rights in Louisiana in 1874 and 1875, his second term was characterized by a growing reluctance to intervene in the South. Signally, amid growing hostility to federal interference in state politics, he "turned a deaf ear to pleas" from Mississippi governor Adelbert Ames to ensure fair elections in that state, which was lost to the Democrats in 1875. "The uproar over Louisiana," where federal troops marched into the state legislature in January 1875, Foner writes, "convinced Grant of the political dangers posed by a close identification with Reconstruction, and made Congressional Republicans extremely wary of further military invention in the South." Eric Foner, *Reconstruction: America's Unfinished Revolution, 1863–1877* (New York: Harper & Row, 1988), 524, 488, 554–55.

House having reluctantly accepted the perpetuation of racial injustice as the price of sectional reconciliation was his tragedy and the nation's failure."[4]

If we seize on the excitable Theodore Roosevelt's claim that "the three great figures of Washington, Lincoln, and Grant" stand "mightiest among the mighty dead" of the nation's past, we risk turning Grant into a myth that will do us little good at a historical moment distinguished by the attempt to dig out from under the crushing weight of all those myths that have naturalized and normalized the Lost Cause Grant knew to be the worst of all.[5] Grant's greatness was his own. Unlike that of Lincoln, it was neither presidential nor political; unlike that of Washington, who combined an aristocratic sensibility with republican commitments, it was entirely, emphatically American. It can be discerned most clearly in his memoirs: in how he wrote, in what he wrote about, in what he chose to pass over.

When Ta-Nehisi Coates tweeted a few years ago, "That's it. Changing my avatar to Ulysses S. Grant," the reputation of the Union general and eighteenth president could be said to have entered a new 140-character chapter as a social media darling. Coates's tweet was prompted by his reading of *Personal Memoirs*, an experience he chronicled in a powerful series of blog posts for the *Atlantic*: "tanner's son . . . turned savior of his country. A slave-holder turned mass emancipator. The warrior transformed into a warrior-poet . . . embracing the hare-brained scheme of black emigration," Coates concluded his series. "It's all just too much. I am a black man, and God only knows what Grant would have made of me. . . . Grant is splendid."[6] Coates astutely perceives in Grant's story an old-fashioned American fable of persistence and reinvention. It has the lineaments of the archetypal tale of self-making inaugurated by Benjamin Franklin and rehearsed by so many other Americans over the centuries. Yet Coates does not stop there. Notably, he refuses to iron out the ambiguities and contradictions that characterized Grant as they do us all. This strikes me as the kind of Grant we most need today.

My acquaintance with Grant's writing has influenced my vision in ways as profound as encounters at various points in my reading life with Virgil, Plutarch, Li Po, Montaigne, Shakespeare, Lincoln, Frederick Douglass, Herman Melville, Leo Tolstoy, Virginia Woolf, and Joan Didion. A friend

4. Brooks D. Simpson, *Let Us Have Peace: Ulysses S. Grant and the Politics of War and Reconstruction, 1861–1868* (Chapel Hill: University of North Carolina Press, 1991), 262–63.

5. Theodore Roosevelt, "Address at the Grant Anniversary at Galena, Illinois," April 27, 1900, State of New York, *Public Papers of Governor Roosevelt* (Albany: Brandow, 1900), 235.

6. Ta-Nehisi Coates, "These Are the Last Days of U.S. Grant," *The Atlantic*, June 29, 2010, https://www.theatlantic.com/entertainment/archive/2010/06/these-are-the-last-days-of-us-grant/58879/.

likes to tease me that there is no conversation into which I cannot smuggle a mention of Grant's name. When it happens—when my mind works itself around from an apparently unrelated subject to the Civil War general—she'll say, "Ah, Grant!" as if he is a mutual friend she hasn't heard news of for a while: "There he is. It was only a matter of time." She's right, of course: Grant is my *idée fixe*. I'll drop his name at what may seem the most unlikely moment. It just seems to me the right connection to make in so many circumstances, especially in recent years, when we have taken to talking about war in ways that differ so sharply from the clear-sighted, plain-speaking mode that was second nature to him.

A Note on the Text

A few comments on my editorial practice might help the reader to navigate this book. The text of *Personal Memoirs* is based on the first edition of 1885–1886. I have largely retained Grant's idiosyncratic spelling and punctuation because that is how his first readers, including the recipients of those wartime letters and telegrams from which he liberally quotes, experienced them. In those instances where the original might provoke confusion, I have made silent corrections. I have also preserved Grant's use of a series of asterisks where he wishes to indicate an ellipsis. For my own ellipses, I have used the conventional format. Next, the first edition includes several footnotes providing long explanations of, or extensive correspondence relating to, events discussed in the text. I preserve the shorter notes as annotations but direct the reader to Appendix 1 for the longer notes. Appendix 2 contains Grant's official final report to the Secretary of War, which also appeared at the end of the first edition.

My annotations provide biographical notes, usually at the first mention, of those who play major roles in Grant's story or are otherwise crucial to an understanding of events. First names, especially for those whose common surnames might provoke confusion, are interpolated in brackets. This practice is not followed for many of the officers of the Army of the Potomac because they appear in the command chart Grant includes in chapter 50, and which readers can consult in Appendix 1 to this edition. With regard to the texts I quote in annotations, I have tried, when feasible, to use translations and editions from the period—books to which Grant and his contemporaries would have had access. So, for example, quotations from Shakespeare come from the first major American edition of the collected works, produced by Richard Grant White in the middle of the nineteenth century and completed immediately after the Civil War.

The first edition of *Personal Memoirs* included several maps that are difficult for the non-specialist to interpret, so I have instead presented modern-day maps, several from the *West Point Atlas of the Civil War*, at key moments in the narrative where illustration of terrain and troop positions might prove especially helpful. Grant's own memory for terrain was remarkable—as his contemporaries attest—but he was not infallible, and there are errors, some of which are explained in the annotations. For accurate casualty numbers and similar statistics, however, readers should consult any of the number of available Civil War histories.

The editorial views expressed in this book are my own and do not reflect the official policy or position of the Department of the Army, the Department of Defense, or the U.S. Government.

Grant with book. Photograph by Matthew Brady. *Library of Congress, Prints and Photographs Division, LC-USZ62-21986.*

Editor's Introduction:
Reintroducing Ulysses S. Grant

Literary Geography: Grant's Prose Style

The routines and habits of celebrated writers provide a subject of perpetual fascination. Readers hunger for the preferably wretched details of artistic creation. Idiosyncrasy is good—John Cheever typing in his underwear, Vladimir Nabokov standing up to shuffle a deck of index cards into *Lolita*, Truman Capote lying down with coffee and a cigarette. Determination under duress or stamina amid deprivation is better: Jean-Paul Marat scratching out revolution atop a box beside the bathtub in which he cooled his scorching psoriasis, the visually impaired James Joyce wearing a white jacket better to illuminate the page, Mavis Gallant pawning her typewriter and starving in Madrid while her agent at the time, Jacques Chambrun, hoarded her *New Yorker* checks.

Perhaps what we admire most in writers is their ability to vanquish the noise of life—from the low hum of the quotidian to the high whine of crisis—by achieving a state of deep concentration that seals them, in the most extreme cases from physical or emotional pain, but more often simply from the insistent, contrary rhythms of responsibility. Consider the case, as so many have done, of the prolific novelist Anthony Trollope, who arose at 5:30 every morning to write steadily for three hours before breakfasting and heading off to a day's work as a postal surveyor.

A world that fetishizes the hyperattention abetted by technology tends to dismiss the sort of deep attention still required for not just the writing life, but all those lives that entail the solving of difficult problems, as antiquated and unfashionable. Despite the warnings of cognitive scientists about crucial limitations to our multitasking capacities and about the overconfidence the practice breeds within us, our commitment to it seems only to grow. Perhaps there is no better test of deep attention than the ability to write while the bombs are falling. The most persuasive instance of such determined focus I know is Ulysses S. Grant, who did much of his writing in war and who composed his *Personal Memoirs* in extremis, deep in debt and dying of cancer.

Grant earned the nickname "Unconditional Surrender" Grant from his refusal to offer any concessions to the Confederate commander at Tennessee's Fort Donelson: "No terms," he wrote his adversary and old acquaintance Simon Bolivar Buckner on February 16, 1862, "except an unconditional and immediate surrender can be accepted. I propose to move immediately upon your works."[1] *Unconditional surrender* might equally well describe Grant's approach to writing, an enterprise to which he gave himself with single-minded focus. Horace Porter, the son of a former governor of Pennsylvania and a member of the West Point class of 1860, who joined the general's staff in 1863, captures this quality in his 1897 account *Campaigning with Grant*:

> His powers of concentration . . . were often shown by the circumstances under which he wrote. Nothing that went on around him . . . could distract his attention or interrupt him. Sometimes, when his tent was filled with officers, talking and laughing at the top of their voices, he would turn to his table and write the most important communications. There would then be an immediate "Hush!" and abundant excuses offered by the company; but he always insisted upon the conversation going on, and after a while his officers came . . . to learn that noise was apparently a stimulus rather than a check to his flow of ideas, and to realize that nothing short of a general attack along the whole line could divert his thoughts from the subject upon which his mind was concentrated.[2]

1. United States War Department, *The War of the Rebellion: A Compilation of the Official Records of the Union and Confederate Armies* (Washington, D.C.: Government Printing Office, 1880–1901), ser. 1, vol. 7, 161 (hereafter cited as *OR*).

2. Horace Porter, *Campaigning with Grant* (New York: Century, 1897), 240.

Grant's February 16, 1862, communiqué to Simon Bolivar Buckner at Fort Donelson. 1884 copy in Grant's hand. *Special Collections, USMA Library.*

On the road Grant hated to retrace his steps. When lost, he would carry right on rather than turning around. He seems to have had a similar superstition about his prose, which he crafted, as Porter documents, with relentless efficiency:

> His work was performed swiftly and uninterruptedly, but without any marked display of nervous energy. His thoughts flowed as freely from his mind as the ink from his pen; he was never at a loss for an expression, and seldom interlined a word or made a material correction. He sat with his head bent low over the table, and when he had occasion to step to another table or desk to get a paper he wanted, he would glide rapidly across the room without straightening himself, and return to his seat with his body still bent over at about the same angle at which he had been sitting when he left his chair.[3]

Fastidious about language, Grant was indifferent to tools and surroundings alike. Nothing could distract him. "He wrote with the first pen he happened to pick up," sharp or blunt, "good or bad." Porter recalls. His desk "was always in a delirious state of confusion," its "local literary geography" baffling everyone except Grant himself, who evidently could find a document

---

3. Porter, *Campaigning*, 7.

"I have my book off my mind now. That [relieves] me
of a tax upon my strength which I could not avoid. Have
the papers any account of Gen. Buckner's visit here
yesterday?" Grant's note to Dr. John H. Douglas, 1885.
Special Collections, USMA Library.

he wanted "even in the dark."[4] The unshakable concentration Grant exhibited in the field also enabled him two decades later to complete the *Personal Memoirs* as he was dying, all the while convinced that in hammering away at the book he was hammering at his coffin, too. "I presume," he wrote to his doctor, "every strain of the mind or body is one more nail in the coffin."[5]

The style of Grant's memoirs, like that of his orders, dispatches, and correspondence, is distinguished by economy and precision. It is unlike much of the writing of his contemporaries and perhaps all the more remarkable given his reading habits as a young man: "Much of the time," Grant writes of his West Point days, "I am sorry to say, was devoted to novels, but not those of a trashy sort. I read all of Bulwer's then published, Cooper's, Marryat's, Scott's, Washington Irving's works, Lever's, and many others that I do not now remember." Even the most well-known authors on Grant's list, James Fenimore Cooper and Walter Scott, are read infrequently today. Nevertheless, as the West Point library circulation records of the era show, Grant's reading was absolutely typical of a cadet, and it duly reflected the national taste. Although now largely forgotten, both Frederick Marryat, who wrote seafaring novels, and Edward Bulwer-Lytton, a versatile writer whose work ranged from novels of manners to crime thrillers, were among the most

4. Porter, *Campaigning*, 241–42.

5. Note to John H. Douglas, June 23, 1885, *Papers of Ulysses S. Grant*, ed. John Y. Simon and John F. Marszalek, 32 vols. (Carbondale: Southern Illinois University Press, 1967–2012), 31:383 n. (hereafter cited as *PUSG*).

popular novelists of the day. Washington Irving, a local celebrity living near West Point in the Hudson Valley during Grant's cadet years, is perhaps best known for the short stories "Rip Van Winkle" and "The Legend of Sleepy Hollow," but he also wrote tales of adventure set on the American frontier and during Spain's medieval occupation by the Moors.

The two American authors on Grant's list, Irving and Cooper, were both heavily influenced by Scott, the sensationally popular Scottish author of poetic romances and historical novels that dramatized everything from the Jacobite rebellions of the Highland clans to medieval and Renaissance England to the Crusades. Full of adventure and antiquarian lore, his plots would inspire bel canto operas such as Gaetano Donizetti's *Lucia di Lammermoor*, Hollywood films like *Ivanhoe* and *Quentin Durward*, and countless imitators, who wrote in a style Grant's publisher Mark Twain described as "full of wordy, windy, flowery 'eloquence,' romanticism, sentimentality."

In *Life on the Mississippi*, published in 1883, about a year before he signed Grant to a contract to write his memoirs for the publishing house he ran with his nephew, Charles L. Webster, Twain diagnosed the South as suffering from "Sir Walter disease." While Scott's influence had waned in the North after the Civil War, Twain argued, the "Southern writer still clings to it." Twain's diagnosis was occasioned by a visit to New Orleans. In the celebration of Mardi Gras and in the spread of similar celebrations to other Southern cities, Twain discovered an anachronistic expression of a romantic soul, apparently dispelled in the Old World and the New by the French Revolution's destruction of the ancien régime yet subsequently revived by the novels of Scott. Twain's reading of Scott is certainly reductive—Scott served as a convenient symbol—but his critique illuminates a sensibility that held sway in much of America and that shaped many prose and verse representations of the Civil War:

> Then comes Sir Walter Scott with his enchantments, and by his single might checks this wave of progress, and even turns it back; sets the world in love with dreams and phantoms; with decayed and swinish forms of religion; with decayed and degraded systems of government; with the sillinesses and emptinesses, sham grandeurs, sham gauds, and sham chivalries of a brainless and worthless long-vanished society. He did measureless harm; more real and lasting harm, perhaps, than any other individual that ever wrote. Most of the world has now outlived good part of these harms, though by no means all of them; but in our South they flourish pretty forcefully still. Not so forcefully as half a gen-

eration ago, perhaps, but still forcefully. There, the genuine and wholesome civilization of the nineteenth century is curiously confused and
commingled with the Walter Scott Middle-Age sham civilization; and
so you have practical common-sense, progressive ideas, and progressive works; mixed up with the duel, the inflated speech, and the jejune
romanticism of an absurd past that is dead, and out of charity ought to
be buried. But for the Sir Walter disease, the character of the Southerner—or Southron, according to Sir Walter's starchier way of phrasing
it—would be wholly modern, in place of modern and mediæval mixed,
and the South would be fully a generation further advanced than it is.
It was Sir Walter that made every gentleman in the South a Major or
a Colonel, or a General or a Judge, before the war; and it was he, also,
that made these gentlemen value these bogus decorations. For it was he
that created rank and caste down there, and also reverence for rank and
caste, and pride and pleasure in them. Enough is laid on slavery, without
fathering upon it these creations and contributions of Sir Walter.

Twain goes on to insist that Scott "had so large a hand in making Southern
character, as it existed before the war, that he is in great measure responsible for
the war," a hyperbolic and "wild proposition" he supports by explaining that
the slaveowning Southerner of the Revolutionary period resembled the slaveowning Southerner of the Civil War "as an Englishman resembles a Frenchman.
The change of character can be traced rather more easily to Sir Walter's influence than to that of any other thing or person." Twain's comic zest should not
obscure the fundamental seriousness of his indictment of the worldview that
gripped the Southern imagination. Twain proposes that an enthusiasm for Scott
stunted Southern writers and prevented them from achieving artistic greatness
after the Civil War. Even today, the sensibility infusing the work of those writers is perceptible in the popular imagining of the Lost Cause as steeped in an
old-fashioned honor no longer current in a degraded world.[6]

---

6. Mark Twain, *Life on the Mississippi* (New York: Harper & Brothers, 1901) 327–29. Among the sem-
inal commentaries on the various traditions of Civil War writing are Edmund Wilson's *Patriotic Gore:
Studies in the Literature of the American Civil War* (New York: Farrar, Straus and Giroux, 1962), and Daniel
Aaron's *The Unwritten War: American Writers and the Civil War* (Madison: University of Wisconsin Press,
1987). More recent studies of note include Stephen Cushman's *Belligerent Muse: Five Northern Writers and
How They Shaped Our Understanding of the Civil War* (Chapel Hill: University of North Carolina Press,
2014), Randall Fuller's *From Battlefields Rising: How the Civil War Transformed American Literature* (New
York: Oxford University Press, 2011), Cynthia Wachtell's *War No More: The Antiwar Impulse in American
Literature, 1861–1914* (Baton Rouge: Louisiana State University Press, 2010), and Martin Griffin's *Ashes
of the Mind: War and Memory in Northern Literature, 1865–1900* (Amherst: University of Massachusetts
Press, 2009). For a survey of literature arising out of the Civil War, see Will Kaufman, "The American

Twain, whose acquaintance with Grant had begun several years before and whose *Innocents Abroad* kept Grant company on his long post-presidential tour of the world, discovered in the general's prose an emphatically different style. When he learned that Grant was planning to publish his memoirs with the Century Company for a modest advance, he persuaded him instead to sign a contract with his own firm for a $10,000 advance and 75 percent of future royalties. This arrangement would be sufficient to rescue Grant's wife, Julia, from the poverty to which Grant's disastrous business partnership with the con artist Ferdinand Ward had consigned the family. More than 300,000 sets of the two-volume first edition were sold by subscription in standard cloth and deluxe leather editions. Many of the salesmen were Union Army veterans, and they were carefully instructed in their work by a thirty-seven-page manual, *How to Introduce the Personal Memoirs of U. S. Grant.*

Even after Twain signed Grant, the path toward publication never lacked for drama. As the correspondence of Twain and his nephew Webster reveals, Grant's precarious health proved a source of constant anxiety to Webster, whose worries about losing the manuscript to theft, fire, or other publishers intensified when Grant decamped to a cottage near Saratoga, New York, where he lived his last several months.[7] As the influence of Twain increased, that of Grant's longtime military secretary Adam Badeau waned. At one point, a jealous Badeau insisted publicly that the bulk of the work was really his, a charge Grant angrily refuted. Over the years there would be others who suspected Twain himself had written the memoirs. Questions of authorship are easily refuted by the existence of the manuscript in Grant's hand at the Library of Congress as well as by even a cursory comparison of the prose with that of Grant's letters. Additionally, Grant's worsening health is reflected in the second volume's occasional lapses, as James M. McPherson and other historians have noted.[8]

In his *Autobiography* Twain recalls being urged by a member of the gen-

---

Civil War," *The Cambridge Companion to War Writing*, ed. Kate McLoughlin (Cambridge, UK: Cambridge University Press, 2009), 148–59.

7. See Mark Twain file, Grant Presidential Library, ser. 2, box 12, folders 22 and 27. For a detailed case study of the selling of the book by canvassers as "one of the largest and most successful campaigns of the nineteenth century," see Walter A. Friedman, *Birth of a Salesman: The Transformation of Selling in America* (Cambridge, MA: Harvard University Press, 2005), 43–49. On Twain's involvement in Grant's last months, see Mark Perry, *Grant and Twain: The Story of an American Friendship* (New York: Random House, 2004).

8. The handwritten manuscript pages and notes at the Library of Congress clearly reveal the effects of Grant's worsening health. For a moving account of this deterioration, see Bruce Catton, *U. S. Grant and the American Military Tradition*, ed. Oscar Handlin (Boston: Little, Brown, 1954), 187–88.

A page from the manuscript of *Personal Memoirs* on which Grant discusses the
advantage of having served during the Mexican War with so many officers who
would go on to fight on both sides in the Civil War. *Library of Congress, Ulysses S.
Grant Papers: Series 4, Personal Memoirs, 1884–1885, Image 266.*

eral's "household" to give some sign of encouragement to Grant while they were in the process of reading page proofs: "I was as much surprised as Columbus's cook could have been," Twain declares, "to learn that Columbus wanted his opinion as to how Columbus was doing his navigating." Capturing Grant's fixity of purpose, he continues: "It could not have occurred to me that General Grant could have any use for anybody's assistance or encouragement in any work which he might undertake to do." Twain nevertheless had an assessment at the ready. He likened *Personal Memoirs* to Caesar's *Commentaries*: both books, he claims to have informed Grant, were distinguished by "clarity of statement, directness, simplicity, unpretentiousness, manifest truthfulness, fairness toward friend and foe alike, soldierly candor and frankness and soldierly avoidance of flowery speech."[9] It was that resistance to flowery speech that Twain seemed to prize above all. In a world seized by an epidemic of Sir Walter disease, Grant was an impervious modern. His prose perhaps owed something to his experience, from boyhood on, in the Methodist Church, which embraced the plain style championed by John Wesley in its hymns and sermons. Grant's clinical descriptions of battle and consistent refusals to romanticize combat were also logical responses to his experience of ordering thousands of men to their deaths.[10]

Although few authors were as committed to demythologizing combat as was Grant, a tension between two modes—romantic and modern—was present during the Civil War. John Beatty, colonel of the 3rd Ohio Volunteer Infantry Regiment, found that the "war stories" featured in the newspapers bore no resemblance to his own experience. In the following entry Beatty describes his response to the popular *Harper's Weekly*, which he read when he returned to camp at Murfreesboro, Tennessee, in January 1863, after the Battle of Stones River:

> I find two numbers of Harper's Weekly on my return. They abound in war stories. The two heroes, of whom I read to-night, received saber cuts on the face and head, obtained leave of absence, returned home, and married forthwith. Saber cuts are very rare in the Army of the Cumberland, and if young officers were compelled to defer entering into wedlock until they got wounds of this kind, there

9. *Autobiography of Mark Twain*, vol. 2, ed. Benjamin Griffin and Harriet Elinor Smith, The Mark Twain Papers (Berkeley: University of California, 2013), 71.

10. I am indebted to Julia Reidhead and Drew Gilpin Faust for their insights on possible factors contributing to the formation of Grant's style. On the role Methodism played in Grant's life more generally, see Ronald C. White, *American Ulysses: A Life of Ulysses S. Grant* (New York: Random House, 2016).

would be precious few soldiers married. Bullet wounds are common enough; but the hand-to-hand encounters, knightly contests of swords, the cleaving of headpieces and shattering of spears, are not incidents of modern warfare.[11]

The tales Beatty encountered in *Harper's Weekly* could not have been further from the reality of Civil War combat or from Grant's way of depicting it. In fact, Grant engages in a kind of stylistic warfare throughout his book with the "romance"—a word he several times repeats—propagated in much contemporaneous writing about the war. Unusual in its own time, Grant's deflationary style can also serve as an antidote to today's prevailing modes of representing war. Our current discourse veers from euphemism—kinetic operations, persistent low-intensity conflict, hearts and minds—to a deeply romanticized, unreflective rhetoric about heroes and values, to the equally and paradoxically romantic language of knowingness, cynicism, and disaffection inherited from pop-culture depictions of Vietnam ("*Apocalypse Now* speak," one might call this last category). It is all or nothing; there is no room for ambiguity.

Caught between gauzy nostalgia for the last "good war" and the current realities of a dubious one, today's discussions are too often muddied by a reluctance to acknowledge what Grant always did: namely, that the deaths of good people in bankrupt causes do nothing to ameliorate those causes and that armies serving just ends comprise soldiers with a wild variety of motives. Grant understood that even a "good war" is never fought for a single good cause alone nor ever won without brutal methods. Beneath the distinctive attributes of a given war, as George Orwell once noted, there is a brutal sameness: "The essential horror of army life . . . is barely affected by the nature of the war you happen to be fighting in. . . . A louse is a louse and a bomb is a bomb, even though the cause you are fighting for happens to be just."[12]

Grant fought in two wars: the Mexican War and the Civil War. The latter he believed a war of principle, the former "one of the most unjust ever waged by a stronger against a weaker nation." Favored by the slave states and deliberately provoked by the American army's incursion into Mexican territory, this unambiguously political war, fought a few years after the U.S.

---

11. John Beatty, *The Citizen-Soldier; or, Memoirs of a Volunteer* (Cincinnati, OH: Wilstach, Baldwin, 1879), 213–14.

12. "Looking Back on the Spanish War," *Essays*, ed. John Carey (New York: Everyman's Library, 2002), 432–33.

annexation of Texas, resulted in Mexico's ceding of more than 50 percent of its territory. But Grant never allowed the fact that brave men died in Mexico to distort his opinion of its politics, nor did he permit his belief in the Union to gild the waste of human life that secured its preservation and the eradication of slavery. More than a century has passed since Grant's death in 1885. We are at war again, or still; his writing reveals another way to talk about it.

The following examples serve to illustrate the tenor of his war writing. During his time in Mexico, Grant wrote frequently to his future wife, Julia Dent, whom he had met while stationed at Jefferson Barracks, in St. Louis, Missouri. He told her how much he missed her; he described Mexico's natural beauty and his wish to return in peace. As the war wore on, he wrote with increasing frequency of the deaths of friends, officers Julia had known in St. Louis. Here he describes to her with typical forthrightness his sensations during his first battle:

> There is no great sport in having bullets flying about one in evry direction but I find they have much less horror when among them than when in anticipation. Now that the war has commenced with such vengence I am in hopes my Dear Julia that we will soon be able to end it.[13]

Of his second battle, the American victory at Resaca de la Palma, he reported in his *Memoirs*:

> [T]he battle of Resaca de la Palma would have been won, just as it was, if I had not been there.

Of his first mission in command during the Civil War, near Florida, Missouri, he admitted:

> I would have given anything then to have been back in Illinois, but I had not the moral courage to call a halt and consider what to do; I kept right on.

Of the character of Zachary Taylor, "Old Rough and Ready," who commanded American forces in Mexico and on whom he would model himself, Grant observed:

---

13. Letter to Julia Dent, May 11, 1846, *PUSG*, 1:86.

No soldier could face either danger or responsibility more calmly than he. These are qualities more rarely found than genius or physical courage.

Of the surrender of Robert E. Lee, Grant wrote not without delight in dispelling a popular myth:

> That much talked of surrendering of Lee's sword and my handing it back, this and much more that has been said about it is the purest romance.

Perhaps Grant's philosophy of composition is best expressed in his description of the letter he sent to Lee accepting his enemy's surrender: "When I put my pen to the paper I did not know the first word that I should make use of in writing the terms. I only knew what was in my mind, and I wished to express it clearly, so that there could be no mistaking it." Grant loves that final phrase: *there could be no mistaking it*. He repeats it several times in his memoirs, initially to describe Taylor's prose style and, later, to describe his own chief aim when writing. Horace Porter attributes the following appraisal to George G. Meade's chief of staff: "There is one striking feature about Grant's orders: no matter how hurriedly he may write them on the field, no one ever has the slightest doubt as to their meaning, or ever has to read them over a second time to understand them."[14] Only on occasion, particularly in the second volume, does that clarity fail, as a result of illness and haste, to dominate Grant's *Personal Memoirs*.

Grant's *Personal Memoirs* falls into several categories of life writing, an activity that of course has a long history. The British writer Robert Southey coined the term *autobiography* in 1809, but writers have been producing accounts of their lives under various names since antiquity. The early autobiographers were often soldiers or saints. Xenophon, Julius Caesar, Saint Augustine, Saint Teresa of Ávila, and the Mughal Emperor Babur all understood that writing a life was different from living one—that they were (skillfully) crafting a self for others to consume—yet they were not writers by profession. The tradition of lives by people who, whatever else they did, imagined their writing selves as largely the point arguably began with Michel de Montaigne

---

14. Porter, *Campaigning*, 241.

in the late sixteenth century, and it includes a range of writers from Jean-Jacques Rousseau to Gertrude Stein, Lillian Hellman, James Baldwin, and Joan Didion.

Its rich international history notwithstanding, life writing occupies perhaps a special place in the cultural history of the United States. "Autobiography," the critic Jay Parini suggests, "could easily be called the essential American genre, a form of writing closely allied to our national self-consciousness."[15] When Grant was coming of age as a reader during the antebellum period, the field already included seventeenth-century Puritan spiritual autobiographies, Indian captivity narratives, and travel memoirs. To these would be added artistically as well as politically significant slave narratives by Harriet Jacobs and Frederick Douglass, among others. There was also the watershed *Autobiography of Benjamin Franklin*, first published in the United States in 1818. Franklin's repurposing of autobiography, which before him had been devoted to spiritual betterment, as a chronicle of intellectual, social, and financial as much as moral self-improvement launched a secular tradition that would eventually encompass Henry Adams, P. T. Barnum, and Grant himself. By the time Grant started writing his memoirs in the mid-1880s, a postbellum flood of Civil War reminiscences had already gathered considerable momentum. Stylistic and political fashions would change in the ensuing decades, but the American enthusiasm for life writing has never diminished.

One thing Grant's *Personal Memoirs* is not, is personal—at least not in the ways a twenty-first-century reader inured to the tell-all mode currently in vogue will recognize. There are only a few chapters devoted to the author's family and childhood and almost no information on his postwar career, including his vexed presidency—he presided over a politically tumultuous period marked by the brief success but ultimate failure of Reconstruction, by increasingly violent westward expansion, and by the greed and concomitant corruption of the Gilded Age—and epic world tour. Some of these

---

15. Jay Parini, Introduction, *The Norton Book of American Autobiography*, ed. Parini (New York: Norton, 1999), 11. On the history of American life writing, see also Daniel B. Shea Jr., *Spiritual Autobiography in Early America* (Princeton: Princeton University Press, 1968); Herbert Leibowitz, *Fabricating Lives: Explorations in American Autobiography* (1975; New York: New Directions, 1989); Albert E. Stone, *Autobiographical Occasions and Original Acts* (Philadelphia: University of Pennsylvania Press, 1982); *American Autobiography: Retrospect and Prospect*, ed. Paul John Eakin (Madison: University of Wisconsin Press, 1991); Susan Clair Imbarrato, *Declarations of Independence in Eighteenth-Century Autobiography* (Knoxville: University of Tennessee Press, 1998); and *Reading African American Autobiography*, ed. Eric D. Lamore (Madison: University of Wisconsin Press, 2017). For a more general survey, see Ben Yagoda's *Memoir: A History* (New York: Riverhead, 2010).

compressions and omissions owe to the fact that Grant ran out of time. Yet he was naturally reticent. His marked aversion to gossip, ridicule, scandal, and rumor is matched by his keenness for deflating pretense and dispelling romance. More to the point, in a gesture of self-protection, Grant expends few words on his emotional life. While reading him one is occasionally reminded of Virginia Woolf's observation that so many memoir writers "leave out the person to whom things happened." These writers, Woolf proposes, "say: 'This is what happened'; but they do not say what the person was like to whom it happened."[16]

What Grant chooses to withhold in fact discloses quite a lot. Attentive readers will discern important aspects of his personality in the self-deprecating references to his youthful ambitions, the terse and resolutely matter-of-fact descriptions of his battlefield experience—accounts further abbreviated by his repulsion at the sight of blood—and in the virtual passing over in the space of a few brief chapters of the period between the Mexican and Civil Wars, during which he endured a series of miserable assignments in the Pacific Northwest. It was in these years that he resigned his commission under somewhat mysterious circumstances owing probably to his drinking, searched fruitlessly for a way to make a living, and ended up a clerk in his father's leather-goods store in Galena, Illinois. Grant's letters from this period to his wife, Julia, which can be found in the first volume of the *Papers of Ulysses S. Grant*, express acute loneliness and frank despair, but this inner life is closed to the reader of the *Personal Memoirs*. Grant was not unique in censoring himself in this fashion, but, unlike, for example, his contemporary and friend William T. Sherman, an excitable extrovert whose own memoirs were published a decade earlier in 1875, he never pushes himself forward as the leading actor of the national drama he is chronicling.

Another reason Grant avoids the intimately personal is that he understands his subject to be war rather than himself. The Civil War is the occasion for his narrative, just as it was the central episode of his life. His book can thus be classified as a species of war writing, a genre that often overlaps with life writing (Julius Caesar, *ipse*, again), but, given that war

16. Virginia Woolf, *A Sketch of the Past, Moments of Being*, ed. Jeanne Schulkind, 2nd ed. (New York: Harcourt Brace, 1985), 65. On Grant's omissions and their significance, see Joan Waugh, "Ulysses S. Grant, Historian," *The Memory of the Civil War in American Culture*, ed. Alice Fahs and Joan Waugh (Chapel Hill: University of North Carolina Press, 2004), 29. Noting the largely impersonal, aloof nature of Grant's account—"an alienation in the midst of action"—Edmund Wilson insists, "the very objectivity of Grant's method of describing the war always works to eliminate its tragedy." *Patriotic Gore* (1962; New York: Norton, 1994), 140, 152.

Julius Caesar trading card, "Great
Generals" series, Allen & Ginter Brand
Cigarettes, 1888. *Metropolitan Museum of
Art, The Jefferson R. Burdick Collection, Gift
of Jefferson R. Burdick.*

is a tragically persistent and ubiquitous human activity, it is a subject that
preoccupies a range of genres, including poetry, drama, novel, and history. It is this dimension of Grant's book—the nature of his war story—
that is its most anomalous. In other respects, his book is a recognizably
nineteenth-century artifact.

Thirteen Ways of Looking at a Battle: The Case of Shiloh

Grant's way of looking at war is, as I have stated, unlike that of many of his
contemporaries. He tends to be ironic where they are sentimental, clinical
where they are romantic, muted where they are melodramatic, parsimonious
where they are verbose. Over the years his book has impressed a surprising
diversity of readers: "Gertrude Stein thought (as I do)," the novelist Gore
Vidal wrote, "that Ulysses S. Grant's memoir was the best American prose,
proof that genius is innate since West Point's English department, in his day,

did not dazzle."[17] (West Point's English department not only did not dazzle, it did not exist in Grant's day; it was established in the 1920s.)

In the process of editing Grant's book I have discovered that what I once conceived to be oppositional modes of representation—nineteenth-century romanticism and Grant's apparent modernity—are not always quite so distinct. Often they compete within the same narrative. In addition, I have encountered among his contemporaries a broader range of approaches to the problem of representing the Civil War than I initially thought available. Following Wallace Stevens's poetic exercise in perspective, "Thirteen Ways of Looking at a Blackbird," one might itemize thirteen ways of looking at a battle. The number thirteen may be arbitrary, although it has a superstitious dread appropriate to an examination of war, but it does help to suggest the multiplicity of perspectives often employed:

I. Cartographic
II. Photographic
III. Lithographic
IV. Statistical
V. Official
VI. Unofficial
VII. Journalistic
VIII. Historical
IX. Biographical or Autobiographical
X. Revisionist
XI. Factual
XII. Fictional
XIII. Memorial

This list is not exhaustive, nor are the categories mutually exclusive—the official is likely to contain statistics and maps, the historical the revisionist, and so forth—but a list of this kind offers at least a plausible set of ways of looking at a subject so difficult to represent accurately that it has become an exceptional case. I am less invested in these or other potential categories per se than in the phenomena that cut across various modes and genres and that can be teased out by reading them in parallel. And while the list includes for the most part nonfictional modes of representation, I am interested equally in the fictive techniques and literary influences that shape purportedly fac-

17. Gore Vidal, Preface, *Norton Book of American Autobiography*, 9.

tual accounts of war. In part, what draws me to a reexamination of Grant's book and the war it depicts—a war that seems never to end in the American mind—is a belief that our ways of looking at war today are myopic and too few at a moment when we can ill afford it, nearly twenty years in to our military commitments in Afghanistan and the Middle East.

Even thirteen is an insufficient number when it comes to looking at the particular battle on which I have chosen to focus here as a kind of case study: Shiloh, fought in southern Tennessee, about ten miles north of the Mississippi border, along the western shore of the Tennessee River, on April 6–7, 1862. There federal troops under Grant's command defeated rebel forces led by General A. S. Johnston, an experienced soldier who was at the time the South's great hope, seconded by the Louisianan P. G. T. Beauregard, who took command after Johnston's death on the first afternoon. When the war broke out, Beauregard was serving as the West Point superintendent. He received the federal surrender of Fort Sumter in April 1861.

Won on the second day by Union forces after near defeat on the first, Shiloh was by no means an unalloyed victory. Although he knew the enemy to be close by, Sherman had been surprised by the initial Confederate attack; Grant, whose headquarters was some miles away, had not ordered the army to entrench; and confusion reigned before Union troops, no few of whom were clustering in a panic along the riverbank, were reorganized by Grant and eventually reinforced by General Don Carlos Buell's Army of the Ohio, which arrived in the evening on April 6. Grant and Sherman's near contemporary at West Point, Buell was later removed from command for failing to pursue the enemy after the Battle of Perryville, in Kentucky. His feud with the other generals over who really saved the day at Shiloh long outlasted the war. As numerous commentators have observed, Shiloh was a battle that revealed the serious inadequacy of Union leadership on several levels even as it pointed the way toward future victories.[18]

Shiloh was a shocking encounter that, like Antietam in the Eastern Theater, altered Americans' attitudes toward the war in which they were engaged. There were almost 24,000 total casualties, a number that outstripped the total deaths of all previous American wars combined. Shiloh reaffirmed for Grant what he had discovered two months before, at Fort Donelson, where he had insisted on the enemy's unconditional surrender, a demand to which the Confederate commander, Grant's old friend Simon

---

18. For a probing analysis of the lessons Grant learned from this battle, see J. F. C. Fuller, *The Generalship of Ulysses S. Grant* (New York: Da Capo, 1991), especially 95–116, 187–88, 202–4, 425–31.

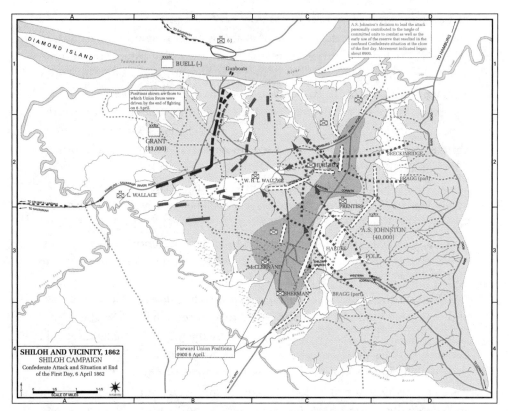

Battle of Shiloh, end of the first day (April 6, 1862). *West Point Atlas of the Civil War.*
Courtesy of Department of History, USMA.

Bolivar Buckner, had been forced to acquiesce despite judging these terms "ungenerous and unchivalrous." It seemed to Buckner, who had known Grant at West Point, fought with him in Mexico, and lent him money at a desperate moment, as if his adversary were playing by a new set of rules. He was. And after Shiloh, Grant explains, he "gave up all idea of saving the Union except by complete conquest."

War, to which chaos is endemic, always poses challenges to those who would plan it and thus also to the structures and forms subsequently recruited to describe it. Prepare all you like, the great nineteenth-century military theorist Carl von Clausewitz tells us: "In the whole range of human activities, war most closely resembles a game of cards" through which good luck and bad both run.[19] The particular opposition of fellow countrymen and

---

19. Carl von Clausewitz, *On War*, ed. and trans. Michael Howard and Peter Paret (Princeton, NJ: Princeton University Press, 1984), 86.

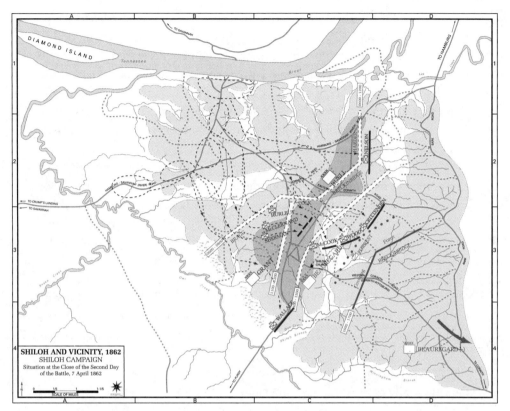

Battle of Shiloh, end of second day. *West Point Atlas of the Civil War. Courtesy of Department of History, USMA.*

former comrades-in-arms in the Civil War made it especially perplexing: an emblem of the confusion, certain units on both sides wore the same color uniform. For a variety of reasons, not the least of which was its unprecedented scale of destruction—other factors were Union unpreparedness on the first day, the Confederate withdrawal on the second, and the timing of Buell's arrival—Shiloh became arguably the most controversial battle of the war, its history among the most contested. As Grant put it, "The battle of Shiloh, or Pittsburg landing, has been perhaps less understood, or, to state the case more accurately, more persistently misunderstood, than any other engagement between National and Confederate troops during the entire rebellion."

The most chronicled battle, Grant might have added. There are no fewer than 229 official ways of looking at Shiloh to be found in *The War of the Rebellion: A Compilation of the Official Records of the Union and Confederate Armies,* a monumental multivolume series published by the War Department from 1880–1901. High-ranking officers on both sides are heavily represented in the *Official Records*, but the chapter on Shiloh is a nesting doll of reports written by everyone from generals to lieutenants—all the way down through regimental, battalion, even battery commanders, who take us closer and closer to a specific action or part of the field. Of course, there are many times that number of unofficial versions, written by the various curators of Civil War memory: participants, eyewitnesses, historians, novelists, journalists, enthusiasts, apologists.

Each official report contains a description of a given unit's position and a chronology of its actions throughout the battle, while most include praise for conspicuously brave soldiers. Almost all close with a summary of casualties, although one officer, Major Ezra Taylor, chief of artillery for the 5th Division, signed off with remarkable zeal: "Trusting that you will not consider this somewhat lengthy report more than is in justice due to those who have sought to do their best to inflict a just chastisement upon these rebellious subjects against the best government under the sun."[20] All of the individual units' casualty tallies were rolled up in a table of field returns submitted by Grant's chief of staff, John Rawlins. "Counting," the literary scholar James Dawes suggests in *The Language of War*, his examination of language and violence in the United States from the Civil War to World War II, "is the epistemology of war."[21] Numbers would become an essential element of the twentieth-century bureaucratic rhetoric about war: a clinical language of statistics, false precision, and misdirection, of which George Orwell and W. H. Auden were among the sharpest critics. This lexicon was enshrined in Vietnam by the "Five O'Clock Follies," the Joint United States Public Affairs Office daily press briefing in Saigon, with its ritual announcement of the body count.

As Dawes notes, Sherman was especially fond of the "actuarial" approach, and statistics play a prominent role in his memoirs. Looking at war as a question of numbers, Dawes suggests, can serve a psychological purpose by depersonalizing loss: counting turns human beings into things.[22] After a battle, the number of the enemy was not infrequently inflated to make the odds against victory seem greater. Numbers were particularly important to Union general John A. McClernand, a political appointee and important

---

20. *OR*, ser. 1, vol. 10, pt. 1, 275.

21. James Dawes, *The Language of War: Literature and Culture in the U.S. from the Civil War through World War II* (Cambridge, MA: Harvard University Press, 2002), 29.

22. Dawes, *Language*, 32.

Miles marched by the different corps of Sherman's army, prepared from maps by an engineer officer. Sherman's own calculations can be seen at lower left. *Special Collections, USMA Library.*

Democratic ally of Lincoln without military experience. McClernand commanded a Union division at Shiloh and proved a constant source of irritation to Grant and others until his eventual relief in 1863.[23] But for McClernand they served a rather different purpose, as this battle report sent directly to Lincoln demonstrates:

> We have just passed through a terrible battle, lasting two days. My division, as usual, has borne or shared in bearing the brunt. I have lost in killed and wounded about every third man of my command. Within a radius of 200 yards of my headquarters some 150 dead bodies were left on the field, the proportion of rebels to Union men being about three to one. Among the killed is General A. S. Johnston (said to be), who fell within 30 yards of my tent. Part of a battery belonging to the enemy was taken within 150 yards of my tent, and some 30 or 40 horses were killed within the same distance. The largely supe-

---

23. In his diary, on October 11, 1864, Lincoln's secretary John Hay described a conversation between the president and Secretary of War Edwin M. Stanton: "They . . . seemed glad to be rid of him [McClernand]. A vain irritable overbearing exacting man who is possessed of the monomania that it was a mere clerical error which placed Grant's name and not his in the Commission of the Lieutenant General." *Inside Lincoln's White House: The Complete Civil War Diary of John Hay*, ed. Michael Burlingame and John R. Turner Ettlinger (Carbondale: Southern Illinois University Press, 1997), 240.

rior number of the enemy enabled him to flank me all day Sunday (the 6th), yet I retook my camp twice, and checked the enemy by repeatedly changing front and meeting him until night-fall, which, together with the arrival of Buell's forces, enabled us to attack the enemy in turn next day and drive him back with great slaughter.

Grant forwarded this statement to Lincoln with the warning that it was "faulty in two particulars," chiefly in its author's tendency to report "too much of other divisions remote" from his own.[24] For the ambitious McClernand, whose personal campaign of self-aggrandizement eventually led to his removal from the Army of the Tennessee, numbers (percentages, body counts of men and horses, distances, days, actions) seem less a measure of horror or an evasion of it than a badge of honor. Henry W. Halleck, the cautious theater commander—well known for his theoretical knowledge of military science but without experience in the field—who was not present at the battle, reacted to the unprecedented casualty numbers reported by Union officers by suggesting to Edwin M. Stanton, Lincoln's irascible, wily, and determined Secretary of War, "There seems to have been a morbid desire on the part of some of our officers to make the loss of their particular commands much greater than it really was."[25]

Thus one theoretically objective kind of representation, numerical, was not, it would seem, entirely reliable. If numbers were sometimes suspect, so too, apparently, were maps. In truth, some of the maps of the day were not very good, but those made of completed battles were also fair game for anyone who wished to reshape the story. In the 1880s, Buell tried to set the record straight about the contribution to the victory made by his Army of the Ohio. In an essay on the battle he accused Sherman of having history redrawn: "Nineteen years after the battle General Sherman revised the official map, and deposited his version with the Society of the Army of the Tennessee for historical use." Thereafter referring to "Sherman's map" or "the Sherman edition," Buell argues that this new cartography, "prepared with such elaboration of detail and introduced with such richness of anecdotal embellishment, was a thorough delusion. . . . General Sherman was in a different place!"[26]

24. *OR*, ser. 1, vol. 10, pt. 1, 113–14.

25. *OR*, ser. 1, vol. 10, pt. 1, 99–100.

26. Don Carlos Buell, "Shiloh Reviewed," *Battles and Leaders of the Civil War*, ed. Robert Underwood Johnson and Clarence Clough Buel, 4 vols. (New York: Century, 1884–1887), 1:509–12 (hereafter cited as *B&L*).

Inflated or deflated numbers; doctored maps; other distortions of time and space caused by obscuring smoke, concealing woods, and deafening explosions; ubiquitous carnage—the field of battle was a site of utter confusion. John A. Cockerill, a sixteen-year-old Union soldier at Shiloh, later recalled, the battle "outstripped my most fanciful dreams of Pandemonium."[27] Sherman wrote to his wife a few days after the battle, "The scenes on this field would have cured anybody of war. Mangled bodies, dead, dying, in every conceivable shape, without heads, legs; and horses!"[28] That Sherman ends his catalogue with horses is no accident: heaps of horse and mule carcasses commonly littered Civil War battlefields. Sherman claims to have buried two thousand at Shiloh. Lew Wallace, the Union general better known as the author of the blockbuster novel *Ben-Hur*, was struck by the overwhelming stench in the aftermath of the battle as he traversed the field in pursuit of the enemy: "Strewn over the surface of the slope clear down to the brook there were dead men, among whom my horse picked his way with reluctance. A sickly smell tainted the air; whether it rose from the bodies or the bloody sod, or was a sulphurous residuum of battle-smoke, I could not tell. In my haste to get rid of it, I plunged inadvertently into a swamp that tried all John's great strength."[29]

The only thing that seemed to thrive in such a landscape was rumor. Sherman, who had a Shakespearean sense of rumor's insidious power, captured a few of the exaggerations and myths decades later in his *Memoirs*: "Probably no single battle of the war gave rise to such wild and damaging reports. It was publicly asserted at the North that our army was taken completely by surprise; that the rebels caught us in our tents; bayoneted the men in their beds; that General Grant was drunk; that Buell's opportune arrival saved the Army of the Tennessee from utter annihilation, etc." According to Sherman, the source of many of these rumors were his fellow generals, chiefly Buell.[30] Like Grant, Sherman was fully aware of the tendency toward hyperbole that war stimulates. Shiloh taught both men to greet the many tall tales that constantly swirled around them with skepticism. On the

---

27. John A. Cockerill, "A Boy at Shiloh," *Battles and Leaders of the Civil War*, ed. Peter Cozzens, vols. 5–6 (Urbana: University of Illinois Press, 2004), 6:128 (hereafter cited as *B&L*, 2nd ser.).

28. Letter to Ellen Ewing Sherman, April 11, 1862, *Home Letters of General Sherman*, ed. M. A. DeWolfe Howe (New York: Scribner's, 1909), 222.

29. In his account of Shiloh Wallace also points out a grave inaccuracy in what Buell called "Sherman's map." Lew Wallace, *Autobiography*, 2 vols. (New York: Harper & Brothers, 1906), 2:568, 547 n. 1.

30. William T. Sherman, *Memoirs of General William T. Sherman*, 2 vols. (New York: D. Appleton, 1875), 1:244.

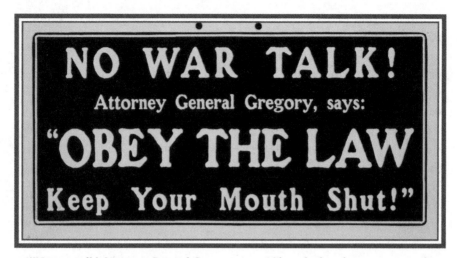

"No war talk! Attorney General Gregory says, 'Obey the law, keep your mouth shut!'" World War I propaganda poster, 1917. *Library of Congress, Prints and Photographs Division, WWI Posters, LC-USZC4-9013.*

battlefield at Shiloh, Grant recounted to Horace Porter, "We learned something . . . about the way in which the reports of losses are sometimes exaggerated in battle." According to Grant, Sherman encountered a demoralized colonel who told him that seven hundred of his eight hundred soldiers had been killed; a few hours later Sherman found the lost seven hundred sheltered under the riverbank, where they were "boiling coffee and eating a hearty meal with an appetite that showed they were still very much alive."[31]

As a young musician detached from his unit, Cockerill wandered the field at Shiloh, a kind of free agent. Cockerill, who later became a journalist, structured his 1893 account of the battle around a rumor. Encountering a "crowd of fear-stricken and dejected soldiers," he identifies a member of his father's regiment who reports that it "had been entirely cut to pieces, and that he had personally witnessed the death of my father—he had seen him shot from his horse." Cockerill later reports this news to his brother, who arrives with Buell's army late on the first day, and his narrative forces the reader likewise to labor under this impression for the duration of his account. Only at the very end of his war story does Cockerill reveal the truth, as he describes the regiment returning to camp: "At its head rode my father, whom I supposed to be dead—pale, and haggard, and worn, but unscathed. He had

---

31. Porter, *Campaigning*, 193.

not seen me nor heard from me for sixty hours." We might be tempted to read in this an anticipation of the modern ironic mode the literary critic Paul Fussell persuasively identified with the literature of World War I in his classic work *The Great War and Modern Memory*. But it coexists with something else in Cockerill, who continues movingly, "He dismounted, and taking me in his arms, gave me the most affectionate embrace that my life had ever known, and I realized then how deeply he loved me."[32]

Grim irony does gain the upper hand in the work of perhaps the most unsentimental of Civil War writers, Ambrose Bierce, a Union soldier and postwar journalist perhaps best known for his satiric compendium *The Devil's Dictionary*. Sentiment appears in Bierce largely to be undermined by the graphic horror of war experience: the temptation to view Shiloh with nostalgia—with the ardor of his younger self—is acknowledged but resisted. The autobiographical sketch "What I Saw of Shiloh" begins with a typically arch claim: "This is a simple story of a battle; such a tale as may be told by a soldier who is no writer to a reader who is no soldier."[33] The hellish grotesque in Bierce's essay culminates in his descent into a ravine "to gratify a reprehensible curiosity" about the damage done by the fires that had erupted in the forest. There he finds

> bodies, half buried in ashes; some in the unlovely looseness of attitude denoting sudden death by the bullet, but by far the greater number in postures of agony that told of the tormenting flame. Their clothing was half burnt away—their hair and beard entirely; the rain had come too late to save their nails. Some were swollen to double girth; others shriveled to manikins. According to the degree of exposure, their faces were bloated and black or yellow and shrunken. The contraction of muscles which had given them claws for hands had cursed each coun-

---

32. Cockerill, "A Boy at Shiloh," *B&L*, 2nd ser., 131–32, 138.

33. Ambrose Bierce, "What I Saw of Shiloh," *The Collected Works of Ambrose Bierce*, 12 vols. (New York: Neale, 1909), 1:234. The critic Randall Fuller calls Bierce's essay "still the most chilling description of the mundane horror and relentless indignity of nineteenth-century warfare." Fuller proposes that Bierce, together with Mark Twain, Stephen Crane, and others, "participated in an epic reimagining of the war in the last third of the nineteenth century. For them, the war was a tragic farce, a sick joke that belied the lofty rhetoric of writers and politicians from the previous generation. Avatars of a new literary realism that would dominate American letters through the end of the nineteenth century," Fuller explains, their "attitude toward the killing" remained "a minority view" in the nation at large, still captivated as the public was by sentimental retellings of the war that skirted politics and glorified battlefield death. See Fuller, *From Battlefields Rising*, 71, 221.

tenance with a hideous grin. Faugh! I cannot catalogue the charms of these gallant gentlemen who had got what they enlisted for.[34]

Bierce's satiric autobiographical and fictional depictions of war anticipate modern literary developments, but his was emphatically not the dominant mode of the time.

The majority of contemporaneous accounts were unequivocally steeped in nostalgia and in the hero worship that is its frequent companion. One that managed to offend readers North and South was William Preston Johnston's contribution to *Battles and Leaders of the Civil War*, a highly successful and influential four-volume collection of articles by high-ranking officers on both sides curated by the editors of the *Century* magazine in the 1880s. Johnston was the son of the Confederate commander A. S. Johnston, and his account of the battle contains this set piece on the death of his father:

> His presence was full of inspiration. He sat his thoroughbred bay, "Fire-eater," with easy command. His voice was persuasive, encouraging, and compelling. His words were few; he said: "Men! They are stubborn; we must use the bayonet." When he reached the center of the line, he turned. "I will lead you!" he cried, and moved toward the enemy. The line was already thrilling and trembling with that irresistible ardor which in battle decides the day. With a mighty shout Bowen's and Statham's brigades moved forward at a charge. A sheet of flame and a mighty roar burst from the Federal stronghold. The Confederate line withered; but there was not an instant's pause. The crest was gained. The enemy were in flight.[35]

---

34. Bierce, "What I Saw of Shiloh," *Collected Works*, 1:261–62. Fuller suggests that this passage and, to an even greater degree, the essay's conclusion "marked the moment when the war came to be seen as the termination of outmoded beliefs and ideals." Fuller, *Battlefields Rising*, 73. Bierce cynically repudiates his own youthful idealism. Yet, as Stephen Cushman notes, in the way in which he chose to write "about the war, Bierce . . . demonstrated repeatedly his devotion to an ethical code of conduct . . . not wholly without higher motives many a cynic would be too embarrassed to acknowledge." *Belligerent Muse: Five Northern Writers and How They Shaped Our Understanding of the Civil War*, 173.

John William De Forest was another important exception to prevailing trends, and his 1867 novel *Miss Ravenel's Conversion from Secession to Loyalty* contains stark depictions of the brutality of war. "With the exception of Bierce," David Blight proposes, "no other American writer wrote of war quite as realistically . . . until after World War I." *Race and Reunion*, 151.

35. William Preston Johnston, "Albert Sidney Johnston at Shiloh," *B&L*, 1:564. Blight calls attention to the reconciliationist agenda of the *Battles and Leaders* series. See *Race and Reunion*, 175.

Grant disparaged Johnston's account, which he read while writing his book:

> The description of the battle of Shiloh given by Colonel Wm. Preston Johnston is very graphic and well told. The reader will imagine that he can see each blow struck, a demoralized and broken mob of Union soldiers, each blow sending the enemy more demoralized than ever towards the Tennessee River, which was a little more than two miles away at the beginning of the onset. If the reader does not stop to inquire why, with such Confederate success for more than twelve hours of hard fighting, the National troops were not all killed, captured or driven into the river, he will regard the pen picture as perfect. But I witnessed the fight from the National side from eight o'clock in the morning until night closed the contest. I see but little in the description that I can recognize.

Grant's claim, "I see but little in the description that I can recognize," has almost as much to do with Johnston's style as it does with his insistence on the rebel domination of the field. In contrast to Johnston's "pen picture," Grant's own description of Shiloh is largely clinical. "His mind," Edmund Wilson noted, "seems so firm and clear that no agony or horror can cloud it." The scene was grotesque; Grant saw no need to heighten it. Blight suggests "tragedy almost grips" Grant, "but only momentarily," in the description of one open field "so covered with the dead that it would have been possible to walk across the clearing, in any direction, stepping on dead bodies, without a foot touching the ground."[36] The image of a battlefield carpeted with corpses is a frequent feature of period war writing. In Grant it comes to seem almost an indulgence, so relentless is his commitment to the businesslike depiction of winning a war. Grant's letters often reveal a different, more emotional attitude, but a public account of battle demanded a different register, one that sounds as if it belongs to the next century. It is no accident that the modernist Gertrude Stein found the general's prose so congenial.

Grant's rejection of Johnston's "pen picture" also reveals a fundamental challenge in representing war. Stendhal, the French novelist who had seen service as an administrator in the French army, captures a similar alienation in his 1839 novel *The Charterhouse of Parma*, which opens with an account of his callow protagonist, Fabrizio del Dongo, searching for adventure in the

---

36. Wilson, *Patriotic Gore*, 152; Blight, *Race and Reunion*, 214.

Napoleonic Wars. Fabrizio ends up sleeping through much of the Battle of Waterloo. He comes away with a saber cut in the thigh and a rather confused sense of what actually transpired. When, laid up in an inn at Amiens, he subsequently reads a newspaper account of the event, he cannot reconcile it with his own experience:

> Fabrizio became an entirely different man, so many and so deep were his reflexions upon the things which had just happened to him. He remained a child only on this one point: had what he had seen been a battle and, furthermore, had this battle been Waterloo? For the first time in his life, he took pleasure in reading; he still hoped to find in the newspapers or in the accounts of battle some description that might allow him to recognize the places he had passed through with Marshal Ney's escort, and later with the other general.[37]

Many Civil War soldiers likewise searched futilely in print for the war in which they had fought.

Grant wasn't the only one dissatisfied with Johnston. Confederate officers couldn't recognize the battle he described either, but their quarrel rested on different grounds. As Grant noted, the loser's narrative is necessarily one of "ifs." Johnston's death left Beauregard in charge. And Beauregard's decision to halt the attack late on the first day—and the order to retreat the next, after his reorganized and reinforced enemy rallied—earned him many critics. The feud between Johnston's partisans, including Confederate president Jefferson Davis, and Beauregard's defenders raged on through the latter half of the century.

The highly partisan yet trenchant South Carolina diarist Mary Chesnut, who as a member of Jefferson and Varina Davis's inner circle had ready access to all the news and gossip, recorded the (in fact, false) reports then circulating in Richmond about Beauregard's behavior on the battlefield: "There is grief enough for Albert Sidney Johnston now," she noted on April 15, 1862, "we begin to see what we have lost. We were pushing them into the river when General Johnston was wounded. Beauregard was lying in his tent, at the rear, in a green sickness—melancholy—but no matter what the name of the malady. He was too slow to move, and lost all the advantage gained by

---

37. Stendhal, *The Charterhouse of Parma*, trans. Richard Howard (New York: Modern Library, 2000), 73.

our dead hero. Without him there is no head to our Western army."[38] This is of a piece with William Preston Johnston's account of Beauregard, who, he maintains, was "two miles in the rear, with the *débris* of the army surging back upon him, the shells bursting around him, sick with his two months' previous malady," imagining "a wreck" at the front. "Complete victory was in his grasp," Johnston insists, "and he threw it away."[39]

One of Beauregard's staff officers, Alexander Robert Chisolm, observed that Johnston's version of events would have been more persuasive had its author actually "been present on the field." Chisolm, who claimed the advantage of "personal knowledge acquired as an eyewitness and aide-de-camp," insisted that Johnston's death did not materially affect the command and control of Confederate forces.[40] Indeed, Private Sam Watkins, who was on the battlefield that day, suggests that the soldiers were largely unaware of the general's death: "Advancing a little further on, we saw General Albert Sidney Johns[t]on. . . . We saw some little commotion among those who surrounded him, but we did not know at the time that he was dead. The fact was kept from the troops."[41]

Beauregard, who was subsequently relieved when a few months after Shiloh he withdrew from Corinth, the railroad junction to which he had retreated after the battle, might have defended his reputation in various ways. What makes the defense he ultimately mounted in an article in the *North American Review* worth lingering over is that it entailed taking responsibility for everything rather than attempting to escape blame for the retreat. Beauregard insists that he was the author of the battle from first to last: "If such a plan was ever devised by General Johnston, he expressed it to no one; gave no instructions to carry it out; and has left no document—not a written line—to prove that such a thought had ever occurred to him. . . . The entire conception of the campaign had been mine." Alluding to William Preston Johnston's article, Beauregard writes, "'Monday,' it has been said, 'was Gen-

38. Mary Boykin Chesnut, *A Diary from Dixie*, ed. Isabella D. Martin and Myrta Lockett Avary (New York: D. Appleton, 1906), 156. Martin and Avary sanitized Chesnut's diary, eliminating some of her most incisive critiques of the slaveholding South. For a more complete edition of the diary, which she continued to revise after the war until her death in 1886, see *Mary Chesnut's Civil War*, ed. C. Vann Woodward (New Haven, CT: Yale University Press, 1981).

39. Johnston, "Albert Sidney Johnston at Shiloh," *B&L*, 1:568.

40. A. R. Chisolm, "The Shiloh Battle-Order and the Withdrawal Sunday Evening," *B&L*, 1:606

41. Sam R. Watkins, *"Co. Aytch," Maury Grays, First Tennessee Regiment; or, A Side Show of the Big War* (Chattanooga, TN: Times Printing, 1900), 33.

Henri de Toulouse-Lautrec, *Napoleon, 1895. Metropolitan Museum of Art, Bequest of Scofield Thayer, 1982.*

eral Beauregard's battle.' It was, unquestionably; but not more than the battle of Sunday, for I directed the general movements of the army on both days." Contributing to Beauregard's frustration was the fact that he later lost control of the battle narrative altogether: "Contrary to all military usage, these reports were sent direct to the War Department, instead of being forwarded through me. Hence the errors, discrepancies, and misinterpretations to be found in certain portions of them."[42] He and many officers on both sides spent the rest of their lives trying to regain their hold on the story of what really happened at Shiloh.

One of the beliefs shared by the otherwise antagonistic champions of Johnston and Beauregard was a confidence in the ability of great men to direct events. This understanding of history was simultaneously coming under attack by Leo Tolstoy in *War and Peace* (1869), written while the American Civil War raged. Tolstoy elsewhere reckoned the martial "greatness of Napoleon, Caesar or Washington" as "only moonlight by the sun of Lincoln," who, Tolstoy explained, "was a universal individualist who wanted

---

42. Pierre G. T. Beauregard, *B&L*, 2nd ser., 5:250, 262–63, 268.

to see himself in the world—not the world in himself."[43] Tolstoy's novel advances a theory in which historical forces eclipse individual agency. It thus calls into question the actual power of the "great man" being celebrated at the time by Thomas Carlyle (the author of a monumental history of the French Revolution), and other nineteenth-century thinkers. Napoleon only seems to be "the force that guides" events, Tolstoy insists in *War and Peace*; in fact, the emperor is like "a child, sitting in a carriage, pulling the straps within it, and fancying he is moving it along."[44] The closest thing to control achieved by Tolstoy's generals is that of Kutuzov, the Russian commander in chief, who understands that his will is subordinate to the spirit of the Russian people, his destiny but a matter of historical contingency.

A century after Tolstoy's novel, in the 1960s, the British historian E. H. Carr would dismiss both Carlyle's notion that "history is the biography of great men"—Carr called it the "Bad King John theory . . . the view that what matters in history is the character and behaviour of individuals"—and also the theories of "divine providence, world spirit, manifest destiny, history with a capital H, or any other of the abstractions which have sometimes been supposed to guide the course of events." Rather, Carr insists, "the actions of individuals are never performed in isolation," nor does a given action always realize an actor's intentions; nevertheless, "social forces" derive from the actions of great numbers of individuals.[45] Perhaps nowhere does the complexity for which Carr advocates appear more frustrating—and what he calls the "childlike" attraction of the Bad King John theory appear more comforting—than in the murky arena of war. Given the chaos of battle, the friction—to borrow Clausewitz's word for "the force that makes the apparently easy so difficult"— who can wonder at the strong, enduring desire to attribute both victory and defeat to the force of individual personality. It is force that dominates the twentieth-century French philosopher Simone Weil's analysis of the relationship between war and individuals. In her analysis of Homer's *Iliad*, Weil contends: "The true hero, the true subject, the center of the *Iliad* is force. Force employed by man, force that enslaves man, force before which man's flesh shrinks away. In this work, at all times, the human spirit is shown as modified by its relations with force, as swept away, blinded, by the very force it imagined

---

43. S. Stakelberg, "Great Russian Tells of Reverence for Lincoln Even Among Barbarians," *New York World*, February 7, 1909; rpt. as "Tolstoi Holds Lincoln World's Greatest Hero," in *The Lincoln Anthology: Great Writers on His Life and Legacy from 1860 to Now*, ed. Harold Holzer (New York: Library of America, 2009), 390–91.

44. Leo Tolstoy, *War and Peace*, trans. Constance Garnett (New York: John Lane, 1911), 1269.

45. Edward Hallett Carr, *What Is History?* (New York: Vintage, 1961), 55–69.

it could handle, as deformed by the weight of the force it submits to."[46] No individual, in Weil's account, can exert himself against the force of war.

Yet Clausewitz, whose treatise *On War* was first published in 1832, and first translated into English in 1873, holds out the possibility that a great general can indeed influence the course of events. The root of "military genius," he argues, is the ambition that fosters in a commander "a personal, almost proprietary interest in every aspect of fighting, so that he turns each opportunity to best advantage" and infuses "this spirit of endeavor" throughout an army to make it "victorious."[47] The figure of the lone military genius—the great general imposing his will on the sweep of battle—has long been a staple of imaginative literature. Take, for example, the eighteenth-century British poet Joseph Addison's commemoration in "The Campaign" of the Duke of Marlborough's generalship at the Battle of Blenheim (1704). "Amidst confusion, horror, and despair," Marlborough, as Addison depicts him, "Examined all the dreadful scenes of war; / In peaceful thought the field of death surveyed, / To fainting squadrons sent the timely aid, / Inspired repulsed battalions to engage, / And taught the doubtful battle where to rage."[48] Marlborough's imposition of will on the battle is echoed in the resistless march of Addison's heroic couplets (rhymed lines of iambic pentameter), and battle lines resolve themselves into a clarity matched by the lines on the page. Poetry possesses an organizing force and imaginative coherence usually unavailable to prose. The flood of memoirs and histories in the half century following the Civil War manifested not only a desire to make sense of the outcome by assigning responsibility to individual heroes and villains but also the impossibility of such explanations.

In the writing of Don Carlos Buell, also a contributor to the *Battles and Leaders* series, we discover yet another combatant fighting to set the record straight. Buell appends a note to his account of Shiloh in which he addresses the question of which perspective he ought to adopt to tell the story of the battle: "When this article was urged upon me . . . I was advised by friends in whose judgment I have great confidence, to write an *impersonal* account of

46. Clausewitz, *On War*, 121. Simone Weil, "The Iliad, or the Poem of Force," *War and the Iliad*, trans. Mary McCarthy (New York: New York Review Books, 2005), 3.

47. Clausewitz, *On War*, 105.

48. *Selections from the Works of Joseph Addison*, ed. Edward Bliss Reed (New York: Henry Holt, 1906), ll. 281–86.

the battle." However, he soon realized that impersonality was "impracticable." An impersonal account, he continues,

> would ignore the characteristics which have made the battle of
> Shiloh the most famous, and to both sides the most interesting of
> the war. The whole theme is full of personality. The battle might be
> called, almost properly, a personal one. It was ushered in by faults
> that were personal, and the resistance that prolonged it until succor
> came was personal.[49]

What makes Shiloh so "interesting," then, is its abundance of personality.
What Buell really means by "interesting," of course, is that the battle was
a near-disaster directly attributable to the personal qualities of Sherman and
Grant, which manifested themselves in unpreparedness and desperation, if also
in "resistance." The "succor" Buell delivers seems somehow to counteract that
personality. Here's how Buell describes his own entrance onto the scene:

> At the moment near the close of the day when the remnant of the
> retrograding army was driven to refuge in the midst of its mag-
> azines, with the triumphant enemy at half-gunshot distance, the
> advance division of a reënforcing army arrived on the opposite bank
> of the river, crossed, and took position under fire at the point of
> attack; the attacking force was checked, and the battle ceased for
> the day. The next morning at dawn the reënforcing army and a
> fresh division belonging to the defeated force advanced against the
> assailants, followed or accompanied by such of the broken columns
> of the previous day as had not lost all cohesion, and after ten hours
> of conflict drove the enemy from the captured camps and the field.

In the years since the battle, however, what seems a straightforward story
had been so thoroughly transformed by "the responsible actors in the critical drama" that, Buell insists, "now it is virtually declared by the principals
themselves, that the Army of the Ohio was an unnecessary intruder in the
battle, and that the blood of more than two thousand of its members shed
on that field was a gratuitous sacrifice."[50] In his obituary of Buell, who died

---

49. Don Carlos Buell, "Shiloh Reviewed," *B&L*, 1:535.

50. Buell, "Shiloh Reviewed," *B&L*, 1:487–88.

in 1898, fellow Union general William Farrar Smith kept the feud alive by alluding to a "malignant hostility" that eventually hounded Buell out of the Civil War army.[51]

It is significant that Buell, rather than claiming the role of military genius, submerges himself within the army he led. He cannot let the record stand because it effectively "left out of their place in the combat" the "twenty thousand . . . soldiers of the Army of the Ohio." This is consistent with his notion that "the ties of discipline" in an army minimize the potentially deleterious effects of personality. In Grant's army at Shiloh he saw only indiscipline: "An unbroken tide of disaster had obliterated the distance between grades, and brought all men to the standard of personal qualities. The feeble groups that still clung together were held by force of individual character more than by discipline, and a disbelief in the ability of the army unaided to extricate itself from the peril that environed it, was, I do not hesitate to affirm, universal. In my opinion, that feeling was shared by the commander himself."[52] War is often regarded, especially but not exclusively by modern writers, as the obliteration of personality—something that representations of it often fight against in their depictions of individual acts of heroism or resistance—yet here in Buell's account we find that the military discipline that achieves victories seems to ensure the successful erasure of personality.

Buell's version has a particular agenda, but it emphasizes what I have been trying to suggest all along, namely that combatant accounts of the Civil War repeatedly call attention to the liability of personal perspective. The unreliability of a representation may owe to the nature of the battle itself: "how little the common soldier knew of the actual situation," Leander Stillwell, a soldier in Buell's army, noted of his experience at Shiloh. Or it may owe to the inherent limits of a soldier's perspective: Buell calls his a "fragmentary treatment," while Ambrose Bierce claims that "incidents" in his narrative "necessarily group themselves about my own personality as a center." As the postwar feuds to which I have alluded suggest, it can also owe to the teller's thwarted ambition, injured reputation, or wounded honor.[53]

If, as the Confederate soldier Sam Watkins suggests in his diary, "about

51. William Farrar Smith, "Don Carlos Buell," *Thirtieth Annual Reunion of the Association of Graduates of the United States Military Academy*, June 7, 1899 (Saginaw, MI: Seemann & Peters, 1899), 116.

52. Buell, "Shiloh Reviewed," *B&L*, 1:529, 522.

53. Leander Stillwell, *The Story of a Common Soldier of Army Life in the Civil War 1861–1865*, 2nd ed. (N.p.: Franklin Hudson, 1920), 51; Buell, "Shiloh Reviewed," *B&L*, 1:535; Bierce, "What I Saw of Shiloh," *Collected Works*, 1:257.

all that a private soldier ever knows of a battle" are the orders he receives—
"He can see the smoke rise and the flash of the enemy's guns, and he can hear
the whistle of the minnie and cannon balls, but he has got to load and shoot
as hard as he can tear and ram cartridge"[54]—it is also true that a commander,
especially in an era of extended battle lines, can never see everything at once,
the way Wellington might have done at Waterloo. Of course there were
some who claimed that no one who was not there could know the truth, but,
as much contemporary writing reveals, the fact of having been there—of
having seen the elephant, in the parlance of the time—served as no guaran-
tor of special insight or understanding.

The Civil War correspondent Sylvanus Cadwallader begins his memoir
Three Years with Grant with a story that illustrates the fundamental unreliability of the war story. He calls attention to a strange phenomenon in the
early days of the war, when veterans were still uncommon. At that time, he
explains, the public accorded to soldiers a "wisdom" commensurate with
"the number of wounds each received in battle." Cadwallader refers to such
men as "Sir Oracles." He then records a fight that took place on a train from
Chicago to Grant's headquarters in Cairo, Illinois, between two men over
what one of them, a captain, calls Grant's "shameful" behavior at Shiloh. It
is at this point that the man sitting opposite Cadwallader, whom he refers to
as "little" and "bilious," intervenes:

> "You seem to know all about the battle of Shiloh," continued
> the little bilious questioner.
>
> "I have a right to know," replied the Captain, bracing up, "I
> went through it from beginning to end." . . .
>
> "I am always willing to overlook and forgive misstatements
> about men and events—"
>
> "But I am not mistaken about what happened, and what came
> under my own observation," hotly replied the Captain.
>
> "—but," continued the little one, "when a man pretending to
> be a gentleman, and an officer, makes slanderous charges against
> a friend of mine; claims to have witnessed what I know never
> occurred; and to have heard orders which I know were never given,
> I intend to clinch his lies on the spot. You are a liar I know. You are

---

54. Watkins, *"Co. Aytch,"* 31.

a coward, I believe. I'll bet ten to one you were not in the battle of Shiloh."

> The Captain sprang to his feet and began to bluster and threaten to fight. . . . Till then but two men had avowed themselves for Gen. Grant. But the audacity of the smaller man, and his determined defense of an absent friend against all odds, struck a responsive chord in most of those present. A general roar of shouts, yells and guffaws burst from all.[55]

Cadwallader subsequently reveals the man's identity as Theodore S. Bowers, a member of Grant's staff.[56] The vignette at once endorses and calls into question the guarantee of eyewitness authenticity. Only eyewitnesses know what really happened, but if anyone can claim to be an eyewitness, who can distinguish false from true reports?

This constellation of accounts suggests how treacherous the representation of war once seemed at least to some of those who wished to record it. Today, by contrast, the cult of experience seems to have a near stranglehold on representations of war. The World War I historian Hew Strachan proposes that the massive scale of warfare in the twentieth century weakened the distinction between combatants and noncombatants and thus also "increased the number of potential war writers with first-hand experience."[57] In the twenty-first century, the phenomenon of limited war fought by comparatively few combatants has yielded a correspondingly small pool of firsthand witnesses who jealously guard their vantage point from a civilian population that for the most part willingly cedes the field and persists in an often-willful ignorance of war. Cadwallader's observation about veteran authority in the very early days of the Civil War, when those veterans made up such a small percentage of the population, might also go some way toward explaining today's atmosphere.

In one of the stories in his 2015 collection *Thirteen Ways of Looking*, "What Time Is It Now, Where Are You?," the Irish-American writer Colum

---

55. Sylvanus Cadwallader, *Three Years with Grant*, ed. Benjamin P. Thomas (Lincoln: University of Nebraska Press, 1996), 7–9.

56. As this anecdote reveals, Bowers was fiercely devoted to Grant. Sadly, Bowers died on March 6, 1866. Late for a train on which he was supposed to join Grant, Bowers attempted to jump from the platform as the consist was rolling out of the station. He was caught between two cars and, as Grant himself described it, "instantly crushed to death." Letter to Lorenzo Bowers, March 7, 1866, *PUSG*, 16:98. Bowers was only thirty-four.

57. Hew Strachan, "The Idea of War," *Cambridge Companion to War Writing*, 8.

McCann enters the consciousness of a civilian writer who has accepted a magazine commission for a New Year's Eve story. McCann's story starts in spring. By early summer his unnamed writer has "landed on the idea that he could perhaps defy his own notions of what a New Year's Eve story could achieve and tell a military tale, perhaps the portrait of a soldier somewhere far away, a young American, say, in a distant land. He could find himself, say, in a barracks on New Year's Eve in Afghanistan." McCann's thought-experiment continues to unspool, effectively working out the "parallel" wars of soldier and poet that Wallace Stevens posits in the final section of "Notes Toward a Supreme Fiction," where he suggests that the two figures meet only as "shadows" or perhaps in a book or a letter or, in the case of McCann's story, through a satellite phone that "rings and rings and rings."[58]

Over the course of the story's several sections the writer pushes further and further into the marine's world as she waits alone in an Afghan outpost. In McCann's several experiments there are perhaps teasing hints of the twentieth-century war story's most common registers: the persistent romance of the exotic, the disaffection inherited from the British poets of World War I and modified into a kind of cynical surrealism by American writers of the Vietnam War experience like Tim O'Brien and Michael Herr, the innocence recovered so that it can be again destroyed. Yet McCann's story, giving itself entirely to the imagination, refuses each of these in turn. In a 2015 *New York Times* review of McCann's book, the novelist Jonathan Dee proposes that this story is in fact "a rebuke" to what he perceives to be the dominant mode of war fiction today. Dee impersonates its voice of exclusivity: "[W]e can't understand what it was like, . . . nobody can possibly understand what it was like, . . . returning vets are constantly victimized by our inability to understand what it was like."[59] The school of exclusivity rests on an abdication of a responsibility to communicate on one hand and to imagine on the other. Nevertheless, as a reading of even a small sampling of Civil War narratives I hope suggests, there is another American tradition of representing war, one in which the near-impossibility of understanding was not the unique curse of the noncombatant but a universal condition.

---

58. Colum McCann, "What Time Is It Now, Where Are You?" *Thirteen Ways of Looking* (New York: Random House, 2016), 147–48, 158; Wallace Stevens, "Notes Toward a Supreme Fiction," *Transport to Summer* (1942), *Collected Poetry & Prose*, ed. Frank Kermode and Joan Richardson (New York: Library of America, 1997), 352.

59. Jonathan Dee, review of *Thirteen Ways of Looking*, by Colum McCann, "Inescapable Rhythms," *New York Times*, November 22, 2015, p. BR13.

Ears to the Rail: Attributes of Grant's Leadership

If Shiloh offers a fine case study in the slipperiness of war narratives, the battle and its aftermath also provide an important window onto the personality and leadership of its putative victor. The North celebrated the Union victory, but if Grant was credited with ultimately bringing some order out of the chaos, he was also blamed for the Union's initial lack of preparedness. Shiloh turned out to be prelude to a period of exile for him. When Halleck arrived a few days after the battle to take command of the federal armies in the West, he shunted Grant off to the extraneous role of "second-in-command," thereby ensuring that he effectively commanded nothing: "I was," Grant recalls, "little more than an observer." In his *Autobiography* General Lew Wallace describes a meeting with Grant during this period: "The conversation was chiefly remarkable in that he made no allusion to his treatment by General Halleck—neither by voice, look, nor manner did he betray any resentment. That very silence on his part touched me the more keenly."[60] This state of affairs persisted until the fall, when Halleck returned to Washington. In the meantime, with Sherman's encouragement, Grant decided not to ask for a transfer but rather to wait and to watch. It is during this time, in the wake of Shiloh, that I would like to pick up the story.

Beauregard's Confederate forces had retreated about twenty miles south, to Corinth, Mississippi. Corinth was at once a miserable backwater— malaria, swamps, dust inches thick in the streets—and a railroad boomtown: the junction of two of the most important Confederate railroads, the Mobile and Ohio and the Memphis and Charleston. The railroads still cross in Corinth: Norfolk Southern and Kansas City freight trains roll through every day. Missing an opportunity to seize the advantage over his defeated enemy, Halleck amassed a force of 100,000 troops before marching south to Corinth on April 30. It took nearly a month to move this vast army approximately twenty miles. And as it inched southward, the Confederates were preparing to evacuate Corinth. In his *Memoirs* Sherman records that on May 29 the Union forces "heard unusual sounds in Corinth, the constant whistling of locomotives, and soon after daylight . . . a series of explosions followed by a dense smoke rising high over the town."[61] Grant suggests that at least to some expert Yankee listeners rebel intentions had become unmistakable a few days before:

---

60. Wallace, *Autobiography*, 2:576.

61. Sherman, *Memoirs*, 1:252–53.

Union Advance from Shiloh to Corinth. *West Point Atlas of the Civil War. Courtesy of Department of History, USMA.*

Trains of cars were heard coming in and going out of Corinth constantly. Some of the men who had been engaged in various capacities on railroads before the war claimed they could tell, by putting their ears to the rail, not only which way the trains were moving but which trains were loaded and which were empty. They said loaded trains had been going out for several days and empty ones coming in. Subsequent events proved the correctness of their judgment.

Halleck was certain he had a fight on his hands, but his army, in Grant's words, in the end "took position without opposition. Everything had been destroyed or carried away." Grant notes that Beauregard even "instructed his soldiers to cheer on the arrival of every train to create the impression

among the Yankees that reinforcements were arriving." Confederate deceptions fooled Halleck and his subordinate John Pope, the strongly antislavery
general who would go east in the fall to command the Army of the Potomac briefly and unsuccessfully. At Corinth, Pope sent nervous dispatches
to Halleck about what he thought was going on in the town. Halleck, the
historian Brooks Simpson observes, "accepted without question reports that
Beauregard's force was growing exponentially."[62] Under duress, Grant, like
the railroad men, customarily kept his ears to the rail and thus kept rumor
and panic at bay. By means of this image of keeping one's ears to the rail I
wish to suggest three interrelated attributes that distinguished Grant's leadership: calm, attentiveness, and imagination of a very particular kind.

Union veteran S. H. M. Byers, who fought at Iuka, Corinth, Vicksburg,
and Chattanooga and thus had ample opportunity to observe Grant in the
field, recalled that the general possessed "true bravery": in other words, he
was neither fearless nor reckless. "He was eminently and above all things a
cool man, and that, I take it, was, in the exciting times in which he lived,
the first great key to his success. He was not made hilarious by victory, nor
was he depressed by defeat." Byers adds, "The war was Grant's opportunity,
and he was at an age and had the disposition to seize it. But his military
renown was not of luck alone. It was earned blow by blow."[63] The staff officer
Horace Porter relates a vignette that reveals Grant's supreme concentration
and almost animal attunement to his surroundings. On the move toward
Richmond after the Battle of the Wilderness, Grant halted at General Winfield Scott Hancock's headquarters. Still recovering from wounds received at
Gettysburg, Hancock, an aggressive career soldier with combat experience
dating to the Mexican War, traveled by ambulance rather than horseback:

> He was reclining upon one of the seats of the ambulance, convers-
> ing with General Grant, who had dismounted and was sitting on
> the ground with his back against a tree, whittling a stick, when the
> sound of firing broke forth directly in front. Hancock sprang up,
> seized his sword, which was lying near him, buckled it around his
> waist, and cried: "My horse! my horse!" The scene was intensely
> dramatic, and recalled vividly to the bystanders the cry of [Shake-

62. Brooks D. Simpson, *Ulysses S. Grant: Triumph over Adversity, 1822–1865* (Minneapolis, MN: Zenith, 2014), 142.

63. S. H. M. Byers, "Some Recollections of Grant," *The Annals of the War, Written by Leading Participants North and South*, ed. Alexander K. McClure (Philadelphia: Times Publishing, 1879), 344–45.

speare's] Richard III on the field of Bosworth. Grant listened a moment without changing his position or ceasing his whittling, and then remarked: "They are not fighting; the firing is all on one side. It takes two sides to start a fight." In a few minutes the firing died away, and it was found that the enemy was not advancing. The incident fairly illustrates the contrast in the temperaments of these two distinguished soldiers.[64]

Grant refused to imagine dangers where there were none, and he greeted real peril with absolute equanimity. After watching Grant coolly resume his writing of a dispatch after a shell exploded right in front of him, soldiers of the 5th Wisconsin acquired the habit of saying, "Ulysses don't scare worth a d—n."[65]

Grant had displayed a similar sangfroid at the Wilderness, his first major engagement in the Eastern Theater of the war, during which exceptional confusion prevailed as a result of the wooded terrain and the fires raging within it. It was a battle, Porter explains, that had to be fought "with the ear, and not with the eye." It therefore demanded a leader who was a good listener—someone who kept his ears to the rail. "Without the change of a muscle of his face, or the slightest alteration in the tones of his voice," Porter observes, Grant "quietly interrogated the officers who brought the reports; then, sifting out the truth from the mass of exaggerations, he gave directions for relieving the situation with the marvelous rapidity which was always characteristic of him when directing movements in the face of an enemy."[66]

The Wilderness clearly posed a specific set of challenges, but to appreciate Grant's powers of discernment fully, it is helpful to be reminded how difficult it is—physiologically—to process and interpret sensory perceptions in any battle. Porter describes, for example, the sights and sounds at Petersburg months later after the explosion of a Union mine there resulted in the gaping hole known as the Crater: "The crater was soon filled with our disorganized men, who were mixed up with the dead and dying of the enemy, and tumbling aimlessly about, or attempting to scramble up the other side. The shouting, screaming, and cheering, mingled with the roar of the artillery and

---

64. Porter, *Campaigning*, 80.

65. Evan Rowland Jones, *Lincoln, Stanton and Grant: Historical Sketches* (London: Frederick Warne, [1875]), 281 n. Also quoted in Porter, *Campaigning*, 97.

66. Porter, *Campaigning*, 72, 69.

the explosion of shells, created a perfect pandemonium, and the crater had become a caldron of hell."[67]

A century later, John Steinbeck, serving as a correspondent during World War II, would emphasize the impossibility of witnessing in battle:

> You can't see much of a battle. Those paintings reproduced in history books which show long lines of advancing troops are either idealized or else times and battles have changed. The account in the morning papers of the battle of yesterday was not seen by the correspondent, but was put together from reports.
>
> What the correspondent really saw was dust and the nasty burst of shells, low bushes and slit trenches. He lay on his stomach, if he had any sense, and watched ants crawling.[68]

Keen observer though he was, in order to keep the vast field of battle in view Grant also needed a particular kind of understanding of the terrain in which he was fighting and the imagination to supply what he could not physically see for himself. In Grant's case this project was complicated by the fact that his enemy knew that terrain far better than he did. Clausewitz suggests that this "special gift" can be found in successful gamekeepers, generals, poets, and painters alike:

> It is the faculty of *quickly and accurately grasping the topography of any area* which enables a man to find his way about at any time. Obviously this is an act of the imagination. Things are perceived, of course, partly by the naked eye and partly by the mind, which fills the gaps

---

67. Porter, *Campaigning*, 264. During World War II Ernie Pyle documented the ways in which the ear was deceived at Anzio:

> People who know the sounds of warfare intimately are puzzled and irritated by the sounds up here. For some reason, you can't tell anything about anything.
> . . . You can't gauge distance at all. One shell may land within your block and sound not much louder than a shotgun. Another landing a quarter mile away makes the earth tremble as in an earthquake, and starts your heart to pounding.
> Sometimes you hear them coming, and sometimes you don't. Sometimes you hear the shell whine after you've heard it explode. Sometimes you hear it whine and it never explodes.

Ernie's War: The Best of Ernie Pyle's World War II Dispatches, ed. David Nichols (New York: Simon & Schuster, 1987), 237–38.

68. John Steinbeck, *Once There Was a War* (1943; New York: Penguin Classics, 2007), 131.

Hippolyte Bellangé, *Battle Scene (Waterloo)*, 1815–66. *Metropolitan Museum of Art, Gift of Mr. and Mrs. E. Powis Jones, 1986.*

with guesswork based on learning and experience, and thus constructs a whole out of the fragments that the eye can see; but if the whole is to be vividly present to the mind, imprinted like a picture, like a map, upon the brain, without fading or blurring in detail, *it can only be achieved by the mental gift that we call imagination.*[69]

Porter noted that Grant "had an extraordinary memory as to anything that was presented to him graphically. After looking critically at a map of a locality, it seemed to become photographed indelibly upon his brain, and he could follow its features without referring to it again. Besides, he possessed an almost intuitive knowledge of topography, and never became confused as to the points of the compass."[70] Grant likely cultivated this faculty in his youth on long solitary journeys on horseback and later refined it at West Point, where he practiced drawing and painting under the tutelage of drawing master Robert Weir.

To see the ways in which this capacity manifested itself in the day-to-day conduct of the war, we can look to Horace Porter's description of his

---

69. Clausewitz, *On War*, 109–10.

70. Porter, *Campaigning*, 66. Porter's invocation of photography signals the importance that medium was to have in recording the Civil War.

first meeting with Grant in the besieged city of Chattanooga in 1863. Porter suggests the ways in which Grant's powers of observation translated into a holistic comprehension of circumstances. "Like nearly all men who speak little," writes Porter, Grant "was a good listener." Various officers reported on the situation to their newly arrived commander:

> Grant sat for some time as immovable as a rock and as silent as the sphinx, but listened attentively to all that was said. After a while he straightened himself up in his chair, his features assumed an air of animation, and in a tone of voice which manifested a deep interest in the discussion, he began to fire whole volleys of questions at the officers present. So intelligent were his inquiries, and so pertinent his suggestions, that he made a profound impression upon every one by the quickness of his perception and the knowledge which he had already acquired regarding important details of the army's condition. . . . [H]ardly anybody was prepared to find one who had the grasp, the promptness of decision, and the general administrative capacity which he displayed at the very start as commander of an extensive military division, in which many complicated problems were presented for immediate solution.[71]

Porter is obviously a partisan, yet the qualities he highlights in Grant are not those we might associate with conventional hero worship: they are eminently unromantic and practical. After the meeting, Grant proceeded to write a mountain of dispatches and orders. The biographer William McFeely, never blind to Grant's flaws, recognizes this moment as emblematic of his subject's particular military genius: These "orders and telegrams . . . demonstrated a grasp of the whole western theater of the war. From the disjointed reports he had been given, he put together a coherent picture of the terrain of an area new to him, and of the vast confused array of men who contended for it."[72]

Grant combined the tactical facility of Clausewitz's gamekeeper with the operational and strategic vision of a commander. Comparing Grant with Lee, Fuller proposes, "*Lee* . . . was an indifferent general-in-chief, not because he failed to win battles, but because his strategy, though it often

---

71. Porter, *Campaigning*, 14, 4–5, 8.

72. William S. McFeely, *Grant* (New York: Norton, 1982), 145–46.

led to brilliant tactical successes, was not of the type which could win the war. . . . Grant understood the meaning of grand strategy, *Lee* did not. . . . He never seems to have been able to focus the war as a whole, as one picture. He could see bits of it clearly enough, but the whole was beyond his vision." The "whole" included, of course, the political and social contexts in which the war was being fought—contexts that Fuller, following Clausewitz, understands as inseparable from war's conduct. It was the difference, Fuller concludes, between a man who "joined the South because he was a Virginian" and a man who "threw in his lot with the North because he believed in the United States."[73]

Grant's style was dictated in part by the kind of war he was fighting. As the military historian John Keegan notes in *The Mask of Command*, by the time of the American Civil War, the battlefield had grown so large that it was becoming increasingly difficult for a commander to see everything for himself, as had Alexander the Great and even Napoleon and the Duke of Wellington as recently as Waterloo: "[I]n 1861–5 it was just possible for a general with the will to do so to ride about his line while his army was in action," Keegan writes. "Grant had the will."[74] Grant's natural preference was to see for himself—in this he followed Zachary Taylor—yet there were still times when he was forced to supplement personal reconnaissance by imagining the terrain represented to him by the imperfect maps of the day. When he commanded the entire army, geography made this ability absolutely vital. Reminding us that before he embarked on the campaign through Virginia, Grant had only eight weeks to study the Eastern Theater, stretching south from Washington, D.C., to the Carolinas, Fuller underscores the complexity and geographic immensity of the general's vast overall command, which ranged from New England to New Mexico, from Minnesota to Mississippi. In addition to the "grand operations" in the East, Fuller explains,

> Grant had to decide on many minor ones, his essential dispersions being as follows: guarding prisoners, protecting railways; hunting down guerillas; holding the Sioux and other Indians in check, and watching the frontier of Canada. . . . [I]t is frequently overlooked by those who criticize Grant's Virginian campaign that he had many

---

73. Fuller, *Generalship*, 373, 378.

74. John Keegan, *The Mask of Command* (New York: Penguin, 1987), 221.

other regions to consider. To me it is quite extraordinary how in this
maze of operations he was able to maintain his object.[75]

In order to supervise the whole show, Grant needed to delegate. He gave
free rein to Sherman on the march through Georgia and the Carolinas and
to Sheridan in the Shenandoah Valley. Fuller discerns the same philosophy
in Grant's decision to leave "the detail of executive command" of the Army
of the Potomac to the competent yet conservative and often prickly George
Meade after taking command of the Union Army so that he would have the
freedom to superintend the strategy of the entire war. "This arrangement
was not a perfect one," Fuller observes, yet Grant "saw that he was confronted by a choice of evils, and what was so characteristic of him was, that
in place of seeking for an ideal solution, he chose what he believed to be the
lesser evil of the two, and at once set to work, leaving all detail to Meade—
the man on the spot."[76]

The inability or unwillingness of some of his army and corps commanders to delegate a corresponding autonomy to their subordinates became a
source of inordinate frustration to Grant. Porter records Grant's criticism
of a general who "neglected to give the necessary directions to his troops"
at the Battle of Chattanooga because he was preoccupied with details that
"could have been better performed by any lieutenant of artillery." Like the
railroad men who could tell which way the empty trains were running at
Corinth, the artillery lieutenant at Chattanooga knew his business best; in
micromanaging his subordinate, the unnamed general was distracted from
the appropriate object of his attention. By contrast, Porter notes, Grant was
"one of the few men holding high position who did not waste valuable hours
by giving his personal attention to petty details. . . . He held subordinates to
a strict accountability in the performance of such duties, and kept his own
time for thought."[77]

Grant offers a case study in failure through micromanagement in General Gouverneur K. Warren. Warren served as Meade's technically profi-
cient and personally courageous Chief of Engineers before taking command
of the 5th Corps. As a corps commander, he seems to have been debilitated
by a need to reassesses and reinterpret every order before he executed it.

---

75. Fuller, *Generalship*, 222–23.

76. Fuller, *Generalship*, 212.

77. Porter, *Campaigning*, 26, 250.

Theodore Lyman, a perceptive young officer on Meade's staff, often had "a great mess" locating Warren in the field: "This was Warren's great way, to go about, looking thus after details and making ingenious plans; but it kept him from generalities, and made it hard to find him, so that he finally came to trouble as much by this as by anything else."[78] Grant, who eventually authorized Warren's relief at the Battle of Five Forks, praised his alacrity in an emergency: "He was a man of fine intelligence, great earnestness, quick perception, and could make his dispositions as quickly as any officer, under difficulties where he was forced to act." Yet when Warren was not under immediate attack, a kind of decisional paralysis set in. Grant's assertion that Warren "could see every danger at a glance before he had encountered it" recalls Clausewitz's description of those "intelligent" yet "irresolute" soldiers who lack the "determination" that will "limit the agonies of doubt and the perils of hesitation."[79] Warren's sound tactical sense and "good ideas" notwithstanding, he did not trust "that division commanders could execute an order without his presence." As a result, he caused interminable delays by his insistence on personally monitoring the movements of each of his divisions in turn.

This debilitating "defect," as Grant calls it, ultimately led to Warren's relief. Yet the sympathetic Lyman reveals that there may have been another factor at work: "Almost all officers grow soon callous in the service; not unfeeling, only accustomed, and unaffected by the suffering they see. But Warren feels it a great deal, and that and the responsibility, and many things of course not going to suit him, all tend to make him haggard." On June 3, 1864, Lyman recorded Warren's response to the brutal federal assault at Cold Harbor, Virginia, which yielded approximately 7,000 casualties in one day: "For thirty days now, it has been one funeral procession, past me; and it is too much! To-day I saw a man burying a comrade, and, within half an hour, he himself was brought in and buried beside him. The men need some rest."[80] Perhaps the crushing burden of ordering so many men to their deaths exacerbated Warren's tendency toward perfectionism and encouraged an excessive oversight of subordinates in the vain hope of preventing further loss of life.

---

78. Theodore Lyman, *Meade's Headquarters, 1863–1865: Letters of Colonel Theodore Lyman from the Wilderness to Appomattox*, ed. George R. Agassiz (Boston: Atlantic Monthly Press, 1922), 146 n. 1.

79. Clausewitz, *On War*, 102–3.

80. Lyman, *Meade's Headquarters*, 147.

Grant's demeanor stands in stark contrast to that of Warren in several respects: he did not give voice to the emotional cost of decision making as Warren did before Lyman; his errors most often stemmed from aggressiveness rather than hesitancy; and he was reluctant to interfere with the decisions of subordinates, a deference that sometimes produced costly results.[81] Contemporaries recognized in Grant someone who not only trusted his subordinates and refused to take fright but was also a good listener and accurate reader of situations. To be a good listener, one has to know how to keep silent. This Grant did, earning the (not-always-complimentary) nicknames "American Sphinx," "Ulysses the Silent," and the "Great Unspeakable" along the way: "The general-in-chief invited the most frank and cordial interchange of views," during meetings, and, according to Porter, he "never failed to listen patiently to the more prominent members of his staff. He seldom joined in the discussions, and usually reserved what he had to say till the end of the argument, when he gave his views and rendered his decision."[82]

To Grant's critics, this silence read as dullness or insensitivity. For example, the historian Henry Adams, grandson of John Quincy Adams, popularized the private views of Grant's military secretary Adam Badeau, who eventually quarreled with Grant over his contributions to the composition of the *Personal Memoirs*:

> [Badeau] said that neither he nor the rest of the staff knew why Grant succeeded; they believed in him because of his success. For stretches of time, his mind seemed torpid. [Grant's chief of staff] Rawlins and the others would systematically talk their ideas into it, for weeks, not directly, but by discussion among themselves, in his presence. In the end, he would announce the idea as his own, without seeming conscious of the discussion; and would give the orders to carry it out with all the energy that belonged to his nature. They could never measure his character or be sure when he would act. They could never follow a mental process in his thought. They were not sure that he did think.

A sharp-tongued lover of political gossip who was certainly embittered by his failure to receive an appointment in Grant's administration, Adams himself

---

81. See, for example, the fiasco of the Battle of the Crater at Petersburg, Virginia, in chapter 57.

82. Porter, *Campaigning*, 196, 114.

was nonetheless alert to the specific circumstances in which Grant thrived: namely, emergency. Adams perceived in Grant a "type" that would have seemed "pre-intellectual, archaic . . . even to cave-dwellers." Grant comes to seem a kind of golem—an automaton involuntarily roused to pitches of energy but ultimately incapable of reflection: "the intellect counted for nothing;—only the energy counted. . . . When in action he was superb and safe to follow; only when torpid he was dangerous."[83]

The faculties I have enumerated enabled Grant to make decisions and to take responsibility for them *in extremis*. That was the nature of his appeal to Lincoln, who had struggled with a series of noisy, indecisive, dilatory generals before giving Grant command of the entire Union army in March of 1864. I have discussed the kind of imagination Grant so clearly possessed, but his decision-making powers owed to his lack of another kind of imagination, which Clausewitz, Fuller, and others describe as the tendency to conjure every possible danger—the very tendency that Grant himself attributed to the otherwise estimable Warren. Of course the one time in his life that Grant did not maintain his silence was in his *Personal Memoirs*, and in its pages one can discern his cultivation of the coolness, common sense, and iron concentration that made victory possible.

Not infrequently, on a Sunday afternoon, as the church bells sound through Morningside Heights, I make my way uptown for a visit to the General Grant National Memorial, a.k.a. "Grant's Tomb." Dedicated in 1897, this massive granite pile was modeled after Mausolus's at Halicarnassus, a marble wonder of the world built to house the remains of a fourth-century BCE king of Caria, in Asia Minor, and subsequently destroyed. Groucho Marx long ago turned the tomb into a joke by asking who was buried there, and the memorial's neglect has periodically provoked Grant's relatives to threaten to

---

83. Henry Adams, *The Education of Henry Adams* (Boston: Houghton Mifflin, 1918), 264–65. In print Badeau was far more complimentary about Grant. He called particular attention to "the steadiness of nerve that bore him up amid carnage and apparent disaster; and, above all, the supreme self-control that preserved him always calm and unruffled, without elation in victory or despondency in adverse fortune." *Military History of Ulysses S. Grant*, vol. 3 (New York: D. Appleton, 1881), 144. On Grant's silence, see also Fuller, *Generalship*, ix, 192. Bruce Catton accounted for the difference between Grant's military and political leadership by proposing, "None of the great qualities that had served him so well during the war was of any use now. The very simplicity of his nature, which made him cut problems down to a few fundamentals, was a handle for the extremists to grip while they struggled to preserve their power." *Grant and the American Military Tradition*, 179.

remove his remains to Ohio. On one occasion I overheard one tourist say to another: "I didn't even know we had a president named Grant, did you?" When I visit, I think chiefly of Grant the writer rather than of the president or even the general. He would have found the place far too quiet: no shells falling, nothing more than the occasional whispered conversation to stimulate his concentration.

Eagle in front of Grant's Tomb, New York, New York. *Photograph by Elizabeth D. Samet.*

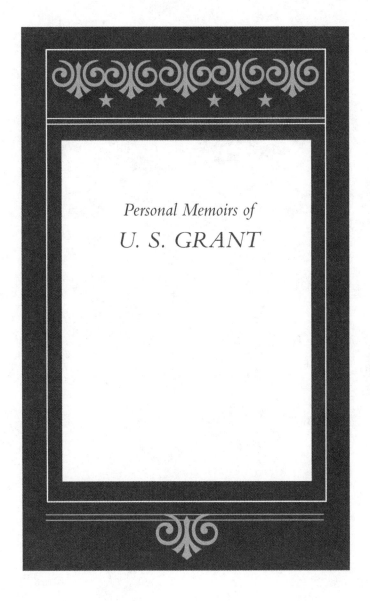

Personal Memoirs of

U. S. GRANT

VOLUME I

These volumes are
dedicated to the American
Soldier and Sailor.

U. S. Grant.

New York City
May 23d 1885.

Dedication page, first edition of *Personal Memoirs*, 1885.

Preface

M an proposes and God disposes."[1] There are but few important events in the affairs of men brought about by their own choice.

Although frequently urged by friends to write my memoirs I had determined never to do so, nor to write anything for publication. At the age of nearly sixty-two I received an injury from a fall, which confined me closely to the house while it did not apparently affect my general health. This made study a pleasant pastime. Shortly after, the rascality of a business partner developed itself by the announcement of a failure.[2] This was

---

1. The expression is proverbial. It can be found across cultures and religions, from the Old Testament to the Hindu *Bhagavadgītā*. A familiar adage in nineteenth-century America, it appears in the writings of Grant's contemporaries, including Abraham Lincoln and the Congregationalist minister and activist Theodore Parker. It is also the title of a gruesome 1864 painting by Sir Edwin Landseer, inspired by Sir John Franklin's disastrous British Royal Navy expedition to the Arctic in 1845.

2. Grant suffered an injury to his leg in late December 1883, when he fell on an icy New York City sidewalk. The unnamed "business partner" was Ferdinand Ward, a missionary's son who became an inveterate con artist. Ward's official partner in the brokerage house of Grant & Ward was actually the former president's second son, Ulysses S. ("Buck") Grant Jr. (1852–1929), but it was Grant himself who invested the capital and ended up losing everything.

Newspapers called Ward the "young Napoleon of finance," but even his own father, as the historian Geoffrey C. Ward notes in a biography of his duplicitous ancestor, admitted he could not be trusted. See *A Disposition to Be Rich: How a Small-Town Pastor's Son Ruined an American President, Brought On a Wall Street Crash, and Made Himself the Best-Hated Man in the United States* (New York: Knopf, 2012), 140.

followed soon after by universal depression of all securities, which seemed to threaten the extinction of a good part of the income still retained, and for which I am indebted to the kindly act of friends. At this juncture the

---

Ward used Grant's name to lure investors. Robust initial returns, satisfying the Gilded Age's hunger for money, delayed discovery of the fraud—as was the case in the more recent Ponzi scheme of Bernard Madoff. Ward was found guilty of grand larceny and sentenced to ten years in Ossining, New York's Sing Sing prison. His trial was front-page news in New York City for months. "Ward in Prison Stripes" announced the *New York Times* after his conviction: "Probably all the ins and outs of Mr. Ferdinand Ward's peculiar financial transactions will never be known unless that gentleman should take it into his head to write an autobiography and therein make a clear breast of the whole business." *New York Times*, November 2, 1885, p. 1.

Of course it was Grant who would write the autobiography; signally, he did not refer to Ward by name within it. Buck's father-in law, the former senator Jerome Chaffee, described Grant's reaction to Ward's "rascality": "No one will ever know the extent of his anguish, not even his own family, for he was the bravest in their presence. I was with him after the exposure of Ward. The General would suffer hours in his large armchair, clutching nervously with his hands at the arm rests, driving his finger-nails into the hard wood. It was a pitiful spectacle. One day he said to me: 'Chaffee, I could kill Ward, as I would a snake. I believe I should do it, too, but I do not wish to be hanged for the killing of such a wretch.'" Chaffee declared that the real cause of Grant's death was not, as the doctors claimed, the cancer in his throat, but rather this betrayal, "a great cancer gnawing at his heart." *The Arizona Sentinel*, September 26, 1885, p. 4.

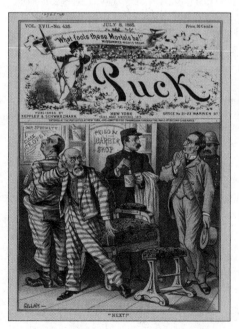

Bernhard Gillam, "NEXT!"
Ferdinand Ward arrives at the prison
barbershop. *Puck*, July 8, 1885.
*Library of Congress, Prints and
Photographs Division, LC-DIG-
ppmsca-28212.*

editor of the *Century Magazine* asked me to write a few articles for him.[3] I consented for the money it gave me; for at that moment I was living upon borrowed money.[4] The work I found congenial, and I determined to continue it. The event is an important one for me, for good or evil; I hope for the former.

In preparing these volumes for the public, I have entered upon the task with the sincere desire to avoid doing injustice to any one, whether on the National or Confederate side, other than the unavoidable injustice of not making mention often where special mention is due. There must be many errors of omission in this work, because the subject is too large to be treated of in two volumes in such way as to do justice to all the officers and men engaged. There were thousands of instances, during the rebellion, of individual, company, regimental and brigade deeds of heroism which deserve special mention and are not here alluded to. The troops engaged in them will have to look to the detailed reports of their individual commanders for the full history of those deeds.[5]

---

3. Grant's article on Shiloh, for which the *Century* paid him $500, was part of a series on the Civil War that ran in the magazine from November 1884–November 1887. The articles, written by high-ranking participants on both sides of the conflict, contributed to a growth in the magazine's circulation from 127,000 to 225,000 within six months. According to the editors, Robert Underwood Johnson and Clarence Clough Buel, this increase translated into an actual readership as large as two million. The series ultimately expanded into a four-volume collection, *Battles and Leaders of the Civil War.* Johnson and Buel explained their aims as follows: "The chief motive has been strict fairness to the testimony of both sides, and the chief endeavors have been to prove every important statement by the "Official Records" and other trustworthy documents, and to spare no pains in the interest of elucidation and accuracy." In addition to capitalizing on the national fascination with the Civil War, Johnson and Buel were eager to instruct the postwar generation as well as to participate in the project of reconciliation between North and South that preoccupied so many Americans during the 1880s and 1890s. The series, the editors explained, "has exerted an influence in bringing about a better understanding between the soldiers who were opposed in that conflict." *B&L*, 1:ix–x.

This grand project of reconciliation between white Americans North and South was made at the expense of African Americans, who were consigned after the official end of Reconstruction in 1877 to the violent midnight of Jim Crow.

4. This "borrowed money" included checks from sympathetic friends and strangers. The most significant loan, $150,000, came from William H. Vanderbilt, to whom Grant then deeded all of his property, including war trophies and memorabilia, which Vanderbilt ultimately donated to the Smithsonian.

5. Readers often comment on Grant's apparently remarkable memory for details. In composing his memoirs, Grant relied on maps and records furnished by his military secretary Adam Badeau and others, but he also had an extraordinary ability to remember

The first volume, as well as a portion of the second, was written before I had reason to suppose I was in a critical condition of health. Later I was reduced almost to the point of death, and it became impossible for me to attend to anything for weeks. I have, however, somewhat regained my strength, and am able, often, to devote as many hours a day as a person should devote to such work.[6] I would have more hope of satisfying the expectation of the public if I could have allowed myself more time. I have used my best

---

features of terrain and other aspects of his war experience. Grenville M. Dodge, an engineer officer in the Civil War, provides an example of Grant's "extraordinary memory":

> During the time General Grant was writing his Memoirs I was in the habit of visiting him when I was in New York, and sitting some hours with him, and he would often read to me some portions of what he had written. Illustrating what an extraordinary memory he had, he read to me a portion of what he had written about me, and the rebuilding of the Nashville & Decatur Railway. As this work had not impressed itself upon my mind as it had upon his, as it was no unusual thing to me, I listened to what he read, and said that my recollection of it was not as he had written it, which seemed to surprise him, and he said if that was so he would have to change it. I said not to change it; that I would go to my office and look over my records, which I did. I had to sit down the next morning and write him a letter, telling him that his recollection of what I had done was absolutely correct, while my own was absolutely wrong, and the chapter stood as he had written it.

Personal Recollections of President Abraham Lincoln, General Ulysses S. Grant and General William T. Sherman (Council Bluffs, IA: Monarch, 1914), 108.

6. Ward's fraud was revealed in May 1884. The Grants spent the summer at their house in Long Branch, New Jersey. Julia Grant describes what happened next:

> It was during that sad summer that the fatal malady first made its appearance in General Grant's throat. There was a plate of delicious peaches on the table, of which the General was very fond. Helping himself, he proceeded to eat the dainty morsel; then he started up as if in great pain and exclaimed: "Oh my. I think something has stung me from that peach." He walked up and down the room and out to the piazza, and rinsed his throat again and again. He was in great pain and said water hurt him like liquid fire. This was the very beginning of his throat trouble.

The Personal Memoirs of Julia Dent Grant (Mrs. Ulysses S. Grant), ed. John Y. Simon (New York: Putnam, 1975; rpt. Carbondale: Southern Illinois University Press, 1988), 328–29.

Grant refused to see a specialist until October, when he was diagnosed with inoperable cancer. He would be dead within the year. The Herculean task of completing the memoirs filled the rest of his days and sustained him through constant pain.

efforts, with the aid of my eldest son, F. D. Grant, assisted by his brothers, to verify from the records every statement of fact given.[7] The comments are my own, and show how I saw the matters treated of whether others saw them in the same light or not.

With these remarks I present these volumes to the public, asking no favor but hoping they will meet the approval of the reader.[8]

U. S. GRANT.

MOUNT MCGREGOR, NEW YORK,

July 1, 1885.

---

7. Julia and Ulysses Grant's oldest child, Frederick Dent Grant (1850–1912), graduated from West Point in 1871. Resigning his commission ten years later, he served in various capacities in civilian life, including minister to Austria and New York City police commissioner. Frederick returned to the army as a volunteer during the Spanish-American War to serve in Puerto Rico and the Philippines. Buck Grant graduated from Harvard University and received a law degree from Columbia. He practiced law in New York City before becoming embroiled with Ward. In 1893, he moved to San Diego, California, where he eventually built the U. S. Grant Hotel. The couple's youngest son, Jesse Root Grant (1858–1934), attended Cornell University and Columbia Law School. In the late 1870s, he joined his parents on their epic world tour, during which he had some remarkable experiences, including supper with Queen Victoria. Jesse published a book about his father in 1925: *In the Days of My Father, General Grant.* Unmentioned here, the Grants' third child, Ellen ("Nellie") Wrenshall Grant Sartoris Jones (1855–1922), was reputed to be her father's favorite. She moved to England after marrying Algernon Sartoris, son of the celebrated English opera singer Adelaide Kemble. The wedding took place in the East Room of the White House in 1874, and made headlines everywhere. But the marriage proved most unhappy, and the couple eventually divorced. Nellie and her children were with Grant at Mount McGregor during his final illness.

8. When P. T. Barnum learned of Grant's financial straits and his decision to make over all of his property, including his memorabilia and trophies, to Vanderbilt, the great promoter came up with a plan:

> Recognizing the fact that people everywhere would feel interested in seeing these trophies, and that I could by exhibiting them in a most elegant and suitable manner throughout the civilized world gratify millions of persons of taste and appreciation, while I could afford to compensate General Grant so liberally for the privilege as to assure him a fine income, I wrote to him. . . .
>
> I called at General Grant's residence soon afterwards, and was politely received by him, his wife, and son, Colonel Frederick Grant.
>
> I said to the General, after our greeting, "General, since your journey around the world you are the best known man on the globe."

"No, sir," replied the General, "your name is familiar to multitudes who never heard of me. Wherever I went, among the most distant nations, the fact that I was an American led to constant inquiries whether I knew Barnum."

Proceeding to the business on which I had called, the General informed me that the trophies were no longer under his control, as Mr. Vanderbilt, after refusing to take them, out of respect to the General, had finally accepted them on condition that after General Grant's decease they should be lodged in some safe public place in Washington, where all could see them.

"After all, Mr. Barnum," said General Grant, "under the present arrangements, everybody who visits Washington can see them."

"Yes, General," I replied, "but millions of persons who will never visit Washington will regret that I had never brought these historical relics where they would see them."

I shall always believe, regardless of any profit (or loss) which might have accrued to me, that my plan was one creditable to all concerned, and that it is to be regretted that it was not carried out.

I was reminded of General Grant's assurance of my name being known to the ends of the earth, when a few weeks later I received a letter addressed to "Mr. Barnum, America."

Life of P. T. Barnum Written by Himself (Buffalo, NY: Courier, 1888), 342–43.

In 2017, Barnum's long-running legacy, the Barnum & Bailey Circus, which began life as P. T. Barnum's Grand Traveling Museum, Menagerie, Caravan & Hippodrome in 1871, finally folded its tent.

Poster for Barnum & Bailey: Greatest Show on Earth, 1915. *From the New York Public Library, http://digitalcollections.nypl.org/items/510d47da-4ecf-a3d9-e040-e00a18064a99.*

Ancestry—Birth—Boyhood

My family is American, and has been for generations, in all its branches, direct and collateral.

Mathew Grant, the founder of the branch in America, of which I am a descendant, reached Dorchester, Massachusetts, in May, 1630.[1] In 1635 he

---

1. Grant's opening chapter is fairly typical of the military memoirs of the period: Sherman, Sheridan, and Longstreet all open their autobiographies with a similar genealogy. Grant's family history accomplishes several things. It marks him as an American of long standing. It also establishes his family's military service, which he traces back to the French and Indian War. Matthew probably sailed on the *Mary and John* from Plymouth, England, in 1630, with the other members of the Dorchester Company. It was the first ship to bring Europeans to Dorchester, Massachusetts. One of the ship's passengers, Roger Clap, describes the harshness of the settlers' early days:

> In our beginning many were in great Straits for want of Provision for themselves and their little Ones. Oh the *Hunger* that many suffered, and saw no hope in an Eye of Reason to be supplied, only by *Clams*, and *Muscles*, and Fish. We did quickly build Boats, and some went a Fishing. But *Bread* was with many a very scarce thing; and *Flesh* of all kinds as scarce. And in those Days, in our Straits, though I cannot say God sent a *Raven* to feed us, as He did the Prophet *Elijah*; yet this I can say to the Praise of God's Glory, that He sent not only poor *ravenous Indians*, which came with their Baskets of Corn on their Backs, to Trade with us, which was a good supply unto many; but also sent *Ships* from *Holland* and from *Ireland* with Provisions, and Indian Corn from *Virginia*, to supply the Wants of his dear Servants in this Wilderness, both for Food and Rayment.

Memoirs of Roger Clap, 1630, Collections of the Dorchester Antiquarian and Historical Society, No. 1. (Boston: Clapp, 1844), 30–31.

moved to what is now Windsor, Connecticut, and was the surveyor for that colony for more than forty years. He was also, for many years of the time, town clerk. He was a married man when he arrived at Dorchester, but his children were all born in this country. His eldest son, Samuel, took lands on the east side of the Connecticut River, opposite Windsor, which have been held and occupied by descendants of his to this day.

I am of the eighth generation from Mathew Grant, and seventh from Samuel. Mathew Grant's first wife died a few years after their settlement in Windsor, and he soon after married the widow Rockwell, who, with her first husband, had been fellow-passengers with him and his first wife, on the ship *Mary and John*, from Dorchester, England, in 1630. Mrs. Rockwell had several children by her first marriage, and others by her second. By intermarriage, two or three generations later, I am descended from both the wives of Mathew Grant.

In the fifth descending generation my great grandfather, Noah Grant, and his younger brother, Solomon, held commissions in the English army, in 1756, in the war against the French and Indians.[2] Both were killed that year.[3]

Understandably, yet evidently to the consternation of the company, some of the original settlers moved further west to Connecticut in 1635. A nineteenth-century record compiled by members of the Dorchester Antiquarian and Historical Society notes that Grant's ancestor was among those who decamped: "Matthew Grant was among the earliest comers, and was made freeman in 1631. He removed to Windsor." *History of the Town of Dorchester, Massachusetts* (Boston: Clapp, 1859), 55.

2. The French and Indian War was the American theater of operations in the Seven Years' War (1756–1763), a global conflict between France and Great Britain. It was also the war that gave George Washington his first experience of combat on a failed expedition to Fort Duquesne, Pennsylvania, where the French had been denying English traders access to routes in the Ohio Valley. Washington informed his brother, "there was something charming in the sound" of whistling bullets. See Letter to John Augustine Washington, May 31, 1754, *The Papers of George Washington: Colonial Series*, vol. 1, ed. W. W. Abbot (Charlottesville: University Press of Virginia, 1983), 119.

In fact, the experience was rather more gruesome than this offhand remark suggests. In the definitive modern history of the war, Fred Anderson proposes that Washington watched helplessly while his Indian allies massacred the French and mutilated their bodies. See *Crucible of War: The Seven Years' War and the Fate of British North America, 1754–1766* (New York: Vintage, 2001), chap 5.

Washington's nineteenth-century hagiographer Mason Weems found even in this sorry episode fodder for myth: "in the *public* mind, he always *rose* as high, or higher, than the others sunk." It was "universally believed," Weems suggests, that had Washington "governed" instead of Virginia governor Robert Dinwiddie, "the fatal Indian war would not have lasted a campaign; and that on the hills of Monongahela, had Washington commanded in place of Braddock, the French and Indians would have been

My grandfather, also named Noah, was then but nine years old. At the breaking out of the war of the Revolution, after the battles of Concord and Lexington, he went with a Connecticut company to join the Continental army, and was present at the battle of Bunker Hill. He served until the fall of Yorktown, or through the entire Revolutionary war.[4] He must, however,

handled very differently." M. L. Weems, *The Life of Washington* (1800; Philadelphia: Allen, 1833), 53–54.

3. Both Solomon and Noah Grant were killed in 1756. Noah saw service as a captain in the Adirondacks with those more celebrated soldiers, Israel Putnam and Robert Rogers (of Rogers' Rangers, a rapidly deployable infantry force employed on scouting missions and other special service). The nineteenth-century historian Francis Parkman provides a dramatic window onto the hardships of the ranging service in this description of a 1759 expedition from his masterpiece, *Montcalm and Wolfe*:

"It is hardly possible," says Rogers, "to describe our grief and consternation." Some gave themselves up to despair. Few but their indomitable chief had strength to go farther. There was scarcely any game, and the barren wilderness yielded no sustenance but a few lily bulbs and the tubers of the climbing plant called in New England the ground-nut. Leaving his party to these miserable resources, and promising to send them relief within ten days, Rogers made a raft of dry pine logs, and drifted on it down the stream, with Captain Ogden, a ranger, and one of the captive Indian boys. They were stopped on the second day by rapids, and gained the shore with difficulty. At the foot of the rapids, while Ogden and the ranger went in search of squirrels, Rogers set himself to making another raft; and, having no strength to use the axe, he burned down the trees, which he then divided into logs by the same process. Five days after leaving his party he reached the first English settlement, Charlestown, or "Number Four," and immediately sent a canoe with provisions to the relief of the sufferers, following himself with other canoes two days later. Most of the men were saved, though some died miserably of famine and exhaustion. Of the few who had been captured, we are told by a French contemporary that they "became victims of the fury of the Indian women," from whose clutches the Canadians tried in vain to save them.

Montcalm and Wolfe, vol. 2, *France and England in North America*, pt. 7 (Boston: Little, Brown, 1888), 257–58.

4. On June 17, 1775, 2,300 British troops under Lord Howe assaulted rebel positions on Breed's Hill on Charlestown's heights. The battle occurred two days after George Washington had been nominated commander of the armies by Congress. Two days after the battle, Washington wrote to a relative, "I am now Imbarkd on a tempestuous Ocean from whence, perhaps, no friendly harbour is to be found." Letter to Burwell Bassett, June 19, 1775, *The Papers of George Washington: Revolutionary War Series*, vol. 1, ed. Philander D. Chase (Charlottesville: University Press of Virginia, 1985), 12.

have been on furlough part of the time—as I believe most of the soldiers of that period were—for he married in Connecticut during the war, had two children, and was a widower at the close. Soon after this he emigrated to Westmoreland County, Pennsylvania, and settled near the town of Greensburg in that county. He took with him the younger of his two children, Peter Grant. The elder, Solomon, remained with his relatives in Connecticut until old enough to do for himself, when he emigrated to the British West Indies.

Grant is effectively claiming that his grandfather served for the duration of the conflict: Bunker Hill followed the opening battle at Lexington and Concord by two months; Yorktown, the final battle of the war, was fought in 1781. While Noah's service may have been a popular family story that later occupied "an important place in adulatory biographies of his grandson," Pulitzer Prize–winning Grant biographer William S. McFeely claims that Noah's service was most probably the stuff of "legend." See McFeely, *Grant: A Biography* (New York: Norton, 1982), 4–5.

The revolutionary generation preoccupied antebellum Americans, and the War for Independence remained a touchstone for both North and South throughout the Civil War. Abraham Lincoln invoked the "iron men" of the Revolution in order to suggest that there had been a falling away from heroic models. See Speech at Chicago, Illinois, July 10, 1858, *The Collected Works of Abraham Lincoln*, ed. Roy P. Basler, 8 vols. (New Brunswick, NJ: Rutgers University Press, 1953), 2:499.

THE LEXINGTON OF 1861.

"The Lexington of 1861," Currier & Ives. *Library of Congress, Prints and Photographs Division, LC-USZC4-1736.*

Not long after his settlement in Pennsylvania, my grandfather, Captain Noah Grant, married a Miss Kelly, and in 1799 he emigrated again, this time to Ohio, and settled where the town of Deerfield now stands. He had now five children, including Peter, a son by his first marriage. My father, Jesse R. Grant, was the second child—oldest son, by the second marriage.

Peter Grant went early to Maysville, Kentucky, where he was very prosperous, married, had a family of nine children, and was drowned at the mouth of the Kanawha River, Virginia, in 1825, being at the time one of the wealthy men of the West.

My grandmother Grant died in 1805, leaving seven children. This broke up the family. Captain Noah Grant was not thrifty in the way of "laying up stores on earth,"[5] and, after the death of his second wife, he went, with the two youngest children, to live with his son Peter, in Maysville. The rest of the family found homes in the neighborhood of Deerfield, my father in the family of Judge Tod, the father of the late Governor Tod, of Ohio. His industry and independence of character were such, that I imagine his labor compensated fully for the expense of his maintenance.

There must have been a cordiality in his welcome into the Tod family, for to the day of his death he looked upon Judge Tod and his wife, with all the reverence he could have felt if they had been parents instead of benefactors. I have often heard him speak of Mrs. Tod as the most admirable woman he had ever known. He remained with the Tod family only a few years, until old enough to learn a trade. He went first, I believe, with his half-brother, Peter Grant, who, though not a tanner himself, owned a tannery in Maysville, Kentucky. Here he learned his trade, and in a few years returned to Deerfield and worked for, and lived in the family of a Mr. Brown, the father of John Brown—"whose body lies mouldering in the grave, while his soul goes marching on."[6] I have often heard my father speak of John Brown, par-

5. The allusion is to Matthew 6:19, here in the King James Version: "Lay not up for yourselves treasures upon earth, where moth and rust doth corrupt, and where thieves break through and steal." It is tempting to wonder whether the thieves alluded to in this verse made Grant think of Ward.

6. The line comes from the "John Brown Song," adapted by soldiers during the war from a contemporary camp-meeting tune. In the tradition of folk music, soldiers added verses as the war went on, and Union and Confederate armies came up with rival versions. It was the same tune to which Julia Ward Howe set "Battle Hymn of the Republic." Biographer Elaine Showalter tells the story of Howe's pivotal encounter with the Union soldiers' rendition:

ticularly since the events at Harper's Ferry. Brown was a boy when they lived in the same house, but he knew him afterwards, and regarded him as a man of great purity of character, of high moral and physical courage, but a fanatic and extremist in whatever he advocated. It was certainly the act of an insane man to attempt the invasion of the South, and the overthrow of slavery, with less than twenty men.[7]

> On November 18, Julia and her companions drove out to watch a parade at Munson's Hill in Northern Virginia. While they were watching, there was an attack by Confederate soldiers on a small group of outliers, and some of the soldiers went to defend them; the parade broke up, and the remaining men were ordered back to their barracks. In the slow drive back to Washington, the Bostonians were surrounded by troops and passed the time by singing army songs including "John Brown's body lies a-mouldering in the ground; his soul is marching on," which had become especially popular with the Massachusetts regiments. "The soldiers seemed to like this," she recalled, "and answered back, 'Good for you!' Mr. Clarke said, 'Mrs. Howe, why do you not write some good words for this stirring tune?' I replied that I had often wished to do this, but as yet had not found in my mind any leading toward it."

Overnight the words apparently came to Howe in a dream. See Elaine Showalter, *The Civil Wars of Julia Ward Howe: A Biography* (New York: Simon & Schuster, 2017), 164.

7. Jesse Grant's frequent talk of Brown suggests the staunchness of his antislavery views. Ulysses's marriage into Julia Dent's slaveholding family would prove a source of family tension; the Grants did not attend the wedding.

The raid on Harpers Ferry took place on October 16–19, 1859, when John Brown and his armed followers seized the federal arsenal. United States Marines commanded by Colonel Robert E. Lee reached the scene on the afternoon of October 17. They besieged Brown's party, which had retreated to the engine house of the arsenal, and captured Brown, who was hanged for treason in December. Brown had already become notorious for his violent campaign in Bleeding Kansas. Herman Melville prefaced his 1866 volume of Civil War poems with "The Portent," a meditation on John Brown written in 1859:

> Hanging from the beam,
>   Slowly swaying (such the law),
> Gaunt the shadow on your green,
>   Shenandoah!
> The cut is on the crown
> (Lo, John Brown),
> And the stabs shall heal no more.
>
> Hidden in the cap
>   Is the anguish none can draw;

My father set up for himself in business, establishing a tannery at Ravenna, the county seat of Portage County. In a few years he removed from Ravenna, and set up the same business at Point Pleasant, Clermont County, Ohio.

During the minority of my father, the West afforded but poor facilities for the most opulent of the youth to acquire an education, and the majority were dependent, almost exclusively, upon their own exertions for whatever learning they obtained. I have often heard him say that his time at school was limited to six months, when he was very young, too young, indeed, to learn

> So your future veils its face,
>   Shenandoah!
> But the streaming beard is shown
> (Weird John Brown),
> The meteor of the war.

Battle-Pieces and Aspects of the War (New York: Harper & Brothers, 1866), 11.

Stephen Vincent Benet would later make the abolitionist Brown the subject of a 15,000-line blank verse epic, *John Brown's Body*, which won the Pulitzer Prize in 1929. Benet's poem was a staple of English classes at West Point for fifty years. For a discussion of its role in the curriculum, see Martin T. Buinicki and David M. Owens, "The Last Campaign of *John Brown's Body*: West Point and America's Forgotten Civil War Epic," *War, Literature & the Arts* 27 (2015): 1–25.

In his novel *Cloudsplitter* Russell Banks offers a vivid explanation of Brown's mission from the perspective of his surviving son Owen:

> Remember, all-out war between the North and the South was unthinkable to us: due to an ancient, deeply ingrained racialism, any war undertaken by the citizens of the North for the purpose of freeing an enslaved people whose skins were black seemed a pure impossibility. We believed instead that the Northerners—when it finally came clear to them what we already knew, that the South now wholly owned the government of the nation—would simply secede from the Union, leaving behind a nation in which a huge number of our fellow Americans and all their unborn progeny were chattel slaves: literal, unrepatriated prisoners-of-war. Before that could happen, we meant to liberate as many of them as possible. And failing that, failing to free our prisoners-of-war prior to the eventual and, as it seemed to us, inevitable cessation of hostilities between the Northern and Southern states, the one side cowardly and the other evil, we meant to slay every slaveholder we could lay our hands on. And those whose throats we could not reach directly or whose heads we could not find in the sights of our guns, we would terrorize from afar, hoping thereby to rouse them to bloody acts of reprisal, which might in turn straighten the spines of our Northern citizenry and bring a few of them over to our side.

Russell Banks, *Cloudsplitter* (New York: HarperPerennial, 1999), 675.

Jesse Grant. *Library of Congress, Prints and Photographs Division, Brady-Handy Collection, LC-DIG-cwpbh-00916.*

much, or to appreciate the advantages of an education, and to a "quarter's schooling" afterwards, probably while living with Judge Tod. But his thirst for education was intense. He learned rapidly, and was a constant reader up to the day of his death—in his eightieth year. Books were scarce in the Western Reserve during his youth, but he read every book he could borrow in the neighborhood where he lived. This scarcity gave him the early habit of studying everything he read, so that when he got through with a book, he knew everything in it. The habit continued through life. Even after reading the daily papers—which he never neglected—he could give all the important information they contained. He made himself an excellent English scholar, and before he was twenty years of age was a constant contributor to Western newspapers, and was also, from that time until he was fifty years old, an able debater in the societies for this purpose, which were common in the West at that time. He always took an active part in politics, but was never a candidate for office, except, I believe, that he was the first Mayor of Georgetown. He supported Jackson for the Presidency; but he was a Whig, a great admirer of Henry Clay, and never voted for any other democrat for high office after Jackson.

My mother's family lived in Montgomery County, Pennsylvania, for several generations. I have little information about her ancestors. Her family took no interest in genealogy, so that my grandfather, who died when I was sixteen years old, knew only back to his grandfather. On the other side, my father took a great interest in the subject, and in his researches, he found that there was an entailed estate in Windsor, Connecticut, belonging to the family, to which his nephew, Lawson Grant—still living—was the heir. He was so much interested in the subject that he got his nephew to empower him to act in the matter, and in 1832 or 1833, when I was a boy ten or eleven years old, he went to Windsor, proved the title beyond dispute, and perfected the claim of the owners for a consideration—three thousand dollars, I think. I remember the circumstance well, and remember, too, hearing him say on his return that he found some widows living on the property, who had little or nothing beyond their homes. From these he refused to receive any recompense.

My mother's father, John Simpson, moved from Montgomery County, Pennsylvania, to Clermont County, Ohio, about the year 1819, taking with him his four children, three daughters and one son. My mother, Hannah Simpson, was the third of these children, and was then over twenty years of age.[8] Her oldest sister was at that time married, and had several children. She still lives in Clermont County at this writing, October 5th, 1884, and is over ninety years of age. Until her memory failed her, a few years ago, she thought the country ruined beyond recovery when the Democratic party lost control in 1860. Her family, which was large, inherited her views, with the exception of one son who settled in Kentucky before the war. He was the only one of the children who entered the volunteer service to suppress the rebellion.

Her brother, next of age and now past eighty-eight, is also still living in Clermont County, within a few miles of the old homestead, and is as active in mind as ever. He was a supporter of the Government during the war, and remains a firm believer, that national success by the Democratic party means irretrievable ruin.

In June, 1821, my father, Jesse R. Grant, married Hannah Simpson. I

8. In comparison to that of her often overbearing husband, the personality of Hannah Grant remains somewhat obscure. Her son rarely mentions her in his letters, and she never visited the White House throughout his presidency. Hypothesizing that she may have suffered from a "psychosomatic disorder," McFeely suggests, "an uncommon detachment existed in the relationship of son to mother." *Grant*, 9.

Nevertheless, Grant's nineteenth-century biographer Hamlin Garland records neighbors' recollections that Grant "got his reticence, his patience, his equable temper," and his good "*sense* from his mother." *Ulysses S. Grant: His Life and Character* (New York: Doubleday & McClure, 1898), 3.

was born on the 27th of April, 1822, at Point Pleasant, Clermont County, Ohio. In the fall of 1823 we moved to Georgetown, the county seat of Brown, the adjoining county east. This place remained my home, until at the age of seventeen, in 1839, I went to West Point.

The schools, at the time of which I write, were very indifferent.[9] There were no free schools, and none in which the scholars were classified. They were all supported by subscription, and a single teacher—who was often a man or a woman incapable of teaching much, even if they imparted all they knew—would have thirty or forty scholars, male and female, from the infant learning the A B C's up to the young lady of eighteen and the boy of twenty, studying the highest branches taught—the three R's, "Reading, 'Riting, 'Rithmetic." I never saw an algebra, or other mathematical work higher than the arithmetic, in Georgetown, until after I was appointed to West Point. I then bought a work on algebra in Cincinnati; but having no teacher it was Greek to me.

My life in Georgetown was uneventful. From the age of five or six until seventeen, I attended the subscription schools of the village, except during the winters of 1836–7 and 1838–9. The former period was spent in Maysville, Kentucky, attending the school of Richardson and Rand; the latter in Ripley, Ohio, at a private sechool. I was not studious in habit, and probably did not make progress enough to compensate for the outlay for board and tuition. At all events both winters were spent in going over the same old arithmetic which I knew every word of before, and repeating: "A noun is the name of a thing," which I had also heard my Georgetown teachers repeat, until I had come to believe it—but I cast no reflections upon my old teacher, Richardson. He turned out bright scholars from his school, many of whom have filled conspicuous places in the service of their States. Two of my contemporaries there—who, I believe, never attended any other institution of learning—have held seats in Congress, and one, if not both, other high offices; these are Wadsworth and Brewster.

---

9. Like that of many of his fellow cadets from the South and West, Grant's schooling was somewhat idiosyncratic, and he was too old to benefit from the Common School movement championed by the reformer Horace Mann in the late 1830s. "Schooling in small-town Ohio in the 1820's and 1830's," Bruce Catton suggests, "was adequate, perhaps, but not fancy." *Grant and the American Military Tradition*, 12.

Jesse's wide reading is noteworthy, and his son's education—culminating in West Point—was clearly central to his father's ambitions for him. In a later chapter Grant mentions his own hopes of one day teaching mathematics.

My father was, from my earliest recollection, in comfortable circumstances, considering the times, his place of residence, and the community in which he lived. Mindful of his own lack of facilities for acquiring an education, his greatest desire in maturer years was for the education of his children. Consequently, as stated before, I never missed a quarter from school from the time I was old enough to attend till the time of leaving home. This did not exempt me from labor. In my early days, every one labored more or less, in the region where my youth was spent, and more in proportion to their private means. It was only the very poor who were exempt. While my father carried on the manufacture of leather and worked at the trade himself, he owned and tilled considerable land. I detested the trade, preferring almost any other labor; but I was fond of agriculture, and of all employment in which horses were used.[10] We had, among other lands, fifty acres of forest

---

10. Tanning was a singularly unpleasant, if profitable, business, which remained largely resistant to mechanization through much of the nineteenth century. The 1840 census estimated that there were 8,229 tanneries in the United States. See Peter C. Welsh, *Tanning in the United States to 1850: A Brief History* (Washington, D.C.: Museum of History and Technology, Smithsonian Institution, 1964), 13.

The labor was filthy, malodorous, and exhausting. The following description of the early nineteenth-century tanning process, from a treatise on manufacturing and trades, gives a good idea of Jesse Grant's work:

> When the hides, which are to be tanned, are raw . . . they are put to steep in water, in order to clear them of the blood and filth they may have collected in the slaughter-house. . . .
>
> After the hides have been well softened they next proceed to cleanse or free them from the hair [by means of] the application of lime. . . .
>
> [A]s soon as it is perceived that the hair is in a fit state to be removed, it is scraped off, on a wooden horse, by means of a crooked knife. . . .
>
> After removing the hair and filth, the next object is to free the hides from the adhesion of any part of the muscle, or fat, and to render them soft and pliant. . . . As soon . . . as they are cleansed and freed from the flesh, &c. they are laid in a pit. . . .
>
> After the skin has been cleaned it is submitted to other operations before it is immersed in the tan liquor. According to Mr. Davy's account of the practices of the art, the large and thick hides which have undergone incipient putrefaction, are introduced for a short time into a strong infusion of oak bark, and after this they are acted on by water impregnated with a little sulphuric or acetic acid; in consequence of which they become harder and denser than before, and fitted after being tanned, for the purpose of forming the stouter kinds of sole leather. The lighter and thinner skins are treated in a different manner: they are macerated for some days in a

within a mile of the village. In the fall of the year choppers were employed to cut enough wood to last a twelvemonth. When I was seven or eight years of age, I began hauling all the wood used in the house and shops. I could not load it on the wagons, of course, at that time, but I could drive, and the choppers would load, and some one at the house unload. When about eleven years old, I was strong enough to hold a plough. From that age until seventeen I did all the work done with horses, such as breaking up the land, furrowing, ploughing corn and potatoes, bringing in the crops when harvested, hauling all the wood, besides tending two or three horses, a cow or two, and sawing wood for stoves, etc., while still attending school. For this I was compensated by the fact that there was never any scolding or punishing by my parents; no objection to rational enjoyments, such as fishing, going to the creek a mile away to swim in summer, taking a horse and visiting my

---

ley formed from the infusion of pigeons' dung in water which contains a little carbonate of ammonia; the skin is thus deprived of its elasticity and becomes more soft.

Thomas Martin, *The Circle of the Mechanical Arts*, 2nd ed. (London: Rees, 1815), 543–44.
    Despite Grant's avowed distaste for tanning, campaign posters and cartoons created during his presidential campaign seized on his familial connection with the trade.

Thomas Worth, "The Great American Tanner." Election-year cartoon. Currier & Ives, 1868. *Library of Congress, Prints and Photographs Division, LC-USZC2-2506.*

grandparents in the adjoining county, fifteen miles off, skating on the ice in winter, or taking a horse and sleigh when there was snow on the ground.

While still quite young I had visited Cincinnati, forty-five miles away, several times, alone; also Maysville, Kentucky, often, and once Louisville. The journey to Louisville was a big one for a boy of that day. I had also gone once with a two-horse carriage to Chilicothe, about seventy miles, with a neighbor's family, who were removing to Toledo, Ohio, and returned alone; and had gone once, in like manner, to Flat Rock, Kentucky, about seventy miles away. On this latter occasion I was fifteen years of age. While at Flat Rock, at the house of a Mr. Payne, whom I was visiting with his brother, a neighbor of ours in Georgetown, I saw a very fine saddle horse, which I rather coveted, and proposed to Mr. Payne, the owner, to trade him for one of the two I was driving. Payne hesitated to trade with a boy, but asking his brother about it, the latter told him that it would be all right, that I was allowed to do as I pleased with the horses. I was seventy miles from home, with a carriage to take back, and Mr. Payne said he did not know that his horse had ever had a collar on. I asked to have him hitched to a farm wagon and we would soon see whether he would work. It was soon evident that the horse had never worn harness before; but he showed no viciousness, and I expressed a confidence that I could manage him. A trade was at once struck, I receiving ten dollars difference.

The next day Mr. Payne, of Georgetown, and I started on our return. We got along very well for a few miles, when we encountered a ferocious dog that frightened the horses and made them run. The new animal kicked at every jump he made. I got the horses stopped, however, before any damage was done, and without running into anything. After giving them a little rest, to quiet their fears, we started again. That instant the new horse kicked, and started to run once more. The road we were on, struck the turnpike within half a mile of the point where the second runaway commenced, and there there was an embankment twenty or more feet deep on the opposite side of the pike. I got the horses stopped on the very brink of the precipice. My new horse was terribly frightened and trembled like an aspen; but he was not half so badly frightened as my companion, Mr. Payne, who deserted me after this last experience, and took passage on a freight wagon for Maysville. Every time I attempted to start, my new horse would commence to kick. I was in quite a dilemma for a time. Once in Maysville I could borrow a horse from an uncle who lived there; but I was more than a day's travel from that point. Finally I took out my bandanna—the style of handkerchief in universal use then—and with this blindfolded my horse. In this way I reached Maysville safely the next day, no doubt much to the surprise of my friend. Here I borrowed a horse from my uncle, and the following day we proceeded on our journey.

About half my school-days in Georgetown were spent at the school of John D. White, a North Carolinian, and the father of Chilton White who represented the district in Congress for one term during the rebellion. Mr. White was always a Democrat in politics, and Chilton followed his father. He had two older brothers—all three being school-mates of mine at their father's school—who did not go the same way. The second brother died before the rebellion began; he was a Whig, and afterwards a Republican. His oldest brother was a Republican and brave soldier during the rebellion. Chilton is reported as having told of an earlier horse-trade of mine. As he told the story, there was a Mr. Ralston living within a few miles of the village, who owned a colt which I very much wanted. My father had offered twenty dollars for it, but Ralston wanted twenty-five. I was so anxious to have the colt, that after the owner left, I begged to be allowed to take him at the price demanded. My father yielded, but said twenty dollars was all the horse was worth, and told me to offer that price; if it was not accepted I was to offer twenty-two and a half, and if that would not get him, to give the twenty-five. I at once mounted a horse and went for the colt. When I got to Mr. Ralston's house, I said to him: "Papa says I may offer you twenty dollars for the colt, but if you won't take that, I am to offer twenty-two and a half, and if you won't take that, to give you twenty-five." It would not require a Connecticut man to guess the price finally agreed upon. This story is nearly true. I certainly showed very plainly that I had come for the colt and meant to have him. I could not have been over eight years old at the time. This transaction caused me great heart-burning. The story got out among the boys of the village, and it was a long time before I heard the last of it. Boys enjoy the misery of their companions, at least village boys in that day did, and in later life I have found that all adults are not free from the peculiarity. I kept the horse until he was four years old, when he went blind, and I sold him for twenty dollars. When I went to Maysville to school, in 1836, at the age of fourteen, I recognized my colt as one of the blind horses working on the tread-wheel of the ferry-boat.

I have described enough of my early life to give an impression of the whole. I did not like to work; but I did as much of it, while young, as grown men can be hired to do in these days, and attended school at the same time. I had as many privileges as any boy in the village, and probably more than most of them. I have no recollection of ever having been punished at home, either by scolding or by the rod. But at school the case was different. The rod was freely used there, and I was not exempt from its influence. I can see John D. White—the school teacher—now, with his long beech switch always in his hand. It was not always the same one, either. Switches were brought in bundles, from a beech wood near the school house, by the boys for whose benefit they were intended. Often a whole bundle would be used up in a single day. I never had any hard feelings against my teacher, either while attending the school, or in later years when reflecting upon my experience. Mr. White was a kind-hearted man, and was much respected by the community in which he lived. He only followed the universal custom of the period, and that under which he had received his own education.[11]

---

11. The two episodes with which Grant closes this chapter on his youth—his inexpert horse trade and the beatings he received from the schoolteacher—suggest a certain vulnerability as well as a source of his aversion to bullying and humiliating others.

2

West Point—Graduation

I n the winter of 1838–9 I was attending school at Ripley, only ten miles distant from Georgetown, but spent the Christmas holidays at home. During this vacation my father received a letter from the Honorable Thomas Morris, then United States Senator from Ohio. When he read it he said to me, "Ulysses, I believe you are going to receive the appointment." "What appointment?" I inquired. "To West Point; I have applied for it." "But I won't go," I said. He said he thought I would, *and I thought so too, if he did.*[1] I really had no objection to going to West Point, except that I had a very exalted idea of the acquirements necessary to get through. I did not believe I possessed them, and could not bear the idea of failing. There had been four boys from our village, or its immediate neighborhood, who had been graduated from West Point, and never a failure of any one appointed from Georgetown, except in the case of the one whose place I was to take. He was the son of Dr. Bailey, our nearest and most intimate neighbor. Young Bailey had been appointed in 1837. Finding before the January examination following, that he could not pass, he resigned and went to a private school, and remained there until the following year, when he was reappointed. Before the next examination he was dismissed. Dr. Bailey was a proud and sensitive

---

1. This anecdote illuminates the tension infusing Grant's relationship with his father. Jesse had high expectations for his eldest son and was disappointed whenever he failed to meet them. He was also quick to capitalize on Ulysses's successes. The uneasiness between them can be discerned perhaps most clearly in the letters Grant wrote to his father in the 1850s, when he was struggling financially and failing at a series of enterprises. His father refused to lend him money.

man, and felt the failure of his son so keenly that he forbade his return home. There were no telegraphs in those days to disseminate news rapidly, no railroads west of the Alleghanies, and but few east; and above all, there were no reporters prying into other people's private affairs. Consequently it did not become generally known that there was a vacancy at West Point from our district until I was appointed. I presume Mrs. Bailey confided to my mother the fact that Bartlett had been dismissed, and that the doctor had forbidden his son's return home.

The Honorable Thomas L. Hamer, one of the ablest men Ohio ever produced, was our member of Congress at the time, and had the right of nomination. He and my father had been members of the same debating society (where they were generally pitted on opposite sides), and intimate personal friends from their early manhood up to a few years before. In politics they differed. Hamer was a life-long Democrat, while my father was a Whig. They had a warm discussion, which finally became angry—over some act of President Jackson, the removal of the deposit of public moneys, I think—after which they never spoke until after my appointment. I know both of them felt badly over this estrangement, and would have been glad at any time to come to a reconciliation; but neither would make the advance. Under these circumstances my father would not write to Hamer for the appointment, but he wrote to Thomas Morris, United States Senator from Ohio, informing him that there was a vacancy at West Point from our district, and that he would be glad if I could be appointed to fill it. This letter, I presume, was turned over to Mr. Hamer, and, as there was no other applicant, he cheerfully appointed me. This healed the breach between the two, never after reopened.

Besides the argument used by my father in favor of my going to West Point—that "he thought I would go"—there was another very strong inducement. I had always a great desire to travel. I was already the best travelled boy in Georgetown, except the sons of one man, John Walker, who had emigrated to Texas with his family, and immigrated back as soon as he could get the means to do so. In his short stay in Texas he acquired a very different opinion of the country from what one would form going there now.

I had been east to Wheeling, Virginia, and north to the Western Reserve, in Ohio, west to Louisville, and south to Bourbon County, Kentucky, besides having driven or ridden pretty much over the whole country within fifty miles of home. Going to West Point would give me the opportunity of visiting the two great cities of the continent, Philadelphia and New York. This was enough. When these places were visited I would have been glad to have had a steamboat or railroad collision, or any other accident happen, by which I might have received a temporary injury sufficient to make me ineligible, for a time, to enter the Academy. Nothing of the kind occurred, and I had to face the music.

Georgetown has a remarkable record for a western village. It is, and has been from its earliest existence, a democratic town. There was probably no time during the rebellion when, if the opportunity could have been afforded, it would not have voted for Jefferson Davis for President of the United States, over Mr. Lincoln, or any other representative of his party; unless it was immediately after some of John Morgan's men, in his celebrated raid through Ohio, spent a few hours in the village.[2] The rebels helped themselves to what-

---

2. General John Hunt Morgan led a raid through Ohio from July 12–26, 1863. Morgan had been ordered to harass Union troops in Kentucky, but he ventured further north with 1,400 cavalry troops. They despoiled several Ohio towns before Union forces captured 750 of them, including Morgan himself, who subsequently escaped imprisonment in the Ohio Penitentiary to rejoin Confederate forces. He was killed the following year in Tennessee. Today a marker in the town of West Point, Ohio, commemorates Morgan's capture. It reads: "This stone marks the spot where the Confederate raider General John H. Morgan surrendered his command to Major General George W. Rue, July 26, 1863, and this is the farthest point north ever reached by any body of Confederate troops during the Civil War." See "Morgan's Raid into Ohio," Carnegie Public Library, East Liverpool, Ohio, https://www.carnegie.lib.oh.us/morgan.

Tennessee military governor Andrew Johnson's telegram announcing the death of John Morgan. Andrew Johnson to Abraham Lincoln and Edwin M. Stanton, September 6, 1864. *Available at Abraham Lincoln Papers at the Library of Congress, Manuscript Division (Washington, D.C.: American Memory Project, [2000–02]), http://memory.loc.gov/ammem/alhtml/alhome.html.*

ever they could find, horses, boots and shoes, especially horses, and many ordered meals to be prepared for them by the families. This was no doubt a far pleasanter duty for some families than it would have been to render a like service for Union soldiers. The line between the Rebel and Union element in Georgetown was so marked that it led to divisions even in the churches.[3] There were churches in that part of Ohio where treason was preached regularly, and where, to secure membership, hostility to the government, to the war and to the liberation of the slaves, was far more essential than a belief in the authenticity or credibility of the Bible. There were men in Georgetown who filled all the requirements for membership in these churches.

Yet this far-off western village, with a population, including old and young, male and female, of about one thousand—about enough for the organization of a single regiment if all had been men capable of bearing arms—furnished the Union army four general officers and one colonel, West Point graduates, and nine generals and field officers of Volunteers, that I can think of. Of the graduates from West Point, all had citizenship elsewhere at the breaking out of the rebellion, except possibly General A. V. Kautz, who had remained in the army from his graduation.[4] Two of the colonels also entered

---

3. The divisions within Georgetown were mirrored in many towns throughout the country. While the conceit of the Civil War as one between brothers has produced some of the most distorted and sentimental accounts of the conflict, it was also an accurate reflection of the circumstances in which some soldiers would find themselves. Grant's friend James Longstreet, who became a prominent Confederate general, tells the story of two brothers-in-law at the Battle of Antietam:

> One of those peculiarly painful personal experiences which are innumerable in war, but seldom get into print (save in fiction), came under my observation in this battle. Colonel H. W. Kingsbury, who was killed while gallantly leading the Eleventh Connecticut Regiment at the ford near the Burnside Bridge, was a brother-in-law of General D. R. Jones, who commanded the Confederates immediately opposing him. His taking-off was a severe blow to Jones, and one from which he never recovered. His health had not been strong for some time. He asked leave of absence shortly after this occurrence, and, gradually but hopelessly sinking, in a few months passed over to the silent majority to join his fallen kinsman.

James Longstreet, *From Manassas to Appomattox: Memoirs of the Civil War in America* (Philadelphia: Lippincott, 1896), 262–63.

4. August V. Kautz was in fact born in Baden, Germany, in 1828. Before entering West Point he served as a private in the Mexican War. After his graduation from the Military Academy in 1852, he did frontier duty in the Pacific Northwest. Kautz served for the entirety of the Civil War, and he was a member of the force that captured John Morgan

in Ohio in 1863. He later served on the Military Commission that tried the conspirators involved in the Lincoln assassination. Kautz remained on active duty until 1892, and he died in 1895. See *Biographical Register of the Officers and Graduates of the United States Military Academy at West Point, N.Y. from Its Establishment in 1802, to 1890*, 3rd ed., 3 vols. (Boston: Houghton, Mifflin, 1891), vol. 2, s.v. "Kautz, August V." (hereafter cited as *Biographical Register*).

The abbreviated service records of West Point graduates in the ensuing notes are drawn primarily from the *cartes de service* contained in the *Register*. This invaluable nineteenth-century resource was compiled, revised, and expanded by George Washington Cullum (1809–1892). Each entry includes a *carte de service* and, in the case of more celebrated graduates, a biographical sketch or obituary.

Cullum graduated from West Point in 1833 and later served as its superintendent (1864–1866). As an engineer officer, he supervised, among other projects, the building of Fort Sumter. In addition to serving as Halleck's aide-de-camp, and subsequently his chief of staff, Cullum continued his work as a military engineer throughout the war. Arguably his most significant legacy, however, was his compilation of the *Register*. This work was done after the Civil War in an attempt to record the contributions of military academy graduates to the nation. It is a monumental reference work infused throughout with many of the stylistic flourishes of the age. West Point's memorial hall is named for Cullum, who bequeathed the money for its construction. It was designed by the architectural firm of McKim, Mead & White.

Cullum Hall, named for George W. Cullum and designed by McKim, Mead, and White. West Point, New York. *Library of Congress, Prints and Photographs Division, HABS NY-5708-4.*

Kautz was the author of a handbook for officers, first published in 1865, and his description there of a successful commanding general contains several of the attributes, including tenacity and preternatural calm, Grant possessed:

> To command a great Army successfully; to be superior to all the obstacles that exist, or the consequences that may follow; to remain alike unmoved at the fall of comrades or the destruction of the enemy, the dangers of battle or the security of success, the fears of defeat or the joys of triumph, indifferent to danger, unwearied by toil, risking all, and fearing no loss, inspiring victory when threatened with defeat, and amid it all the mind clear, every knowledge at command, making no errors, and directing all aright, is unquestionably the highest attribute of man, and a perfection to be found only in how few of the great soldiers of the past!

Customs of the Service for Officers of the Army (Philadelphia: Lippincott, 1866), 322.

the service from other localities. The other seven, General McGroierty, Colonels White, Fyffe, Loudon and Marshall, Majors King and Bailey, were all residents of Georgetown when the war broke out, and all of them, who were alive at the close, returned there. Major Bailey was the cadet who had preceded me at West Point. He was killed in West Virginia, in his first engagement. As far as I know, every boy who has entered West Point from that village since my time has been graduated.

I took passage on a steamer at Ripley, Ohio, for Pittsburg, about the middle of May, 1839. Western boats at that day did not make regular trips at stated times, but would stop anywhere, and for any length of time, for passengers or freight. I have myself been detained two or three days at a place after steam was up, the gang planks, all but one, drawn in, and after the time advertised for starting had expired. On this occasion we had no vexatious delays, and in about three days Pittsburg was reached. From Pittsburg I chose passage by the canal to Harrisburg, rather than by the more expeditious stage. This gave a better opportunity of enjoying the fine scenery of Western Pennsylvania, and I had rather a dread of reaching my destination at all. At that time the canal was much patronized by travellers, and, with the comfortable packets of the period, no mode of conveyance could be more pleasant, when time was not an object. From Harrisburg to Philadelphia there was a railroad, the first I had ever seen, except the one on which I had just crossed the summit of the Alleghany Mountains, and over which canal boats were transported. In travelling by the road from Harrisburg, I thought the perfection of rapid transit had been reached. We travelled at least eighteen miles an hour, when at full speed, and made the whole distance averaging probably as much as twelve miles an hour. This seemed like annihilating space.[5] I stopped five

---

5. Rebecca Solnit's *River of Shadows* offers a probing discussion of the ways in which the nineteenth-century technologies of the railroad and photography forever altered American understandings of temporal and geographic realities. Solnit notes that Grant's description of the railroad as having succeeded in "annihilating space" was one of many "variations on one of the stock phrases of the day." In addition to shrinking space and time, the railroads eroded local peculiarities, the most important of which was local time: "railroad time" began to eclipse "solar time." "Many railroad stations had two clocks, one for local solar time, another for railroad time," but "so powerful were the railroads that their time became the universally recognized time of the United States and Canada, and solar time virtually disappeared." See *River of Shadows: Eadweard Muybridge and the Technological Wild West* (New York: Penguin, 2004), 11, 61.

The sensation of radical yet exhilarating dislocation produced by train travel finds a twentieth-century analogue in the movement of the automobile and the airplane. Virginia Woolf powerfully represents the former in her novel *Orlando*:

days in Philadelphia, saw about every street in the city, attended the theatre, visited Girard College (which was then in course of construction), and got reprimanded from home afterwards, for dallying by the way so long. My sojourn in New York was shorter, but long enough to enable me to see the city very well. I reported at West Point on the 30th or 31st of May, and about two weeks later passed my examination for admission, without difficulty, very much to my surprise.

A military life had no charms for me, and I had not the faintest idea of staying in the army even if I should be graduated, which I did not expect.[6]

The Old Kent Road was very crowded on Thursday, the eleventh of October, 1928. People spilt off the pavement. There were women with shopping bags. Children ran out. There were sales at drapers' shops. Streets widened and narrowed. Long vistas steadily shrunk together. Here was a market. Here a funeral. Here a procession with banners upon which was written in great letters "Ra—Un," but what else? Meat was very red. Butchers stood at the door. Women almost had their heels sliced off. Amor Vin— that was over a porch. A woman looked out of a bedroom window, profoundly contemplative, and very still. Applejohn and Applebed, Undert—. Nothing could be seen whole or read from start to finish. What was seen begun—like two friends starting to meet each other across the street—was never seen ended. After twenty minutes the body and mind were like scraps of torn paper tumbling from a sack and, indeed, the process of motoring fast out of London so much resembles the chopping up small of body and mind, which precedes unconsciousness and perhaps death itself that it is an open question in what sense Orlando can be said to have existed at the present moment.

Orlando: A Biography (1928; New York: Harcourt, Harvest, 2006), 224–25.

In his 1939 meditation on flight, the aviator Antoine de Saint-Exupéry also describes the work of machines, airplanes among them, as that of "annihilating time and space." See *Wind, Sand and Stars*, trans. Lewis Galantière (New York: Harcourt, Harvest, 2002), 44.

6. After Grant had been at West Point a few months, he sent a letter to a cousin full of playful self-deprecation (and his customarily idiosyncratic spelling):

If I were to come home now with my uniform on. They way you would laugh at my appearance would be curious. My pants sit as tight to my skin as the bark to a tree and if I do not walk *military.* that is if I bend over quickly or run. they are very apt to crack with a report as loud as a pistol. my coat must always be buttoned up tight to the chin. it is made of sheeps grey cloth all covered with big round buttens. it makes me look very singulir. If you were to see me at a distance. the first question you would ask would be. "is that a Fish or an animal"? You must give my very best love and respects to all my friends particulaly you[r] brothers. Uncle Ross & Sam'l Simpson.

View of the Hudson River, ca. 1845. Painted by Cadet Truman Seymour, who graduated from West Point in 1846, fought in the Mexican and Civil Wars, retired from the Army in 1876, and devoted the rest of his life to painting. *Special Collections, USMA Library.*

The encampment which preceded the commencement of academic studies was very wearisome and uninteresting. When the 28th of August came—the date for breaking up camp and going into barracks—I felt as though I had been at West Point always, and that if I staid to graduation, I would have to remain always.[7] I did not take hold of my studies with avidity, in fact I rarely

You must also write me a long. long letter in reply to this and till me about evry thing and every body including yourself. If you happen to see my folks just till them that I am happy, *alive* and *kicking.*

Letter to R. McKinstry Griffith, September 22, 1839, Ulysses S. Grant Papers, Special Collections, USMA Library.

7. In 1843, the year Grant graduated, Cadet William Dutton, a member of the class of 1846, described his room in a letter to his cousin:

I believe I have never given you a description of our room—etc. If not it may not be uninteresting to give you an "Order" posted on every door—"Bedsteads—against door—Trunks—under iron bedsteads—Lamps—clean on mantle—Dress Caps—Neatly arranged behind door—

"Dear cousin we have a great deal of rough times here, drilling, walking post + pouring [*sic*] over our dry studies." Grant's letter to R. McKinstry Griffith, July 18, 1840. *Special Collections, USMA Library.*

Looking-Glass—between washstand & door—Books—neatly arranged on shelf farthest from door—Broom—Hanging behind door—Drawing books—under shelf farthest from door—Muskets—in gun rack and locks sprung—Bayonets in scabbards—Accouterments—Hanging over muskets—Sabres—Cutlasses & swords—hanging over muskets—Candle Box—for scrubbing utensils—Against wall under shelf nearest door, & fire place—clothes—neatly hung on pegs over—bedsteads—Mattress & Blankets neatly folded—Orderly Board—over mantle—chairs—when not used under tables—Orderlies of rooms are held responsible for the observance

ever read over a lesson the second time during my entire cadetship. I could not sit in my room doing nothing. There is a fine library connected with the Academy from which cadets can get books to read in their quarters. I devoted more time to these, than to books relating to the course of studies. Much of the time, I am sorry to say, was devoted to novels, but not those of a trashy sort. I read all of Bulwer's then published, Cooper's, Marryat's, Scott's, Washington Irving's works, Lever's, and many others that I do not now remember.[8] Mathematics was very easy to me, so that when January came, I passed the examination, taking a good standing in that branch. In French, the only other study at that time in the first year's course, my standing was very low. In fact, if the class had been turned the other end foremost I should have been near head. I never succeeded in getting squarely at either end of my class, in any one study, during the four years. I came near it in French,

---

of the above mentioned arrangement. By order of Lieut. E. J. Steptoe—1st Lieut. 1st Art. & commd't A compy."

Letter to Lucy J. Mathews, February 18, 1843, William Dutton Papers, Special Collections, USMA Library.

8. Grant was also the president of the Dialectic Society, a cadet literary club the activities of which remain somewhat obscure. To supplement the books in the library, which did include some fiction as well as literary periodicals, cadets undoubtedly shared personal copies of books. One of the surviving letters from Grant's cadet days is a query to a Philadelphia publishing house regarding an unfilled order for two novels: *Charles O'Malley* and *The Confessions of Harry Lorrequer*, picaresque narratives of military life by Charles Lever. See Letter to Carey and Hart, April 8, 1843, *PUSG*, 1:11.

In Cooper, the first name on his list of novelists, Grant encountered portraits of frontier life that featured rugged heroes such as Hawk-eye (Natty Bumppo), abundant scenes of hunting—an activity Grant found repellent—and episodes from the French and Indian War. In this representative passage from Cooper's blockbuster *The Last of the Mohicans*, Hawk-eye grapples with a Native American ally of the French:

> With ready skill, Hawk-eye and his antagonist each grasped that uplifted arm of the other, which held the dangerous knife. For near a minute, they stood looking one another in the eye, and gradually exerting the power of their muscles for the mastery. At length, the toughened sinews of the white man prevailed over the less practiced limbs of the native. The arm of the latter slowly gave way before the increasing force of the scout, who suddenly wresting his armed hand from the grasp of the foe, drove the sharp weapon through his naked bosom to the heart.

J. Fenimore Cooper, *The Last of the Mohicans, Or, A Narrative of 1757* (Cambridge, MA: Houghton, Mifflin, 1876), 76.

Cadet Grant's demerits, 1839–1843. *Special Collections, USMA Library.*

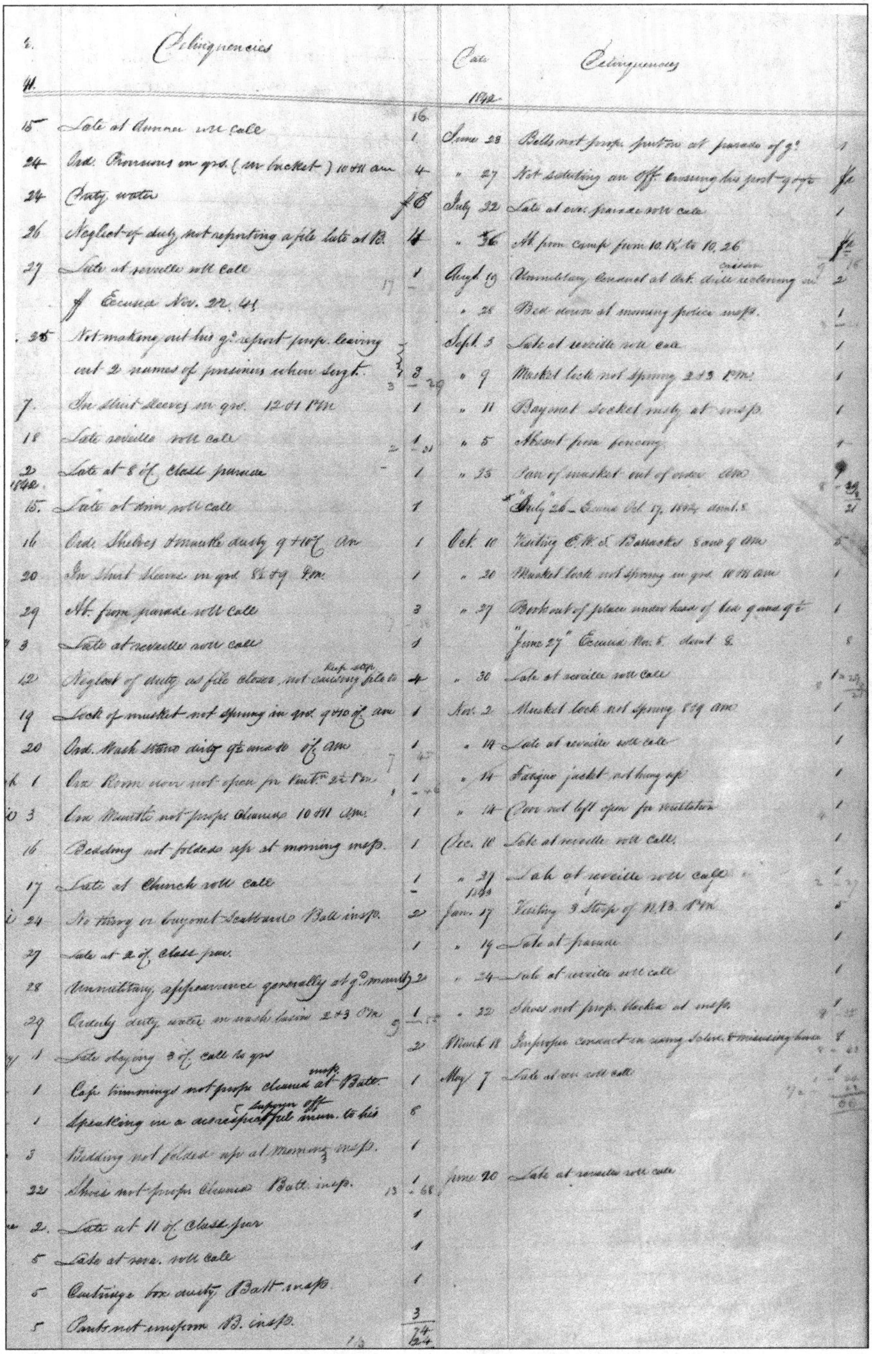

West Point Library circulation records showing the names of Cadets Grant and Simon Bolivar Buckner, October 29, 1842. *Special Collections, USMA Library.*

artillery, infantry and cavalry tactics, and conduct.[9]

Early in the session of the Congress which met in December, 1839, a bill was discussed abolishing the Military Academy. I saw in this an honorable way to obtain a discharge, and read the debates with much interest, but with impatience at the delay in taking action, for I was selfish enough to favor the bill.[10] It never

9. Grant does not mention drawing classes, for which he clearly had an aptitude. Professor Robert W. Weir was the drawing master at West Point for decades; he taught Grant, Sherman, and many others. Weir was himself an accomplished artist of the Hudson River School. In addition to drawing and painting a variety of scenes for Weir, cadets executed maps and mathematical designs as part of their studies.

Professor Robert W. Weir. *Library of Congress, Prints and Photographs Division, Brady-Handy Collection, LC-DIG-cwpbh-02462.*

10. The congressional debates at this time focused on the constitutionality of the academy, the size of the army, and the wisdom of relying so heavily on a single federal institution to supply its officers. Fears of an officer caste, inherited from the revolutionary period, also informed the debate. In July 1840, for example, Senator John Reynolds of Illinois, "denounced the institution as establishing a distinct order in the community." On the other side, Senator James Monroe of New York spoke "with ardor in defence of the Military Academy, insisting on the necessity of scientific cultivation to ensure success in war to the highest gallantry." Senator John Pope of Kentucky likewise "remonstrated against such an attempt to destroy an institution which had existed nearly half a century, and which was an ornament to the country." *Congressional Globe,* 26th Congress, 1st Session 544 (1840).

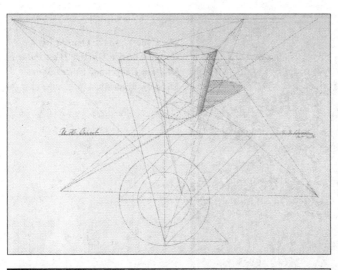

One of Grant's drawings for his mathematics course. *Special Collections, USMA Library.*

Example of map drawn by cadets during Grant's era. *Special Collections, USMA Library.*

passed, and a year later, although the time hung drearily with me, I would have been sorry to have seen it succeed. My idea then was to get through the course, secure a detail for a few years as assistant professor of mathematics at the Academy, and afterwards obtain a permanent position as professor in some respectable college; but circumstances always did shape my course different from my plans.

At the end of two years the class received the usual furlough, extending from the close of the June examination to the 28th of August. This I enjoyed beyond any other period of my life. My father had sold out his business in Georgetown—where my youth had been spent, and to which my day-dreams carried me back as my future home, if I should ever be able to retire

"Le Cadet," 1842. **Drawn by Cadet George Derby.** *West Point Museum Collection, United States Military Academy.*

on a competency. He had moved to Bethel, only twelve miles away, in the adjoining county of Clermont, and had bought a young horse that had never been in harness, for my special use under the saddle during my furlough. Most of my time was spent among my old school-mates—these ten weeks were shorter than one week at West Point.

Persons acquainted with the Academy know that the corps of cadets is divided into four companies for the purpose of military exercises. These companies are officered from the cadets, the superintendent and commandant selecting the officers for their military bearing and qualifications. The adjutant, quartermaster, four captains and twelve lieutenants are taken from the first, or Senior class; the sergeants from the second, or Junior class; and the corporals from the third, or Sophomore class. I had not been "called out" as a corporal, but when I returned from furlough I found myself the last but one—about my standing in all the tactics—of eighteen sergeants. The promotion was too much for me. That year my standing in the class— as shown by the number of demerits of the year—was about the same as it was among the sergeants, and I was dropped, and served the fourth year as a private.

During my first year's encampment General Scott visited West Point, and reviewed the cadets. With his commanding figure, his quite colossal size and showy uniform, I thought him the finest specimen of manhood my eyes had ever beheld, and the most to be envied.[11] I could never resemble him in appearance, but I believe I did have a presentiment for a moment that some day I should occupy his place on review—although I had no intention then of remaining in the army. My experience in a horse-trade ten years before, and the ridicule it caused me, were too fresh in my mind for me to communicate this presentiment to even my most intimate chum. The next summer Martin Van Buren, then President of the United States, visited West Point and reviewed the cadets; he did not impress me with the awe which Scott had inspired.[12] In fact I regarded General Scott and Captain

---

11. Winfield Scott (1786–1866) was the most visible soldier of his age. Grant would serve under him in the Mexican War. A hero of the War of 1812, he was still commanding general of the army at the beginning of the Civil War. When the superannuated Scott resigned in November 1861, Lincoln replaced him with George B. McClellan. As a boy, the novelist Henry James encountered the magnificent general in New York City:

> I distinguish in the earlier twilight of Fourteenth Street my father's return to us one November day—we knew he had been out to vote—with the news that General Winfield Scott, his and the then "Whig" candidate, had been defeated for the Presidency; just as I rescue from the same limbo my afterwards proud little impression of having "met" that high-piled hero of the Mexican War, whom the Civil War was so soon and with so little ceremony to extinguish, literally met him, at my father's side, in Fifth Avenue, where he had just emerged from a cross-street. I remain vague as to what had then happened and scarce suppose I was, at the age probably of eight or nine, "presented"; but we must have been for some moments face to face while from under the vast amplitude of a dark blue military cloak with a big velvet collar and loosened silver clasp, which spread about him like a symbol of the tented field, he greeted my parent—so clear is my sense of the time it took me to gape *all* the way up to where he towered aloft.

A Small Boy and Others (New York: Scribner's, 1913), 50–51.

12. West Point plebes were for many years required to memorize the following bit of self-congratulatory prose, known as "Scott's Fixed Opinion": "I give it as my fixed opinion, that but for our graduated cadets, the war between the United States and Mexico might, and probably would have lasted some four or five years, with, in its first half, more defeats than victories falling to our share; whereas, in less than two campaigns, we conquered a great country and a peace without the loss of a single battle or skirmish." This and other pieces of lore are reproduced in *Bugle Notes*, a handbook issued to new cadets.

C. F. Smith, the Commandant of Cadets, as the two men most to be envied in the nation. I retained a high regard for both up to the day of their death.[13]

---

13. Charles Ferguson Smith (1807–1862), Grant's commanding officer at West Point, graduated from the military academy in 1825. The son of an army surgeon and the grandson of a colonel in the Continental Army, Smith served gallantly in the Mexican War, and was later stationed on the frontier. He commanded the Department of Utah at the outbreak of the Civil War, during which he would serve under Grant. Smith's professionalism ensured that there was no awkwardness in this reversal of roles, and his premature death in 1862 robbed Grant of a most capable soldier. The feeling Smith awakened in fellow soldiers is reflected in this rather overheated tribute in Cullum's *Biographical Register*:

> On the 25th of April, 1862, this brave and noble paladin, who was as intrepid as Ney, as chivalric as Murat, and as rock-fast as Macdonald, breathed his last. The Army could boast of no better general. His stately and commanding presence inspired his soldiers with respect and almost fear. In his rigid discipline, though severe, he was always just, requiring no greater subordination from inferiors than he was ready to yield to superiors. The call of duty was to him a magic sound for which he was always ready to make every sacrifice and endure any fatigue. He was the very model of a soldier, calm, prudent, and self-poised, yet, in the hour of danger, bold almost to rashness. Had he lived he would have held a high niche in the Temple of Fame, whose doors were already opened to him. Sherman said that, "had C. F. Smith lived, Grant would have disappeared to history after Donelson."

Biographical Register, vol. 1, s.v. "Smith, Charles F."
    Smith died of an infection resulting from a foot injury received while jumping from one boat to another at Savannah, Tennessee, during an expedition up the Tennessee River. On April 21, four days before his death, Smith wrote a remarkable and revealing letter to Grant:

> I shall leave here in a few days and doubt if the accidents of life throw us together again. But I trust you will believe to the fullest extent my sense of appreciation of the kindness and consideration I have ever received at your hands during our service together in this land of Egyptian darkness.
> I do not know that I should attempt to express myself thus if I did not think I perceived in the newspaper press a studied attempt on the part of heartless politicians to strike down your well deserved honors. I do not know what your aspirations for the future may be; but there is evidently a class of political intelligencers who joined to some of your friends, thinking you an available candidate for the presidency, would seek to place you in that office. I must confess I think too well of you as a modest christian gentleman to run the gauntlet for the office, still successes attend you in that or any other line you may desire.

Charles F. Smith Papers, Special Collections, USMA Library.

The last two years wore away more rapidly than the first two, but they still seemed about five times as long as Ohio years, to me.[14] At last all the examinations were passed, and the members of the class were called upon to record their choice of arms of service and regiments. I was anxious to enter the cavalry, or dragoons as they were then called, but there was only one regiment of dragoons in the Army at that time, and attached to that, besides the full complement of officers, there were at least four brevet second lieutenants. I recorded therefore my first choice, dragoons; second, 4th infantry; and got the latter.[15] Again there was a furlough—or, more properly speak-

14. Studying at West Point in the early 1840s, Grant was less than sixty years removed from the various intrigues that had occurred in the Hudson Highlands during the Revolutionary War. The Hudson River Valley's inhabitants had been deeply divided in their allegiances, many of them fiercely loyal to the crown. In this respect, the region was not dissimilar to the border states during the Civil War. The most celebrated action to take place in the Highlands was the defection of Benedict Arnold and the capture of his British contact, Major John André, who was hanged as a spy by Washington and who became, strangely, an object of great public sympathy among American colonists. It was in the same locale that Cooper, one of Cadet Grant's favorite authors, chose to set his first novel, *The Spy,* a tale of revolutionary-era espionage.

15. Grant's middling class rank limited his choice of branch. Class rank still largely determines a cadet's branch today.

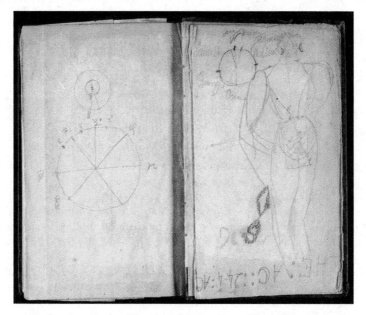

Cadet Grant's doodling in John Gummere's 1837 *Elementary Treatise on Geometry.* **Special Collections, USMA Library.**

ing, leave of absence for the class were now commissioned officers—this time to the end of September. Again I went to Ohio to spend my vacation among my old school-mates; and again I found a fine saddle horse purchased for my special use, besides a horse and buggy that I could drive—but I was not in a physical condition to enjoy myself quite as well as on the former occasion. For six months before graduation I had had a desperate cough ("Tyler's grip" it was called), and I was very much reduced, weighing but one hundred and seventeen pounds, just my weight at entrance, though I had grown six inches in stature in the mean time. There was consumption in my father's family, two of his brothers having died of that disease, which made my symptoms more alarming. The brother and sister next younger than myself died, during the rebellion, of the same disease, and I seemed the most promising subject for it of the three in 1843.[16]

Having made alternate choice of two different arms of service with different uniforms, I could not get a uniform suit until notified of my assignment. I left my measurement with a tailor, with directions not to make the uniform until I notified him whether it was to be for infantry or dragoons. Notice did not reach me for several weeks, and then it took at least a week to get the letter of instructions to the tailor and two more to make the clothes and have them sent to me. This was a time of great suspense. I was impatient to get on my uniform and see how it looked, and probably wanted my old school-mates, particularly the girls, to see me in it.

The conceit was knocked out of me by two little circumstances that happened soon after the arrival of the clothes, which gave me a distaste for military uniform that I never recovered from. Soon after the arrival of the suit I donned it, and put off for Cincinnati on horseback. While I was riding along a street of that city, imagining that every one was looking at me, with a feeling akin to mine when I first saw General Scott, a little urchin, bareheaded, barefooted, with dirty and ragged pants held up by a single gallows—that's what suspenders were called then—and a shirt that

16. *Consumption* was the common nineteenth-century term for tuberculosis, a devastating killer that would claim the lives of Grant's sister Clara and brother Simpson as well as that of his chief-of-staff, John A. Rawlins, who died shortly after the Civil War. Before the discovery of the bacillus, the disease was erroneously believed to be hereditary. At the end of the nineteenth century, tuberculosis was a leading cause of death in the United States. Grant clearly feared contracting the disease himself. What he refers to as the "grip," a persistent cough and fever that bothered him at West Point and returned in the late 1850s, when he was trying to make a go of farming near St. Louis, mimicked some of the symptoms of tuberculosis.

had not seen a wash-tub for weeks, turned to me and cried: "Soldier! will you work? No, sir—ee; I'll sell my shirt first!!" The horse trade and its dire consequences were recalled to mind.[17]

17. This incident may have helped to forge Grant's dislike for uniform, but the example of Zachary Taylor in the Mexican War was probably a more profound influence. In later chapters Grant notes Taylor's preference for civilian clothes even on the battlefield. Much has been made of the simplicity of Grant's uniform, but the Civil War surgeon J. Franklin Dyer insisted in his journal, "The gossip about his extreme simplicity is nonsense. He dresses as becomes his position, no more, no less." April 22, 1864, *The Diary of a Civil War Surgeon*, ed. Michael B. Chesson (Lincoln: University of Nebraska Press, 2003), 145.

Grant's playful, rather literary vignette calls to mind a moment in Charles Dickens's *Great Expectations*, written during the Civil War and serially published in America alongside engravings of battles in *Harper's Weekly*. In the following passage, the novel's protagonist, Pip, a blacksmith's apprentice who acquires a mysterious benefactor determined to make him a gentleman, has just emerged from a tailor's shop dressed in a brand-new set of clothes, only to be mocked by the tailor's assistant (Trabb's boy), in the High Street:

> Casting my eyes along the street at a certain point of my progress, I beheld Trabb's boy approaching, lashing himself with an empty blue bag. Deeming that a serene and unconscious contemplation of him would best beseem me, and would be most likely to quell his evil mind, I advanced with that expression of countenance, and was rather congratulating myself on my success, when suddenly the knees of Trabb's boy smote together, his hair uprose, his cap fell off, he trembled violently in every limb, staggered out into the road, and crying to the populace, "Hold me! I'm so frightened!" feigned to be in a paroxysm of terror and contrition, occasioned by the dignity of my appearance. As I passed him, his teeth loudly chattered in his head, and with every mark of extreme humiliation, he prostrated himself in the dust.
>
> This was a hard thing to bear, but this was nothing. I had not advanced another two hundred yards, when, to my inexpressible terror, amazement, and indignation, I again beheld Trabb's boy approaching. He was coming round a narrow corner. His blue bag was slung over his shoulder, honest industry beamed in his eyes, a determination to proceed to Trabb's with cheerful briskness was indicated in his gait. With a shock he became aware of me, and was severely visited as before; but this time his motion was rotatory, and he staggered round and round me with knees more afflicted, and with uplifted hands as if beseeching for mercy. His sufferings were hailed with the greatest joy by a knot of spectators, and I felt utterly confounded.
>
> I had not got as much further down the street as the post-office, when I again beheld Trabb's boy shooting round by a back way. This time, he was entirely changed. He wore the blue bag in the manner of my great-coat, and was strutting along the pavement towards me on the

The other circumstance occurred at home. Opposite our house in Bethel stood the old stage tavern where "man and beast" found accommodation. The stable-man was rather dissipated, but possessed of some humor. On my return I found him parading the streets, and attending in the stable, barefooted, but in a pair of sky-blue nankeen pantaloons—just the color of my uniform trousers—with a strip of white cotton sheeting sewed down the outside seams in imitation of mine. The joke was a huge one in the mind of many of the people, and was much enjoyed by them; but I did not appreciate it so highly.

During the remainder of my leave of absence, my time was spent in visiting friends in Georgetown and Cincinnati, and occasionally other towns in that part of the State.

---

opposite side of the street, attended by a company of delighted young friends to whom he from time to time exclaimed, with a wave of his hand, "Don't know yah!" Words cannot state the amount of aggravation and injury wreaked upon me by Trabb's boy, when, passing abreast of me, he pulled up his shirt-collar, twined his side-hair, stuck an arm akimbo, and smirked extravagantly by, wriggling his elbows and body, and drawling to his attendants, "Don't know yah, don't know yah, pon my soul don't know yah!" The disgrace attendant on his immediately afterwards taking to crowing and pursuing me across the bridge with crows, as from an exceedingly dejected fowl who had known me when I was a blacksmith, culminated the disgrace with which I left the town, and was, so to speak, ejected by it into the open country.

Charles Dickens, *Great Expectations*, 3 vols. (London: Chapman and Hall, 1861), 2:181–83.

3

Army Life—Causes of the Mexican War— Camp Salubrity

On the 30th of September I reported for duty at Jefferson Barracks, St. Louis, with the 4th United States infantry. It was the largest military post in the country at that time, being garrisoned by sixteen companies of infantry, eight of the 3d regiment, the remainder of the 4th.[1] Colonel Steven Kearney, one of the ablest officers of the day, commanded the post, and under him discipline was kept at a high standard, but without vexatious rules or regulations.[2] Every drill and roll-call had to be attended, but in the

---

1. For a fuller picture of life at Jefferson Barracks, see the early chapters of Longstreet's *From Manassas to Appomattox.*

2. Stephen Watts Kearny (1794–1848), whose name Grant misspells, served in the army from the War of 1812 until his death from yellow fever. He spent most of his career on frontier duty. During the Mexican War, he captured the territory of New Mexico; eventually he served as military governor of California. Kearny also became the object of vitriolic attacks by the powerful Missouri senator Thomas Hart Benton after the officer court-martialed the senator's son-in-law, the volatile and incompetent John C. Frémont. As a result, argues the historian Bernard DeVoto,

> Kearny has never had his due. . . . Kearny's service to the United States at a decisive turning point in history is great—was itself decisive. He did the jobs assigned him, quietly, completely, authoritatively. He took New Mexico and organized it. He completed the conquest and began the organization of California. . . . He succeeded at everything he set out to do: he was an expert. He kept his temper and he held his tongue. He wrote no letter to politicians or the press. He conducted no intrigues and was not

intervals officers were permitted to enjoy themselves, leaving the garrison, and going where they pleased, without making written application to state where they were going for how long, etc., so that they were back for their next duty. It did seem to me, in my early army days, that too many of the older officers, when they came to command posts, made it a study to think what orders they could publish to annoy their subordinates and render them uncomfortable. I noticed, however, a few years later, when the Mexican war broke out, that most of this class of officers discovered they were possessed of disabilities which entirely incapacitated them for active field service. They had the moral courage to proclaim it, too. They were right; but they did not always give their disease the right name.[3]

At West Point I had a class-mate—in the last year of our studies he was

---

interested in politics. Few of those in high places we have had to deal with were capable of putting the republic before themselves. Kearny served it without trying to serve himself. He was a man, a gentleman, and a soldier. The enmity of an adventurer's father-in-law should not be permitted to obscure his achievement any longer.

The Year of Decision: 1846 (1942; New York: St. Martin's, 2000), 482–83.

Grant's observation about Kearny's ability to maintain discipline without being a martinet reveals his admiration for a particular style of command, one which he was ultimately to adopt in the Civil War.

3. The name, of course, is *cowardice*, a term Grant rarely and never cavalierly invoked. Grant's clear-eyed, practical analysis of military life and the character of soldiers contrasts sharply with his youthful enthusiasm for romantic writers like Cooper and Walter Scott. Scott himself gives a sense of his attitudes in the 1829 preface to the Waverley novels:

I must refer to a very early period of my life, were I to point out my first achievements as a tale-teller—but I believe some of my old schoolfellows can still bear witness that I had a distinguished character for that talent, at a time when the applause of my companions was my recompense for the disgraces and punishments which the future romance-writer incurred for being idle himself, and keeping others idle, during hours that should have been employed on our tasks. The chief enjoyment of my holidays was to escape with a chosen friend, who had the same taste with myself, and alternately to recite to each other such wild adventures as we were able to devise. We told, each in turn, interminable tales of knight-errantry and battles and enchantments, which were continued from one day to another as opportunity offered, without our ever thinking of bringing them to a conclusion.

Preface, *Waverley Novels*, vol. 1 (Edinburgh: Adam and Charles Black, 1860), 6.

Julia Dent Grant. *Library of Congress, Prints and Photographs Division, Brady-Handy Collection, LC-DIG-cwpbh-05123.*

room-mate also—F[rederick]. T. Dent, whose family resided some five miles west of Jefferson Barracks. Two of his unmarried brothers were living at home at that time, and as I had taken with me from Ohio, my horse, saddle and bridle, I soon found my way out to White Haven, the name of the Dent estate. As I found the family congenial my visits became frequent. There were at home, besides the young men, two daughters, one a school miss of fifteen, the other a girl of eight or nine. There was still an older daughter of seventeen, who had been spending several years at boarding-school in St. Louis, but who, though through school, had not yet returned home. She was spending the winter in the city with connections, the family of Colonel John O'Fallon, well known in St. Louis. In February she returned to her country home. After that I do not know but my visits became more frequent; they certainly did become more enjoyable. We would often take walks, or go on horseback to visit the neighbors, until I became quite well acquainted in that vicinity. Sometimes one of the brothers would accompany us, sometimes one of the younger sisters. If the 4th infantry had remained at Jefferson Barracks it is possible, even probable, that this life might have continued for some years without my finding out that there was anything serious the matter with me; but in the following May a circumstance occurred which developed my sentiment so palpably that there was no mistaking it.[4]

4. Grant is speaking here of course about his future wife, Julia Dent. Of the couple's first meeting, Longstreet writes,

The annexation of Texas was at this time the subject of violent discussion in Congress, in the press, and by individuals.[5] The administration of President Tyler, then in power, was making the most strenuous efforts to effect the annexation, which was, indeed, the great and absorbing question of the day. During these discussions the greater part of the single rifle regiment in the army—the 2d dragoons, which had been dismounted a year or two before, and designated "Dismounted Rifles"—was stationed at Fort Jessup, Louisiana, some twenty-five miles east of the Texas line, to observe the frontier. About the 1st of May the 3d infantry was ordered from Jefferson Barracks to Louisiana, to go into camp in the neighborhood of Fort Jessup, and there await further orders. The troops were embarked on steamers and were on their way down the Mississippi within a few days after the receipt of this order. About the time they started I obtained a leave of absence for twenty days to go to Ohio to visit my parents. I was obliged to go to St. Louis to take a steamer for Louisville or Cincinnati, or the first steamer going up the Ohio River to any point. Before I left St. Louis orders were received at Jefferson Barracks for the 4th infantry to follow the 3d. A messenger was sent after me to stop my leaving; but before he could reach me I was off, totally ignorant of these events. A day or two after my arrival at Bethel I received a letter from a class-mate and fellow lieutenant in the 4th, informing me of the circumstances related above, and advising me not to open any letter post marked St. Louis or Jefferson Barracks, until the expiration of my leave, and saying that he would pack up my things and take them along for me. His advice was not necessary, for no other letter was sent to me. I now discovered that I was exceedingly anxious to get back to Jefferson Barracks, and I understood the reason without explanation from any one. My leave of absence required me

---

Of the class of 1843, Ulysses S. Grant joined the Fourth Regiment as brevet lieutenant, and I had the pleasure to ride with him on our first visit to Mr. Frederick Dent's home, a few miles from the garrison, where we first met Miss Julia Dent, the charming woman who, five years later, became Mrs. Grant. Miss Dent was a frequent visitor at the garrison balls and hops, where Lieutenant Hoskins, who was something of a tease, would inquire of her if she could tell where he might find "the small lieutenant with the large epaulettes."

Longstreet, *Manassas to Appomattox*, 18.

5. Congress's 1845 annexation of Texas, which white settlers from the United States had declared a republic in 1836, increased tensions with Mexico and set the stage for war the following year.

to report for duty, at Jefferson Barracks, at the end of twenty days. I knew my regiment had gone up the Red River, but I was not disposed to break the letter of my leave; besides, if I had proceeded to Louisiana direct, I could not have reached there until after the expiration of my leave. Accordingly, at the end of the twenty days, I reported for duty to Lieutenant Ewell, commanding at Jefferson Barracks, handing him at the same time my leave of absence. After noticing the phraseology of the order—leaves of absence were generally worded, "at the end of which time he will report for duty with his proper command"—he said he would give me an order to join my regiment in Louisiana. I then asked for a few days' leave before starting, which he readily granted. This was the same Ewell who acquired considerable reputation as a Confederate general during the rebellion. He was a man much esteemed, and deservedly so, in the old army, and proved himself a gallant and efficient officer in two wars—both in my estimation unholy.[6]

I immediately procured a horse and started for the country, taking no baggage with me, of course. There is an insignificant creek—the Gravois—between Jefferson Barracks and the place to which I was going, and at that day there was not a bridge over it from its source to its mouth. There is not water enough in the creek at ordinary stages to run a coffee mill, and at low water there is none running whatever. On this occasion it had been raining heavily, and, when the creek was reached, I found the banks full to overflowing, and the current rapid. I looked at it a moment to consider what to do. One of my superstitions had always been when I started to go any where, or to do anything, not to turn back, or stop until the thing intended was accomplished. I have frequently started to go to places where I had never been and to which I did not know the way, depending upon making inquiries on the road, and if I got past the place without knowing it, instead of turning back, I would go on until a road was found turning in the right direction, take that, and come in by the other side. So I struck into the

6. Richard S. Ewell (1817–1872) graduated from West Point in 1840. As an officer in the 1st Dragoons, he served on frontier duty before and after the Mexican War, and he was wounded during a skirmish with Apaches in 1859. He resigned in 1861 to join the rebellion. He is perhaps best known for his controversial role in the Battle of Gettysburg. After forcing Union troops back through the Pennsylvania town on the first day of the battle, Ewell, who had received contradictory orders from Robert E. Lee—Lee also refused Ewell reinforcements—and who saw how well-defended the Union position on Cemetery Hill was, did not push on to take the high ground. After the war, devotees of the cult of Lee made Ewell the scapegoat for this critical Confederate loss.

stream, and in an instant the horse was swimming and I being carried down by the current.[7] I headed the horse towards the other bank and soon reached it, wet through and without other clothes on that side of the stream. I went on, however, to my destination and borrowed a dry suit from my—future— brother-in-law. We were not of the same size, but the clothes answered every purpose until I got more of my own.

Before I returned I mustered up courage to make known, in the most awkward manner imaginable, the discovery I had made on learning that the 4th infantry had been ordered away from Jefferson Barracks. The young lady afterwards admitted that she too, although until then she had never looked upon me other than as a visitor whose company was agreeable to her, had experienced a depression of spirits she could not account for when the regiment left. Before separating it was definitely understood that at a convenient time we would join our fortunes, and not let the removal of a regiment

7. Commentators have remarked on Grant's peculiar superstition about retracing his steps and suggested that it translated into his way of making war, which was characterized by its relentless forward momentum. Unsurprisingly, soldiers are often superstitious, given to ritual in places of hazard and unpredictability. Joseph Heller suggests at once the reasons for—and the futility of—such superstition in his satirical novel of World War II, *Catch-22*:

> Nothing could save the men in Pianosa from the mission to Bologna. They were trapped.
> . . . All through the day, they looked at the bomb line on the big, wobbling easel map of Italy. . . . The bomb line was a scarlet band of narrow satin ribbon that delineated the forwardmost position of the Allied ground forces in every sector. . . .
> . . . When night fell, they congregated in the darkness with flashlights, continuing their macabre vigil at the bomb line in brooding entreaty as though hoping to move the ribbon up by the collective weight of their sullen prayers.
> "I really can't believe it," Clevinger exclaimed to Yossarian in a voice rising and falling in protest and wonder. "It's a complete reversion to primitive superstition. They're confusing cause and effect. It makes as much sense as knocking on wood or crossing your fingers. They really believe that we wouldn't have to fly that mission tomorrow if someone would only tiptoe up to the map in the middle of the night and move the bomb line over Bologna. Can you imagine? You and I must be the only rational ones left."
> In the middle of the night Yossarian knocked on wood, crossed his fingers, and tiptoed out of his tent to move the bomb line up over Bologna. . . .
> Moving the bomb line did not fool the Germans.

Catch-22 (New York: Simon & Schuster, 2011), 118–19, 131.

trouble us. This was in May, 1844. It was the 22d of August, 1848, before the fulfilment of this agreement. My duties kept me on the frontier of Louisiana with the Army of Observation during the pendency of Annexation; and afterwards I was absent through the war with Mexico, provoked by the action of the army, if not by the annexation itself. During that time there was a constant correspondence between Miss Dent and myself, but we only met once in the period of four years and three months. In May, 1845, I procured a leave for twenty days, visited St. Louis, and obtained the consent of the parents for the union, which had not been asked for before.

As already stated, it was never my intention to remain in the army long, but to prepare myself for a professorship in some college. Accordingly, soon after I was settled at Jefferson Barracks, I wrote a letter to Professor Church—Professor of Mathematics at West Point—requesting him to ask my designation as his assistant, when next a detail had to be made. Assistant professors at West Point are all officers of the army, supposed to be selected for their special fitness for the particular branch of study they are assigned to teach. The answer from Professor Church was entirely satisfactory, and no doubt I should have been detailed a year or two later but for the Mexican War coming on.[8] Accordingly I laid out for myself a course of studies to be

---

8. Albert E. Church (1807–1878) graduated first in the West Point class of 1828. After several years of service as an artillery officer, he returned to the academy to teach mathematics for half a century. Church's West Point obituary suggests something of his personality and its appeal to the young Grant:

> Being thoroughly familiar with his subject, understanding all its difficult and doubtful points, all its real and imaginary perplexities, with a distinct and pleasant voice, a kind and urbane manner, he had the happy faculty of making his subject and his method of treating it attractive to his pupils. Both by the unity and detail of his expositions he led them easily on to the mastery of the subject, and many a "fundler" left the recitation room in a cheerful mood, by reason of the patient and gracious manner with which he had been helped to understand some intricate problem, so that he almost persuaded himself that he had solved it by his own ingenuity. One needed to be dull or idle to be "found deficient" under such instruction.

Geo. W. Holley, "Albert E. Church," *Ninth Annual Reunion of the Association of the Graduates of the United States Military Academy*, June 13, 1878 (New York: A. S. Barnes, 1878), 53.

Knowing that Julia's father was not overly impressed with a young lieutenant's prospects, Grant had written to "Colonel Dent" in October 1845, before the Mexican War broke out:

pursued in garrison, with regularity, if not persistency. I reviewed my West Point course of mathematics during the seven months at Jefferson Barracks, and read many valuable historical works, besides an occasional novel.[9] To help my memory I kept a book in which I would write up, from time to time, my recollections of all I had read since last posting it. When the regiment was ordered away, I being absent at the time, my effects were packed up by Lieutenant Haslett [Robert Hazlitt], of the 4th infantry, and taken along. I never saw my journal after, nor did I ever keep another, except for a portion of the time while travelling abroad. Often since a fear has crossed my mind lest that book might turn up yet, and fall into the hands of some malicious person who would publish it. I know its appearance would cause me as much heart-burning as my youthful horse-trade, or the later rebuke for wearing uniform clothes.[10]

The 3d infantry had selected camping grounds on the reservation at Fort Jessup, about midway between the Red River and the Sabine. Our orders required us to go into camp in the same neighborhood, and await further instructions. Those authorized to do so selected a place in the pine woods, between the old town of Natchitoches and Grand Ecore, about three miles from each, and on high ground back from the river. The place was given the name of Camp Salubrity, and proved entitled to it. The camp was on a high, sandy, pine ridge, with spring branches in the valley, in front and rear. The springs furnished an abundance of cool, pure water, and the ridge was above

---

Your Pa asks what I could do out of the Army? I can tell you: I have at this time the offer of a professorship of mathematics in a tolerably well endowed College in Hillsboro, Ohio, a large and flourishing town, where my salery would probably equal or exceed my present pay. The Principle of the Institution got my father to write to me on the subject; he says I can have until next spring to think of this matter. The last letter I wrote was to make all the enquiries I could about the situation and if the answer proves favorable I shall give this matter serious concideration.

PUSG, 1:59.

9. In the same letter to Julia in which he shared his ambitions of becoming a professor of mathematics, Grant reported that he was reading *The Wandering Jew*, a popular and strongly anti-Catholic novel by Eugène Sue. See *PUSG*, 1:60.

10. This passing reference to the lost journal and the allusion to other embarrassing incidents he has already narrated reveal a persistent sensitivity, which is the keynote of McFeely's biography of Grant. McFeely perhaps overemphasizes these psychological wounds, but Grant's vulnerability manifests itself at those moments later in the text where he expresses a concern for doing justice to the reputations of others.

the flight of mosquitoes, which abound in that region in great multitudes and of great voracity. In the valley they swarmed in myriads, but never came to the summit of the ridge. The regiment occupied this camp six months before the first death occurred, and that was caused by an accident.

There was no intimation given that the removal of the 3d and 4th regiments of infantry to the western border of Louisiana was occasioned in any way by the prospective annexation of Texas, but it was generally understood that such was the case. Ostensibly we were intended to prevent filibustering into Texas, but really as a menace to Mexico in case she appeared to contemplate war. Generally the officers of the army were indifferent whether the annexation was consummated or not; but not so all of them. For myself, I was bitterly opposed to the measure, and to this day regard the war, which resulted, as one of the most unjust ever waged by a stronger against a weaker nation. It was an instance of a republic following the bad example of European monarchies, in not considering justice in their desire to acquire additional territory.[11]

Texas was originally a state belonging to the republic of Mexico. It extended from the Sabine River on the east to the Rio Grande on the west, and from the Gulf of Mexico on the south and east to the territory of the United States and New Mexico—another Mexican state at that time—on the north and west. An empire in territory, it had but a very sparse popula-

---

11. The Mexican War, provoked in large part by the Southern slave power, is generally regarded as a prelude to the American Civil War. Grant was not alone in his condemnation of it. As Amy S. Greenberg explains in an excellent history, the conflict with Mexico sparked "America's first national antiwar movement." See *A Wicked War: Clay, Lincoln, and the 1846 U.S. Invasion of Mexico* (New York: Knopf, 2012), xvi.

Antiwar sentiment found notably fervent expression in the theologian Theodore Parker's oration at Boston's Faneuil Hall on February 4, 1847:

> We are in a war; the signs of war are seen here in Boston. Men, needed to hew wood and honestly serve society, are marching about your streets; they are learning to kill men, men who never harmed us nor them; learning to kill their brothers. It is a mean and infamous war we are fighting. It is a great boy fighting a little one, and that little one feeble and sick. What makes it worse is, the little boy is in the right, and the big boy is in the wrong, and tells solemn lies to make his side seem right. He wants, besides, to make the small boy pay the expenses of the quarrel.

"Speech Delivered at the Anti-War Meeting in Faneuil Hall," February 4, 1847, *The Collected Works of Theodore Parker*, ed. Frances Power Cobbe, vol. 4, *Discourses of Politics* (London: Trübner, 1863), 32.

tion, until settled by Americans who had received authority from Mexico to colonize. These colonists paid very little attention to the supreme government, and introduced slavery into the state almost from the start, though the constitution of Mexico did not, nor does it now, sanction that institution. Soon they set up an independent government of their own, and war existed, between Texas and Mexico, in name from that time until 1836, when active hostilities very nearly ceased upon the capture of Santa Anna, the Mexican President.[12] Before long, however, the same people—who with permission of Mexico had colonized Texas, and afterwards set up slavery there, and then seceded as soon as they felt strong enough to do so—offered themselves and the State to the United States, and in 1845 their offer was accepted. The occupation, separation and annexation were, from the inception of the movement to its final consummation, a conspiracy to acquire territory out of which slave states might be formed for the American Union.

Statue of Theodore Parker,
Theodore Parker Church,
West Roxbury, Massachusetts.
Photograph by Elizabeth D. Samet.

12. Antonio López de Santa Anna (1794–1876) led Mexican forces against Texas in 1835. He supervised the slaughter at the Alamo and later lost the Battle of San Jacinto to Sam Houston.

Even if the annexation itself could be justified, the manner in which
the subsequent war was forced upon Mexico cannot. The fact is, annex-
ationists wanted more territory than they could possibly lay any claim to,
as part of the new acquisition. Texas, as an independent State, never had
exercised jurisdiction over the territory between the Nueces River and the
Rio Grande. Mexico had never recognized the independence of Texas, and
maintained that, even if independent, the State had no claim south of the
Nueces. I am aware that a treaty, made by the Texans with Santa Anna while
he was under duress, ceded all the territory between the Nueces and the Rio
Grande; but he was a prisoner of war when the treaty was made, and his life
was in jeopardy. He knew, too, that he deserved execution at the hands of
the Texans, if they should ever capture him. The Texans, if they had taken
his life, would have only followed the example set by Santa Anna himself a
few years before, when he executed the entire garrison of the Alamo and the
villagers of Goliad.

In taking military possession of Texas after annexation, the army of
occupation, under General Taylor, was directed to occupy the disputed territory. The army did not stop at the Nueces and offer to negotiate for a
settlement of the boundary question, but went beyond, apparently in order
to force Mexico to initiate war. It is to the credit of the American nation,
however, that after conquering Mexico, and while practically holding the
country in our possession, so that we could have retained the whole of it,
or made any terms we chose, we paid a round sum for the additional territory taken; more than it was worth, or was likely to be, to Mexico. To us
it was an empire and of incalculable value; but it might have been obtained
by other means. The Southern rebellion was largely the outgrowth of the
Mexican war. Nations, like individuals, are punished for their transgres-
sions. We got our punishment in the most sanguinary and expensive war of
modern times.

The 4th infantry went into camp at Salubrity in the month of May,
1844, with instructions, as I have said, to await further orders. At first, officers and men occupied ordinary tents. As the summer heat increased these
were covered by sheds to break the rays of the sun. The summer was whiled
away in social enjoyments among the officers, in visiting those stationed at,
and near, Fort Jessup, twenty-five miles away, visiting the planters on the
Red River, and the citizens of Natchitoches and Grand Ecore. There was
much pleasant intercourse between the inhabitants and the officers of the
army. I retain very agreeable recollections of my stay at Camp Salubrity, and
of the acquaintances made there, and no doubt my feeling is shared by the

few officers living who were there at the time. I can call to mind only two officers of the 4th infantry, besides myself, who were at Camp Salubrity with the regiment, who are now alive.[13]

With a war in prospect, and belonging to a regiment that had an unusual number of officers detailed on special duty away from the regiment, my hopes of being ordered to West Point as instructor vanished. At the time of which I now write, officers in the quartermaster's, commissary's and adjutant-general's departments were appointed from the line of the army, and did not vacate their regimental commissions until their regimental and staff commissions were for the same grades. Generally lieutenants were appointed to captaincies to fill vacancies in the staff corps. If they should reach a captaincy in the line before they arrived at a majority in the staff, they would elect which commission they would retain. In the 4th infantry, in 1844, at least six line officers were on duty in the staff, and therefore permanently detached from the regiment. Under these circumstances I gave up everything like a special course of reading, and only read thereafter for my own amusement, and not very much for that, until the war was over. I kept a horse and rode, and staid out of doors most of the time by day, and entirely recovered from the cough which I had carried from West Point, and from all indications of consumption. I have often thought that my life was saved, and my health restored, by exercise and exposure, enforced by an administrative act, and a war, both of which I disapproved.

As summer wore away, and cool days and colder nights came upon us, the tents we were occupying ceased to afford comfortable quarters; and "further orders" not reaching us, we began to look about to remedy the hardship. Men were put to work getting out timber to build huts, and in a very short time all were comfortably housed—privates as well as officers. The outlay by the government in accomplishing this was nothing, or nearly nothing. The winter was spent more agreeably than the summer had been. There were occasional parties given by the planters along the "coast"—as the bottom lands on the Red River were called. The climate was delightful.

Near the close of the short session of Congress of 1844–5, the bill for

---

13. Grant's passing remark that most officers were no longer alive generalizes the very particular loss of his friend and classmate Robert Hazlitt, with whom, as he revealed in a letter to Julia, he spent most of his time at Camp Salubrity: "Hazlitt and me visit each other, at our linen Mansions about three times per day, and our calls are so unfashionable that the three calls lasts from morning until bed time." Letter to Julia Dent, July 28, 1844, *PUSG*, 1:31.

the annexation of Texas to the United States was passed. It reached President Tyler on the 1st of March, 1845, and promptly received his approval. When the news reached us we began to look again for "further orders." They did not arrive promptly, and on the 1st of May following I asked and obtained a leave of absence for twenty days, for the purpose of visiting St. Louis. The object of this visit has been before stated.

Early in July the long expected orders were received, but they only took the regiment to New Orleans Barracks. We reached there before the middle of the month, and again waited weeks for still further orders. The yellow fever was raging in New Orleans during the time we remained there, and the streets of the city had the appearance of a continuous well-observed Sunday.[14] I recollect but one occasion when this observance seemed to be broken by the inhabitants. One morning about daylight I happened to be awake, and, hearing the discharge of a rifle not far off, I looked out to ascertain where the sound came from. I observed a couple of clusters of men near by, and learned afterwards that "it was nothing; only a couple of gentlemen deciding a difference of opinion with rifles, at twenty paces." I do not remember if either was killed, or even hurt, but no doubt the question of difference was settled satisfactorily, and "honorably," in the estimation of the parties engaged. I do not believe I ever would have the courage to fight a duel. If any man should wrong me to the extent of my being willing to kill him, I would not be willing to give him the choice of weapons with which it should be done, and of the time, place and distance separating us, when I executed him. If I should do another such a wrong as to justify him in killing me, I would make any reasonable atonement within my power, if convinced of the wrong done. I place my opposition to duelling on higher grounds than

---

14. For a gripping cinematic treatment of a yellow fever epidemic in New Orleans in the 1850s, see the Warner Brothers film *Jezebel* (1938), directed by William Wyler and starring Bette Davis, Henry Fonda, Fay Bainter, and George Brent. The film also offers a more nuanced portrait of antebellum Southern life than does the more celebrated film *Gone with the Wind*, released the following year.

In 1900, U.S. Army physician Walter Reed (1851–1902) finally proved that mosquitos were the vector for yellow fever and disproved the theory that the disease was caused by contact with infected air or with "fomites," clothing or bedding used by infected people. Reed did his research in Cuba, where, during the Spanish-American War, more American soldiers died of disease than of combat wounds. Reed is celebrated for the elegance of his experiment, which involved placing subjects in two adjacent rooms separated only by a screen, which allowed air but not infected mosquitos to circulate. Sadly, some of his human subjects died after being infected.

any here stated. No doubt a majority of the duels fought have been for want of moral courage on the part of those engaged to decline.[15]

At Camp Salubrity, and when we went to New Orleans Barracks, the 4th infantry was commanded by Colonel Vose, then an old gentleman who had not commanded on drill for a number of years. He was not a man to discover infirmity in the presence of danger. It now appeared that war was imminent, and he felt that it was his duty to brush up his tactics. Accordingly, when we got settled down at our new post, he took command of the regiment at a battalion drill. Only two or three evolutions had been gone through when he dismissed the battalion, and, turning to go to his own quarters, dropped dead. He had not been complaining of ill health, but no doubt died of heart disease. He was a most estimable man, of exemplary habits, and by no means the author of his own disease.

---

15. This is the first of several times Grant uses the phrase "moral courage." It proved to be an important concept for him. This discussion about dueling reveals his lack of sympathy for old-fashioned concepts of honor and chivalry that dominated military culture at the time and to which many Southern officers in particular would continue to cling. Grant's impatience with this code was to manifest itself again in his exchange with Confederate commander Simon Bolivar Buckner at Fort Donelson in 1862.

One of the most energetic critiques of dueling as a way of settling differences among gentlemen in an honor culture can be found in a 1709 essay by Richard Steele: the sense of "resentment" that motivates dueling, Steele argues, "neither has its foundation from true reason or solid fame; but is an imposture, made up of cowardice, falsehood, and want of understanding. . . . Most of the quarrels I have ever known, have proceeded from some valiant coxcomb's persisting, in the wrong, to defend some prevailing folly, and preserve himself from the ingenuity of owning a mistake." No. 25, *The Tatler*, ed. George A. Aitken (London: Duckworth, 1898), 1:208–209.

4

Corpus Christi—Mexican Smuggling—
Spanish Rule in Mexico—
Supplying Transportation

Early in September the regiment left New Orleans for Corpus Christi, now in Texas. Ocean steamers were not then common, and the passage was made in sailing vessels. At that time there was not more than three feet of water in the channel at the outlet of Corpus Christi Bay; the debarkation, therefore, had to take place by small steamers, and at an island in the channel called Shell Island, the ships anchoring some miles out from shore. This made the work slow, and as the army was only supplied with one or two steamers, it took a number of days to effect the landing of a single regiment with its stores, camp and garrison equipage, etc. There happened to be pleasant weather while this was going on, but the land-swell was so great that when the ship and steamer were on opposite sides of the same wave they would be at considerable distance apart. The men and baggage were let down to a point higher than the lower deck of the steamer, and when ship and steamer got into the trough between the waves, and were close together, the load would be drawn over the steamer and rapidly run down until it rested on the deck.

After I had gone ashore, and had been on guard several days at Shell Island, quite six miles from the ship, I had occasion for some reason or other to return on board. While on the *Suviah*—I think that was the name of our vessel—I heard a tremendous racket at the other end of the ship, and much and excited sailor language, such as "damn your eyes," etc. In a moment or two the captain, who was an excitable little man, dying with consumption, and not weighing much over a hundred pounds, came running out, carrying a sabre nearly as large and as heavy as he was, and crying, that his men had

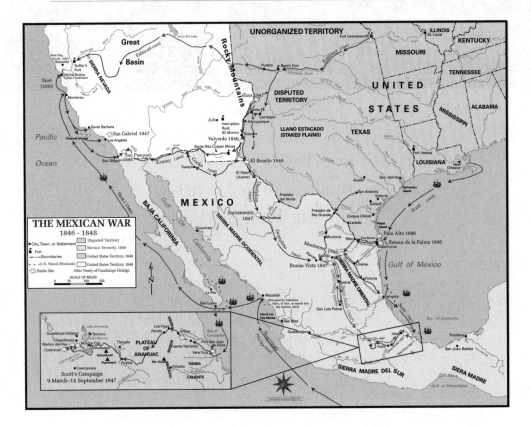

Mexican War Overview Map. *West Point Atlas of the Mexican War.*
Courtesy of Department of History, USMA.

mutinied. It was necessary to sustain the captain without question, and in a few minutes all the sailors charged with mutiny were in irons. I rather felt for a time a wish that I had not gone aboard just then. As the men charged with mutiny submitted to being placed in irons without resistance, I always doubted if they knew that they had mutinied until they were told.

By the time I was ready to leave the ship again I thought I had learned enough of the working of the double and single pulley, by which passengers were let down from the upper deck of the ship to the steamer below, and determined to let myself down without assistance. Without saying anything of my intentions to any one, I mounted the railing, and taking hold of the centre rope, just below the upper block, I put one foot on the hook below the lower block, and stepped off. Just as I did so some one called out "hold on." It was too late. I tried to "hold on" with all my might, but my heels went up,

Captain D. P. Whiting, 7th Infantry, "Birds-eye View of the Camp of the Army of Occupation," Corpus Christi, Texas, October 1845. *Library of Congress, Prints and Photographs Division, LC-DIG-pga-06205.*

and my head went down so rapidly that my hold broke, and I plunged head foremost into the water, some twenty-five feet below, with such velocity that it seemed to me I never would stop. When I came to the surface again, being a fair swimmer, and not having lost my presence of mind, I swam around until a bucket was let down for me, and I was drawn up without a scratch or injury. I do not believe there was a man on board who sympathized with me in the least when they found me uninjured. I rather enjoyed the joke myself. The captain of the *Suviah* died of his disease a few months later, and I believe before the mutineers were tried. I hope they got clear, because, as before stated, I always thought the mutiny was all in the brain of a very weak and sick man.

After reaching shore, or Shell Island, the labor of getting to Corpus Christi was slow and tedious. There was, if my memory serves me, but one small steamer to transport troops and baggage when the 4th infantry arrived. Others were procured later. The distance from Shell Island to Corpus Christi was some sixteen or eighteen miles. The channel to the bay was so shallow that the steamer, small as it was, had to be dragged over the bottom when loaded. Not more than one trip a day could be effected. Later this was remedied, by deepening the channel and increasing the number of vessels suitable to its navigation.

Corpus Christi is near the head of the bay of the same name, formed by the entrance of the Nueces River into tide-water, and is on the west bank of that bay. At the time of its first occupancy by United States troops there was a small Mexican hamlet there, containing probably less than one hundred souls. There was, in addition, a small American trading post, at which goods were sold to Mexican smugglers. All goods were put up in compact packages of about one hundred pounds each, suitable for loading on pack mules. Two of these packages made a load for an ordinary Mexican mule, and three for the larger ones. The bulk of the trade was in leaf tobacco, and domestic cotton-cloths and calicoes. The Mexicans had, before the arrival of the army, but little to offer in exchange except silver. The trade in tobacco was enormous, considering the population to be supplied. Almost every Mexican above the age of ten years, and many much younger, smoked the cigarette. Nearly every Mexican carried a pouch of leaf tobacco, powdered by rolling in the hands, and a roll of corn husks to make wrappers. The cigarettes were made by the smokers as they used them.[1]

---

1. Grant omits a discussion of the ways in which the soldiers occupied their days during this long period of waiting for the war to begin. We have to look elsewhere, in this case to Longstreet, to obtain a more detailed portrait of life in camp:

> Near our camps were extensive plains well adapted to military manoeuvres which were put to prompt use for drill and professional instruction. There were many advantages too in the way of amusement, game on the wild prairies and fish in the broad gulf were plentiful, and there was the salt water for bathing. On one occasion during the winter a violent north wind forced the waters over the beach, in some places far enough to disturb our camps, and when they receded, quantities of fish were found in the little puddles left behind, and turtles more than enough to supply the army.
>
> The officers built a theatre, depending upon their own efforts to reimburse them. As there was no one outside the army except two rancheros within a hundred miles, our dramatic company was organized from among the officers, who took both male and female characters. In farce and comedy we did well enough, and soon collected funds to pay for the building and incidental expenses. The house was filled every night. General Worth always encouraging us, General Taylor sometimes, and General Twiggs occasionally, we found ourselves in funds sufficient to send over to New Orleans for costumes, and concluded to try tragedy. The "Moor of Venice" was chosen, Lieutenant Theoderic Porter to be the Moor, and Lieutenant U. S. Grant to be the daughter of Brabantio. But after rehearsal Porter protested that male heroines could not support the character nor give

sentiment to the hero, so we sent over to New Orleans and secured Mrs. Hart, who was popular with the garrisons in Florida. Then all went well, and life through the winter was gay.

Longstreet, *Manassas to Appomattox*, 19–20.

The young George Gordon Meade was not quite so enthusiastic about the camp's entertainments: "I have had a rather stupid day of it," he wrote to his wife on January 1, 1846:

> In the morning I was engaged making official complimentary visits to the "big-bugs" of the camp, all of whom had egg-nogg and cake for their visitors; then we had a race, gotten up by the officers for their amusement; and then I dined with a party who endeavored to be as merry as they could be under the circumstances; and, in the evening, I accompanied them to the theatre; for you must know that since our arrival here they have built a theatre and imported a company of strolling actors, who murder tragedy, burlesque comedy, and render farce into buffoonery, in the most approved style.

The Life and Letters of George Gordon Meade (New York: Charles Scribner's Sons, 1913), 1:43–44.

Although *Othello* is staged today as a serious tragedy, during the nineteenth century it was often performed, in both Great Britain and the United States, in one of a few burlesque adaptations of the original. For a discussion of issues of race and performance as manifested in nineteenth-century American productions of *Othello*, see Coppélia Kahn, "Forbidden Mixtures: Shakespeare in Blackface Minstrelsy, 1844," *Shakespeare and the Cultures of Performance*, ed. Paul Yachnin and Patricia Badir (Aldershot, UK: Ashgate, 2008).

An example of a nineteenth-century staging of *Othello* as burlesque. J. W. Gear, "Mr. W. J. Hammond and Ms. Daly as Othello and Desdemona at the New Strand Theatre." *Yale Center for British Art, Paul Mellon Fund.*

In a January 12, 1846, letter to Julia, Grant does mention that two theaters had been built—and that there was a per-

Up to the time of which I write, and for years afterwards—I think until the administration of President [Benito] Juarez [Juárez]—the cultivation, manufacture and sale of tobacco constituted a government monopoly, and paid the bulk of the revenue collected from internal sources. The price was enormously high, and made successful smuggling very profitable. The difficulty of obtaining tobacco is probably the reason why everybody, male and female, used it at that time. I know from my own experience that when I was at West Point, the fact that tobacco, in every form, was prohibited, and the mere possession of the weed severely punished, made the majority of the cadets, myself included, try to acquire the habit of using it. I failed utterly at the time and for many years afterward; but the majority accomplished the object of their youthful ambition.[2]

---

formance every night—but he does not allude to his own participation in the amateur theatricals. See *PUSG*, 1:69.

2. Grant overcame this aversion to tobacco to become an inveterate smoker, a habit that was likely a contributing factor in his fatal cancer. He was a pipe smoker at the beginning of the Civil War until his victory at Fort Donelson in 1862, when the public flooded him with gifts of cigar boxes after reading newspapers stories that he had been smoking a cigar during the attack. See Bruce Catton, *Grant Moves South* (1960; Boston: Little Brown, 1988), 181. Army surgeon John Brinton records his first meeting with the pipe-smoking Grant early in the war at his headquarters at Cairo, Illinois:

> He did nothing carelessly, but worked slowly, every now and then stopping and taking his pipe out of his mouth.
>
> But this reminds me, that I have not yet spoken of his pipe. The man in after days became so thoroughly identified with the cigar, that people could scarcely believe that he was once an assiduous smoker of the pipe. Well, the pipe which he first used was a meerschaum with a curved stem eight or ten inches long, which allowed the pipe to hang down. He smoked steadily and slowly and evidently greatly enjoyed his tobacco.

Personal Memoirs of John H. Brinton, Major and Surgeon U. S. V. 1861–1865 (New York: Neale, 1914), 37–38.

Horace Porter offers this account of Grant's record-breaking day of smoking at the Battle of the Wilderness in 1864:

> [Winfield Scott] Hancock came to headquarters about 8 P.M., and had a conference with the general-in-chief and General Meade. . . . General Grant, in offering him a cigar, found that only one was left in his pocket. Deducting the number he had given away from the supply he had started out with in the morning showed that he had smoked that day about twenty, all very strong and of formidable size. But it must remembered that it was

Under Spanish rule Mexico was prohibited from producing anything that the mother-country could supply. This rule excluded the cultivation of the grape, olive and many other articles to which the soil and climate were well adapted. The country was governed for "revenue only;" and tobacco, which cannot be raised in Spain, but is indigenous to Mexico, offered a fine instrumentality for securing this prime object of government. The native population had been in the habit of using "the weed" from a period, back of any recorded history of this continent. Bad habits—if not restrained by law or public opinion—spread more rapidly and universally than good ones, and the Spanish colonists adopted the use of tobacco almost as generally as the natives. Spain, therefore, in order to secure the largest revenue from this source, prohibited the cultivation, except in specified localities—and in these places farmed out the privilege at a very high price. The tobacco when raised could only be sold to the government, and the price to the consumer was limited only by the avarice of the authorities, and the capacity of the people to pay.

All laws for the government of the country were enacted in Spain, and the officers for their execution were appointed by the Crown, and sent out to the New El Dorado.[3] The Mexicans had been brought up ignorant of

---

a particularly long day. He never afterward equaled that record in the use of tobacco.

Porter, *Campaigning*, 70.

3. El Dorado was a mythical city of gold celebrated in literature. Edgar Allan Poe's poem "Eldorado" provides one version of the legend:

Gayly bedight,
A gallant knight,
In sunshine and in shadow,
Had journeyed long,
Singing a song,
In search of Eldorado.

But he grew old,—
This knight so bold,—
And o'er his heart a shadow
Fell as he found
No spot of ground
That looked like Eldorado.

And, as his strength
Failed him at length,

how to legislate or how to rule. When they gained their independence, after many years of war, it was the most natural thing in the world that they should adopt as their own the laws then in existence. The only change was, that Mexico became her own executor of the laws and the recipient of the revenues. The tobacco tax, yielding so large a revenue under the law as it stood, was one of the last, if not the very last, of the obnoxious imposts to be repealed. Now, the citizens are allowed to cultivate any crops the soil will yield. Tobacco is cheap, and every quality can be produced. Its use is by no means so general as when I first visited the country.[4]

Gradually the "Army of Occupation" assembled at Corpus Christi. When it was all together it consisted of seven companies of the 2d regiment of dragoons, four companies of light artillery, five regiments of infantry—the 3d, 4th, 5th, 7th and 8th—and one regiment of artillery acting as infantry—not more than three thousand men in all. General Zachary Taylor commanded the whole. There were troops enough in one body to establish a drill and discipline sufficient to fit men and officers for all they were capable of in case of battle. The rank and file were composed of men who had enlisted in time of peace, to serve for seven dollars a month, and were necessarily inferior as material to the average volunteers enlisted later in the war expressly to fight, and also to the volunteers in the war for the preservation of the Union. The men engaged in the Mexican war were brave, and the officers of the regular army, from highest to lowest, were educated in their profession. A more efficient army for its number and armament, I do not believe ever fought a battle than the one commanded by General Taylor in his first two engagements on Mexican—or Texan soil.

The presence of United States troops on the edge of the disputed ter-

---

He met a pilgrim Shadow.
"Shadow," said he,
"Where can it be—
This land of Eldorado?"

"Over the Mountains
Of the Moon,
Down the Valley of the Shadow,
Ride, boldly ride,"
The Shade replied,—
"If you seek for Eldorado!"

Edgar Allan Poe, *Poems* (New York: Crowell, 1882), 98.

4. Grant never lost his affection for Mexico and returned for a visit with Julia in 1880.

ritory furthest from the Mexican settlements, was not sufficient to provoke hostilities. We were sent to provoke a fight, but it was essential that Mexico should commence it. It was very doubtful whether Congress would declare war; but if Mexico should attack our troops, the Executive could announce, "Whereas, war exists by the acts of, etc.," and prosecute the contest with vigor. Once initiated there were but few public men who would have the courage to oppose it. Experience proves that the man who obstructs a war in which his nation is engaged, no matter whether right or wrong, occupies no enviable place in life or history. Better for him, individually, to advocate "war, pestilence, and famine," than to act as obstructionist to a war already begun. The history of the defeated rebel will be honorable hereafter, compared with that of the Northern man who aided him by conspiring against his government while protected by it. The most favorable posthumous history the stay-at-home traitor can hope for is—oblivion.

Mexico showing no willingness to come to the Nueces to drive the invaders from her soil, it became necessary for the "invaders" to approach to within a convenient distance to be struck. Accordingly, preparations were begun for moving the army to the Rio Grande, to a point near Matamoras. It was desirable to occupy a position near the largest centre of population possible to reach, without absolutely invading territory to which we set up no claim whatever.[5]

---

5. Among those with the courage to declare their opposition were Theodore Parker, Henry David Thoreau, Thomas Corwin, and, belatedly, U.S. Representative Abraham Lincoln, whose introduction of the so-called Spot Resolutions, which attempted to show that the United States had provoked the war by invading Mexican territory, earned him the sobriquet "Spotty Lincoln." In a speech before the House Lincoln argued that the public had been seduced by "the exceeding brightness of military glory—that attractive rainbow that rises in showers of blood—that serpent's eye that charms to destroy." *Appendix to Congressional Globe*, 30th Congress, 1st Session 95 (January 12, 1848).

Proponents of the war were inspired in part by an expansionist doctrine given impassioned voice in the writings of John L. O'Sullivan, who popularized the term *manifest destiny* in 1845:

> Why, were other reasoning wanting, in favor of now elevating this question of the reception of Texas into the Union, out of the lower region of our past party dissensions, up to its proper level of a high and broad nationality, it surely is to be found, found abundantly, in the manner in which other nations have undertaken to intrude themselves into it, between us and the proper parties to the case, in a spirit of hostile interference against us, for the avowed object of thwarting our policy and hampering our power, limiting our greatness and checking the fulfillment of our manifest destiny to

The distance from Corpus Christi to Matamoras is about one hundred and fifty miles. The country does not abound in fresh water, and the length of the marches had to be regulated by the distance between water supplies. Besides the streams, there were occasional pools, filled during the rainy season, some probably made by the traders, who travelled constantly between Corpus Christi and the Rio Grande, and some by the buffalo. There was not at that time a single habitation, cultivated field, or herd of domestic animals, between Corpus Christi and Matamoras. It was necessary, therefore, to have a wagon train sufficiently large to transport the camp and garrison equipage, officers' baggage, rations for the army, and part rations of grain for the artillery horses and all the animals taken from the north, where they had been accustomed to having their forage furnished them. The army was but indifferently supplied with transportation. Wagons and harness could easily be supplied from the north; but mules and horses could not so readily be brought. The American traders and Mexican smugglers came to the relief. Contracts were made for mules at from eight to eleven dollars each. The smugglers furnished the animals, and took their pay in goods of the description before mentioned. I doubt whether the Mexicans received in value from the traders five dollars per head for the animals they furnished, and still more, whether they paid anything but their own time in procuring them. Such is trade; such is war. The government paid in hard cash to the contractor the stipulated price.

Between the Rio Grande and the Nueces there was at that time a large band of wild horses feeding; as numerous, probably, as the band of buffalo roaming further north was before its rapid extermination commenced. The Mexicans used to capture these in large numbers and bring them into the American settlements and sell them. A picked animal could be purchased at from eight to twelve dollars, but taken at wholesale, they could be bought for thirty-six dollars a dozen. Some of these were purchased for the army, and answered a most useful purpose. The horses were generally very strong, formed much like the Norman horse, and with very heavy manes and tails. A number of officers supplied themselves with these, and they generally ren-

---

overspread the continent allotted by Providence for the free development of our yearly multiplying millions.

"Annexation," *The United States Magazine and Democratic Review* 17, no. 1 (July–August 1845): 5.

George Catlin, *Catching the Wild Horse,* from *Catlin's North American Indian Portfolio,* 1845. *From The New York Public Library, https://digitalcollections.nypl.org/items/510d47da-dbe9-a3d9-e040-e00a18064a99.*

dered as useful service as the northern animal; in fact they were much better when grazing was the only means of supplying forage.

There was no need for haste, and some months were consumed in the necessary preparations for a move. In the meantime the army was engaged in all the duties pertaining to the officer and the soldier. Twice, that I remember, small trains were sent from Corpus Christi, with cavalry escorts, to San Antonio and Austin, with paymasters and funds to pay off small detachments of troops stationed at those places. General Taylor encouraged officers to accompany these expeditions. I accompanied one of them in December, 1845. The distance from Corpus Christi to San Antonio was then computed at one hundred and fifty miles. Now that roads exist it is probably less. From San Antonio to Austin we computed the distance at one hundred and ten miles, and from the latter place back to Corpus Christi at over two hundred miles. I know the distance now from San Antonio to Austin is but little over eighty miles, so that our computation was probably too high.

There was not at the time an individual living between Corpus Christi and San Antonio until within about thirty miles of the latter point, where there were a few scattering Mexican settlements along the San Antonio River. The people in at least one of these hamlets lived underground for protection against the Indians. The country abounded in game, such as deer and antelope, with abundance of wild turkeys along the streams and where there were nut-bearing woods. On the Nueces, about twenty-five miles up from Corpus Christi, were a few log cabins, the remains of a town called San Patricio, but the inhabitants had all been massacred by the Indians, or driven away.

San Antonio was about equally divided in population between Americans and Mexicans. From there to Austin there was not a single residence except at New Braunfels, on the Guadalupe River. At that point was a settlement of Germans who had only that year come into the State. At all events they were living in small huts, about such as soldiers would hastily construct for temporary occupation. From Austin to Corpus Christi there was only a small settlement at Bastrop, with a few farms along the Colorado River; but after leaving that, there were no settlements except the home of one man, with one female slave, at the old town of Goliad. Some of the houses were still standing. Goliad had been quite a village for the period and region, but some years before there had been a Mexican massacre, in which every inhabitant had been killed or driven away. This, with the massacre of the prisoners in the Alamo, San Antonio, about the same time, more than three hundred men in all, furnished the strongest justification the Texans had for carrying on the war with so much cruelty.[6] In fact, from that time until the Mexican

---

6. Texans, led by Sam Houston and Stephen Austin, declared their independence from Mexico in 1835. The massacre of Americans by Mexican troops under Santa Anna at the Alamo and Goliad followed. In the ensuing decade, after the Texans' victory at San Jacinto, Texas existed as an independent republic; its attempts to join the United States as a slave state intensified the national debate over slavery.

Among those killed at the Alamo was Davy Crockett, whose legend was stoked in part by the publication of *Col. Crockett's Exploits and Adventures in Texas*, which was in fact written by the playwright Richard Penn Smith. Theodore Roosevelt later relied on it for his adulatory essay "Remember the Alamo." Smith renders Crockett's last diary entry as follows: "*March 5*. Pop, pop, pop! Bom, bom, bom! throughout the day.—No time for memorandums now.—Go ahead!—Liberty and independence for ever!" Here Penn renders Congressman Crockett's explanation of his decision to go to Texas to his Tennessee constituents: "I concluded my speech by telling them that I was done with politics for the present, and that they might all go to hell, and I would go to Texas." Smith's Crockett wants "to give the Texians a helping hand, on the high road to freedom." Crockett loved the white man's freedom, as he made clear in Mississippi, where he stopped on the way to Texas:

war, the hostilities between Texans and Mexicans was so great that neither was safe in the neighborhood of the other who might be in superior numbers or possessed of superior arms. The man we found living there seemed like an old friend; he had come from near Fort Jessup, Louisiana, where the officers of the 3d and 4th infantry and the 2d dragoons had known him and his family. He had emigrated in advance of his family to build up a home for them.

> "Well, gentlemen," says I, "being called upon for a toast, and being in a slave-holding state, in order to avoid giving offence and running the risk of being Lynched, it may be necessary to premise that I am neither an abolitionist nor a colonizationist, but simply Colonel Crockett, of Tennessee, now bound for Texas." When they heard my name they gave three cheers for Colonel Crockett; and silence being restored, I continued. "Now, gentlemen, I will offer you a toast, hoping, after what I have stated, that it will give offence to no one present; but should I be mistaken, I must imitate the 'old Roman' and take the responsibility. I offer, gentlemen, The abolition of slavery: Let the work first begin in the two houses of Congress. There are no slaves in the country more servile than the party slaves in Congress. The wink or the nod of their masters is all sufficient for the accomplishment of the most dirty work."

Col. Crockett's Exploits and Adventures in Texas . . . Written by Himself (New York: Wm. H. Graham, 1848), 202, 31, 33, 82.

5

Trip to Austin—Promotion to Full Second Lieutenant—Army of Occupation

When our party left Corpus Christi it was quite large, including the cavalry escort, Paymaster, Major Dix, his clerk and the officers who, like myself, were simply on leave; but all the officers on leave, except Lieutenant Benjamin—afterwards killed in the valley of Mexico—Lieutenant, now General, Augur, and myself, concluded to spend their allotted time at San Antonio and return from there.[1] We were all to be back at Corpus Christi by the end of the month. The paymaster was detained in Austin so long that, if we had waited for him, we would have exceeded our leave. We concluded, therefore, to start back at once with the animals we had, and having to rely principally on grass for their food, it was a good six days' journey. We had to sleep on the prairie every night, except at Goliad, and possibly one night on the Colorado, without shelter and with only such food as we carried with us, and prepared ourselves. The journey was hazardous on account of Indians, and there were white men in Texas whom I would not have cared to meet in a secluded place.[2] Lieutenant Augur was taken seriously

---

1. Christopher Columbus Augur (1821–1898) was Grant's classmate at West Point. He served in Mexico, on frontier duty, in the Civil War, and in various departments in the South and West until his retirement from active duty in 1885. During the Civil War he was seriously wounded at the battle of Cedar Mountain in the summer of 1862. Later, he commanded the left wing of the army during the siege of Port Hudson, May 22–July 8, 1863.

2. Smith's Davy Crockett gives a flavor of the lawless life of Texas at the time in a story of his encounter with a character he calls "the Bee hunter":

Drawing of Native Americans made by Cadet Grant,
ca. 1842. *West Point Museum Collection, United States Military Academy.*

sick before we reached Goliad and at a distance from any habitation. To add
to the complication, his horse—a mustang that had probably been captured
from the band of wild horses before alluded to, and of undoubted longevity
at his capture—gave out. It was absolutely necessary to get forward to Goliad
to find a shelter for our sick companion. By dint of patience and exceedingly
slow movements, Goliad was at last reached, and a shelter and bed secured
for our patient. We remained over a day, hoping that Augur might recover
sufficiently to resume his travels. He did not, however, and knowing that
Major Dix would be along in a few days, with his wagon-train, now empty,

In order to afford me some idea of the state of society in the more
thickly settled parts of Texas, the Bee hunter told me that he had set down
to the breakfast table, one morning at an inn, at San Felipe, and among
the small party around the board were eleven who had fled from the states
charged with having committed murder. So accustomed are the inhabitants
to the appearance of fugitives from justice that they are particularly careful
to make inquiries of the characters of newcomers, and generally obtain
early and circumstantial information concerning strangers. "Indeed," said
he, "it is very common to hear the inquiry made, 'What did he do that
made him leave home?' or, 'What have you come to Texas for?' intimating
almost an assurance of one's being a criminal."

Smith, *Exploits and Adventures*, 124.

and escort, we arranged with our Louisiana friend to take the best of care of the sick lieutenant until thus relieved, and went on.

I had never been a sportsman in my life; had scarcely ever gone in search of game, and rarely seen any when looking for it. On this trip there was no minute of time while travelling between San Patricio and the settlements on the San Antonio River, from San Antonio to Austin, and again from the Colorado River back to San Patricio, when deer or antelope could not be seen in great numbers. Each officer carried a shot-gun, and every evening, after going into camp, some would go out and soon return with venison and wild turkeys enough for the entire camp. I, however, never went out, and had no occasion to fire my gun; except, being detained over a day at Goliad, Benjamin and I concluded to go down to the creek—which was fringed with timber, much of it the pecan—and bring back a few turkeys. We had scarcely reached the edge of the timber when I heard the flutter of wings overhead, and in an instant I saw two or three turkeys flying away. These were soon followed by more, then more, and more, until a flock of twenty or thirty had left from just over my head. All this time I stood watching the turkeys to see where they flew—with my gun on my shoulder, and never once thought of levelling it at the birds. When I had time to reflect upon the matter, I came to

John James Audubon, "Wild Turkey (Male)," *The Birds of America*, 1840. *From The New York Public Library, https:// digitalcollections.nypl.org/items/510d47d9– 7341–a3d9–e040–e00a18064a99.*

the conclusion that as a sportsman I was a failure, and went back to the house. Benjamin remained out, and got as many turkeys as he wanted to carry back.[3]

After the second night at Goliad, Benjamin and I started to make the remainder of the journey alone. We reached Corpus Christi just in time to avoid "absence without leave." We met no one—not even an Indian—during the remainder of our journey, except at San Patricio. A new settlement had been started there in our absence of three weeks, induced possibly by the fact that there were houses already built, while the proximity of troops gave protection against the Indians. On the evening of the first day out from Goliad we heard the most unearthly howling of wolves, directly in our front. The prairie grass was tall and we could not see the beasts, but the sound indicated that they were near. To my ear it appeared that there must have been enough of them to devour our party, horses and all, at a single meal. The part of Ohio that I hailed from was not thickly settled, but wolves had been driven out long before I left. Benjamin was from Indiana, still less populated, where the wolf yet roamed over the prairies. He understood the nature of the animal and the capacity of a few to make believe there was an unlimited number of them. He kept on towards the noise, unmoved. I followed in his trail, lacking moral courage to turn back and join our sick companion. I have no doubt that if Benjamin had proposed returning to Goliad, I would not only have "seconded the motion" but have suggested that it

---

3. The notion that hunting is good preparation for war is a commonplace of military writing. It can be found in authorities ranging from Xenophon to Clausewitz. In *Cyropedia*, or *The Education of Cyrus*, a treatise on the preparation of the Persian emperor for his duties, Xenophon writes:

> Here is why they take care that hunting be a matter of public concern, and why, just as he is also in war, the king is their leader, and he himself joins the hunt and also takes care that they do: It seems to them that hunting is the truest of the exercises that pertain to war. For it habituates them to rise at dawn and to endure cold and heat, it exercises them in marches and in running, and it is necessary both to shoot wild animals with the bow and to spear them whenever one comes close. It is necessary that, whenever one of the mightier wild animals turns up, as often happens, even the soul be whetted, for surely one must strike the wild animal that comes to close quarters and be on one's guard against the one that approaches. Consequently, it is not easy to find anything missing from hunting that is present in war.

The Education of Cyrus, trans. and ed. Wayne Ambler (Ithaca, NY: Cornell University Press, 2001), 25.

John James Audubon, Canis Latrans (Prairie Wolf, Males), *The Viviparous Quadrupeds of North America*, 1845–1848. *From The New York Public Library, https://digitalcollections.nypl.org/items/510d47da-7839-a3d9-e040-e00a18064a99.*

was very hard-hearted in us to leave Augur sick there in the first place; but Benjamin did not propose turning back. When he did speak it was to ask: "Grant, how many wolves do you think there are in that pack?" Knowing where he was from, and suspecting that he thought I would over-estimate the number, I determined to show my acquaintance with the animal by putting the estimate below what possibly could be correct, and answered: "Oh, about twenty," very indifferently. He smiled and rode on. In a minute we were close upon them, and before they saw us. There were just *two* of them. Seated upon their haunches, with their mouths close together, they had made all the noise we had been hearing for the past ten minutes. I have often thought of this incident since when I have heard the noise of a few disappointed politicians who had deserted their associates. There are always more of them before they are counted.[4]

A week or two before leaving Corpus Christi on this trip, I had been promoted from brevet second lieutenant, 4th infantry, to full second lieutenant,

---

4. This is Grant at his folksiest. He shared with Lincoln the ability to tell a story on himself.

7th infantry. Frank Gardner,[5] of the 7th, was promoted to the 4th in the same orders. We immediately made application to be transferred, so as to get back to our old regiments. On my return, I found that our application had been approved at Washington. While in the 7th infantry I was in the company of Captain Holmes, afterwards a Lieutenant-general in the Confederate army. I never came in contact with him in the war of the Rebellion, nor did he render any very conspicuous service in his high rank. My transfer carried me to the company of Captain McCall, who resigned from the army after the Mexican war and settled in Philadelphia. He was prompt, however, to volunteer when the rebellion broke out, and soon rose to the rank of major-general in the Union army. I was not fortunate enough to meet him after he resigned. In the old army he was esteemed very highly as a soldier and gentleman. Our relations were always most pleasant.[6]

The preparations at Corpus Christi for an advance progressed as rapidly in the absence of some twenty or more lieutenants as if we had been there. The principal business consisted in securing mules, and getting them broken to harness. The process was slow but amusing. The animals sold to the government were all young and unbroken, even to the saddle, and were quite as wild as the wild horses of the prairie. Usually a number would be brought in by a company of Mexicans, partners in the delivery. The mules were first driven into a stockade, called a *corral*, inclosing an acre or more of ground. The Mexicans,—who were all experienced in throwing the lasso,—would go into the *corral* on horseback, with their lassos attached to the pommels of their saddles. Soldiers detailed as teamsters and blacksmiths would also enter the *corral*, the former with ropes to serve as halters, the latter with branding irons and a fire to keep the irons heated. A lasso was then thrown over the neck of a mule, when he would immediately go to the length of his tether, first one end, then the other in the air. While he was thus plunging and gyrating, another lasso would be thrown by another Mexican, catching the

---

5. Afterwards General Gardner, C.S.A. [Note to the first edition.]

Franklin Gardner (1823–1873) was another of Grant's West Point classmates. He would go on to command the Confederate fort at Port Hudson, which was besieged by Union forces under the command of General Nathaniel Banks in the summer of 1863. There he would face Christopher Augur, whom Grant mentions in the previous chapter.

6. Theophilus H. Holmes (1804–1880) graduated from West Point in 1829. George A. McCall (1802–1868), West Point class of 1822, fought in several Civil War engagements, was captured at the Battle of New Market, and imprisoned in Richmond's notorious Libby Prison during the summer of 1862, before being exchanged. He died in 1868.

**Edwin Forbes, "A Tough Customer." Army mules,
Rappahannock Station, Virginia, 1864.** *Library of Congress,
Prints and Photographs Division, Morgan Collection of
Civil War Drawings, LC-DIG-ppmsca-20658.*

animal by a fore-foot. This would bring the mule to the ground, when he
was seized and held by the teamsters while the blacksmith put upon him,
with hot irons, the initials "U. S." Ropes were then put about the neck, with
a slip-noose which would tighten around the throat if pulled. With a man on
each side holding these ropes, the mule was released from his other bindings
and allowed to rise. With more or less difficulty he would be conducted to
a picket rope outside and fastened there. The delivery of that mule was then
complete. This process was gone through with every mule and wild horse
with the army of occupation.

The method of breaking them was less cruel and much more amusing.
It is a well-known fact that where domestic animals are used for specific
purposes from generation to generation, the descendants are easily, as a rule,
subdued to the same uses. At that time in Northern Mexico the mule, or
his ancestors, the horse and the ass, was seldom used except for the saddle or
pack. At all events the Corpus Christi mule resisted the new use to which he
was being put. The treatment he was subjected to in order to overcome his
prejudices was summary and effective.

The soldiers were principally foreigners who had enlisted in our large
cities, and, with the exception of a chance drayman among them, it is not
probable that any of the men who reported themselves as competent teamsters had ever driven a mule-team in their lives, or indeed that many had
had any previous experience in driving any animal whatever to harness.

Numbers together can accomplish what twice their number acting individually could not perform. Five mules were allotted to each wagon. A teamster would select at the picket rope five animals of nearly the same color and general appearance for his team. With a full corps of assistants, other teamsters, he would then proceed to get his mules together. In two's the men would approach each animal selected, avoiding as far as possible its heels. Two ropes would be put about the neck of each animal, with a slip-noose, so that he could be choked if too unruly. They were then led out, harnessed by force and hitched to the wagon in the position they had to keep ever after. Two men remained on either side of the leader, with the lassos about its neck, and one man retained the same restraining influence over each of the others. All being ready, the hold would be slackened and the team started. The first motion was generally five mules in the air at one time, backs bowed, hind feet extended to the rear. After repeating this movement a few times the leaders would start to run. This would bring the breeching tight against the mules at the wheels, which these last seemed to regard as a most unwarrantable attempt at coercion and would resist by taking a seat, sometimes going so far as to lie down. In time all were broken in to do their duty submissively if not cheerfully, but there never was a time during the war when it was safe to let a Mexican mule get entirely loose. Their drivers were all teamsters by the time they got through.

I recollect one case of a mule that had worked in a team under the saddle, not only for some time at Corpus Christi, where he was broken, but all the way to the point opposite Matamoras, then to Camargo, where he got loose from his fastenings during the night. He did not run away at first, but staid in the neighborhood for a day or two, coming up sometimes to the feed trough even; but on the approach of the teamster he always got out of the way. At last, growing tired of the constant effort to catch him, he disappeared altogether. Nothing short of a Mexican with his lasso could have caught him. Regulations would not have warranted the expenditure of a dollar in hiring a man with a lasso to catch that mule; but they did allow the expenditure "of the mule," on a certificate that he had run away without any fault of the quartermaster on whose returns he was borne, and also the purchase of another to take his place. I am a competent witness, for I was regimental quartermaster at the time.

While at Corpus Christi all the officers who had a fancy for riding kept horses. The animals cost but little in the first instance, and when picketed they would get their living without any cost. I had three not long before the army moved, but a sad accident bereft me of them all at one time. A colored boy who gave them all the attention they got—besides looking after my tent and that of a class-mate and fellow-lieutenant and cooking for us, all for about eight dollars per month, was riding one to water and leading the other two. The led horses pulled him from his seat and all three ran away. They never were heard of afterwards. Shortly after that some one told Captain Bliss, General Taylor's Adjutant-General, of my misfortune. "Yes; I heard Grant lost five or six dollars' worth of horses the other day," he replied. That was a slander; they were broken to the saddle when I got them and cost nearly twenty dollars. I never suspected the colored boy of malicious intent in letting them get away, because, if they had not escaped, he could have had one of them to ride on the long march then in prospect.

6

Advance of the Army—Crossing the Colorado—The Rio Grande

At last the preparations were complete and orders were issued for the advance to begin on the 8th of March. General Taylor had an army of not more than three thousand men. One battery, the siege guns and all the convalescent troops were sent on by water to Brazos Santiago, at the mouth of the Rio Grande. A guard was left back at Corpus Christi to look after public property and to take care of those who were too sick to be removed.[1] The remainder of the army, probably not more than twenty five hundred men, was divided into three brigades, with the cavalry independent. Colonel Twiggs, with seven companies of dragoons and a battery of light artillery, moved on the 8th. He was followed by the three infantry brigades, with a day's interval between the commands. Thus the rear brigade did not move from Corpus Christi until the 11th of March. In view of the immense bodies of men moved on the same day over narrow roads, through dense forests and across large streams, in our late war, it seems strange now that a body of less than three thousand men should have been broken into four columns, separated by a day's march.

---

1. Of the approximately 90,000 U.S. soldiers who participated in the war, scholars estimate that a little over 12,000 died of diseases including yellow fever and dysentery. The ratio of death from disease to death in combat in the Mexican War was approximately seven to one; moreover, by several measures, this was the deadliest American war. See *The Encyclopedia of the Mexican-American War: A Political, Social, and Military History*, ed. Spencer C. Tucker, 2 vols. (Santa Barbara: ABC–CLIO, 2013), s.v. "Casualties, United States."

General Taylor was opposed to anything like plundering by the troops, and in this instance, I doubt not, he looked upon the enemy as the aggrieved party and was not willing to injure them further than his instructions from Washington demanded. His orders to the troops enjoined scrupulous regard for the rights of all peaceable persons and the payment of the highest price for all supplies taken for the use of the army.

All officers of foot regiments who had horses were permitted to ride them on the march when it did not interfere with their military duties. As already related, having lost my "five or six dollars' worth of horses" but a short time, before I determined not to get another, but to make the journey on foot. My company commander, Captain McCall, had two good American horses, of considerably more value in that country, where native horses were cheap, than they were in the States. He used one himself and wanted the other for his servant. He was quite anxious to know whether I did not intend to get me another horse before the march began. I told him No; I belonged to a foot regiment. I did not understand the object of his solicitude at the time, but, when we were about to start, he said: "There, Grant, is a horse for you." I found that he could not bear the idea of his servant riding on a long march while his lieutenant went a-foot. He had found a mustang, a three-year-old colt only recently captured, which had been purchased by one of the colored servants with the regiment for the sum of three dollars. It was probably the only horse at Corpus Christi that could have been purchased just then for any reasonable price. Five dollars, sixty-six and two-thirds per cent. advance, induced the owner to part with the mustang. I was sorry to take him, because I really felt that, belonging to a foot regiment, it was my duty to march with the men. But I saw the Captain's earnestness in the matter, and accepted the horse for the trip. The day we started was the first time the horse had ever been under saddle. I had, however, but little difficulty in breaking him, though for the first day there were frequent disagreements between us as to which way we should go, and sometimes whether we should go at all. At no time during the day could I choose exactly the part of the column I would march with; but after that, I had as tractable a horse as any with the army, and there was none that stood the trip better.[2] He never

2. Horse stories abound in Grant's book. His fondness for these animals is clear from the start, and his skill at managing them was well known throughout the army. His classmate Rufus Ingalls, later Quartermaster General of the army, told Horace Porter of Grant's equestrian excellence at West Point:

"Jeff Davis," a pony Grant used during the Civil War, 1865. *Library of Congress, Prints and Photographs Division, LC-DIG-stereo-1s02753.*

ate a mouthful of food on the journey except the grass he could pick within the length of his picket rope.

A few days out from Corpus Christi, the immense herd of wild horses that ranged at that time between the Nueces and the Rio Grande was seen directly in advance of the head of the column and but a few miles off. It was the very band from which the horse I was riding had been captured but a few weeks before. The column was halted for a rest, and a number of officers, myself among them, rode out two or three miles to the right to see the extent of the herd. The country was a rolling prairie, and, from the higher ground, the vision was obstructed only by the earth's curvature. As far as the eye could reach to our right, the herd extended. To the left, it extended equally. There was no estimating the number of animals in it; I have no idea

---

At cavalry drill he excelled every one in his class. He used to take great delight in mounting and breaking in the most intractable of the new horses that were purchased from time to time and put in the squad. He succeeded in this, not by punishing the animal he had taken in hand, but by patience and tact, and his skill in making the creature know what he wanted to have it do. He was a particularly daring jumper. In jumping hurdles, when Grant's turn came the soldiers in attendance would, at an indication from him, raise the top bar a foot or so higher than usual, and he would generally manage to clear it.

Porter, *Campaigning*, 341–42.

that they could all have been corralled in the State of Rhode Island, or Delaware, at one time. If they had been, they would have been so thick that the pasturage would have given out the first day. People who saw the Southern herd of buffalo, fifteen or twenty years ago, can appreciate the size of the Texas band of wild horses in 1846.[3]

---

3. The warriors of literature and legend frequently prove themselves by taming unmanageable horses. Plutarch writes of Alexander the Great's breaking of Bucephalus. Like Grant, Alexander treats the animal with gentleness:

> Philonicus the Thessalian brought the horse Bucephalus to Philip, offering to sell him for thirteen talents; but when they went into the field to try him, they found him so very vicious and unmanageable, that he reared up when they endeavoured to mount him, and would not so much as endure the voice of any of Philip's attendants. Upon which, as they were leading him away as wholly useless and untractable, Alexander, who stood by, said, "What an excellent horse do they lose for want of address and boldness to manage him!" Philip at first took no notice of what he said; but when he heard him repeat the same thing several times, and saw he was much vexed to see the horse sent away, "Do you reproach," said he to him, "those who are older than yourself, as if you knew more, and were better able to manage him than they?" "I could manage this horse," replied he, "better than others do." "And if you do not," said Philip, "what will you forfeit for your rashness?" "I will pay," answered Alexander, "the whole price of the horse." At this the whole company fell a laughing; and as soon as the wager was settled amongst them, he immediately ran to the horse, and taking hold of the bridle, turned him directly towards the sun, having, it seems, observed that he was disturbed at and afraid of the motion of his own shadow; then letting him go forward a little, still keeping the reins in his hands, and stroking him gently when he found him begin to grow eager and fiery, he let fall his upper garment softly, and with one nimble leap securely mounted him, and when he was seated, by little and little drew in the bridle, and curbed him without either striking or spurring him. Presently, when he found him free from all rebelliousness, and only impatient for the course, he let him go at full speed, inciting him now with a commanding voice, and urging him also with his heel. Philip and his friends looked on at first in silence and anxiety for the result, till seeing him turn at the end of his career, and come back rejoicing and triumphing for what he had performed, they all burst out into acclamations of applause; and his father shedding tears, it is said, for joy, kissed him as he came down from his horse, and in his transport said, "O my son, look thee out a kingdom equal to and worthy of thyself, for Macedonia is too little for thee."

Plutarch's Lives: The Translation Called Dryden's, rev. Arthur Hugh Clough (Boston: Little, Brown, 1859), 4:165–66.

Léon Davent, *Alexander Mastering Bucephalus,*
after Francesco Primaticcio, ca. 1540–45.
*Metropolitan Museum of Art, The Elisha
Whittelsey Collection, The Elisha Whittelsey
Fund, 1949.*

Below an artist depicts a similar episode from the *Shahnameh* (*Book of Kings*), the
great Persian epic, in which the young warrior Rostam proves his mettle by lassoing
a wondrous foal "Of mountain size and weight, of mammoth force," and successfully
removing him from his mother, who "attacks like a lioness" whenever someone attempts
to take him away. Rostam outroars the mare and seizes the horse, Rakhsh, who proves
a fierce, invaluable companion to the hero. See Abolqasem Ferdowsi, *Shahnameh*, trans.
Dick Davis (New York: Penguin Classics, 2006), 131–132.

"Rustam Lassos Rakhsh," folio from
Shahnama (by Abu'l Qasim Firdausi), ca.
1450. *Metropolitan Museum of Art, Rogers Fund,
1972.*

At the point where the army struck the Little Colorado River, the stream was quite wide and of sufficient depth for navigation. The water was brackish and the banks were fringed with timber. Here the whole army concentrated before attempting to cross. The army was not accompanied by a pontoon train, and at that time the troops were not instructed in bridge building. To add to the embarrassment of the situation, the army was here, for the first time, threatened with opposition. Buglers, concealed from our view by the brush on the opposite side, sounded the "assembly," and other military calls. Like the wolves before spoken of, they gave the impression that there was a large number of them and that, if the troops were in proportion to the noise, they were sufficient to devour General Taylor and his army. There were probably but few troops, and those engaged principally in watching the movements of the "invader." A few of our cavalry dashed in, and forded and swam the stream, and all opposition was soon dispersed. I do not remember that a single shot was fired.

The troops waded the stream, which was up to their necks in the deepest part. Teams were crossed by attaching a long rope to the end of the wagon tongue, passing it between the two swing mules and by the side of the leader, hitching his bridle as well as the bridle of the mules in rear to it, and carrying the end to men on the opposite shore. The bank down to the water was steep on both sides. A rope long enough to cross the river, therefore, was attached to the back axle of the wagon, and men behind would hold the rope to prevent the wagon "beating" the mules into the water. This latter rope also served the purpose of bringing the end of the forward one back, to be used over again. The water was deep enough for a short distance to swim the little Mexican mules which the army was then using, but they, and the wagons, were pulled through so fast by the men at the end of the rope ahead, that no time was left them to show their obstinacy. In this manner the artillery and transportation of the "army of occupation" crossed the Little Colorado River.

About the middle of the month of March the advance of the army reached the Rio Grande and went into camp near the banks of the river, opposite the city of Matamoras and almost under the guns of a small fort at the lower end of the town. There was not at that time a single habitation from Corpus Christi until the Rio Grande was reached.

The work of fortifying was commenced at once. The fort was laid out by the engineers, but the work was done by the soldiers under the supervision of their officers, the chief engineer retaining general directions. The Mexi-

What Taylor lacked in Mexico: pontoon train, Civil War. *Library of Congress, Prints and Photographs Division, LC-DIG-ppmsca-33372.*

cans now became so incensed at our near approach that some of their troops crossed the river above us, and made it unsafe for small bodies of men to go far beyond the limits of camp. They captured two companies of dragoons, commanded by Captains Thornton and Hardee. The latter figured as a general in the late war, on the Confederate side, and was author of the tactics first used by both armies.[4] Lieutenant Theodric Porter, of the 4th infantry, was killed while out with a small detachment; and Major Cross, the assistant quartermaster-general, had also been killed not far from camp.

There was no base of supplies nearer than Point Isabel, on the coast, north of the mouth of the Rio Grande and twenty-five miles away. The enemy, if the Mexicans could be called such at this time when no war had been declared, hovered about in such numbers that it was not safe to send a wagon train after supplies with any escort that could be spared. I have already said that General Taylor's whole command on the Rio Grande num-

---

4. William J. Hardee (1815–1873) graduated from West Point in 1838 and later served as commandant of cadets. Hardee's *Rifle and Light Infantry Tactics* (1861)—usually identified as *Hardee's Tactics*—was largely translated from French manuals. This book replaced an earlier manual written by Winfield Scott. As Grant notes, the Union Army continued to use a version of it even after Hardee defected to the Southern cause.

bered less than three thousand men. He had, however, a few more troops at Point Isabel or Brazos Santiago. The supplies brought from Corpus Christi in wagons were running short. Work was therefore pushed with great vigor on the defences, to enable the minimum number of troops to hold the fort. All the men who could be employed, were kept at work from early dawn until darkness closed the labors of the day. With all this the fort was not completed until the supplies grew so short that further delay in obtaining more could not be thought of. By the latter part of April the work was in a partially defensible condition, and the 7th infantry, Major Jacob Brown commanding, was marched in to garrison it, with some few pieces of artillery. All the supplies on hand, with the exception of enough to carry the rest of the army to Point Isabel, were left with the garrison, and the march was commenced with the remainder of the command, every wagon being taken with the army. Early on the second day after starting the force reached its destination, without opposition from the Mexicans. There was some delay in getting supplies ashore from vessels at anchor in the open roadstead.

7

The Mexican War—The Battle of Palo Alto—The Battle of Resaca de la Palma— Army of Invasion—General Taylor— Movement on Camargo

While General Taylor was away with the bulk of his army, the little garrison up the river was besieged. As we lay in our tents upon the sea-shore, the artillery at the fort on the Rio Grande could be distinctly heard.

The war had begun.

There were no possible means of obtaining news from the garrison, and information from outside could not be otherwise than unfavorable. What General Taylor's feelings were during this suspense I do not know; but for myself, a young second lieutenant who had never heard a hostile gun before, I felt sorry that I had enlisted. A great many men, when they smell battle afar off, chafe to get into the fray. When they say so themselves they generally fail to convince their hearers that they are as anxious as they would like to make believe, and as they approach danger they become more subdued. This rule is not universal, for I have known a few men who were always aching for a fight when there was no enemy near, who were as good as their word when the battle did come. But the number of such men is small.[1]

---

1. One might contrast the bravado of George Washington's claim that bullets had a "charming" sound with Grant's gentle self-mockery here and later in this chapter or with Lincoln's description of his own brief militia service in the Black Hawk War. Lincoln told his comic war story during a discussion of the presidential race in which partisans of the Democratic candidate Lewis Cass, the governor of the Michigan territory, talked up Cass's war record:

On the 7th of May the wagons were all loaded and General Taylor started on his return, with his army reinforced at Point Isabel, but still less than three thousand strong, to relieve the garrison on the Rio Grande. The road from Point Isabel to Matamoras is over an open, rolling, treeless prairie, until the timber that borders the bank of the Rio Grande is reached. This river, like the Mississippi, flows through a rich alluvial valley in the most meandering manner, running towards all points of the compass at times within a few miles. Formerly the river ran by Resaca de la Palma, some four or five miles east of the present channel. The old bed of the river at Resaca had become filled at places, leaving a succession of little lakes. The timber that had formerly grown upon both banks, and for a considerable distance out, was still standing. This timber was struck six or eight miles out from the besieged garrison, at a point known as Palo Alto—"Tall trees" or "woods."

Early in the forenoon of the 8th of May as Palo Alto was approached, an army, certainly outnumbering our little force, was seen, drawn up in line of battle just in front of the timber. Their bayonets and spearheads glistened in the sunlight formidably. The force was composed largely of cavalry armed with lances. Where we were the grass was tall, reaching nearly to the shoulders of the men, very stiff, and each stock was pointed at the top, and hard and almost as sharp as a darning-needle. General Taylor halted his army before the head of column came in range of the artillery of the Mexicans. He then formed a line of battle, facing the enemy. His artillery, two batteries and

---

By the way, Mr. Speaker, did you know I am a military hero? Yes, sir, in the days of the Black Hawk war, I fought, bled, and came away. Speaking of General Cass's career, reminds me of my own. I was not at Stillman's defeat, but I was about as near it as Cass was to Hull's surrender; and, like him, I saw the place very soon afterwards. It is quite certain I did not break my sword, for I had none to break; but I bent a musket pretty badly on one occasion. If Cass broke his sword, the idea is, he broke it in desperation; I bent the musket by accident. If General Cass went in advance of me in picking whortleberries, I guess I surpassed him in charges upon the wild onions. If he saw any live fighting Indians, it was more than I did, but I had a good many bloody struggles with the musquitoes; and although I never fainted from loss of blood, I can truly say I was often very hungry.

Mr. Speaker, if I should ever conclude to doff whatever our Democratic friends may suppose there is of black-cockade Federalism about me, and, thereupon, they shall take me up as their candidate for the Presidency, I protest they shall not make fun of me, as they have of General Cass, by attempting to write me into a military hero.

Appendix to the Congressional Globe, 30th Congress, 1st Session 1042 (July 27, 1848).

two eighteen-pounder iron guns, drawn by oxen, were placed in position at intervals along the line. A battalion was thrown to the rear, commanded by Lieutenant-Colonel Childs, of the artillery, as reserves. These preparations completed, orders were given for a platoon of each company to stack arms and go to a stream off to the right of the command, to fill their canteens and also those of the rest of their respective companies. When the men were all back in their places in line, the command to advance was given. As I looked down that long line of about three thousand armed men, advancing towards a larger force also armed, I thought what a fearful responsibility General Taylor must feel, commanding such a host and so far away from friends.[2] The Mexicans immediately opened fire upon us, first with artillery and then with infantry. At first their shots did not reach us, and the advance was continued. As we got nearer, the cannon balls commenced going through the ranks. They hurt no one, however, during this advance, because they would strike the ground long before they reached our line, and ricochetted through the tall grass so slowly that the men would see them and open ranks and let them pass. When we got to a point where the artillery could be used with effect, a halt was called, and the battle opened on both sides.

The infantry under General Taylor was armed with flint-lock muskets, and paper cartridges charged with powder, buck-shot and ball. At the distance of a few hundred yards a man might fire at you all day without your finding it out. The artillery was generally six-pounder brass guns throwing only solid shot; but General Taylor had with him three or four twelve-pounder howitzers throwing shell, besides his eighteen-pounders before spoken of, that had a long range. This made a powerful armament. The Mexicans were armed about as we were so far as their infantry was concerned, but their artillery only fired solid shot. We had greatly the advantage in this arm.[3]

---

2. Grant will return to the question of a commander's moral responsibility in chapter 18, when he describes his first time in command of a regiment during the pursuit of Colonel Thomas Harris near Florida, Missouri.

3. The ancient sage Archimedes supposedly invented artillery, which he put in the service of the Syracusans when they were besieged by the Roman Marcellus:

> When, therefore, the Romans assaulted the walls in two places at once, fear and consternation stupefied the Syracusans, believing that nothing was able to resist that violence and those forces. But when Archimedes began to ply his engines, he at once shot against the land forces all sorts of missile weapons, and immense masses of stone that came down with incredible noise and violence, against which no man could stand; for they knocked down those upon whom they fell, in heaps, breaking all their ranks and

The artillery was advanced a rod or two in front of the line, and opened fire. The infantry stood at order arms as spectators, watching the effect of our shots upon the enemy, and watching his shots so as to step out of their way. It could be seen that the eighteen-pounders and the howitzers did a great deal of execution. On our side there was little or no loss while we occupied this position. During the battle Major Ringgold, an accomplished and brave artillery officer, was mortally wounded, and Lieutenant Luther, also of the artillery, was struck.[4] During the day several advances were made, and just

files. In the mean time huge poles thrust out from the walls over the ships, sunk some by the great weights which they let down from on high upon them; others they lifted up into the air by an iron hand or beak like a crane's beak, and, when they had drawn them up by the prow, and set them on end upon the poop, they plunged them to the bottom of the sea; or else the ships, drawn by engines within, and whirled about, were dashed against steep rocks that stood jutting out under the walls, with great destruction of the soldiers that were aboard them. A ship was frequently lifted up to a great height in the air (a dreadful thing to behold), and was rolled to and fro, and kept swinging, until the mariners were all thrown out, when at length it was dashed against the rocks, or let fall.

Marcellus, Plutarch's Lives, 2:254.

4. Grant's account of the death of Major Ringgold lacks entirely the drama accorded it by visual artists of the day. Several quickly produced engravings of his death,

Edward Williams Clay, Major Ringgold: mortally wounded at the Battle of Palo Alto. 1846. *Library of Congress, Prints and Photographs Division, LC-DIG-pga-04932.*

while composers wrote "Major Ringgold's Quick Step" and a vocal quartette, "The Death of Major Ringgold." Grant's laconic description of this battle and so many others is the antithesis of the chivalric combat contained in the novels he favored as a young man. Here, in a representative scene, Sir Walter Scott depicts a hand-to-hand contest between his Scottish hero Quentin Durward and the French champion De la Marck:

> "Hola! gentlemen of Scotland," said the ruffian but undaunted chief, waving his mace, "who longs to gain a coronet—who strikes at the Boar of Ardennes?—You, young man, have, methinks, a hankering; but you must win ere you wear it."
>
> Quentin heard but imperfectly the words, which were partly lost in the hollow helmet; but the action could not be mistaken, and he had but time to bid his uncle and comrades, as they were gentlemen, to stand back, when De la Marck sprang upon him with a bound like a tiger, aiming, at the same time a blow with his mace, so as to make his hand and foot keep time together, and giving his stroke full advantage of the descent of his leap, but, light of foot and quick of eye, Quentin leaped aside, and disappointed an aim which would have been fatal had it taken effect.
>
> They then closed, like the wolf and the wolf dog, their comrades on either side remaining inactive spectators, for Le Balafré roared out for fair play, adding "that he would venture his nephew on him were he as wight as Wallace."
>
> Neither was the experienced soldier's confidence unjustified; for, although the blows of the despairing robber fell like those of the hammer on the anvil, yet the quick motions, and dexterous swordsmanship of the young Archer enabled him to escape, and to requite them with the point of his less noisy, though more fatal weapon; and that so often, and so effectually, that the huge strength of his antagonist began to give way to fatigue, while the ground on which he stood became a puddle of blood. Yet, still unabated in courage and ire, the wild Boar of Ardennes fought on with as much mental energy as at first, and Quentin's victory seemed dubious and distant, when a female voice behind him called him by his name, ejaculating, "Help! help! for the sake of the blessed Virgin!"
>
> He turned his head, and with a single glance beheld Gertrude Pavillon, her mantle stripped from her shoulders, dragged forcibly along by a French soldier; one of several who, breaking into the chapel close by, had seized, as their prey, on the terrified females who had taken refuge there.
>
> "Wait for me but one moment," exclaimed Quentin to De la Marck, and sprang to extricate his benefactress from a situation of which he conjectured all the dangers.
>
> "I wait no man's pleasure," said De la Marck, flourishing his mace, and beginning to retreat—glad, no doubt, at being free of so formidable an assailant. "You shall wait mine, though, by your leave," said Balafré; "I will not have my nephew baulked." So saying, he instantly assaulted De la Marck with his two-handed sword.

at dusk it became evident that the Mexicans were falling back. We again advanced, and occupied at the close of the battle substantially the ground held by the enemy at the beginning. In this last move there was a brisk fire upon our troops, and some execution was done. One cannon-ball passed through our ranks, not far from me. It took off the head of an enlisted man, and the under jaw of Captain Page of my regiment, while the splinters from the musket of the killed soldier, and his brains and bones, knocked down two or three others, including one officer, Lieutenant Wallen,—hurting them more or less. Our casualties for the day were nine killed and forty-seven wounded.[5]

Quentin found, in the meanwhile, that the rescue of Gertrude was a task more difficult than could be finished in one moment.

Quentin Durward, vol. 2, *The Waverley Novels,* 32:385–87.

5. Zachary Taylor's official report on the Battle of Palo Alto listed "nine killed, forty-four wounded, and two missing." Letter to the Adjutant-General of the Army, May 16, 1846, *The American Quarterly Register and Magazine,* 1, no. 1 (1848): 60.

Grant mentions four of the casualties by name: Major Samuel Ringgold, Lieutenant Luther, Captain John B. Page, and Lieutenant Henry Wallen. Grant characteristically refuses to linger on the fate of any of his comrades, but his correspondence from the period reveals the way in which one of the wounded men, Captain Page, preoccupied him at the time. Page's was, of course, only one of the many grievous woundings and deaths Grant would witness in Mexico. In the aftermath of the battle Grant wrote to Julia with news of Page:

Although the balls were whizing thick and fast about me I did not feel a sensation of fear until nearly the close of the firing a ball struck close by me killing one man instantly, it nocked Capt. Page's under Jaw entirely off and broke in the roof of his mouth, and nocked Lt. Wallen and one Sergeant down besides, but they were not much hurt. Capt. Page is still alive.

Letter to Julia Dent, May 11, 1846, *PUSG,* 1:85.
Several weeks later he reported to a friend back in Ohio:

During the days fight I scarsely thought of the probability or possibility of being touched myself (although 9 lb. shots were whistling all round,) until near the close of the evening a shot struck the ranks a little ways in front of me and nocked one man's head off, nocked the under Jaw of Capt. Page entirely away, and brought several others to the ground. Although Capt. Page rec'd so terrible a wound he is recovering from it. The under jaw is gone to the wind pipe and the tongue hangs down upon the throat. He will never be able to speak or to eat.

Letter to John W. Lowe, June 26, 1846, *PUSG,* 1:96.

At the break of day on the 9th, the army under Taylor was ready to renew the battle; but an advance showed that the enemy had entirely left our front during the night.[6] The chaparral before us was impenetrable except

---

The captain died on July 12, 1846, a few weeks after Grant's second letter. Born in Maine, Page had joined the army in 1818 and spent most of his career in the southern United States enforcing the government's Indian Removal policy. The wounded Page became newsworthy: papers across the country carried updates on his condition. "POOR CAPTAIN PAGE!!!" read the headline in the *Philadelphia Sun* on June 13, 1846. Years later, in 1861, the *Philadelphia Public Ledger* republished the eyewitness account of a soldier who had been at the battle: "The blood of poor Page was the first blood I saw; he was knocked down in the grass, and as he endeavored to raise himself, he presented such a ghastly spectacle that a sickly, fainting sensation came over me." For a detailed account of the media attention to this episode, see "A Forgotten American Hero: Capt. John B. Page," *Historical Society of Pennsylvania Newsletter* 2008, https://hsp.org/blogs/hidden-histories/a-forgotten-american-hero-capt-john-b-page.

Ambrose Bierce offers a far more graphic description of the kind of wound suffered by Page in his short story "Chickamauga," in which a young boy, mistakenly believing the soldier crawling toward him is playing a game, leaps on his back only to be thrown off:

> The man sank upon his breast, recovered, flung the small boy fiercely to the ground as an unbroken colt might have done, then turned upon him a face that lacked a lower jaw—from the upper teeth to the throat was a great red gap fringed with hanging shreds of flesh and splinters of bone. The unnatural prominence of nose, the absence of chin, the fierce eyes, gave this man the appearance of a great bird of prey crimsoned in throat and breast by the blood of its quarry. The man rose to his knees, the child to his feet. The man shook his fist at the child; the child, terrified at last, ran to a tree near by, got upon the farther side of it, and took a more serious view of the situation. And so the uncanny multitude dragged itself slowly and painfully along in hideous pantomime—moved forward down the slope like a swarm of great black beetles, with never a sound of going—in silence profound, absolute.

Tales of Soldiers and Civilians (San Francisco: E. L. G. Steele, 1891), 47–48.

6. Grant wrote to his friend John Lowe, "During that night I believe all slept as soundly on the ground at Palo Alto as if they had been in a palace. For my own part I dont think I even dreamed of battles." *PUSG*, 1:95–96.

Shakespeare imagines what a soldier's dreams might consist of in *1 Henry IV*, in which Kate, the wife of the ferocious warrior Hotspur—a soldier who has rebelled against his king and who will be as good as his word when the fight comes—reports that she has overheard his nightmares:

> LADY PERCY. O good my lord, why are you thus alone?
>   For what offence have I this fortnight been

where there were roads or trails, with occasionally clear or bare spots of small dimensions. A body of men penetrating it might easily be ambushed. It was better to have a few men caught in this way than the whole army, yet it was necessary that the garrison at the river should be relieved. To get to them the chaparral had to be passed. Thus I assume General Taylor reasoned. He halted the army not far in advance of the ground occupied by the Mexicans the day before, and selected Captain C. F. Smith, of the artillery, and Captain McCall, of my company, to take one hundred and fifty picked men each and find where the enemy had gone. This left me in command of the company, an honor and responsibility I thought very great.

Smith and McCall found no obstruction in the way of their advance

---

> A banish'd woman from my Harry's bed?
> Tell me, sweet lord, what is't that takes from thee
> Thy stomach, pleasure and thy golden sleep?
> Why dost thou bend thine eyes upon the earth,
> And start so often when thou sit'st alone?
> Why hast thou lost the fresh blood in thy cheeks;
> And given my treasures and my rights of thee
> To thick-eyed musing and curs'd melancholy?
> In thy faint slumbers I by thee have watch'd,
> And heard thee murmur tales of iron wars;
> Speak terms of manage to thy bounding steed;
> Cry "Courage! to the field!" And thou hast talk'd
> Of sallies and retires, of trenches, tents,
> Of palisadoes, frontiers, parapets,
> Of basilisks, of cannon, culverin,
> Of prisoners' ransom and of soldiers slain,
> And all the currents of a heady fight.
> Thy spirit within thee hath been so at war
> And thus hath so bestirr'd thee in thy sleep,
> That beads of sweat have stood upon thy brow,
> Like bubbles in a late-disturbed stream;
> And in thy face strange motions have appear'd,
> Such as we see when men restrain their breath
> On some great sudden hest. O, what portents are these?
> Some heavy business hath my lord in hand,
> And I must know it, else he loves me not.

1 Henry IV 3.2.31–58. All quotations from Shakespeare come from the nineteenth-century edition of Richard Grant White, *Mr. William Shakespeare's Comedies, Histories, Tragedies and Poems*. One of the earliest significant American editions of Shakespeare, White's twelve volumes were originally published from 1857 to 1866. They were reprinted as *The Riverside Shakespeare*, 6 vols. (Boston: Houghton, Mifflin, 1883).

until they came up to the succession of ponds, before described, at Resaca. The Mexicans had passed them and formed their lines on the opposite bank. This position they had strengthened a little by throwing up dead trees and brush in their front, and by placing artillery to cover the approaches and open places. Smith and McCall deployed on each side of the road as well as they could, and engaged the enemy at long range. Word was sent back, and the advance of the whole army was at once commenced. As we came up we were deployed in like manner. I was with the right wing, and led my company through the thicket wherever a penetrable place could be found, taking advantage of any clear spot that would carry me towards the enemy. At last I got pretty close up without knowing it. The balls commenced to whistle very thick overhead, cutting the limbs of the chaparral right and left. We could not see the enemy, so I ordered my men to lie down, an order that did not have to be enforced. We kept our position until it became evident that the enemy were not firing at us, and then withdrew to find better ground to advance upon.

By this time some progress had been made on our left. A section of artillery had been captured by the cavalry, and some prisoners had been taken. The Mexicans were giving way all along the line, and many of them had, no doubt, left early. I at last found a clear space separating two ponds. There seemed to be a few men in front and I charged upon them with my company. There was no resistance, and we captured a Mexican colonel, who had been wounded, and a few men. Just as I was sending them to the rear with a guard of two or three men, a private came from the front bringing back one of our officers, who had been badly wounded in advance of where I was. The ground had been charged over before. My exploit was equal to that of the soldier who boasted that he had cut off the leg of one of the enemy. When asked why he did not cut off his head, he replied: "Some one had done that before." This left no doubt in my mind but that the battle of Resaca de la Palma would have been won, just as it was, if I had not been there.[7]

---

7. Here Grant lampoons the figure of the vainglorious soldier—the braggadocio, or *miles gloriosus*, a type dating back to ancient Roman literature. Shakespeare's Falstaff is perhaps the quintessential English example. In this scene from *1 Henry IV*, Falstaff, who has been tricked by his two friends, Poins and Prince Hal (the future King Henry V), tells the story of being robbed of his own ill-gotten gains by a band of fearsome thieves:

> PRINCE. Pray God you have not murthered some of them.

> FALSTAFF. Nay, that's past praying for: I have pepper'd two of them; two I am
> sure I have paid, two rogues in buckram suits. I tell thee what, Hal, if I tell

thee a lie, spit in my face, call me horse. Thou knowest my old ward; here I lay, and thus I bore my point. Four rogues in buckram let drive at me—

PRINCE. What, four? thou saidst but two even now.

FALSTAFF. Four, Hal; I told thee four.

POINS. Ay, ay, he said four.

FALSTAFF. These four came all a-front, and mainly thrust at me. I made me no more ado but took all their seven points in my target, thus.

PRINCE. Seven? why, there were but four even now.

FALSTAFF. In buckram?

POINS. Ay, four, in buckram suits.

FALSTAFF. Seven, by these hilts, or I am a villain else.

PRINCE. Prithee, let him alone; we shall have more anon.

FALSTAFF. Dost thou hear me, Hal?

PRINCE. Ay, and mark thee too, Jack.

FALSTAFF. Do so, for it is worth the listening to. These nine in buckram that I told thee of—

PRINCE. So, two more already.

FALSTAFF. Their points being broken,—

POINS. Down fell their hose.

FALSTAFF. Began to give me ground: but I followed me close, came in foot and hand; and with a thought seven of the eleven I paid.

PRINCE. O monstrous! eleven buckram men grown out of two!

FALSTAFF. But, as the Devil would have it, three misbegotten knaves in Kendal green came at my back and let drive at me; for it was so dark, Hal, that thou couldst not see thy hand.

American actor James Hackett as Falstaff. *From the New York Public Library, https://digitalcollections.nypl. org/items/d221aa10-58de-0134-22c3- 00505686a51c.*

There was no further resistance. The evening of the 9th the army was encamped on its old ground near the Fort, and the garrison was relieved. The siege had lasted a number of days, but the casualties were few in number. Major Jacob Brown, of the 7th infantry, the commanding officer, had been killed, and in his honor the fort was named. Since then a town of considerable importance has sprung up on the ground occupied by the fort and troops, which has also taken his name.[8]

The battles of Palo Alto and Resaca de la Palma seemed to us engaged, as pretty important affairs; but we had only a faint conception of their magnitude until they were fought over in the North by the Press and the reports came back to us. At the same time, or about the same time, we learned that war existed between the United States and Mexico, by the acts of the latter country. On learning this fact General Taylor transferred our camps to the south or west bank of the river, and Matamoras was occupied. We then became the "Army of Invasion."

> PRINCE. These lies are like their father that begets them; gross as a mountain, open, palpable. Why, thou clay-brain'd guts, thou knotty-pated fool, thou whoreson, obscene, greasy tallow-keech,—
>
> FALSTAFF. What, art thou mad? art thou mad? is not the truth the truth?
>
> . . .
>
> PRINCE. We two saw you four set on four and bound them, and were masters of their wealth. Mark now, how a plain tale shall put you down. Then did we two set on you four; and, with a word, out-fac'd you from your prize, and have it; yea, and can show it you here in the house: and, Falstaff, you carried your guts away as nimbly, with as quick dexterity, and roar'd for mercy and still run and roar'd, as ever I heard bull-calf. What a slave art thou, to hack thy sword as thou hast done, and then say it was in fight! What trick? what device? what starting-hole? canst thou now find out to hide thee from this open and apparent shame?
>
> POINS. Come, let's hear, Jack, what trick hast thou now?
>
> FALSTAFF. By the Lord, I knew ye as well as he that made ye. Why, hear you, my masters: was it for me to kill the heir-apparent? should I turn upon the true Prince? why, thou knowest I am as valiant as Hercules: but beware instinct; the lion will not touch the true Prince. Instinct is a great matter; I was now a coward on instinct. I shall think the better of myself and thee during my life; I for a valiant lion, and thou for a true Prince. But, by the Lord, lads, I am glad you have the money.

1 Henry IV 2.4.172–209, 230–49.

8. Brownsville, Texas.

Zachary Taylor. Photograph by Mathew
Brady, ca. 1844–1849. *Library of Congress,
Prints and Photographs Division, LC-
USZ62-110067.*

Up to this time Taylor had none but regular troops in his command;
but now that invasion had already taken place, volunteers for one year commenced arriving. The army remained at Matamoras until sufficiently reinforced to warrant a movement into the interior. General Taylor was not
an officer to trouble the administration much with his demands, but was
inclined to do the best he could with the means given him. He felt his
responsibility as going no further. If he had thought that he was sent to perform an impossibility with the means given him, he would probably have
informed the authorities of his opinion and left them to determine what
should be done. If the judgment was against him he would have gone on and
done the best he could with the means at hand without parading his grievance before the public. No soldier could face either danger or responsibility
more calmly than he. These are qualities more rarely found than genius or
physical courage.[9]

9. Taylor was Grant's model in many respects, especially in his ability to write with
clarity and directness, or, as Grant will phrase it in chapter 10, "to put his meaning so
plainly there could be no mistaking it." Bruce Catton notes that Grant's enthusiasm
for both Taylor and the volunteers was unusual among regular army officers. See *Grant
and the American Military Tradition,* 34. Taylor evidently saw something to admire in the
young lieutenant as well. Interviewed after Grant's death, former Confederate general
Lafayette McLaws, who graduated from West Point a year ahead of Grant, shared this
revealing story about the young lieutenant:

General Taylor never made any great show or parade, either of uniform or retinue. In dress he was possibly too plain, rarely wearing anything in the field to indicate his rank, or even that he was an officer; but he was known to every soldier in his army, and was respected by all. I can call to mind only one instance when I saw him in uniform, and one other when I heard of his wearing it. On both occasions he was unfortunate.[10] The first was at Corpus Christi. He had concluded to review his army before starting on the march and gave orders accordingly. Colonel Twiggs was then second in rank with the army, and to him was given the command of the review. Colonel and Brevet Brigadier-General Worth, a far different soldier from Taylor in the use of the uniform, was next to Twiggs in rank, and claimed superiority by virtue of his brevet rank when the accidents of service threw them where one or the other had to command. Worth declined to attend the review as subordinate to Twiggs until the question was settled by the highest authority. This broke up the review, and the question was referred to Washington for final decision.

General Taylor was himself only a colonel, in real rank, at that time, and a brigadier-general by brevet. He was assigned to duty, however, by the President, with the rank which his brevet gave him. Worth was not so assigned, but by virtue of commanding a division he must, under the army regulations of that day, have drawn the pay of his brevet rank. The question was

---

Gen. Zachary Taylor once told me an anecdote of Grant, which occurred during the Mexican war. Lieut. Grant was in charge of a party of men detailed to clear the way for the advance of boats laden with troops from Aransas Bay to Corpus Christi by removing the oyster beds and other obstructions. Failing either by words or signs to [make] those under him understand him, Lieut. Grant jumped into the water, which was up to his waist, and worked with his men. Some dandy officers began making fun of him for his zeal, when Gen. Taylor came upon the scene, and rebuked it by saying:

"I wish I had more officers like Grant, who would stand ready to set a personal example when needed."

"Gen. Grant and the South," *New York Times*, July 24, 1885, p. 6. See also Jean Edward Smith, *Grant* (New York: Simon & Schuster, 2001), 40.

10. When Lew Wallace, the future Civil War general who also fought in Mexico, was told that Taylor was arriving to review the troops, he could not identify him. "That General Taylor?" Wallace later explained to a colonel displeased that no one had saluted the general as he passed: "I took him to be a teamster." Wallace, *Autobiography*, 1:154.

submitted to Washington, and no response was received until after the army had reached the Rio Grande. It was decided against General Worth, who at once tendered his resignation and left the army, going north, no doubt, by the same vessel that carried it. This kept him out of the battles of Palo Alto and Resaca de la Palma. Either the resignation was not accepted, or General Worth withdrew it before action had been taken. At all events he returned to the army in time to command his division in the battle of Monterey, and served with it to the end of the war.[11]

The second occasion on which General Taylor was said to have donned his uniform, was in order to receive a visit from the Flag Officer of the naval squadron off the mouth of the Rio Grande. While the army was on that river the Flag Officer sent word that he would call on the General to pay his respects on a certain day. General Taylor, knowing that naval officers habitually wore all the uniform the "law allowed" on all occasions of ceremony, thought it would be only civil to receive his guest in the same style. His uniform was therefore got out, brushed up, and put on, in advance of the visit. The Flag Officer, knowing General Taylor's aversion to the wearing of the uniform, and feeling that it would be regarded as a compliment should he meet him in civilian's dress, left off his uniform for this occasion. The

11. Brevet rank is a temporary rank. It was awarded in the nineteenth-century American army to an officer assigned a particular duty or command. Confusion of the kind Grant documents here was not uncommon either in Mexico or in the Civil War.

David E. Twiggs (1790–1862) began his military career in the War of 1812. At the outbreak of the Civil War, he surrendered his command of federal forces in Texas and joined the Confederate States Army (C.S.A.). He died of illness in the second year of the war. William J. Worth (1794–1849) served as aide-de-camp to Winfield Scott during the War of 1812, and he later commanded the 8th Infantry in the Seminole Wars of 1838. From 1820 to 1828, Worth was commandant at West Point, where cadets have traditionally memorized Worth's Battalion Orders, which, like Scott's Fixed Opinion, is contained in *Bugle Notes*:

But an officer on duty knows no one—to be partial is to dishonor both himself and the object of his ill-advised favor. What will be thought of him who exacts of his friends that which disgraces him? Look at him who winks at and overlooks offenses in one, which he causes to be punished in another, and contrast him with the inflexible soldier who does his duty faithfully, notwithstanding it occasionally wars with his private feelings. The conduct of one will be venerated and emulated, the other detested as a satire upon soldiership and honor.

Worth died of cholera in Texas after his service in the Mexican War. His body is buried in Manhattan, in Worth Square, at the corner of Broadway and Twenty-fourth Street.

meeting was said to have been embarrassing to both, and the conversation was principally apologetic.[12]

Relief, Worth Monument, built in 1857, New York, New York.
Photograph by Elizabeth D. Samet.

12. This episode anticipates some of the vanity and preoccupation with regulations and seniority that would continue to plague the Union army during the Civil War. Leo Tolstoy has a little fun with military ceremony in this marvelous scene from *War and Peace*, published in 1869, and composed during the American Civil War. The Russian commander in chief's request to review the troops in their marching attire, for the purpose of showing his Austrian allies the battle-weary state of his troops, has been misunderstood as an order for a full-dress parade:

> In the evening, on the last stage of the march, the order had been received that the commander-in-chief would inspect the regiment on the march. Though the wording of the order did not seem quite clear to the general in command of the regiment, and the question arose whether they were to take it to mean, in marching order or not, it was decided on a consultation between the majors to present the regiment in parade order on the ground, since, as the saying is, it is better to bow too low than not bow low enough. And the soldiers after a twenty-mile march had not closed their eyes, but had spent the night mending and cleaning, while the adjutants and officers had been reckoning up and calculating. And by the morning the regiment, instead of the straggling, disorderly crowd it had been on the last march, the previous evening, presented the spectacle of an organised mass of two thousand men, of whom everyone knew his part and his duty, and had every button and every strap in its proper position, and shining with cleanliness. . . .

The time was whiled away pleasantly enough at Matamoras, while we were waiting for volunteers. It is probable that all the most important people of the territory occupied by our army left their homes before we got there, but with those remaining the best of relations apparently existed. It was the policy of the Commanding General to allow no pillaging, no taking of private property for public or individual use without satisfactory compensation, so that a better market was afforded than the people had ever known before.

Among the troops that joined us at Matamoras was an Ohio regiment, of which Thomas L. Hamer, the Member of Congress who had given me my appointment to West Point, was major. He told me then that he could have had the colonelcy, but that as he knew he was to be appointed a brigadier-general, he preferred at first to take the lower grade. I have said before that Hamer was one of the ablest men Ohio ever produced. At that time he was in the prime of life, being less than fifty years of age, and possessed an admirable physique, promising long life. But he was taken

---

. . . The general was unmistakably admiring his regiment, and happy in it, and it was evident that his whole brain was engrossed by the regiment. . . .

At that moment two figures on horseback came into sight on the road from the town, where sentinels had been posted to give the signal. They were an adjutant, and a Cossack riding behind him.

The adjutant had been sent by the commander-in-chief to confirm to the commander what had not been clearly stated in the previous order, namely, that the commander-in-chief wished to inspect the regiment exactly in the order in which it had arrived—wearing their overcoats, and carrying their baggage, and without any sort of preparation. . . .

On hearing this the general's head sank; he shrugged his shoulders, and flung up his hands with a choleric gesture.

"Here's a mess we've made of it," he said. "Why, didn't I tell you, Mihail Mitritch, that on the march meant in their overcoats," he said reproachfully to the major. "Ah, my God!" he added, and stepped resolutely forward. "Captains of the companies!" he shouted in a voice used to command. "Sergeants! . . . Will his excellency be coming soon?" he said, turning to the adjutant with an expression of respectful deference, that related obviously only to the person he was speaking of.

"In an hour's time, I believe."

"Have we time to change clothes?"

"I can't say, general. . . ."

War and Peace, 130–32.

sick before Monterey, and died within a few days. I have always believed that had his life been spared, he would have been President of the United States during the term filled by President Pierce. Had Hamer filled that office his partiality for me was such, there is but little doubt I should have been appointed to one of the staff corps of the army—the Pay Department probably—and would therefore now be preparing to retire. Neither of these speculations is unreasonable, and they are mentioned to show how little men control their own destiny.

Reinforcements having arrived, in the month of August the movement commenced from Matamoras to Camargo, the head of navigation on the Rio Grande. The line of the Rio Grande was all that was necessary to hold, unless it was intended to invade Mexico from the North. In that case the most natural route to take was the one which General Taylor selected. It entered a pass in the Sierra Madre Mountains, at Monterey, through which the main road runs to the City of Mexico. Monterey itself was a good point to hold, even if the line of the Rio Grande covered all the territory we desired to occupy at that time. It is built on a plain two thousand feet above tide water, where the air is bracing and the situation healthy.

On the 19th of August the army started for Monterey, leaving a small garrison at Matamoras. The troops, with the exception of the artillery, cavalry, and the brigade to which I belonged, were moved up the river to Camargo on steamers. As there were but two or three of these, the boats had to make a number of trips before the last of the troops were up. Those who marched did so by the south side of the river. Lieutenant-Colonel [John] Garland, of the 4th infantry, was the brigade commander, and on this occasion commanded the entire marching force. One day out convinced him that marching by day in that latitude, in the month of August, was not a beneficial sanitary measure, particularly for Northern men. The order of marching was changed and night marches were substituted with the best results.

When Camargo was reached, we found a city of tents outside the Mexican hamlet. I was detailed to act as quartermaster and commissary to the regiment. The teams that had proven abundantly sufficient to transport all supplies from Corpus Christi to the Rio Grande over the level prairies of Texas, were entirely inadequate to the needs of the reinforced army in a mountainous country. To obviate the deficiency, pack mules were hired, with Mexicans to pack and drive them. I had charge of the few wagons allotted to the 4th infantry and of the pack train to supplement them. There were not men enough in the army to manage that train without the help of Mexicans who had learned how. As it was the difficulty was great enough. The troops would take up their march at an early hour each day. After they had started, the tents and cooking utensils had to be made into packages, so that they could be lashed to the backs of the mules. Sheet-iron kettles, tent-poles and mess chests were inconvenient articles to transport in that way. It took several hours to get ready to start each morning, and by the time we were ready some of the mules first loaded would be tired of standing so long with their loads on their backs. Sometimes one would start to run, bowing his back and kicking up until he scattered his load; others would lie down and try to disarrange their loads by attempting to get on the top of them by rolling on them; others with tent-poles for part of their loads would manage to run a tent-pole on one side of a sapling while they would take the other. I am not aware of ever having used a profane expletive in my life; but I would have the charity to excuse those who may have done so, if they were in charge of a train of Mexican pack mules at the time.

8

Advance on Monterey—The Black Fort—The Battle of Monterey—Surrender of the City

The advance from Camargo was commenced on the 5th of September.[1] The army was divided into four columns, separated from each other

---

1. The letters of Lieutenant Grant reveal youthful attitudes and expectations masked in the memoirs by the maturity of the dying general. On September 6, he expressed weariness but also disappointment that Mexico seemed to be a war without battles: "Julia aint you geting tired of hearing of war, war, war? I am truly tired of it. here it is now five months that we have been at war and as yet but two battles. I do wish this would close. If we have to fight I would like to do it all at once and then make friends—" *PUSG*, 1:109.

The following description—from a letter to an unknown addressee—of the assault on Jalapa in 1847, is about as enthusiastic as Grant's war writing got:

> It was war pyrotechnics of the most serious and brilliant character. While it was a most inspiring sight, it was a painful one to me. I stood there watching the brigade slowly climbing those ragged heights, each minute nearer and nearer the works of the enemy with our missiles flying over their heads, while white puffs of smoke spitefully flashed out in rapid succession along the enemy's line and I knew that every discharge sent death into our ranks. As our men finally swept over and into the works, my heart was sad at the fate that held me from sharing in that brave and brilliant assault. But our batteries did their duty, and no doubt helped in achieving the glorious result.

April 24, 1847, *PUSG*, 1:134.

The naïveté of inexperienced soldiers is the frequent subject of modern war fiction, where it is generally established in order to be destroyed: "A few of his friends were soldiers and he wanted to volunteer too." Thus the novelist Hans Herbert

by one day's march. The advance reached Cerralvo in four days and halted for the remainder of the troops to come up. By the 13th the rear-guard had arrived, and the same day the advance resumed its march, followed as before, a day separating the divisions. The forward division halted again at Marin, twenty-four miles from Monterey. Both this place and Cerralvo were nearly deserted, and men, women and children were seen running and scattered over the hills as we approached; but when the people returned they found all their abandoned property safe, which must have given them a favorable opinion of *Los Grengos*—"the Yankees." From Marin the movement was in mass. On the 19th General Taylor, with his army, was encamped at Walnut Springs, within three miles of Monterey.

The town is on a small stream coming out of the mountain-pass, and is backed by a range of hills of moderate elevation. To the north, between the city and Walnut Springs, stretches an extensive plain. On this plain, and entirely outside of the last houses of the city, stood a strong fort, enclosed on all sides, to which our army gave the name of "Black Fort." Its guns commanded the approaches to the city to the full extent of their range. There were two detached spurs of hills or mountains to the north and north-west of the city, which were also fortified. On one of these stood the Bishop's Palace. The road to Saltillo leaves the upper or western end of the city under the fire of the guns from these heights. The lower or eastern end was defended by two or three small detached works, armed with artillery and infantry. To the south was the mountain stream before mentioned, and back of that the range of foot-hills. The plaza in the centre of the city was the citadel, properly

---

Grimm describes the mindset of the eponymous seventeen-year-old protagonist of his World War I novel *Schlump*:

> He could picture himself in a field-grey uniform, the girls eyeing him up and offering him cigarettes. Then he would go to war. He pictured the sun shining, the grey uniforms charging, one man falling, the others surging forward further with their cries and cheers, and pair after pair of red trousers vanishing beneath green hedges. In the evenings the soldiers would sit around a campfire and chat about life at home. One would sing a melancholy song. Out in the darkness the double sentries would stand at their posts, leaning on the muzzles of their rifles, dreaming of home and being reunited with loved ones. In the morning they'd break camp and march singing into battle, where some would fall and others be wounded. Eventually the war would be won and they'd return home victorious. Girls would throw flowers from windows and the celebrations would never end.

Schlump, trans. Jamie Bulloch (New York: New York Review Books, 2015), 6–7.

speaking. All the streets leading from it were swept by artillery, cannon being intrenched behind temporary parapets. The house-tops near the plaza were converted into infantry fortifications by the use of sand-bags for parapets. Such were the defences of Monterey in September, 1846. General [Pedro de] Ampudia, with a force of certainly ten thousand men, was in command.

General Taylor's force was about six thousand five hundred strong, in three divisions, under Generals Butler, Twiggs and Worth.[2] The troops

---

2. William O. Butler (1791–1880) was a Kentuckian who fought in the Battle of New Orleans during the War of 1812, and later represented his state in Congress. Butler also served as a delegate to the peace convention of 1861, when American politicians met in Washington, D.C., in a failed attempt to avert war. In his biography of Butler, Frank P. Blair Jr., who would later serve under Grant in the Civil War, tells the story of the young Ensign Butler's exploits in the War of 1812 in the Great Lakes region. Blair's prose exemplifies the style of the age:

> There were two battles at the river Raisin—one on the 18th, the other on the 22d of January [1813]. In the first, the whole body of Indian warriors, drawn together from all the lakes tribes for the defence of Upper Canada against the approaching Kentuckians, were encountered. In moving to the attack of this formidable force of the fiercest, and bravest, and most expert warriors on the continent, a strong party of them were descried from the line with which Ensign Butler advanced, running forward to reach a fence, as a cover from which to ply their rifles. Butler instantly proposed, and was permitted, to anticipate them. Calling upon some of the most alert and active men of the company, he ran directly to meet the Indians at the fence. He and his comrades outstripped the enemy; and, getting possession of the fence, kept the advantage of the position for their advancing friends. This incident, of however little importance as to results, is worth remembrance in giving the traits of a young soldier's character. It is said that the hardiest veteran, at the opening of the fire in battle, feels, for the moment, somewhat appalled; and Gen. Wolfe, one of the bravest of men, declared that the "horrid yell of the Indian strikes the boldest heart with affright." The strippling student, who, for the first time, beheld a field of battle on the snows of the river Raisin, presenting in bold relief, long files of those terrible enimies, whose massacres had filled his native State with tales of horror, must have felt some stirring sensations. But the crack of the Indian rifle, and his savage yell, awoke in him the chivalric instincts of his nature; and the promptitude with which he communicated his enthusiasm to a few comrades around, and rushed forward to meet danger in its most appalling form, risking himself to save others, and to secure a triumph which he could scarcely hope to share, gave earnest of the military talent, the self-sacrificing courage, and the soldierly sympathies which have drawn to him the nation's esteem.

Francis P. Blair, *The Life and Public Services of Gen. William O. Butler* (Baltimore, MD: N. Hickman, 1848), 7.

went into camp at Walnut Springs, while the engineer officers, under Major Mansfield—a General in the late war—commenced their reconnoissance.[3] Major Mansfield found that it would be practicable to get troops around, out of range of the Black Fort and the works on the detached hills to the north-west of the city, to the Saltillo road. With this road in our possession, the enemy would be cut off from receiving further supplies, if not from all communication with the interior. General Worth, with his division somewhat reinforced, was given the task of gaining possession of the Saltillo road, and of carrying the detached works outside the city, in that quarter. He started on his march early in the afternoon of the 20th. The divisions under Generals Butler and Twiggs were drawn up to threaten the east and north sides of the city and the works on those fronts, in support of the movement under General Worth. Worth's was regarded as the main attack on Monterey, and all other operations were in support of it. His march this day was uninterrupted; but the enemy was seen to reinforce heavily about the Bishop's Palace and the other outside fortifications on their left. General Worth reached a defensible position just out of range of the enemy's guns on the heights north-west of the city, and bivouacked for the night. The engineer officers with him—Captain Sanders and Lieutenant George G. Meade, afterwards the commander of the victorious National army at the battle of Gettysburg— made a reconnoissance to the Saltillo road under cover of night.

3. Joseph K. F. Mansfield (1803–1862), Taylor's chief engineer in the Mexican War, graduated from West Point in 1822. He worked on many fortifications, largely in the South, and superintended the construction of Fort Pulaski, Georgia. Mansfield was still on active duty at the outbreak of the Civil War. He superintended the defenses of Washington, D.C., and was killed in command of the 12th Army Corps at the Battle of Antietam. A biographical sketch in Cullum's *Biographical Register* describes his end:

> Reaching the headquarters of the Army of the Potomac, he was at once assigned to the command of the Twelfth Army Corps, which he led into action at Antietam, Sep. 17, 1862, on the extreme right of the line of battle, in support of Hooker's Corps, which was visibly melting away. Mansfield's division, mostly composed of raw troops, met a most galling fire from the defenders of Dunker Church. Seeing his men waver, he pressed forward where the battle was hottest, throwing the whole ardor of his soul into the conflict. His towering form and flowing white locks made him so conspicuous to the enemy that rider and horse soon fell, the former pierced by one and the latter by three minie balls. The General, mortally wounded, died the next morning, saying, "It is the Lord's will, and it is all right."

Biographical Register, vol. 1, s.v. "Butler, William O."

During the night of the 20th General Taylor had established a battery, consisting of two twenty-four-pounder howitzers and a ten-inch mortar, at a point from which they could play upon Black Fort. A natural depression in the plain, sufficiently deep to protect men standing in it from the fire from the fort, was selected and the battery established on the crest nearest the enemy. The 4th infantry, then consisting of but six reduced companies, was ordered to support the artillerists while they were intrenching themselves and their guns. I was regimental quartermaster at the time and was ordered to remain in charge of camp and the public property at Walnut Springs. It was supposed that the regiment would return to its camp in the morning.

The point for establishing the siege battery was reached and the work performed without attracting the attention of the enemy. At daylight the next morning fire was opened on both sides and continued with, what seemed to me at that day, great fury. My curiosity got the better of my judgment, and I mounted a horse and rode to the front to see what was going on. I had been there but a short time when an order to charge was given, and lacking the moral courage to return to camp—where I had been ordered to stay—I charged with the regiment. As soon as the troops were out of the depression they came under the fire of Black Fort. As they advanced they got under fire from batteries guarding the east, or lower, end of the city, and of musketry. About one-third of the men engaged in the charge were killed or wounded in the space of a few minutes. We retreated to get out of fire, not backward, but eastward and perpendicular to the direct road running into the city from Walnut Springs. I was, I believe, the only person in the 4th infantry in the charge who was on horseback. When we got to a place of safety the regiment halted and drew itself together—what was left of it. The adjutant of the regiment, Lieutenant [Charles W.] Hoskins, who was not in robust health, found himself very much fatigued from running on foot in the charge and retreat, and, seeing me on horseback, expressed a wish that he could be mounted also. I offered him my horse and he accepted the offer. A few minutes later I saw a soldier, a quartermaster's man, mounted, not far away. I ran to him, took his horse and was back with the regiment in a few minutes. In a short time we were off again; and the next place of safety from the shots of the enemy that I recollect of being in, was a field of cane or corn to the northeast of the lower batteries. The adjutant to whom I had loaned my horse was killed, and I was designated to act in his place.

This charge was ill-conceived, or badly executed. We belonged to the brigade commanded by Lieutenant-Colonel Garland, and he had received orders to charge the lower batteries of the city, and carry them if he could without too much loss, for the purpose of creating a diversion in favor of Worth, who was conducting the movement which it was intended should be decisive. By a movement by the left flank Garland could have led his men beyond the range of the fire from Black Fort and advanced towards the north-east angle of the city, as well covered from fire as could be expected. There was no undue loss of life in reaching the lower end of Monterey, except that sustained by Garland's command.

Meanwhile Quitman's brigade, conducted by an officer of engineers, had reached the eastern end of the city, and was placed under cover of the houses without much loss. Colonel Garland's brigade also arrived at the suburbs, and, by the assistance of some of our troops that had reached house-tops from which they could fire into a little battery covering the approaches to the lower end of the city, the battery was speedily captured and its guns were turned upon another work of the enemy. An entrance into the east end of the city was now secured, and the houses protected our troops so long as they were inactive.[4]

On the west General Worth had reached the Saltillo road after some fighting but without heavy loss. He turned from his new position and captured the forts on both heights in that quarter. This gave him possession of the upper or west end of Monterey. Troops from both Twiggs's and Butler's divisions were in possession of the east end of the town, but the Black Fort to the north of the town and the plaza in the centre were still in the possession of the enemy. Our camps at Walnut Springs, three miles away, were guarded by a company from each regiment. A regiment of Kentucky volunteers guarded the mortars and howitzers engaged against Black Fort. Practically Monterey was invested.

There was nothing done on the 22d by the United States troops; but the enemy kept up a harmless fire upon us from Black Fort and the batteries still in their possession at the east end of the city. During the night they evacu-

---

4. John Garland (1792–1861) began his military service in the War of 1812 and went on to serve in Florida as well as Mexico. A native of Virginia and the father-in-law of the Confederate general James Longstreet, Garland died in New York City just a few months after the beginning of the Civil War on June 5, 1861. Colorado's Fort Garland (1858–1883) was named for him. John A. Quitman (1798–1858) was born in New York but eventually moved to Mississippi, where he became involved in state politics. He went to Texas when the 1836 Revolution broke out and ultimately volunteered for the Mexican War.

ated these; so that on the morning of the 23d we held undisputed possession of the east end of Monterey.

Twiggs's division was at the lower end of the city, and well covered from the fire of the enemy. But the streets leading to the plaza—all Spanish or Spanish-American towns have near their centres a square called a plaza—were commanded from all directions by artillery. The houses were flat-roofed and but one or two stories high, and about the plaza the roofs were manned with infantry, the troops being protected from our fire by parapets made of sand-bags. All advances into the city were thus attended with much danger. While moving along streets which did not lead to the plaza, our men were protected from the fire, and from the view, of the enemy except at the crossings; but at these a volley of musketry and a discharge of grape-shot were invariably encountered. The 3d and 4th regiments of infantry made an advance nearly to the plaza in this way and with heavy loss. The loss of the 3d infantry in commissioned officers was especially severe. There were only five companies of the regiment and not over twelve officers present, and five of these officers were killed. When within a square of the plaza this small command, ten companies in all, was brought to a halt. Placing themselves under cover from the shots of the enemy, the men would watch to detect a head above the sand-bags on the neighboring houses. The exposure of a single head would bring a volley from our soldiers.

We had not occupied this position long when it was discovered that our ammunition was growing low. I volunteered to go back[5] to the point we had started from, report our position to General Twiggs, and ask for ammunition to be forwarded. We were at this time occupying ground off from the street, in rear of the houses. My ride back was an exposed one. Before starting I adjusted myself on the side of my horse furthest from the enemy, and with only one foot holding to the cantle of the saddle, and an arm over the neck of the horse exposed, I started at full run. It was only at street crossings that my horse was under fire, but these I crossed at such a flying rate that generally I was past and under cover of the next block of houses before the enemy fired. I got out safely without a scratch.

At one place on my ride, I saw a sentry walking in front of a house, and

5. General Garland expressed a wish to get a message back to General Twiggs, his division commander, or General Taylor, to the effect that he was nearly out of ammunition and must have more sent to him, or otherwise be reinforced. Deeming the return dangerous he did not like to order any one to carry it, so he called for a volunteer. Lieutenant Grant offered his services, which were accepted.—PUBLISHERS. [Note to the first edition.]

stopped to inquire what he was doing there. Finding that the house was full of wounded American officers and soldiers, I dismounted and went in. I found there Captain Williams, of the Engineer Corps, wounded in the head, probably fatally, and Lieutenant Territt, also badly wounded, his bowels protruding from his wound. There were quite a number of soldiers also. Promising them to report their situation, I left, readjusted myself to my horse, recommenced the run, and was soon with the troops at the east end. Before ammunition could be collected, the two regiments I had been with were seen returning, running the same gauntlet in getting out that they had passed in going in, but with comparatively little loss. The movement was countermanded and the troops were withdrawn. The poor wounded officers and men I had found, fell into the hands of the enemy during the night, and died.[6]

6. In his biography of Grant, Hamlin Garland energetically describes his subject's courageous but ultimately unnecessary ride:

> The command could neither go forward nor back, and the battle hung poised till Colonel Garland at last discovered his ammunition to be running low. It then became necessary to get word to General Twiggs, his division commander, calling for ammunition or reinforcements. The colonel called for volunteers.
> "Men, I've got to send some one back to General Twiggs. It's a dangerous job, and I don't like to order any man to do it. Who'll volunteer?"
> "I will," said Quartermaster Grant, promptly. "I've got a horse."
> "You're just the man to do it. Keep on the side streets, and ride hard."
> Grant needed no direction, for he was among the best horsemen in the entire command, and had been instructed by the Comanches. He swung himself over his saddle, and, with one heel behind the cantle, and one hand wound in his horse's mane, dashed at full gallop down a side street leading to the north, a street which looked like a dry canal. At every crossing he was exposed to view, and the enemy, getting his range, sent a slash of bullets after him as he flashed past. Hanging thus, he forced his horse to leap a four-foot wall. He rode to the north till safely out of fire; then, regaining his seat, he turned to the east, and in a few moments' time drew rein before General Twiggs, and breathlessly uttered his message.
> Twiggs gave the order to collect the ammunition, but before it could be done the troops came pouring back.

Garland, *Grant*, 79–80.

Taylor noted in dispatches the deaths of both the officers Grant mentions: William G. Williams, West Point class of 1824, and J. C. Terrett. Of the former he wrote to the Adjutant General in Washington on October 9, 1846: "Captain Williams, Topographical Engineers, to my great regret and the loss of the service, was mortally wounded

While this was going on at the east, General Worth, with a small division of troops, was advancing towards the plaza from the opposite end of the city. He resorted to a better expedient for getting to the plaza—the citadel—than we did on the east. Instead of moving by the open streets, he advanced through the houses, cutting passage-ways from one to another. Without much loss of life, he got so near the plaza during the night that before morning, Ampudia, the Mexican commander, made overtures for the surrender of the city and garrison. This stopped all further hostilities. The terms of surrender were soon agreed upon. The prisoners were paroled and permitted to take their horses and personal property with them.

My pity was aroused by the sight of the Mexican garrison of Monterey marching out of town as prisoners, and no doubt the same feeling was experienced by most of our army who witnessed it. Many of the prisoners were cavalry, armed with lances, and mounted on miserable little half-starved horses that did not look as if they could carry their riders out of town. The men looked in but little better condition. I thought how little interest the men before me had in the results of the war, and how little knowledge they had of "what it was all about."[7]

After the surrender of the garrison of Monterey a quiet camp life was led until midwinter. As had been the case on the Rio Grande, the people who remained at their homes fraternized with the "Yankees" in the pleasantest manner. In fact, under the humane policy of our commander, I question whether the great majority of the Mexican people did not regret our departure as much as they had regretted our coming. Property and person were thoroughly protected, and a market was afforded for all the products of the country such as the people had never enjoyed before. The educated and wealthy portion of the population here, as elsewhere, abandoned their homes and remained away from them as long as they were in the possession of the invaders; but this class formed a very small percentage of the whole population.

---

while fearlessly exposing himself in the attack of the 21st." Taylor numbered Williams and Terrett among "our most gallant and accomplished officers" lost on that day. See "Storming of Monterey—Gen. Taylor's Report, October 9, 1846," *The American Quarterly Register and Magazine* 1, no. 1 (1848): 70, 67.

7. Grant's discussion of his enemy here is typical in its lack of vindictiveness and bloodlust.

9

Political Intrigue—Buena Vista—
Movement against Vera Cruz—Siege and
Capture of Vera Cruz

he Mexican war was a political war, and the administration conducting it desired to make party capital out of it.[1] General Scott was at the
head of the army, and, being a soldier of acknowledged professional capacity,
his claim to the command of the forces in the field was almost indisputable
and does not seem to have been denied by President Polk, or [William L.]
Marcy, his Secretary of War.[2] Scott was a Whig and the administration was

---

1. Some have argued that Grant's laconic descriptions of war's bloody results suggest a
lack of feeling, but one might also interpret his restraint as a recognition that dwelling
on gruesome details perversely offers but another way of glorifying the experience.
There was little worth celebrating about the Mexican War. Henry James recalled, "The
not very glorious smoke of the Mexican War . . . had been in the air when I was a . . .
boy." *A Small Boy and Others*, 52.

2. This is the second time that Grant explicitly condemns the war in which he fought.
The nature of military obedience is such that those who find themselves in uniform
when a war breaks out may well end up fighting for a cause they judge bankrupt—if
they inquire after causes at all. The Mexican War inspired Henry David Thoreau to
civil disobedience, and in the treatise he wrote to defend his refusal to pay taxes to support the war effort or slavery, he portrayed the soldier as a victim, the prime example of
all those citizens "who serve the state . . . as machines, with their bodies" only. Thoreau
imagines a column marching off to war:

> A common and natural result of an undue respect for law is, that you may
> see a file of soldiers, colonel, captain, corporal, privates, powder-monkeys,
> and all, marching in admirable order over hill and dale to the wars, against
> their wills, ay, against their common sense and consciences, which makes it

democratic. General Scott was also known to have political aspirations, and nothing so popularizes a candidate for high civil positions as military victories.[3] It would not do therefore to give him command of the "army of conquest." The plans submitted by Scott for a campaign in Mexico were disapproved by the administration, and he replied, in a tone possibly a little disrespectful, to the effect that, if a soldier's plans were not to be supported by the administration, success could not be expected. This was on the 27th of May, 1846. Four days later General Scott was notified that he need not go to Mexico. General [Edmund P.] Gaines was next in rank, but he was too old and feeble to take the field. Colonel Zachary Taylor—a brigadier-general by brevet—was therefore left in command. He, too, was a Whig, but was not supposed to entertain any political ambitions; nor did he; but after the fall of Monterey, his third battle and third complete victory, the Whig papers at home began to speak of him as the candidate of their party for the Presidency. Something had to be done to neutralize his growing popularity. He could not be relieved from duty in the field where all his battles had been victories: the design would have been too transparent. It was finally decided to send General Scott to Mexico in chief command, and to authorize him to carry out his own original plan: that is, capture Vera Cruz and march upon the capital of the country. It was no doubt supposed that Scott's ambition would lead him to slaughter Taylor or destroy his chances for the Presidency, and yet it was hoped that he would not make sufficient capital himself to secure the prize.

The administration had indeed a most embarrassing problem to solve. It was engaged in a war of conquest which must be carried to a successful issue, or the political object would be unattained. Yet all the capable officers of the requisite rank belonged to the opposition, and the man selected for his lack of political ambition had himself become a prominent candidate for the Presidency. It was necessary to destroy his chances promptly. The problem

---

very steep marching indeed, and produces a palpitation of the heart. They have no doubt that it is a damnable business in which they are concerned; they are all peaceably inclined. Now, what are they? Men at all? or small movable forts and magazines, at the service of some unscrupulous man in power?

"Civil Disobedience," *A Yankee in Canada, with Anti-Slavery and Reform Papers* (Boston: Ticknor and Fields, 1866), 125–26.

3. Grant of course knew at first hand what it meant to be catapulted to political office through military heroism.

was to do this without the loss of conquest and without permitting another general of the same political party to acquire like popularity. The fact is, the administration of Mr. Polk made every preparation to disgrace Scott, or, to speak more correctly, to drive him to such desperation that he would disgrace himself.[4]

General Scott had opposed conquest by the way of the Rio Grande, Matamoras and Saltillo from the first. Now that he was in command of all the forces in Mexico, he withdrew from Taylor most of his regular troops and left him only enough volunteers, as he thought, to hold the line then in possession of the invading army. Indeed Scott did not deem it important to hold anything beyond the Rio Grande, and authorized Taylor to fall back to that line if he chose. General Taylor protested against the depletion of his army, and his subsequent movement upon Buena Vista would indicate that he did not share the views of his chief in regard to the unimportance of conquest beyond the Rio Grande.

Scott had estimated the men and material that would be required to capture Vera Cruz and to march on the capital of the country, two hundred and sixty miles in the interior. He was promised all he asked and seemed to have not only the confidence of the President, but his sincere good wishes. The promises were all broken. Only about half the troops were furnished that had been pledged, other war material was withheld and Scott had scarcely started for Mexico before the President undertook to supersede him by the

---

4. Scott did not disgrace himself: instead, he commandeered Taylor's army, executed an ambitious amphibious landing on the Mexican coast, captured Veracruz, and, cutting his supply line, boldly marched 260 miles west into the hostile interior toward Mexico City. In his autobiography Scott notes, "The Duke of Wellington, with whom the autobiographer was slightly acquainted, took quite an interest in the march of this army from Vera Cruz, and at every arrival caused its movements to be marked on a map. Admiring its triumphs up to the basin of Mexico, he now said to a common friend: 'Scott is lost. He has been carried away by successes. He can't take the city, and he can't fall back upon his base.'" *Memoirs*, 2 vols. (New York: Sheldon, 1864), 2:466, n.

Catton notes that Grant learned a vital strategic lesson from Scott's march—a lesson that would pay dividends during the Vicksburg campaign. See Catton, *Grant and the American Military Tradition*, 41–42, 101–2. See also Lloyd Lewis, *Captain Sam Grant* (Boston: Little, Brown, 1950), 204.

On the various ways in which the ambitions of generals and the incessant political maneuvering of President James K. Polk shaped the conduct of the war from first to last, see Greenberg, *A Wicked War*. It was in the same waters off Veracruz that the Spanish conquistador Hernán Cortés, making retreat impossible, scuttled his own ships in 1519. He then advanced into the interior to terrorize the inhabitants and ultimately destroy the Aztec kingdom of Moctezuma.

Edward Clay Williams, "Distinguished Military Operations with a Hasty Bowl of Soup," 1846. *Library of Congress, Prints and Photographs Division, LC-USZ62-62676.*

appointment of Senator Thomas H. Benton as lieutenant-general. This being refused by Congress, the President asked legislative authority to place a junior over a senior of the same grade, with the view of appointing Benton to the rank of major-general and then placing him in command of the army, but Congress failed to accede to this proposition as well, and Scott remained in command: but every general appointed to serve under him was politically opposed to the chief, and several were personally hostile.

General Scott reached Brazos Santiago or Point Isabel, at the mouth of the Rio Grande, late in December, 1846, and proceeded at once up the river to Camargo, where he had written General Taylor to meet him. Taylor, however, had gone to, or towards Tampico, for the purpose of establishing a post there. He had started on this march before he was aware of General Scott being in the country. Under these circumstances Scott had to issue his orders designating the troops to be withdrawn from Taylor, without the personal consultation he had expected to hold with his subordinate.

General Taylor's victory at Buena Vista, February 22d, 23d, and 24th, 1847, with an army composed almost entirely of volunteers who had not been in battle before, and over a vastly superior force numerically, made his nomination for the Presidency by the Whigs a foregone conclusion. He was nominated and elected in 1848. I believe that he sincerely regretted this turn in his fortunes, preferring the peace afforded by a quiet life free from abuse to the honor of filling the highest office in the gift of any people, the Presidency of the United States.

When General Scott assumed command of the army of invasion, I was in the division of General David Twiggs, in Taylor's command; but under the new orders my regiment was transferred to the division of General William Worth, in which I served to the close of the war. The troops withdrawn from Taylor to form part of the forces to operate against Vera Cruz, were assembled at the mouth of the Rio Grande preparatory to embarkation for their destination. I found General Worth a different man from any I had before served directly under. He was nervous, impatient and restless on the march, or when important or responsible duty confronted him. There was not the least reason for haste on the march, for it was known that it would take weeks to assemble shipping enough at the point of our embarkation to carry the army, but General Worth moved his division with a rapidity that would have been commendable had he been going to the relief of a beleaguered garrison. The length of the marches was regulated by the distances between places affording a supply of water for the troops, and these distances were sometimes long and sometimes short. General Worth on one occasion at least, after having made the full distance intended for the day, and after the troops were in camp and preparing their food, ordered tents struck and made the march that night which had been intended for the next day. Some commanders can move troops so as to get the maximum distance out of them without fatigue, while others can wear them out in a few days without accomplishing so much. General Worth belonged to this latter class. He enjoyed, however, a fine reputation for his fighting qualities, and thus attached his officers and men to him.[5]

The army lay in camp upon the sand-beach in the neighborhood of the mouth of the Rio Grande for several weeks, awaiting the arrival of transports to carry it to its new field of operations. The transports were all sailing vessels. The passage was a tedious one, and many of the troops were on shipboard over thirty days from the embarkation at the mouth of the Rio Grande to the time of debarkation south of Vera Cruz. The trip was a comfortless one for officers and men. The transports used were built for carrying freight and possessed but limited accommodations for passengers, and the climate added to the discomfort of all.

The transports with troops were assembled in the harbor of Anton Lizardo, some sixteen miles south of Vera Cruz, as they arrived, and there

---

5. This is the first of many nuanced portraits of fellow officers that appear throughout the *Memoirs*, and it reveals Grant's ability to delineate precisely an individual's strengths and weaknesses. During the Civil War, ambivalence about a given officer—the recognition of certain failings—did not prevent Grant from acknowledging and exploiting that officer's strengths.

awaited the remainder of the fleet, bringing artillery, ammunition and supplies of all kinds from the North. With the fleet there was a little steam propeller dispatch-boat—the first vessel of the kind I had ever seen, and probably the first of its kind ever seen by any one then with the army. At that day ocean steamers were rare, and what there were were sidewheelers. This little vessel, going through the fleet so fast, so noiselessly and with its propeller under water out of view, attracted a great deal of attention. I recollect that Lieutenant Sidney Smith, of the 4th infantry, by whom I happened to be standing on the deck of a vessel when this propeller was passing, exclaimed, "Why, the thing looks as if it was propelled by the force of circumstances."[6]

Finally on the 7th of March, 1847, the little army of ten or twelve thousand men, given Scott to invade a country with a population of seven or eight millions, a mountainous country affording the greatest possible natural advantages for defence, was all assembled and ready to commence the perilous task of landing from vessels lying in the open sea.

The debarkation took place inside of the little island of Sacrificios, some three miles south of Vera Cruz. The vessels could not get anywhere near shore, so that everything had to be landed in lighters or surf-boats; Gen-

6. Sidney Smith of Virginia, previously wounded at Molino del Rey, died on September 16, 1847, of wounds suffered during the storming of Mexico City. Grant wrote to Julia that same month: "The idea of staying longer in this country is to me insupportable. Just think of the three long years that have passed since we met. My health has always been good, but exposure to weather and a Tropicle Sun had added ten years to my apparent age. At this rate I will soon be old.—Out of all the officers that left Jefferson Barracks with the 4th Infantry but three besides myself now remains with us, besides this four or five who joined since, are gone. Poor Sidney Smith was the last one killed." Letter to Julia Dent, September 1847, *PUSG*, 1:146–47.

This sense of war's endlessness is a common feature of soldiers' accounts. Take, for example, the following observation from Edmund Blunden's World War I memoir:

One of the first ideas that established themselves in my inquiring mind was the prevailing sense of the endlessness of war. No one here appeared to conceive any end to it. . . . Such as it was, the Old British Line at Festubert had the appearance of great age and perpetuity; its weather-beaten sandbag wall was already venerable. It shared the past with the defences of Troy. The skulls which spades disturbed about it were in a manner coeval with those of the most distant wars; there is an obstinate remoteness about a skull. And, as for the future, one of the first hints that came home to me was implied in a machine-gun emplacement stubbornly built in brick and cement, as one might build a house.

Undertones of War (Chicago: University of Chicago Press, 2007), 11–12.

eral Scott had provided these before leaving the North. The breakers were sometimes high, so that the landing was tedious. The men were got ashore rapidly, because they could wade when they came to shallow water; but the camp and garrison equipage, provisions, ammunition and all stores had to be protected from the salt water, and therefore their landing took several days. The Mexicans were very kind to us, however, and threw no obstacles in the way of our landing except an occasional shot from their nearest fort. During the debarkation one shot took off the head of Major Albertis [Alburtis]. No other, I believe, reached anywhere near the same distance. On the 9th of March the troops were landed and the investment of Vera Cruz, from the Gulf of Mexico south of the city to the Gulf again on the north, was soon and easily effected. The landing of stores was continued until everything was got ashore.

Vera Cruz, at the time of which I write and up to 1880, was a walled city. The wall extended from the water's edge south of the town to the water again on the north. There were fortifications at intervals along the line and at the angles. In front of the city, and on an island half a mile out in the Gulf, stands San Juan de Ulloa, an enclosed fortification of large dimensions and great strength for that period. Against artillery of the present day the land forts and walls would prove elements of weakness rather than strength. After the invading army had established their camps out of range of the fire from the city, batteries were established, under cover of night, far to the front of the line where the troops lay. These batteries were intrenched and the approaches sufficiently protected. If a sortie had been made at any time by the Mexicans, the men serving the batteries could have been quickly reinforced without great exposure to the fire from the enemy's main line. No serious attempt was made to capture the batteries or to drive our troops away.

The siege continued with brisk firing on our side till the 27th of March, by which time a considerable breach had been made in the wall surrounding the city. Upon this General Morales, who was Governor of both the city and of San Juan de Ulloa, commenced a correspondence with General Scott looking to the surrender of the town, forts and garrison. On the 29th Vera Cruz and San Juan de Ulloa were occupied by Scott's army. About five thousand prisoners and four hundred pieces of artillery, besides large amounts of small arms and ammunition, fell into the hands of the victorious force. The casualties on our side during the siege amounted to sixty-four officers and men, killed and wounded.

10

March to Jalapa—Battle of Cerro Gordo—
Perote—Puebla—Scott and Taylor

General Scott had less than twelve thousand men at Vera Cruz. He had been promised by the administration a very much larger force, or claimed that he had, and he was a man of veracity. Twelve thousand was a very small army with which to penetrate two hundred and sixty miles into an enemy's country, and to besiege the capital; a city, at that time, of largely over one hundred thousand inhabitants. Then, too, any line of march that could be selected led through mountain passes easily defended. In fact, there were at that time but two roads from Vera Cruz to the City of Mexico that could be taken by an army; one by Jalapa and Perote, the other by Cordova and Orizaba, the two coming together on the great plain which extends to the City of Mexico after the range of mountains is passed.

It was very important to get the army away from Vera Cruz as soon as possible, in order to avoid the yellow fever, or vomito, which usually visits that city early in the year, and is very fatal to persons not acclimated; but transportation, which was expected from the North, was arriving very slowly. It was absolutely necessary to have enough to supply the army to Jalapa, sixty-five miles in the interior and above the fevers of the coast. At that point the country is fertile, and an army of the size of General Scott's could subsist there for an indefinite period.[1] Not counting the sick, the

---

1. In addition to outrunning the fever by reaching higher ground, Scott was attempting to outrace Santa Anna. Scott's decision to live off the "fertile" land of the interior

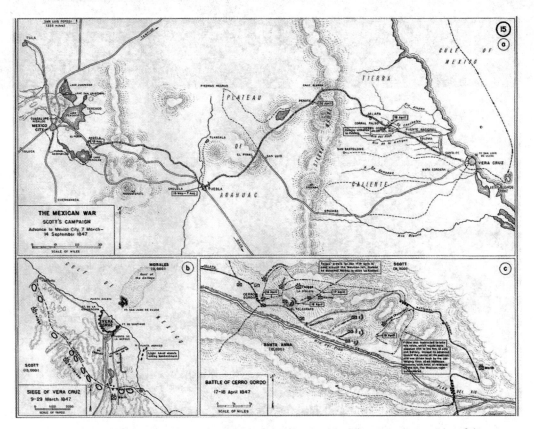

Scott's campaign to Mexico City, March 7–September 14, 1847. *West Point Atlas of the Mexican War. Courtesy of Department of History, USMA.*

weak and the garrisons for the captured city and fort, the moving column was now less than ten thousand strong. This force was composed of three divisions, under Generals Twiggs, Patterson, and Worth. The importance of escaping the vomito was so great that as soon as transportation enough could be got together to move a division the advance was commenced. On the 8th of April, Twiggs's division started for Jalapa. He was followed very soon by Patterson, with his division. General Worth was to bring up the rear with his command as soon as transportation enough was assembled to carry six days' rations for his troops with the necessary ammunition and camp and garrison equipage. It was the 13th of April before this division left Vera Cruz.

would be an important model for Grant, who would eventually cut loose from his base of supply during the 1863 Vicksburg campaign.

The leading division ran against the enemy at Cerro Gordo, some fifty miles west, on the road to Jalapa, and went into camp at Plan del Rio, about three miles from the fortifications. General Patterson reached Plan del Rio with his division soon after Twiggs arrived. The two were then secure against an attack from Santa Anna, who commanded the Mexican forces. At all events they confronted the enemy without reinforcements and without molestation, until the 18th of April. General Scott had remained at Vera Cruz to hasten preparations for the field; but on the 12th, learning the situation at the front, he hastened on to take personal supervision. He at once commenced his preparations for the capture of the position held by Santa Anna and of the troops holding it.

Cerro Gordo is one of the higher spurs of the mountains some twelve to fifteen miles east of Jalapa, and Santa Anna had selected this point as the easiest to defend against an invading army. The road, said to have been built by Cortez, zigzags around the mountain-side and was defended at every turn by artillery. On either side were deep chasms or mountain walls. A direct attack along the road was an impossibility. A flank movement seemed equally impossible. After the arrival of the commanding-general upon the scene, reconnoissances were sent out to find, or to make, a road by which the rear of the enemy's works might be reached without a front attack. These reconnoissances were made under the supervision of Captain Robert E. Lee, assisted by Lieutenants P. G. T. Beauregard, Isaac I. Stevens, Z. B. Tower, G. W. Smith, George B. McClellan, and J. G. Foster, of the corps of engineers, all officers who attained rank and fame, on one side or the other, in the great conflict for the preservation of the unity of the nation.[2] The reconnoissance was completed, and the labor of cutting out and making roads by the flank of the enemy was effected by the 17th of the month. This was accomplished without the knowledge of Santa Anna or his army, and over ground where he supposed it impossible. On the same day General Scott issued his order for the attack on the 18th.

The attack was made as ordered, and perhaps there was not a battle of the Mexican war, or of any other, where orders issued before an engagement were nearer being a correct report of what afterwards took place. Under

2. This list of officers gives an excellent sense of the intimacy of the regular army before the Civil War and of the ways in which relationships of long standing textured the interactions between comrades and adversaries during the Civil War. It is also noteworthy how many of these experienced officers violated the oaths they had sworn in order to fight for the South.

the supervision of the engineers, roadways had been opened over chasms to the right where the walls were so steep that men could barely climb them. Animals could not. These had been opened under cover of night, without attracting the notice of the enemy. The engineers, who had directed the opening, led the way and the troops followed. Artillery was let down the steep slopes by hand, the men engaged attaching a strong rope to the rear axle and letting the guns down, a piece at a time, while the men at the ropes kept their ground on top, paying out gradually, while a few at the front directed the course of the piece. In like manner the guns were drawn by hand up the opposite slopes. In this way Scott's troops reached their assigned position in rear of most of the intrenchments of the enemy, unobserved.[3] The attack was made, the Mexican reserves behind the works beat a hasty retreat, and those occupying them surrendered. On the left General Pillow's command made a formidable demonstration, which doubtless held a part of the enemy in his front and contributed to the victory.[4] I am not pretending to give full details of all the battles fought, but of the portion that I saw. There were troops engaged on both sides at other points in which both sustained losses; but the battle was won as here narrated.

The surprise of the enemy was complete, the victory overwhelming; some three thousand prisoners fell into Scott's hands, also a large amount of ordnance and ordnance stores. The prisoners were paroled, the artillery parked and the small arms and ammunition destroyed. The battle of Buena Vista was probably very important to the success of General Scott at Cerro Gordo and in his entire campaign from Vera Cruz to the great plains reaching to the City of Mexico. The only army Santa Anna had to protect his capital and the mountain passes west of Vera Cruz, was the one he had with him confronting General Taylor. It is not likely that he would have gone as

---

3. At Cerro Gordo, and not for the last time, Robert E. Lee discovered a route of approach for the army to attack a heavily fortified position. As Grant admiringly explains, Lee and his engineers widened the road and moved equipment under cover of darkness. For a superb account of the significance of this episode and Lee's Mexican War service more generally, see Elizabeth Pryor, *Reading the Man: A Portrait of Robert E. Lee Through His Private Letters* (New York: Penguin, 2007), chapter 10.

4. The wealthy Tennessee Democrat Gideon J. Pillow (1806–1878) was appointed a brigadier general of volunteers in 1846. He was a political powerbroker who received his commission as a reward for helping Polk to the presidency. A relentless self-promoter, Pillow would remain a center of controversy during the Civil War, when he joined the C.S.A. Pillow will reenter the picture in later chapters recounting Grant's operations in Tennessee in 1862.

far north as Monterey to attack the United States troops when he knew his country was threatened with invasion further south. When Taylor moved to Saltillo and then advanced on to Buena Vista, Santa Anna crossed the desert confronting the invading army, hoping no doubt to crush it and get back in time to meet General Scott in the mountain passes west of Vera Cruz. His attack on Taylor was disastrous to the Mexican army, but, notwithstanding this, he marched his army to Cerro Gordo, a distance not much short of one thousand miles by the line he had to travel, in time to intrench himself well before Scott got there. If he had been successful at Buena Vista his troops would no doubt have made a more stubborn resistance at Cerro Gordo. Had the battle of Buena Vista not been fought Santa Anna would have had time to move leisurely to meet the invader further south and with an army not demoralized nor depleted by defeat.

After the battle the victorious army moved on to Jalapa, where it was in a beautiful, productive and healthy country, far above the fevers of the coast. Jalapa, however, is still in the mountains, and between there and the great plain the whole line of the road is easy of defence. It was important, therefore, to get possession of the great highway between the sea-coast and the capital up to the point where it leaves the mountains, before the enemy could have time to re-organize and fortify in our front. Worth's division was selected to go forward to secure this result. The division marched to Perote on the great plain, not far from where the road debouches from the mountains. There is a low, strong fort on the plain in front of the town, known as the Castle of Perote. This, however, offered no resistance and fell into our hands, with its armament.

General Scott having now only nine or ten thousand men west of Vera Cruz, and the time of some four thousand of them being about to expire, a long delay was the consequence. The troops were in a healthy climate, and where they could subsist for an indefinite period even if their line back to Vera Cruz should be cut off. It being ascertained that the men whose time would expire before the City of Mexico could possibly fall into the hands of the American army, would not remain beyond the term for which they had volunteered, the commanding-general determined to discharge them at once, for a delay until the expiration of their time would have compelled them to pass through Vera Cruz during the season of the vomito. This reduced Scott's force in the field to about five thousand men.

Early in May, Worth, with his division, left Perote and marched on to Puebla. The roads were wide and the country open except through one pass in a spur of mountains coming up from the south, through which the road runs. Notwithstanding this the small column was divided into two bodies, moving a day apart. Nothing occurred on the march of special note, except that while lying at the town of Amozoque—an easy day's march east of Puebla—a body of the enemy's cavalry, two or three thousand strong, was seen to our right, not more than a mile away. A battery or two, with two or three infantry regiments, was sent against them and they soon disappeared. On the 15th of May we entered the city of Puebla.

General Worth was in command at Puebla until the latter end of May, when General Scott arrived. Here, as well as on the march up, his restlessness, particularly under responsibilities, showed itself. During his brief command he had the enemy hovering around near the city, in vastly superior numbers to his own. The brigade to which I was attached changed quarters three different times in about a week, occupying at first quarters near the plaza, in the heart of the city; then at the western entrance; then at the extreme east. On one occasion General Worth had the troops in line, under arms, all day, with three days' cooked rations in their haversacks. He galloped from one command to another proclaiming the near proximity of Santa Anna with an army vastly superior to his own. General Scott arrived upon the scene the latter part of the month, and nothing more was heard of Santa Anna and his myriads. There were, of course, bodies of mounted Mexicans hovering around to watch our movements and to pick up stragglers, or small bodies of troops, if they ventured too far out. These always withdrew on the approach of any considerable number of our soldiers. After the arrival of General Scott I was sent, as quartermaster, with a large train of wagons, back two days' march at least, to procure forage. We had less than a thousand men as escort, and never thought of danger. We procured full loads for our entire train at two plantations, which could easily have furnished as much more.

There had been great delay in obtaining the authority of Congress for the raising of the troops asked for by the administration. A bill was before the National Legislature from early in the session of 1846–7, authorizing the creation of ten additional regiments for the war to be attached to the regular army, but it was the middle of February before it became a law. Appointments of commissioned officers had then to be made; men had to be enlisted, the regiments equipped and the whole transported to Mexico. It was August before General Scott received reinforcement sufficient to warrant an advance. His moving column, not even now more than ten thousand strong, was in four divisions, commanded by Generals Twiggs, Worth, Pillow and Quitman. There was also a cavalry corps under General Harney, composed of detachments of the 1st, 2d, and 3d dragoons.[5] The advance commenced on the 7th of August with Twiggs's division in front. The remaining three divisions followed, with an interval of a day between. The marches were short, to make concentration easier in case of attack.

I had now been in battle with the two leading commanders conducting armies in a foreign land.[6] The contrast between the two was very marked. General Taylor never wore uniform, but dressed himself entirely for comfort. He moved about the field in which he was operating to see through his own eyes the situation. Often he would be without staff officers, and when he was accompanied by them there was no prescribed order in which they followed. He was very much given to sit his horse side-ways—with both feet on one side—particularly on the battle-field. General Scott was the reverse in all these particulars. He always wore all the uniform prescribed or allowed by law when he inspected his lines; word would be sent to all division and brigade commanders in advance, notifying them of the hour when the commanding general might be expected. This was done so that all the army might be under arms to salute their chief as he passed. On these occasions he wore his dress uniform, cocked hat, aiguillettes, sabre and spurs.[7] His staff

---

5. William S. Harney (1800–1889) was commissioned in 1818, fought in the Florida Indian Wars, and was given a brevet promotion to brigadier general for his services at Cerro Gordo. Harney retired in 1863, but not before being relieved of command of the Department of the West in 1861, after cosigning an agreement with the Southern-sympathizing Missouri State Guard commander Sterling Price, who counted on this agreement to buy time to rally secessionist elements in the state: "General Harney publicly declares," the document read, "that . . . he can have no occasion, as he has no wish, to make military movements, which might otherwise create excitements and jealousies which he most earnestly desires to avoid." *OR,* ser. 1, vol. 3, 375.

6. One of the great set pieces of Grant's book, this double portrait of Scott ("Old Fuss and Feathers") and Taylor ("Old Rough and Ready") reveals not only the author's sense of humor and ability to parse finely when appraising character but also his discovery of a model in Taylor. His description of Taylor's ability to "put his meaning so plainly there could be no mistaking it" will recur, almost verbatim, in his account of writing the terms of surrender for Lee's army at Appomattox.

7. In the first chapter ("The General Is Older than the Capital") of her magisterial history of wartime Washington, Margaret Leech offers an unforgettable portrait of the superannuated Scott on the eve of war in 1861, ensconced, after years of living in New York City, in new living quarters in Washington, D.C., with a French chef:

> From his splendid prime, the General had retained, not only a discriminating palate, but the defects suitable to a proud and ambitious nature.

Zachary Taylor in broad-brimmed hat and civilian dress. H. R. Robinson. *Library of Congress, Prints and Photographs Division, LC-DIG-pga-02530.*

proper, besides all officers constructively on his staff—engineers, inspectors, quartermasters, etc., that could be spared—followed, also in uniform and in prescribed order. Orders were prepared with great care and evidently with the view that they should be a history of what followed.

In their modes of expressing thought, these two generals contrasted quite as strongly as in their other characteristics. General Scott was precise in language, cultivated a style peculiarly his own; was proud of his rhetoric; not averse to speaking of himself, often in the third person, and he could bestow praise upon the person he was talking about without the least embarrassment. Taylor was not a conversationalist, but on paper he could put his meaning so plainly that there could be no mistaking it. He knew how to express what he wanted to say in the fewest well-chosen words, but would not sacrifice meaning to the construction of high-sounding sentences. But with their opposite characteristics both were great and successful soldiers; both were true, patriotic and upright in all their dealings. Both

He had always been vain, pompous, exacting, jealous and high-tempered. Now that his sick old body could no longer support the racking of its wounds, his irascibility had dwindled to irritation, and his imperiousness to petulance. . . .

. . . His eye had lost its fire and he could no longer sit a horse, but in huge epaulettes and yellow sash he was still his country's hero. . . . The General was as magnificent as a monument, and no one was troubled by the circumstance that he was nearly as useless.

Reveille in Washington (Garden City, NY: Garden City Publishing, 1945), 1–2.

Winfield Scott and his staff during the Civil War. *Library of Congress, Prints and Photographs Division, Civil War Photographs, LC–DIG–ppmsca-34127.*

were pleasant to serve under—Taylor was pleasant to serve with. Scott saw more through the eyes of his staff officers than through his own. His plans were deliberately prepared, and fully expressed in orders. Taylor saw for himself, and gave orders to meet the emergency without reference to how they would read in history.[8]

8. Taylor was hugely popular—his name was used to sell soap and cigars, and one of the fastest racehorses of the day was called "Zachary Taylor"—yet he was not immune to criticism rooted in his prosecution of the war in Mexico and, before that, his campaigns against the Seminoles in Florida. One contemporary cartoon depicted a composite figure, with Taylor's face and Scott's elaborate uniform, atop a tower of skulls. Such towers had been associated with the Aztec capital of Tenochtitlan (Mexico City) by Andrés de Tapia, a soldier with Cortés's army in 1521, and later by Bernal Diaz del Castillo, who wrote that such towers—*tzompantli*—contained over 100,000 skulls. This was an exaggeration; however, in 2015, archaeologists discovered a tower near the site of the Templo Mayor, and the excavation has thus far unearthed almost 700 skulls. See Cleve R. Wootson Jr., "Archaeologists Unearth a 500-Year-Old Tower of Skulls—and Another Gruesome Aztec Mystery," *Washington Post*, July 4, 2017; and Jason Daley, "Aztec 'Skull Tower' Contains Remains of Women and Children," Smithsonian.com, July 3, 2017, http://www.smithsonianmag.com/smart-news/aztec-skull-tower-contains-remains-women-and-children-180963905/.

N. Currier, "An Available Candidate."
A political cartoon suggesting "the one
qualification for a Whig president" is the brutal
building of a tower of skulls. The general could
be Taylor or Scott. *Library of Congress, Prints and
Photographs Division, LC-DIG-pga-04723.*

Babur, the founder of the Mughal dynasty, also constructed these towers to intimidate
his "infidel" enemies and commemorate his victories during his conquests of Afghanistan and India in the sixteenth century: "Many fell slain in battle," Babur wrote of a
victory against Hindu forces in India: "Many others lost their heads and headed off into
the wilderness of aimlessness to become morsels for crows and ravens. There were piles of
the slain, and towers of skulls were erected." *The Baburnama: Memoirs of Babur, Prince and
Emperor,* trans. Wheeler M. Thackston (New York: Modern Library, 2002), 393.

"Meeting between Babur and Sultan
'Ali Mirza near Samarqand," folio from
Baburnama (The Book of Babur), ca. 1590.
*Metropolitan Museum of Art, Louis V. Bell
Fund, 1967.*

11

Advance on the City of Mexico—Battle of Contreras—Assault at Churubusco—Negotiations for Peace—Battle of Molino del Rey—Storming of Chapultepec—San Cosme—Evacuation of the City—Halls of the Montezumas

The route followed by the army from Puebla to the City of Mexico was over Rio Frio mountain, the road leading over which, at the highest point, is about eleven thousand feet above tide water. The pass through this mountain might have been easily defended, but it was not; and the advanced division reached the summit in three days after leaving Puebla. The City of Mexico lies west of Rio Frio mountain, on a plain backed by another mountain six miles farther west, with others still nearer on the north and south. Between the western base of Rio Frio and the City of Mexico there are three lakes, Chalco and Xochimilco on the left and Texcoco on the right, extending to the east end of the City of Mexico.[1] Chalco and Texcoco are divided by

1. The lakes of the Basin of Mexico had been vital to the Mesoamerican civilizations destroyed by the Spanish conquistadors. Here, in a 1520 letter to Charles V, Hernán Cortés describes the valley through which Grant advanced as part of Scott's army. This 1843 translation would have been available to Grant and his contemporaries:

> Before I begin to describe this great city and the others already mentioned, it may be well for the better understanding of the subject to say something of the configuration of Mexico, in which they are situated, it being the principal seat of Muteczuma's power. This Province is in the form of a circle, surrounded on all sides by lofty and rugged mountains; its level surface comprises an area of about seventy leagues in circumference, including two lakes, that overspread nearly the whole valley, being navi-

a narrow strip of land over which the direct road to the city runs. Xochimilco is also to the left of the road, but at a considerable distance south of it, and is connected with Lake Chalco by a narrow channel. There is a high rocky mound, called El Peñon, on the right of the road, springing up from the low flat ground dividing the lakes. This mound was strengthened by intrenchments at its base and summit, and rendered a direct attack impracticable.

Scott's army was rapidly concentrated about Ayotla and other points near the eastern end of Lake Chalco. Reconnoissances were made up to within gun-shot of El Peñon, while engineers were seeking a route by the south side of Lake Chalco to flank the city, and come upon it from the south and south-west. A way was found around the lake, and by the 18th of August troops were in St. Augustin Tlalpam, a town about eleven miles due south from the plaza of the capital. Between St. Augustin Tlalpam and the city lie the hacienda of San Antonio and the village of Churubusco, and south-west of them is Contreras. All these points, except St. Augustin Tlalpam, were intrenched and strongly garrisoned. Contreras is situated on the side of a mountain, near its base, where volcanic rocks are piled in great confusion, reaching nearly to San Antonio. This made the approach to the city from the south very difficult.

The brigade to which I was attached—Garland's, of Worth's division—was sent to confront San Antonio, two or three miles from St. Augustin Tlalpam, on the road to Churubusco and the City of Mexico. The ground on which San Antonio stands is completely in the valley, and the surface of the land is only a little above the level of the lakes, and, except to the south-west, it was cut up by deep ditches filled with water. To the south-west is the Pedregal—the volcanic rock before spoken of—over which cavalry or

---

gated by boats more than fifty leagues round. One of these lakes contains fresh and the other, which is the larger of the two, salt water. On one side of the lakes, in the middle of the valley, a range of highlands divides them from one another, with the exception of a narrow strait which lies between the highlands and the lofty sierras. This strait is a bow-shot wide, and connects the two lakes; and by this means a trade is carried on between the cities and other settlements on the lakes in canoes without the necessity of traveling by land. As the salt lake rises and falls with its tides like the sea, during the time of high water it pours into the other lake with the rapidity of a powerful stream; and on the other hand, when the tide has ebbed, the water runs from the fresh into the salt lake.

The Despatches of Hernando Cortés, trans. and ed. George Folsom (New York: Wiley and Putnam, 1843), 110–11.

artillery could not be passed, and infantry would make but poor progress if confronted by an enemy. From the position occupied by Garland's brigade, therefore, no movement could be made against the defences of San Antonio except to the front, and by a narrow causeway, over perfectly level ground, every inch of which was commanded by the enemy's artillery and infantry. If Contreras, some three miles west and south, should fall into our hands, troops from there could move to the right flank of all the positions held by the enemy between us and the city. Under these circumstances General Scott directed the holding of the front of the enemy without making an attack until further orders.

On the 18th of August, the day of reaching San Augustin Tlalpam, Garland's brigade secured a position within easy range of the advanced intrenchments of San Antonio, but where his troops were protected by an artificial embankment that had been thrown up for some other purpose than defense. General Scott at once set his engineers reconnoitring the works about Contreras, and on the 19th movements were commenced to get troops into positions from which an assault could be made upon the force occupying that place. The Pedregal on the north and north-east, and the mountain on the south, made the passage by either flank of the enemy's defences difficult, for their work stood exactly between those natural bulwarks; but a road was completed during the day and night of the 19th, and troops were got to the north and west of the enemy.

This affair, like that of Cerro Gordo, was an engagement in which the officers of the engineer corps won special distinction. In fact, in both cases, tasks which seemed difficult at first sight were made easier for the troops that had to execute them than they would have been on an ordinary field. The very strength of each of these positions was, by the skill of the engineers, converted into a defence for the assaulting parties while securing their positions for final attack.[2] All the troops with General Scott in the valley of Mexico, except a part of the division of General Quitman at San Augustin Tlalpam and the brigade of Garland (Worth's division) at San Antonio, were engaged at the battle of Contreras, or were on their way, in obedience to the orders of their chief, to reinforce those who were engaged. The assault was made on the morning of the 20th, and in less than half an hour from the sound of the advance the position was in our hands, with many prisoners and large quantities of ordnance and other stores. The brigade commanded by

---

2. Grant's appreciation for the work of the engineers anticipates his reliance on their skill during the Civil War.

General Riley was from its position the most conspicuous in the final assault, but all did well, volunteers and regulars.[3]

From the point occupied by Garland's brigade we could see the progress made at Contreras and the movement of troops toward the flank and rear of the enemy opposing us. The Mexicans all the way back to the city could see the same thing, and their conduct showed plainly that they did not enjoy the sight. We moved out at once, and found them gone from our immediate front. Clarke's brigade of Worth's division now moved west over the point of the Pedregal, and after having passed to the north sufficiently to clear San Antonio, turned east and got on the causeway leading to Churubusco and the City of Mexico. When he approached Churubusco his left, under Colonel Hoffman, attacked a tête-de-pont [bridgehead] at that place and brought on an engagement.[4] About an hour after, Garland was ordered to advance directly along the causeway, and got up in time to take part in the engagement. San Antonio was found evacuated, the evacuation having probably taken place immediately upon the enemy seeing the stars and stripes waving over Contreras.

The troops that had been engaged at Contreras, and even then on their way to that battle-field, were moved by a causeway west of, and parallel to the one by way of San Antonio and Churubusco. It was expected by the commanding general that these troops would move north sufficiently far to flank the enemy out of his position at Churubusco, before turning east to reach the San Antonio road, but they did not succeed in this, and Churubusco proved to be about the severest battle fought in the valley of Mexico. General Scott coming upon the battle-field about this juncture, ordered two brigades, under Shields, to move north and turn the right of the enemy. This Shields did, but not without hard fighting and heavy loss.[5] The enemy

3. Bennett C. Riley (1790–1853), another veteran of the War of 1812, was recognized for meritorious service at Cerro Gordo and Contreras. Riley subsequently commanded the Department of Upper California and acted as Provincial Governor there during the Gold Rush. His obituary noted, "In this position he fully sustained his character for probity, humanity and energy." *New York Times*, June 11, 1853, p. 4.

4. William Hoffman (1807–1884) graduated from West Point in 1829. On frontier duty at the outbreak of the Civil War, he was initially taken prisoner by rebels. After his exchange on August 27, 1862, he served as Commissary-General of Prisoners in Washington, D.C., until the end of the Civil War. He retired from active service in 1870.

5. Unlike his contemporaries, Grant largely omits the details of battle, a technique akin to the Chinese poetic practice called the ellipsis of battle, in which the battle itself, judged unworthy of heroic representation, is largely passed over. Only the preparations

finally gave way, leaving in our hands prisoners, artillery and small arms. The balance of the causeway held by the enemy, up to the very gates of the city, fell in like manner. I recollect at this place that some of the gunners who had stood their ground, were deserters from General Taylor's army on the Rio Grande.[6]

Both the strategy and tactics displayed by General Scott in these various engagements of the 20th of August, 1847, were faultless as I look upon them now, after the lapse of so many years. As before stated, the work of the engineer officers who made the reconnoissances and led the different commands to their destinations, was so perfect that the chief was able to give his orders to his various subordinates with all the precision he could use on an ordinary

---

and aftermath are described. The lyric "Battle," by Ch'ü Yüan (332–295 BCE), provides an excellent example of this style of indirection:

> "We grasp our battle-spears: we don our breast-plates of hide.
> The axles of our chariots touch: our short swords meet.
> Standards obscure the sun: the foe roll up like clouds.
> Arrows fall thick: the warriors press forward.
> They menace our ranks: they break our line.
> The left-hand trace-horse is dead: the one on the right is smitten.
> The fallen horses block our wheels: they impede the yoke-horses!"
>
> They grasp their jade drum-sticks: they beat the sounding drums.
> Heaven decrees their fall: the dread Powers are angry.
>
> The warriors are all dead: they lie on the moor-field.
> They issued but shall not enter: they went but shall not return.
> The plains are flat and wide; the way home is long.
> Their swords lie beside them: their black bows, in their hand.
> Though their limbs were torn, their hearts could not be repressed.
> They were more than brave: they were inspired with the spirit of "Wu."
> Steadfast to the end, they could not be daunted.
> Their bodies were stricken, but their souls have taken Immortality—
> Captains among the ghosts, heroes among the dead.

"Wu" is the term for "military genius." *A Hundred and Seventy Chinese Poems*, trans. Arthur Waley (New York: Knopf, 1919), 39–40.

6. The deserters to whom Grant refers came from the so-called St. Patrick's Battalion, *El Batallón de los San Patricios*, a group of Irish soldiers led by Sergeant John Riley, who were so alienated by the harsh treatment they received at the hands of anti-Irish, anti-Catholic U.S. officers that they deserted and fought bravely for Mexico. Many were captured at Churubusco. Thirty of them were hanged at Chapultepec, after being found guilty at a court-martial presided over by Bennett Riley.

march. I mean, up to the points from which the attack was to commence. After that point is reached the enemy often induces a change of orders not before contemplated. The enemy outside the city outnumbered our soldiery quite three to one, but they had become so demoralized by the succession of defeats this day, that the City of Mexico could have been entered without much further bloodshed.[7] In fact, Captain Philip Kearney [Kearny]— afterwards a general in the war of the rebellion—rode with a squadron of cavalry to the very gates of the city, and would no doubt have entered with

---

7. Cortés described at length the Aztec city Temixititan (Mexico City), which was situated in a great salt lake and which he destroyed in 1521. Temixititan was, he said, "as large as Seville or Cordova," and he estimated that more than 60,000 citizens convened in its markets each day, buying and selling "all kinds of merchandise that the world affords": gold, silver and other precious metals; bricks, timber, and pottery; cotton; produce; maize; honey, wax, and a kind of wine; eggs, fish, game birds, rabbits, deer, and Chihuahuas; herbs, roots, and medicines. He saw barber shops and what he called restaurants. He encountered magistrates regulating trade and administering justice. Here Cortés describes the main temple, "whose grandeur of architectural details no human tongue is able to describe," and his actions on entering it:

> There are three halls in this grand temple, which contain the principal idols; these are of wonderful extent and height, and admirable workmanship, adorned with figures sculptured in stone and wood; leading from the halls are chapels with very small doors, to which the light is not admitted, nor are any persons except the priests. . . . In these chapels are the images or idols . . . ; the principal ones, in which the people have greatest faith and confidence, I precipitated from their pedestals, and cast them down the steps of the temple, purifying the chapels in which they had stood, as they were all polluted with human blood, shed in the sacrifices. In the place of these I put images of Our Lady and the Saints, which excited not a little feeling in Muteczuma and the inhabitants, who at first remonstrated, declaring that if my proceedings were known throughout the country, the people would rise against me; for they believed that their idols bestowed on them all temporal good, and if they permitted them to be ill-treated, they would be angry and withhold their gifts, and by this means the people would be deprived of the fruits of the earth and perish with famine. I answered, through the interpreters, that they were deceived in expecting any favors from idols, the work of their own hands, formed of unclean things; and that they must learn there was but one God, the universal Lord of all, who had created the heavens and earth, and all things else, and had made them and us; that He was without beginning and immortal, and they were bound to adore and believe Him, and no other creature or thing.

Despatches, 111–17.

General Philip Kearny, 1815–1862. *From the New York Public Library, https://digitalcollections.nypl.org/ items/510d47da-f1e3-a3d9-e040-e00a18064a99.*

his little force, only at that point he was badly wounded, as were several of his officers. He had not heard the call for a halt.[8]

8. Philip Kearny (1815–1862) was the nephew of Stephen W. Kearny, the commander at Jefferson Barracks whose leadership Grant so admired. The younger Kearny was widely respected for his personal valor. Winfield Scott, for whom Kearny served like his uncle before him as aide-de-camp, called him "the bravest man I ever knew, and a perfect soldier." John Watts De Peyster, *Personal and Military History of Philip Kearny* (New York: Rice and Gage, 1869), 33.

The following account of Kearny's actions at Mexico City, written by a participant in the battle, provides a sense of his personal heroism and also serves to show just how atypical Grant's matter-of-fact representations of combat were. Kearny and his cavalry troop have just passed a unit of cheering New York infantry when the latter receive an order to halt from a staff officer. They obey it only when their own lieutenant insists:

> The order came upon the men like a bomb-shell, projected from the rear. Stop the pursuit! What did it mean? They had put the enemy to flight; and they knew he would not again make stand to oppose them that side the city—nor even in the city; for the scare upon his scattered troops would be sure to carry them clear through it, especially when chased by Kearny. Stop the pursuit! What could it mean? The lieutenant-colonel could not tell. He could only beg of them to obey. They laughed at him, for he had not led them; and only looked to the lieutenant who had. The latter listened to the order from the aide-de-camp, for it was at length directed to him, as the only one who had the power to enforce obedience to it. . . . "Halt!"

cried the New York lieutenant, flinging himself in front of the pursuers, and raising his sword with an air of determination. It was a command that came only from a sense of military duty, and the word faltered upon his lips, as he pronounced it. "Halt did yez say, liftinant?" "Halt!" repeated the officer in a firmer tone. "If *you* say halt, begorrah, we'll do it; but not for any other officer in the Amirekean army!" With the sword held at point, the lieutenant stood determinedly pointing them; and the men came reluctantly to a stand. They had scarce done so, when a spectacle commenced passing before their eyes that made every man of them sad—almost mad. Back along the road came riding the squadron [troop] of Kearny, not as they had passed before, at full gallop in the flush of a vigorous charge; but slow and dejected as if returning from a reverse. And in the rear rode their leader, his left arm no longer grasping the reins, but hanging by his side like the sling jacket of a hussar!

The tale was soon told. Some half-mile beyond the spot where the aide-de-camp halted us, the enemy had cut the Acapulco road and thrown a parapet across it, with the usual fosse outside. Here a few of their bravest men had determined to make a last stand. But Kearny, braver than they, riding at wild gallop, had leaped into the work—with one spring, clearing both ditch and parapet! His faithful sergeant had followed him; both, as soon as they alighted, plying their sabres upon the enemy inside! At that moment sounded the recall bugle . . . and the American dragoons, trained to the signal, pulled up short outside.

It was a terrible predicament! Alone within the entrenchment, surrounded by a score of assailants, Kearny and his sergeant had no other alternative but retreat; and, wheeling right about, both headed their horses to releap the ditch. Their gallant grays carried them across—the sergeant safe; but the best cavalry officer in the American army received a [canister] shot in his left arm that caused him instantaneously to let go his bridle rein. It pained me to see it hanging loose, as he and his squadron filed past going back along the Acapulco road. But the cheer that saluted his return was far more sympathetic and not less enthusiastic than that sent after him in his impetuous charge.

Mayne Reid, "A Dashing Dragoon: The Murat of the American Army," rpt. in *Service with the French Troops in Africa*, by Philip Kearny (New York, 1844; rpt. 1889), 93–95.

Although his arm was later amputated, Kearny remained undaunted. Resigning from the army, he sought further experience in Europe, where in the 1840s he had been sent to cavalry school and seen combat with the French Chasseurs d'Afrique. He returned to fight with the French at the Battle of Solferino in 1859, and he was given the Legion of Honor for his services. Kearny joined the Union army in 1861 and commanded the 1st New Jersey Brigade, whose troops nicknamed him "The One-Armed Devil" for his ferocity. He was killed at the Battle of Chantilly in 1862. James Longstreet, who fought on the other side, tells the story of Kearny's death:

I moved my troops out and occupied the lines . . . , relieving the few men who were on picket. Just as we reached there General Kearny, a Federal

General Franklin Pierce[9] had joined the army in Mexico, at Puebla, a short time before the advance upon the capital commenced. He had consequently not been in any of the engagements of the war up to the battle of Contreras. By an unfortunate fall of his horse on the afternoon of the 19th he was painfully injured. The next day, when his brigade, with the other troops engaged on the same field, was ordered against the flank and rear of the enemy guarding the different points of the road from San Augustin Tlalpam to the city, General Pierce attempted to accompany them. He was not sufficiently recovered to do so, and fainted. This circumstance gave rise to exceedingly unfair and unjust criticisms of him when he became a candidate for the Presidency. Whatever General Pierce's qualifications may have been for the Presidency, he was a gentleman and a man of courage. I was not a supporter of him politically, but I knew him more intimately than I did any other of the volunteer generals.

General Scott abstained from entering the city at this time, because Mr. Nicholas P. Trist, the commissioner on the part of the United States to negotiate a treaty of peace with Mexico, was with the army, and either he or General Scott thought—probably both of them—that a treaty would be more possible while the Mexican government was in possession of the capital than if it was scattered and the capital in the hands of an invader. Be this as it may,

---

officer, came along looking for his line, that had disappeared. It was raining in the woods, and was so late in the day that a Federal was not easily distinguished from a Confederate. Kearny did not seem to know that he was in the Confederate line, and our troops did not notice that he was a Federal. He began to inquire about some command, and in a moment or so the men saw that he was a Federal officer. At the same moment he realized where he was. He was called upon to surrender, but instead of doing so he wheeled his horse, lay flat on the animal's neck, clapped spurs into his sides and dashed off. Instantly a half-dozen shots rang out, and before he had gone thirty steps he fell. He had been in the army all his life, and we knew him and respected him. His body was sent over the lines under a flag of truce.

"Our March against Pope," *B&L*, 2:521–22.

9. In 1853, in the wake of the Compromise of 1850, Franklin Pierce (1804–1869) became the second veteran of the Mexican War, after Zachary Taylor, to be elected president. Despite his New England background—Pierce was from New Hampshire—he seemed to many rather eager to appease the Southern slave power. The passage of the Kansas-Nebraska Act in 1854, which allowed popular sovereignty to settle the question of slavery in each new state, together with the government's purchase of Arizona and New Mexico, reignited tensions, especially in "Bleeding Kansas," where abolitionists, including John Brown, clashed in open violence with proslavery settlers.

we did not enter at that time. The army took up positions along the slopes of the mountains south of the city, as far west as Tacubaya. Negotiations were at once entered into with Santa Anna, who was then practically *the Government* and the immediate commander of all the troops engaged in defence of the country. A truce was signed which denied to either party the right to strengthen its position, or to receive reinforcements during the continuance of the armistices, but authorized General Scott to draw supplies for his army from the city in the meantime.

Negotiations were commenced at once and were kept up vigorously, between Mr. Trist and the commissioners appointed on the part of Mexico, until the 2d of September.[10] At that time Mr. Trist handed in his ultimatum. Texas was to be given up absolutely by Mexico, and New Mexico and California ceded to the United States for a stipulated sum to be afterwards determined. I do not suppose Mr. Trist had any discretion whatever in regard to boundaries. The war was one of conquest, in the interest of an institution, and the probabilities are that private instructions were for the acquisition of territory out of which new States might be carved. At all events the Mexicans felt so outraged at the terms proposed that they commenced preparations for defence, without giving notice of the termination of the armistice. The terms of the truce had been violated before, when teams had been sent into the city to bring out supplies for the army. The first train entering the city was very severely threatened by a mob. This, however, was apologized for by the authorities and all responsibility for it denied; and thereafter, to avoid exciting the Mexican people and soldiery, our teams with their escorts were sent in at night, when the troops were in barracks and the citizens in bed. The circumstance was overlooked and negotiations continued. As soon as the news reached General Scott of the second violation of the armistice, about the 4th of September, he wrote a vigorous note to President Santa Anna, calling his attention to it, and, receiving an unsatisfactory reply, declared the armistice at an end.

General Scott, with Worth's division, was now occupying Tacubaya, a village some four miles south-west of the City of Mexico, and extending from the base up the mountain-side for the distance of half a mile. More than a mile west, and also a little above the plain, stands Molino del Rey. The mill

---

10. Nicholas Trist (1800–1874), chief clerk at the State Department, fluent in Spanish, tutored in his youth by Thomas Jefferson, did not get along with Winfield Scott and was eventually recalled by Polk. He ignored this presidential summons in order to conclude a peace. For a detailed account of Trist's negotiations, see Greenberg, *A Wicked War*.

is a long stone structure, one story high and several hundred feet in length. At the period of which I speak General Scott supposed a portion of the mill to be used as a foundry for the casting of guns. This, however, proved to be a mistake. It was valuable to the Mexicans because of the quantity of grain it contained. The building is flat roofed, and a line of sand-bags over the outer walls rendered the top quite a formidable defence for infantry. Chapultepec is a mound springing up from the plain to the height of probably three hundred feet, and almost in a direct line between Molino del Rey and the western part of the city. It was fortified both on the top and on the rocky and precipitous sides.

The City of Mexico is supplied with water by two aqueducts, resting on strong stone arches. One of these aqueducts draws its supply of water from a mountain stream coming into it at or near Molino del Rey, and runs north close to the west base of Chapultepec; thence along the centre of a wide road, until it reaches the road running east into the city by the Garita San Cosme; from which point the aqueduct and road both run east to the city. The second aqueduct starts from the east base of Chapultepec, where it is fed by a spring, and runs north-east to the city. This aqueduct, like the other, runs in the middle of a broad road-way, thus leaving a space on each side. The arches supporting the aqueduct afforded protection for advancing troops as well as to those engaged defensively. At points on the San Cosme road parapets were thrown across, with an embrasure for a single piece of artillery in each. At the point where both road and aqueduct turn at right angles from north to east, there was not only one of these parapets supplied by one gun and infantry supports, but the houses to the north of the San Cosme road, facing south and commanding a view of the road back to Chapultepec, were covered with infantry, protected by parapets made of sand-bags. The roads leading to garitas (the gates) San Cosme and Belen, by which these aqueducts enter the city, were strongly intrenched. Deep, wide ditches, filled with water, lined the sides of both roads. Such were the defences of the City of Mexico in September, 1847, on the routes over which General Scott entered.

Prior to the Mexican war General Scott had been very partial to General Worth—indeed he continued so up to the close of hostilities—but, for some reason, Worth had become estranged from his chief. Scott evidently took this coldness somewhat to heart. He did not retaliate, however, but on the contrary showed every disposition to appease his subordinate. It was understood at the time that he gave Worth authority to plan and execute the battle of Molino del Rey without dictation or interference from any one, for the very purpose of restoring their former relations. The effort failed, and the two generals remained ever after cold and indifferent towards each other, if not actually hostile.

The battle of Molino del Rey was fought on the 8th of September. The night of the 7th, Worth sent for his brigade and regimental commanders, with their staffs, to come to his quarters to receive instructions for the morrow. These orders contemplated a movement up to within striking distance of the Mills before daylight. The engineers had reconnoitred the ground as well as possible, and had acquired all the information necessary to base proper orders both for approach and attack.

By daylight on the morning of the 8th, the troops to be engaged at Molino were all at the places designated. The ground in front of the Mills, to the south, was commanded by the artillery from the summit of Chapultepec as well as by the lighter batteries at hand; but a charge was made, and soon all was over. Worth's troops entered the Mills by every door, and the enemy beat a hasty retreat back to Chapultepec. Had this victory been followed up promptly, no doubt Americans and Mexicans would have gone over the defences of Chapultepec so near together that the place would have fallen into our hands without further loss. The defenders of the works could not have fired upon us without endangering their own men. This was not done, and five days later more valuable lives were sacrificed to carry works which had been so nearly in our possession on the 8th. I do not criticise the failure to capture Chapultepec at this time. The result that followed the first assault could not possibly have been foreseen, and to profit by the unexpected advantage, the commanding general must have been on the spot and given the necessary instructions at the moment, or the troops must have kept on without orders. It is always, however, in order to follow a retreating foe, unless stopped or otherwise directed. The loss on our side at Molino del Rey was severe for the numbers engaged. It was especially so among commissioned officers.

I was with the earliest of the troops to enter the Mills. In passing through to the north side, looking towards Chapultepec, I happened to notice that there were armed Mexicans still on top of the building, only a few feet from many of our men. Not seeing any stairway or ladder reaching to the top of the building, I took a few soldiers, and had a cart that happened to be standing near brought up, and, placing the shafts against the wall and chocking the wheels so that the cart could not back, used the shafts as a sort of ladder extending to within three or four feet of the top. By this I climbed to the roof of the building, followed by a few men, but found a private soldier had preceded me by some other way. There were still quite a number of Mexicans on the roof, among them a major and five or six officers of lower grades,

Confederate brass mountain howitzers of the type Grant used at Molino del Rey. Richmond, Virginia, 1865. *Library of Congress, Prints and Photographs Division, Civil War Photographs, LC-DIG-cwpb-02492.*

who had not succeeded in getting away before our troops occupied the building. They still had their arms, while the soldier before mentioned was walking as sentry, guarding the prisoners he had *surrounded*, all by himself. I halted the sentinel, received the swords from the commissioned officers, and proceeded, with the assistance of the soldiers now with me, to disable the muskets by striking them against the edge of the wall, and throw them to the ground below.

Molino del Rey was now captured, and the troops engaged, with the exception of an appropriate guard over the captured position and property, were marched back to their quarters in Tacubaya. The engagement did not last many minutes, but the killed and wounded were numerous for the number of troops engaged.

During the night of the 11th batteries were established which could play upon the fortifications of Chapultepec. The bombardment commenced early on the morning of the 12th, but there was no further engagement during this day than that of the artillery. General Scott assigned the capture of Chapultepec to General Pillow, but did not leave the details to his judgment. Two assaulting columns, two hundred and fifty men each, composed of volunteers for the occasion, were formed. They were commanded by Captains [Samuel] McKinzie [Mackenzie] and [Silas] Casey respectively. The assault was successful, but bloody.

In later years, if not at the time, the battles of Molino del Rey and Chapultepec have seemed to me to have been wholly unnecessary. When the assaults upon the garitas of San Cosme and Belen were determined upon, the road running east to the former gate could have been reached easily, without an engagement, by moving along south of the Mills until west of them suf-ficiently far to be out of range, thence north to the road above mentioned; or, if desirable to keep the two attacking columns nearer together, the troops could have been turned east so as to come on the aqueduct road out of range of the guns from Chapultepec. In like manner, the troops designated to act against Belen could have kept east of Chapultepec, out of range, and come on to the aqueduct, also out of range of Chapultepec. Molino del Rey and Chapultepec would both have been necessarily evacuated if this course had been pursued, for they would have been turned.

General Quitman, a volunteer from the State of Mississippi, who stood well with the army both as a soldier and as a man, commanded the column acting against Belen. General Worth commanded the column against San Cosme. When Chapultepec fell the advance commenced along the two aqueduct roads. I was on the road to San Cosme, and witnessed most that took place on that route. When opposition was encountered our troops sheltered themselves by keeping under the arches supporting the aqueduct, advancing an arch at a time. We encountered no serious obstruction until within gun-shot of the point where the road we were on intersects that running east to the city, the point where the aqueduct turns at a right angle. I have described the defences of this position before. There were but three commissioned officers besides myself, that I can now call to mind, with the advance when the above position was reached. One of these officers was a Lieutenant Semmes, of the Marine Corps.[11] I think Captain [John H.] Gore, and Lieutenant [Henry M.] Judah, of the 4th infantry, were the

11. Raphael Semmes (1809–1877) commanded the brig USS *Somers*, which foundered in a gale off the coast of Veracruz. His ship lost, Semmes attached himself to Scott's land force and marched with it all the way to Mexico City. At San Cosme, Semmes hauled a howitzer into a tower to train it on the enemy. He was in Mobile, Alabama, when the Civil War broke out, and he resigned his commission to join the Confederate States Navy. He was captain of the CSS *Alabama*, a notorious raider that attacked Union merchant ships. The Alabama lost a battle to the USS *Kearsage* off the coast of Cherbourg, France, in 1864. In 1851 Semmes published an account of his Mexican War experiences, in which he described the Battle of Molino del Rey as the least understood battle of the war and the "most sanguinary struggle that ever took place on the American continent." Semmes blamed Scott for his imprudence in joining battle in the first place as well as for his subsequent vanity and jealousy of Worth. Worth, for his part, received Scott's congratulations for the ultimate victory, according to Semmes, "courteously, but with a clouded brow, and a troubled heart, as he had lost the flower of his division, and some of his most devoted friends, in this ill-advised contest." *Service Afloat and Ashore during the Mexican War* (Cincinnati, OH: Wm. H. Moore, 1851), 444, 442.

CSS *Alabama* (1862–1864), Captain Raphael Semmes in the foreground, Capetown, August 1863. *NH 57256-KN. Courtesy of the Naval History and Heritage Command.*

Edouard Manet, *The "Kearsage" at Boulogne.* Manet painted the victorious ship at anchor after the battle, 1864. *Metropolitan Museum of Art, Gift of Peter H. B. Frelinghuysen, and Purchase, Mr. and Mrs. Richard J. Bernhard Gift, by exchange, Gifts of Mr. and Mrs. Richard Rodgers and Joanne Toor Cummings, by exchange, and Drue Heinz Trust, The Dillon Fund, The Vincent Astor Foundation, Mr. and Mrs. Henry R. Kravis, The Charles Engelhard Foundation, and Florence and Herbert Irving Gifts, 1999.*

others. Our progress was stopped for the time by the single piece of artillery at the angle of the roads and the infantry occupying the house-tops back from it.

West of the road from where we were, stood a house occupying the south-west angle made by the San Cosme road and the road we were moving upon. A stone wall ran from the house along each of these roads for a considerable distance and thence back until it joined, enclosing quite a yard about the house. I watched my opportunity and skipped across the road and behind the south wall. Proceeding cautiously to the west corner of the enclosure, I peeped around and seeing nobody, continued, still cautiously, until the road running east and west was reached. I then returned to the troops, and called for volunteers. All that were close to me, or that heard me, about a dozen, offered their services. Commanding them to carry their arms at a trail, I watched our opportunity and got them across the road and under cover of the wall beyond, before the enemy had a shot at us. Our men under cover of the arches kept a close watch on the intrenchments that crossed our path and the house-tops beyond, and whenever a head showed itself above the parapets they would fire at it. Our crossing was thus made practicable without loss.

When we reached a safe position I instructed my little command again to carry their arms at a trail, not to fire at the enemy until they were ordered, and to move very cautiously following me until the San Cosme road was reached; we would then be on the flank of the men serving the gun on the road, and with no obstruction between us and them. When we reached the south-west corner of the enclosure before described, I saw some United States troops pushing north through a shallow ditch near by, who had come up since my reconnoissance. This was the company of Captain Horace Brooks, of the artillery, acting as infantry.[12] I explained to Brooks briefly what I had

12. Horace Brooks (1814–1894) had been assistant professor of mathematics at West Point just prior to Grant's cadetship. After the Mexican War, he served on the frontier and in the Civil War before retiring from active service in 1877. An obituary in the *Army and Navy Journal* relates a memorable vignette from Brooks's service at Fort Jefferson, Florida, early in the Civil War:

> Gen. Brooks belonged to the old school of officers. He was a man of small stature, but as full of pluck as an egg is full of meat. It is related of him, that during the war, being in command at Fort Jefferson, Dry Tortugas, "Billy Wilson's Zouaves," then there, commenced a riot in the barracks, smashing things right and left. Gen. Brooks strode fearlessly into their barracks, saying: "I understand you wanted to see me. Here I am; what do you

discovered and what I was about to do. He said, as I knew the ground and he did not, I might go on and he would follow. As soon as we got on the road leading to the city the troops serving the gun on the parapet retreated, and those on the house-tops near by followed; our men went after them in such close pursuit—the troops we had left under the arches joining—that a second line across the road, about half-way between the first and the garita, was carried. No reinforcements had yet come up except Brooks's company, and the position we had taken was too advanced to be held by so small a force. It was given up, but retaken later in the day, with some loss.

Worth's command gradually advanced to the front now open to it. Later in the day in reconnoitring I found a church off to the south of the road, which looked to me as if the belfry would command the ground back of the garita San Cosme. I got an officer of the voltigeurs, with a mountain howitzer and men to work it, to go with me. The road being in possession of the enemy, we had to take the field to the south to reach the church. This took us over several ditches breast deep in water and grown up with water plants. These ditches, however, were not over eight or ten feet in width. The howitzer was taken to pieces and carried by the men to its destination. When I knocked for admission a priest came to the door who, while extremely polite, declined to admit us. With the little Spanish then at my command, I explained to him that he might save property by opening the door, and he certainly would save himself from becoming a prisoner, for a time at least; and besides, I intended to go in whether he consented or not. He began to see his duty in the same light that I did, and opened the door, though he did not look as if it gave him special pleasure to do so. The gun was carried to the belfry and put together. We were not more than two or three hundred yards from San Cosme. The shots from our little gun dropped in upon the enemy and created great confusion. Why they did not send out a small party and capture us, I do not know. We had no infantry or other defences besides our one gun.

The effect of this gun upon the troops about the gate of the city was so marked that General Worth saw it from his position.[13] He was so pleased that he sent a staff officer, Lieutenant Pemberton—later Lieutenant-General

---

want?" The men, struck at seeing so small a man so perfectly fearless, gave three cheers for Brooks, and at once quieted down.

Army and Navy Journal 31, no. 22 (January 20, 1894): 365.

13. Mentioned in the reports of Major Lee, Colonel Garland and General Worth.—PUBLISHERS. [Note to the first edition.]

commanding the defences of Vicksburg—to bring me to him. He expressed his gratification at the services the howitzer in the church steeple was doing, saying that every shot was effective, and ordered a captain of voltigeurs to report to me with another howitzer to be placed along with the one already rendering so much service. I could not tell the General that there was not room enough in the steeple for another gun, because he probably would have looked upon such a statement as a contradiction from a second lieutenant. I took the captain with me, but did not use his gun.[14]

The night of the 13th of September was spent by the troops under General Worth in the houses near San Cosme, and in line confronting the general line of the enemy across to Belen. The troops that I was with were in the houses north of the road leading into the city, and were engaged during the night in cutting passage-ways from one house to another towards the town. During the night Santa Anna, with his army—except the deserters—left the city. He liberated all the convicts confined in the town, hoping, no doubt, that they would inflict upon us some injury before daylight; but several hours after Santa Anna was out of the way, the city authorities sent a delegation to General Scott to ask—if not demand—an armistice, respecting church property, the rights of citizens and the supremacy of the city government in the management of municipal affairs. General Scott declined to trammel himself with conditions, but gave assurances that those who chose to remain within our lines would be protected so long as they behaved themselves properly.

General Quitman had advanced along his line very successfully on the 13th, so that at night his command occupied nearly the same position at Belen that Worth's troops did about San Cosme. After the interview above related between General Scott and the city council, orders were issued for the cautious entry of both columns in the morning. The troops under Worth were to stop at the Alameda, a park near the west end of the city. Quitman was to go directly to the Plaza, and take possession of the Palace—a mass of buildings on the east side in which Congress has its sessions, the national courts are held, the public offices are all located, the President resides, and much room is left for museums, receptions, etc. This is the building generally designated as the "Halls of the Montezumas."

---

14. John C. Pemberton (1814–1881) graduated from West Point in 1837. He served in the Seminole War (1837–1838) and was involved in almost every major engagement of the Mexican War. Although Pemberton was a Pennsylvanian, his wife hailed from Virginia, and he joined the rebellion. Some of his fellow Confederates, however, questioned his loyalty. He surrendered Vicksburg to Grant on July 4, 1863.

12

Promotion to First Lieutenant—Capture
of the City of Mexico—The Army—
Mexican Soldiers—Peace Negotiations

On entering the city the troops were fired upon by the released convicts, and possibly by deserters and hostile citizens.[1] The streets were deserted, and the place presented the appearance of a "city of the dead," except for this firing by unseen persons from house-tops, windows, and around corners.[2] In this firing the lieutenant-colonel of my regiment, Gar-

---

1. It had been a favorite idea with General Scott for a great many years before the Mexican War to have established in the United States a soldiers' home, patterned after something of the kind abroad, particularly, I believe, in France. He recommended this uniformly, or at least frequently, in his annual reports to the Secretary of War, but never got any hearing. Now, as he had conquered the state, he made assessments upon the different large towns and cities occupied by our troops, in proportion to their capacity to pay, and appointed officers to receive the money. In addition to the sum thus realized he had derived, through capture at Cerro Gordo, sales of captured government tobacco, etc., sums which swelled the fund to a total of about $220,000. Portions of this fund were distributed among the rank and file, given to the wounded in hospital, or applied in other ways, leaving a balance of some $118,000 remaining unapplied at the close of the war. After the war was over and the troops all home, General Scott applied to have this money, which had never been turned into the Treasury of the United States, expended in establishing such homes as he had previously recommended. This fund was the foundation of the Soldiers' Home at Washington City, and also one at Harrodsburgh, Kentucky.

The latter went into disuse many years ago. In fact it never had many soldiers in it, and was, I believe, finally sold. [Note to the first edition.]

2. Grant's allusion to the Halls of the Montezumas recalls that earlier conquest of the city by the Spanish in 1521, about which Bartolomé de Las Casas, a soldier who took

land, was badly wounded, Lieutenant Sidney Smith, of the 4th infantry, was also wounded mortally. He died a few days after, and by his death I was promoted to the grade of first lieutenant. I had gone into the battle of Palo Alto in May, 1846, a second lieutenant, and I entered the city of Mexico sixteen months later with the same rank, after having been in all the engagements possible for any one man and in a regiment that lost more officers during the war than it ever had present at any one engagement. My regiment lost four commissioned officers, all senior to me, by steamboat explosions during the Mexican war. The Mexicans were not so discriminating. They sometimes picked off my juniors.

General Scott soon followed the troops into the city, in state. I wonder that he was not fired upon, but I believe he was not; at all events he was not hurt. He took quarters at first in the "Halls of the Montezumas," and from there issued his wise and discreet orders for the government of a conquered city, and for suppressing the hostile acts of liberated convicts already spoken of—orders which challenge the respect of all who study them. Lawlessness was soon suppressed, and the City of Mexico settled down into a quiet, law-abiding place. The people began to make their appearance upon the streets without fear of the invaders. Shortly afterwards the bulk of the troops were sent from the city to the villages at the foot of the mountains, four or five miles to the south and south-west.

Whether General Scott approved of the Mexican war and the manner in which it was brought about, I have no means of knowing. His orders to troops indicate only a soldierly spirit, with probably a little regard for the perpetuation of his own fame. On the other hand, General Taylor's, I think, indicate that he

---

part in the expedition and later became a priest sympathetic to the Mexicans, offered one of the most powerful indictments in 1542:

> It was upon these gentle lambs, imbued by the Creator with all the qualities we have mentioned, that from the very first day they clapped eyes on them the Spanish fell like ravening wolves upon the fold, or like tigers and savage lions who have not eaten meat for days. The pattern established at the outset has remained unchanged to this day, and the Spaniards still do nothing save tear the natives to shreds, murder them and inflict upon them untold misery, suffering and distress, tormenting, harrying and persecuting them mercilessly. We shall in due course describe some of the many ingenious methods of torture they have invented and refined for this purpose.

A Short Account of the Destruction of the Indies, ed. and trans. Nigel Griffin (New York: Penguin Classics, 2004), 11.

considered the administration accountable for the war, and felt no responsibility resting on himself further than for the faithful performance of his duties. Both generals deserve the commendations of their countrymen and to live in the grateful memory of this people to the latest generation.

Earlier in this narrative I have stated that the plain, reached after passing the mountains east of Perote, extends to the cities of Puebla and Mexico. The route travelled by the army before reaching Puebla, goes over a pass in a spur of mountain coming up from the south. This pass is very susceptible of defence by a smaller against a larger force. Again, the highest point of the road-bed between Vera Cruz and the City of Mexico is over Rio Frio mountain, which also might have been successfully defended by an inferior against a superior force. But by moving north of the mountains, and about thirty miles north of Puebla, both of these passes would have been avoided. The road from Perote to the City of Mexico, by this latter route, is as level as the prairies in our West. Arriving due north from Puebla, troops could have been detached to take possession of that place, and then proceeding west with the rest of the army no mountain would have been encountered before reaching the City of Mexico. It is true this road would have brought troops in by Guadalupe—a town, church and detached spur of mountain about two miles north of the capital, all bearing the same general name—and at this point Lake Texcoco comes near to the mountain, which was fortified both at the base and on the sides: but troops could have passed north of the mountain and come in only a few miles to the north-west, and so flanked the position, as they actually did on the south.

It has always seemed to me that this northern route to the City of Mexico, would have been the better one to have taken. But my later experience has taught me two lessons: first, that things are seen plainer after the events have occurred; second, that the most confident critics are generally those who know the least about the matter criticised. I know just enough about the Mexican war to approve heartily of most of the generalship, but to differ with a little of it.[3] It is natural that an important city like Puebla should not

---

3. Grant's discussion raises important questions regarding individual perspective and the obstacles to obtaining accurate knowledge on the battlefield. A popular memoir of the Civil War, Confederate soldier Sam Watkins's "Co. Aytch," offers one of the more evocative accounts of the individual's experience in this passage on Shiloh:

> This was the first big battle in which our regiment had ever been engaged. I do not pretend to tell of what command distinguished itself; of heroes; of blood and wounds; of shrieks and groans; of brilliant charges; of

have been passed with contempt; it may be natural that the direct road to it should have been taken; but it could have been passed, its evacuation insured and possession acquired without danger of encountering the enemy in intricate mountain defiles. In this same way the City of Mexico could have been approached without any danger of opposition, except in the open field.

But General Scott's successes are an answer to all criticism. He invaded a populous country, penetrating two hundred and sixty miles into the interior, with a force at no time equal to one-half of that opposed to him; he was without a base; the enemy was always intrenched, always on the defensive; yet he won every battle, he captured the capital, and conquered the government. Credit is due to the troops engaged, it is true, but the plans and the strategy were the general's.

I had now made marches and been in battle under both General Scott and General Taylor. The former divided his force of 10,500 men into four columns, starting a day apart, in moving from Puebla to the capital of the nation, when it was known that an army more than twice as large as his own stood ready to resist his coming. The road was broad and the country open except in crossing the Rio Frio mountain. General Taylor pursued the same course in marching toward an enemy. He moved even in smaller bodies. I never thought at the time to doubt the infallibility of these two generals in all matters pertaining to their profession. I supposed they moved in small bodies because more men could not be passed over a single road on the same day with their artillery and necessary trains. Later I found the fallacy of this

---

cannon captured, etc. I was but a private soldier, and if I happened to look to see if I could find out anything, "Eyes right, guide center," was the order. "Close up, guide right, halt, forward, right oblique, left oblique, halt, forward, guide center, eyes right, dress up promptly in the rear, steady, double quick, charge bayonets, fire at will," is about all that a private soldier ever knows of a battle. He can see the smoke rise and the flash of the enemy's guns, and he can hear the whistle of the minnie and cannon balls, but he has got to load and shoot as hard as he can tear and ram cartridge, or he will soon find out, like the Irishman who had been shooting blank cartridges, when a ball happened to strike him, and he hallooed out, "Faith, Pat, and be jabbers, them fellows are shooting bullets." But I nevertheless remember many things that came under my observation in this battle. I remember a man by the name of Smith stepping deliberately out of the ranks and shooting his finger off to keep out of the fight; of another poor fellow who was accidentally shot and killed by the discharge of another person's gun, and of others suddenly taken sick with colic.

Watkins,"*Co. Aytch,*" 31.

belief. The rebellion, which followed as a sequence to the Mexican war, never could have been suppressed if larger bodies of men could not have been moved at the same time than was the custom under Scott and Taylor.

The victories in Mexico were, in every instance, over vastly superior numbers. There were two reasons for this. Both General Scott and General Taylor had such armies as are not often got together. At the battles of Palo Alto and Resaca de la Palma, General Taylor had a small army, but it was composed exclusively of regular troops, under the best of drill and discipline. Every officer, from the highest to the lowest, was educated in his profession, not at West Point necessarily, but in the camp, in garrison, and many of them in Indian wars. The rank and file were probably inferior, as material out of which to make an army, to the volunteers that participated in all the later battles of the war; but they were brave men, and then drill and discipline brought out all there was in them. A better army, man for man, probably never faced an enemy than the one commanded by General Taylor in the earliest two engagements of the Mexican war. The volunteers who followed were of better material, but without drill or discipline at the start. They were associated with so many disciplined men and professionally educated officers, that when they went into engagements it was with a confidence they would not have felt otherwise. They became soldiers themselves almost at once. All these conditions we would enjoy again in case of war.[4]

---

4. Grant would continue to be more understanding of volunteers than some of his fellow officers, including Sherman. Nevertheless, in his correspondence, Grant offered a quite different assessment of the volunteers' behavior in Mexico:

> Since we have been in Matamoras a great many murders have been committed, and what is strange there seemes to be but very week means made use of to prevent frequent repetitions. Some of the volunteers and about all the Texans seem to think it perfectly right to impose upon the people of a conquered City to any extent, and even to murder them where the act can be covered by the dark. And how much they seem to enjoy acts of violence too! I would not pretend to guess the number of murders that have been committed upon the persons of poor Mexicans and our soldiers, since we have been here, but the number would startle you.

Letter to Julia Dent, July 25, 1846, *PUSG*, 1:102; also quoted in Greenberg, *Wicked War*, 131.

The volunteers, Amy Greenberg notes, "lacking both training and discipline, were not only less reliable under fire than the regulars, and disproportionately susceptible to communicable disease, in part because of their poor sanitation practices, but also committed atrocities against Mexican civilians that would come to shock Americans back

The Mexican army of that day was hardly an organization. The private soldier was picked up from the lower class of the inhabitants when wanted; his consent was not asked; he was poorly clothed, worse fed, and seldom paid. He was turned adrift when no longer wanted. The officers of the lower grades were but little superior to the men. With all this I have seen as brave stands made by some of these men as I have ever seen made by soldiers. Now Mexico has a standing army larger than that of the United States. They have a military school modelled after West Point. Their officers are educated and, no doubt, generally brave. The Mexican war of 1846–8 would be an impossibility in this generation.

The Mexicans have shown a patriotism which it would be well if we would imitate in part, but with more regard to truth. They celebrate the anniversaries of Chapultepec and Molino del Rey as of very great victories. The anniversaries are recognized as national holidays. At these two battles, while the United States troops were victorious, it was at very great sacrifice of life compared with what the Mexicans suffered. The Mexicans, as on many other occasions, stood up as well as any troops ever did. The trouble seemed to be the lack of experience among the officers, which led them after a certain time to simply quit, without being particularly whipped, but because they had fought enough. Their authorities of the present day grow enthusiastic over their theme when telling of these victories, and speak with pride of the large sum of money they forced us to pay in the end. With us, now twenty years after the close of the most stupendous war ever known, we have writers—who profess devotion to the nation—engaged in trying to prove that the Union forces were not victorious; practically, they say, we were slashed around from Donelson to Vicksburg and to Chattanooga; and in the East from Gettysburg to Appomattox, when the physical rebellion gave out from sheer exhaustion. There is no difference in the amount of romance in the two stories.

I would not have the anniversaries of our victories celebrated, nor those of our defeats made fast days and spent in humiliation and prayer; but I would like to see truthful history written. Such history will do full credit to the

home." Greenberg adds, "None of this should have been surprising. As youths, most of the volunteers had thrilled to tales of Texas heroism and Alamo martyrs. . . . Many who volunteered felt deep enmity for the people of Mexico, and conflated them with Indians and African American slaves. Lacking training and discipline, with little knowledge of military codes, many ran wild." *Wicked War,* 131–32.

courage, endurance and soldierly ability of the American citizen, no matter what section of the country he hailed from, or in what ranks he fought. The justice of the cause which in the end prevailed, will, I doubt not, come to be acknowledged by every citizen of the land, in time. For the present, and so long as there are living witnesses of the great war of sections, there will be people who will not be consoled for the loss of a cause which they believed to be holy. As time passes, people, even of the South, will begin to wonder how it was possible that their ancestors ever fought for or justified institutions which acknowledged the right of property in man.

After the fall of the capital and the dispersal of the government of Mexico, it looked very much as if military occupation of the country for a long time might be necessary. General Scott at once began the preparation of orders, regulations and laws in view of this contingency. He contemplated making the country pay all the expenses of the occupation, without the army becoming a perceptible burden upon the people. His plan was to levy a direct tax upon the separate states, and collect, at the ports left open to trade, a duty on all imports. From the beginning of the war private property had not been taken, either for the use of the army or of individuals, without full compensation. This policy was to be pursued. There were not troops enough in the valley of Mexico to occupy many points, but now that there was no organized army of the enemy of any size, reinforcements could be got from the Rio Grande, and there were also new volunteers arriving from time to time, all by way of Vera Cruz. Military possession was taken of Cuernavaca, fifty miles south of the City of Mexico; of Toluca, nearly as far west; and of Pachuca, a mining town of great importance, some sixty miles to the north-east. Vera Cruz, Jalapa, Orizaba, and Puebla were already in our possession.

Meanwhile the Mexican government had departed in the person of Santa Anna, and it looked doubtful for a time whether the United States commissioner, Mr. Trist, would find anybody to negotiate with. A temporary government, however, was soon established at Queretaro, and Trist began negotiations for a conclusion of the war. Before terms were finally agreed upon he was ordered back to Washington, but General Scott prevailed upon him to remain, as an arrangement had been so nearly reached, and the administration must approve his acts if he succeeded in making such a treaty as had been contemplated in his instructions. The treaty was finally signed the 2d of February, 1848, and accepted by the government at Washington. It is that known as the "Treaty of Guadalupe Hidalgo," and secured to the United States the Rio Grande as the boundary of Texas, and the whole territory then included in New Mexico and Upper California, for the sum of $15,000,000.[5]

Soon after entering the city of Mexico, the opposition of Generals Pillow, Worth and Colonel [James] Duncan to General Scott became very marked. Scott claimed that they had demanded of the President his removal. I do not know whether this is so or not, but I do know of their unconcealed hostility to their chief. At last he placed them in arrest, and preferred charges against them of insubordination and disrespect. This act brought on a crisis in the career of the general commanding. He had asserted from the beginning that the administration was hostile to him; that it had failed in its promises of men and war material; that the President himself had shown duplicity if not treachery in the endeavor to procure the appointment of Benton: and the administration now gave open evidence of its enmity. About the middle of February orders came convening a court of inquiry, composed of Brevet

---

5. The Treaty of Guadalupe Hidalgo, signed on February 2, 1848, followed by the Gadsden Purchase of 1853, added huge swaths of territory to the Southwestern United States. An 1846 treaty with Great Britain had secured territory in the Pacific Northwest.

"Mapa de los Estados Unidos de Méjico." 1847. *Library of Congress, Geography and Map Division.*

Brigadier-General [Nathan] Towson, the paymaster-general of the army, Brigadier-General [Caleb] Cushing and Colonel [William G.] Belknap, to inquire into the conduct of the accused and the accuser, and shortly afterwards orders were received from Washington, relieving Scott of the command of the army in the field and assigning Major-General William O. Butler of Kentucky to the place. This order also released Pillow, Worth and Duncan from arrest.[6]

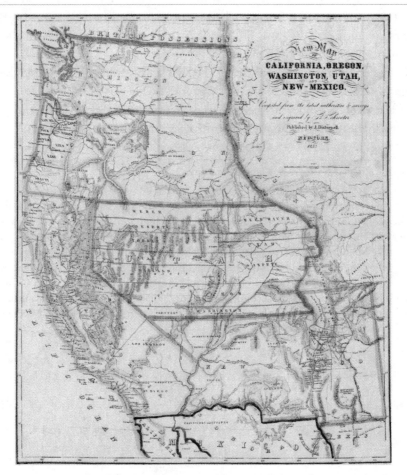

**"New map of California, Oregon, Washington, Utah, and New Mexico,"
by G. Schroeter and John Disturnell, 1853.** *Library of Congress,
Geography and Map Division.*

6. For accounts of this political infighting, see Richard Bruce Winders, *Mr. Polk's Army: The American Experience in the Mexican War* (College Station: Texas A&M University Press, 1997), chapter 3; and John S. D. Eisenhower, *So Far from God: The U.S. War with Mexico 1846–1848* (New York: Random House, 1989), chapter 28.

If a change was to be made the selection of General Butler was agreeable to every one concerned, so far as I remember to have heard expressions on the subject. There were many who regarded the treatment of General Scott as harsh and unjust. It is quite possible that the vanity of the General had led him to say and do things that afforded a plausible pretext to the administration for doing just what it did and what it had wanted to do from the start. The court tried the accuser quite as much as the accused. It was adjourned before completing its labors, to meet in Frederick, Maryland. General Scott left the country, and never after had more than the nominal command of the army until early in 1861. He certainly was not sustained in his efforts to maintain discipline in high places.

The efforts to kill off politically the two successful generals, made them both candidates for the Presidency. General Taylor was nominated in 1848, and was elected. Four years later General Scott received the nomination but was badly beaten, and the party nominating him died with his defeat.[7]

---

7. The Mexican war made three presidential candidates, Scott, Taylor and Pierce—and any number of aspirants for that high office. It made also governors of States, members of the cabinet, foreign ministers and other officers of high rank both in state and nation. The rebellion, which contained more war in a single day, at some critical periods, than the whole Mexican war in two years, has not been so fruitful of political results to those engaged on the Union side. On the other side, the side of the South, nearly every man who holds office of any sort whatever, either in the state or in the nation, was a Confederate soldier; but this is easily accounted for from the fact that the South was a military camp, and there were very few people of a suitable age to be in the army who were not in it. [Note to the first edition.]

13

Treaty of Peace—Mexican Bull Fights—
Regimental Quartermaster—Trip to
Popocatapetl—Trip to the Caves of Mexico

The treaty of peace between the two countries was signed by the commissioners of each side early in February, 1848. It took a considerable time for it to reach Washington, receive the approval of the administration, and be finally ratified by the Senate. It was naturally supposed by the army that there would be no more fighting, and officers and men were of course anxious to get home, but knowing there must be delay they contented themselves as best they could.[1] Every Sunday there was a bull fight

---

1. During a war, the intensity of actual combat is often punctuated by long periods of inactivity and boredom. Grant took the opportunity peaceful interludes afforded to learn more about Mexico and its peoples. To the extent that Grant and his contemporaries knew anything about the history of the land they had invaded, they would probably have learned it from William H. Prescott's *History of the Conquest of Mexico*, a monumental study of the Aztecs and the Spanish conquest published in 1843, the year that Grant graduated from West Point. The academy's library had a copy of Prescott's book. Prescott shared Grant's appreciation for the country; he also admired its conqueror. "Of all that extensive empire which once acknowledged the authority of Spain in the New World," Prescott's history begins,

> no portion, for interest and importance, can be compared with Mexico;—
> and this equally, whether we consider the variety of its soil and climate; the
> inexhaustible stores of its mineral wealth; its scenery, grand and picturesque
> beyond example; the character of its ancient inhabitants, not only far surpassing in intelligence that of the other North American races, but reminding us, by their monuments, of the primitive civilization of Egypt and
> Hindostan; or, lastly, the peculiar circumstances of its Conquest, adven-

for the amusement of those who would pay their fifty cents. I attended one of them—just one—not wishing to leave the country without having witnessed the national sport. The sight to me was sickening. I could not see how human beings could enjoy the sufferings of beasts, and often of men, as they seemed to do on these occasions.[2]

At these sports there are usually from four to six bulls sacrificed. The audience occupies seats around the ring in which the exhibition is given, each seat but the foremost rising higher than the one in front, so that every one can get a full view of the sport. When all is ready a bull is turned into the ring. Three or four men come in, mounted on the merest skeletons of horses blind or blind-folded and so weak that they could not make a sudden turn with their riders without danger of falling down. The men are armed with spears having a point as sharp as a needle. Other men enter the arena on foot, armed with red flags and explosives about the size of a musket cartridge. To each of these explosives is fastened a barbed needle which serves the purpose of attaching them to the bull by running the needle into the skin. Before

---

turous and romantic as any legend devised by Norman or Italian bard of chivalry. It is the purpose of the present narrative to exhibit the history of this Conquest, and that of the remarkable man by whom it was achieved.

History of the Conquest of Mexico, ed. John Foster Kirk, 2 vols. (Philadelphia: Lippincott, 1873), 1:1-2.

2. The only time his staff officer Horace Porter saw Grant lose his temper during the war was when the general saw a teamster beating his horses with the butt-end of a whip:

Putting both spurs into "Egypt's" flanks, he dashed toward the teamster, and raising his clenched fist, called out to him: "What does this conduct mean, you scoundrel? Stop beating those horses!" The teamster looked at him, and said coolly, as he delivered another blow aimed at the face of the wheel-horse: "Well, who's drivin' this team anyhow—you or me?" The general was now thoroughly angered, and his manner was by no means as angelic as that of the celestial being who called a halt when Balaam was disciplining the ass. "I'll show you, you infernal villain!" he cried, shaking his fist in the man's face. Then calling to an officer of the escort, he said: "Take this man in charge, and have him tied up to a tree for six hours as a punishment for his brutality." . . . During the stirring scenes of that day's battle the general twice referred to the incident in vehement language, showing that the recollection of it was still rankling in his mind. This was the one exhibition of temper manifested by him during the entire campaign, and the only one I ever witnessed during my many years of service with him.

Porter, *Campaigning*, 164–65.

the animal is turned loose a lot of these explosives are attached to him. The pain from the pricking of the skin by the needles is exasperating; but when the explosions of the cartridges commence the animal becomes frantic. As he makes a lunge towards one horseman, another runs a spear into him. He turns towards his last tormentor when a man on foot holds out a red flag; the bull rushes for this and is allowed to take it on his horns. The flag drops and covers the eyes of the animal so that he is at a loss what to do; it is jerked from him and the torment is renewed. When the animal is worked into an uncontrollable frenzy, the horsemen withdraw, and the matadores—literally murderers—enter, armed with knives having blades twelve or eighteen inches long, and sharp. The trick is to dodge an attack from the animal and stab him to the heart as he passes. If these efforts fail the bull is finally lassoed, held fast and killed by driving a knife blade into the spinal column just back of the horns. He is then dragged out by horses or mules, another is let into the ring, and the same performance is renewed.

On the occasion when I was present one of the bulls was not turned aside by the attacks in the rear, the presentations of the red flag, etc., etc., but kept right on, and placing his horns under the flanks of a horse threw him and his rider to the ground with great force. The horse was killed and the rider lay prostrate as if dead. The bull was then lassoed and killed in the manner above described. Men came in and carried the dead man off in a litter. When the slaughtered bull and horse were dragged out, a fresh bull was turned into the ring. Conspicuous among the spectators was the man who had been carried out on a litter but a few minutes before. He was only dead so far as that performance went; but the corpse was so lively that it could not forego the chance of witnessing the discomfiture of some of his brethren who might not be so fortunate. There was a feeling of disgust manifested by the audience to find that he had come to life again. I confess that I felt sorry to see the cruelty to the bull and the horse. I did not stay for the conclusion of the performance; but while I did stay, there was not a bull killed in the prescribed way.

Bull fights are now prohibited in the Federal District—embracing a territory around the City of Mexico, somewhat larger than the District of Columbia—and they are not an institution in any part of the country. During one of my recent visits to Mexico, bull fights were got up in my honor at Puebla and at Pachuca. I was not notified in advance so as to be able to decline and thus prevent the performance; but in both cases I civilly declined to attend.

Another amusement of the people of Mexico of that day, and one which nearly all indulged in, male and female, old and young, priest and layman, was Monte playing. Regular feast weeks were held every year at what was then known as St. Augustin Tlalpam, eleven miles out of town. There were dealers to suit every class and condition of people. In many of the booths *tlacos*—the copper coin of the country, four of them making six and a quarter cents of our money—were piled up in great quantities, with some silver, to accommodate the people who could not bet more than a few pennies at a time. In other booths silver formed the bulk of the capital of the bank, with a few doubloons to be changed if there should be a run of luck against the bank. In some there was no coin except gold. Here the rich were said to bet away their entire estates in a single day. All this is stopped now.[3]

---

3. The 1868 edition of *Hoyle* describes Monte as follows:

This is the national game of the Mexicans, and is extensively played in California; but all attempts to establish it on this side of the Continent have signally failed. It is played with cards made expressly for the game, and which are known as Monte cards. They are thinner than other cards, and number but thirty-two, as in Euchre, those of the same denomination being discarded.

The Monte banker, or dealer must have the whole of his bank, or money which he risks at the game, in sight upon the table. After shuffling the cards, which is done in a peculiar manner, from the bottom of the pack, he deals out two, one at a time, and places them side by side upon the table, with their faces up. This is called the "*lay-out*," and upon these cards the players place their bets.

The two cards thus constituting the *lay-out* may be, for example, a King and a Ten, upon either of which the player may place his money; the bets being made, the dealer turns up the pack, exposing the bottom card, which is called the *port* card. Now, if this card happen to be of like denomination to either one of the *lay-out* cards, the dealer takes the money which may have been bet upon it.

We will suppose the *port* card to be a King—the dealer, having taken the money upon it, removes the King, and puts another card, taken from the pack, in its stead. Suppose that card to be an Ace: the players having again made their bets, the dealer proceeds with the game, which he does by taking the cards from the top of the pack and throwing them face up upon the table. In thus dealing, if the Ten shows before the Ace, the Ace wins, and the Ten loses, when the cards are again shuffled, and dealt as before.

The *lay-out* is not confined to *two* cards, but may be four, or more, as desired.

In this game, the *limit* is the bank, the player having the right at any time, to bet the whole amount, which is called "tapping the bank," which the player indicates by turning over the card upon which he bets, and placing his money thereupon.

The Modern Pocket Hoyle (New York: Dick & Fitzgerald, 1868), s.v. "Monte."

Mexican Monte, 1908. *Library of Congress, Prints and Photographs Division, LC-USZ62-64628.*

Cards have long been a recreation for soldiers—and sometimes, perhaps especially in literature, the cause of their ruin. This is the case in Alexander Pushkin's story "The Queen of Spades" (1834), in which an officer named Hermann, not normally a gambler, learns of the existence of a secret formula for winning at faro and ends up killing an old woman to get it. After Hermann still fails to win, he is committed to an asylum, where he monomaniacally "mutters with extraordinary rapidity" what would have been the winning hand and the slightly different hand he actually played: "Three, seven, ace! Three, seven, queen! . . ." "The Queen of Spades," *Novels, Tales, Journeys: The Complete Prose of Alexander Pushkin*, trans. Richard Pevear and Larissa Volokhonsky (New York: Knopf, 2016), 224.

War and Peace also contains a set piece involving a desperate faro game, in which the young soldier Nikolay Rostov, as if in a fever, racks up a monstrous debt of 43,000 rubles that contributes to the ruin of his family's fortune. See *War and Peace*, 413–19.

Soldiers from the 134th Illinois Volunteer Infantry playing cards at Columbus, Kentucky. Photograph by John Carbutt, 1864. *Library of Congress, Prints and Photographs Division, LC-DIG-ppmsca-33525.*

For myself, I was kept somewhat busy during the winter of 1847–8. My regiment was stationed in Tacubaya. I was regimental quartermaster and commissary. General Scott had been unable to get clothing for the troops from the North. The men were becoming—well, they needed cloth- ing. Material had to be purchased, such as could be obtained, and people employed to make it up into "Yankee uniforms." A quartermaster in the city was designated to attend to this special duty; but clothing was so much needed that it was seized as fast as made up. A regiment was glad to get a dozen suits at a time. I had to look after this matter for the 4th infantry. Then our regimental fund had run down and some of the musicians in the band had been without their extra pay for a number of months.

The regimental bands at that day were kept up partly by pay from the government, and partly by pay from the regimental fund. There was author- ity of law for enlisting a certain number of men as musicians. So many could receive the pay of non-commissioned officers of the various grades, and the remainder the pay of privates. This would not secure a band leader, nor good players on certain instruments. In garrison there are various ways of keep- ing up a regimental fund sufficient to give extra pay to musicians, establish libraries and ten-pin alleys, subscribe to magazines and furnish many extra comforts to the men.[4] The best device for supplying the fund is to issue

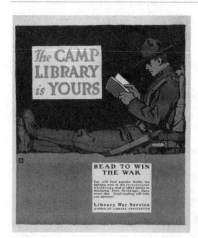

World War I–era American Library Association poster by C. B. Falls, 1917. *Library of Congress, Prints and Photographs Division, WWI Posters, LC-DIG-ppmsca-40831.*

4. In the nineteenth century, soldiers had to shift for themselves when it came to sup- plying most comforts. During the twentieth century, the military began to recognize that it could do something to improve morale during the doldrums, and camp libraries were established. At the outbreak of World War I, however, morale was still left largely to civilian organizations. Because their efforts were not always predictable, by World War II the military had taken over their functions. The Army's Special Services—which

"Wanted! 500 Bakers for the U.S. Army." By World War I organization had replaced the improvisation of Grant's days, 1917. *Library of Congress, Prints and Photographs Division, WWI Posters, LC-DIG-ppmsca-40986.*

bread to the soldiers instead of flour. The ration used to be eighteen ounces per day of either flour or bread; and one hundred pounds of flour will make one hundred and forty pounds of bread. This saving was purchased by the commissary for the benefit of the fund. In the emergency the 4th infantry was laboring under, I rented a bakery in the city, hired bakers—Mexicans—bought fuel and whatever was necessary, and I also got a contract from the chief commissary of the army for baking a large amount of hard bread. In two months I made more money for the fund than my pay amounted to during the entire war. While stationed at Monterey I had relieved the post

incidentally offered an ideal home for all of the entertainers and athletes who were mobilized—trained recreation officers in "devising, planning, and supervising practicable recreation and welfare activities for combat troops in Theaters of Operations, domestic and overseas." These activities ranged from providing sports equipment to mounting theatrical productions. Fort Meade, Maryland, was the original home of the Special Services, and *The Fort Meade Post* carried numerous stories on the good work done by the Special Services. Today, Morale, Welfare, and Recreation (MWR) facilities ranging from libraries to gymnasiums are available to soldiers even in the theater of war. The Army Library Program furnishes paperbacks and other reading material to deployed soldiers and maintains temporary libraries and e-library kiosks in theater, while librarians staff a network of libraries at posts, camps, and stations around the globe.

fund in the same way. There, however, was no profit except in the saving of flour by converting it into bread.[5]

In the spring of 1848 a party of officers obtained leave to visit Popocata-petl, the highest volcano in America, and to take an escort. I went with the party, many of whom afterwards occupied conspicuous positions before the country. Of those who "went south," and attained high rank, there was Lieutenant Richard Anderson, who commanded a corps at Spottsylvania; Captain Sibley, a major-general, and, after the war, for a number of years in the employ of the Khédive of Egypt; Captain George Crittenden, a rebel general; S. B. Buckner, who surrendered Fort Donelson; and Mansfield Lovell, who commanded at New Orleans before that city fell into the hands of the National troops. Of those who remained on our side there were Captain Andrew Porter, Lieutenant C. P. Stone and Lieutenant Z. B. Tower. There were quite a number of other officers, whose names I cannot recollect.[6]

---

5. Jean Edward Smith observes that Grant learned invaluable lessons from this unwelcome assignment: "it taught him the intricacies of military logistics from the bottom up. For a man who would go on to command large armies, no training could have been more valuable. During the Civil War Grant's armies might occasionally have straggled, discipline might sometimes have been lax, but food and ammunition trains were always expertly handled. While Grant's military fame deservedly rests on his battlefield victories, those victories depended in no small measure on his skill as a quartermaster. Unlike many Union armies, the forces he led never wanted for the tools of war." Smith, *Grant*, 52–53.

6. Richard H. Anderson (1821–1879) graduated from West Point in 1842, served on the frontier before the Mexican War, and later joined the C.S.A.

Henry H. Sibley (1816–1886), West Point class of 1828, was a native of Louisiana. He served in the Seminole War; after the Mexican War, he remained on frontier duty until he resigned in May 1861, to join the C.S.A. He later served for several years in the Egyptian army. He was also the inventor of the Sibley tent, which was based on a Comanche design.

George B. Crittenden (1812–1880) was born in Kentucky and graduated from West Point in 1832. He resigned from the army the following year and returned to Kentucky to practice law, a civilian career interrupted briefly by service in the Texas Army. He rejoined the army during the Mexican War and remained in the service until 1861, when he resigned his commission to join the C.S.A.

Mansfield Lovell (1822–1884) graduated from West Point in 1842. After service in the Mexican War and various assignments, he resigned in 1854. Born in Washington, D.C., and a resident of New York in 1861, he nevertheless fought for the Confederacy.

Andrew Porter (1820–1872) was born in Lancaster, Pennsylvania. He was the cousin of Grant's staff officer Horace Porter and also a first cousin once removed of Mary Todd Lincoln. He fought at First Bull Run and served as provost marshal of the Army of the Potomac before retiring for health reasons in 1864. In 1848, Porter, who was "then said

At a little village (Ozumba) near the base of Popocatapetl, where we purposed to commence the ascent, we procured guides and two pack mules with forage for our horses. High up on the mountain there was a deserted house of one room, called the Vaqueria, which had been occupied years before by men in charge of cattle ranging on the mountain. The pasturage

---

to be the best shot in the United States army," wounded future Confederate general James J. Archer, with whom he had served in Mexico, in a duel, according to an article in the *Confederate Veteran*, a newsletter "published monthly in the interest of confederate veterans and kindred topics." The magazine was instrumental in postwar Southern revisionism. See *Confederate Veteran* 8, no. 2 (February 1900): 65.

The wonderfully named Zealous B. Tower (1819–1900), West Point class of 1841, worked in the Corps of Engineers on fortifications from Alcatraz Island, California, to the Harbor Defenses of Portland, Maine. By the end of the Civil War he was the chief engineer of the Military Division of the Tennessee. He retired in 1883 after a forty-year career.

Charles P. Stone (1824–1887) had perhaps the most bizarre career of any of the officers Grant mentions here. After graduating from West Point in 1845 and serving in Mexico, he was an ordnance officer at various arsenals before resigning in 1854. Despite his commitment to the Union—he volunteered for service on January 2, 1861—his anti-abolitionist sentiments did not sit well with the Massachusetts soldiers he commanded. This unpopularity made him an easy scapegoat for various Union Army failures on the battlefield. He was arrested and sent to Fort Lafayette, a military prison in New York, where suspected secessionists were imprisoned. He spent seven months there before his name was cleared, and he returned to duty in the field until his resignation in 1864. Cullum's biographical sketch staunchly defends Stone, who was made a scapegoat for Union failures at the Battle of Ball's Bluff:

> Congress was much excited, and the Committee on the Conduct of the War demanded a victim, the choice falling upon poor Stone, who was arrested and incarcerated in Fort Lafayette, N. Y., without any charges against him, denied all intercourse with others, and treated as a common felon. This disgraceful transaction [finds a parallel] only in the annals of Eastern despots. . . .
>
> . . . [In 1886 Stone] became Engineer-in-Chief of the Committee for the Construction of the Pedestal of the Colossal Statue of "Liberty Enlightening the World" . . . on Bedloe's Island, New York harbor, and in sight of that military prison where for over half a year he was cruelly deprived *of his own liberty*. Hardly had the completion of this noble monument been celebrated, on which occasion Stone acted as Grand Marshal, before he died, January 24, 1887.

Biographical Register, vol. 2, s.v. "Stone, Charles P."

For a full account of Stone's travail, see Stephen W. Sears, "The Ordeal of General Stone," *Controversies and Commanders: Dispatches from the Army of the Potomac* (Boston: Houghton Mifflin, 1999).

up there was very fine when we saw it, and there were still some cattle, descendants of the former domestic herd, which had now become wild. It was possible to go on horseback as far as the Vaqueria, though the road was somewhat hazardous in places. Sometimes it was very narrow with a yawning precipice on one side, hundreds of feet down to a roaring mountain torrent below, and almost perpendicular walls on the other side. At one of these places one of our mules loaded with two sacks of barley, one on each side, the two about as big as he was, struck his load against the mountain-side and was precipitated to the bottom. The descent was steep but not perpendicular. The mule rolled over and over until the bottom was reached, and we supposed of course the poor animal was dashed to pieces. What was our surprise, not long after we had gone into bivouac, to see the lost mule, cargo and owner coming up the ascent. The load had protected the animal from serious injury; and his owner had gone after him and found a way back to the path leading up to the hut where we were to stay.

The night at the Vaqueria was one of the most unpleasant I ever knew. It was very cold and the rain fell in torrents. A little higher up the rain ceased and snow began. The wind blew with great velocity. The log-cabin we were in had lost the roof entirely on one side, and on the other it was hardly better then a sieve. There was little or no sleep that night. As soon as it was light the next morning, we started to make the ascent to the summit. The wind continued to blow with violence and the weather was still cloudy, but there was neither rain nor snow. The clouds, however, concealed from our view the country below us, except at times a momentary glimpse could be got through a clear space between them. The wind carried the loose snow around the mountain-sides in such volumes as to make it almost impossible to stand up against it. We labored on and on, until it became evident that the top could not be reached before night, if at all in such a storm, and we concluded to return. The descent was easy and rapid, though dangerous, until we got below the snow line. At the cabin we mounted our horses, and by night were at Ozumba.

The fatigues of the day and the loss of sleep the night before drove us to bed early. Our beds consisted of a place on the dirt-floor with a blanket under us. Soon all were asleep; but long before morning first one and then another of our party began to cry out with excruciating pain in the eyes. Not one escaped it. By morning the eyes of half the party were so swollen that they were entirely closed. The others suffered pain equally. The feeling was about what might be expected from the prick of a sharp needle at a white heat. We remained in quarters until the afternoon bathing our eyes in cold water. This relieved us very much, and before night the pain had entirely left. The swelling, however, continued, and about half the party still had their eyes entirely closed; but we concluded to make a start back, those who could see a little leading the horses of those who could not see at all. We moved back to the village of Ameca Ameca, some six miles, and stopped again for the night. The next morning all were entirely well and free from pain. The weather was clear and Popocatapetl stood out in all its beauty, the top looking as if not a mile away, and inviting us to return. About half the party were anxious to try the ascent again, and concluded to do so. The remainder—I was with the remainder—concluded that we had got all the pleasure there was to be had out of mountain climbing, and that we would visit the great caves of Mexico, some ninety miles from where we then were, on the road to Acapulco.

The party that ascended the mountain the second time succeeded in reaching the crater at the top, with but little of the labor they encountered in their first attempt. Three of them—Anderson, Stone and Buckner—wrote accounts of their journey, which were published at the time. I made no notes of this excursion, and have read nothing about it since, but it seems to me that I can see the whole of it as vividly as if it were but yesterday. I have been back at Ameca Ameca, and the village beyond, twice in the last five years. The scene had not changed materially from my recollection of it.[7]

---

7. Simon Bolivar Buckner, Grant's friend and the man who would surrender to him at Fort Donelson, did make it to the top of the volcano, an experience he described in an unsigned article in *Putnam's Monthly Magazine*:

> At twenty minutes past ten o'clock, having attached a small flag to one of the poles which had been used in making the ascent, we took formal possession of the subjacent country and planted the "stars and stripes" firmly on the highest peak of the Popocatepetl, overlooking the dark crater which was smoking below.
>
> The view from this point is unsurpassed in extent and magnificence. The eye looked, in every direction, far as human vision can extend, over almost boundless tracts of diversified and enchanting prospect. . . .
>
> Wherever our future wanderings may lead us, it will be no inconsiderable source of gratification to know that we were the first Americans who ever stood upon the snowy peak of the "Smoking Mountain," and planted our national color within the tropics, in a clime of eternal winter, over a region of perpetual fire; where it is greeted by the first beams of the sun as he rises from the Atlantic, and receives his last parting look as he sinks behind the waves of the great Southern Ocean.

"A Visit to Popocatepetl," *Putnam's Monthly Magazine* (April 1853): 415–16.

The Mexican War began a vogue in American tourism and travel writing about Mexico. In her study of the origins of this trend, Andrea Boardman notes that the

The party which I was with moved south down the valley to the town of Cuantla, some forty miles from Ameca Ameca. The latter stands on the plain at the foot of Popocatapetl, at an elevation of about eight thousand feet above tide water. The slope down is gradual as the traveller moves south, but one would not judge that, in going to Cuantla, descent enough had been made to occasion a material change in the climate and productions of the soil; but such is the case. In the morning we left a temperate climate where the cereals and fruits are those common to the United States, we halted in the evening in a tropical climate where the orange and banana, the coffee and the sugar-cane were flourishing. We had been travelling, apparently, on a plain all day, but in the direction of the flow of water.

Soon after the capture of the City of Mexico an armistice had been agreed to, designating the limits beyond which troops of the respective armies were not to go during its continuance. Our party knew nothing about these limits. As we approached Cuantla bugles sounded the assembly, and soldiers rushed from the guard-house in the edge of the town towards us. Our party halted, and I tied a white pocket handkerchief to a stick and, using it as a flag of truce, proceeded on to the town. Captains Sibley and Porter followed a few hundred yards behind. I was detained at the guard-house until a messenger could be dispatched to the quarters of the commanding general, who authorized that I should be conducted to him. I had been with the general but a few minutes when the two officers following announced themselves. The Mexican general reminded us that it was a violation of the truce for us to be there. However, as we had no special authority from our own commanding general, and as we knew nothing about the terms of the truce, we were permitted to occupy a vacant house outside the guard for the night, with the promise of a guide to put us on the road to Cuernavaca the next morning.

Cuernavaca is a town west of Cuantla. The country through which we passed, between these two towns, is tropical in climate and productions and rich in scenery. At one point, about half-way between the two places, the road goes over a low pass in the mountains in which there is a very quaint old town,

"soldier-tourists" who "wrote about their experiences during and after the war, sharing their wonderment at the landscape and antiquities and descriptions of people and places . . . kept Mexico's tourist attractions in the American imagination for several decades." "The U.S.-Mexican War and the Beginnings of American Tourism in Mexico," *Holiday in Mexico: Critical Reflections on Tourism and Tourist Encounters*, ed. Diane Berger and Andrew Grant Wood (Durham, NC: Duke University Press, 2010), 22.

Grant's extended descriptions of the Mexican scenery, unusual in a book characterized by narrative drive, suggest the degree to which he was taken with the country.

the inhabitants of which at that day were nearly all full-blooded Indians. Very few of them even spoke Spanish. The houses were built of stone and generally only one story high. The streets were narrow, and had probably been paved before Cortez visited the country. They had not been graded, but the paving had been done on the natural surface. We had with us one vehicle, a cart, which was probably the first wheeled vehicle that had ever passed through that town.

On a hill overlooking this town stands the tomb of an ancient king; and it was understood that the inhabitants venerated this tomb very highly, as well as the memory of the ruler who was supposed to be buried in it. We ascended the mountain and surveyed the tomb; but it showed no particular marks of architectural taste, mechanical skill or advanced civilization. The next day we went into Cuernavaca.

After a day's rest at Cuernavaca our party set out again on the journey to the great caves of Mexico. We had proceeded but a few miles when we were stopped, as before, by a guard and notified that the terms of the existing armistice did not permit us to go further in that direction. Upon convincing the guard that we were a mere party of pleasure seekers desirous of visiting the great natural curiosities of the country which we expected soon to leave, we were conducted to a large hacienda near by, and directed to remain there until the commanding general of that department could be communicated with and his decision obtained as to whether we should be permitted to pursue our journey. The guard promised to send a messenger at once, and expected a reply by night. At night there was no response from the commanding general, but the captain of the guard was sure he would have a reply by morning. Again in the morning there was no reply. The second evening the same thing happened, and finally we learned that the guard had sent no message or messenger to the department commander. We determined therefore to go on unless stopped by a force sufficient to compel obedience.

After a few hours' travel we came to a town where a scene similar to the one at Cuantla occurred. The commanding officer sent a guide to conduct our party around the village and to put us upon our road again. This was the last interruption: that night we rested at a large coffee plantation, some eight miles from the cave we were on the way to visit. It must have been a Saturday night; the peons had been paid off, and spent part of the night in gambling away their scanty week's earnings. Their coin was principally copper, and I do not believe there was a man among them who had received as much as twenty-five cents in money. They were as much excited, however, as if they had been staking thousands. I recollect one poor fellow, who had lost his last *tlaco*, pulled off his shirt and, in the most excited manner, put that up on the turn of a card. Monte was the game played, the place out of doors, near the window of the room occupied by the officers of our party.

The next morning we were at the mouth of the cave at an early hour, provided with guides, candles and rockets. We explored to a distance of about three miles from the entrance, and found a succession of chambers of great dimensions and of great beauty when lit up with our rockets. Stalactites and stalagmites of all sizes were discovered. Some of the former were many feet in diameter and extended from ceiling to floor; some of the latter were but a few feet high from the floor; but the formation is going on constantly, and many centuries hence these stalagmites will extend to the ceiling and become complete columns. The stalagmites were all a little concave, and the cavities were filled with water. The water percolates through the roof, a drop at a time—often the drops several minutes apart—and more or less charged with mineral matter. Evaporation goes on slowly, leaving the mineral behind. This in time makes the immense columns, many of them thousands of tons in weight, which serve to support the roofs over the vast chambers. I recollect that at one point in the cave one of these columns is of such huge proportions that there is only a narrow passage left on either side of it. Some of our party became satisfied with their explorations before we had reached the point to which the guides were accustomed to take explorers, and started back without guides. Coming to the large column spoken of, they followed it entirely around, and commenced retracing their steps into the bowels of the mountain, without being aware of the fact. When the rest of us had completed our explorations, we started out with our guides, but had not gone far before we saw the torches of an approaching party. We could not conceive who these could be, for all of us had come in together, and there were none but ourselves at the entrance when we started in. Very soon we found it was our friends. It took them some time to conceive how they had got where they were. They were sure they had kept straight on for the mouth of the cave, and had gone about far enough to have reached it.

14

Return of the Army—Marriage—Ordered to the Pacific Coast—Crossing the Isthmus—Arrival at San Francisco

My experience in the Mexican war was of great advantage to me afterwards. Besides the many practical lessons it taught, the war brought nearly all the officers of the regular army together so as to make them personally acquainted. It also brought them in contact with volunteers, many of whom served in the war of the rebellion afterwards.[1] Then,

---

1. In his novel of World War I, *Under Fire*, Henri Barbusse, who fought as a volunteer, describes the psychology of the amateur soldier:

> These are not soldiers, these are men. They are not adventurers or warriors, designed for human butchery—as butchers or cattle. They are the ploughmen or workers that one recognizes even in their uniforms. They are uprooted civilians. They are ready, waiting for the signal for death or murder, but when you examine their faces between the vertical ranks of bayonets, they are nothing but men.
>
> Each one knows that he will be presenting his head, his chest, his belly, the whole of his body, naked, to the rifles that are already fixed, the shells, the heaps of ready-prepared grenades and, above all, the methodical, almost infallible machine-gun . . . before he finds the other soldiers that he must kill. They are not careless of their lives, like bandits, or blind with fury, like savages. Despite all the propaganda, they are not inflamed. . . . Fully conscious of what they are doing, fully fit and in good health, they have massed there to throw themselves once more into that madman's role that is imposed on each of them by the folly of the human race. . . . They are not the sort of heroes that people think they are, but their sacri-

in my particular case, I had been at West Point at about the right time to meet most of the graduates who were of a suitable age at the breaking out of the rebellion to be trusted with large commands. Graduating in 1843, I was at the military academy from one to four years with all cadets who graduated between 1840 and 1846—seven classes. These classes embraced more than fifty officers who afterwards became generals on one side or the other in the rebellion, many of them holding high commands. All the older officers, who became conspicuous in the rebellion, I had also served with and known in Mexico: Lee, J. E. Johnston, A. S. Johnston, Holmes, [Paul O.] Hebért [Hébert] and a number of others on the Confederate side; McCall, Mansfield, Phil. Kearney and others on the National side. The acquaintance thus formed was of immense service to me in the war of the rebellion—I mean what I learned of the characters of those to whom I was afterwards opposed. I do not pretend to say that all movements, or even many of them, were made with special reference to the characteristics of the commander against whom they were directed. But my appreciation of my enemies was certainly affected by this knowledge. The natural disposition of most people is to clothe a commander of a large army whom they do not know, with almost superhuman abilities. A large part of the National army, for instance, and most of the press of the country, clothed

---

fice has greater value than those who have not seen them will ever be able to understand.

Under Fire, trans. Robin Buss (New York: Penguin Classics, 2004), 223.

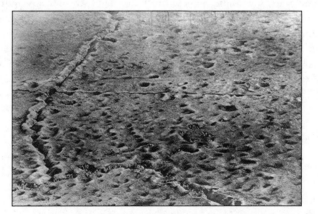

**Aerial photograph taken by French aviator of a battlefield on the
Somme front. Central News Photo Service, January 19, 1917.**
Library of Congress, Prints and Photographs Division, LC-DIG-ppmsca-40796.

General Lee with just such qualities, but I had known him personally, and knew that he was mortal; and it was just as well that I felt this.[2]

The treaty of peace was at last ratified, and the evacuation of Mexico by United States troops was ordered. Early in June the troops in the City of Mexico began to move out. Many of them, including the brigade to which I belonged, were assembled at Jalapa, above the vomito, to await the arrival of transports at Vera Cruz: but with all this precaution my regiment and others were in camp on the sand beach in a July sun, for about a week before embarking, while the fever raged with great virulence in Vera Cruz, not two miles away. I can call to mind only one person, an officer, who died of the disease. My regiment was sent to Pascagoula, Mississippi, to spend the summer. As soon as it was settled in camp I obtained a leave of absence for four months and proceeded to St. Louis. On the 22d of August, 1848, I was married to Miss Julia Dent, the lady of whom I have before spoken.[3] We visited my parents and relations in Ohio, and, at the end of my leave, proceeded to my post at Sackett's Harbor, New York. In April following I was ordered to Detroit, Michigan, where two years were spent with but few important incidents.[4]

---

2. This paragraph offers an excellent lens through which to read the narrative of the Civil War, which begins in chapter 17 and occupies the rest of the book.

3. Julia writes in her memoirs, "My wedding was necessarily a simple one. The season was unfavorable for a large gathering, and our temporary home in St. Louis was small. We were married about eight o'clock, and received during the evening all of our *old* friends in the city. . . . A table was set at the end of the back parlor upon which were served ices, fruits, and all that papa's hospitality and good taste could suggest for the occasion. My wedding cake, I was assured, was a marvel of beauty." *Personal Memoirs of Julia Dent Grant*, 55.

The marriage was a happy one, and Grant's separation from Julia and their children was one of the chief factors contributing to his misery in California. His letters throughout this period are full of longing and unhappiness.

4. Eunice Tripler, the wife Charles Tripler (1806–1866), an army doctor assigned to Fort Wayne, recalled meeting the Grants in Detroit:

The Grants came to Detroit in 1849. Mrs. Grant and I exchanged calls. U. S. Grant was then a Lieutenant in the Army and his pay was about $60 per month. Dr. Tripler was at this time a Major. Mrs. Grant always had a great lump of a baby in her arms. Dr. Tripler pointed out Grant to me in the street one day. "That's Grant over there. How he does drive that little rat of a horse" (a French pony, a pacer—though the best he could afford. At this very time, as I well remember, Dr. Tripler was driving his pair of Vermont Morgan mares). Grant used to drive furiously on Jefferson Avenue then unpaved and on the River Rouge when frozen. And we met the Grants in

The present constitution of the State of Michigan was ratified during this time. By the terms of one of its provisions, all citizens of the United States residing within the State at the time of the ratification became citizens of Michigan also. During my stay in Detroit there was an election for city officers. Mr. Zachariah Chandler was the candidate of the Whigs for the office of Mayor, and was elected, although the city was then reckoned democratic. All the officers stationed there at the time who offered their votes were permitted to cast them. I did not offer mine, however, as I did not wish to consider myself a citizen of Michigan. This was Mr. Chandler's first entry into politics, a career he followed ever after with great success, and in which he died enjoying the friendship, esteem and love of his countrymen.

In the spring of 1851 the garrison at Detroit was transferred to Sackett's Harbor, and in the following spring the entire 4th infantry was ordered to the Pacific Coast. It was decided that Mrs. Grant should visit my parents at first for a few months, and then remain with her own family at their St. Louis home until an opportunity offered of sending for her. In the month of April the regiment was assembled at Governor's Island, New York Harbor, and on the 5th of July eight companies sailed for Aspinwall.[5] We numbered a little over seven hundred persons, including the families of officers and soldiers. Passage was secured for us on the old steamer *Ohio*, commanded at the time by Captain Schenck, of the navy.[6] It had not been determined, until a day

company occasionally. I recall, in particular, a large party at Gen. Brady's where they were present. Most of the time Lieut. Grant was standing rather aloof from the company and uncommunicative with his hands behind his back, impassive. He always gave me the impression of a school-boy who had not learned his lesson, but he was always very devoted and tender to his wife. She, as I think, was his salvation. My cousin, Capt. Lewis Hunt, a class-mate of Grant at West Point, had said to me, "There's more in Grant than you think."

Eunice Tripler, *Some Notes of Her Personal Recollections* (New York: Grafton Press, 1910), 103–4.

5. Present-day Colón; the name was changed in 1890.

6. The SS *Ohio* was owned by the U.S. Mail and Steam Ship Company (1848–1868). Its captain was James F. Schenck (1807–1882), a naval officer who had served in the Mexican War and "raised with his own hands the first American flag to fly in California." Schenck would later serve in the Civil War. See *Dictionary of American Naval Fighting Ships* (*DANFS*), vol. 6 (Washington, D.C.: Naval History Division, Department of the Navy, 1976), s.v. "*Schenck.*"

When a fire and mechanical difficulties disrupted an earlier voyage of the *Ohio*, Schenck was credited for his "excellent . . . discipline." A newspaper reported, "There were upwards of three hundred souls on board, and had they had a less cool and experienced commander than Captain Schenck, there is no telling what, between the fire and machinery, would have been their fate." "Accident to the Steamship Ohio," *Daily Alta California*, September 8, 1851.

Rear Admiral James F. Schenck, U.S. Navy, 1868 or 1869. *NH 46097. Courtesy of the Naval History and Heritage Command.*

A Wickes-class destroyer was named for Schenck. Commissioned in 1919, Destroyer No. 159 served in a variety of capacities, according to *DANFS*:

> The high point of *Schenck*'s war service came on Christmas Eve, 1943, when the group located a concentration of U-boats. After stalking radar and sound contacts for most of the night and making six attacks, *Schenck* heard an underwater explosion and saw an oil slick which marked the end of *U-645*. Almost immediately, another submarine sank *Schenck*'s squadronmate, *Leary* (DD-158). *Schenck* continued her ASW operations and was later commended by the task group commander for her role in preventing a concentrated wolfpack attack on [the escort carrier] *Card*; for her continued aggressive action after the sinking of *Leary,* despite having only fourteen depth charges left; and for her skillful rescue of *Leary*'s survivors.

After the war, *Schenck* was sold for scrap.

USS *Schenck* (DD-159). *NH 108704. Courtesy of the Naval History and Heritage Command.*

or two before starting, that the 4th infantry should go by the *Ohio*; consequently, a complement of passengers had already been secured. The addition
of over seven hundred to this list crowded the steamer most uncomfortably,
especially for the tropics in July.

In eight days Aspinwall was reached. At that time the streets of the town
were eight or ten inches under water, and foot passengers passed from place
to place on raised foot-walks. July is at the height of the wet season, on the
Isthmus. At intervals the rain would pour down in streams, followed in not
many minutes by a blazing, tropical summer's sun. These alternate changes,
from rain to sunshine, were continuous in the afternoons. I wondered how
any person could live many months in Aspinwall, and wondered still more
why any one tried.

In the summer of 1852 the Panama railroad was completed only to the
point where it now crosses the Chagres River. From there passengers were
carried by boats to Gorgona, at which place they took mules for Panama,
some twenty-five miles further. Those who travelled over the Isthmus in
those days will remember that boats on the Chagres River were propelled
by natives not inconveniently burdened with clothing. These boats carried
thirty to forty passengers each. The crews consisted of six men to a boat,
armed with long poles. There were planks wide enough for a man to walk
on conveniently, running along the sides of each boat from end to end. The
men would start from the bow, place one end of their poles against the river
bottom, brace their shoulders against the other end, and then walk to the
stern as rapidly as they could. In this way from a mile to a mile and a half an
hour could be made, against the current of the river.[7]

I, as regimental quartermaster, had charge of the public property and had
also to look after the transportation. A contract had been entered into with
the steamship company in New York for the transportation of the regiment
to California, including the Isthmus transit. A certain amount of baggage
was allowed per man, and saddle animals were to be furnished to commissioned officers and to all disabled persons. The regiment, with the exception

7. The railroad was completed in 1855, the Panama Canal opened in 1914. The historian
David McCullough notes that as president Grant, no doubt recalling his own arduous
crossing, would be "more keenly interested in an isthmian canal than any of his predecessors had been." Grant entrusted his childhood friend Daniel Ammen, a retired
admiral whom he had appointed the head of the Bureau of Navigation, with organizing
exploratory expeditions to the region. See *The Path Between the Seas: The Creation of the
Panama Canal* (New York: Simon & Schuster, 1978), 26.

of one company left as guards to the public property—camp and garrison equipage principally—and the soldiers with families, took boats, propelled as above described, for Gorgona. From this place they marched to Panama, and were soon comfortably on the steamer anchored in the bay, some three or four miles from the town. I, with one company of troops and all the soldiers with families, all the tents, mess chests and camp kettles, was sent to Cruces, a town a few miles higher up the Chagres River than Gorgona. There I found an impecunious American who had taken the contract to furnish transportation for the regiment at a stipulated price per hundred pounds for the freight and so much for each saddle animal. But when we reached Cruces there was not a mule, either for pack or saddle, in the place. The contractor promised that the animals should be on hand in the morning. In the morning he said that they were on the way from some imaginary place, and would arrive in the course of the day. This went on until I saw that he could not procure the animals at all at the price he had promised to furnish them for. The unusual number of passengers that had come over on the steamer, and the large amount of freight to pack, had created an unprecedented demand for mules. Some of the passengers paid as high as forty dollars for the use of a mule to ride twenty-five miles, when the mule would not have sold for ten dollars in that market at other times. Meanwhile the cholera had broken out, and men were dying every hour. To diminish the food for the disease, I permitted the company detailed with me to proceed to Panama. The captain and the doctors accompanied the men, and I was left alone with the sick and the soldiers who had families. The regiment at Panama was also affected with the disease; but there were better accommodations for the well on the steamer, and a hospital, for those taken with the disease, on an old hulk anchored a mile off. There were also hospital tents on shore on the island of Flamingo, which stands in the bay.

I was about a week at Cruces before transportation began to come in. About one-third of the people with me died, either at Cruces or on the way to Panama. There was no agent of the transportation company at Cruces to consult, or to take the responsibility of procuring transportation at a price which would secure it. I therefore myself dismissed the contractor and made a new contract with a native, at more than double the original price. Thus we finally reached Panama. The steamer, however, could not proceed until the cholera abated, and the regiment was detained still longer. Altogether, on the Isthmus and on the Pacific side, we were delayed six weeks. About one-seventh of those who left New York harbor with the 4th infantry on the

5th of July, now lie buried on the Isthmus of Panama or on Flamingo island in Panama Bay.

One amusing circumstance occurred while we were lying at anchor in Panama Bay. In the regiment there was a Lieutenant Slaughter who was very liable to sea-sickness. It almost made him sick to see the wave of a table-cloth when the servants were spreading it. Soon after his graduation, Slaughter was ordered to California and took passage by a sailing vessel going around Cape Horn. The vessel was seven months making the voyage, and Slaughter was sick every moment of the time, never more so than while lying at anchor after reaching his place of destination. On landing in California he found orders which had come by the Isthmus, notifying him of a mistake in his assignment; he should have been ordered to the northern lakes. He started back by the Isthmus route and was sick all the way. But when he arrived at the East he was again ordered to California, this time definitely, and at this date was making his third trip. He was as sick as ever, and had been so for more than a month while lying at anchor in the bay. I remember him well, seated with his elbows on the table in front of him, his chin between his hands, and looking the picture of despair. At last he broke out, "I wish I had taken my father's advice; he wanted me to go into the navy; if I had done so, I should not have had to go to sea so much." Poor Slaughter! it was his last sea voyage. He was killed by Indians in Oregon.[8]

---

8. Grant's "amusing circumstance" leavens the seriousness of the foregoing paragraph. The suffering was appalling—a third of the passengers died—and Grant responded to the cholera epidemic with coolness and efficiency. Lloyd Lewis suggests that this episode reinforced for Grant, who had already witnessed Taylor's neglect of camp sanitation during the Mexican War, the reality "that disease, not gunpowder, was the greatest killer of soldiers. As long as he would live he would talk more of Panama than of any of his battles, even of that murderous day in the leaden hell of San Cosme. The sick and dying men, the rain and the mud, the burdens thrown upon him by the incompetent Bonneville [his commanding officer in Panama] had, however, lifted him from his own homesickness and had revealed to him his unguessed powers at this business of managing a command of military men." Lewis, *Captain Sam Grant*, 307.

William A. Slaughter (1827–1855) survived the crossing to be killed by White River Indians while on a scouting expedition in 1855. Slaughter was fondly remembered by Elwood Evans in his *History of the Pacific Northwest*:

It was the fortune of the writer of these annals to have enjoyed the intimate personal acquaintance of the late Lieutenant Slaughter. His death

By the last of August the cholera had so abated that it was deemed safe to start. The disease did not break out again on the way to California, and we reached San Francisco early in September.

---

was certainly one of the saddest events of that war. . . . As an officer, he was brave to a fault. As an Indian campaigner, he had been remarkably successful. No man had more endeared himself to his command. None had a more happy faculty of inspiring men with enthusiasm. Small in frame and delicate in person, his powers of endurance were wonderful. He had led almost all the expeditions to check the Indians during his stay in the country, and had been actively in the field from the commencement of hostilities till he met his untimely death. Brilliant he was as a soldier; and, as the citizen, he had rendered himself equally dear to the people of the territory in which he had been assigned to duty. In the walks of social life, who that enjoyed his friendship or acquaintance can ever forget him?

History of the Pacific Northwest: Oregon and Washington (Portland, OR: North Pacific History Company, 1889), 1:548.

George Crook, a future Civil War general known mainly for his later role in the Indian Wars, crossed the isthmus the following year and documented the misery of the journey. See *General George Crook: His Autobiography*, ed. Martin F. Schmitt (Norman: University of Oklahoma Press, 1946), 3–6.

15

San Francisco—Early California Experiences—Life on the Pacific Coast—Promoted Captain—Flush Times in California[1]

San Francisco at that day was a lively place. Gold, or placer digging as it was called, was at its height. Steamers plied daily between San Francisco and both Stockton and Sacramento. Passengers and gold from the southern mines came by the Stockton boat; from the northern mines by Sacramento.

---

1. This is the second of only two chapters Grant devotes to the time between the wars, a period of some dozen years. Even by Grant's standards, a great deal is left unsaid. In fact, his experience in California was, despite his enthusiasm for its natural beauty and climate, arguably the most miserable of his life. His sojourn in the Pacific was dominated by loneliness and punctuated by one failed money-making scheme after another. It was also during this assignment that Grant earned the reputation for drunkenness that would dog him throughout his life and that has become for the casual inquirer his most salient attribute. Several historians, including McFeely, Smith, White, and Chernow, have written well and at length about Grant's depression in California and his resultant abuse of alcohol. This response to a letter from Julia suggests the depths of his misery:

> The Mail has just arrived bringing me a very short and very unsatisfactory letter. You speak of not joining me on this coast in a manner that would indicate that you have been reflecting upon a dream which you say you have had until you really imagine that it is true. Do not write so any more dearest. It is hard enough for us to be seperated so far without borrowing immaginary troubles. You know that it was entirely out of the question for you to have come with me at the time I had to come. I am doing all I can to put up a penny not only to enable you and our dear little

In the evening when these boats arrived, Long Wharf—there was but one wharf in San Francisco in 1852—was alive with people crowding to meet the miners as they came down to sell their "dust" and to "have a time." Of these some were runners for hotels, boarding houses or restaurants; others belonged to a class of impecunious adventurers, of good manners and good presence, who were ever on the alert to make the acquaintance of people with some ready means, in the hope of being asked to take a meal at a restaurant. Many were young men of good family, good education and gentlemanly instincts. Their parents had been able to support them during their minority, and to give them good educations, but not to maintain them afterwards. From 1849 to 1853 there was a rush of people to the Pacific coast, of the class described. All thought that fortunes were to be picked up, without effort, in the gold fields on the Pacific. Some realized more than their most sanguine expectations; but for one such there were hundreds disappointed, many of whom now fill unknown graves; others died wrecks of their former selves, and many, without a vicious instinct, became criminals and outcasts. Many of the real scenes in early California life exceed in strangeness and interest any of the mere products of the brain of the novelist.[2]

---

boys to get here comfortably, but to enable you to be comfortable after you do get here.

Letter to Julia Dent Grant, March 31, 1853, *PUSG*, 1:296–97.

In another letter Grant complains of "a very sever cold" as well as of Julia's silence: "By this Mail I recieved no letter from you, nor from any one at your house. Where Mails come but twice per month it does seem as though I might expect news from you and our dear little boys." Letter to Julia Dent Grant, June 28, 1853, *PUSG*, 1:303.

For an engaging and detailed account of army life in the Pacific Northwest at roughly the same time, see the early chapters of Crook's *Autobiography.*

2. The transformation wrought by the Gold Rush has receded into historical memory, but the discovery of gold in large quantities turned San Francisco from a remote outpost into a boomtown. Grant intimates the mania for gold that Frank Norris depicts in *McTeague: A Story of San Francisco.* Norris's novel, on which Erich von Stroheim based his monumental film *Greed* (1924), captures elements of life in the city during this period as well as the obsession with gold that possessed so many. Gold is everywhere in Norris's novel: in the ground as well as in the characters' frenzied imaginations. Here McTeague, a dentist who fills teeth with gold in San Francisco, returns to the mines from which he came to the city:

At turns of the road, on the higher points, cañons disclosed themselves far away, gigantic grooves in the landscape, deep blue in the distance, opening

Those early days in California brought out character. It was a long way off then, and the journey was expensive. The fortunate could go by Cape Horn or by the Isthmus of Panama; but the mass of pioneers crossed the plains with their ox-teams. This took an entire summer. They were very lucky when they got through with a yoke of worn-out cattle. All other means were exhausted in procuring the outfit on the Missouri River. The immigrant, on arriving, found himself a stranger, in a strange land, far from friends. Time pressed, for the little means that could be realized from the sale of what was left of the outfit would not support a man long at California prices. Many became discouraged. Others would take off their coats and look for a job, no matter what it might be. These succeeded as a rule. There were many young men who had studied professions before they went to California, and who had never done a day's manual labor in their lives, who took in the situation at once and went to work to make a start at anything they could get to do. Some supplied carpenters and masons with material—carrying plank, brick, or mortar, as the case might be; others drove stages, drays, or baggage wagons, until they could do better. More became discouraged early and spent their time looking up people who would "treat," or lounging about

---

one into another, ocean-deep, silent, huge, and suggestive of colossal primeval forces held in reserve. At their bottoms they were solid, massive; on their crests they broke delicately into fine serrated edges where the pines and redwoods outlined their million of tops against the high white horizon. Here and there the mountains lifted themselves out of the narrow river beds in groups like giant lions rearing their heads after drinking. The entire region was untamed. . . .

But there were men in these mountains, like lice on mammoths' hides, fighting them stubbornly, now with hydraulic "monitors," now with drill and dynamite, boring into the vitals of them, or tearing away great yellow gravelly scars in the flanks of them, sucking their blood, extracting gold.

Here and there at long distances upon the cañon sides rose the head-gear of a mine, surrounded with its few unpainted houses, and topped by its never-failing feather of black smoke. On near approach one heard the prolonged thunder of the stamp-mill, the crusher, the insatiable monster, gnashing the rocks to powder with its long iron teeth, vomiting them out again in a thin stream of wet gray mud. Its enormous maw, fed night and day with the car-boys' loads, gorged itself with gravel, and spat out the gold, grinding the rocks between its jaws, glutted, as it were, with the very entrails of the earth, and growling over its endless meal, like some savage animal, some legendary dragon, some fabulous beast, symbol of inordinate and monstrous gluttony.

McTeague: A Novel of San Francisco (New York: Doubleday & McClure, 1899), 379–80.

restaurants and gambling houses where free lunches were furnished daily. They were welcomed at these places because they often brought in miners who proved good customers.[3]

My regiment spent a few weeks at Benicia [Benecia] barracks, and then was ordered to Fort Vancouver, on the Columbia River, then in Oregon Territory. During the winter of 1852–3 the territory was divided, all north of the Columbia River being taken from Oregon to make Washington Territory.

Prices for all kinds of supplies were so high on the Pacific coast from 1849 until at least 1853—that it would have been impossible for officers of the army to exist upon their pay, if it had not been that authority was given them to purchase from the commissary such supplies as he kept, at New Orleans wholesale prices. A cook could not be hired for the pay of a captain. The cook could do better. At Benicia, in 1852, flour was 25 cents per pound; potatoes were 16 cents; beets, turnips and cabbage, 6 cents; onions, 37½ cents; meat and other articles in proportion. In 1853 at Vancouver vegetables were a little lower. I with three other officers concluded that we would raise a crop for ourselves, and by selling the surplus realize something handsome. I bought a pair of horses that had crossed the plains that summer and were very poor. They recuperated rapidly, however, and proved a good team to break up the ground with. I performed all the labor of breaking up the ground while the other officers planted the potatoes. Our crop was enormous. Luckily for us the Columbia River rose to a great height from the melting of the snow in the mountains in June, and overflowed and killed

3. In addition to Norris's novel and Bret Harte's short story "The Luck of Roaring Camp," the most evocative literary representations of the "strange things done . . . / By the men who moil for gold" are probably those of Jack London and Robert W. Service, both of whom wrote about the Klondike Gold Rush of the 1890s. The opening stanza of Service's "The Cremation of Sam McGee" evokes the frenzied spirit that attaches to all such rushes:

> There are strange things done in the midnight sun
>   By the men who moil for gold;
> The Arctic trails have their secret tales
>   That would make your blood run cold;
> The Northern Lights have seen queer sights,
>   But the queerest they ever did see
> Was that night on the marge of Lake Lebarge
>   I cremated Sam McGee.

Songs of a Sourdough (Toronto: William Briggs, 1908), 55.

most of our crop. This saved digging it up, for everybody on the Pacific coast seemed to have come to the conclusion at the same time that agriculture would be profitable. In 1853 more than three-quarters of the potatoes raised were permitted to rot in the ground, or had to be thrown away. The only potatoes we sold were to our own mess.[4]

While I was stationed on the Pacific coast we were free from Indian wars.[5] There were quite a number of remnants of tribes in the vicinity of

---

4. This was only one of several schemes Grant devised for making money: all of them failed. In one instance, he was swindled of $500 by a man named Elijah Camp. Having returned to New York after his resignation in 1854, Grant tried, to no avail, to track Camp down in Sackets Harbor. He returned to New York City, where he did not have enough money to pay his hotel bill or to buy a ticket home; Buckner kindly bailed him out. Grant's letters to Julia, recounting a variety of ill-fated schemes and counting the days since he has last heard from her, offer a prosaic modern analogue to the predicament of that archetypal military wanderer, Odysseus, stranded after the Trojan War on the nymph Calypso's island and faced with the prospect of never reaching home:

> The nymph, obedient to divine command,
> To seek Ulysses, paced along the sand.
> Him pensive on the lonely beach she found,
> With streaming eyes in briny torrents drown'd,
> And inly pining for his native shore;
> For now the soft enchantress pleased no more;
> For now, reluctant, and constrain'd by charms,
> Absent he lay in her desiring arms,
> In slumber wore the heavy night away,
> On rocks and shores consumed the tedious day;
> There sat all desolate, and sigh'd alone,
> With echoing sorrows made the mountains grown,
> And roll'd his eyes o'er all the restless main,
> Till dimm'd with rising grief they stream'd again.

Homer, trans. Alexander Pope, vol. 3 (New York: Harper & Brothers, 1836), pp. 10–11; bk. 5, ll. 191–204.

5. George Catlin, who documented his extensive visits to Indian tribes throughout the country in the 1830s in a series of paintings, which he displayed in a traveling art exhibition called "Catlin's Indian Gallery," predicted the imminent extinction of Native Americans in his journals, first published in 1841:

> A numerous nation of human beings, whose origin is beyond the reach of human investigation,—whose early history is lost—whose term of national existence is nearly expired—three-fourths of whose country has fallen into the possession of civilized man within the short space of 250 years—twelve millions of whose bodies have fattened the soil in the mean time; who have

Portland in Oregon, and of Fort Vancouver in Washington Territory. They had generally acquired some of the vices of civilization, but none of the virtues, except in individual cases. The Hudson's Bay Company had held the North-west with their trading posts for many years before the United States was represented on the Pacific coast. They still retained posts along the Columbia River and one at Fort Vancouver, when I was there. Their treatment of the Indians had brought out the better qualities of the savages. Farming had been undertaken by the company to supply the Indians with bread and vegetables; they raised some cattle and horses; and they had now taught the Indians to do the labor of the farm and herd. They always compensated them for their labor, and always gave them goods of uniform quality and at uniform price.

Before the advent of the American, the medium of exchange between the Indian and the white man was pelts. Afterward it was silver coin. If an Indian received in the sale of a horse a fifty dollar gold piece, not an infre-

---

fallen victims to whiskey, the small-pox, and the bayonet; leaving at this time but a meager proportion to live a short time longer, in the certain apprehension of soon sharing a similar fate.

Letter No. 1, *Letters and Notes on the Manners, Customs and Condition of the North American Indians*, 2 vols. (New York: Wiley and Putnam, 1841), 1:4–5.

Of the particular depredations of the fur traders in the United States and Canada, Catlin wrote,

Besides the many thousands who are daily and hourly selling whiskey and rum, and useless gewgaws, to the Indians . . . [thousands more] pervade the countries of the wildest tribes they can reach, with guns and gunpowder in their hands, and other instruments of death . . . calculated to terrify and coerce him to favourable terms in his trade. . . .

These traders, in addition to the terror, and sometimes death, that they carry into these remote realms, at the muzzles of their guns, as well as by the whiskey and the small-pox, are continually arming tribe after tribe with fire-arms; who are able thereby, to bring their unsuspecting enemies into unequal combats, where they are slain by thousands, and who have no way to heal the awful wound but by arming themselves in turn; and in a similar manner reeking [*sic*] their vengeance upon *their* defenceless enemies on the West. In this wholesale way, and by whiskey and disease, tribe after tribe sink their heads and lose their better, proudest half, before the next and succeeding waves of civilization flow on, to see or learn anything definite of them.

Letter No. 58, *Letters and Notes*, 2:250–51.

quent occurrence, the first thing he did was to exchange it for American half dollars. These he could count. He would then commence his purchases, paying for each article separately, as he got it. He would not trust any one to add up the bill and pay it all at once. At that day fifty dollar gold pieces, not the issue of the government, were common on the Pacific coast. They were called slugs.

The Indians, along the lower Columbia as far as the Cascades and on the lower Willamette, died off very fast during the year I spent in that section; for besides acquiring the vices of the white people they had acquired also their diseases. The measles and the small-pox were both amazingly fatal. In their wild state, before the appearance of the white man among them, the principal complaints they were subject to were those produced by long involuntary fasting, violent exercise in pursuit of game, and over-eating. Instinct more than reason had taught them a remedy for these ills. It was the steam bath. Something like a bake-oven was built, large enough to admit a man lying down. Bushes were stuck in the ground in two rows, about six feet long and some two or three feet apart; other bushes connected the rows at one end. The tops of the bushes were drawn together to interlace, and confined in that position; the whole was then plastered over with wet clay until every opening was filled. Just inside the open end of the oven the floor was scooped out so as to make a hole that would hold a bucket or two of water. These ovens were always built on the banks of a stream, a big spring, or pool of water. When a patient required a bath, a fire was built near the oven and a pile of stones put upon it. The cavity at the front was then filled with water. When the stones were sufficiently heated, the patient would draw himself into the oven; a blanket would be thrown over the open end, and hot stones put into the water until the patient could stand it no longer. He was then withdrawn from his steam bath and doused into the cold stream near by. This treatment may have answered with the early ailments of the Indians. With the measles or small-pox it would kill every time.[6]

---

6. The 1853 epidemic in the Pacific Northwest was devastating to Native Americans. Cortés's expedition had introduced smallpox into the New World in the sixteenth century; it is estimated that a third of the Aztecs died from the disease. The earliest attempts at inoculation took place in China or India; by the early eighteenth century the practice was beginning to find support in the West. Lady Mary Wortley Montague, who first witnessed the practice in 1717, when she accompanied her husband, the British ambassador to Constantinople, to Turkey, inoculated her children when she returned to England. Here she describes the practice to a correspondent:

"The Cow-Pock—or—the Wonderful Effects of the New Inoculation," James
Gillray's caricature of Dr. Jenner's vaccination program at the Smallpox and
Inoculation Hospital at St. Pancras, 1802. *Library of Congress, Prints and Photographs
Division, LC-USZC4-3147.*

A propos of distempers, I am going to tell you a thing that I am sure
will make you wish yourself here. The small-pox, so fatal, and so general
amongst us, is here entirely harmless by the invention of *ingrafting*, which is
the term they give it. There is a set of old women who make it their business to perform the operation every autumn, in the month of September,
when the great heat is abated. People send to one another to know if any
of their family has a mind to have the small-pox: they make parties for this
purpose, and when they are met (commonly fifteen or sixteen together),
the old woman comes with a nut-shell full of the matter of the best sort of
small-pox, and asks what veins you please to have opened. She immediately
rips open that you offer to her with a large needle (which gives you no more
pain than a common scratch), and puts into the vein as much venom as can
lye upon the head of her needle, and after binds up the little wound with a
hollow bit of shell; and in this manner opens four or five veins. . . . Every
year thousands undergo this operation; and the French embassador says
pleasantly, that they take the small-pox here by way of diversion, as they
take the waters in other countries. There is no example of any one that has
died in it; and you may believe I am very well satisfied of the safety of the
experiment, since I intend to try it on my dear little son.

I am patriot enough to take pains to bring this useful invention into

During my year on the Columbia River, the small-pox exterminated one small remnant of a band of Indians entirely, and reduced others materially. I do not think there was a case of recovery among them, until the doctor with the Hudson Bay Company took the matter in hand and established a hospital. Nearly every case he treated recovered. I never, myself, saw the treatment described in the preceding paragraph, but have heard it described by persons who have witnessed it. The decimation among the Indians I knew of personally, and the hospital, established for their benefit, was a Hudson's Bay building not a stone's throw from my own quarters.

The death of Colonel Bliss, of the Adjutant General's department, which occurred July 5th, 1853, promoted me to the captaincy of a company then stationed at Humboldt Bay, California. The notice reached me in September of the same year, and I very soon started to join my new command. There was no way of reaching Humboldt at that time except to take passage on a San Francisco sailing vessel going after lumber. Red wood, a species of cedar, which on the Pacific coast takes the place filled by white pine in the East, then abounded on the banks of Humboldt Bay. There were extensive saw-mills engaged in preparing this lumber for the San Francisco market, and sailing vessels, used in getting it to market, furnished the only means of communication between Humboldt and the balance of the world.

I was obliged to remain in San Francisco for several days before I found

---

fashion in England; and I should not fail to write to some of our doctors very particularly about it, if I knew any one of them that I thought had virtue enough to destroy such a considerable branch of their revenue for the good of mankind. But that distemper is too beneficial to them, not to expose to all their resentment the hardy wight that should undertake to put an end to it. Perhaps, if I live to return, I may, however, have courage to war with them.

Letter to Mrs. S[arah]. C[hiswell], April 1, O.S. [1714], *The Letters and Works of Lady Mary Wortley Montagu*, ed. Lord Wharncliffe, 3 vols. (London: Richard Bentley, 1837), 1:391–93. ·

Meanwhile, in New England, Cotton Mather, who learned about the practice from his Libyan slave Onesimus, advocated for widespread inoculation. Although vaccination increasingly found proponents, it was still controversial in 1777, when George Washington took the bold step of inoculating the Continental Army: "You will pardon my observations upon the smallpox," he wrote to Patrick Henry, "because I know it is more destructive to an army in the natural way, than the enemy's sword, and because I shudder whenever I reflect upon the difficulties of keeping it out." Letter to Patrick Henry, April 13, 1777, *The Writings of George Washington*, ed. Jared Sparks (New York: Harper & Brothers, 1847), vol. 4, pt. 2, 390–91.

a vessel. This gave me a good opportunity of comparing the San Francisco of 1852 with that of 1853. As before stated, there had been but one wharf in front of the city in 1852—Long Wharf. In 1853 the town had grown out into the bay beyond what was the end of this wharf when I first saw it. Streets and houses had been built out on piles where the year before the largest vessels visiting the port lay at anchor or tied to the wharf. There was no filling under the streets or houses. San Francisco presented the same general appearance as the year before; that is, eating, drinking and gambling houses were conspicuous for their number and publicity. They were on the first floor, with doors wide open. At all hours of the day and night in walking the streets, the eye was regaled, on every block near the water front, by the sight of players at faro. Often broken places were found in the street, large enough to let a man down into the water below. I have but little doubt that many of the people who went to the Pacific coast in the early days of the gold excitement, and have never been heard from since, or who were heard from for a time and then ceased to write, found watery graves beneath the houses or streets built over San Francisco Bay.

Besides the gambling in cards there was gambling on a larger scale in city lots. These were sold "On Change," much as stocks are now sold on Wall Street. Cash, at time of purchase, was always paid by the broker; but the purchaser had only to put up his margin. He was charged at the rate of two or three per cent. a month on the difference, besides commissions. The sand hills, some of them almost inaccessible to foot-passengers, were surveyed off and mapped into fifty vara lots—a vara being a Spanish yard. These were sold at first at very low prices, but were sold and resold for higher prices until they went up to many thousands of dollars. The brokers did a fine business, and so did many such purchasers as were sharp enough to quit purchasing before the final crash came. As the city grew, the sand hills back of the town furnished material for filling up the bay under the houses and streets, and still further out. The temporary houses, first built over the water in the harbor, soon gave way to more solid structures. The main business part of the city now is on solid ground, made where vessels of the largest class lay at anchor in the early days. I was in San Francisco again in 1854. Gambling houses had disappeared from public view. The city had become staid and orderly.

16

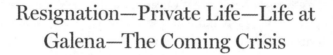

Resignation—Private Life—Life at Galena—The Coming Crisis

My family, all this while, was at the East. It consisted now of a wife and two children. I saw no chance of supporting them on the Pacific coast out of my pay as an army officer. I concluded, therefore, to resign, and in March applied for a leave of absence until the end of the July following, tendering my resignation to take effect at the end of that time.[1] I left

---

1. Grant says little here about the circumstances surrounding his resignation, which he submitted to the adjutant-general in Washington, on April 11, 1854, on the very same day he accepted his captaincy. As McFeely proposes, this episode became the prime source of stories about Grant's excessive drinking: "All the rivers of alcohol—imagined or real—flow down from the Fort Humboldt days." *Grant*, 55.

Ronald White endorses the version of events told by Grant's friend Rufus Ingalls: after a drinking binge, Grant was evidently given an ultimatum by the commander at Fort Humboldt, Major Robert C. Buchanan (1811–1878). See White, *American Ulysses: A Life of Ulysses S. Grant* (New York: Random House, 2016), 120. See also Jean Edward Smith, *Grant*, 86–88. Both White and Smith draw on Hamlin Garland's account.

Grant's letters to Julia during this period clearly reveal the abundant provocations to drink at Fort Humboldt. On his arrival at the fort in January, he wrote, "Imagine a place closed in by the sea having thrown up two tongues of land, closed in a bay that can be entered only with certain winds." On February 2, he began his letter: "You do not know how forsaken I feel here!" Although he reported that Humboldt Bay appeared to be a "very healthy place," the mail was irregular on account of the rough weather, he had trouble with his teeth, and he was just about ready to resign were it not for the fact that "*poverty poverty*, begins to stare me in the face." Letters to Julia Dent, January 18, February, 2, and March 6, 1854, *PUSG* 1:315, 316, 323.

Buchanan was an old nemesis: He had taken over for Kearny at Jefferson Barracks

the Pacific coast very much attached to it, and with the full expectation of making it my future home. That expectation and that hope remained uppermost in my mind until the Lieutenant-Generalcy bill was introduced into Congress in the winter of 1863–4. The passage of that bill, and my promotion, blasted my last hope of ever becoming a citizen of the further West.[2]

In the late summer of 1854 I rejoined my family, to find in it a son whom I had never seen, born while I was on the Isthmus of Panama. I was now to commence, at the age of thirty-two, a new struggle for our support. My wife had a farm near St. Louis, to which we went, but I had no means to stock it. A house had to be built also. I worked very hard, never losing a day because of bad weather, and accomplished the object in a moderate way. If nothing else could be done I would load a cord of wood on a wagon and take it to the city for sale. I managed to keep along very well until 1858, when I was attacked by fever and ague. I had suffered very severely and for a long time from this disease, while a boy in Ohio. It lasted now over a year, and, while it did not keep me in the house, it did interfere greatly with the amount of work I was able to perform. In the fall of 1858 I sold out my stock, crops and farming utensils at auction, and gave up farming.

In the winter I established a partnership with Harry Boggs, a cousin of Mrs. Grant, in the real estate agency business. I spent that winter at St. Louis

and upbraided Grant for being late to dinner on several occasions. As even the largely complimentary Cullum acknowledges, Buchanan was an old-school martinet: "General Buchanan was one of the most prominent Infantry officers of the Army, in which he performed long, faithful, and honorable service. Though a rigid disciplinarian, he was always kind and considerate to subordinates; just and incorruptible in all his dealings; dignified and courtly in his demeanor; gallant and chivalrous on the battlefield; and ever a worthy and noble exemplar to his profession." *Biographical Register*, vol. 1, s.v. "Buchanan, Robert C."

George Crook, who as a new second lieutenant encountered Buchanan the same year, offers a far less generous portrait: "Our commander seemed particularly elated at his own importance, and his fitness for the duties assigned him, and lost no opportunity to impress on all of us subordinates how far we fell short of what he expected. He seemed to take delight in wounding the feelings of those under him, and succeeded pretty generally in making himself unpopular amongst the citizens as well as the army." Crook escaped the many "petty tyrants," drunken officers and soldiers, and incompetents he encountered in the West by going hunting whenever he could—a recreation Grant did not enjoy. See *Autobiography*, 9, 10, 18–19.

2. Swept on a tide of celebrity to the presidency, the most well-known American of his day, Grant nevertheless seemed in certain important senses to have less control over his destiny than he might otherwise have done, while his fame never brought the wealth that would have solved the problem still facing him at the end: providing for his family.

myself, but did not take my family into town until the spring. Our business might have become prosperous if I had been able to wait for it to grow. As it was, there was no more than one person could attend to, and not enough to support two families. While a citizen of St. Louis and engaged in the real estate agency business, I was a candidate for the office of county engineer, an office of respectability and emolument which would have been very acceptable to me at that time. The incumbent was appointed by the county court, which consisted of five members. My opponent had the advantage of birth over me (he was a citizen by adoption) and carried off the prize. I now withdrew from the co-partnership with Boggs, and, in May, 1860, removed to Galena, Illinois, and took a clerkship in my father's store.[3]

While a citizen of Missouri, my first opportunity for casting a vote at a Presidential election occurred. I had been in the army from before attaining my majority and had thought but little about politics, although I was a Whig by education and a great admirer of Mr. Clay. But the Whig party had ceased to exist before I had an opportunity of exercising the privilege of casting a ballot; the Know-Nothing party had taken its place, but was on the wane; and the Republican party was in a chaotic state and had not yet received a name. It had no existence in the Slave States except at points on the borders next to Free States. In St. Louis City and County, what afterwards became the Republican party was known as the Free-Soil Democracy, led by the Honorable Frank P. Blair.[4] Most of my neighbors had known me as an officer

---

3. Almost destitute after failing at farming and real estate, unable to gain an appointment as a county engineer—he even pawned his watch in 1857—Grant was eventually compelled to work for his brothers as a clerk in his father's leather-goods store in Galena. Surely this solution exacerbated his already difficult relationship with Jesse. The great Southern diarist Mary Chesnut records an encounter between Grant and one of his army acquaintances during this period: "General Edward Johnston says he got Grant a place—*esprit de corps*, you know. He could not bear to see an old army man driving a wagon; that was when he found him out West, put out of the army for habitual drunkenness." January 1, 1864, *Diary*, 269.

Lloyd Lewis is more succinct about Grant's interwar period: "Sam Grant was becoming the ghost of a soldier." *Captain Sam Grant*, 358.

4. Republican congressman Frank P. Blair (1821–1875) organized the St. Louis branch of the militaristic national political movement called the Wide Awakes in support of Abraham Lincoln's campaign for president. Blair's armed Wide Awakes clashed with the secessionist Missouri State Militia at Camp Jackson. He would later be rewarded for his loyalty with a general's appointment in the Civil War. Blair was rare among the men Grant mostly disparages as "political generals" in his battlefield competence. McPherson suggests that Blair developed into a "first-class" corps commander. See McPherson, *Battle Cry of Freedom: The Civil War Era* (New York: Ballantine, 1989), 329. On the

of the army with Whig proclivities. They had been on the same side, and, on
the death of their party, many had become Know-Nothings, or members of
the American party. There was a lodge near my new home, and I was invited
to join it. I accepted the invitation; was initiated; attended a meeting just one
week later, and never went to another afterwards.

I have no apologies to make for having been one week a member of the
American party; for I still think native-born citizens of the United States
should have as much protection, as many privileges in their native country,
as those who voluntarily select it for a home. But all secret, oath-bound
political parties are dangerous to any nation, no matter how pure or how
patriotic the motives and principles which first bring them together. No
political party can or ought to exist when one of its corner-stones is opposition to freedom of thought and to the right to worship God "according
to the dictate of one's own conscience," or according to the creed of any
religious denomination whatever. Nevertheless, if a sect sets up its laws as
binding above the State laws, wherever the two come in conflict this claim
must be resisted and suppressed at whatever cost.[5]

Up to the Mexican war there were a few out and out abolitionists, men
who carried their hostility to slavery into all elections, from those for a justice of the peace up to the Presidency of the United States. They were noisy
but not numerous. But the great majority of people at the North, where
slavery did not exist, were opposed to the institution, and looked upon its
existence in any part of the country as unfortunate. They did not hold the
States where slavery existed responsible for it; and believed that protection
should be given to the right of property in slaves until some satisfactory
way could be reached to be rid of the institution. Opposition to slavery was
not a creed of either political party. In some sections more anti-slavery men
belonged to the Democratic party, and in others to the Whigs. But with the
inauguration of the Mexican war, in fact with the annexation of Texas, "the
inevitable conflict" commenced.[6]

Wide Awakes, see Jon Grinspan, "'Young Men for War': The Wide Awakes and Lincoln's 1860 Presidential Campaign," *Journal of American History* 96 (September 2009):
357–78.

5. Grant's awkwardness about his very brief flirtation with the Know-Nothings owes
almost certainly to the fact that their ugly platform was strongly nativist, anti-Catholic,
and anti-immigrant. The party also refused to declare a position on the slavery question.

6. Grant referred in an earlier chapter to his father's acquaintance with John Brown.
Abolitionist sentiment gathered momentum in the years after the Mexican War. Harriet
Beecher Stowe's 1852 novel *Uncle Tom's Cabin* gave further impetus to antislavery feel-

As the time for the Presidential election of 1856—the first at which I had the opportunity of voting—approached, party feeling began to run high. The Republican party was regarded in the South and the border States not only as opposed to the extension of slavery, but as favoring the compulsory abolition of the institution without compensation to the owners. The most horrible visions seemed to present themselves to the minds of people who, one would suppose, ought to have known better. Many educated and, otherwise, sensible persons appeared to believe that emancipation meant social equality. Treason to the Government was openly advocated and was not

---

ing in the country by making an abstract argument personal, immediate, and dramatic, especially for white Americans living in free states who could ignore their own complicity in the original national sin of slavery. Lincoln's apocryphal comment on meeting Stowe, "Is this the little woman who made the great war?" reveals something about the novel's perceived power. On the provenance of this quotation, see *Recollected Words of Abraham Lincoln*, ed. Don E. Fehrenbacher and Virginia Fehrenbacher (Stanford, CA: Stanford University Press, 1996), s.v. "Stowe, Harriet Beecher."

Here Stowe describes the attic of horrors in the house of the brutal overseer Simon Legree, a transplanted New Englander:

> The garret of the house that Legree occupied, like most other garrets, was a great, desolate space, dusty, hung with cobwebs, and littered with cast-off lumber. . . . Altogether, it was a weird and ghostly place; but, ghostly as it was, it wanted not in legends, among the superstitious negroes, to increase its terrors. Some few years before, a negro woman, who had incurred Legree's displeasure, was confined there for several weeks. What passed there we do not say; the negroes used to whisper darkly to each other; but it was known that the body of the unfortunate creature was one day taken down from there, and buried; and, after that, it was said that oaths, and cursings, and the sound of violent blows used to ring through that old garret, and mingled with wailings and groans of despair. Once, when Legree chanced to overhear something of this kind, he flew into a violent passion, and swore that the next one that told stories about that garret should have an opportunity of knowing what was there, for he would chain him up there for a week. This hint was enough to repress talking, though, of course, it did not disturb the credit of the story in the least.

Uncle Tom's Cabin; or, Life among the Lowly (Boston: John P. Jewett, 1853), 498–99.

Stowe's book ratcheted up defenses of slavery as well: not only "Anti-Tom" novels but also critical reviews and essays, including Louisa S. McCord's influential "Uncle Tom's Cabin," *Southern Quarterly Review* 7, no. 13 (1853): 81–120. Mary Chesnut, who reread the book in 1862, faulted Stowe on several points, including her sentimentalized characterizations of slaves. But the chief complaint recorded in the diary is that Stowe ignored what Chesnut herself regarded as the most damning aspect of slavery: the sexual abuse of female slaves by their white masters.

rebuked. It was evident to my mind that the election of a Republican President in 1856 meant the secession of all the Slave States, and rebellion. Under these circumstances I preferred the success of a candidate whose election would prevent or postpone secession, to seeing the country plunged into a war the end of which no man could foretell. With a Democrat elected by the unanimous vote of the Slave States, there could be no pretext for secession for four years. I very much hoped that the passions of the people would subside in that time, and the catastrophe be averted altogether; if it was not, I believed the country would be better prepared to receive the shock and to resist it. I therefore voted for James Buchanan for President. Four years later the Republican party was successful in electing its candidate to the Presidency. The civilized world has learned the consequence. Four millions of human beings held as chattels have been liberated; the ballot has been given to them; the free schools of the country have been opened to their children. The nation still lives, and the people are just as free to avoid social intimacy with the blacks as ever they were, or as they are with white people.[7]

Harriet Beecher Stowe. Photograph by William R. Howell, ca. 1870. *Library of Congress, Prints and Photographs Division, LC-DIG-ppmsca-49808.*

7. In contrast to the overt racism of contemporaries such as Sherman, for example, Grant's attitudes on race were moderate for his day. Like Lincoln, he remained somewhat skeptical about the possibilities of social equality and integration of the races, but he worked with Lincoln to ensure the enforcement of the Emancipation Proclamation. Grant emancipated William Jones, the slave he had acquired from his father-in-law. "Grant's views on slavery were ambivalent," Jean Edward Smith writes of Grant's prewar sentiments, "and Jones was the only slave he ever owned. When he moved to St. Louis, Grant was initially tempted to rent the man out, but soon decided against it. On March 29, 1859, he went to circuit court and filed the manumission papers to

While living in Galena I was nominally only a clerk supporting myself and family on a stipulated salary. In reality my position was different. My father had never lived in Galena himself, but had established my two brothers there, the one next younger than myself in charge of the business, assisted by the youngest. When I went there it was my father's intention to give up all connection with the business himself, and to establish his three sons in it: but the brother who had really built up the business was sinking with consumption, and it was not thought best to make any change while he was in this condition. He lived until September, 1861, when he succumbed to that insidious disease which always flatters its victims into the belief that they are growing better up to the close of life. A more honorable man never transacted business. In September, 1861, I was engaged in an employment which required all my attention elsewhere.

During the eleven months that I lived in Galena prior to the first call for volunteers, I had been strictly attentive to my business, and had made but few acquaintances other than customers and people engaged in the same line with myself. When the election took place in November, 1860, I had not been a resident of Illinois long enough to gain citizenship and could not, therefore, vote. I was really glad of this at the time, for my pledges would have compelled me to vote for Stephen A. Douglas, who had no possible chance of election. The contest was really between Mr. Breckinridge and Mr. Lincoln; between minority rule and rule by the majority. I wanted, as between these candidates, to see Mr. Lincoln elected. Excitement ran high during the canvass, and torch-light processions enlivened the scene in the generally quiet streets of Galena many nights during the campaign. I did not parade with either party, but occasionally met with the "wide awakes"—Republicans—in their rooms, and superintended their drill. It was evident, from the time of the Chicago nomination to the close of the canvass, that the election of the Republican candidate would be the signal for some of the Southern States to secede. I still had hopes that the four years which had elapsed since the first nomination of a Presidential candidate by a party distinctly opposed to slavery extension, had given time for the extreme pro-slavery sentiment to cool down; for the Southerners to think well before they took the awful leap which they had so vehemently threatened. But I was mistaken.

The Republican candidate was elected, and solid substantial people of the

emancipate Jones. Grant never discussed his motives, but the action speaks for itself. Able-bodied slaves sold for a thousand dollars or more, and Grant surely could have used the money. Instead, he set Jones free." *Grant*, 94.

"Grand procession of Wide-Awakes at New York on the evening of October 3, 1860," *Harper's Weekly*, October 13, 1860. *Library of Congress, Prints and Photographs Division, LC-USZ62-59401.*

North-west, and I presume the same order of people throughout the entire North, felt very serious, but determined, after this event. It was very much discussed whether the South would carry out its threat to secede and set up a separate government, the corner-stone of which should be, protection to the "Divine" institution of slavery. For there were people who believed in the "divinity" of human slavery, as there are now people who believe Mormonism and Polygamy to be ordained by the Most High.[8] We forgive them for

8. One of the most active and prolific defenders of slavery as a positive good—not simply, as other defenders argued, a necessary evil—was George Fitzhugh (1806–1881), a planter from Virginia. "The negro slaves of the South are the happiest, and, in some sense, the freest people in the world," Fitzhugh proposes while arguing that the truest American bondage is that of Northern wage-slavery:

> The children and the aged and infirm work not at all, and yet have all the comforts and necessaries of life provided for them. They enjoy liberty, because they are oppressed neither by care nor labor. The women do little hard work, and are protected from the despotism of their husbands by their masters. The negro men and stout boys work, on the average, in good

entertaining such notions, but forbid their practice. It was generally believed that there would be a flurry; that some of the extreme Southern States would go so far as to pass ordinances of secession. But the common impression was that this step was so plainly suicidal for the South, that the movement would not spread over much of the territory and would not last long.

Doubtless the founders of our government, the majority of them at least, regarded the confederation of the colonies as an experiment. Each colony considered itself a separate government; that the confederation was for mutual protection against a foreign foe, and the prevention of strife and war among themselves. If there had been a desire on the part of any single State to withdraw from the compact at any time while the number of States was limited to the original thirteen, I do not suppose there would have been any to contest the right, no matter how much the determination might have been regretted. The problem changed on the ratification of the Constitution by all the colonies; it changed still more when amendments were added; and if the right of any one State to withdraw continued to exist at all after the ratification of the Constitution, it certainly ceased on the formation of new States, at least so far as the new States themselves were concerned. It was never possessed at all by Florida or the States west of the Mississippi, all of which were purchased by the treasury of the entire nation. Texas and the territory brought into the Union in consequence of annexation, were purchased with both blood and treasure; and Texas, with a domain greater than that of any European state except Russia, was permitted to retain as state property all the public lands within its borders. It would have been ingratitude and injustice of the most flagrant sort for this State to withdraw from the Union after all that had been spent and done to introduce her; yet, if separation had actually occurred, Texas must necessarily have gone with

---

weather, not more than nine hours a day. The balance of their time is spent in perfect abandon. Besides, they have their Sabbaths and holidays. White men, with so much of license and liberty, would die of ennui; but negroes luxuriate in corporeal and mental repose. With their faces upturned to the sun, they can sleep at any hour; and quiet sleep is the greatest of human enjoyments. "Blessed be the man who invented sleep." 'Tis happiness in itself—and results from contentment with the present, and confident assurance of the future.

Cannibals All! or, Slaves without Masters (Richmond, VA: A. Morris, 1857), 29–30.

For a full survey of proslavery arguments, see *The Ideology of Slavery: Proslavery Thought in the Antebellum South, 1830–1860*, ed. Drew Gilpin Faust (Baton Rouge: Louisiana State University Press, 1981).

the South, both on account of her institutions and her geographical position. Secession was illogical as well as impracticable; it was revolution.

Now, the right of revolution is an inherent one. When people are oppressed by their government, it is a natural right they enjoy to relieve themselves of the oppression, if they are strong enough, either by withdrawal from it, or by overthrowing it and substituting a government more acceptable. But any people or part of a people who resort to this remedy, stake their lives, their property, and every claim for protection given by citizenship—on the issue. Victory, or the conditions imposed by the conqueror—must be the result.

In the case of the war between the States it would have been the exact truth if the South had said,—"We do not want to live with you Northern people any longer; we know our institution of slavery is obnoxious to you, and, as you are growing numerically stronger than we, it may at some time in the future be endangered. So long as you permitted us to control the government, and with the aid of a few friends at the North to enact laws constituting your section a guard against the escape of our property, we were willing to live with you. You have been submissive to our rule heretofore; but it looks now as if you did not intend to continue so, and we will remain in the Union no longer." Instead of this the seceding States cried lustily,—"Let us alone; you have no constitutional power to interfere with us." Newspapers and people at the North reiterated the cry. Individuals might ignore the constitution; but the Nation itself must not only obey it, but must enforce the strictest construction of that instrument; the construction put upon it by the Southerners themselves. The fact is the constitution did not apply to any such contingency as the one existing from 1861 to 1865. Its framers never dreamed of such a contingency occurring. If they had foreseen it, the probabilities are they would have sanctioned the right of a State or States to withdraw rather than that there should be war between brothers.

The framers were wise in their generation and wanted to do the very best possible to secure their own liberty and independence, and that also of their descendants to the latest days. It is preposterous to suppose that the people of one generation can lay down the best and only rules of government for all who are to come after them, and under unforeseen contingencies. At the time of the framing of our constitution the only physical forces that had been subdued and made to serve man and do his labor, were the currents in the streams and in the air we breathe. Rude machinery, propelled by water power, had been invented; sails to propel ships upon the waters had been set to catch the passing breeze—but the application of steam to propel vessels against both wind and current, and machinery to do all manner of work had not been thought of. The instantaneous transmission of messages around the world by means of electricity would probably at that day have been attributed to witchcraft or a league with the Devil. Immaterial circumstances had changed as greatly as material ones. We could not and ought not to be rigidly bound by the rules laid down under circumstances so different for emergencies so utterly unanticipated. The fathers themselves would have been the first to declare that their prerogatives were not irrevocable. They would surely have resisted secession could they have lived to see the shape it assumed.

I travelled through the Northwest considerably during the winter of 1860–1. We had customers in all the little towns in south-west Wisconsin, south-east Minnesota and north-east Iowa. These generally knew I had been a captain in the regular army and had served through the Mexican war. Consequently wherever I stopped at night, some of the people would come to the public-house where I was, and sit till a late hour discussing the probabilities of the future. My own views at that time were like those officially expressed by Mr. Seward at a later day, that "the war would be over in ninety days."[9] I continued to entertain these views until after the battle of Shiloh. I believe now that there would have been no more battles at the West after the capture of Fort Donelson if all the troops in that region had been under a single commander who would have followed up that victory.

There is little doubt in my mind now that the prevailing sentiment of the South would have been opposed to secession in 1860 and 1861, if there had been a fair and calm expression of opinion, unbiased by threats, and if the ballot of one legal voter had counted for as much as that of any other. But there was no calm discussion of the question. Demagogues who were too old to enter the army if there should be a war, others who entertained so high an opinion of their own ability that they did not believe they could be spared from the direction of the affairs of state in such an event, declaimed vehemently and unceasingly against the North; against its aggressions upon

9. William H. Seward (1801–1872) was secretary of state in the Lincoln administration. He insisted that his commitment to abolition began in his youth in Florida, where his father was a slave owner: "I early came to the conclusion that something was wrong, and the 'gradual emancipation' laws of the State, soon after coming into debate, enabled me to solve the mystery, and determined me, at that early age, to be an abolitionist." *Autobiography of William H. Seward, from 1801–1834, with a Memoir of His Life, and Selections from His Letters from 1831–1846* (New York: D. Appleton, 1877), 28.

the South; its interference with Southern rights, etc., etc. They denounced the Northerners as cowards, poltroons, negro-worshippers; claimed that one Southern man was equal to five Northern men in battle; that if the South would stand up for its rights the North would back down. Mr. Jefferson Davis said in a speech, delivered at La Grange, Mississippi, before the secession of that State, that he would agree to drink all the blood spilled south of Mason and Dixon's line if there should be a war.[10] The young men who would have the fighting to do in case of war, believed all these statements, both in regard to the aggressiveness of the North and its cowardice. They, too, cried out for a separation from such people. The great bulk of the legal voters of the South were men who owned no slaves; their homes were generally in the hills and poor country; their facilities for educating their children, even up to the point of reading and writing, were very limited; their interest in the contest was very meagre—what there was, if they had been capable of seeing it, was with the North; they too needed emancipation. Under the old régime they were looked down upon by those who controlled all the affairs

10. McPherson notes that there is no evidence of Jefferson Davis ever having said this. "Grant's memory," he suggests, "probably confused this alleged statement by Davis with similar statements made by other Southern leaders during the secession winter of 1860–61." James M. McPherson, ed. *Personal Memoirs*, by Ulysses S. Grant (New York: Penguin, 1999), 646 n. 31.

   Such boasts and their deflation are the stuff of poetry. Witness the French peers' mockery of the zealous Dauphin before the Battle of Agincourt in Shakespeare's *Henry V*:

> DAUPHIN. Would I were able to load him with his desert! Will it never be day? I will trot to-morrow a mile, and my way shall be paved with English faces.
>
> CONSTABLE. I will not say so, for fear I should be fac'd out of my way: but I would it were morning; for I would fain be about the ears of the English.
>
> RAMBURES. Who will go to hazard with me for twenty prisoners?
>
> CONSTABLE. You must first go yourself to hazard, ere you have them.
>
> DAUPHIN. 'T is midnight; I'll go arm myself.   [*Exit.*
>
> ORLEANS. The Dolphin longs for morning.
>
> RAMBURES. He longs to eat the English.
>
> CONSTABLE. I think he will eat all he kills.
>
> . . . .
>
> ORLEANS. He never did harm, that I heard of.
>
> CONSTABLE. Nor will do none to-morrow: he will keep that good name still.

Henry V 3.7.72–83, 88–90.

in the interest of slave-owners, as poor white trash who were allowed the ballot so long as they cast it according to direction.

I am aware that this last statement may be disputed and individual testimony perhaps adduced to show that in ante-bellum days the ballot was as untrammelled in the south as in any section of the country; but in the face of any such contradiction I reassert the statement. The shot-gun was not resorted to. Masked men did not ride over the country at night intimidating voters; but there was a firm feeling that a class existed in every State with a sort of divine right to control public affairs. If they could not get this control by one means they must by another. The end justified the means. The coercion, if mild, was complete.

There were two political parties, it is true, in all the States, both strong in numbers and respectability, but both equally loyal to the institution which stood paramount in Southern eyes to all other institutions in state or nation. The slave-owners were the minority, but governed both parties. Had politics ever divided the slave-holders and the non-slave-holders, the majority would have been obliged to yield, or internecine war would have been the consequence. I do not know that the Southern people were to blame for this condition of affairs. There was a time when slavery was not profitable, and the discussion of the merits of the institution was confined almost exclusively to the territory where it existed. The States of Virginia and Kentucky came near abolishing slavery by their own acts, one State defeating the measure by a tie vote and the other only lacking one. But when the institution became profitable, all talk of its abolition ceased where it existed; and naturally, as human nature is constituted, arguments were adduced in its support. The cotton-gin probably had much to do with the justification of slavery.

The winter of 1860–1 will be remembered by middle-aged people of to-day as one of great excitement. South Carolina promptly seceded after the result of the Presidential election was known. Other Southern States proposed to follow. In some of them the Union sentiment was so strong that it had to be suppressed by force. Maryland, Delaware, Kentucky and Missouri, all Slave States, failed to pass ordinances of secession; but they were all represented in the so-called congress of the so-called Confederate States. The Governor and Lieutenant-Governor of Missouri, in 1861, [Claiborne F.] Jackson and [Thomas C.] Reynolds, were both supporters of the rebellion and took refuge with the enemy. The governor soon died, and the lieutenant-governor assumed his office; issued proclamations as governor of the State; was recognized as such by the Confederate Government, and continued his pretensions until the collapse of the rebellion. The South claimed the sovereignty of States, but claimed the right to coerce into their confederation such States as they wanted, that is, all the States where slavery existed. They did not seem to think this course inconsistent. The fact is, the Southern slave-owners believed that, in some way, the ownership of slaves conferred a sort of patent of nobility—a right to govern independent of the interest or wishes of those who did not hold such property. They convinced themselves, first, of the divine origin of the institution and, next, that that particular institution was not safe in the hands of any body of legislators but themselves.

Meanwhile the Administration of President Buchanan looked helplessly on and proclaimed that the general government had no power to interfere; that the Nation had no power to save its own life. Mr. Buchanan had in his cabinet two members at least, who were as earnest—to use a mild term—in the cause of secession as Mr. Davis or any Southern statesman. One of them, [John B.] Floyd, the Secretary of War, scattered the army so that much of it could be captured when hostilities should commence, and distributed the cannon and small arms from Northern arsenals throughout the South so as to be on hand when treason wanted them. The navy was scattered in like manner. The President did not prevent his cabinet preparing for war upon their government, either by destroying its resources or storing them in the South until a de facto government was established with Jefferson Davis as its President, and Montgomery, Alabama, as the Capital. The secessionists had then to leave the cabinet. In their own estimation they were aliens in the country which had given them birth. Loyal men were put into their places. Treason in the executive branch of the government was estopped. But the harm had already been done. The stable door was locked after the horse had been stolen.[11]

During all of the trying winter of 1860–1, when the Southerners were so defiant that they would not allow within their borders the expression of a sentiment hostile to their views, it was a brave man indeed who could

11. Margaret Leech summarizes the full range of opinion on Buchanan: "Mr. Buchanan later protested that during this period his mood had been serene, and that he had 'not lost an hour's sleep or a single meal.' Unsympathetic observers, on the other hand, described him as a broken old man, who did nothing but cry and pray. The first picture seems nearly as exaggerated as the second." Leech concludes: "In the end, his sundered country was united only in the opinion that Mr. Buchanan was a coward and a fool. Sinking heavily into a chair in Scott's headquarters, he exclaimed, 'The office of President of the United States is not fit for a gentleman to hold.'" *Reveille in Washington*, 24–25.

stand up and proclaim his loyalty to the Union. On the other hand men at the North—prominent men—proclaimed that the government had no power to coerce the South into submission to the laws of the land; that if the North undertook to raise armies to go south, these armies would have to march over the dead bodies of the speakers. A portion of the press of the North was constantly proclaiming similar views. When the time arrived for the President-elect to go to the capital of the Nation to be sworn into office, it was deemed unsafe for him to travel, not only as a President-elect, but as any private citizen should be allowed to do. Instead of going in a special car, receiving the good wishes of his constituents at all the stations along the road, he was obliged to stop on the way and to be smuggled into the capital. He disappeared from public view on his journey, and the next the country knew, his arrival was announced at the capital. There is little doubt that he would have been assassinated if he had attempted to travel openly throughout his journey.[12]

---

12. Apprised of a plot to assassinate the president-elect in Baltimore, Lincoln's advisors persuaded him to travel from Philadelphia incognito, in the company of detective Allan Pinkerton and bodyguard Ward Lamon, in a sleeping compartment that had been designated for an "invalid passenger." Mary Chesnut recorded the observation of an acquaintance: "Brewster says Lincoln passed through Baltimore, disguised, and at night, and that he did well, for just now Baltimore is dangerous ground. He says he hears from all quarters that the vulgarity of Lincoln, his wife, and his son is beyond credence—a thing you must see before you can believe it." March 1, 1861, *Diary*, 12.

As Lincoln biographer David Herbert Donald notes, despite the veracity of the assassination threat, the papers exploited this escapade to mock the president-elect. See *Lincoln* (London: Jonathan Cape, 1995), 277–79. *New York Times* correspondent Joseph Howard embellished the details by suggesting that Lincoln wore "a Scotch plaid cap and a very long military cloak, so that he was entirely unrecognizable." *New York Times*, February 25, 1861, p.1.

Cartoons of Lincoln in outlandish costumes soon began to surface. In the next century the story would become the subject of an MGM movie, *The Tall Target* (1951), directed by Anthony Mann, with Dick Powell as a police detective and Adolphe Menjou as a secessionist masquerading as a loyal Union officer.

17

Outbreak of the Rebellion—Presiding at a Union Meeting—Mustering Officer of State Troops—Lyon at Camp Jackson— Services Tendered to the Government

The 4th of March, 1861, came, and Abraham Lincoln was sworn to maintain the Union against all its enemies. The secession of one State after another followed, until eleven had gone out. On the 11th of April Fort Sumter, a National fort in the harbor of Charleston, South Carolina, was fired upon by the Southerners and a few days after was captured.[1] The Confederates proclaimed themselves aliens, and thereby

---

1. Arguably, the mist of romance that continues to enshroud the Civil War first rose at Fort Sumter, where P. G. T. Beauregard (1818–1893) faced Major Robert Anderson (1805–1871), who had been an artillery instructor at West Point from 1835–37, when Beauregard was a cadet. Narratives of their encounter in the spring of 1861 emphasize its cordiality, chivalry, and correct military etiquette. Beauregard sent cigars and whiskey, which Anderson politely refused; the Union garrison was permitted to march out of the fort under arms saluting the national flag. Anderson himself saw fit to emphasize that latter detail in his dispatch to the War Department:

> Having defended Fort Sumter for thirty-four hours, until the quarters were entirely burned, the main gate destroyed by fire, the gorge-wall seriously injured, the magazine surrounded by flame, and its door closed from the effect of the heat, four barrels and three cartridges of powder only being available, and no provisions but pork remaining, I accepted the terms of evacuation offered by General Beauregard, being the same offered by him on the 11th inst., prior to the commencement of hostilities, and marched out of Fort Sumter Sunday afternoon, the 14th inst., with colors flying and

drums beating, bringing away company and private property, and saluting my flag with fifty guns.

Biographical Register, vol. 1, s.v. "Anderson, Robert."

Isolated in the hostile and volatile state of South Carolina, their supplies dwindling, "Anderson and his men," suggests James McPherson, "became in northern eyes the defenders of a modern Thermopylae." *Battle Cry*, 266–67. Rebels, too, saw the ancient parallel. At a meeting of a survivors' association of the Charleston District in 1890, for example, one officer declared, "The defenders of Fort Sumter are worthy to stand in history alongside those who held the pass at Thermopylae." "The Defense of Charleston Harbor," *Proceedings at a Special Meeting of The Survivors' Association, of Charleston District*, July 25, 1890 ([Charleston]: Walker, Evans & Cogswell, 1890), 9.

Thermopylae was the mountain pass where a small contingent of Spartans under the command of Leonidas made a last stand against the invading Persian army of Xerxes in 480 BCE. Classical analogues were common in nineteenth-century discussions of Civil War battles. Another engagement, the Battle of Pilot Knob, where Confederates under Sterling Price made a vain stand in Missouri in 1864, came to be called the "Thermopylae of the West." In book 7 of his *History* Herodotus narrates the Spartans' brave, ultimately fatal defense of the mountain pass:

> [T]he Greeks, reckless of their own safety and desperate, since they knew that, as the mountain had been crossed, their destruction was nigh at hand, exerted themselves with the most furious valour against the barbarians.
>
> By this time the spears of the greater number were all shivered, and with their swords they hewed down the ranks of the Persians; and here, as they strove, Leonidas fell fighting bravely, together with many other famous Spartans. . . .
>
> . . . And now there arose a fierce struggle between the Persians and the Lacedæmonians over the body of Leonidas, in which the Greeks four times drove back the enemy, and at last by their great bravery succeeded in bearing off the body. This combat was scarcely ended when the Persians with Ephialtes approached; and the Greeks, informed that they drew nigh, made a change in the manner of their fighting. Drawing back into the narrowest part of the pass, and retreating even behind the cross wall, they posted themselves upon a hillock, where they stood all drawn up together in one close body, except only the Thebans. The hillock whereof I speak is at the entrance of the straits, where the stone lion stands which was set up in honour of Leonidas. Here they defended themselves to the last, such as still had swords using them, and the others resisting with their hands and teeth; till the barbarians, who in part had pulled down the wall and attacked them in front, in part had gone round and now encircled them upon every side, overwhelmed and buried the remnant left beneath showers of missile weapons. . . .
>
> The slain were buried where they fell; and in their honour, nor less in honour of those who died before Leonidas sent the allies away, an inscription was set up, which said,—

debarred themselves of all right to claim protection under the Constitution of the United States. We did not admit the fact that they were aliens, but all the same, they debarred themselves of the right to expect better treatment than people of any other foreign state who make war upon an independent nation. Upon the firing on Sumter President Lincoln issued his first call for troops and soon after a proclamation convening Congress in extra session. The call was for 75,000 volunteers for ninety days' service. If the shot fired at Fort Sumter "was heard around the world," the call of the President for 75,000 men was heard throughout the Northern States. There was not a state in the North of a million of inhabitants that would not have furnished the entire number faster than arms could have been supplied to them, if it had been necessary.[2]

> "Here did four thousand men from Pelops' land
> Against three hundred myriads bravely stand."

This was in honour of all. Another was for the Spartans alone:—

> "Go, stranger, and to Lacedaemon tell
> That here, obeying her behests, we fell."

The History of Herodotus, trans. George Rawlinson, 4 vols. (New York: D. Appleton, 1882), 4:150–53.

2. Fannie Beers, married to a Southerner but living with her mother in the North because of her health when the war broke out, suggests what all this patriotic fervor looked like to partisans of the South:

> Rumors of an engagement in Virginia intensified my suspense until it seemed unbearable. One day I received a kindly warning from an old friend concerning a small Confederate flag which had been sent to me by my husband. It was a tiny silken affair, which I kept in my prayer-book. This harmless possession was magnified by the people of the town into an immense rebel banner, which would eventually float over my mother's house. I had still a few friends whose temperate counsel had hitherto protected me. The note referred to warned me that while I retained possession of the flag I might at any time expect the presence of a mob. I would not have destroyed my treasure for worlds, and how to conceal it became a subject of constant thought. The discovery one day of a jar of "perpetual paste" in mother's secretary suggested an idea which was at once carried out. Applying this strongly adhesive mixture to one side of the flag, I pasted it upon the naked flesh just over my heart. One morning the mail brought certain news of a Confederate victory at Big Bethel. This so exasperated the people that on their way from the post-office an excited crowd halted under my window, crying out, "Where's that rebel woman?" "Let's have that flag," "Show your

Wall of Fort Sumter with shell holes. *From the New York Public Library, https://digitalcollections.nypl .org/items/510d47e0-ba18-a3d9-e040- e00a18064a99.*

As soon as the news of the call for volunteers reached Galena, posters were stuck up calling for a meeting of the citizens at the court-house in the evening. Business ceased entirely; all was excitement; for a time there were no party distinctions; all were Union men, determined to avenge the insult to the national flag. In the evening the court-house was packed. Although a comparative stranger I was called upon to preside; the sole reason, possibly,

---

colors," etc. Carried away by intense excitement, I threw open the blinds, and, waving the newspaper above my head, shouted, "Hurrah Hurrah for Big Bethel! Hurrah for the brave rebels." A perfect howl of rage arose from below, and greater evil might have befallen but for the timely appearance of the venerable village doctor, who now rode hastily in among the excited men, and, standing up in his buggy, cried out, "Friends, she is but a frail, defenceless woman. Be thankful if your morning's work be not her death." Slowly and sullenly the crowd dispersed, while the good doctor hastily ascended to my chamber. I lay with fevered cheeks and burning eyes among the pillows where my mother had placed me. The terrible excitement under which I labored forbade all blame or any allusion to my act of imprudence. I was soothed and tenderly cared for until, under the influence of a sedative, I fell asleep.

Beers reports that this ordeal transformed her from a girl to "a *woman*, full of courage and hope." She put that newfound spirit to use as a nurse working in Alabama, Georgia, and elsewhere. See Fannie A. Beers, *Memories: A Record of Personal Experience and Adventure during Four Years of War* (Philadelphia: J. B. Lippincott, 1889), 10–11.

was that I had been in the army and had seen service. With much embarrassment and some prompting I made out to announce the object of the meeting. Speeches were in order, but it is doubtful whether it would have been safe just then to make other than patriotic ones. There was probably no one in the house, however, who felt like making any other. The two principal speeches were by B. B. Howard, the post-master and a Breckinridge Democrat at the November election the fall before, and John A. Rawlins, an elector on the Douglas ticket. E. B. Washburne, with whom I was not acquainted at that time, came in after the meeting had been organized, and expressed, I understood afterwards, a little surprise that Galena could not furnish a presiding officer for such an occasion without taking a stranger. He came forward and was introduced, and made a speech appealing to the patriotism of the meeting.[3]

After the speaking was over volunteers were called for to form a company.

---

3. Illinois congressman Elihu B. Washburne (1816–1887), the man who met Lincoln's train at the station in Washington at the end of the president-elect's journey, incognito, from Pennsylvania, was Lincoln's longtime champion and friend. He would continue to be Grant's ally throughout the war. His support was invaluable in the wake of Shiloh, when there were many voices in Lincoln's ear calling for the general's dismissal. Grant's staff officer James Harrison Wilson later recalled, "Notwithstanding his tremendous success, Grant was but little known in Washington, and there was among the leading members of the cabinet and of the Senate a lingering doubt as to his entire trustworthiness. . . . Washburne, the member of Congress from his district, was the most potent and aggressive factor in the scheme of reviving the lieutenant generalcy and giving it to Grant." *Under the Old Flag*, 2 vols. (New York: D. Appleton, 1912), 1:345.

Alexander K. McClure is the source for one of the more popular (if probably apocryphal) Lincoln quotations about Grant:

> Lincoln remained silent for what seemed a very long time. He then gathered himself up in his chair and said in a tone of earnestness that I shall never forget: "*I can't spare this man; he fights.*" That was all he said, but I knew that it was enough, and that Grant was safe in Lincoln's hands against his countless hosts of enemies. The only man in all the nation who had the power to save Grant was Lincoln, and he had decided to do it. . . . It seemed to me impossible for him to save Grant without taking a crushing load of condemnation upon himself; but Lincoln was wiser than all those around him, and he not only saved Grant, but he saved him by such well-concerted effort that he soon won popular applause from those who were most violent in demanding Grant's dismissal."

A. K. McClure, *Abraham Lincoln and Men of War-Times* (Philadelphia: Times Publishing, 1892), 180.

The quota of Illinois had been fixed at six regiments; and it was supposed that one company would be as much as would be accepted from Galena. The company was raised and the officers and non-commissioned officers elected before the meeting adjourned. I declined the captaincy before the balloting, but announced that I would aid the company in every way I could and would be found in the service in some position if there should be a war. I never went into our leather store after that meeting, to put up a package or do other business.[4]

The ladies of Galena were quite as patriotic as the men.[5] They could not enlist, but they conceived the idea of sending their first company to the field uniformed. They came to me to get a description of the United States uniform for infantry; subscribed and bought the material; procured tailors to cut out the garments, and the ladies made them up. In a few days the company was in uniform and ready to report at the State capital for assignment. The men all turned out the morning after their enlistment, and I took charge, divided them into squads and superintended their drill. When they were ready to go to Springfield I went with them and remained there until they were assigned to a regiment.

There were so many more volunteers than had been called for that the question whom to accept was quite embarrassing to the governor, Richard

---

4. Grant sounds a decidedly triumphant note in his announcement that he never had to do another piece of business in his father's leather-goods store.

5. As volunteers and paid laborers, women made significant contributions to both the Union and Confederate war efforts. While some served in disguise in the armed forces, many thousands more raised money, produced essential supplies at home, or worked in nursing and other capacities at the front; some worked as spies. For an account of the war work women performed, see Jane E. Schultz, *Women at the Front: Hospital Workers in Civil War America* (Chapel Hill: University of North Carolina Press, 2004). For a detailed examination of the role of women in the South, see Drew Gilpin Faust, *Mothers of Invention: Women of the Slaveholding South in the American Civil War* (Chapel Hill: University of North Carolina Press, 1996). As Margaret Leech notes in *Reveille in Washington*, women also served in various government departments including Treasury, at the Printing Office, and at the Arsenal and Navy Yard manufacturing cartridges. After the war, especially in the South, women were also heavily involved in the project of memorialization. Official government recruiting efforts directed at women to serve in uniform or as civilians, with a particular focus on nursing and clerical work, gathered momentum in the twentieth century.

Yates.[6] The legislature was in session at the time, however, and came to his relief. A law was enacted authorizing the governor to accept the services of ten additional regiments, one from each congressional district, for one month, to be paid by the State, but pledged to go into the service of the United States if there should be a further call during their term. Even with this relief the governor was still very much embarrassed. Before the war was over he was like the President when he was taken with the varioloid: "at last he had something he could give to all who wanted it."[7]

In time the Galena company was mustered into the United States service, forming a part of the 11th Illinois volunteer infantry. My duties, I thought, had ended at Springfield, and I was prepared to start home by the evening train, leaving at nine o'clock. Up to that time I do not think I had been introduced to Governor Yates, or had ever spoken to him. I knew him

World War I–era recruiting poster for government stenographers. Art by Roy Hull Still, ca. 1918. *Library of Congress, Prints and Photographs Division, WWI Posters, LC-DIG-ppmsca-50014.*

World War II–era recruiting poster for the Women's Army Corps, 1943. *Library of Congress, Prints and Photographs Division, LC-USZC4-1653.*

6. Richard Yates (1818–1873), governor of Illinois throughout the war, was a vigorous recruiter and a staunch supporter of Lincoln and the Emancipation Proclamation. After the war, he was elected to the U.S. Senate for one term.

7. Varioloid is a mild form of smallpox that Lincoln caught not long after he delivered the Gettysburg Address in November 1863.

by sight, however, because he was living at the same hotel and I often saw him at table. The evening I was to quit the capital I left the supper room before the governor and was standing at the front door when he came out. He spoke to me, calling me by my old army title "Captain," and said he understood that I was about leaving the city. I answered that I was. He said he would be glad if I would remain over-night and call at the Executive office the next morning. I complied with his request, and was asked to go into the Adjutant-General's office and render such assistance as I could, the governor saying that my army experience would be of great service there. I accepted the proposition.

My old army experience I found indeed of very great service. I was no clerk, nor had I any capacity to become one. The only place I ever found in my life to put a paper so as to find it again was either a side coat-pocket or the hands of a clerk or secretary more careful than myself. But I had been quartermaster, commissary and adjutant in the field. The army forms were familiar to me and I could direct how they should be made out. There was a clerk in the office of the Adjutant-General who supplied my deficiencies. The ease with which the State of Illinois settled its accounts with the government at the close of the war is evidence of the efficiency of Mr. [John S.] Loomis as an accountant on a large scale. He remained in the office until that time.

As I have stated, the legislature authorized the governor to accept the services of ten additional regiments. I had charge of mustering these regiments into the State service. They were assembled at the most convenient railroad centres in their respective congressional districts. I detailed officers to muster in a portion of them, but mustered three in the southern part of the State myself. One of these was to assemble at Belleville, some eighteen miles south-east of St. Louis. When I got there I found that only one or two companies had arrived. There was no probability of the regiment coming together under five days. This gave me a few idle days which I concluded to spend in St. Louis.

There was a considerable force of State militia at Camp Jackson, on the outskirts of St. Louis, at the time. There is but little doubt that it was the design of Governor Claiborn[e] Jackson to have these troops ready to seize the United States arsenal and the city of St. Louis. Why they did not do so I do not know. There was but a small garrison, two companies I think, under Captain N. Lyon at the arsenal, and but for the timely services of the Hon. F. P. Blair, I have little doubt that St. Louis would have gone into rebel hands, and with it the arsenal with all its arms and ammunition.

STRAYED.

From the neighbourhood of Boonville, Mo. on the 18th inst a mischievous JACK who was frightened and run away from his Leader by the sudden appearance of a Lion. He is of no value whatever and only a low PRICE can be given for his capture. Sam

"Strayed," a cartoon showing Lyon routing forces under Sterling Price and Claiborne Fox Jackson, near Boonville, Missouri, 1861. *Library of Congress, Prints and Photographs Division, LC-USZ62-14953.*

Blair was a leader among the Union men of St. Louis in 1861. There was no State government in Missouri at the time that would sanction the raising of troops or commissioned officers to protect United States property, but Blair had probably procured some form of authority from the President to raise troops in Missouri and to muster them into the service of the United States. At all events, he did raise a regiment and took command himself as Colonel. With this force he reported to Captain Lyon and placed himself and regiment under his orders. It was whispered that Lyon thus reinforced intended to break up Camp Jackson and capture the militia. I went down to the arsenal in the morning to see the troops start out. I had known Lyon for two years at West Point and in the old army afterwards. Blair I knew very well by sight. I had heard him speak in the canvass of 1858, possibly several times, but I had never spoken to him. As the troops marched out of the enclosure around the arsenal, Blair was on his horse outside forming them into line preparatory to their march. I introduced myself to him and had a few moments' conversation and expressed my sympathy with his purpose. This was my first personal acquaintance with the Honorable—afterwards

Major-General F. P. Blair. Camp Jackson surrendered without a fight and the garrison was marched down to the arsenal as prisoners of war.

Up to this time the enemies of the government in St. Louis had been bold and defiant, while Union men were quiet but determined. The enemies had their head-quarters in a central and public position on Pine Street, near Fifth—from which the rebel flag was flaunted boldly. The Union men had a place of meeting somewhere in the city, I did not know where, and I doubt whether they dared to enrage the enemies of the government by placing the national flag outside their head-quarters. As soon as the news of the capture of Camp Jackson reached the city the condition of affairs was changed. Union men became rampant, aggressive, and, if you will, intolerant. They proclaimed their sentiments boldly, and were impatient at anything like disrespect for the Union. The secessionists became quiet but were filled with suppressed rage. They had been playing the bully. The Union men ordered the rebel flag taken down from the building on Pine Street. The command was given in tones of authority and it was taken down, never to be raised again in St. Louis.[8]

---

8. Twenty-eight people died in the violence in St. Louis after Blair's contingent of Wide Awakes came to Nathaniel Lyon's assistance in the breaking up of Camp Jackson and the defense of the large federal arsenal. For a lively account of Lyon's actions, which included a scouting expedition in which he disguised himself as Blair's mother-in-law, see McPherson, *Battle Cry*, 290–92. It was this violence that led the commander of the military Department of the West, William S. Harney, to seek a truce with pro-secessionist elements in the state.

Lyon (1818–1861) graduated from West Point a year ahead of Grant. After fighting in the Florida and Mexican Wars, he served on frontier duty in the west. Not long after these events, he was killed at the Battle of Wilson's Creek, Missouri, on August 10, 1861. Lyon was a fervid Unionist: "I would rather see the country lighted up with the flames of war from the centre to its remotest border," he wrote, "than that the great rights and hopes of the human race expire before the arrogance of Secessionists. Of this, however, there is no danger. They are at war with nature and the human heart, and cannot succeed." Cullum describes him as follows:

> Nathaniel Lyon was the Andrew Jackson type of soldier, ever ready to dare all things and take the responsibility. He was well named, for he was as bold as a lion and an utter stranger to fear. This iron-souled man was endued with a genius for war, for to personal he added moral courage, inspired those under him with his own intense enthusiasm, and was cool and rock-fast amid the greatest dangers. Though apparently rash, his intuitive judgment, steady self-possession, and untiring energy crowned his enterprises with success. He pursued his ends, not by soft and pliant means, but by the most direct and audacious measures, having a sublime confi-

I witnessed the scene. I had heard of the surrender of the camp and that the garrison was on its way to the arsenal. I had seen the troops start out in the morning and had wished them success. I now determined to go to the arsenal and await their arrival and congratulate them. I stepped on a car standing at the corner of 4th and Pine streets, and saw a crowd of people standing quietly in front of the head-quarters, who were there for the purpose of hauling down the flag. There were squads of other people at intervals down the street. They too were quiet but filled with suppressed rage, and muttered their resentment at the insult to, what they called, "their" flag. Before the car I was in had started, a dapper little fellow—he would be called a dude at this day—stepped in. He was in a great state of excitement and used adjectives freely to express his contempt for the Union and for those who had just perpetrated such an outrage upon the rights of a free people. There was only one other passenger in the car besides myself when this young man entered. He evidently expected to find nothing but sympathy when he got away from the "mud sills" engaged in compelling a "free people" to pull down a flag they adored. He turned to me saying: "Things have come to a —— pretty pass when a free people can't choose their own flag. Where I came from if a man dares to say a word in favor of the Union we hang him to a limb of the first tree we come to." I replied that "after all we were not so intolerant in St. Louis as we might be; I had not seen a single rebel hung yet, nor heard of one; there were plenty of them who ought to be, however." The

dence in himself and believing in the justice of his cause. A sterner warrior rarely ever trod a battlefield, and a truer patriot never more freely shed his blood in advocacy of his principles. Tenacity of purpose continued till life's end, and his heroic death crowned the martyrdom to his faith. The termination to his brief and brilliant career in Missouri, where Secession held high carnival, saddened millions of Northern hearts, for the nation had looked hopefully to him as one of the most intrepid paladins in its defense.

Biographical Register, vol. 2, s.v. "Lyon, Nathaniel."

After Lyon's death later that summer, Melville celebrated his valor in verse:

> Some hearts there are of deeper sort,
>   Prophetic, sad,
> Which yet for cause are trebly clad;
>   Known death they fly on:
> This wizard-heart and heart-of-oak had Lyon.

"Lyon," *Battle-Pieces*, 24.

young man subsided. He was so crestfallen that I believe if I had ordered him to leave the car he would have gone quietly out, saying to himself: "More Yankee oppression."

By nightfall the late defenders of Camp Jackson were all within the walls of the St. Louis arsenal, prisoners of war. The next day I left St. Louis for Mattoon, Illinois, where I was to muster in the regiment from that congressional district. This was the 21st Illinois infantry, the regiment of which I subsequently became colonel. I mustered one regiment afterwards, when my services for the State were about closed.

Brigadier-General John Pope was stationed at Springfield, as United States mustering officer, all the time I was in the State service.[9] He was a native of Illinois and well acquainted with most of the prominent men in the State. I was a carpet-bagger and knew but few of them. While I was on duty at Springfield the senators, representatives in Congress, ex-governors and the State legislators were nearly all at the State capital. The only acquaintance I made among them was with the governor, whom I was serving, and, by chance, with Senator S. A. Douglas. The only members of Congress I knew were Washburne and Philip Foulk [Fouke]. With the former, though he represented my district and we were citizens of the same town, I only became acquainted at the meeting when the first company of Galena volunteers was raised. Foulk I had known in St. Louis when I was a citizen of that city. I had been three years at West Point with Pope and had served with him a short time during the Mexican war, under General Taylor. I saw a good deal of him during my service with the State. On one occasion he said to me that I ought to go into the United States service. I told him I intended to do so if there was a war. He spoke of his acquaintance with the public men of the State, and said he could get them to recommend me for a position and that

9. A member of the West Point class of 1842, John Pope (1822–1892) was a topographical engineer who served in a number of capacities including the superintending of the Pacific Railroad Survey in the early 1850s. He fought in both theaters of the Civil War and was noted for capturing Island No. 10 in the Mississippi on April 8, 1862. After the war, he commanded the Department of the Missouri and the Division of the Pacific and the Department of California. Cadet Pope once complained to his mother: "The skin is coming off my face up to my nose on account of standing Guard yesterday for four hours during the most intense heat and we are obliged to wear those tall bell crowned leather Caps which with the brass trimmings weigh about 5 Pounds and hurt my head extremely and the rim also coming just to the nose." Seeking to "console" himself with a line from Alexander Pope's *Essay on Man* (1733–34)— "Whatever is, is right"—he found it "but poor Consolation." Letter to Mrs. Lucretia Pope, July 7, 1838, John Pope Papers, Special Collections, USMA Library.

he would do all he could for me. I declined to receive endorsement for permission to fight for my country.[10]

Going home for a day or two soon after this conversation with General Pope, I wrote from Galena the following letter to the Adjutant-General of the Army.

GALENA, ILLINOIS,
May 24, 1861.

COL. L. THOMAS,
Adjt. Gen. U. S. A.,
Washington, D. C.

SIR:—Having served for fifteen years in the regular army, including four years at West Point, and feeling it the duty of every one who has been educated at the Government expense to offer their services for the support of that Government, I have the honor, very respectfully, to tender my services, until the close of the war, in such capacity as may be offered. I would say, in view of my present age and length of service, I feel myself competent to command a regiment, if the President, in his judgment, should see fit to intrust one to me.

Since the first call of the President I have been serving on the staff of the Governor of this State, rendering such aid as I could in the

---

10. "No one sent for Ulysses Simpson Grant no one indeed," Gertrude Stein wrote in her idiosyncratic celebration of Grant as an unlikely American hero:

No indeed. Not at all while anybody went.

No one sent, listen to this, no one sent for Ulysses Simpson Grant as long that is while anybody went.

He could remember that he did not feel that he was sad and never had been.

Is this Ulysses Simpson. Yes it is Ulysses Simpson.

Is this Hiram Ulysses.

Well yes perhaps it is. . . .

How could I know if I were to say so that there is a difference between Hiram Ulysses Grant and Ulysses Simpson Grant.

Who was Grant. . . .

Grant was a general so they said and they knew and he was, he was married, he was a father, he was a general, he was a president, he was a traveler, he was a writer and a reader and he was dead. This is what they said.

Four in America (New Haven, CT: Yale University Press, 1947), 42–44.

organization of our State militia, and am still engaged in that capacity. A letter addressed to me at Springfield, Illinois, will reach me.

I am very respectfully,

Your obt. svt.,

U. S. GRANT.

This letter failed to elicit an answer from the Adjutant-General of the Army. I presume it was hardly read by him, and certainly it could not have been submitted to higher authority. Subsequent to the war General Badeau having heard of this letter applied to the War Department for a copy of it. The letter could not be found and no one recollected ever having seen it. I took no copy when it was written. Long after the application of General Badeau, General Townsend, who had become Adjutant-General of the Army, while packing up papers preparatory to the removal of his office, found this letter in some out-of-the-way place. It had not been destroyed, but it had not been regularly filed away.[11]

11. Adam Badeau (1831–1895) served as Grant's military secretary for years. Badeau began his career as a journalist. He was a friend of the great actor Edwin Booth, brother of John Wilkes Booth, and of the historian Henry Adams, as well as the reputed lover of the cavalryman James Harrison Wilson, who also served for a time on Grant's staff. Badeau and Grant had a falling out over the general's memoirs, in the composition of which Badeau wanted, and would eventually claim, a greater role than was warranted. The final break came when Badeau sent a letter full of criticism of Grant's literary abilities and suffused with disappointment that Grant's book would eclipse the biography he had published a few years earlier. In his reply to the letter's claims about Grant's incompetence to complete a literary project and Badeau's own indispensability, Grant revealed a clear sense of himself as a writer. The letter is reproduced as Grant wrote it, with his strikethroughs, as well as with the editor John Y. Simon's attempts to decipher the handwriting. The latter's interpolations appear in brackets:

In answer to this I have only to say that for the last twenty-fou[r] years I have been very much emplo[yed] in writing. As a soldier I wrote my own orders, directions and reports. They were n[ot] edited nor assistance rendered. As President [I] wrote every official document, I believe, bearing my name. (Messages of course contained abstracts from report of heads of departments, made out and sent to me before the reports themselves were compiled. The I assume no President ever wrote out him self.) All these have been published and widely circulated. The public ~~have~~ has become accustomed to them and ~~no~~ [know] my style of writing. They know that it is not even an attempt to imitate either a literary ~~style nor~~ [or clasical style] and that it is just what it is pure and simple and nothing else. If I succeed

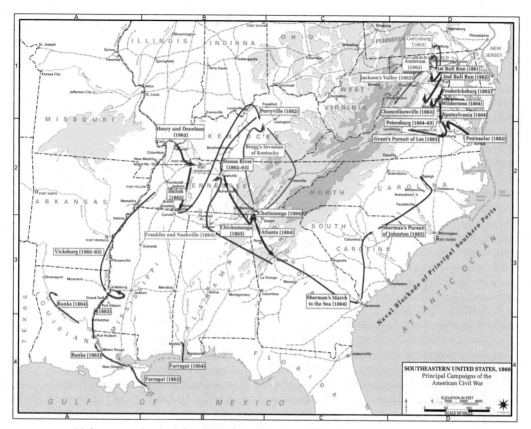

Major campaigns of the Civil War. *West Point Atlas of the Civil War. Courtesy of Department of History, USMA.*

I felt some hesitation in suggesting rank as high as the colonelcy of a regiment, feeling somewhat doubtful whether I would be equal to the position. But I had seen nearly every colonel who had been mustered in from the State

> in telling my story so that others can see, as I do, what I attempt to shew, I will be satisfied. The reader must [also be satisfied] be for he knew from the begining just what to ~~accept~~ [expect].

Letter to Adam Badeau, May 2–5, 1885, *PUSG*, 31:355–56.

On the relationship between Badeau and Grant and its rupture, see McFeely, *Grant*, chapter 28, and White, *Grant*, 642–46. The unpleasant end to the relationship between Grant and Badeau notwithstanding, the latter's three-volume *Military History of Ulysses S. Grant* and his subsequent memoir *Grant in Peace* contain valuable insights and often provide details of a kind Grant omits.

of Illinois, and some from Indiana, and felt that if they could command a regiment properly, and with credit, I could also.

Having but little to do after the muster of the last of the regiments authorized by the State legislature, I asked and obtained of the governor leave of absence for a week to visit my parents in Covington, Kentucky, immediately opposite Cincinnati. General McClellan had been made a major-general and had his headquarters at Cincinnati. In reality I wanted to see him. I had known him slightly at West Point, where we served one year together, and in the Mexican war. I was in hopes that when he saw me he would offer me a position on his staff. I called on two successive days at his office but failed to see him on either occasion, and returned to Springfield.[12]

---

12. George B. McClellan (1826–1885) graduated from West Point in 1846 as an engineering officer. He served in the Mexican War and in the West, and some surmise that the snub to which Grant alludes had its origins in McClellan's encounter with a drunken Grant in the Pacific Northwest, when the latter had been responsible for outfitting McClellan's railroad survey expedition. See Simpson, *Triumph over Adversity*, 58.

McClellan was later a member of the Delafield Commission (1855–56), a group of army officers sent to observe the Crimean War. The knowledge these officers brought back contributed to the increased professionalization of the American army. For a comprehensive discussion of the commission's impact, see Matthew Moten, *The Delafield Commission and the American Military Profession* (College Station: Texas A&M University Press, 2000).

On his return to the United States, McClellan resigned and went to work for the railroads. A controversial and self-aggrandizing figure, McClellan rose to general-in-chief of the Armies before his failure to deliver a decisive blow to Lee in Virginia led Lincoln to relieve him. The disgruntled McClellan ran for president in the 1864 election on the Democratic ticket. Although he was a War Democrat who promised to prosecute the conflict successfully, the party platform called for a negotiated peace.

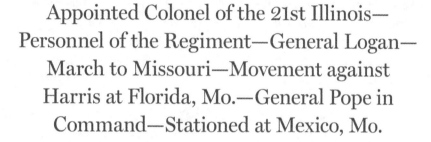

18

Appointed Colonel of the 21st Illinois— Personnel of the Regiment—General Logan— March to Missouri—Movement against Harris at Florida, Mo.—General Pope in Command—Stationed at Mexico, Mo.

While I was absent from the State capital on this occasion the President's second call for troops was issued. This time it was for 300,000 men, for three years or the war. This brought into the United States service all the regiments then in the State service. These had elected their officers from highest to lowest and were accepted with their organizations as they were, except in two instances. A Chicago regiment, the 19th infantry, had elected a very young man to the colonelcy. When it came to taking the field the regiment asked to have another appointed colonel and the one they had previously chosen made lieutenant-colonel. The 21st regiment of infantry, mustered in by me at Mattoon, refused to go into the service with the colonel of their selection in any position. While I was still absent Governor Yates appointed me colonel of this latter regiment. A few days after I was in charge of it and in camp on the fair grounds near Springfield.

My regiment was composed in large part of young men of as good social position as any in their section of the State. It embraced the sons of farmers, lawyers, physicians, politicians, merchants, bankers and ministers, and some men of maturer years who had filled such positions themselves. There were also men in it who could be led astray; and the colonel, elected by the votes of the regiment, had proved to be fully capable of developing all there was in his men of recklessness. It was said that he even went so far at times as to take the guard from their posts and go with them to the village near by and make a night of it. When there came a prospect of battle the regiment wanted to have some one else to lead them. I found it very hard work for a few days to bring all the men into anything like subordination; but the great majority favored discipline, and by the application of a little regular army punishment all were reduced to as good discipline as one could ask.[1]

The ten regiments which had volunteered in the State service for thirty days, it will be remembered, had done so with a pledge to go into the National service if called upon within that time. When they volunteered the government had only called for ninety days' enlistments. Men were called now for three years or the war. They felt that this change of period released them from the obligation of re-volunteering. When I was appointed colonel, the 21st regiment was still in the State service. About the time they were to be mustered into the United States service, such of them as would go, two members of Congress from the State, McClernand and Logan, appeared at the capital and I was introduced to them.[2] I had never seen either of them before, but I had read a great deal about them, and particularly about Logan, in the newspapers. Both were democratic members of Congress, and Logan had been elected from the southern district of the State, where he had a majority of eighteen thousand over his Republican competitor. His district had been settled originally by people from the Southern States, and at the breaking out of secession they sympathized with the South. At the first outbreak of war some of them joined the Southern army; many others were preparing to do so; others rode over the country at night denouncing the Union, and made it as necessary to guard railroad bridges over which National troops had to pass in southern Illinois, as it was in Kentucky or any of the border slave states. Logan's popularity in this district was unbounded.

1. On Grant's ability to take command of this disorderly regiment, Jean Edward Smith observes that no West Point officer better "understood the nature of the Union's volunteer army better than Grant." *Grant*, 108.

For a vivid description of the discipline Grant imposed upon arrival, see Fuller, *Generalship*, 72–75. Lloyd Lewis notes that the regiment had already earned the embarrassing nickname of "Yates's Hellions." *Captain Sam Grant*, 427.

2. John A. McClernand (1812–1900) and Senator John A. Logan (1826–1886) both became what was referred to as "political generals," officers appointed for their ability to recruit soldiers and bring in votes. Logan, who had also been a volunteer in the Mexican War, proved himself a capable military commander. By contrast, McClernand, an inveterate intriguer, proved a thorn in Grant's side until his circulation of a self-aggrandizing report on his exploits at Vicksburg in the summer of 1863 gave Grant the pretext he needed for relieving him.

He knew almost enough of the people in it by their Christian names, to form an ordinary congressional district. As he went in politics, so his district was sure to go. The Republican papers had been demanding that he should announce where he stood on the questions which at that time engrossed the whole of public thought. Some were very bitter in their denunciations of his silence. Logan was not a man to be coerced into an utterance by threats. He did, however, come out in a speech before the adjournment of the special session of Congress which was convened by the President soon after his inauguration, and announced his undying loyalty and devotion to the Union. But I had not happened to see that speech, so that when I first met Logan my impressions were those formed from reading denunciations of him. McClernand, on the other hand, had early taken strong grounds for the maintenance of the Union and had been praised accordingly by the Republican papers. The gentlemen who presented these two members of Congress asked me if I would have any objections to their addressing my regiment. I hesitated a little before answering. It was but a few days before the time set for mustering into the United States service such of the men as were willing to volunteer for three years or the war. I had some doubt as to the effect a speech from Logan might have; but as he was with McClernand, whose sentiments on the all-absorbing questions of the day were well known, I gave my consent. McClernand spoke first; and Logan followed in a speech which he has hardly equalled since for force and eloquence. It breathed a loyalty and devotion to the Union which inspired my men to such a point that they would have volunteered to remain in the army as long as an enemy of the country continued to bear arms against it. They entered the United States service almost to a man.

General Logan went to his part of the State and gave his attention to raising troops. The very men who at first made it necessary to guard the roads in southern Illinois became the defenders of the Union. Logan entered the service himself as colonel of a regiment and rapidly rose to the rank of major-general. His district, which had promised at first to give much trouble to the government, filled every call made upon it for troops, without resorting to the draft. There was no call made when there were not more volunteers than were asked for. That congressional district stands credited at the War Department to-day with furnishing more men for the army than it was called on to supply.

I remained in Springfield with my regiment until the 3d of July, when I was ordered to Quincy, Illinois. By that time the regiment was in a good state of discipline and the officers and men were well up in the company drill. There was direct railroad communication between Springfield and Quincy, but I thought it would be good preparation for the troops to march there. We had no transportation for our camp and garrison equipage, so wagons were hired for the occasion and on the 3d of July we started. There was no hurry, but fair marches were made every day until the Illinois River was crossed. There I was overtaken by a dispatch saying that the destination of the regiment had been changed to Ironton, Missouri, and ordering me to halt where I was and await the arrival of a steamer which had been dispatched up the Illinois River to take the regiment to St. Louis. The boat, when it did come, grounded on a sand-bar a few miles below where we were in camp. We remained there several days waiting to have the boat get off the bar, but before this occurred news came that an Illinois regiment was surrounded by rebels at a point on the Hannibal and St. Joe Railroad some miles west of Palmyra, in Missouri, and I was ordered to proceed with all dispatch to their relief. We took the cars and reached Quincy in a few hours.

When I left Galena for the last time to take command of the 21st regiment I took with me my oldest son, Frederick D. Grant, then a lad of eleven years of age. On receiving the order to take rail for Quincy I wrote to Mrs. Grant, to relieve what I supposed would be her great anxiety for one so young going into danger, that I would send Fred home from Quincy by river. I received a prompt letter in reply decidedly disapproving my proposition, and urging that the lad should be allowed to accompany me. It came too late. Fred was already on his way up the Mississippi bound for Dubuque, Iowa, from which place there was a railroad to Galena.

My sensations as we approached what I supposed might be "a field of battle" were anything but agreeable. I had been in all the engagements in Mexico that it was possible for one person to be in; but not in command. If some one else had been colonel and I had been lieutenant-colonel I do not think I would have felt any trepidation. Before we were prepared to cross the Mississippi River at Quincy my anxiety was relieved; for the men of the besieged regiment came straggling into town. I am inclined to think both sides got frightened and ran away.

I took my regiment to Palmyra and remained there for a few days, until relieved by the 19th Illinois infantry. From Palmyra I proceeded to Salt River, the railroad bridge over which had been destroyed by the enemy. Colonel John M. Palmer at that time commanded the 13th Illinois, which was acting as a guard to workmen who were engaged in rebuilding this bridge. Palmer was my senior and commanded the two regiments as long as we remained together. The bridge was finished in about two weeks, and I received orders to move against Colonel Thomas Harris, who was said to be encamped at the little town of Florida, some twenty-five miles south of where we then were.

At the time of which I now write we had no transportation and the country about Salt River was sparsely settled, so that it took some days to collect teams and drivers enough to move the camp and garrison equipage of a regiment nearly a thousand strong, together with a week's supply of provision and some ammunition. While preparations for the move were going on I felt quite comfortable; but when we got on the road and found every house deserted I was anything but easy. In the twenty-five miles we had to march we did not see a person, old or young, male or female, except two horsemen who were on a road that crossed ours. As soon as they saw us they decamped as fast as their horses could carry them. I kept my men in the ranks and forbade their entering any of the deserted houses or taking anything from them. We halted at night on the road and proceeded the next morning at an early hour. Harris had been encamped in a creek bottom for the sake of being near water. The hills on either side of the creek extend to a considerable height, possibly more than a hundred feet. As we approached the brow of the hill from which it was expected we could see Harris' camp, and possibly find his men ready formed to meet us, my heart kept getting higher and higher until it felt to me as though it was in my throat. I would have given anything then to have been back in Illinois, but I had not the moral courage to halt and consider what to do; I kept right on. When we reached a point from which the valley below was in full view I halted. The place where Harris had been encamped a few days before was still there and the marks of a recent encampment were plainly visible, but the troops were gone. My heart resumed its place. It occurred to me at once that Harris had been as much afraid of me as I had been of him. This was a view of the question I had never taken before; but it was one I never forgot afterwards. From that event to the close of the war, I never experienced trepidation upon confronting an enemy, though I always felt more or less anxiety. I never forgot that he had as much reason to fear my forces as I had his. The lesson was valuable.[3]

3. This is a pivotal moment in the narrative: Grant comes to realize what it means to assume the responsibility of command in the way that he had watched Taylor accept it in Mexico. The episode also illustrates something larger about the development of ideas regarding military leadership, specifically attitudes toward the kinds of personal risk commanders ought to take in battle. Grant falls somewhere along the continuum stretching from ancient commanders who led from the front and the so-called chateau

Inquiries at the village of Florida divulged the fact that Colonel Harris, learning of my intended movement, while my transportation was being collected took time by the forelock and left Florida before I had started from Salt River. He had increased the distance between us by forty miles. The next day I started back to my old camp at Salt River bridge. The citizens living on the line of our march had returned to their houses after we passed, and finding everything in good order, nothing carried away, they were at their front doors ready to greet us now. They had evidently been led to believe that the National troops carried death and devastation with them wherever they went.

In a short time after our return to Salt River bridge I was ordered with my regiment to the town of Mexico. General Pope was then commanding the district embracing all of the State of Missouri between the Mississippi and Missouri rivers, with his headquarters in the village of Mexico. I was assigned to the command of a sub-district embracing the troops in the immediate neighborhood, some three regiments of infantry and a section of artillery. There was one regiment encamped by the side of mine. I assumed command of the whole and the first night sent the commander of the other regiment the parole and countersign. Not wishing to be outdone in courtesy, he immediately sent me the countersign for his regiment for the night. When he was informed that the countersign sent to him was for use with his

---

generals of the First World War. He certainly took risks and came under fire repeatedly during the Civil War; however, as the military historian John Keegan explains, he did not expose himself recklessly in an era in which the rifle had increased both the density and range of fire on the battlefield:

> Grant usually rode alone, and he was often alone on the battlefield, just as Wellington was at the close of Waterloo. But unlike Wellington, and even more unlike Alexander, he felt no need to share the risks of the individual soldier. Quite the contrary. To the questions In front always? sometimes? or never? Grant would probably have tried to avoid giving an answer but, if pressed, would have uttered a grudging "Never if I can help it."

Keegan, *Mask of Command* (New York: Penguin, 1987), 208.

William Styron offers insight into the psychology of competing fears in his short story about a Marine in the Pacific during World War II, "Elobey, Annobón, and Corisco": "I found myself in a conflict I had never anticipated: afraid of going into battle, yet even more afraid of betraying my fear, which would be an ugly prelude to the most harrowing fear of all—that when forced to the test in combat I would demonstrate my absolute terror, fall apart and fail my fellow Marines." *The Suicide Run* (New York: Random House, 2009), 192.

regiment as well as mine, it was difficult to make him understand that this was not an unwarranted interference of one colonel over another. No doubt he attributed it for the time to the presumption of a graduate of West Point over a volunteer pure and simple. But the question was soon settled and we had no further trouble.

My arrival in Mexico had been preceded by that of two or three regiments in which proper discipline had not been maintained, and the men had been in the habit of visiting houses without invitation and helping themselves to food and drink, or demanding them from the occupants. They carried their muskets while out of camp and made every man they found take the oath of allegiance to the government. I at once published orders prohibiting the soldiers from going into private houses unless invited by the inhabitants, and from appropriating private property to their own or to government uses. The people were no longer molested or made afraid. I received the most marked courtesy from the citizens of Mexico as long as I remained there.

Up to this time my regiment had not been carried in the school of the soldier beyond the company drill, except that it had received some training on the march from Springfield to the Illinois River. There was now a good opportunity of exercising it in the battalion drill. While I was at West Point the tactics used in the army had been Scott's and the musket the flint lock. I had never looked at a copy of tactics from the time of my graduation. My standing in that branch of studies had been near the foot of the class. In the Mexican war in the summer of 1846, I had been appointed regimental quartermaster and commissary and had not been at a battalion drill since. The arms had been changed since then and Hardee's tactics had been adopted. I got a copy of tactics and studied one lesson, intending to confine the exercise of the first day to the commands I had thus learned. By pursuing this course from day to day I thought I would soon get through the volume.[4]

---

4. George Sherston, Siegfried Sassoon's alter ego, describes an analogous experience familiarizing himself with the latest British Army manual on the Western Front in the third volume of Sassoon's fictionalized memoir:

> Sitting in the Company Mess on a fine breezy afternoon copying out and assimilating a lecture on Consolidation of Captured Trenches, which I shall spout to the Company as though it came out of my head, though it is all from the recently issued *Manual for the training and employment of Platoons* which I spent yesterday evening in studying. I now feel rather "on

Troops drilling near Washington, D.C. *Library of Congress, Prints and Photographs Division, Civil War Photographs, LC-DIG-ppmsca-33193.*

We were encamped just outside of town on the common, among scattering suburban houses with enclosed gardens, and when I got my regiment in line and rode to the front I soon saw that if I attempted to follow the lesson I had studied I would have to clear away some of the houses and garden fences to make room. I perceived at once, however, that Hardee's tactics—a mere translation from the French with Hardee's name attached—was nothing more than common sense and the progress of the age applied to Scott's system. The commands were abbreviated and the movement expedited. Under the old tactics almost every change in the order of march was

---

my toes" about being in France, and am resolved to make a good job of it this time. The manual (a 32 page pamphlet) is a masterpiece of common sense, clearness, and condensation, and entirely supersedes the academic old *Infantry Training 1914* which was based on Boer War experience and caused me much mystification. . . . I tell myself that I simply must become an efficient company commander. It is the only way I can do the men any good, and they are such a decent well-behaved lot that it is a pleasure to work with them and do what one can for their comfort.

Sherston's Progress (1936; New York: Penguin Classics, 2013), 100–1.

preceded by a "halt," then came the change, and then the "forward march."
With the new tactics all these changes could be made while in motion. I
found no trouble in giving commands that would take my regiment where
I wanted it to go and carry it around all obstacles. I do not believe that the
officers of the regiment ever discovered that I had never studied the tactics
that I used.[5]

5. Grant was no martinet. Here he displays a characteristic amalgamation of humor and
common sense—and an impatience with what Paul Fussell would label "chickenshit" in
his analysis of World War II:

> Chickenshit . . . refers to behavior that makes military life worse than it
> need be: petty harassment of the weak by the strong; open scrimmage for
> power and authority and prestige; sadism thinly disguised as necessary dis-
> cipline; a constant "paying off of old scores"; and insistence on the letter
> rather than the spirit of ordinances. Chickenshit is so called—instead of
> horse- or bull- or elephant shit—because it is small-minded and ignoble
> and takes the trivial seriously. Chickenshit can be recognized instantly
> because it never has anything to do with winning the war.

Wartime: Understanding and Behavior in the Second World War (New York: Oxford University Press, 1989), 80.

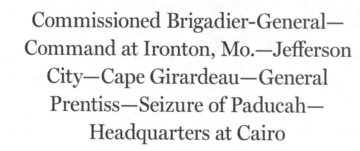

Commissioned Brigadier-General— Command at Ironton, Mo.—Jefferson City—Cape Girardeau—General Prentiss—Seizure of Paducah— Headquarters at Cairo

I had not been in Mexico many weeks when, reading a St. Louis paper, I found the President had asked the Illinois delegation in Congress to recommend some citizens of the State for the position of brigadier-general, and that they had unanimously recommended me as first on a list of seven. I was very much surprised because, as I have said, my acquaintance with the Congressmen was very limited and I did not know of anything I had done to inspire such confidence. The papers of the next day announced that my name, with three others, had been sent to the Senate, and a few days after our confirmation was announced.

When appointed brigadier-general I at once thought it proper that one of my aides should come from the regiment I had been commanding, and so selected Lieutenant C. B. Lagow. While living in St. Louis, I had had a desk in the law office of McClellan, Moody and Hillyer. Difference in views between the members of the firm on the questions of the day, and general hard times in the border cities, had broken up this firm. Hillyer was quite a young man, then in his twenties, and very brilliant. I asked him to accept a place on my staff. I also wanted to take one man from my new home, Galena. The canvass in the Presidential campaign the fall before had brought out a young lawyer by the name of John A. Rawlins, who proved himself one of the ablest speakers in the State. He was also a candidate for elector on the Douglas ticket. When Sumter was fired upon and the integrity of the Union

Members of Grant's staff, with the photographer Mathew Brady at far left, City Point, Virginia, 1864. *Library of Congress, Prints and Photographs Division, LC-DIG-cwpb-02958.*

threatened, there was no man more ready to serve his country than he. I wrote at once asking him to accept the position of assistant adjutant-general with the rank of captain, on my staff. He was about entering the service as major of a new regiment then organizing in the north-western part of the State; but he threw this up and accepted my offer.

Neither Hillyer nor Lagow proved to have any particular taste or special qualifications for the duties of the soldier, and the former resigned during the Vicksburg campaign; the latter I relieved after the battle of Chattanooga. Rawlins remained with me as long as he lived, and rose to the rank of brigadier general and chief-of-staff to the General of the Army—an office created for him—before the war closed. He was an able man, possessed of

great firmness, and could say "no" so emphatically to a request which he
thought should not be granted that the person he was addressing would
understand at once that there was no use of pressing the matter. General
Rawlins was a very useful officer in other ways than this. I became very
much attached to him.[1]

Shortly after my promotion I was ordered to Ironton, Missouri, to command a district in that part of the State, and took the 21st Illinois, my old
regiment, with me. Several other regiments were ordered to the same destination about the same time. Ironton is on the Iron Mountain railroad, about
seventy miles south of St. Louis, and situated among hills rising almost to
the dignity of mountains. When I reached there, about the 8th of August,
Colonel B. Gratz Brown—afterwards Governor of Missouri and in 1872
Vice-Presidential candidate—was in command. Some of his troops were
ninety days' men and their time had expired some time before.[2] The men

1. John A. Rawlins (1831–1869) eventually became Grant's chief of staff and remained
with him after the war until his death of tuberculosis. Biographers suggest that Rawlins, a devout temperance advocate, was a steadying influence on Grant throughout the
war and was largely successful in preventing him from drinking. For a contemporary
account of Rawlins's role as well as of the workings of Grant's staff more generally, see
Horace Porter, *Campaigning with Grant*. For the views of modern historians, see Simpson, *Triumph over Adversity*, and Keegan, *Mask of Command*, 194–202.

2. The ninety-day enlistment period suggests how long the government thought the war
would last. Walt Whitman captured the eagerness of those early volunteers in "Drum-
Taps," which depicts new recruits tramping through the city to the "wild cheers of the
crowd." "How good they look," Whitman observes, "with their guns on their shoulders! / . . . Mannahatta a-march—and it's O to sing it well! / It's O for a manly life in
the camp!" *Drum-Taps* (New York, 1865), 6–7.

Few volunteers anticipated the daily horrors of the war. For a detailed account of
the hardships they faced, see Michael C. C. Adams, *Living Hell: The Dark Side of the Civil
War* (Baltimore, MD: Johns Hopkins University Press, 2005).

John Beatty, colonel of the 3rd Ohio Regiment, testifies to the indiscipline of the
volunteers and reveals the challenges he faced, in the absence of the regimental commander, in attempting to gain control of his troops in camp during January 1862:

> To-day a soldier about half drunk was arrested for leaving camp
> without permission and brought to my quarters; he had two canteens of
> whisky on his person. I remonstrated with him mildly, but he grew saucy,
> insubordinate, and finally insolent and insulting; he said he did not care a
> damn for what I thought or did, and was ready to go to the guard-house;
> in fact wanted to go there. Finally, becoming exasperated, I took the can-
> teens from him, poured out the whisky, and directed Captain Patterson to
> strap him to a tree until he cooled off somewhat. The Captain failing in

had no clothing but what they had volunteered in, and much of this was so worn that it would hardly stay on. General Hardee—the author of the tactics I did not study—was at Greenville, some twenty-five miles further south, it was said, with five thousand Confederate troops. Under these circumstances Colonel Brown's command was very much demoralized. A squadron of cavalry could have ridden into the valley and captured the entire force. Brown

his efforts to fasten him securely, I took my saddle girth, backed him up to the tree, buckled him to it, and returned to my quarters. This proved to be the last straw which broke the unfortunate camel's back. It was a high-handed outrage upon the person of a volunteer soldier; the last and worst of the many arbitrary and severe acts of which I had been guilty. The regiment seemed to arise *en masse*, and led on by a few reckless men who had long disliked me, advanced with threats and fearful oaths toward my tent. The bitter hatred which the men entertained for me had now culminated. It being Sunday the whole regiment was off duty, and while some, and perhaps many, of the boys had no desire to resort to violent measures, yet all evidently sympathized with the prisoner, and regarded my action as arbitrary and cruel. The position of the soldier was a humiliating one, but it gave him no bodily pain. Possibly I had no authority for punishing him in this way; and had I taken time for reflection it is more than probable I should have found some other and less objectionable mode; confinement in the guard-house, however, would have been no punishment for such a man; on the contrary it would have afforded him that relief from disagreeable duty which he desired. At any rate the act, whether right or wrong, had been done, and I must either stand by it now or abandon all hope of controlling the regiment hereafter. I watched the mob, unobserved by it, from an opening in my tent door. Saw it gather, consult, advance, and could hear the boisterous and threatening language very plainly. Buckling my pistol belt under my coat where it could not be seen, I stepped out just as the leaders advanced to the tree for the purpose of releasing the man. I asked them very quietly what they proposed to do. Then I explained to them how the soldier had violated orders, which I was bound by my oath to enforce; how, when I undertook to remonstrate kindly against such unsoldierly conduct, he had insulted and defied me. Then I continued as calmly as I ever spoke, "I understand you have come here to untie him; let the man who desires to undertake the work begin—if there be a dozen men here who have it in their minds to do this thing—let them step forward—I dare them to do it." They saw before them a quiet, plain man who was ready to die if need be; they could not doubt his honesty of purpose. He gave them time to act and answer, they stood irresolute and silent; with a wave of the hand he bade them go to their quarters, and they went.

Citizen-Soldier, 91–93.

himself was gladder to see me on that occasion than he ever has been since. I relieved him and sent all his men home, within a day or two, to be mustered out of service.[3]

---

3. Sherman tells the story of a mutinous ninety-day man, a lawyer turned captain, who decided after the debacle of Bull Run, which changed everyone's understanding about the nature of this war, that he was going home. For Sherman (as for his untested volunteers), battle was a new and harrowing experience: "for the first time in my life I saw cannonballs strike men and crash through the trees and saplings above and around us, and realized the always sickening confusion as one approaches a fight from the rear," he records in his *Memoirs*. Thoroughly disgusted by the army's chaotic flight from Bull Run, he subsequently attempted to restore some order in camp at Fort Corcoran:

> The Sixty-ninth still occupied Fort Corcoran, and one morning, after reveille, when I had just received the report, had dismissed the regiment, and was leaving, I found myself in a crowd of men crossing the drawbridge on their way to a barn close by, where they had their sinks; among them was an officer, who said: "Colonel, I am going to New York today. What can I do for you?" I answered: "How can you go to New York? I do not remember to have signed a leave for you." He said, "No; he did not want a leave. He had engaged to serve three months, and had already served more than that time. If the Government did not intend to pay him, he could afford to lose the money; that he was a lawyer, and had neglected his business long enough, and was then going home." I noticed that a good many of the soldiers had paused about us to listen, and knew that, if this officer could defy me, they also would. So I turned on him sharp, and said: "Captain, this question of your term of service has been submitted to the rightful authority, and the decision has been published in orders. You are a soldier, and must submit to orders till you are properly discharged. If you attempt to leave without orders, it will be mutiny, and I will shoot you like a dog! Go back into the fort *now*, instantly, and don't dare to leave without my consent." I had on an overcoat, and may have had my hand about the breast, for he looked at me hard, paused a moment, and then turned back into the fort. The men scattered, and I returned to the house where I was quartered, close by.

Later that day, Lincoln visited the various encampments and gave speeches to the assembled soldiers. When they cheered, he told them, "Don't cheer, boys. I confess I rather like it myself, but Colonel Sherman here says it is not military; and I guess we had better defer to his opinion." At each stop Lincoln offered "redress in case of grievance," and at Fort Corcoran he encountered the obstreperous captain:

> This officer forced his way through the crowd to the carriage, and said: "Mr. President, I have a cause of grievance. This morning I went to speak to Colonel Sherman, and he threatened to shoot me." Mr. Lincoln, who was still standing, said, "Threatened to shoot you?" "Yes, sir, he threatened

Within ten days after reaching Ironton I was prepared to take the offensive against the enemy at Greenville. I sent a column east out of the valley we were in, with orders to swing around to the south and west and come into the Greenville road ten miles south of Ironton. Another column marched on the direct road and went into camp at the point designated for the two columns to meet. I was to ride out the next morning and take per-

to shoot me." Mr. Lincoln looked at him, then at me, and stooping his tall, spare form toward the officer, said to him in a loud stage-whisper, easily heard for some yards around: "Well, if I were you, and he threatened to shoot, I would not trust him, for I believe he would do it." The officer turned about and disappeared, and the men laughed at him. Soon the carriage drove on, and, as we descended the hill, I explained the facts to the President, who answered, "Of course I didn't know any thing about it, but I thought you knew your own business best." I thanked him for his confidence, and assured him that what he had done would go far to enable me to maintain good discipline, and it did.

Sherman, *Memoirs*, 1:186, 188–91.

Federal Cavalry at Sudley Ford, Bull Run, Virginia. Photograph by George Barnard, 1862. *Library of Congress, Prints and Photographs Division, Civil War Photographs, LC-DIG-cwpb-00955.*

Battlefield dead after First Bull Run. *Library of Congress, Prints and Photographs Division, Civil War Photographs, LC-DIG-cwpbh-03383.*

sonal command of the movement. My experience against Harris, in northern Missouri, had inspired me with confidence. But when the evening train came in, it brought General B. M. Prentiss with orders to take command of the district.[4] His orders did not relieve me, but I knew that by law I was senior, and at that time even the President did not have the authority to assign a junior to command a senior of the same grade. I therefore gave General Prentiss the situation of the troops and the general condition of affairs, and started for St. Louis the same day. The movement against the rebels at Greenville went no further.

From St. Louis I was ordered to Jefferson City, the capital of the State, to take command. General Sterling Price, of the Confederate army, was thought to be threatening the capital, Lexington, Chillicothe and other comparatively large towns in the central part of Missouri. I found a good many troops in Jefferson City, but in the greatest confusion, and no one person knew where they all were. Colonel Mulligan, a gallant man, was in command, but he had not been educated as yet to his new profession and did not know how to maintain discipline. I found that volunteers had obtained permission from the department commander, or claimed they had, to raise, some of them, regiments; some battalions; some companies—the officers to be commissioned according to the number of men they brought into the service. There were recruiting stations all over town, with notices, rudely lettered on boards over the doors, announcing the arm of service and length of time for which recruits at that station would be received. The law required all volunteers to serve for three years or the war. But in Jefferson City in August, 1861, they were recruited for different periods and on different conditions; some were enlisted for six months, some for a year, some without any condition as to where they were to serve, others were not to be sent out of the State. The recruits were principally men from regiments stationed there and already in the service, bound for three years if the war lasted that long.

The city was filled with Union fugitives who had been driven by guerilla bands to take refuge with the National troops. They were in a deplorable condition and must have starved but for the support the government gave them. They had generally made their escape with a team or two, sometimes a yoke of oxen with a mule or a horse in the lead. A little bedding

---

4. Benjamin M. Prentiss (1819–1901) would later make a valiant stand at the Hornet's Nest at the Battle of Shiloh, where he was surrounded and captured by the rebels. Subsequently exchanged, he would go on to fight in Mississippi and Arkansas.

besides their clothing and some food had been thrown into the wagon. All else of their worldly goods were abandoned and appropriated by their former neighbors; for the Union man in Missouri who staid at home during the rebellion, if he was not immediately under the protection of the National troops, was at perpetual war with his neighbors. I stopped the recruiting service, and disposed the troops about the outskirts of the city so as to guard all approaches. Order was soon restored.

I had been at Jefferson City but a few days when I was directed from department headquarters to fit out an expedition to Lexington, Booneville and Chillicothe, in order to take from the banks in those cities all the funds they had and send them to St. Louis. The western army had not yet been supplied with transportation. It became necessary therefore to press into the service teams belonging to sympathizers with the rebellion or to hire those of Union men. This afforded an opportunity of giving employment to such of the refugees within our lines as had teams suitable for our purposes. They accepted the service with alacrity. As fast as troops could be got off they were moved west some twenty miles or more. In seven or eight days from my assuming command at Jefferson City, I had all the troops, except a small garrison, at an advanced position and expected to join them myself the next day.

But my campaigns had not yet begun, for while seated at my office door, with nothing further to do until it was time to start for the front, I saw an officer of rank approaching, who proved to be Colonel Jefferson C. Davis.[5] I

H. Mosler, "The Assassination of General Nelson by General Jefferson C. Davis," *Harper's Weekly*, October 18, 1862.

5. On September 29, 1862, more than a half-century after Alexander Hamilton met Aaron Burr in Weehawken, New Jersey, in a fatal duel, the same sensitivity and nervous readiness to detect perceived slights led to the shooting of William "Bull" Nelson (1824–1862) by fellow Union general Jefferson C. Davis (1828–1879) in the Galt House hotel in Louisville, Kentucky. These two experienced officers quarreled over preparations to defend Louisville against a potential Confederate attack. Nelson lost his temper

and humiliated Davis by cursing at him and threatening to have the provost marshal forcibly remove him to Cincinnati. Davis evidently replied by insisting that he, too, was a general officer and merited the respect owed a gentleman. Brooding over the injury for several days, Davis determined to confront Nelson. He found him in the hotel lobby and demanded an apology. As the war correspondent Alf Burnett, at the Galt House that day, reported, when "Davis advanced and demanded an explanation, Nelson turned and cursed him, calling him an infamous puppy, and using other violent language unfit for publication. Upon [Davis's] pressing his demand for an explanation, Nelson, who was an immensely powerful and large man, took the back of his hand and deliberately slapped General Davis's face." Turning to Burnett, Davis demanded, "Did your hear that d—d insolent scoundrel insult me, Sir? I suppose, he don't know me, Sir. I'll teach him a lesson, Sir." Borrowing a pistol from a captain who happened to be walking by, Davis—"Davis's face was livid, and such a look of mingled indignation, mortification, and determination I never before beheld," Burnett attested—walked toward Nelson, by then on his way upstairs, called to him to halt, and shot him in the chest. Davis was arrested but later released after two witnesses (both officers on Nelson's staff), were killed in action. He served out the rest of the war with distinction. Burnett offers the opinion of another bystander: "had not Davis acted as he did, after the gross provocation he received, Davis would have deserved to have been shot himself." Significantly, Burnett concludes his account by condemning not Davis, but Nelson: "It is a great pity so brave a man should have had so little control over his temper." *Incidents of the War: Humorous, Pathetic, and Descriptive* (Cincinnati, OH: Rickey & Carroll, 1863), 28–29.

There is something grotesque about this incident: a self-described officer and gentleman, in the midst of a war, expending the same deadly energy on a comrade that he ought to have done on their common enemy. This is the kind of soldier Jaques describes in his speech on the seven ages of man in Shakespeare's comedy *As You Like It*: "Jealous in honour, sudden and quick in quarrel, / Seeking the bubble reputation / Even in the cannon's mouth." 2.7.152–53.

In his volume of *Military Miscellanies*, published in 1889, Colonel James B. Fry reported that Davis remained unapologetic: "I never heard that he expressed, and I do not believe that he felt, any regret for having killed Nelson." But Fry, alive to the paradox of the gentleman's code, goes on to say that early versions of the episode unjustly favored Davis:

> Though Davis was aggrieved, it is difficult to see now, even if it was not then, how he can be justified in provoking the final quarrel and committing the foul deed of death. The facts will not sustain the theory of self-defence; and the military law, as he well knew, offered prompt and ample redress for all the wrong Nelson had done him at their first meeting. But he made no appeal to law. On the contrary he deliberately took all law into his own hands.

Military Miscellanies (New York: Brentano's, 1889), 497, 500.

Another officer, Richard W. Johnson, who regarded both men as "distinguished officers," noted, "the killing of Nelson did not seem to lessen [Davis's] standing as an officer or interfere with his military advancement." *A Soldier's Reminiscences in Peace and War* (Philadelphia: J. B. Lippincott, 1886), 256–57.

Davis served for the duration of the war and was mustered out in 1866.

had never met him before, but he introduced himself by handing me an order for him to proceed to Jefferson City and relieve me of the command. The orders directed that I should report at department headquarters at St. Louis without delay, to receive important special instructions. It was about an hour before the only regular train of the day would start. I therefore turned over to Colonel Davis my orders, and hurriedly stated to him the progress that had been made to carry out the department instructions already described. I had at that time but one staff officer,[6] doing myself all the detail work usually performed by an adjutant-general. In an hour after being relieved from the command I was on my way to St. Louis, leaving my single staff officer to follow the next day with our horses and baggage.

The "important special instructions" which I received the next day, assigned me to the command of the district of south-east Missouri, embracing all the territory south of St. Louis, in Missouri, as well as all southern Illinois. At first I was to take personal command of a combined expedition that had been ordered for the capture of Colonel Jeff. Thompson, a sort of independent or partisan commander who was disputing with us the possession of south-east Missouri.[7] Troops had been ordered to move from Ironton

---

6. C. B. Lagow, the others not yet having joined me. [Note to the first edition.]

7. Frémont proclaimed martial law in Missouri, on August 30, 1861, citing the "crimes and outrages" of "bands of murderers and marauders, who infest nearly every county in the State, and avail themselves of the public misfortunes and the vicinity of a hostile force to gratify private and neighborhood vengeance, and who find an enemy wherever they find plunder." *OR*, ser. 1, vol. 3, 466.

In response to this declaration, the Missouri raider Meriwether Jeff Thompson (1826–1876), sometimes known as the Swamp Fox, published his own proclamation on September 2, 1861:

Whereas, Maj. Gen. John C. Frémont, commanding the minions of Abraham Lincoln in the State of Missouri, has seen fit to declare martial law throughout the whole State, and has threatened to shoot any citizen soldier found in arms within certain limits; also to confiscate the property and free the negroes belonging to members of the Missouri State Guard:

Therefore, know ye, that I, M. Jeff. Thompson, brigadier-general of the First Military District of Missouri, having not only the military authority of brigadier-general, but certain police powers, granted by Acting Governor Thomas C. Reynolds, and confirmed afterward by Governor Jackson, do most solemnly promise that for every member of the Missouri State Guard, or soldier of our allies, the armies of the Confederate States, who shall be put to death in pursuance of this said order of General Frémont, I will "*hang, draw* and quarter" a minion of said Abraham Lincoln.

While I am anxious that this unfortunate war shall be conducted, if

to Cape Girardeau, sixty or seventy miles to the south-east, on the Mississippi River; while the forces at Cape Girardeau had been ordered to move to Jacksonville, ten miles out towards Ironton; and troops at Cairo and Bird's Point, at the junction of the Ohio and Mississippi rivers, were to hold themselves in readiness to go down the Mississippi to Belmont, eighteen miles below, to be moved west from there when an officer should come to command them. I was the officer who had been selected for this purpose. Cairo was to become my headquarters when the expedition terminated.

In pursuance of my orders I established my temporary headquarters at Cape Girardeau and sent instructions to the commanding officer at Jackson, to inform me of the approach of General Prentiss from Ironton. Hired wagons were kept moving night and day to take additional rations to Jackson, to supply the troops when they started from there. Neither General Prentiss nor Colonel Marsh, who commanded at Jackson, knew their destination. I drew up all the instructions for the contemplated move, and kept them in my pocket until I should hear of the junction of our troops at Jackson. Two or three days after my arrival at Cape Girardeau, word came that General Prentiss was approaching that place (Jackson). I started at once to meet him there and to give him his orders. As I turned the first corner of a street after starting, I saw a column of cavalry passing the next street in front of me. I turned and rode around the block the other way, so as to meet the head of the column. I found there General Prentiss himself, with a large escort. He

possible, upon the most liberal principles of civilized warfare, and every order that I have issued has been with that object yet, if this rule is to be abandoned (it must first be done by our enemies), I intend to exceed General Frémont in his excesses and will make all tories that come in my reach rue the day that a different policy was adopted by their leaders.

Already mills, barns, warehouses, and other private property have been wastefully and wantonly destroyed by the enemy in this district, while we have taken nothing except articles strictly contraband or absolutely necessary. Should these things be repeated, I will retaliate tenfold, so help me God!

OR, ser. 1, vol. 3, 693.

This exchange reveals the vicious nature of guerrilla warfare in regions like Missouri and Kansas. When Thompson was defeated by Union forces at Frederickton, Missouri, the New York Times declared it fit punishment: "The chastisement of the semi-savage, THOMPSON, who so lately talked in his gasconading proclamation of 'hanging, drawing and quartering' Unionists, will diffuse intense delight in Missouri. He will fall back now, and Winter, perhaps, in the swamps of Arkansas." "Jeff. Thompson CHASTISED," New York Times, October 24, 1861, p. 5.

had halted his troops at Jackson for the night, and had come on himself to Cape Girardeau, leaving orders for his command to follow him in the morning. I gave the General his orders—which stopped him at Jackson—but he was very much aggrieved at being placed under another brigadier-general, particularly as he believed himself to be the senior. He had been a brigadier, in command at Cairo, while I was mustering officer at Springfield without any rank. But we were nominated at the same time for the United States service, and both our commissions bore date May 17th, 1861. By virtue of my former army rank I was, by law, the senior. General Prentiss failed to get orders to his troops to remain at Jackson, and the next morning early they were reported as approaching Cape Girardeau. I then ordered the General very peremptorily to countermarch his command and take it back to Jackson. He obeyed the order, but bade his command adieu when he got them to Jackson, and went to St. Louis and reported himself. This broke up the expedition. But little harm was done, as Jeff. Thompson moved light and had no fixed place for even nominal headquarters. He was as much at home in Arkansas as he was in Missouri and would keep out of the way of a superior force. Prentiss was sent to another part of the State.

General Prentiss made a great mistake on the above occasion, one that he would not have committed later in the war. When I came to know him better, I regretted it much. In consequence of this occurrence he was off duty in the field when the principal campaign at the West was going on, and his juniors received promotion while he was where none could be obtained. He would have been next to myself in rank in the district of south-east Missouri, by virtue of his services in the Mexican war. He was a brave and very earnest soldier. No man in the service was more sincere in his devotion to the cause for which we were battling; none more ready to make sacrifices or risk life in it.

On the 4th of September I removed my headquarters to Cairo and found Colonel Richard Oglesby in command of the post.[8] We had never

---

8. Four days after his arrival, Grant issued General Order No. 5:

> It is with regret the Genl Comdg sees and learns that the closest intimacy exists between many of the officers and soldiers of his command; that they visit together the lowest drinking and dancing saloons; quarrel, curse, drink and carouse generally on the lowest level of equality, and neglect generally the interests of the Government they are sworn to serve[.]

> Such conduct is totally subversive of good ~~conduct~~ order and Military Disipline and must be discontinued.

met, at least not to my knowledge. After my promotion I had ordered my
brigadier-general's uniform from New York, but it had not yet arrived, so
that I was in citizen's dress. The Colonel had his office full of people, mostly
from the neighboring States of Missouri and Kentucky, making complaints
or asking favors. He evidently did not catch my name when I was presented,
for on my taking a piece of paper from the table where he was seated and
writing the order assuming command of the district of south-east Missouri,
Colonel Richard J. Oglesby to command the post at Bird's Point, and handing it to him, he put on an expression of surprise that looked a little as if
he would like to have some one identify me. But he surrendered the office
without question.[9]

> In future it will be the duty of every Commanding officer of a Regi-
> ment or detachment to at once arrest any one of their commands guilty of
> such conduct and prefer charges against them, and the duty of all officers
> who have a decent respect for themselves and the service they have entered
> into to report everything of the kind.
>
> Disipline cannot be maintained where the officers do not command
> respect and such conduct cannot insure it.
>
> In this military District Disipline shall be maintained even if it is at the
> expense of the commission of all officers who stand in the way of attaining
> that end.

PUSG, 2:207–8.

9. Richard J. Oglesby (1824–1899) would serve until 1864, when he succeeded Yates
as governor of Illinois. Oglesby had served in the Mexican War and later went to California to prospect for gold. In her book on Decatur's famous sons, Jane Martin Johns
wrote of Oglesby's Civil War service on guard duty with the Eighth Illinois in Cairo:

> Naturally fond of ease and luxury, he shared the fare and the fate of enlisted
> men. His active spirit chafed under the restraint of mere guard duty. But he
> too had learned that a soldier's duty was to obey orders and let his superiors
> do the thinking. He was anxious that a more aggressive policy should be
> adopted, and had little faith in the loyalty of the border states.
>
> Especially distasteful to Oglesby was the necessity of enforcing the
> Fugitive Slave Law. Kentucky slave owners came boldly into his camp and
> demanded the arrest of their "runaway niggers," and when he was obliged
> by military rule to order a fugitive slave arrested, conducted outside the
> lines and turned over to his master by a corporal's guard he said, "It was the
> bitterest pill that I ever swallowed; I actually shed tears."

Later, at the Battle of Corinth, Oglesby was "shot through the left lung by an ounce
ball," but he survived this serious wound and stayed on active service until 1864. See

The day after I assumed command at Cairo a man came to me who said he was a scout of General Fremont.[10] He reported that he had just come from Columbus, a point on the Mississippi twenty miles below on the Kentucky side, and that troops had started from there, or were about to start, to seize Paducah, at the mouth of the Tennessee. There was no time for delay; I reported by telegraph to the department commander the information I had received, and added that I was taking steps to get off that night to be in advance of the enemy in securing that important point. There was a large number of steamers lying at Cairo and a good many boatmen were staying in the town. It was the work of only a few hours to get the boats manned, with coal aboard and steam up. Troops were also designated to go aboard. The distance from Cairo to Paducah is about forty-five miles. I did not wish to get there before daylight of the 6th, and directed therefore that the boats should lie at anchor out in the stream until the time to start.

Personal Recollections of Early Decatur, Abraham Lincoln, Richard J. Oglesby and The Civil War (Decatur Chapter, Daughters of the American Revolution, 1912), 112–14.

10. Nicknamed the Pathfinder, John C. Frémont (1813–1890) was commissioned in 1838 as a topographical engineer and made his name as a surveyor and cartographer in the American West. His military career was punctuated by controversy and serial resignation. Relieved from command in the Shenandoah Valley in 1862, he left military service for good. A strong Unionist, Frémont also ran for president on several occasions. His father-in-law, the powerful Missouri Senator Thomas Hart Benton, promoted his career and defended his reputation, while his wife, Jessie Benton Frémont, a committed abolitionist, assisted him with his political campaign and with his writing, including *Memoirs of My Life*. For a detailed account of Frémont's life and significance, see Tom Chaffin, *Pathfinder: John C. Frémont and the Path of American Empire* (Norman: University of Oklahoma Press, 2002).

Grant once described Frémont's style to the journalist John Russell Young, who accompanied the Grants on their post-presidential world tour:

> Fremont had as much state as a sovereign, and was as difficult to approach. His head-quarters alone required as much transportation as a division of troops. I was under his command a part of the time, and remember how imposing was his manner of doing business. He sat in a room in full uniform, with his maps before him. When you went in, he would point out one line or another in a mysterious manner, never asking you to take a seat. You left without the least idea of what he meant or what he wanted you to do.

John Russell Young, *Around the World with Grant*, 2 vols. (New York: American News Company, 1879), 2:215.

Not having received an answer to my first dispatch, I again telegraphed to department headquarters that I should start for Paducah that night unless I received further orders. Hearing nothing, we started before midnight and arrived early the following morning, anticipating the enemy by probably not over six or eight hours. It proved very fortunate that the expedition against Jeff. Thompson had been broken up. Had it not been, the enemy would have seized Paducah and fortified it, to our very great annoyance.

When the National troops entered the town the citizens were taken by surprise. I never after saw such consternation depicted on the faces of the people.[11] Men, women and children came out of their doors looking pale and frightened at the presence of the invader. They were expecting rebel troops that day. In fact, nearly four thousand men from Columbus were at that time within ten or fifteen miles of Paducah on their way to occupy the place. I had but two regiments and one battery with me; but the enemy did not know this and returned to Columbus. I stationed my troops at the best points to guard the roads leading into the city, left gunboats to guard the river fronts and by noon was ready to start on my return to Cairo. Before leaving, however, I addressed a short printed proclamation to the citizens of Paducah assuring them of our peaceful intentions, that we had come among them to protect them against the enemies of our country, and that all who chose could continue their usual avocations with assurance of the protection of the government. This was evidently a relief to them; but the majority would

---

11. Grant's proclamation to the citizens of Paducah reads as follows:

> I have come among you, not as an enemy, but as your friend and fellow-citizen, not to injure or annoy you, but to respect the rights, and to defend and enforce the rights of all loyal citizens. An enemy, in rebellion against our common Government, has taken possession of, and planted its guns upon the soil of Kentucky and fired upon our flag. Hickman and Columbus are in his hands. He is moving upon your city. I am here to defend you against this enemy and to assert and maintain the authority and sovereignty of your Government and mine. I have nothing to do with opinions. I shall deal only with armed rebellion and its aiders and abetors. You can pursue your usual avocations without fear or hindrance. The strong arm of the Government is here to protect its friends, and to punish only its enemies. Whenever it is manifest that you are able to defend yourselves, to maintain the authority of your Government and protect the rights of all its loyal citizens, I shall withdraw the forces under my command from your city.

PUSG, 2:194–95.

Telegram from Grant to C. F. Smith. *Special Collections, USMA Library.*

have much preferred the presence of the other army. I reinforced Paducah rapidly from the troops at Cape Girardeau; and a day or two later General C. F. Smith, a most accomplished soldier, reported at Cairo and was assigned to the command of the post at the mouth of the Tennessee.[12] In a short time

---

12. Lew Wallace, who had limited military experience, sought the advice of Smith, the career soldier, whom he greatly admired :

> He was a person of superb physique, very tall, perfectly proportioned, straight, square-shouldered, ruddy-faced, with eyes of perfect blue, and long snow-white mustaches. He seemed to know the army regulations by heart, and caught a tactical mistake, whether of command or execution, by a kind of mental *coup d'œil.* He was naturally kind, genial, communicative, and never failed to answer when information was sought of him. . . . On the occasion of a review General Smith had the bearing of a marshal of France. He could ride along a line of volunteers in the regulation uniform of a brigadier-general, plume, chapeau, epaulets and all, without exciting laughter—something nobody else could do in the beginning of the war. He was at first accused of disloyalty, and when told of it, his eyes flashed wickedly; then he laughed, and said, "Oh, never mind! They'll take it back after our first battle." And they did.

"The Capture of Fort Donelson," *B&L,* 1:405.

Grant's letter of condolence to Smith's wife moves swiftly from the formulaic to the personal:

> It becomes my painful duty to announce to you the death of your lamented husband, Major Gen. Charles F. Smith. He died at 4 o'clock P.M. yesterday at Savanna Tennessee.

> In his death the nation has lost one of its most gallant and most able defenders.

it was well fortified and a detachment was sent to occupy Smithland, at the mouth of the Cumberland.

The State government of Kentucky at that time was rebel in sentiment, but wanted to preserve an armed neutrality between the North and the South, and the governor really seemed to think the State had a perfect right to maintain a neutral position. The rebels already occupied two towns in the State, Columbus and Hickman, on the Mississippi; and at the very moment the National troops were entering Paducah from the Ohio front, General Lloyd Tilghman—a Confederate—with his staff and a small detachment of men, were getting out in the other direction, while, as I have already said, nearly four thousand Confederate troops were on Kentucky soil on their way to take possession of the town. But, in the estimation of the governor and of those who thought with him, this did not justify the National authorities in invading the soil of Kentucky. I informed the legislature of the State of what I was doing, and my action was approved by the majority of that body. On my return to Cairo I found authority from department headquarters for me to take Paducah "if I felt strong enough," but very soon after I was reprimanded from the same quarters for my correspondence with the legislature and warned against a repetition of the offence.

Soon after I took command at Cairo, General Fremont entered into arrangements for the exchange of the prisoners captured at Camp Jackson in the month of May. I received orders to pass them through my lines to Columbus as they presented themselves with proper credentials. Quite a number of these prisoners I had been personally acquainted with before the

---

It was my fortune to have gone through West Point with the Gen. then Captain, as Commandant of Cadets, and to have served with him in all his battles in Mexico, and in this rebellion, and I can bear honest testimony to his great worth as a soldier and friend. Where an entire Nation condoles with you in your berievement no one can do so with more heartfelt grief than my self.

Letter to Mrs. C. F. Smith, April 26, 1862, Charles F. Smith Papers, Special Collections, USMA Library.

After the war, in a note to Smith's daughter on the appointment of her brother as a second lieutenant, Grant wrote of his "great pleasure" at being "able to serve in any way within my power the family of one who I highly respected, I might say loved as your father. My great respect for him commenced when he was Commandant of Cadets and I a *Plebe*. This respect ripened as I knew him better in later years." Letter to Miss Louisa Smith, July 21, 1866, Charles F. Smith Papers, Special Collections, USMA Library.

war. Such of them as I had so known were received at my headquarters as old acquaintances, and ordinary routine business was not disturbed by their presence. On one occasion when several were present in my office my intention to visit Cape Girardeau the next day, to inspect the troops at that point, was mentioned. Something transpired which postponed my trip; but a steamer employed by the government was passing a point some twenty or more miles above Cairo, the next day, when a section of rebel artillery with proper escort brought her to. A major, one of those who had been at my headquarters the day before, came at once aboard and after some search made a direct demand for my delivery. It was hard to persuade him that I was not there. This officer was Major Barrett, of St. Louis. I had been acquainted with his family before the war.

General Fremont in Command—Movement against Belmont—Battle of Belmont— A Narrow Escape—After the Battle

From the occupation of Paducah up to the early part of November nothing important occurred with the troops under my command. I was reinforced from time to time and the men were drilled and disciplined preparatory for the service which was sure to come. By the 1st of November I had not fewer than 20,000 men, most of them under good drill and ready to meet any equal body of men who, like themselves, had not yet been in an engagement. They were growing impatient at lying idle so long, almost in hearing of the guns of the enemy they had volunteered to fight against. I asked on one or two occasions to be allowed to move against Columbus. It could have been taken soon after the occupation of Paducah; but before November it was so strongly fortified that it would have required a large force and a long siege to capture it.

In the latter part of October General Fremont took the field in person and moved from Jefferson City against General Sterling Price, who was then in the State of Missouri with a considerable command.[1] About the first of

---

1. Sterling Price (1809–1867) was a Virginian who served in Mexico as a brigadier general of volunteers. The victor at Wilson's Creek, where Lyon died, Price became a major general in the C.S.A. and suffered losses at Pea Ridge, Iuka, and Corinth. In 1864, based in Arkansas, he launched one final raid into Missouri and Kansas before his command disintegrated. Before returning to Missouri, where he died of cholera, Price for a time joined those rebels who attempted to start a colony in Mexico. For a detailed account of Price's career, see Albert Castel, *General Sterling Price and the Civil War in the West* (Baton Rouge: Louisiana State University Press, 1968).

November I was directed from department headquarters to make a demonstration on both sides of the Mississippi River with the view of detaining the rebels at Columbus within their lines. Before my troops could be got off, I was notified from the same quarter that there were some 3,000 of the enemy on the St. Francis River about fifty miles west, or south-west, from Cairo, and was ordered to send another force against them. I dispatched Colonel Oglesby at once with troops sufficient to compete with the reported number of the enemy. On the 5th word came from the same source that the rebels were about to detach a large force from Columbus to be moved by boats down the Mississippi and up the White River, in Arkansas, in order to reinforce Price, and I was directed to prevent this movement if possible. I accordingly sent a regiment from Bird's Point under Colonel W. H. L. Wallace[2] to overtake and reinforce Oglesby, with orders to march to New Madrid, a point some distance below Columbus, on the Missouri side. At the same time I directed General C. F. Smith to move all the troops he could spare from Paducah directly against Columbus, halting them, however, a few miles from the town to await further orders from me. Then I gathered up all the troops at Cairo and Fort Holt, except suitable guards, and moved them down the river on steamers convoyed by two gunboats, accompanying them myself. My force consisted of a little over 3,000 men and embraced five regiments of infantry, two guns and two companies of cavalry. We dropped down the river on the 6th to within about six miles of Columbus, debarked a few men on the Kentucky side and established pickets to connect with the troops from Paducah.[3]

I had no orders which contemplated an attack by the National troops, nor did I intend anything of the kind when I started out from Cairo; but after we started I saw that the officers and men were elated at the prospect of at last having the opportunity of doing what they had volunteered to do—fight the enemies of their country. I did not see how I could main-

2. William Hervey Lamme Wallace (1821–1862), a private at the start of the war, ended it as a division commander at the Battle of Shiloh, where he died of wounds suffered in defense of the Hornet's Nest.

3. This movement, which preceded the Battle of Belmont, was Grant's first significant operation with the federal navy. Grant would enjoy effective working relationships with naval officers, including Andrew Foote, his counterpart in this expedition, David Farragut, David Dixon Porter, and William "Dirty Bill" Porter. For a detailed account of naval operations during the war, see James M. McPherson, *War on the Waters: The Union & Confederate Navies, 1861–1865* (Chapel Hill: University of North Carolina Press, 2012).

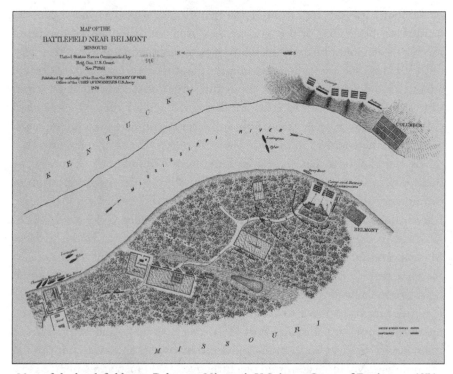

Map of the battlefield near Belmont, Missouri, U.S Army Corps of Engineers, 1876.
Library of Congress, Geography and Map Division.

tain discipline, or retain the confidence of my command, if we should
return to Cairo without an effort to do something. Columbus, besides
being strongly fortified, contained a garrison much more numerous than
the force I had with me. It would not do, therefore, to attack that point.
About two o'clock on the morning of the 7th, I learned that the enemy
was crossing troops from Columbus to the west bank to be dispatched, presumably, after Oglesby. I knew there was a small camp of Confederates at
Belmont, immediately opposite Columbus, and I speedily resolved to push
down the river, land on the Missouri side, capture Belmont, break up the
camp and return. Accordingly, the pickets above Columbus were drawn in
at once, and about daylight the boats moved out from shore. In an hour we
were debarking on the west bank of the Mississippi, just out of range of the
batteries at Columbus.

The ground on the west shore of the river, opposite Columbus, is low
and in places marshy and cut up with sloughs. The soil is rich and the timber
large and heavy. There were some small clearings between Belmont and
the point where we landed, but most of the country was covered with the

native forests. We landed in front of a cornfield. When the debarkation commenced, I took a regiment down the river to post it as a guard against surprise. At that time I had no staff officer who could be trusted with that duty. In the woods, at a short distance below the clearing, I found a depression, dry at the time, but which at high water became a slough or bayou. I placed the men in the hollow, gave them their instructions and ordered them to remain there until they were properly relieved. These troops, with the gunboats, were to protect our transports.

Up to this time the enemy had evidently failed to divine our intentions. From Columbus they could, of course, see our gunboats and transports loaded with troops. But the force from Paducah was threatening them from the land side, and it was hardly to be expected that if Columbus was our object we would separate our troops by a wide river. They doubtless thought we meant to draw a large force from the east bank, then embark ourselves, land on the east bank and make a sudden assault on Columbus before their divided command could be united.

About eight o'clock we started from the point of debarkation, marching by the flank. After moving in this way for a mile or a mile and a half, I halted where there was marshy ground covered with a heavy growth of timber in our front, and deployed a large part of my force as skirmishers. By this time the enemy discovered that we were moving upon Belmont and sent out troops to meet us. Soon after we had started in line, his skirmishers were encountered and fighting commenced. This continued, growing fiercer and fiercer, for about four hours, the enemy being forced back gradually until he was driven into his camp. Early in this engagement my horse was shot under me, but I got another from one of my staff and kept well up with the advance until the river was reached.

The officers and men engaged at Belmont were then under fire for the first time. Veterans could not have behaved better than they did up to the moment of reaching the rebel camp. At this point they became demoralized from their victory and failed to reap its full reward. The enemy had been followed so closely that when he reached the clear ground on which his camp was pitched he beat a hasty retreat over the river bank, which protected him from our shots and from view. This precipitate retreat at the last moment enabled the National forces to pick their way without hinderance through the abatis—the only artificial defence the enemy had. The moment the camp was reached our men laid down their arms and commenced rummaging the tents to pick up trophies. Some of the higher officers were little better than the privates. They galloped about from one cluster of men to another and at every halt delivered a short eulogy upon the Union cause and the achievements of the command.

All this time the troops we had been engaged with for four hours, lay crouched under cover of the river bank, ready to come up and surrender if summoned to do so; but finding that they were not pursued, they worked their way up the river and came up on the bank between us and our transports. I saw at the same time two steamers coming from the Columbus side towards the west shore, above us, black—or gray—with soldiers from boiler-deck to roof. Some of my men were engaged in firing from captured guns at empty steamers down the river, out of range, cheering at every shot. I tried to get them to turn their guns upon the loaded steamers above and not so far away. My efforts were in vain. At last I directed my staff officers to set fire to the camps. This drew the fire of the enemy's guns located on the heights of Columbus. They had abstained from firing before, probably because they were afraid of hitting their own men; or they may have supposed, until the camp was on fire, that it was still in the possession of their friends. About this time, too, the men we had driven over the bank were seen in line up the river between us and our transports. The alarm "surrounded" was given. The guns of the enemy and the report of being surrounded, brought officers and men completely under control. At first some of the officers seemed to think that to be surrounded was to be placed in a hopeless position, where there was nothing to do but surrender. But when I announced that we had cut our way in and could cut our way out just as well, it seemed a new revelation to officers and soldiers. They formed line rapidly and we started back to our boats, with the men deployed as skirmishers as they had been on entering camp. The enemy was soon encountered, but his resistance this time was feeble. Again the Confederates sought shelter under the river banks. We could not stop, however, to pick them up, because the troops we had seen crossing the river had debarked by this time and were nearer our transports than we were. It would be prudent to get them behind us; but we were not again molested on our way to the boats.

From the beginning of the fighting our wounded had been carried to the houses at the rear, near the place of debarkation. I now set the troops to bringing their wounded to the boats.[4] After this had gone on for some little

---

4. Grant alludes to the wounded on several occasions—we know the mere sight of blood distressed him—but he offers no satisfactory description of their care. The surgeon John H. Brinton supplies details on what happened in the wake of Belmont. His account suggests the speed with which underprepared surgeons necessarily learned on the job:

time I rode down the road, without even a staff officer, to visit the guard I had stationed over the approach to our transports. I knew the enemy had crossed over from Columbus in considerable numbers and might be expected to attack us as we were embarking. This guard would be encountered first and, as they were in a natural intrenchment, would be able to hold the enemy for a considerable time. My surprise was great to find there was not a single man in the trench. Riding back to the boat I found the officer who had commanded the guard and learned that he had withdrawn his force when the main body fell back. At first I ordered the guard to return, but finding that it would take some time to get the men together and march them back to their position, I countermanded the order. Then fearing that the enemy we had seen crossing the river below might be coming upon us unawares,

---

Here let me relate a little anecdote of one of my surgeons, a member of one of the Illinois regiments. He was a very earnest man, but at that time rather deficient in professional, or at all events, surgical training. In his hospital lay a patient whose leg, seriously injured, demanded amputation. The surgeon came to my office one afternoon, confessing that he had never done, and had never seen an amputation, and moreover had no idea how one should be done, and begged me, at the appointed time, to perform the operation for him. I explained to him that this would never do; his position in the regiment demanded that he himself should remove the limb. And then I explained to him how the amputation should be done, and made him go through the motions, promising him that I would help him through when the time came. On the following morning I did so, and he operated very well, and to the satisfaction of the lookers on. Somehow or other this amputation established his reputation. He at once took rank as an experienced surgeon; nor, better still, did his newborn confidence desert him, for at the battle before Fort Donelson, some months afterwards, I was informed by one of the hospital stewards that a great surgeon was busy operating in one of the field hospitals in the rear of our lines. I at once rode over to see who this person was, and found the operator busy in the second story of a little country house, to which many wounded men were being carried.

I found bloodstained footmarks on the crooked stairs, and in the second-story room stood my friend of Cairo memory; amputated arms and legs seemed almost to litter the floor; beneath the operating table was a pool of blood, the operator was smeared with it and the surroundings were ghastly beyond all limits of surgical propriety. "Ah, Doctor," said the new-fledged surgeon, "I am getting on, just look at these," pointing to his trophies on the floor with a right royal gesture. And after all he seemed to have done good work, and from that time he was a recognized surgical authority among his confrères.

Brinton, *Personal Memoirs*, 90–91.

I rode out in the field to our front, still entirely alone, to observe whether the enemy was passing. The field was grown up with corn so tall and thick as to cut off the view of even a person on horseback, except directly along the rows. Even in that direction, owing to the overhanging blades of corn, the view was not extensive. I had not gone more than a few hundred yards when I saw a body of troops marching past me not fifty yards away. I looked at them for a moment and then turned my horse towards the river and started back, first in a walk, and when I thought myself concealed from the view of the enemy, as fast as my horse could carry me. When at the river bank I still had to ride a few hundred yards to the point where the nearest transport lay.

The cornfield in front of our transports terminated at the edge of a dense forest. Before I got back the enemy had entered this forest and had opened a brisk fire upon the boats. Our men, with the exception of details

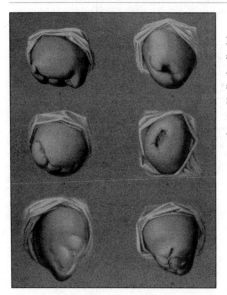

Examples of thigh stumps after amputation from *The Medical and Surgical History of the War of the Rebellion*, **an extensive history produced by the Surgeon-General's Office in the 1870s.** *Courtesy of NIH U.S. National Library of Medicine.*

A little more than a century later James Sterba quoted the musings of the chief medical officer on a hospital ship receiving wounded soldiers from Vietnam:

> The bulk of the injuries we are getting now are mines and booby-traps, whereas in the past incidents of grenade and rifle fire represented the bulk. In the past four or five months, there appears to have been a four- or five-fold increase in multiple amputees.
>
> I hope this is all incredible some day. Right now, it's all too damn credible.

"Scraps of Paper from Vietnam," *New York Times Magazine*, October 18, 1970. p. 116.

that had gone to the front after the wounded, were now either aboard the transports or very near them. Those who were not aboard soon got there, and the boats pushed off. I was the only man of the National army between the rebels and our transports. The captain of a boat that had just pushed out but had not started, recognized me and ordered the engineer not to start the engine; he then had a plank run out for me. My horse seemed to take in the situation. There was no path down the bank and every one acquainted with the Mississippi River knows that its banks, in a natural state, do not vary at any great angle from the perpendicular. My horse put his fore feet over the bank without hesitation or urging, and with his hind feet well under him, slid down the bank and trotted aboard the boat, twelve or fifteen feet away, over a single gang plank. I dismounted and went at once to the upper deck.

The Mississippi River was low on the 7th of November, 1861, so that the banks were higher than the heads of men standing on the upper decks of the steamers. The rebels were some distance back from the river, so that their fire was high and did us but little harm. Our smoke-stack was riddled with bullets, but there were only three men wounded on the boats, two of whom were soldiers. When I first went on deck I entered the captain's room adjoining the pilot-house, and threw myself on a sofa. I did not keep that position a moment, but rose to go out on the deck to observe what was going on. I had scarcely left when a musket ball entered the room, struck the head of the sofa, passed through it and lodged in the foot.

When the enemy opened fire on the transports our gunboats returned it with vigor. They were well out in the stream and some distance down, so that they had to give but very little elevation to their guns to clear the banks of the river. Their position very nearly enfiladed the line of the enemy while he was marching through the cornfield. The execution was very great, as we could see at the time and as I afterwards learned more positively. We were very soon out of range and went peacefully on our way to Cairo, every man feeling that Belmont was a great victory and that he had contributed his share to it.

Our loss at Belmont was 485 in killed, wounded and missing. About 125 of our wounded fell into the hands of the enemy. We returned with 175 prisoners and two guns, and spiked four other pieces. The loss of the enemy, as officially reported, was 642 men, killed, wounded and missing. We had engaged about 2,500 men, exclusive of the guard left with the transports. The enemy had about 7,000; but this includes the troops brought over from Columbus who were not engaged in the first defence of Belmont.

The two objects for which the battle of Belmont was fought were fully accomplished. The enemy gave up all idea of detaching troops from Columbus. His losses were very heavy for that period of the war. Columbus was beset by people looking for their wounded or dead kin, to take them home for medical treatment or burial. I learned later, when I had moved further south, that Belmont had caused more mourning than almost any other battle up to that time. The National troops acquired a confidence in themselves at Belmont that did not desert them through the war.

The day after the battle I met some officers from General Polk's command, arranged for permission to bury our dead at Belmont and also commenced negotiations for the exchange of prisoners. When our men went to bury their dead, before they were allowed to land they were conducted below the point where the enemy had engaged our transports. Some of the officers expressed a desire to see the field; but the request was refused with the statement that we had no dead there.[5]

While on the truce-boat I mentioned to an officer, whom I had known both at West Point and in the Mexican war, that I was in the cornfield near their troops when they passed; that I had been on horseback and had worn a soldier's overcoat at the time. This officer was on General Polk's staff. He said both he and the general had seen me and that Polk had said to his men, "There is a Yankee; you may try your marksmanship on him if you wish," but nobody fired at me.[6]

---

5. Sassoon's George Sherston suggests some of the sensory horrors of a battle's aftermath in this description of the Western Front in 1916:

> For the first time I was among the débris of an attack. After going a very short distance we made the first of many halts, and I saw, arranged by the roadside, about fifty of the British dead. Many of them were Gordon highlanders. There were Devons and South Staffordshires among them, but they were beyond regimental rivalry now—their fingers mingled in bloodstained bunches, as though acknowledging the companionship of death. There was much battle gear lying about, and some dead horses. There were rags and shreds of clothing, boots riddled and torn, and when we came to the old German front-line, a sour pervasive stench which differed from anything my nostrils had known before. Meanwhile we made our continually retarded progress up the hill, and I scrutinized these battle effects with partially complacent curiosity. I wanted to be able to say that I had seen "the horrors of war"; and here they were, nearly three days old.

Memoirs of an Infantry Officer (1930; New York: Penguin Classics, 2013), 59–60.

6. This is the second of two near misses Grant records in this chapter; there are others scattered through the *Memoirs*, where they are presented with a deadpan style and usu-

Belmont was severely criticised in the North as a wholly unnecessary battle, barren of results, or the possibility of them from the beginning. If it had not been fought, Colonel Oglesby would probably have been captured or destroyed with his three thousand men. Then I should have been culpable indeed.[7]

---

ally serve to illustrate the role of chance in war. They may also suggest Grant's proximity to the fight, but they are never accompanied by a self-aggrandizing moral. One might compare Theodore Roosevelt's handling in *The Rough Riders* of an analogous incident in Cuba during the Spanish-American War:

> A curious incident happened as I was getting the men started forward. Always when men have been lying down under cover for some time, and are required to advance, there is a little hesitation, each looking to see whether the others are going forward. As I rode down the line, calling to the troopers to go forward; and rasping brief directions to the captains and lieutenants, I came upon a man lying behind a little bush, and I ordered him to jump up. I do not think he understood that we were making a forward move, and he looked up at me for a moment with hesitation, and I again bade him rise, jeering him and saying: "Are you afraid to stand up when I am on horseback?" As I spoke, he suddenly fell forward on his face, a bullet having struck him and gone through him lengthwise. I suppose the bullet had been aimed at me; at any rate, I, who was on horseback in the open was unhurt, and the man lying flat on the ground in the cover beside me was killed.

The Rough Riders (New York: P. F. Collier & Son, 1899), 125–26.

Roosevelt's self-congratulatory, melodramatic account, written at the turn of the twentieth century, highlights Grant's anomalous style. As Paul Fussell documents so vividly in *The Great War and Modern Memory*, accident would become a staple, irony the dominant mode, of the writing to emerge from World War I.

7. For a comprehensive account of Belmont, the first battle in the West, see Nathaniel Cheairs Hughes Jr., *The Battle of Belmont: Grant Strikes South* (Chapel Hill: University of North Carolina Press, 2008).

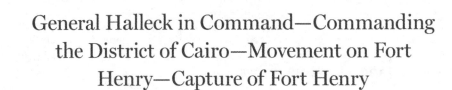

General Halleck in Command—Commanding the District of Cairo—Movement on Fort Henry—Capture of Fort Henry

While at Cairo I had frequent opportunities of meeting the rebel officers of the Columbus garrison. They seemed to be very fond of coming up on steamers under flags of truce. On two or three occasions I went down in like manner. When one of their boats was seen coming up carrying a white flag, a gun would be fired from the lower battery at Fort Holt, throwing a shot across the bow as a signal to come no farther. I would then take a steamer and, with my staff and occasionally a few other officers, go down to receive the party. There were several officers among them whom I had known before, both at West Point and in Mexico. Seeing these officers who had been educated for the profession of arms, both at school and in actual war, which is a far more efficient training, impressed me with the great advantage the South possessed over the North at the beginning of the rebellion. They had from thirty to forty per cent. of the educated soldiers of the Nation. They had no standing army and, consequently, these trained soldiers had to find employment with the troops from their own States. In this way what there was of military education and training was distributed throughout their whole army. The whole loaf was leavened.[1]

---

1. West Point produced 977 lieutenants between 1833 and 1861; 259 of them would join the Confederacy, 638 the Union. See "West Point in the Making of America," Smithsonian National Museum of American History, http://americanhistory.si.edu/westpoint/history_3a.html.

Such familiarity produced not only occasional cordiality between enemies, as Grant documents here, but also rivalry—even animosity—between comrades. After witness-

The North had a greater number of educated and trained soldiers, but the bulk of them were still in the army and were retained, generally with their old commands and rank, until the war had lasted many months. In the Army of the Potomac there was what was known as the "regular brigade," in which, from the commanding officer down to the youngest second lieutenant, every one was educated to his profession. So, too, with many of the batteries; all the officers, generally four in number to each, were men educated for their profession. Some of these went into battle at the beginning under division commanders who were entirely without military training. This state of affairs gave me an idea which I expressed while at Cairo; that the government ought to disband the regular army, with the exception of the staff corps, and notify the disbanded officers that they would receive no compensation while the war lasted except as volunteers. The register should be kept up, but the names of all officers who were not in the volunteer service at the close, should be stricken from it.

On the 9th of November, two days after the battle of Belmont, Major-General H. W. Halleck superseded General Fremont in command of the Department of the Missouri.[2] The limits of his command took in

---

ing "the wrath of a young West Pointer" during a conversation about which of two other Military Academy graduates, Alfred Torbert or Philip Sheridan, should get credit for a particular success, Union volunteer John De Forest compared "regular officers" to "a singing choir or an opera troupe" in their penchant for jealousy. See *A Volunteer's Adventures: A Union Captain's Record of the Civil War*, ed. James H. Crushore (Baton Rouge: Louisiana State University Press, 1996), 198.

Dennis Hart Mahan, a West Point professor who had taught many of these officers, was so disgusted by the infighting that he wrote to William T. Sherman in the summer of 1863 of his desire to send a *"confidential circular"* to his former students soliciting their cooperation in defense of the Union. As Brooks Simpson and Jean Berlin note, Mahan "thought that quarrels among them should be arbitrated in private by mutual friends. He had done what he could to defend his graduates in print until they started going after each other." Brooks D. Simpson and Jean V. Berlin, eds. *Sherman's Civil War: Selected Correspondence of William T. Sherman, 1860–1865* (Chapel Hill: University of North Carolina Press, 1999), 543 n. 2.

2. The relationship between Grant and Henry Wager Halleck (1815–1872) was fraught from the start. Halleck, whose nickname was "Old Brains," was regarded as a master theoretician who lacked experience in the field. He graduated from West Point in 1839, and served as an engineer, mostly in California. After resigning in 1854, he worked as a lawyer and railroad president. He also wrote and translated books on mining, law, and military theory. Reappointed as a major general in 1861, Halleck, commanding first the Department of the Missouri and then the Department of the Mississippi, was in charge of the Western Theater until he was made general-in-chief of the armies in July 1862. In the field, Halleck was cautious to the point of inaction, and his communication with

Arkansas and west Kentucky east to the Cumberland River. From the battle of Belmont until early in February, 1862, the troops under my command did little except prepare for the long struggle which proved to be before them.

The enemy at this time occupied a line running from the Mississippi River at Columbus to Bowling Green and Mill Springs, Kentucky. Each of these positions was strongly fortified, as were also points on the Tennessee and Cumberland rivers near the Tennessee state line. The works on the Tennessee were called Fort Heiman and Fort Henry, and that on the Cumberland was Fort Donelson. At these points the two rivers approached within eleven miles of each other. The lines of rifle pits at each place extended back from the water at least two miles, so that the garrisons were in reality only seven miles apart. These positions were of immense importance to the enemy; and of course correspondingly important for us to possess ourselves of.[3] With Fort Henry in our hands we had a navigable stream open to us

---

Grant, as the ensuing chapters reveal, began to deteriorate after Fort Donelson. John Russell Young recorded the general's thoughts about Halleck:

> When I was made Lieutenant-General, General Halleck became chief of staff to the army. He was very useful, and was loyal and industrious, sincerely anxious for the success of his country, and without any feeling of soreness at being superseded. In this respect Halleck was a contrast to other officers of equal ability, who felt that unless they had the commands they craved they were not needed. Halleck's immense knowledge of military science was of great use in the War office to those of us in the field. His fault—and this prevented his being a successful commander in the field— was timidity in taking responsibilities. I do not mean timid personally, because no one ever doubted his courage, but timid in reaching conclusions. He would never take a chance in a battle. A general who will never take a chance in a battle will never fight one. When I was in the field, I had on two or three occasions to come to Washington to see that Halleck carried out my orders. I found that there was some panic about the rebels coming between our army and the capitol, and Halleck had changed or amended my orders to avoid some such danger. I would say, "I don't care anything about that. I do not care if the rebels do get between my troops and Washington, so that they get into a place where I can find them."

Around the World with Grant, 2:216.

3. Admiral David Porter emphasizes Grant's strategic grasp and fixity of purpose: "Grant knew the nature of these works better than any other officer, and saw that Bowling Green and Columbus could both be turned as soon as Henry and Donelson fell. Halleck and others were making great strategic movements, which amounted to nothing, but Grant kept his mind steadily fixed on these two forts, knowing the effect

up to Muscle Shoals, in Alabama. The Memphis and Charleston Railroad strikes the Tennessee at Eastport, Mississippi, and follows close to the banks of the river up to the shoals. This road, of vast importance to the enemy, would cease to be of use to them for through traffic the moment Fort Henry became ours. Fort Donelson was the gate to Nashville—a place of great military and political importance—and to a rich country extending far east in Kentucky. These two points in our possession, the enemy would necessarily be thrown back to the Memphis and Charleston road, or to the boundary of the cotton states, and, as before stated, that road would be lost to them for through communication.

The designation of my command had been changed after Halleck's arrival, from the District of South-east Missouri to the District of Cairo, and the small district commanded by General C. F. Smith, embracing the mouths of the Tennessee and Cumberland rivers, had been added to my jurisdiction. Early in January, 1862, I was directed by General McClellan, through my department commander, to make a reconnoissance in favor of Brigadier-General Don Carlos Buell, who commanded the Department of the Ohio, with headquarters at Louisville, and who was confronting General S. B. Buckner with a larger Confederate force at Bowling Green.[4] It was supposed that Buell was about to make some move against the enemy, and my demonstration was intended to prevent the sending of troops from Columbus, Fort Henry or Donelson to Buckner. I at once ordered General Smith to send a force up the west bank of the Tennessee to threaten forts Heiman and Henry; McClernand at the same time with a force of 6,000 men was sent out into west Kentucky, threatening Columbus with one column and the Tennessee River with another. I went with McClernand's command. The weather was very bad; snow and rain fell; the roads, never good in that section, were intolerable. We were out more than a week splashing through the mud, snow and rain, the men suffering very much. The object of the expedition was accomplished. The enemy did not send reinforcements to

---

their fall would have." David D. Porter, *The Naval History of the Civil War* (New York: Sherman, 1886), 141.

4. Don Carlos Buell (1818–1898) graduated from West Point a year ahead of Grant. He served on frontier duty and in the Mexican War. His most important command in the Civil War was the Army of the Ohio, which began to arrive on the field on the evening of the first day of the Battle of Shiloh. The timing of his army's appearance and the nature of its contribution to the ultimate Union victory provided fodder for controversy for the rest of the century.

Bowling Green, and General George H. Thomas fought and won the battle of Mill Springs before we returned.[5]

As a result of this expedition General Smith reported that he thought it practicable to capture Fort Heiman. This fort stood on high ground, completely commanding Fort Henry on the opposite side of the river, and its possession by us, with the aid of our gunboats, would insure the capture of Fort Henry. This report of Smith's confirmed views I had previously held, that the true line of operations for us was up the Tennessee and Cumberland rivers. With us there, the enemy would be compelled to fall back on the east and west entirely out of the State of Kentucky. On the 6th of January, before receiving orders for this expedition, I had asked permission of the general commanding the department to go to see him at St. Louis. My object was to lay this plan of campaign before him. Now that my views had been confirmed by so able a general as Smith, I renewed my request to go to St. Louis

---

5. George H. Thomas (1816–1870) was appointed to West Point from the state of Virginia. After graduating in 1840, he served in the Florida War and the Mexican War. He was on frontier duty at the beginning of the Civil War. Thomas had several nicknames: "Old Slow Trot," supposedly earned while a cavalry instructor at West Point because he prohibited cadets from galloping; "Pap"; and the "Rock of Chickamauga," bestowed after he held the line and mitigated the disaster of the Union defeat there by covering the retreat to Chattanooga. All of them suggest the nature of his soldiering. *"Where will I find you, General, when I return?"* an aide asks Thomas in Kate Brownlee Sherwood's nineteenth-century poem "Thomas at Chickamauga." Thomas, "like a lion turned, his pale lips set and sere, / And shook his mane, and stamped his foot, and fiercely answered, *'Here!'"* *Camp-Fire, Memorial-Day, and Other Poems* (Chicago: Jansen, McClurg, 1885), 34–35.

Thomas rose to command the Army of the Cumberland and won a vital victory at Nashville late in the war. So slow was he to attack there, however, that Grant almost relieved him. Cullum writes of this episode:

> Grant, impatient and unreasonable, urged Thomas to strike at once, threatening his removal from command if he did not; but nothing could induce the cool, calm, sturdy, resolute, common-sense old warrior to fight a battle prematurely, or by possibility defeat the sacred cause for the Union which had cost nearly four years of bloody war. Silently and patiently the firm patriot bore all reproach, and, serenely resolute, telegraphed that he had done everything in his power to strike the enemy as quickly as possible, but that he could not control the elements nor get troops ready by magic, and that, if the General-in-Chief deemed it necessary to relieve him, he would submit without a murmur. Noble Roman! preferring to sacrifice himself rather than his country!

Biographical Register, vol. 2, s.v. "Thomas, George H."

on what I deemed important military business. The leave was granted, but not graciously. I had known General Halleck but very slightly in the old army, not having met him either at West Point or during the Mexican war. I was received with so little cordiality that I perhaps stated the object of my visit with less clearness than I might have done, and I had not uttered many sentences before I was cut short as if my plan was preposterous. I returned to Cairo very much crestfallen.

Flag-officer Foote commanded the little fleet of gunboats then in the neighborhood of Cairo and, though in another branch of the service, was subject to the command of General Halleck.[6] He and I consulted freely upon military matters and he agreed with me perfectly as to the feasibility of the campaign up the Tennessee. Notwithstanding the rebuff I had received from my immediate chief, I therefore, on the 28th of January, renewed the suggestion by telegraph that "if permitted, I could take and hold Fort Henry on the Tennessee." This time I was backed by Flag-officer Foote, who sent a similar dispatch. On the 29th I wrote fully in support of the proposition. On the 1st of February I received full instructions from department headquarters to move upon Fort Henry. On the 2d the expedition started.

In February, 1862, there were quite a good many steamers laid up at Cairo for want of employment, the Mississippi River being closed against navigation below that point. There were also many men in the town whose occupation had been following the river in various capacities, from captain down to deck hand. But there were not enough of either boats or men to move at one time the 17,000 men I proposed to take with me up the Tennessee. I loaded the boats with more than half the force, however, and sent General McClernand in command. I followed with one of the later boats and found McClernand had stopped, very properly, nine miles below Fort Henry. Seven gunboats under Flag-officer Foote had accompanied the advance. The transports we had with us had to return to Paducah to bring up a division from there, with General C. F. Smith in command.

Before sending the boats back I wanted to get the troops as near to the enemy as I could without coming within range of their guns. There was a stream emptying into the Tennessee on the east side, apparently at about long range distance below the fort. On account of the narrow water-shed separat-

---

6. Andrew Foote (1806–1863) was a Connecticut native who joined the navy in 1822; when the war broke out he was in command of the Brooklyn Navy Yard. Foote was a temperance advocate and gave voice to his antislavery sentiments in the book *Africa and the American Flag* (1854).

ing the Tennessee and Cumberland rivers at that point, the stream must be insignificant at ordinary stages, but when we were there, in February, it was a torrent. It would facilitate the investment of Fort Henry materially if the troops could be landed south of that stream. To test whether this could be done I boarded the gunboat *Essex* and requested Captain Wm. Porter commanding it, to approach the fort to draw its fire.[7] After we had gone some distance past the mouth of the stream we drew the fire of the fort, which fell much short of us. In consequence I had made up my mind to return and bring the troops to the upper side of the creek, when the enemy opened upon us with a rifled gun that sent shot far beyond us and beyond the stream. One shot passed very near where Captain Porter and I were standing, struck the deck near the stern, penetrated and passed through the cabin and so out into the river. We immediately turned back, and the troops were debarked below the mouth of the creek.

When the landing was completed I returned with the transports to Paducah to hasten up the balance of the troops. I got back on the 5th with the advance, the remainder following as rapidly as the steamers could carry them. At ten o'clock at night, on the 5th, the whole command was not yet up. Being anxious to commence operations as soon as possible before the enemy could reinforce heavily, I issued my orders for an advance at 11 A.M. on the 6th. I felt sure that all the troops would be up by that time.

Fort Henry occupies a bend in the river which gave the guns in the water battery a direct fire down the stream. The camp outside the fort was intrenched, with rifle pits and outworks two miles back on the road to Donelson and Dover. The garrison of the fort and camp was about 2,800, with strong reinforcements from Donelson halted some miles out. There were seventeen heavy guns in the fort. The river was very high, the banks being overflowed except where the bluffs come to the water's edge. A portion of the ground on which Fort Henry stood was two feet deep in water. Below, the water extended into the woods several hundred yards back from the bank on the east side. On the west bank Fort Heiman stood on high ground, completely commanding Fort Henry. The distance from Fort Henry to Donelson is but eleven miles. The two positions were so important to the enemy, *as he saw his interest*, that it was natural to suppose that reinforcements would

---

7. William D. "Dirty Bill" Porter (1809–1864) proved another important partner for Grant in this phase of the war. In command of the *Essex* during the Battle of Fort Henry, Porter was badly injured when shot pierced the ship's bow shield and burst the boilers.

come from every quarter from which they could be got. Prompt action on our part was imperative.

The plan was for the troops and gunboats to start at the same moment. The troops were to invest the garrison and the gunboats to attack the fort at close quarters. General Smith was to land a brigade of his division on the west bank during the night of the 5th and get it in rear of Heiman.

At the hour designated the troops and gunboats started. General Smith found Fort Heiman had been evacuated before his men arrived. The gunboats soon engaged the water batteries at very close quarters, but the troops which were to invest Fort Henry were delayed for want of roads, as well as by the dense forest and the high water in what would in dry weather have been unimportant beds of streams. This delay made no difference in the result. On our first appearance Tilghman had sent his entire command, with the exception of about one hundred men left to man the guns in the fort, to the outworks on the road to Dover and Donelson, so as to have them out of range of the guns of our navy; and before any attack on the 6th he had ordered them to retreat on Donelson. He stated in his subsequent report that the defence was intended solely to give his troops time to make their escape.

Tilghman was captured with his staff and ninety men, as well as the armament of the fort, the ammunition and whatever stores were there. Our cavalry pursued the retreating column towards Donelson and picked up two guns and a few stragglers; but the enemy had so much the start, that the pursuing force did not get in sight of any except the stragglers.

All the gunboats engaged were hit many times. The damage, however, beyond what could be repaired by a small expenditure of money, was slight, except to the *Essex*. A shell penetrated the boiler of that vessel and exploded it, killing and wounding forty-eight men, nineteen of whom were soldiers who had been detailed to act with the navy.[8] On several occasions during the

---

8. In his description of the scene, James Laning, the second master of the *Essex*, reveals several of the hazards of naval combat:

> In the twinkling of an eye the scene was changed from a blaze of glory to a carnival of death and destruction. A shot from the enemy pierced the casemate just above the port-hole on the port side, then through the middle boiler, killing Acting Master's Mate S. B. Brittan, Jr., in its flight, and opening a chasm for the escape of the scalding steam and water. The scene which followed was almost indescribable. The writer, who had gone aft in obedience to orders only a few moments before (thus providentially saved), was met by Fourth Master Walker, followed by a crowd of men rushing

war such details were made when the complement of men with the navy was insufficient for the duty before them. After the fall of Fort Henry Captain Walke, commanding the iron-clad *Carondelet*, at my request ascended the Tennessee River and thoroughly destroyed the bridge of the Memphis and Ohio Railroad.[9]

---

aft. Walker called to me to go back; that a shot from the enemy had carried away the steam pipe. I at once ran to the stern of the vessel, and looking out of the stern port saw a number of our brave fellows struggling in the water. The steam and hot water in the forward gun deck had driven all who were able to get out of the ports overboard, except a few who were fortunate enough to cling to the casemate outside. . . .

In a very few minutes after the explosion our gallant ship (which had, in the language of Flag-officer Foote, fought most effectually through two-thirds of the engagement) was drifting slowly away from the field of glory; her commander badly wounded, a number of her officers and crew dead at their posts, whilst many others were writhing in their last agony.

Quoted in Porter, *Naval History*, 146.

Henry Walke, U.S. Navy. *Library of Congress, Prints and Photographs Division, Civil War Photographs, LC-DIG-cwpb-05252.*

9. Henry Walke (1809–1896), commander of the *Carondelet*, later recalled a humorous moment in the battle when his ship inadvertently got ahead of the flag-officer's vessel:

In approaching to take possession of Fort Henry, the "St. Louis" ran ahead and with frantic cheers some of her crew landed at the fort, contrary to the express orders of the flag-officer. The "Cincinnati" and "Carondelet" steamed up and flanked the batteries; the latter, being nearest to the fort, ran aground in that position, just as the order was given for their engines to be stopped, and the "Cincinnati" began to drift down the river. At first sight the "Carondelet" appeared to be steaming ahead of the flag-officer, and Foote immediately hailed her commander, with a few sharp technicalities to keep in his station; but the "Carondelet" was immovable: sticking fast to the flats, she stubbornly remained in her position ahead of the other boats, notwithstanding all that her commander could say or the engines do to back her off. Here was a scene! The flag-officer in the midst of the excitement came forward in haste, trumpet in hand, and called out again and again to stop the "Carondelet" (unaware of the fact that his own vessel was all the time drifting down the river) until at last he gave up the under-taking in favor of a junior officer, whose lungs poor fellow proved quite inadequate to the task of moving the "Carondelet;" which with the cheers, orders, groans and general confusion; all the captain's efforts to explain his queer situation were confounded. At length the pantomime transformed itself into a comedy; but a satisfactory explanation was finally afforded by the action of the gunboat sliding off the bank into deep water.

USS *Cairo*, Mississippi River gunboat fleet. *Library of Congress, Prints and Photographs Division, Civil War Photographs, LC-DIG-ppmsca-34040.*

The *Carondolet* fired 101 64- and 84-pound shells and one solid shot into the fort. Walke describes the carnage thus produced among the Confederate defenders:

> The surgeon of the fort labored with the few he could get to help him, to save the bleeding and dying. The scene was one which robbed us of all feelings of exultation. Some of our shell had pierced entirely through the breastwork; throwing tons of earth over the prostrated gunners, and then plunging ten feet into the earth beyond, or through the cabins in the rear: afterwards setting fire to them by their explosions. After the wounded were cared for, and the excitement had subsided, our men proceeded instinctively and quietly to draw the dead bodies of the victims from the water and the earth, and then buried them as well as they could.

H. Walke, *Naval Scenes and Reminiscences of the Civil War in the United States* (New York: F. R. Reed, 1877), 56–59.

22

Investment of Fort Donelson—The Naval Operations—Attack of the Enemy—Assaulting the Works—Surrender of the Fort

I informed the department commander of our success at Fort Henry and that on the 8th I would take Fort Donelson. But the rain continued to fall so heavily that the roads became impassable for artillery and wagon trains. Then, too, it would not have been prudent to proceed without the gunboats. At least it would have been leaving behind a valuable part of our available force.

On the 7th, the day after the fall of Fort Henry, I took my staff and the cavalry—a part of one regiment—and made a reconnoissance to within about a mile of the outer line of works at Donelson. I had known General Pillow in Mexico, and judged that with any force, no matter how small, I could march up to within gunshot of any intrenchments he was given to hold. I said this to the officers of my staff at the time. I knew that Floyd was in command, but he was no soldier, and I judged that he would yield to Pillow's pretensions. I met, as I expected, no opposition in making the reconnoissance and, besides learning the topography of the country on the way and around Fort Donelson, found that there were two roads available for marching; one leading to the village of Dover, the other to Donelson.

Fort Donelson is two miles north, or down the river, from Dover. The fort, as it stood in 1861, embraced about one hundred acres of land. On the east it fronted the Cumberland; to the north it faced Hickman's creek, a small stream which at that time was deep and wide because of the back-water from the river; on the south was another small stream, or rather a ravine, opening into the Cumberland. This also was filled with back-water from the river.

The fort stood on high ground, some of it as much as a hundred feet above the Cumberland. Strong protection to the heavy guns in the water batteries had been obtained by cutting away places for them in the bluff. To the west there was a line of rifle-pits some two miles back from the river at the farthest point. This line ran generally along the crest of high ground, but in one place crossed a ravine which opens into the river between the village and the fort. The ground inside and outside of this intrenched line was very broken and generally wooded. The trees outside of the rifle-pits had been cut down for a considerable way out, and had been felled so that their tops lay outwards from the intrenchments. The limbs had been trimmed and pointed, and thus formed an abatis in front of the greater part of the line. Outside of this intrenched line, and extending about half the entire length of it, is a ravine running north and south and opening into Hickman creek at a point north of the fort. The entire side of this ravine next to the works was one long abatis.

General Halleck commenced his efforts in all quarters to get reinforcements to forward to me immediately on my departure from Cairo. General Hunter sent men freely from Kansas, and a large division under General [William "Bull"] Nelson, from Buell's army, was also dispatched.[1] Orders went out from the War Department to consolidate fragments of companies that were being recruited in the Western States so as to make full companies, and to consolidate companies into regiments. General Halleck did not approve or disapprove of my going to Fort Donelson. He said nothing whatever to me on the subject. He informed Buell on the 7th that I would march against Fort Donelson the next day; but on the 10th he directed me to fortify Fort Henry strongly, particularly to the land side, saying that he forwarded me intrenching tools for that purpose. I received this dispatch in front of Fort Donelson.

I was very impatient to get to Fort Donelson because I knew the importance of the place to the enemy and supposed he would reinforce it rapidly. I felt that 15,000 men on the 8th would be more effective than 50,000 a month later. I asked Flag-officer Foote, therefore, to order his gunboats still

---

1. David Hunter (1802–1886), committed abolitionist and son of an army chaplain, spent the early part of his career on frontier duty. He resigned and then rejoined the army in the early 1840s and subsequently fought in Mexico. Hunter commanded the Sixth Cavalry at First Bull Run, where he was wounded. He made news the following year when, commanding the Department of the South, he prematurely emancipated the slaves within his region, an order Lincoln forced him to rescind. Hunter later presided over the trial of the conspirators in the Lincoln assassination.

about Cairo to proceed up the Cumberland River and not to wait for those gone to Eastport and Florence; but the others got back in time and we started on the 12th. I had moved McClernand out a few miles the night before so as to leave the road as free as possible.

Just as we were about to start, the first reinforcement reached me on transports. It was a brigade composed of six full regiments commanded by Colonel Thayer, of Nebraska. As the gunboats were going around to Donelson by the Tennessee, Ohio and Cumberland rivers, I directed Thayer to turn about and go under their convoy.

I started from Fort Henry with 15,000 men, including eight batteries and part of a regiment of cavalry, and, meeting with no obstruction to detain us, the advance arrived in front of the enemy by noon. That afternoon and the next day were spent in taking up ground to make the investment as complete as possible. General Smith had been directed to leave a portion of his division behind to guard forts Henry and Heiman. He left General Lew. Wallace with 2,500 men.[2] With the remainder of his division he occupied our left,

---

2. Today Lewis Wallace (1827–1905) is known primarily for two things: getting lost on his way to the Battle of Shiloh and writing the novel *Ben-Hur: A Tale of the Christ* (1880). Wallace volunteered for the Mexican War, practiced law and served in the Illinois State Senate, and again volunteered for military service in 1861. For Wallace's extended defense of his actions at Shiloh, see chapter 53 of his *Autobiography*.

His novel was a sensation. Harper sold a million copies by 1912. The following year, Sears, Roebuck ordered another million. "Through Sears," note Robert E. Morsberger and Katharine M. Morsberger, "*Ben-Hur* became available to even the most isolated households in rural areas." *Lew Wallace: Militant Romantic* (New York: McGraw Hill, 1980), 447–48.

The novel was subsequently dramatized on stage and screen, most recently in William Wyler's 1959 film, starring Charlton Heston as the title character, in which the chariot race was made even more thrilling through the use of widescreen technology. This description of the pivotal chariot race between Ben-Hur and his old friend Messala gives a flavor of Wallace's prose style:

> At the moment chosen for the dash, Messala was moving in a circle round the goal. To pass him, Ben-Hur had to cross the track, and good strategy required the movement to be in a forward direction; that is, on a like circle limited to the least possible increase. The thousands on the benches understood it all: they saw the signal given—the magnificent response; the four close outside Messala's outer wheel; Ben-Hur's inner wheel behind the other's car—all this they saw. Then they heard a crash loud enough to send a thrill through the Circus, and, quicker than thought, out over the course a spray of shining white and yellow flinders flew. Down on its right side toppled the bed of the Roman's chariot. There was a rebound as of the axle

extending to Hickman creek. McClernand was on the right and covered the roads running south and south-west from Dover. His right extended to the back-water up the ravine opening into the Cumberland south of the village. The troops were not intrenched, but the nature of the ground was such that they were just as well protected from the fire of the enemy as if rifle-pits had been thrown up. Our line was generally along the crest of ridges. The artillery was protected by being sunk in the ground. The men who were not

hitting the hard earth; another and another; then the car went to pieces; and Messala, entangled in the reins, pitched forward headlong. . . .

The people arose, and leaped upon the benches, and shouted and screamed. Those who looked that way caught glimpses of Messala, now under the trampling of the fours, now under the abandoned cars. He was still; they thought him dead; but far the greater number followed Ben-Hur in his career. They had not seen the cunning touch of the reins by which, turning a little to the left, he caught Messala's wheel with the iron-shod point of his axle, and crushed it; but they had seen the transformation of the man, and themselves felt the heat and glow of his spirit, the heroic res-olution, the maddening energy of action with which, by look, word, and gesture, he so suddenly inspired his Arabs. And such running! It was rather the long leaping of lions in harness; but for the lumbering chariot, it seemed the four were flying. When the Byzantine and Corinthian were half-way down the course, Ben-Hur turned the first goal.

And the race was WON!

Lew Wallace, *Ben-Hur: A Tale of the Christ* (New York: Harper & Brothers, 1908), 369–70.

Poster advertising a theatrical adaptation of *Ben-Hur*, ca. 1901.
Library of Congress, Prints and Photographs Division, LC-USZ62-50782.

serving the guns were perfectly covered from fire on taking position a little back from the crest. The greatest suffering was from want of shelter. It was midwinter and during the siege we had rain and snow, thawing and freezing alternately. It would not do to allow camp-fires except far down the hill out of sight of the enemy, and it would not do to allow many of the troops to remain there at the same time. In the march over from Fort Henry numbers of the men had thrown away their blankets and overcoats. There was therefore much discomfort and absolute suffering.

During the 12th and 13th, and until the arrival of Wallace and Thayer on the 14th, the National forces, composed of but 15,000 men, without intrenchments, confronted an intrenched army of 21,000, without conflict further than what was brought on by ourselves. Only one gunboat had arrived. There was a little skirmishing each day, brought on by the movement of our troops in securing commanding positions; but there was no actual fighting during this time except once, on the 13th, in front of McClernand's command. That general had undertaken to capture a battery of the enemy which was annoying his men. Without orders or authority he sent three regiments to make the assault. The battery was in the main line of the enemy, which was defended by his whole army present. Of course the assault was a failure, and of course the loss on our side was great for the number of men engaged. In this assault Colonel William Morrison fell badly wounded. Up to this time the surgeons with the army had no difficulty in finding room in the houses near our line for all the sick and wounded; but now hospitals were overcrowded. Owing, however, to the energy and skill of the surgeons the suffering was not so great as it might have been. The hospital arrangements at Fort Donelson were as complete as it was possible to make them, considering the inclemency of the weather and the lack of tents, in a sparsely settled country where the houses were generally of but one or two rooms.[3]

3. Working conditions for surgeons in the field were often primitive. The surgeon J. Franklin Dyer described his experience during the Peninsular Campaign in Virginia in the summer of 1862:

> I performed amputations on the ground by the light of a single candle stuck in a bayonet, but had not sufficient time to perform all that were necessary, when we were ordered to move and leave our killed and wounded on the field and in hospital, with a detail of surgeons to remain with them.

By July of 1863, Dyer thought that the ambulance and surgical service had become

On the return of Captain Walke to Fort Henry on the 10th, I had requested him to take the vessels that had accompanied him on his expedition up the Tennessee, and get possession of the Cumberland as far up towards Donelson as possible. He started without delay, taking, however, only his own gunboat, the *Carondelet*, towed by the steamer *Alps*. Captain Walke arrived a few miles below Donelson on the 12th, a little after noon. About the time the advance of troops reached a point within gunshot of the fort on the land side, he engaged the water batteries at long range. On the 13th I informed him of my arrival the day before and of the establishment of most of our batteries, requesting him at the same time to attack again that day so that I might take advantage of any diversion. The attack was made and many shots fell within the fort, creating some consternation, as we now know. The investment on the land side was made as complete as the number of troops engaged would admit of.[4]

During the night of the 13th Flag-officer Foote arrived with the iron-clads *St. Louis, Louisville* and *Pittsburg* and the wooden gunboats *Tyler* and *Conestoga*, convoying Thayer's brigade. On the morning of the 14th Thayer

---

"probably . . . better organized" than any "in the world," but terrible suffering remained "inseparable" from war. See *Journal*, 28, 105.

4. Walke himself suggests that, as important as the navy's contributions were, the credit for the defeat of Fort Donelson belonged to the Army: "A few particulars are called for from those who were present on that occasion to dispel the idea that Fort Donelson was captured by our fleet under Admiral Foote, for in reality it was taken by General Grant, with the army." Walke also recounts a memorable scene on the *Carondelet* on the morning of the 14th:

> Next morning the "Carondelet" replenished her stock of ammunition and partly repaired her damages, and again "shifted berth" by orders from the flag-officer, when a startling instance of inebriety occurred.
>
> At this critical period, the gunner at the magazine, in a fit of intoxication, threatened to blow up the "Carondelet," and send her with all her hands to ———. He was immediately ironed and confined in his room, under a guard in charge of the third master, but, during the battle, he succeeded in eluding his guard and reached the magazine hatch, where he was stopped by the surgeon Dr. McNeily, and others, and again secured. The third master, who was also intemperate and disaffected, was discharged a few days after the battle.

Naval Scenes, 74, 76.

Charles F. Smith as a colonel. *Library of Congress, Prints and Photographs Division, Civil War Photographs, LC-DIG-cwpb-05691.*

was landed.[5] Wallace, whom I had ordered over from Fort Henry, also arrived about the same time. Up to this time he had been commanding a brigade belonging to the division of General C. F. Smith. These troops were now restored to the division they belonged to, and General Lew. Wallace

5. On this day Halleck wrote to C. F. Smith with news of his promotion to major general. Halleck's telegram alludes to some difficulty in the matter of the promotion. Smith had been accused of disloyalty, but he had been ably defended by Grant and others.

"The fight has been a hard one, and the victory complete." Halleck's telegram to Smith informing him of his promotion to major general, February 14, 1862. *Special Collections, USMA Library.*

was assigned to the command of a division composed of the brigade of Colonel Thayer and other reinforcements that arrived the same day. This new division was assigned to the centre, giving the two flanking divisions an opportunity to close up and form a stronger line.

The plan was for the troops to hold the enemy within his lines, while the gunboats should attack the water batteries at close quarters and silence his guns if possible. Some of the gunboats were to run the batteries, get above the fort and above the village of Dover. I had ordered a reconnoissance made with the view of getting troops to the river above Dover in case they should be needed there. That position attained by the gunboats it would have been but a question of time—and a very short time, too—when the garrison would have been compelled to surrender.

By three in the afternoon of the 14th Flag-officer Foote was ready, and advanced upon the water batteries with his entire fleet. After coming in range of the batteries of the enemy the advance was slow, but a constant fire was delivered from every gun that could be brought to bear upon the fort. I occupied a position on shore from which I could see the advancing navy. The leading boat got within a very short distance of the water battery, not further off I think than two hundred yards, and I soon saw one and then another of them dropping down the river, visibly disabled. Then the whole fleet followed and the engagement closed for the day. The gunboat which Flag-officer Foote was on, besides having been hit about sixty times, several of the shots passing through near the water-line, had a shot enter the pilot-house which killed the pilot, carried away the wheel and wounded the flag-officer himself. The tiller-ropes of another vessel were carried away and she, too, dropped helplessly back. Two others had their pilot-houses so injured that they scarcely formed a protection to the men at the wheel.[6]

---

6. Walke describes the scene on the decks of the *Carondelet* as it drifted helplessly:

> She was terribly cut up, not a mast or spar was standing. All our barges, boats, stanchions and hammock nettings, had been cut to pieces, with the pilot house and smoke pipes riddled; port side cut open fifteen feet, and decks ripped up, in many places plowed up; rifled gun and anchors in fragments; with four men killed and fifteen wounded, two mortally, and two solid shots in her bow between wind and water. In this condition the "Carondelet" drifted slowly out of battle without turning; and her bow guns were playing on the enemy as long as our shell could reach him.
>
> Our decks were so slippery with the blood of the brave men who had fallen, that we could hardly stand until we covered them with sand. While thus drifting we received a 32-pounder from the enemy on a ricochet in

The enemy had evidently been much demoralized by the assault, but they were jubilant when they saw the disabled vessels dropping down the river entirely out of the control of the men on board. Of course I only witnessed the falling back of our gunboats and felt sad enough at the time over the repulse. Subsequent reports, now published, show that the enemy telegraphed a great victory to Richmond. The sun went down on the night of the 14th of February, 1862, leaving the army confronting Fort Donelson anything but comforted over the prospects. The weather had turned intensely cold; the men were without tents and could not keep up fires where most of them had to stay, and, as previously stated, many had thrown away their overcoats and blankets. Two of the strongest of our gunboats had been disabled, presumably beyond the possibility of rendering any present assistance. I retired this night not knowing but that I would have to intrench my position, and bring up tents for the men or build huts under the cover of the hills.

On the morning of the 15th, before it was yet broad day, a messenger from Flag-officer Foote handed me a note, expressing a desire to see me on the flag-ship and saying that he had been injured the day before so much that he could not come himself to me. I at once made my preparations for starting. I directed my adjutant-general to notify each of the division commanders of my absence and instruct them to do nothing to bring on an engagement until they received further orders, but to hold their positions. From the heavy rains that had fallen for days and weeks preceding and from the constant use of the roads between the troops and the landing four to seven miles below, these roads had become cut up so as to be hardly passable. The intense cold of the night of the 14th–15th had frozen the ground solid. This made travel on horseback even slower than through the mud; but I went as fast as the roads would allow.

When I reached the fleet I found the flag-ship was anchored out in the stream. A small boat, however, awaited my arrival and I was soon on board with the flag-officer. He explained to me in short the condition in which he was left by the engagement of the evening before, and suggested that I should intrench while he returned to Mound City with his disabled boats, expressing at the time the belief that he could have the necessary repairs made and

the starboard bow port, which beheaded two seamen and cut another in two, sending blood and brains over the captain, officers and men who were standing near them.

Naval Scenes, 78.

be back in ten days. I saw the absolute necessity of his gunboats going into hospital and did not know but I should be forced to the alternative of going through a siege. But the enemy relieved me from this necessity.

When I left the National line to visit Flag-officer Foote I had no idea that there would be any engagement on land unless I brought it on myself. The conditions for battle were much more favorable to us than they had been for the first two days of the investment. From the 12th to the 14th we had but 15,000 men of all arms and no gunboats. Now we had been reinforced by a fleet of six naval vessels, a large division of troops under General L. Wallace and 2,500 men brought over from Fort Henry belonging to the division of C. F. Smith. The enemy, however, had taken the initiative. Just as I landed I met Captain Hillyer of my staff, white with fear, not for his personal safety, but for the safety of the National troops. He said the enemy had come out of his lines in full force and attacked and scattered McClernand's division, which was in full retreat. The roads, as I have said, were unfit for making fast time, but I got to my command as soon as possible. The attack had been made on the National right. I was some four or five miles north of our left. The line was about three miles long. In reaching the point where the disaster had occurred I had to pass the divisions of Smith and Wallace. I saw no sign of excitement on the portion of the line held by Smith; Wallace was nearer the scene of conflict and had taken part in it. He had, at an opportune time, sent Thayer's brigade to the support of McClernand and thereby contributed to hold the enemy within his lines.

I saw everything favorable for us along the line of our left and centre. When I came to the right appearances were different. The enemy had come out in full force to cut his way out and make his escape. McClernand's division had to bear the brunt of the attack from this combined force. His men had stood up gallantly until the ammunition in their cartridge-boxes gave out. There was abundance of ammunition near by lying on the ground in boxes, but at that stage of the war it was not all of our commanders of regiments, brigades, or even divisions, who had been educated up to the point of seeing that their men were constantly supplied with ammunition during an engagement. When the men found themselves without ammunition they could not stand up against troops who seemed to have plenty of it. The division broke and a portion fled, but most of the men, as they were not pursued, only fell back out of range of the fire of the enemy. It must have been about this time that Thayer pushed his brigade in between the enemy and those of our troops that were without ammunition. At all events the enemy fell back within his intrenchments and was there when I got on the field.

I saw the men standing in knots talking in the most excited manner. No officer seemed to be giving any directions. The soldiers had their muskets, but no ammunition, while there were tons of it close at hand. I heard some of the men say that the enemy had come out with knapsacks, and haversacks filled with rations. They seemed to think this indicated a determination on his part to stay out and fight just as long as the provisions held out. I turned to Colonel J. D. Webster, of my staff, who was with me, and said: "Some of our men are pretty badly demoralized, but the enemy must be more so, for he has attempted to force his way out, but has fallen back: the one who attacks first now will be victorious and the enemy will have to be in a hurry if he gets ahead of me." I determined to make the assault at once on our left. It was clear to my mind that the enemy had started to march out with his entire force, except a few pickets, and if our attack could be made on the left before the enemy could redistribute his forces along the line, we would find but little opposition except from the intervening abatis. I directed Colonel Webster to ride with me and call out to the men as we passed: "Fill your cartridge-boxes, quick, and get into line; the enemy is trying to escape and he must not be permitted to do so." This acted like a charm. The men only wanted some one to give them a command. We rode rapidly to Smith's quarters, when I explained the situation to him and directed him to charge the enemy's works in his front with his whole division, saying at the same time that he would find nothing but a very thin line to contend with. The general was off in an incredibly short time, going in advance himself to keep his men from firing while they were working their way through the abatis intervening between them and the enemy. The outer line of rifle-pits was passed, and the night of the 15th General Smith, with much of his division, bivouacked within the lines of the enemy. There was now no doubt but that the Confederates must surrender or be captured the next day.

There seems from subsequent accounts to have been much consternation, particularly among the officers of high rank, in Dover during the night of the 15th. General Floyd, the commanding officer, who was a man of talent enough for any civil position, was no soldier and, possibly, did not possess the elements of one. He was further unfitted for command, for the reason that his conscience must have troubled him and made him afraid. As Secretary of War he had taken a solemn oath to maintain the Constitution of the United States and to uphold the same against all its enemies. He had betrayed that trust. As Secretary of War he was reported through the northern press to have scattered the little army the country had so that the most of it could be picked up in detail when secession occurred. About a year before leaving the

Cabinet he had removed arms from northern to southern arsenals. He continued in the Cabinet of President Buchanan until about the 1st of January, 1861, while he was working vigilantly for the establishment of a confederacy made out of United States territory. Well may he have been afraid to fall into the hands of National troops. He would no doubt have been tried for misappropriating public property, if not for treason, had he been captured. General Pillow, next in command, was conceited, and prided himself much on his services in the Mexican war. He telegraphed to General Johnston, at Nashville, after our men were within the rebel rifle-pits, and almost on the eve of his making his escape, that the Southern troops had had great success all day. Johnston forwarded the dispatch to Richmond. While the authorities at the capital were reading it Floyd and Pillow were fugitives.

A council of war was held by the enemy at which all agreed that it would be impossible to hold out longer. General Buckner, who was third in rank in the garrison but much the most capable soldier, seems to have regarded it a duty to hold the fort until the general commanding the department, A. S. Johnston, should get back to his headquarters at Nashville. Buckner's report shows, however, that he considered Donelson lost and that any attempt to hold the place longer would be at the sacrifice of the command. Being assured that Johnston was already in Nashville, Buckner too agreed that surrender was the proper thing. Floyd turned over the command to Pillow, who declined it. It then devolved upon Buckner, who accepted the responsibility of the position. Floyd and Pillow took possession of all the river transports at Dover and before morning both were on their way to Nashville, with the brigade formerly commanded by Floyd and some other troops, in all about 3,000. Some marched up the east bank of the Cumberland; others went on the steamers. During the night Forrest also, with his cavalry and some other troops about a thousand in all, made their way out, passing between our right and the river.[7]

---

7. The Tennessean Nathan Bedford Forrest (1821–1877) was a formidable commander who specialized in guerrilla tactics. He had made a fortune before the war in various enterprises, including the slave trade. He was also responsible for the slaughter of African American troops at Fort Pillow. After the war, he was the first grand wizard of the Ku Klux Klan. For a detailed account of his life, see Jack Hurst, *Nathan Bedford Forrest: A Biography* (New York: Vintage, 1994).

Lew Wallace offers some insight into the dysfunctional relationship among the three Confederate commanders at Donelson:

Having taken the resolution to defend Nashville at Donelson, he [Albert Sidney Johnston] intrusted the operation to three chiefs of brigade—John

They had to ford or swim over the back-water in the little creek just south of Dover.

Before daylight General Smith brought to me the following letter from General Buckner:

> HEADQUARTERS, FORT DONELSON,
> *February* 16, 1862.
>
> SIR:—In consideration of all the circumstances governing the present situation of affairs at this station, I propose to the Commanding Officer of the Federal forces the appointment of Commissioners to agree upon terms of capitulation of the forces and fort under my command, and in that view suggest an armistice until 12 o'clock to-day.
>
> I am, sir, very respectfully,
> Your ob't se'v't,
> S. B. BUCKNER,
> Brig. Gen. C. S. A.
>
> To Brigadier-General U. S. Grant,

B. Floyd, Gideon J. Pillow, and Simon B. Buckner. Of these, the first was ranking officer, and he was at the time under indictment by a grand jury at Washington for malversation as Secretary of War under President Buchanan, and for complicity in an embezzlement of public funds. As will be seen, there came a crisis when the recollection of the circumstance exerted an unhappy influence over his judgment. The second officer had a genuine military record; but it is said of him that he was of a jealous nature, insubordinate, and quarrelsome. His bold attempt to supersede General Scott in Mexico was green in the memories of living men. To give pertinency to the remark, there is reason to believe that a personal misunderstanding between him and General Buckner, older than the rebellion, was yet unsettled when the two met at Donelson. All in all, therefore, there is little doubt that the junior of the three commanders was the fittest for the enterprise intrusted to them. He was their equal in courage; while in devotion to the cause and to his profession of arms, in tactical knowledge, in military bearing, in the faculty of getting the most service out of his inferiors, and inspiring them with confidence in his ability,—as a soldier in all the higher meanings of the word,—he was greatly their superior.

"The Capture of Fort Donelson," *B&L*, 1:401.

For a modern historian's interpretation of the bizarre departures of Pillow and Floyd, see Jean Edward Smith, *Grant*, 160–61.

Com'ding U. S. Forces,
Near Fort Donelson.

To this I responded as follows:

HEADQUARTERS ARMY IN THE FIELD,
Camp near Donelson,
February 16, 1862.

General S. B. BUCKNER,
Confederate Army.

SIR:—Yours of this date, proposing armistice and appointment
of Commissioners to settle terms of capitulation, is just received.
No terms except an unconditional and immediate surrender can be
accepted. I propose to move immediately upon your works.

I am, sir, very respectfully,
Your ob't se'v't,
U. S. GRANT,
Brig. Gen.

To this I received the following reply:

HEADQUARTERS, DOVER, TENNESSEE,
February 16, 1862.

To Brig. Gen'l U. S. GRANT,
U. S. Army.

SIR:—The distribution of the forces under my command,
incident to an unexpected change of commanders, and the
overwhelming force under your command, compel me,
notwithstanding the brilliant success of the Confederate arms
yesterday, to accept the ungenerous and unchivalrous terms which
you propose.

I am, sir,
Your very ob't se'v't,
S. B. BUCKNER,
Brig. Gen. C. S. A.

General Buckner, as soon as he had dispatched the first of the above letters,
sent word to his different commanders on the line of rifle-pits, notifying them
that he had made a proposition looking to the surrender of the garrison, and

directing them to notify National troops in their front so that all fighting might be prevented. White flags were stuck at intervals along the line of rifle-pits, but none over the fort. As soon as the last letter from Buckner was received I mounted my horse and rode to Dover. General Wallace, I found, had preceded me an hour or more. I presume that, seeing white flags exposed in his front, he rode up to see what they meant and, not being fired upon or halted, he kept on until he found himself at the headquarters of General Buckner.[8]

I had been at West Point three years with Buckner and afterwards served with him in the army, so that we were quite well acquainted. In the course of our conversation, which was very friendly, he said to me that if he had been in command I would not have got up to Donelson as easily as I did. I told him that if he had been in command I should not have tried in the way I did: I had invested their lines with a smaller force than they had to defend them, and at the same time had sent a brigade full 5,000 strong, around by water; I had relied very much upon their commander to allow me to come

---

8. Grant's exchange with Buckner reveals two radically different understandings of war. Melville began his poem "Donelson" with a reference to Grant's "hard countermand" as "wormwood in the mouth." *Battle-Pieces*, 33.

Buckner's expectations that his old friend would offer some accommodation—and his resentful acceptance of the "ungenerous and unchivalrous terms"—contrasts sharply with Grant's rather brusque and businesslike way of making war. A not-insignificant element of the South's critique of the North—both during and after the war—focused on this lack of chivalry and on an absence of manners and social tact. Mary Chesnut's diary, for example, is full of condemnations of ill-mannered Yankees: She calls Grant a "brutal" and "bull-headed Suwarrow [Suvorov]. He don't care a snap if men fall like the leaves fall; he fights to win, that chap does. He is not distracted by a thousand side issues; he does not see them. He is narrow and sure—sees only in a straight line." March 12, 1864, and January 1, 1864, *Diary*, 299, 269–70.

Buckner's disappointed reply, evoking as it does the vocabulary of chivalry, helps to illuminate the role of self-deception in sustaining the soldier. In her meditation on Homer's *Iliad*, the French philosopher Simone Weil explains the enduring power of the belief that war is a game, an illusion "the first contact of war does not immediately destroy. . . . War's necessity is terrible, altogether different in kind from the necessity of peace. So terrible is it that the human spirit will not submit to it so long as it can possibly escape. . . . Danger then becomes an abstraction, the lives you destroy are like toys being broken by a child, and quite as incapable of feeling; heroism is but a theatrical gesture and smirched with boastfulness." "The Iliad, or the Poem of Force," *War and the Iliad*, trans. Mary McCarthy (New York: New York Review Books, 2005), 21–22.

On the fundamental hollowness and hypocrisy of the chivalric code, see Eugen Weber, "The Ups and Downs of Honor," *The American Scholar* 68, no. 1 (Winter 1999): 79–92; and the story of the 1351 Combat of the Thirty in Barbara W. Tuchman's *A Distant Mirror: The Calamitous 14th Century* (New York: Ballantine, 1979), 131–32.

safely up to the outside of their works. I asked General Buckner about what force he had to surrender. He replied that he could not tell with any degree of accuracy; that all the sick and weak had been sent to Nashville while we were about Fort Henry; that Floyd and Pillow had left during the night, taking many men with them; and that Forrest, and probably others, had also escaped during the preceding night: the number of casualties he could not tell; but he said I would not find fewer than 12,000, nor more than 15,000.[9]

---

9. Buckner, now a prisoner of war, refused Grant's offer of a loan. Hamlin Garland records the two adversaries' meeting soon after the surrender:

> Buckner grumbled at these "unchivalrous terms," but yielded, and when he met Grant within the defenses he said, with a bow and smile:
> "General, as they say in Mexico, this house and all it contains is yours."
> A moment later Grant said: "I thought Pillow was in command."
> "He was," replied Buckner.
> "Where is he now?"
> "Gone."
> "Why did he go?"
> "Well, he thought you'd rather get hold of him than any other man in the Southern Confederacy."
> "Oh," said Grant, quickly, with a smile, "if I'd got him I'd let him go again. He would do us more good commanding you fellows!"

Garland, *Grant*, 192.

After five months at Fort Warren, on Georges Island in Boston Harbor, Buckner was exchanged and returned to the fight. Despite events at Donelson, he would be one of the last visitors to the dying Grant, who asked his doctor the next day whether the papers carried news of his old friend's visit.

In another example of the "old-time ties" connecting enemies, James Longstreet tells the story of being invited to dinner by an old friend at the beginning of the war:

> We were provokingly near Washington, with orders not to attempt to advance even to Alexandria. Well-chosen and fortified positions, with soldiers to man them, soon guarded all approaches to the capital. We had frequent little brushes with parties pushed out to reconnoitre. Nevertheless, we were neither so busy nor so hostile as to prevent the reception of a cordial invitation to a dinner-party on the other side, to be given to me at the headquarters of General Richardson. He was disappointed when I refused to accept this amenity, and advised him to be more careful lest the politicians should have him arrested for giving aid and comfort to the enemy. He was my singularly devoted friend and admirer before the war, and had not ceased to be conscious of old-time ties.

Manassas to Appomattox, 59.

He asked permission to send parties outside of the lines to bury his dead, who had fallen on the 15th when they tried to get out. I gave directions that his permit to pass our limits should be recognized. I have no reason to believe that this privilege was abused, but it familiarized our guards so much with the sight of Confederates passing to and fro that I have no doubt many got beyond our pickets unobserved and went on. The most of the men who went in that way no doubt thought they had had war enough, and left with the intention of remaining out of the army. Some came to me and asked permission to go, saying that they were tired of the war and would not be caught in the ranks again, and I bade them go.

The actual number of Confederates at Fort Donelson can never be given with entire accuracy. The largest number admitted by any writer on the Southern side, is by Colonel Preston Johnston. He gives the number at 17,000. But this must be an underestimate. The commissary general of prisoners reported having issued rations to 14,623 Fort Donelson prisoners at Cairo, as they passed that point. General Pillow reported the killed and wounded at 2,000; but he had less opportunity of knowing the actual numbers than the officers of McClernand's division, for most of the killed and wounded fell outside their works, in front of that division, and were buried or cared for by Buckner after the surrender and when Pillow was a fugitive. It is known that Floyd and Pillow escaped during the night of the 15th, taking with them not less than 3,000 men. Forrest escaped with about 1,000 and others were leaving singly and in squads all night. It is probable that the Confederate force at Donelson, on the 15th of February, 1862, was 21,000 in round numbers.

On the day Fort Donelson fell I had 27,000 men to confront the Confederate lines and guard the road four or five miles to the left, over which all our supplies had to be drawn on wagons. During the 16th, after the surrender, additional reinforcements arrived.

During the siege General Sherman had been sent to Smithland, at the mouth of the Cumberland River, to forward reinforcements and supplies to me.[10] At that time he was my senior in rank and there was no authority of law

---

10. William. T. Sherman (1818–1891) graduated from West Point two years before Grant. He was on duty in California during the Mexican War and did not serve with Grant until the Civil War. Sherman's was the most important professional friendship Grant had. Different though the two men were temperamentally, they had mutual understanding, loyalty, and trust. After the Civil War, Sherman succeeded Grant as general-in-chief of the army. Sherman's *Memoirs*, published in 1875, is a penetrat-

to assign a junior to command a senior of the same grade. But every boat that came up with supplies or reinforcements brought a note of encouragement from Sherman, asking me to call upon him for any assistance he could render and saying that if he could be of service at the front I might send for him and he would waive rank.[11]

---

ing, engaging account; it offers an ideal companion—and stylistic counterpoint—to Grant's book.

Drawing of Theseus and the Centaur, after a sculpture by Canova, made by Cadet Sherman, May 1, 1838. *West Point Museum Collection, United States Military Academy.*

11. One of the soldiers who fought for the Union at Fort Donelson was a woman named Frances Clayton. Disguised as Jack Williams, Clayton served alongside her husband, who was killed at Stones River, in a number of battles. Sheridan reports the presence of two women discovered in the Fifteenth Missouri regiment during a foraging expedition southwest of Murfreesboro, Tennessee, in the winter of 1863:

> The officer in direct command always reported to me personally whatever had happened during the time he was out . . . and on one occasion the colonel in command, Colonel Conrad, of the Fifteenth Missouri, informed me that he got through without much difficulty; in fact, that everything had gone all right and been eminently satisfactory, except that in returning he had been mortified greatly by the conduct of *the two females belonging to the detachment and division train at my headquarters.* These women, he said, had given much annoyance by getting drunk, and to some extent demoralizing his men. To say that I was astonished at his statement would be a mild way of putting it, and had I not known him to be a most upright

man and of sound sense, I should have doubted not only his veracity, but
his sanity. Inquiring who they were and for further details, I was informed
that there certainly were in the command two females, that in some mysterious manner had attached themselves to the service as soldiers; that one,
an East Tennessee woman, was a teamster in the division wagon-train and
the other a private soldier in a cavalry company temporarily attached to
my headquarters for escort duty. While out on the foraging expedition
these Amazons had secured a supply of "apple-jack" by some means, got
very drunk, and on the return had fallen into Stone River and been nearly
drowned. After they had been fished from the water, in the process of
resuscitation their sex was disclosed, though up to this time it appeared
to be known only to each other. The story was straight and the circumstance clear, so, convinced of Conrad's continued sanity, I directed the
provost-marshal to bring in arrest to my headquarters the two disturbers
of Conrad's peace of mind. After some little search the East Tennessee
woman was found in camp, somewhat the worse for the experiences of
the day before, but awaiting her fate content idly smoking a cob-pipe. She
was brought to me, and put in duress under charge of the division surgeon
until her companion could be secured. To the doctor she related that the
year before she had "refugeed" from East Tennessee, and on arriving in
Louisville assumed men's apparel and sought and obtained employment
as a teamster in the quartermaster's department. Her features were very
large, and so coarse and masculine was her general appearance that she
would readily have passed as a man, and in her case the deception was
no doubt easily practiced. Next day the "she dragoon" was caught, and
proved to be a rather prepossessing young woman, and though necessarily
bronzed and hardened by exposure, I doubt if, even with these marks of
campaigning, she could have deceived as readily as did her companion.
How the two got acquainted, I never learned, and though they had joined
the army independently of each other, yet an intimacy had sprung up
between them long before the mishaps of the foraging expedition. They
both were forwarded to army headquarters, and, when provided with
clothing suited to their sex, sent back to Nashville, and thence beyond
our lines to Louisville.

Personal Memoirs of P. H. Sheridan, 2 vols. (New York: Charles L. Webster, 1888),
1:253–55.

Sheridan's account dismisses as a humorous oddity what was in fact a more widespread phenomenon. It is estimated that some four hundred women served in the Union
and Confederate armies. For a detailed account, see DeAnne Blanton and Lauren M.
Cook, *They Fought Like Demons: Women Soldiers in the Civil War* (Baton Rouge: Louisiana State University Press, 2002).

Today, at a moment when issues of gender in the military have become the subject
of national interest and debate, it is worth noting the long history of women forced to
serve incognito if they wished to fight. The identity of Mother Ross, a soldier in the
British Army, was discovered only while she was undergoing an operation to repair a

skull fracture received in the Battle of Ramilies in 1706. Hannah Snell, who enlisted under the name James Gray, fought in the East Indies at the siege of Pondicherry in the 1740s.

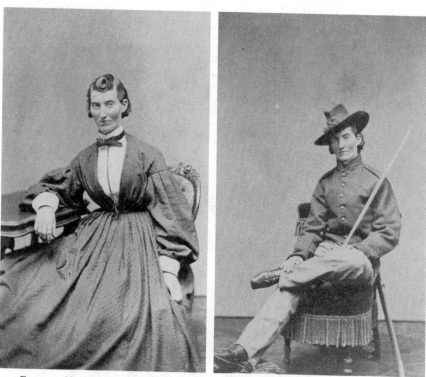

Frances Clayton, veteran of Fort Donelson, Shiloh, and Stones River. Photograph by S. Masury, ca. 1865. *Library of Congress, Prints and Photographs Division, LC-DIG-ppmsca-30980.*

Frances Clayton in uniform as "Jack Williams." Photograph by S. Masury, ca. 1865. *Library of Congress, Prints and Photographs Division, LC-DIG-ppmsca-40533.*

Mary Edwards Walker, the first woman to serve as a contract civilian surgeon with the U.S. Army, never sought to conceal her identity as a woman even as she dressed like a man. During the war she wore a Bloomer costume, which involved a tunic over trousers and was more practical than a dress. By the 1870s, she was dressing entirely in men's clothing in part as a political statement in favor of women's rights. Walker was awarded the Congressional Medal of Honor for her courageous work. In 1897 she declared:

> I am the original new woman. . . . Why, before Lucy Stone, Mrs. Bloomer, Elizabeth Cady Stanton and Susan B. Anthony were—before they were, I am. In the early '40's, when they began their work in dress reform, I

was already wearing pants. . . . I have made it possible for the bicycle girl to wear the abbreviated skirt, and I have prepared the way for the girl in knickerbockers.

Biography of Dr. Mary Edwards Walker, NIH Physician Biographies, https://cfmedicine.nlm.nih.gov/physicians/biography_325.html.

Dr. Mary Edwards Walker, 1832–1919.
Library of Congress, Prints and Photographs Division,
LC-DIG-bellcm-25836.

Women warriors have featured in literature since the Greek myths introduced Penthesilea, Queen of the Amazons. Their presence often occasions great uneasiness among the male soldiers against whom they fight. Book 11 of Virgil's *Aeneid* contains the magnificent portrait of the Volscian Camilla, whom the poet likens to Penthesilea. A swift runner and a formidable "Warrior Queen," Camilla fights against Italy's Trojan invaders at the head of a band of women. Camilla's victories in the one-on-one combat that dominates epic battle shame the men, and she is finally vanquished by a strategem: coveting another adversary's splendid golden armor—distracted, as it were, by martial finery—she allows herself to be surprised by Aruns. The former's misogyny emerges in the prayer he makes before launching the javelin that kills her: "Let me, by stealth, this female plague o'ercome." Virgil gives Camilla a splendid death scene, which concludes:

> Short, and more short, she pants; by slow degrees
> Her mind the passage from her body frees.
> She drops her sword; she nods her plumy crest,
> Her drooping head declining on her breast:
> In the last sigh her struggling soul expires,
> And, murm'ring with disdain, to Stygian sounds retires.

Virgil's Æneid, trans. John Dryden, vol. 13 of *The Harvard Classics*, ed. Charles W. Eliot (New York: P. F. Collier & Son, 1909), bk. 11, ll. 754, 1163, 1205–10.

23

Promoted Major-General of Volunteers—
Unoccupied Territory—Advance upon
Nashville—Situation of the Troops—Confederate
Retreat—Relieved of the Command—Restored
to the Command—General Smith

The news of the fall of Fort Donelson caused great delight all over the North.[1] At the South, particularly in Richmond, the effect was correspondingly depressing. I was promptly promoted to the grade of Major-General of Volunteers, and confirmed by the Senate. All three of my division commanders were promoted to the same grade and the colonels who commanded brigades were made brigadier-generals in the volunteer service. My chief, who was in St. Louis, telegraphed his congratulations to General Hunter in Kansas for the services he had rendered in securing the fall of Fort Donelson by sending reinforcements so rapidly. To Washington he telegraphed that the victory was due to General C. F. Smith; "promote him," he

---

1. Grant captured Fort Donelson at a moment when the Union was searching desperately for heroes. The victory and the ensuing celebration of it by the press and the public, changed Grant's relationship with Halleck, among others. Regarding Americans' craving for heroes, Lew Wallace observed: "A peculiarity of the most democratic people in the world is their hunger for heroes. The void in that respect had never been so gaping as in 1861. General Scott was then old and passing away, and the North caught eagerly at the promise held out by George B. McClellan; while the South, with as much precipitation, pinned its faith and hopes on Albert Sidney Johnston." "The Capture of Fort Donelson," *B&L*, 1:399.

   Newspaper pictures of the victorious Grant smoking a cigar prompted grateful citizens to deluge him with thousands. His name and likeness would be used, as had Zachary Taylor's before him, to sell tobacco.

said, "and the whole country will applaud." On the 19th there was published at St. Louis a formal order thanking Flag-officer Foote and myself, and the forces under our command, for the victories on the Tennessee and the Cumberland. I received no other recognition whatever from General Halleck. But General Cullum, his chief of staff, who was at Cairo, wrote me a warm congratulatory letter on his own behalf. I approved of General Smith's promotion highly, as I did all the promotions that were made.[2]

My opinion was and still is that immediately after the fall of Fort Donelson the way was opened to the National forces all over the South-west without much resistance. If one general who would have taken the responsibility had been in command of all the troops west of the Alleghanies, he could have marched to Chattanooga, Corinth, Memphis and Vicksburg with the troops we then had, and as volunteering was going on rapidly over the North there would soon have been force enough at all these centres to operate offensively against any body of the enemy that might be found near them. Rapid movements and the acquisition of rebellious territory would have promoted volunteering, so that reinforcements could have been had as fast as

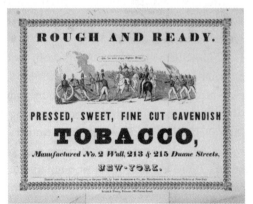

Label for "Rough and Ready" tobacco, which pictures Taylor ordering Braxton Bragg, "Give 'em more grape," at the Battle of Buena Vista, 1847. *Library of Congress, Prints and Photographs Division, LC-DIG-ds-00855.*

Label for Grant's tobacco, 1874. *Library of Congress, Prints and Photographs Division, LC-USZC4-4421.*

2. Grant's recollection of Halleck's silence suggests some lingering resentment.

transportation could have been obtained to carry them to their destination. On the other hand there were tens of thousands of strong able-bodied young men still at their homes in the South-western States, who had not gone into the Confederate army in February, 1862, and who had no particular desire to go. If our lines had been extended to protect their homes, many of them never would have gone. Providence ruled differently. Time was given the enemy to collect armies and fortify his new positions; and twice afterwards he came near forcing his north-western front up to the Ohio River.[3]

I promptly informed the department commander of our success at Fort Donelson and that the way was open now to Clarksville and Nashville; and that unless I received orders to the contrary I should take Clarksville on the 21st and Nashville about the 1st of March. Both these places are on the Cumberland River above Fort Donelson. As I heard nothing from head-quarters on the subject, General C. F. Smith was sent to Clarksville at the time designated and found the place evacuated. The capture of forts Henry and Donelson had broken the line the enemy had taken from Columbus to Bowling Green, and it was known that he was falling back from the east-ern point of this line and that Buell was following, or at least advancing. I should have sent troops to Nashville at the time I sent to Clarksville, but my transportation was limited and there were many prisoners to be for-warded north.

None of the reinforcements from Buell's army arrived until the 24th of February. Then General Nelson came up, with orders to report to me with two brigades, he having sent one brigade to Cairo. I knew General Buell was advancing on Nashville from the north, and I was advised by scouts that the rebels were leaving that place, and trying to get out all the supplies they could. Nashville was, at that time, one of the best provisioned posts in the South. I had no use for reinforcements now, and thinking Buell would like to have his troops again, I ordered Nelson to proceed to Nashville without debarking at Fort Donelson. I sent a gunboat also as a convoy. The Cumber-land River was very high at the time; the railroad bridge at Nashville had been burned, and all river craft had been destroyed, or would be before the enemy left. Nashville is on the west bank of the Cumberland, and Buell was approaching from the east. I thought the steamers carrying Nelson's division would be useful in ferrying the balance of Buell's forces across. I ordered

---

3. Grant was repeatedly frustrated at his fellow commanders' failure to seize initia-tive and take risks. His own errors—his lack of defensive preparedness at Shiloh, for example—were most often the products of aggressiveness.

Nelson to put himself in communication with Buell as soon as possible, and if he found him more than two days off from Nashville to return below the city and await orders. Buell, however, had already arrived in person at Edgefield, opposite Nashville, and [Ormsby M.] Mitchell [Mitchel]'s division of his command reached there the same day. Nelson immediately took possession of the city.

After Nelson had gone and before I had learned of Buell's arrival, I sent word to department headquarters that I should go to Nashville myself on the 28th if I received no orders to the contrary. Hearing nothing, I went as I had informed my superior officer I would do. On arriving at Clarksville I saw a fleet of steamers at the shore—the same that had taken Nelson's division—and troops going aboard. I landed and called on the commanding officer, General C. F. Smith. As soon as he saw me he showed an order he had just received from Buell in these words:

> NASHVILLE,
> *February* 25, 1862.
>
> GENERAL C. F. SMITH,
> Commanding U. S. Forces, Clarksville.
>
> GENERAL:—The landing of a portion of our troops, contrary to
> my intentions, on the south side of the river has compelled me to hold
> this side at every hazard. If the enemy should assume the offensive,
> and I am assured by reliable persons that in view of my position
> such is his intention, my force present is altogether inadequate,
> consisting of only 15,000 men. I have to request you, therefore, to
> come forward with all the available force under your command. So
> important do I consider the occasion that I think it necessary to give
> this communication all the force of orders, and I send four boats, the
> *Diana*, *Woodford*, *John Rain*, and *Autocrat*, to bring you up. In five or six
> days my force will probably be sufficient to relieve you.
>
> Very respectfully, your ob't srv't,
> D. C. BUELL,
> Brigadier-General Comd'g.
> P. S.—The steamers will leave here at 12 o'clock to-night.

General Smith said this order was nonsense. But I told him it was better to obey it. The General replied, "of course I must obey," and said his men were embarking as fast as they could. I went on up to Nashville and inspected the position taken by Nelson's troops. I did not see Buell during the day, and wrote him a note saying that I had been in Nashville since early morning and had hoped to meet him. On my return to the boat we met. His troops were still east of the river, and the steamers that had carried Nelson's division up were mostly at Clarksville to bring Smith's division. I said to General Buell my information was that the enemy was retreating as fast as possible. General Buell said there was fighting going on then only ten or twelve miles away. I said: "Quite probably; Nashville contained valuable stores of arms, ammunition and provisions, and the enemy is probably trying to carry away all he can. The fighting is doubtless with the rear-guard who are trying to protect the trains they are getting away with." Buell spoke very positively of the danger Nashville was in of an attack from the enemy. I said, in the absence of positive information, I believed my information was correct. He responded that he "knew." "Well," I said, "I do not know; but as I came by Clarksville General Smith's troops were embarking to join you."

Smith's troops were returned the same day. The enemy were trying to get away from Nashville and not to return to it.

At this time General Albert Sidney Johnston commanded all the Confederate troops west of the Alleghany Mountains, with the exception of those in the extreme south.[4] On the National side the forces confronting him

---

4. Albert Sidney Johnston (1803–1862) graduated from West Point in 1826 and fought in the Black Hawk War before resigning from the army in 1834. He later volunteered for the Mexican War. Reappointed as a major in the regular army in 1849, he served on frontier duty, and the beginning of the Civil War found him in command of the Department of the Pacific. Resigning his commission, Johnston led what would become a legendary march across the Mojave and Sonora deserts with the Los Angeles Mounted Rifles, a state militia group that joined the rebellion. After his death at the Battle of Shiloh, Johnston became a lost savior to some Southerners, his death one of the reasons the war was lost. Mary Chesnut, no fan of Johnston's successor, Beauregard, laments his loss repeatedly in her diary. William Preston Johnston, A. S. Johnston's adoring son, described his march across the desert as the stuff of epic:

> General Johnston's letters, written to his wife on the road, do not convey a full conception of the sufferings of this midsummer march. His stoicism and the wish to relieve his wife's solicitude caused him to treat lightly annoyances that in the aggregate amounted to torture; torrid heat, swarms of flies and mosquitoes, clouds of stifling dust, brackish drinking-water, wearing vigils, prolonged night marches, and exhausting fatigue, are but a part of the ills undergone. The route lay through one of the hottest regions in the world, where the thermometer often marked over 120° in the shade, when shade could be found. The Colorado Desert, through which their route lay, is a depressed basin, treeless, arid, and cut off from moisture and the cooling breath of the sea-breeze. One hundred and thirty miles across,

were divided into, at first three, then four separate departments. Johnston had greatly the advantage in having supreme command over all troops that could possibly be brought to bear upon one point, while the forces similarly situated on the National side, divided into independent commands, could not be brought into harmonious action except by orders from Washington.

At the beginning of 1862 Johnston's troops east of the Mississippi occupied a line extending from Columbus, on his left, to Mill Springs, on his right. As we have seen, Columbus, both banks of the Tennessee River, the west bank of the Cumberland and Bowling Green, all were strongly fortified. Mill Springs was intrenched. The National troops occupied no territory south of the Ohio, except three small garrisons along its bank and a force thrown out from Louisville to confront that at Bowling Green. Johnston's strength was no doubt numerically inferior to that of the National troops; but this was compensated for by the advantage of being sole commander of all the Confederate forces at the West, and of operating in a country where his friends would take care of his rear without any detail of soldiers. But when General George H. Thomas moved upon the enemy at Mill Springs and totally routed him, inflicting a loss of some 300 killed and wounded, and forts Henry and Heiman fell into the hands of the National forces, with their armaments and about 100 prisoners, those losses seemed to dishearten the Confederate commander so much that he immediately commenced a retreat from Bowling Green on Nashville. He reached this latter place on the 14th of February, while Donelson was still besieged. Buell followed with a portion of the Army of the Ohio, but he had to march and did not reach the east bank of the Cumberland opposite Nashville until the 24th of the month, and then with only one division of his army.

The bridge at Nashville had been destroyed and all boats removed or disabled, so that a small garrison could have held the place against any National troops that could have been brought against it within ten days after the arrival of the force from Bowling Green. Johnston seemed to lie quietly at Nashville to await the result at Fort Donelson, on which he had staked the possession of most of the territory embraced in the States

---

sixty miles of waste stretch away without a drop of water, or a sign of animal or vegetable life. The struggling mules sometimes sank to the knee in its dry sands; and the hot blast of the sirocco lifted the loose, moving soil, in clouds and pillars of dust, that fell like the showers of ashes that buried Pompeii.

The Life of Gen. Albert Sidney Johnston (New York: D. Appleton, 1878), 281.

of Kentucky and Tennessee. It is true, the two generals senior in rank at Fort Donelson were sending him encouraging dispatches, even claiming great Confederate victories up to the night of the 16th when they must have been preparing for their individual escape. Johnston made a fatal mistake in intrusting so important a command to Floyd, who he must have known was no soldier even if he possessed the elements of one. Pillow's presence as second was also a mistake. If these officers had been forced upon him and designated for that particular command, then he should have left Nashville with a small garrison under a trusty officer, and with the remainder of his force gone to Donelson himself. If he had been captured the result could not have been worse than it was.

Johnston's heart failed him upon the first advance of National troops. He wrote to Richmond on the 8th of February, "I think the gunboats of the enemy will probably take Fort Donelson without the necessity of employing their land force in co-operation." After the fall of that place he abandoned Nashville and Chattanooga without an effort to save either, and fell back into northern Mississippi, where, six weeks later, he was destined to end his career.

From the time of leaving Cairo I was singularly unfortunate in not receiving dispatches from General Halleck. The order of the 10th of February directing me to fortify Fort Henry strongly, particularly to the land side, and saying that intrenching tools had been sent for that purpose, reached me after Donelson was invested. I received nothing direct which indicated that the department commander knew we were in possession of Donelson. I was reporting regularly to the chief of staff, who had been sent to Cairo, soon after the troops left there, to receive all reports from the front and to telegraph the substance to the St. Louis headquarters. Cairo was at the southern end of the telegraph wire. Another line was started at once from Cairo to Paducah and Smithland, at the mouths of the Tennessee and Cumberland respectively. My dispatches were all sent to Cairo by boat, but many of those addressed to me were sent to the operator at the end of the advancing wire and he failed to forward them. This operator afterwards proved to be a rebel; he deserted his post after a short time and went south taking his dispatches with him. A telegram from General McClellan to me of February 16th, the day of the surrender, directing me to report in full the situation, was not received at my headquarters until the 3d of March.

On the 2d of March I received orders dated March 1st to move my command back to Fort Henry, leaving only a small garrison at Donelson. From Fort Henry expeditions were to be sent against Eastport, Mississippi, and

Paris, Tennessee. We started from Donelson on the 4th, and the same day I was back on the Tennessee River. On March 4th I also received the following dispatch from General Halleck:

> MAJ.-GEN. U. S. GRANT,
> Fort Henry:
>   You will place Maj.-Gen. C. F. Smith in command of expedition, and remain yourself at Fort Henry. Why do you not obey my orders to report strength and positions of your command?
>   H. W. HALLECK,
>   Major-General.

I was surprised. This was the first intimation I had received that General Halleck had called for information as to the strength of my command. On the 6th he wrote to me again. "Your going to Nashville without authority, and when your presence with your troops was of the utmost importance, was a matter of very serious complaint at Washington, so much so that I was advised to arrest you on your return." This was the first I knew of his objecting to my going to Nashville. That place was not beyond the limits of my command, which, it had been expressly declared in orders, were "not defined." Nashville is west of the Cumberland River, and I had sent troops that had reported to me for duty to occupy the place. I turned over the command as directed and then replied to General Halleck courteously, but asked to be relieved from further duty under him.

Later I learned that General Halleck had been calling lustily for more troops, promising that he would do something important if he could only be sufficiently reinforced. McClellan asked him what force he then had. Halleck telegraphed me to supply the information so far as my command was concerned, but I received none of his dispatches. At last Halleck reported to Washington that he had repeatedly ordered me to give the strength of my force, but could get nothing out of me; that I had gone to Nashville, beyond the limits of my command, without his authority, and that my army was more demoralized by victory than the army at Bull Run had been by defeat. General McClellan, on this information, ordered that I should be relieved from duty and that an investigation should be made into any charges against me. He even authorized my arrest. Thus in less than two weeks after the victory at Donelson, the two leading generals in the army were in correspondence as to what disposition should be made of me, and in less than three weeks I was virtually in arrest and without a command.

On the 13th of March I was restored to command, and on the 17th Halleck sent me a copy of an order from the War Department which stated that accounts of my misbehavior had reached Washington and directed him to investigate and report the facts. He forwarded also a copy of a detailed dispatch from himself to Washington entirely exonerating me; but he did not inform me that it was his own reports that had created all the trouble. On the contrary, he wrote to me, "Instead of relieving you, I wish you, as soon as your new army is in the field, to assume immediate command, and lead it to new victories." In consequence I felt very grateful to him, and supposed it was his interposition that had set me right with the government. I never knew the truth until General Badeau unearthed the facts in his researches for his history of my campaigns.

General Halleck unquestionably deemed General C. F. Smith a much fitter officer for the command of all the forces in the military district than I was, and, to render him available for such command, desired his promotion to antedate mine and those of the other division commanders. It is probable that the general opinion was that Smith's long services in the army and distinguished deeds rendered him the more proper person for such command. Indeed I was rather inclined to this opinion myself at that time, and would have served as faithfully under Smith as he had done under me. But this did not justify the dispatches which General Halleck sent to Washington, or his subsequent concealment of them from me when pretending to explain the action of my superiors.[5]

On receipt of the order restoring me to command I proceeded to Savannah on the Tennessee, to which point my troops had advanced. General Smith was delighted to see me and was unhesitating in his denunciation of the treatment I had received. He was on a sick bed at the time, from which he never came away alive. His death was a severe loss to our western army. His personal courage was unquestioned, his judgment and professional acquirements were unsurpassed, and he had the confidence of those he commanded as well as of those over him.

5. To John Russell Young, Grant somewhat exaggerated the trouble in which he found himself: "And yet after Donelson I was in disgrace and under arrest, and practically without a command, because of some misunderstanding on the part of Halleck." But the public adulation that followed Donelson helped considerably: "I hardly know what would have come of it, as far as I was concerned, had not the country interfered. You see Donelson was our first clear victory, and you will remember the enthusiasm that came with it. The country saved me from Halleck's displeasure." Young, *Around the World with Grant*, 2:452.

The Army at Pittsburg Landing—Injured
by a Fall—The Confederate Attack at
Shiloh—The First Day's Fight at Shiloh—
General Sherman—Condition of the
Army—Close of the First Day's Fight—The
Second Day's Fight—Retreat and Defeat
of the Confederates[1]

When I reassumed command on the 17th of March I found the army divided, about half being on the east bank of the Tennessee at Savannah, while one division was at Crump's landing on the west bank about four miles higher up, and the remainder at Pittsburg landing, five miles above Crump's. The enemy was in force at Corinth, the junction of the two most important railroads in the Mississippi valley—one connecting Memphis and the Mississippi River with the East, and the other leading south to all the cotton states. Still another railroad connects Corinth with Jackson, in west Tennessee. If we obtained possession of Corinth the enemy would have no railroad for the transportation of armies or supplies until that running east from Vicksburg was reached. It was the great strategic position at the West between the Tennessee and the Mississippi rivers and between Nashville and Vicksburg.

I at once put all the troops at Savannah in motion for Pittsburg landing, knowing that the enemy was fortifying at Corinth and collecting an army

---

1. See the introduction for a detailed account of the many competing narratives of Shiloh. Chapters 24 and 25 are revisions of the article Grant contributed to the *Century* magazine.

Railroad crossing, Corinth, Mississippi, 2016. *Photograph by Elizabeth D. Samet.*

there under Johnston. It was my expectation to march against that army as soon as Buell, who had been ordered to reinforce me with the Army of the Ohio, should arrive; and the west bank of the river was the place to start from. Pittsburg is only about twenty miles from Corinth, and Hamburg landing, four miles further up the river, is a mile or two nearer. I had not been in command long before I selected Hamburg as the place to put the Army of the Ohio when it arrived. The roads from Pittsburg and Hamburg to Corinth converge some eight miles out. This disposition of the troops would have given additional roads to march over when the advance commenced, within supporting distance of each other.

Before I arrived at Savannah, Sherman, who had joined the Army of the Tennessee and been placed in command of a division, had made an expedition on steamers convoyed by gunboats to the neighborhood of Eastport, thirty miles south, for the purpose of destroying the railroad east of Corinth. The rains had been so heavy for some time before that the low-lands had become impassable swamps. Sherman debarked his troops and started out to accomplish the object of the expedition; but the river was rising so rapidly that the back-water up the small tributaries threatened to cut off the possibility of getting back to the boats, and the expedition had to return without reaching the railroad. The guns had to be hauled by hand through the water to get back to the boats.

On the 17th of March the army on the Tennessee River consisted of five divisions, commanded respectively by Generals C. F. Smith, McClernand, L. Wallace, Hurlbut and Sherman. General W. H. L. Wallace was temporarily in command of Smith's division, General Smith, as I have said, being confined to his bed. Reinforcements were arriving daily and as they came up they were organized, first into brigades, then into a division, and the command given to General Prentiss, who had been ordered to report to me. General Buell was on his way from Nashville with 40,000 veterans. On the 19th of March he was at Columbia, Tennessee, eighty-five miles from Pittsburg. When all reinforcements should have arrived I expected to take the initiative by marching on Corinth, and had no expectation of needing fortifications, though this subject was taken into consideration. McPherson, my only military engineer, was directed to lay out a line to intrench.[2] He did so, but reported that it would have to be made in rear of the line of encampment as it then ran. The new line, while it would be nearer the river, was yet too far away from the Tennessee, or even from the creeks, to be easily supplied with water, and in case of attack these creeks would be in the hands of the enemy. The fact is, I regarded the campaign we were engaged in as an offensive one and had no idea that the enemy would leave strong intrenchments to take the initiative when he knew he would be attacked where he was if he remained. This view, however, did not prevent every precaution being taken and every effort made to keep advised of all movements of the enemy.

Johnston's cavalry meanwhile had been well out towards our front, and occasional encounters occurred between it and our outposts. On the 1st of April this cavalry became bold and approached our lines, showing that an advance of some kind was contemplated. On the 2d Johnston left Corinth in force to attack my army. On the 4th his cavalry dashed down and captured a small picket guard of six or seven men, stationed some five miles out from Pittsburg on the Corinth road. Colonel Buckland sent relief to the guard at once and soon followed in person with an entire regiment, and General Sherman followed Buckland taking the remainder of a brigade. The pur-

---

2. The Union troops did not entrench at Shiloh, however, and the Civil War historian James M. McPherson suggests, "Grant had evidently forgotten the lesson of Fort Donelson, for once again he focused his mind so intently on plans for attacking the rebels that he could spare no thoughts for war the rebels might be planning to do to him." *Battle Cry*, 407.

James B. McPherson (1828–1864) graduated from West Point in 1853 and served in the Corps of Engineers on projects ranging from the defenses of New York Harbor to Alcatraz Island. His services were highly valued by Grant and Sherman, who deeply felt his loss when he was killed making a reconnaissance in Atlanta in the summer of 1864.

suit was kept up for some three miles beyond the point where the picket guard had been captured, and after nightfall Sherman returned to camp and reported to me by letter what had occurred.

At this time a large body of the enemy was hovering to the west of us, along the line of the Mobile and Ohio railroad. My apprehension was much greater for the safety of Crump's landing than it was for Pittsburg. I had no apprehension that the enemy could really capture either place. But I feared it was possible that he might make a rapid dash upon Crump's and destroy our transports and stores, most of which were kept at that point, and then retreat before Wallace could be reinforced. Lew. Wallace's position I regarded as so well chosen that he was not removed.

At this time I generally spent the day at Pittsburg and returned to Savannah in the evening. I was intending to remove my headquarters to Pittsburg, but Buell was expected daily and would come in at Savannah. I remained at this point, therefore, a few days longer than I otherwise should have done, in order to meet him on his arrival. The skirmishing in our front, however, had been so continuous from about the 3d of April that I did not leave Pittsburg each night until an hour when I felt there would be no further danger before the morning.[3]

On Friday the 4th, the day of Buckland's advance, I was very much injured by my horse falling with me, and on me, while I was trying to get to the front where firing had been heard.[4] The night was one of impenetrable

3. J. F. C. Fuller, who lauds Grant for his military genius, nevertheless declares Shiloh "one of the most complete surprises recorded in the history of this war." Yet Grant learned from his errors this time, and in the Vicksburg campaign, Fuller notes, "he prepared one of the most elaborate and successful suprisals ever effected in war." *Generalship*, 104, 188.

4. Grant's attempt to get to the front to see for himself not only recalls his model Zachary Taylor but also reveals the confusion endemic to the Civil War battlefield. Writing to William Dean Howells after the war, Union veteran John De Forest proposed that making sense of a battle in which one participated was a nearly hopeless task:

> You do right to praise Tolstoï. Something that you wrote a while ago sent me to his *Peace and War*. . . . Let me tell you that nobody but he has written the whole truth about war and battle. *I* tried, and I told all I dared, and perhaps all I could. But there was one thing I did not dare tell. Lest the world should infer that I was naturally a coward, and so could not know the feelings of a brave man. I actually did not dare state the extreme horror of battle, and the anguish with which the bravest soldiers struggle through it. His story of *Borodino*—the soldiers sitting hungry and white under that

darkness, with rain pouring down in torrents; nothing was visible to the eye except as revealed by the frequent flashes of lightning. Under these circumstances I had to trust to the horse, without guidance, to keep the road. I had not gone far, however, when I met General W. H. L. Wallace and Colonel (afterwards General) McPherson coming from the direction of the front. They said all was quiet so far as the enemy was concerned. On the way back to the boat my horse's feet slipped from under him, and he fell with my leg under his body. The extreme softness of the ground, from the excessive rains of the few preceding days, no doubt saved me from a severe injury and protracted lameness. As it was, my ankle was very much injured, so much so that my boot had to be cut off. For two or three days after I was unable to walk except with crutches.

On the 5th General Nelson, with a division of Buell's army, arrived at Savannah and I ordered him to move up the east bank of the river, to be in a position where he could be ferried over to Crump's landing or Pittsburg as occasion required. I had learned that General Buell himself would be at Savannah the next day, and desired to meet me on his arrival. Affairs at Pittsburg landing had been such for several days that I did not want to be away during the day. I determined, therefore, to take a very early breakfast and ride out to meet Buell, and thus save time. He had arrived on the eve-

storm of death; the desperate struggles to keep the mind away from the horrors of the situation; the poor brave Prince pacing the meadow, counting his steps, etc.—it is the actual truth about the glories of war. I say it on the faith of a man who has seen it all a great many times by the hour together. . . . Oddly enough, the truth is not true to the uninformed. I recommended Tolstoï's *Borodino* to an educated bright man of my acquaintance. He returned it with the remark that it seemed "confused." Well, that is just the truth, the supereminent, vital fact of the description. Nothing is more confounding, fragmentary, incomprehensible than a battle as one sees it. And you see so little, too, unless you are a staff officer and ride about, or perhaps a general. No two spectators ever fully agree in their story of a battle. Tolstoï must have been engaged many times. There are a thousand little touches which nobody could have guessed: the general who gives Pierre an angry glare; the staff officer who yells, "What are you here for?" and rides off; the view of the charging enemy whom Pierre supposes to be Russians, and wonders why they are coming back—are touches which go to make up the picture of the haste, flurry, confusion, which a battle is. I am glad to have found Tolstoï.

Quoted in Howells, "Editor's Study," *Harper's New Monthly Magazine* 74, no. 444 (May 1887): 987.

ning of the 5th, but had not advised me of the fact and I was not aware of it until some time after. While I was at breakfast, however, heavy firing was heard in the direction of Pittsburg landing, and I hastened there, sending a hurried note to Buell informing him of the reason why I could not meet him at Savannah. On the way up the river I directed the dispatch-boat to run in close to Crump's landing, so that I could communicate with General Lew. Wallace. I found him waiting on a boat apparently expecting to see me, and I directed him to get his troops in line ready to execute any orders he might receive. He replied that his troops were already under arms and prepared to move.

Up to that time I had felt by no means certain that Crump's landing might not be the point of attack. On reaching the front, however, about eight A.M., I found that the attack on Pittsburg was unmistakable, and that nothing more than a small guard, to protect our transports and stores, was needed at Crump's. Captain Baxter, a quartermaster on my staff, was accordingly directed to go back and order General Wallace to march immediately to Pittsburg by the road nearest the river. Captain Baxter made a memorandum of this order. About one P.M., not hearing from Wallace and being much in need of reinforcements, I sent two more of my staff, Colonel McPherson and Captain Rowley, to bring him up with his division. They reported finding him marching towards Purdy, Bethel, or some point west from the river, and farther from Pittsburg by several miles than when he started. The road from his first position to Pittsburg landing was direct and near the river. Between the two points a bridge had been built across Snake Creek by our troops, at which Wallace's command had assisted, expressly to enable the troops at the two places to support each other in case of need. Wallace did not arrive in time to take part in the first day's fight. General Wallace has since claimed that the order delivered to him by Captain Baxter was simply to join the right of the army, and that the road over which he marched would have taken him to the road from Pittsburg to Purdy where it crosses Owl Creek on the right of Sherman; but this is not where I had ordered him nor where I wanted him to go.

I never could see and do not now see why any order was necessary further than to direct him to come to Pittsburg landing, without specifying by what route. His was one of three veteran divisions that had been in battle, and its absence was severely felt. Later in the war General Wallace would not have made the mistake that he committed on the 6th of April, 1862. I presume his idea was that by taking the route he did he would be able to come around on the flank or rear of the enemy, and thus perform an act of heroism that would redound to the credit of his command, as well as to the benefit of his country.

Some two or three miles from Pittsburg landing was a log meeting-house called Shiloh. It stood on the ridge which divides the waters of Snake and Lick creeks, the former emptying into the Tennessee just north of Pittsburg landing, and the latter south. This point was the key to our position and was held by Sherman. His division was at that time wholly raw, no part of it ever having been in an engagement; but I thought this deficiency was more than made up by the superiority of the commander. McClernand was on Sherman's left, with troops that had been engaged at forts Henry and Donelson and were therefore veterans so far as western troops had become such at that stage of the war. Next to McClernand came Prentiss with a raw division, and on the extreme left, Stuart with one brigade of Sherman's division. Hurlbut was in rear of Prentiss, massed, and in reserve at the time of the onset. The division of General C. F. Smith was on the right, also in reserve. General Smith was still sick in bed at Savannah, but within hearing of our guns. His services would no doubt have been of inestimable value had his health permitted his presence. The command of his division devolved upon Brigadier-General W. H. L. Wallace, a most estimable and able officer; a veteran too, for he had served a year in the Mexican war and had been with his command at Henry and Donelson. Wallace was mortally wounded in the first day's engagement, and with the change of commanders thus necessarily effected in the heat of battle the efficiency of his division was much weakened.

The position of our troops made a continuous line from Lick Creek on the left to Owl Creek, a branch of Snake Creek, on the right, facing nearly south and possibly a little west. The water in all these streams was very high at the time and contributed to protect our flanks. The enemy was compelled, therefore, to attack directly in front. This he did with great vigor, inflicting heavy losses on the National side, but suffering much heavier on his own.

The Confederate assaults were made with such a disregard of losses on their own side that our line of tents soon fell into their hands. The ground on which the battle was fought was undulating, heavily timbered with scattered clearings, the woods giving some protection to the troops on both sides. There was also considerable underbrush. A number of attempts were made by the enemy to turn our right flank, where Sherman was posted, but every effort was repulsed with heavy loss. But the front attack was kept up so vigorously that, to prevent the success of these attempts to get on our flanks, the National troops were compelled, several times, to take positions to the rear nearer Pittsburg landing. When the firing ceased at night the National line was all of a mile in rear of the position it had occupied in the morning.

In one of the backward moves, on the 6th, the division commanded by General Prentiss did not fall back with the others. This left his flanks exposed and enabled the enemy to capture him with about 2,200 of his officers and men. General Badeau gives four o'clock of the 6th as about the time this capture took place. He may be right as to the time, but my recollection is that the hour was later. General Prentiss himself gave the hour as half-past five. I was with him, as I was with each of the division commanders that day, several times, and my recollection is that the last time I was with him was about half-past four, when his division was standing up firmly and the General was as cool as if expecting victory. But no matter whether it was four or later, the story that he and his command were surprised and captured in their camps is without any foundation whatever. If it had been true, as currently reported at the time and yet believed by thousands of people, that Prentiss and his division had been captured in their beds, there would not have been an all-day struggle, with the loss of thousands killed and wounded on the Confederate side.[5]

---

5. The explorer Henry Morton Stanley, who fought with the Confederates at Shiloh, contradicts Grant's version of events while also offering insight into the state of Confederate troops:

> Generals Johnston and Beauregard proposed to hurl into the Tennessee River an army of nearly 50,000 rested and well-fed troops, by means of 40,000 soldiers, who, for two days, had subsisted on sodden biscuit and raw bacon, who had been exposed for two nights to rain and dew, and had marched twenty-three miles! Considering that at least a fourth of our force were lads under twenty, and that such a strenuous task was before them, it suggests itself to me that the omission to take the physical powers of those youths into their calculation had as much to do with the failure of the project as the obstinate courage of General Grant's troops. . . .
>
> "They fly!" was echoed from lip to lip. It accelerated our pace, and filled us with a noble rage. Then I knew what the Berserker passion was! It deluged us with rapture, and transfigured each Southerner into an exulting victor. At such a moment, nothing could have halted us. . . .
>
> . . . Then we caught sight of their beautiful array of tents, before which they had made their stand, after being roused from their Sunday-morning sleep, and huddled into line, at hearing their pickets challenge our skirmishers. The half-dressed dead and wounded showed what a surprise our attack had been. We drew up in the enemy's camp, panting and breathing hard. Some precious minutes were thus lost in recovering our breaths, indulging our curiosity, and re-forming our line. Signs of a hasty rouse to

With the single exception of a few minutes after the capture of Prentiss, a continuous and unbroken line was maintained all day from Snake Creek or its tributaries on the right to Lick Creek or the Tennessee on the left above Pittsburg. There was no hour during the day when there was not heavy firing and generally hard fighting at some point on the line, but seldom at all points at the same time. It was a case of Southern dash against Northern pluck and endurance. Three of the five divisions engaged on Sunday were entirely raw, and many of the men had only received their arms on the way from their States to the field. Many of them had arrived but a day or two before and were hardly able to load their muskets according to the manual. Their officers were equally ignorant of their duties. Under these circumstances it is not astonishing that many of the regiments broke at the first fire. In two cases, as I now remember, colonels led their regiments from the field on first hearing the whistle of the enemy's bullets. In these cases the colonels were constitutional cowards, unfit for any military position; but not so the officers and men led out of danger by them. Better troops never went upon a battle-field than many of these, officers and men, afterwards proved themselves to be, who fled panic-stricken at the first whistle of bullets and shell at Shiloh.[6]

---

the battle were abundant. Military equipments, uniform-coats, half-packed knapsacks, bedding, of a new and superior quality, littered the company streets.

Meantime, a series of other camps lay behind the first array of tents. The resistance we had met, though comparatively brief, enabled the brigades in rear of the advance camp to recover from the shock of the surprise; but our delay had not been long enough to give them time to form in proper order of battle. There were wide gaps between their divisions, into which the quick-flowing tide of elated Southerners entered, and compelled them to fall back lest they should be surrounded. Prentiss's brigade, despite their most desperate efforts, were thus hemmed in on all sides, and were made prisoners.

I had a momentary impression that, with the capture of the first camp, the battle was well-nigh over; but, in fact, it was only a brief prologue of the long and exhaustive series of struggles which took place that day.

The Autobiography, ed. Dorothy Stanley (Boston: Houghton Mifflin, 1909), 186–87, 191.

6. The novelist Stephen Crane illuminates the contagion of fear in his protagonist Henry Fleming's flight from Chancellorsville in *The Red Badge of Courage*:

The youth stared. Surely, he thought, this impossible thing was not about to happen. He waited as if he expected the enemy to suddenly stop, apologize, and retire bowing. It was all a mistake.

But the firing began somewhere on the regimental line and ripped along in both directions. The level sheets of flame developed great clouds of smoke that tumbled and tossed in the mild wind near the ground for a moment, and then rolled through the ranks as through a gate. The clouds were tinged an earthlike yellow in the sunrays and in the shadow were a sorry blue. The flag was sometimes eaten and lost in this mass of vapor, but more often it projected, sun-touched, resplendent.

Into the youth's eyes there came a look that one can see in the orbs of a jaded horse. His neck was quivering with nervous weakness and the muscles of his arms felt numb and bloodless. His hands, too, seemed large and awkward as if he was wearing invisible mittens. And there was a great uncertainty about his knee joints.

The words that comrades had uttered previous to the firing began to recur to him. "Oh, say, this is too much of a good thing! What do they take us for—why don't they send supports? I didn't come here to fight the hull damned rebel army."

He began to exaggerate the endurance, the skill, and the valor of those who were coming. Himself reeling from exhaustion, he was astonished beyond measure at such persistency. They must be machines of steel. It was very gloomy struggling against such affairs, wound up perhaps to fight until sundown.

He slowly lifted his rifle and catching a glimpse of the thickspread field he blazed at a cantering cluster. He stopped then and began to peer as best as he could through the smoke. He caught changing views of the ground covered with men who were all running like pursued imps, and yelling.

To the youth it was an onslaught of redoubtable dragons. He became like the man who lost his legs at the approach of the red and green monster. He waited in a sort of a horrified, listening attitude. He seemed to shut his eyes and wait to be gobbled.

A man near him who up to this time had been working feverishly at his rifle suddenly stopped and ran with howls. A lad whose face had borne an expression of exalted courage, the majesty of he who dares give his life, was, at an instant, smitten abject. He blanched like one who has come to the edge of a cliff at midnight and is suddenly made aware. There was a revelation. He, too, threw down his gun and fled. There was no shame in his face. He ran like a rabbit.

The Red Badge of Courage: An Episode of the American Civil War (New York: D. Appleton, 1895), 66–68.

In the 1951 preface to his World War I novel *Fear*, first published in 1930, the French writer Gabriel Chevallier insisted on the moral obligation to write about a soldier's fear:

> When I was young we were taught—when we were at the front—that war was edifying, purifying and redemptive. We have all seen the repercussions of such twaddle: profiteers, arms dealers, the black market, denunciations, betrayals, firing squads, torture; not to mention famines, tuberculosis, typhus, terror, sadism. And heroism, I agree. But the small, exceptional amount of heroism does not make up for the immensity of evil. . . .

During the whole of Sunday I was continuously engaged in passing from one part of the field to another, giving directions to division commanders. In thus moving along the line, however, I never deemed it important to stay long with Sherman. Although his troops were then under fire for the first time, their commander, by his constant presence with them, inspired a confidence in officers and men that enabled them to render services on that bloody battle-field worthy of the best of veterans. McClernand was next to Sherman, and the hardest fighting was in front of these two divisions. McClernand told me on that day, the 6th, that he profited much by having so able a commander supporting him. A casualty to Sherman that would have taken him from the field that day would have been a sad one for the troops engaged at Shiloh. And how near we came to this! On the 6th Sherman was shot twice, once in the hand, once in the shoulder, the ball cutting his coat and making a slight wound, and a third ball passed through his hat. In addition to this he had several horses shot during the day.

The nature of this battle was such that cavalry could not be used in front; I therefore formed ours into line in rear, to stop stragglers—of whom there were many. When there would be enough of them to make a show, and after they had recovered from their fright, they would be sent to reinforce some part of the line which needed support, without regard to their companies, regiments or brigades.

On one occasion during the day I rode back as far as the river and met General Buell, who had just arrived; I do not remember the hour, but at that time there probably were as many as four or five thousand stragglers lying under cover of the river bluff, panic-stricken, most of whom would have been shot where they lay, without resistance, before they would have taken muskets and marched to the front to protect themselves. This meeting between General Buell and myself was on the dispatch-boat used to run

The great novelty of this book . . . is that its narrator declared: I am afraid. In all the "war books" I had read, fear was indeed sometimes mentioned, but it was other people's fear. . . .

The author of the present book believed that it would be dishonest to speak of his comrades' fear without mentioning his. That is why he decided to admit, indeed to proclaim, his own fear. To have written about the war without writing about fear, without emphasizing it, would have been a farce. You do not spend time in places where at any moment you may be blown to pieces without experiencing a degree of apprehension.

Fear, trans. Malcolm Imrie (New York: New York Review Books, 2011), xiii–xiv.

Captain Adolph Metzner, 32nd Indiana Volunteer Infantry Regiment, War casualties at Shiloh (Pittsburg Landing), April 7, 1862. Metzner sketched throughout the war.
Library of Congress, Prints and Photographs Division, LC-DIG-ppmsca-51284.

between the landing and Savannah. It was brief, and related specially to his getting his troops over the river. As we left the boat together, Buell's attention was attracted by the men lying under cover of the river bank. I saw him berating them and trying to shame them into joining their regiments. He even threatened them with shells from the gunboats near by.[7] But it was all to no effect. Most of these men afterward proved themselves as gallant as any of those who saved the battle from which they had deserted. I have no doubt that this sight impressed General Buell with the idea that a line of retreat would be a good thing just then. If he had come in by the front instead of

---

7. Admiral David Porter explains the gunboats' role in the battle:

> We will only refer to the moment when our troops, having been driven by the enemy from point to point and ridge to ridge, had reached the river bank and were brought to bay. Here the gun-boats "Lexington" and "Taylor" rendered good service, and the national troops, rallying under the cover of their guns, made a superb resistance, and although the enemy flung himself fiercely upon the Union lines he was again and again driven back.

Naval History, 152–53.

through the stragglers in the rear, he would have thought and felt differently. Could he have come through the Confederate rear, he would have witnessed there a scene similar to that at our own. The distant rear of an army engaged in battle is not the best place from which to judge correctly what is going on in front. Later in the war, while occupying the country between the Tennessee and the Mississippi, I learned that the panic in the Confederate lines had not differed much from that within our own. Some of the country people estimated the stragglers from Johnston's army as high as 20,000. Of course this was an exaggeration.

The situation at the close of Sunday was as follows: along the top of the bluff just south of the log-house which stood at Pittsburg landing, Colonel J. D. Webster, of my staff, had arranged twenty or more pieces of artillery facing south or up the river. This line of artillery was on the crest of a hill overlooking a deep ravine opening into the Tennessee. Hurlbut with his division intact was on the right of this artillery, extending west and possibly a little north. McClernand came next in the general line, looking more to the west. His division was complete in its organization and ready for any duty. Sherman came next, his right extending to Snake Creek. His command, like the other two, was complete in its organization and ready, like its chief, for any service it might be called upon to render. All three divisions were, as a matter of course, more or less shattered and depleted in numbers from the terrible battle of the day. The division of W. H. L. Wallace, as much from the disorder arising from changes of division and brigade commanders, under heavy fire, as from any other cause, had lost its organization and did not occupy a place in the line as a division. Prentiss' command was gone as a division, many of its members having been killed, wounded or captured; but it had rendered valiant services before its final dispersal, and had contributed a good share to the defence of Shiloh.

The right of my line rested near the bank of Snake Creek, a short distance above the bridge which had been built by the troops for the purpose of connecting Crump's landing and Pittsburg landing. Sherman had posted some troops in a log-house and out-buildings which overlooked both the bridge over which Wallace was expected and the creek above that point. In this last position Sherman was frequently attacked before night, but held the point until he voluntarily abandoned it to advance in order to make room for Lew. Wallace, who came up after dark.

There was, as I have said, a deep ravine in front of our left. The Tennessee River was very high and there was water to a considerable depth in the ravine. Here the enemy made a last desperate effort to turn our flank, but was repelled. The gunboats *Tyler* and *Lexington*, Gwin and Shirk command-ing, with the artillery under Webster, aided the army and effectually checked their further progress. Before any of Buell's troops had reached the west bank of the Tennessee, firing had almost entirely ceased; anything like an attempt on the part of the enemy to advance had absolutely ceased. There was some artillery firing from an unseen enemy, some of his shells passing beyond us; but I do not remember that there was the whistle of a single musket-ball heard. As his troops arrived in the dusk General Buell marched several of his regiments part way down the face of the hill where they fired briskly for some minutes, but I do not think a single man engaged in this firing received an injury. The attack had spent its force.

General Lew. Wallace, with 5,000 effective men, arrived after firing had ceased for the day, and was placed on the right. Thus night came, Wal-lace came, and the advance of Nelson's division came; but none—unless night—in time to be of material service to the gallant men who saved Shiloh on that first day against large odds. Buell's loss on the 6th of April was two men killed and one wounded, all members of the 36th Indiana infantry. The Army of the Tennessee lost on that day at least 7,000 men. The presence of two or three regiments of Buell's army on the west bank before firing ceased had not the slightest effect in preventing the capture of Pittsburg landing.

So confident was I before firing had ceased on the 6th that the next day would bring victory to our arms if we could only take the initiative, that I visited each division commander in person before any reinforcements had reached the field. I directed them to throw out heavy lines of skirmishers in the morning as soon as they could see, and push them forward until they found the enemy, following with their entire divisions in supporting dis-tance, and to engage the enemy as soon as found. To Sherman I told the story of the assault at Fort Donelson, and said that the same tactics would win at Shiloh. Victory was assured when Wallace arrived, even if there had been no other support. I was glad, however, to see the reinforcements of Buell and credit them with doing all there was for them to do. During the night of the 6th the remainder of Nelson's division, Buell's army, crossed the river and were ready to advance in the morning, forming the left wing. Two other divisions, [Thomas L.] Crittenden's and [Alexander M.] McCook's, came up the river from Savannah in the transports and were on the west bank early on the 7th. Buell commanded them in person. My command was thus nearly doubled in numbers and efficiency.

During the night rain fell in torrents and our troops were exposed to the storm without shelter. I made my headquarters under a tree a few hundred yards back from the river bank. My ankle was so much swollen from the fall of my horse the Friday night preceding, and the bruise was so painful, that I could get no rest. The drenching rain would have precluded the possibility of sleep without this additional cause. Some time after midnight, growing restive under the storm and the continuous pain, I moved back to the log-house under the bank. This had been taken as a hospital, and all night wounded men were being brought in, their wounds dressed, a leg or an arm amputated as the case might require, and everything being done to save life or alleviate suffering. The sight was more unendurable than encountering the enemy's fire, and I returned to my tree in the rain.[8]

8. In his autobiographical sketch "What I Saw of Shiloh," Ambrose Bierce offers this eerie description of a Union field hospital:

> Hidden in hollows and behind clumps of rank brambles were large tents, dimly lighted with candles, but looking comfortable. The kind of comfort they supplied was indicated by pairs of men entering and reappearing, bearing litters; by low moans from within and by long rows of dead with covered faces outside. These tents were constantly receiving the wounded, yet were never full; they were continually ejecting the dead, yet were never empty. It was as if the helpless had been carried in and murdered, that they might not hamper those whose business it was to fall to-morrow.

Collected Works, 1:246–47.

John W. De Forest included a graphic description of field hospital surgery in his novel *Miss Ravenel's Conversion from Secession to Loyalty*:

> Deep in the profound and solemn woods, a full mile and a half from the fighting line, they came to the field hospital of the division. It was simply an immense collection of wounded men in every imaginable condition of mutilation, every one stained more or less with his own blood, every one of a ghastly yellowish pallor, all lying in the open air on the bare ground, or on their own blankets, with no shelter except the friendly foliage of the oaks and beeches. In the centre of this mass of suffering stood several operating tables, each burdened by a grievously wounded man and surrounded by surgeons and their assistants. Underneath were great pools of clotted blood, amidst which lay amputated fingers, hands, arms, feet and legs, only a little more ghastly in color than the faces of those who waited their turn on the table. The surgeons, who never ceased their awful labor, were daubed with blood to the elbows; and a smell of blood drenched the stifling air, overpowering even the pungent odor of chloroform. The place resounded with groans, notwithstanding that most of the injured men who retained their senses exhibited the heroic endurance so common on the battle-field. One man, whose leg was amputated close to his body, uttered an

The advance on the morning of the 7th developed the enemy in the camps occupied by our troops before the battle began, more than a mile back from the most advanced position of the Confederates on the day before. It is known now that they had not yet learned of the arrival of Buell's command. Possibly they fell back so far to get the shelter of our tents during the rain, and also to get away from the shells that were dropped upon them by the gunboats every fifteen minutes during the night.[9]

> inarticulate jabber of broken screams, and rolled, or rather bounced from side to side of a pile of loose cotton, with such violence that two hospital attendants were fully occupied in holding him. Another, shot through the body, lay speechless and dying, but quivering from head to foot with a prolonged though probably unconscious agony. He continued to shudder thus for half an hour, when he gave one superhuman throe, and then lay quiet for ever.

Miss Ravenel's Conversion from Secession to Loyalty (New York: Harper & Brothers, 1867), 292.

For another contemporary account, based on the author's own service in a Civil War hospital, see Louisa May Alcott's *Hospital Sketches* (Boston: James Redpath, 1863). Of particular poignancy is Alcott's account in her fourth chapter of a Union soldier named John, wounded at the Battle of Fredericksburg. Alcott comforts him during a lingering death. For a modern account of the war's impact on medical science, see Shauna Devine, *Learning from the Wounded: The Civil War and the Rise of American Medical Science* (Chapel Hill: University of North Carolina Press, 2014).

9. In the 1890s, various news outlets carried Sherman's tale of his encounter with Grant on the evening of the first day:

> "After that terrible Sunday at Shiloh," Gen. Sherman said one day to the writer, "I started out to find Grant and see how we were to get across the river. It was pouring rain and pitch dark, there was considerable confusion, and the only thing just then possible, as it seemed to me, was to put the river between us and the enemy and recuperate. Full of only this idea, I ploughed around in the mud until at last I found him standing backed up against a wet tree, his hat well slouched down and coat well pulled up around his ears, an old tin lantern in his hand, the rain pelting on us both, and the inevitable cigar glowing between his teeth, having retired, evidently, for the night. Some wise and sudden instinct impelled me to a more cautious and less impulsive proposition than at first intended, and I opened up with, 'Well, Grant, we've had the devil's own day, haven't we?'
>
> " 'Yes,' he said, with a short, sharp puff of the cigar, 'lick 'em tomorrow, though.' "

Reprinted as "Grant's Pertinacity," *Army and Navy Journal* 31, no. 19 (December 30, 1893): 317.

The position of the Union troops on the morning of the 7th was as follows: General Lew. Wallace on the right; Sherman on his left; then McClernand and then Hurlbut. Nelson, of Buell's army, was on our extreme left, next to the river. Crittenden was next in line after Nelson and on his right, McCook followed and formed the extreme right of Buell's command. My old command thus formed the right wing, while the troops directly under Buell constituted the left wing of the army. These relative positions were retained during the entire day, or until the enemy was driven from the field.

In a very short time the battle became general all along the line. This day everything was favorable to the Union side. We had now become the attacking party. The enemy was driven back all day, as we had been the day before, until finally he beat a precipitate retreat. The last point held by him was near the road leading from the landing to Corinth, on the left of Sherman and right of McClernand. About three o'clock, being near that point and seeing that the enemy was giving way everywhere else, I gathered up a couple of regiments, or parts of regiments, from troops near by, formed them in line of battle and marched them forward, going in front myself to prevent premature or long-range firing. At this point there was a clearing between us and the enemy favorable for charging, although exposed. I knew the enemy were ready to break and only wanted a little encouragement from us to go quickly and join their friends who had started earlier. After marching to within musket-range I stopped and let the troops pass. The command, *Charge,* was given, and was executed with loud cheers and with a run; when the last of the enemy broke.[10]

---

10. For Grant's correspondence with Lew Wallace's wife, which appeared in a note to the first edition, see Appendix 1, chapter 24, note 1.

25

Struck by a Bullet—Precipitate Retreat of the Confederates—Intrenchments at Shiloh—General Buell—General Johnston—Remarks on Shiloh

During this second day of the battle I had been moving from right to left and back, to see for myself the progress made. In the early part of the afternoon, while riding with Colonel McPherson and Major Hawkins, then my chief commissary, we got beyond the left of our troops. We were moving along the northern edge of a clearing, very leisurely, toward the river above the landing. There did not appear to be an enemy to our right, until suddenly a battery with musketry opened upon us from the edge of the woods on the other side of the clearing. The shells and balls whistled about our ears very fast for about a minute. I do not think it took us longer than that to get out of range and out of sight. In the sudden start we made, Major Hawkins lost his hat. He did not stop to pick it up. When we arrived at a perfectly safe position we halted to take an account of damages. McPherson's horse was panting as if ready to drop. On examination it was found that a ball had struck him forward of the flank just back of the saddle, and had gone entirely through. In a few minutes the poor beast dropped dead; he had given no sign of injury until we came to a stop. A ball had struck the metal scabbard of my sword, just below the hilt, and broken it nearly off; before the battle was over it had broken off entirely. There were three of us: one had lost a horse, killed; one a hat and one a sword-scabbard.[1] All were thankful that it was no worse.

---

1. Writing in the *Overland Monthly* in 1899, the former *New York Times* war correspondent Ben C. Truman declared:

Adolph Metzner, Sergeant Frederick Woehler,
Company A, 32nd Indiana Volunteers. Killed at
Shiloh. *Library of Congress, Prints and Photographs
Division, LC-DIG-ppmsca-51198.*

After the rain of the night before and the frequent and heavy rains for
some days previous, the roads were almost impassable. The enemy carrying his

---

This battle singularly illustrates how far the fortunes of war depend
upon what we call accident. If General Johnston had lived he would have
pursued on Monday the aggressive policy of Sunday, and his army would
have either won a magnificent victory or suffered a tremendous defeat.
And that he did not live was due to accident. A stray shot cut an artery
in his leg. An extemporized tourniquet would have stopped the bleeding.
But half an hour earlier he had dismissed his surgeon-in-chief—who up
to that time had accompanied him—to attend wounded Federal prisoners.
There was no one present at the moment who knew enough to tie up the
artery, and General Johnston bled to death. It may be gloriously said of the
distinguished Confederate commander that his lofty humanity to Federal
prisoners cost him his life. On the other hand, General Grant, Colonel
McPherson, and Major Hawkins, reconnoitering the field together, suddenly found themselves subjected to a sharp musket fire from a concealed
battery. Major Hawkins lost his hat, Colonel McPherson's horse was shot
through the body and lived just long enough to take him out of danger,
and the scabbard of General Grant's sword was taken off by a ball. If the
one ball had missed General Johnston, and the other had struck General
Grant, the commander of the Federal forces, not of the Confederate forces,
would have been changed, and the issue of the battle of Shiloh might have
been altogether different. What a great contribution Shiloh has been to the
achievements of war! What a glowing chapter on the eloquent impotence
of "Ifs"!

"A Spectacular Battle and Its 'Ifs,'" *Overland Monthly,* 2nd ser., 34, no. 200 (August
1899): 158–59.

artillery and supply trains over them in his retreat, made them still worse for troops following. I wanted to pursue, but had not the heart to order the men who had fought desperately for two days, lying in the mud and rain whenever not fighting, and I did not feel disposed to positively order Buell, or any part of his command, to pursue. Although the senior in rank at the time I had been so only a few weeks. Buell was, and had been for some time past, a department commander, while I commanded only a district. I did not meet Buell in person until too late to get troops ready and pursue with effect; but had I seen him at the moment of the last charge I should have at least requested him to follow.[2]

I rode forward several miles the day after the battle, and found that the enemy had dropped much, if not all, of their provisions, some ammunition and the extra wheels of their caissons, lightening their loads to enable them to get off their guns. About five miles out we found their field hospital abandoned. An immediate pursuit must have resulted in the capture of a considerable number of prisoners and probably some guns.

Shiloh was the severest battle fought at the West during the war, and but few in the East equalled it for hard, determined fighting. I saw an open field, in our possession on the second day, over which the Confederates had made repeated charges the day before, so covered with dead that it would have been possible to walk across the clearing, in any direction, stepping on dead bodies, without a foot touching the ground.[3] On our side National and Confederate

---

2. In an article on the battle of Shiloh which I wrote for the *Century* Magazine, I stated that General A. McD. McCook, who commanded a division of Buell's army, expressed some unwillingness to pursue the enemy on Monday, April 7th, because of the condition of his troops. General Badeau, in his history, also makes the same statement, on my authority. Out of justice to General McCook and his command, I must say that they left a point twenty-two miles east of Savannah on the morning of the 6th. From the heavy rains of a few days previous and the passage of trains and artillery, the roads were necessarily deep in mud, which made marching slow. The division had not only marched through this mud the day before, but it had been in the rain all night without rest. It was engaged in the battle of the second day and did as good service as its position allowed. In fact an opportunity occurred for it to perform a conspicuous act of gallantry which elicited the highest commendation from division commanders in the Army of the Tennessee. General Sherman both in his memoirs and report makes mention of this fact. General McCook himself belongs to a family which furnished many volunteers to the army. I refer to these circumstances with minuteness because I did General McCook injustice in my article in the *Century*, though not to the extent one would suppose from the public press. I am not willing to do any one an injustice, and if convinced that I have done one, I am always willing to make the fullest admission. [Note to the first edition.]

3. The description of battlefields blanketed by the dead is a frequent feature of Civil War reminiscences. "The sheer number of bodies requiring disposal after a Shiloh, an Antie-

tam, or a Gettysburg defied both administrative imagination and logistical capacity," Drew Gilpin Faust explains in her history of Civil War death. "Burying the dead after a Civil War battle seemed always to be an act of improvisation, one that called upon the particular resources of the moment and circumstance: available troops to be detailed, prisoners of war to be deployed, civilians to be enlisted." *This Republic of Suffering: Death and the American Civil War* (New York: Vintage, 2008), 61, 65.

The corpse-covered battlefield is also a common literary trope. Here the epic poet Ludovico Ariosto describes the field at Ravenna: "The horses, fetlock-deep, can scarce advance / For human blood which saturates the weald— / The dead so many, and so small the trench / For Germans, Spaniards, Greeks, Italians, French." *Orlando Furioso*, trans. Barbara Reynolds (New York: Penguin Classics, 1975), 3:55, 171.

General Orders No. 80, responding to reports of disrespectful picnickers at the national cemetery, Shiloh, Tennessee, 1875. *Photograph by Elizabeth D. Samet.*

The carnage was brought home to the public through word and image during the Civil War. In addition to engravings in *Harper's Weekly*, Frank Leslie's *Illustrated News*, and other sources, photographic representation changed the way Americans looked at war. When Mathew Brady mounted a show of photographs in New York City in 1862, shortly after Antietam, the *New York Times* took note:

> We recognize the battle-field as a reality, but it stands as a remote one. It is like a funeral next door. . . . It attracts your attention, but does not enlist your sympathy. But it is very different when the hearse stops at your own door, and the corpse is carried out over your own threshold—you know whether it is a wedding or a funeral then, without looking at the color of gloves worn. Those who lose friends in battle know what battle-fields are, and our Marylanders, with their door-yards strewn with the dead and dying, and their houses turned into hospitals for the wounded, know what battle-fields are.
>
> Mr. BRADY has done something to bring home to us the terrible

troops were mingled together in about equal proportions; but on the remainder of the field nearly all were Confederates. On one part, which had evidently not been ploughed for several years, probably because the land was poor, bushes had grown up, some to the height of eight or ten feet. There was not one of these left standing unpierced by bullets. The smaller ones were all cut down.[4]

Contrary to all my experience up to that time, and to the experience of the army I was then commanding, we were on the defensive. We were without intrenchments or defensive advantages of any sort, and more than

---

reality and earnestness of war. If he has not brought bodies and laid them in our dooryards and along the streets, he has done something very like it.

"Pictures of the Dead at Antietam," *New York Times*, October 20, 1862, p. 5.

This initial attention notwithstanding, the public soon lost interest, and Brady eventually went bankrupt with his collection of Civil War photographs.

What may have been the first photographs of battlefield dead were taken by Felice Beato at Lucknow in 1858 during the Indian Mutiny. Beato also documented the Crimean War and the massacre at Peking during the Second Opium War.

**"After the capture of the Taku forts,"
massacre at Peking. Photograph
by Felice Beato, 1860.** *Metropolitan
Museum of Art, Gilman Collection,
Museum Purchase, 2005.*

4. Isaac Rosenberg would describe the carnage of the prolonged trench warfare of the Western Front, full of wrecked machines and mangled men, as a "Dead Man's Dump":

> The wheels lurched over sprawled dead
> But pained them not, though their bones crunched,
> Their shut mouths made no moan.
> They lie there huddled, friend and foeman,
> Man born of man, and born of woman,
> And shells go crying over them
> From night till night and now.

Poems by Isaac Rosenberg, ed. Gordon Bottomley (London: Heinemann, 1922), 105.

half the army engaged the first day was without experience or even drill as soldiers. The officers with them, except the division commanders and possibly two or three of the brigade commanders, were equally inexperienced in war.[5] The result was a Union victory that gave the men who achieved it great confidence in themselves ever after.

The enemy fought bravely, but they had started out to defeat and destroy an army and capture a position. They failed in both, with very heavy loss in killed and wounded, and must have gone back discouraged and convinced that the "Yankee" was not an enemy to be despised.

After the battle I gave verbal instructions to division commanders to let the regiments send out parties to bury their own dead, and to detail parties, under commissioned officers from each division, to bury the Confederate dead in their respective fronts and to report the numbers so buried. The latter part of these instructions was not carried out by all; but they were by those sent from Sherman's division, and by some of the parties sent out by McClernand. The heaviest loss sustained by the enemy was in front of these two divisions.

The criticism has often been made that the Union troops should have been intrenched at Shiloh.[6] Up to that time the pick and spade had been but

---

5. What Erich Maria Remarque suggests of the neophyte's inexperience in World War I could also describe the Civil War recruit:

> Attack, counter-attack, charge, repulse—these are words, but what things they signify! We have lost a good many men, mostly recruits. Reinforcements have again been sent up to our sector. They are one of the new regiments, composed almost entirely of young fellows just called up. They have had hardly any training, and are sent into the field with only a theoretical knowledge. . . .
>
> . . . They are helpless in this grim fighting area, they fall like flies. Modern trench-warfare demands knowledge and experience; a man must have a feeling for the contours of the ground, an ear for the sound and character of the shells, must be able to decide beforehand where they will drop, how they will burst, and how to shelter from them.

All Quiet on the Western Front, trans. A. W. Wheen (New York: Ballantine, 1982), 129.

6. The war correspondent Henry V. Boynton blamed Sherman for this failure in a book published in response to Sherman's *Memoirs*: "Where General Sherman argues against the idea of a surprise at Shiloh, the records prove it to have been complete, and due mainly to his own blindness and neglect. Where he seeks to detract from the service rendered there by Buell and his army, the records set that service in clear light." H. V. Boynton, *Sherman's Historical Raid: The Memoirs in the Light of the Record* (Cincinnati, OH: Wilstach, Baldwin, 1875), 272–73.

little resorted to at the West. I had, however, taken this subject under consideration soon after re-assuming command in the field, and, as already stated, my only military engineer reported unfavorably. Besides this, the troops with me, officers and men, needed discipline and drill more than they did experience with the pick, shovel and axe. Reinforcements were arriving almost daily, composed of troops that had been hastily thrown together into companies and regiments—fragments of incomplete organizations, the men and officers strangers to each other. Under all these circumstances I concluded that drill and discipline were worth more to our men than fortifications.

General Buell was a brave, intelligent officer, with as much professional pride and ambition of a commendable sort as I ever knew. I had been two years at West Point with him, and had served with him afterwards, in garrison and in the Mexican war, several years more. He was not given in early life or in mature years to forming intimate acquaintances. He was studious by habit, and commanded the confidence and respect of all who knew him. He was a strict disciplinarian, and perhaps did not distinguish sufficiently between the volunteer who "enlisted for the war" and the soldier who serves in time of peace. One system embraced men who risked life for a principle, and often men of social standing, competence, or wealth and independence of character. The other includes, as a rule, only men who could not do as well in any other occupation. General Buell became an object of harsh criticism later, some going so far as to challenge his loyalty. No one who knew him ever believed him capable of a dishonorable act, and nothing could be more dishonorable than to accept high rank and command in war and then betray the trust. When I came into command of the army in 1864, I requested the Secretary of War to restore General Buell to duty.

After the war, during the summer of 1865, I travelled considerably through the North, and was everywhere met by large numbers of people. Every one had his opinion about the manner in which the war had been conducted: who among the generals had failed, how, and why. Correspondents of the press were ever on hand to hear every word dropped, and were not always disposed to report correctly what did not confirm their preconceived notions, either about the conduct of the war or the individuals concerned in it.[7] The opportunity frequently occurred for me to defend General Buell

7. Grant expresses his frustration with reporters on several occasions in the *Memoirs*. Franker still in his correspondence, he was often frustrated and personally wounded by the false stories that circulated in newspapers about his incompetence and, worse yet, his drinking. See Simpson, *Triumph over Adversity*. Today the presence of reporters on the

against what I believed to be most unjust charges. On one occasion a correspondent put in my mouth the very charge I had so often refuted—of disloyalty. This brought from General Buell a very severe retort, which I saw in the New York *World* some time before I received the letter itself. I could very well understand his grievance at seeing untrue and disgraceful charges apparently sustained by an officer who, at the time, was at the head of the army. I replied to him, but not through the press. I kept no copy of my letter, nor did I ever see it in print; neither did I receive an answer.

General Albert Sidney Johnston, who commanded the Confederate forces at the beginning of the battle, was disabled by a wound on the afternoon of the first day. This wound, as I understood afterwards, was not necessarily fatal, or even dangerous. But he was a man who would not abandon what he deemed an important trust in the face of danger and consequently continued in the saddle, commanding, until so exhausted by the loss of blood that he had to be taken from his horse, and soon after died. The news was not long in reaching our side and I suppose was quite an encouragement to the National soldiers.

I had known Johnston slightly in the Mexican war and later as an officer in the regular army. He was a man of high character and ability. His contemporaries at West Point, and officers generally who came to know him personally later and who remained on our side, expected him to prove the most formidable man to meet that the Confederacy would produce.

I once wrote that nothing occurred in his brief command of an army to prove or disprove the high estimate that had been placed upon his military ability; but after studying the orders and dispatches of Johnston I am compelled to materially modify my views of that officer's qualifications as a soldier. My judgment now is that he was vacillating and undecided in his actions.

All the disasters in Kentucky and Tennessee were so discouraging to the authorities in Richmond that Jefferson Davis wrote an unofficial letter to Johnston expressing his own anxiety and that of the public, and saying that he had made such defence as was dictated by long friendship, but that in the absence of a report he needed facts. The letter was not a reprimand in direct

---

battlefield is unsurprising, but the phenomenon of the war correspondent was born in the Crimea with William Howard Russell, a British newspaperman who also reported on the American Civil War. Phillip Knightley has documented the history of this specialized profession in *The First Casualty: The War Correspondent as Hero and Myth-Maker from the Crimea to Iraq* (Baltimore, MD: Johns Hopkins University Press, 2004).

terms, but it was evidently as much felt as though it had been one. General Johnston raised another army as rapidly as he could, and fortified or strongly intrenched at Corinth. He knew the National troops were preparing to attack him in his chosen position. But he had evidently become so disturbed at the results of his operations that he resolved to strike out in an offensive campaign which would restore all that was lost, and if successful accomplish still more. We have the authority of his son and biographer for saying that his plan was to attack the forces at Shiloh and crush them; then to cross the Tennessee and destroy the army of Buell, and push the war across the Ohio River. The design was a bold one; but we have the same authority for saying that in the execution Johnston showed vacillation and indecision. He left Corinth on the 2d of April and was not ready to attack until the 6th. The distance his army had to march was less than twenty miles. Beauregard, his second in command, was opposed to the attack for two reasons: first, he thought, if let alone the National troops would attack the Confederates in their intrenchments; second, we were in ground of our own choosing and would necessarily be intrenched. Johnston not only listened to the objection of Beauregard to an attack, but held a council of war on the subject on the morning of the 5th. On the evening of the same day he was in consultation with some of his generals on the same subject, and still again on the morning of the 6th. During this last consultation, and before a decision had been reached, the battle began by the National troops opening fire on the enemy. This seemed to settle the question as to whether there was to be any battle of Shiloh. It also seems to me to settle the question as to whether there was a surprise.[8]

---

8. The feud between the partisans of Johnston and Beauregard raged on throughout the rest of the century and into the next. Beauregard had not helped himself by writing a triumphant telegram to Jefferson Davis on the night of April 6. It was sent the following day: "We this morning attacked the enemy in strong position in front of Pittsburg, and after a severe battle of ten hours, thanks be to the Almighty, gained a complete victory, driving the enemy from every position. Loss on both sides heavy, including our commander-in-chief, General A. S. Johnston, who fell gallantly leading his troops into the thickest of the fight." *OR*, ser. 1, vol. 10, pt. 1, 384.

Beauregard continued to feud with Jefferson Davis throughout the war, but he found a defender in the Confederate officer and poet John Esten Cooke, who had great personal affection for him and thought him the luckiest of Confederate generals: "Often he appeared to be outgeneralled, checkmated, and driven to the 'last ditch,' but ever some fortunate circumstance intervened to change the whole situation. More than once fortune seemed to go against him, but he always retrieved the day by some surprising movement." *Wearing of the Gray: Being Personal Portraits, Scenes, and Adventures of War* (New York: E. B. Treat & Co, 1867), 83.

I do not question the personal courage of General Johnston, or his ability. But he did not win the distinction predicted for him by many of his friends. He did prove that as a general he was over-estimated.

General Beauregard was next in rank to Johnston and succeeded to the command, which he retained to the close of the battle and during the subsequent retreat on Corinth, as well as in the siege of that place. His tactics have been severely criticised by Confederate writers, but I do not believe his fallen chief could have done any better under the circumstances. Some of these critics claim that Shiloh was won when Johnston fell, and that if he had not fallen the army under me would have been annihilated or captured. *Ifs* defeated the Confederates at Shiloh. There is little doubt that we would have been disgracefully beaten *if* all the shells and bullets fired by us had passed harmlessly over the enemy and *if* all of theirs had taken effect. Commanding generals are liable to be killed during engagements; and the fact that when he was shot Johnston was leading a brigade to induce it to make a charge which had been repeatedly ordered, is evidence that there was neither the universal demoralization on our side nor the unbounded confidence on theirs which has been claimed. There was, in fact, no hour during the day when I doubted the eventual defeat of the enemy, although I was disappointed that reinforcements so near at hand did not arrive at an earlier hour.

The description of the battle of Shiloh given by Colonel Wm. Preston Johnston is very graphic and well told.[9] The reader will imagine that he can

9. William Preston Johnston's account occurs in a biography of his father. The following example of its tone and character reveals a style wholly different from Grant's and entirely typical of the period:

> As he looked around on his soldiers he might well feel more like the chieftain who leads his clansmen to battle than the mere general of an army. Everywhere he beheld men bound to him by ties of ancient friendship or of service on other fields. . . . He looked upon them with the tenderness of a patriarchal regard—of an Abraham or a Jephthah. In the dread holocaust of war, in which perish the bravest and best, he was ready to make his offering, as a sacrifice for his people and for constitutional liberty. In this spirit he sent, in this spirit he led, the sons of the South to the field of death and victory, on which he himself was to fall a victim.

Life of Johnston, 584–85.

Johnston's reputation would be enshrined in Lost Cause literature such as Mary Jervey's hagiographic poem "General Albert Sidney Johnston":

> In thickest fight triumphantly he fell,

see each blow struck, a demoralized and broken mob of Union soldiers, each blow sending the enemy more demoralized than ever towards the Tennessee River, which was a little more than two miles away at the beginning of the onset. If the reader does not stop to inquire why, with such Confederate success for more than twelve hours of hard fighting, the National troops were not all killed, captured or driven into the river, he will regard the pen picture as perfect. But I witnessed the fight from the National side from eight o'clock in the morning until night closed the contest. I see but little in the description that I can recognize. The Confederate troops fought well and deserve commendation enough for their bravery and endurance on the 6th of April, without detracting from their antagonists or claiming anything more than their just dues.

The reports of the enemy show that their condition at the end of the first day was deplorable; their losses in killed and wounded had been very heavy, and their stragglers had been quite as numerous as on the National side, with the difference that those of the enemy left the field entirely and were not

---

While into victory's arms he led us on;
A death so glorious our grief should quell:
We mourn him, yet his battle-crown is won.

No slanderous tongue can vex his spirit now,
No bitter taunts can stain his blood-bought fame;
Immortal honor rests upon his brow,
And noble memories cluster round his name.

For hearts shall thrill and eyes grow dim with tears,
To read the story of his touching fate;
How in his death the gallant soldier wears
The crown that came for earthly life too late.

Ye people! guard his memory—sacred keep
The garlands green above his hero-grave;
Yet weep, for praise can never wake his sleep,
To tell him he is shrined among the brave!

This poem was collected together with similar effusions by Henry M. Wharton, who had served as a private in John B. Gordon's brigade of the Army of Northern Virginia. See *War Songs and Poems of the Southern Confederacy, 1861–1865* (Philadelphia: John C. Winston, 1904), 46.

For another romantic account of the battle—this one from the opposite side—see Union officer Wills de Hass's "The Battle of Shiloh," *Annals of the War*, ed. McClure, 677–92.

brought back to their respective commands for many days. On the Union side but few of the stragglers fell back further than the landing on the river, and many of these were in line for duty on the second day. The admissions of the highest Confederate officers engaged at Shiloh make the claim of a victory for them absurd. The victory was not to either party until the battle was over. It was then a Union victory, in which the Armies of the Tennessee and the Ohio both participated. But the Army of the Tennessee fought the entire rebel army on the 6th and held it at bay until near night; and night alone closed the conflict and not the three regiments of Nelson's division.

The Confederates fought with courage at Shiloh, but the particular skill claimed I could not and still cannot see; though there is nothing to criticise except the claims put forward for it since. But the Confederate claimants for superiority in strategy, superiority in generalship and superiority in dash and prowess are not so unjust to the Union troops engaged at Shiloh as are many Northern writers. The troops on both sides were American, and united they need not fear any foreign foe. It is possible that the Southern man started in with a little more dash than his Northern brother; but he was correspondingly less enduring.

The endeavor of the enemy on the first day was simply to hurl their men against ours—first at one point, then at another, sometimes at several points at once. This they did with daring and energy, until at night the rebel troops were worn out. Our effort during the same time was to be prepared to resist assaults wherever made. The object of the Confederates on the second day was to get away with as much of their army and material as possible. Ours then was to drive them from our front, and to capture or destroy as great a part as possible of their men and material. We were successful in driving them back, but not so successful in captures as if farther pursuit could have been made. As it was, we captured or recaptured on the second day about as much artillery as we lost on the first; and, leaving out the one great capture of Prentiss, we took more prisoners on Monday than the enemy gained from us on Sunday. On the 6th Sherman lost seven pieces of artillery, McClernand six, Prentiss eight, and Hurlbut two batteries. On the 7th Sherman captured seven guns, McClernand three and the Army of the Ohio twenty.

At Shiloh the effective strength of the Union forces on the morning of the 6th was 33,000 men. Lew. Wallace brought 5,000 more after nightfall. Beauregard reported the enemy's strength at 40,955. According to the custom of enumeration in the South, this number probably excluded every man enlisted as musician or detailed as guard or nurse, and all commissioned officers—everybody who did not carry a musket or serve a cannon. With us everybody in the field receiving pay from the government is counted. Excluding the troops who fled, panic-stricken, before they had fired a shot, there was not a time during the 6th when we had more than 25,000 men in line. On the 7th Buell brought 20,000 more. Of his remaining two divisions, Thomas's did not reach the field during the engagement; Wood's arrived before firing had ceased, but not in time to be of much service.

Our loss in the two days' fight was 1,754 killed, 8,408 wounded and 2,885 missing. Of these, 2,103 were in the Army of the Ohio. Beauregard reported a total loss of 10,699, of whom 1,728 were killed, 8,012 wounded and 957 missing. This estimate must be incorrect. We buried, by actual count, more of the enemy's dead in front of the divisions of McClernand and Sherman alone than here reported, and 4,000 was the estimate of the burial parties of the whole field. Beauregard reports the Confederate force on the 6th at over 40,000, and their total loss during the two days at 10,699; and at the same time declares that he could put only 20,000 men in battle on the morning of the 7th.

The navy gave a hearty support to the army at Shiloh, as indeed it always did both before and subsequently when I was in command. The nature of the ground was such, however, that on this occasion it could do nothing in aid of the troops until sundown on the first day. The country was broken and heavily timbered, cutting off all view of the battle from the river, so that friends would be as much in danger from fire from the gunboats as the foe. But about sundown, when the National troops were back in their last position, the right of the enemy was near the river and exposed to the fire of the two gunboats, which was delivered with vigor and effect. After nightfall, when firing had entirely ceased on land, the commander of the fleet informed himself, approximately, of the position of our troops and sug- gested the idea of dropping a shell within the lines of the enemy every fifteen minutes during the night. This was done with effect, as is proved by the Confederate reports.

Up to the battle of Shiloh I, as well as thousands of other citizens, believed that the rebellion against the Government would collapse sud- denly and soon, if a decisive victory could be gained over any of its armies. Donelson and Henry were such victories. An army of more than 21,000 men was captured or destroyed. Bowling Green, Columbus and Hickman, Kentucky, fell in consequence, and Clarksville and Nashville, Tennessee, the last two with an immense amount of stores, also fell into our hands. The Tennessee and Cumberland rivers, from their mouths to the head of naviga- tion, were secured. But when Confederate armies were collected which not only attempted to hold a line farther south, from Memphis to Chattanooga, Knoxville and on to the Atlantic, but assumed the offensive and made such a gallant effort to regain what had been lost, then, indeed, I gave up all idea of saving the Union except by complete conquest.[10] Up to that time it had been the policy of our army, certainly of that portion commanded by me, to protect the property of the citizens whose territory was invaded, without regard to their sentiments, whether Union or Secession. After this,

---

10. The war had many turning points, but the evolution in Grant's thinking at this moment marks a crucial shift. "Rapid conclusion of a war undoubtedly constitutes the greatest kindness," wrote the German military theorist Helmuth von Moltke (Moltke the Elder). "All means not absolutely reprehensible must be used to accomplish this end. This involves both weakening the hostile fighting forces and making use of all the resources of the hostile environment: finances, railroads, provisions, and even prestige. . . . Modern wars call whole peoples to arms." *Moltke on the Art of War: Selected Writings*, ed. Daniel Hughes (New York: Ballantine, Presidio, 1995), 24, 26.

Sherman, in his march through Georgia and the Carolinas, and Sheridan, in his Shenandoah Valley campaign, would put the concept of total war into action with energy and efficiency. Regarding "Grant's instructions to destroy the valley," Sheridan writes:

> He had rightly concluded that it was time to bring the war home to a people engaged in raising crops from a prolific soil to feed the country's enemies, and devoting to the Confederacy its best youth. I endorsed the programme in all its parts, for the stores of meat and grain that the valley provided, and the men it furnished for Lee's depleted regiments, were the strongest auxiliaries he possessed in the whole insurgent section. In a war a territory like this is a factor of great importance, and whichever adversary controls it permanently reaps all the advantages of its prosperity. . . . I do not hold war to mean simply that lines of men shall engage each other in battle, and material interests be ignored. This is but a duel, in which one combatant seeks the other's life; war means much more, and is far worse than this. Those who rest at home in peace and plenty see but little of the horrors attending such a duel, and even grow indifferent to them as the struggle goes on, contenting themselves with encouraging all who are able-bodied to enlist in the cause, to fill up the shattered ranks as death thins them. It is another matter, however, when deprivation and suffering are brought to their own doors. Then the case appears much graver, for the loss of property weighs heavy with the most of mankind; heavier often, than the sacrifices made on the field of battle. Death is popularly considered the maximum of punishment in war, but it is not; reduction to poverty brings prayers for peace more surely and more quickly than does the destruction of human life, as the selfishness of man has demonstrated in more than one great conflict.

Sheridan, *Personal Memoirs*, 1:485–88.

National Cemetery, Shiloh
Battlefield, Tennessee, 2016.
Photograph by Elizabeth D. Samet.

however, I regarded it as humane to both sides to protect the persons of those found at their homes, but to consume everything that could be used to support or supply armies. Protection was still continued over such supplies as were within lines held by us and which we expected to continue to hold; but such supplies within the reach of Confederate armies I regarded as much contraband as arms or ordnance stores. Their destruction was accomplished without bloodshed and tended to the same result as the destruction of armies. I continued this policy to the close of the war. Promiscuous pillaging, however, was discouraged and punished. Instructions were always given to take provisions and forage under the direction of commissioned officers who should give receipts to owners, if at home, and turn the property over to officers of the quartermaster or commissary departments to be issued as if furnished from our Northern depots. But much was destroyed without receipts to owners, when it could not be brought within our lines and would otherwise have gone to the support of secession and rebellion.

This policy I believe exercised a material influence in hastening the end.

The battle of Shiloh, or Pittsburg landing, has been perhaps less understood, or, to state the case more accurately, more persistently misunderstood, than any other engagement between National and Confederate troops during the entire rebellion. Correct reports of the battle have been published, notably by Sherman, Badeau and, in a speech before a meeting of veterans, by General Prentiss; but all of these appeared long subsequent to the close of the rebellion and after public opinion had been most erroneously formed.[11]

---

11. A few days after the battle Sherman wrote a letter to his wife that revealed the psychological impact of the slaughter:

I myself made no report to General Halleck, further than was contained in a letter, written immediately after the battle informing him that an engagement had been fought and announcing the result. A few days afterwards General Halleck moved his headquarters to Pittsburg landing and assumed command of the troops in the field. Although next to him in rank, and nominally in command of my old district and army, I was ignored as much as if I had been at the most distant point of territory within my jurisdiction; and although I was in command of all the troops engaged at Shiloh I was not permitted to see one of the reports of General Buell or his subordinates in that battle, until they were published by the War Department long after the event. For this reason I never made a full official report of this engagement.

The first man killed in the battle was my orderly close by my side, a young, handsome, faithful soldier who carried his carbine ever ready to defend me. His name was Holliday, and the shot that killed him was meant for me. After the battle was over I had him brought to my camp and buried by a tree scarred with balls and its top carried off by a cannon ball. . . .

. . . The scenes on this field would have cured anybody of war. Mangled bodies, dead, dying, in every conceivable shape, without heads, legs; and horses! . . . All I can say this was a battle, and you will receive so many graphic accounts that my picture would be tame. . . . I still feel the horrid nature of this war, and the piles of dead and wounded and maimed makes me more anxious than ever for some hope of an end, but I know such a thing cannot be for a long, long time. Indeed I never expect it, or to survive it.

Letter to Ellen Ewing Sherman, April 11, 1862, *Home Letters*, 220–23.

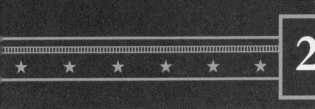

26

Halleck Assumes Command in the Field— The Advance upon Corinth—Occupation of Corinth—The Army Separated

General Halleck arrived at Pittsburg landing on the 11th of April and immediately assumed command in the field. On the 21st General Pope arrived with an army 30,000 strong, fresh from the capture of Island Number Ten in the Mississippi River. He went into camp at Hamburg landing five miles above Pittsburg. Halleck had now three armies: the Army of the Ohio, Buell commanding; the Army of the Mississippi, Pope commanding; and the Army of the Tennessee. His orders divided the combined force into the right wing, reserve, centre and left wing. Major-General George H. Thomas, who had been in Buell's army, was transferred with his division to the Army of the Tennessee and given command of the right wing, composed of all of that army except McClernand's and Lew. Wallace's divisions. McClernand was assigned to the command of the reserve, composed of his own and Lew. Wallace's divisions. Buell commanded the centre, the Army of the Ohio; and Pope the left wing, the Army of the Mississippi. I was named second in command of the whole, and was also supposed to be in command of the right wing and reserve.[1]

Orders were given to all the commanders engaged at Shiloh to send in

---

1. Halleck now took command in the field, and Grant's temporary exile began. Although Grant had been heralded as a hero after Donelson, Northern newspapers were now full of stories of his unpreparedness. He became, as James McPherson notes, "a bigger goat than Albert Sidney Johnston had been in the South after his retreat from Tennessee." *Battle Cry*, 414.

Arthur Lumley, Soldiers building corduroy roadway, Virginia. *Library of Congress, Prints and Photographs Division, LC-DIG-ppmsca-20775.*

their reports without delay to department headquarters. Those from officers of the Army of the Tennessee were sent through me; but from the Army of the Ohio they were sent by General Buell without passing through my hands. General Halleck ordered me, verbally, to send in my report, but I positively declined on the ground that he had received the reports of a part of the army engaged at Shiloh without their coming through me. He admitted that my refusal was justifiable under the circumstances, but explained that he had wanted to get the reports off before moving the command, and as fast as a report had come to him he had forwarded it to Washington.

Preparations were at once made upon the arrival of the new commander for an advance on Corinth. Owl Creek, on our right, was bridged, and expeditions were sent to the north-west and west to ascertain if our position was being threatened from those quarters; the roads towards Corinth were corduroyed and new ones made; lateral roads were also constructed, so that in case of necessity troops marching by different routes could reinforce each other.[2] All commanders were cautioned against bringing on an engagement

---

2. A corduroy road consisted of transverse logs laid across swampy terrain. The word *corduroy* is, according to the *Oxford English Dictionary*, an English coinage: an attempt to reproduce the French-sounding phrase *corde du roi*, the king's cord. Its use to describe

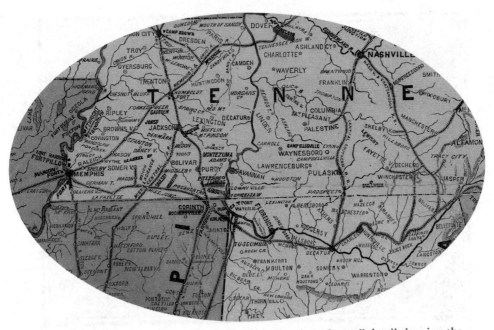

"Lloyd's New Military Map of the Border & Southern States," detail showing the junction at Corinth in northeast Mississippi, 1862. *Library of Congress, Geography and Map Division.*

and informed in so many words that it would be better to retreat than to fight.[3] By the 30th of April all preparations were complete; the country west to the Mobile and Ohio railroad had been reconnoitred, as well as the road to Corinth as far as Monterey twelve miles from Pittsburg. Everywhere small

corded fabrics arose in the eighteenth century, while its application to a corded road originated in the United States during the antebellum period. It was not until 1862, however, that it was first used as a verb—as in to corduroy a road—by British war correspondent William Howard Russell and others. War tends to accelerate linguistic change.

3. Halleck's caution was a source of immense frustration for Grant and many others. It took nearly a month to move his vast army—he had amassed a force of 100,000 men— the twenty miles to Corinth. In the interim, Beauregard was able to move his supplies and escape with his army further south to Tupelo, Mississippi. As the historian Peter Cozzens notes, Corinth was "less important" to the Confederates and more important to Halleck than was warranted. Instead of trying to destroy Beauregard's army, Cozzens argues, Halleck concentrated exclusively on the town. Committed, as his own treatise *Elements of Military Art and Science* attested, to "eighteenth-century theories of 'strategic points' as the keys to victory and to Baron Henri Jomini's emphasis on movement over annihilation, Halleck hesitated to give battle." Cozzens, *The Darkest Days of the War: The Battles of Iuka & Corinth* (Chapel Hill: University of North Carolina, 1997), 18.

bodies of the enemy had been encountered, but they were observers and not in force to fight battles.

Corinth, Mississippi, lies in a south-westerly direction from Pittsburg landing and about nineteen miles away as the bird would fly, but probably twenty-two by the nearest wagon-road. It is about four miles south of the line dividing the States of Tennessee and Mississippi, and at the junction of the Mississippi and Chattanooga railroad with the Mobile and Ohio road which runs from Columbus to Mobile.[4] From Pittsburg to Corinth the land is rolling, but at no point reaching an elevation that makes high hills to pass over. In 1862 the greater part of the country was covered with forest with intervening clearings and houses. Underbrush was dense in the low grounds along the creeks and ravines, but generally not so thick on the high land as to prevent men passing through with ease. There are two small creeks running from north of the town and connecting some four miles south, where they form Bridge Creek which empties into the Tuscumbia River. Corinth is on the ridge between these streams and is a naturally strong defensive position. The creeks are insignificant in volume of water, but the stream to the east widens out in front of the town into a swamp, impassable in the presence of an enemy. On the crest of the west bank of this stream the enemy was strongly intrenched.

Corinth was a valuable strategic point for the enemy to hold, and consequently a valuable one for us to possess ourselves of. We ought to have seized it immediately after the fall of Donelson and Nashville, when it could have been taken without a battle, but failing then it should have been taken, without delay, on the concentration of troops at Pittsburg landing after the battle of Shiloh. In fact the arrival of Pope should not have been awaited. There was no time from the battle of Shiloh up to the evacuation of Corinth when the enemy would not have left if pushed. The demoralization among the Confederates from their defeats at Henry and Donelson; their long marches from Bowling Green, Columbus, and Nashville, and their failure at Shiloh; in fact from having been driven out of Kentucky and Tennessee, was so great that a stand for the time would have been impossible. Beauregard made strenuous efforts to reinforce himself and partially succeeded. He appealed

---

4. Corinth was at once a miserable backwater—malarial swamps, dust inches thick in the streets, mosquitoes, disease—and a railroad boomtown. It was the junction of two of the most important Confederate railroads: the Mobile & Ohio and the Memphis & Charleston. For a fuller description, see chapter 2 of Cozzens, *Darkest Days*. The railroads still cross in Corinth: Norfolk Southern and Kansas City freight trains roll through every day.

to the people of the South-west for new regiments, and received a few. A. S. Johnston had made efforts to reinforce in the same quarter, before the battle of Shiloh, but in a different way. He had negroes sent out to him to take the place of teamsters, company cooks and laborers in every capacity, so as to put all his white men into the ranks. The people, while willing to send their sons to the field, were not willing to part with their negroes. It is only fair to state that they probably wanted their blacks to raise supplies for the army and for the families left at home.

Beauregard, however, was reinforced by Van Dorn immediately after Shiloh with 17,000 men.[5] Interior points, less exposed, were also depleted to add to the strength at Corinth. With these reinforcements and the new regiments, Beauregard had, during the month of May, 1862, a large force on paper, but probably not much over 50,000 effective men. We estimated his strength at 70,000. Our own was, in round numbers, 120,000. The defensible nature of the ground at Corinth, and the fortifications, made 50,000 then enough to maintain their position against double that number for an indefinite time but for the demoralization spoken of.

On the 30th of April the grand army commenced its advance from Shiloh upon Corinth. The movement was a siege from the start to the close. The National troops were always behind intrenchments, except of course the

---

5. Earl Van Dorn (1820–1863) was Grant's West Point classmate, and they were involved in many of the same engagements in Mexico. Van Dorn subsequently served on frontier duty until resigning in 1861 to join the C.S.A. On his "quixotic" exploits, see Cozzens, *Darkest Days*, 10, 44–47. In 1861, in letters to his wife, rebel artillery officer Thomas Henry Carter offered the following impressions of Van Dorn's personality:

> Van Dorn is much annoyed at having no cavalry. I begin to like him better. He comes with a great reputation for success & is full of dash & fight. He talks I hear of asking for a transfer to the West. I suppose he thinks the times too slow here for him.

> Van Dorn I like too, he is a gentleman, not profound or striking in any way. You have seen thousands equal to him in every respect except perhaps Tactics & for ought I know some hidden military talents which explain his success hitherto. He is very dressy & fond of reviews. Rides a superb horse presented by the Texans, & just received. His manners are pleasant.

Letters to Sarah Ludlow Carter, October 22, 1861, and November 23, 1861, *A Gunner in Lee's Army: The Civil War Letters of Thomas Henry Carter*, ed. Graham T. Dozier (Chapel Hill: University of North Carolina, 2014), 43, 61.

small reconnoitring parties sent to the front to clear the way for an advance. Even the commanders of these parties were cautioned, "not to bring on an engagement." "It is better to retreat than to fight." The enemy were constantly watching our advance, but as they were simply observers there were but few engagements that even threatened to become battles. All the engagements fought ought to have served to encourage the enemy. Roads were again made in our front, and again corduroyed; a line was intrenched, and the troops were advanced to the new position. Cross roads were constructed to these new positions to enable the troops to concentrate in case of attack. The National armies were thoroughly intrenched all the way from the Tennessee River to Corinth.

For myself I was little more than an observer. Orders were sent direct to the right wing or reserve, ignoring me, and advances were made from one line of intrenchments to another without notifying me. My position was so embarrassing in fact that I made several applications during the siege to be relieved.

General Halleck kept his headquarters generally, if not all the time, with the right wing. Pope being on the extreme left did not see so much of his chief, and consequently got loose as it were at times. On the 3d of May he was at Seven Mile Creek with the main body of his command, but threw forward a division to Farmington, within four miles of Corinth. His troops had quite a little engagement at Farmington on that day, but carried the place with considerable loss to the enemy. There would then have been no difficulty in advancing the centre and right so as to form a new line well up to the enemy, but Pope was ordered back to conform with the general line. On the 8th of May he moved again, taking his whole force to Farmington, and pushed out two divisions close to the rebel line. Again he was ordered back. By the 4th of May the centre and right wing reached Monterey, twelve miles out. Their advance was slow from there, for they intrenched with every forward movement. The left wing moved up again on the 25th of May and intrenched itself close to the enemy. The creek with the marsh before described, separated the two lines. Skirmishers thirty feet apart could have maintained either line at this point.

Our centre and right were, at this time, extended so that the right of the right wing was probably five miles from Corinth and four from the works in their front. The creek, which was a formidable obstacle for either side to pass on our left, became a very slight obstacle on our right. Here the enemy occupied two positions. One of them, as much as two miles out from his main line, was on a commanding elevation and defended by an intrenched battery with infantry supports. A heavy wood intervened between this work and the National forces. In rear to the south there was a clearing extending a mile or more, and south of this clearing a log-house which had been loop-holed and was occupied by infantry. Sherman's division carried these two positions with some loss to himself, but with probably greater to the enemy, on the 28th of May, and on that day the investment of Corinth was complete, or as complete as it was ever made. Thomas' right now rested west of the Mobile and Ohio railroad. Pope's left commanded the Memphis and Charleston railroad east of Corinth.

Some days before I had suggested to the commanding general that I thought if he would move the Army of the Mississippi at night, by the rear of the centre and right, ready to advance at daylight, Pope would find no natural obstacle in his front and, I believed, no serious artificial one. The ground, or works, occupied by our left could be held by a thin picket line, owing to the stream and swamp in front. To the right the troops would have a dry ridge to march over. I was silenced so quickly that I felt that possibly I had suggested an unmilitary movement.

Later, probably on the 28th of May, General Logan, whose command was then on the Mobile and Ohio railroad, said to me that the enemy had been evacuating for several days and that if allowed he could go into Corinth with his brigade. Trains of cars were heard coming in and going out of Corinth constantly. Some of the men who had been engaged in various capacities on railroads before the war claimed that they could tell, by putting their ears to the rail, not only which way the trains were moving but which trains were loaded and which were empty.[6] They said loaded trains had been going out for several days and empty ones coming in. Subsequent events proved the correctness of their judgment. Beauregard published his orders for the evacuation of Corinth on the 26th of May and fixed the 29th for the departure of his troops, and on the 30th of May General Halleck had his whole army drawn up prepared for battle and announced in orders that there was every indication that our left was to be attacked that morning. Corinth

---

6. One of the great advantages an army of citizen-soldiers brings is the wealth of knowledge of various trades and professions. Later in the war, a regiment full of Pennsylvania miners at Petersburg would devise the idea of tunneling under and exploding the Confederate defenses. The plan had merit, but Grant and Meade gave only halfhearted support, and poor execution resulted in the debacle of the Crater.

had already been evacuated and the National troops marched on and took possession without opposition. Everything had been destroyed or carried away. The Confederate commander had instructed his soldiers to cheer on the arrival of every train to create the impression among the Yankees that reinforcements were arriving. There was not a sick or wounded man left by the Confederates, nor stores of any kind. Some ammunition had been blown up—not removed—but the trophies of war were a few Quaker guns, logs of about the diameter of ordinary cannon, mounted on wheels of wagons and pointed in the most threatening manner towards us.[7]

7. The use of Quaker guns—logs mounted on carriages to simulate cannon—was only one of Beauregard's deceptions.

A battery of "Quaker guns," Port Royal Island, South Carolina, 1861. Photograph by Timothy O'Sullivan. *Library of Congress, Prints and Photographs Division, LC-DIG-stereo-1s02734.*

John Pope wrote to Halleck at 1:20 a.m. on May 30: "The enemy is re-enforcing heavily, by trains, in my front and on my left. The cars are running constantly, and the cheering is immense every time they unload in front of me. I have no doubt, from all appearances, that I shall be attacked in heavy force at daylight." *OR*, ser. 1, vol. 10, pt. 2, 225.

When Sherman wrote to Halleck's headquarters asking for an explanation of the explosions and smoke emanating from Corinth early in the morning, Halleck replied: "I cannot explain. General Pope telegraphed me about 1 o'clock this morning that the enemy opposite his left were receiving large reinforcements, each train load as it landed being received with cheers." He then added: "It is the impression that Corinth is to be given up, and a stand made in the angle between the two railroads." The cheers in fact welcomed the empty cars rolling in to evacuate the soldiers overnight. Before he left, Beauregard burned whatever he did not take with him. See *OR*, ser. 1, vol. 10, pt. 2, 228.

The possession of Corinth by the National troops was of strategic importance, but the victory was barren in every other particular. It was nearly bloodless. It is a question whether the *morale* of the Confederate troops engaged at Corinth was not improved by the immunity with which they were permitted to remove all public property and then withdraw themselves. On our side I know officers and men of the Army of the Tennessee—and I presume the same is true of those of the other commands—were disappointed at the result. They could not see how the mere occupation of places was to close the war while large and effective rebel armies existed. They believed that a well-directed attack would at least have partially destroyed the army defending Corinth. For myself I am satisfied that Corinth could have been captured in a two days' campaign commenced promptly on the arrival of reinforcements after the battle of Shiloh.

General Halleck at once commenced erecting fortifications around Corinth on a scale to indicate that this one point must be held if it took the whole National army to do it. All commanding points two or three miles to the south, south-east and south-west were strongly fortified. It was expected in case of necessity to connect these forts by rifle-pits. They were laid out on a scale that would have required 100,000 men to fully man them. It was probably thought that a final battle of the war would be fought at that point. These fortifications were never used. Immediately after the occupation of Corinth by the National troops, General Pope was sent in pursuit of the retreating garrison and General Buell soon followed. Buell was the senior of the two generals and commanded the entire column. The pursuit was kept up for some thirty miles, but did not result in the capture of any material of war or prisoners, unless a few stragglers who had fallen behind and were willing captives. On the 10th of June the pursuing column was all back at Corinth. The Army of the Tennessee was not engaged in any of these movements.

The Confederates were now driven out of West Tennessee, and on the 6th of June, after a well-contested naval battle, the National forces took possession of Memphis and held the Mississippi river from its source to that point. The railroad from Columbus to Corinth was at once put in good condition and

---

When Halleck rode into the town in the next morning in disguise, he was greeted by Confederate graffiti on some of the buildings: "These premises to let; inquire of G. T. Beauregard." William Conant Church, *Ulysses S. Grant and the Period of National Preservation and Reconstruction* (New York: G. P. Putnam's Sons, 1899), 145. See also Stephen E. Ambrose, *Halleck: Lincoln's Chief of Staff* (Baton Rouge: Louisiana State University Press, 1998), 52–53.

held by us. We had garrisons at Donelson, Clarksville and Nashville, on the Cumberland River, and held the Tennessee River from its mouth to Eastport. New Orleans and Baton Rouge had fallen into the possession of the National forces, so that now the Confederates at the west were narrowed down for all communication with Richmond to the single line of road running east from Vicksburg. To dispossess them of this, therefore, became a matter of the first importance. The possession of the Mississippi by us from Memphis to Baton Rouge was also a most important object. It would be equal to the amputation of a limb in its weakening effects upon the enemy.

After the capture of Corinth a movable force of 80,000 men, besides enough to hold all the territory acquired, could have been set in motion for the accomplishment of any great campaign for the suppression of the rebellion. In addition to this fresh troops were being raised to swell the effective force. But the work of depletion commenced. Buell with the Army of the Ohio was sent east, following the line of the Memphis and Charleston railroad. This he was ordered to repair as he advanced—only to have it destroyed by small guerilla bands or other troops as soon as he was out of the way. If he had been sent directly to Chattanooga as rapidly as he could march, leaving two or three divisions along the line of the railroad from Nashville forward, he could have arrived with but little fighting, and would have saved much of the loss of life which was afterwards incurred in gaining Chattanooga. Bragg[8] would then not have had time to raise an army to contest the possession of middle and east Tennessee and Kentucky; the battles of Stone River and Chickamauga would not necessarily have been fought; Burnside would not have been besieged in Knoxville without the power of helping himself or escaping; the battle of Chattanooga would not have been fought.[9] These

---

8. Braxton Bragg (1817–1876) graduated from West Point in 1837. After serving in the wars in Florida and Mexico and on frontier duty, he retired in 1856 to become a sugar planter in Louisiana until the outbreak of the Civil War. Bragg was born in North Carolina, and the U.S. Army's Fort Bragg, in Fayetteville, is named for him. The convention of naming federal military installations—to say nothing of the streets and buildings found throughout them—after officers who fought against the United States was a postwar development that gathered momentum during the twentieth century. The army has not yet addressed the full significance of its naming conventions.

9. Ambrose E. Burnside (1824–1881) graduated from West Point in 1847. He was one of the series of commanders Lincoln appointed to lead the Army of the Potomac and subsequently found wanting. A sense of the carnage of Stones River can be gleaned from Sheridan's *Memoirs*:

As soon as possible after the Confederate retreat I went over the battle-field to collect such of my wounded as had not been carried off to the South and to bury my dead. In the cedars and on the ground where I had been so fiercely assaulted when the battle opened on the morning of the 31st, evidences of the bloody struggle appeared on every hand in the form of broken fire-arms, fragments of accoutrements, and splintered trees. The dead had nearly all been left unburied, but as there was likelihood of their mutilation by roving swine, the bodies had mostly been collected in piles at different points and inclosed by rail fences. The sad duties of interment and of caring for the wounded were completed by the 5th.

Sheridan, *Personal Memoirs*, 1: 239–40.

Approximately a month after the battle, John Beatty of the 3rd Ohio Volunteer Infantry Regiment, still stationed in the area, toured the field, and his thoughts ran to Thomas Gray's *Elegy Written in a Country Churchyard*, arguably the most popular poem of the eighteenth century:

For miles through the woods evidences of the terrible conflict meet one at every step. Trees peppered with bullet and buckshot, and now and then one cut down by cannon ball; unexploded shell, solid shot, dead horses, broken caissons, haversacks, old shoes, hats, fragments of muskets, and unused cartridges, are to be seen everywhere. In an open space in the oak woods is a long strip of fresh earth, in which forty-one sticks are standing, with intervals between them of perhaps a foot. Here forty-one poor fellows lie under the fresh earth, with nothing but the forty-one little sticks above to mark the spot. Just beyond this are twenty-five sticks, to indicate the last resting-place of twenty-five brave men; and so we found these graves in the woods, meadows, corn-fields, cotton-fields, everywhere. We stumbled on one grave in a solitary spot in the thick cedars, where the sunshine never penetrates. At the head of the little mound of fresh earth a round stick was standing, and on the top of this was an old felt hat; the hat still doing duty over the head, if not on the head, of the dead soldier who lay there. The rain and sun and growing vegetation of one summer will render it impossible to find these graves. The grass will cover the fresh earth, the sticks will either rot or become displaced, and then there will be nothing to indicate that—

"Perhaps in this neglected spot is laid
Some heart once pregnant with celestial fire;
Hands that the rod of empire might have swayed,
Or waked to ecstasy the living lyre."

Beatty, *Citizen-Soldier*, 219–20.

This was the same poem that the British General Wolfe recited to his staff on the eve of the Battle of Quebec in 1759. Francis Parkman immortalized the episode in his history of the French and Indian War. The elegiac mood that characterizes Beatty's passage similarly dominates Parkman's set piece:

are the negative advantages, if the term negative is applicable, which would probably have resulted from prompt movements after Corinth fell into the possession of the National forces. The positive results might have been: a bloodless advance to Atlanta, to Vicksburg, or to any other desired point south of Corinth in the interior of Mississippi.

For full two hours the procession of boats, borne on the current, steered silently down the St. Lawrence. The stars were visible, but the night was moonless and sufficiently dark. The general was in one of the foremost boats, and near him was a young midshipman, John Robison, afterwards professor of natural philosophy in the University of Edinburgh. He used to tell in his later life how Wolfe, with a low voice, repeated Gray's "Elegy in a Country Churchyard" to the officers about him. Probably it was to relive the intense strain of his thoughts. Among the rest was the verse which his own fate was soon to illustrate,—

"The paths of glory lead but to the grave."

"Gentlemen," he said, as his recital ended, "I would rather have written those lines than take Quebec." None were there to tell him that the hero is greater than the poet.

Montcalm and Wolfe, vol. 2, pt. 7 of *France and England in North America*, vol. 9 of *Francis Parkman's Works*, New Library Edition (Boston: Little, Brown, 1898), 297.

Headquarters Moved to Memphis—
On the Road to Memphis—Escaping
Jackson—Complaints and Requests—
Halleck Appointed Commander-In-
Chief—Return to Corinth—Movements
of Bragg—Surrender of Clarksville—The
Advance upon Chattanooga—Sheridan
Colonel of a Michigan Regiment

My position at Corinth, with a nominal command and yet no command, became so unbearable that I asked permission of Halleck to remove my headquarters to Memphis. I had repeatedly asked, between the fall of Donelson and the evacuation of Corinth, to be relieved from duty under Halleck; but all my applications were refused until the occupation of the town. I then obtained permission to leave the department, but General Sherman happened to call on me as I was about starting and urged me so strongly not to think of going, that I concluded to remain. My application to be permitted to remove my headquarters to Memphis was, however, approved, and on the 21st of June I started for that point with my staff and a cavalry escort of only a part of one company. There was a detachment of two or three companies going some twenty-five miles west to be stationed as a guard to the railroad. I went under cover of this escort to the end of their march, and the next morning proceeded to La Grange with no convoy but the few cavalry men I had with me.

From La Grange to Memphis the distance is forty-seven miles. There were no troops stationed between these two points, except a small force guarding a working party which was engaged in repairing the railroad. Not knowing where this party would be found I halted at La Grange. General Hurlbut was in command there at the time and had his headquarters tents pitched on the lawn of a very commodious country house. The proprietor was at home and, learning of my arrival, he invited General Hurlbut and me to dine with him. I accepted the invitation and spent a very pleasant afternoon with my host, who was a thorough Southern gentleman fully convinced of the justice of secession. After dinner, seated in the capacious porch, he entertained me with a recital of the services he was rendering the cause. He was too old to be in the ranks himself—he must have been quite seventy then—but his means enabled him to be useful in other ways. In ordinary times the homestead where he was now living produced the bread and meat to supply the slaves on his main plantation, in the low-lands of Mississippi. Now he raised food and forage on both places, and thought he would have that year a surplus sufficient to feed three hundred families of poor men who had gone into the war and left their families dependent upon the "patriotism" of those better off. The crops around me looked fine, and I had at the moment an idea that about the time they were ready to be gathered the "Yankee" troops would be in the neighborhood and harvest them for the benefit of those engaged in the suppression of the rebellion instead of its support. I felt, however, the greatest respect for the candor of my host and for his zeal in a cause he thoroughly believed in, though our views were as wide apart as it is possible to conceive.

The 23d of June, 1862, on the road from La Grange to Memphis was very warm, even for that latitude and season. With my staff and small escort I started at an early hour, and before noon we arrived within twenty miles of Memphis. At this point I saw a very comfortable-looking white-haired gentleman seated at the front of his house, a little distance from the road. I let my staff and escort ride ahead while I halted and, for an excuse, asked for a glass of water. I was invited at once to dismount and come in. I found my host very genial and communicative, and staid longer than I had intended, until the lady of the house announced dinner and asked me to join them. The host, however, was not pressing, so that I declined the invitation and, mounting my horse, rode on.

About a mile west from where I had been stopping a road comes up from the south-east, joining that from La Grange to Memphis. A mile west of this junction I found my staff and escort halted and enjoying the shade of forest trees on the lawn of a house located several hundred feet back from the road, their horses hitched to the fence along the line of the road. I, too, stopped and we remained there until the cool of the afternoon, and then rode into Memphis.

The gentleman with whom I had stopped twenty miles from Memphis was a Mr. [Josiah] De Loche [Deloach], a man loyal to the Union. He had not pressed me to tarry longer with him because in the early part of my visit a neighbor, a Dr. Smith, had called and, on being presented to me, backed off the porch as if something had hit him. Mr. De Loche knew that the rebel General [William H.] Jackson was in that neighborhood with a detachment of cavalry. His neighbor was as earnest in the southern cause as was Mr. De Loche in that of the Union. The exact location of Jackson was entirely unknown to Mr. De Loche; but he was sure that his neighbor would know it and would give information of my presence, and this made my stay unpleasant to him after the call of Dr. Smith.

I have stated that a detachment of troops was engaged in guarding workmen who were repairing the railroad east of Memphis. On the day I entered Memphis, Jackson captured a small herd of beef cattle which had been sent east for the troops so engaged. The drovers were not enlisted men and he released them. A day or two after one of these drovers came to my headquarters and, relating the circumstances of his capture, said Jackson was very much disappointed that he had not captured me; that he was six or seven miles south of the Memphis and Charleston railroad when he learned that I was stopping at the house of Mr. De Loche, and had ridden with his command to the junction of the road he was on with that from La Grange and Memphis, where he learned that I had passed three-quarters of an hour before. He thought it would be useless to pursue with jaded horses a well-mounted party with so much of a start. Had he gone three-quarters of a mile farther he would have found me with my party quietly resting under the shade of trees and without even arms in our hands with which to defend ourselves.

General Jackson of course did not communicate his disappointment at not capturing me to a prisoner, a young drover; but from the talk among the soldiers the facts related were learned. A day or two later Mr. De Loche called on me in Memphis to apologize for his apparent incivility in not insisting on my staying for dinner. He said that his wife accused him of marked discourtesy, but that, after the call of his neighbor, he had felt restless until I got away. I never met General Jackson before the war, nor during it, but have met him since at his very comfortable summer home at Manitou Springs, Colorado. I reminded him of the above incident, and this drew from him the response that he was thankful now he had not captured me. I certainly was very thankful too.

My occupation of Memphis as district headquarters did not last long. The period, however, was marked by a few incidents which were novel to me. Up to that time I had not occupied any place in the South where the citizens were at home in any great numbers. Dover was within the fortifications at Fort Donelson, and, as far as I remember, every citizen was gone. There were no people living at Pittsburg landing, and but very few at Corinth. Memphis, however, was a populous city, and there were many of the citizens remaining there who were not only thoroughly impressed with the justice of their cause, but who thought that even the "Yankee soldiery" must entertain the same views if they could only be induced to make an honest confession. It took hours of my time every day to listen to complaints and requests. The latter were generally reasonable, and if so they were granted; but the complaints were not always, or even often, well founded. Two instances will mark the general character. First: the officer who commanded at Memphis immediately after the city fell into the hands of the National troops had ordered one of the churches of the city to be opened to the soldiers. Army chaplains were authorized to occupy the pulpit. Second: at the beginning of the war the Confederate Congress had passed a law confiscating all property of "alien enemies" at the South, including the debts of Southerners to Northern men. In consequence of this law, when Memphis was occupied the provost-marshal had forcibly collected all the evidences he could obtain of such debts.

Almost the first complaints made to me were these two outrages. The gentleman who made the complaints informed me first of his own high standing as a lawyer, a citizen and a Christian. He was a deacon in the church which had been defiled by the occupation of Union troops, and by a Union chaplain filling the pulpit. He did not use the word "defile," but he expressed the idea very clearly. He asked that the church be restored to the former congregation. I told him that no order had been issued prohibiting the congregation attending the church. He said of course the congregation could not hear a Northern clergyman who differed so radically with them on questions of government. I told him the troops would continue to occupy that church for the present, and that they would not be called upon to hear disloyal sentiments proclaimed from the pulpit. This closed the argument on the first point.

Then came the second. The complainant said that he wanted the papers restored to him which had been surrendered to the provost-marshal under protest; he was a lawyer, and before the establishment of the "Confederate States Government" had been the attorney for a number of large business houses at the North; that "his government" had confiscated all debts due "alien enemies," and appointed commissioners, or officers, to collect such debts and pay them over to the "government": but in his case, owing to his high standing, he had been permitted to hold these claims for collection, the responsible officials knowing that he would account to the "government" for every dollar received. He said that his "government," when it came in possession of all its territory, would hold him personally responsible for the claims he had surrendered to the provost-marshal. His impudence was so sublime that I was rather amused than indignant. I told him, however, that if he would remain in Memphis I did not believe the Confederate government would ever molest him. He left, no doubt, as much amazed at my assurance as I was at the brazenness of his request.

On the 11th of July General Halleck received telegraphic orders appointing him to the command of all the armies, with headquarters in Washington. His instructions pressed him to proceed to his new field of duty with as little delay as was consistent with the safety and interests of his previous command. I was next in rank, and he telegraphed me the same day to report at department headquarters at Corinth. I was not informed by the dispatch that my chief had been ordered to a different field and did not know whether to move my headquarters or not. I telegraphed asking if I was to take my staff with me, and received word in reply: "This place will be your headquarters. You can judge for yourself." I left Memphis for my new field without delay, and reached Corinth on the 15th of the month. General Halleck remained until the 17th of July; but he was very uncommunicative, and gave me no information as to what I had been called to Corinth for.[1]

When General Halleck left to assume the duties of general-in-chief I remained in command of the district of West Tennessee. Practically I became a department commander, because no one was assigned to that position over me and I made my reports direct to the general-in-chief; but I was not assigned to the position of department commander until the 25th of October. General Halleck while commanding the Department of the Mississippi had had control as far east as a line drawn from Chattanooga north. My district only embraced West Tennessee and Kentucky west of the Cumberland River. Buell, with the Army of the Ohio, had, as previously stated, been

---

1. Grant's period of exile had ended, and Halleck's removal to Washington largely freed Grant to conduct the war in the West as he judged best.

ordered east towards Chattanooga, with instructions to repair the Memphis and Charleston railroad as he advanced. Troops had been sent north by Halleck along the line of the Mobile and Ohio railroad to put it in repair as far as Columbus. Other troops were stationed on the railroad from Jackson, Tennessee, to Grand Junction, and still others on the road west to Memphis.

The remainder of the magnificent army of 120,000 men which entered Corinth on the 30th of May had now become so scattered that I was put entirely on the defensive in a territory whose population was hostile to the Union. One of the first things I had to do was to construct fortifications at Corinth better suited to the garrison that could be spared to man them. The structures that had been built during the months of May and June were left as monuments to the skill of the engineer, and others were constructed in a few days, plainer in design but suited to the command available to defend them.

I disposed the troops belonging to the district in conformity with the situation as rapidly as possible. The forces at Donelson, Clarksville and Nashville, with those at Corinth and along the railroad eastward, I regarded as sufficient for protection against any attack from the west. The Mobile and Ohio railroad was guarded from Rienzi, south of Corinth, to Columbus; and the Mississippi Central railroad from Jackson, Tennessee, to Bolivar. Grand Junction and La Grange on the Memphis railroad were abandoned.

South of the Army of the Tennessee, and confronting it, was Van Dorn, with a sufficient force to organize a movable army of thirty-five to forty thousand men, after being reinforced by Price from Missouri. This movable force could be thrown against either Corinth, Bolivar or Memphis; and the best that could be done in such event would be to weaken the points not threatened in order to reinforce the one that was. Nothing could be gained on the National side by attacking elsewhere, because the territory already occupied was as much as the force present could guard. The most anxious period of the war, to me, was during the time the Army of the Tennessee was guarding the territory acquired by the fall of Corinth and Memphis and before I was sufficiently reinforced to take the offensive. The enemy also had cavalry operating in our rear, making it necessary to guard every point of the railroad back to Columbus, on the security of which we were dependent for all our supplies. Headquarters were connected by telegraph with all points of the command except Memphis and the Mississippi below Columbus. With these points communication was had by the railroad to Columbus, then down the river by boat. To reinforce Memphis would take three or four days, and to get an order there for troops to move elsewhere would have taken at least two days. Memphis therefore was practically isolated from the balance of the command. But it was in Sherman's hands. Then too the troops were well intrenched and the gunboats made a valuable auxiliary.

During the two months after the departure of General Halleck there was much fighting between small bodies of the contending armies, but these encounters were dwarfed by the magnitude of the main battles so as to be now almost forgotten except by those engaged in them. Some of them, however, estimated by the losses on both sides in killed and wounded, were equal in hard fighting to most of the battles of the Mexican war which attracted so much of the attention of the public when they occurred. About the 23d of July Colonel [Leonard] Ross, commanding at Bolivar, was threatened by a large force of the enemy so that he had to be reinforced from Jackson and Corinth. On the 27th there was skirmishing on the Hatchie River, eight miles from Bolivar. On the 30th I learned from Colonel P. H. Sheridan, who had been far to the south, that Bragg in person was at Rome, Georgia, with his troops moving by rail (by way of Mobile) to Chattanooga and his wagon train marching overland to join him at Rome. Price was at this time at Holly Springs, Mississippi, with a large force, and occupied Grand Junction as an outpost. I proposed to the general-in-chief to be permitted to drive him away, but was informed that, while I had to judge for myself, the best use to make of my troops *was not to scatter them*, but hold them ready to reinforce Buell.

The movement of Bragg himself with his wagon trains to Chattanooga across country, while his troops were transported over a long round-about road to the same destination, without need of guards except when in my immediate front, demonstrates the advantage which troops enjoy while acting in a country where the people are friendly. Buell was marching through a hostile region and had to have his communications thoroughly guarded back to a base of supplies. More men were required the farther the National troops penetrated into the enemy's country. I, with an army sufficiently powerful to have destroyed Bragg, was purely on the defensive and accomplishing no more than to hold a force far inferior to my own.

On the 2d of August I was ordered from Washington to live upon the country, on the resources of citizens hostile to the government, so far as practicable. I was also directed to "handle rebels within our lines without gloves," to imprison them, or to expel them from their homes and from our lines. I do not recollect having arrested and confined a citizen (not a soldier) during the entire rebellion. I am aware that a great many were sent to northern prisons, particularly to Joliet, Illinois, by some of my subordinates with the statement that it was my order. I had all such released the moment I learned of their arrest; and finally sent a staff officer north to release every prisoner who was said to be confined by my order. There were many citizens at home who deserved punishment because they were soldiers when an opportunity was afforded to inflict an injury to the National cause. This class was not of the kind that were apt to get arrested, and I deemed it better that a few guilty men should escape than that a great many innocent ones should suffer.

On the 14th of August I was ordered to send two more divisions to Buell. They were sent the same day by way of Decatur. On the 22d Colonel Rodney Mason surrendered Clarksville with six companies of his regiment.

Colonel Mason was one of the officers who had led their regiments off the field at almost the first fire of the rebels at Shiloh. He was by nature and education a gentleman, and was terribly mortified at his action when the battle was over. He came to me with tears in his eyes and begged to be allowed to have another trial. I felt great sympathy for him and sent him, with his regiment, to garrison Clarksville and Donelson. He selected Clarksville for his headquarters, no doubt because he regarded it as the post of danger, it being nearer the enemy. But when he was summoned to surrender by a band of guerillas, his constitutional weakness overcame him. He inquired the number of men the enemy had, and receiving a response indicating a force greater than his own he said if he could be satisfied of that fact he would surrender.[2] Arrangements were made for him to count the guerillas, and having satisfied himself that the enemy had the greater force he surrendered and informed his subordinate at Donelson of the fact, advising him to do the same. The guerillas paroled their prisoners and moved upon Donelson, but the officer in command at that point marched out to meet them and drove them away.

Among other embarrassments, at the time of which I now write, was the fact that the government wanted to get out all the cotton possible from the South and directed me to give every facility toward that end.[3] Pay in gold

2. Grant's treatment of Mason here is gentle, but he was always alert to the behavior of commanders in combat and to the potentially deadly consequences of their failures.

3. The historian Sven Beckert has illuminated the global cotton trade and slavery's position at its center: "The outbreak of the Civil War," Beckert argues, "severed in one stroke the relationships that had underpinned the worldwide web of cotton production and global capitalism since the 1780s. In an effort to force British diplomatic recognition, the Confederate government banned all cotton exports. By the time the Confederacy realized this policy was doomed, a northern blockade effectively kept most cotton from leaving the South. . . . The effects of the resulting 'cotton famine,' as it came to be known, quickly rippled outward, reshaping industry—and the larger society—in places

was authorized, and stations on the Mississippi River and on the railroad in our possession had to be designated where cotton would be received. This opened to the enemy not only the means of converting cotton into money, which had a value all over the world and which they so much needed, but it afforded them means of obtaining accurate and intelligent information in regard to our position and strength. It was also demoralizing to the troops. Citizens obtaining permits from the treasury department had to be protected within our lines and given facilities to get out cotton by which they realized enormous profits. Men who had enlisted to fight the battles of their country did not like to be engaged in protecting a traffic which went to the support of an enemy they had to fight, and the profits of which went to men who shared none of their dangers.

On the 30th of August Colonel M. D. Leggett, near Bolivar, with the 20th and 29th Ohio volunteer infantry, was attacked by a force supposed to be about 4,000 strong. The enemy was driven away with a loss of more than one hundred men. On the 1st of September the bridge guard at Medon was attacked by guerillas. The guard held the position until reinforced, when the enemy were routed leaving about fifty of their number on the field dead or wounded, our loss being only two killed and fifteen wounded. On the same day Colonel Dennis, with a force of less than 500 infantry and two pieces of artillery, met the cavalry of the enemy in strong force, a few miles west of Medon, and drove them away with great loss. Our troops buried 179 of the enemy's dead, left upon the field. Afterwards it was found that all the houses in the vicinity of the battle-field were turned into hospitals for the wounded. Our loss, as reported at the time, was forty-five killed and wounded. On the 2d of September I was ordered to send more reinforcements to Buell. Jackson and Bolivar were yet threatened, but I sent the reinforcements. On the 4th I received direct orders to send [Gordon] Granger's division also to Louisville, Kentucky.

General Buell had left Corinth about the 10th of June to march upon Chattanooga; Bragg, who had superseded Beauregard in command, sent one division from Tupelo on the 27th of June for the same place. This gave Buell about seventeen days' start. If he had not been required to repair the railroad as he advanced, the march could have been made in eighteen days at the outside, and Chattanooga must have been reached by the National forces before the rebels could have possibly got there. The road between Nashville

ranging from Manchester to Alexandria." *Empire of Cotton: A Global History* (New York: Vintage, 2014), 246.

and Chattanooga could easily have been put in repair by other troops, so that communication with the North would have been opened in a short time after the occupation of the place by the National troops. If Buell had been permitted to move in the first instance, with the whole of the Army of the Ohio and that portion of the Army of the Mississippi afterwards sent to him, he could have thrown four divisions from his own command along the line of road to repair and guard it.

Granger's division was promptly sent on the 4th of September. I was at the station at Corinth when the troops reached that point, and found General P. H. Sheridan with them. I expressed surprise at seeing him and said that I had not expected him to go. He showed decided disappointment at the prospect of being detained. I felt a little nettled at his desire to get away and did not detain him.

Sheridan was a first lieutenant in the regiment in which I had served eleven years, the 4th infantry, and stationed on the Pacific coast when the war broke out. He was promoted to a captaincy in May, 1861, and before the close of the year managed in some way, I do not know how, to get East. He went to Missouri. Halleck had known him as a very successful young officer in managing campaigns against the Indians on the Pacific coast, and appointed him acting-quartermaster in south-west Missouri. There was no difficulty in getting supplies forward while Sheridan served in that capacity; but he got into difficulty with his immediate superiors because of his stringent rules for preventing the use of public transportation for private purposes. He asked to be relieved from further duty in the capacity in which he was engaged and his request was granted. When General Halleck took the field in April, 1862, Sheridan was assigned to duty on his staff. During the advance on Corinth a vacancy occurred in the colonelcy of the 2d Michigan cavalry. Governor Blair, of Michigan, telegraphed General Halleck asking him to suggest the name of a professional soldier for the vacancy, saying he would appoint a good man without reference to his State. Sheridan was named; and was so conspicuously efficient that when Corinth was reached he was assigned to command a cavalry brigade in the Army of the Mississippi.[4] He was in command at Booneville on the 1st of July with two small

4. Horace Porter certainly admired Grant, but he was utterly dazzled by Sheridan's dash and style:

> No one could look at Sheridan . . . without a sentiment of undisguised admiration. . . . Bold in conception, self-reliant, demonstrating by his acts that "much danger makes great hearts most resolute," fertile in resources,

Detail, Equestrian Statue of Philip Sheridan, Washington, D.C., 2017. *Photograph by Elizabeth D. Samet.*

regiments, when he was attacked by a force full three times as numerous as his own. By very skilful manœuvres and boldness of attack he completely routed the enemy. For this he was made a brigadier-general and became a conspicuous figure in the army about Corinth. On this account I was sorry to see him leaving me. His departure was probably fortunate, for he rendered distinguished services in his new field.

Granger and Sheridan reached Louisville before Buell got there, and on the night of their arrival Sheridan with his command threw up works around the railroad station for the defence of troops as they came from the front.

---

combining the restlessness of a Hotspur with the patience of a Fabius, it is no wonder that he should have been looked upon as the wizard of the battle-field. Generous of his life, gifted with the ingenuity of a Hannibal, the dash of a Murat, the courage of a Ney, the magnetism of his presence roused his troops to deeds of individual heroism, and his unconquerable columns rushed to victory with all the confidence of Cæsar's Tenth Legion. Wherever blows fell thickest, there was his crest. Despite the valor of the defense, opposing ranks went down before the fierceness of his onsets, never to rise again, and he would not pause till the folds of his banners waved above the strongholds he had wrested from the foe. Brave Sheridan! I can almost see him now, his silent clay again quickened into life, once more riding "Rienzi" through a fire of hell, leaping opposing earthworks at a single bound, and leaving nothing of those who barred his way except the fragments scattered in his path. As long as manly courage is talked of, or heroic deeds are honored, the hearts of a grateful people will beat responsive to the mention of the talismanic name of Sheridan.

Porter, *Campaigning,* 468–69.

28

Advance of Van Dorn and Price—
Price Enters Iuka—Battle of Iuka

A t this time, September 4th, I had two divisions of the Army of the Mississippi stationed at Corinth, Rienzi, Jacinto and Danville. There were at Corinth also Davies' division and two brigades of McArthur's, besides cavalry and artillery. This force constituted my left wing, of which Rosecrans was in command. General Ord commanded the centre, from Bethel to Humboldt on the Mobile and Ohio railroad and from Jackson to Bolivar where the Mississippi Central is crossed by the Hatchie River.[1] General Sherman commanded on the right at Memphis with two of his brigades back at Brownsville, at the crossing of the Hatchie River by the Memphis and Ohio railroad. This made the most convenient arrangement I could devise for concentrating all my spare forces upon any threatened point. All the troops of the command were within telegraphic communication of each other, except those under Sherman. By bringing a portion of his command to Brownsville, from which point there was a railroad and

---

1. Ohioan William S. Rosecrans (1819–1898) graduated from West Point in 1842, a year ahead of Grant. He served in various capacities in the Corps of Engineers before leaving the army to become a civil engineer, architect, and businessman. He volunteered for military service in 1861 and served throughout the war. His varied postwar positions included two terms in the House of Representatives (representing California). Edward O. C. Ord (1818–1883) graduated from West Point in 1839. He served as an artillery officer first in Florida and then in California. After the Civil War, serving in the West, he commanded the Department of Arkansas, the Fourth Military District, and the Departments of California, the Platte, and Texas successively before retiring in 1880.

Detail, plinth, Soldiers and
Sailors' Monument, New
York, New York, 2016.
*Photograph by Elizabeth D.
Samet.*

telegraph back to Memphis, communication could be had with that part of
my command within a few hours by the use of couriers. In case it became
necessary to reinforce Corinth, by this arrangement all the troops at Bolivar,
except a small guard, could be sent by rail by the way of Jackson in less than
twenty-four hours; while the troops from Brownsville could march up to
Bolivar to take their place.[2]

On the 7th of September I learned of the advance of Van Dorn and Price,
apparently upon Corinth. One division was brought from Memphis to Bolivar to meet any emergency that might arise from this move of the enemy.
I was much concerned because my first duty, after holding the territory
acquired within my command, was to prevent further reinforcing of Bragg
in Middle Tennessee. Already the Army of Northern Virginia had defeated
the army under General Pope and was invading Maryland. In the Centre
General Buell was on his way to Louisville and Bragg marching parallel to
him with a large Confederate force for the Ohio River.

I had been constantly called upon to reinforce Buell until at this time
my entire force numbered less than 50,000 men, of all arms. This included

---

2. In his history of the railroad in the United States Christian Wolmar calculates that
there were 30,000 miles of track throughout the country in 1861. The nine thousand
miles in Confederate territory were seriously inferior to Northern railroads because
there were few junctions and little gauge standardization. This disadvantage was crucial in what Wolmar calls the "world's first railroad war." By 1865, "the United States
Military Railroad, a government agency, was bigger than any private company of the
age, operating 2,105 miles of line with 419 locomotives and 6,330 cars. The railroads
afforded the armies unprecedented mobility, which, as the war progressed, they learned
to exploit to the fullest. The scale of destruction and carnage," Wolmar maintains, "can
be directly attributed to the railroads." Wolmar, *The Great Railroad Revolution* (New
York: PublicAffairs, 2013), 91–92, 94, 118.

everything from Cairo south within my jurisdiction. If I too should be driven back, the Ohio River would become the line dividing the belligerents west of the Alleghanies, while at the East the line was already farther north than when hostilities commenced at the opening of the war. It is true Nashville was never given up after its first capture, but it would have been isolated and the garrison there would have been obliged to beat a hasty retreat if the troops in West Tennessee had been compelled to fall back. To say at the end of the second year of the war the line dividing the contestants at the East was pushed north of Maryland, a State that had not seceded, and at the West beyond Kentucky, another State which had been always loyal, would have been discouraging indeed. As it was, many loyal people despaired in the fall of 1862 of ever saving the Union. The administration at Washington was much concerned for the safety of the cause it held so dear. But I believe there was never a day when the President did not think that, in some way or other, a cause so just as ours would come out triumphant.

Up to the 11th of September Rosecrans still had troops on the railroad east of Corinth, but they had all been ordered in. By the 12th all were in except a small force under Colonel [Robert C.] Murphy of the 8th Wisconsin. He had been detained to guard the remainder of the stores which had not yet been brought in to Corinth.

On the 13th of September General Sterling Price entered Iuka, a town about twenty miles east of Corinth on the Memphis and Charleston railroad. Colonel Murphy with a few men was guarding the place. He made no resistance, but evacuated the town on the approach of the enemy.[3] I was apprehensive lest the object of the rebels might be to get troops into Tennessee to reinforce Bragg, as it was afterwards ascertained to be. The authorities at Washington, including the general-in-chief of the army, were very anxious, as I have said, about affairs both in East and Middle Tennessee; and my anxiety was quite as great on their account as for any danger threatening my command. I had not force enough at Corinth to attack Price even by stripping everything; and there was danger that before troops could be got from other points he might be far on his way across the Tennessee. To prevent this all spare forces at Bolivar and Jackson were ordered to Corinth, and cars were concentrated at Jackson for their transportation. Within twenty-four hours from the transmission of the order the troops were at their destination, although there had been a delay of four hours

---

3. Grant and Rosecrans were both infuriated by Murphy's speedy retreat; Rosecrans court-martialed him for it.

resulting from the forward train getting off the track and stopping all the others. This gave a reinforcement of near 8,000 men, General Ord in command. General Rosecrans commanded the district of Corinth with a movable force of about 9,000, independent of the garrison deemed necessary to be left behind. It was known that General Van Dorn was about a four days' march south of us, with a large force. It might have been part of his plan to attack at Corinth, Price coming from the east while he came up from the south. My desire was to attack Price before Van Dorn could reach Corinth or go to his relief.[4]

---

4. James McPherson suggests Grant's attempt to fix the Confederates in a pincer movement failed largely because of the necessity of relying on couriers for communication. When the Confederates engaged Rosecrans's troops, Ord, three miles away, claimed that he did not advance because terrain features and wind direction prevented him from hearing the sounds of battle. Price withdrew from Iuka—Rosecrans had not blocked that avenue of retreat—to regroup and link up with Van Dorn for an attack on Corinth. See *Battle Cry*, 522–23.

As Grant was not present at the battle, his account is sparse. In his regimental history of the 4th Minnesota Infantry Volunteers Alonzo L. Brown supplies details that suggest the intensity of the fight:

> Volleys could not be distinguished, and until the end of the engagement it was like one continued roar or clap of thunder, and although Ord and Grant, six or seven miles on the north side of Iuka, say they did not hear it, the wind being from the north, the citizens at Jacinto, eighteen miles distant, heard it, so they informed us, as plainly as if it had been only a mile away from their village. . . .
>
> The next morning, on going forward to the ground on which the battle occurred, we found the guns of the Eleventh Ohio Battery standing in the road between the two lines of battle, and about one hundred yards in front of the position where they were when captured, the enemy spiked the guns with ten-penny board nails in their vents. The dead lay thickly scattered on the little ridge occupied by the Fifth Iowa and the battery, and also in the woods to the left and rear, where our troops had been engaged in slaughtering each other. In the low ground behind the battery twelve horses belonging to two caissons had become tangled together and piled up like a pyramid. Some below were wounded; others, dead, and over and above all, with his hind feet entangled down among the dead and wounded beneath him, stood a noble looking animal with head and ears erect, his right fore leg bent over the neck of a horse beneath him, his eyes wide open and out of his nostrils there extended, like a great white beard, a foam fully a foot long and streaked with purple. He was dead. This scene, and with it that of our dead heroes and those of the enemy lying thickly over the ground and the look of destruction and desolation that abounded in the

General Rosecrans had previously had his headquarters at Iuka, where his command was spread out along the Memphis and Charleston railroad eastward. While there he had a most excellent map prepared showing all the roads and streams in the surrounding country. He was also personally familiar with the ground, so that I deferred very much to him in my plans for the approach. We had cars enough to transport all of General Ord's command, which was to go by rail to Burnsville, a point on the road about seven miles west of Iuka. From there his troops were to march by the north side of the railroad and attack Price from the north-west, while Rosecrans was to move eastward from his position south of Corinth by way of the Jacinto road. A small force was to hold the Jacinto road where it turns to the north-east, while the main force moved on the Fulton road which comes into Iuka further east. This plan was suggested by Rosecrans.

Bear Creek, a few miles to the east of the Fulton road, is a formidable obstacle to the movement of troops in the absence of bridges, all of which, in September, 1862, had been destroyed in that vicinity. The Tennessee, to the north-east, not many miles away, was also a formidable obstacle for an army

---

vicinity, was the grandest and most awful spectacle of war that I viewed during a service of four and a half years.

Brown, *History of the Regiment of Minnesota Infantry Volunteers during the Great Rebellion 1861–1865* (St. Paul, MN: Pioneer Press, 1892), 91, 96–97.

The tangle of humans and horses Brown describes was common on the Civil War battlefield, where it is estimated that 1.5 million horses and mules were killed. See Drew Gilpin Faust, "Equine Relics of the Civil War," *Southern Cultures* 6 (Spring 2000): 23–49. Time and conditions permitting, the horses were customarily burned after the battle, while the soldiers were buried but not necessarily identified.

Burying horses, battlefield of Haelen, Belgium, 1914. The challenge of disposing of large numbers of animal carcasses after battle persisted into the twentieth century. *Library of Congress, Prints and Photographs Division, LC-DIG-ggbain-17380.*

followed by a pursuing force. Ord was on the north-west, and even if a rebel movement had been possible in that direction it could have brought only temporary relief, for it would have carried Price's army to the rear of the National forces and isolated it from all support. It looked to me that, if Price would remain in Iuka until we could get there, his annihilation was inevitable.

On the morning of the 18th of September General Ord moved by rail to Burnsville, and there left the cars and moved out to perform his part of the programme. He was to get as near the enemy as possible during the day and intrench himself so as to hold his position until the next morning. Rosecrans was to be up by the morning of the 19th on the two roads before described, and the attack was to be from all three quarters simultaneously. Troops enough were left at Jacinto and Rienzi to detain any cavalry that Van Dorn might send out to make a sudden dash into Corinth until I could be notified. There was a telegraph wire along the railroad, so there would be no delay in communication. I detained cars and locomotives enough at Burnsville to transport the whole of Ord's command at once, and if Van Dorn had moved against Corinth instead of Iuka I could have thrown in reinforcements to the number of 7,000 or 8,000 before he could have arrived. I remained at Burnsville with a detachment of about 900 men from Ord's command and communicated with my two wings by courier. Ord met the advance of the enemy soon after leaving Burnsville. Quite a sharp engagement ensued, but he drove the rebels back with considerable loss, including one general officer killed. He maintained his position and was ready to attack by daylight the next morning. I was very much disappointed at receiving a dispatch from Rosecrans after midnight from Jacinto, twenty-two miles from Iuka, saying that some of his command had been delayed, and that the rear of his column was not yet up as far as Jacinto. He said, however, that he would still be at Iuka by two o'clock the next day. I did not believe this possible because of the distance and the condition of the roads, which was bad; besides, troops after a forced march of twenty miles are not in a good condition for fighting the moment they get through. It might do in marching to relieve a beleaguered garrison, but not to make an assault. I immediately sent Ord a copy of Rosecrans' dispatch and ordered him to be in readiness to attack the moment he heard the sound of guns to the south or south-east. He was instructed to notify his officers to be on the alert for any indications of battle. During the 19th the wind blew in the wrong direction to transmit sound either towards the point where Ord was, or to Burnsville where I had remained.

A couple of hours before dark on the 19th Rosecrans arrived with the head of his column at Barnets, the point where the Jacinto road to Iuka leaves

Major General E. O. C. Ord and staff. *Library of Congress, Prints and Photographs Division, Civil War Photographs, LC-DIG-ppmsca-34120.*

the road going east. He here turned north without sending any troops to the Fulton road. While still moving in column up the Jacinto road he met a force of the enemy and had his advance badly beaten and driven back upon the main road. In this short engagement his loss was considerable for the number engaged, and one battery was taken from him. The wind was still blowing hard and in the wrong direction to transmit sounds towards either Ord or me. Neither he nor I nor any one in either command heard a gun that was fired upon the battle-field. After the engagement Rosecrans sent me a dispatch announcing the result. This was brought by a courier. There was no road between Burnsville and the position then occupied by Rosecrans and the country was impassable for a man on horseback. The courier bearing the message was compelled to move west nearly to Jacinto before he found a road leading to Burnsville. This made it a late hour of the night before I learned of the battle that had taken place during the afternoon. I at once notified Ord of the fact and ordered him to attack early in the morning. The next morning Rosecrans himself renewed the attack and went into Iuka with but little resistance. Ord also went in according to orders, without hearing a gun from the south of town but supposing the troops coming from the south-west must be up by that time. Rosecrans, however, had put no troops upon the Fulton road, and the enemy had taken advantage of this neglect and retreated by that road during the night. Word was soon brought to me that our troops were in Iuka. I immediately rode into town and found that the enemy was not being pursued even by the cavalry. I ordered pursuit by the whole of Rosecrans' command and went on with him a few miles in person. He followed only a few miles after I left him and then went into camp, and the pursuit was continued no further. I was disappointed at the result of the battle of Iuka—but I had so high an opinion of General Rosecrans that I found no fault at the time.[5]

5. Despite Grant's generous words about Rosecrans at the close of this chapter, the two men had a somewhat acrimonious relationship dating to the Battles of Iuka and Corinth. On the evening of the former, Rosecrans was heard asking, "Where, in the name of God, is Grant?" Cozzens, *Darkest Days*, 122.

"The Old Lion and the Ass," *Puck*, 1885. Bernhard Gillem satirized Rosecrans for attempting to diminish Grant's reputation while Congress was debating a bill for restoring to Grant the military pension he had surrendered when he was elected president. *Library of Congress, Prints and Photographs Division, LC-DIG-ppmsca-28278.*

29

Van Dorn's Movements—Battle of Corinth—Command of the Department of the Tennessee

On the 19th of September General Geo. H. Thomas was ordered east to reinforce Buell. This threw the army at my command still more on the defensive. The Memphis and Charleston railroad was abandoned, except at Corinth, and small forces were left at Chewalla and Grand Junction. Soon afterwards the latter of these two places was given up and Bolivar became our most advanced position on the Mississippi Central railroad. Our cavalry was kept well to the front and frequent expeditions were sent out to watch the movements of the enemy. We were in a country where nearly all the people, except the negroes, were hostile to us and friendly to the cause we were trying to suppress.[1] It was easy, therefore, for the enemy to get early

---

1. The slaves' anticipation at the approach of the Union army—and the ambivalence of some Union soldiers—is depicted in Frances Ellen Watkins Harper's 1892 novel *Iola Leroy*, in which the brutal Southern home guard stands between the enslaved Robert Johnson and the freedom of the Union lines:

> Robert waited eagerly and hopefully his chance to join the Union army; and was ready and willing to do anything required of him by which he could earn his freedom and prove his manhood. He conducted his plans with the greatest secrecy. A few faithful and trusted friends stood ready to desert with him when the Union army came within hailing distance. When it came, there was a stampede to its ranks of men ready to serve in any capacity, to labor in the tents, fight on the fields, or act as scouts.

African American Scouts, Secret Service Headquarters, City Point, Virginia. *Library of Congress, Prints and Photographs Division, Civil War Photographs, LC-DIG-cwpb-02159.*

information of our every move. We, on the contrary, had to go after our information in force, and then often returned without it.[2]

On the 22d Bolivar was threatened by a large force from south of Grand Junction, supposed to be twenty regiments of infantry with cavalry and artillery. I reinforced Bolivar, and went to Jackson in person to superintend the movement of troops to whatever point the attack might be made upon.

Later, Robert encounters a sympathetic Union captain, to whom he remarks, "I think that some of these Northern soldiers do two things—hate slavery and hate niggers." The captain agrees but then suggests that the performance of the Massachusetts 54th at Fort Wagner succeeded in changing "public opinion." Frances Ellen Watkins Harper, *Iola Leroy* (New York: Penguin Classics, 2010), 29, 38.

2. Despite the evident precariousness of the situation, Grant minimized the danger in his communiqués with Halleck and traveled to St. Louis after Iuka, ostensibly to coordinate for the destruction of some Confederate ironclads being built on the Yazoo River in Louisiana. See Cozzens, *Darkest Days*, 143–45.

The troops from Corinth were brought up in time to repel the threatened movement without a battle. Our cavalry followed the enemy south of Davis' mills in Mississippi.

On the 30th I found that Van Dorn was apparently endeavoring to strike the Mississippi River above Memphis. At the same time other points within my command were so threatened that it was impossible to concentrate a force to drive him away. There was at this juncture a large Union force at Helena, Arkansas, which, had it been within my command, I could have ordered across the river to attack and break up the Mississippi Central railroad far to the south. This would not only have called Van Dorn back, but would have compelled the retention of a large rebel force far to the south to prevent a repetition of such raids on the enemy's line of supplies. Geographical lines between the commands during the rebellion were not always well chosen, or they were too rigidly adhered to.

Van Dorn did not attempt to get upon the line above Memphis, as had apparently been his intention. He was simply covering a deeper design; one much more important to his cause. By the 1st of October it was fully apparent that Corinth was to be attacked with great force and determination, and that Van Dorn, Lovell, Price, Villepigue and Rust had joined their strength for this purpose. There was some skirmishing outside of Corinth with the advance of the enemy on the 3d. The rebels massed in the north-west angle of the Memphis and Charleston and the Mobile and Ohio railroads, and were thus between the troops at Corinth and all possible reinforcements. Any fresh troops for us must come by a circuitous route.

On the night of the 3d, accordingly, I ordered General McPherson, who was at Jackson, to join Rosecrans at Corinth with reinforcements picked up along the line of the railroad equal to a brigade. Hurlbut had been ordered from Bolivar to march for the same destination; and as Van Dorn was coming upon Corinth from the north-west some of his men fell in with the advance of Hurlbut's and some skirmishing ensued on the evening of the 3d. On the 4th Van Dorn made a dashing attack, hoping, no doubt, to capture Rosecrans before his reinforcements could come up. In that case the enemy himself could have occupied the defences of Corinth and held at bay all the Union troops that arrived. In fact he could have taken the offensive against the reinforcements with three or four times their number and still left a sufficient garrison in the works about Corinth to hold them. He came near success, some of his troops penetrating the National lines at least once, but the works that were built after Halleck's departure enabled Rosecrans to hold his position until the troops of both McPherson and Hurlbut approached towards the rebel front and rear. The enemy was finally driven back with great slaughter: all their charges, made with great gallantry, were repulsed. The loss on our side was heavy, but nothing to compare with Van Dorn's. McPherson came up with the train of cars bearing his command as close to the enemy as was prudent, debarked on the rebel flank and got in to the support of Rosecrans just after the repulse. His approach, as well as that of Hurlbut, was known to the enemy and had a moral effect. General Rosecrans, however, failed to follow up the victory, although I had given specific orders in advance of the battle for him to pursue the moment the enemy was repelled. He did not do so, and I repeated the order after the battle. In the first order he was notified that the force of 4,000 men which was going to his assistance would be in great peril if the enemy was not pursued.

General Ord had joined Hurlbut on the 4th and being senior took command of his troops. This force encountered the head of Van Dorn's retreating column just as it was crossing the Hatchie by a bridge some ten miles out from Corinth. The bottom land here was swampy and bad for the operations of troops, making a good place to get an enemy into. Ord attacked the troops that had crossed the bridge and drove them back in a panic. Many were killed, and others were drowned by being pushed off the bridge in their hurried retreat. Ord followed and met the main force. He was too weak in numbers to assault, but he held the bridge and compelled the enemy to resume his retreat by another bridge higher up the stream. Ord was wounded in this engagement and the command devolved on Hurlbut.[3]

Rosecrans did not start in pursuit till the morning of the 5th and then took the wrong road. Moving in the enemy's country he travelled with a wagon train to carry his provisions and munitions of war. His march was therefore slower than that of the enemy, who was moving towards his supplies. Two or three hours of pursuit on the day of battle, without anything except what the men carried on their persons, would have been worth more than any pursuit commenced the next day could have possibly been. Even when he did start, if Rosecrans had followed the route taken by the enemy, he would have come upon Van Dorn in a swamp with a stream in front and

---

3. Stephen A. Hurlbut (1815–1882) was a lawyer and Lincoln supporter who volunteered in 1861. Observing that Hurlbut "brought to the army a talent for politics, a taste for the bottle, and a lack of ethics," Cozzens suggests that he did not pursue the Confederates after the engagement on the Hatchie River because he was drunk. See *Darkest Days*, 280, 299–300. By the following summer, in command at Memphis, Hurlbut almost resigned amid accusations of incompetence and corruption that would continue to follow him throughout the war.

Ord holding the only bridge; but he took the road leading north and towards Chewalla instead of west, and, after having marched as far as the enemy had moved to get to the Hatchie, he was as far from battle as when he started. Hurlbut had not the numbers to meet any such force as Van Dorn's if they had been in any mood for fighting, and he might have been in great peril.

I now regarded the time to accomplish anything by pursuit as past and, after Rosecrans reached Jonesboro, I ordered him to return. He kept on to Ripley, however, and was persistent in wanting to go farther. I thereupon ordered him to halt and submitted the matter to the general-in-chief, who allowed me to exercise my judgment in the matter, but inquired "why not pursue?" Upon this I ordered Rosecrans back. Had he gone much farther he would have met a greater force than Van Dorn had at Corinth and behind intrenchments or on chosen ground, and the probabilities are he would have lost his army.

The battle of Corinth was bloody, our loss being 315 killed, 1,812 wounded and 232 missing. The enemy lost many more. Rosecrans reported 1,423 dead and 2,225 prisoners. We fought behind breastworks, which accounts in some degree for the disparity. Among the killed on our side was General Hackelman. General Oglesby was badly, it was for some time supposed mortally, wounded. I received a congratulatory letter from the President, which expressed also his sorrow for the losses.[4]

This battle was recognized by me as being a decided victory, though not so complete as I had hoped for, nor nearly so complete as I now think was within the easy grasp of the commanding officer at Corinth.[5] Since the

4. This terse statistical summary of the Battle of Corinth belies the intensity of the slaughter there. For a painstaking account of the conflict, see Cozzens, *Darkest Days*. Doc Quinn, a slave who was one of the many "servants and bodyguards" attached to a Confederate regiment, described the battle's aftermath: "I 'member dat after de battle of Corinth, Mississippi, a five acre field was so thickly covered with de dead and wounded dat you couldn't touch de ground in walkin' across it. And de onliest way to bury dem was to cut a deep furrow with a plow, lay de soldiers head to head, and plow de dirt back on dem." *Voices from Slavery: 100 Authentic Slave Narratives*, ed. Norman R. Yetman (Mineola, NY: Dover, 2000), 244.

5. Grant's veiled criticism of Rosecrans here does not give an adequate sense of the degree to which—egged on by members of their respective staffs—they had fallen out by this time. McPherson, Hurlbut, Rawlins, and possibly other officers even went so far as to involve Julia Grant in the quarrel. Her protestations about Rosecrans's disloyalty, however, did little to impress her husband, who was nevertheless delighted when Rosecrans was transferred to the command of the Army of the Cumberland. See *Personal Memoirs of Julia Dent Grant*, 104.

"Confederate Dead at Fort Robinette, Corinth," Mississippi, 1862. Photograph by Nicholas Brown. *Library of Congress, Prints and Photographs Division, LC-DIG-stereo-1s04685.*

war it is known that the result, as it was, was a crushing blow to the enemy, and felt by him much more than it was appreciated at the North. The battle relieved me from any further anxiety for the safety of the territory within my jurisdiction, and soon after receiving reinforcements I suggested to the general-in-chief a forward movement against Vicksburg.

On the 23d of October I learned of Pemberton's being in command at Holly Springs and much reinforced by conscripts and troops from Alabama and Texas. The same day General Rosecrans was relieved from duty with my command, and shortly after he succeeded Buell in the command of the army in Middle Tennessee. I was delighted at the promotion of General Rosecrans to a separate command, because I still believed that when independent of an immediate superior the qualities which I, at that time, credited him with possessing, would show themselves. As a subordinate I found that I could not make him do as I wished, and had determined to relieve him from duty that very day.

At the close of the operations just described my force, in round numbers, was 48,500. Of these 4,800 were in Kentucky and Illinois, 7,000 in Memphis, 19,200 from Mound City south, and 17,500 at Corinth. General McClernand had been authorized from Washington to go north and organize troops to be used in opening the Mississippi. These new levies with other reinforcements now began to come in.

On the 25th of October I was placed in command of the Department of the Tennessee. Reinforcements continued to come from the north and by the 2d of November I was prepared to take the initiative. This was a great relief after the two and a half months of continued defence over a large district of country, and where nearly every citizen was an enemy ready to give information of our every move. I have described very imperfectly a few of the battles and skirmishes that took place during this time. To describe all would take more space than I can allot to the purpose; to make special mention of all the officers and troops who distinguished themselves, would take a volume.[6]

---

6. For gallantry in the various engagements, from the time I was left in command down to 26th of October and on my recommendation, Generals McPherson and C. S. Hamilton were promoted to be Major-Generals, and Colonels C. C. Marsh, 20th Illinois, M. M. Crocker, 13th Iowa, J. A. Mower, 11th Missouri, M. D. Leggett, 78th Ohio, J. D. Stevenson, 7th Missouri, and John E. Smith, 45th Illinois, to be Brigadiers. [Note to the first edition.]

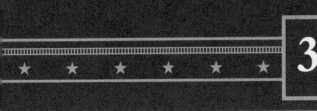

30

The Campaign against Vicksburg— Employing the Freedmen—Occupation of Holly Springs—Sherman Ordered to Memphis—Sherman's Movements down the Mississippi—Van Dorn Captures Holly Springs—Collecting Forage and Food

Vicksburg was important to the enemy because it occupied the first high ground coming close to the river below Memphis. From there a railroad runs east, connecting with other roads leading to all points of the Southern States. A railroad also starts from the opposite side of the river, extending west as far as Shreveport, Louisiana. Vicksburg was the only channel, at the time of the events of which this chapter treats, connecting the parts of the Confederacy divided by the Mississippi. So long as it was held by the enemy, the free navigation of the river was prevented. Hence its importance. Points on the river between Vicksburg and Port Hudson were held as dependencies; but their fall was sure to follow the capture of the former place.

The campaign against Vicksburg commenced on the 2d of November as indicated in a dispatch to the general-in-chief in the following words: "I have commenced a movement on Grand Junction, with three divisions from Corinth and two from Bolivar. Will leave here [Jackson, Tennessee] to-morrow, and take command in person. If found practicable, I will go to Holly Springs, and, may be, Grenada, completing railroad and telegraph as I go."

At this time my command was holding the Mobile and Ohio railroad from about twenty-five miles south of Corinth, north to Columbus, Kentucky; the Mississippi Central from Bolivar north to its junction with the Mobile and Ohio; the Memphis and Charleston from Corinth east to Bear Creek, and the Mississippi River from Cairo to Memphis. My entire command was no more than was necessary to hold these lines, and hardly that if kept on the defensive. By moving against the enemy and into his unsubdued, or not yet captured, territory, driving their army before us, these lines would nearly hold themselves; thus affording a large force for field operations. My moving force at that time was about 30,000 men, and I estimated the enemy confronting me, under Pemberton, at about the same number. General McPherson commanded my left wing and General C. S. Hamilton the centre, while Sherman was at Memphis with the right wing.[1] Pemberton was fortified at the Tallahatchie, but occupied Holly Springs and Grand Junction on the Mississippi Central railroad. On the 8th we occupied Grand Junction and La Grange, throwing a considerable force seven or eight miles south, along the line of the railroad. The road from Bolivar forward was repaired and put in running order as the troops advanced.

Up to this time it had been regarded as an axiom in war that large bodies of troops must operate from a base of supplies which they always covered and guarded in all forward movements. There was delay therefore in repairing the road back, and in gathering and forwarding supplies to the front.

By my orders, and in accordance with previous instructions from Washington, all the forage within reach was collected under the supervision of the chief quartermaster and the provisions under the chief commissary, receipts being given when there was any one to take them; the supplies in any event to be accounted for as government stores. The stock was bountiful, but still it gave me no idea of the possibility of supplying a moving column in an enemy's country from the country itself.[2]

---

1. Grant's classmate Charles S. Hamilton (1822–1891) served in Mexico, was wounded at the Battle of Molino del Rey, and resigned in 1853. He began the Civil War as colonel of the 3rd Wisconsin Volunteers. One of his subordinates, the cavalryman Benjamin Grierson, wrote that Hamilton "was the most disagreeable man I had served under. He lacked many things which I had been taught to believe were essential to a gentleman. He was tyrannical, dogmatic, and repulsive in his manner and seemed to arrogate to himself the assumption of being one of the great men of the age; was always dissatisfied with the commands assigned to him and had few friends among the officers of the army in the District of West Tennessee." *A Just and Righteous Cause: Benjamin H. Grierson's Civil War Memoir*, ed. Bruce J. Dinges and Shirley A. Leckie (Carbondale: University of Southern Illinois Press, 2008), 139.

2. Grant's eventual decision to cut loose from his supply lines was to be his boldest logistical stroke. The decision would at first alarm Sherman, who ended up being Grant's

It was at this point, probably, where the first idea of a "Freedman's Bureau" took its origin.[3] Orders of the government prohibited the expulsion of the negroes from the protection of the army, when they came in voluntarily. Humanity forbade allowing them to starve. With such an army of them, of all ages and both sexes, as had congregated about Grand Junction, amounting to many thousands, it was impossible to advance. There was no special authority for feeding them unless they were employed as teamsters, cooks and pioneers with the army; but only able-bodied young men were suitable for such work. This labor would support but a very limited percentage of them. The plantations were all deserted; the cotton and corn were ripe: men, women and children above ten years of age could be employed in saving these crops. To do this work with contrabands, or to have it done,

---

most apt pupil. This strategy—employed to effect, as Keegan notes, by Napoleon in Spain—violated the principles of war articulated by Jomini and other influential theorists studied so assiduously by Halleck, Sherman, and others. See Keegan, *Mask of Command*, 219–20.

3. The War Department did not set up the Freedmen's Bureau until almost the end of the war, in 1865, to assist the approximately four million freed slaves. Grant and his contemporaries customarily referred to freed slaves as "contrabands," a custom started in Virginia in 1861, when the Union general Benjamin F. Butler designated those slaves who escaped to Union lines "contrabands of war." The Act to establish a Bureau for the Relief of Freedmen and Refugees began:

> That there is hereby established in the War Department, to continue during the present war of rebellion, and for one year thereafter, a bureau of refugees, freedmen, and abandoned lands, to which shall be committed, as hereinafter provided, the supervision and management of all abandoned lands, and the control of all subjects relating to refugees and freedmen from rebel states, or from any district of country within the territory embraced in the operations of the army, under such rules and regulations as may be prescribed by the head of the bureau and approved by the President.

The Statutes at Large, Treaties, and Proclamations of the United States of America, vol. 13 (Boston: Little, Brown, 1866), 507–8.

With General O. O. Howard (1830–1909) as its first commissioner, the Bureau worked primarily to secure labor, social services, education, and justice for the once enslaved. Howard, a Historically Black University, is named for the general, who graduated from West Point in 1854, after attending Bowdoin College in Maine. He lost his arm at the Battle of Fair Oaks in June 1862, but he returned to serve out the rest of the war. After his tenure as the Commissioner of the Bureau of Refugees, Freedmen, and Abandoned Lands (1865–1875), he served on the frontier and was there involved in various military actions against—and earnest attempts to secure peace with—Native American tribes.

African American
army cook, City Point,
Virginia, 1864–65. *Library
of Congress, Prints and
Photographs Division, Civil
War Photographs, LC-DIG-
cwpb-02010.*

organization under a competent chief was necessary. On inquiring for such a man, Chaplain [John] Eaton, now and for many years the very able United States Commissioner of Education, was suggested. He proved as efficient in that field as he has since done in his present one. I gave him all the assistants and guards he called for. We together fixed the prices to be paid for the negro labor, whether rendered to the government or to individuals. The cotton was to be picked from abandoned plantations, the laborers to receive the stipulated price (my recollection is twelve and a half cents per pound for picking and ginning) from the quartermaster, he shipping the cotton north to be sold for the benefit of the government. Citizens remaining on their plantations were allowed the privilege of having their crops saved by freedmen on the same terms.

At once the freedmen became self-sustaining. The money was not paid to them directly, but was expended judiciously and for their benefit. They gave me no trouble afterwards.

Later the freedmen were engaged in cutting wood along the Mississippi River to supply the large number of steamers on that stream. A good price was paid for chopping wood used for the supply of government steamers (steamers chartered and which the government had to supply with fuel). Those supplying their own fuel paid a much higher price. In this way a fund was created not only sufficient to feed and clothe all, old and young, male

African American Burial Detail, Cold Harbor, Virginia, 1865.
Photograph by John Reekie. *Library of Congress, Prints and*
Photographs Division, Civil War Photographs, LC-DIG-cwpb-04324.

and female, but to build them comfortable cabins, hospitals for the sick, and to supply them with many comforts they had never known before.

At this stage of the campaign against Vicksburg I was very much disturbed by newspaper rumors that General McClernand was to have a separate and independent command within mine, to operate against Vicksburg by way of the Mississippi River. Two commanders on the same field are always one too many, and in this case I did not think the general selected had either the experience or the qualifications to fit him for so important a position. I feared for the safety of the troops intrusted to him, especially as he was to raise new levies, raw troops, to execute so important a trust. But on the 12th I received a dispatch from General Halleck saying that I had command of all the troops sent to my department and authorizing me to fight the enemy where I pleased. The next day my cavalry was in Holly Springs, and the enemy fell back south of the Tallahatchie.

Holly Springs I selected for my depot of supplies and munitions of war, all of which at that time came by rail from Columbus, Kentucky, except the few stores collected about La Grange and Grand Junction. This was a long line (increasing in length as we moved south) to maintain in an enemy's country. On the 15th of November, while I was still at Holly Springs, I sent word to Sherman to meet me at Columbus. We were but forty-seven miles apart, yet the most expeditious way for us to meet was for me to take the rail to Columbus and Sherman a steamer for the same place. At that meeting, besides talking over my general plans I gave him his orders to join me with two divisions and to march them down the Mississippi Central railroad if he could. Sherman, who was always prompt, was up by the 29th to Cottage Hill, ten miles north of Oxford. He brought three divisions with him, leaving a garrison of only four regiments of infantry, a couple of pieces of artillery and a small detachment of cavalry. Further reinforcements he knew were on their way from the north to Memphis. About this time General Halleck ordered troops from Helena, Arkansas (territory west of the Mississippi was not under my command then), to cut the road in Pemberton's rear. The expedition was under Generals [Alvin P.] Hovey and C. C. Washburn and was successful so far as reaching the railroad was concerned, but the damage done was very slight and was soon repaired.

The Tallahatchie, which confronted me, was very high, the railroad bridge destroyed and Pemberton strongly fortified on the south side. A crossing would have been impossible in the presence of an enemy. I sent the cavalry higher up the stream and they secured a crossing. This caused the enemy to evacuate their position, which was possibly accelerated by the expedition of Hovey and Washburn. The enemy was followed as far south as Oxford by the main body of troops, and some seventeen miles farther by McPherson's command. Here the pursuit was halted to repair the railroad from the Tallahatchie northward, in order to bring up supplies. The piles on which the railroad bridge rested had been left standing. The work of constructing a roadway for the troops was but a short matter, and, later, rails were laid for cars.

During the delay at Oxford in repairing railroads I learned that an expedition down the Mississippi now was inevitable and, desiring to have a competent commander in charge, I ordered Sherman on the 8th of December back to Memphis to take charge. The following were his orders:

Headquarters 13th Army Corps, Department of the Tennessee.
OXFORD, MISSISSIPPI, *December* 8,1862.
MAJOR-GENERAL W. T. SHERMAN,
Commanding Right Wing:
You will proceed, with as little delay as possible, to Memphis, Tennessee, taking with you one division of your present command. On your arrival at Memphis you will assume command of all the

troops there, and that portion of General Curtis's forces at present east of the Mississippi River, and organize them into brigades and divisions in your own army. As soon as possible move with them down the river to the vicinity of Vicksburg, and with the co-operation of the gunboat fleet under command of Flag-officer Porter proceed to the reduction of that place in such a manner as circumstances, and your own judgment, may dictate.

The amount of rations, forage, land transportation, etc., necessary to take, will be left entirely with yourself. The Quartermaster at St. Louis will be instructed to send you transportation for 30,000 men; should you still find yourself deficient, your quartermaster will be authorized to make up the deficiency from such transports as may come into the port of Memphis.

On arriving in Memphis, put yourself in communication with Admiral Porter, and arrange with him for his co-operation.

Inform me at the earliest practicable day of the time when you will embark, and such plans as may then be matured. I will hold the forces here in readiness to co-operate with you in such manner as the movements of the enemy may make necessary.

Leave the District of Memphis in the command of an efficient officer, and with a garrison of four regiments of infantry, the siege guns, and whatever cavalry may be there.

U. S. GRANT,
Major-General.

This idea had presented itself to my mind earlier, for on the 3d of December I asked Halleck if it would not be well to hold the enemy south of the Yallabusha and move a force from Helena and Memphis on Vicksburg. On the 5th again I suggested, from Oxford, to Halleck that if the Helena troops were at my command I thought it would be possible to take them and the Memphis forces south of the mouth of the Yazoo River, and thus secure Vicksburg and the State of Mississippi. Halleck on the same day, the 5th of December, directed me not to attempt to hold the country south of the Tallahatchie, but to collect 25,000 troops at Memphis by the 20th for the Vicksburg expedition. I sent Sherman with two divisions at once, informed the general-in-chief of the fact, and asked whether I should command the expedition down the river myself or send Sherman. I was authorized to do as I thought best for the accomplishment of the great object in view. I sent Sherman and so informed General Halleck.

As stated, my action in sending Sherman back was expedited by a desire to get him in command of the forces separated from my direct supervision. I feared that delay might bring McClernand, who was his senior and who had authority from the President and Secretary of War to exercise that particular command,—and independently. I doubted McClernand's fitness; and I had good reason to believe that in forestalling him I was by no means giving offence to those whose authority to command was above both him and me.

Neither my orders to General Sherman, nor the correspondence between us or between General Halleck and myself, contemplated at the time my going further south than the Yallabusha. Pemberton's force in my front was the main part of the garrison of Vicksburg, as the force with me was the defence of the territory held by us in West Tennessee and Kentucky. I hoped to hold Pemberton in my front while Sherman should get in his rear and into Vicksburg. The further north the enemy could be held the better.

It was understood, however, between General Sherman and myself that our movements were to be co-operative; if Pemberton could not be held away from Vicksburg I was to follow him; but at that time it was not expected to abandon the railroad north of the Yallabusha. With that point as a secondary base of supplies, the possibility of moving down the Yazoo until communications could be opened with the Mississippi was contemplated.

It was my intention, and so understood by Sherman and his command, that if the enemy should fall back I would follow him even to the gates of Vicksburg. I intended in such an event to hold the road to Grenada on the Yallabusha and cut loose from there, expecting to establish a new base of supplies on the Yazoo, or at Vicksburg itself, with Grenada to fall back upon in case of failure. It should be remembered that at the time I speak of it had not been demonstrated that an army could operate in an enemy's territory depending upon the country for supplies. A halt was called at Oxford with the advance seventeen miles south of there, to bring up the road to the latter point and to bring supplies of food, forage and munitions to the front.

On the 18th of December I received orders from Washington to divide my command into four army corps, with General McClernand to command one of them and to be assigned to that part of the army which was to operate down the Mississippi.[4] This interfered with my plans, but probably resulted

---

4. Grant does not allude here to what became his most notorious order. Frustrated by the illegal trade in cotton, Grant sought to ban traders from his Department. Some of those traders happened to be Jewish, and on December 17 Grant issued General Order No. 11:

in my ultimately taking the command in person. McClernand was at that time in Springfield, Illinois. The order was obeyed without any delay. Dispatches were sent to him the same day in conformity.

On the 20th General Van Dorn appeared at Holly Springs, my secondary base of supplies, captured the garrison of 1,500 men commanded by Colonel Murphy, of the 8th Wisconsin regiment, and destroyed all our munitions of war, food and forage. The capture was a disgraceful one to the officer commanding but not to the troops under him.[5] At the same time

---

I. The Jews, as a class, violating every regulation of trade established by the Treasury Department, and also Department orders, are hereby expelled from the Department.

II. Within twenty-four hours from the receipt of this order by Post Commanders, they will see that all of this class of people are furnished with passes and required to leave, and any one returning after such notification, will be arrested and held in confinement until an opportunity occurs of sending them out as prisoners unless furnished with permits from these Head Quarters.

III. No permits will be given these people to visit Head Quarters for the purpose of making personal application for trade permits.

PUSG, 7:50.

Julia Grant called the order "obnoxious." *Memoirs*, 107. Jean Edward Smith describes it as "one of the most blatant examples of state-sponsored anti-Semitism in American history." He emphasizes that it was issued on Grant's initiative alone, over the objections of his chief of staff John Rawlins. Smith argues that Grant's linguistic precision calls into question any interpretation of his use of "Jew" as merely a substitute for "cotton trader." Smith further suggests that the order is consistent with "a streak of nativism that ran deep in Grant." Those nativist impulses were expressed in Grant's brief flirtation with the Know-Nothings, which he alludes to in chapter 16. Lincoln ordered the policy rescinded as soon as he heard about it. *Grant*, 225–27.

For a comprehensive account of this episode, see Jonathan D. Sarna, *When General Grant Expelled the Jews* (New York: Nextbook/Schocken, 2012).

5. Dabney Herndon Maury, who served on Van Dorn's staff, gives a sense of the general's personality in this account of an exchange with the insubordinate Nathan Bedford Forrest:

Bragg sent orders through Van Dorn to Forrest, to turn over all his captured horses, arms, etc., to the ordnance and quartermaster officers of the army. The property not being forthcoming, the general wrote peremptorily to Van Dorn to call on Forrest to obey the order, and explain his delay in doing so. Van Dorn sent for him to come to his office, and in a tone of authority demanded of him immediate compliance, saying, "Why have you not turned in those captured horses?" Forrest replied defiantly, "Because I haven't got 'em." Van Dorn said, "That statement differs from your written

Forrest got on our line of railroad between Jackson, Tennessee, and Columbus, Kentucky, doing much damage to it. This cut me off from all communication with the north for more than a week, and it was more than two
weeks before rations or forage could be issued from stores obtained in the
regular way. This demonstrated the impossibility of maintaining so long a
line of road over which to draw supplies for an army moving in an enemy's
country. I determined, therefore, to abandon my campaign into the interior
with Columbus as a base, and returned to La Grange and Grand Junction
destroying the road to my front and repairing the road to Memphis, making
the Mississippi river the line over which to draw supplies. Pemberton was
falling back at the same time.

The moment I received the news of Van Dorn's success I sent the cavalry at the front back to drive him from the country. He had start enough
to move north destroying the railroad in many places, and to attack several small garrisons intrenched as guards to the railroad. All these he found

---

report, sir." Forrest, white with rage, said, "General Van Dorn, the time
will come when your rank will not protect you, and you shall account
to me for this outrage!" Van Dorn, with his blue eyes blazing, retorted,
"General Forrest, my rank shall never protect me from any man who feels
aggrieved by me, and I await your pleasure now, sir." Forrest slowly passed
his hand over his face; then he said: "General Van Dorn, I think there are
Yankees enough for you and me to fight without our fighting each other.
I am sorry for what I said, and respectfully ask your pardon." Van Dorn
replied: "General Forrest, I am glad to hear you speak so. No man can ever
doubt your readiness to fight any man or any thing, but while under my
command you must obey my orders, and I have important orders for you
to execute at once." He then ordered him to pursue the raiding party of
Colonel Straight, which had just passed down into Alabama.

Recollections of a Virginian in the Mexican, Indian, and Civil Wars (New York: Scribner's,
1894), 207–8.

Van Dorn's career was decidedly mixed, but Maury elsewhere contributed the following encomium: "I believe that in him we lost the greatest cavalry soldier of his time.
His knowledge of roads and country was wonderful. He knew how to care for his men
and horses. His own wants were few; his habits simple; he was energetic and enduring;
he deferred everything to his military duty; he craved glory beyond everything—high
glory; there was no stain of vain glory about anything he ever said or did. As the bravest
are ever the gentlest, so was he simple and kind, and gentle as a child. . . . Take him for
all in all he was the most gallant soldier I have ever known." "Recollections of General
Earl Van Dorn," *Southern Historical Society Papers* 19 (1891): 197–98.

Van Dorn was killed in 1863 by the husband of a woman with whom he was
rumored to be having an affair.

warned of his coming and prepared to receive him. Van Dorn did not succeed in capturing a single garrison except the one at Holly Springs, which was larger than all the others attacked by him put together. Murphy was also warned of Van Dorn's approach, but made no preparations to meet him. He did not even notify his command.[6]

---

6. Confederate cavalryman Victor M. Rose provided the following reminiscence of the Confederate commander John S. Griffith's exuberant entry into Holly Springs:

> Upon one occasion he was detailing the exciting scenes attendant upon the Confederate entry into Holly Springs, and especially the earnest welcome extended the rebels by the ladies, when his auditor asked: "And how did you feel, General?" "Feel!" exclaimed the excited veteran; "I felt as if I could have charged hell, and captured the devil, if the Almighty had commanded me to do so!"

Although Julia Grant had decamped the previous evening, Southern writers invented a story that served the ends of their chivalric romance of the war. Here is Rose's version:

> Colonel Griffith sent guards to arrest all the officers domiciled in houses, and to the house occupied by Mrs. Grant, at which were several of the General's staff. Griffith detailed ten men, in the special charge of Colonel Boggess, as a guarantee that the ladies should be treated with deference and respect. But a few minutes elapsed when a messenger from Boggess announced to Colonel Griffith that three ladies denied him entrance to the house. Griffith, fearing some rudeness might be committed, repaired to the scene immediately, when Colonel Boggess exclaimed: "I can not execute your orders without the exercise of violence to these ladies!" Mrs. Grant, stepping forward, said: "And you, sir, make war upon women, do you?" "On the contrary, madam," replied the knightly Griffith, doffing his plumed chapeau, and bowing profoundly to the lady; "we leave that to our enemies!" But the ladies continued to "hold the fort," and Griffith, addressing the soldiers, said: "Men, offer no rudeness to the ladies; if they will not allow you to pass through the gate, tear off a picket from the fence, and flank them; if you are denied admittance at the door, go around them, and find ingress through a window. You must search the house for concealed prisoners, but do not touch the hem of the garment of one of these ladies." The men commenced tearing off the pickets to the right and left of the gate, when Mrs. Grant relented, and politely invited them to enter through the gate, at the same time protesting that there were no men in the house. One officer was found in the house. Colonel Griffith placed a guard over the house, for the protection of the ladies, while the command remained in town.

Victor M. Rose, *Ross' Texas Brigade* (Louisville: Courier-Journal, 1881), 136, 87.

Colonel Murphy was the officer who, two months before, had evacuated Iuka on the approach of the enemy. General Rosecrans denounced him for the act and desired to have him tried and punished. I sustained the colonel at the time because his command was a small one compared with that of the enemy—not one-tenth as large—and I thought he had done well to get away without falling into their hands. His leaving large stores to fall into Price's possession I looked upon as an oversight and excused it on the ground of inexperience in military matters. He should, however, have destroyed them. This last surrender demonstrated to my mind that Rosecrans' judgment of Murphy's conduct at Iuka was correct. The surrender of Holly Springs was most reprehensible and showed either the disloyalty of Colonel Murphy to the cause which he professed to serve, or gross cowardice.[7]

---

7. The December 20 raid against Holly Springs, the mercurial Van Dorn's star turn, was a great blow to Grant: the loss of supplies was enormous, the damage to the railroads significant. Forced to abandon his overland campaign against Vicksburg, Grant fell back before committing to his new strategy of cutting loose from his supply base. Robert C. Murphy (1827–1888), colonel of the 8th Wisconsin, was the same officer who had so quickly abandoned Iuka without destroying the supply depot. He closed his report to Rawlins as follows:

> General Van Dorn burned up all the stores, depot buildings, armory, and ordnance buildings; in fact a large portion of the business part of the town is in ruins. There are no supplies here for the paroled prisoners and the sick, and what shall be done for them? My fate is most mortifying. I have wished a hundred times to-day that I had been killed. I have done all in my power—in truth, my force was inadequate. I have foreseen this and have so advised. No works here, and no force to put in them if they were here, and yet I know General Grant is not to blame; he has done all for the best, and so did I. I have obeyed orders, and have been unfortunate in so doing. The misfortune of war is mine. This railroad line cannot be maintained without an immense force. They make a feint on Jackson and the real attack on Holly Springs. The first depletes the latter and makes the move almost certain. Colonel, I send this by an officer who was here and knows the facts; he can tell you many things I cannot write.

OR, ser. 1, vol. 17, pt. 1, 509.

Having been court-martialed but acquitted for his actions at Iuka, Murphy was now summarily dismissed from the service for "his cowardly and disgraceful conduct." *OR*, ser.1, vol. 17, pt. 1, 516.

One of Murphy's subordinates, Major John J. Mudd, concluded his official report to Rawlins: "I cannot close this report without expressing the opinion that this disaster is another added to the long list occasioned by the drunkenness or inefficiency of commanding officers." *OR*, ser. 1, vol. 17, pt. 1, 513.

After the war was over I read from the diary of a lady who accompanied General Pemberton in his retreat from the Tallahatchie, that the retreat was almost a panic. The roads were bad and it was difficult to move the artillery and trains. Why there should have been a panic I do not see. No expedition had yet started down the Mississippi River. Had I known the demoralized condition of the enemy, or the fact that central Mississippi abounded so in all army supplies, I would have been in pursuit of Pemberton while his cavalry was destroying the roads in my rear.

After sending cavalry to drive Van Dorn away, my next order was to dispatch all the wagons we had, under proper escort, to collect and bring in all supplies of forage and food from a region of fifteen miles east and west of the road from our front back to Grand Junction, leaving two months' supplies for the families of those whose stores were taken. I was amazed at the quantity of supplies the country afforded. It showed that we could have subsisted off the country for two months instead of two weeks without going beyond the limits designated. This taught me a lesson which was taken advantage of later in the campaign when our army lived twenty days with the issue of only five days' rations by the commissary. Our loss of supplies was great at Holly Springs, but it was more than compensated for by those taken from the country and by the lesson taught.

The news of the capture of Holly Springs and the destruction of our supplies caused much rejoicing among the people remaining in Oxford. They came with broad smiles on their faces, indicating intense joy, to ask what I was going to do now without anything for my soldiers to eat. I told them that I was not disturbed; that I had already sent troops and wagons to collect all the food and forage they could find for fifteen miles on each side of the road. Countenances soon changed, and so did the inquiry. The next was, "What are *we* to do?" My response was that we had endeavored to feed ourselves from our own northern resources while visiting them; but their friends in gray had been uncivil enough to destroy what we had brought along, and it could not be expected that men, with arms in their hands, would starve in the midst of plenty. I advised them to emigrate east, or west, fifteen miles and assist in eating up what we left.

31

Headquarters Moved to Holly Springs—
General McClernand in Command—
Assuming Command at Young's Point—
Operations above Vicksburg—
Fortifications about Vicksburg—The Canal—
Lake Providence—Operations at Yazoo Pass

his interruption in my communications north—I was really cut off
from communication with a great part of my own command during
this time—resulted in Sherman's moving from Memphis before McClernand could arrive, for my dispatch of the 18th did not reach McClernand.

John A. McClernand. *Library of Congress, Prints
and Photographs Division, Civil War Photographs,
LC-DIG-cwpb-07371.*

Pemberton got back to Vicksburg before Sherman got there. The rebel positions were on a bluff on the Yazoo River, some miles above its mouth. The waters were high so that the bottoms were generally overflowed, leaving only narrow causeways of dry land between points of debarkation and the high bluffs. These were fortified and defended at all points. The rebel position was impregnable against any force that could be brought against its front. Sherman could not use one-fourth of his force. His efforts to capture the city, or the high ground north of it, were necessarily unavailing.

Sherman's attack was very unfortunate, but I had no opportunity of communicating with him after the destruction of the road and telegraph to my rear on the 20th.[1] He did not know but what I was in the rear of the enemy and depending on him to open a new base of supplies for the troops with me. I had, before he started from Memphis, directed him to take with him a few small steamers suitable for the navigation of the Yazoo, not knowing but that I might want them to supply me after cutting loose from my base at Grenada.

On the 23d I removed my headquarters back to Holly Springs. The troops were drawn back gradually, but without haste or confusion, finding supplies abundant and no enemy following. The road was not damaged south of Holly Springs by Van Dorn, at least not to an extent to cause any delay. As I had resolved to move headquarters to Memphis, and to repair the road to that point, I remained at Holly Springs until this work was completed.

On the 10th of January, the work on the road from Holly Springs to Grand Junction and thence to Memphis being completed, I moved my headquarters to the latter place. During the campaign here described, the losses

---

1. This was a consequence both of Van Dorn's raid, in which he also succeeded in destroying part of the Memphis and Charleston Railroad, and of the movement of Forrest through Western Tennessee, during which Confederate cavalry successfully cut up sections of track on the Mobile and Ohio, severed telegraph lines, and either seized or destroyed materiel. Sherman defended his actions and resented the subsequent criticism in the Northern press that came in the wake of McClernand's appointment to the command: "Still, my relief, on the heels of a failure, raised the usual cry, at the North, of 'repulse, failure, and bungling.' There was no bungling on my part, for I never worked harder or with more intensity of purpose in my life." Sherman also gives a clear sense of the difficulty of attacking the well-situated and well-defended fort: "The men of the Sixth Missouri actually scooped out with their hands caves in the bank, which sheltered them against the fire of the enemy, who, right over their heads, held their muskets outside the parapet vertically, and fired down. So critical was the position, that we could not recall the men till after dark, and then one at a time." *Memoirs*, 1:295, 292.

(mostly captures) were about equal, crediting the rebels with their Holly Springs capture, which they could not hold.

When Sherman started on his expedition down the river he had 20,000 men, taken from Memphis, and was reinforced by 12,000 more at Helena, Arkansas. The troops on the west bank of the river had previously been assigned to my command. McClernand having received the orders for his assignment reached the mouth of the Yazoo on the 2d of January, and immediately assumed command of all the troops with Sherman, being a part of his own corps, the 13th, and all of Sherman's, the 15th. Sherman, and Admiral Porter with the fleet, had withdrawn from the Yazoo. After consultation they decided that neither the army nor navy could render service to the cause where they were, and learning that I had withdrawn from the interior of Mississippi, they determined to return to the Arkansas River and to attack Arkansas Post, about fifty miles up that stream and garrisoned by about five or six thousand men. Sherman had learned of the existence of this force through a man who had been captured by the enemy with a steamer loaded with ammunition and other supplies intended for his command. The man had made his escape. McClernand approved this move reluctantly, as Sherman says.[2] No obstacle was encountered until the gunboats and transports

2. Grant had a copy of Sherman's *Memoirs* on his desk when he was writing his book. In it, Sherman tells an anecdote about a Confederate officer who was reluctant to surrender at Fort Hindman:

I soon found General Churchill, in conversation with Admiral Porter and General A. J. Smith, and about this time my adjutant-general, Major J. H. Hammond, came and reported that General Deshler, who commanded the rebel brigade facing and opposed to Steele, had refused to stack arms and surrender, on the ground that he had received no orders from his commanding general; that nothing separated this brigade from Steele's men except the light parapet, and that there might be trouble there at any moment. I advised General Churchill to send orders at once, because a single shot might bring the whole of Steele's division on Deshler's brigade, and I would not be responsible for the consequences; soon afterward, we both concluded to go in person. General Churchill had the horses of himself and staff in the ditch; they were brought in, and we rode together to where Garland was standing, and Churchill spoke to him in an angry tone, "Why did you display the white flag!" Garland replied, "I received orders to do so from one of your staff." Churchill denied giving such an order, and angry words passed between them. I stopped them, saying that it made little difference then, as they were in our power. We continued

were within range of the fort. After three days' bombardment by the navy an assault was made by the troops and marines, resulting in the capture of

---

to ride down the line to its extreme point, where we found Deshler in person, and his troops were still standing to the parapet with their muskets in hand. Steele's men were on the outside. I asked Deshler: "What does this mean? You are a regular officer, and ought to know better." He answered, snappishly, that "he had received no orders to surrender;" when General Churchill said: "You see, sir, that we are in their power, and you may surrender." Deshler turned to his staff-officers, and ordered them to repeat the command to "stack arms," etc., to the colonels of his brigade. I was on my horse, and he was on foot. Wishing to soften the blow of defeat, I spoke to him kindly, saying that I knew a family of Deshlers in Columbus, Ohio, and inquired if they were relations of his. He disclaimed any relation with people living north of the Ohio, in an offensive tone, and I think I gave him a piece of my mind that he did not relish. He was a West Point graduate, small but very handsome, and was afterward killed in battle. I never met him again.

Memoirs, 1:300–1.

Pages from a draft of Sherman's account of the capture of Arkansas Post for his *Memoirs. Library of Congress, Manuscript Division, William T. Sherman Papers.*

the place, and in taking 5,000 prisoners and 17 guns. I was at first disposed to disapprove of this move as an unnecessary side movement having no especial bearing upon the work before us; but when the result was understood I regarded it as very important. Five thousand Confederate troops left in the rear might have caused us much trouble and loss of property while navigating the Mississippi.

Immediately after the reduction of Arkansas Post and the capture of the garrison, McClernand returned with his entire force to Napoleon, at the mouth of the Arkansas River. From here I received messages from both Sherman and Admiral Porter, urging me to come and take command in person, and expressing their distrust of McClernand's ability and fitness for so important and intricate an expedition.

On the 17th I visited McClernand and his command at Napoleon. It was here made evident to me that both the army and navy were so distrustful of McClernand's fitness to command that, while they would do all they could to insure success, this distrust was an element of weakness.[3] It would have

---

3. Sherman gives a window onto McClernand's personality in this vignette about their meeting after the capture of Arkansas Post:

> I found General McClernand on the Tigress, in high spirits. He said repeatedly: "Glorious! glorious! my star is ever in the ascendant!" He spoke complimentarily of the troops, but was extremely jealous of the navy. He said: "I'll make a splendid report;" "I had a man up a tree;" etc. I was very hungry and tired and fear I did not appreciate the honors in reserve for us and asked for something to eat and drink.

Sherman, *Memoirs*, 1:301.

Admiral David Porter, who writes of himself in the third person, offers a similarly damning assessment of McClernand:

> After the troops were settled in their tents opposite Vicksburg, it became apparent that there could be no harmonious cooperation while McClernand remained in command of all the military forces. His peculiarities unfitted him for such a command, and these peculiarities became so offensive to Generals Sherman and McPherson, and to Admiral Porter, that they urged General Grant to take command himself as the only chance for the success of the enterprise, and in consequence the latter hastened to Milliken's Bend or Young's Point and assumed the command of all the forces, which he was entitled to do being military commander of the department.

Naval History, 293.

been criminal to send troops under these circumstances into such danger. By this time I had received authority to relieve McClernand, or to assign any person else to the command of the river expedition, or to assume command in person. I felt great embarrassment about McClernand. He was the senior major-general after myself within the department. It would not do, with his rank and ambition, to assign a junior over him. Nothing was left, therefore, but to assume the command myself. I would have been glad to put Sherman in command, to give him an opportunity to accomplish what he had failed in the December before; but there seemed no other way out of the difficulty, for he was junior to McClernand. Sherman's failure needs no apology.

On the 20th I ordered General McClernand with the entire command, to Young's Point and Milliken's Bend, while I returned to Memphis to make all the necessary preparation for leaving the territory behind me secure. General Hurlbut with the 16th corps was left in command. The Memphis and Charleston railroad was held, while the Mississippi Central was given up. Columbus was the only point between Cairo and Memphis, on the river, left with a garrison. All the troops and guns from the posts on the abandoned railroad and river were sent to the front.

On the 29th of January I arrived at Young's Point and assumed command the following day. General McClernand took exception in a most characteristic way—for him. His correspondence with me on the subject was more in the nature of a reprimand than a protest. It was highly insubordinate, but I overlooked it, as I believed, for the good of the service. General McClernand was a politician of very considerable prominence in his State; he was a member of Congress when the secession war broke out; he belonged to that political party which furnished all the opposition there was to a vigorous prosecution of the war for saving the Union; there was no delay in his declaring himself for the Union at all hazards, and there was no uncertain sound in his declaration of where he stood in the contest before the country. He also gave up his seat in Congress to take the field in defence of the principles he had proclaimed.

The real work of the campaign and siege of Vicksburg now began. The problem was to secure a footing upon dry ground on the east side of the river from which the troops could operate against Vicksburg. The Mississippi River, from Cairo south, runs through a rich alluvial valley of many miles in width, bound on the east by land running from eighty up to two or more hundred feet above the river. On the west side the highest land, except in a few places, is but little above the highest water. Through this valley the river meanders in the most tortuous way, varying in direction to all points of the compass. At places it runs to the very foot of the bluffs. After leaving Memphis, there are no such highlands coming to the water's edge on the east shore until Vicksburg is reached.

The intervening land is cut up by bayous filled from the river in high water—many of them navigable for steamers. All of them would be, except for overhanging trees, narrowness and tortuous course, making it impossible to turn the bends with vessels of any considerable length. Marching across this country in the face of an enemy was impossible; navigating it proved equally impracticable. The strategical way according to the rule, therefore, would have been to go back to Memphis; establish that as a base of supplies; fortify it so that the storehouses could be held by a small garrison, and move from there along the line of railroad, repairing as we advanced, to the Yallabusha, or to Jackson, Mississippi. At this time the North had become very much discouraged. Many strong Union men believed that the war must prove a failure. The elections of 1862 had gone against the party which was for the prosecution of the war to save the Union if it took the last man and the last dollar. Voluntary enlistments had ceased throughout the greater part of the North, and the draft had been resorted to to fill up our ranks. It was my judgment at the time that to make a backward movement as long as that from Vicksburg to Memphis, would be interpreted, by many of those yet full of hope for the preservation of the Union, as a defeat, and that the draft would be resisted, desertions ensue and the power to capture and punish deserters lost.[4] There was nothing left to be done but to *go forward to a decisive*

---

4. John G. B. Adams, a captain in the 19th Massachusetts, reveals what it meant to punish a deserter. At Spotsylvania Adams was ordered to superintend a punishment he found just yet so odious that he exchanged it for picket duty:

> John D. Starbird of Company K was one of the three deserters who returned with the regiment. The charges against him had been placed on file on condition that he serve faithfully to the end of the war. While he had promised to do this, he did not intend to, and was only kept in battle at the Wilderness by fear of death from the officers. On the 8th he deserted while under fire, was captured the 19th, tried by drum-head court-martial the 20th, and ordered to be shot at 7 A.M. on the 21st. Early in the morning of that day Adjutant Curtis came to me and said, "Jack, you are detailed to take charge of the shooting of Starbird." I was not pleased with the order, and Captain Mumford, who was ever ready to do a kind act for a friend, exchanged duty with me, I going on picket for him. The detail consisted

victory. This was in my mind from the moment I took command in person at Young's Point.

The winter of 1862–3 was a noted one for continuous high water in the Mississippi and for heavy rains along the lower river. To get dry land, or rather land above the water, to encamp the troops upon, took many miles of river front. We had to occupy the levees and the ground immediately behind. This was so limited that one corps, the 17th, under General McPherson, was at Lake Providence, seventy miles above Vicksburg.

It was in January the troops took their position opposite Vicksburg. The water was very high and the rains were incessant. There seemed no possibility of a land movement before the end of March or later, and it would not do to lie idle all this time. The effect would be demoralizing to the troops and injurious to their health. Friends in the North would have grown more and more discouraged, and enemies in the same section more and more insolent in their gibes and denunciation of the cause and those engaged in it.

I always admired the South, as bad as I thought their cause, for the boldness with which they silenced all opposition and all croaking, by press or by individuals, within their control.[5] War at all times, whether a civil war

---

of eight men from our regiment. Their muskets were loaded by Captain Mumford, seven with ball cartridges, one with a blank. Starbird was seated on his coffin, blindfolded. The order was given to fire. Six shots struck him near the heart; the other musket hung fire, and the ball entered his leg. He died at once.

Those who read this, and do not understand the situation at the time, may think the killing of Starbird unjust and cruel, but it was not. At that time there were in the ranks of every regiment, men who had no interest in the cause. They had enlisted for the bounty, and did not intend to render any service. They not only shirked duty, but their acts and conversation were demoralizing good men. The shooting of Starbird changed all this. Men who had straggled and kept out of battle now were in the ranks, and the result to our corps alone was as good as if we had been re-enforced by a full regiment.

John G. B. Adams, *Reminiscences of the Nineteenth Massachusetts Regiment* (Boston: Wright & Potter, 1899), 94.

5. Press coverage could be merely negative, of course, but it could also violate what is today called operational security—or OPSEC—by revealing plans still in progress. Armies have experimented with a variety of approaches to reporters. Annoyed by censors during World War II, John Steinbeck tried a cheeky experiment:

Correspondents had no quarrel with censors. They had a tough job. They didn't know what might be brought up against them. No one could dis-

between sections of a common country or between nations, ought to be avoided, if possible with honor.[6] But, once entered into, it is too much for human nature to tolerate an enemy within their ranks to give aid and comfort to the armies of the opposing section or nation.

Vicksburg, as stated before, is on the first high land coming to the river's edge, below that on which Memphis stands. The bluff, or high land, follows the left bank of the Yazoo for some distance and continues in a southerly direction to the Mississippi River, thence it runs along the Mississippi to Warrenton, six miles below. The Yazoo River leaves the high land a short distance below Haines' Bluff and empties into the Mississippi nine miles above Vicksburg. Vicksburg is built on this high land where the Mississippi washes the base of the hill. Haines' Bluff, eleven miles from Vicksburg, on

---

cipline them for eliminating, and so in self-preservation they eliminated pretty deeply. Navy censors were particularly sensitive to names of places, whether they had any military importance or not. It was the safest way. Once when I felt a little bruised by censorship I sent through Herodotus's account of the battle of Salamis fought between the Greeks and Persians in 480 B.C., and since there were place names involved, albeit classical ones, the Navy censors killed the whole story.

John Steinbeck, *Once There Was a War* (New York: Penguin Classics, 2007), 5.
During the Vietnam War the United States Public Affairs office gave a bizarre daily press briefing at Saigon's Rex Hotel. The event, which featured a ritual announcement of the body count, was known derisively as the "five o'clock follies." Richard Pyle, the Saigon Bureau Chief for the Associated Press, described the follies as "the longest-playing tragicomedy in Southeast Asia's theater of the absurd." "The Press: Farewell to the Follies," *Time Magazine*, February 12, 1973.
Our most recent conflicts in Iraq and Afghanistan have featured the practice of "embedding" reporters with particular units. The work to emerge from these journalists and others has been invaluable to our understanding of the war. See especially Dexter Filkins, *The Forever War* (New York: Random House, 2008); David Finkel, *The Good Soldiers* (New York: Farrar, Straus and Giroux, 2009), and George Packer, *The Assassins' Gate: America in Iraq* (New York: Farrar, Straus and Giroux, 2005).

6. The particular kind of savagery attendant on a civil war has been the topic of historians, philosophers, and poets from most of the world's traditions. The *Bhagavadgītā*—a vital part of the *Mahābhārata*, the Hindu epic—is occasioned by the warrior Arjuna's scruples about fighting his relatives. Seeing many of his kinsmen opposing one another on the battlefield, he loses his taste for the fight, lays down his weapons, and sits on the ground. It is at this point that the god Krishna reprimands Arjuna for his weakness and offers the *Bhagavadgītā* as spiritual guidance to help Arjuna overcome his reluctance "to perform a terrible action." Civil war thus gives rise to one of the core texts of the Hindu tradition. See *The Mahābhārata*, abridged and trans. John D. Smith (New York: Penguin Classics, 2009), 354–55.

the Yazoo River, was strongly fortified. The whole distance from there to Vicksburg and thence to Warrenton was also intrenched, with batteries at suitable distances and rifle-pits connecting them.

From Young's Point the Mississippi turns in a north-easterly direction to a point just above the city, when it again turns and runs south-westerly, leaving vessels, which might attempt to run the blockade, exposed to the fire of batteries six miles below the city before they were in range of the upper batteries. Since then the river has made a cut-off, leaving what was the peninsula in front of the city, an island. North of the Yazoo was all a marsh, heavily timbered, cut up with bayous, and much overflowed. A front attack was therefore impossible, and was never contemplated; certainly not by me. The problem then became, how to secure a landing on high ground east of the Mississippi without an apparent retreat. Then commenced a series of experiments to consume time, and to divert the attention of the enemy, of my troops and of the public generally. I, myself, never felt great confidence that any of the experiments resorted to would prove successful. Nevertheless I was always prepared to take advantage of them in case they did.

In 1862 General Thomas Williams had come up from New Orleans and cut a ditch ten or twelve feet wide and about as deep, straight across from Young's Point to the river below. The distance across was a little over a mile. It was Williams' expectation that when the river rose it would cut a navigable channel through; but the canal started in an eddy from both ends, and, of course, it only filled up with water on the rise without doing any execution in the way of cutting. Mr. Lincoln had navigated the Mississippi in his younger days and understood well its tendency to change its channel, in places, from time to time. He set much store accordingly by this canal. General McClernand had been, therefore, directed before I went to Young's Point to push the work of widening and deepening this canal. After my arrival the work was diligently pushed with about 4,000 men—as many as could be used to advantage—until interrupted by a sudden rise in the river that broke a dam at the upper end, which had been put there to keep the water out until the excavation was completed. This was on the 8th of March.

Even if the canal had proven a success, so far as to be navigable for steamers, it could not have been of much advantage to us. It runs in a direction almost perpendicular to the line of bluffs on the opposite side, or east bank, of the river. As soon as the enemy discovered what we were doing he established a battery commanding the canal throughout its length. This battery soon drove out our dredges, two in number, which were doing the work of thousands of men. Had the canal been completed it might have proven of some use in running transports through, under the cover of night, to use below; but they would yet have to run batteries, though for a much shorter distance.

While this work was progressing we were busy in other directions, trying to find an available landing on high ground on the east bank of the river, or to make water-ways to get below the city, avoiding the batteries.

On the 30th of January, the day after my arrival at the front, I ordered General McPherson, stationed with his corps at Lake Providence, to cut the levee at that point. If successful in opening a channel for navigation by this route, it would carry us to the Mississippi River through the mouth of the Red River, just above Port Hudson and four hundred miles below Vicksburg by the river.

Lake Providence is a part of the old bed of the Mississippi, about a mile from the present channel. It is six miles long and has its outlet through Bayou Baxter, Bayou Macon, and the Tensas, Washita and Red Rivers. The last three are navigable streams at all seasons. Bayous Baxter and Macon are narrow and tortuous, and the banks are covered with dense forests over-hanging the channel. They were also filled with fallen timber, the accumulation of years. The land along the Mississippi River, from Memphis down, is in all instances highest next to the river, except where the river washes the bluffs which form the boundary of the valley through which it winds. Bayou Baxter, as it reaches lower land, begins to spread out and disappears entirely in a cypress swamp before it reaches the Macon. There was about two feet of water in this swamp at the time. To get through it, even with vessels of the lightest draft, it was necessary to clear off a belt of heavy timber wide enough to make a passage way. As the trees would have to be cut close to the bottom—under water—it was an undertaking of great magnitude.

On the 4th of February I visited General McPherson, and remained with him several days. The work had not progressed so far as to admit the water from the river into the lake, but the troops had succeeded in drawing a small steamer, of probably not over thirty tons' capacity, from the river into the lake. With this we were able to explore the lake and bayou as far as cleared. I saw then that there was scarcely a chance of this ever becoming a practicable route for moving troops through an enemy's country. The distance from Lake Providence to the point where vessels going by that route

Theodore R. Davis, "Cutting the Canal Opposite Vicksburg," *Harper's Weekly*, August 2, 1862.

would enter the Mississippi again, is about four hundred and seventy miles by the main river. The distance would probably be greater by the tortuous bayous through which this new route would carry us. The enemy held Port Hudson, below where the Red River debouches, and all the Mississippi above to Vicksburg. The Red River, Washita and Tensas were, as has been said, all navigable streams, on which the enemy could throw small bodies of men to obstruct our passage and pick off our troops with their sharpshooters. I let the work go on, believing employment was better than idleness for the men.[7] Then, too, it served as a cover for other efforts which gave a

---

7. Grant claims that his "experiments" were designed to keep his army occupied. The conditions under which the troops worked, however, were arduous, the labor exhausting, and the swamps fever ridden. In Xenophon's *The Education of Cyrus* the eponymous pupil receives the following advice from his father: "How difficult it is to maintain even one idle human being, and still more difficult, son, a whole household, but it is most

better prospect of success. This work was abandoned after the canal proved a failure.

Lieutenant-Colonel Wilson[8] of my staff was sent to Helena, Arkansas, to examine and open a way through Moon Lake and the Yazoo Pass if possible. Formerly there was a route by way of an inlet from the Mississippi River into Moon Lake, a mile east of the river, thence east through Yazoo Pass to Coldwater, along the latter to the Tallahatchie, which joins the Yallabusha about two hundred and fifty miles below Moon Lake and forms the Yazoo River. These were formerly navigated by steamers trading with the rich plantations along their banks; but the State of Mississippi had built a strong levee across the inlet some years before, leaving the only entrance for vessels into this rich region the one by way of the mouth of the Yazoo several hundreds of miles below.

On the 2d of February this dam, or levee, was cut. The river being high, the rush of water through the cut was so great that in a very short time the entire obstruction was washed away. The bayous were soon filled and much of the country was overflowed. This pass leaves the Mississippi River but a few miles below Helena. On the 24th General Ross, with his brigade of about 4,500 men on transports, moved into this new water-way. The rebels had obstructed the navigation of Yazoo Pass and the Coldwater by felling trees into them. Much of the timber in this region being of greater specific gravity than water, and being of great size, their removal was a matter of great labor; but it was finally accomplished, and on the 11th of March Ross found himself, accompanied by two gunboats under the command of Lieutenant-Commander Watson Smith, confronting a fortification at Greenwood, where the Tallahatchie and Yallabusha unite and the Yazoo begins. The bends of the rivers are such at this point as to almost form an island, scarcely above water at that stage of the river. This island was fortified and manned. It was named Fort Pemberton after the commander at Vicksburg. No land approach was accessible. The troops,

---

difficult of all to maintain an idle army. For there are very many mouths in an army, it sets out with very few supplies, and it uses up most extravagantly whatever it takes, so that an army ought never be idle." Xenophon, *Education of Cyrus*, 51.

8. James Harrison Wilson (1837–1925) graduated from West Point in 1860 and spent the first years of the war as a topographical engineer in the Army of the Potomac. After moving west to serve with Grant, he became Sherman's chief engineer. Wilson went to Washington to organize the Cavalry Bureau in 1864. This administrative service was a prelude to his own cavalry commands under Sheridan and later Sherman.

therefore, could render no assistance towards an assault further than to establish a battery on a little piece of ground which was discovered above water. The gunboats, however, attacked on the 11th and again on the 13th of March. Both efforts were failures and were not renewed. One gunboat was disabled and we lost six men killed and twenty-five wounded. The loss of the enemy was less.

Fort Pemberton was so little above the water that it was thought that a rise of two feet would drive the enemy out. In hope of enlisting the elements on our side, which had been so much against us up to this time, a second cut was made in the Mississippi levee, this time directly opposite Helena, or six miles above the former cut. It did not accomplish the desired result, and Ross, with his fleet, started back. On the 22d he met [Isaac F.] Quinby with a brigade at Yazoo Pass. Quinby was the senior of Ross, and assumed command. He was not satisfied with returning to his former position without seeing for himself whether anything could be accomplished. Accordingly Fort Pemberton was revisited by our troops; but an inspection was sufficient this time without an attack. Quinby, with his command, returned with but little delay. In the meantime I was much exercised for the safety of Ross, not knowing that Quinby had been able to join him. Reinforcements were of no use in a country covered with water, as they would have to remain on board of their transports. Relief had to come from another quarter. So I determined to get into the Yazoo below Fort Pemberton.

Steel's Bayou empties into the Yazoo River between Haines' Bluff and its mouth. It is narrow, very tortuous, and fringed with a very heavy growth of timber, but it is deep. It approaches to within one mile of the Mississippi at Eagle Bend, thirty miles above Young's Point. Steel's Bayou connects with Black Bayou, Black Bayou with Deer Creek, Deer Creek with Rolling Fork, Rolling Fork with the Big Sunflower River, and the Big Sunflower with the Yazoo River about ten miles above Haines' Bluff in a right line but probably twenty or twenty-five miles by the winding of the river. All these waterways are of about the same nature so far as navigation is concerned, until the Sunflower is reached; this affords free navigation.

Admiral Porter explored this waterway as far as Deer Creek on the 14th of March, and reported it navigable. On the next day he started with five gunboats and four mortar-boats. I went with him for some distance. The heavy, overhanging timber retarded progress very much, as did also the short turns in so narrow a stream. The gunboats, however, ploughed their way through without other damage than to their appearance. The transports did not fare so well although they followed behind. The road was somewhat cleared for them by the gunboats. In the evening I returned to headquarters to hurry up reinforcements. Sherman went in person on the 16th, taking with him Stuart's division of the 15th corps. They took large river transports to Eagle Bend on the Mississippi, where they debarked and marched across to Steel's Bayou, where they re-embarked on the transports. The river steamers, with their tall smoke-stacks and light guards extending out, were so much impeded that the gunboats got far ahead. Porter, with his fleet, got within a few hundred yards of where the sailing would have been clear and free from the obstructions caused by felling trees into the water, when he encountered rebel sharpshooters, and his progress was delayed by obstructions in his front. He could do nothing with gunboats against sharpshooters. The rebels, learning his route, had sent in about 4,000 men—many more than there were sailors in the fleet.

Sherman went back, at the request of the admiral, to clear out Black Bayou and to hurry up reinforcements, which were far behind. On the night of the 19th he received notice from the admiral that he had been attacked by sharpshooters and was in imminent peril. Sherman at once returned through Black Bayou in a canoe, and passed on until he met a steamer, with the last of the reinforcements he had, coming up. They tried to force their way through Black Bayou with their steamer, but, finding it slow and tedious work, debarked and pushed forward on foot. It was night when they landed, and intensely dark. There was but a narrow strip of land above water, and that was grown up with underbrush or cane. The troops lighted their way through this with candles carried in their hands for a mile and a half, when they came to an open plantation. Here the troops rested until morning. They made twenty-one miles from this resting-place by noon the next day, and were in time to rescue the fleet. Porter had fully made up his mind to blow up the gunboats rather than have them fall into the hands of the enemy. More welcome visitors he probably never met than the "boys in blue" on this occasion. The vessels were backed out and returned to their rendezvous on the Mississippi; and thus ended in failure the fourth attempt to get in rear of Vicksburg.[9]

---

9. Sherman vividly recounts this episode in his *Memoirs*, while the American novelist Winston Churchill made it a set piece of his popular 1901 book *The Crisis*:

The General slept lightly. It was three o'clock Saturday morning when the sharp challenge of a sentry broke the silence. A negro, white eyed, bedraggled, and muddy, stood in the candle light under the charge of a young lieutenant. The officer saluted, and handed the General a roll of tobacco.

"I found this man in the swamp, sir. He has a message from the Admiral—"

The General tore open the roll and took from it a piece of tissue paper which he spread out and held under the candle. He turned to a staff officer who had jumped from his bed and was hurrying into his coat.

"Porter's surrounded," he said. The order came in a flash. "Kilby Smith and all men here across creek to relief at once. I'll take canoe through bayou to Hill's and hurry reënforcements."

The staff officer paused, his hand on the latch of the door.

"But your escort, General. You're not going through that sewer in a canoe without an escort!"

"I guess they won't look for a needle in that haystack," the General answered. For a brief second he eyed the lieutenant. "Get back to your regiment, Brice, if you want to go," he said.

Stephen saluted and went out. All through the painful march that followed, though soaked in swamp water and bruised by cypress knees, he thought of Sherman in his canoe, winding unprotected through the black labyrinth, risking his life that more men might be brought to the rescue of the gunboats. . . .

The force swept forward, with the three picket companies in the swamp on the right. And presently they came in sight of the shapeless ironclads with their funnels belching smoke, a most remarkable spectacle. How Porter had pushed them there was one of the miracles of the war.

Then followed one of a thousand memorable incidents in the life of a memorable man. General Sherman, jumping on the bare back of a scrawny horse, cantered through the fields. And the bluejackets, at sight of that familiar figure, roared out a cheer that might have shaken the drops from the wet boughs. The Admiral and the General stood together on the deck, their hands clasped. And the Colonel astutely remarked, as he rode up in answer to a summons, that if Porter was the only man whose daring could have pushed a fleet to that position, Sherman was certainly the only man who could have got him out of it.

The Crisis (New York: Macmillan, 1901), 418–20.

32

The Bayous West of the Mississippi— Criticisms of the Northern Press— Running the Batteries—Loss of the *Indianola*—Disposition of the Troops

The original canal scheme was also abandoned on the 27th of March. The effort to make a waterway through Lake Providence and the connecting bayous was abandoned as wholly impracticable about the same time.

At Milliken's Bend, and also at Young's Point, bayous or channels start, which connecting with other bayous passing Richmond, Louisiana, enter the Mississippi at Carthage twenty-five or thirty miles above Grand Gulf. The Mississippi levee cuts the supply of water off from these bayous or channels, but all the rainfall behind the levee, at these points, is carried through these same channels to the river below. In case of a crevasse in this vicinity, the water escaping would find its outlet through the same channels. The dredges and laborers from the canal having been driven out by overflow and the enemy's batteries, I determined to open these other channels, if possible. If successful the effort would afford a route, away from the enemy's batteries, for our transports. There was a good road back of the levees, along these bayous, to carry the troops, artillery and wagon trains over whenever the water receded a little, and after a few days of dry weather. Accordingly, with the abandonment of all the other plans for reaching a base heretofore described, this new one was undertaken.

As early as the 4th of February I had written to Halleck about this route, stating that I thought it much more practicable than the other undertaking (the Lake Providence route), and that it would have been accomplished with much less labor if commenced before the water had got all over the country.

The upper end of these bayous being cut off from a water supply, further than the rainfall back of the levees, was grown up with dense timber for a distance of several miles from their source. It was necessary, therefore, to clear this out before letting in the water from the river. This work was continued until the waters of the river began to recede and the road to Richmond, Louisiana, emerged from the water. One small steamer and some barges were got through this channel, but no further use could be made of it because of the fall in the river. Beyond this it was no more successful than the other experiments with which the winter was whiled away. All these failures would have been very discouraging if I had expected much from the efforts; but I had not. From the first the most I hoped to accomplish was the passage of transports, to be used below Vicksburg, without exposure to the long line of batteries defending that city.

This long, dreary and, for heavy and continuous rains and high water, unprecedented winter was one of great hardship to all engaged about Vicksburg. The river was higher than its natural banks from December, 1862, to the following April. The war had suspended peaceful pursuits in the South, further than the production of army supplies, and in consequence the levees were neglected and broken in many places and the whole country was covered with water. Troops could scarcely find dry ground on which to pitch their tents. Malarial fevers broke out among the men. Measles and small-pox also attacked them. The hospital arrangements and medical attendance were so perfect, however, that the loss of life was much less than might have been expected. Visitors to the camps went home with dismal stories to relate; Northern papers came back to the soldiers with these stories exaggerated.[1]

1. In April 1863 Frederick Law Olmsted, known today primarily for his work as a landscape architect, was visiting Grant's army in his capacity as general secretary of the United States Sanitary Commission (1861–1879), a civilian charitable organization that provided medical care and other kinds of relief to the Union army. Here he reflects in a letter to his father on the condition of McPherson's soldiers and those in Sherman's corps, who were, he noted, amply supplied with food, clothing and shoes. They were also perched on a strip of land no higher than the water and only fifty feet wide:

The water had risen an inch and a half during the night and you would say it was about the most dismal place and the most dismal prospect upon which an army could be put. So here of Sherman's corps: the ground all asoak and water backing up on them in every direction except where the levee restrained it. The levee itself was lined with graves; there being no other place where the dead could be buried, on account of the water, which at once fills every cavity. These graves, which must be seen by everyone, there being no other road to travel near the camps, have helped, I suppose, to give the impression that Grant's army was in a terribly diseased state. . . .

Because I would not divulge my ultimate plans to visitors, they pronounced me idle, incompetent and unfit to command men in an emergency, and clamored for my removal. They were not to be satisfied, many of them, with my simple removal, but named who my successor should be. McClernand, Fremont, Hunter and McClellan were all mentioned in this connection. I took no steps to answer these complaints, but continued to do my duty, as I understood it, to the best of my ability. Every one has his superstitions. One of mine is that in positions of great responsibility every one should do his duty to the best of his ability where assigned by competent authority, without application or the use of influence to change his position. While at Cairo I had watched with very great interest the operations of the Army of the Potomac, looking upon that as the main field of the war. I had no idea, myself, of ever having any large command, nor did I suppose that I was equal to one; but I had the vanity to think that as a cavalry officer I might succeed very well in the command of a brigade. On one occasion, in talking about this to my staff officers, all of whom were civilians without any military education whatever, I said that I would give anything if I were commanding a brigade of cavalry in the Army of the Potomac and I believed I could do some good. Captain Hillyer spoke up and suggested that I make application to be transferred there to command the cavalry. I then told him that I would cut my right arm off first, and mentioned this superstition.

In time of war the President, being by the Constitution Commander-in-chief of the Army and Navy, is responsible for the selection of commanders. He should not be embarrassed in making his selections. I having been selected, my responsibility ended with my doing the best I knew how. If I had sought the place, or obtained it through personal or political influence, my belief is that I would have feared to undertake any plan of my own conception, and would probably have awaited direct orders from my distant superiors. Persons obtaining important commands by application or political influence are apt to keep a written record of complaints and predictions of defeat, which are shown in case of disaster. Somebody must be responsible for their failures.

In fact the health of the army, tho' not quite as good as that of the army in general, is amazingly good. You can not conceive how well and happy the men in general looked. They are mostly now well broken in, and know how to take care of themselves.

Letter to John Olmsted, April 1, 1863, *Writings on Landscape, Culture, and Society*, ed. Charles E. Beveridge (New York: Library of America, 2015), 255.

With all the pressure brought to bear upon them, both President Lincoln and General Halleck stood by me to the end of the campaign. I had never met Mr. Lincoln, but his support was constant.

At last the waters began to recede; the roads crossing the peninsula behind the levees of the bayous, were emerging from the waters; the troops were all concentrated from distant points at Milliken's Bend preparatory to a final move which was to crown the long, tedious and discouraging labors with success.

I had had in contemplation the whole winter the movement by land to a point below Vicksburg from which to operate, subject only to the possible but not expected success of some one of the expedients resorted to for the purpose of giving us a different base. This could not be undertaken until the waters receded. I did not therefore communicate this plan, even to an officer of my staff, until it was necessary to make preparations for the start. My recollection is that Admiral Porter was the first one to whom I mentioned it. The co-operation of the navy was absolutely essential to the success (even to the contemplation) of such an enterprise. I had no more authority to command Porter than he had to command me. It was necessary to have part of his fleet below Vicksburg if the troops went there. Steamers to use as ferries were also essential. The navy was the only escort and protection for these steamers, all of which in getting below had to run about fourteen miles of batteries. Porter fell into the plan at once, and suggested that he had better superintend the preparation of the steamers selected to run the batteries, as sailors would probably understand the work better than soldiers. I was glad to accept his proposition, not only because I admitted his argument, but because it would enable me to keep from the enemy a little longer our designs. Porter's fleet was on the east side of the river above the mouth of the Yazoo, entirely concealed from the enemy by the dense forests that intervened. Even spies could not get near him, on account of the undergrowth and overflowed lands. Suspicions of some mysterious movements were aroused.[2] Our river

---

2. Grenville Dodge, in command at Corinth at around this time, offers insight into the running of spies:

> From the beginning of the war I had made considerable use of spies and scouts within the enemy's lines, and had obtained a very reliable force, mostly Southern men living in Northern Alabama and Mississippi. They had relatives enlisted in the First Alabama Cavalry, a regiment I raised while in command at Corinth. These scouts were instructed how to obtain the number of troops in any command, company, regiment, brigade, division

guards discovered one day a small skiff moving quietly and mysteriously up the river near the east shore, from the direction of Vicksburg, towards the fleet. On overhauling the boat they found a small white flag, not much larger than a handkerchief, set up in the stern, no doubt intended as a flag of truce in case of discovery. The boat, crew and passengers were brought ashore to me. The chief personage aboard proved to be Jacob Thompson, Secretary of the Interior under the administration of President Buchanan. After a pleasant conversation of half an hour or more I allowed the boat and crew, passengers and all, to return to Vicksburg, without creating a suspicion that there was a doubt in my mind as to the good faith of Mr. Thompson and his flag.

Admiral Porter proceeded with the preparation of the steamers for their hazardous passage of the enemy's batteries.[3] The great essential was to pro-

---

or corps, and I placed them at Chattanooga, Atlanta. Selma, Montgomery, Mobile, Meridian, Jackson and Vicksburg, for the purpose of watching the movements of the enemy, and especially to report any force that should move towards Vicksburg, and, after Vicksburg was invested, to report the force sent to Johnston, who was moving an army to relieve Vicksburg. It is a singular fact that from their reports Grant was notified of every movement in his rear, and he ordered reinforcements from the North, of as many men as were sent to Johnston, and placed them under Sherman on the Big Black, ready to meet Johnston.

These secret-service men never gave a larger force than 30,000 men with Johnston, which was about the size of Johnston's army. These spies never left their stations. They communicated with me through their relatives, often through their wives, who would come into Corinth to see their relatives in the Alabama Cavalry, and thus throw off suspicion. In one or two cases of emergency they reported directly to Grant.

Personal Recollections, 50.

3. In his account of the operation Admiral Porter included a revealing episode that occurred at Carthage, ten miles below Vicksburg:

The plantation at this place was owned by an ultra Confederate who exulted over the expected loss of all the gun-boats when he heard that they were to attempt the passage of the batteries, but when at two o'clock he saw them one after another heave in sight their night numbers up and signaling to the flag-ship, "all's well," he went off in despair, got drunk, set fire to his house and all the negro cabins, and departed to parts unknown. The negroes had already joined the Union Army, having no attachment to their brutal master, who had become so debased that he scarcely bore resemblance to a man.

Naval History, 311–12.

Admiral David Dixon Porter. *NH47204. Courtesy of the Naval History and Heritage Command.*

tect the boilers from the enemy's shot, and to conceal the fires under the boilers from view. This he accomplished by loading the steamers, between the guards and boilers on the boiler deck up to the deck above, with bales of hay and cotton, and the deck in front of the boilers in the same way, adding sacks of grain. The hay and grain would be wanted below, and could not be transported in sufficient quantity by the muddy roads over which we expected to march.

Before this I had been collecting, from St. Louis and Chicago, yawls and barges to be used as ferries when we got below. By the 16th of April Porter was ready to start on his perilous trip. The advance, flagship *Benton*, Porter commanding, started at ten o'clock at night, followed at intervals of a few minutes by the *Lafayette* with a captured steamer, the *Price*, lashed to her side, the *Louisville, Mound City, Pittsburgh* and *Carondelet*—all of these being naval vessels. Next came the transports—*Forest Queen, Silver Wave* and *Henry Clay*, each towing barges loaded with coal to be used as fuel by the naval and transport steamers when below the batteries. The gunboat *Tuscumbia* brought up the rear. Soon after the start a battery between Vicksburg and Warrenton

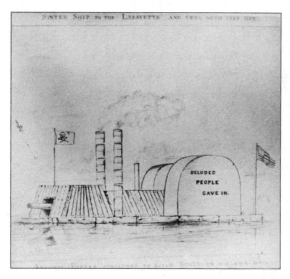

Porter's "Dummy Ironclad,"
sent to attack Vicksburg on
March 9, 1863. *NH95021.*
*Courtesy of the Naval History
and Heritage Command.*

opened fire across the intervening peninsula, followed by the upper batteries, and then by batteries all along the line. The gunboats ran up close under the bluffs, delivering their fire in return at short distances, probably without much effect. They were under fire for more than two hours and every vessel was struck many times, but with little damage to the gunboats. The transports did not fare so well. The *Henry Clay* was disabled and deserted by her crew. Soon after a shell burst in the cotton packed about the boilers, set the vessel on fire and burned her to the water's edge. The burning mass, however, floated down to Carthage before grounding, as did also one of the barges in tow.

The enemy were evidently expecting our fleet, for they were ready to light up the river by means of bonfires on the east side and by firing houses on the point of land opposite the city on the Louisiana side. The sight was magnificent, but terrible. I witnessed it from the deck of a river transport, run out into the middle of the river and as low down as it was prudent to go. My mind was much relieved when I learned that no one on the transports had been killed and but few, if any, wounded. During the running of the batteries men were stationed in the holds of the transports to partially stop with cotton shot-holes that might be made in the hulls. All damage was afterwards soon repaired under the direction of Admiral Porter.[4]

4. Melville imagined what the scene would have looked like from an anchorage above the city in his poem "Running the Batteries," where he refers to the golden flames of a burning transport as "The fair, false, Circe light of cruel War." *Battle-Pieces*, 78.

The experiment of passing batteries had been tried before this, however, during the war. Admiral Farragut had run the batteries at Port Hudson with the flagship *Hartford* and one iron-clad and visited me from below Vicksburg. The 13th of February Admiral Porter had sent the gunboat *Indianola*, Lieutenant-Commander George Brown commanding, below. She met Colonel Ellet of the Marine brigade below Natchez on a captured steamer. Two of the Colonel's fleet had previously run the batteries, producing the greatest consternation among the people along the Mississippi from Vicksburg[5] to the Red River.[6]

The *Indianola* remained about the mouth of the Red River some days, and then started up the Mississippi. The Confederates soon raised the *Queen of the West*,[7] and repaired her.[8] With this vessel and the ram *Webb*, which they

---

5. Colonel Ellet reported having attacked a Confederate battery on the Red River two days before with one of his boats, the *De Soto*. Running aground, he was obliged to abandon his vessel. However, he reported that he set fire to her and blew her up. Twenty of his men fell into the hands of the enemy. With the balance he escaped on the small captured steamer, the *New Era*, and succeeded in passing the batteries at Grand Gulf and reaching the vicinity of Vicksburg. [Note to the first edition.]

6. David Glasgow Farragut (1801–1870) went to sea at the age of nine and commanded his first vessel during the War of 1812.

7. One of Colonel Ellet's vessels which had run the blockade on February the 2d and been sunk in the Red River. [Note to the first edition.]

8. The commander of the *Queen of the West* was Charles Rivers Ellet (1843–1863). At nineteen, Ellet was then the youngest colonel in the army. He was the son of Charles Ellet (1810–1862), an accomplished civil engineer who waged war on Confederate gunboats on the Mississippi with his Union Ram Fleet. The elder Ellet, who designed this fleet, used it to greatest effect during the Battle of Memphis in June 1862, where he was fatally wounded. During the Vicksburg Campaign, the younger Ellet fought in the Marine Brigade, commanded by his uncle Alfred, before the latter's death in the fall of 1863. The Marine Brigade became notorious for burning towns and plantations. David Porter thought Ellet "gallant and daring" but also impetuous: "The only trouble I have," he wrote to Secretary of the Navy Gideon Welles, "is to hold him in and keep him out of danger." *Queen of the West* was lost on the Red River, where Ellet successfully engaged several Confederate vessels before imprudently heading further upriver into an ambush. Had Ellet only "waited patiently," Porter communicated to Welles on February 22, he would have had support from the *Indianola*, a brand-new ironclad. When the ship ran aground, it was at the time piloted by a Mr. Garvey, who was most likely a saboteur, according to Ellet. On February 21 he wrote to Porter of the crew's escape: "Some person had already taken the yawl, however, and it was gone; the other yawl was on the *De Soto*, a short distance below. Fortunately the cotton bales with which the *Queen* was protected afforded an avenue of escape, and the majority of the men and officers succeeded in reaching the *De Soto*." The captured *Queen* and another Confed-

Currier & Ives, "Admiral Farragut's Fleet Engaging the Rebel Batteries at Port Hudson, March 14, 1863." *Library of Congress, Prints and Photographs Division, LC-DIG-pga-05757.*

erate gunboat presently sank the *Indianola* in water shallow enough for them to attempt to render her serviceable once again. Enclosing an informative newspaper report, Porter telegraphed the rest of the story to Welles on March 10:

> I have been pretty well assured for some time that the *Indianola*, had been blown up in consequence of the appearance of a wooden imitation mortar, which enemy sunk with their batteries. The mortar was a valuable aid to us. It forced away the *Queen of the West* and caused the blowing up of the *Indianola*. The following is an account of the affair taken from the *Vicksburg Whig* of the 5th instant:
>
> "*Destruction of the Indianola.*—We stated a day or two since that we would not then enlighten our readers in regard to a matter which was puzzling them very much. We allude to the loss of the gunboat Indianola, recently captured from the enemy. We were loath to acknowledge she had been destroyed, but such is the case.
>
> The Yankee barge sent down the river last week was reported to be an ironclad gunboat. The authorities, thinking that this monster would retake the *Indianola*, immediately issued an order to blow her up. The order was sent down by a courier to the officer in charge of the boat. A few hours afterwards another order was sent down countermanding the first, it being ascertained that the monstrous craft was only a coal boat. But before it reached the *Indianola* she had been blown to atoms; not even a gun was saved. Who is to blame for this piece [of] folly? This precipitancy? It would really seem we had no use for gunboats on the Mississippi, as a coal barge is

had had for some time in the Red River, and two other steamers, they followed the *Indianola*. The latter was encumbered with barges of coal in tow, and consequently could make but little speed against the rapid current of the Mississippi. The Confederate fleet overtook her just above Grand Gulf, and attacked her after dark on the 24th of February. The *Indianola* was superior to all the others in armament, and probably would have destroyed them or driven them away, but for her encumbrance. As it was she fought them for an hour and a half, but, in the dark, was struck seven or eight times by the ram and other vessels, and was finally disabled and reduced to a sinking condition. The armament was thrown overboard and the vessel run ashore. Officers and crew then surrendered.

I had started McClernand with his corps of four divisions on the 29th of March, by way of Richmond, Louisiana, to New Carthage, hoping that he might capture Grand Gulf before the balance of the troops could get there; but the roads were very bad, scarcely above water yet. Some miles from New Carthage the levee to Bayou Vidal was broken in several places, overflowing the roads for the distance of two miles. Boats were collected from the surrounding bayous, and some constructed on the spot from such material as could be collected, to transport the troops across the overflowed interval. By the 6th of April McClernand had reached New Carthage with one division and its artillery, the latter ferried through the woods by these boats. On the 17th I visited New Carthage in person, and saw that the process of getting troops through in the way we were doing was so tedious that a better method must be devised. The water was falling, and in a few days there would not be depth enough to use boats; nor would the land be dry enough to march over. McClernand had already found a new route from Smith's plantation where the crevasse occurred, to Perkins' plantation, eight to twelve miles below New Carthage. This increased the march from Milliken's Bend from twenty-seven to nearly forty miles. Four bridges had to be built across bayous, two of them each over six hundred feet long, making about two thousand feet of bridging in all. The river falling made the current in these bayous very rapid, increasing the difficulty of building and permanently fas-

magnified into a monster, and our authorities immediately order a boat that would have been worth a small army to us to be blown up."

Official Records of the Union and Confederate Navies in the War of the Rebellion, ser. 1, vol. 24 (Washington, D.C.: Government Printing Office, 1911), 218, 382, 385, 397.

For a detailed account of this episode and its context in the larger river war, see McPherson, *War on the Waters*, chapter 8.

tening these bridges; but the ingenuity of the "Yankee soldier" was equal to any emergency. The bridges were soon built of such material as could be found near by, and so substantial were they that not a single mishap occurred in crossing all the army with artillery, cavalry and wagon trains, except the loss of one siege gun (a thirty-two pounder). This, if my memory serves me correctly, broke through the only pontoon bridge we had in all our march across the peninsula. These bridges were all built by McClernand's command, under the supervision of Lieutenant [Peter C.] Hains of the Engineer Corps.

I returned to Milliken's Bend on the 18th or 19th, and on the 20th issued the following final order for the movement of troops:

HEADQUARTERS DEPARTMENT OF THE TENNESSEE,
MILLIKEN'S BEND, LOUISIANA,
April 20, 1863.

Special Orders, No. 110.

★ ★ ★ ★ ★ ★ ★

VIII. The following orders are published for the information and guidance of the "Army in the Field," in its present movement to obtain a foothold on the east bank of the Mississippi River, from which Vicksburg can be approached by practicable roads.

First.—The Thirteenth army corps, Major-General John A. McClernand commanding, will constitute the right wing.

Second.—The Fifteenth army corps, Major-General W. T. Sherman commanding, will constitute the left wing.

Third.—The Seventeenth army corps, Major-General James B. McPherson commanding, will constitute the centre.

Fourth.—The order of march to New Carthage will be from right to left.

Fifth.—Reserves will be formed by divisions from each army corps; or, an entire army corps will be held as a reserve, as necessity may require. When the reserve is formed by divisions, each division will remain under the immediate command of its respective corps commander, unless otherwise specially ordered for a particular emergency.

Sixth.—Troops will be required to bivouac, until proper facilities can be afforded for the transportation of camp equipage.

Seventh.—In the present movement, one tent will be allowed to each company for the protection of rations from rain; one wall tent for each regimental headquarters; one wall tent for each brigade headquarters; and one wall tent for each division headquarters; corps commanders having the books and blanks of their respective commands to provide for, are authorized to take such tents as are absolutely necessary, but not to exceed the number allowed by General Orders No. 160, A. G. O., series of 1862.

Eighth.—All the teams of the three army corps, under the immediate charge of the quartermasters bearing them on their returns, will constitute a train for carrying supplies and ordnance and the authorized camp equipage of the army.

Ninth.—As fast as the Thirteenth army corps advances, the Seventeenth army corps will take its place; and it, in turn, will be followed in like manner by the Fifteenth army corps.

Tenth.—Two regiments from each army corps will be detailed by corps commanders, to guard the lines from Richmond to New Carthage.

Eleventh.—General hospitals will be established by the medical director between Duckport and Milliken's Bend. All sick and disabled soldiers will be left in these hospitals. Surgeons in charge of hospitals will report convalescents as fast as they become fit for duty. Each corps commander will detail an intelligent and good drill officer, to remain behind and take charge of the convalescents of their respective corps; officers so detailed will organize the men under their charge into squads and companies, without regard to the regiments they belong to; and in the absence of convalescent commissioned officers to command them, will appoint non-commissioned officers or privates. The force so organized will constitute the guard of the line from Duckport to Milliken's Bend. They will furnish all the guards and details required for general hospitals, and with the contrabands that may be about the camps, will furnish all the details for loading and unloading boats.

Twelfth.—The movement of troops from Milliken's Bend to New Carthage will be so conducted as to allow the transportation of ten days' supply of rations, and one-half the allowance of ordnance, required by previous orders.

Thirteenth.—Commanders are authorized and enjoined to collect all the beef cattle, corn and other necessary supplies on the line of march; but wanton destruction of property, taking of articles useless for military purposes, insulting citizens, going into and searching houses without proper orders from division commanders, are positively prohibited. All such irregularities must be summarily punished.

Fourteenth.—Brigadier-General J. C. Sullivan is appointed to the command of all the forces detailed for the protection of the line from here to New Carthage. His particular attention is called to General Orders, No. 69, from Adjutant-General's Office, Washington, of date March 20, 1863.

By order of

MAJOR-GENERAL U. S. GRANT.

McClernand was already below on the Mississippi.[9] Two of McPherson's divisions were put upon the march immediately. The third had not yet arrived from Lake Providence; it was on its way to Milliken's Bend and was to follow on arrival.

Sherman was to follow McPherson. Two of his divisions were at Duckport and Young's Point, and the third under [Frederick] Steele was under orders to return from Greenville, Mississippi, where it had been sent to expel a rebel battery that had been annoying our transports.

It had now become evident that the army could not be rationed by a wagon train over the single narrow and almost impassable road between Milliken's Bend and Perkins' plantation. Accordingly six more steamers were protected as before, to run the batteries, and were loaded with supplies. They took twelve barges in tow, loaded also with rations. On the night of the 22d of April they ran the batteries, five getting through more or less disabled while one was sunk. About half the barges got through with their needed freight.

When it was first proposed to run the blockade at Vicksburg with river steamers there were but two captains or masters who were willing to accompany their vessels, and but one crew. Volunteers were called for from the army, men who had had experience in any capacity in navigating the

---

9. By now, David Porter had lost all faith in McClernand: "General McClernand had been ordered by Grant to push forward with his division, and with the help of the Navy, to seize upon Grand Gulf. . . . McClernand had been given the advance to satisfy his ambition, but he was not equal to the occasion, and this desire of General Grant to show McClernand that he was anxious to give him an opportunity for distinction, might have hazarded the success of the campaign. . . . McClernand, wrapped in his dignity, scorned all advice." *Naval History*, 312–13.

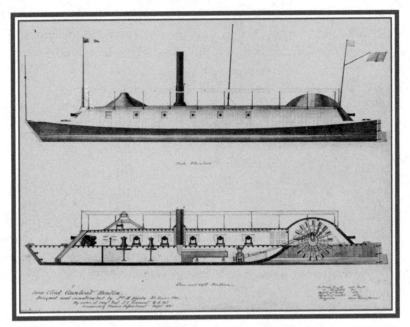

Blueprint of iron gunboat USS *Benton*, flagship of Admiral Porter. *NH68439.*
Courtesy of the Naval History and Heritage Command.

western rivers. Captains, pilots, mates, engineers and deck-hands enough presented themselves to take five times the number of vessels we were moving through this dangerous ordeal. Most of them were from Logan's division, composed generally of men from the southern part of Illinois and from Missouri. All but two of the steamers were commanded by volunteers from the army, and all but one so manned. In this instance, as in all others during the war, I found that volunteers could be found in the ranks and among the commissioned officers to meet every call for aid whether mechanical or professional.[10] Colonel W. S. Oliver was master of transportation on this occasion by special detail.

---

10. Here again Grant's account reveals the value of the volunteers and the diversity of life experience they brought to the army.

33

Attack on Grand Gulf—Operations below Vicksburg

On the 24th my headquarters were with the advance at Perkins' plantation. Reconnoissances were made in boats to ascertain whether there
was high land on the east shore of the river where we might land above
Grand Gulf. There was none practicable. Accordingly the troops were set
in motion for Hard Times, twenty-two miles farther down the river and
nearly opposite Grand Gulf. The loss of two steamers and six barges reduced
our transportation so that only 10,000 men could be moved by water. Some
of the steamers that had got below were injured in their machinery, so that
they were only useful as barges towed by those less severely injured. All
the troops, therefore, except what could be transported in one trip, had to
march. The road lay west of Lake St. Joseph. Three large bayous had to be
crossed. They were rapidly bridged in the same manner as those previously
encountered.[1]

On the 27th McClernand's corps was all at Hard Times, and McPherson's was following closely. I had determined to make the attempt to effect
a landing on the east side of the river as soon as possible. Accordingly, on
the morning of the 29th, McClernand was directed to embark all the troops
from his corps that our transports and barges could carry. About 10,000 men
were so embarked. The plan was to have the navy silence the guns at Grand

---

1. On this occasion Governor Richard Yates, of Illinois, happened to be on a visit to the
army, and accompanied me to Carthage. I furnished an ambulance for his use and that
of some of the State officers who accompanied him. [Note to the first edition.]

Major General James Birdseye McPherson.
Library of Congress, Prints and Photographs Division,
Civil War Photographs, LC-DIG-cwpb-07051.

Gulf, and to have as many men as possible ready to debark in the shortest possible time under cover of the fire of the navy and carry the works by storm. The following order was issued:

PERKINS PLANTATION, LA.,
April 27, 1863.

MAJOR-GENERAL J. A. MCCLERNAND,
Commanding 13th A. C.

Commence immediately the embarkation of your corps, or so much of it as there is transportation for. Have put aboard the artillery and every article authorized in orders limiting baggage, except the men, and hold them in readiness, with their places assigned, to be moved at a moment's warning.

All the troops you may have, except those ordered to remain behind, send to a point nearly opposite Grand Gulf, where you see, by special orders of this date, General McPherson is ordered to send one division.

The plan of the attack will be for the navy to attack and silence all the batteries commanding the river. Your corps will be on the river, ready to run to and debark on the nearest eligible land below the promontory first brought to view passing down the river. Once on shore, have each commander instructed beforehand to form his men the best the ground will admit of, and take possession of the most commanding points, but avoid separating your command so that it cannot support itself. The first object is to get a foothold where our troops can maintain themselves until such time as preparations can be made and troops collected for a forward movement.

Admiral Porter has proposed to place his boats in the position indicated to you a few days ago, and to bring over with them such troops as may be below the city after the guns of the enemy are silenced.

It may be that the enemy will occupy positions back from the city, out of range of the gunboats, so as to make it desirable to run past Grand Gulf and land at Rodney. In case this should prove the plan, a signal will be arranged and you duly informed, when the transports are to start with this view. Or, it may be expedient for the boats to run past, but not the men. In this case, then, the transports would have to be brought back to where the men could land and move by forced marches to below Grand Gulf, re-embark rapidly and proceed to the latter place. There will be required, then, three signals; one, to indicate that the transports can run down and debark the troops at Grand Gulf; one, that the transports can run by without the troops; and the last, that the transports can run by with the troops on board.

Should the men have to march, all baggage and artillery will be left to run the blockade.

If not already directed, require your men to keep three days' rations in their haversacks, not to be touched until a movement commences.

U. S. GRANT,
Major-General.

At 8 o'clock A.M., 29th, Porter made the attack with his entire strength present, eight gunboats. For nearly five and a half hours the attack was kept up without silencing a single gun of the enemy. All this time McClernand's 10,000 men were huddled together on the transports in the stream ready to attempt a landing if signalled. I occupied a tug from which I could see the effect of the battle on both sides, within range of the enemy's guns; but a small tug, without armament, was not calculated to attract the fire of batteries while they were being assailed themselves. About half-past one the fleet withdrew, seeing their efforts were entirely unavailing. The enemy ceased firing as soon as we withdrew. I immediately signalled the Admiral and went aboard his ship. The navy lost in this engagement eighteen killed and fifty-six wounded. A large proportion of these were of the crew of the flagship, and most of those from a single shell which penetrated the ship's side and exploded between decks where the men were working their guns.[2] The sight of the mangled and dying men which met my eye as I boarded the ship was sickening.[3]

2. Porter notes that his flagship, the *Benton*, "was badly cut up . . . struck forty-seven times in the casemates, and seventy times in all by heavy shot, the three-quarter inch iron was perforated twelve times, the two and-a-half inch, four times. A hundred pound shot passed through the pilot-house, smashing the wheel and severely wounding the pilot, nine men were killed and nineteen wounded." *Naval History*, 315.

3. In Frederick Marryat's *Mr Midshipman Easy* Grant would have encountered the following description of naval warfare. In this scene the *Aurora*, the hero's ship, engages a Russian frigate:

> The *Aurora* was put about, and her broadside poured into the stern of the Russian frigate—for such she was. It was almost dark, but the enemy, who appeared as anxious as the *Aurora* to come to action, hauled up her courses to await her coming up. In five minutes the two vessels were alongside, exchanging murderous broadsides at little more than pistol-shot— running slowly in for the land, then not more than five miles distant. . . .
>
> The moon now burst out from a low bank of clouds, and enabled them to accomplish their work with more precision. In a quarter of an hour the Russian was totally dismasted. . . . Observing that the fire from her antagonist had ceased, the *Aurora* also discontinued, and the jolly-boat astern being still uninjured, the second lieutenant was deputed to pull alongside of the frigate to ascertain if she had struck. . . .
>
> . . . Still the pertinacity and decided courage of the Russian captain convinced Captain Wilson, that, in all probability, he would sink at his anchor before he would haul down his colours; and not only would he lose more of the *Aurora*'s men, but also the Russian vessel, without he took a more decided step. Captain Wilson, therefore, resolved to try her by the board. Having poured in a raking fire, he stood off for a few moments, during which he called the officers and men on deck, and stated his intention. He then went about, and himself conning the *Aurora*, ran her on board the Russian, pouring in his reserved broadside as the vessels came into collision, and heading his men as they leaped on the enemy's decks. . . .
>
> Our hero, who had the good fortune to be still unhurt, was for a little while close to Captain Wilson when he boarded, and was about to oppose his unequal force against that of the Russian captain, when he was pulled back by the collar by Mr Hawkins, the chaplain, who rushed in advance with a sabre in his hand. The opponents were well matched, and it may be said that, with little interruption, a hand-to-hand conflict ensued, for the moon lighted up the scene of carnage, and they were well able to distinguish each other's faces. At last, the chaplain's sword broke: he rushed in, drove the hilt into his antagonist's face, closed with him, and they both

Grand Gulf is on a high bluff where the river runs at the very foot of it. It is as defensible upon its front as Vicksburg and, at that time, would have been just as impossible to capture by a front attack. I therefore requested Porter to run the batteries with his fleet that night, and to take charge of the transports, all of which would be wanted below.

There is a long tongue of land from the Louisiana side extending towards Grand Gulf, made by the river running nearly east from about three miles above and nearly in the opposite direction from that point for about the same distance below. The land was so low and wet that it would not have been practicable to march an army across but for a levee. I had had this explored before, as well as the east bank below to ascertain if there was a possible

---

fell down the hatchway together. After this, the deck was gained, or rather cleared, by the crew of the *Aurora*, for few could be said to have resisted, and in a minute or two the frigate was in their possession. The chaplain and the Russian captain were hoisted up, still clinging to each other, both senseless from the fall, but neither of them dead, although bleeding from several wounds.

As soon as the main deck had been cleared, Captain Wilson ordered the hatches to be put on, and left a party on board while he hastened to attend to the condition of his own ship and ship's company.

It was daylight before anything like order had been restored to the decks of the *Aurora*; the water was still smooth, and instead of letting go her own anchor, she had hung on with a hawser to the prize, but her sails had been furled, her decks cleared, guns secured, and the buckets were dashing away the blood from her planks and the carriages of the guns, when the sun rose and shone upon them. The numerous wounded had, by this time, been put into their hammocks, although there were still one or two cases of amputation to be performed. . . .

. . . It was not until the *Aurora* presented a more cheerful appearance that Captain Wilson went over to the other ship, whose deck, now that the light of heaven enabled them to witness all the horrors even to minuteness, presented a shocking spectacle of blood and carnage. Body after body was thrown over; the wounded were supplied with water and such assistance as could be rendered until the surgeons could attend them; the hatches were then taken off, and the remainder of her crew ordered on deck; about two hundred obeyed the summons, but the lower deck was as crowded with killed and wounded as was the upper. For the present the prisoners were handed over down into the fore-hold of the *Aurora*, which had been prepared for their reception, and the work of separation of the dead from the living then underwent.

Mr Midshipman Easy, vol. 7 of *The Novels of Captain Marryat*, ed. R. Brimley Johnson (London: Dent, 1896), 300–304.

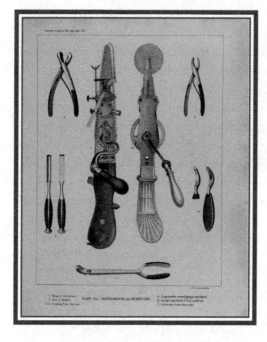

"Instruments for Resection," *The Medical and Surgical History of the War of the Rebellion (1861–1865). Courtesy of NIH U.S. National Library of Medicine.*

point of debarkation north of Rodney. It was found that the top of the levee afforded a good road to march upon.

Porter, as was always the case with him, not only acquiesced in the plan, but volunteered to use his entire fleet as transports. I had intended to make this request, but he anticipated me. At dusk, when concealed from the view of the enemy at Grand Gulf, McClernand landed his command on the west bank. The navy and transports ran the batteries successfully. The troops marched across the point of land under cover of night, unobserved. By the time it was light the enemy saw our whole fleet, iron-clads, gunboats, river steamers and barges, quietly moving down the river three miles below them, black, or rather blue, with National troops.

When the troops debarked, the evening of the 29th, it was expected that we would have to go to Rodney, about nine miles below, to find a landing; but that night a colored man came in who informed me that a good landing would be found at Bruinsburg, a few miles above Rodney, from which point there was a good road leading to Port Gibson some twelve miles in the interior. The information was found correct, and our landing was effected without opposition.

Sherman had not left his position above Vicksburg yet. On the morning of the 27th I ordered him to create a diversion by moving his corps up the Yazoo and threatening an attack on Haines' Bluff.

My object was to compel Pemberton to keep as much force about Vicksburg as I could, until I could secure a good footing on high land east of the river. The move was eminently successful and, as we afterwards learned, created great confusion about Vicksburg and doubts about our real design. Sherman moved the day of our attack on Grand Gulf, the 29th, with ten regiments of his command and eight gunboats which Porter had left above Vicksburg.

He debarked his troops and apparently made every preparation to attack the enemy while the navy bombarded the main forts at Haines' Bluff. This move was made without a single casualty in either branch of the service. On the first of May Sherman received orders from me (sent from Hard Times the evening of the 29th of April) to withdraw from the front of Haines' Bluff and follow McPherson with two divisions as fast as he could.

I had established a depot of supplies at Perkins' plantation. Now that all our gunboats were below Grand Gulf it was possible that the enemy might fit out boats in the Big Black with improvised armament and attempt to destroy these supplies. McPherson was at Hard Times with a portion of his corps, and the depot was protected by a part of his command. The night of the 29th I directed him to arm one of the transports with artillery and send it up to Perkins' plantation as a guard; and also to have the siege guns we had brought along moved there and put in position.

The embarkation below Grand Gulf took place at De Shroon's, Louisiana, six miles above Bruinsburg, Mississippi. Early on the morning of 30th of April McClernand's corps and one division of McPherson's corps were speedily landed.

When this was effected I felt a degree of relief scarcely ever equalled since.[4] Vicksburg was not yet taken it is true, nor were its defenders demoralized by any of our previous moves. I was now in the enemy's country, with a vast river and the stronghold of Vicksburg between me and my base of supplies. But I was on dry ground on the same side of the river with the enemy. All the campaigns, labors, hardships and exposures from the month of December previous to this time that had been made and endured, were for the accomplishment of this one object.

4. James M. McPherson suggests the magnitude of what transpired in the three weeks between the landing at Grand Gulf and the investment of Vicksburg: "Grant's army marched 130 miles, won five battles over detachments of the Confederate Army of Mississippi that if united would have been nearly as large as the 44,000 men in Grant's Army of the Tennessee, and penned up the Confederates in the Vicksburg defenses." *War on the Waters*, 166–67.

I had with me the 13th corps, General McClernand commanding, and two brigades of Logan's division of the 17th corps, General McPherson commanding—in all not more than twenty thousand men to commence the campaign with. These were soon reinforced by the remaining brigade of Logan's division and Crocker's division of the 17th corps.[5] On the 7th of May I was further reinforced by Sherman with two divisions of his, the 15th corps. My total force was then about thirty-three thousand men.

The enemy occupied Grand Gulf, Haines' Bluff and Jackson with a force of nearly sixty thousand men. Jackson is fifty miles east of Vicksburg and is connected with it by a railroad. My first problem was to capture Grand Gulf to use as a base.

Bruinsburg is two miles from high ground. The bottom at that point is higher than most of the low land in the valley of the Mississippi, and a good road leads to the bluff. It was natural to expect the garrison from Grand Gulf to come out to meet us and prevent, if they could, our reaching this solid base. Bayou Pierre enters the Mississippi just above Bruinsburg and, as it is a navigable stream and was high at the time, in order to intercept us they had to go by Port Gibson, the nearest point where there was a bridge to cross upon. This more than doubled the distance from Grand Gulf to the high land back of Bruinsburg. No time was to be lost in securing this foothold. Our transportation was not sufficient to move all the army across the river at one trip, or even two; but the landing of the 13th corps and one division of the 17th was effected during the day, April 30th, and early evening. McClernand was advanced as soon as ammunition and two days' rations (to last five) could be issued to his men. The bluffs were reached an hour before sunset and McClernand was pushed on, hoping to reach Port Gibson and save the bridge spanning the Bayou Pierre before the enemy could get there; for crossing a stream in the presence of an enemy is always difficult. Port Gibson, too, is the starting point of roads to Grand Gulf, Vicksburg and Jackson.

McClernand's advance met the enemy about five miles west of Port Gibson at Thompson's plantation. There was some firing during the night, but nothing rising to the dignity of a battle until daylight. The enemy had taken a strong natural position with most of the Grand Gulf garrison, numbering about seven or eight thousand men, under General Bowen. His hope

5. Marcellus M. Crocker (1830–1865) had organized a private militia in Iowa before the war had even begun. He proved to be a highly competent officer. Crocker rendered noteworthy service at Shiloh and Corinth, and he had become a division commander by the time of the Vicksburg campaign. Crocker died of tuberculosis.

was to hold me in check until reinforcements under Loring could reach him from Vicksburg; but Loring did not come in time to render much assistance south of Port Gibson. Two brigades of McPherson's corps followed McClernand as fast as rations and ammunition could be issued, and were ready to take position upon the battle-field whenever the 13th corps could be got out of the way.

The country in this part of Mississippi stands on edge, as it were, the roads running along the ridges except when they occasionally pass from one ridge to another. Where there are no clearings the sides of the hills are covered with a very heavy growth of timber and with undergrowth, and the ravines are filled with vines and canebrakes, almost impenetrable. This makes it easy for an inferior force to delay, if not defeat, a far superior one.

Near the point selected by Bowen to defend, the road to Port Gibson divides, taking two ridges which do not diverge more than a mile or two at the widest point. These roads unite just outside the town. This made it necessary for McClernand to divide his force. It was not only divided, but it was separated by a deep ravine of the character above described. One flank could not reinforce the other except by marching back to the junction of the roads. McClernand put the divisions of Hovey, Carr and A. J. Smith upon the right-hand branch and Osterhaus on the left. I was on the field by ten A.M., and inspected both flanks in person. On the right the enemy, if not being pressed back, was at least not repulsing our advance. On the left, however, Osterhaus was not faring so well. He had been repulsed with some loss. As soon as the road could be cleared of McClernand's troops I ordered up McPherson, who was close upon the rear of the 13th corps, with two brigades of Logan's division. This was about noon. I ordered him to send one brigade (General John E. Smith's was selected) to support Osterhaus, and to move to the left and flank the enemy out of his position. This movement carried the brigade over a deep ravine to a third ridge and, when Smith's troops were seen well through the ravine, Osterhaus was directed to renew his front attack. It was successful and unattended by heavy loss. The enemy was sent in full retreat on their right, and their left followed before sunset. While the movement to our left was going on, McClernand, who was with his right flank, sent me frequent requests for reinforcements, although the force with him was not being pressed. I had been upon the ground and knew it did not admit of his engaging all the men he had. We followed up our victory until night overtook us about two miles from Port Gibson; then the troops went into bivouac for the night.

34

Capture of Port Gibson—Grierson's Raid—Occupation of Grand Gulf— Movement up the Big Black—Battle of Raymond

W e started next morning for Port Gibson as soon as it was light enough to see the road. We were soon in the town, and I was delighted to find that the enemy had not stopped to contest our crossing further at the bridge, which he had burned. The troops were set to work at once to construct a bridge across the South Fork of the Bayou Pierre. At this time the water was high and the current rapid. What might be called a raft-bridge was soon constructed from material obtained from wooden buildings, stables, fences, etc., which sufficed for carrying the whole army over safely. Colonel J. H. Wilson, a member of my staff, planned and super-intended the construction of this bridge, going into the water and working as hard as any one engaged. Officers and men generally joined in this work. When it was finished the army crossed and marched eight miles beyond to the North Fork that day. One brigade of Logan's division was sent down the stream to occupy the attention of a rebel battery, which had been left behind with infantry supports to prevent our repairing the burnt railroad bridge. Two of his brigades were sent up the bayou to find a crossing and reach the North Fork to repair the bridge there. The enemy soon left when he found we were building a bridge elsewhere. Before leaving Port Gibson we were reinforced by Crocker's division, McPherson's corps, which had crossed the Mississippi at Bruinsburg and come up without stopping except to get two days' rations. McPherson still had one division west of the Mississippi River, guarding the road from Milliken's Bend to the river below until Sherman's command should relieve it.

On leaving Bruinsburg for the front I left my son Frederick, who had joined me a few weeks before, on board one of the gunboats asleep, and hoped to get away without him until after Grand Gulf should fall into our hands; but on waking up he learned that I had gone, and being guided by the sound of the battle raging at Thompson's Hill—called the Battle of Port Gibson—found his way to where I was. He had no horse to ride at the time, and I had no facilities for even preparing a meal. He, therefore, foraged around the best he could until we reached Grand Gulf. Mr. C. A. Dana, then an officer of the War Department, accompanied me on the Vicksburg campaign and through a portion of the siege.[1] He was in the same situation as Fred so far as transportation and mess arrangements were concerned. The first time I call to mind seeing either of them, after the battle, they were mounted on two enormous horses, grown white from age, each equipped with dilapidated saddles and bridles.

Our trains arrived a few days later, after which we were all perfectly equipped.

My son accompanied me throughout the campaign and siege, and caused no anxiety either to me or to his mother, who was at home. He looked out for himself and was in every battle of the campaign. His age, then not quite

1. Stanton sent the journalist Charles A. Dana (1819–1897) to Grant's headquarters during the Vicksburg campaign in order to verify reports that continued to circulate regarding Grant's drinking and unreliability. As assistant secretary of war, Dana provided daily intelligence to Stanton and Lincoln. His postwar account, published in 1898, offers valuable glimpses into the daily workings of the Vicksburg campaign and other important Civil War events. Dana, impressed with Grant's equanimity during the Grand Gulf operations, was won over:

The night was pitch dark, and, as we rode side by side, Grant's horse suddenly gave a nasty stumble. I expected to see the general go over the animal's head, and I watched intently, not to see if he was hurt, but if he would show any anger. I had been with Grant daily now for three weeks, and I had never seen him ruffled or heard him swear. His equanimity was becoming a curious spectacle to me. When I saw his horse lunge my first thought was, "Now he will swear." For an instant his moral status was on trial; but Grant was a tenacious horseman, and instead of going over the animal's head, as I imagined he would, he kept his seat. Pulling up his horse, he rode on, and, to my utter amazement, without a word or sign of impatience.

Recollections of the Civil War: With the Leaders at Washington and in the Field in the Sixties (New York: D. Appleton, 1902), 43.

thirteen, enabled him to take in all he saw, and to retain a recollection of it that would not be possible in more mature years.[2]

When the movement from Bruinsburg commenced we were without a wagon train. The train still west of the Mississippi was carried around with proper escort, by a circuitous route from Milliken's Bend to Hard Times seventy or more miles below, and did not get up for some days after the battle of Port Gibson. My own horses, headquarters' transportation, servants, mess chest, and everything except what I had on, was with this train. General A. J. Smith happened to have an extra horse at Bruinsburg which I borrowed, with a saddle-tree without upholstering further than stirrups. I had no other for nearly a week.

It was necessary to have transportation for ammunition. Provisions could be taken from the country; but all the ammunition that can be carried on the person is soon exhausted when there is much fighting. I directed, therefore, immediately on landing that all the vehicles and draft animals, whether horses, mules, or oxen, in the vicinity should be collected and loaded to their capacity with ammunition. Quite a train was collected during the 30th, and a motley train it was. In it could be found fine carriages, loaded nearly to the top with boxes of cartridges that had been pitched in promiscuously, drawn

---

2. The presence of young boys at the front was not so unusual as it would seem today. Later in the war, Julia brought all the children to visit Grant at his headquarters at City Point, Virginia. Sherman's family visited him in Mississippi after the fall of Vicksburg. His nine-year-old son Willie was a popular presence in the Mississippi camp Sherman occupied before being sent to Chattanooga. Willie died of typhoid in Memphis in the fall of 1863.

Although the youth of Civil War drummer boys has been somewhat exaggerated, many were under eighteen when they began their service. John Cockerill, who survived the war to become a well-known journalist, wrote about his experiences as a sixteen-year-old musician at Shiloh. The youngest of all is said to have been John Clem, who attached himself to a company at the age of nine. For more information, see Elizabeth Collins, "The Beats of Battle: Images of Army Drummer Boys Endure," *Soldiers: The Official U.S. Army Magazine*, http://soldiers.dodlive.mil/2013/12/the-beats-of-battle-images-of-army-drummer-boys-endure/; and Cate Lineberry, "The Boys of War," *New York Times*, October 4, 2011, https://opinionator.blogs.nytimes.com/2011/10/04/the-boys-of-war/.

Lincoln wrote to Stanton on March 15, 1864, asking him to help find a "suitable" appointment for one Robert H. Hendershot, a "gallant Drummer-boy . . . whose history is briefly written on the fine drum presented to him which he now carries." Hendershot, of the 8th Michigan Volunteers, was apparently twelve years old at the Battle of Fredericksburg and had been recently discharged from the service because of disability. See Letter to Edwin M. Stanton, March 15, 1864, *Collected Works*, ed. Basler, 7:249.

by mules with plough, harness, straw collars, rope-lines, etc.; long-coupled wagons, with racks for carrying cotton bales, drawn by oxen, and everything that could be found in the way of transportation on a plantation, either for use or pleasure. The making out of provision returns was stopped for the time. No formalities were to retard our progress until a position was secured when the time could be spared to observe them.

It was at Port Gibson I first heard through a Southern paper of the complete success of Colonel Grierson, who was making a raid through central Mississippi. He had started from La Grange April 17th with three regiments of about 1,700 men. On the 21st he had detached Colonel Hatch with one regiment to destroy the railroad between Columbus and Macon and then return to La Grange. Hatch had a sharp fight with the enemy at Columbus and retreated along the railroad, destroying it at Okalona and Tupelo, and arriving in La Grange April 26. Grierson continued his movement with about 1,000 men, breaking the Vicksburg and Meridian railroad and the New Orleans and Jackson railroad, arriving at Baton Rouge May 2d. This raid was of great importance, for Grierson had attracted the attention of the enemy from the main movement against Vicksburg.[3]

---

3. Benjamin H. Grierson (1826–1911) led a two-week cavalry raid through Mississippi, during which he damaged railroad lines supplying Vicksburg, destroyed supplies, and distracted Pemberton's attention from Grant's operations. After the war, Grierson went on to command the 10th Cavalry, a regiment of African American soldiers. Grierson's memoir, *A Just and Righteous Cause*, contains a spirited narrative of the raid, which involved a series of deceptions, including the use of Confederate uniforms, which earned his soldiers the sobriquet "Butternut Guerillas"; happy accidents; and a hair-breadth escape back to federal lines. S. A. Forbes, who had been a captain in the 7th Illinois Cavalry, describes the essence of a raid:

> A cavalry raid at its best is essentially a *game* of strategy and speed, with personal violence as an incidental complication. It is played according to more or less definite rules, not inconsistent, indeed, with the players' killing each other if the game cannot be won in any other way; but it is commonly a strenuous game rather than a bloody one, intensely exciting, but not necessarily very dangerous. This narrative will consequently be without the grim and gory features of most tales of war, but will tell instead of the rapid march, the subtle ruse, the gallant dash, the sudden surprise, and the quick and cunning retreat which leaves an opponent miles in the rear before he knows that the fight is over.

"Grierson's Cavalry Raid," *Transactions of the Illinois State Historical Society for the Year 1907* 12 (1908): 102–3.

During the night of the 2d of May the bridge over the North Fork was repaired, and the troops commenced crossing at five the next morning. Before the leading brigade was over it was fired upon by the enemy from a commanding position; but they were soon driven off. It was evident that the enemy was covering a retreat from Grand Gulf to Vicksburg. Every commanding position from this (Grindstone) crossing to Hankinson's ferry over the Big Black was occupied by the retreating foe to delay our progress. McPherson, however, reached Hankinson's ferry before night, seized the ferry boat, and sent a detachment of his command across and several miles north on the road to Vicksburg. When the junction of the road going to Vicksburg with the road from Grand Gulf to Raymond and Jackson was reached, Logan with his division was turned to the left towards Grand Gulf. I went with him a short distance from this junction. McPherson had encountered the largest force yet met since the battle of Port Gibson and had a skirmish nearly approaching a battle; but the road Logan had taken enabled him to come up on the enemy's right flank, and they soon gave way. McPherson was ordered to hold Hankinson's ferry and the road back to Willow Springs with one division; McClernand, who was now in the rear, was to join in this as well as to guard the line back down the bayou. I did not want to take the chances of having an enemy lurking in our rear.

On the way from the junction to Grand Gulf, where the road comes into the one from Vicksburg to the same place six or seven miles out, I learned that the last of the enemy had retreated past that place on their way to Vicksburg. I left Logan to make the proper disposition of his troops for the night, while I rode into the town with an escort of about twenty cavalry. Admiral Porter had already arrived with his fleet. The enemy had abandoned his heavy guns and evacuated the place.

When I reached Grand Gulf May 3d I had not been with my baggage since the 27th of April and consequently had had no change of underclothing, no meal except such as I could pick up sometimes at other headquarters, and no tent to cover me. The first thing I did was to get a bath, borrow some fresh underclothing from one of the naval officers and get a good meal on the flag-ship. Then I wrote letters to the general-in-chief informing him of our present position, dispatches to be telegraphed from Cairo, orders to General Sullivan commanding above Vicksburg, and gave orders to all my corps

---

Grierson's exploits also provided fodder for Harrison Sinclair's novel *The Horse Soldiers*, on which the 1959 John Ford film of the same name is based. It starred John Wayne and William Holden.

commanders. About twelve o'clock at night I was through my work and started for Hankinson's ferry, arriving there before daylight. While at Grand Gulf I heard from Banks, who was on the Red River, and who said that he could not be at Port Hudson before the 10th of May and then with only 15,000 men. Up to this time my intention had been to secure Grand Gulf, as a base of supplies, detach McClernand's corps to Banks and co-operate with him in the reduction of Port Hudson.[4]

4. The siege of Port Hudson, Louisiana—the longest siege in American history—began on May 22, 1863, and the surrender took place on July 9, five days after that of Vicksburg. By the end, the Confederate garrison was evidently living on mules and rats. See McPherson, *Battle Cry*, 638. Union officer John William De Forest called it "forty days and nights in the wilderness of death." *A Volunteer's Adventures*, 116.

Detritus of war: Earthworks after the surrender of the Confederates at Port Hudson, Louisiana. *Library of Congress, Prints and Photographs Division, LC-DIG-stereo-1s04326.*

The abject misery of a city under siege is perhaps nowhere more powerfully expressed than in this set piece on the Roman siege of Jerusalem in 70 AD by the Jewish general Josephus:

> All egress being now intercepted, every hope of safety to the Jews was utterly cut off; and famine, with distended jaws, was devouring the people by houses and families. The roofs were filled with women and babes in the last stage: the streets with old men already dead. Children and youths, swollen up, huddled together like spectres in the market-places; and fell down wherever the pangs of death seized them. To inter their relations, they who were themselves affected had not strength; and those still in health and vigour were deterred by the multitude of the dead, and by the uncertainty that hung over themselves. For many expired while burying others; and many repaired to the cemeteries ere the fatal hour arrived.

The news from Banks forced upon me a different plan of campaign from the one intended. To wait for his co-operation would have detained me at least a month. The reinforcements would not have reached ten thousand men after deducting casualties and necessary river guards at all high points close to the river for over three hundred miles. The enemy would have strengthened his position and been reinforced by more men than Banks could have brought. I therefore determined to move independently of Banks, cut loose from my base, destroy the rebel force in rear of Vicksburg and invest or capture the city.

Grand Gulf was accordingly given up as a base and the authorities at Washington were notified. I knew well that Halleck's caution would lead him to disapprove of this course; but it was the only one that gave any chance of success. The time it would take to communicate with Washington and get a reply would be so great that I could not be interfered with until it was demonstrated whether my plan was practicable. Even Sherman, who afterwards ignored bases of supplies other than what were afforded by the country while marching through four States of the Confederacy with an army more than twice as large as mine at this time, wrote me from Hankinson's ferry, advising me of the impossibility of supplying our army over a single road. He urged me to "stop all troops till your army is partially supplied with wagons, and then act as quick as possible; for this road will be jammed, as sure as life." To this I replied: "I do not calculate upon the possibility of supplying

---

Amidst these calamities there was neither lamentation, nor wailing: famine overpowered the affections. With dry eyes and gaping mouths, the slowly-dying gazed on those who had gone to their rest before them. Profound silence reigned through the city, and a night pregnant with death, and the brigands more dreadful still than these. For bursting open the houses, as they would a sepulcher, they plundered the dead, and dragging off the coverings from the bodies, departed with laughter. They even tried the points of their swords in the carcases, and, to prove the temper of the blades, would run them through some of those who were stretched still breathing on the ground; others, who implored them to lend them their hand and sword, they abandoned disdainfully to the famine. They all expired with their eyes intently fixed on the temple, averting them from the insurgents whom they left alive. These at first, finding the stench of the bodies insupportable, ordered that they should be buried at the public expense; but afterwards when unequal to the task, they threw them from the walls into the ravines below.

The Jewish War of Flavius Josephus, trans. Robert Traill, ed. Isaac Taylor, (London: Houlston and Stoneman, 1851), 2:160–61.

the army with full rations from Grand Gulf. I know it will be impossible without constructing additional roads. What I do expect is to get up what rations of hard bread, coffee and salt we can, and make the country furnish the balance." We started from Bruinsburg with an average of about two days' rations, and received no more from our own supplies for some days; abundance was found in the mean time. A delay would give the enemy time to reinforce and fortify.[5]

McClernand's and McPherson's commands were kept substantially as they were on the night of the 2d, awaiting supplies sufficient to give them three days' rations in haversacks. Beef, mutton, poultry and forage were found in abundance. Quite a quantity of bacon and molasses was also secured from the country, but bread and coffee could not be obtained in quantity sufficient for all the men. Every plantation, however, had a run of stone, propelled by mule power, to grind corn for the owners and their slaves. All these were kept running while we were stopping, day and night, and when we were marching, during the night, at all plantations covered by the troops. But the product was taken by the troops nearest by, so that the majority of the command was destined to go without bread until a new base was established on the Yazoo above Vicksburg.

While the troops were awaiting the arrival of rations I ordered reconnoissances made by McClernand and McPherson, with the view of leading the enemy to believe that we intended to cross the Big Black and attack the city at once.

On the 6th Sherman arrived at Grand Gulf and crossed his command that night and the next day. Three days' rations had been brought up from Grand Gulf for the advanced troops and were issued. Orders were given for a forward movement the next day. Sherman was directed to order up Blair, who had been left behind to guard the road from Milliken's Bend to Hard Times with two brigades.

The quartermaster at Young's Point was ordered to send two hundred wagons with Blair, and the commissary was to load them with hard bread, coffee, sugar, salt and one hundred thousand pounds of salt meat.

On the 3d Hurlbut, who had been left at Memphis, was ordered to send

---

5. This is yet another instance of Grant's conviction that delay inevitably helped the enemy as much as it did him. Sherman, who still had not grasped the boldness of his commander's plan, wrote Grant a letter of caution: "It is useless to push out men here till their supplies are regulated, unless you intend to live on the country." *OR*, ser. 1, vol. 24, pt. 3, 284.

four regiments from his command to Milliken's Bend to relieve Blair's division, and on the 5th he was ordered to send Lauman's division in addition, the latter to join the army in the field. The four regiments were to be taken from troops near the river so that there would be no delay.

During the night of the 6th McPherson drew in his troops north of the Big Black and was off at an early hour on the road to Jackson, via Rocky Springs, Utica and Raymond. That night he and McClernand were both at Rocky Springs ten miles from Hankinson's ferry. McPherson remained there during the 8th, while McClernand moved to Big Sandy and Sherman marched from Grand Gulf to Hankinson's ferry. The 9th, McPherson moved to a point within a few miles west of Utica; McClernand and Sherman remained where they were. On the 10th McPherson moved to Utica, Sherman to Big Sandy; McClernand was still at Big Sandy. The 11th, McClernand was at Five Mile Creek; Sherman at Auburn; McPherson five miles advanced from Utica. May 12th, McClernand was at Fourteen Mile Creek; Sherman at Fourteen Mile Creek; McPherson at Raymond after a battle.

After McPherson crossed the Big Black at Hankinson's ferry Vicksburg could have been approached and besieged by the south side. It is not probable, however, that Pemberton would have permitted a close besiegement. The broken nature of the ground would have enabled him to hold a strong defensible line from the river south of the city to the Big Black, retaining possession of the railroad back to that point. It was my plan, therefore, to get to the railroad east of Vicksburg, and approach from that direction. Accordingly, McPherson's troops that had crossed the Big Black were withdrawn and the movement east to Jackson commenced.

As has been stated before, the country is very much broken and the roads generally confined to the tops of the hills. The troops were moved one (sometimes two) corps at a time to reach designated points out parallel to the railroad and only from six to ten miles from it. McClernand's corps was kept with its left flank on the Big Black guarding all the crossings. Fourteen Mile Creek, a stream substantially parallel with the railroad, was reached and crossings effected by McClernand and Sherman with slight loss. McPherson was to the right of Sherman, extending to Raymond. The cavalry was used in this advance in reconnoitring to find the roads: to cover our advances and to find the most practicable routes from one command to another so they could support each other in case of an attack. In making this move I estimated Pemberton's movable force at Vicksburg at about eighteen thousand men, with smaller forces at Haines' Bluff and Jackson. It would not be possible for Pemberton to attack me with all his troops at one place, and I determined to throw my army between his and fight him in detail. This was done with success, but I found afterwards that I had entirely under-estimated Pemberton's strength.

Up to this point our movements had been made without serious opposition. My line was now nearly parallel with the Jackson and Vicksburg railroad and about seven miles south of it. The right was at Raymond eighteen miles from Jackson, McPherson commanding; Sherman in the centre on Fourteen Mile Creek, his advance thrown across; McClernand to the left, also on Fourteen Mile Creek, advance across, and his pickets within two miles of Edward's station, where the enemy had concentrated a considerable force and where they undoubtedly expected us to attack. McClernand's left was on the Big Black. In all our moves, up to this time, the left had hugged the Big Black closely, and all the ferries had been guarded to prevent the enemy throwing a force on our rear.

McPherson encountered the enemy, five thousand strong with two batteries under General [John] Gregg, about two miles out of Raymond. This was about two P.M. Logan was in advance with one of his brigades. He deployed and moved up to engage the enemy. McPherson ordered the road in rear to be cleared of wagons, and the balance of Logan's division, and Crocker's, which was still farther in rear, to come forward with all dispatch. The order was obeyed with alacrity. Logan got his division in position for assault before Crocker could get up, and attacked with vigor, carrying the enemy's position easily, sending Gregg flying from the field not to appear against our front again until we met at Jackson.

In this battle McPherson lost 66 killed, 339 wounded, and 37 missing— nearly or quite all from Logan's division. The enemy's loss was 100 killed, 305 wounded, besides 415 taken prisoners.

I regarded Logan and Crocker as being as competent division commanders as could be found in or out of the army and both equal to a much higher command. Crocker, however, was dying of consumption when he volunteered. His weak condition never put him on the sick report when there was a battle in prospect, as long as he could keep on his feet. He died not long after the close of the rebellion.

35

Movement against Jackson—Fall of Jackson—Intercepting the Enemy—Battle of Champion's Hill

When the news reached me of McPherson's victory at Raymond about sundown my position was with Sherman. I decided at once to turn the whole column towards Jackson and capture that place without delay.

Pemberton was now on my left, with, as I supposed, about 18,000 men; in fact, as I learned afterwards, with nearly 50,000. A force was also collecting on my right, at Jackson, the point where all the railroads communicating with Vicksburg connect. All the enemy's supplies of men and stores would come by that point. As I hoped in the end to besiege Vicksburg I must first destroy all possibility of aid. I therefore determined to move swiftly towards Jackson, destroy or drive any force in that direction and then turn upon Pemberton. But by moving against Jackson, I uncovered my own communication. So I finally decided to have none—to cut loose altogether from my base and move my whole force eastward. I then had no fears for my communications, and if I moved quickly enough could turn upon Pemberton before he could attack me in the rear.[1]

Accordingly, all previous orders given during the day for movements on the 13th were annulled by new ones. McPherson was ordered at daylight to move on Clinton, ten miles from Jackson; Sherman was notified of my determination to capture Jackson and work from there westward. He was

---

1. J. F. C. Fuller suggests that the "audacity" of Grant's plan to abandon his communications "completely bewildered" the Confederate commander, John Pemberton, who proceeded under the mistaken belief that "such an action was impossible." *Generalship*, 142.

ordered to start at four in the morning and march to Raymond. McClernand was ordered to march with three divisions by Dillon's to Raymond. One was left to guard the crossing of the Big Black.

On the 10th I had received a letter from Banks, on the Red River, asking reinforcements. Porter had gone to his assistance with a part of his fleet on the 3d, and I now wrote to him describing my position and declining to send any troops. I looked upon side movements as long as the enemy held Port Hudson and Vicksburg as a waste of time and material.

General Joseph E. Johnston arrived at Jackson in the night of the 13th from Tennessee, and immediately assumed command of all the Confederate troops in Mississippi.[2] I knew he was expecting reinforcements from the south and east. On the 6th I had written to General Halleck: "Information from the other side leaves me to believe the enemy are bringing forces from Tullahoma."[3]

Up to this time my troops had been kept in supporting distances of each other, as far as the nature of the country would admit. Reconnoissances were constantly made from each corps to enable them to acquaint themselves with the most practicable routes from one to another in case a union became necessary.

McPherson reached Clinton with the advance early on the 13th and immediately set to work destroying the railroad. Sherman's advance reached Raymond before the last of McPherson's command had got out of the town. McClernand withdrew from the front of the enemy, at Edward's station,

---

2. Joseph E. Johnston (1807–1891) was an 1829 West Point graduate who served briefly as Winfield Scott's aide-de-camp during the Florida War of 1836–38, in which he was cited for gallantry. He subsequently fought in the Mexican War and was wounded at Cerro Gordo. Johnston resigned from the U.S. Army on April 22, 1861, less than two weeks after the fall of Fort Sumter, to join the C.S.A. He is usually described as a competent if defensive-minded commander. In chapter 59 Grant praises Johnston's prudence and husbanding of resources.

3. It was Dodge's network of "spies and scouts" that ferreted out this information for Grant. Dodge later heard from Frederick Grant that on the morning of the battle Dodge's agents "reported . . . General Johnston's position and force, and General Grant said he could attack and defeat Pemberton and reach Vicksburg before General Johnston could aid or reinforce Pemberton. General Grant acted on their information, and speaks of it in his dispatches and Memoirs, and as I take the Rebellion Records," Dodge continues, "and read my dispatches to Hurlbut at Memphis, who sent them by boat to Grant, I am surprised at the accuracy of the reports of these scouts. Of course they were often detected and lost their lives, but there were always others ready to take their places." *Personal Recollections*, 50–51.

Civil War courier. *Library of Congress, Prints and Photographs Division, LC-DIG-ppmsca-27220.*

with much skill and without loss, and reached his position for the night in good order. On the night of the 13th, McPherson was ordered to march at early dawn upon Jackson, only fifteen miles away. Sherman was given the same order; but he was to move by the direct road from Raymond to Jackson, which is south of the road McPherson was on and does not approach within two miles of it at the point where it crossed the line of intrenchments which, at that time, defended the city. McClernand was ordered to move one division of his command to Clinton, one division a few miles beyond Mississippi Springs following Sherman's line, and a third to Raymond. He was also directed to send his siege guns, four in number with the troops going by Mississippi Springs. McClernand's position was an advantageous one in any event. With one division at Clinton he was in position to reinforce McPherson, at Jackson, rapidly if it became necessary; the division beyond Mississippi Springs was equally available to reinforce Sherman; the one at Raymond could take either road. He still had two other divisions farther back now that Blair had come up, available within a day at Jackson. If this last command should not be wanted at Jackson, they were already one day's march from there on their way to Vicksburg and on three different roads leading to the latter city. But the most important consideration in my mind was to have a force confronting Pemberton if he should come out to attack my rear. This I expected him to do; as shown further on, he was directed by Johnston to make this very move.

I notified General Halleck that I should attack the State capital on the 14th. A courier carried the dispatch to Grand Gulf through an unprotected country.

Sherman and McPherson communicated with each other during the night and arranged to reach Jackson at about the same hour. It rained in torrents during the night of the 13th and the fore part of the day of the 14th. The roads were intolerable, and in some places on Sherman's line, where the land was low, they were covered more than a foot deep with water. But the troops never murmured. By nine o'clock Crocker, of McPherson's corps, who was now in advance, came upon the enemy's pickets and speedily drove them in upon the main body. They were outside of the intrenchments in a strong position, and proved to be the troops that had been driven out of Raymond. Johnston had been reinforced; during the night by Georgia and South Carolina regiments, so that his force amounted to eleven thousand men, and he was expecting still more.

Sherman also came upon the rebel pickets some distance out from the town, but speedily drove them in. He was now on the south and south-west of Jackson confronting the Confederates behind their breastworks, while McPherson's right was nearly two miles north, occupying a line running north and south across the Vicksburg railroad. Artillery was brought up and reconnoissances made preparatory to an assault. McPherson brought up Logan's division while he deployed Crocker's for the assault. Sherman made similar dispositions on the right. By eleven A.M. both were ready to attack. Crocker moved his division forward, preceded by a strong skirmish line. These troops at once encountered the enemy's advance and drove it back on the main body, when they returned to their proper regiment and the whole division charged, routing the enemy completely and driving him into this main line. This stand by the enemy was made more than two miles outside of his main fortifications. McPherson followed up with his command until within range of the guns of the enemy from their intrenchments, when he halted to bring his troops into line and reconnoitre to determine the next move. It was now about noon.

While this was going on Sherman was confronting a rebel battery which enfiladed the road on which he was marching—the Mississippi Springs road—and commanded a bridge spanning a stream over which he had to pass. By detaching right and left the stream was forced and the enemy flanked and speedily driven within the main line. This brought our whole line in front of the enemy's line of works, which was continuous on the north, west and south sides from the Pearl River north of the city to the same river south. I was with Sherman. He was confronted by a force sufficient to hold us back. Appearances did not justify an assault where we were. I had directed Sherman to send a force to the right, and to reconnoitre as far as to the Pearl River. This force, Tuttle's division, not returning I rode to the right with my staff, and soon found that the enemy had left that part of the line. Tuttle's movement or McPherson's pressure had no doubt led Johnston to order a retreat, leaving only the men at the guns to retard us while he was getting away. Tuttle had seen this and, passing through the lines without resistance, came up in the rear of the artillerists confronting Sherman and captured them with ten pieces of artillery. I rode immediately to the State House, where I was soon followed by Sherman. About the same time McPherson discovered that the enemy was leaving his front, and advanced Crocker, who was so close upon the enemy that they could not move their guns or destroy them. He captured seven guns and, moving on, hoisted the National flag over the rebel capital of Mississippi. [Carter] Stevenson's brigade was sent to cut off the rebel retreat, but was too late or not expeditious enough.

Our loss in this engagement was: McPherson, 37 killed, 228 wounded; Sherman, 4 killed and 21 wounded and missing. The enemy lost 845 killed, wounded and captured. Seventeen guns fell into our hands, and the enemy destroyed by fire their store-houses, containing a large amount of commissary stores.

On this day Blair reached New Auburn and joined McClernand's 4th division. He had with him two hundred wagons loaded with rations, the only commissary supplies received during the entire campaign.

I slept that night in the room that Johnston was said to have occupied the night before.

About four in the afternoon I sent for the corps commanders and directed the dispositions to be made of their troops. Sherman was to remain in Jackson until he destroyed that place as a railroad centre, and manufacturing city of military supplies. He did the work most effectually. Sherman and I went together into a manufactory which had not ceased work on account of the battle nor for the entrance of Yankee troops. Our presence did not seem to attract the attention of either the manager or the operatives, most of whom were girls. We looked on for a while to see the tent cloth which they were making roll out of the looms, with "C. S. A." woven in each bolt. There was an immense amount of cotton, in bales, stacked outside. Finally I told Sherman I thought they had done work enough. The operatives were told they could leave and take with them what cloth they could carry. In a few minutes cotton and factory were in a blaze. The proprietor visited Washington while

I was President to get his pay for this property, claiming that it was private. He asked me to give him a statement of the fact that his property had been destroyed by National troops, so that he might use it with Congress where he was pressing, or proposed to press, his claim. I declined.[4]

On the night of the 13th Johnston sent the following dispatch to Pemberton at Edward's station: "I have lately arrived, and learn that Major-General Sherman is between us with four divisions at Clinton. It is important to establish communication, that you may be reinforced. If practicable, come up in his rear at once. To beat such a detachment would be of immense value. All the troops you can quickly assemble should be brought. Time is all-important." This dispatch was sent in triplicate, by different messengers. One of the messengers happened to be a loyal man who had been expelled from Memphis some months before by Hurlbut for uttering disloyal and threatening sentiments. There was a good deal of parade about his expulsion, ostensibly as a warning to those who entertained the

---

4. Sherman tells the following story about the destruction of Jackson:

> I was ordered to remain one day to break up railroads, to destroy the arsenal, a foundery, the cotton-factory of the Messrs. Green, etc., etc., and then to follow McPherson.
>
> McPherson left Jackson early on the 15th, and General Grant during the same day. I kept my troops busy in tearing up railroad-tracks, etc. . . . Just as I was leaving Jackson, a very fat man came to see me, to inquire if his hotel, a large, frame-building near the depot, were doomed to be burned. I told him we had no intention to burn it, or any other house, except the machine-shops, and such buildings as could easily be converted to hostile uses. He professed to be a law-abiding Union man, and I remember to have said that this fact was manifest from the sign of his hotel, which was the "Confederate Hotel;" the sign "United States" being faintly painted out, and "Confederate" painted over it! I remembered that hotel, as it was the supper-station for the New Orleans trains when I used to travel the road before the war. I had not the least purpose, however, of burning it, but, just as we were leaving the town, it burst out in flames and was burned to the ground. I never found out exactly who set it on fire, but was told that in one of our batteries were some officers and men who had been made prisoners at Shiloh, with Prentiss's division, and had been carried past Jackson in a railroad-train; they had been permitted by the guard to go to this very hotel for supper, and had nothing to pay but greenbacks, which were refused, with insult, by this same law-abiding landlord. These men, it was said, had quietly and stealthily applied the fire underneath the hotel just as we were leaving the town.

Sherman, *Memoirs*, 1:321–22.

Poster for *Secret Service*, William Gillette's hugely popular 1896 play about a Union spy who poses as a Confederate. RKO turned it into a movie starring Richard Dix in 1931. *Library of Congress, Prints and Photographs Division, LC-USZ62-99701.*

sentiments he expressed; but Hurlbut and the expelled man understood each other. He delivered his copy of Johnston's dispatch to McPherson who forwarded it to me.[5]

Receiving this dispatch on the 14th I ordered McPherson to move promptly in the morning back to Bolton, the nearest point where Johnston could reach the road. Bolton is about twenty miles west of Jackson. I also informed McClernand of the capture of Jackson and sent him the following order: "It is evidently the design of the enemy to get north of us and cross the Big Black, and beat us into Vicksburg. We must not allow them to do this. Turn all your forces towards Bolton station, and make all dispatch in getting

---

5. The use of spies and agents grew during the war. The Confederacy had the initial advantage largely because the war was fought on southern terrain; however, the use of spies in the North developed as the conflict wore on. Allan Pinkerton—the self-styled detective who got wind of the plot to assassinate the president-elect in Baltimore—is probably the most celebrated Union spymaster. McClellan, who met Pinkerton before the war while he was working for the railroads, asked him to organize an intelligence service for the Army of the Ohio. On the development of Pinkerton's service and a detailed account of espionage on both sides, see "Intelligence in the Civil War," a publication of the Central Intelligence Agency, https://www.cia.gov/library/publications/intelligence-history/civil-war/Intel_in_the_CW1.pdf.

there. Move troops by the most direct road from wherever they may be on the receipt of this order."

And to Blair I wrote: "Their design is evidently to cross the Big Black and pass down the peninsula between the Big Black and Yazoo rivers. We must beat them. Turn your troops immediately to Bolton; take all the trains with you. Smith's division, and any other troops now with you, will go to the same place. If practicable, take parallel roads, so as to divide your troops and train."

Johnston stopped on the Canton road only six miles north of Jackson, the night of the 14th. He sent from there to Pemberton dispatches announcing the loss of Jackson, and the following order:

"As soon as the reinforcements are all up, they must be united to the rest of the army. I am anxious to see a force assembled that may be able to inflict a heavy blow upon the enemy. Can Grant supply himself from the Mississippi? Can you not cut him off from it, and above all, should he be compelled to fall back for want of supplies, beat him."

The concentration of my troops was easy, considering the character of the country. McPherson moved along the road parallel with and near the railroad. McClernand's command was, one division (Hovey's) on the road McPherson had to take, but with a start of four miles. One (Osterhaus) was at Raymond, on a converging road that intersected the other near Champion's Hill; one (Carr's) had to pass over the same road with Osterhaus, but being back at Mississippi Springs, would not be detained by it; the fourth (Smith's) with Blair's division, was near Auburn with a different road to pass over. McClernand faced about and moved promptly. His cavalry from Raymond seized Bolton by half-past nine in the morning, driving out the enemy's pickets and capturing several men.

The night of the 15th Hovey was at Bolton; Carr and Osterhaus were about three miles south, but abreast, facing west; Smith was north of Raymond with Blair in his rear.

McPherson's command, with Logan in front, had marched at seven o'clock, and by four reached Hovey and went into camp; Crocker bivouacked just in Hovey's rear on the Clinton road. Sherman with two divisions, was in Jackson, completing the destruction of roads, bridges and military factories. I rode in person out to Clinton. On my arrival I ordered McClernand to move early in the morning on Edward's station, cautioning him to watch for the enemy and not bring on an engagement unless he felt very certain of success.

I naturally expected that Pemberton would endeavor to obey the orders of his superior, which I have shown were to attack us at Clinton. This, indeed, I knew he could not do; but I felt sure he would make the attempt to reach that point. It turned out, however, that he had decided his superior's plans were impracticable, and consequently determined to move south from Edward's station and get between me and my base. I, however, had no base, having abandoned it more than a week before. On the 15th Pemberton had actually marched south from Edward's station, but the rains had swollen Baker's Creek, which he had to cross so much that he could not ford it, and the bridges were washed away. This brought him back to the Jackson road, on which there was a good bridge over Baker's Creek. Some of his troops were marching until midnight to get there. Receiving here early on the 16th a repetition of his order to join Johnston at Clinton, he concluded to obey, and sent a dispatch to his chief, informing him of the route by which he might be expected.

About five o'clock in the morning (16th) two men, who had been employed on the Jackson and Vicksburg railroad, were brought to me. They reported that they had passed through Pemberton's army in the night, and that it was still marching east. They reported him to have eighty regiments of infantry and ten batteries; in all, about twenty-five thousand men.

I had expected to leave Sherman at Jackson another day in order to complete his work; but getting the above information I sent him orders to move with all dispatch to Bolton, and to put one division with an ammunition train on the road at once, with directions to its commander to march with all possible speed until he came up to our rear. Within an hour after receiving this order Steele's division was on the road. At the same time I dispatched to Blair, who was near Auburn, to move with all speed to Edward's station. McClernand was directed to embrace Blair in his command for the present. Blair's division was a part of the 15th army corps (Sherman's); but as it was on its way to join its corps, it naturally struck our left first, now that we had faced about and were moving west. The 15th corps, when it got up, would be on our extreme right. McPherson was directed to get his trains out of the way of the troops, and to follow Hovey's division as closely as possible. McClernand had two roads about three miles apart, converging at Edward's station, over which to march his troops. Hovey's division of his corps had the advance on a third road (the Clinton) still farther north. McClernand was directed to move Blair's and A. J. Smith's divisions by the southernmost of these roads, and Osterhaus and Carr by the middle road. Orders were to move cautiously with skirmishers to the front to feel for the enemy.

Smith's division on the most southern road was the first to encounter the enemy's pickets, who were speedily driven in. Osterhaus, on the middle road, hearing the firing, pushed his skirmishers forward, found the enemy's pickets and forced them back to the main line. About the same time Hovey encountered the enemy on the northern or direct wagon road from Jackson to Vicksburg. McPherson was hastening up to join Hovey, but was embarrassed by Hovey's trains occupying the roads. I was still back at Clinton. McPherson sent me word of the situation, and expressed the wish that I was up. By half-past seven I was on the road and proceeded rapidly to the front, ordering all trains that were in front of troops off the road. When I arrived Hovey's skirmishing amounted almost to a battle.

McClernand was in person on the middle road and had a shorter distance to march to reach the enemy's position than McPherson. I sent him word by a staff officer to push forward and attack. These orders were repeated several times without apparently expediting McClernand's advance.

Champion's Hill, where Pemberton had chosen his position to receive us, whether taken by accident or design, was well selected. It is one of the highest points in that section, and commanded all the ground in range. On the east side of the ridge, which is quite precipitous, is a ravine running first north, then westerly, terminating at Baker's Creek. It was grown up thickly with large trees and undergrowth, making it difficult to penetrate with troops, even when not defended. The ridge occupied by the enemy terminated abruptly where the ravine turns westerly. The left of the enemy occupied the north end of this ridge. The Bolton and Edward's station wagon-road turns almost due south at this point and ascends the ridge, which it follows for about a mile; then turning west, descends by a gentle declivity to Baker's Creek, nearly a mile away. On the west side the slope of the ridge is gradual and is cultivated from near the summit to the creek. There was, when we were there, a narrow belt of timber near the summit west of the road.

From Raymond there is a direct road to Edward's station, some three miles west of Champion's Hill. There is one also to Bolton. From this latter road there is still another, leaving it about three and a half miles before reaching Bolton and leads direct to the same station. It was along these two roads that three divisions of McClernand's corps, and Blair of Sherman's, temporarily under McClernand, were moving. Hovey of McClernand's command was with McPherson, farther north on the road from Bolton direct to Edward's station. The middle road comes into the northern road at the point where the latter turns to the west and descends to Baker's Creek; the southern road is still several miles south and does not intersect the others until it reaches Edward's station. Pemberton's lines covered all these roads, and faced east. Hovey's line, when it first drove in the enemy's pickets, was formed parallel to that of the enemy and confronted his left.

By eleven o'clock the skirmishing had grown into a hard-contested battle. Hovey alone, before other troops could be got to assist him, had captured a battery of the enemy. But he was not able to hold his position and had to abandon the artillery. McPherson brought up his troops as fast as possible, Logan in front, and posted them on the right of Hovey and across the flank of the enemy. Logan reinforced Hovey with one brigade from his division; with his other two he moved farther west to make room for Crocker, who was coming up as rapidly as the roads would admit. Hovey was still being heavily pressed, and was calling on me for more reinforcements. I ordered Crocker, who was now coming up, to send one brigade from his division. McPherson ordered two batteries to be stationed where they nearly enfiladed the enemy's line, and they did good execution.

From Logan's position now a direct forward movement carried him over open fields, in rear of the enemy and in a line parallel with them. He did make exactly this move, attacking, however, the enemy through the belt of woods covering the west slope of the hill for a short distance. Up to this time I had kept my position near Hovey where we were the most heavily pressed; but about noon I moved with a part of my staff by our right around, until I came up with Logan himself. I found him near the road leading down to Baker's Creek. He was actually in command of the only road over which the enemy could retreat; Hovey, reinforced by two brigades from McPherson's command, confronted the enemy's left; Crocker, with two brigades, covered their left flank; McClernand two hours before, had been within two miles and a half of their centre with two divisions, and the two divisions, Blair's and A. J. Smith's, were confronting the rebel right; Ransom, with a brigade of McArthur's division of the 17th corps (McPherson's), had crossed the river at Grand Gulf a few days before, and was coming up on their right flank. Neither Logan nor I knew that we had cut off the retreat of the enemy. Just at this juncture a messenger came from Hovey, asking for more reinforcements. There were none to spare. I then gave an order to move McPherson's command by the left flank around to Hovey. This uncovered the rebel line of retreat, which was soon taken advantage of by the enemy.

During all this time, Hovey, reinforced as he was by a brigade from Logan and another from Crocker, and by Crocker gallantly coming up with two other brigades on his right, had made several assaults, the last one about the time the road was opened to the rear. The enemy fled precipitately.

This was between three and four o'clock. I rode forward, or rather back, to where the middle road intersects the north road, and found the skirmishers of Carr's division just coming in. Osterhaus was farther south and soon after came up with skirmishers advanced in like manner. Hovey's division, and McPherson's two divisions with him, had marched and fought from early dawn, and were not in the best condition to follow the retreating foe. I sent orders to Osterhaus to pursue the enemy, and to Carr, whom I saw personally, I explained the situation and directed him to pursue vigorously as far as the Big Black, and to cross it if he could; Osterhaus to follow him. The pursuit was continued until after dark.

The battle of Champion's Hill lasted about four hours, hard fighting, preceded by two or three hours of skirmishing, some of which almost rose to the dignity of battle. Every man of Hovey's division and of McPherson's two divisions was engaged during the battle. No other part of my command was engaged at all, except that as described before.[6] Osterhaus's and A. J. Smith's divisions had encountered the rebel advanced pickets as early as half-past seven. Their positions were admirable for advancing upon the enemy's line. McClernand, with two divisions, was within a few miles of the battle-field long before noon and in easy hearing. I sent him repeated orders by staff

6. Charles A. Dana relates a peculiar encounter with John A. Logan after the Battle of Champion's Hill:

> After the battle I started out on horseback with Colonel Rawlins to visit the field. When we reached Logan's command we found him greatly excited. He declared the day was lost, and that he would soon be swept from his position. I contested the point with him. "Why, general," I said, "we have gained the day."
>
> He could not see it. "Don't you hear the cannon over there?" he answered. "They will be down on us right away! In an hour I will have twenty thousand men to fight."
>
> I found afterward that this was simply a curious idiosyncrasy of Logan's. In the beginning of a fight he was one of the bravest men that could be, saw no danger, went right on fighting until the battle was over. Then, after the battle was won, his mind gained the immovable conviction that it was lost. Where we were victorious, he thought that we were defeated. I had a very interesting conversation with Logan on this day, when he attempted to convince me that we had lost the battle of Champion's Hill. It was merely an intellectual peculiarity. It did not in the least impair his value as a soldier or commanding officer. He never made any mistake on account of it.

Recollections, 53–54.

officers fully competent to explain to him the situation. These traversed the wood separating us, without escort, and directed him to push forward; but he did not come. It is true, in front of McClernand there was a small force of the enemy and posted in a good position behind a ravine obstructing his advance; but if he had moved to the right by the road my staff officers had followed the enemy must either have fallen back or been cut off. Instead of this he sent orders to Hovey, who belonged to his corps, to join on to his right flank. Hovey was bearing the brunt of the battle at the time. To obey the order he would have had to pull out from the front of the enemy and march back as far as McClernand had to advance to get into battle and substantially over the same ground. Of course I did not permit Hovey to obey the order of his intermediate superior.

We had in this battle about 15,000 men absolutely engaged. This excludes those that did not get up, all of McClernand's command except Hovey. Our loss was 410 killed, 1,844 wounded and 187 missing. Hovey alone lost 1,200 killed, wounded and missing—more than one-third of his division.

Had McClernand come up with reasonable promptness, or had I known the ground as I did afterwards, I cannot see how Pemberton could have escaped with any organized force. As it was he lost over three thousand killed and wounded and about three thousand captured in battle and in pursuit. Loring's division, which was the right of Pemberton's line, was cut off from the retreating army and never got back into Vicksburg. Pemberton himself fell back that night to the Big Black River. His troops did not stop before midnight and many of them left before the general retreat commenced, and no doubt a good part of them returned to their homes.[7] Logan alone cap-

---

7. Grant several times mentions how eager Confederate soldiers were to get home, yet many returned to the ranks to fight again. The soldier's melancholy and homesickness has been an enduring theme of literature. It finds eloquent voice in the Tang Dynasty poet Li Po's "Lament of the Frontier Guard," here in Ezra Pound's translation:

> By the North Gate, the wind blows full of sand,
> Lonely from the beginning of time until now!
> Trees fall, the grass goes yellow with autumn.
> I climb the towers and towers
>   to watch out the barbarous land:
> Desolate castle, the sky, the wide desert.
> There is no wall left to this village.
> Bones white with a thousand frosts,
> High heaps, covered with trees and grass;

tured 1,300 prisoners and eleven guns. Hovey captured 300 under fire and about 700 in all, exclusive of 500 sick and wounded whom he paroled, thus making 1,200.

McPherson joined in the advance as soon as his men could fill their cartridge-boxes, leaving one brigade to guard our wounded. The pursuit was continued as long as it was light enough to see the road. The night of the 16th of May found McPherson's command bivouacked from two to six miles west of the battle-field, along the line of the road to Vicksburg. Carr and Osterhaus were at Edward's station, and Blair was about three miles southeast; Hovey remained on the field where his troops had fought so bravely and bled so freely. Much war material abandoned by the enemy was picked up on the battle-field, among it thirty pieces of artillery. I pushed through the advancing column with my staff and kept in advance until after night. Finding ourselves alone we stopped and took possession of a vacant house. As no troops came up we moved back a mile or more until we met the head of the column just going into bivouac on the road. We had no tents, so we occupied the porch of a house which had been taken for a rebel hospital and which was filled with wounded and dying who had been brought from the battle-field we had just left.

While a battle is raging one can see his enemy mowed down by the thousand, or the ten thousand, with great composure; but after the battle

---

Who brought this to pass?
Who has brought the flaming imperial anger?
Who has brought the army with drums and with kettle-drums?
Barbarous kings.
A gracious spring, turned to blood-ravenous autumn,
A turmoil of wars-men, spread over the middle kingdom,
Three hundred and sixty thousand,
And sorrow, sorrow like rain.
Sorrow to go, and sorrow, sorrow returning,
Desolate, desolate fields,
And no children of warfare upon them,
        No longer the men for offence and defence.
Ah, how shall you know the dreary sorrow at the North Gate,
With Rihoku's name forgotten,
And we guardsmen fed to the tigers.

Ezra Pound, *Lustra* (London: Elkin Mathews, 1916), 78–79.

"Ambulance drill in the field—the newly organized corps soon after Antietam," *The Photographic History of the Civil War. Review of Reviews. 1911.*

these scenes are distressing, and one is naturally disposed to do as much to alleviate the suffering of an enemy as a friend.[8]

8. Here Grant points to an important psychological dimension of warfare: the temporary numbing of human feeling that often accompanies the witnessing of carnage. Dana illustrates the reawakening of feeling after battle in this portrait of Rawlins after Champion's Hill:

> On the hill where the thickest of the fight had taken place we stopped, and were looking around at the dead and dying men lying all about us, when suddenly a man, perhaps forty-five or fifty years old, who had a Confederate uniform on, lifted himself up on his elbow, and said:
>
> "For God's sake, gentlemen, is there a Mason among you?"
>
> "Yes," said Rawlins, "I am a Mason." He got off his horse and kneeled by the dying man, who gave him some letters out of his pocket. When he came back Rawlins had tears on his cheeks. The man, he told us, wanted him to convey some souvenir—a miniature or a ring, I do not remember what—to his wife, who was in Alabama. Rawlins took the package, and some time afterward he succeeded in sending it to the woman.

Recollections, 54–55.

36

Battle of Black River Bridge—Crossing the Big Black—Investment of Vicksburg— Assaulting the Works

We were now assured of our position between Johnston and Pemberton, without a possibility of a junction of their forces. Pemberton might have made a night march to the Big Black, crossed the bridge there and, by moving north on the west side, have eluded us and finally returned to Johnston. But this would have given us Vicksburg. It would have been his proper move, however, and the one Johnston would have made had he been in Pemberton's place. In fact it would have been in conformity with Johnston's orders to Pemberton.

Sherman left Jackson with the last of his troops about noon on the 16th and reached Bolton, twenty miles west, before halting. His rear guard did not get in until two A.M. the 17th, but renewed their march by daylight. He paroled his prisoners at Jackson, and was forced to leave his own wounded in care of surgeons and attendants. At Bolton he was informed of our victory. He was directed to commence the march early next day, and to diverge from the road he was on to Bridgeport on the Big Black River, some eleven miles above the point where we expected to find the enemy. Blair was ordered to join him there with the pontoon train as early as possible.

This movement brought Sherman's corps together, and at a point where I hoped a crossing of the Big Black might be effected and Sherman's corps used to flank the enemy out of his position in our front, thus opening a crossing for the remainder of the army. I informed him that I would endeavor to hold the enemy in my front while he crossed the river.

The advance division, Carr's (McClernand's corps), resumed the pursuit at half-past three A.M. on the 17th, followed closely by Osterhaus, McPherson bringing up the rear with his corps. As I expected, the enemy was found in position on the Big Black. The point was only six miles from that where my advance had rested for the night, and was reached at an early hour. Here the river makes a turn to the west, and has washed close up to the high land; the east side is a low bottom, sometimes overflowed at very high water, but was cleared and in cultivation. A bayou runs irregularly across this low land, the bottom of which, however, is above the surface of the Big Black at ordinary stages. When the river is full water runs through it, converting the point of land into an island. The bayou was grown up with timber, which the enemy had felled into the ditch. At this time there was a foot or two of water in it. The rebels had constructed a parapet along the inner bank of this bayou by using cotton bales from the plantation close by and throwing dirt over them. The whole was thoroughly commanded from the height west of the river. At the upper end of the bayou there was a strip of uncleared land which afforded a cover for a portion of our men. Carr's division was deployed on our right, Lawler's brigade forming his extreme right and reaching through these woods to the river above. Osterhaus' division was deployed to the left of Carr and covered the enemy's entire front. McPherson was in column on the road, the head close by, ready to come in wherever he could be of assistance.

While the troops were standing as here described an officer from Banks' staff came up and presented me with a letter from General Halleck, dated the 11th of May. It had been sent by the way of New Orleans to Banks to be forwarded to me. It ordered me to return to Grand Gulf and to co-operate from there with Banks against Port Hudson, and then to return with our combined forces to besiege Vicksburg. I told the officer that the order came too late, and that Halleck would not give it now if he knew our position. The bearer of the dispatch insisted that I ought to obey the order, and was giving arguments to support his position when I heard great cheering to the right of our line and, looking in that direction, saw Lawler in his shirt sleeves leading a charge upon the enemy. I immediately mounted my horse and rode in the direction of the charge, and saw no more of the officer who delivered the dispatch; I think not even to this day.[1]

The assault was successful. But little resistance was made. The enemy fled from the west bank of the river, burning the bridge behind him and

---

1. With this anecdote Grant reveals another of the advantages to cutting loose from communications.

Major General Henry W. Halleck. Photograph by J. A. Scholten. *Library of Congress, Prints and Photographs Division, Civil War Photographs, LC-DIG-cwpb-06956.*

leaving the men and guns on the east side to fall into our hands. Many tried to escape by swimming the river. Some succeeded and some were drowned in the attempt. Eighteen guns were captured and 1,751 prisoners. Our loss was 39 killed, 237 wounded and 3 missing. The enemy probably lost but few men except those captured and drowned. But for the successful and complete destruction of the bridge, I have but little doubt that we should have followed the enemy so closely as to prevent his occupying his defences around Vicksburg.[2]

As the bridge was destroyed and the river was high, new bridges had to be built. It was but little after nine o'clock A.M. when the capture took place. As soon as work could be commenced, orders were given for the construction of three bridges. One was taken charge of by Lieutenant Hains,[3] of the

2. For the diarist Emilie McKinley this retreat signaled the beginning of the end: "Yesterday was one of the saddest days it has ever been my fate to have experienced," her entry for Monday, May 18, 1863, reads: "our troops retreated from Big Black bridge to Vicksburg. They could have held it but were afraid of being flanked as they would have been—Oh! my heart ached, as I hope it never will again." *From the Pen of a She-Rebel: The Civil War Diary of Emilie Riley McKinley*, ed. Gordon A. Cotton (Columbia: University of South Carolina Press, 2001), 6.

3. After Major Samuel Lockett, C.S.A., burned the railroad bridge over the Big Black River, Peter C. Hains and others worked overnight to superintend the building of three crossings, including a two-hundred-foot pontoon bridge. Hains went on to build the tidal basin reservoir at Washington, D.C. He was the lone Civil War officer still on active duty at the beginning of World War I. For a detailed account of his engi-

Engineer Corps, one by General McPherson himself and one by General Ransom, a most gallant and intelligent volunteer officer. My recollection is that Hains built a raft bridge; McPherson a pontoon, using cotton bales in large numbers, for pontoons; and that Ransom felled trees on opposite banks of the river, cutting only on one side of the tree, so that they would fall with their tops interlacing in the river, without the trees being entirely severed from their stumps. A bridge was then made with these trees to support the roadway. Lumber was taken from buildings, cotton gins and wherever found, for this purpose. By eight o'clock in the morning of the 18th all three bridges were complete and the troops were crossing.

Sherman reached Bridgeport about noon of the 17th and found Blair with the pontoon train already there. A few of the enemy were intrenched on the west bank, but they made little resistance and soon surrendered. Two divisions were crossed that night and the third the following morning.

On the 18th I moved along the Vicksburg road in advance of the troops and as soon as possible joined Sherman. My first anxiety was to secure a base of supplies on the Yazoo River above Vicksburg. Sherman's line of march led him to the very point on Walnut Hills occupied by the enemy the December before when he was repulsed. Sherman was equally anxious with myself. Our impatience led us to move in advance of the column and well up with the advanced skirmishers. There were some detached works along the crest of the hill. These were still occupied by the enemy, or else the garrison from Haines' Bluff had not all got past on their way to Vicksburg. At all events the bullets of the enemy whistled by thick and fast for a short time. In a few minutes Sherman had the pleasure of looking down from the spot coveted so much by him the December before on the ground where his command had lain so helpless for offensive action. He turned to me, saying that up to this minute he had felt no positive assurance of success. This, however, he said was the end of one of the greatest campaigns in history and I ought to make a report of it at once. Vicksburg was not yet captured, and there was no telling what might happen before it was taken; but whether captured or not, this was a complete and successful campaign. I do not claim to quote Sherman's language; but the substance only. My reason for mentioning this incident will appear further on.

neering feat and those of the entire campaign, see Terry Winschel, "The Engineers at Vicksburg," U.S. Army Corps of Engineers Engineer Research and Development Center, http://www.erdc.usace.army.mil/Media/News-Stories/Article/1108324/the-engineers-at-vicksburg-part-18-bridging-the-big-black-river/.

McPherson, after crossing the Big Black, came into the Jackson and Vicksburg road which Sherman was on, but to his rear. He arrived at night near the lines of the enemy, and went into camp. McClernand moved by the direct road near the railroad to Mount Albans, and then turned to the left and put his troops on the road from Baldwin's ferry to Vicksburg. This brought him south of McPherson. I now had my three corps up the works built for the defence of Vicksburg, on three roads—one to the north, one to the east and one to the south-east of the city. By the morning of the 19th the investment was as complete as my limited number of troops would allow. Sherman was on the right, and covered the high ground from where it over-looked the Yazoo as far south-east as his troops would extend. McPherson joined on to his left, and occupied ground on both sides of the Jackson road. McClernand took up the ground to his left and extended as far towards War-renton as he could, keeping a continuous line.

On the 19th there was constant skirmishing with the enemy while we were getting into better position. The enemy had been much demoralized by his defeats at Champion's Hill and the Big Black, and I believed he would not make much effort to hold Vicksburg. Accordingly, at two o'clock I ordered an assault. It resulted in securing more advanced positions for all our troops where they were fully covered from the fire of the enemy.

The 20th and 21st were spent in strengthening our position and in making roads in rear of the army, from Yazoo River or Chickasaw Bayou. Most of the army had now been for three weeks with only five days' rations issued by the commissary. They had an abundance of food, however, but began to feel the want of bread. I remember that in passing around to the left of the line on the 21st, a soldier, recognizing me, said in rather a low voice, but yet so that I heard him, "Hard tack." In a moment the cry was taken up all along the line, "Hard tack! Hard tack!" I told the men nearest to me that we had been engaged ever since the arrival of the troops in building a road over which to supply them with everything they needed. The cry was instantly changed to cheers. By the night of the 21st all the troops had full rations issued to them. The bread and coffee were highly appreciated.[4]

---

4. Hard tack was a baked biscuit so dense it was difficult to eat. In his culinary history of the Civil War William C. Davis explains, "The problems with hardtack commenced almost from the moment they cooled after baking and were packed into wooden crates for shipment to the central commissary depots." In addition to being "hard as bricks," Davis writes, they were often infested with insects. Soldiers tried to break the crackers with rifle butts "only to find them teeming with worms." Among the nicknames given to the crackers were "worm castles," "tooth dullers," and "sheet-

I now determined on a second assault. Johnston was in my rear, only fifty miles away, with an army not much inferior in numbers to the one I had with me, and I knew he was being reinforced. There was danger of his coming to the assistance of Pemberton, and after all he might defeat my anticipations of capturing the garrison if, indeed, he did not prevent the capture of the city. The immediate capture of Vicksburg would save sending me the reinforcements which were so much wanted elsewhere, and would set free the army under me to drive Johnston from the State. But the first consideration of all was—the troops believed they could carry the works in their front, and would not have worked so patiently in the trenches if they had not been allowed to try.[5]

iron crackers." *A Taste for War: The Culinary History of the Blue and the Gray* (Mechanicsburg, PA: Stackpole, 2003), 42–43.

The Union Army was on the whole far better fed than its opponent. One of the consequences of insufficient food among Confederate soldiers was their tendency—documented at Shiloh, Cedar Creek, and other battles—to halt their advance when they passed Union camps full of food, clothing, and other supplies.

In 1862, James M. Sanderson, who worked for the Sanitary Commission and saw firsthand how soldiers prepared their mess, wrote *Camp Fires and Camp Cooking; or, Culinary Hints for the Soldier*, a guide for soldiers in the field. The book contained "The Cook's Creed," which suggests several of the pitfalls of field kitchens:

> Cleanliness is next to godliness both in persons and kettles: be ever industrious then in scouring your pots. Much elbow grease, a few ashes, and a little water are capital aids to the careful cook. Better wear out your pans with scouring than your stomachs with purging; and it is less dangerous to work your elbows than your comrade's bowels. Dirt and grease betray the poor cook, and destroy the poor soldier; whilst health, content, and good cheer should ever reward him who does his duty and keeps his kettles clean. In military life, punctuality is not only a duty, but a necessity, and the cook should always endeavor to be exact in time. Be sparing with sugar and salt, as a deficiency can be better remedied than an overplus.
>
> Remember that beans, badly boiled, kill more than bullets; and fat is more fatal than powder. In cooking, more than in anything else in this world, always make haste slowly. One hour too much is vastly better than five minutes too little, with rare exceptions. A big fire scorches your soup, burns your face, and crisps your temper. Skim, simmer, and scour, are the true secrets of good cooking.

Camp Fires and Camp Cooking; or Culinary Hints for the Soldier (Washington, D.C.: Government Printing Office, 1862), 4–5.

5. The attacks on May 19 and May 22 resulted in more than three thousand Union casualties. As is the case with every costly and unsuccessful assault, questions were sub-

"Hard tack." Captain J. W. Forsyth sitting atop a crate of hardtack, Aquia Creek, Virginia. *Library of Congress, Prints and Photographs Division, LC-DIG-stereo-1s02737.*

The attack was ordered to commence on all parts of the line at ten o'clock A.M. on the 22d with a furious cannonade from every battery in position. All the corps commanders set their time by mine so that all might open the engagement at the same minute. The attack was gallant, and portions of each of the three corps succeeded in getting up to the very parapets of the enemy and in planting their battle flags upon them; but at no place were we able to enter. General McClernand reported that he had gained the enemy's intrenchments at several points, and wanted reinforcements. I occupied a position from which I believed I could see as well as he what took place in his front, and I did not see the success he reported. But his request for reinforcements being repeated I could not ignore it, and sent him Quinby's division of the 17th corps. Sherman and McPherson were both ordered to renew their assaults as a diversion in favor of McClernand. This last attack only served to increase our casualties without giving any benefit whatever. As soon as it was dark our troops that had reached the enemy's line and been obliged to remain there for security all day, were withdrawn; and thus ended the last assault upon Vicksburg.

---

sequently raised about the necessity of these attacks. Grant certainly thought he had a psychological advantage over the reeling Pemberton, but Jean Edward Smith suggests that the explanation he provides here is merely "self-justification." *Grant*, 252–53.

37

Siege of Vicksburg

Inow determined upon a regular siege—to "out-camp the enemy," as it were, and to incur no more losses. The experience of the 22d convinced officers and men that this was best, and they went to work on the defences and approaches with a will. With the navy holding the river, the investment of Vicksburg was complete. As long as we could hold our position the enemy was limited in supplies of food, men and munitions of war to what they had on hand. These could not last always.[1]

---

1. Mary Ann Loughborough, who elected to stay with her husband, then stationed in Vicksburg, describes the hunger of soldiers and civilians alike in the besieged city:

> I never was made to exist under ground; and when I am obliged to, what wonder that I vegetate, like other unfortunate plants—grow wan, spindling, and white! . . .
>
> The hill opposite our cave might be called "death's point" from the number of animals that had been killed in eating the grass on the sides and summit. In all directions I can see the turf turned up, from the shells that have gone ploughing into the earth. Horses or mules that are tempted to mount the hill by the promise of grass that grows profusely there, invariably come limping down wounded, to die at the base, or are brought down dead from the summit.
>
> A certain number of mules are killed each day by the commissaries, and are issued to the men, all of whom prefer the fresh meat, though it be of mule, to the bacon and salt rations that they have eaten for so long a time without change. There have already been some cases of scurvy: the soldiers have a horror of the disease; therefore, I suppose, the mule meat is all the

The crossing of troops at Bruinsburg commenced April 30th. On the 18th of May the army was in rear of Vicksburg. On the 19th, just twenty days after the crossing, the city was completely invested and an assault had been made: five distinct battles (besides continuous skirmishing) had been fought and won by the Union forces; the capital of the State had fallen and its arsenals, military manufactories and everything useful for military purposes had been destroyed; an average of about one hundred and eighty miles had been marched by the troops engaged; but five days' rations had been issued, and no forage; over six thousand prisoners had been captured, and as many more of the enemy had been killed or wounded; twenty-seven heavy cannon and sixty-one field-pieces had fallen into our hands; and four hundred miles of the river, from Vicksburg to Port Hudson, had become ours.[2] The Union

more welcome. Indeed, I petitioned M—— to have some served on our table. He said: "No; wait a little longer." He did not like to see me eating mule until I was obliged to; that he trusted Providence would send us some change shortly.

Providence ended up sending the Loughboroughs sustenance in the form of a cow that was hit by a shell later that day. See *My Cave Life in Vicksburg* (New York: D. Appleton, 1864), 114, 116–17.

2. As was the case at Vicksburg, the siege of Port Hudson was punctuated by costly Union assaults on the earthworks, on May 27 and June 14. Both were repulsed. Among the Union forces participating was a sizable contingent of African American troops. The attack of the Massachusetts 54th on South Carolina's Fort Wagner may be the most celebrated action involving African American soldiers in the war, but two months earlier the 1st and 3rd Louisiana Native Guards had been conspicuous for their bravery in the May 27 Union assault on Port Hudson. The Native Guards were composed of—and at least initially officered by—free black men from New Orleans. By May 1863, all of the black officers had been forced out except for those of the 1st Regiment, which had been confined, as was the custom, to noncombat roles. At Port Hudson these soldiers were wasted in a fruitless attack on the heavily defended fort. One Native Guards officer, Captain André Cailloux, E Company, 1st Louisiana Native Guards, who liked to boast that he was "the blackest man in the crescent city," became a symbol of African American heroism. In *A History of the Negro in the American Rebellion* William Wells Brown describes him as follows: "Whether in the drawing-room or on the parade, he was ever the center of attraction. Finely educated, polished in his manner, a splendid horseman, a good boxer, bold, athletic, and daring, he never lacked admirers. His men were ready at any time to follow him to the cannon's mouth; and he was ready to lead them. The regiment petitioned their commander to allow them to occupy the post of danger in the battle, and it was granted." *A History of the Negro in the American Rebellion: His Heroism and His Fidelity* (Boston: Lee & Shepard, 1867), 169.

Cailloux was killed in front of the Confederate works. Because the enemy refused to extend their truce to the part of the battlefield on which black soldiers had fallen, no

force that had crossed the Mississippi River up to this time was less than forty-three thousand men. One division of these, Blair's, only arrived in time to take part in the battle of Champion's Hill, but was not engaged there; and one brigade, Ransom's of McPherson's corps, reached the field after the battle. The enemy had at Vicksburg, Grand Gulf, Jackson, and on the roads between these places, over sixty thousand men. They were in their own country, where no rear guards were necessary. The country is admirable

---

one could collect his body, which decomposed together with those of his fellow soldiers until the siege was lifted. In the end, the only way his corpse could be identified was by a ring that he wore. For detailed accounts, see Stephen J. Ochs, *A Black Patriot and a White Priest: André Cailloux and Claude Paschal Maistre in Civil War New Orleans* (Baton Rouge: Louisiana State University Press, 2002), and James G. Hollandsworth Jr., *The Louisiana Native Guards: The Black Military Experience During the Civil War* (Baton Rouge: Louisiana State University Press, 1995).

Thomas Wentworth Higginson, who commanded a regiment of liberated slaves in South Carolina, argued eloquently for their commitment and competence. In his memoir *Army Life in a Black Regiment* he explains the Southern black soldier's added incentive:

> They fought with ropes round their necks, and when orders were issued that the officers of colored troops should be put to death on capture, they took a grim satisfaction. It helped their *esprit de corps* immensely. With us, at least, there was to be no play-soldier. Though they had begun with a slight feeling of inferiority to the white troops, this compliment substituted a peculiar sense of self-respect. And even when the new colored regiments began to arrive from the North my men still pointed out this difference,—that in case of ultimate defeat, the Northern troops, black or white, would go home, while the First South Carolina must fight it out or be re-enslaved. . . .
>
>   . . . Till the blacks were armed, there was no guaranty of their freedom. It was their demeanor under arms that shamed the nation into recognizing them as men.

Army Life in a Black Regiment and Other Writings, ed. R. D. Madison (New York: Penguin Classics, 1997), 194–95, 206.

For the first years of the war, black soldiers fought for less money than did their white counterparts: $10 per month as opposed to $13. Many black soldiers proudly refused to accept any pay until they were given the same salary as their white comrades. "Are we *Soldiers*, or are we *Labourers?*" James Henry Gooding, a corporal in the Massachusetts 54th, demanded in a letter to Lincoln in 1863: "Now your Excellency, we have done a Soldier's Duty. Why Can't we have a Soldier's pay?" *On the Altar of Freedom: A Black Soldier's Civil War Letters from the Front*, ed. Virginia Matzke Adams (Amherst: University of Massachusetts Press, 1991), 119.

for defence, but difficult for the conduct of an offensive campaign. All their troops had to be met. We were fortunate, to say the least, in meeting them in detail: at Port Gibson seven or eight thousand; at Raymond, five thousand; at Jackson, from eight to eleven thousand; at Champion's Hill, twenty-five thousand; at the Big Black, four thousand. A part of those met at Jackson were all that was left of those encountered at Raymond. They were beaten in detail by a force smaller than their own, upon their own ground. Our loss up to this time was:

AT	KILLED	WOUNDED	MISSING
Port Gibson	131	719	25
South Fork Bayou Pierre		1	
Skirmishes, May 3	1	9	
Fourteen Mile Creek	6	24	
Raymond	66	339	37
Jackson	42	251	7
Champion's Hill	410	1,844	187
Big Black	39	237	3
Bridgeport		1	
TOTAL	695	3,425	259

Of the wounded many were but slightly so, and continued on duty. Not half of them were disabled for any length of time.

After the unsuccessful assault of the 22d the work of the regular siege began. Sherman occupied the right starting from the river above Vicksburg, McPherson the centre (McArthur's division now with him) and McClernand the left, holding the road south to Warrenton. Lauman's division arrived at this time and was placed on the extreme left of the line.

In the interval between the assaults of the 19th and 22d, roads had been completed from the Yazoo River and Chickasaw Bayou, around the rear of the army, to enable us to bring up supplies of food and ammunition; ground had been selected and cleared on which the troops were to be encamped, and tents and cooking utensils were brought up. The troops had been without these from the time of crossing the Mississippi up to this time. All was now ready for the pick and spade. Prentiss and Hurlbut were ordered to send forward every man that could be spared. Cavalry especially was wanted to watch the fords along the Big Black, and to observe Johnston. I knew that Johnston was receiving reinforcements from Bragg, who was confronting Rosecrans in Tennessee. Vicksburg was so important to the enemy that I believed he would make the most strenuous efforts to raise the siege, even at the risk of losing ground elsewhere.

My line was more than fifteen miles long, extending from Haines' Bluff to Vicksburg, thence to Warrenton. The line of the enemy was about seven. In addition to this, having an enemy at Canton and Jackson, in our rear, who was being constantly reinforced, we required a second line of defence facing the other way. I had not troops enough under my command to man these. General Halleck appreciated the situation and, without being asked, forwarded reinforcements with all possible dispatch.

The ground about Vicksburg is admirable for defence. On the north it is about two hundred feet above the Mississippi River at the highest point and very much cut up by the washing rains; the ravines were grown up with cane and underbrush, while the sides and tops were covered with a dense forest. Farther south the ground flattens out somewhat, and was in cultivation. But here, too, it was cut up by ravines and small streams. The enemy's line of defence followed the crest of a ridge from the river north of the city eastward, then southerly around to the Jackson road, full three miles back of the city; thence in a southwesterly direction to the river. Deep ravines of the description given lay in front of these defences. As there is a succession of gullies, cut out by rains along the side of the ridge, the line was necessarily very irregular. To follow each of these spurs with intrenchments, so as to command the slopes on either side, would have lengthened their line very much. Generally therefore, or in many places, their line would run from near the head of one gully nearly straight to the head of another, and an outer work triangular in shape, generally open in the rear, was thrown up on the point; with a few men in this outer work they commanded the approaches to the main line completely.

The work to be done, to make our position as strong against the enemy as his was against us, was very great. The problem was also complicated by our wanting our line as near that of the enemy as possible. We had but four engineer officers with us. Captain Prime, of the Engineer Corps, was the chief, and the work at the beginning was mainly directed by him. His health soon gave out, when he was succeeded by Captain Comstock, also of the Engineer Corps. To provide assistants on such a long line I directed that all officers who had graduated at West Point, where they had necessarily to study military engineering, should in addition to their other duties assist in the work.[3]

The chief quartermaster and the chief commissary were graduates. The chief commissary, now the Commissary-General of the Army, begged off, however, saying that there was nothing in engineering that he was good for unless he would do for a sap-roller. As soldiers require rations while working in the ditches as well as when marching and fighting, and as we would be sure to lose him if he was used as a sap-roller, I let him off. The general is a large man; weighs two hundred and twenty pounds, and is not tall.[4]

We had no siege guns except six thirty-two pounders, and there were none at the West to draw from. Admiral Porter, however, supplied us with a battery of navy-guns of large calibre, and with these, and the field artillery used in the campaign, the siege began.[5] The first thing to do was to get the

3. Cyrus Ballou Comstock (1831–1888) was a West Point graduate and trained engineer who commanded the Civil War Balloon Corps until its dissolution amid Comstock's disagreements with the chief aeronaut, Thaddeus S. C. Lowe.

Professor Lowe's Military Balloon, near Gaines Mill, Virginia. Photograph by Mathew Brady. *Library of Congress, Prints and Photographs Division, Civil War Photographs, LC-DIG-ppmsca-33091.*

4. The officers referred to are Judson D. Bingham and Robert MacFeely, both West Point graduates. A sap roller was a large cylindrical basket full of wood, cotton bales, or other material that protected sappers from enemy fire.

5. After the war Varina Davis, the wife of Confederate president Jefferson Davis, included in a memoir about her husband a proud and defiant account of the life of women inside the besieged city:

How to dispose of the women and children during the siege was a problem which could be solved in only one way, viz., they must stay at home. Their fathers, husbands, brothers, or sons were many of them in

artillery in batteries where they would occupy commanding positions; then establish the camps, under cover from the fire of the enemy but as near up as possible; and then construct rifle-pits and covered ways, to connect the entire command by the shortest route. The enemy did not harass us much while we were constructing our batteries. Probably their artillery ammunition was short; and their infantry was kept down by our sharpshooters, who were always on the alert and ready to fire at a head whenever it showed itself above the rebel works.[6]

In no place were our lines more than six hundred yards from the enemy. It was necessary, therefore, to cover our men by something more than the ordinary parapet. To give additional protection sand bags, bullet-proof, were placed along the tops of the parapets far enough apart to make loop-holes

---

the army of Northern Virginia, or in the West. The money left with their families was all exhausted; all industries were at a standstill. The interior of Mississippi had been desolated by fire and sword, and the women and children could not exist there unprotected and without food; so they grappled with the ills they knew, and remained at home. Caves were dug in the high clay hills, and there the non-combatants dwelt in darkness while the shells were flying. By the light of lamps they mended, patched, and darned for the soldiers, knitted them socks, and rendered every other service that brave and tender women learn to perform in the hour of danger. I saw one bright young bride, whose arm had been shattered by a piece of shell and afterward amputated; and a man who was there during the siege said, on July 26th: "We noticed one man with his wife in his arms—she having fainted with fright at the explosion of a shell within a few feet of her. A shell burst in the midst of several children who were making their way out of danger, and the dirt thrown up by the explosion knocked three of them down, but fortunately did no injury. The little ones picked themselves up as quick as possible, and wiping the dust from their eyes, hastened on."

The women nursed the sick and wounded, ate mule and horse meat, and bread made of spoiled flour, with parched corn boiled for coffee; but they listened to the whistling shells undaunted, nothing fearing except for the lives of those who were fighting far and near.

Jefferson Davis, Ex-President of the Confederate States of America (New York: Belford, 1890), 2: 420–21.

6. Loughborough describes what it looked like at the other end of the rifle: "So they [the Confederate soldiers] sat cramped up all day in the pits—their rations cooked in the valley and brought to them—scarcely daring to change their positions and stand erect, for the Federal sharpshooters were watching for their heads; and to rise above the breastworks was almost certain death." *My Cave Life*, 106–7.

for musketry. On top of these, logs were put. By these means the men were enabled to walk about erect when off duty, without fear of annoyance from sharpshooters.[7] The enemy used in their defence explosive musket-balls, no doubt thinking that, bursting over our men in the trenches, they would do some execution; but I do not remember a single case where a man was injured by a piece of one of these shells. When they were hit and the ball exploded, the wound was terrible. In these cases a solid ball would have hit

---

7. Civil War sharpshooters, who had the ability to hit a target at nearly a half-mile, and some of whom wore a kind of camouflage, had a dubious reputation because they violated certain expectations of fair play: "To shoot a man as he defecated, or slept, or sat cooking or eating" or reading "could not easily be rationalized as an act of self-defense," Drew Gilpin Faust observes. "The cool calculation, the purposefulness, and the asymmetry of risk involved in sharpshooting rendered it even more threatening to basic principles of humanity than the frenzied excesses of heated battle." *Republic of Suffering*, 42.

The idea that it was somehow obscene furtively to shoot an enemy engaged in daily activities persisted well into the twentieth century. George Orwell addresses this issue in his essay "Looking Back on the Spanish War," when he describes what happened when he went "out to snipe at the Fascists" in an enemy trench approximately a hundred yards distant:

> Some of our aeroplanes were coming over. At this moment a man, presumably carrying a message to an officer, jumped out of the trench and ran along the top of the parapet in full view. He was half-dressed and was holding up his trousers with both hands as he ran. I refrained from shooting at him. It is true that I am a poor shot and unlikely to hit a running man at a hundred yards, and also that I was thinking chiefly about getting back to our trench while the Fascists had their attention fixed on the aeroplanes. Still, I did not shoot partly because of that detail about the trousers. I had come here to shoot at "Fascists"; but a man who is holding up his trousers isn't a "Fascist", he is visibly a fellow-creature, similar to yourself, and you don't feel like shooting at him.

Orwell, "Looking Back on the Spanish War," *Essays*, 436–37.

By contrast, today's sharpshooters—or snipers—fighting in wars asymmetrical by definition, perfectly embody our age's fascination with seemingly superheroic powers. Accustomed over the last decade to a cinema filled with comic book heroes and high-tech weaponry, the public has been receptive to the sniper, a figure who has become a staple of popular culture through memoirs, which often chronicle the arduous training and peculiar rituals of sniper school in as much detail as they do battlefield action, and through the film *American Sniper*, based on Chris Kyle's memoir of the same name. In June 2017, headlines and tweets announced excitedly that a Canadian sniper had set a record by hitting a human target—an alleged Islamic State militant—at a distance of more than two miles.

as well. Their use is barbarous, because they produce increased suffering without any corresponding advantage to those using them.[8]

---

8. S. H. Lockett, Chief Engineer of Defenses at Vicksburg, denied that the Confederates used "explosive bullets" and thought that Grant was confused about the rebel response to Union sap-rollers:

> By the 8th of June, in spite of all efforts to prevent them, the enemy's sap-rollers had approached within sixty feet of two of our works. A private soldier suggested a novel expedient by which we succeeded in destroying the rollers. He took a piece of port-fire, stuffed it with cotton saturated with turpentine, and fired it from an old-fashioned large-bore musket into the roller, and thus set it on fire. Thus the enemy's sappers were exposed and forced to leave their sap and begin a new one some distance back. After this they kept their sap-rollers wet, forcing us to other expedients.

"The Defense of Vicksburg," *B&L*, 3:491.

This dispute was part of a larger postwar controversy over the use of explosive bullets. Whether or not such rounds were used at Vicksburg, there is evidence that both sides manufactured and employed explosive musket shells. During the war, ordnance and weapons expert Colonel Berkeley Lewis explains,

> the claim was made in the North that the Confederates were using explosive bullets, certainly a shocking accusation. After the war a Congressional Committee cleared the South of this charge, and the whole affair was dismissed as wartime propaganda. Explosive bullets were really used during the war, but by the North as well as the South. European observers were so impressed by the performance of such ammunition that a convention held at St. Petersburg in 1868 outlawed the use of explosive filler in projectiles weighing less than 400 grams. The United States did not subscribe.

Berkeley R. Lewis, *Small Arms and Ammunition in the United States Service*, Smithsonian Miscellaneous Collections, vol. 129 (Washington, D.C.: Smithsonian Institution, 1956), 126.

Robert Graves meditated on the changing definition of atrocity during World War I:

> As for atrocities against soldiers—where should one draw the line? The British soldier, at first, regarded as atrocious the use of bowie-knifes by German patrols. After a time, he learned to use them himself; they were cleaner killing weapons than revolvers or bombs. The Germans regarded as equally atrocious the British Mark VII rifle-bullet, which was more apt to turn on striking than the German bullet.

Good-bye to All That (New York: Anchor, Doubleday, 1985), 183.

The enemy could not resort to our method to protect their men, because we had an inexhaustible supply of ammunition to draw upon and used it freely. Splinters from the timber would have made havoc among the men behind.

There were no mortars with the besiegers, except what the navy had in front of the city; but wooden ones were made by taking logs of the toughest wood that could be found, boring them out for six or twelve pound shells and binding them with strong iron bands. These answered as coehorns, and shells were successfully thrown from them into the trenches of the enemy.[9]

The World War II correspondent Sergeant Mack Morriss describes another kind of atrocity he encountered in the Huertgen Forest in November 1944:

> The man lay there, but he wasn't able to bandage his own wounds. The medics tried to reach him but were fired upon. One was hit, and the trees around the man were white with scars of the machine-gun bullets that kept the medics away. Finally—after 70 hours—they managed to reach him.
>
> He was still conscious, and for the medics it was a blessing that he was conscious; and for the man himself it was a blessing. For during the darkness the Germans had moved up to the wounded man. They took his field jacket from him, and his cigarettes. They booby-trapped him by setting a charge under his back, so that whoever lifted him would die. So the wounded man, knowing this, lay quietly on the charge and told the men who came to help him what the Germans had done. They cut the wires of the booby trap and carried him away.
>
> The green monument of Huertgen is a bitter thing.

"War in the Huertgen Forest," *Yank*, January 5, 1945.

9. A coehorn is a small, portable mortar designed to provide "plunging 'vertical' fire" angled to crest defenses impregnable to direct fire. Such mortars were first employed by the Dutch commander Manno, Baron von Coehoorn, against the French at the siege of Namur in 1692. See James C. Halett et al., *Field Artillery Weapons of the Civil War*, rev. ed. (Urbana: University of Illinois Press, 2004), 139–40.

The effects of constant shelling on the nerves would be documented more fully during World War I, which gave rise to the rolling, or creeping, barrage, intended to soften the enemy before an infantry assault, and to the term *shell-shock*. The practice continued on the Eastern Front in World War II. Gert Ledig's novel *The Stalin Front* offers a powerful description of the physiological response to a barrage of artillery:

> The rolling barrage. The Captain looked into the staring eyes of the Runner and screamed. They both opened their mouths, and then the air pressure hurled them into the shelter. The red sky, the darkness, the other man's face—everything spun at baffling speed like the numbers on a roulette wheel round an invisible centre. Their lungs had nothing to breathe.

The labor of building the batteries and intrenching was largely done by the pioneers, assisted by negroes who came within our lines and who were paid for their work; but details from the troops had often to be made.[10] The work was pushed forward as rapidly as possible, and when an advanced position was secured and covered from the fire of the enemy the batteries were advanced. By the 30th of June there were two hundred and twenty guns in position, mostly light field-pieces, besides a battery of heavy guns belonging to, manned and commanded by the navy. We were now as strong for defence against the garrison of Vicksburg as they were against us; but I knew that

---

They flopped against the walls, like bundles of clothing. That was the end. Or the beginning.

  The Runner went into a dream. . . . His consciousness returned, with pitiless clarity. He was gripped by fear. His fingers were gummy with blood. It was trickling out of his body into the darkness, and suddenly he understood what was happening: the arcs of shells, parabola by parabola. Projectiles calculated to land bang on the trench. A wave of steel, drilling itself into the ground, even as the next one was flying through the air, and the one after was erupting from the guns. The attack of a regiment, a division, an entire army, and the focus of the attack was just in front of his own trenches.

The Stalin Front, trans. Michael Hofmann (New York: New York Review Books, 2004), 48.

  The U.S. Marine E. B. Sledge, who served in the Pacific during World War II, is more succinct: "To be killed by a bullet seemed so clean and surgical. But shells would not only tear and rip the body, they tortured one's mind almost beyond the brink of sanity. After each shell I was wrung out, limp and exhausted." *With the Old Breed: At Peleliu and Okinawa* (New York: Ballantine, Presidio, 2010), 74.

10. Freed slaves flooded Union lines in both theaters, where they were employed (sometimes forcibly) at manual labor. Some joined the army. John Finnely, a slave from Alabama encouraged by the approach of federal troops to escape about a year into the war, describes the kinds of work he performed at Nashville after being sent there on a freight train by the Union army:

  I'se water toter dere for de army and dere am no fightin' at first but before long dey starts de battle. Dat battle am a experience for me. De noise am awful, just one steady roar of guns and de cannons. De window glass in Nashville am all shook out from de shakement of de cannons. Dere dead mens all over de ground and lots of wounded and some cussin' and some prayin'. Some am moanin' and did and dat one cry for de water and, God-a-mighty I don't want any such again. Dere am men carryin' de dead off de field, but dy can't keep up with de cannons. I helps bury de dead and den I gets sent to Murfreesboro and dere it am just the same.

Yetman, ed., *Voices from Slavery*, 126.

Johnston was in our rear, and was receiving constant reinforcements from the east. He had at this time a larger force than I had had at any time prior to the battle of Champion's Hill.[11]

As soon as the news of the arrival of the Union army behind Vicksburg reached the North, floods of visitors began to pour in. Some came to gratify curiosity; some to see sons or brothers who had passed through the terrible

---

11. The seventeenth-century English poet John Milton, following the Italian Renaissance poet Ariosto, reckoned with the impact of technology on modern warfare in his epic *Paradise Lost*. In the account in book 6 of the war in Heaven between the loyal angels and Lucifer's rebellious host, Milton makes artillery a Satanic invention—he refers to Satan's "devilish engines" in the book's explanatory argument—for which the traditional arms of God's loyal legions are no match:

> A triple mounted row of pillars laid
> On wheels (for like to pillars most they seem'd,
> Or hollow'd bodies made of oak and fir,
> With branches lopt, in wood or mountain fell'd)
> Brass, iron, stony mold, had not their mouths
> With hideous orifice gaped on us wide,
> Portending hollow truce. At each, behind,
> A Seraph stood, and in his hand a reed
> Stood waving, tipt with fire: while we suspense,
> Collected stood within our thoughts amused,
> Not long, for sudden all at once their reeds
> Put forth, and to a narrow vent apply'd
> With nicest touch. Immediate in a flame,
> But soon obscured with smoke, all Heav'n appear'd,
> From those deep-throated engines belch'd, whose roar
> Imbowel'd with outrageous noise the air,
> And all her entrails tore, disgorging foul
> Their dev'lish glut, chain'd thunderbolts and hail
> Of iron globes; which on the victor host
> Levell'd with such impetuous fury smote,
> That whom they hit, none on their feet might stand,
> Though standing else as rocks, but down they fell
> By thousands, Angel on Archangel roll'd;
> The sooner for their arms; unarm'd they might
> Have easily as Spirits evaded swift
> By quick contraction or remove; but now
> Foul dissipation follow'd and forced rout;
> Nor served it to relax their serried files.

"To this uproar," Milton writes, traditional warfare "seem'd a civil Game." See *Paradise Lost*, ed. Henry Stebbing (New York: D. Appleton, 1845), bk. 6, ll. 572–99, 666–67.

THE ANNOTATED MEMOIRS OF ULYSSES S. GRANT

ordeal; members of the Christian and Sanitary Associations came to minister to the wants of the sick and the wounded.[12] Often those coming to see a son or brother would bring a dozen or two of poultry. They did not know how little the gift would be appreciated. Many of the soldiers had lived so much on chickens, ducks and turkeys without bread during the march, that the sight of poultry, if they could get bacon, almost took away their appetite. But the intention was good.

Among the earliest arrivals was the Governor of Illinois, with most of the State officers. I naturally wanted to show them what there was of most interest. In Sherman's front the ground was the most broken and most wooded, and more was to be seen without exposure. I therefore took them to Sherman's headquarters and presented them. Before starting out to look at the lines—possibly while Sherman's horse was being saddled—there were many questions asked about the late campaign, about which the North had been so imperfectly informed. There was a little knot around Sherman and another around me, and I heard Sherman repeating, in the most animated manner, what he had said to me when we first looked down from Walnut Hills upon the land below on the 18th of May, adding: "Grant is entitled to every bit of the credit for the campaign; I opposed it. I wrote him a letter about it." But for this speech it is not likely that Sherman's opposition would have ever been heard of. His untiring energy and great efficiency during the

---

12. An unofficial history of the United States Sanitary Commission, written by a former member, Katharine Prescott Wormeley, gives a sense of the organization's contributions throughout the siege:

> The supplies which it issued to the Army before Vicksburg during the months of May and June were as follows:—Quilts, 1504; pillows, 2220; sheets, 1840; drawers, 5376; towels, &c., 7484; farina, &c., 266 lbs.; sago, &c., 1044 lbs.; bed sacks, 758; pillow-cases, 2830; shirts, 7909; dressing-gowns, 422; socks, 2453 pairs; slippers, 1190 pairs; corn starch, 275 lbs.; cloths and bandages, 50 bbls.; fruit, 5114 cans; concentrated beef, 771 cans; dried fruit, 16,430 lbs.; dried beef, 888 lbs.; groceries, 1882 lbs.; wines and liquors, 1979 bottles; butter, 3557 lbs.; apple-butter, 30 gallons; eggs, 2401 doz.; pickles, 2376 gallons; molasses, 85 gallons; sour krout, 1532 gallons; potatoes, 5762 bushels; ale and cider, 1031 gallons; ice, 27,367 lbs.; crackers, 6898 lbs.; codfish, 6777 lbs.; cornmeal, 2485 lbs.; tea, 532 lbs.; pickles, 301 bottles; lemons, 13,200; hospital furniture, 1747 articles; fans, 2347; crutches, 65 pairs; cots and mattresses, 199; spices, 2006 papers; quinine, 200 oz.

The United States Sanitary Commission: A Sketch of Its Purposes and Its Work (Boston: Little, Brown, 1863), 180–81.

campaign entitle him to a full share of all the credit due for its success. He could not have done more if the plan had been his own.[13]

On the 26th of May I sent Blair's division up the Yazoo to drive out a force of the enemy supposed to be between the Big Black and the Yazoo. The country was rich and full of supplies of both food and forage. Blair was instructed to take all of it. The cattle were to be driven in for the use of our army, and the food and forage to be consumed by our troops or destroyed by fire; all bridges were to be destroyed, and the roads rendered as nearly impassable as possible. Blair went forty-five miles and was gone almost a week. His work was effectually done. I requested Porter at this time to send the marine brigade, a floating nondescript force which had been assigned to his command and which proved very useful, up to Haines' Bluff to hold it until reinforcements could be sent.

On the 26th I also received a letter from Banks, asking me to reinforce him with ten thousand men at Port Hudson. Of course I could not comply with his request, nor did I think he needed them. He was in no danger of an attack by the garrison in his front, and there was no army organizing in his rear to raise the siege.

On the 3d of June a brigade from Hurlbut's command arrived, General Kimball commanding. It was sent to Mechanicsburg, some miles north-east of Haines' Bluff and about midway between the Big Black and the Yazoo. A brigade of Blair's division and twelve hundred cavalry had already, on Blair's return from the Yazoo, been sent to the same place with instructions to watch the crossings of the Big Black River, to destroy the roads in his (Blair's) front, and to gather or destroy all supplies.

On the 7th of June our little force of colored and white troops across the Mississippi, at Milliken's Bend, were attacked by about 3,000 men from Richard Taylor's trans-Mississippi command.[14] With the aid of the

---

13. For the discussion of Sherman's dissent, which appeared in a note to the first edition, see Appendix 1, chapter 37, note 1.

14. By 1865, nearly 180,000 African Americans had served in the Union Army (10 percent of the total force), while 19,000 had served in the U.S. Navy. There were practical as well as principled considerations behind the decision to form the United States Colored Troops. By the summer of 1863, white volunteers for the Union cause had precipitously declined. Frederick Douglass and others advanced eloquent, passionate arguments in favor of black military service as a path to citizenship: "Once let the black man get upon his person the brass letters U.S.; let him get an eagle on his button, and a musket on his shoulder, and bullets in his pocket," Douglass wrote on July 6, 1863, two days after the fall of Vicksburg and the Union victory at Gettysburg, "and there

gunboats they were speedily repelled. I sent Mower's brigade over with instructions to drive the enemy beyond the Tensas Bayou; and we had no further trouble in that quarter during the siege. This was the first important engagement of the war in which colored troops were under fire. These men were very raw, having all been enlisted since the beginning of the siege, but they behaved well.[15]

---

is no power on earth which can deny that he has earned the right of citizenship in the United States." "Address for the Promotion of Colored Enlistments," *The Civil War, 1861–1865*, vol. 3 of *The Life and Writings of Frederick Douglass*, ed. Philip S. Foner (New York: International Publishers, 1952), 365.

Paul Laurence Dunbar meditated on the only partially fulfilled legacy of African American sacrifice in his poem "The Colored Soldiers," which concludes,

> They were comrades then and brothers,
>   Are they more or less to-day?
> They were good to stop a bullet
>   And to front the fearful fray.
> They were citizens and soldiers,
>   When rebellion raised its head;
> And the traits that made them worthy,—
>   Ah! those virtues are not dead.
>
> They have shared your nightly vigils,
>   They have shared your daily toil;
> And their blood with yours commingling
>   Has enriched the Southern soil.
>
> They have slept and marched and suffered
>   'Neath the same dark skies as you,
> They have met as fierce a foeman,
>   And have been as brave and true.
>
> And their deeds shall find a record
>   In the registry of Fame;
> For their blood has cleansed completely
>   Every blot of Slavery's shame.
> So all honor and all glory
>   To those noble sons of Ham—
> The gallant colored soldiers
>   Who fought for Uncle Sam!

The Complete Poems of Paul Laurence Dunbar, ed. W. D. Howells (New York: Dodd, Mead, 1922), 51–52.

15. In late June, just after the Battle of Milliken's Bend, the American Freedmen's Inquiry Commission made a *Preliminary Report Touching the Condition and Management of*

Emancipated Refugees to the Secretary of War. The report made the following argument in favor of African American military service:

> There is an additional reason why a considerable portion of the Union armies should be made up of persons of African descent. The transformation of the slave society of the South into free society, no longer properly a question, has become a necessity of our national existence. Reflecting men have already readied the conclusion, and the mass of our people are attaining to it day by day, that the sole condition of permanent peace on this continent is the eradication of negro slavery. But the history of the world furnishes no example of an enslaved race which won its freedom without exertion of its own. That the indiscriminate massacres of a servile insurrection have been spared us, as addition to the horrors of a civil war, is due, it would seem, rather to that absence of revenge and blood thirstiness which characterizes this race, than to the lack either of courage or of any other quality that makes the hardy combatant; for these the negro appears so far as we have tried him in civilized warfare to possess. And in such warfare is it fitting that the African race seek its own social salvation. The negro must fight for emancipation if he is to be emancipated.

The authors of the report also included a letter written by Captain M. M. Miller, a white officer of the 9th Louisiana, a regiment of black troops that fought at Milliken's Bend, testifying to the courage of the troops he commanded:

> We had about 50 men killed in the regiment and 80 wounded; so you can judge of what part of the fight my company sustained. I never felt more grieved and sick at heart than when I saw how my brave soldiers had been slaughtered—one with six wounds, all the rest with two or three, none less than two wounds. Two of my colored sergeants were killed, both brave, noble men; always prompt, vigilant, and ready for the fray. I never more wish to hear the expression, "The niggers won't fight." Come with me 100 yards from where I sit, and I can show you the wounds that cover the bodies of 16 as brave, loyal, and patriotic soldiers as ever drew bead on a Rebel. . . .
>
> It was a horrible fight, the worst I was ever engaged in—not even excepting Shiloh. The enemy cried, "No quarter!" but some of them were very glad to take it when made prisoners. . . .
>
> My wound is not serious but troublesome. What few men I have left seem to think much of me because I stood up with them in the fight. I can say for them that I never saw a braver company of men in my life.
>
> Not one of them offered to leave his place until ordered to fall back; in fact, very few ever did fall back. I went down to the hospital, three miles, to-day, to see the wounded. Nine of them were there, two having died of their wounds. A boy I had cooking for me came and begged a gun when the Rebels were advancing, and took his place with the company, and when we re-took the breastworks, I found him badly wounded with one gunshot and two bayonet wounds. A new recruit I had issued a gun to the day before the fight was found dead, with a firm grasp on his gun, the bayonet

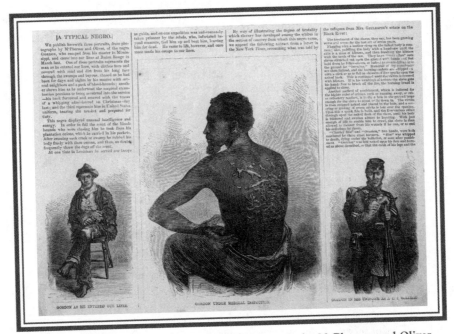

"A Typical Negro," with drawings from photographs by McPherson and Oliver. This article appeared opposite a depiction of African American soldiers at Milliken's Bend, *Harper's Weekly*, July 4, 1863. *Library of Congress, Prints and Photographs Division, LC-USZ62-98515.*

On the 8th of June a full division arrived from Hurlbut's command, under General [William] Sooy Smith. It was sent immediately to Haines' Bluff, and General C. C. Washburn was assigned to the general command at that point.

On the 11th a strong division arrived from the Department of the Missouri under General Herron, which was placed on our left. This cut off the last possible chance of communication between Pemberton and Johnston, as it enabled Lauman to close up on McClernand's left while Herron intrenched from Lauman to the water's edge. At this point the water recedes a few hundred yards from the high land. Through this opening no doubt

---

of which was broken in three pieces. So they fought and died defending the cause that we revere. They met death coolly, bravely—not rashly did they expose themselves, but all were steady and obedient to orders.

Preliminary Report touching the Condition and Management of Emancipated Refugees; made to the Secretary of War by the American Freedmen's Inquiry Commission, June 30, 1863 (New York: John F. Trow, 1863), 36–38.

the Confederate commanders had been able to get messengers under cover of night.

On the 14th General Parke arrived with two divisions of Burnside's corps, and was immediately dispatched to Haines' Bluff. These latter troops—Herron's and Parke's—were the reinforcements already spoken of sent by Halleck in anticipation of their being needed. They arrived none too soon.

I now had about seventy-one thousand men. More than half were disposed across the peninsula, between the Yazoo at Haines' Bluff and the Big Black, with the division of Osterhaus watching the crossings of the latter river farther south and west from the crossing of the Jackson road to Baldwin's ferry and below.

There were eight roads leading into Vicksburg, along which and their immediate sides, our work was specially pushed and batteries advanced; but no commanding point within range of the enemy was neglected.

On the 17th I received a letter from General Sherman and one on the 18th from General McPherson, saying that their respective commands had complained to them of a fulsome, congratulatory order published by General McClernand to the 13th corps, which did great injustice to the other troops engaged in the campaign. This order had been sent North and published, and now papers containing it had reached our camps. The order had not been heard of by me, and certainly not by troops outside of McClernand's command until brought in this way. I at once wrote to McClernand, directing him to send me a copy of this order. He did so, and I at once relieved him from the command of the 13th army corps and ordered him back to Springfield, Illinois. The publication of his order in the press was in violation of War Department orders and also of mine.[16]

16. One of Sherman's division commanders gave him a copy of the June 13 *Memphis Evening Bulletin*, in which McClernand's "Congratulatory Order" to his troops had been printed. McClernand, in addition to offering congratulations to his own corps, had been highly critical of his fellow corps commanders. Sherman thought it "a catalogue of nonsense—such an effusion of vain-glory and hypocrisy." Letter to John Rawlins, June 17, 1863, *Sherman's Civil War*, 485.

This is the action that prompted McClernand's relief; Lincoln did not reinstate him until 1864. On McClernand and the phenomenon of the political general, see Brooks D. Simpson, "Lincoln and His Political Generals," *Journal of the Abraham Lincoln Association* 21, no. 1 (Winter 2000): 63–77.

38

Johnston's Movements—Fortifications at
Haines' Bluff—Explosion of the Mine—
Explosion of the Second Mine—Preparing
for the Assault—The Flag of Truce—Meeting
with Pemberton—Negotiations for
Surrender—Accepting the Terms—
Surrender of Vicksburg

On the 22d of June positive information was received that Johnston had crossed the Big Black River for the purpose of attacking our rear, to raise the siege and release Pemberton. The correspondence between Johnston and Pemberton shows that all expectation of holding Vicksburg had by this time passed from Johnston's mind. I immediately ordered Sherman to the command of all the forces from Haines' Bluff to the Big Black River. This amounted now to quite half the troops about Vicksburg. Besides these, Herron and A. J. Smith's divisions were ordered to hold themselves in readiness to reinforce Sherman. Haines' Bluff had been strongly fortified on the land side, and on all commanding points from there to the Big Black at the railroad crossing batteries had been constructed. The work of connecting by rifle-pits where this was not already done, was an easy task for the troops that were to defend them.

We were now looking west, besieging Pemberton, while we were also looking east to defend ourselves against an expected siege by Johnston. But as against the garrison of Vicksburg we were as substantially protected as they were against us. Where we were looking east and north we were strongly fortified, and on the defensive. Johnston evidently took in the situation and wisely, I think, abstained from making an assault on us because it would simply have inflicted loss on both sides without accomplishing any result. We were strong enough to have taken the offensive against him; but I did not feel disposed to take any risk of losing our hold upon Pemberton's army, while I would have rejoiced at the opportunity of defending ourselves against an attack by Johnston.

From the 23d of May the work of fortifying and pushing forward our position nearer to the enemy had been steadily progressing. At three points on the Jackson road, in front of Leggett's brigade, a sap was run up to the enemy's parapet, and by the 25th of June we had it undermined and the mine charged. The enemy had countermined, but did not succeed in reaching our mine. At this particular point the hill on which the rebel work stands rises abruptly. Our sap ran close up to the outside of the enemy's parapet. In fact this parapet was also our protection. The soldiers of the two sides occasionally conversed pleasantly across this barrier; sometimes they exchanged the hard bread of the Union soldiers for the tobacco of the Confederates; at other times the enemy threw over hand-grenades, and often our men, catching them in their hands, returned them.[1]

Our mine had been started some distance back down the hill; consequently when it had extended as far as the parapet it was many feet below it. This caused the failure of the enemy in his search to find and destroy it. On the 25th of June at three o'clock, all being ready, the mine was exploded.

---

1. The proximity of enemies is a common feature of trench warfare and one of the defining characteristics of the Western Front. Here an unknown soldier of the Queen's Westminster Rifles describes the Christmas truce of 1914: "It seemed the weirdest thing in the world that you should be talking to the men you were trying to shoot the day before and to crown all a German officer got a camera and took our photos in a group. All tonight there wasn't a shot fired." Quoted in *The Imperial War Museum Book of the Western Front*, ed. Malcolm Brown (London: Pan Macmillan, 2001), 53.

In the American Civil War, of course, the closeness between trenches was not simply physical but also linguistic and cultural. Stephen Crane depicts such a conversation across the lines at the beginning of *The Red Badge of Courage*. In this respect, the experience shared something with other civil wars, including those of ancient Rome. Caesar describes the fraternization between pickets in Spain: "Gaining by their commanders' absence the chance to communicate freely, the soldiers came out in crowds, looking for and calling out the names of any acquaintances or fellow townsmen" in Caesar's camp. The soldiers "lamented . . . because they had fought against men who were their friends and kinsmen." Later in the wars, when the camps of Caesar and Pompey were separated only by a stream of the Apsus River, enemies again talked with one another and agreed to hurl no weapons while conversations were in progress. See *Civil War*, trans. John Carter (Oxford, UK: Oxford World's Classics, 2008), 41, 86.

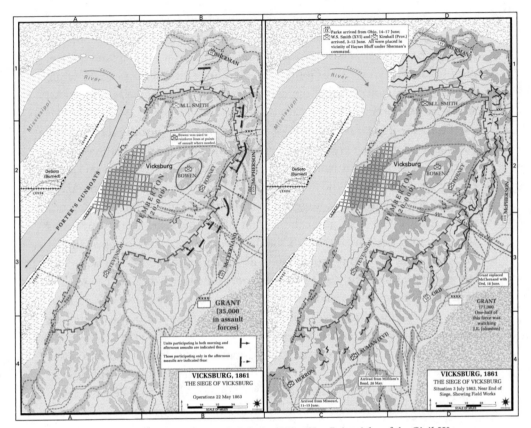

The Siege of Vicksburg, May 22–July 3, 1863. *West Point Atlas of the Civil War. Courtesy of Department of History, USMA.*

A heavy artillery fire all along the line had been ordered to open with the explosion. The effect was to blow the top of the hill off and make a crater where it stood. The breach was not sufficient to enable us to pass a column of attack through. In fact, the enemy having failed to reach our mine had thrown up a line farther back, where most of the men guarding that point were placed. There were a few men, however, left at the advance line, and others working in the countermine, which was still being pushed to find ours. All that were there were thrown into the air, some of them coming down on our side, still alive. I remember one colored man, who had been under ground at work when the explosion took place, who was thrown to our side. He was not much hurt, but terribly frightened. Some one asked him how high he had gone up. "Dun no, massa, but t'ink 'bout t'ree mile," was his reply. General Logan commanded at this point and took this colored man to his quarters, where he did service to the end of the siege.

As soon as the explosion took place the crater was seized by two regiments of our troops who were near by, under cover, where they had been placed for the express purpose. The enemy made a desperate effort to expel them, but failed, and soon retired behind the new line. From here, however, they threw hand-grenades, which did some execution. The compliment was returned by our men, but not with so much effect. The enemy could lay their grenades on the parapet, which alone divided the contestants, and roll them down upon us; while from our side they had to be thrown over the parapet, which was at considerable elevation. During the night we made efforts to secure our position in the crater against the missiles of the enemy, so as to run trenches along the outer base of their parapet, right and left; but the enemy continued throwing their grenades, and brought boxes of field ammunition (shells), the fuses of which they would light with port-fires, and throw them by hand into our ranks. We found it impossible to continue this work. Another mine was consequently started which was exploded on the 1st of July, destroying an entire rebel redan, killing and wounding a considerable number of its occupants and leaving an immense chasm where it stood. No attempt to charge was made this time, the experience of the 25th admonishing us. Our loss in the first affair was about thirty killed and wounded. The enemy must have lost more in the two explosions than we did in the first. We lost none in the second.

From this time forward the work of mining and pushing our position nearer to the enemy was prosecuted with vigor, and I determined to explode no more mines until we were ready to explode a number at different points and assault immediately after. We were up now at three different points, one in front of each corps, to where only the parapet of the enemy divided us.

At this time an intercepted dispatch from Johnston to Pemberton informed me that Johnston intended to make a determined attack upon us in order to relieve the garrison at Vicksburg. I knew the garrison would make no formidable effort to relieve itself. The picket lines were so close to each other—where there was space enough between the lines to post pickets—that the men could converse. On the 21st of June I was informed, through this means, that Pemberton was preparing to escape, by crossing to the Louisiana side under cover of night; that he had employed workmen in making boats for that purpose; that the men had been canvassed to ascertain if they would make an assault on the "Yankees" to cut their way out; that they had refused, and almost mutinied, because their commander would not surrender and relieve their sufferings, and had only been pacified by the assurance that boats enough would be finished in a week to carry them all over. The rebel pickets also said that houses in the city had been pulled down to get material to build these boats with. Afterwards this story was verified: on entering the city we found a large number of very rudely constructed boats.

All necessary steps were at once taken to render such an attempt abortive. Our pickets were doubled; Admiral Porter was notified, so that the river might be more closely watched; material was collected on the west bank of the river to be set on fire and light up the river if the attempt was made; and batteries were established along the levee crossing the peninsula on the Louisiana side. Had the attempt been made the garrison of Vicksburg would have been drowned, or made prisoners on the Louisiana side. General Richard Taylor was expected on the west bank to co-operate in this movement, I believe, but he did not come, nor could he have done so with a force sufficient to be of service. The Mississippi was now in our possession from its source to its mouth, except in the immediate front of Vicksburg and of Port Hudson. We had nearly exhausted the country, along a line drawn from Lake Providence to opposite Bruinsburg. The roads west were not of a character to draw supplies over for any considerable force.

By the 1st of July our approaches had reached the enemy's ditch at a number of places. At ten points we could move under cover to within from five to one hundred yards of the enemy. Orders were given to make all preparations for assault on the 6th of July. The debouches were ordered widened to afford easy egress, while the approaches were also to be widened to admit the troops to pass through four abreast. Plank, and bags filled with cotton packed in tightly, were ordered prepared, to enable the troops to cross the ditches.

On the night of the 1st of July Johnston was between Brownsville and the Big Black, and wrote Pemberton from there that about the 7th of the month an attempt would be made to create a diversion to enable him to cut his way out. Pemberton was a prisoner before this message reached him.

On July 1st Pemberton, seeing no hope of outside relief, addressed the following letter to each of his four division commanders:

> "Unless the siege of Vicksburg is raised, or supplies are thrown in,
> it will become necessary very shortly to evacuate the place. I see no
> prospect of the former, and there are many great, if not insuperable
> obstacles in the way of the latter. You are, therefore, requested to

inform me with as little delay as possible, as to the condition of your troops and their ability to make the marches and undergo the fatigues necessary to accomplish a successful evacuation."

Two of his generals suggested surrender, and the other two practically did the same. They expressed the opinion that an attempt to evacuate would fail. Pemberton had previously got a message to Johnston suggesting that he should try to negotiate with me for a release of the garrison with their arms. Johnston replied that it would be a confession of weakness for him to do so; but he authorized Pemberton to use his name in making such an arrangement.

On the 3d about ten o'clock A.M. white flags appeared on a portion of the rebel works. Hostilities along that part of the line ceased at once. Soon two persons were seen coming towards our lines bearing a white flag. They proved to be General Bowen, a division commander, and Colonel Montgomery, aide-de-camp to Pemberton, bearing the following letter to me:

"I have the honor to propose an armistice for —— hours, with the view to arranging terms for the capitulation of Vicksburg. To this end, if agreeable to you, I will appoint three commissioners, to meet a like number to be named by yourself at such place and hour to-day as you may find convenient. I make this proposition to save the further effusion of blood, which must otherwise be shed to a frightful extent, feeling myself fully able to maintain my position for a yet indefinite period. This communication will be handed you under a flag of truce, by Major-General John S. Bowen."

It was a glorious sight to officers and soldiers on the line where these white flags were visible, and the news soon spread to all parts of the command. The troops felt that their long and weary marches, hard fighting, ceaseless watching by night and day, in a hot climate, exposure to all sorts of weather, to diseases and, worst of all, to the gibes of many Northern papers that came to them saying all their suffering was in vain, that Vicksburg would never be taken, were at last at an end and the Union sure to be saved.

Bowen was received by General A. J. Smith, and asked to see me. I had been a neighbor of Bowen's in Missouri, and knew him well and favorably before the war; but his request was refused. He then suggested that I should meet Pemberton. To this I sent a verbal message saying that, if Pemberton desired it, I would meet him in front of McPherson's corps at three o'clock that afternoon. I also sent the following written reply to Pemberton's letter:

> "Your note of this date is just received, proposing an armistice for several hours, for the purpose of arranging terms of capitulation through commissioners, to be appointed, etc. The useless effusion of blood you propose stopping by this course can be ended at any time you may choose, by the unconditional surrender of the city and garrison. Men who have shown so much endurance and courage as those now in Vicksburg, will always challenge the respect of an adversary, and I can assure you will be treated with all the respect due to prisoners of war. I do not favor the proposition of appointing commissioners to arrange the terms of capitulation, because I have no terms other than those indicated above."

At three o'clock Pemberton appeared at the point suggested in my verbal message, accompanied by the same officers who had borne his letter of the morning. Generals Ord, McPherson, Logan and A. J. Smith, and several officers of my staff, accompanied me. Our place of meeting was on a hillside within a few hundred feet of the rebel lines. Near by stood a stunted oak-tree, which was made historical by the event. It was but a short time before the last vestige of its body, root and limb had disappeared, the fragments taken as trophies. Since then the same tree has furnished as many cords of wood, in the shape of trophies, as "The True Cross."[2]

---

2. Here is another example of Grant's impulse to demythologize: not only does he describe the tree as "stunted" but he also implies that, in the style of counterfeit saints' relics, many more souvenirs had been fashioned than a small tree could possibly yield. In its guide to the battlefield as it stood in 1914, Wisconsin's Vicksburg Monument Commission noted souvenir hunters' destruction of the tree as well as of the stone monument that replaced it:

> From the place where the Jackson road passes through the Confederate works, an avenue named after General Pemberton crosses over to Union Avenue. By the side of this driveway, a little way down the hillside, there stands on end, pointing upward, a big siege gun. This is known as "Surrender Monument." It marks the spot where Generals Grant and Pemberton met on the 3d of July to consider terms of surrender. Long ago a stone monument was erected there, but tourists and others chipped off and carried away so much of it that it was thought best to remove it to the national cemetery—where it now stands—and put the big cannon in its place. It was not long after the surrender before the oak tree which marked the spot where

"The capture of Vicksburg—interview between Generals Grant and
Pemberton, to settle the terms of surrender," *Harper's Weekly*, August 1, 1863.

Pemberton and I had served in the same division during part of the
Mexican War. I knew him very well therefore, and greeted him as an old
acquaintance. He soon asked what terms I proposed to give his army if it
surrendered. My answer was the same as proposed in my reply to his letter.
Pemberton then said, rather snappishly, "The conference might as well end,"
and turned abruptly as if to leave. I said, "Very well." General Bowen, I saw,
was very anxious that the surrender should be consummated. His manner
and remarks while Pemberton and I were talking, showed this. He now
proposed that he and one of our generals should have a conference. I had
no objection to this, as nothing could be made binding upon me that they
might propose. Smith and Bowen accordingly had a conference, during
which Pemberton and I, moving a short distance away towards the enemy's
lines were in conversation. After a while Bowen suggested that the Confederate army should be allowed to march out with the honors of war, carrying
their small arms and field artillery. This was promptly and unceremoniously
rejected. The interview here ended, I agreeing, however, to send a letter
giving final terms by ten o'clock that night.

Grant and Pemberton met disappeared root and branch as relics. I do not
suppose that any place in the park is of greater interest to visitors than this.

Wisconsin at Vicksburg, compiled by Hosea W. Rood (Madison, WI, 1914), 196.

Word was sent to Admiral Porter soon after the correspondence with Pemberton commenced, so that hostilities might be stopped on the part of both army and navy. It was agreed on my parting with Pemberton that they should not be renewed until our correspondence ceased.

When I returned to my headquarters I sent for all the corps and division commanders with the army immediately confronting Vicksburg. Half the army was from eight to twelve miles off, waiting for Johnston. I informed them of the contents of Pemberton's letters, of my reply and the substance of the interview, and that I was ready to hear any suggestion; but would hold the power of deciding entirely in my own hands. This was the nearest approach to a "council of war" I ever held.[3] Against the general, and almost unanimous judgment of the council I sent the following letter:

"In conformity with agreement of this afternoon, I will submit the following proposition for the surrender of the City of Vicksburg, public stores, etc. On your accepting the terms proposed, I will march in one division as a guard, and take possession at eight A.M. to-morrow. As soon as rolls can be made out, and paroles be signed by officers and men, you will be allowed to march out of our lines, the officers taking with them their side-arms and clothing, and the field, staff and cavalry officers one horse each. The rank and file will be allowed all their clothing, but no other property. If these conditions are accepted, any amount of rations you may deem necessary can be taken from the stores you now have, and also the necessary cooking utensils for preparing them. Thirty wagons also, counting two two-horse or mule teams as one, will be allowed to transport such articles as cannot be carried along. The same conditions will be allowed to all sick and wounded officers and soldiers as fast as they become able to travel. The paroles for these latter must be signed, however, whilst officers present are authorized to sign the roll of prisoners."

By the terms of the cartel then in force, prisoners captured by either army were required to be forwarded as soon as possible to either Aiken's landing below Dutch Gap on the James River, or to Vicksburg, there to be exchanged, or paroled until they could be exchanged. There was a Confederate commissioner at Vicksburg, authorized to make the exchange. I did not

3. The "council of war" is a set piece of ancient and medieval chronicles.

propose to take him a prisoner, but to leave him free to perform the functions of his office. Had I insisted upon an unconditional surrender, there would have been over thirty thousand men to transport to Cairo, very much to the inconvenience of the army on the Mississippi. Thence the prisoners would have had to be transported by rail to Washington or Baltimore; thence again by steamer to Aiken's—all at very great expense. At Aiken's they would have had to be paroled, because the Confederates did not have Union prisoners to give in exchange. Then again Pemberton's army was largely composed of men whose homes were in the South-west; I knew many of them were tired of the war and would get home just as soon as they could. A large number of them had voluntarily come into our lines during the siege, and requested to be sent north where they could get employment until the war was over and they could go to their homes.

Late at night I received the following reply to my last letter:

"I have the honor to acknowledge the receipt of your communication of this date, proposing terms of capitulation for this garrison and post. In the main your terms are accepted; but, in justice both to the honor and spirit of my troops, manifested in the defence of Vicksburg, I have to submit the following amendments, which, if acceded to by you, will perfect the agreement between us. At ten o'clock A.M. to-morrow, I propose to evacuate the works in and around Vicksburg, and to surrender the city and garrison under my command, by marching out with my colors and arms, stacking them in front of my present lines. After which you will take possession. Officers to retain their side-arms and personal property, and the rights and property of citizens to be respected."

This was received after midnight. My reply was as follows:

"I have the honor to acknowledge the receipt of your communication of 3d July. The amendment proposed by you cannot be acceded to in full. It will be necessary to furnish every officer and man with a parole signed by himself, which, with the completion of the roll of prisoners, will necessarily take some time. Again, I can make no stipulations with regard to the treatment of citizens and their private property. While I do not propose to cause them any undue annoyance or loss, I cannot consent to leave myself under any restraint by stipulations. The property which officers will be allowed to take with them will be as stated in my proposition of last evening; that is, officers will be allowed their private baggage and side-arms, and mounted officers one horse each. If you mean by your proposition for each brigade to march to the front of the lines now occupied by it, and stack arms at ten o'clock A.M., and then return to the inside and there remain as prisoners until properly paroled, I will make no objection to it. Should no notification be received of your acceptance of my terms by nine o'clock A.M. I shall regard them as having been rejected, and shall act accordingly. Should these terms be accepted, white flags should be displayed along your lines to prevent such of my troops as may not have been notified, from firing upon your men."

Pemberton promptly accepted these terms.[4]

During the siege there had been a good deal of friendly sparring between the soldiers of the two armies, on picket and where the lines were close together. All rebels were known as "Johnnies," all Union troops as "Yanks." Often "Johnny" would call: "Well, Yank, when are you coming into town?" The reply was sometimes: "We propose to celebrate the 4th of July there." Sometimes it would be: "We always treat our prisoners with kindness and do not want to hurt them;" or, "We are holding you as prisoners of war while you are feeding yourselves." The garrison, from the commanding general down, undoubtedly expected an assault on the fourth. They knew from the temper of their men it would be successful when made; and that would be a greater humiliation than to surrender. Besides it would be attended with severe loss to them.

The Vicksburg paper, which we received regularly through the courtesy of the rebel pickets, said prior to the fourth, in speaking of the "Yankee" boast that they would take dinner in Vicksburg that day, that the best receipt for cooking a rabbit was "First ketch your rabbit." The paper at this time

---

4. Having earned the nickname "Unconditional Surrender" at Fort Donelson, Grant here defied expectation and accepted Pemberton's terms, which included paroles: promises soldiers made (in lieu of imprisonment) not to fight again until formally exchanged. On July 3, having received a dispatch from Grant about the proposed meeting with Pemberton, Sherman telegraphed: "If you are in Vicksburg, glory, hallelujah! the best Fourth of July since 1776. Of course we must not rest idle, only don't let us brag too soon." *OR*, ser. 1, vol. 24, pt. 3, 461.

and for some time previous was printed on the plain side of wall paper. The last number was issued on the fourth and announced that we had "caught our rabbit."

I have no doubt that Pemberton commenced his correspondence on the third with a two-fold purpose: first, to avoid an assault, which he knew would be successful, and second, to prevent the capture taking place on the great national holiday, the anniversary of the Declaration of American Independence. Holding out for better terms as he did he defeated his aim in the latter particular.

At the appointed hour the garrison of Vicksburg marched out of their works and formed line in front, stacked arms and marched back in good order. Our whole army present witnessed this scene without cheering. Logan's division, which had approached nearest the rebel works, was the first to march in; and the flag of one of the regiments of his division was soon floating over the court-house. Our soldiers were no sooner inside the lines than the two armies began to fraternize. Our men had had full rations from the time the siege commenced, to the close. The enemy had been suffering, particularly towards the last. I myself saw our men taking bread from their haversacks and giving it to the enemy they had so recently been engaged in starving out. It was accepted with avidity and with thanks.

Pemberton says in his report:

"If it should be asked why the 4th of July was selected as the day for surrender, the answer is obvious. I believed that upon that day I should obtain better terms. Well aware of the vanity of our foe, I knew they would attach vast importance to the entrance on the 4th of July into the stronghold of the great river, and that, to gratify their national vanity, they would yield then what could not be extorted from them at any other time."

This does not support my view of his reasons for selecting the day he did for surrendering. But it must be recollected that his first letter asking terms was received about 10 o'clock A.M., July 3d. It then could hardly be expected that it would take twenty-four hours to effect a surrender. He knew that Johnston was in our rear for the purpose of raising the siege, and he naturally would want to hold out as long as he could. He knew his men would not resist an assault, and one was expected on the fourth. In our interview he told me he had rations enough to hold out for some time—my recollection is two weeks. It was this statement that induced me to insert in the terms that he was to draw rations for his men from his own supplies.

On the 4th of July General Holmes, with an army of eight or nine thousand men belonging to the trans-Mississippi department, made an attack upon Helena, Arkansas. He was totally defeated by General Prentiss, who was holding Helena with less than forty-two hundred soldiers. Holmes reported his loss at 1,636, of which 173 were killed; but as Prentiss buried 400, Holmes evidently understated his losses. The Union loss was 57 killed, 127 wounded, and between 30 and 40 missing. This was the last effort on the part of the Confederacy to raise the siege of Vicksburg.

On the third, as soon as negotiations were commenced, I notified Sherman and directed him to be ready to take the offensive against Johnston, drive him out of the State and destroy his army if he could. Steele and Ord were directed at the same time to be in readiness to join Sherman as soon as the surrender took place. Of this Sherman was notified.

I rode into Vicksburg with the troops, and went to the river to exchange congratulations with the navy upon our joint victory. At that time I found that many of the citizens had been living under ground. The ridges upon which Vicksburg is built, and those back to the Big Black, are composed of a deep yellow clay of great tenacity. Where roads and streets are cut through, perpendicular banks are left and stand as well as if composed of stone. The magazines of the enemy were made by running passage-ways into this clay at places where there were deep cuts. Many citizens secured places of safety for their families by carving out rooms in these embankments. A door-way in these cases would be cut in a high bank, starting from the level of the road or street, and after running in a few feet a room of the size required was carved out of the clay, the dirt being removed by the door-way. In some instances I saw where two rooms were cut out, for a single family, with a door-way in the clay wall separating them. Some of these were carpeted and furnished with considerable elaboration. In these the occupants were fully secure from the shells of the navy, which were dropped into the city night and day without intermission.[5]

---

5. Mary Ann Loughborough describes what it felt like to be on the receiving end of a federal barrage in one of the caves:

> Terror stricken, we remained crouched in the cave, while shell after shell followed each other in quick succession. I endeavored by constant prayer to prepare myself for the sudden death I was almost certain awaited me.

I returned to my old headquarters outside in the afternoon, and did not move into the town until the sixth. On the afternoon of the fourth I sent Captain Wm. M. Dunn of my staff to Cairo, the nearest point where the telegraph could be reached, with a dispatch to the general-in-chief. It was as follows:

> "The enemy surrendered this morning. The only terms allowed is their parole as prisoners of war. This I regard as a great advantage to us at this moment. It saves, probably, several days in the capture, and leaves troops and transports ready for immediate service. Sherman, with a large force, moves immediately on Johnston, to drive him from the State. I will send troops to the relief of Banks, and return the 9th army corps to Burnside."

> My heart stood still as we would hear the reports from the guns, and the rushing and fearful sound of the shell as it came toward us. As it neared, the noise became more deafening; the air was full of the rushing sound; pains darted through my temples; my ears were full of confusing noise; and, as it exploded, the report flashed through my head like an electric shock, leaving me in a quiet state of terror the most painful that I can imagine—cowering in a corner, holding my child to my heart—the only feeling of my life being the choking throbs of my heart, that rendered me almost breathless. As singly they fell short, or beyond the cave, I was aroused by a feeling of thankfulness that was of short duration. Again and again the terrible fright came over us in that night.

My Cave Life, 56–57.

A century later during the Blitz, Londoners would descend into modern caves, Underground stations. Ernie Pyle was there to describe the horror:

> In my first days in England I had seen terrible bomb damage. . . .
> I had talked with wounded soldiers. I had gone through London's great night of fire-bombing. I had listened for hours to the crack of guns and the crunch of bombs. And although I didn't especially know it at the time, none of these things went clear down deep inside and made me hurt.
> It was not until I went down seventy feet into the bowels of the Liverpool Street tube and saw humanity sprawled there in childlike helplessness that my heart first jumped and my throat caught. . . .
> . . . Think of that as your destiny—every night, every night from now on.

Ernie's War, 52–53.

This news, with the victory at Gettysburg won the same day, lifted a great load of anxiety from the minds of the President, his Cabinet and the loyal people all over the North. The fate of the Confederacy was sealed when Vicksburg fell. Much hard fighting was to be done afterwards and many precious lives were to be sacrificed; but the *morale* was with the supporters of the Union ever after.

I at the same time wrote to General Banks informing him of the fall and sending him a copy of the terms; also saying I would send him all the troops he wanted to insure the capture of the only foothold the enemy now had on the Mississippi River. General Banks had a number of copies of this letter printed, or at least a synopsis of it, and very soon a copy fell into the hands of General Gardner, who was then in command of Port Hudson. Gardner at once sent a letter to the commander of the National forces saying that he had been informed of the surrender of Vicksburg and telling how the information reached him. He added that if this was true, it was useless for him to hold out longer. General Banks gave him assurances that Vicksburg had been surrendered, and General Gardner surrendered unconditionally on the 9th of July. Port Hudson with nearly 6,000 prisoners, 51 guns, 5,000 small-arms and other stores fell into the hands of the Union forces: from that day to the close of the rebellion the Mississippi River, from its source to its mouth, remained in the control of the National troops.

Pemberton and his army were kept in Vicksburg until the whole could be paroled. The paroles were in duplicate, by organization (one copy for each, Federals and Confederates), and signed by the commanding officers of the companies or regiments. Duplicates were also made for each soldier and signed by each individually, one to be retained by the soldier signing and one to be retained by us. Several hundred refused to sign their paroles, preferring to be sent to the North as prisoners to being sent back to fight again. Others again kept out of the way, hoping to escape either alternative.[6]

6. Many paroled soldiers returned to the ranks to fight again. The situation is reminiscent of the contests of chivalric romance in which knights grant mercy to their adversaries only to encounter them again in the course of their wanderings. For example, confronting one adversary a second time, Lancelot rejects his cry for mercy: "Having once set you free, I'll never again show you mercy, even if it were to ensure my eternal salvation." Chrétien de Troyes, *Arthurian Romances*, trans. William W. Kibler (New York: Penguin Classics, 2004), 243.

This is the sort of chivalric inanity satirized so brilliantly in the film *Monty Python and the Holy Grail* (1975).

Pemberton appealed to me in person to compel these men to sign their paroles, but I declined. It also leaked out that many of the men who had signed their paroles, intended to desert and go to their homes as soon as they got out of our lines. Pemberton hearing this, again appealed to me to assist him. He wanted arms for a battalion, to act as guards in keeping his men together while being marched to a camp of instruction, where he expected to keep them until exchanged. This request was also declined. It was precisely what I expected and hoped that they would do. I told him, however, that I would see that they marched beyond our lines in good order. By the eleventh, just one week after the surrender, the paroles were completed and the Confederate garrison marched out. Many deserted, and fewer of them were ever returned to the ranks to fight again than would have been the case had the surrender been unconditional and the prisoners sent to the James River to be paroled.

As soon as our troops took possession of the city guards were established along the whole line of parapet, from the river above to the river below. The prisoners were allowed to occupy their old camps behind the intrenchments. No restraint was put upon them, except by their own commanders. They were rationed about as our own men, and from our supplies. The men of the two armies fraternized as if they had been fighting for the same cause. When they passed out of the works they had so long and so gallantly defended, between lines of their late antagonists, not a cheer went up, not a remark was made that would give pain. Really, I believe there was a feeling of sadness just then in the breasts of most of the Union soldiers at seeing the dejection of their late antagonists.

The day before the departure the following order was issued:

> "Paroled prisoners will be sent out of here to-morrow. They will be authorized to cross at the railroad bridge, and move from there to Edward's Ferry,[7] and on by way of Raymond. Instruct the commands to be orderly and quiet as these prisoners pass, to make no offensive remarks, and not to harbor any who fall out of ranks after they have passed."

---

7. Meant Edward's Station. [Note to the first edition.]

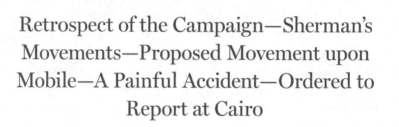

Retrospect of the Campaign—Sherman's Movements—Proposed Movement upon Mobile—A Painful Accident—Ordered to Report at Cairo

The capture of Vicksburg, with its garrison, ordnance and ordnance stores, and the successful battles fought in reaching them, gave new spirit to the loyal people of the North. New hopes for the final success of the cause of the Union were inspired. The victory gained at Gettysburg, upon the same day, added to their hopes. Now the Mississippi River was entirely in the possession of the National troops; for the fall of Vicksburg gave us Port Hudson at once. The army of northern Virginia was driven out of Pennsylvania and forced back to about the same ground it occupied in 1861. The Army of the Tennessee united with the Army of the Gulf, dividing the Confederate States completely.

The first dispatch I received from the government after the fall of Vicksburg was in these words:

> "I fear your paroling the prisoners at Vicksburg, without actual delivery to a proper agent as required by the seventh article of the cartel, may be construed into an absolute release, and that the men will immediately be placed in the ranks of the enemy. Such has been the case elsewhere. If these prisoners have not been allowed to depart, you will detain them until further orders."

Halleck did not know that they had already been delivered into the hands of Major Watts, Confederate commissioner for the exchange of prisoners. At Vicksburg 31,600 prisoners were surrendered, together with 172 cannon, about 60,000 muskets and a large amount of ammunition. The small-arms of the enemy were far superior to the bulk of ours. Up to this time our troops at the West had been limited to the old United States flint-lock muskets changed into percussion, or the Belgian musket imported early in the war—almost as dangerous to the person firing it as to the one aimed at—and a few new and improved arms. These were of many different calibers, a fact that caused much trouble in distributing ammunition during an engagement.[1] The enemy had generally new arms which had run the blockade and were of uniform caliber. After the surrender I authorized all colonels whose regiments were armed with inferior muskets, to place them in the stack of captured arms and replace them with the latter. A large number of arms turned in to the Ordnance Department as captured, were thus arms that had really been used by the Union army in the capture of Vicksburg.

In this narrative I have not made the mention I should like of officers, dead and alive, whose services entitle them to special mention. Neither have I made that mention of the navy which its services deserve. Suffice it to say, the close of the siege of Vicksburg found us with an army unsurpassed, in proportion to its numbers, taken as a whole of officers and men. A military education was acquired which no other school could have given. Men who thought a company was quite enough for them to command properly at the beginning, would have made good regimental or brigade commanders; most of the brigade commanders were equal to the command of a division, and one, Ransom, would have been equal to the command of a corps at least. Logan and Crocker ended the campaign fitted to command independent armies.

General F. P. Blair joined me at Milliken's Bend a full-fledged general, without having served in a lower grade. He commanded a division in the campaign. I had known Blair in Missouri, where I had voted against him in 1858 when he ran for Congress. I knew him as a frank, positive and generous man, true to his friends even to a fault, but always a leader. I dreaded his coming; I knew from experience that it was more difficult to command two generals desiring to be leaders than it was to command one army officered intelligently and with subordination. It affords me the greatest pleasure to record now my agreeable disappointment in respect to his character. There was no man braver than he, nor was there any who obeyed all orders of his

---

1. On the impact of the war on the gun industry and the limited use of repeating rifles in the conflict, see Pamela Haag, *The Gunning of America: Business and the Making of American Gun Culture* (New York: Basic Books, 2016), chapter 4.

General Francis P. Blair
and his staff. *Library
of Congress, Prints and
Photographs Division, Civil
War Photographs, LC-DIG-
cwpbh-03137.*

superior in rank with more unquestioning alacrity. He was one man as a soldier, another as a politician.

The navy under Porter was all it could be, during the entire campaign. Without its assistance the campaign could not have been successfully made with twice the number of men engaged. It could not have been made at all, in the way it was, with any number of men without such assistance. The most perfect harmony reigned between the two arms of the service. There never was a request made, that I am aware of, either of the flag-officer or any of his subordinates, that was not promptly complied with.

The campaign of Vicksburg was suggested and developed by circumstances.[2] The elections of 1862 had gone against the prosecution of the war. Voluntary enlistments had nearly ceased and the draft had been resorted to; this was resisted, and a defeat or backward movement would have made its execution impossible. A forward movement to a decisive victory was necessary.[3] Accordingly I resolved to get below Vicksburg, unite with Banks

---

2. As the explicit aims of the war enlarged with the issuing of the Emancipation Proclamation, so, too, did the means of making it. On Grant's grasp of political context, see Fuller, *The Generalship of Ulysses S. Grant.* In contrast to generals who regarded military action as unconnected to policy or who tried to make the latter somehow serve the former, Grant understood what was axiomatic for Clausewitz, that war could never be regarded in isolation from its social, cultural, and political contexts. "The political object," Clausewitz writes, "the original motive for war—will thus determine both the military objective to be reached and the amount of effort it requires." Clausewitz, *On War,* 81.

3. The discontent would explode on July 13, soon after the victories at Gettysburg and Vicksburg, in the New York City draft riots, during which the Colored Orphan Asylum was burned to the ground. Herman Melville captured the significance of the riots for the future in one of his best Civil War poems, "The House-top. A Night Piece":

against Port Hudson, make New Orleans a base and, with that base and Grand Gulf as a starting point, move our combined forces against Vicksburg. Upon reaching Grand Gulf, after running its batteries and fighting a battle, I received a letter from Banks informing me that he could not be at Port Hudson under ten days, and then with only fifteen thousand men. The time was worth more than the reinforcements; I therefore determined to push into the interior of the enemy's country.

With a large river behind us, held above and below by the enemy, rapid movements were essential to success. Jackson was captured the day after a new commander had arrived, and only a few days before large reinforcements were expected. A rapid movement west was made; the garrison of Vicksburg was met in two engagements and badly defeated, and driven back into its stronghold and there successfully besieged. It looks now as though

No sleep. The sultriness pervades the air
And binds the brain—a dense oppression, such
As tawny tigers feel in matted shades,
Vexing their blood and making apt for ravage.
Beneath the stars the roofy desert spreads
Vacant as Libya. All is hushed near by.
Yet fitfully from far breaks a mixed surf
Of muffled sound, the Atheist roar of riot.
Yonder, where parching Sirius set in drought,
Balefully glares red Arson—there—and there.
The Town is taken by its rats—ship-rats.
And rats of the wharves. All civil charms
And priestly spells which late held hearts in awe—
Fear-bound, subjected to a better sway
Than sway of self; these like a dream dissolve,
And man rebounds whole æons back in nature.
Hail to the low dull rumble, dull and dead,
And ponderous drag that shakes the wall.
Wise Draco comes, deep in the midnight roll
Of black artillery; he comes, though late;
In code corroborating Calvin's creed
And cynic tyrannies of honest kings;
He comes, nor parlies; and the Town, redeemed,
Give thanks devout; nor, being thankful, heeds
The grimy slur on the Republic's faith implied,
Which holds that Man is naturally good,
And—more—is Nature's Roman, never to be scourged.

Battle-Pieces, 86–87.

Providence had directed the course of the campaign while the Army of the Tennessee executed the decree.

Upon the surrender of the garrison of Vicksburg there were three things that required immediate attention. The first was to send a force to drive the enemy from our rear, and out of the State. The second was to send reinforcements to Banks near Port Hudson, if necessary, to complete the triumph of opening the Mississippi from its source to its mouth to the free navigation of vessels bearing the Stars and Stripes. The third was to inform the authorities at Washington and the North of the good news, to relieve their long suspense and strengthen their confidence in the ultimate success of the cause they had so much at heart.

Soon after negotiations were opened with General Pemberton for the surrender of the city, I notified Sherman, whose troops extended from Haines' Bluff on the left to the crossing of the Vicksburg and Jackson road over the Big Black on the right, and directed him to hold his command in readiness to advance and drive the enemy from the State as soon as Vicksburg surrendered. Steele and Ord were directed to be in readiness to join Sherman in his move against General Johnston, and Sherman was advised of this also. Sherman moved promptly, crossing the Big Black at three different points with as many columns, all concentrating at Bolton, twenty miles west of Jackson.

Johnston heard of the surrender of Vicksburg almost as soon as it occurred, and immediately fell back on Jackson. On the 8th of July Sherman was within ten miles of Jackson and on the 11th was close up to the defences of the city and shelling the town. The siege was kept up until the morning of the 17th, when it was found that the enemy had evacuated during the night. The weather was very hot, the roads dusty and the water bad. Johnston destroyed the roads as he passed and had so much the start that pursuit was useless; but Sherman sent one division, Steele's, to Brandon, fourteen miles east of Jackson.

The National loss in the second capture of Jackson was less than one thousand men, killed, wounded and missing. The Confederate loss was probably less, except in captured. More than this number fell into our hands as prisoners.

Medicines and food were left for the Confederate wounded and sick who had to be left behind. A large amount of rations was issued to the families that remained in Jackson. Medicine and food were also sent to Raymond for the destitute families as well as the sick and wounded, as I thought it only fair that we should return to these people some of the articles we had taken

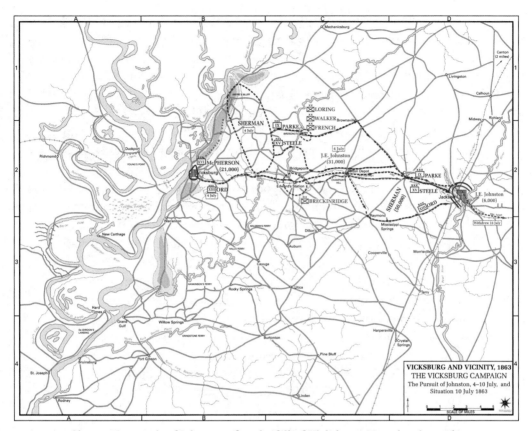

Sherman's pursuit of Johnston after the fall of Vicksburg. Map also shows the complex network of bayous and waterways surrounding Vicksburg. *West Point Atlas of the Civil War. Courtesy of Department of History, USMA.*

while marching through the country. I wrote to Sherman: "Impress upon the men the importance of going through the State in an orderly manner, abstaining from taking anything not absolutely necessary for their subsistence while travelling. They should try to create as favorable an impression as possible upon the people." Provisions and forage, when called for by them, were issued to all the people, from Bruinsburg to Jackson and back to Vicksburg, whose resources had been taken for the supply of our army. Very large quantities of groceries and provisions were so issued.[4]

---

4. Someone profits from every war. Contractors—Halliburton, KBR, and Blackwater among them—have assumed a highly visible role in the most recent U.S. conflicts and raised vital questions about the privatizing of war. Profiteering was a significant problem during the Civil War. Colonel Henry S. Olcott, an officer who investigated dishonest contractors, later described the extent of their malfeasance: "Nay, so vile was

Sherman was ordered back to Vicksburg, and his troops took much the same position they had occupied before—from the Big Black to Haines' Bluff.

Having cleaned up about Vicksburg and captured or routed all regular Confederate forces for more than a hundred miles in all directions, I felt that the troops that had done so much should be allowed to do more before the enemy could recover from the blow he had received, and while important points might be captured without bloodshed. I suggested to the General-in-chief the idea of a campaign against Mobile, starting from Lake Pontchartrain. Halleck preferred another course. The possession of the trans-Mississippi by the Union forces seemed to possess more importance in his mind than almost any campaign east of the Mississippi. I am well aware that the President was very anxious to have a foothold in Texas, to stop the clamor of some of the foreign governments which seemed to be seeking a pretext to interfere in the war, at least so far as to recognize belligerent rights to the Confederate States. This, however, could have been easily done without wasting troops in western Louisiana and eastern Texas, by sending a garrison at once to Brownsville on the Rio Grande.

Halleck disapproved of my proposition to go against Mobile, so that I was obliged to settle down and see myself put again on the defensive as I had been a year before in west Tennessee. It would have been an easy thing to capture Mobile at the time I proposed to go there. Having that as a base of operations, troops could have been thrown into the interior to operate against General Bragg's army. This would necessarily have compelled Bragg to detach in order to meet this fire in his rear. If he had not done this the troops from Mobile could have inflicted inestimable damage upon much of the country from which his army and Lee's were yet receiving their supplies. I was so much impressed with this idea that I renewed my request later in July and again about the 1st of August, and proposed sending all the troops necessary, asking only the assistance of the navy to protect the debarkation of troops at or near Mobile. I also asked for a leave of absence to visit New Orleans, particularly if my suggestion to move against Mobile should be

---

the scramble for money," Olcott insisted, "so debasing its influence, that our dead heroes were followed into the very grave by the plundering contractor, who cheated in the coffin that was to hold the sacred dust, and amassed fortunes by supplying rotten headstones in defiance of accepted stipulations. What shall we call this wretched episode of national history but a Carnival of Fraud. This was the Augean stable to cleanse which the broom of authority was placed in my hands." "The War's Carnival of Fraud," *Annals of the War*, ed. McClure, 708.

approved. Both requests were refused. So far as my experience with General Halleck went it was very much easier for him to refuse a favor than to grant one. But I did not regard this as a favor. It was simply in line of duty, though out of my department.

The General-in-chief having decided against me, the depletion of an army, which had won a succession of great victories, commenced, as had been the case the year before after the fall of Corinth when the army was sent where it would do the least good. By orders, I sent to Banks a force of 4,000 men; returned the 9th corps to Kentucky and, when transportation had been collected, started a division of 5,000 men to Schofield in Missouri where Price was raiding the State. I also detached a brigade under Ransom to Natchez, to garrison that place permanently. This latter move was quite fortunate as to the time when Ransom arrived there. The enemy happened to have a large number, about 5,000 head, of beef cattle there on the way from Texas to feed the Eastern armies, and also a large amount of munitions of war which had probably come through Texas from the Rio Grande and which were on the way to Lee's and other armies in the East.

The troops that were left with me around Vicksburg were very busily and unpleasantly employed in making expeditions against guerilla bands and small detachments of cavalry which infested the interior, and in destroying mills, bridges and rolling stock on the railroads. The guerillas and cavalry were not there to fight but to annoy, and therefore disappeared on the first approach of our troops.

The country back of Vicksburg was filled with deserters from Pemberton's army and, it was reported, many from Johnston's also. The men determined not to fight again while the war lasted. Those who lived beyond the reach of the Confederate army wanted to get to their homes. Those who did not, wanted to get North where they could work for their support till the war was over. Besides all this there was quite a peace feeling, for the time being, among the citizens of that part of Mississippi, but this feeling soon subsided. It is not probable that Pemberton got off with over 4,000 of his army to the camp where he proposed taking them, and these were in a demoralized condition.[5]

5. Grant frequently mentions deserters as evidence of a lack of Confederate will to fight, and he does not express skepticism here with regard to their tales. Of course, as Grant well knew, deserters could also be sources of deliberate misinformation. Albion Tourgée, a lieutenant in the 105th Ohio Infantry, observed this phenomenon. "The Confederate deserter was an institution which has received too little consideration. Taken altogether he was of far greater service to the southern cause than the best corps

On the 7th of August I further depleted my army by sending the 13th corps, General Ord commanding, to Banks. Besides this I received orders to co-operate with the latter general in movements west of the Mississippi. Having received this order I went to New Orleans to confer with Banks about the proposed movement. All these movements came to naught.

During this visit I reviewed Banks' army a short distance above Carrollton. The horse I rode was vicious and but little used, and on my return to New Orleans ran away and, shying at a locomotive in the street, fell, probably on me. I was rendered insensible, and when I regained consciousness I found myself in a hotel near by with several doctors attending me. My leg was swollen from the knee to the thigh, and the swelling, almost to the point of bursting, extended along the body up to the arm-pit. The pain was almost beyond endurance. I lay at the hotel something over a week without being able to turn myself in bed. I had a steamer stop at the nearest point possible, and was carried to it on a litter. I was then taken to Vicksburg, where I remained unable to move for some time afterwards.[6]

in the Confederate army," Tourgée writes. "He was ubiquitous, willing, and altogether inscrutable. Whether he told the truth or a lie, he was almost equally certain to deceive. He was sometimes a real deserter and sometimes a mock deserter. In either case, he was sure to be loaded." Tourgée's analysis of the Confederate deserter goes on to address issues of regional and class bias:

> The northern officer was wholly unacquainted with the character of the southern "poor-white." With the usual arrogance of the well-informed, he looked with contempt on any man who could not read and write; who made small pretense of tidiness; who spoke the vernacular of the South with a drawl, and seemed more concerned about his supply of "terbacker" than the outcome of the war. These men, simple-minded but true as steel and cunning as foxes, needed no padding of pretense to make themselves believed. They were not thought capable of deception. They came into our lines; told the stories they were instructed to tell; hung about for a while; were sent to the rear or slipped away; stayed at home a month or two, and then found their way back to their regiments.

"The Story of a Thousand," *The Cosmopolitan* 18, no. 6 (April 1895): 731.

6. The fall in New Orleans led to more stories about Grant's drunkenness. General Thomas Kilby Smith, who was riding with Grant at the time, offered the following explanation to his wife:

> Our reception in New Orleans was very brilliant—serenades, calls, a magnificent evening reception or levee by General Banks, and yesterday

Adolph Metzner,
Lost on the Field
of Chickamauga.
*Library of
Congress, Prints
and Photographs
Division,
LC-DIG-
ppmsca-51225.*

While I was absent General Sherman declined to assume command because, he said, it would confuse the records; but he let all the orders be made in my name, and was glad to render any assistance he could. No orders were issued by my staff, certainly no important orders, except upon consultation with and approval of Sherman.

On the 13th of September, while I was still in New Orleans, Halleck telegraphed to me to send all available forces to Memphis and thence to Tuscumbia, to co-operate with Rosecrans for the relief of Chattanooga. On the 15th he telegraphed again for all available forces to go to Rosecrans. This was received on the 27th. I was still confined to my bed, unable to rise from it without assistance; but I at once ordered Sherman to send one division to Memphis as fast as transports could be provided. The division of McPherson's

---

a grand review. The parade grounds are some eight miles from the city. We rode out on horseback, and I am sorry to say our festivities were or are interrupted by a rather serious accident. The two generals and their staff made a large cavalcade. General Grant was riding a fine but unbroken horse and on our return the animal shied upon a carriage and fell; he was in advance and at rapid speed; the officer following was out of place, and rode over him and the trampling of the horse bruised him severely. We took him in a state of insensibility into a roadside inn before which the accident occurred, and where he now lies in the room in which I write. His thigh is badly injured and he cannot move his leg, but he is better this morning and I think can be moved in a day or two; with the residue of his staff, I remain to take care of him.

Letter to Elizabeth B. Smith, September 6, 1863, *Life and Letters of Thomas Kilby Smith*, ed. Walter George Smith (New York: G. P. Putnam's Sons, 1898), 334–35.

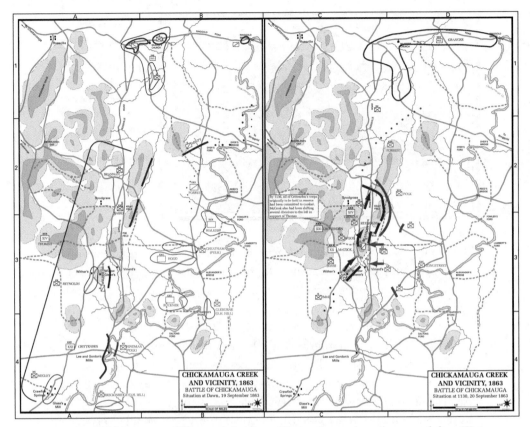

Battle of Chickamauga. Map on right shows Thomas's stand on the second day. *West Point Atlas of the Civil War. Courtesy of Department of History, USMA.*

corps, which had got off and was on the way to join Steele in Arkansas, was recalled and sent, likewise, to report to Hurlbut at Memphis. Hurlbut was directed to forward these two divisions with two others from his own corps at once, and also to send any other troops that might be returning there. Halleck suggested that some good man, like Sherman or McPherson, should be sent to Memphis to take charge of the troops going east. On this I sent Sherman, as being, I thought, the most suitable person for an independent command, and besides he was entitled to it if it had to be given to any one. He was directed to take with him another division of his corps. This left one back, but having one of McPherson's divisions he had still the equivalent.

Before the receipt by me of these orders the battle of Chickamauga had been fought and Rosecrans forced back into Chattanooga. The administration as well as the General-in-chief was nearly frantic at the situation of affairs there. Mr. Charles A. Dana, an officer of the War Department, was

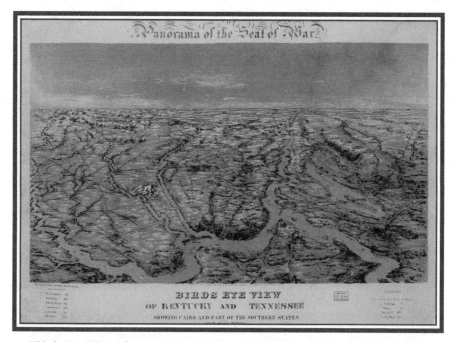

"Birds Eye View of Kentucky and Tennessee, Showing Cairo and the Southern States," 1862. *Library of Congress, Geography and Map Division.*

sent to Rosecrans' headquarters. I do not know what his instructions were, but he was still in Chattanooga when I arrived there at a later period.

It seems that Halleck suggested that I should go to Nashville as soon as able to move and take general direction of the troops moving from the west. I received the following dispatch dated October 3d: "It is the wish of the Secretary of War that as soon as General Grant is able he will come to Cairo and report by telegraph." I was still very lame, but started without delay. Arriving at Columbus on the 16th I reported by telegraph: "Your dispatch from Cairo of the 3d directing me to report from Cairo was received at 11.30 on the 10th. Left the same day with staff and headquarters and am here en route for Cairo."

End of Volume I

VOLUME II

Civil War Cannon Balls, Soldiers and Sailors'
Monument, New York, New York. *Photograph by
Elizabeth D. Samet.*

40

First Meeting with Secretary Stanton— General Rosecrans—Commanding Military Division of Mississippi—Andrew Johnson's Address—Arrival at Chattanooga

The reply (to my telegram of October 16, 1863, from Cairo, announcing my arrival at that point) came on the morning of the 17th, directing me to proceed immediately to the Galt House, Louisville, where I would meet an officer of the War Department with my instructions. I left Cairo within an hour or two after the receipt of this dispatch, going by rail via Indianapolis. Just as the train I was on was starting out of the depot at Indianapolis a messenger came running up to stop it, saying the Secretary of War was coming into the station and wanted to see me.

I had never met Mr. [Edwin M.] Stanton up to that time, though we had held frequent conversations over the wires the year before, when I was in Tennessee. Occasionally at night he would order the wires between the War Department and my headquarters to be connected, and we would hold a conversation for an hour or two. On this occasion the Secretary was accompanied by Governor [John] Brough of Ohio, whom I had never met, though he and my father had been old acquaintances. Mr. Stanton dismissed the special train that had brought him to Indianapolis, and accompanied me to Louisville.

Up to this time no hint had been given me of what was wanted after I left Vicksburg, except the suggestion in one of Halleck's dispatches that I had better go to Nashville and superintend the operation of troops sent to relieve Rosecrans. Soon after we started the Secretary handed me two orders, saying that I might take my choice of them. The two were identical in all but one particular. Both created the "Military Division of Mississippi," (giving me

Secretary of War Edwin M. Stanton. *Library of Congress, Prints and Photographs Division, LC-DIG-cwpbh-00958.*

the command) composed of the Departments of the Ohio, the Cumberland, and the Tennessee, and all the territory from the Alleghanies to the Mississippi River north of Banks's command in the south-west. One order left the department commanders as they were, while the other relieved Rosecrans and assigned Thomas to his place. I accepted the latter. We reached Louisville after night and, if I remember rightly, in a cold, drizzling rain. The Secretary of War told me afterwards that he caught a cold on that occasion from which he never expected to recover. He never did.[1]

A day was spent in Louisville, the Secretary giving me the military news at the capital and talking about the disappointment at the results of some of the campaigns. By the evening of the day after our arrival all matters of discussion seemed exhausted, and I left the hotel to spend the evening away, both Mrs. Grant (who was with me) and myself having relatives living in Louisville. In the course of the evening Mr. Stanton received a dispatch from Mr. C. A. Dana, then in Chattanooga, informing him that

---

1. This sentence is rather puzzling. Stanton (1814–1869) recovered to serve out the rest of the war. He did, however, suffer from increasingly severe asthma. He had taken over for Lincoln's first Secretary of War, Simon Cameron, in 1862. Stanton was a Democrat and an abolitionist; he was exceptionally competent, if interpersonally difficult. Stanton biographer William Marvel notes that the secretary was mistrustful of Grant and his reputation for drunkenness. It was Stanton who sent Charles Dana out to inform on the general. On Stanton's health and his meeting with Grant, see Marvel, *Lincoln's Autocrat: The Life of Edwin Stanton* (Chapel Hill: University of North Carolina Press, 2015), 354, 277–78, 305–6.

unless prevented Rosecrans would retreat, and advising peremptory orders against his doing so.[2]

As stated before, after the fall of Vicksburg I urged strongly upon the government the propriety of a movement against Mobile. General Rosecrans had been at Murfreesboro, Tennessee, with a large and well-equipped army from early in the year 1863, with Bragg confronting him with a force quite equal to his own at first, considering it was on the defensive. But after the investment of Vicksburg Bragg's army was largely depleted to strengthen Johnston, in Mississippi, who was being reinforced to raise the siege. I frequently wrote General Halleck suggesting that Rosecrans should move against Bragg. By so doing he would either detain the latter's troops where they were or lay Chattanooga open to capture. General Halleck strongly approved the suggestion, and finally wrote me that he had repeatedly ordered Rosecrans to advance, but that the latter had constantly failed to comply with the order, and at last, after having held a council of war, had replied in effect that it was a military maxim "not to fight two decisive battles at the same time." If true, the maxim was not applicable in this case. It would be bad to be defeated in two decisive battles fought the same day, but it would not be bad to win them. I, however, was fighting no battle, and the siege of Vicksburg had drawn from Rosecrans' front so many of the enemy that his chances of victory were much greater than they would be if he waited until the siege was over, when these troops could be returned. Rosecrans was ordered to move against the army that was detaching troops to raise the siege. Finally he did move, on the 24th of June, but ten days afterwards Vicksburg surrendered, and the troops sent from Bragg were free to return.[3]

---

2. Dana recalled his first meeting with an irascible Rosecrans at Chattanooga. After reading Dana's letter of introduction from Stanton, the general evidently "burst out in angry abuse of the Government at Washington. He had not been sustained, he said. His requests had been ignored, his plans thwarted. Both Stanton and Halleck had done all they could, he declared, to prevent his success." Dana replied, "I have no authority to listen to complaints against the Government. I was sent here for the purpose of finding out what the Government could do to aid you, and have no right to confer with you on other matters." This seemed to calm the general, who then proceeded to explain the situation to Dana. See *Recollections*, 107.

3. Grant expresses little patience with "maxims" and "axioms" of war. He was, as he freely admits, no great student of military theory. James Harrison Wilson recorded Sherman's observations on Grant's lack of military knowledge:

> "Wilson, I am a damned sight smarter man than Grant; I know a great deal more about war, military history, strategy, and grand tactics than he does;

It was at this time that I recommended to the general-in-chief the movement against Mobile. I knew the peril the Army of the Cumberland was in, being depleted continually, not only by ordinary casualties, but also by having to detach troops to hold its constantly extending line over which to draw supplies, while the enemy in front was as constantly being strengthened. Mobile was important to the enemy, and in the absence of a threatening force was guarded by little else than artillery. If threatened by land and from the water at the same time the prize would fall easily, or troops would have to be sent to its defence. Those troops would necessarily come from Bragg. My judgment was overruled, and the troops under my command were dissipated over other parts of the country where it was thought they could render the most service.[4]

Soon it was discovered in Washington that Rosecrans was in trouble and required assistance. The emergency was now too immediate to allow us to give this assistance by making an attack in rear of Bragg upon Mobile. It was therefore necessary to reinforce directly, and troops were sent from every available point.

Rosecrans had very skilfully manœuvred Bragg south of the Tennessee River, and through and beyond Chattanooga. If he had stopped and intrenched, and made himself strong there, all would have been right and the

---

I know more about organization, supply, and administration and about everything else than he does; but I'll tell you where he beats me and where he beats the world. He don't care a damn for what the enemy does out of his sight, but it scares me like hell!" He added: "I am more nervous than he is. I am more likely to change my orders or to countermarch my command than he is. He uses such information as he has according to his best judgment; he issues his orders and does his level best to carry them out without much reference to what is going on about him and, so far, experience seems to have fully justified him."

Wilson praises the accuracy of Sherman's assessment before concluding, "While Sherman was in many ways much more brilliant than Grant, those who knew both will have long since settled down to the conclusion that Grant was a far saner and safer general than Sherman." *Under the Old Flag*, 2:17.

Sherman's observation that Grant "uses such information as he has" points to his friend's success in avoiding one of the pitfalls to which commanders are liable: a desire to acquire perfect information in war. This desire, exacerbated by technological advances in intelligence gathering and communication, tends to paralyze. "Perfect information" is a fantasy that can never be realized.

4. Grant continued to push for the capture of Mobile, but it was not until August 5, 1864, that Farragut reduced the forts at the Battle of Mobile Bay.

mistake of not moving earlier partially compensated. But he pushed on, with his forces very much scattered, until Bragg's troops from Mississippi began to join him. Then Bragg took the initiative. Rosecrans had to fall back in turn, and was able to get his army together at Chickamauga, some miles south-east of Chattanooga, before the main battle was brought on. The battle was fought on the 19th and 20th of September, and Rosecrans was badly defeated, with a heavy loss in artillery and some sixteen thousand men killed, wounded and captured. The corps under Major-General George H. Thomas stood its ground, while Rosecrans, with Crittenden and McCook, returned to Chattanooga.[5] Thomas returned also, but later, and with his troops in good order. Bragg followed and took possession of Missionary Ridge, overlooking Chattanooga. He also occupied Lookout Mountain, west of the town, which Rosecrans had abandoned, and with it his control of the river and the river road as far back as Bridgeport. The National troops were now strongly intrenched in Chattanooga Valley, with the Tennessee River behind them and the enemy occupying commanding heights to the east and west, with a strong line across the valley from mountain to mountain, and with Chattanooga Creek, for a large part of the way, in front of their line.

On the 29th Halleck telegraphed me the above results, and directed

---

5. The Confederate evacuation of Chattanooga in September had been a deep blow to the South. Desertions climbed, and a desperate Jefferson Davis determined that Braxton Bragg should go on the offensive just as Lee had done in the East. He detached divisions from Joseph Johnston's army in Mississippi and from Lee's Army of Northern Virginia to come to Bragg's aid in the mountains of north Georgia. The latter division, led by Longstreet, was forced to take a nine-hundred-mile train trip to detour around Union positions in eastern Tennessee. According to Albion Tourgée, the tales of a Confederate retreat told by the deserters coming into federal lines during this period were part of a ruse. Bragg "knew his opponent's weakness and made it the prime element of his game," Tourgée surmised. "He had two instruments with which to carry out his deceptions—his army and numerous deserters. He made his army serve his purpose by marching in hot haste toward Lafayette, until he had crossed West Chickamauga creek, and then cunningly hiding behind the wooded heights of the Pigeon mountain range. The business of the deserter was to make General Rosecrans believe this headlong haste was to continue until the rear-guard of his army reached Rome and the last wagon was parked in the valley of the Coosa, out of the reach." "The Story of a Thousand," 731.

The ensuing Battle of Chickamauga proved a debacle for Rosecrans. The battle, which took place in the mountains of northern Georgia on September 19–20, resulted in more than 34,000 casualties altogether. It was for covering the Union retreat that George H. Thomas earned his nickname, "The Rock of Chickamauga."

One of the most harrowing retreats of the following century would be that of the Italians from Caporetto, in 1917. It is brilliantly evoked in chapter 30 of Ernest Hemingway's *A Farewell to Arms* (New York: Scribner's, 1929).

all the forces that could be spared from my department to be sent to Rose-crans. Long before this dispatch was received Sherman was on his way, and McPherson was moving east with most of the garrison of Vicksburg.

A retreat at that time would have been a terrible disaster.[6] It would not only have been the loss of a most important strategic position to us, but it would have been attended with the loss of all the artillery still left with the Army of the Cumberland and the annihilation of that army itself, either by capture or demoralization.

All supplies for Rosecrans had to be brought from Nashville. The railroad between this base and the army was in possession of the government up to Bridgeport, the point at which the road crosses to the south side of the Tennessee River; but Bragg, holding Lookout and Raccoon mountains west of Chattanooga, commanded the railroad, the river and the shortest and best wagon-roads, both south and north of the Tennessee, between Chattanooga and Bridgeport. The distance between these two places is but twenty-six miles by rail; but owing to the position of Bragg, all supplies for Rosecrans had to be hauled by a circuitous route north of the river and over a mountainous country, increasing the distance to over sixty miles.

This country afforded but little food for his animals, nearly ten thousand of which had already starved, and not enough were left to draw a single piece of artillery or even the ambulances to convey the sick. The men had been on half rations of hard bread for a considerable time, with but few other supplies except beef driven from Nashville across the country. The region along the road became so exhausted of food for the cattle that by the time they reached Chattanooga they were much in the condition of the few animals left alive there—"on the lift." Indeed, the beef was so poor that the soldiers were in the habit of saying, with a faint facetiousness, that they were living on "half rations of hard bread and *beef dried on the hoof*."

Nothing could be transported but food, and the troops were without sufficient shoes or other clothing suitable for the advancing season. What they had was well worn. The fuel within the Federal lines was exhausted, even to the stumps of trees. There were no teams to draw it from the opposite bank, where it was abundant. The only way of supplying fuel, for some time before my arrival, had been to cut trees on the north bank of the river at a considerable distance up the stream, form rafts of it and float it down with the current, effecting a landing on the south side within our lines by

---

6. The strategic importance of Chattanooga lay in the fact that it was the only railroad link between the Confederacy's eastern and western armies.

Edwin Forbes, "Beef for the Army—on the march," Rappahannock Station, Virginia. *Library of Congress, Prints and Photographs Division, LC-DIG-ppmsca-20663.*

the use of paddles or poles. It would then be carried on the shoulders of the men to their camps.

If a retreat had occurred at this time it is not probable that any of the army would have reached the railroad as an organized body, if followed by the enemy.

On the receipt of Mr. Dana's dispatch Mr. Stanton sent for me. Finding that I was out he became nervous and excited, inquiring of every person he met, including guests of the house, whether they knew where I was, and bidding them find me and send me to him at once. About eleven o'clock I returned to the hotel, and on my way, when near the house, every person met was a messenger from the Secretary, apparently partaking of his impatience to see me. I hastened to the room of the Secretary and found him pacing the floor rapidly in his dressing-gown. Saying that the retreat must be prevented, he showed me the dispatch. I immediately wrote an order assuming command of the Military Division of the Mississippi, and telegraphed it to General Rosecrans. I then telegraphed to him the order from Washington assigning Thomas to the command of the Army of the Cumberland; and to Thomas that he must hold Chattanooga at all hazards, informing him at the same time that I would be at the front as soon as possible. A prompt reply was received from Thomas, saying, "We will hold the town till we starve."[7] I appreciated the force of this dispatch later when I witnessed the condition of affairs which prompted it. It looked, indeed, as if but two courses were open: one to starve, the other to surrender or be captured.

On the morning of the 20th of October I started, with my staff, and proceeded as far as Nashville. At that time it was not prudent to travel beyond that point by night, so I remained in Nashville until the next morning. Here I met for the first time Andrew Johnson, Military Governor of Tennessee.[8] He delivered a speech of welcome. His composure showed that it was by no means his maiden effort. It was long, and I was in torture while he was delivering it, fearing something would be expected from me in response. I was

---

7. Thomas's determination in desperate circumstances finds a twentieth-century analogue in General Anthony C. McAuliffe's response to the news that the Germans were demanding the surrender of the besieged Bastogne: "Nuts!" Unable to come up with a pithier reply, his staff typed it up and presented it to the Germans on December 22, 1944. McAuliffe's troops held out until Patton's 3rd Army arrived. For an account of McAuliffe's answer to the Germans, see Rick Atkinson, *The Guns at Last Light* (New York: Picador, 2013), 455–56.

Troops of the 101st Airborne Division watch C-47s drop supplies, December 26, 1944, Bastogne, Belgium. *Courtesy of U.S. Army Center of Military History.*

8. Andrew Johnson (1808–1875) was a Jacksonian Democrat and a strong proponent of states' rights. A senator from Tennessee when the war broke out, he remained in office even after the state seceded. Recognizing the importance of such an ally, Lincoln made Johnson the military governor of this strategically vital state in 1862. Johnson's status as a War Democrat made him a shrewd addition as vice president on the 1864 Republican ticket. After Lincoln's assassination, Johnson clashed repeatedly with the Radical Republicans over Reconstruction policies. His attempt to remove Stanton, a supporter of Radical Reconstruction, from office precipitated a crisis, and he was subsequently impeached for his alleged violation of the Tenure of Office Act in 1868. Johnson was acquitted, but the rest of his brief time in office was dominated by the Radical Republicans, who overrode his vetoes of their Reconstruction legislation.

relieved, however, the people assembled having apparently heard enough. At all events they commenced a general hand-shaking, which, although trying where there is so much of it, was a great relief to me in this emergency.

From Nashville I telegraphed to Burnside, who was then at Knoxville, that important points in his department ought to be fortified, so that they could be held with the least number of men; to Admiral Porter at Cairo, that Sherman's advance had passed Eastport, Mississippi, that rations were probably on their way from St. Louis by boat for supplying his army, and requesting him to send a gunboat to convoy them; and to Thomas, suggesting that large parties should be put at work on the wagon-road then in use back to Bridgeport.

On the morning of the 21st we took the train for the front, reaching Stevenson Alabama, after dark. Rosecrans was there on his way north. He came into my car and we held a brief interview, in which he described very clearly the situation at Chattanooga, and made some excellent suggestions as to what should be done. My only wonder was that he had not carried them out. We then proceeded to Bridgeport, where we stopped for the night. From here we took horses and made our way by Jasper and over Waldron's Ridge to Chattanooga. There had been much rain, and the roads were almost impassable from mud, knee-deep in places, and from wash-outs on the mountain sides. I had been on crutches since the time of my fall in New Orleans, and had to be carried over places where it was not safe to cross on horseback. The roads were strewn with the *débris* of broken wagons and the carcasses of thousands of starved mules and horses. At Jasper, some ten or twelve miles from Bridgeport, there was a halt. General O. O. Howard had his headquarters there.[9] From this point I telegraphed Burnside to make

9. Howard tells the story of his first encounter with Grant at Chattanooga:

> One day I was at Stevenson and, while at the railroad station, the Nashville train brought Grant, Rawlins, and one or two more of his staff. On his car I was introduced to him. He gave me his hand and said pleasantly: "I am glad to see you, General." Then I had to do the talking. In a few minutes a staff officer from Hooker came in and offered Grant a carriage to take him to Hooker's headquarters, a quarter of a mile distant—extending also an invitation to the general to stay and partake of Hooker's hospitality. Grant replied: "If General Hooker wishes to see *me* he will find me on this train!" The answer and the manner of it surprised me; but it was Grant's way of maintaining his ascendency where a subordinate was likely to question it. Hooker soon entered the car and paid his respects in person. Grant that day went on with me to Bridgeport and stayed with me in my tent overnight.

every effort to secure five hundred rounds of ammunition for his artillery and small-arms. We stopped for the night at a little hamlet some ten or twelve miles farther on. The next day we reached Chattanooga a little before dark. I went directly to General Thomas's headquarters, and remaining there a few days, until I could establish my own.[10]

During the evening most of the general officers called in to pay their respects and to talk about the condition of affairs. They pointed out on the map the line, marked with a red or blue pencil, which Rosecrans had contemplated falling back upon. If any of them had approved the move they did not say so to me. I found General W. F. Smith occupying the position of chief engineer of the Army of the Cumberland. I had known Smith as a cadet at West Point, but had no recollection of having met him after my graduation, in 1843, up to this time. He explained the situation of the two armies and the topography of the country so plainly that I could see it without an inspection.[11] I found that he had established a saw-mill on the banks of the river, by utilizing an old engine found in the neighborhood; and, by rafting logs from the north side of the river above, had got out the lumber and completed pon-

It was there he said to me: "If I should seek a command higher than that intrusted to me by my Government I should be flying in the face of Providence." Grant was very lame then, suffering from a fall of his horse. The next day at sunrise Rawlins lifted him into his saddle. Then with a small escort Grant rode off by the most dangerous route via Jasper and along the shore of the Tennessee to Chattanooga. By this journey he set in motion the entire fall campaign against Bragg.

Autobiography of Oliver Otis Howard (New York: Baker & Taylor, 1907), 1:460–61.

10. Grant arrived in Chattanooga on October 23. McFeely explains the significance of this initial meeting: "After listening to each of his subordinates, Grant turned to the table and, ignoring their presence, began to write. They stood by uselessly as he composed orders and telegrams that demonstrated a grasp of the whole of the Western Theater of the war. From the disjointed reports he had been given, he put together a coherent picture of the terrain of an area that was new to him, and of the vast confused array of men who contended for it." *Grant*, 145–46.

11. William Farrar "Baldy" Smith (1824–1903) graduated from West Point in 1845, two years behind Grant. Smith spent the time between his graduation and the Civil War on various surveying, exploration, and engineering assignments and as a teacher of mathematics at West Point. Serving well at Chattanooga, Smith would become something of a disappointment at Petersburg, where he squandered his initial advantage over Beauregard. Smith went on to have a most interesting postwar career, which included serving as the President of the International Telegraph Company and Commissioner of Police in New York City.

**Equestrian Statue of George
H. Thomas, Washington, D.C.**
Photograph by Elizabeth D. Samet.

toons and roadway plank for a second bridge, one flying bridge being there already. He was also rapidly getting out the materials and constructing the boats for a third bridge. In addition to this he had far under way a steamer for plying between Chattanooga and Bridgeport whenever we might get possession of the river. This boat consisted of a scow, made of the plank sawed out at the mill, housed in, and a stern wheel attached which was propelled by a second engine taken from some shop or factory.

I telegraphed to Washington this night, notifying General Halleck of my arrival, and asking to have General Sherman assigned to the command of the Army of the Tennessee, headquarters in the field. The request was at once complied with.

41

Assuming the Command at Chattanooga— Opening a Line of Supplies—Battle of Wauhatchie—On the Picket Line

The next day, the 24th, I started out to make a personal inspection, taking Thomas and Smith with me, besides most of the members of my personal staff. We crossed to the north side of the river, and, moving to the north of detached spurs of hills, reached the Tennessee at Brown's Ferry, some three miles below Lookout Mountain, unobserved by the enemy. Here we left our horses back from the river and approached the water on foot. There was a picket station of the enemy on the opposite side, of about twenty men, in full view, and we were within easy range. They did not fire upon us nor seem to be disturbed by our presence. They must have seen that we were all commissioned officers. But, I suppose, they looked upon the garrison of Chattanooga as prisoners of war, feeding or starving themselves, and thought it would be inhuman to kill any of them except in self-defence.[1]

That night I issued orders for opening the route to Bridgeport—*a cracker*

---

1. Thomas Hardy (1840–1928) captured the strange predicament of enemies who might in other circumstances be friends in his 1902 poem "The Man He Killed," which concludes,

> "Yes; quaint and curious war is!
> You shoot a fellow down
> You'd treat if met where any bar is,
> Or help to half-a-crown."

Collected Poems of Thomas Hardy, vol. 1 of *The Poetical Works of Thomas Hardy* (London: Macmillan, 1920), 269.

Grant and members of his staff on Lookout Mountain after the Battle of Chattanooga, Tennessee. *Library of Congress, Prints and Photographs Division, LC-DIG-ppmsca-32399.*

line, as the soldiers appropriately termed it. They had been so long on short rations that my first thought was the establishment of a line over which food might reach them.[2]

---

2. By the time Grant arrived, horses were already dying of starvation, evidently so weak that they could not even move to nearby water sources. The entire Army of the Cumberland was close to starving after enduring a month-long siege. Peter Cozzens describes the desperation:

> A lack of decent clothing and an early onset of autumn, which brought with it cold, drenching rains, compounded the soldiers' misery. . . . Clothing grew threadbare, and shoes gave out altogether. . . .
>
> Hunger indeed drove the men to pathetic extremes. Unloading boxes of crackers, they sifted the dirt beneath supply wagons for crumbs. Canine mascots began to disappear. Soldiers would loiter in groups around the slaughter yards, quarreling with one another for the offal of cattle.

The Shipwreck of Their Hopes: The Battles for Chattanooga (Urbana: University of Illinois Press, 1996), 9–10.

Major S. H. M. Byers, adjutant of the 5th Iowa, later wrote of what he saw on the march toward Chattanooga with Sherman's army:

> The enemy sat around on the hill-tops like crows waiting to devour a carcass. Ten thousand of them sat on top of Lookout, 25,000 sat on top of Missionary Ridge; still other thousands occupied Raccoon Mountain, almost behind the Union army, thus cutting off its line of supplies. Rosecrans's

Chattanooga is on the south bank of the Tennessee, where that river runs nearly due west. It is at the northern end of a valley five or six miles in width, through which Chattanooga Creek runs. To the east of the valley is Missionary Ridge, rising from five to eight hundred feet above the creek and terminating somewhat abruptly a half mile or more before reaching the Tennessee. On the west of the valley is Lookout Mountain, twenty-two hundred feet above tide-water. Just below the town the Tennessee makes a turn to the south and runs to the base of Lookout Mountain, leaving no level ground between the mountain and river. The Memphis and Charleston Railroad passes this point, where the mountain stands nearly perpendicular. East of Missionary Ridge flows the South Chickamauga River; west of Lookout Mountain is Lookout Creek; and west of that, Raccoon Mountains. Lookout Mountain, at its northern end, rises almost perpendicularly for some distance, then breaks off in a gentle slope of cultivated fields to near the summit, where it ends in a palisade thirty or more feet in height. On the gently sloping ground, between the upper and lower palisades, there is a single farmhouse, which is reached by a wagon-road from the valley east.[3]

---

army was living on a cracker a day. To be exact, the men had four crackers and a quarter of a pound of bacon for three days. The horses, except at headquarters, had nothing but the bark of trees and dead leaves. Thousands of them lay dead. Along the one muddy wagon road to Bridgeport 10,000 dead mules filled the air with an unbearable stench.

Byers had marched east from the vicinity of Corinth, where he had been repairing railroads, far more pleasant duty than that of the men in the besieged city. Here he describes a particular find:

We made short marches, and when not working on the railroad had good times in bivouac. A mail was to go back North, and thousands were writing letters home. Books, too, from plantation houses that had fallen under the ban, furnished those who cared for it something to read. I still have in my possession a handsome morocco-bound volume, called "Great Truths by Great Authors," that I picked up on the lawn of a burning home near Oxford, Miss. It afforded me delightful reading there in bivouac on the banks of the Tennessee. On its flyleaf is dimly written the name of "Rupert Hughes, Dec. 25, 1855." It was probably a Christmas gift. I carried it with me to the end of the war, and after these 40 years if Hughes or any of his kindred will identify the volume it shall be returned.

"War's Mighty Cost," *National Tribune*, October 26, 1905, p. 1.

3. Until one visits a Civil War battlefield and sees perhaps the foundations of a house that once stood there, it is easy to lose sight of the fact that the fighting frequently took place

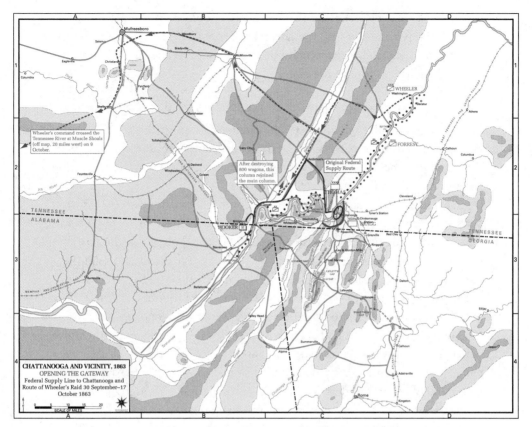

Opening the Gateway: Federal Supply Line to Chattanooga and Route of Wheeler's Raid, September 30–October 17, 1863. *West Point Atlas of the Civil War. Courtesy of Department of History, USMA.*

The intrenched line of the enemy commenced on the north end of Missionary Ridge and extended along the crest for some distance south, thence across Chattanooga valley to Lookout Mountain. Lookout Mountain was also fortified and held by the enemy, who also kept troops in Lookout valley west, and on Raccoon Mountain, with pickets extending down the river so as to command the road on the north bank and render it useless to us. In addition to this there was an intrenched line in Chattanooga valley extending from the river east of the town to Lookout Mountain, to make the investment complete. Besides the fortifications on Mission[ary] Ridge, there was a line at the base of the hill, with occasional spurs of rifle-pits half-way up the front. The enemy's pickets extended out into the valley towards the

amid civilian habitation: through the active pastures, fields, and orchards on which citizens were still practicing the arts of peace.

town, so far that the pickets of the two armies could converse. At one point they were separated only by the narrow creek which gives its name to the valley and town, and from which both sides drew water. The Union lines were shorter than those of the enemy.

Thus the enemy, with a vastly superior force, was strongly fortified to the east, south, and west, and commanded the river below. Practically, the Army of the Cumberland was besieged. The enemy had stopped with his cavalry north of the river the passing of a train loaded with ammunition and medical supplies. The Union army was short of both, not having ammunition enough for a day's fighting.

General Halleck had, long before my coming into this new field, ordered parts of the 11th and 12th corps, commanded respectively by Generals Howard and Slocum, Hooker in command of the whole, from the Army of the Potomac to reinforce Rosecrans.[4] It would have been folly to send them to Chattanooga to help eat up the few rations left there. They were consequently left on the railroad, where supplies could be brought to them. Before my arrival, Thomas ordered their concentration at Bridgeport.

General W. F. Smith had been so instrumental in preparing for the move which I was now about to make, and so clear in his judgment about the manner of making it, that I deemed it but just to him that he should have command of the troops detailed to execute the design, although he was then acting as a staff officer and was not in command of troops.

On the 24th of October, after my return to Chattanooga, the following details were made: General Hooker, who was now at Bridgeport, was ordered to cross to the south side of the Tennessee and march up by Whitesides and Wauhatchie to Brown's Ferry.[5] General Palmer, with a division

4. Henry W. Slocum (1826–1894) graduated from West Point in 1852 and fought against the Seminoles in Florida. He resigned from the army in 1856 and later joined the Civil War as a colonel of volunteers. He lived in Brooklyn, New York, where he is commemorated with an equestrian statue at Grand Army Plaza.

5. Joseph Hooker (1814–1879) was one of the war's more colorful and controversial generals. After graduating from West Point in 1837, he served in various posts from Florida to the Maine border. He served in the Mexican War and in California before resigning in 1853. Hooker returned to the army as a brigadier general of volunteers. During the war he would become both hero and goat. When, after agitating against Burnside, he was given the command of the Army of the Potomac in 1863, Lincoln wrote him the following letter:

I have placed you at the head of the Army of the Potomac. Of course I have done this upon what appear to me to be sufficient reasons. And yet I

of the 14th corps, Army of the Cumberland, was ordered to move down the river on the north side, by a back road, until opposite Whitesides, then cross and hold the road in Hooker's rear after he had passed. Four thousand

---

think it best for you to know that there are some things in regard to which, I am not quite satisfied with you. I believe you to be a brave and a skilful soldier, which, of course, I like. I also believe you do not mix politics with your profession, in which you are right. You have confidence in yourself, which is a valuable, if not an indispensable quality. You are ambitious, which, within reasonable bounds, does good rather than harm. But I think that during Gen. Burnside's command of the Army, you have taken counsel of your ambition, and thwarted him as much as you could, in which you did a great wrong to the country, and to a most meritorious and honorable brother officer. I have heard, in such way as to believe it, of your recently saying that both the Army and the Government needed a Dictator. Of course it was not *for* this, but in spite of it, that I have given you the command. Only those generals who gain successes, can set up dictators. What I now ask of you is military success, and I will risk the dictatorship. The government will support you to the utmost of it's [*sic*] ability, which is neither more nor less than it has done and will do for all commanders. I much fear that the spirit which you have aided to infuse into the Army, of criticising their Commander, and withholding confidence from him, will now turn upon you. I shall assist you as far as I can, to put it down. Neither you, nor Napoleon, if he were alive again, could get any good out of an army, while such a spirit prevails in it.

And now, beware of rashness. Beware of rashness, but with energy, and sleepless vigilance, go forward, and give us victories.

Letter to Joseph Hooker, January 26, 1863, available at Abraham Lincoln Papers at the Library of Congress, Manuscript Division (Washington, D.C.: American Memory Project, [2000–02]), https://www.loc.gov/item/scsm000601/.

Equestrian statue of Joseph Hooker, Boston, Massachusetts.
Photograph by Elizabeth D. Samet.

men were at the same time detailed to act under General Smith directly from Chattanooga. Eighteen hundred of them, under General [William B.] Hazen, were to take sixty pontoon boats, and under cover of night float by the pickets of the enemy at the north base of Lookout, down to Brown's Ferry, then land on the south side and capture or drive away the pickets at that point.[6] Smith was to march with the remainder of the detail, also under cover of night, by the north bank of the river to Brown's Ferry, taking with him all the material for laying the bridge as soon as the crossing was secured.

On the 26th, Hooker crossed the river at Bridgeport and commenced his eastward march. At three o'clock on the morning of the 27th, Hazen moved into the stream with his sixty pontoons and eighteen hundred brave and well-equipped men. Smith started enough in advance to be near the river when Hazen should arrive. There are a number of detached spurs of hills north of the river at Chattanooga, back of which is a good road parallel to the stream, sheltered from the view from the top of Lookout. It was over this road Smith marched. At five o'clock Hazen landed at Brown's Ferry, surprised the picket guard, and captured most of it. By seven o'clock the whole of Smith's force was ferried over and in possession of a height commanding the ferry. This was speedily fortified, while a detail was laying the pontoon bridge. By ten o'clock the bridge was laid, and our extreme right, now in Lookout valley, was fortified and connected with the rest of the army. The two bridges over the Tennessee River—a flying one at Chattanooga and the new one at Brown's Ferry—with the road north of the river, covered from both the fire and the view of the enemy, made the connection complete. Hooker found but slight obstacles in his way, and on the afternoon of the 28th emerged into Lookout valley at Wauhatchie. Howard marched on to Brown's Ferry, while Geary, who commanded a division in the 12th corps, stopped three miles south. The pickets of the enemy on the river below were now cut off, and soon came in and surrendered.

The river was now opened to us from Lookout valley to Bridgeport.

---

6. Writing about his experience in Vietnam, Tim O'Brien asserts the continuity across time and place of the picket's nocturnal watch: "The night was clear. We ate C rations and drank some beer. Then the guard started, the ritual came alive from our pagan past—Thucydides and Polybius and Julius Caesar, tales of encampment, tales of night terror—the long silent stare into an opaque shell of shadows and dark. Three men to a foxhole: two asleep and one awake. No smoking: The enemy will see the light and blow your lungs out. Stay alert: Courts-martial for those dozing on guard. All the rules passed down from ancient warfare, the lessons of dead men." *If I Die in a Combat Zone: Box Me Up and Ship Me Home* (New York: Broadway Books, 1999), 130.

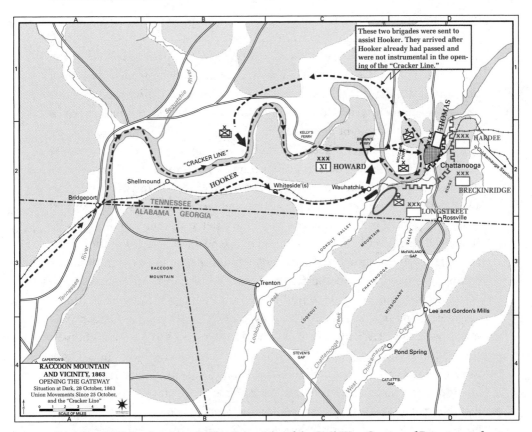

These two brigades were sent to assist Hooker. They arrived after Hooker already had passed and were not instrumental in the opening of the "Cracker Line."

"CRACKER LINE"

KELLY'S FERRY

BROWN'S FERRY

MOCCASIN POINT

HARDEE

XXX

Chickamauga Station

Chattanooga

XXX

XXX

XI HOWARD

HOOKER

Shellmound

Whiteside'(s)

Wauhatchie

BRECKINRIDGE

Bridgeport

TENNESSEE
ALABAMA | GEORGIA

XXX

LONGSTREET

Rossville

RIDGE

VALLEY

LOOKOUT VALLEY

MOUNTAIN

McFARLAND'S GAP

RACCOON MOUNTAIN

Trenton

CHATTANOOGA

Lookout Creek

LOOKOUT

MISSIONARY

Lee and Gordon's Mills

Chattanooga Creek

West Chickamauga Creek

Pond Spring

STEVEN'S GAP

CATLETT'S GAP

CAPERTON'S

RACCOON MOUNTAIN AND VICINITY, 1863
OPENING THE GATEWAY
Situation at Dark, 28 October, 1863
Union Movements Since 25 October,
and the "Cracker Line"

0 1 2 3 4 5
SCALE OF MILES

Opening the "Cracker Line." *West Point Atlas of the Civil War. Courtesy of Department of History, USMA.*

Between Brown's Ferry and Kelly's Ferry the Tennessee runs through a narrow gorge in the mountains, which contracts the stream so much as to increase the current beyond the capacity of an ordinary steamer to stem it. To get up these rapids, steamers must be cordelled; that is, pulled up by ropes from the shore. But there is no difficulty in navigating the stream from Bridgeport to Kelly's Ferry. The latter point is only eight miles from Chattanooga and connected with it by a good wagon-road, which runs through a low pass in the Raccoon Mountains on the south side of the river to Brown's Ferry, thence on the north side to the river opposite Chattanooga. There were several steamers at Bridgeport, and abundance of forage, clothing and provisions.

On the way to Chattanooga I had telegraphed back to Nashville for a good supply of vegetables and small rations, which the troops had been so long deprived of. Hooker had brought with him from the east a full supply of land transportation. His animals had not been subjected to hard work on bad roads without forage, but were in good condition.[7] In five days from my arrival in Chattanooga the way was open to Bridgeport and, with the aid of steamers and Hooker's teams, in a week the troops were receiving full rations. It is hard for any one not an eye-witness to realize the relief this brought. The men were soon reclothed and also well fed; an abundance of ammunition was brought up, and a cheerfulness prevailed not before enjoyed in many weeks. Neither officers nor men looked upon themselves any longer as doomed. The weak and languid appearance of the troops, so visible before, disappeared at once. I do not know what the effect was on the other side, but assume it must have been correspondingly depressing. Mr. Davis had visited Bragg but a short time before, and must have perceived our condition to be about as Bragg described it in his subsequent report. "These dispositions," he said, "faithfully sustained, insured the enemy's speedy evacuation of Chattanooga for want of food and forage. Possessed of the shortest route to his depot, and the one by which reinforcements must reach him, we held him at our mercy, and his destruction was only a question of time." But the dispositions were not "faithfully sustained," and I doubt not but thousands of men engaged in trying to "sustain" them now rejoice that they were not. There was no time during the rebellion when I did not think, and often say, that the South was more to be benefited by its defeat than the North. The latter had the people, the institutions, and the territory to make a great and prosperous nation. The former was burdened with an institution abhorrent to all civilized people not brought up under it, and one which degraded labor, kept it in ignorance, and enervated the governing class. With the outside world at war with this institution, they could not have extended their territory. The labor of the country was not skilled, nor allowed to become so. The whites could not toil without becoming degraded, and those who did were denominated "poor white trash." The system of labor would have soon exhausted the soil and left the people poor. The non-slaveholders would have left the country, and the small slaveholder must have sold out to his more fortunate

7. Assistant Quartermaster William G. Le Duc disagreed with this assessment, reporting that the excellent animals Hooker had used in the east were "against protest . . . ordered to be turned into the corrals at Alexandria and Washington. These choice and efficient trains, that could be relied on to do effective work day and night, were thus broken up, and the want of them was soon after most seriously felt on the Tennessee. Hooker's troops were supplied from the corral at Nashville with all sorts of animals, young and old, broken and unbroken. Many died on the road before reaching Bridgeport." "The Little Steamboat that Opened the 'Cracker Line,'" *B&L*, 3:676 n.

neighbor. Soon the slaves would have outnumbered the masters, and, not being in sympathy with them, would have risen in their might and exterminated them. The war was expensive to the South as well as to the North, both in blood and treasure, but it was worth all it cost.

The enemy was surprised by the movements which secured to us a line of supplies. He appreciated its importance, and hastened to try to recover the line from us. His strength on Lookout Mountain was not equal to Hooker's command in the valley below. From Missionary Ridge he had to march twice the distance we had from Chattanooga, in order to reach Lookout Valley; but on the night of the 28th and 29th an attack was made on Geary at Wauhatchie by Longstreet's corps. When the battle commenced, Hooker ordered Howard up from Brown's Ferry. He had three miles to march to reach Geary. On his way he was fired upon by rebel troops from a foot-hill to the left of the road and from which the road was commanded. Howard turned to the left, charged up the hill and captured it before the enemy had time to intrench, taking many prisoners. Leaving sufficient men to hold this height, he pushed on to reinforce Geary. Before he got up, Geary had been engaged for about three hours against a vastly superior force. The night was so dark that the men could not distinguish one from another except by the light of the flashes of their muskets. In the darkness and uproar Hooker's teamsters became frightened and deserted their teams. The mules also became frightened, and breaking loose from their fastenings stampeded directly towards the enemy. The latter, no doubt, took this for a charge, and stampeded in turn. By four o'clock in the morning the battle had entirely ceased, and our "cracker line" was never afterward disturbed.[8]

---

8. The successful landing of the first steamboat laden with supplies during the night of October 30–31 opened the cracker line. In a November 11 diary entry John Beatty of the 3rd Ohio Infantry described the relief felt by the troops:

> There has been much suffering among the men. They have for weeks been reduced to quarter rations, and at times so eager for food that the commissary store-rooms would be thronged, and the few crumbs which fell from broken boxes of hard-bread carefully gathered up and eaten. Men have followed the forage wagons and picked up the grains of corn which fell from them, and in some instances they have picked up the grains of corn from the mud where mules have been fed. The suffering among the animals has been intense. Hundreds of mules and horses have died of starvation. Now, however, that we have possession of the river, the men are fully supplied, but the poor horses and mules are still suffering. A day or two more will, I trust, enable us to provide well for them also. Two steamboats are

In securing possession of Lookout Valley, Smith lost one man killed and four or five wounded. The enemy lost most of his pickets at the ferry, captured. In the night engagement of the 28th–9th Hooker lost 416 killed and wounded. I never knew the loss of the enemy, but our troops buried over one hundred and fifty of his dead and captured more than a hundred.

After we had secured the opening of a line over which to bring our supplies to the army, I made a personal inspection to see the situation of the pickets of the two armies. As I have stated, Chattanooga Creek comes down the centre of the valley to within a mile or such a matter of the town of Chattanooga, then bears off westerly, then north-westerly, and enters the Tennessee River at the foot of Lookout Mountain. This creek, from its mouth up to where it bears off west, lay between the two lines of pickets, and the guards of both armies drew their water from the same stream. As I would be under short-range fire and in an open country, I took nobody with me, except, I believe, a bugler, who stayed some distance to the rear. I rode from our right around to our left. When I came to the camp of the picket guard of our side, I heard the call, "Turn out the guard for the commanding general." I replied, "Never mind the guard," and they were dismissed and went back to their tents. Just back of these, and about equally distant from the creek, were the guards of the Confederate pickets. The sentinel on their post called out in like manner, "Turn out the guard for the commanding general," and, I believe, added, "General Grant." Their line in a moment front-faced to the north, facing me, and gave a salute, which I returned.

The most friendly relations seemed to exist between the pickets of the two armies.[9] At one place there was a tree which had fallen across the stream,

---

plying between this and Chattanooga, and one immense wagon train is also busy. Supplies are coming forward with a reasonable degree of rapidity. The men appear to be in good health and excellent spirits.

Citizen-Soldier, 352–53.

9. The proximity of enemy camps before the Battle of Agincourt offers Shakespeare an opportunity to have a little fun in *Henry V* at the expense of Fluellen, the Welsh captain who strictly observes the rules of war. Here he encounters his fellow captain, Gower, on the eve of the battle:

GOWER. Captain Fluellen!

FLUELLEN. So! in the name of Jesu Christ, speak lower. It is the greatest admiration of the universal world, when the true and aunchient prerogatifes and laws of the wars is not kept: if you would take the pains but to examine the wars of Pompey the Great, you shall find, I warrant you, that there is no

and which was used by the soldiers of both armies in drawing water for their camps. General Longstreet's corps was stationed there at the time, and wore blue of a little different shade from our uniform. Seeing a soldier in blue on this log, I rode up to him, commenced conversing with him, and asked whose corps he belonged to. He was very polite, and, touching his hat to me, said he belonged to General Longstreet's corps. I asked him a few questions—but not with a view of gaining any particular information—all of which he answered, and I rode off.[10]

> tiddle taddle nor pibble pabble in Pompey's camp; I warrant you, you shall find the ceremonies of the wars, and the cares of it, and the forms of it, and the sopriety of it, and the modesty of it, to be otherwise.
>
> GOWER. Why, the enemy is loud; you hear him all night.
>
> FLUELLEN. If the enemy is an ass and a fool and a prating coxcomb, is it meet, think you, that we should also, look you, be an ass and a fool and a prating coxcomb? in your own conscience, now?
>
> GOWER. I will speak lower.
>
> FLUELLEN. I pray you and peseech you that you will.

Henry V 4.1.64–80.

Joseph S. Fullerton, the aide-de-camp to the 4th Corps commander, General Gordon Granger, described a kind of detente between the picket lines during the siege:

> The two lines of pickets were not more than three hundred yards apart; but, by common consent, there was no picket firing. On a still night, standing on the picket line, one could hear the old negro song "Dixie," adopted by the Confederates as their national music; while from our line came, in swelling response, "Hail Columbia" and "The Star-spangled Banner." With a glass Bragg's headquarters on Missionary Ridge, even the movement of his officers and orderlies, could be seen; while from the ridge or Lookout Mountain our whole camp was clearly in view. By daylight our troops could be counted, our reveille heard, our roll-call noted, our scanty meals of half rations seen—the last without envy. And we were not only heard and seen, but the enemy's signal-flag on Lookout talked, over our heads, with the signal-flag on Missionary Ridge.

"The Army of the Cumberland at Chattanooga," *B&L*, 3:719.

10. Today we have become so accustomed to thinking of the Civil War as a contest between blue and gray that it is easy to overlook the fact that, especially during the early days, uniforms were hardly regular or even clearly distinguishable. In addition to prewar uniforms, some units on both sides patterned themselves after the French Zouaves of North Africa, who wore striped or red uniforms. Meanwhile, Berdan's Sharpshooters wore green, while the 2nd Wisconsin wore gray—not atypical for state militias—at First Bull Run and were accidentally fired on by the 79th New York as a

result. Militia company nicknames such as "Barnesville Blues," for a Confederate unit from Georgia, suggest the confusion of color abounding on the battlefield. The devout Christian Lew Wallace noted approvingly that his own Zouave regiment eschewed the excesses of the French (and, incidentally, of Union Army regiments from New York, New Jersey, Pennsylvania, Illinois, and other states):

Vincent van Gogh, *The Zouave*, 1888. *Metropolitan Museum of Art, Gift of Emanie Philips, 1962.*

There was nothing of the flashy, Algerian colors in the uniform of the Eleventh Indiana; no red fez, a head-gear exclusively Mohammedan, and therefore to be religiously avoided by Christians; no red breeches, no red or yellow sash with tassels big as early cab-bages. Our outfit was of the tamest gray twilled goods, not unlike home-made jeans—a visor cap, French in pattern, its top of red cloth not larger than the palm of one's hand; a blue flannel shirt with open neck; a jacket Greekish in form, edged with narrow binding, the red scarcely noticeable; breeches baggy, but not petticoated; button gaiters connect-ing below the knees with the breeches, and strapped over the shoe. The effect was to magnify the men, though in line two thousand yards off they looked like a smoky ribbon long-drawn out.

Autobiography, 1:270.

Wounded Zouave with another soldier. Photograph by Mathew Brady. *Library of Congress, Prints and Photographs Division, LC-DIG-ppmsca-33112.*

On the significance and symbolism of uniforms more generally, see Paul Fussell, *Uniforms: Why We Are What We Wear* (New York: Mariner, 2003).

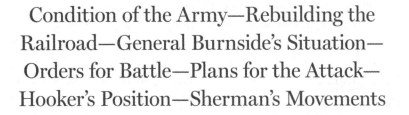

42

Condition of the Army—Rebuilding the Railroad—General Burnside's Situation— Orders for Battle—Plans for the Attack— Hooker's Position—Sherman's Movements

Having got the Army of the Cumberland in a comfortable position, I now began to look after the remainder of my new command. Burnside was in about as desperate a condition as the Army of the Cumberland had been, only he was not yet besieged. He was a hundred miles from the nearest possible base, Big South Fork of the Cumberland River, and much farther from any railroad we had possession of. The roads back were over mountains, and all supplies along the line had long since been exhausted. His animals, too, had been starved, and their carcasses lined the road from Cumberland Gap, and far back towards Lexington, Ky. East Tennessee still furnished supplies of beef, bread and forage, but it did not supply ammunition, clothing, medical supplies, or small rations, such as coffee, sugar, salt and rice.

Sherman had started from Memphis for Corinth on the 11th of October. His instructions required him to repair the road in his rear in order to bring up supplies. The distance was about three hundred and thirty miles through a hostile country. His entire command could not have maintained the road if it had been completed. The bridges had all been destroyed by the enemy, and much other damage done. A hostile community lived along the road; guerilla bands infested the country, and more or less of the cavalry of the enemy was still in the West. Often Sherman's work was destroyed as soon as completed, and he only a short distance away.[1]

---

1. John Marszalek argues that Sherman's experience with guerrillas in the late spring of 1862, while he was commanding the garrison at Memphis after the Union occupation

The Memphis and Charleston Railroad strikes the Tennessee River at Eastport, Mississippi. Knowing the difficulty Sherman would have to supply himself from Memphis, I had previously ordered supplies sent from St. Louis on small steamers, to be convoyed by the navy, to meet him at Eastport. These he got. I now ordered him to discontinue his work of repairing roads and to move on with his whole force to Stevenson, Alabama, without delay. This order was borne to Sherman by a messenger, who paddled down the Tennessee in a canoe and floated over Muscle Shoals; it was delivered at Iuka on the 27th. In this Sherman was notified that the rebels were moving a force towards Cleveland, East Tennessee, and might be going to Nashville, in which event his troops were in the best position to beat them there. Sherman, with his characteristic promptness, abandoned the work he was engaged upon and pushed on at once. On the 1st of November he crossed the Tennessee at Eastport, and that day was in Florence, Alabama, with the head of column, while his troops were still crossing at Eastport, with Blair bringing up the rear.

Sherman's force made an additional army, with cavalry, artillery, and trains, all to be supplied by the single track road from Nashville. All indications pointed also to the probable necessity of supplying Burnside's command in East Tennessee, twenty-five thousand more, by the same route. A single track could not do this. I gave, therefore, an order to Sherman to halt General G. M. Dodge's command, of about eight thousand men, at Athens, and subsequently directed the latter to arrange his troops along the railroad from Decatur north towards Nashville, and to rebuild that road. The road from Nashville to Decatur passes over a broken country, cut up with innumerable streams, many of them of considerable width, and with valleys far below the road-bed. All the bridges over these had been destroyed, and the rails taken up and twisted by the enemy. All the cars and

---

of Corinth in the late spring of 1862, worked a crucial change in his "perception of the rules of war." From this period, Sherman "saw nothing wrong with collective pillage, condemning only the private kind, a distinction his soldiers could hardly have been expected to understand." *Sherman: A Soldier's Passion for Order* (New York: Free Press, 2003), 195.

Michael Fellman notes that the language of Sherman's orders became "casually brutal" during this period as he gradually raised "the stakes of guerrilla war" and broadened his counterinsurgency campaign into a policy of "making war so terrible to Southerners" that they would surrender. See *Citizen Sherman: A Life of William Tecumseh Sherman* (New York: Random House, 1995), 140–42.

locomotives not carried off had been destroyed as effectually as they knew how to destroy them. All bridges and culverts had been destroyed between Nashville and Decatur, and thence to Stevenson, where the Memphis and Charleston and the Nashville and Chattanooga roads unite. The rebuilding of this road would give us two roads as far as Stevenson over which to supply the army. From Bridgeport, a short distance farther east, the river supplements the road.

General Dodge, besides being a most capable soldier, was an experienced railroad builder. He had no tools to work with except those of the pioneers—axes, picks, and spades. With these he was able to intrench his men and protect them against surprises by small parties of the enemy. As he had no base of supplies until the road could be completed back to Nashville, the first matter to consider after protecting his men was the getting in of food and forage from the surrounding country. He had his men and teams bring in all the grain they could find, or all they needed, and all the cattle for beef, and such other food as could be found. Millers were detailed from the ranks to run the mills along the line of the army. When these were not near enough to the troops for protection they were taken down and moved up to the line of the road. Blacksmith shops, with all the iron and steel found in them, were moved up in like manner. Blacksmiths were detailed and set to work making the tools necessary in railroad and bridge building. Axemen were put to work getting out timber for bridges and cutting fuel for locomotives when the road should be completed. Car-builders were set to work repairing the locomotives and cars. Thus every branch of railroad building, making tools to work with, and supplying the workmen with food, was all going on at once, and without the aid of a mechanic or laborer except what the command itself furnished. But rails and cars the men could not make without material, and there was not enough rolling stock to keep the road we already had worked to its full capacity. There were no rails except those in use. To supply these deficiencies I ordered eight of the ten engines General McPherson had at Vicksburg to be sent to Nashville, and all the cars he had except ten. I also ordered the troops in West Tennessee to points on the river and on the Memphis and Charleston road, and ordered the cars, locomotives and rails from all the railroads except the Memphis and Charleston to Nashville. The military manager of railroads also was directed to furnish more rolling stock and, as far as he could, bridge material. General Dodge had the work assigned him finished within forty days after receiving his orders. The number of bridges to rebuild was one hun-

Men repairing railroad track after the Battle of Stones River, near Murfreesboro, Tennessee, 1863. *Library of Congress, Prints and Photographs Division, Civil War Photographs, LC-DIG-cwpb-02135.*

dred and eighty-two, many of them over deep and wide chasms; the length of road repaired was one hundred and two miles.[2]

---

2. Grenville Dodge, who went on to work for the Union Pacific Railroad after the war, recalls the nature of his assignment in Tennessee in the ensuing months: "During this winter my command was in the Department of the Cumberland, but not reporting to or under the command of any officer of that Department. As General Grant states, I lived off the country, and brought upon myself and my command the complaints of every rebel from whom I took forage or provisions." Dodge was accused by another Union officer of "disgraceful conduct," including the impressment of African Americans. Grant dismissed the charges and ordered the arrest of Dodge's accuser. Dodge defended himself to his commander as follows:

> It is galling to any officer to have his command designated as mobs, thieves and banditti, and have these sweeping charges go up through Departments where he and his command are entire strangers. I do not know that I am a bandit when I forage, subsist, and mount my command out of a country, and when I press negroes to rebuild railroads. My orders are to do this, and I consider it not only right but that my orders and duty require it. This entire country was full of everything when I came here, and that was the only inducement to Bragg or any other rebel General to secure possession of it again, and you can depend upon it, he will never turn his army towards Middle Tennessee after I am through with it. Subsisting my force off the country was a military necessity. I have simply obeyed orders and feel that I should be protected, and request that you send an officer of your staff here to investigate.

Personal Recollections, 61–62.

The enemy's troops, which it was thought were either moving against Burnside or were going to Nashville, went no farther than Cleveland. Their presence there, however, alarmed the authorities at Washington, and, on account of our helpless condition at Chattanooga, caused me much uneasiness. Dispatches were constantly coming, urging me to do something for Burnside's relief; calling attention to the importance of holding East Tennessee; saying the President was much concerned for the protection of the loyal people in that section, etc. We had not at Chattanooga animals to pull a single piece of artillery, much less a supply train. Reinforcements could not help Burnside, because he had neither supplies nor ammunition sufficient for them; hardly, indeed, bread and meat for the men he had. There was no relief possible for him except by expelling the enemy from Missionary Ridge and about Chattanooga.

On the 4th of November Longstreet left our front with about fifteen thousand troops, besides Wheeler's cavalry, five thousand more, to go against Burnside.[3] The situation seemed desperate, and was more aggravating because nothing could be done until Sherman should get up. The authorities at Washington were now more than ever anxious for the safety of Burnside's army, and plied me with dispatches faster than ever, urging that something should be done for his relief. On the 7th, before Longstreet could possibly have reached Knoxville, I ordered Thomas peremptorily to attack the enemy's right, so as to force the return of the troops that had gone up the valley. I directed him to take mules, officers' horses, or animals wherever he could get them to move the necessary artillery. But he persisted in the declaration that he could not move a single piece of artillery, and could not see how he could possibly comply with the order. Nothing was left to be done but to answer Washington dispatches as best I could; urge Sherman forward, although he was making every effort to get forward, and encourage Burnside to hold on, assuring him that in a short time he should be relieved. All of Burnside's dispatches showed the greatest confidence in his ability to hold his position as long as his ammunition held out. He even suggested the propriety of abandoning the territory he held south and west of Knoxville, so as

3. The original version of this account, which appeared in *Battles and Leaders*, includes an editorial footnote to this sentence: "In the course of the preparation of this paper we asked General Grant, whether the detachment of Longstreet for the attack on Knoxville was not, in his opinion, a great mistake on the part of Bragg. He replied in the affirmative; and when it was further presumed that Bragg doubtless thought his position impregnable, the Victor of Chattanooga answered, with a shrewd look that accented the humor of his words: 'Well, it *was* impregnable.'" *B&L*, 3:693 n.

to draw the enemy farther from his base and make it more difficult for him to get back to Chattanooga when the battle should begin.

Longstreet had a railroad as far as Loudon; but from there to Knoxville he had to rely on wagon trains. Burnside's suggestion, therefore, was a good one, and it was adopted. On the 14th I telegraphed him:

> "Sherman's advance has reached Bridgeport. His whole force will be ready to move from there by Tuesday at farthest. If you can hold Longstreet in check until he gets up, or by skirmishing and falling back can avoid serious loss to yourself and gain time, I will be able to force the enemy back from here and place a force between Longstreet and Bragg that must inevitably make the former take to the mountain-passes by every available road, to get to his supplies. Sherman would have been here before this but for high water in Elk River driving him some thirty miles up that river to cross."

And again later in the day, indicating my plans for his relief, as follows:

> "Your dispatch and Dana's just received. Being there, you can tell better how to resist Longstreet's attack than I can direct. With your showing you had better give up Kingston at the last moment and save the most productive part of your possessions. Every arrangement is now made to throw Sherman's force across the river, just at and below the mouth of Chickamauga Creek, as soon as it arrives. Thomas will attack on his left at the same time, and together it is expected to carry Missionary Ridge, and from there push a force on to the railroad between Cleveland and Dalton. Hooker will at the same time attack, and, if he can, carry Lookout Mountain. The enemy now seems to be looking for an attack on his left flank. This favors us. To further confirm this, Sherman's advance division will march direct from Whiteside to Trenton. The remainder of his force will pass over a new road just made from Whiteside to Kelly's Ferry, thus being concealed from the enemy, and leave him to suppose the whole force is going up Lookout Valley. Sherman's advance has only just reached Bridgeport. The rear will only reach there on the 16th. This will bring it to the 19th as the earliest day for making the combined movement as desired. Inform me if you think you can sustain yourself until this time. I can hardly conceive of the enemy breaking through at Kingston and pushing for Kentucky. If they should, however, a new

problem would be left for solution. Thomas has ordered a division of cavalry to the vicinity of Sparta. I will ascertain if they have started, and inform you. It will be entirely out of the question to send you ten thousand men, not because they cannot be spared, but how would they be fed after they got even one day east from here?"

Longstreet, for some reason or other, stopped at Loudon until the 13th. That being the terminus of his railroad communications, it is probable he was directed to remain there awaiting orders. He was in a position threatening Knoxville, and at the same time where he could be brought back speedily to Chattanooga. The day after Longstreet left Loudon, Sherman reached Bridgeport in person and proceeded on to see me that evening, the 14th, and reached Chattanooga the next day.

My orders for battle were all prepared in advance of Sherman's arrival,[4] except the dates, which could not be fixed while troops to be engaged were so far away. The possession of Lookout Mountain was of no special advantage to us now. Hooker was instructed to send Howard's corps to the north side of the Tennessee, thence up behind the hills on the north side, and to go into camp opposite Chattanooga; with the remainder of the command, Hooker was, at a time to be afterwards appointed, to ascend the western slope between the upper and lower palisades, and so get into Chattanooga valley.

The plan of battle was for Sherman to attack the enemy's right flank, form a line across it, extend our left over South Chickamauga River so as to threaten or hold the railroad in Bragg's rear, and thus force him either to weaken his lines elsewhere or lose his connection with his base at Chickamauga Station. Hooker was to perform like service on our right. His problem was to get from Lookout Valley to Chattanooga Valley in the most expeditious way possible; cross the latter valley rapidly to Rossville, south of Bragg's line on Missionary Ridge, form line there across the ridge facing north, with his right flank extended to Chickamauga Valley east of the ridge, thus threatening the enemy's rear on that flank and compelling him to reinforce this also. Thomas, with the Army of the Cumberland, occupied the centre, and was to assault while the enemy was engaged with most of his forces on his two flanks.

To carry out this plan, Sherman was to cross the Tennessee at Brown's

4. For correspondence included in a note to the first edition, see Appendix 1, chapter 42, note 1.

Ferry and move east of Chattanooga to a point opposite the north end of Mission Ridge, and to place his command back of the foot-hills out of sight of the enemy on the ridge. There are two streams called Chickamauga emptying into the Tennessee River east of Chattanooga—North Chickamauga, taking its rise in Tennessee, flowing south, and emptying into the river some seven or eight miles east; while the South Chickamauga, which takes its rise in Georgia, flows northward, and empties into the Tennessee some three or four miles above the town. There were now one hundred and sixteen pontoons in the North Chickamauga River, their presence there being unknown to the enemy.

At night a division was to be marched up to that point, and at two o'clock in the morning moved down with the current, thirty men in each boat. A few were to land east of the mouth of the South Chickamauga, capture the pickets there, and then lay a bridge connecting the two banks of the river. The rest were to land on the south side of the Tennessee, where Missionary Ridge would strike it if prolonged, and a sufficient number of men to man the boats were to push to the north side to ferry over the main body of Sherman's command while those left on the south side intrenched themselves. Thomas was to move out from his lines facing the ridge, leaving enough of Palmer's corps to guard against an attack down the valley. Lookout Valley being of no present value to us, and being untenable by the enemy if we should secure Missionary Ridge, Hooker's orders were changed. His revised orders brought him to Chattanooga by the established route north of the Tennessee. He was then to move out to the right to Rossville.

Hooker's position in Lookout Valley was absolutely essential to us so long as Chattanooga was besieged. It was the key to our line for supplying the army. But it was not essential after the enemy was dispersed from our front, or even after the battle for this purpose was begun. Hooker's orders, therefore, were designed to get his force past Lookout Mountain and Chattanooga Valley, and up to Missionary Ridge. By crossing the north face of Lookout the troops would come into Chattanooga Valley in rear of the line held by the enemy across the valley, and would necessarily force its evacuation. Orders were accordingly given to march by this route. But days before the battle began the advantages as well as the disadvantages of this plan of action were all considered. The passage over the mountain was a difficult one to make in the face of an enemy. It might consume so much time as to lose us the use of the troops engaged in it at other points where they were more wanted. After reaching Chattanooga Valley, the creek of the same name, quite a formidable stream to get an army over, had to be crossed. I was perfectly willing that the enemy should keep Lookout Mountain until we got through with the troops on Missionary Ridge. By marching Hooker to the north side of the river, thence up the stream, and recrossing at the town, he could be got in position at any named time; when in this new position, he would have Chattanooga Creek behind him, and the attack on Missionary Ridge would unquestionably cause the evacuation by the enemy of his line across the valley and on Lookout Mountain. Hooker's order was changed accordingly. As explained elsewhere, the original order had to be reverted to, because of a flood in the river rendering the bridge at Brown's Ferry unsafe for the passage of troops at the exact juncture when it was wanted to bring all the troops together against Missionary Ridge.

The next day after Sherman's arrival I took him, with Generals Thomas and Smith and other officers, to the north side of the river, and showed them the ground over which Sherman had to march, and pointed out generally what he was expected to do.[5] I, as well as the authorities in Washington,

---

5. O. O. Howard's account of Sherman's arrival highlights the mutual affection Grant and Sherman had for each other as well as the differences in their personalities:

> Grant in command was, as everybody then said, habitually reticent. Sherman was never so. Grant meditated on the situation, withholding his opinion till his plan was well matured. Sherman quickly, brilliantly gave you half a dozen. Grant, once speaking of Sherman in cadet phrase, said: "He bones all the time while he is awake; as much on horseback as in camp or at his quarters." It was true. Sherman had remarkable topographical ability. A country that he once saw he could not forget. The cities, the villages, the streams, the mountains, hills, and divides—these were as easily seen by him as human faces, and the features were always on hand for use. It made him ever playing at draughts with his adversary. Let the enemy move and Sherman's move was instant and well chosen.
>
> Grant appeared more inclined to systematize and simplify; bring up sufficient force to outnumber; do unexpected things; take promptly the offensive; follow up a victory. It was a simple, straightforward calculus, which avoided too much complication. It made Grant the man for campaign and battle. Sherman was always at his best in campaign—in general maneuvers—better than in actual battle. His great knowledge of history, his topographical scope, his intense suggestive faculties seemed often to be impaired by the actual conflict. And the reason is plain; such a mind and body as his, full of impulse, full of fire, are more likely to be perturbed by excitement than is the more ironbound constitution of a Grant or a Thomas.
>
> Sherman, patriotic all through, was very self-reliant. He believed in neglecting fractions and was not afraid of responsibility. Grant, probably much influenced by his earliest teachings, relied rather on Providence than

was still in a great state of anxiety for Burnside's safety. Burnside himself, I believe, was the only one who did not share in this anxiety. Nothing could be done for him, however, until Sherman's troops were up. As soon, therefore, as the inspection was over, Sherman started for Bridgeport to hasten matters, rowing a boat himself, I believe, from Kelly's Ferry. Sherman had left Bridgeport the night of the 14th, reached Chattanooga the evening of the 15th, made the above-described inspection on the morning of the 16th, and started back the same evening to hurry up his command, fully appreciating the importance of time.

His march was conducted with as much expedition as the roads and season would admit of. By the 20th he was himself at Brown's Ferry with the head of column, but many of his troops were far behind, and one division (Ewing's) was at Trenton, sent that way to create the impression that Lookout was to be taken from the south. Sherman received his orders at the ferry, and was asked if he could not be ready for the assault the following morning. News had been received that the battle had been commenced at Knoxville.[6] Burnside had been cut off from telegraphic communications.

---

simply on himself; he gathered up the fragments for use, and was also strong to dare, because somehow, without saying so, he struck the blows of a persistent faith.

As I watched the countenances of those two men that evening I gathered hope for our cause. Grant's faculty of gaining the ascendency over his generals without pretension or assumption then appeared. He chose, then he trusted his leaders. They grew great because he did not desert them even in disaster.

Autobiography, 1:474–76.

6. Davis's order to Longstreet to move against Knoxville after the victory at Chickamauga puzzled many. Taking great advantage of the city's natural topography, Union engineer Orlando M. Poe (1832–1885) supervised the strengthening of the city's fortifications—he would later serve as Sherman's chief engineer in the march through Georgia—in a display of great technical accomplishment. For Poe's own account, see "The Defense of Knoxville," *B&L,* 3:731–45. Holding out against the siege, assisted by the strongly loyal civilians in the area, the garrison ultimately thwarted Longstreet's attack on November 29, 1863. On Poe's life, see Paul Taylor, *Orlando M. Poe: Civil War General and Great Lakes Engineer* (Kent, OH: Kent State University Press, 2009).

In his contribution to the *Battles and Leaders* series Edward Porter Alexander describes both the brutality of the fighting and the condition of the Confederate troops after they were ordered to raise the siege and march back to Chattanooga:

We were so badly off for horse-shoes that on the advance to Knoxville we stripped the shoes from all the dead horses, and we killed for the pur-

The President, the Secretary of War, and General Halleck, were in an agony of suspense. My suspense was also great, but more endurable, because I was where I could soon do something to relieve the situation. It was impossible to get Sherman's troops up for the next day. I then asked him if they could not be got up to make the assault on the morning of the 22d, and ordered Thomas to move on that date. But the elements were against us. It rained all the 20th and 21st. The river rose so rapidly that it was difficult to keep the pontoons in place.

General Orlando B. Willcox, a division commander under Burnside, was at this time occupying a position farther up the valley than Knoxville—about Maynardville—and was still in telegraphic communication with the North. A dispatch was received from him saying that he was threatened from the east. The following was sent in reply:

> "If you can communicate with General Burnside, say to him that our attack on Bragg will commence in the morning. If successful, such a move will be made as I think will relieve East Tennessee, if he can hold out. Longstreet passing through our lines to Kentucky need not cause alarm. He would find the country so bare that he would lose his transportation and artillery before reaching Kentucky, and would meet such a force before he got through, that he could not return."

Meantime, Sherman continued his crossing without intermission as fast as his troops could be got up. The crossing had to be effected in full view of the enemy on the top of Lookout Mountain. Once over, however, the troops soon disappeared behind the detached hills on the north side, and would not come to view again, either to watchmen on Lookout Mountain or Missionary Ridge, until they emerged between the hills to strike the bank of the river. But when Sherman's advance reached a point opposite the town

---

pose the wounded and broken-down animals, both our own and those left behind by the enemy. During the siege the river brought down to us a number of dead horses and mules, thrown in within the town. We watched for them, took them out, and got the shoes and nails from their feet. Our men were nearly as badly off as the animals—perhaps worse, as they did not have hoofs. I have myself seen bloody stains on frozen ground, left by the barefooted where our infantry had passed. We of the artillery took the shoes off the drivers and gave them to the cannoneers who had to march.

"Longstreet at Knoxville," *B&L*, 3:750.

Sherman and his generals: (*l. to r.*) Oliver O. Howard, John A. Logan, William B. Hazen, William T. Sherman, Jefferson C. Davis, Henry W. Slocum, Joseph A. Mower. *Library of Congress, Prints and Photographs Division, Civil War Photographs, LC-DIG-cwpbh-03225.*

of Chattanooga, Howard, who, it will be remembered, had been concealed behind the hills on the north side, took up his line of march to join the troops on the south side. His crossing was in full view both from Missionary Ridge and the top of Lookout, and the enemy of course supposed these troops to be Sherman's. This enabled Sherman to get to his assigned position without discovery.

43

Preparations for Battle—Thomas Carries the First Line of the Enemy—Sherman Carries Missionary Ridge—Battle of Lookout Mountain—General Hooker's Fight

On the 20th, when so much was occurring to discourage—rains falling so heavily as to delay the passage of troops over the river at Brown's Ferry and threatening the entire breaking of the bridge; news coming of a battle raging at Knoxville; of Willcox being threatened by a force from the east—a letter was received from Bragg which contained these words: "As there may still be some non-combatants in Chattanooga, I deem it proper to notify you that prudence would dictate their early withdrawal." Of course, I understood that this was a device intended to deceive; but I did not know what the intended deception was. On the 22d, however, a deserter came in who informed me that Bragg was leaving our front, and on that day Buckner's division was sent to reinforce Longstreet at Knoxville, and another division started to follow but was recalled. The object of Bragg's letter, no doubt, was in some way to detain me until Knoxville could be captured, and his troops there be returned to Chattanooga.[1]

---

1. In this case the deserter was apparently honest, but it is the deserter telling false tales of retreat who captures the literary imagination and finds archetypal literary expression in book two of Virgil's *Aeneid*, when the Trojan hero Aeneas recounts for the Carthaginian queen Dido the story of his city's fall. When the walls of the city proved impregnable to the Greeks, the besiegers decided to employ a ruse. They appeared to depart from Troy leaving behind a monstrous wooden horse. Hidden inside were Greek warriors under the command of Odysseus, mastermind of the scheme. While the Trojans debate whether to burn the horse or wheel it into the city, a deserter, Sinon, appears:

> Trembling the miscreant stood, unarm'd and bound;
> He star'd, and roll'd his haggard eyes around,
> Then said: "Alas! what earth remains, what sea
> Is open to receive unhappy me?
> What fate a wretched fugitive attends,
> Scorn'd by my foes, abandon'd by my friends?"
> He said, and sigh'd, and cast a rueful eye:
> Our pity kindles, and our passions die.

Sinon then tells a tale of false accusation and betrayal—"False tears true pity move"—insisting that killing him would only please the Greeks. He explains that the horse is an offering left by the Greeks to appease the offended goddess Athena and should therefore be welcomed into the city:

> With such deceits he gain'd their easy hearts,
> Too prone to credit his perfidious arts.
> What Diomede, nor Thetis' greater son,
> A thousand ships, nor ten years' siege, had done—
> False tears and fawning words the city won.

Virgil's Æneid, trans. Dryden, bk. 2, ll. 85–92, 259–63.

Jean Mignon, *The Trojans Bring the Wooden Horse into Their City*, etching, after Luca Penni, 1535–55. *Metropolitan Museum of Art, Harris Brisbane Dick Fund, 1932.*

    This is the story that the gangster Cody Jarrett (James Cagney), in the 1949 film *White Heat*, directed by Raoul Walsh, invokes to explain to his gang a heist in which they will hide themselves in an empty fuel tanker in order to get inside a chemical plant to steal the payroll:

> And that brings me to a little story Ma used to tell me when I was a kid. A story about a horse. . . . 'Way back there was a whole army tryin' to knock over a place called Troy and gettin' nowhere fast. Couldn't put a dent in the walls. Then one morning the people of Troy wake up and look over the walls—and the army's taken a powder. Men, boats, the works.

During the night of the 21st the rest of the pontoon boats, completed, one hundred and sixteen in all, were carried up to and placed in North Chickamauga. The material for the roadway over these was deposited out of view of the enemy within a few hundred yards of the bank of the Tennessee, where the north end of the bridge was to rest.

Hearing nothing from Burnside, and hearing much of the distress in Washington on his account, I could no longer defer operations for his relief. I determined, therefore, to do on the 23d, with the Army of the Cumberland, what had been intended to be done on the 24th.

The position occupied by the Army of the Cumberland had been made very strong for defence during the months it had been besieged. The line was about a mile from the town, and extended from Citico Creek, a small stream running near the base of Missionary Ridge and emptying into the Tennessee about two miles below the mouth of the South Chickamauga, on the left, to Chattanooga Creek on the right. All commanding points on the line were well fortified and well equipped with artillery. The important elevations within the line had all been carefully fortified and supplied with a proper armament. Among the elevations so fortified was one to the east of the town, named Fort Wood. It owed its importance chiefly to the fact that it lay between the town and Missionary Ridge, where most of the strength of the enemy was. Fort Wood had in it twenty-two pieces of artillery, most of which would reach the nearer points of the enemy's line. On the morning of the 23d Thomas, according to instructions, moved Granger's corps of two divisions, Sheridan and T. J. Wood commanding, to the foot of Fort Wood, and formed them into line as if going on parade, Sheridan on the right, Wood to the left, extending to or near Citico Creek. Palmer, commanding the 14th corps, held that part of our line facing south and south-west. He supported Sheridan with one division (Baird's), while his other division under Johnson remained in the trenches, under arms, ready to be moved to any point. Howard's corps was moved in rear of the centre. The picket lines were within a few hundred yards of each other. At two o'clock in the afternoon all were ready to advance. By this time the clouds had lifted so that the enemy could see from his elevated position all that was going on. The signal

Just one thing they left behind: a big wooden horse. (Licks his lips.) Well, according to Ma . . .

Ivan Goff, *White Heat*, ed. Patrick McGilligan (Madison: University of Wisconsin Press, 1984), 160.

for advance was given by a booming of cannon from Fort Wood and other points on the line. The rebel pickets were soon driven back upon the main guards, which occupied minor and detached heights between the main ridge and our lines. These too were carried before halting, and before the enemy had time to reinforce their advance guards. But it was not without loss on both sides. This movement secured to us a line fully a mile in advance of the one we occupied in the morning, and the one which the enemy had occupied up to this time. The fortifications were rapidly turned to face the other way. During the following night they were made strong. We lost in this preliminary action about eleven hundred killed and wounded, while the enemy probably lost quite as heavily, including the prisoners that were captured. With the exception of the firing of artillery, kept up from Missionary Ridge and Fort Wood until night closed in, this ended the fighting for the first day.

The advantage was greatly on our side now, and if I could only have been assured that Burnside could hold out ten days longer I should have rested more easily. But we were doing the best we could for him and the cause.[2]

By the night of the 23d Sherman's command was in a position to move, though one division (Osterhaus's) had not yet crossed the river at Brown's Ferry. The continuous rise in the Tennessee had rendered it impossible to keep the bridge at that point in condition for troops to cross; but I was determined to move that night even without this division. Orders were sent to Osterhaus accordingly to report to Hooker, if he could not cross by eight o'clock on the morning of the 24th. Because of the break in the bridge, Hooker's orders were again changed, but this time only back to those first given to him.

General W. F. Smith had been assigned to duty as Chief Engineer of the Military Division. To him were given the general direction of moving

---

2. S. H. M. Byers of the 5th Iowa described his feelings on the eve of the Battle of Chattanooga:

> I had lately returned to the Army of the Tennessee, after a very short furlough, from my home in the West. How well I remember it—ten days of furlough out of four years of war! It was the only time in the whole four years that I slept in a bed. We had helped to capture Vicksburg after a hundred days' siege, and felt entitled to a rest. My regiment, the 5th Iowa, had already marched 2000 miles in two years. But Rosecrans was in straits, Sherman was called for, and we made the forced march of four hundred miles from Memphis to Chattanooga without a murmur.

"Sherman's Attack at the Tunnel," *B&L*, 3:712.

troops by the boats from North Chickamauga, laying the bridge after they reached their position, and generally all the duties pertaining to his office of chief engineer. During the night General Morgan L. Smith's division was marched to the point where the pontoons were, and the brigade of Giles A. Smith was selected for the delicate duty of manning the boats and surprising the enemy's pickets on the south bank of the river. During this night also General J. M. Brannan, chief of artillery, moved forty pieces of artillery, belonging to the Army of the Cumberland, and placed them on the north side of the river so as to command the ground opposite, to aid in protecting the approach to the point where the south end of the bridge was to rest. He had to use Sherman's artillery horses for this purpose, Thomas having none.

At two o'clock in the morning, November 24th, Giles A. Smith pushed out from the North Chickamauga with his one hundred and sixteen boats, each loaded with thirty brave and well-armed men. The boats with their precious freight dropped down quietly with the current to avoid attracting the attention of any one who could convey information to the enemy, until arriving near the mouth of South Chickamauga. Here a few boats were landed, the troops debarked, and a rush was made upon the picket guard known to be at that point. The guard were surprised, and twenty of their number captured. The remainder of the troops effected a landing at the point where the bridge was to start, with equally good results. The work of ferrying over Sherman's command from the north side of the Tennessee was at once commenced, using the pontoons for the purpose. A steamer was also brought up from the town to assist. The rest of M. L. Smith's division came first, then the division of John E. Smith. The troops as they landed were put to work intrenching their position. By daylight the two entire divisions were over, and well covered by the works they had built.

The work of laying the bridge, on which to cross the artillery and cavalry, was now begun. The ferrying over the infantry was continued with the steamer and the pontoons, taking the pontoons, however, as fast as they were wanted to put in their place in the bridge. By a little past noon the bridge was completed, as well as one over the South Chickamauga connecting the troops left on that side with their comrades below, and all the infantry and artillery were on the south bank of the Tennessee.

Sherman at once formed his troops for assault on Missionary Ridge. By one o'clock he started with M. L. Smith on his left, keeping nearly the course of Chickamauga River; J. E. Smith next to the right and a little to the rear; and Ewing still farther to the right and also a little to the rear of J. E. Smith's command, in column, ready to deploy to the right if an enemy should come from that direction. A good skirmish line preceded each of these columns. Soon the foot of the hill was reached; the skirmishers pushed directly up, followed closely by their supports. By half-past three Sherman was in possession of the height without having sustained much loss. A brigade from each division was now brought up, and artillery was dragged to the top of the hill by hand.[3] The enemy did not seem to be aware of this movement until the top of the hill was gained. There had been a drizzling rain during the day, and the clouds were so low that Lookout Mountain and the top of Missionary Ridge were obscured from the view of persons in the valley. But now the enemy opened fire upon their assailants, and made several attempts

---

3. Civil War artillery was a dirty, hot, deafening business into which Ambrose Bierce gives insight in his harrowing short story "The Affair at Coulter's Notch." A Union battery is ordered to place a gun in a notch on a hillcrest, where it alone will face a dozen enemy guns:

> Within that defile, barely broad enough for a single gun, were piled the wrecks of no fewer than four. They had noted the silencing of only the last one disabled—there had been a lack of men to replace it quickly with another. The débris lay on both sides of the road; the men had managed to keep an open way between, through which the fifth piece was now firing. The men?—they looked like demons of the pit! All were hatless, all stripped to the waist, their reeking skins black with blotches of powder and spattered with gouts of blood. They worked like madmen, with rammer and cartridge, lever and lanyard. They set their swollen shoulders and bleeding hands against the wheels at each recoil and heaved the heavy gun back to its place. There were no commands; in that awful environment of whooping shot, exploding shells, shrieking fragments of iron, and flying splinters of wood, none could have been heard. Officers, if officers there were, were indistinguishable; all worked together—each while he lasted—governed by the eye. When the gun was sponged, it was loaded; when loaded, aimed and fired. The colonel observed something new to his military experience—something horrible and unnatural: the gun was bleeding at the mouth! In temporary default of water, the man sponging had dipped his sponge into a pool of his comrade's blood. In all this work there was no clashing; the duty of the instant was obvious. When one fell, another, looking a trifle cleaner, seemed to rise from the earth in the dead man's tracks, to fall in his turn.

Tales of Soldiers and Civilians, 115–17.

In *War and Peace* Tolstoy offers another of literature's most memorable depictions of artillerymen in action in his description of the eccentric, unflappable Captain Tushin, the shoeless battery commander, deafened by the firing, who inspires his men amid the carnage and refuses several orders to retreat at the Battle of Schöngrabern.

with their skirmishers to drive them away, but without avail. Later in the day a more determined attack was made, but this, too, failed, and Sherman was left to fortify what he had gained.

Sherman's cavalry took up its line of march soon after the bridge was completed, and by half-past three the whole of it was over both bridges and on its way to strike the enemy's communications at Chickamauga Station. All of Sherman's command was now south of the Tennessee. During the afternoon General Giles A. Smith was severely wounded and carried from the field.

Thomas having done on the 23d what was expected of him on the 24th, there was nothing for him to do this day except to strengthen his position. Howard, however, effected a crossing of Citico Creek and a junction with Sherman, and was directed to report to him. With two or three regiments of his command he moved in the morning along the banks of the Tennessee, and reached the point where the bridge was being laid. He went out on the bridge as far as it was completed from the south end, and saw Sherman superintending the work from the north side and moving himself south as fast as an additional boat was put in and the roadway put upon it. Howard reported to his new chief across the chasm between them, which was now narrow and in a few minutes closed.

While these operations were going on to the east of Chattanooga, Hooker was engaged on the west. He had three divisions: Osterhaus's, of the 15th corps, Army of the Tennessee; Geary's, 12th corps, Army of the Potomac; and Cruft's, 14th corps, Army of the Cumberland. Geary was on the right at Wauhatchie, Cruft at the centre, and Osterhaus near Brown's Ferry. These troops were all west of Lookout Creek. The enemy had the east bank of the creek strongly picketed and intrenched, and three brigades of troops in the rear to reinforce them if attacked. These brigades occupied the summit of the mountain. General Carter L. Stevenson was in command of the whole. Why any troops, except artillery with a small infantry guard, were kept on the mountain-top, I do not see. A hundred men could have held the summit—which is a palisade for more than thirty feet down—against the assault of any number of men from the position Hooker occupied.

The side of Lookout Mountain confronting Hooker's command was rugged, heavily timbered, and full of chasms, making it difficult to advance with troops, even in the absence of an opposing force. Farther up, the ground becomes more even and level, and was in cultivation. On the east side the slope is much more gradual, and a good wagon road, zigzagging up it, connects the town of Chattanooga with the summit.

Early on the morning of the 24th Hooker moved Geary's division, supported by a brigade of Cruft's, up Lookout Creek, to effect a crossing. The remainder of Cruft's division was to seize the bridge over the creek, near the crossing of the railroad. Osterhaus was to move up to the bridge and cross it. The bridge was seized by Gross's brigade after a slight skirmish with the pickets guarding it. This attracted the enemy so that Geary's movement farther up was not observed. A heavy mist obscured him from the view of the troops on the top of the mountain. He crossed the creek almost unobserved, and captured the picket of over forty men on guard near by. He then commenced ascending the mountain directly in his front. By this time the enemy was seen coming down from their camps on the mountain slope, and filing into their rifle-pits to contest the crossing of the bridge. By eleven o'clock the bridge was complete. Osterhaus was up, and after some sharp skirmishing the enemy was driven away with considerable loss in killed and captured.

While the operations at the bridge were progressing, Geary was pushing up the hill over great obstacles, resisted by the enemy directly in his front, and in face of the guns on top of the mountain. The enemy, seeing their left flank and rear menaced, gave way, and were followed by Cruft and Osterhaus. Soon these were up abreast of Geary, and the whole command pushed up the hill, driving the enemy in advance. By noon Geary had gained the open ground on the north slope of the mountain, with his right close up to the base of the upper palisade, but there were strong fortifications in his front. The rest of the command coming up, a line was formed from the base of the upper palisade to the mouth of Chattanooga Creek.

Thomas and I were on the top of Orchard Knob. Hooker's advance now made our line a continuous one. It was in full view, extending from the Tennessee River, where Sherman had crossed, up Chickamauga River to the base of Mission Ridge, over the top of the north end of the ridge to Chattanooga Valley, then along parallel to the ridge a mile or more, across the valley to the mouth of Chattanooga Creek, thence up the slope of Lookout Mountain to the foot of the upper palisade. The day was hazy, so that Hooker's operations were not visible to us except at moments when the clouds would rise. But the sound of his artillery and musketry was heard incessantly. The enemy on his front was partially fortified, but was soon driven out of his works. During the afternoon the clouds, which had so obscured the top of Lookout all day as to hide whatever was going on from the view of those below, settled down and made it so dark where Hooker was as to stop operations for the time. At four o'clock Hooker reported his position as impregnable. By a little after five direct communication was established, and a brigade of troops was sent from Chattanooga to reinforce him. These troops had to cross Chattanooga Creek and met with some opposition, but soon overcame it, and by night the commander, General Carlin, reported to Hooker and was assigned to his left. I now telegraphed to Washington: "The fight to-day progressed favorably. Sherman carried the end of Missionary Ridge, and his right is now at the tunnel, and his left at Chickamauga Creek. Troops from Lookout Valley carried the point of the mountain, and now hold the eastern slope and a point high up. Hooker reports two thousand prisoners taken, besides which a small number have fallen into our hands from Missionary Ridge." The next day the President replied: "Your dispatches as to fighting on Monday and Tuesday are here. Well done. Many thanks to all. Remember Burnside." And Halleck also telegraphed: "I congratulate you on the success thus far of your plans. I fear that Burnside is hard pushed, and that any further delay may prove fatal. I know you will do all in your power to relieve him."[4]

The division of Jefferson C. Davis, Army of the Cumberland, had been sent to the North Chickamauga to guard the pontoons as they were deposited in the river, and to prevent all ingress or egress of citizens. On the night of the 24th his division, having crossed with Sherman, occupied our extreme left from the upper bridge over the plain to the north base of Missionary Ridge. Firing continued to a late hour in the night, but it was not connected with an assault at any point.

---

4. Owing to the fog and haze that Grant describes, the struggle for Lookout Mountain would come to be called the Battle above the Clouds.

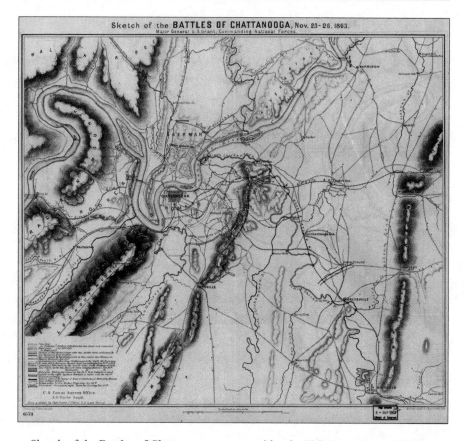

Sketch of the Battles of Chattanooga, prepared by the U.S. Coast Survey Office.
Library of Congress, Geography and Map Division.

Battle of Chattanooga—A Gallant
Charge—Complete Rout of the Enemy—
Pursuit of the Confederates—General
Bragg—Remarks on Chattanooga

At twelve o'clock at night, when all was quiet, I began to give orders for the next day, and sent a dispatch to Willcox to encourage Burnside. Sherman was directed to attack at daylight. Hooker was ordered to move at the same hour, and endeavor to intercept the enemy's retreat if he still remained; if he had gone, then to move directly to Rossville and operate against the left and rear of the force on Missionary Ridge. Thomas was not to move until Hooker had reached Missionary Ridge. As I was with him on Orchard Knob, he would not move without further orders from me.

The morning of the 25th opened clear and bright, and the whole field was in full view from the top of Orchard Knob. It remained so all day. Bragg's headquarters were in full view, and officers—presumably staff officers—could be seen coming and going constantly.

The point of ground which Sherman had carried on the 24th was almost disconnected from the main ridge occupied by the enemy. A low pass, over which there is a wagon road crossing the hill, and near which there is a railroad tunnel, intervenes between the two hills. The problem now was to get to the main ridge. The enemy was fortified on the point; and back farther, where the ground was still higher, was a second fortification commanding the first. Sherman was out as soon as it was light enough to see, and by sunrise his command was in motion. Three brigades held the hill already gained. Morgan L. Smith moved along the east base of Missionary Ridge; Loomis along the west base, supported by two brigades of John E. Smith's division; and Corse with his brigade was between the two, moving directly towards

Missionary Ridge, Chattanooga, Tennessee. *Library of Congress, Prints and Photographs Division, Civil War Photographs, LC-DIG-ppmsca-32821.*

the hill to be captured. The ridge is steep and heavily wooded on the east side, where M. L. Smith's troops were advancing, but cleared and with a more gentle slope on the west side. The troops advanced rapidly and carried the extreme end of the rebel works. Morgan L. Smith advanced to a point which cut the enemy off from the railroad bridge and the means of bringing up supplies by rail from Chickamauga Station, where the main depot was located. The enemy made brave and strenuous efforts to drive our troops from the position we had gained, but without success. The contest lasted for two hours. Corse, a brave and efficient commander, was badly wounded in this assault. Sherman now threatened both Bragg's flank and his stores, and made it necessary for him to weaken other points of his line to strengthen his right. From the position I occupied I could see column after column of Bragg's forces moving against Sherman. Every Confederate gun that could be brought to bear upon the Union forces was concentrated upon him. J. E. Smith, with two brigades, charged up the west side of the ridge to the support of Corse's command, over open ground and in the face of a heavy fire of both artillery and musketry, and reached the very parapet of the enemy. He lay here for a time, but the enemy coming with a heavy force upon his right flank, he was compelled to fall back, followed by the foe. A few hundred yards brought Smith's troops into a wood, where they were speedily reformed, when they charged and drove the attacking party back to his intrenchments.

Seeing the advance, repulse, and second advance of J. E. Smith from the position I occupied, I directed Thomas to send a division to reinforce him. Baird's division was accordingly sent from the right of Orchard Knob. It had to march a considerable distance directly under the eyes of the enemy to reach its position. Bragg at once commenced massing in the same direction. This was what I wanted. But it had now got to be late in the afternoon, and

I had expected before this to see Hooker crossing the ridge in the neighborhood of Rossville and compelling Bragg to mass in that direction also.

The enemy had evacuated Lookout Mountain during the night, as I expected he would. In crossing the valley he burned the bridge over Chattanooga Creek, and did all he could to obstruct the roads behind him. Hooker was off bright and early, with no obstructions in his front but distance and the destruction above named. He was detained four hours crossing Chattanooga Creek, and thus was lost the immediate advantage I expected from his forces. His reaching Bragg's flank and extending across it was to be the signal for Thomas's assault of the ridge. But Sherman's condition was getting so critical that the assault for his relief could not be delayed any longer.

Sheridan's and Wood's divisions had been lying under arms from early morning, ready to move the instant the signal was given. I now directed Thomas to order the charge at once.[1] I watched eagerly to see the effect, and became impatient at last that there was no indication of any charge being made. The centre of the line which was to make the charge was near where Thomas and I stood, but concealed from view by an intervening forest. Turning to Thomas to inquire what caused the delay, I was surprised to see Thomas J. Wood, one of the division commanders who was to make the charge, standing talking to him. I spoke to General Wood, asking him why he did not charge as ordered an hour before. He replied very promptly that this was the first he had heard of it, but that he had been ready all day to move at a moment's notice. I told him to make the charge at once. He was off in a moment, and in an incredibly short time loud cheering was heard, and he and Sheridan were driving the enemy's advance before them towards Missionary Ridge. The Confederates were strongly intrenched on the crest of the ridge in front of us, and had a second line half-way down and another at the base. Our men drove the troops in front of the lower line of rifle-pits so rapidly, and followed them so closely, that rebel and Union troops went over the first line of works almost at the same time. Many rebels were captured and sent to the rear under the fire of their own friends higher up the hill. Those that were not captured retreated, and were pursued. The retreating hordes being between friends and pursuers caused the enemy to fire high to avoid killing their own men. In fact, on that occasion the Union soldier nearest the enemy was in the safest position. Without awaiting further orders or stopping to reform, on our troops went to the second line of works; over

---

1. In this order authority was given for the troops to reform after taking the first line of rifle-pits preparatory to carrying the ridge. [Note to the first edition.]

that and on for the crest—thus effectually carrying out my orders of the 18th
for the battle and of the 24th[2] for this charge.[3]

I watched their progress with intense interest.[4] The fire along the rebel

---

2. For correspondence included in a note to the first edition, see Appendix 1, chapter
44, note 1.

3. Joseph S. Fullerton, who was on Orchard Knob with Grant, Thomas, and the other
commanders, wrote,

> The order of the commanding general had now been fully and most suc-
> cessfully carried out. But it did not go far enough to satisfy these brave men,
> who thought the time had come to finish the battle of Chickamauga. There
> was a halt of but a few minutes, to take breath and to re-form lines; then,
> with a sudden impulse, and without orders, all started up the ridge. Offi-
> cers, catching their spirit, first followed, then led. There was no thought
> of supports or of protecting flanks, though the enemy's line could be seen,
> stretching on either side.
>
> As soon as this movement was seen from Orchard Knob, Grant quickly
> turned to Thomas, who stood by his side, and I heard him say angrily:
> "Thomas, who ordered those men up the ridge?" Thomas replied, in his
> usual slow, quiet manner: "I don't know; I did not." Then, addressing Gen-
> eral Gordon Granger, he said, "Did you order them up, Granger?" "No,"
> said Granger; "they started up without orders. When those fellows get
> started all hell can't stop them." General Grant said something to the effect
> that somebody would suffer if it did not turn out well, and then, turning,
> stoically watched the ridge. He gave no further orders.

Granger then sent Fullerton up to ask Sheridan what exactly was going on:

> As soon as I reached General Wood, Captain Avery got to General Sher-
> idan, and delivered his message. "I didn't order them up," said Sheridan;
> "but we are going to take the ridge!" He then asked Avery for his flask and
> waved it at a group of Confederate officers, standing just in front of Bragg's
> headquarters, with the salutation, "Here's at you!" At once two guns—the
> "Lady Breckinridge" and the "Lady Buckner"—in front of Bragg's head-
> quarters were fired at Sheridan and the group of officers about him. One
> shell struck so near as to throw dirt over Sheridan and Avery. "Ah!" said the
> general, "that is ungenerous; I shall take those guns for that!"

By evening, the field was littered with corpses, the victors seized by "the wildest confusion. . . . Some madly shouted; some wept from very excess of joy; some grotesquely
danced out their delight—even our wounded forgot their pain, to join in the general
hurrah." "The Army of the Cumberland at Chattanooga," *B&L*, 3:725–26.

4. Grant is here describing what came to be known in Civil War lore as the Miracle
of Missionary Ridge. Melville immortalized it in the following stanzas from his poem
"Chattanooga":

line was terrific. Cannon and musket balls filled the air: but the damage done was in small proportion to the ammunition expended. The pursuit continued until the crest was reached, and soon our men were seen climbing over the Confederate barriers at different points in front of both Sheridan's and Wood's divisions. The retreat of the enemy along most of his line was

> A kindling impulse seized the host
>   Inspired by heaven's elastic air;
> Their hearts outran their General's plan,
>   Though Grant commanded there—
>   Grant, who without reserve can dare;
> And, "Well, go on and do your will,"
>   He said, and measured the mountain then:
> So master-riders fling the rein—
>   But you must know your men.
>   . . . .
> From right to left, from left to right
>   They roll the rallying cheer—
> Vie with each other, brother with brother,
>   Who shall the first appear—
>   What color-bearer with colors clear
> In sharp relief, like sky-drawn Grant,
>   Whose cigar must now be near the stump—
> While in solicitude his back
>   Heaps slowly to a hump.

In a note to the poem Melville adds:

Although the month was November, the day was in character an October one—cool, clear, bright, intoxicatingly invigorating; one of those days peculiar to the ripest hours of our American autumn. This weather must have had much to do with the spontaneous enthusiasm which seized the troops—an enthusiasm aided, doubtless, by glad thoughts of the victory of Look-out Mountain won the day previous, and also by the elation attending the capture, after a fierce struggle, of the long ranges of rifle-pits at the mountain's base, where orders for the time should have stopped the advance. But there and then it was that the army took the bit between its teeth, and ran away with the generals to the victory commemorated. General Grant, at Culpepper, a few weeks prior to crossing the Rapidan for the Wilderness, expressed to a visitor his impression of the impulse and the spectacle: Said he: "I never saw any thing like it": language which seems curiously undertoned, considering its application; but from the taciturn Commander it was equivalent to a superlative or hyperbole from the talkative.

Battle-Pieces, 90–92, 249–50 n. j.

Adolph Metzner, Captain Louis von Trebra, Missionary Ridge. *Library of Congress, Prints and Photographs Division, LC-DIG-ppmsca-51285.*

precipitate and the panic so great that Bragg and his officers lost all control over their men. Many were captured, and thousands threw away their arms in their flight.

Sheridan pushed forward until he reached the Chickamauga River at a point above where the enemy crossed. He met some resistance from troops occupying a second hill in rear of Missionary Ridge, probably to cover the retreat of the main body and of the artillery and trains. It was now getting dark, but Sheridan, without halting on that account pushed his men forward up this second hill slowly and without attracting the attention of the men placed to defend it, while he detached to the right and left to surround the position. The enemy discovered the movement before these dispositions were complete, and beat a hasty retreat, leaving artillery, wagon trains, and many prisoners in our hands. To Sheridan's prompt movement the Army of the Cumberland, and the nation, are indebted for the bulk of the capture of prisoners, artillery, and small-arms that day. Except for his prompt pursuit, so much in this way would not have been accomplished.

While the advance up Mission Ridge was going forward, General Thomas with staff, General Gordon Granger, commander of the corps making the assault, and myself and staff occupied Orchard Knob, from which the entire field could be observed.[5] The moment the troops were seen going over the last line of rebel defences, I ordered Granger to join his command, and mounting my horse I rode to the front. General Thomas left about the same time. Sheridan on the extreme right was already in pursuit of the enemy east of the ridge. Wood, who commanded the division to the left of Sheridan, accompanied his men on horseback in the charge, but did not join Sheridan in the pursuit. To the left, in Baird's front where Bragg's troops had massed against Sherman, the resistance was more stubborn and the contest lasted longer. I ordered Granger to follow the enemy with Wood's division, but he was so much excited, and kept up such a roar of musketry in the direction the enemy had taken, that by the time I could stop the firing the enemy had got well out of the way. The enemy confronting Sherman, now seeing everything to their left giving way, fled also. Sherman, however, was not aware of the extent of our success until after nightfall, when he received orders to pursue at daylight in the morning.[6]

---

5. Fullerton notes that it "was impossible to keep a regular line of battle" owing to the steepness of the hill and the broken ground; instead, the men's "movements were in shape like the flight of migratory birds—sometimes in line, sometimes in mass, mostly in V-shaped groups, with the points toward the enemy. At these points the regimental flags were flying, sometimes drooping as the bearers were shot, but never reaching the ground, for other brave hands were there to seize them. Sixty flags were advancing up the hill." "The Army of the Cumberland at Chattanooga," *B&L*, 3:725.

6. At two o'clock in the afternoon Byers's regiment fixed bayonets and joined the attack on the ridge. After crossing a half-mile of open ground, they found themselves subject to murderous fire. As Thomas's troops continued to push ahead, Byers was captured:

> In a moment I reflected that I was a prisoner, and horrible pictures of Libby and Andersonville flashed through my mind—and with them the presentiment of evil I had had the night before the assault. I took a blanket from one of my dead comrades lying near me, and at the point of the bayonet I was hurried on up the mountain, the fire from our own guns constantly increasing. I passed numerous lines of the enemy standing or lying in the rifle-pits with which the whole mountain-side was honeycombed, both in front of Sherman and in front of Thomas. Once I glanced back and to the right. Glorious sight! The troops of Thomas were storming up the slopes of Missionary Ridge. In a hollow, back of the lines, I was mustered with others of my brigade who had been captured. Three of that night's messmates were among them. We were relieved of our watches, our money, our knives, even our pocket-combs, by a chivalrous young officer of the guard. . . .
>
> . . . In five minutes, prisoners and guards, infantry, artillery, and wagons were on the run pell-mell to the rear. Missionary Ridge had been taken.

As soon as Sherman discovered that the enemy had left his front he directed his reserves, Davis's division of the Army of the Cumberland, to push over the pontoon-bridge at the mouth of the Chickamauga, and to move forward to Chickamauga Station. He ordered Howard to move up the stream some two miles to where there was an old bridge, repair it during the night, and follow Davis at four o'clock in the morning. Morgan L. Smith was ordered to reconnoitre the tunnel to see if that was still held. Nothing was found there but dead bodies of men of both armies. The rest of Sherman's command was directed to follow Howard at daylight in the morning to get on to the railroad towards Graysville.

Hooker, as stated, was detained at Chattanooga Creek by the destruction of the bridge at that point. He got his troops over, with the exception of the artillery, by fording the stream at a little after three o'clock. Leaving his artillery to follow when the bridge should be reconstructed, he pushed on with the remainder of his command. At Rossville he came upon the flank of a division of the enemy, which soon commenced a retreat along the ridge. This threw them on Palmer. They could make but little resistance in the position they were caught in, and as many of them as could do so escaped. Many, however, were

---

Byers spent fifteen months in several prisons, including the notorious Libby, in Richmond, Virginia, before he succeeded in escaping at Columbia, South Carolina. He reports that at the time of his escape, only sixteen of the sixty men captured in his regiment, and only two from his company, were still alive. Most of the enlisted men had died in Andersonville. See "Sherman's Attack at the Tunnel," *B&L*, 3:713.

In *Who Would Have Thought It?* (1872) the Mexican American novelist María Amparo Ruiz De Burton suggests the dearth of Southern resources through the following exchange between a civilian and a soldier recently returned from prison in the South:

> "But didn't the rebels give you any other kind of food at all?" again asked Mrs. Cackle.
> "Yes, ma'am, a little. They gave us corn or flour sometimes, and a bit of bacon, or molasses, but not much of anything."
> "The wicked, horrid creatures!" exclaimed Mrs. C.
> "The truth is, ma'am, that they didn't have much to give, and nothing to spare. They complained that we were there eating them up, because we helped to consume the little they had, and so we were starving them. When I was first taken prisoner, they gave me some kind of bread made of oats and corn meal. It was very hard, and I threw mine away, and the reb sentinel taking care of us picked it up and began to eat it. I asked him how could he eat such dry husks, and he said to me, 'When you have been longer in the Confederacy, you will be mighty glad to get such dry husks as these;' and so I would, afterwards. They are all starving down there."

Who Would Have Thought It? (New York: Penguin Classics, 2009), 162.

captured. Hooker's position during the night of the 25th was near Rossville, extending east of the ridge. Palmer was on his left, on the road to Graysville.

During the night I telegraphed to Willcox that Bragg had been defeated, and that immediate relief would be sent to Burnside if he could hold out; to Halleck I sent an announcement of our victory, and informed him that forces would be sent up the valley to relieve Burnside.

Before the battle of Chattanooga opened I had taken measures for the relief of Burnside the moment the way should be clear. Thomas was directed to have the little steamer that had been built at Chattanooga loaded to its capacity with rations and ammunition. Granger's corps was to move by the south bank of the Tennessee River to the mouth of the Holston, and up that to Knoxville accompanied by the boat. In addition to the supplies transported by boat, the men were to carry forty rounds of ammunition in their cartridge-boxes, and four days' rations in haversacks.

In the battle of Chattanooga, troops from the Army of the Potomac, from the Army of the Tennessee, and from the Army of the Cumberland participated. In fact, the accidents growing out of the heavy rains and the sudden rise in the Tennessee River so mingled the troops that the organizations were not kept together, under their respective commanders, during the battle. Hooker, on the right, had Geary's division of the 12th corps, Army of the Potomac; Osterhaus's division of the 15th corps, Army of the Tennessee; and Cruft's division of the Army of the Cumberland. Sherman had three divisions of his own army, Howard's corps from the Army of the Potomac, and Jefferson C. Davis's division of the Army of the Cumberland. There was no jealousy—hardly rivalry. Indeed, I doubt whether officers or men took any note at the time of the fact of this intermingling of commands. All saw a defiant foe surrounding them, and took it for granted that every move was intended to dislodge him, and it made no difference where the troops came from so that the end was accomplished.

The victory at Chattanooga was won against great odds, considering the advantage the enemy had of position, and was accomplished more easily than was expected by reason of Bragg's making several grave mistakes: first, in sending away his ablest corps commander with over twenty thousand troops; second, in sending away a division of troops on the eve of battle; third, in placing so much of a force on the plain in front of his impregnable position.[7]

---

7. By this time the full significance of the Union army's western victories was understood throughout the Confederacy, as Mary Chesnut's diary entry for January 1, 1864, reveals: "Yes, as with Lincoln, they have ceased to carp at him [Grant] as a rough clown, no gentleman, etc. You never hear now of Lincoln's nasty fun; only of his wisdom. Doesn't take much soap and water to wash the hands that the rod of empire sway. They talked of Lincoln's drunkenness, too. Now, since Vicksburg they have not a word to say

It was known that Mr. Jefferson Davis had visited Bragg on Missionary Ridge a short time before my reaching Chattanooga. It was reported and believed that he had come out to reconcile a serious difference between Bragg and Longstreet, and finding this difficult to do, planned the campaign against Knoxville, to be conducted by the latter general. I had known both Bragg and Longstreet before the war, the latter very well. We had been three years at West Point together, and, after my graduation, for a time in the same regiment. Then we served together in the Mexican War. I had known Bragg in Mexico, and met him occasionally subsequently. I could well understand how there might be an irreconcilable difference between them.[8]

---

against Grant's habits. He has the disagreeable habit of not retreating before irresistible veterans." *Diary*, 270.

By the spring of 1864, after Grant had taken command in the East, it was becoming clear to the Confederate cartographer Oscar Hinrichs that Lee, no longer "the man for the times," was unable to respond effectively to Grant's strategy. "Lee seems to be afraid of Grant," he noted, "who seems only fooling and playing with him." Grant, Hinrichs concluded, "is much of the Bull dog and has his tenacity of purpose in fighting us." June 11, June 9, August 20, *Stonewall's Prussian Mapmaker: The Journals of Captain Oscar Hinrichs*, ed. Richard Brady Williams (Chapel Hill: University of North Carolina press, 2014), 135, 134, 158.

Grant would employ a strategy similar to the one Pompey used against Caesar in the Roman civil wars. Pompey, however, was persuaded by those less prudent to change his approach:

> Pompeius . . . thought it was too risky to stake everything on a single engagement against men who were well trained and desperate and against Caesar's famous good luck. It would be more effective and less dangerous to wear them down through lack of supplies, as they were neither in control of productive territory, nor did they have the use of the sea, nor did they possess ships to make a speedy escape. On the basis of this excellent analysis he decided to conduct a war of attrition, and reduce his enemies from victims of hunger to victims of disease. . . . [But many powerful men] urged Pompeius to fight, constantly drawing his attention to Caesar, who kept on forming up his army and offering battle; but from that very fact he drew the lesson for them, that Caesar was forced to do this because of his shortage of supplies, and precisely for this reason it was the right moment for them to do nothing, because Caesar was driven to act by necessity. All the troops protested against his decision . . . and [Pompeius] prepared unwillingly for battle, to his own detriment and that of those who were misleading him.

Appian, *The Civil War*, trans. John Carter (New York: Penguin Classics, 1996), 104–5.

8. Varina Davis writes, "Wherever it was possible, the President went to the battle-field, and was present during the engagement, and at these times he bitterly regretted his executive office, and longed to engage actively in the fight." *Jefferson Davis*, 2:498.

Braxton Bragg, in a presumably less querulous mood, with a postwar sightseeing party, Paint Rock, French Broad River, North Carolina, 1870. Photograph by Rufus Morgan. *Library of Congress, Prints and Photographs Division, LC-DIG-stereo-1s04495.*

Bragg was a remarkably intelligent and well-informed man, professionally and otherwise. He was also thoroughly upright. But he was possessed of an irascible temper, and was naturally disputatious. A man of the highest moral character and the most correct habits, yet in the old army he was in frequent trouble. As a subordinate he was always on the lookout to catch his commanding officer infringing his prerogatives; as a post commander he was equally vigilant to detect the slightest neglect, even of the most trivial order.

I have heard in the old army an anecdote very characteristic of Bragg. On one occasion, when stationed at a post of several companies commanded by a field officer, he was himself commanding one of the companies and at the same time acting as post quartermaster and commissary. He was first lieutenant at the time, but his captain was detached on other duty. As commander of the company he made a requisition upon the quartermaster—himself—for something he wanted. As quartermaster he declined to fill the requisition, and endorsed on the back of it his reasons for so doing. As company commander he responded to this, urging that his requisition called for nothing but what he was entitled to, and that it was the duty of the quartermaster to fill it. As quartermaster he still persisted that he was right. In this condition of affairs Bragg referred the whole matter to the commanding officer of the post. The latter, when he saw the nature of the matter referred, exclaimed: "My God, Mr. Bragg, you have quarrelled with every officer in the army, and now you are quarrelling with yourself!"

Longstreet was an entirely different man. He was brave, honest, intelligent, a very capable soldier, subordinate to his superiors, just and kind to his subordinates, but jealous of his own rights, which he had the courage to maintain. He was never on the lookout to detect a slight, but saw one as soon as anybody when intentionally given.

It may be that Longstreet was not sent to Knoxville for the reason stated, but because Mr. Davis had an exalted opinion of his own military genius, and thought he saw a chance of "killing two birds with one stone." On several occasions during the war he came to the relief of the Union army by means of his *superior military genius.*

I speak advisedly when I say Mr. Davis prided himself on his military capacity. He says so himself, virtually, in his answer to the notice of his nomination to the Confederate presidency. Some of his generals have said so in their writings since the downfall of the Confederacy.

My recollection is that my first orders for the battle of Chattanooga were as fought.[9] Sherman was to get on Missionary Ridge, as he did; Hooker to

---

9. In claiming that everything went according to plan, Grant seemed, at least to some, to be slighting Thomas and his soldiers. The editors of *Battles and Leaders* saw fit to include alternate narratives and rejoinders alongside Grant's article. Baldy Smith, for example, insisted Thomas's "assault on the center before either flank was turned was never seriously contemplated, and was made without plan, without orders." "Comments on General Grant's 'Chattanooga,'" *B&L*, 3:717.

Hooker and Sherman's flanking movements were to take precedence, with Thomas's center, comprising the troops who had run from Chickamauga, in support in the center. "Success had not followed Sherman's movement," Fullerton writes. "The battle as planned had not been won." He continues, "Late on this memorable afternoon there was an accident—an accident like the charge at Balaklava; though, unlike this theme for poetry, it called for greater daring, and was attended by complete success, and yielded most important results, for it led to the complete shattering of the enemy's army, and drove him from the field." *B&L*, 3:724.

Fullerton here alludes to the moment at Balaclava when the Greys, ordered to seize Russian artillery, were mowed down by enfilading fire. Alfred, Lord Tennyson, inspired by a London *Times* editorial that called the charge not an accident but a "hideous blunder," immortalized it in the "The Charge of the Light Brigade." The second stanza alludes to the blunder:

> "Forward, the Light Brigade!"
> Was there a man dismay'd?
> Not tho' the soldier knew
>   Some one had blunder'd:
> Theirs not to make reply,
> Theirs not to reason why,

Private Henry McCollum and fellow soldiers, 78th Pennsylvania Infantry Regiment, posing on Point Lookout, Tennessee. *Library of Congress, Prints and Photographs Division, LC-DIG-ppmsca-31696.*

cross the north end of Lookout Mountain, as he did, sweep across Chattanooga Valley and get across the south end of the ridge near Rossville. When Hooker had secured that position the Army of the Cumberland was to assault in the centre. Before Sherman arrived, however, the order was so changed as that Hooker was directed to come to Chattanooga by the north bank of the Tennessee River. The waters in the river, owing to heavy rains, rose so fast that the bridge at Brown's Ferry could not be maintained in a condition to be used in crossing troops upon it. For this reason Hooker's orders were changed by telegraph back to what they were originally.[10]

> Theirs but to do and die:
> Into the valley of Death
>   Rode the six hundred.

The Poetical Works of Alfred Tennyson (Chicago: National Library Association, 1887), 568.

10. From this point on this volume was written (with the exception of the campaign in the Wilderness, which had been previously written) by General Grant, after his great illness in April, and the present arrangement of the subject-matter was made by him between the 10th and 18th of July, 1885. [Note to the first edition.]

45

The Relief of Knoxville—Headquarters Moved to Nashville—Visiting Knoxville—Cipher Dispatches—Withholding Orders

Chattanooga now being secure to the National troops beyond any doubt, I immediately turned my attention to relieving Knoxville, about the situation of which the President, in particular, was very anxious.[1] Prior to the battles, I had made preparations for sending troops to the relief of Burnside at the very earliest moment after securing Chattanooga. We had there two little steamers which had been built and fitted up from the remains of old boats and put in condition to run. General Thomas was directed to have one of these boats loaded with rations and ammunition and move up the Tennessee River to the mouth of the Holston, keeping the boat all the time abreast of the troops. General Granger, with the 4th corps reinforced to make twenty thousand men, was to start the moment Missionary Ridge was carried, and under no circumstances were the troops to return to their old camps. With the provisions carried, and the little that could be got in the country, it was supposed he could hold out until Longstreet was driven away, after which event East Tennessee would furnish abundance of food for Burnside's army and his own also.

While following the enemy on the 26th, and again on the morning of the 27th, part of the time by the road to Ringgold, I directed Thomas, verbally, not to start Granger until he received further orders from me; advising

---

1. On November 25, Lincoln telegraphed from Washington: "Your dispatches as to fighting on Monday and Tuesday are here. Well done. Many thanks to all. Remember Burnside." *OR*, ser. 1, vol. 31, pt. 3, 25.

him that I was going to the front to more fully see the situation. I was not right sure but that Bragg's troops might be over their stampede by the time they reached Dalton. In that case Bragg might think it well to take the road back to Cleveland, move thence towards Knoxville, and, uniting with Longstreet, make a sudden dash upon Burnside.

When I arrived at Ringgold, however, on the 27th, I saw that the retreat was most earnest. The enemy had been throwing away guns, caissons and small-arms, abandoning provisions, and, altogether, seemed to be moving like a disorganized mob, with the exception of Cleburne's division, which was acting as rear-guard to cover the retreat.[2]

2. Patrick Ronayne Cleburne (1828–1864) emigrated from Ireland to the United States, where he made his home in Arkansas. From colonel of the 15th Arkansas Infantry, he eventually rose to the rank of major general in command of a division. Cleburne's division fought fiercely at Chickamauga and again at Chattanooga. In the face of serious manpower shortages in 1864, Cleburne proposed arming slaves, a recommendation quashed by Jefferson Davis. Later that year, Cleburne was killed at the Battle of Franklin, Tennessee. Irving A. Buck, a captain in Cleburne's division, dismissed the many myths surrounding his commander's death: "There have been numerous sensational and dramatic accounts of Cleburne's death written, the most of them purely fanciful or imaginative, such as his horse being killed just when his fore feet were over the top of the Federal entrenchments, and the General himself falling 'pierced by forty-nine balls.'" Buck then presented the testimony of General Daniel C. Govan, the last to speak with Cleburne:

> General Cleburne seemed to be more despondent than I ever saw him. I was the last one to receive any instructions from him, and as I saluted and bade him good-bye I remarked, "Well, General, there will not be many of us that will get back to Arkansas," and he replied, "Well, Govan, if we are to die, let us die like men." After receiving his final orders we were directed to advance, which was about 2 o'clock in the afternoon. We had to advance across an old open common, subjected to the heavy fire of the Federal forces. We met the enemy in a short space of time and carried the first line commanded by General Wagner. When that line was broken, General Cleburne's object seemed to be to run into the rear line with the fleeing Federals from Wagner's division. About that time General Cleburne's horse was killed. His courier brought him another, and as he was in the act of mounting, this horse was killed. He then disappeared in the smoke of battle, and that was the last time I ever saw him alive. I spoke to his aide-de-camp, Mangum, and told him I was sure the General would be killed, as I did not see how he could escape with his life under such terrific fire, and as he never again appeared in the lines, confirmed my opinion that he was dead. The above is the substance of what I am able to recall after a space of forty odd years.

In another letter Govan saluted Cleburne's heroism in language typical of the age:

When Hooker moved from Rossville toward Ringgold Palmer's division took the road to Graysville, and Sherman moved by the way of Chickamauga Station toward the same point. As soon as I saw the situation at Ringgold I sent a staff officer back to Chattanooga to advise Thomas of the condition of affairs, and direct him by my orders to start Granger at once. Feeling now that the troops were already on the march for the relief of Burnside I was in no hurry to get back, but stayed at Ringgold through the day to prepare for the return of our troops.

Ringgold is in a valley in the mountains, situated between East Chickamauga Creek and Taylor's Ridge, and about twenty miles south-east from Chattanooga. I arrived just as the artillery that Hooker had left behind at Chattanooga Creek got up. His men were attacking Cleburne's division, which had taken a strong position in the adjacent hills so as to cover the retreat of the Confederate army through a narrow gorge which presents itself at that point. Just beyond the gorge the valley is narrow, and the creek so tortuous that it has to be crossed a great many times in the course of the first mile. This attack was unfortunate, and cost us some men unnecessarily. Hooker captured, however, 3 pieces of artillery and 230 prisoners, and 130 rebel dead were left upon the field.

I directed General Hooker to collect the flour and wheat in the neighboring mills for the use of the troops, and then to destroy the mills and all other property that could be of use to the enemy, but not to make any wanton destruction.

At this point Sherman came up, having reached Graysville with his troops, where he found Palmer had preceded him. Palmer had picked up many prisoners and much abandoned property on the route. I went back in the evening to Graysville with Sherman, remained there over night and did not return to Chattanooga until the following night, the 29th. I then

---

General Cleburne then moved forward on foot, waving his cap, and I lost sight of him in the smoke and din of battle, and he must have met his death in a few seconds afterwards. All of this occurred near the intersection of the pike, and his body was found within 20 yards of where I saw him last waving his cap and urging his command forward. Never in any attack during the war did troops display greater gallantry—not Pickett's division at Gettysburg, nor the Old Guard at Waterloo—than when the heroic commander of the Arkansas division fell, sword in hand, near the entrenchments in that desperate and ill-fated attack on Franklin.

Cleburne and His Command (New York: Neale, 1908), 338–41.

found that Thomas had not yet started Granger, thus having lost a full day which I deemed of so much importance in determining the fate of Knoxville. Thomas and Granger were aware that on the 23d of the month Burnside had telegraphed that his supplies would last for ten or twelve days and during that time he could hold out against Longstreet, but if not relieved within the time indicated he would be obliged to surrender or attempt to retreat. To effect a retreat would have been an impossibility. He was already very low in ammunition, and with an army pursuing he would not have been able to gather supplies.

Finding that Granger had not only not started but was very reluctant to go, he having decided for himself that it was a very bad move to make, I sent word to General Sherman of the situation and directed him to march to the relief of Knoxville. I also gave him the problem that we had to solve—that Burnside had now but four to six days supplies left, and that he must be relieved within that time.

Sherman, fortunately, had not started on his return from Graysville, having sent out detachments on the railroad which runs from Dalton to Cleveland and Knoxville to thoroughly destroy that road, and these troops had not yet returned to camp. I was very loath to send Sherman, because his men needed rest after their long march from Memphis and hard fighting at Chattanooga. But I had become satisfied that Burnside would not be rescued if his relief depended upon General Granger's movements.

Sherman had left his camp on the north side of the Tennessee River, near Chattanooga, on the night of the 23d, the men having two days' cooked rations in their haversacks. Expecting to be back in their tents by that time and to be engaged in battle while out, they took with them neither overcoats nor blankets. The weather was already cold, and at night they must have suffered more or less. The two days' rations had already lasted them five days; and they were now to go through a country which had been run over so much by Confederate troops that there was but little probability of finding much food. They did, however, succeed in capturing some flour. They also found a good deal of bran in some of the mills, which the men made up into bread; and in this and other ways they eked out an existence until they could reach Knoxville.[3]

---

3. Sherman kept going, but without a great deal of enthusiasm:

General Wilson and Mr. Dana arrived last night and brought me yours of November 29. I have already crossed the Hiwassee, and am marching for

I was so very anxious that Burnside should get news of the steps being taken for his relief, and thus induce him to hold out a little longer if it became necessary, that I determined to send a message to him. I therefore sent a member of my staff, Colonel J. H. Wilson, to get into Knoxville if he could, report to Burnside the situation fully, and give him all the encouragement possible. Mr. Charles A. Dana was at Chattanooga during the battle, and had been there even before I assumed command. Mr. Dana volunteered to accompany Colonel Wilson, and did accompany him. I put the information of what was being done for the relief of Knoxville into writing, and directed that in some way or other it must be secretly managed so as to have a copy of this fall into the hands of General Longstreet.[4] They made the trip safely; General Longstreet did learn of Sherman's coming in advance of his reaching there, and Burnside was prepared to hold out even for a longer time if it had been necessary.

Burnside had stretched a boom across the Holston River to catch scows and flats as they floated down. On these, by previous arrangements with the loyal people of East Tennessee, were placed flour and corn, with forage and provisions generally, and were thus secured for the use of the Union troops. They also drove cattle into Knoxville by the east side, which was not covered

Loudon and Knoxville. I have sent a messenger down to mouth of Hiwassee to communicate with Granger, but I think I can beat him in moving fast. I will have if possible Burnside hear my guns on the 3d or 4th at furthest.

Recollect that East Tennessee is my horror. That any military man should send a force into East Tennessee puzzles me. Burnside is there and must be relieved, but when relieved I want to get out, and he should come out too.

I think of course its railroad should be absolutely destroyed, its provisions eaten up or carried away, and all troops brought out. Cumberland Gap should be held simply as an outpost of Kentucky, but Burnside must be relieved first and these other things after.

OR, ser. 1, vol. 31, pt. 3, 297.

4. It is useful to remember that Grant is here attempting to outfox a friend he knew well and to whom he had emotional ties forged at West Point, at Jefferson Barracks, and in Mexico. Longstreet offered the following estimation of Grant at the time of his promotion to general-in-chief: "An officer of the Union service had worked his way during three years of severe field service from obscure position with a regiment, to command of armies, and had borne his banners in triumph through battle and siege, over the prejudice of higher officers, until President Lincoln's good judgment told him that Grant was the man for the times . . . assigned as commander over half a million of men, to the surprise of many." *Manassas to Appomattox*, 543.

General James Longstreet, C.S.A.
Library of Congress Prints and Photographs
Division, LC-DIG-cwpbh-04698.

by the enemy; so that when relief arrived Burnside had more provisions on hand than when he had last reported.

Our total loss (not including Burnside's) in all these engagements amounted to 757 killed, 4,529 wounded and 330 missing. We captured 6,142 prisoners—about 50 per cent. more than the enemy reported for their total loss—40 pieces of artillery, 69 artillery carriages and caissons and over 7,000 stands of small-arms. The enemy's loss in arms was probably much greater than here reported, because we picked up a great many that were found abandoned.

I had at Chattanooga, in round numbers, about 60,000 men. Bragg had about half this number, but his position was supposed to be impregnable. It was his own fault that he did not have more men present. He had sent Longstreet away with his corps swelled by reinforcements up to over twenty thousand men, thus reducing his own force more than one-third and depriving himself of the presence of the ablest general of his command. He did this, too, after our troops had opened a line of communication by way of Brown's and Kelly's ferries with Bridgeport, thus securing full rations and supplies of every kind; and also when he knew reinforcements were coming to me. Knoxville was of no earthly use to him while Chattanooga was in our hands. If he should capture Chattanooga, Knoxville with its garrison would have fallen into his hands without a struggle. I have never been able to see the wisdom of this move.

Then, too, after Sherman had arrived, and when Bragg knew that he was

Assault on Fort Sanders,
Knoxville, Tennessee.
*Library of Congress, Prints
and Photographs Division,
LC-DIG-pga-01839.*

Orlando M. Poe and
Orville E. Babcock at Fort
Sanders after the battle,
Knoxville, Tennessee.
*Library of Congress, Prints
and Photographs Division,
Civil War Photographs, LC-
DIG-ppmsca-35175.*

on the north side of the Tennessee River, he sent Buckner's division to reinforce Longstreet. He also started another division a day later, but our attack
having commenced before it reached Knoxville Bragg ordered it back. It had
got so far, however, that it could not return to Chattanooga in time to be of
service there. It is possible this latter blunder may have been made by Bragg
having become confused as to what was going on on our side. Sherman had,
as already stated, crossed to the north side of the Tennessee River at Brown's
Ferry, in full view of Bragg's troops from Lookout Mountain, a few days
before the attack. They then disappeared behind foot hills, and did not come
to the view of the troops on Missionary Ridge until they met their assault.
Bragg knew it was Sherman's troops that had crossed, and, they being so
long out of view, may have supposed that they had gone up the north bank
of the Tennessee River to the relief of Knoxville and that Longstreet was
therefore in danger. But the first great blunder, detaching Longstreet, cannot
be accounted for in any way I know of. If he had captured Chattanooga, East
Tennessee would have fallen without a struggle. It would have been a victory

for us to have got our army away from Chattanooga safely. It was a manifold greater victory to drive away the besieging army; a still greater one to defeat that army in his chosen ground and nearly annihilate it.

The probabilities are that our loss in killed was the heavier, as we were the attacking party. The enemy reported his loss in killed at 361: but as he reported his missing at 4,146, while we held over 6,000 of them as prisoners, and there must have been hundreds if not thousands who deserted, but little reliance can be placed on this report. There was certainly great dissatisfaction with Bragg on the part of the soldiers for his harsh treatment of them, and a disposition to get away if they could. Then, too, Chattanooga, following in the same half year with Gettysburg in the East and Vicksburg in the West, there was much the same feeling in the South at this time that there had been in the North the fall and winter before. If the same license had been allowed the people and press in the South that was allowed in the North, Chattanooga would probably have been the last battle fought for the preservation of the Union.

General William F. Smith's services in these battles had been such that I thought him eminently entitled to promotion. I was aware that he had previously been named by the President for promotion to the grade of major-general, but that the Senate had rejected the nomination. I was not aware of the reasons for this course, and therefore strongly recommended him for a major-generalcy. My recommendation was heeded and the appointment made.

Upon the raising of the siege of Knoxville I, of course, informed the authorities at Washington—the President and Secretary of War—of the fact, which caused great rejoicing there. The President especially was rejoiced that Knoxville had been relieved[5] without further bloodshed. The safety of Burnside's army and the loyal people of East Tennessee had been the subject of much anxiety to the President for several months, during which time he was doing all he could to relieve the situation; sending a new commander[6] with a few thousand troops by the way of Cumberland Gap, and telegraphing me daily, almost hourly, to "remember Burnside," "do something for Burnside," and other appeals of like tenor. He saw no escape for East Tennessee until after our victory at Chattanooga. Even then he was afraid that Burnside might be out of ammunition, in a starving condition, or overpow-

5. For the correspondence included in a note in the first edition, see Appendix 1, chapter 45, note 1.

6. General John G. Foster. [Note to the first edition.]

ered: and his anxiety was still intense until he heard that Longstreet had been driven from the field.

Burnside followed Longstreet only to Strawberry Plains, some twenty miles or more east, and then stopped, believing that Longstreet would leave the State. The latter did not do so, however, but stopped only a short distance farther on and subsisted his army for the entire winter off East Tennessee. Foster now relieved Burnside. Sherman made disposition of his troops along the Tennessee River in accordance with instructions. I left Thomas in command at Chattanooga, and, about the 20th of December, moved my headquarters to Nashville, Tennessee.[7]

---

7. Dodge relates a wonderful tale about an evening on the town with Grant, Sherman, and other officers in December 1863:

> After our return to headquarters, Sherman's first suggestion was that we should go to the theater. We were all dressed in our rough, campaigning clothes, in fact we had nothing else with us, as we had not been able to get any supplies since we left the Mississippi River. That night we went to the theater, paid our way in, and obtained seats in the front row in the balcony. The play of "Hamlet" was upon the boards. You all know what a fine Shakespearean critic Sherman was. The play was simply being butchered—to the great amusement of a theater full of soldiers, who were either coming from leave of absence or going upon one. No one in the audience seemed to recognize us, and we sat there quite a while. Sherman, who was sitting next to me, talked so loudly about the play that everybody could hear him. He said: "Dodge, that is no way to play Hamlet!" and he went on so excitedly that I said to him two or three times, "General, don't talk so loud, some of the boys will discover us, and there will be a scene." But he was so indignant at the butchery of the play that he could not keep still. During the grave-digger's scene, where Hamlet picks up the skull of Yorick and soliloquizes upon it, a soldier in the back part of the audience rose up and hallooed out at the top of his voice. "Say pard, what is it, Yank or Reb?" Of course the whole house came down, and Grant said, "We had better get out of here." We left, and no one knew that the two great soldiers of the age had been listening.

Personal Recollections, 140–41.

Nashville had an active theater scene both before and during the war. The celebrated actor Laura Keene, who was in *Our American Cousin* the night Lincoln was assassinated at Ford's Theatre, had played the New Theatre in October. Dodge seems to have gotten the date wrong: *Hamlet*, starring Edwin Adams, was played on December 21, at the Old Theatre, according to the *Nashville Daily Union*, which also carried a notice for *Macbeth*, starring "the distinguished young tragedian" Adams on December 23. The paper's impression was much more positive than Dodge's: Adams, it declared, "played Macbeth last night to a splendid audience, and deepened the fine impression he

Nashville was the most central point from which to communicate with my entire military division, and also with the authorities at Washington. While remaining at Chattanooga I was liable to have my telegraphic communications cut so as to throw me out of communication with both my command and Washington.

Nothing occurred at Nashville worthy of mention during the winter,[8]

---

had already made as a tragedian, by his happy impersonation of Hamlet. If there were previously any skeptics, there can be none now. All, we opine, will unite in awarding him the praise due to true genius and worth; and in anticipating for him a most brilliant career." Tickets cost 50 cents for the dress circle and 25 cents for the gallery.

Despite his confusion regarding the date, Dodge's memory of the graveyard scene is resonant: the contemplation of skulls was not an unknown activity to that theater audience. John Beatty encountered one on the field at Chickamauga three months after the battle:

> To day we picked up, on the battle-field of Chickamauga, the skull of a man who had been shot in the head. It was smooth, white, and glossy. A little over three months ago this skull was full of life, hope, and ambition. He who carried it into battle had, doubtless, mother, sisters, friends, whose happiness was, to some extent, dependent upon him. They mourn for him now, unless, possibly, they hope still to hear that he is safe and well. Vain hope. Sun, rain, and crows have united in the work of stripping the flesh

The actor Laura Keene. *Library of Congress Prints and Photographs Division, LC-DIG-cwpbh-01959.*

from his bones, and while the greater part of these lay whitening where they fell, the skull has been rolling about the field the sport and plaything, of the winds. This is war, and amid such scenes we are supposed to think of the amount of our salary, and of what the newspapers may say of us.

Citizen-Soldier, 365–66.

8. During this winter the citizens of Jo Davies County, Ill., subscribed for and had a diamond-hilted sword made for General Grant, which was always known as the Chattanooga sword. The scabbard was of gold, and was ornamented with a scroll running nearly its entire length, displaying in engraved letters the names of the battles in which General Grant had participated.

Congress also gave him a vote of thanks for the victories at Chattanooga, and voted him a gold medal for Vicksburg and Chattanooga. All such things are now in the possession of the government at Washington. [Note to the first edition.]

One consequence of having headquarters at Nashville was proximity to Military

so I set myself to the task of having troops in positions from which they could move to advantage, and in collecting all necessary supplies so as to be ready to claim a due share of the enemy's attention upon the appearance of the first good weather in the spring. I expected to retain the command I then had, and prepared myself for the campaign against Atlanta. I also had great hopes of having a campaign made against Mobile from the Gulf. I expected after Atlanta fell to occupy that place permanently, and to cut off Lee's army from the West by way of the road running through Augusta to Atlanta and thence south-west. I was preparing to hold Atlanta with a small garrison, and it was my expectation to push through to Mobile if that city was in our possession: if not, to Savannah; and in this manner to get possession of the only east and west railroad that would then be left to the enemy. But the spring campaign against Mobile was not made.

The Army of the Ohio had been getting supplies over Cumberland Gap until their animals had nearly all starved. I now determined to go myself to see if there was any possible chance of using that route in the spring, and if not to abandon it.[9] Accordingly I left Nashville in the latter part of December by

Governor Andrew Johnson. Dodge offers his impression of the volatile future president, with whom Grant would tangle after the war over Reconstruction policy:

> On our arrival General Grant took us to call upon Andrew Johnson, the Military Governor of Tennessee. We found him in a fine new residence. General Grant excused our appearance by saying we had not had time to change our clothes, and after a short conversation, Governor Johnson opened up with a great tirade against the rebels and how he would treat them. He brought his fist down on the piano with such force that one could have heard it sound all over the house, and declared: "No rebel need hope for mercy from me." We left, all of us rather disgusted, as his tirade was uncalled for, and while I was in command of Middle Tennessee I hardly ever put my hand on a rebel, taking his stock or forage, but Johnson tried to stop it and protect him.

Personal Recollections, 139–40.

9. The Cumberland Gap, a vital natural gateway to the west, has furnished material for song and story for centuries. Bison, Native American tribes, Kentucky-bound settlers under the protection of Daniel Boone have all passed through it—an estimated 300,000 people in the century before the war. The Gap changed hands several times during the Civil War. In June 1862, George W. Morgan took it from Confederate troops under the command of Felix K. Zollicoffer but did not occupy it long. In his report to Stanton, Morgan grandly called the Gap "this American Gibraltar." *OR,* ser. 1, vol. 10, pt. 1, 56.

Its topographical advantages also made it difficult to supply. Morgan was pushed out, but Burnside later repossessed the Gap, and it remained in Union hands for the rest of the war. The traditional Appalachian folksong "Cumberland Gap" chronicles the

rail for Chattanooga. From Chattanooga I took one of the little steamers previously spoken of as having been built there, and, putting my horses aboard,
went up to the junction of the Clinch with the Tennessee. From that point
the railroad had been repaired up to Knoxville and out east to Strawberry
Plains. I went by rail therefore to Knoxville, where I remained for several
days. General John G. Foster was then commanding the Department of the
Ohio. It was an intensely cold winter, the thermometer being down as low
as zero every morning for more than a week while I was at Knoxville and
on my way from there on horseback to Lexington, Kentucky, the first point
where I could reach rail to carry me back to my headquarters at Nashville.

The road over Cumberland Gap, and back of it, was strewn with *débris*
of broken wagons and dead animals, much as I had found it on my first trip
to Chattanooga over Waldron's Ridge. The road had been cut up to as great
a depth as clay could be by mules and wagons, and in that condition frozen;
so that the ride of six days from Strawberry Plains to Lexington over these
holes and knobs in the road was a very cheerless one, and very disagreeable.

I found a great many people at home along that route, both in Tennessee
and Kentucky, and, almost universally, intensely loyal. They would collect in
little places where we would stop of evenings, to see me, generally hearing
of my approach before we arrived. The people naturally expected to see the
commanding general the oldest person in the party. I was then forty-one
years of age, while my medical director was gray-haired and probably twelve
or more years my senior. The crowds would generally swarm around him,
and thus give me an opportunity of quietly dismounting and getting into the
house. It also gave me an opportunity of hearing passing remarks from one
spectator to another about their general. Those remarks were apt to be more
complimentary to the cause than to the appearance of the supposed general,

---

history of the region from Boone's crossing to Morgan's withdrawal before rebel forces
under Bragg in the fall of 1862. The folklorists John A. Lomax and Alan Lomax compiled a version from interviews with local musicians for inclusion in *American Ballads
and Folksongs* (New York: Macmillan, 1934), 274–76. Most variants of the ballad share
this refrain:

> La-a-ay down, boys,
>   Le's take a nap:
> Thar's goin' to be trouble
>   In the Cumberland Gap—

For an account of an early twentieth-century performance, see Horace Kephart, *Our
Southern Highlanders* (New York: Outing, 1913), 82.

owing to his being muffled up, and also owing to the travel-worn condition we were all in after a hard day's ride. I was back in Nashville by the 13th of January, 1864.

When I started on this trip it was necessary for me to have some person along who could turn dispatches into cipher, and who could also read the cipher dispatches which I was liable to receive daily and almost hourly. Under the rules of the War Department at that time, Mr. Stanton had taken entire control of the matter of regulating the telegraph and determining how it should be used, and of saying who, and who alone, should have the ciphers. The operators possessed of the ciphers, as well as the ciphers used, were practically independent of the commanders whom they were serving immediately under, and had to report to the War Department through General [Anson] Stager all the dispatches which they received or forwarded.

I was obliged to leave the telegraphic operator back at Nashville, because that was the point at which all dispatches to me would come, to be forwarded from there. As I have said, it was necessary for me also to have an operator during this inspection who had possession of this cipher to enable me to telegraph to my division and to the War Department without my dispatches being read by all the operators along the line of wires over which they were transmitted. Accordingly I ordered the cipher operator [Samuel H. Beckwith] to turn over the key to Captain Cyrus B. Comstock, of the Corps of Engineers, whom I had selected as a wise and discreet man who certainly could be trusted with the cipher if the operator at my headquarters could.

The operator refused point blank to turn over the key to Captain Comstock as directed by me, stating that his orders from the War Department were not to give it to anybody—the commanding general or any one else. I told him I would see whether he would or not. He said that if he did he would be punished. I told him if he did not he most certainly would be punished. Finally, seeing that punishment was certain if he refused longer to obey my order, and being somewhat remote (even if he was not protected altogether from the consequences of his disobedience to his orders) from the War Department, he yielded. When I returned from Knoxville I found quite a commotion. The operator had been reprimanded very severely and ordered to be relieved. I informed the Secretary of War, or his assistant secretary in charge of the telegraph, Stager, that the man could not be relieved, for he had only obeyed my orders. It was absolutely necessary for me to have the cipher, and the man would most certainly have been punished if he had not delivered it; that they would have to punish me if they punished anybody, or words to that effect.

This was about the only thing approaching a disagreeable difference between the Secretary of War and myself that occurred until the war was over, when we had another little spat. Owing to his natural disposition to assume all power and control in all matters that he had anything whatever to do with, he boldly took command of the armies, and, while issuing no orders on the subject, prohibited any order from me going out of the adjutant-general's office until he had approved it. This was done by directing the adjutant-general to hold any orders that came from me to be issued from the adjutant-general's office until he had examined them and given his approval. He never disturbed himself, either, in examining my orders until it was entirely convenient for him; so that orders which I had prepared would often lie there three or four days before he would sanction them. I remonstrated against this in writing, and the Secretary apologetically restored me to my rightful position of General-in-Chief of the Army. But he soon lapsed again and took control much as before.

After the relief of Knoxville Sherman had proposed to Burnside that he should go with him to drive Longstreet out of Tennessee; but Burnside assured him that with the troops which had been brought by Granger, and which were to be left, he would be amply prepared to dispose of Longstreet without availing himself of this offer. As before stated Sherman's command had left their camps north of the Tennessee, near Chattanooga, with two days' rations in their haversacks, without coats or blankets, and without many wagons, expecting to return to their camps by the end of that time. The weather was now cold and they were suffering, but still they were ready to make the further sacrifice, had it been required, for the good of the cause which had brought them into service. Sherman, having accomplished the object for which he was sent, marched back leisurely to his old camp on the Tennessee River.

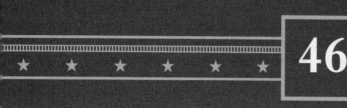

Operations in Mississippi—Longstreet in East Tennessee—Commissioned Lieutenant-General—Commanding the Armies of the United States—First Interview with President Lincoln

Soon after his return from Knoxville I ordered Sherman to distribute his forces from Stevenson to Decatur and thence north to Nashville; Sherman suggested that he be permitted to go back to Mississippi, to the limits of his own department and where most of his army still remained, for the purpose of clearing out what Confederates might still be left on the east bank of the Mississippi River to impede its navigation by our boats. He expected also to have the co-operation of Banks to do the same thing on the west shore. Of course I approved heartily.

About the 10th of January Sherman was back in Memphis, where Hurlbut commanded, and got together his Memphis men, or ordered them collected and sent to Vicksburg. He then went to Vicksburg and out to where McPherson was in command, and had him organize his surplus troops so as to give him about 20,000 men in all.

Sherman knew that General (Bishop) Polk was occupying Meridian with his headquarters, and had two divisions of infantry with a considerable force of cavalry scattered west of him.[1] He determined, therefore, to move directly upon Meridian.

---

1. Leonidas Polk (1806–1864) was a bishop in the Episcopal Church before the war. An 1827 West Point graduate—and a classmate of Jefferson Davis—Polk resigned his commission after only a few months to pursue his spiritual vocation. Known as the

I had sent some 2,500 cavalry under General Sooy Smith to Sherman's department, and they had mostly arrived before Sherman got to Memphis. Hurlbut had 7,000 cavalry, and Sherman ordered him to reinforce Smith so as to give the latter a force of about 7,000 with which to go against Forrest, who was then known to be south-east from Memphis. Smith was ordered to move about the 1st of February.

While Sherman was waiting at Vicksburg for the arrival of Hurlbut with his surplus men, he sent out scouts to ascertain the position and strength of the enemy and to bring back all the information they could gather. When these scouts returned it was through them that he got the information of General Polk's being at Meridian, and of the strength and disposition of his command.

Forrest had about 4,000 cavalry with him, composed of thoroughly well-disciplined men, who under so able a leader were very effective. Smith's command was nearly double that of Forrest, but not equal, man to man, for the lack of a successful experience such as Forrest's men had had. The fact is, troops who have fought a few battles and won, and followed up their victories, improve upon what they were before to an extent that can hardly be counted by percentage. The difference in result is often decisive victory instead of inglorious defeat. This same difference, too, is often due to the way troops are officered, and for the particular kind of warfare which

---

Fighting Bishop, Polk was a zealot of limited martial ability: he made poor strategic decisions, arbitrarily disobeyed orders that did not suit him, and was given to quarrels and intrigue. He was killed during the Atlanta campaign at Pine Mountain, Georgia. The historian Thomas Connelly argues that at the start of the war Polk was indubitably "the most dangerous man in the Army of Tennessee." *Army of the Heartland: The Army of Tennessee, 1861–1862* (Baton Rouge: Louisiana State University Press, 1967), 47.

Despite his obvious shortcomings as a commander, Polk somehow inspired the confidence and affection of his soldiers. In Sam Watkins's account, Polk's death acquires elements of the saintly and miraculous:

> I saw him while the infirmary corps were bringing him off the field. He was as white as a piece of marble, and a most remarkable thing about him was, that not a drop of blood was ever seen to come out of the place through which the cannon ball had passed. My pen and ability is inadequate to the task of doing his memory justice. . . . "Bishop Polk" was ever a favorite with the army, and when any position was to be held, it was known that "Bishop Polk" was there, we knew and felt that "all was well."

Watkins, *"Co. Aytch,"* 133.

Forrest had carried on neither army could present a more effective officer than he was.[2]

---

2. Fighting in North Africa in World War II, the American general Omar Bradley, presented with a division others wanted to send back to the United States for retraining, recognized that the problem was a lack of the "successful experience" that Grant discusses here rather than some inherent deficiency. As a result, he decided to give them a key assignment in battle in Tunisia in 1943. "I wanted that gap for the Thirty-fourth," Bradley later recollected to the journalist A. J. Liebling: "It had its tail between its legs. I said, 'Leave it to me and I'll guarantee that it carries its first important objective, if I have to give it every gun in the Corps.'" Bradley observed that after taking Hill 609, "the Thirty-fourth had its tail over the dashboard. You couldn't hold it." Liebling explained:

> The Thirty-fourth was the division components of which had been so messed around with in the fighting between Sened and Maknassy, while other components had subsequently been set out on hills near Kasserine like goats set out to lure a tiger. Then, when the tiger, in the form of German armor, came, the American armored division that had been cast in the role of big-game hunter lost its nerve and the let the Germans scoop up the infantry goats, along with about 100 of our tanks. The residue of the Thirty-fourth was left with a goat mentality, which it imparted to the replacements. Old Dr. Bradley's psychotherapy fixed it up. Confusion, though normal, is not inevitable.

"For Boots Norgaard," *Mollie and Other War Pieces* (Lincoln: University of Nebraska Press, 2004), 131–32.

Forrest practiced a particular kind of warfare, and the experience of his guerrillas differs markedly from that of more conventional units. Toward the end of *War and Peace* Tolstoy describes the brutality of partisan warfare as conducted between the Russians—civilians and soldiers, some of the latter disguised in enemy uniforms—against the retreating French army of Napoleon:

> Before this irregular warfare was officially recognised by our government many thousands of the enemy's soldiers—straggling, marauding, or foraging parties—had been slain by Cossacks and peasants, who killed these men as instinctively as dogs set upon a stray mad dog. Denis Davydov was the first to feel with his Russian instinct the value of this terrible cudgel which belaboured the French, and asked no questions about the etiquette of the military art; and to him belongs the credit of the first step towards the recognition of this method of warfare. . . .
> The irregulars destroyed the Grand Armée piecemeal. They swept up the fallen leaves that were dropping of themselves from the withered tree, and sometimes they shook the tree itself."

War and Peace, 1303–4.

Sherman got off on the 3d of February and moved out on his expedition, meeting with no opposition whatever until he crossed the Big Black, and with no great deal of opposition after that until he reached Jackson, Mississippi. This latter place he reached on the 6th or 7th, Brandon on the 8th, and Morton on the 9th. Up to this time he moved in two columns to enable him to get a good supply of forage, etc., and expedite the march. Here, however, there were indications of the concentration of Confederate infantry, and he was obliged to keep his army close together. He had no serious engagement; but he met some of the enemy who destroyed a few of his wagons about Decatur, Mississippi, where, by the way, Sherman himself came near being picked up.

He entered Meridian on the 14th of the month, the enemy having retreated toward Demopolis, Alabama. He spent several days in Meridian in thoroughly destroying the railroad to the north and south, and also for the purpose of hearing from Sooy Smith, who he supposed had met Forrest before this time and he hoped had gained a decisive victory because of a superiority of numbers. Hearing nothing of him, however, he started on his return trip to Vicksburg. There he learned that Smith, while waiting for a few of his men who had been ice-bound in the Ohio River, instead of getting off on the 1st as expected, had not left until the 11th. Smith did meet Forrest, but the result was decidedly in Forrest's favor.[3]

Sherman had written a letter to Banks, proposing a co-operative movement with him against Shreveport, subject to my approval. I disapproved of Sherman's going himself, because I had other important work for him to do, but consented that he might send a few troops to the aid of Banks, though their time to remain absent must be limited. We must have them for the spring campaign. The trans-Mississippi movement proved abortive.

My eldest son, who had accompanied me on the Vicksburg campaign and siege, had while there contracted disease, which grew worse, until he had grown so dangerously ill that on the 24th of January I obtained permission to go to St. Louis, where he was staying at the time, to see him, hardly expecting to find him alive on my arrival. While I was permitted to

---

3. Writing from Memphis on December 19, Hurlbut was optimistic: "Forrest is at Jackson; forces estimated about 4,000," he informed Grant. "Grierson moves to-morrow on Purdy and Bolivar, and [W. Sooy] Smith from Columbus on Monday. Forrest must fight or run. Roads dreadful from rain. I think we shall cure Forrest of his ambition to command West Tennessee." Yet on the very same day Sherman wrote to Grant: "I deem General W. Sooy Smith too mistrustful of himself for a leader against Forrest; Mower is the better man for this duty." *OR*, ser. 1, vol. 31, pt. 3, 449, 445.

go, I was not permitted to turn over my command to any one else, but was directed to keep the headquarters with me and to communicate regularly with all parts of my division and with Washington, just as though I had remained at Nashville.

When I obtained this leave I was at Chattanooga, having gone there again to make preparations to have the troops of Thomas in the southern part of Tennessee co-operate with Sherman's movement in Mississippi. I directed Thomas, and Logan who was at Scottsboro, Alabama, to keep up a threatening movement to the south against J. E. Johnston, who had again relieved Bragg, for the purpose of making him keep as many troops as possible there.

I learned through Confederate sources that Johnston had already sent two divisions in the direction of Mobile, presumably to operate against Sherman, and two more divisions to Longstreet in East Tennessee. Seeing that Johnston had depleted in this way, I directed Thomas to send at least ten thousand men, besides [David S.] Stanley's division which was already to the east, into East Tennessee, and notified Schofield, who was now in command in East Tennessee, of this movement of troops into his department and also of the reinforcements Longstreet had received.[4] My object was to drive Longstreet out of East Tennessee as a part of the preparations for my spring campaign.

---

4. John M. Schofield (1831–1906) graduated from West Point in 1853 and served most of his prewar career on the Military Academy faculty. At the outbreak of war in 1861, he was on a leave of absence serving as a professor of physics at Washington University in St. Louis. His wartime service was spent in the Western Theater and on Sherman's march. Later, as the superintendent of West Point, Schofield articulated a powerful, progressive definition of discipline, memorized, if not perhaps always practiced, by generations of cadets:

> The discipline which makes the soldiers of a free country reliable in battle is not to be gained by harsh or tyrannical treatment. On the contrary, such treatment is far more likely to destroy than to make an army. It is possible to impart instruction and to give commands in such a manner and such a tone of voice to inspire in the soldier no feeling but an intense desire to obey, while the opposite manner and tone of voice cannot fail to excite strong resentment and a desire to disobey. The one mode or the other of dealing with subordinates springs from a corresponding spirit in the breast of the commander. He who feels the respect which is due to others cannot fail to inspire in them regard for himself, while he who feels, and hence manifests, disrespect toward others, especially his inferiors, cannot fail to inspire hatred against himself.

Address to the Corps of Cadets, August 11, 1879, *Bugle Notes*.

About this time General Foster, who had been in command of the Department of the Ohio after Burnside until Schofield relieved him,[5] advised me that he thought it would be a good thing to keep Longstreet just where he was; that he was perfectly quiet in East Tennessee, and if he was forced to leave there, his whole well-equipped army would be free to go to any place where it could effect the most for their cause. I thought the advice was good, and, adopting that view, countermanded the orders for pursuit of Longstreet.

On the 12th of February I ordered Thomas to take Dalton and hold it, if possible; and I directed him to move without delay. Finding that he had not moved, on the 17th I urged him again to start, telling him how important it was, that the object of the movement was to co-operate with Sherman, who was moving eastward and might be in danger. Then again on the 21st, he not yet having started, I asked him if he could not start the next day. He finally got off on the 22d or 23d. The enemy fell back from his front without a battle, but took a new position quite as strong and farther to the rear. Thomas reported that he could not go any farther, because it was impossible with his poor teams, nearly starved, to keep up supplies until the railroads were repaired. He soon fell back.

Schofield also had to return for the same reason. He could not carry supplies with him, and Longstreet was between him and the supplies still left in the country. Longstreet, in his retreat, would be moving towards his supplies, while our forces, following, would be receding from theirs. On the 2d of March, however, I learned of Sherman's success, which eased my mind very much. The next day, the 3d, I was ordered to Washington.

The bill restoring the grade of lieutenant-general of the army had passed through Congress and became a law on the 26th of February. My nomination had been sent to the Senate on the 1st of March and confirmed the next day (the 2d). I was ordered to Washington on the 3d to receive my commission, and started the day following that. The commission was handed to me on the 9th. It was delivered to me at the Executive Mansion by President Lincoln in the presence of his Cabinet, my eldest son, those of my staff who were with me and a few other visitors.[6]

---

5. For the correspondence appearing in a note to the first edition, see Appendix 1, chapter 46, note 1.

6. Today, there are approximately fifty lieutenant generals and twelve generals in the U.S. Army. When Grant received his third star, the rank had not been used since George Washington (although Winfield Scott had held the brevet, or temporary, rank of lieutenant general) and had to be revived. Grant and his son Fred stayed at Willard's Hotel

Abraham Lincoln, 1863. Photograph by Alexander Gardner. *Metropolitan Museum of Art, Warner Communications Inc. Purchase Fund, 1976.*

The President in presenting my commission read from a paper—stating, however, as a preliminary, and prior to the delivery of it, that he had drawn that up on paper, knowing my disinclination to speak in public, and handed me a copy in advance so that I might prepare a few lines of reply. The President said:

"General Grant, the nation's appreciation of what you have done, and its reliance upon you for what remains to be done in the existing great struggle, are now presented, with this commission constituting you lieutenant-general in the Army of the United States. With this high honor, devolves upon you, also, a corresponding responsibility. As the country herein trusts you, so, under God, it will sustain you. I scarcely need to add, that, with what I here speak for the nation, goes my own hearty personal concurrence."

To this I replied: "Mr. President, I accept the commission, with gratitude for the high honor conferred. With the aid of the noble armies that have fought in so many fields for our common country, it will be my earnest endeavor not to disappoint your expectations. I feel the full weight of the responsibilities now devolving on me; and I know that if they are met, it will

at 1401 Pennsylvania Avenue. Margaret Leech describes the hotel as the capital's "great meeting place," where important government business was reputed to be transacted and where "a procession of celebrities" dined prodigiously on various delicacies: "Englishmen, themselves no inconsiderable feeders, were appalled by the meals that the American guests, ladies as well as gentlemen, were able to consume." *Reveille in Washington*, 8.

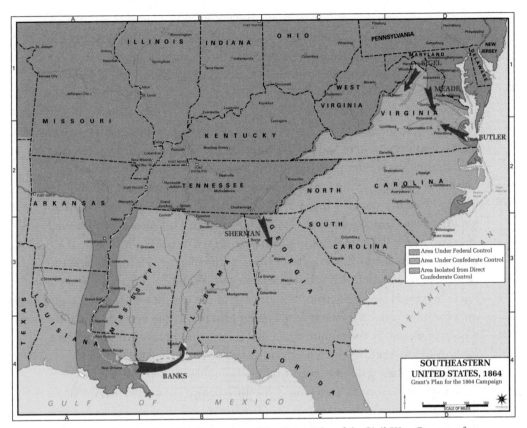

Grant's plan for the 1864 Campaign. *West Point Atlas of the Civil War. Courtesy of Department of History, USMA.*

be due to those armies, and above all, to the favor of that Providence which leads both nations and men."

On the 10th I visited the headquarters of the Army of the Potomac at Brandy Station; then returned to Washington, and pushed west at once to make my arrangements for turning over the commands there and giving general directions for the preparations to be made for the spring campaign.

It had been my intention before this to remain in the West, even if I was made lieutenant-general; but when I got to Washington and saw the situation it was plain that here was the point for the commanding general to be. No one else could, probably, resist the pressure that would be brought to bear upon him to desist from his own plans and pursue others. I determined, therefore, before I started back to have Sherman advanced to my late position, McPherson to Sherman's in command of the department, and Logan to the command of McPherson's corps. These changes were all made on my recommendation and without hesitation. My commission as lieu-tenant-general was given to me on the 9th of March, 1864. On the following day, as already stated, I visited General Meade, commanding the Army of the Potomac, at his headquarters at Brandy Station, north of the Rapidan. I had known General Meade slightly in the Mexican war, but had not met him since until this visit. I was a stranger to most of the Army of the Potomac, I might say to all except the officers of the regular army who had served in the Mexican war. There had been some changes ordered in the organization of that army before my promotion. One was the consolidation of five corps into three, thus throwing some officers of rank out of important commands. Meade evidently thought that I might want to make still one more change not yet ordered. He said to me that I might want an officer who had served with me in the West, mentioning Sherman specially, to take his place. If so, he begged me not to hesitate about making the change. He urged that the work before us was of such vast importance to the whole nation that the feel-ing or wishes of no one person should stand in the way of selecting the right men for all positions. For himself, he would serve to the best of his ability wherever placed. I assured him that I had no thought of substituting any one for him. As to Sherman, he could not be spared from the West.

This incident gave me even a more favorable opinion of Meade than did his great victory at Gettysburg the July before. It is men who wait to be selected, and not those who seek, from whom we may always expect the most efficient service.

Meade's position afterwards proved embarrassing to me if not to him. He was commanding an army and, for nearly a year previous to my taking command of all the armies, was in supreme command of the Army of the Potomac—except from the authorities at Washington. All other general offi-cers occupying similar positions were independent in their commands so far as any one present with them was concerned. I tried to make General Meade's position as nearly as possible what it would have been if I had been in Washington or any other place away from his command. I therefore gave all orders for the movements of the Army of the Potomac to Meade to have them executed. To avoid the necessity of having to give orders direct, I established my headquarters near his, unless there were reasons for locating them elsewhere. This sometimes happened, and I had on occasions to give orders direct to the troops affected.[7] On the 11th I returned to Washington

7. Some historians have judged Grant's decision to leave George G. Meade in com-mand of the Army of the Potomac an awkward solution, but J. F. C. Fuller proposes

and, on the day after, orders were published by the War Department placing me in command of all the armies. I had left Washington the night before to return to my old command in the West and to meet Sherman whom I had telegraphed to join me in Nashville.

Sherman assumed command of the military division of the Mississippi on the 18th of March, and we left Nashville together for Cincinnati. I had Sherman accompany me that far on my way back to Washington so that we could talk over the matters about which I wanted to see him, without losing any more time from my new command than was necessary. The first point which I wished to discuss was particularly about the co-operation of his command with mine when the spring campaign should commence. There were also other and minor points, minor as compared with the great importance of the question to be decided by sanguinary war—the restoration to duty of officers who had been relieved from important commands, namely McClellan, Burnside and Fremont in the East, and Buell, McCook, Negley and Crittenden in the West.

Some time in the winter of 1863–64 I had been invited by the general-in-chief to give my views of the campaign I thought advisable for the command under me—now Sherman's. General J. E. Johnston was defending Atlanta and the interior of Georgia with an army, the largest part of which was stationed at Dalton, about 38 miles south of Chattanooga. Dalton is at the junction of the railroad from Cleveland with the one from Chattanooga to Atlanta.

There could have been no difference of opinion as to the first duty of the armies of the military division of the Mississippi. Johnston's army was the first objective, and that important railroad centre, Atlanta, the second. At the time I wrote General Halleck giving my views of the approaching campaign, and at the time I met General Sherman, it was expected that General Banks would be through with the campaign which he had been ordered upon before

---

that by thus allowing Meade to retain administrative control Grant freed himself to focus on the larger strategic picture. See *Generalship*, 212.

Bruce Catton meanwhile argues, "Grant's Virginia campaign . . . makes sense only when viewed as part of the total picture—for which, it must be remembered, Grant bore the responsibility." Catton continues: "That hard advance from the Rapidan to the James, made at such a frightful cost, and those dreary weeks in the Petersburg trenches that had seemed to be sheer useless waste and tragedy—these had been essential in the grand strategy of the last years of the war. They had compelled the Richmond government to keep facing north while Sherman and Thomas took the Confederacy to pieces behind its back." *Grant and the American Military Tradition*, 124–25.

my appointment to the command of all the armies, and would be ready to co-operate with the armies east of the Mississippi, his part in the programme being to move upon Mobile by land while the navy would close the harbor and assist to the best of its ability.[8] The plan therefore was for Sherman to attack Johnston and destroy his army if possible, to capture Atlanta and hold it, and with his troops and those of Banks to hold a line through to Mobile, or at least to hold Atlanta and command the railroad running east and west, and the troops from one or other of the armies to hold important points on the southern road, the only east and west road that would be left in the possession of the enemy. This would cut the Confederacy in two again, as our gaining possession of the Mississippi River had done before. Banks was not ready in time for the part assigned to him, and circumstances that could not be foreseen determined the campaign which was afterwards made, the success and grandeur of which has resounded throughout all lands.

In regard to restoring officers who had been relieved from important commands to duty again, I left Sherman to look after those who had been removed in the West while I looked out for the rest. I directed, however, that he should make no assignment until I could speak to the Secretary of War about the matter. I shortly after recommended to the Secretary the assignment of General Buell to duty. I received the assurance that duty would be offered to him; and afterwards the Secretary told me that he had offered Buell an assignment and that the latter had declined it, saying that it would be degradation to accept the assignment offered. I understood afterwards that he refused to serve under either Sherman or [E. R. S.] Canby because he had ranked them both. Both graduated before him and ranked him in the old army. Sherman ranked him as a brigadier-general. All of them ranked me in the old army, and Sherman and Buell did as brigadiers. The worst excuse a soldier can make for declining service is that he once ranked the commander he is ordered to report to.

On the 23d of March I was back in Washington, and on the 26th took up my headquarters at Culpeper Court-House, a few miles south of the headquarters of the Army of the Potomac.

Although hailing from Illinois myself, the State of the President, I never met Mr. Lincoln until called to the capital to receive my commission as lieutenant-general. I knew him, however, very well and favorably from the accounts given by officers under me at the West who had known him all

---

8. A note to the first edition directs readers to consult the letter to Banks included in Grant's official report. See Appendix 2.

WPA poster for a centennial reenactment of the Lincoln-Douglas Debate, August 27, 1936, West Chicago, Illinois. Library of Congress, Prints and Photographs Division, WPA Poster Collection, LC-USZC2-5233.

their lives.[9] I had also read the remarkable series of debates between Lincoln and Douglas a few years before, when they were rival candidates for the United States Senate. I was then a resident of Missouri, and by no means a "Lincoln man" in that contest; but I recognized then his great ability.

In my first interview with Mr. Lincoln alone he stated to me that he had never professed to be a military man or to know how campaigns should be conducted, and never wanted to interfere in them: but that procrastination on the part of commanders, and the pressure from the people at the North and Congress, *which was always with him*, forced him into issuing his series of "Military Orders"—one, two, three, etc. He did not know but they were all wrong, and did know that some of them were. All he wanted or had ever wanted was some one who would take the responsibility and act, and call on him for all the assistance needed, pledging himself to use all the power of the

9. Theodore Roosevelt would later make much of the fact that Grant and Lincoln were both men of the West: "In speaking to you, men of the greatest city of the West," Roosevelt began "The Strenuous Life," his speech at Chicago's Hamilton Club on April 10, 1899, "men of the State which gave to the country Lincoln and Grant, men who preëminently and distinctly embody all that is most American in the American character, I wish to preach, not the doctrine of ignoble ease, but the doctrine of the strenuous life." *The Strenuous Life: Essays and Addresses* (New York: Century, 1902), 1.

government in rendering such assistance. Assuring him that I would do the best I could with the means at hand, and avoid as far as possible annoying him or the War Department, our first interview ended.[10]

---

10. In his paraphrase of what he told Lincoln—"Assuring him that I would do the best I could with the means at hand . . ."—Grant echoes an earlier passage on his model Zachary Taylor in chapter 7: "General Taylor was not an officer to trouble the administration much with his demands, but was inclined to do the best he could with the means given him."

Grant and Lincoln developed a very good working relationship, full of mutual respect. Having read the Lincoln-Douglas debates, Grant would have had at least some sense of how the president's mind worked and of his fundamental principles. Horace Porter describes the first encounter between the two men at the White House:

Secretary of State William H. Seward. *Library of Congress, Prints and Photographs Division, Civil War Photographs, LC-DIG-cwpb-04948.*

The President, who was eight inches taller, looked down with beaming countenance upon his guest. . . . In a great crisis of their country's history both had entered the public service from the same State. Both were conspicuous for the possession of that most uncommon of all virtues common sense. Both despised the arts of the demagogue and shrank from posing for effect, or indulging in mock heroics. . . .

. . . The visitors had by this time become so curious to catch a sight of the general that their eagerness knew no bounds and they became altogether unmanageable. Mr. Seward's consummate knowledge of the wiles of diplomacy now came to the rescue and saved the situation. He succeeded in struggling through the crowd with the general until they reached the large East Room, where the people could circulate more freely. This, however, was only a temporary relief. The people by this time had worked themselves up to a state of uncontrollable excitement. The vast throng surged and swayed and crowded until alarm was felt for the safety of the ladies. Cries now arose of "Grant! Grant! Grant!" Then came cheer after cheer. Seward after some persuasion induced the general to stand upon a sofa, thinking the visitors would be satisfied with a view of him and retire; but as soon as they caught sight of him their shouts were renewed, and a rush was made to shake his hand. The President sent word that he and the Secretary of War would await the general's return in one of the small drawing-rooms, but it was

The Secretary of War I had met once before only, but felt that I knew him better.

While commanding in West Tennessee we had occasionally held conversations over the wires, at night, when they were not being otherwise used. He and General Halleck both cautioned me against giving the President my plans of campaign, saying that he was so kind-hearted, so averse to refusing anything asked of him, that some friend would be sure to get from him all he knew. I should have said that in our interview the President told me he did not want to know what I proposed to do. But he submitted a plan of campaign of his own which he wanted me to hear and then do as I pleased about. He brought out a map of Virginia on which he had evidently marked every position occupied by the Federal and Confederate armies up to that time. He pointed out on the map two streams which empty into the Potomac, and suggested that the army might be moved on boats and landed between the mouths of these streams. We would then have the Potomac to bring our supplies, and the tributaries would protect our flanks while we moved out. I listened respectfully, but did not suggest that the same streams would protect Lee's flanks while he was shutting us up.

I did not communicate my plans to the President, nor did I to the Secretary of War or to General Halleck.

March the 26th my headquarters were, as stated, at Culpeper, and the work of preparing for an early campaign commenced.[11]

fully an hour before he was able to make his way there, and then only with the aid of several officers and ushers.

Porter, *Campaigning*, 19–21.

11. After this initial visit to Washington, Grant returned to Nashville, where he told the story of his reception at the White House and shared with the western commanders his first impressions of the Army of the Potomac: "General Grant also told us of his visit to the Army of the Potomac," Dodge writes, "and what a splendid Army it was—how finely equipped and provisioned as compared to our armies. General Sherman naturally asked him in relation to some of the officers of that army whom they mutually knew, and General Grant said in answer to him, that they had said to him (Grant), 'You have not yet met Bobby Lee,' intimating to him their doubts as to his ability to win the same victories there as he had won in the West." *Personal Recollections*, 70.

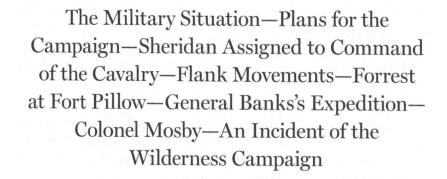

The Military Situation—Plans for the
Campaign—Sheridan Assigned to Command
of the Cavalry—Flank Movements—Forrest
at Fort Pillow—General Banks's Expedition—
Colonel Mosby—An Incident of the
Wilderness Campaign

When I assumed command of all the armies the situation was about this: the Mississippi River was guarded from St. Louis to its mouth; the line of the Arkansas was held, thus giving us all the North-west north of that river. A few points in Louisiana not remote from the river were held by the Federal troops, as was also the mouth of the Rio Grande. East of the Mississippi we held substantially all north of the Memphis and Charleston Railroad as far east as Chattanooga, thence along the line of the Tennessee and Holston rivers, taking in nearly all of the State of Tennessee. West Virginia was in our hands; and that part of old Virginia north of the Rapidan and east of the Blue Ridge we also held. On the sea-coast we had Fortress Monroe[1] and Norfolk in Virginia; Plymouth, Washington and New Berne in North

---

1. Fort Monroe would become Jefferson Davis's prison house for two years. Varina Davis, who eventually came to live with her husband there, claimed that he was subjected to "tortures"—put in leg irons, inadequately fed, kept in filth in a noxious cell—by General Nelson Miles, the Union commander. His treatment, she noted, "led him to the conclusion that it was not the belief that these things were necessary to prevent his escape, but a purpose to inflict physical pain, and perhaps to deprive him of life." In the following description of her first visit to Fort Monroe Varina portrays her husband as an exquisite gentleman whose rarified sensibility is injured as much by the boorishness of his captors as by the physical deprivations of prison life:

Carolina; Beaufort, Folly and Morris islands, Hilton Head, Port Royal and Fort Pulaski in South Carolina and Georgia; Fernandina, St. Augustine, Key West and Pensacola in Florida. The balance of the Southern territory, an empire in extent, was still in the hands of the enemy.[2]

> Through the bars of the inner room I saw Mr. Davis's shrunken form and glassy eyes; his cheek bones stood out like those of a skeleton. Merely crossing the room made his breath come in short gasps, and his voice was scarcely audible.
>
> His room had a rough screen in one corner, a horse-bucket for water, a basin and pitcher that stood on a chair with the back sawn off for a wash-stand, and a hospital towel, a little iron bedstead with a hard mattress, one pillow, and a square wooden table, a wooden-seated chair that had one short leg and rocked from side to side unexpectedly, and a Boston rocker, which had been sent in a few weeks before. His table-cloth was a copy of the New York *Herald* spread on the little table. I was locked in with him and sent the baby home with Frederick.
>
> The bed was so infested with insects as to give a perceptible odor to the room. He knew so little of such things that he could not imagine what annoyed him so at night, and insisted it was some cutaneous affection. His dinner was brought after a while by one of the men, and was good enough, had it not been slopped from one dish to another in the carriage and covered by a gray hospital towel. To a fastidious taste, rendered much more so by illness, this was very offensive. Mrs. Cooper had, however, added oysters to the menu that day, and he ate one and nothing else, but his vitality was so low that even this small amount gave him intense gastric pain. The passing of the three sentinels by the doors and window rendered me, though in strong health, so nervous I could scarcely keep my eyes still.
>
> He was bitter at no earthly creature, but expressed supreme contempt for the petty insults inflicted hourly upon him by General Miles, who, he said, had exhausted his ingenuity to find something more afflicting to visit upon him. Among other things, he told me that General Miles never walked with him on the ramparts, in enforced companionship, without saying something so offensive and irritating as to render the exercise a painful effort.

Jefferson Davis, 2:655, 759–60.

2. When Dodge came east, he found the atmosphere of the Army of the Potomac decidedly less congenial than that of the Army of the Tennessee:

> McPherson had said to us the night before the attack on Kenesaw, when Logan criticized the order as leading us to destruction, "So much the more reason that we should put our energies and hearts into carrying it out, so that it shall not fail on account of our disapproval," that being the only time I ever heard an order even criticised. But I must say I heard it in the Army

Sherman, who had succeeded me in the command of the military division of the Mississippi, commanded all the troops in the territory west of the Alleghanies and north of Natchez, with a large movable force about Chattanooga. His command was subdivided into four departments, but the commanders all reported to Sherman and were subject to his orders. This arrangement, however, insured the better protection of all lines of communication through the acquired territory, for the reason that these different department commanders could act promptly in case of a sudden or unexpected raid within their respective jurisdictions without awaiting the orders of the division commander.

In the East the opposing forces stood in substantially the same relations towards each other as three years before, or when the war began; they were both between the Federal and Confederate capitals. It is true, footholds had been secured by us on the sea-coast, in Virginia and North Carolina, but, beyond that, no substantial advantage had been gained by either side. Battles had been fought of as great severity as had ever been known in war, over ground from the James River and Chickahominy, near Richmond, to Gettysburg and Chambersburg, in Pennsylvania, with indecisive results, sometimes favorable to the National army, sometimes to the Confederate army; but in every instance, I believe, claimed as victories for the South by the Southern press if not by the Southern generals. The Northern press, as a whole, did not discourage these claims; a portion of it always magnified rebel success and belittled ours, while another portion, most sincerely earnest in their desire for the preservation of the Union and the overwhelming success of the Federal armies, would nevertheless generally express dissatisfaction with whatever victories were gained because they were not more complete.[3]

That portion of the Army of the Potomac not engaged in guarding lines of communication was on the northern bank of the Rapidan. The Army of Northern Virginia confronting it on the opposite bank of the same river, was strongly intrenched and commanded by the acknowledged ablest general in

---

of the Potomac, and anything but kindly comments by one commander upon another, and, as this was in the dark days of the war, I had many misgivings about what I heard. Rawlins had won my confidence, and on my return to camp in the evening I used to tell him what I had heard, and he would laugh and say, "General, this is not the old Army of the Tennessee."

Personal Recollections, 77.

3. As Grant notes, the land over which his army would march to victory over the next year had all been fought over before. It was seeded with the dead.

the Confederate army. The country back to the James River is cut up with many streams, generally narrow, deep, and difficult to cross except where bridged. The region is heavily timbered, and the roads narrow, and very bad after the least rain. Such an enemy was not, of course, unprepared with adequate fortifications at convenient intervals all the way back to Richmond, so that when driven from one fortified position they would always have another farther to the rear to fall back into.

To provision an army, campaigning against so formidable a foe through such a country, from wagons alone seemed almost impossible. System and discipline were both essential to its accomplishment.

The Union armies were now divided into nineteen departments, though four of them in the West had been concentrated into a single military division. The Army of the Potomac was a separate command and had no territorial limits. There were thus seventeen distinct commanders. Before this time these various armies had acted separately and independently of each other, giving the enemy an opportunity often of depleting one command, not pressed, to reinforce another more actively engaged. I determined to stop this. To this end I regarded the Army of the Potomac as the centre, and all west to Memphis along the line described as our position at the time, and north of it, the right wing; the Army of the James, under General [Benjamin F.] Butler, as the left wing, and all the troops south, as a force in rear of the enemy. Some of these latter were occupying positions from which they could not render service proportionate to their numerical strength. All such were depleted to the minimum necessary to hold their positions as a guard against blockade runners; where they could not do this their positions were abandoned altogether. In this way ten thousand men were added to the Army of the James from South Carolina alone, with General Gillmore in command.[4] It was not contemplated that General Gillmore should leave his

---

4. Quincy A. Gillmore (1825–1888), West Point class of 1849, served in various assignments with the Army Corps of Engineers. During the Civil War he ultimately rose to command the Department of the South and the 10th Army Corps, in which capacity he executed the reduction of Fort Sumter and the siege and capture of Fort Wagner, in Charleston Harbor, during the summer of 1863. It was at Fort Wagner that the Massachusetts 54th, the war's most celebrated regiment of African American soldiers, lost about half its strength and its colonel, the white abolitionist Robert Gould Shaw, in a frontal assault. The film *Glory* tells the story of the 54th, whose actions helped prove to many skeptics the worth of black soldiers. It is a cruel irony that African American soldiers had to prove their fundamental humanity by demonstrating their capacity for being slaughtered on a battlefield.

department; but as most of his troops were taken, presumably for active service, he asked to accompany them and was permitted to do so. Officers and soldiers on furlough, of whom there were many thousands, were ordered to their proper commands; concentration was the order of the day, and to have it accomplished in time to advance at the earliest moment the roads would permit was the problem.

As a reinforcement to the Army of the Potomac, or to act in support of it, the 9th army corps, over twenty thousand strong, under General Burnside, had been rendezvoused at Annapolis, Maryland. This was an admirable position for such a reinforcement. The corps could be brought at the last moment as a reinforcement to the Army of the Potomac, or it could be thrown on the sea-coast, south of Norfolk, in Virginia or North Carolina, to operate against Richmond from that direction. In fact Burnside and the War Department both thought the 9th corps was intended for such an expedition up to the last moment.

My general plan now was to concentrate all the force possible against

Augustus Saint-Gaudens, Shaw Memorial (detail), Boston, Massachusetts. *Photograph by Elizabeth D. Samet.*

Currier & Ives, "The Gallant Charge of the Fifty Fourth Massachusetts (Colored) Regiment," July 18, 1863, Fort Wagner, South Carolina. *Library of Congress, Prints and Photographs Division, Popular Graphic Arts, LC-DIG-ppmsca-35357.*

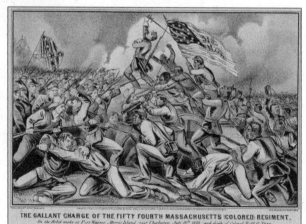

Robert E. Lee trading card, "Great Generals" series, Allen & Ginter Cigarette Brands, Richmond, Virginia, 1888. *Metropolitan Museum of Art, The Jefferson R. Burdick Collection, Gift of Jefferson R. Burdick.*

George R. Crook trading card "Great Generals" series, Allen & Ginter Cigarettes Brands, Richmond, Virginia, 1888. *Metropolitan Museum of Art, The Jefferson R. Burdick Collection, Gift of Jefferson R. Burdick.*

Joseph E. Johnston trading card, "Great Generals" series, Allen & Ginter Cigarette Brands, Richmond, Virginia, 1888. *Metropolitan Museum of Art, The Jefferson R. Burdick Collection, Gift of Jefferson R. Burdick.*

the Confederate armies in the field. There were but two such, as we have seen, east of the Mississippi River and facing north. The Army of Northern Virginia, General Robert E. Lee commanding, was on the south bank of the Rapidan, confronting the Army of the Potomac; the second, under General Joseph E. Johnston, was at Dalton, Georgia, opposed to Sherman who was still at Chattanooga. Beside these main armies the Confederates had to guard the Shenandoah Valley, a great storehouse to feed their armies from, and their line of communications from Richmond to Tennessee. Forrest, a brave and intrepid cavalry general, was in the West with a large force; making a larger command necessary to hold what we had gained in Middle and West Tennessee. We could not abandon any territory north of the line held by the enemy because it would lay the Northern States open to invasion. But as the Army of the Potomac was the principal garrison for the protection of Washington even while it was moving on Lee, so all the forces to the west, and the Army of the James, guarded their special trusts when advancing them from as well as when remaining at them. Better indeed, for they forced the enemy to guard his own lines and resources at a greater distance from ours, and with a greater force. Little expeditions could not so well be sent out to destroy a bridge or tear up a few miles of railroad track, burn a storehouse, or inflict other little annoyances. Accordingly I arranged for a simultaneous movement all along the line. Sherman was to move from Chattanooga, Johnston's army and Atlanta being his objective points.[5] [George] Crook, commanding in West Virginia, was to move from the mouth of the Gauley River with a cavalry force and some artillery, the Virginia and Tennessee Railroad to be his objective. Either the enemy would have to keep a large force to protect their communications, or see them destroyed and a large amount of forage and provision, which they so much needed, fall into our hands. [Franz] Sigel was in command in the Valley of Virginia.[6] He was to advance up the valley, covering the North from an invasion through that channel as well while advancing as by remaining near Harper's Ferry. Every mile he advanced also gave us possession of stores on which Lee relied. Butler was to advance by the James River, having Richmond and Petersburg as his objective.

Before the advance commenced I visited Butler at Fort Monroe. This was the first time I had ever met him.[7] Before giving him any order as to the

---

5. For the correspondence appearing in a note to the first edition, see Appendix 1, chapter 47, note 1.

6. Like Peter J. Osterhaus and Carl Schurz, Franz Sigel (1824–1902) was a German refugee from the failed revolution of 1848. Sigel was an effective recruiter but a poor soldier, as the following chapter documents.

7. "Beast," Benjamin F. Butler's nickname, suggests something of the controversy he stirred up over the course of his Civil War service. A volunteer general from Massachusetts without military experience, Butler earned this sobriquet in 1862, in command of the occupying force of New Orleans, where he responded vigorously and sternly to a virulently hostile population—even hanging a citizen named Mumford for tearing up the national flag. Almost as provocative in certain quarters of a Southern city preoccupied with honor, was his General Order No. 28, issued on May 15, 1862: "As the officers and soldiers of the United States have been subject to repeated insults from the women (calling themselves ladies) of New Orleans, in return for the most scrupulous non-interference and courtesy on our part, it is ordered that hereafter when any female shall, by word, gesture, or movement, insult or show contempt for any officer or soldier of the United States, she shall be regarded and held liable to be treated as a woman of the town plying her avocation." A politically influential Democrat, Butler was allowed to muddle through several commands before Grant was finally able to relieve him without fear of political backlash toward the end of the war. About the Mumford affair, Butler writes in his self-serving apologia: "It was said that Butler would never dare hang him . . . and that if he was executed Butler should die the death by any and every possible

part he was to play in the approaching campaign I invited his views. They were very much such as I intended to direct, and as I did direct,[8] in writing, before leaving.

General W. F. Smith, who had been promoted to the rank of major-general shortly after the battle of Chattanooga on my recommendation, had not yet been confirmed. I found a decided prejudice against his confirmation by a majority of the Senate, but I insisted that his services had been such that he should be rewarded. My wishes were now reluctantly

means." Despite many threats to his life, Butler persisted. His narrative reveals a rather sadistic delight:

> [I]t was agreed that I should be notified by anonymous letters, and accordingly they sent me forty or fifty the next morning, in almost every language and every degree of literature, accompanied by illustrations of pistols and coffins and cross-bones and skulls, to intimidate me.
>
> Indeed, their performances frightened one man besides myself. He was my secret service man, who had attended the meeting and made a speech in behalf of my being shot. He was rather unmerciful. He returned from the gathering about ten o'clock at night, and told me what had taken place and said that I was in the utmost danger if I had Mumford executed. I told him that was where we differed; I thought I should be in the utmost danger if I did not have him executed, for the question was now to be determined whether I commanded that city or whether the mob commanded it. . . .
>
> On the afternoon of the next day I got a note saying that Mrs. Mumford and her children wished me to see them. . . . Mrs. Mumford in a proper way began to intercede for her husband and the father of her children. She wept bitterly, as did the children, who fell about my knees, adding all those moving acts which perhaps they had been instructed to say and do, or which perhaps naturally came to them. I was obliged to answer their mother that I wished it could be permitted to my sense of duty to reprieve her husband, but that it could not be. . . .
>
> "I hear Mumford believes he will not be executed," I said, "and I am told he is making no preparations for his death. Now, I think the greatest kindness you can do him is to let me ring for my carriage and send you to the jail. I will give an order for your admission to his room, or that you and your family may meet him in any room in the jail that will be most convenient for you. I wish you to convince him that he is mistaken and that he will be executed. Whether I live or die he will die; and let him in the few hours he has to live look to his God for pardon."

Butler's Book: Autobiography and Personal Reminiscences of Major-General Benjamin F. Butler (Boston: A. M. Thayer, 1892), 418, 439–40.

8. A note to the first edition directs readers to consult the instructions to Butler included in Grant's official report. See Appendix 2.

complied with, and I assigned him to the command of one of the corps under General Butler. I was not long in finding out that the objections to Smith's promotion were well founded.

In one of my early interviews with the President I expressed my dissatisfaction with the little that had been accomplished by the cavalry so far in the war, and the belief that it was capable of accomplishing much more than it had done if under a thorough leader. I said I wanted the very best man in the army for that command. Halleck was present and spoke up, saying: "How would Sheridan do?" I replied: "The very man I want." The President said I could have anybody I wanted. Sheridan was telegraphed for that day, and on his arrival was assigned to the command of the cavalry corps with the Army of the Potomac. This relieved General Alfred Pleasonton. It was not a reflection on that officer, however, for I did not know but that he had been as efficient as any other cavalry commander.

Banks in the Department of the Gulf was ordered to assemble all the troops he had at New Orleans in time to join in the general move, Mobile to be his objective.

At this time I was not entirely decided as to whether I should move the Army of the Potomac by the right flank of the enemy, or by his left. Each plan presented advantages.[9] If by his right—my left—the Potomac, Chesapeake Bay and tributaries would furnish us an easy line over which to bring all supplies to within easy hauling distance of every position the army could occupy from the Rapidan to the James River. But Lee could, if he chose, detach or move his whole army north on a line rather interior to the one I would have to take in following. A movement by his left—our right—would obviate this; but all that was done would have to be done with the supplies and ammunition we started with. All idea of adopting this latter plan was abandoned when the limited quantity of supplies possible to take with us was considered. The country over which we would have to pass was so exhausted of all food or forage that we would be obliged to carry everything with us.

While these preparations were going on the enemy was not entirely idle. In the West Forrest made a raid in West Tennessee up to the northern border, capturing the garrison of four or five hundred men at Union City, and followed it up by an attack on Paducah, Kentucky, on the banks of the Ohio. While he was able to enter the city he failed to capture the forts or any part of the garrison. On the first intelligence of Forrest's raid I telegraphed

9. For the correspondence appearing in a note to the first edition, see Appendix 1, chapter 47, note 2.

Sherman to send all his cavalry against him, and not to let him get out of the trap he had put himself into. Sherman had anticipated me by sending troops against him before he got my order.

Forrest, however, fell back rapidly, and attacked the troops at Fort Pillow, a station for the protection of the navigation of the Mississippi River. The garrison consisted of a regiment of colored troops, infantry, and a detachment of Tennessee cavalry. These troops fought bravely, but were overpowered. I will leave Forrest in his dispatches to tell what he did with them.

"The river was dyed," he says, "with the blood of the slaughtered for two hundred yards. The approximate loss was upward of five hundred killed, but few of the officers escaping. My loss was about twenty killed. It is hoped that these facts will demonstrate to the Northern people that negro soldiers cannot cope with Southerners." Subsequently Forrest made a report in which he left out the part which shocks humanity to read.[10]

---

10. This quotation comes from Forrest's initial report:

> Arrived there [Fort Pillow] on the morning of the 12th and attacked the place with a portion of McCulloch's and Bell's brigades, numbering about 1,500 men, and after a sharp contest captured the garrison and all of its stores. A demand was made for the surrender, which was refused. The victory was complete, and the loss of the enemy will never be known from the fact that large numbers ran into the river and were shot and drowned. The force was composed of about 500 negroes and 200 white soldiers (Tennessee Tories). The river was dyed with the blood of the slaughtered for 200 yards. There was in the fort a large number of citizens who had fled there to escape the conscript law. Most of these ran into the river and were drowned. The approximate loss was upward of 500 killed, but few of the officers escaping.
>
> It is hoped that these facts will demonstrate to the Northern people that negro soldiers cannot cope with Southerners. We still hold the fort.

OR, ser. 1, vol. 32, pt. 1, 610.

One rebel soldier present at Pillow, Sergeant Achilles Clark of the 20th Tennessee Cavalry, C.S.A., likened the fort to an abattoir slicked with blood and brains. He claimed the killing continued until the Confederates became sickened by their own butchery. For Clark's letter and a documentary history of the incident, see "Fort Pillow Revisited: New Evidence about an Old Controversy," ed. John Cimprich and Robert C. Mainfort Jr., *Civil War History* 28.4 (December 1982): 297–99. Southern apologists would continue to dismiss the charge of atrocity as Yankee propaganda. Varina Davis, for instance, called it a "so-called massacre." See *Jefferson Davis*, 2:485.

The *Richmond Dispatch* refuted the charges in several articles, perhaps none so revealing as "Remember Fort Pillow," which was prompted by the tragic assault on the Crater at Petersburg, in which African American troops were once again slaughtered together with their white comrades. The article contains essential ingredients of what would become the Lost Cause myth after the war:

> The poor deluded negroes—deluded by the unscrupulous and brutal Yankees with cunning lies and bad whiskey—entered the breach in the Confederate works near Petersburg, on Saturday, with the cry of "Remember Fort Pillow! No quarter!" To reasonable and reflecting minds, the scene and the circumstances afford abundant cause of the most unutterable disgust for the Yankee character; utterly dissolute, as it is, of every sentiment of honor or humanity. With the odds of three or four to one against the South . . . the Yankees have, besides, enlisted the slaves of the South to fight against their masters; and they endeavor to fill the hearts of these confiding poor creatures with vindictive rage and thirst for revenge against their people, their masters, who have ever treated them with kindness and humanity. Now, they do this by the most extravagant falsehoods concerning the conduct of our men, under Forrest, at Fort Pillow. Thus exciting those ill-fated blacks (whom they have robbed of homes such as they never can give them,) with imaginary wrongs and outrages, and making them drunk with liquor, they hound them on to the attack of the Southern soldiers—to attack the men commanded by Robert E. Lee, the soldier without reproach, and the Christian gentleman without stain and without dishonor. In the whole history of this war not one act of unnecessary harshness even can be charged to this peerless commander.—His humanity is overflowing, and his desire to spare the effusion of blood has lost him many advantages which he permitted, for that sentiment, unavailed to pass by. He governs an army of heroes—a braver or more chivalrous body of men were never ranged in line of battle. Against such a chieftain and such high-spirited veterans these unprincipled and heartless Yankees send forward their black regiments with the savage cry of "Remember Fort Pillow! No Quarter!"

Richmond Dispatch, August 2, 1864, p. 2.

"The War in Tennessee—Rebel Massacre of the Union Troops after the Surrender of Fort Pillow, April 12," *Frank Leslie's Illustrated Newspaper*, May 7, 1864. *Library of Congress, Prints and Photographs Division, LC-DIG-ds-07662.*

Long before the events at Fort Pillow, black soldiers of the Massachusetts 54th were desperate not to allow their comrades to be taken prisoner at Fort Wagner because they

At the East, also, the rebels were busy. I had said to Halleck that Plymouth and Washington, North Carolina, were unnecessary to hold. It would be better to have the garrisons engaged there added to Butler's command. If success attended our arms, both places, and others too, would fall into our hands naturally. These places had been occupied by Federal troops before I took command of the armies, and I knew that the Executive would be reluctant to abandon them, and therefore explained my views; but before my views were carried out the rebels captured the garrison at Plymouth. I then ordered the abandonment of Washington, but directed the holding of New Berne at all hazards. This was essential because New Berne was a port into which blockade runners could enter.

General Banks had gone on an expedition up the Red River long before my promotion to general command. I had opposed the movement strenuously, but acquiesced because it was the order of my superior at the time. By direction of Halleck I had reinforced Banks with a corps of about ten thousand men from Sherman's command. This reinforcement was wanted back badly before the forward movement commenced. But Banks had got so far that it seemed best that he should take Shreveport on the Red River, and turn over the line of that river to Steele, who commanded in Arkansas, to hold instead of the line of the Arkansas. Orders were given accordingly, and with the expectation that the campaign would be ended in time for Banks to return A. J. Smith's command to where it belonged and get back to New Orleans himself in time to execute his part in the general plan. But the expedition was a failure.[11] Banks did not get back in time to take part in the

knew the fate that likely awaited them in Confederate hands. See Luis F. Emilio, *A Brave Black Regiment* (New York: Da Capo, 1995), 103. See also Higginson, *Army Life in a Black Regiment*.

11. The joint expedition up Louisiana's Red River in March 1864, sponsored by the administration as a way to strengthen the Unionist state government then being formed by Nathaniel Banks—the cotton bales also provided an incentive—yet only reluctantly supported by Grant and Sherman, who were more interested in moving against Mobile, failed utterly. See McPherson, *War on the Waters*, 192.

The campaign was doomed by many things, among them the incompetence of Banks and the hubris of Admiral David Porter. Confederate commander Richard Taylor, the son of Zachary Taylor, repeatedly engaged federal troops, whom Banks had led too far from the river to benefit from naval support. The most significant engagement took place near Mansfield on April 8. Taylor's account of the battle concludes: "With a much smaller force on the field, we invariably outnumbered the enemy at the fighting point; and foreseeing the possibility of this, I was justified in my confidence of success. The defeat of the Federal army was largely due to the ignorance and arrogance of its com-programme as laid down. Nor was Smith returned until long after the movements of May, 1864, had been begun. The services of forty thousand veteran troops, over and above the number required to hold all that was necessary

mander, General Banks, who attributed my long retreat to his own wonderful strategy." Banks's troops did manage to hold the Confederates off at Pleasant Hill the following day, but Taylor had insufficient support from his commander, Kirby Smith, who was preoccupied with safeguarding Shreveport and distracted by the reported advance of Union troops from Arkansas. With the river rise lower than usual, the Union fleet was in immediate danger of being stranded. Taylor seethes with contempt for Kirby Smith:

> Granted that he was alarmed for Shreveport, sacred to him and his huge staff as Benares, dwelling-place of many gods, to the Hindoo. . . . To pursue a retreating foe, numbering six thousand men, he took over seven thousand infantry, and left me twelve hundred to operate against twenty odd thousand and a powerful fleet. From the evening of the 21st of April, when I returned to the front near Grand Ecore, to the 13th of May the day on which Porter and Banks escaped from Alexandria, I kept him advised of the enemy's movements and condition. Couriers and staff officers were sent to implore him to return and reap the fruits of Mansfield and Pleasant Hill, whose price had been paid in blood. Not a man was sent me . . . . From first to last, General Kirby Smith seemed determined to throw a protecting shield around the Federal army and fleet.

Taylor excoriates Smith by means of a hyperbolic comparison: "In all the ages since the establishment of the Assyrian monarchy no commander has possessed equal power to destroy a cause." Richard Taylor, *Destruction and Reconstruction: Personal Experiences of the Late War* (New York: D. Appleton, 1879), 164, 188–89.

Perhaps the only real positive on either side was the ingenious engineering of Lieutenant Colonel Joseph Bailey, who in the nick of time found a way to get Porter's gunboats over the rapids at Alexandria by building a complex of dams. Twentieth-century photos reveal the remnants of Bailey's original structure.

Remnants of Bailey's Dam still visible a century after it was built, Red River, Alexandria, Rapides Parish, Louisiana. *Library of Congress, Prints and Photographs Division, HAER LA-6.*

in the Department of the Gulf, were thus paralyzed. It is but just to Banks, however, to say that his expedition was ordered from Washington and he was in no way responsible except for the conduct of it. I make no criticism on this point. He opposed the expedition.[12]

By the 27th of April spring had so far advanced as to justify me in fixing a day for the great move. On that day Burnside left Annapolis to occupy Meade's position between Bull Run and the Rappahannock. Meade was notified and directed to bring his troops forward to his advance. On the following day Butler was notified of my intended advance on the 4th of May, and he was directed to move the night of the same day and get as far up the James River as possible by daylight, and push on from there to accomplish the task given him. He was also notified that reinforcements were being collected in Washington City, which would be forwarded to him should the enemy fall back into the trenches at Richmond. The same day Sherman was directed to get his forces up ready to advance on the 5th. Sigel was in Winchester and was notified to move in conjunction with the others.

The criticism has been made by writers on the campaign from the Rapidan to the James River that all the loss of life could have been obviated by moving the army there on transports. Richmond was fortified and intrenched so perfectly that one man inside to defend was more than equal to five outside besieging or assaulting. To get possession of Lee's army was the first great object. With the capture of his army Richmond would necessarily follow. It was better to fight him outside of his stronghold than in it. If the Army of the Potomac had been moved bodily to the James River by water Lee could have moved a part of his forces back to Richmond, called Beauregard from the south to reinforce it, and with the balance moved on to Washington. Then, too, I ordered a move, simultaneous with that of the Army of the Potomac, up the James River by a formidable army already collected at the mouth of the river.

While my headquarters were at Culpeper, from the 26th of March to

---

12. In a passage suggestive of the tension and infighting that textured everyday life for Civil War commanders, David Porter wrote less diplomatically of his counterpart: "Most of the civilians who undertook the command of armies were wise enough to select a capable soldier as chief-of-staff and surrounded themselves with as much military talent as possible; but Banks having previously succeeded in all that he had undertaken, having been a popular Governor and Speaker of the House of Representatives, thought himself equal in military abilities to any army officer; and although in every operation of consequence undertaken by him he failed of success, yet he assumed as much as Caesar did after he had conquered the world." *Naval History*, 536.

Colonel John S. Mosby. C.S.A. *Library of Congress, Prints and Photographs Division, Civil War Photographs, LC-DIG-cwpbh-03240.*

the 4th of May, I generally visited Washington once a week to confer with the Secretary of War and President. On the last occasion, a few days before moving, a circumstance occurred which came near postponing my part in the campaign altogether. Colonel John S. Mosby had for a long time been commanding a partisan corps, or regiment, which operated in the rear of the Army of the Potomac. On my return to the field on this occasion, as the train approached Warrenton Junction, a heavy cloud of dust was seen to the east of the road as if made by a body of cavalry on a charge. Arriving at the junction the train was stopped and inquiries made as to the cause of the dust. There was but one man at the station, and he informed us that Mosby had crossed a few minutes before at full speed in pursuit of Federal cavalry. Had he seen our train coming, no doubt he would have let his prisoners escape to capture the train. I was on a special train, if I remember correctly, without any guard.

Since the close of the war I have come to know Colonel Mosby personally, and somewhat intimately. He is a different man entirely from what I had supposed. He is slender, not tall, wiry, and looks as if he could endure any amount of physical exercise. He is able, and thoroughly honest and truthful. There were probably but few men in the South who could have commanded successfully a separate detachment in the rear of an opposing army, and so near the border of hostilities, as long as he did without losing his entire command.[13]

On this same visit to Washington I had my last interview with the President before reaching the James River. He had of course become acquainted with the fact that a general movement had been ordered all along the line, and seemed to think it a new feature in war. I explained to him that it was necessary to have a great number of troops to guard and hold the territory we had captured, and to prevent incursions into the Northern States. These troops could perform this service just as well by advancing as by remaining

---

13. John S. Mosby (1833–1913), known as the "Gray Ghost," was himself the author of two Civil War memoirs, *Mosby's War Reminiscences and Stuart's Cavalry Campaigns* and *The Memoirs of Colonel John S. Mosby*. The first, as Edmund Wilson notes in his monumental study of Civil War literature, *Patriotic Gore*, "reads almost like the imaginary adventures of some character of the Conan Doyle era," while the latter offers a rich portrait of an effective soldier and a window onto a mind that revealed a Jeffersonian "ideal of education" realized "in unpredictable ways." *Patriotic Gore* (1962; New York: Norton, 1994), 307–8.

Mosby fascinated North and South. Walt Whitman included a story of Mosby's savage attack on a federal ambulance train in *Specimen Days* (1882), while the energetic John Esten Cooke noted the ways in which legend tended to eclipse the truth about Mosby:

> I was reading the other day a work entitled "Jack Mosby, the Guerilla," by a certain "Lieutenant-Colonel ——," of the United States Army. The book is exceedingly sanguinary. Colonel Mosby is therein represented as a tall, powerful, black-bearded, cruel, and remorseless brigand of the Fra Diavolo order, whose chief amusement was to hang up Federal soldiers by their arms, and kindle fires under their feet—for what reason is not explained; and when not thus pleasantly engaged, he is described as cutting down the unfortunate bluecoats with a tremendous sabre, or riddling them with bullets from an extensive assortment of pistols in his belt. . . . The question of most interest is—Was Colonel Mosby a partisan officer, engaged in a perfectly legitimate warfare, or was he a mere robber? The present writer regards any imputations upon the character of this officer, or upon the nature of the warfare which he carried on, as absurd. . . . [T]here was no officer in that army who occupied a more formally official position than Mosby, or whose operations more perfectly conformed to the rules of civilized warfare.

Cooke, *Wearing of the Gray*, 113, 119.

Mosby, like James Longstreet, did more than simply profess his allegiance to the United States after the war; he worked constructively to promote federal policies and was vilified by many in the South as a result.

still; and by advancing they would compel the enemy to keep detachments to hold them back, or else lay his own territory open to invasion. His answer was: "Oh, yes! I see that. As we say out West, if a man can't skin he must hold a leg while somebody else does."

There was a certain incident connected with the Wilderness campaign of which it may not be out of place to speak; and to avoid a digression further on I will mention it here.

A few days before my departure from Culpeper the Honorable E. B. Washburne visited me there, and remained with my headquarters for some distance south, through the battle in the Wilderness and, I think, to Spottsylvania. He was accompanied by a Mr. Swinton, whom he presented as a literary gentleman who wished to accompany the army with a view of writing a history of the war when it was over. He assured me—and I have no doubt Swinton gave him the assurance—that he was not present as a correspondent of the press. I expressed an entire willingness to have him (Swinton) accompany the army, and would have allowed him to do so as a correspondent, restricted, however, in the character of the information he could give. We received Richmond papers with about as much regularity as if there had been no war, and knew that our papers were received with equal regularity by the Confederates. It was desirable, therefore, that correspondents should not be privileged spies of the enemy within our lines.

Probably Mr. Swinton expected to be an invited guest at my headquarters, and was disappointed that he was not asked to become so. At all events he was not invited, and soon I found that he was corresponding with some paper (I have now forgotten which one), thus violating his word either expressed or implied. He knew of the assurance Washburne had given as to the character of his mission. I never saw the man from the day of our introduction to the present that I recollect. He accompanied us, however, for a time at least.

The second night after crossing the Rapidan (the night of the 5th of May) Colonel W. R. Rowley, of my staff, was acting as night officer at my headquarters. A short time before midnight I gave him verbal instructions for the night. Three days later I read in a Richmond paper a verbatim report of these instructions.

A few nights still later (after the first, and possibly after the second, day's fighting in the Wilderness) General Meade came to my tent for consultation, bringing with him some of his staff officers. Both his staff and mine retired to the camp-fire some yards in front of the tent, thinking our conversation should be private. There was a stump a little to one side, and between the front of the tent and camp-fire. One of my staff, Colonel T. S. Bowers, saw what he took to be a man seated on the ground and leaning against the stump, listening to the conversation between Meade and myself. He called the attention of Colonel Rowley to it. The latter immediately took the man by the shoulder and asked him, in language more forcible than polite, what he was doing there. The man proved to be Swinton, the "historian," and his replies to the question were evasive and unsatisfactory, and he was warned against further eaves-dropping.

The next I heard of Mr. Swinton was at Cold Harbor. General Meade came to my headquarters saying that General Burnside had arrested Swinton, who at some previous time had given great offence, and had ordered him to be shot that afternoon. I promptly ordered the prisoner to be released, but that he must be expelled from the lines of the army not to return again on pain of punishment.[14]

14. Swinton was a correspondent for the *New York Times*. He would go on to publish the war history mentioned, *Campaigns of the Army of the Potomac*, in 1866. A revised reissue in 1882 carried testimonials from men on both sides of the conflict, including William H. Seward, Jefferson Davis, and Henry Ward Beecher, the last of whom proclaimed, "If any one will know the mechanism and anatomy of battle, let him read our American Napier, William Swinton." Swinton's treatment of Grant's generalship and of the abilities of the Union armies more generally provoked angry responses from Adam Badeau and others.

48

Commencement of the Grand Campaign—General Butler's Position—Sheridan's First Raid

The armies were now all ready to move for the accomplishment of a single object. They were acting as a unit so far as such a thing was possible over such a vast field. Lee, with the capital of the Confederacy, was the main end to which all were working. Johnston, with Atlanta, was an important obstacle in the way of our accomplishing the result aimed at, and was therefore almost an independent objective. It was of less importance only because the capture of Johnston and his army would not produce so immediate and decisive a result in closing the rebellion as would the possession of Richmond, Lee and his army. All other troops were employed exclusively in support of these two movements. This was the plan; and I will now endeavor to give, as concisely as I can, the method of its execution, outlining first the operations of minor detached but co-operative columns.

As stated before, Banks failed to accomplish what he had been sent to do on the Red River, and eliminated the use of forty thousand veterans whose co-operation in the grand campaign had been expected—ten thousand with Sherman and thirty thousand against Mobile.

Sigel's record is almost equally brief. He moved out, it is true, according to programme; but just when I was hoping to hear of good work being done in the valley I received instead the following announcement from Halleck: "Sigel is in full retreat on Strasburg. He will do nothing but run; never did anything else." The enemy had intercepted him about New Market and handled him roughly, leaving him short six guns, and some nine hundred men out of his six thousand.

The plan had been for an advance of Sigel's forces in two columns. Though the one under his immediate command failed ingloriously the other proved more fortunate. Under Crook and Averell his western column advanced from the Gauley in West Virginia at the appointed time, and with more happy results. They reached the Virginia and Tennessee Railroad at Dublin and destroyed a depot of supplies, besides tearing up several miles of road and burning the bridge over New River. Having accomplished this they recrossed the Alleghanies to Meadow Bluffs and there awaited further orders.

Butler embarked at Fort Monroe with all his command, except the cavalry and some artillery which moved up the south bank of the James River. His steamers moved first up Chesapeake Bay and York River as if threatening the rear of Lee's army. At midnight they turned back, and Butler by daylight was far up the James River. He seized City Point and Bermuda Hundred early in the day, without loss and, no doubt, very much to the surprise of the enemy.

This was the accomplishment of the first step contemplated in my instructions to Butler. He was to act from here, looking to Richmond as his objective point. I had given him to understand that I should aim to fight Lee between the Rapidan and Richmond if he would stand; but should Lee fall back into Richmond I would follow up and make a junction of the armies of the Potomac and the James on the James River. He was directed to secure a footing as far up the south side of the river as he could at as early a date as possible.

Butler was in position by the 6th of May and had begun intrenching, and on the 7th he sent out his cavalry from Suffolk to cut the Weldon Railroad. He also sent out detachments to destroy the railroad between Petersburg and Richmond, but no great success attended these latter efforts. He made no great effort to establish himself on that road and neglected to attack Petersburg, which was almost defenceless. About the 11th he advanced slowly until he reached the works at Drury's Bluff, about half way between Bermuda Hundred and Richmond. In the mean time Beauregard had been gathering reinforcements. On the 16th he attacked Butler with great vigor, and with such success as to limit very materially the further usefulness of the Army of the James as a distinct factor in the campaign. I afterward ordered a portion of it to join the Army of the Potomac, leaving a sufficient force with Butler to man his works, hold securely the footing he had already gained and maintain a threatening front toward the rear of the Confederate capital.

The position which General Butler had chosen between the two rivers, the James and Appomattox, was one of great natural strength, one where a large area of ground might be thoroughly inclosed by means of a single intrenched line, and that a very short one in comparison with the extent of territory which it thoroughly protected. His right was protected by the James River, his left by the Appomattox, and his rear by their junction—the two streams uniting near by. The bends of the two streams shortened the line that had been chosen for intrenchments, while it increased the area which the line inclosed.

Previous to ordering any troops from Butler I sent my chief engineer, General [John G.] Barnard, from the Army of the Potomac to that of the James to inspect Butler's position and ascertain whether I could again safely make an order for General Butler's movement in co-operation with mine, now that I was getting so near Richmond; or, if I could not, whether his position was strong enough to justify me in withdrawing some of his troops and having them brought round by water to White House to join me and reinforce the Army of the Potomac. General Barnard reported the position very strong for defensive purposes, and that I could do the latter with great security; but that General Butler could not move from where he was, in co-operation, to produce any effect. He said that the general occupied a place between the James and Appomattox rivers which was of great strength, and where with an inferior force he could hold it for an indefinite length of time against a superior; but that he could do nothing offensively. I then asked him why Butler could not move out from his lines and push across the Richmond and Petersburg Railroad to the rear and on the south side of Richmond. He replied that it was impracticable, because the enemy had substantially the same line across the neck of land that General Butler had. He then took out his pencil and drew a sketch of the locality, remarking that the position was like a bottle and that Butler's line of intrenchments across the neck represented the cork; that the enemy had built an equally strong line immediately in front of him across the neck; and it was therefore as if Butler was in a bottle. He was perfectly safe against an attack; but, as Barnard expressed it, the enemy had corked the bottle and with a small force could hold the cork in its place. This struck me as being very expressive of his posi-tion, particularly when I saw the hasty sketch which General Barnard had drawn; and in making my subsequent report I used that expression without adding quotation marks, never thinking that anything had been said that would attract attention—as this did, very much to the annoyance, no doubt, of General Butler and, I know, very much to my own. I found afterwards that this was mentioned in the notes of General Badeau's book, which, when

"As if he had been in a bottle
strongly corked," cartoon of Butler
by William H. Tevis, 1865. *Library
of Congress, Prints and Photographs
Division, LC-DIG-ppmsca-34863.*

they were shown to me, I asked to have stricken out; yet it was retained there, though against my wishes.[1]

I make this statement here because, although I have often made it before, it has never been in my power until now to place it where it will correct history; and I desire to rectify all injustice that I may have done to individuals, particularly to officers who were gallantly serving their country during the trying period of the war for the preservation of the Union. General Butler certainly gave his very earnest support to the war; and he gave his own best efforts personally to the suppression of the rebellion.[2]

The further operations of the Army of the James can best be treated of in connection with those of the Army of the Potomac, the two being so intimately associated and connected as to be substantially one body in which the individuality of the supporting wing is merged.

Before giving the reader a summary of Sherman's great Atlanta campaign, which must conclude my description of the various co-operative movements preparatory to proceeding with that of the operations of the centre, I will briefly mention Sheridan's first raid upon Lee's communications which, though an incident of the operations on the main line and not specifically marked out in the original plan, attained in its brilliant execution and results all the proportions of an independent campaign. By thus anticipating, in point of time, I will be able to more perfectly observe the continuity of events occurring in my immediate front when I shall have undertaken to describe our advance from the Rapidan.

---

1. For Grant's use of the phrase "bottle strongly corked" in his General Report of July 22, 1865, see *OR* ser. 1, vol. 34, pt. 1, 17. For Butler's frustration at being known ever after as "Bottled-up-Butler," see *Butler's Book*, chapter 18.

2. Butler makes sure to quote as many exculpatory statements as he can in his autobiography.

On the 8th of May, just after the battle of the Wilderness and when we were moving on Spottsylvania I directed Sheridan verbally to cut loose from the Army of the Potomac, pass around the left of Lee's army and attack his cavalry: to cut the two roads—one running west through Gordonsville, Charlottesville and Lynchburg, the other to Richmond, and, when compelled to do so for want of forage and rations, to move on to the James River and draw these from Butler's supplies. This move took him past the entire rear of Lee's army. These orders were also given in writing through Meade.

The object of this move was three-fold. First, if successfully executed, and it was, he would annoy the enemy by cutting his line of supplies and telegraphic communications, and destroy or get for his own use supplies in store in the rear and coming up. Second, he would draw the enemy's cavalry after him, and thus better protect our flanks, rear and trains than by remaining with the army. Third, his absence would save the trains drawing his forage and other supplies from Fredericksburg, which had now become our base. He started at daylight the next morning, and accomplished more than was expected. It was sixteen days before he got back to the Army of the Potomac.

The course Sheridan took was directly to Richmond. Before night Stuart, commanding the Confederate cavalry, came on to the rear of his command.[3] But the advance kept on, crossed the North Anna, and at Beaver

---

3. J. E. B. Stuart (1833–1864) graduated from West Point in 1854. A cavalry officer, he served on frontier duty and was sent to Kansas to help put down the disturbances of 1855–57. Stuart resigned his commissioned and joined the Rebellion in May 1861. By the time of his death on May 12, 1864, from wounds received at the Battle of Yellow Tavern, he had risen to command the cavalry corps of Lee's Army of Northern Virginia. O. O. Howard tells a revealing story about his future adversary that also illuminates the tensions that characterized West Point in the 1850s:

> Against me certain things were alleged: First, that I was an abolitionist; second, that I associated with "cut men"; third, that I visited and made companions of enlisted men; and fourth, that I had joined the Bible class and curried favor with the professor of ethics. We were accustomed to salute each other as we passed, or give some sign of pleasant recognition. I now saw that individuals who belonged to the small conspiracy passed me without recognition or took some other method of showing that my society was not desirable. . . .
>
> . . . Seeing how matters went, Captain Alden at last sent for me and said that he had noticed how I was being treated and how unjustly demerit was being given me and he said, "Now, Mr. Howard, I want to give you some advice. Mind you, I do not give you this advice as Commandant of

Dam, a station on the Virginia Central Railroad, recaptured four hundred Union prisoners on their way to Richmond, destroyed the road and used and destroyed a large amount of subsistence and medical stores.

Stuart, seeing that our cavalry was pushing towards Richmond, abandoned the pursuit on the morning of the 10th and, by a detour and an exhausting march, interposed between Sheridan and Richmond at Yellow Tavern, only about six miles north of the city. Sheridan destroyed the railroad and more supplies at Ashland, and on the 11th arrived in Stuart's front. A severe engagement ensued in which the losses were heavy on both sides, but the rebels were beaten, their leader mortally wounded, and some guns and many prisoners were captured.[4]

Cadets, for I shall punish you for any infraction of regulations. Yes, sir, I shall punish you severely, but I give it to you as a father to his son. If I were in your place I would knock some man down."

I understood Captain Alden thoroughly, and from that time on my friends had nothing to complain of from my want of spirit. I had some conflicts, some wounds, and was reasonably punished for breaking the regulations, and my demerits increased.

My friends might be curious to know if I had any following in my own class. Indeed I did, and it wasn't long before I had nine-tenths of the class in sympathy with me and my defenders. I never can forget the manliness of J. E. B. Stuart, of Virginia, who became, in the Civil War, the leader of the Southern cavalry. He spoke to me, he visited me, and we became warm friends, often, on Saturday afternoons, visiting the young ladies of the post together. While I was made to feel keenly the hatred which accompanies ostracism, yet by a straightforward course I first robbed it of its sting; and finally the majority of those who opposed me were ashamed of the course they had pursued and before graduation there were few indeed with whom I was not on good terms. I did not go to the offenders and ask any favors, but one by one they came to me.

J. E. B. Stuart, C.S.A.
Library of Congress, Prints and Photographs Division, Civil War Photographs, LC-DIG-cwpb-07546.

Autobiography, 1:52–54.

4. Sheridan gives credit to George Armstrong Custer for the victory at Yellow Tavern: Stuart had gotten there first and pinned down the Union cavalry with enfilading fire when Custer launched a mounted charge: "Custer's charge," Sheridan writes,

Sheridan passed through the outer defences of Richmond, and could, no doubt, have passed through the inner ones. But having no supports near he could not have remained. After caring for his wounded he struck for the James River below the city, to communicate with Butler and to rest his men and horses as well as to get food and forage for them.

He moved first between the Chickahominy and the James, but in the morning (the 12th) he was stopped by batteries at Mechanicsville. He then turned to cross to the north side of the Chickahominy by Meadow Bridge. He found this barred, and the defeated Confederate cavalry, reorganized, occupying the opposite side. The panic created by his first entrance within the outer works of Richmond having subsided troops were sent out to attack his rear.

He was now in a perilous position, one from which but few generals could have extricated themselves. The defences of Richmond, manned, were to the right, the Chickahominy was to the left with no bridge remain-

---

was brilliantly executed. Beginning at a walk, he increased his gait to a trot, and then at full speed rushed at the enemy. At the same moment the dismounted troops along my whole front moved forward, and as Custer went through the battery, capturing two of the guns with their cannoneers and breaking up the enemy's left, Gibbs and Devin drove his centre and right from the field. Gregg meanwhile, with equal success, charged the force in his rear—Gordon's brigade—and the engagement ended by giving us complete control of the road to Richmond. We captured a number of prisoners, and the casualties on both sides were quite severe, General Stuart himself falling mortally wounded, and General James B. Gordon, one of his brigade commanders, being killed.

Sheridan, *Personal Memoirs*, 1:378.

Varina Davis's version of Stuart's death sounds a more romantic note:

The Federals came thundering down, recognized Stuart, and fired twelve shots at him; he wheeled upon them and emptied his revolver, then checked his horse and rode for our lines, knowing he had been mortally wounded. His death-wound is said to have been dealt by a skulker concealed in a fence corner. A bullet struck him in the hip and passed through the abdomen. Like the Cid, he felt the menace to the foe his presence would be, and asked his staff to hold him upon the saddle, that the enemy might not see he was wounded. Thus supported, he rode into our lines to die, confident of having done his whole duty, at peace with God, and willing, if it was His will, to leave the struggle and the end to His good pleasure.

Jefferson Davis, 2:499.

ing and the opposite bank guarded, to the rear was a force from Richmond. This force was attacked and beaten by Wilson's and [David M.] Gregg's divisions, while Sheridan turned to the left with the remaining division and hastily built a bridge over the Chickahominy under the fire of the enemy, forced a crossing and soon dispersed the Confederates he found there. The enemy was held back from the stream by the fire of the troops not engaged in bridge building.

On the 13th Sheridan was at Bottom's Bridge, over the Chickahominy. On the 14th he crossed this stream and on that day went into camp on the James River at Haxall's Landing. He at once put himself into communication with General Butler, who directed all the supplies he wanted to be furnished.

Sheridan had left the Army of the Potomac at Spottsylvania, but did not know where either this or Lee's army was now. Great caution therefore had to be exercised in getting back. On the 17th, after resting his command for three days, he started on his return. He moved by the way of White House. The bridge over the Pamunkey had been burned by the enemy, but a new one was speedily improvised and the cavalry crossed over it. On the 22d he was at Aylett's on the Matapony, where he learned the position of the two

George Armstrong Custer and Alfred Pleasonton, 1863. Photograph by Timothy H. O'Sullivan. *Metropolitan Museum of Art, Gilman Collection, Museum Purchase, 2005.*

armies. On the 24th he joined us on the march from North Anna to Cold Harbor, in the vicinity of Chesterfield.

Sheridan in this memorable raid passed entirely around Lee's army: encountered his cavalry in four engagements, and defeated them in all; recaptured four hundred Union prisoners and killed and captured many of the enemy; destroyed and used many supplies and munitions of war; destroyed miles of railroad and telegraph, and freed us from annoyance by the cavalry of the enemy for more than two weeks.

49

Sherman's Campaign in Georgia—Siege of Atlanta—Death of General McPherson— Attempt to Capture Andersonville— Capture of Atlanta

After separating from Sherman in Cincinnati I went on to Washington, as already stated, while he returned to Nashville to assume the duties of his new command. His military division was now composed of four departments and embraced all the territory west of the Alleghany Mountains and east of the Mississippi River, together with the State of Arkansas in the trans-Mississippi. The most easterly of these was the Department of the Ohio, General Schofield commanding; the next was the Department of the Cumberland, General Thomas commanding; the third the Department of the Tennessee, General McPherson commanding; and General Steele still commanded the trans-Mississippi, or Department of Arkansas. The last-named department was so far away that Sherman could not communicate with it very readily after starting on his spring campaign, and it was therefore soon transferred from his military division to that of the Gulf, where General Canby, who had relieved General Banks, was in command.

The movements of the armies, as I have stated in a former chapter, were to be simultaneous, I fixing the day to start when the season should be far enough advanced, it was hoped, for the roads to be in a condition for the troops to march.

General Sherman at once set himself to work preparing for the task which was assigned him to accomplish in the spring campaign. McPherson lay at Huntsville with about twenty-four thousand men, guarding those points of Tennessee which were regarded as most worth holding; Thomas, with over sixty thousand men of the Army of the Cumberland, was at Chat-

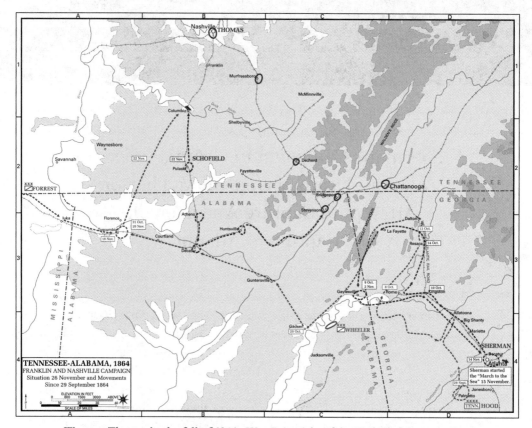

Western Theater in the fall of 1864. *West Point Atlas of the Civil War. Courtesy of Department of History, USMA.*

tanooga; and Schofield, with about fourteen thousand men, was at Knox-ville. With these three armies, numbering about one hundred thousand men in all, Sherman was to move on the day fixed for the general advance, with a view of destroying Johnston's army and capturing Atlanta. He visited each of these commands to inform himself as to their condition, and it was found to be, speaking generally, good.

One of the first matters to turn his attention to was that of getting, before the time arrived for starting, an accumulation of supplies forward to Chattanooga, sufficiently large to warrant a movement. He found, when he got to that place, that the trains over the single-track railroad, which was frequently interrupted for a day or two at a time, were only sufficient to meet the daily wants of the troops without bringing forward any surplus of any kind. He found, however, that trains were being used to transport all the beef cattle, horses for the cavalry, and even teams that were being brought to the front. He at once changed all this, and required beef cattle, teams, cavalry horses, and everything that could travel, even the troops, to be marched, and used the road exclusively for transporting supplies. In this way he was able to accumulate an abundance before the time finally fixed upon for the move, the 4th of May.

As I have said already, Johnston was at Dalton, which was nearly one-fourth of the way between Chattanooga and Atlanta. The country is mountainous all the way to Atlanta, abounding in mountain streams, some of them of considerable volume. Dalton is on ground where water drains towards Atlanta and into one of the main streams rising north-east from there and flowing south-west—this being the general direction which all the main streams of that section take, with smaller tributaries entering into them. Johnston had been preparing himself for this campaign during the entire winter. The best positions for defence had been selected all the way from Dalton back to Atlanta, and very strongly intrenched; so that, as he might be forced to fall back from one position, he would have another to fall into in his rear. His position at Dalton was so very strongly intrenched that no doubt he expected, or at least hoped, to hold Sherman there and prevent him from getting any further. With a less skilful general, and one disposed to take no risks, I have no doubt that he would have succeeded.

Sherman's plan was to start Schofield, who was farthest back, a few days in advance from Knoxville, having him move on the direct road to Dalton. Thomas was to move out to Ringgold. It had been Sherman's intention to cross McPherson over the Tennessee River at Huntsville or Decatur, and move him south from there so as to have him come into the road running from Chattanooga to Atlanta a good distance to the rear of the point Johnston was occupying; but when that was contemplated it was hoped that McPherson alone would have troops enough to cope with Johnston, if the latter should move against him while unsupported by the balance of the army. In this he was disappointed. Two of McPherson's veteran divisions had re-enlisted on the express provision that they were to have a furlough. This furlough had not yet expired, and they were not back.

Then, again, Sherman had lent Banks two divisions under A. J. Smith, the winter before, to co-operate with the trans-Mississippi forces, and this with the express pledge that they should be back by a time specified, so as to be prepared for this very campaign. It is hardly necessary to say they were not returned. That department continued to absorb troops to no purpose to the end of the war. This left McPherson so weak that the part of the plan above indicated had to be changed. He was therefore brought up to Chat-

Adolph Metzner, Inside Confederate fortifications after the Battle of Resaca, Georgia, May 1864. *Library of Congress, Prints and Photographs Division, LC-DIG-ppmsca-51289.*

tanooga and moved from there on a road to the right of Thomas—the two coming together about Dalton. The three armies were abreast, all ready to start promptly on time.

Sherman soon found that Dalton was so strongly fortified that it was useless to make any attempt to carry it by assault; and even to carry it by regular approaches was impracticable. There was a narrowing up in the mountain, between the National and Confederate armies, through which a stream, a wagon road and a railroad ran. Besides, the stream had been dammed so that the valley was a lake. Through this gorge the troops would have to pass. McPherson was therefore sent around by the right, to come out by the way of Snake Creek Gap into the rear of the enemy. This was a surprise to Johnston, and about the 13th he decided to abandon his position at Dalton.

On the 15th there was very hard fighting about Resaca; but our cavalry having been sent around to the right got near the road in the enemy's rear. Again Johnston fell back, our army pursuing. The pursuit was continued to Kingston, which was reached on the 19th with very little fighting, except that Newton's division overtook the rear of Johnston's army and engaged it. Sherman was now obliged to halt for the purpose of bringing up his railroad trains. He was depending upon the railroad for all of his supplies, and as of

A somewhat more sanitized view than Metzner provides of a Confederate fort in front of Atlanta. Sherman can be seen in the background leaning on the earthworks. Photograph by George Barnard. *Library of Congress, Prints and Photographs Division, Civil War Photographs, LC-DIG-ppmsca-34008.*

course the railroad was wholly destroyed as Johnston fell back, it had to be rebuilt. This work was pushed forward night and day, and caused much less delay than most persons would naturally expect in a mountainous country where there were so many bridges to be rebuilt.

The campaign to Atlanta was managed with the most consummate skill, the enemy being flanked out of one position after another all the way there. It is true this was not accomplished without a good deal of fighting—some of it very hard fighting, rising to the dignity of very important battles—neither were single positions gained in a day. On the contrary, weeks were spent at some; and about Atlanta more than a month was consumed.

It was the 23d of May before the road was finished up to the rear of Sherman's army and the pursuit renewed. This pursuit brought him up to the vicinity of Allatoona. This place was very strongly intrenched, and naturally a very defensible position. An assault upon it was not thought of, but preparations were made to flank the enemy out of it. This was done by sending a large force around our right, by the way of Dallas, to reach the rear of the enemy. Before reaching there, however, they found the enemy fortified in their way, and there resulted hard fighting for about a week at a place called New Hope Church. On the left our troops also were fortified, and as close up to the enemy as they could get. They kept working still farther around to the left toward the railroad. This was the case more particularly with the cavalry. By the 4th of June Johnston found that he was being hemmed in so rapidly that he drew off and Allatoona was left in our possession.

Allatoona, being an important place, was strongly intrenched for occupation by our troops before advancing farther, and made a secondary base of supplies. The railroad was finished up to that point, the intrenchments completed, store-houses provided for food, and the army got in readiness for a further advance. The rains, however, were falling in such torrents that it was impossible to move the army by the side roads which they would have to move upon in order to turn Johnston out of his new position.

While Sherman's army lay here, General F. P. Blair returned to it, bringing with him the two divisions of veterans who had been on furlough.

Johnston had fallen back to Marietta and Kenesaw Mountain, where strong intrenchments awaited him. At this latter place our troops made an assault upon the enemy's lines after having got their own lines up close to him, and failed, sustaining considerable loss. But during the progress of the battle Schofield was gaining ground to the left; and the cavalry on his left were gaining still more toward the enemy's rear. These operations were completed by the 3d of July, when it was found that Johnston had evacuated the place. He was pursued at once. Sherman had made every preparation to abandon the railroad, leaving a strong guard in his intrenchments. He had intended, moving out with twenty days' rations and plenty of ammunition, to come in on the railroad again at the Chattahoochee River. Johnston frustrated this plan by himself starting back as above stated. This time he fell back to the Chattahoochee.

About the 5th of July he was besieged again, Sherman getting easy possession of the Chattahoochee River both above and below him. The enemy was again flanked out of his position, or so frightened by flanking movements that on the night of the 9th he fell back across the river.

Here Johnston made a stand until the 17th, when Sherman's old tactics prevailed again and the final movement toward Atlanta began. Johnston was now relieved of the command, and Hood superseded him.

Johnston's tactics in this campaign do not seem to have met with much favor, either in the eyes of the administration at Richmond, or of the people of that section of the South in which he was commanding. The very fact of a change of commanders being ordered under such circumstances was an indication of a change of policy, and that now they would become the aggressors—the very thing our troops wanted.[1]

---

1. Grant's enthusiasm for the Confederate change of commanders owed to the fact that in contrast to the defensive-minded Johnston, who was willing to adopt a Fabian strategy of delay—at this stage, the best hope remaining to the South—John B. Hood (1831–1879) prosecuted the war vigorously and squandered precious Confederate manpower in several ill-advised offensives against Sherman. Hood began the war in command of the Texas Brigade, whose soldiers developed a reputation for their ferocity in battle and a roughness honed on the frontier. The brigade association's tribute to him can be found in *The Life and Character of Gen. John B. Hood*, by Mrs. C. M. Winkler (Austin, Texas: Draughton & Lambert, 1885). Wounded at Gettysburg, losing a leg at Chickamauga, Hood commanded his last action at Nashville against George Thomas; it failed.

Hood graduated from West Point in 1853, a class of fifty-one cadets, ten of whom would fight for the Confederacy. Others, including McPherson, Schofield, and Sheridan, would fight on the opposite side. Hood spent the years after graduation on frontier duty, and his impetuosity as a leader was evident from the start. Growing "weary of the routine duties of camp life" at Fort Mason, Texas, he "determined to change the scene and start on a scouting expedition in search of the red men and the forests." It was on this expedition, in July 1857, that his company encountered a party of Comanche and Lipan Indians. "I was young and buoyant in spirit," Hood recalled, "my men were well mounted and all eager for a chase as well as a fray." He was also poorly prepared for the hardships that awaited him on the plains. Soon Hood and his soldiers were out of water and game. With men and horses in a weakened condition, a suspicious Hood nevertheless approached a group of Indians who were waving a white flag—one group of Indians, who were headed to a reservation, had been directed to wave a flag if they encountered cavalry. The Indians fired, and a skirmish began near Devil's River:

> The quick and sharp report of our rifles, the smoke and cracking noise of the fire, together with the great odds against us, the shouts of the soldiers and the yells of the Indians, betokened the deadly peril from which seemingly naught but a miracle could effect our deliverance. Each man, after discharging his rifle, drew his revolver and used it with terrible effect as the warriors, in many instances, were within a few feet of the muzzle of our arms. Stubbornly did my brave men hold their ground; again and again they drove the enemy back to the edge and in rear of the burning mass of weeds in our front, when finally the Indians charged desperately and forced our line back a few paces in the centre. Having discharged my shot-gun, I rode at once with revolver in hand to that point, rallied the soldiers, who again drove them back, whilst our horses, in some instances, were beaten over the head with shields. . . . At this juncture I was pierced in the left hand with an arrow which passed through the reins and the fourth finger, pinning my hand to the bridle. I instantly broke the spear head and threw it aside. Unmindful of the fact that the feathers could not pass through the wound, I pulled the arrow in the direction in which it had been shot, and

was compelled finally in order to free myself of it to seize the feathered in lieu of the barbed end.

Thus raged this hand to hand conflict until all our shots were expended, and it was found that owing to the restiveness of the horses we could not reload while mounted. We then fell back about fifty yards and dismounted for that purpose. Soon afterward arose from beyond the burning heap one continuous mourning howl, such as can alone come forth from the heart of the red man in deep distress. These sounds of sorrow revealed to me that we were in little danger of a renewal of the assault, and I was, I may in truth say, most thankful for the truce thus proclaimed. Two of our men had been killed and four, besides myself, severely wounded; we had also one horse killed and several disabled. Had the combat been renewed I would have had, after leaving a guard with the horses, but five or six men to fight on foot.

Nightfall was approaching; the Indians gathered up their dead and wounded, and moved off toward the Rio Grande. Our thirst, which was great at the beginning of the combat, had now become intense from excitement and loss of blood. I therefore moved at once to Devil's river, where we bivouacked about 10 p.m., and sent a messenger to Camp Hudson for supplies and medical aid.

Thus closed this terrible scene. . . . We were nigh meeting a similar fate to that of the gallant Custer and his noble band.

Advance and Retreat: Personal Experiences in the United States and Confederate Armies (New Orleans, LA: G. T. Beauregard, Hood Orphan Memorial Fund, 1880), 8–13.

Hood's narrative reveals a great deal about his rashness—and suggests why Grant was so pleased by the news that he had replaced Johnston. Mary Chesnut found in Hood a figure of romance and charm:

When Hood came with his sad Quixote face, the face of an old Crusader, who believed in his cause, his cross, and his crown, we were not prepared for such a man as a beau-ideal of the wild Texans. He is tall, thin, and shy; has blue eyes and light hair; a tawny beard, and a vast amount of it, covering the lower part of his face, the whole appearance that of awkward strength. Some one said that his great reserve of manner he carried only into the society of ladies. Major Venable added that he had often heard of the light of battle shining in a man's eyes. He had seen it once—when he carried to Hood orders from Lee, and found in the hottest of the fight that the man was transfigured. The fierce light of Hood's eyes I can never forget.

After Hood lost his leg at Chickamauga, Chesnut glimpsed him in a large drawing-room in Richmond: "Hood, solitary, sad, with crutches by his chair. . . . Mrs. Buckner came in and her little girl who, when she spied Hood, bounded into the next room, and sprang into his lap. Hood smoothed her little dress down and held her close to him." See August 10, 1863 and March 12, 1864, *Diary*, 230, 298.

In an example of the force of the spell exerted by Hood and other Confederate officers, who perversely endure as symbols of honor and gallantry in a country against which they took up arms, the U.S. Army's Fort Hood, in Texas, is named in his honor.

John Bell Hood. Drawing by Alfred R. Waud. *Library of Congress, Prints and Photographs Division, LC-DIG-cwpb-03391.*

For my own part, I think that Johnston's tactics were right. Anything that could have prolonged the war a year beyond the time that it did finally close, would probably have exhausted the North to such an extent that they might then have abandoned the contest and agreed to a separation.

Atlanta was very strongly intrenched all the way around in a circle about a mile and a half outside of the city. In addition to this, there were advanced intrenchments which had to be taken before a close siege could be commenced.

Sure enough, as indicated by the change of commanders, the enemy was about to assume the offensive. On the 20th he came out and attacked the Army of the Cumberland most furiously. Hooker's corps, and Newton's and Johnson's divisions were the principal ones engaged in this contest, which lasted more than an hour; but the Confederates were then forced to fall back inside their main lines. The losses were quite heavy on both sides. On this day General Gresham, since our Postmaster-General, was very badly wounded. During the night Hood abandoned his outer lines, and our troops were advanced. The investment had not been relinquished for a moment during the day.

During the night of the 21st Hood moved out again, passing by our left flank, which was then in motion to get a position farther in rear of him, and a desperate battle ensued, which lasted most of the day of the 22d. At first the battle went very much in favor of the Confederates, our troops being somewhat surprised. While our troops were advancing they were struck in flank, and their flank was enveloped. But they had become too thorough veterans to be thrown into irreparable confusion by an unexpected attack when off their guard, and soon they were in order and engaging the enemy, with the advantage now of knowing where their antagonist was. The field of battle continued to expand until it embraced about seven miles of ground. Finally, however, and before night, the enemy was driven back into the city.[2]

It was during this battle that McPherson, while passing from one column to another, was instantly killed. In his death the army lost one of its ablest, purest and best generals.[3]

Garrard had been sent out with his cavalry to get upon the railroad east of Atlanta and to cut it in the direction of Augusta. He was successful in this, and returned about the time of the battle. Rousseau had also come up

---

2. General John A. Logan, upon whom devolved the command of the Army of the Tennessee during this battle, in his report gave our total loss in killed, wounded and missing at 3,521; and estimated that of the enemy to be not less than 10,000: and General G. M. Dodge, graphically describing to General Sherman the enemy's attack, the full weight of which fell first upon and was broken by his depleted command, remarks: "The disparity of forces can be seen from the fact that in the charge made by my two brigades under Fuller and Mersy they took 351 prisoners, representing forty-nine different regiments, eight brigades and three divisions; and brought back eight battle flags from the enemy." [Note to the first edition.]

3. McPherson had just left a conference with Sherman to investigate sounds of artillery coming from an unexpected direction. Riding to the sound of the guns, McPherson neared the battle and, according to Sherman, "disappeared" in some "woods, doubtless with a sense of absolute security. The sound of musketry was there heard, and McPherson's horse came back, bleeding, wounded, and riderless." Sherman describes McPherson as "then in his prime . . . over six feet high, and a very handsome man in every way, was universally liked, and had many noble qualities." *Memoirs*, 2:76–77.

About a month after his death, the *New York Times* reprinted an exchange of letters between Grant and McPherson's grandmother, Lydia Slocum, originally published in the *Fremont Sentinel* of Ohio. Slocum wished to acknowledge Grant's affection for her grandson: "When it was announced at his funeral, from the public print, that, when Gen. GRANT heard of his death, he went into his tent and wept like a child, my heart went out in thanks to you for the interest you manifested in him while he was with you." In his reply Grant expressed his deep sorrow: "I knew him well. To know him was but to love him. It may be some consolation to you, his aged grandmother, to know that every officer and every soldier who served under your grandson, felt the highest reverence for his patriotism, his zeal, his great, almost unequaled ability, and all the manly virtues that can adorn a commander. Your bereavement is great, but cannot exceed mine." "The Late Gen. McPherson," *New York Times*, August 27, 1864, p. 2.

from Tennessee with a small division of cavalry, having crossed the Tennessee River about Decatur and made a raid into Alabama. Finally, when hard pressed, he had come in, striking the railroad in rear of Sherman, and reported to him about this time.

The battle of the 22d is usually known as the Battle of Atlanta, although the city did not fall into our hands until the 2d of September. Preparations went on, as before, to flank the enemy out of his position. The work was tedious, and the lines that had to be maintained were very long. Our troops were gradually worked around to the east until they struck the road between Decatur and Atlanta. These lines were strongly fortified, as were those to the north and west of the city—all as close up to the enemy's lines as practicable—in order to hold them with the smallest possible number of men, the design being to detach an army to move by our right and try to get upon the railroad down south of Atlanta.

On the 27th the movement by the right flank commenced. On the 28th the enemy struck our right flank, General Logan commanding, with great vigor. Logan intrenched himself hastily, and by that means was enabled to resist all assaults and inflict a great deal of damage upon the enemy. These assaults were continued to the middle of the afternoon, and resumed once or twice still later in the day. The enemy's losses in these unsuccessful assaults were fearful.

During that evening the enemy in Logan's front withdrew into the town. This now left Sherman's army close up to the Confederate lines, extending from a point directly east of the city around by the north and west of it for a distance of fully ten miles; the whole of this line being intrenched, and made stronger every day they remained there.

In the latter part of July Sherman sent Stoneman to destroy the railroads to the south, about Macon. He was then to go east and, if possible, release our prisoners about Andersonville.[4] There were painful stories current at the

---

4. For a fictionalized account of life at the prison, see MacKinlay Kantor's blockbuster novel of the 1950s, *Andersonville*. Quoting from the account of one of the Union prisoners, a Dr. T. H. Mann, Varina Davis characteristically suggests that blame for the harshness of the prison rested with the degenerate Yankee inmates themselves rather than with their chivalrous captors. Mann had described the various "classes and grades of society . . . represented" in the prison population in an article in the *Century* magazine. Through selective quotation, Davis turns Mann's catalogue into a rogues' gallery featuring "Negro soldiers; *Bowery roughs*, the worst class of all; mechanics, farmers, *gamblers*, etc." *Jefferson Davis*, 2:538.

time about the great hardships these prisoners had to endure in the way of general bad treatment, in the way in which they were housed, and in the way in which they were fed. Great sympathy was felt for them; and it was thought that even if they could be turned loose upon the country it would be a great relief to them. But the attempt proved a failure. McCook, who commanded a small brigade, was first reported to have been captured; but he got back, having inflicted a good deal of damage upon the enemy.[5] He had also taken some prisoners; but encountering afterwards a largely superior force of the enemy he was obliged to drop his prisoners and get back as best he could with what men he had left. He had lost several hundred men out of his small command. On the 4th of August Colonel Adams, commanding a little brigade of about a thousand men, returned reporting Stoneman and all but himself as lost. I myself had heard around Richmond of the capture of Stoneman, and had sent Sherman word, which he received. The rumor was confirmed there, also, from other sources. A few days after Colonel Adams's return Colonel Capron also got in with a small detachment and confirmed the report of the capture of Stoneman with something less than a thousand men.

It seems that Stoneman, finding the escape of all his force was impossible, had made arrangements for the escape of two divisions. He covered the movement of these divisions to the rear with a force of about seven hundred men, and at length surrendered himself and this detachment to the commanding Confederate. In this raid, however, much damage was inflicted upon the enemy by the destruction of cars, locomotives, army wagons, manufactories of military supplies, etc.

On the 4th and 5th Sherman endeavored to get upon the railroad to our right, where Schofield was in command, but these attempts failed utterly. General Palmer was charged with being the cause of this failure, to a great extent, by both General Sherman and General Schofield; but I am not prepared to say this, although a question seems to have arisen with Palmer as to whether Schofield had any right to command him. If he did raise this question while an action was going on, that act alone was exceedingly reprehensible.

For context, see Mann's original two-part article, "A Yankee in Andersonville," *The Century Illustrated Monthly Magazine* 40, new ser. 18 (1890): 447–61 and 606–22.

5. Edward M. McCook (1833–1909) was one of the members of an extended Ohio family that supplied so many soldiers to the cause they came to be known as the Fighting McCooks.

About the same time Wheeler got upon our railroad north of Resaca and destroyed it nearly up to Dalton. This cut Sherman off from communication with the North for several days. Sherman responded to this attack on his lines of communication by directing one upon theirs.

Kilpatrick started on the night of the 18th of August to reach the Macon road about Jonesboro. He succeeded in doing so, passed entirely around the Confederate lines of Atlanta, and was back again in his former position on our left by the 22d. These little affairs, however, contributed but very little to the grand result. They annoyed, it is true, but any damage thus done to a railroad by any cavalry expedition is soon repaired.

Sherman made preparations for a repetition of his tactics; that is, for a flank movement with as large a force as could be got together to some point in the enemy's rear. Sherman commenced this last movement on the 25th of August, and on the 1st of September was well up towards the railroad twenty miles south of Atlanta. Here he found Hardee intrenched, ready to meet him. A battle ensued, but he was unable to drive Hardee away before night set in. Under cover of the night, however, Hardee left of his own accord. That night Hood blew up his military works, such as he thought would be valuable in our hands, and decamped.

The next morning at daylight General H. W. Slocum, who was commanding north of the city, moved in and took possession of Atlanta, and notified Sherman. Sherman then moved deliberately back, taking three days to reach the city, and occupied a line extending from Decatur on the left to Atlanta in the centre, with his troops extending out of the city for some distance to the right.

The campaign had lasted about four months, and was one of the most memorable in history. There was but little if anything in the whole campaign, now that it is over, to criticise at all, and nothing to criticise severely. It was creditable alike to the general who commanded and the army which had executed it. Sherman had on this campaign some bright, wide-awake division and brigade commanders whose alertness added a host to the efficiency of his command.[6]

---

6. Sherman's march soon assumed the status of myth. Georgia diarist Eliza Andrews captured both the devastation—"there was not even a chicken left in the country"—and the corresponding Southern rage:

About three miles from Sparta we struck the "Burnt Country," as it is well named by the natives, and then I could better understand the wrath

The troops now went to work to make themselves comfortable, and to enjoy a little rest after their arduous campaign. The city of Atlanta was turned into a military base. The citizens were all compelled to leave.[7] Sher-

---

and desperation of these poor people. I almost felt as if I should like to hang a Yankee myself. There was hardly a fence left standing all the way from Sparta to Gordon. The fields were trampled down and the road was lined with carcasses of horses, hogs, and cattle that the invaders, unable either to consume or to carry away with them, had wantonly shot down to starve out the people and prevent them from making their crops. The stench in some places was unbearable; every few hundred yards we had to hold our noses or stop them with the cologne Mrs. Elzey had given us, and it proved a great boon. The dwellings that were standing all showed signs of pillage, and on every plantation we saw the charred remains of the gin-house and packing-screw, while here and there, lone chimney-stacks, "Sherman's Sentinels," told of homes laid in ashes. The infamous wretches!

The War-Time Journal of a Georgia Girl, 1864–1865 (New York: D. Appleton, 1908), 32–33.

Sherman was well aware of the reputation he had acquired in the South, and part of him seemed frankly to relish it. In a letter to his eleven-year-old daughter Minnie, written when he was still in Memphis, he explained, "I am here the Stern & Cruel tyrant, slave of a Despotic Master, Lincoln. Hundreds of children like yourself are daily taught to curse my name, and each night thousands Kneel in prayer & beseech the almighty to consign me to Perdition. Such is war." Letter to Maria Boyle Ewing Sherman, August 6, 1862, *Sherman's Civil War*, 262.

7. On September 12, in response to a protest by the mayor and city council about the evacuation of Atlanta, Sherman wrote a letter that contains one of the more celebrated articulations of his philosophy of war:

You cannot qualify war in harsher terms than I will. War is cruelty, and you cannot refine it; and those who brought war into our country deserve all the curses and maledictions a people can pour out. I know I had no hand in making this war, and I know I will make more sacrifices to-day than any of you to secure peace. But you cannot have peace and a division of our country. . . . Once admit the Union, once more acknowledge the authority of the national Government, and, instead of devoting your houses and streets and roads to the dread uses of war, I and this army become at once your protectors and supporters, shielding you from danger, let it come from what quarter it may. I know that a few individuals cannot resist a torrent of error and passion, such as swept the South into rebellion, but you can point out, so that we may know those who desire a government, and those who insist on war and its desolation.

man also very wisely prohibited the assembling of the army of sutlers and traders who always follow in the wake of an army in the field, if permitted to do so, from trading with the citizens and getting the money of the soldiers for articles of but little use to them, and for which they are made to pay most exorbitant prices. He limited the number of these traders to one for each of his three armies.

The news of Sherman's success reached the North instantaneously, and set the country all aglow. This was the first great political campaign for the Republicans in their canvass of 1864. It was followed later by Sheridan's campaign in the Shenandoah Valley; and these two campaigns probably had more effect in settling the election of the following November than all the speeches, all the bonfires, and all the parading with banners and bands of music in the North.[8]

> You might as well appeal against the thunder-storm as against these terrible hardships of war. They are inevitable, and the only way the people of Atlanta can hope once more to live in peace and quiet at home, is to stop the war, which can only be done by admitting that it began in error and is perpetuated in pride.
>
> We don't want your negroes, or your horses, or your houses, or your lands, or any thing you have, but we do want and will have a just obedience to the laws of the United States. That we will have, and, if it involves the destruction of your improvements, we cannot help it. . . .
>
> But, my dear sirs, when peace does come, you may call on me for any thing. Then will I share with you the last cracker, and watch with you to shield your homes and families against danger from every quarter.
>
> Now you must go, and take with you the old and feeble, feed and nurse them, and build for them, in more quiet places, proper habitations to shield them against the weather until the mad passions of men cool down, and allow the Union and peace once more to settle over your old homes at Atlanta.

Memoirs, 2:126–27.

8. The conquest of Atlanta received its most celebrated popular treatment in Margaret Mitchell's *Gone With the Wind* and the film subsequently made from it. Mitchell describes the burning of Atlanta with a sentimentality—indicated by the preoccupation with dogs and cats—that has long dominated the Southern war story. When Scarlett's second husband Frank Kennedy tries to tell Scarlett and Melanie what has happened to Atlanta, he cannot, Mitchell writes, "bring himself to tell the worst" because "upsetting ladies . . . made him feel helpless." She continues:

> He could not tell them what the army saw when it marched back into

Atlanta, the acres and acres of chimneys standing blackly above ashes, piles of half-burned rubbish and tumbled heaps of brick clogging the streets, old trees dying from fire, their charred limbs tumbling to the ground in the cold wind. He remembered how the sight had turned him sick, remembered the bitter curses of the Confederates when they saw the remains of the town. He hoped the ladies would never hear of the horrors of the looted cemetery, for they'd never get over that. . . . The sight of that cemetery still gave Frank nightmares. Hoping to find jewelry buried with the dead, the Yankee soldiers had broken open vaults, dug up graves. They had robbed the bodies, stripped from the coffins gold and silver name plates, silver trimmings and silver handles. The skeletons and corpses, flung helter-skelter among their splintered caskets, lay exposed and so pitiful.

And Frank couldn't tell them about the dogs and the cats. Ladies set such a store by pets. But the thousands of starving animals, left homeless when their masters had been so rudely evacuated, had shocked him almost as much as the cemetery, for Frank loved cats and dogs. The animals had been frightened, cold, ravenous, wild as forest creatures, the strong attacking the weak, the weak waiting for the weaker to die so they could eat them.

Gone with the Wind (1936; New York: Pocket, 2008), 666.

David O. Selznick's sensational 1939 film dramatized the devastation of Atlanta in a spectacular montage of flames and tramping soldiers over which is superimposed in bold white letters the name, "SHERMAN!" One of the film's most powerful shots is that of Scarlett amid thousands of wounded Confederate soldiers lying helpless on the ground at the railroad depot. When the film premiered at the Loew's Grand Theater in the segregated city of Atlanta, Hattie McDaniel, the African American actor who would win an Oscar for her performance as Mammy, was prohibited from attending.

Grand Movement of the Army of the Potomac—Crossing the Rapidan—Entering the Wilderness—Battle of the Wilderness

Soon after midnight, May 3d–4th, the Army of the Potomac moved out from its position north of the Rapidan, to start upon that memorable campaign, destined to result in the capture of the Confederate capital and the army defending it. This was not to be accomplished, however, without as desperate fighting as the world has ever witnessed; not to be consummated in a day, a week, a month, or a single season. The losses inflicted, and endured, were destined to be severe; but the armies now confronting each other had already been in deadly conflict for a period of three years, with immense losses in killed, by death from sickness, captured and wounded; and neither had made any real progress accomplishing the final end. It is true the Confederates had, so far, held their capital, and they claimed this to be their sole object. But previously they had boldly proclaimed their intention to capture Philadelphia, New York, and the National Capital, and had made several attempts to do so, and once or twice had come fearfully near making their boast good—too near for complacent contemplation by the loyal North. They had also come near losing their own capital on at least one occasion. So here was a stand-off. The campaign now begun was destined to result in heavier losses, to both armies, in a given time, than any previously suffered; but the carnage was to be limited to a single year, and to accomplish all that had been anticipated or desired at the beginning in that time. We had to have hard fighting to achieve this. The two armies had been confronting each other so long, without any decisive result, that they hardly knew which could whip.

Ten days' rations, with a supply of forage and ammunition were taken in wagons. Beef cattle were driven with the trains, and butchered as wanted. Three days' rations in addition, in haversacks, and fifty rounds of cartridges, were carried on the person of each soldier.

The country over which the army had to operate, from the Rapidan to the crossing of the James River, is rather flat, and is cut by numerous streams which make their way to the Chesapeake Bay. The crossings of these streams by the army were generally made not far above tide-water, and where they formed a considerable obstacle to the rapid advance of troops even when the enemy did not appear in opposition. The country roads were narrow and poor. Most of the country is covered with a dense forest, in places, like the Wilderness and along the Chickahominy, almost impenetrable even for infantry except along the roads. All bridges were naturally destroyed before the National troops came to them.

The Army of the Potomac was composed of three infantry and one cavalry corps, commanded respectively by Generals W. S. Hancock, G. K. Warren, John Sedgwick and P. H. Sheridan. The artillery was commanded by General Henry J. Hunt. This arm was in such abundance that the fourth of it could not be used to advantage in such a country as we were destined to pass through.[1] The surplus was much in the way, taking up as it did so much of the narrow and bad roads, and consuming so much of the forage and other stores brought up by the trains.[2]

---

1. Flavius Vegetius, the author of a highly influential book on Roman military practice, warned of the danger of excessively large armies:

> An army too numerous is subject to many dangers and inconveniences. Its bulk makes it slow and unwieldy in its motions; and as it is obliged to march in columns of great length, it is exposed to the risk of being continually harassed and insulted by inconsiderable parties of the enemy. The incumbrance of the baggage is often an occasion of its being surprised in its passage through difficult places or over rivers. The difficulty of providing forage for such numbers of horses and other beasts of burden is very great. Besides, scarcity of provisions . . . soon ruins such large armies. . . . And sometimes they unavoidably will be distressed for want of water. . . .
>
> The ancients, taught by experience, preferred discipline to numbers.

Flavius Vegetius Renatus, *The Military Institutions of the Romans*, trans. John Clark, ed. Thomas R. Phillips (Harrisburg, PA: Military Service Publishing, 1944), 69.

2. For the command charts of the Union and Confederate armies included at this point in the first edition, see Appendix 1, chapter 50, note 1.

Such tables and lists of personnel are a common feature of Civil War memoirs,

The 5th corps, General Warren commanding, was in advance on the right, and marched directly for Germania Ford, preceded by one division of cavalry, under General J. H. Wilson. General Sedgwick followed Warren with the 6th corps. Germania Ford was nine or ten miles below the right of Lee's line. Hancock, with the 2d corps, moved by another road, farther east, directly upon Ely's Ford, six miles below Germania, preceded by Gregg's division of cavalry, and followed by the artillery. Torbert's division of cavalry was left north of the Rapidan, for the time, to picket the river and pre-

---

where they can be found within the narrative itself, after the discussion of a battle, or in appendices. Their purpose is primarily informational, but they also serve as a roll of honor. Their literary ancestor is the catalogue of ships in book 2 of Homer's *Iliad*, a three-hundred-line excursion that has intrigued and sometimes frustrated readers for centuries. Why, they ask, does Homer spend so much time enumerating the members of the Greek alliance? One of the effects of this relentless list of names is to underscore the war's magnitude. The roll call of individual soldiers also works against what the poem acknowledges to be the great leveling force of war. Here is a representative sample of Homer's catalogue:

> What crowded armies, from what climes, they bring,
> Their names, their numbers, and their chiefs, I sing.

THE CATALOGUE OF THE SHIPS

> The hardy warriors whom Bœotia bred,
> Peneleus, Leitus, Prothoënor led:
> With these Arcesilaus and Clonius stand,
> Equal in arms, and equal in command.
> . . . .
> Great Agamemnon rules the numerous band,
> A hundred vessels in long order stand,
> And crowded nations wait his dread command.
> High on the deck the king of men appears,
> And his refulgent arms in triumph wears;
> Proud of his host, unrivalled in his reign,
> In silent pomp he moves along the main.
> . . . .
> Last under Prothous the Magnesians stood,
> Prothous the swift, of old Tenthredon's blood;
> . . . .
> In forty sable barks they stemmed the main;
> Such were the chiefs, and such the Grecian train.

Iliad, trans. Alexander Pope, ed. A. J. Church (London: John Lane, 1907), bk. 2, ll. 584–89, 694–700, 916–17, 922–23.

vent the enemy from crossing and getting into our rear. The cavalry seized the two crossings before daylight, drove the enemy's pickets guarding them away, and by six o'clock A.M. had the pontoons laid ready for the crossing of the infantry and artillery. This was undoubtedly a surprise to Lee. The fact that the movement was unopposed proves this.

Burnside, with the 9th corps, was left back at Warrenton, guarding the railroad from Bull Run forward to preserve control of it in case our crossing the Rapidan should be long delayed. He was instructed, however, to advance at once on receiving notice that the army had crossed; and a dispatch was sent to him a little after one P.M. giving the information that our crossing had been successful.

The country was heavily wooded at all the points of crossing, particularly on the south side of the river. The battle-field from the crossing of the Rapidan until the final movement from the Wilderness toward Spottsylvania was of the same character. There were some clearings and small farms within what might be termed the battle-field; but generally the country was covered with a dense forest. The roads were narrow and bad. All the conditions were favorable for defensive operations.

There are two roads, good for that part of Virginia, running from Orange Court House to the battle-field. The most southerly of these roads is known as the Orange Court House Plank Road, the northern one as the Orange Turnpike. There are also roads from east of the battle-field running to Spottsylvania Court House, one from Chancellorsville, branching at Aldrich's; the western branch going by Piney Branch Church, Alsop's, thence by the Brock Road to Spottsylvania; the east branch goes by Gates's, thence to Spottsylvania. The Brock Road runs from Germania Ford through the battle-field and on to the Court House. As Spottsylvania is approached the country is cut up with numerous roads, some going to the town direct, and others crossing so as to connect the farms with roads going there.

Lee's headquarters were at Orange Court House. From there to Fredericksburg he had the use of the two roads above described running nearly parallel to the Wilderness. This gave him unusual facilities, for that country, for concentrating his forces to his right. These roads strike the road from Germania Ford in the Wilderness.

As soon as the crossing of the infantry was assured, the cavalry pushed forward, Wilson's division by Wilderness Tavern to Parker's store, on the Orange Plank Road; Gregg to the left towards Chancellorsville. Warren followed Wilson and reached the Wilderness Tavern by noon, took position there and intrenched. Sedgwick followed Warren. He was across the river and in camp

Federal wagon train, Petersburg, Virginia. *Library of Congress, Prints and Photographs Division, LC-DIG-stereo-1s02787.*

on the south bank, on the right of Warren, by sundown. Hancock, with the 2d corps, moved parallel with Warren and camped about six miles east of him. Before night all the troops, and by the evening of the 5th the trains of more than four thousand wagons, were safely on the south side of the river.

There never was a corps better organized than was the quartermaster's corps with the Army of the Potomac in 1864. With a wagon-train that would have extended from the Rapidan to Richmond, stretched along in single file and separated as the teams necessarily would be when moving, we could still carry only three days' forage and about ten to twelve days' rations, besides a supply of ammunition. To overcome all difficulties, the chief quartermaster, General Rufus Ingalls, had marked on each wagon the corps badge with the division color and the number of the brigade.[3] At a glance, the particular brigade to which any wagon belonged could be told. The wagons were also marked to note the contents: if ammunition, whether for artillery or infantry; if forage, whether grain or hay; if rations, whether, bread, pork, beans, rice, sugar, coffee or whatever it might be. Empty wagons were never allowed to follow the army or stay in camp. As soon as a wagon was empty it would return to the base of supply for a load of precisely the same article that had been taken from it. Empty trains were obliged to leave the road free for loaded ones. Arriving near the army they would be parked in fields nearest to the brigades they belonged to. Issues, except of ammunition, were made at night in all cases. By this system the

3. Grant's West Point classmate Rufus Ingalls (1818–1893) served on frontier duty, in Mexico, and in California and Washington before the Civil War, during which he served exclusively as a quartermaster.

hauling of forage for the supply train was almost wholly dispensed with. They consumed theirs at the depots.

I left Culpeper Court House after all the troops had been put in motion, and passing rapidly to the front, crossed the Rapidan in advance of Sedgwick's corps; and established headquarters for the afternoon and night in a deserted house near the river.

Orders had been given, long before this movement began, to cut down the baggage of officers and men to the lowest point possible. Notwithstanding this I saw scattered along the road from Culpeper to Germania Ford wagon-loads of new blankets and overcoats, thrown away by the troops to lighten their knapsacks; an improvidence I had never witnessed before.

Lee, while his pickets and signal corps must have discovered at a very early hour on the morning of the 4th of May, that the Army of the Potomac was moving, evidently did not learn until about one o'clock in the afternoon by what route we would confront his army. This I judge from the fact that at 1.15 P.M., an hour and a quarter after Warren had reached Old Wilderness Tavern, our officers took off rebel signals which, when translated, were seen to be an order to his troops to occupy their intrenchments at Mine Run.

Here at night dispatches were received announcing that Sherman, Butler and Crook had moved according to programme.

On discovering the advance of the Army of the Potomac, Lee ordered Hill, Ewell and Longstreet, each commanding corps, to move to the right to attack us, Hill on the Orange Plank Road, Longstreet to follow on the same road.[4] Longstreet was at this time—middle of the afternoon—at Gordonsville, twenty or more miles away. Ewell was ordered by the Orange Pike. He was near by and arrived some four miles east of Mine Run before bivouacking for the night.

---

4. Ambrose P. Hill (1825–1865) graduated from West Point in 1847; Ambrose Burnside was one of his classmates. Hill went on to serve as an artillery officer in the Mexican War. He subsequently fought against the Seminoles in Florida. He resigned his commision on March 1, 1861, to join the C.S.A., in which he ultimately became a corps commander in the Army of Northern Virginia. Hill fought in several of the major battles of the Eastern Theater, including the Seven Days, Antietam, Chancellorsville, and Gettysburg. He was killed near Petersburg a week before the end of the war. The U.S. Army's Fort A. P. Hill, established in 1941 in Caroline County, Virginia, is named in "honor" of this "American soldier" because, as the Installation Diary makes clear, of his distinguished career in the "Confederate Service," rather than for anything he accomplished while wearing the uniform of the federal army. See Installation Diary, June 1941–1961, 2, http://www.aphill.army.mil/docs/History/Installation%20Diary%20Jun%201941-1961.pdf.

My orders were given through General Meade for an early advance on the morning of the 5th. Warren was to move to Parker's store, and Wilson's cavalry—then at Parker's store—to move on to Craig's meeting-house. Sedgwick followed Warren, closing in on his right. The Army of the Potomac was facing to the west, though our advance was made to the south, except when facing the enemy. Hancock was to move south-westward to join on the left of Warren, his left to reach to Shady Grove Church.

At six o'clock, before reaching Parker's store, Warren discovered the enemy. He sent word back to this effect, and was ordered to halt and prepare to meet and attack him. Wright, with his division of Sedgwick's corps, was ordered, by any road he could find, to join on to Warren's right, and Getty with his division, also of Sedgwick's corps, was ordered to move rapidly by Warren's rear and get on his left. This was the speediest way to reinforce Warren, who was confronting the enemy on both the Orange plank and turnpike roads.

Burnside had moved promptly on the 4th, on receiving word that the Army of the Potomac had safely crossed the Rapidan. By making a night march, although some of his troops had to march forty miles to reach the river, he was crossing with the head of his column early on the morning of the 5th.

Meade moved his headquarters on to Old Wilderness Tavern, four miles south of the river, as soon as it was light enough to see the road. I remained to hasten Burnside's crossing and to put him in position. Burnside at this time was not under Meade's command, and was his senior in rank. Getting information of the proximity of the enemy, I informed Meade, and without waiting to see Burnside, at once moved forward my headquarters to where Meade was.

It was my plan then, as it was on all other occasions, to take the initiative whenever the enemy could be drawn from his intrenchments if we were not intrenched ourselves. Warren had not yet reached the point where he was to halt, when he discovered the enemy near by. Neither party had any advantage of position. Warren was, therefore, ordered to attack as soon as he could prepare for it. At nine o'clock Hancock was ordered to come up to the support of Getty. He himself arrived at Getty's front about noon, but his troops were yet far in the rear. Getty was directed to hold his position at all hazards until relieved. About this hour Warren was ready, and attacked with favorable though not decisive results. Getty was somewhat isolated from Warren and was in a precarious condition for a time. Wilson, with his division of cavalry, was farther south, and was cut off from the rest of the army. At two o'clock Hancock's troops began to arrive, and immediately he was ordered to join Getty and attack the enemy. But the heavy timber and narrow roads prevented him from getting into position for attack as promptly as he generally did when receiving such orders. At four o'clock he again received his orders to attack, and General Getty received orders from Meade a few minutes later to attack whether Hancock was ready or not. He met the enemy under Heth within a few hundred yards.

Hancock immediately sent two divisions, commanded by Birney and Mott, and later two brigades, Carroll's and Owen's, to the support of Getty. This was timely and saved Getty. During the battle Getty and Carroll were wounded, but remained on the field. One of Birney's most gallant brigade commanders—Alexander Hays—was killed.

I had been at West Point with Hays for three years, and had served with him through the Mexican war, a portion of the time in the same regiment. He was a most gallant officer, ready to lead his command wherever ordered. With him it was "Come, boys," not "Go."[5]

Wadsworth's division and Baxter's brigade of the 2d division were sent to reinforce Hancock and Getty; but the density of the intervening forest was such that, there being no road to march upon, they did not get up with the head of column until night, and bivouacked where they were without getting into position.

During the afternoon Sheridan sent Gregg's division of cavalry to Todd's Tavern in search of Wilson. This was fortunate. He found Wilson engaged with a superior force under General Rosser, supported by infantry, and falling back before it. Together they were strong enough to turn the tables upon the enemy and themselves become aggressive. They soon drove the rebel cavalry back beyond Corbin's Bridge.

---

5. Grant had known Alexander Hays well for years. Hays (1819–1864) graduated from West Point in 1844 and served on frontier duty in Louisiana until the outbreak of the Mexican War. He resigned at its conclusion but began organizing a regiment of Pennsylvania volunteers in April 1861. Hays fought exclusively in the Eastern Theater before being killed at the Battle of the Wilderness: "Up came Hays's brigade, disappeared in the woods, and, in a few minutes, General Hays was carried past me, covered with blood, shot through the head," Meade's aide-de-camp Theodore Lyman reported to his wife. "Hays . . . was a strong-built, rough sort of man, with red hair, and a tawny full beard; a braver man never went into action, and the wonder only is that he was not killed before, as he always rode at the very head of his men, shouting to them and waving his sword." Letters to Elizabeth Lyman, May 15 and 16, 1864, *1863–1865: Letters of Colonel Theodore Lyman from the Wilderness to Appomattox*, ed. George R. Agassiz (Boston: Massachusetts Historical Society, 1922), 92–93.

Lieutenants Ulysses Grant and Alexander Hays, 1845. *Special Collections, United States Military Academy Library.*

Fighting between Hancock and Hill continued until night put a close to it. Neither side made any special progress.

After the close of the battle of the 5th of May my orders were given for the following morning.[6] We knew Longstreet with 12,000 men was on

---

6. The journalist William Swinton captured the particular confusions of the battlefield at the Wilderness:

> The troops could only receive direction by a point of the compass; for not only were the lines of battle entirely hidden from the sight of the commander, but no officer could see ten files on each side of him. Artillery was wholly ruled out of use; the massive concentration of three hundred guns stood silent, and only an occasional piece or section could be brought into play in the road-sides. Cavalry was still more useless. But in that horrid thicket there lurked two hundred thousand men, and through it lurid fires played; and, though no array of battle could be seen, there came out of its depths the crackle and roll of musketry like the noisy boiling of some hell-caldron that told the dread story of death.

Swinton, *Campaigns*, 429.

Horace Porter describes the Wilderness as "a battle fought with the ear, and not with the eye." The senses of sound and touch "guided the movements" of the actors in a "scene . . . of unutterable horror." Porter also notes that Grant responded to an anxious, excitable officer who came to him in the middle of the battle with theories about what Lee was going to do: "Oh, I am heartily tired of hearing about what Lee is going to do. Some of you always seem to think he is suddenly going to turn a double sommersault, and land in our rear and on both of our flanks at the same time. Go back to your command, and try to think what we are going to do ourselves, instead of what Lee is going to do." Porter, *Campaigning*, 72, 70.

his way to join Hill's right, near the Brock Road, and might arrive during the night. I was anxious that the rebels should not take the initiative in the morning, and therefore ordered Hancock to make an assault at 4.30 o'clock. Meade asked to have the hour changed to six. Deferring to his wishes as far as I was willing, the order was modified and five was fixed as the hour to move.

Hancock had now fully one-half of the Army of the Potomac. Wadsworth with his division, which had arrived the night before, lay in a line perpendicular to that held by Hill, and to the right of Hancock. He was directed to move at the same time, and to attack Hill's left.

Burnside, who was coming up with two divisions, was directed to get in between Warren and Wadsworth, and attack as soon as he could get in position to do so. Sedgwick and Warren were to make attacks in their front, to detain as many of the enemy as they could and to take advantage of any attempt to reinforce Hill from that quarter. Burnside was ordered if he should succeed in breaking the enemy's centre, to swing around to the left and envelop the right of Lee's army. Hancock was informed of all the movements ordered.

Burnside had three divisions, but one of them—a colored division—was sent to guard the wagon train, and he did not see it again until July.

Lee was evidently very anxious that there should be no battle on his right until Longstreet got up. This is evident from the fact that notwithstanding the early hour at which I had ordered the assault, both for the purpose of being the attacking party and to strike before Longstreet got up, Lee was ahead in his assault on our right. His purpose was evident, but he failed.

Hancock was ready to advance by the hour named, but learning in time that Longstreet was moving a part of his corps by the Catharpin Road, thus threatening his left flank, sent a division of infantry, commanded by General Barlow, with all his artillery, to cover the approaches by which Longstreet was expected. This disposition was made in time to attack as ordered. Hancock moved by the left of the Orange Plank Road, and Wadsworth by the right of it. The fighting was desperate for about an hour, when the enemy began to break up in great confusion.

I believed then, and see no reason to change that opinion now, that if the country had been such that Hancock and his command could have seen the confusion and panic in the lines of the enemy, it would have been taken advantage of so effectually that Lee would not have made another stand outside of his Richmond defences.

Gibbon commanded Hancock's left, and was ordered to attack, but was not able to accomplish much.

On the morning of the 6th Sheridan was sent to connect with Hancock's left and attack the enemy's cavalry who were trying to get on our left and rear. He met them at the intersection of the Furnace and Brock roads and at Todd's Tavern, and defeated them at both places. Later he was attacked, and again the enemy was repulsed.

Hancock heard the firing between Sheridan and Stuart, and thinking the enemy coming by that road, still further reinforced his position guarding the entrance to the Brock Road. Another incident happened during the day to further induce Hancock to weaken his attacking column. Word reached him that troops were seen moving towards him from the direction of Todd's Tavern, and Brooke's brigade was detached to meet this new enemy; but the troops approaching proved to be several hundred convalescents coming from Chancellorsville, by the road Hancock had advanced upon, to join their respective commands. At 6.50 o'clock A.M., Burnside, who had passed Wilderness Tavern at six o'clock, was ordered to send a division to the support of Hancock, but to continue with the remainder of his command in the execution of his previous order. The difficulty of making a way through the dense forests prevented Burnside from getting up in time to be of any service on the forenoon of the sixth.

Hancock followed Hill's retreating forces, in the morning, a mile or more. He maintained this position until, along in the afternoon, Longstreet came upon him. The retreating column of Hill meeting reinforcements that had not yet been engaged, became encouraged and returned with them. They were enabled, from the density of the forest, to approach within a few hundred yards of our advance before being discovered. Falling upon a brigade of Hancock's corps thrown to the advance, they swept it away almost instantly. The enemy followed up his advantage and soon came upon Mott's division, which fell back in great confusion. Hancock made dispositions to hold his advanced position, but after holding it for a time, fell back into the position that he had held in the morning, which was strongly intrenched. In this engagement the intrepid Wadsworth while trying to rally his men was mortally wounded and fell into the hands of the enemy.[7] The enemy followed up, but made no immediate attack.

7. James S. Wadsworth (1807–1864) was a wealthy, politically influential abolitionist from New York and a volunteer without previous military experience. He carried the saber his grandfather had worn in the Revolution. See Leech, *Reveille in Washington*, 167. Grant's use of the epithet "the intrepid Wadsworth" is uncharacteristic. Lincoln, too, was deeply "affected" by the general's death: "no man," the president remarked, according to his secretary John Hay, "has given himself up to the war with such self

The Confederate General Jenkins was killed and Longstreet seriously wounded in this engagement. Longstreet had to leave the field, not to resume command for many weeks. His loss was a severe one to Lee, and compensated in a great measure for the mishap, or misapprehensions, which had fallen to our lot during the day.

After Longstreet's removal from the field Lee took command of his right in person. He was not able, however, to rally his men to attack Hancock's position, and withdrew from our front for the purpose of reforming. Hancock sent a brigade to clear his front of all remnants that might be left of Longstreet's or Hill's commands. This brigade having been formed at right angles to the intrenchments held by Hancock's command, swept down the whole length of them from left to right. A brigade of the enemy was encountered in this move; but it broke and disappeared without a contest.

Firing was continued after this, but with less fury. Burnside had not yet been able to get up to render any assistance. But it was now only about nine in the morning, and he was getting into position on Hancock's right.

At 4.15 in the afternoon Lee attacked our left. His line moved up to within a hundred yards of ours and opened a heavy fire. This status was maintained for about half an hour. Then a part of Mott's division and Ward's brigade of Birney's division gave way and retired in disorder. The enemy under R. H. Anderson took advantage of this and pushed through our line, planting their flags on a part of the intrenchments not on fire. But owing to the efforts of Hancock, their success was but temporary. Carroll, of Gibbon's division, moved at a double quick with his brigade and drove back the enemy,

---

sacrificing patriotism as Genl. Wadsworth. He went into the service not wishing or expecting great success or distinction in his military career & profoundly indifferent to popular applause, actuated only by a sense of duty which he neither evaded nor sought to evade." May 14, 1864, *Inside Lincoln's White House*, 196.

Alfred R. Waud, "General Wadsworth just before his death." *Library of Congress, Prints and Photographs Division, LC-DIG-ppmsca-20047.*

inflicting great loss. Fighting had continued from five in the morning some-times along the whole line, at other times only in places. The ground fought over had varied in width, but averaged three-quarters of a mile. The killed, and many of the severely wounded, of both armies, lay within this belt where it was impossible to reach them. The woods were set on fire by the bursting shells, and the conflagration raged. The wounded who had not strength to move themselves were either suffocated or burned to death. Finally the fire communicated with our breastworks, in places. Being constructed of wood, they burned with great fury. But the battle still raged, our men firing through the flames until it became too hot to remain longer.[8]

8. In his regimental history of the 121st New York Infantry ("Upton's Regulars"), Isaac O. Best records the eyewitness testimony of Colonel Clinton Beckwith about the fire and its devastating effects:

> [A] good many wounded were scattered through the woods and thickets, which were on fire in front and on both sides of us. Many wounded on both sides must have perished in the flames, as partially burned bodies were seen scattered about on the burned-over ground. The balance of our division was formed on our right, and by night our lines were formed. We lay in line of battle upon our arms, and shortly after dark when the firing slack-ened, the cries of the wounded between the lines, which were not far apart, was something terrible to hear. Some prayed, some cursed, some cried and some asked to be killed and put out of their misery.

History of the 121st New York State Infantry (Chicago: Privately printed, 1921), 120–21.

The Roman historian Livy depicts the similarly horrific scene that greeted Hannibal's victorious Carthaginians as they surveyed the field at Cannae on the morning after the battle:

> At dawn next morning the Carthaginians applied themselves to col-lecting the spoils and viewing the carnage, which even to an enemy's eyes was a shocking spectacle. All over the field Roman soldiers lay dead in their thousands, horse and foot mingled, as the shifting phases of the battle, or the attempt to escape, had brought them together. Here and there wounded men, covered with blood, who had been roused to consciousness by the morning cold, were dispatched by a quick blow as they struggled to rise from amongst the corpses; others were found still alive with the sinews in their thighs and behind their knees sliced through, baring their throats and necks and begging who would to spill what little blood they had left. Some had their heads buried in the ground, having apparently dug themselves holes and by smothering their faces with earth had choked themselves to death. Most strange of all was a Numidian soldier, still living, and lying, with nose and ears horribly lacerated, underneath the body of a Roman

Lee was now in distress. His men were in confusion, and his personal efforts failed to restore order. These facts, however, were learned subsequently, or we would have taken advantage of his condition and no doubt gained a decisive success. His troops were withdrawn now, but I revoked the order, which I had given previously to this assault, for Hancock to attack, because his troops had exhausted their ammunition and did not have time to replenish from the train, which was at some distance.

Burnside, Sedgwick, and Warren had all kept up an assault during all this time; but their efforts had no other effect than to prevent the enemy from reinforcing his right from the troops in their front.

I had, on the 5th, ordered all the bridges over the Rapidan to be taken up except one at Germania Ford.

The troops on Sedgwick's right had been sent to reinforce our left. This left our right in danger of being turned, and us of being cut off from all present base of supplies. Sedgwick had refused his right and intrenched it for protection against attack. But late in the afternoon of the 6th [Jubal A.] Early came out from his lines in considerable force and got in upon Sedgwick's right, notwithstanding the precautions taken, and created considerable confusion. Early captured several hundred prisoners, among them two general officers. The defence, however, was vigorous; and night coming on, the enemy was thrown into as much confusion as our troops, engaged, were. Early says in his Memoirs that if we had discovered the confusion in his lines we might have brought fresh troops to his great discomfort. Many officers, who had not been attacked by Early, continued coming to my headquarters even after Sedgwick had rectified his lines a little farther to the rear, with news of the disaster, fully impressed with the idea that the enemy was pushing on and would soon be upon me.

During the night all of Lee's army withdrew within their intrenchments. On the morning of the 7th General Custer drove the enemy's cavalry from Catharpin Furnace to Todd's Tavern.[9] Pickets and skirmishers were sent

---

who, when his useless hands had no longer been able to grasp his sword,
had died in the act of tearing his enemy, in bestial fury, with his teeth.

The War with Hannibal, Books XXI–XXX of *The History of Rome from Its Foundation*, trans. Aubrey de Sélincourt, ed. Betty Radice (New York: Penguin Classics, 1972), 151–52.

9. George Armstrong Custer (1839–1876) is best known for his defeat at the Battle of Little Big Horn, in Montana, at the age of thirty-seven. However, he learned his trade in the Civil War. Custer graduated from West Point in 1861; by 1865 he was a brevet

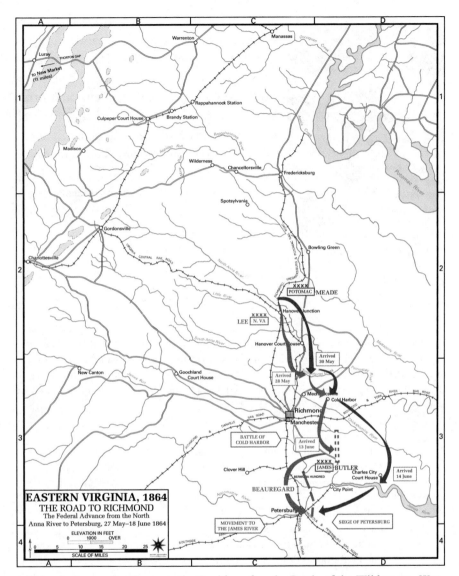

A   B   C   D

Warrenton   Manassas

Luray
THORTON GAP
to New Market
(11 miles)

Rappahannock Station

Culpeper Court House   Brandy Station

Madison

Wilderness   Chancellorsville   Fredericksburg

Spotsylvania

Potomac River

Gordonsville

Bowling Green

Charlottesville

XXXX
POTOMAC   MEADE

Hanover Junction
XXXX
LEE   N. VA

Hanover Court House

New Canton

Goochland
Court House

Arrived
30 May

Arrived
28 May

Mechanicsville   Cold Harbor

Richmond
Manchester

BATTLE OF
COLD HARBOR

Arrived
13 June

Clover Hill

XXXX
JAMES   BUTLER
Charles City
Court House

Arrived
14 June

BEAUREGARD

City Point

Petersburg

EASTERN VIRGINIA, 1864
THE ROAD TO RICHMOND
The Federal Advance from the North
Anna River to Petersburg, 27 May–18 June 1864

ELEVATION IN FEET
0   1000   OVER

N

0   5   10   15   20   25
SCALE OF MILES

MOVEMENT TO
THE JAMES RIVER

SIEGE OF PETERSBURG

Federal advance South across the Rapidan after the Battle of the Wilderness. *West
Point Atlas of the Civil War. Courtesy of Department of History, USMA.*

major general. Flamboyant, audacious, energetic, vain, Custer has been a subject of
controversy and fascination ever since his death. On first seeing Custer in August 1863,
the surgeon J. Franklin Dyer recorded this delightful portrait in his journal: "General
Custer . . . is a gorgeous-looking young man—smart though—his dress a black velvet
jacket and pants, double knot of lace on sleeves, and two gold stripes on the legs, and
light flaxen hair falling in curls on his shoulders. Some men can dress like circus riders
without making themselves ridiculous." *Journal*, 114.

Burial place of Stonewall Jackson's arm, Wilderness Battlefield, Virginia. *Photograph by Elizabeth D. Samet.*

along our entire front to find the position of the enemy. Some went as far as a mile and a half before finding him. But Lee showed no disposition to come out of his Works. There was no battle during the day, and but little firing except in Warren's front; he being directed about noon to make a reconnoissance in force. This drew some sharp firing, but there was no attempt on the part of Lee to drive him back. This ended the Battle of the Wilderness.[10]

10. An incident that subsequently became the stuff of legend occurred on the second day. Lee, energized by the arrival of the Texas Brigade, began to lead them toward the enemy when the soldiers, alarmed for their commander, stopped him crying: "Lee to the rear!" Soldiers escorted him back to safety. The moment was commemorated by John Reuben Thompson in "Lee to the Rear."

> The grand old gray-beard rode to the space,
> Where Death and his victims stood face to face,
> And silently waved his old slouch hat—
> A world of meaning there was in that!
>
> "Follow me! Steady! We'll save the day!"
> This was what he seemed to say:
> And to the light of his glorious eye
> The bold brigades thus made reply:
>
> "We'll go forward, but you must go back,"
> And they moved not an inch in the perilous track
> "Go to the rear and we'll send them to h—"
> And the sound of the battle was lost in their yell.
>
> Turning his bridle, Robert Lee
> Rode to the rear. . . .

Library of Southern Literature, vol. 12, ed. Edwin Anderson Alderman and Joel Chandler Harris (Atlanta: Martin & Hoyt, 1910), 5249–250.

After the Battle—Telegraph and Signal Service—Movement by the Left Flank

More desperate fighting has not been witnessed on this continent than that of the 5th and 6th of May. Our victory consisted in having successfully crossed a formidable stream, almost in the face of an enemy, and in getting the army together as a unit. We gained an advantage on the morning of the 6th, which, if it had been followed up, must have proven very decisive. In the evening the enemy gained an advantage; but was speedily repulsed. As we stood at the close, the two armies were relatively in about the same condition to meet each other as when the river divided them. But the fact of having safely crossed was a victory.[1]

Our losses in the Wilderness were very severe. Those of the Confederates must have been even more so; but I have no means of speaking with

---

1. On the morning of May 7, the two armies having fought to an exhausted standstill at the Wilderness, Grant surprised the Army of the Potomac by deciding to go forward rather than backward, as his predecessors had done in succession. John G. B. Adams, a captain in the 19th Massachusetts, remarked: "Most of us thought it was another Chancellorsville, and that the next day we should recross the river; but when the order came, 'By the left flank, march!' we found that Grant was not made that way, and we must continue the fight." *Reminiscences*, 88.

The decision to advance in the wake of a bloody stalemate manifested the attribute Theodore Lyman thought distinguished Grant: "He habitually wears an expression as if he had determined to drive his head through a brick wall, and was about to do it. I have much confidence in him." Letter to Elizabeth Lyman, April 12, 1864, *Meade's Headquarters*, 81.

accuracy upon this point. The Germania Ford bridge was transferred to Ely's Ford to facilitate the transportation of the wounded to Washington.

It may be as well here as elsewhere to state two things connected with all movements of the Army of the Potomac: first, in every change of position or halt for the night, whether confronting the enemy or not, the moment arms were stacked the men intrenched themselves. For this purpose they would build up piles of logs or rails if they could be found in their front, and dig a ditch, throwing the dirt forward on the timber. Thus the digging they did counted in making a depression to stand in, and increased the elevation in front of them. It was wonderful how quickly they could in this way construct defences of considerable strength.[2] When a halt

---

2. The entrenched warfare of Grant's Overland Campaign produced tremendous casualties. By contrast, Sherman's army, which could rely on maneuver, managed to avoid attacking entrenched positions on their march. One exception was Atlanta. O. O. Howard's account reveals the costliness of the assault on Johnston's heavily fortified, "almost impregnable" position in the Kenesaw mountains:

> For reasons similar to those which influenced Lee to strike twice for Little Round Top, Sherman ordered an assault here with the hope of carrying the southern slope of Kenesaw, or of penetrating Johnston's long front at some weak point. Schofield, well southward, advanced and crossed Olley's Creek, and kept up enough fire and effort to hold a large force in his front. McPherson, on the left, did the same, a serious engagement being sustained by Logan's corps advancing straight against the mountain. Logan lost heavily from the trenches in his front, and from artillery that raked his men as they advanced. Seven regimental commanders fell, killed or wounded. But the dreadful battle, hard to describe, was left to Thomas. . . . Like Pickett's charge at Gettysburg, the movement was preceded by a heavy cannonade. Then our skirmishers sprang forward and opened; and quickly the enemy's skirmish-line was drawn back to their main work. . . . The enemy's fire was terrific. Our men did not stop till they had gained the edge of the felled trees; a few penetrated to fall close to the enemy's parapet; but most sought shelter behind logs and rocks in rifle-holes or depressions. Harker, moving with them, cheered on his men; when they were forced to stop, he rallied them again and made a second vigorous effort, in which he fell mortally wounded. Davis's effort was like Newton's; he met the same withering fire from rifle-balls and shells. But his men managed to make a shelter, which they kept, close up to the hostile works. Here they staid and intrenched. . . . Our losses in this assault were heavy indeed, and our gain was nothing. We realized now as never before, the futility of direct assaults upon intrenched lines already well prepared and well manned.

"The Struggle for Atlanta," *B&L*, 4:310–11.

was made with the view of assaulting the enemy, or in his presence, these would be strengthened or their positions changed under the direction of engineer officers. The second was, the use made of the telegraph and signal corps. Nothing could be more complete than the organization and discipline of this body of brave and intelligent men. Insulated wires—insulated so that they would transmit messages in a storm, on the ground or under water—were wound upon reels, making about two hundred pounds weight of wire to each reel. Two men and one mule were detailed to each reel. The pack-saddle on which this was carried was provided with a rack like a saw-buck placed crosswise of the saddle, and raised above it so that the reel, with its wire, would revolve freely. There was a wagon, supplied with a telegraph operator, battery and telegraph instruments for each division, each corps, each army, and one for my headquarters. There were wagons also loaded with light poles, about the size and length of a wall tent pole, supplied with an iron spike in one end, used to hold the wires up when laid, so that wagons and artillery would not run over them. The mules thus loaded were assigned to brigades, and always kept with the command they were assigned to. The operators were also assigned to particular headquarters, and never changed except by special orders.[3]

Such assaults were an all-too-common feature of the Civil War—at Vicksburg, Atlanta, Cold Harbor, Petersburg—and their lethality would only increase in the next century as the mass infantry attacks of World War I's Western Front—preceded, as in this case, with artillery bombardment—were met with machine-gun fire.

3. John Keegan argues that Grant "had a particular aptitude" for the telegraph. See *Mask of Command*, 212. Samuel F. B. Morse telegraphed his first message, "What hath God wrought?" from Washington to Baltimore in 1844. The telegraph network grew extensively throughout the country and the world in the ensuing decades. The transatlantic cable was laid in 1858, and by 1860 there were fifty thousand miles of telegraph lines in the United States. In 1861, efforts were made to organize the Military Telegraph as part of the Quartermaster Corps. It was divided into regional departments commanded by officers, with Colonel Anson Stager at their head. Operators, however, were civilians. The service's first historian, William Plum, who was an operator in the Western Theater, writes, "Thus organized, the United States Military Telegraph became the medium of communication by which hundreds of thousands of armed men were directed from point to point, commissary subsistence and ordnance stores ordered, and the innumerable necessities of great armies made known, as well as the story of their victories and defeats." Plum also took exception to what he regarded as Grant's undue interference with the organization of the telegraph service in the Western Theater. See *The Military Telegraph during the Civil War in the United States*, 2 vols. (Chicago: Jansen, McClurg, 1882), 1:131, 242–72.

Military Telegraph Construction Corps, April 1864. Photograph by Timothy L. O'Sullivan. *Library of Congress, Prints and Photographs Division, Civil War Photographs, LC-DIG-ppmsca-33168.*

Alfred Waud, "Grant writing out the telegram that communicates the crossing of the Rapidan, May 1864." *Library of Congress, Prints and Photographs Division, LC-DIG-ppmsca-21342.*

Field telegraph station, Wilcox's Landing, Virginia, 1864. *Library of Congress, Prints and Photographs Division, Civil War Photographs, Reproduction Number: LC-DIG-cwpb-01564.*

The moment the troops were put in position to go into camp all the men connected with this branch of service would proceed to put up their wires. A mule loaded with a coil of wire would be led to the rear of the nearest flank of the brigade he belonged to, and would be led in a line parallel thereto, while one man would hold an end of the wire and uncoil it as the mule was led off. When he had walked the length of the wire the whole of it would be on the ground. This would be done in rear of every brigade at the same time. The ends of all the wires would then be joined, making a continuous wire in the rear of the whole army. The men, attached to brigades or divisions, would all commence at once raising the wires with their telegraph poles. This was done by making a loop in the wire and putting it over the spike and raising the pole to a perpendicular position. At intervals the wire would be attached to trees, or some other permanent object, so that one pole was sufficient at a place. In the absence of such a support two poles would have to be used, at intervals, placed at an angle so as to hold the wire firm in its place. While this was being done the telegraph wagons would take their positions near where the headquarters they belonged to were to be established, and would connect with the wire. Thus, in a few minutes longer time than it took a mule to walk the length of its coil, telegraphic communication would be effected between all the headquarters of the army. No orders ever had to be given to establish the telegraph.

The signal service was used on the march. The men composing this corps were assigned to specified commands. When movements were made, they would go in advance, or on the flanks, and seize upon high points of ground giving a commanding view of the country, if cleared, or would climb tall trees on the highest points if not cleared, and would denote, by signals, the positions of different parts of our own army, and often the movements of the enemy. They would also take off the signals of the enemy and transmit them. It would sometimes take too long a time to make translations of intercepted dispatches for us to receive any benefit from them. But sometimes they gave useful information.

On the afternoon of the 7th I received news from Washington announcing that Sherman had probably attacked Johnston that day, and that Butler had reached City Point safely and taken it by surprise on the 5th. I had given orders for a movement by the left flank, fearing that Lee might move rapidly to Richmond to crush Butler before I could get there.

My order for this movement was as follows:

HEADQUARTERS ARMIES OF THE U.S.,
May 7, 1864, 6.30 A.M.

MAJOR-GENERAL MEADE,
Commanding A. P.

Make all preparations during the day for a night march to take
position at Spottsylvania C. H. with one army corps, at Todd's Tavern
with one, and another near the intersection of the Piney Branch and
Spottsylvania road with the road from Alsop's to Old Court House.
If this move is made the trains should be thrown forward early in the
morning to the Ny River.

I think it would be advisable in making the change to leave
Hancock where he is until Warren passes him. He could then
follow and become the right of the new line. Burnside will move
to Piney Branch Church. Sedgwick can move along the pike to
Chancellorsville and on to his destination. Burnside will move
on the plank road to the intersection of it with the Orange and
Fredericksburg plank road, then follow Sedgwick to his place of
destination.

All vehicles should be got out of hearing of the enemy before the
troops move, and then move off quietly.

It is more than probable that the enemy concentrate for a heavy
attack on Hancock this afternoon. In case they do we must be
prepared to resist them, and follow up any success we may gain,
with our whole force. Such a result would necessarily modify these
instructions.

All the hospitals should be moved to-day to Chancellorsville.

U. S. GRANT,
Lieut.-General.

During the 7th Sheridan had a fight with the rebel cavalry at Todd's
Tavern, but routed them, thus opening the way for the troops that were to
go by that route at night. Soon after dark Warren withdrew from the front
of the enemy, and was soon followed by Sedgwick. Warren's march carried
him immediately behind the works where Hancock's command lay on the
Brock Road. With my staff and a small escort of cavalry I preceded the
troops. Meade with his staff accompanied me. The greatest enthusiasm was
manifested by Hancock's men as we passed by. No doubt it was inspired by
the fact that the movement was south. It indicated to them that they had
passed through the "beginning of the end" in the battle just fought. The

Example of the gangrenous
decomposition that often resulted
from Civil War wounds, *The Medical
and Surgical History of the War of the
Rebellion. Courtesy of NIH U.S. National
Library of Medicine.*

cheering was so lusty that the enemy must have taken it for a night attack. At all events it drew from him a furious fusillade of artillery and musketry, plainly heard but not felt by us.

Meade and I rode in advance. We had passed but a little way beyond our left when the road forked. We looked to see, if we could, which road Sheridan had taken with his cavalry during the day. It seemed to be the right-hand one, and accordingly we took it. We had not gone far, however, when Colonel C. B. Comstock, of my staff, with the instinct of the engineer, suspecting that we were on a road that would lead us into the lines of the enemy, if he, too, should be moving, dashed by at a rapid gallop and all alone. In a few minutes he returned and reported that Lee was moving, and that the road we were on would bring us into his lines in a short distance. We returned to the forks of the road, left a man to indicate the right road to the head of Warren's column when it should come up, and continued our journey to Todd's Tavern, where we arrived after midnight.

My object in moving to Spottsylvania was two-fold: first, I did not want Lee to get back to Richmond in time to attempt to crush Butler before I could get there; second, I wanted to get between his army and Richmond if possible; and, if not, to draw him into the open field. But Lee, by accident, beat us to Spottsylvania. Our wagon trains had been ordered easterly of the roads the troops were to march upon before the movement commenced. Lee interpreted this as a semi-retreat of the Army of the Potomac to Fredericksburg, and so informed his government. Accordingly he ordered Longstreet's corps—now commanded by Anderson—to move in the morning (the 8th) to Spottsylvania. But the woods being still on fire, Anderson could not go into bivouac, and marched directly on to his destination that night. By this accident Lee got possession of Spottsylvania. It is impossible to say now what would have been the result if Lee's orders had been obeyed as given; but it is certain that we would have been in Spottsylvania, and between him and his capital. My belief is that there would have been a race between the two armies to see which could reach Richmond first, and the Army of the Potomac would have had the shorter line. Thus, twice since crossing the Rapidan we came near closing the campaign, so far as battles were concerned, from the Rapidan to the James River or Richmond. The first failure was caused by our not following up the success gained over Hill's corps on the morning of the 6th, as before described; the second, when fires caused by that battle drove Anderson to make a march during the night of the 7th–8th which he was ordered to commence on the morning of the 8th. But accident often decides the fate of battle.[4]

---

4. Moltke the Elder emphasized the role of chance and the predominance of ignorance in battle:

> Certainly the commander in chief (*Feldherr*) will keep his great objective (*Zweck*) continuously in mind, undisturbed by the vicissitudes of events. But the path on which he hopes to reach it can never be firmly established in advance. Throughout the campaign he must make a series of decisions on the basis of situations that cannot be foreseen. The successive acts of the war are thus not premeditated designs, but on the contrary are spontaneous acts guided by military measures. Everything depends on penetrating the uncertainty of veiled situations to evaluate the facts, to clarify the unknown, to make decisions rapidly, and then to carry them out with strength and constancy.
>
> To the calculation of a known and an unknown quantity, one's own will and that of the enemy, enter yet other factors. These are the fully unforeseeable: weather, illnesses, railway accidents, misunderstandings, and disappointments—in short, all the influences that one may call luck, fate, or higher providence, which mankind neither creates nor dominates.

Moltke on the Art of War, 45–46.

Caesar, too, insisted on the crucial role of luck: "luck, a force universally powerful but particularly so in war, brings about great changes by slight adjustments of her balance." *Civil War*, 113.

Sheridan's cavalry had had considerable fighting during the afternoon of the 7th, lasting at Todd's Tavern until after night, with the field his at the close. He issued the necessary orders for seizing Spottsylvania and holding the bridge over the Po River, which Lee's troops would have to cross to get to Spottsylvania. But Meade changed Sheridan's orders to [Wesley] Merritt—who was holding the bridge—on his arrival at Todd's Tavern, and thereby left the road free for Anderson when he came up. Wilson, who was ordered to seize the town, did so, with his division of cavalry; but he could not hold it against the Confederate corps which had not been detained at the crossing of the Po, as it would have been but for the unfortunate change in Merritt's orders. Had he been permitted to execute the orders Sheridan gave him, he would have been guarding with two brigades of cavalry the bridge over the Po River which Anderson had to cross, and must have detained him long enough to enable Warren to reinforce Wilson and hold the town.

Anderson soon intrenched himself—if indeed the intrenchments were not already made—immediately across Warren's front. Warren was not aware of his presence, but probably supposed it was the cavalry which Merritt had engaged earlier in the day. He assaulted at once, but was repulsed. He soon organized his men, as they were not pursued by the enemy, and made a second attack, this time with his whole corps. This time he succeeded in gaining a position immediately in the enemy's front, where he intrenched. His right and left divisions—the former Crawford's, the latter Wadsworth's, now commanded by Cutler—drove the enemy back some distance.

At this time my headquarters had been advanced to Piney Branch Church. I was anxious to crush Anderson before Lee could get a force to his support. To this end Sedgwick who was at Piney Branch Church, was ordered to Warren's support. Hancock, who was at Todd's Tavern, was notified of Warren's engagement, and was directed to be in readiness to come up. Burnside, who was with the wagon trains at Aldrich's on our extreme left, received the same instructions. Sedgwick was slow in getting up for some reason—probably unavoidable, because he was never at fault when serious work was to be done—so that it was near night before the combined forces were ready to attack. Even then all of Sedgwick's command did not get into the engagement. Warren led the last assault, one division at a time, and of course it failed.

Warren's difficulty was twofold: when he received an order to do anything, it would at once occur to his mind how all the balance of the army should be engaged so as properly to co-operate with him. His ideas were generally good, but he would forget that the person giving him orders had thought of others at the time he had of him. In like manner, when he did get ready to execute an order, after giving most intelligent instructions to division commanders, he would go in with one division, holding the others in reserve until he could superintend their movements in person also, forgetting that division commanders could execute an order without his presence. His difficulty was constitutional and beyond his control. He was an officer of superior ability, quick perceptions, and personal courage to accomplish anything that could be done with a small command.

Lee had ordered Hill's corps—now commanded by Early—to move by the very road we had marched upon. This shows that even early in the morning of the 8th Lee had not yet become acquainted with my move, but still thought that the Army of the Potomac had gone to Fredericksburg. Indeed, he informed the authorities at Richmond that he had possession of Spottsylvania and was thus on my flank. Anderson was in possession of Spottsylvania, through no foresight of Lee, however. Early only found that he had been following us when he ran against Hancock at Todd's Tavern. His coming detained Hancock from the battle-field of Spottsylvania for that day; but he, in like manner, kept Early back and forced him to move by another route.

Had I ordered the movement for the night of the 7th by my left flank, it would have put Hancock in the lead. It would also have given us an hour or more earlier start. It took all that time for Warren to get the head of his column to the left of Hancock after he had got his troops out of their line confronting the enemy. This hour, and Hancock's capacity to use his whole force when necessary, would, no doubt, have enabled him to crush Anderson before he could be reinforced. But the movement made was tactical. It kept the troops in mass against a possible assault by the enemy. Our left occupied its intrenchments while the two corps to the right passed. If an attack had been made by the enemy he would have found the 2d corps in position, fortified, and, practically, the 5th and 6th corps in position as reserves, until his entire front was passed. By a left flank movement the army would have been scattered while still passing the front of the enemy, and before the extreme right had got by it would have been very much exposed. Then, too, I had not yet learned the special qualifications of the different corps commanders. At that time my judgment was that Warren was the man I would suggest to succeed Meade should anything happen to that gallant soldier to take him from the field. As I have before said, Warren was a gallant soldier, an able man; and he was beside thoroughly imbued with the solemnity and importance of the duty he had to perform.[5]

5. The story of Gouverneur K. Warren (1830–1882) has a rather sad ending, which was in large part the result of the tendency to micromanage Grant calls attention to here and again in chapter 64. Following graduation from West Point in 1850, Warren served in a variety of engineer assignments from the Mississippi Delta to the Dakota Territory, and he was teaching mathematics at his alma mater when the Civil War broke out. He served in all of the major campaigns in the Eastern Theater up to Petersburg. His hesitancy is symptomatic of a certain type of military mind described by O. O. Howard in this reflection on some of his West Point classmates: "Many officers fail with large commands, and the reason is traceable to their encumbering their minds with the detail." *Autobiography*, 1:57.

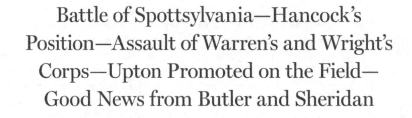

Battle of Spottsylvania—Hancock's Position—Assault of Warren's and Wright's Corps—Upton Promoted on the Field— Good News from Butler and Sheridan

The Mattapony River is formed by the junction of the Mat, the Ta, the Po and the Ny rivers, the last being the northernmost of the four. It takes its rise about a mile south and a little east of the Wilderness Tavern. The Po rises south-west of the same place, but farther away. Spottsylvania is on the ridge dividing these two streams, and where they are but a few miles apart. The Brock Road reaches Spottsylvania without crossing either of these streams. Lee's army coming up by the Catharpin Road, had to cross the Po at Wooden Bridge. Warren and Hancock came by the Brock Road. Sedgwick crossed the Ny at Catharpin Furnace. Burnside coming by Aldrich's to Gates's house, had to cross the Ny near the enemy. He found pickets at the bridge, but they were soon driven off by a brigade of Willcox's division, and the stream was crossed. This brigade was furiously attacked; but the remainder of the division coming up, they were enabled to hold their position, and soon fortified it.

About the time I received the news of this attack, word came from Hancock that Early had left his front. He had been forced over to the Catharpin Road, crossing the Po at Corbin's and again at Wooden Bridge. These are the bridges Sheridan had given orders to his cavalry to occupy on the 8th, while one division should occupy Spottsylvania. These movements of the enemy gave me the idea that Lee was about to make the attempt to get to, or towards, Fredericksburg to cut off my supplies. I made arrangements to attack his right and get between him and Richmond if he should try to execute this design. If he had any such intention it was abandoned as soon as Burnside was established south of the Ny.

The Po and the Ny are narrow little streams, but deep, with abrupt banks, and bordered by heavily wooded and marshy bottoms—at the time we were there—and difficult to cross except where bridged. The country about was generally heavily timbered, but with occasional clearings. It was a much better country to conduct a defensive campaign in than an offensive one.[1]

---

1. Adams of the 19th Massachusetts describes a solid week of skirmishing between the Battle of the Wilderness and his regiment's arrival at Spotsylvania, where they found further "hot work" at the Bloody Angle:

> We marched to Williams's Tavern, where we went into line of battle and threw up works. From this time on we were engaged every day. The 8th, we had a lively brush at Todd's Tavern, and drove the rebels a mile; the 9th, crossed Po River; the 10th, recrossed and engaged the enemy at Laurel Hill. We found them strongly intrenched and a charge was ordered. The opinion of every officer and man was that we could not dislodge them, as we must charge a long distance over an open field. General Barlow was to lead and the 19th was to be the directing battalion. The order to our division was, "Follow the colors of the 19th." With cheers for General Barlow we advanced over the crest of the hill, the rebels opening on us with a terrible fire. Grape and cannister ploughed through our ranks. Both color-bearers were shot down, and for a moment our line melted away; but other hands grasped the colors, and we renewed the charge, only to be again repulsed. No army on earth could capture the works with such odds against it, but we charged once more, then gave it up. . . .
>
> We remained here until the night of the 11th, when men were detailed to keep up the skirmish firing while the brigade was withdrawn. It was a dark, dreary night, and we fell over stumps and fallen trees as we moved to the left. At four o'clock on the morning of the 12th we formed in line. Our orders were to give commands in whispers, have dippers so hung that they would not rattle against bayonets, and move forward. We were soon in front of the rebel works which were protected by abatis. We tore these aside and passed on. One regiment, forgetting the orders, gave a cheer, and the rebels were aroused, yet over the works we went, and the fiercest hand-to-hand fight of the war ensued. We captured Gen. Bushrod Johnson and his entire division, including twenty-two pieces of artillery and seventeen stands of colors. . . .
>
> While engaged here the rebels had recaptured a small part of their works on our right, and we were ordered to move to that point. Collecting as many men of the regiment as we could find we marched by the flank to what has since been known as the "Bloody Angle;" here we found hot work. While we were firing the rebels ran up a white flag, and we advanced

By noon of the 9th the position of the two armies was as follows: Lee occupied a semicircle facing north, north-west and north-east, inclosing the town. Anderson was on his left extending to the Po, Ewell came next, then Early. Warren occupied our right, covering the Brock and other roads converging at Spottsylvania; Sedgwick was to his left and Burnside on our extreme left. Hancock was yet back at Todd's Tavern, but as soon as it was known that Early had left Hancock's front the latter was ordered up to War-ren's right. He formed a line with three divisions on the hill overlooking the Po early in the afternoon, and was ordered to cross the Po and get on the enemy's flank. The fourth division of Hancock's corps, Mott commanding, was left at Todd's when the corps first came up; but in the afternoon it was brought up and placed to the left of Sedgwick's—now Wright's—6th corps. In the morning General Sedgwick had been killed near the right of his intrenchments by rebel sharpshooters.[2] His loss was a severe one to the Army

---

to receive their surrender, but as soon as we were over the brow of the little hill that had protected us, they fired a volley killing several of our men. From that time until dark the cry was "No quarter."

Adams, *Reminiscences*, 89–91.

2. John Sedgwick (1813–1864), a member of the West Point class of 1837, was commis-sioned as an artillery officer. He fought against the Seminoles in Florida and accompa-nied the forced westward migration of tribes along the Trail of Tears in 1838. He was present at most of the major engagements of the Mexican War. In the years leading up to the Civil War, Sedgwick was posted to "Bleeding Kansas" and then to the frontier, where he commanded an expedition against the Kiowa and Comanche. Sedgwick saw further action in the Eastern Theater of the Civil War, where he was wounded at Antie-tam. His chief of staff, Martin T. McMahon, wrote an exceptionally vivid account of Sedgwick's death at Spotsylvania:

Death of General Sedgwick at Spotsylvania, Virginia. The sharpshooter can be seen in the background at left of the relief. West Point, New York. *Photograph by Elizabeth D. Samet.*

He was an inveterate tease, and I at once suspected that he had some joke on the staff which he was leading up to. He was interrupted in his comments by observing that the troops, who during this time had been filing from the left into the rifle-pits, had come to a halt and were lying down, while the left of the line partly overlapped the position of the section of artillery. He stopped abruptly and said, "That is wrong. Those troops must be moved farther to the right; I don't wish them to overlap that battery." I started out to execute the order, and he rose at the same moment, and we sauntered out slowly to the gun on the right. About an hour before, I had remarked to the general, pointing to the two pieces in a half-jesting manner, which he well understood, "General, do you see that section of artillery? Well, you are not to go near it to-day." He answered good-naturedly, "McMahon, I would like to know who commands this corps, you or I?" I said, playfully, "Well, General, sometimes I am in doubt myself"; but added, "Seriously, General, I beg of you not to go to that angle; every officer who has shown himself there has been hit, both yesterday and to-day." He answered quietly, "Well, I don't know that there is any reason for my going there." When afterward we walked out to the position indicated, this conversation had entirely escaped the memory of both.

I gave the necessary order to move the troops to the right, and as they rose to execute the movement the enemy opened a sprinkling fire, partly from sharp-shooters. As the bullets whistled by, some of the men dodged. The general said laughingly, "What! what! men, dodging this way for single bullets! What will you do when they open fire along the whole line? I am ashamed of you. They couldn't hit an elephant at this distance." A few seconds after, a man who had been separated from his regiment passed directly in front of the general, and at the same moment a sharp-shooter's bullet passed with a long shrill whistle very close, and the soldier, who was then just in front of the general, dodged to the ground. The general touched him gently with his foot, and said, "Why, my man, I am ashamed of you, dodging that way," and repeated the remark, "They couldn't hit an elephant at this distance." The man rose and saluted and said good-na-turedly, "General, I dodged a shell once, and if I hadn't, it would have taken my head off. I believe in dodging." The general laughed and replied, "All right, my man; go to your place."

For a third time the same shrill whistle, closing with a dull, heavy stroke, interrupted our talk; when, as I was about to resume, the general's face turned slowly to me, the blood spurting from his left cheek under the eye in a steady stream. He fell in my direction; I was so close to him that my effort to support him failed, and I fell with him. . . .

. . . A smile remained upon his lips but he did not speak. The doctor poured water from a canteen over the general's face. The blood still poured upward in a little fountain. The men in the long line of rifle-pits, retaining their places from force of discipline, were all kneeling with heads raised and faces turned toward the scene; for the news had already passed along the line.

"The Death of General John Sedgwick," *B&L*, 4:175.

"California Joe," a member of Berdan's Sharpshooters, *Harper's Weekly,* August 2, 1862.

of the Potomac and to the Nation. General H. G. Wright succeeded him in the command of his corps.

Hancock was now, nine P.M. of the 9th of May, across the left flank of Lee's army, but separated from it, and also from the remainder of Meade's army, by the Po River. But for the lateness of the hour and the darkness of the night he would have attempted to cross the river again at Wooden Bridge, thus bringing himself on the same side with both friend and foe.

The Po at the points where Hancock's corps crossed runs nearly due east. Just below his lower crossing—the troops crossed at three points—it turns due south, and after passing under Wooden Bridge soon resumes a more easterly direction. During the night this corps built three bridges over the Po; but these were in rear.

The position assumed by Hancock's corps forced Lee to reinforce his left during the night. Accordingly on the morning of the 10th, when Hancock renewed his effort to get over the Po to his front, he found himself confronted by some of Early's command, which had been brought from the extreme right of the enemy during the night. He succeeded in effecting a crossing with one brigade, however, but finding the enemy intrenched in his front, no more were crossed.

Hancock reconnoitred his front on the morning of the 10th, with the view of forcing a crossing, if it was found that an advantage could be gained. The enemy was found strongly intrenched on the high ground overlooking

A statue of Sedgwick was erected at West Point not long after the war. There was a time when cadets in danger of failing their exams would don full-dress uniforms at midnight and race across the parade field to the statue to spin its spurs for luck.

the river, and commanding the Wooden Bridge with artillery. Anderson's left rested on the Po, where it turns south; therefore, for Hancock to cross over—although it would bring him to the same side of the stream with the rest of the army—would still farther isolate him from it. The stream would have to be crossed twice in the face of the enemy to unite with the main body. The idea of crossing was therefore abandoned.

Lee had weakened the other parts of his line to meet this movement of Hancock's, and I determined to take advantage of it. Accordingly in the morning, orders were issued for an attack in the afternoon on the centre by Warren's and Wright's corps, Hancock to command all the attacking force. Two of his divisions were brought to the north side of the Po. Gibbon was placed to the right of Warren, and Birney in his rear as a reserve. Barlow's division was left south of the stream, and Mott of the same corps was still to the left of Wright's corps. Burnside was ordered to reconnoitre his front in force, and, if an opportunity presented, to attack with vigor. The enemy seeing Barlow's division isolated from the rest of the army, came out and attacked with fury. Barlow repulsed the assault with great slaughter, and with considerable loss to himself. But the enemy reorganized and renewed the assault. Birney was now moved to the high ground overlooking the river crossings built by our troops, and covered the crossings. The second assault was repulsed, again with severe loss to the enemy, and Barlow was withdrawn without further molestation. General T. G. Stevenson was killed in this move.

Between the lines, where Warren's assault was to take place, there was a ravine grown up with large trees and underbrush, making it almost impenetrable by man. The slopes on both sides were also covered with a heavy growth of timber. Warren, before noon, reconnoitred his front twice, the first time with one and the second with two divisions. He was repulsed on both occasions, but gained such information of the ground as to induce him to report recommending the assault.

Wright also reconnoitred his front and gained a considerably advanced position from the one he started from. He then organized a storming party, consisting of twelve regiments, and assigned Colonel Emory Upton, of the 121st New York Volunteers, to the command of it.[3] About four o'clock in the

---

3. The site Grant describes is the Muleshoe, a salient in the Confederate line that came to be called the Bloody Angle. The fighting there lasted for twenty hours. Emory Upton (1839–1881) had graduated from West Point only three years earlier, in May

1861. While a cadet, he had gotten into a fight with South Carolinian Wade Gibbes. Morris Schaff, a member of the class of 1862, describes the atmosphere in the Corps of Cadets during the period:

> It is true there had been instances where combats had been more or less tinged by sectional feeling . . . but this one, between Wade Hampton Gibbes of South Carolina and Emery Upton of New York, was distinctly political in every feature. It was the most thrilling event in my life as a cadet; and, in my judgment, it was the most significant in that of West Point itself. . . .
>
> Now Upton, before coming to West Point, had been a student at Oberlin, an institution hated and despised by the South for its pronounced attitude on slavery, and more than all for admitting negroes as students. When he was being quizzed on his arrival as a new cadet, . . . he openly and frankly declared that he . . . was an Abolitionist, the first and, I believe, the only cadet who ever had the temerity to plant himself squarely in the ranks of that unpopular band of liberty-loving dreamers. . . . Upton's sincere declaration of his position . . . at once made him a marked man.
>
> Under the natural exasperation over the Brown Raid [at Harper's Ferry], men from the South . . . gave vent to their feelings; and, in the course of some talk with his fellows, Gibbes, in referring to Upton . . . made remarks on his intimate association with negroes, of a character keenly offensive, such as no self-respecting cadet could stand for a moment. . . . Upton promptly called for an explanation. . . . and soon the word passed through our companies . . . that Gibbes and Upton were to fight. . . .
>
> The national significance of the affair was interpreted at once; there were more than personal matters involved; and a crowd soon gathered on the pavement, on the stoop, and packed into the hall. I made my way . . . [and] gained a place on the stairway. . . . Personally I do not know what took place in that room; but there are those living who do. . . .
>
> . . . I do remember this, however, that when the fight was over, I saw Upton's resolute face bleeding. . . .
>
> . . . I am satisfied that the South then and there beheld what iron and steel there was in the Northern blood when once it was up.

The Spirit of Old West Point, 1858–1862 (Boston: Houghton Mifflin, 1907), 143–47.

In addition to his heroic attack on the Muleshoe at Spotsylvania, Upton fought in almost every major engagement in the East: from First Bull Run, where he was wounded, to Antietam, Fredericksburg, Gettysburg, Cold Harbor, Petersburg, Third Winchester, where he was again wounded, and Selma. After the war, he traveled to Asia and Europe to study military tactics, and he subsequently wrote several books. Upton was in command of the Presidio in San Francisco when, plagued by unendurable headaches, he killed himself in 1881. For a modern diagnosis of his case using nineteenth-century medical records, see J. M. Hyson Jr. et al., "The Suicide of General Emory Upton: A Case Report," *Military Medicine* 155, no. 10 (October 1990): 445–52.

General Emory Upton.
*Library of Congress, Prints and
Photographs Division, Civil
War Photographs, LC-DIG-
cwpb-05762.*

afternoon the assault was ordered, Warren's and Wright's corps, with Mott's division of Hancock's corps, to move simultaneously. The movement was prompt, and in a few minutes the fiercest of struggles began. The battle-field was so densely covered with forest that but little could be seen, by any one person, as to the progress made. Meade and I occupied the best position we could get, in rear of Warren.

Warren was repulsed with heavy loss, General J. C. Rice being among the killed. He was not followed, however, by the enemy, and was thereby enabled to reorganize his command as soon as covered from the guns of the enemy. To the left our success was decided, but the advantage was lost by the

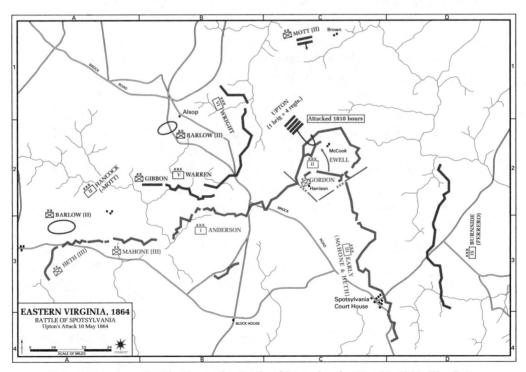

Upton's attack on the Bloody Angle, Battle of Spotsylvania, May 10, 1864. *West Point Atlas of the Civil War. Courtesy of Department of History, USMA.*

feeble action of Mott. Upton with his assaulting party pushed forward and crossed the enemy's intrenchments. Turning to the right and left he captured several guns and some hundreds of prisoners. Mott was ordered to his assistance but failed utterly. So much time was lost in trying to get up the troops which were in the right position to reinforce, that I ordered Upton to withdraw; but the officers and men of his command were so averse to giving up the advantage they had gained that I withdrew the order. To relieve them, I ordered a renewal of the assault. By this time Hancock, who had gone with Birney's division to relieve Barlow, had returned, bringing the division with him. His corps was now joined with Warren's and Wright's in this last assault. It was gallantly made, many men getting up to, and over, the works of the enemy; but they were not able to hold them. At night they were withdrawn. Upton brought his prisoners with him, but the guns he had captured he was obliged to abandon. Upton had gained an important advantage, but a lack in others of the spirit and dash possessed by him lost it to us. Before leaving Washington I had been authorized to promote officers on the field for special acts of gallantry. By this authority I conferred the rank of brigadier-general upon Upton on the spot, and this act was confirmed by the President. Upton had been badly wounded in this fight.

Burnside on the left had got up to within a few hundred yards of Spottsylvania Court House, completely turning Lee's right. He was not aware of the importance of the advantage he had gained, and I, being with the troops where the heavy fighting was, did not know of it at the time. He had gained his position with but little fighting, and almost without loss. Burnside's position now separated him widely from Wright's corps, the corps nearest to him. At night he was ordered to join on to this. This brought him back about a mile, and lost to us an important advantage. I attach no blame to Burnside for this, but I do to myself for not having had a staff officer with him to report to me his position.

The enemy had not dared to come out of his line at any point to follow up his advantage, except in the single instance of his attack on Barlow. Then he was twice repulsed with heavy loss, though he had an entire corps against two brigades. Barlow took up his bridges in the presence of this force.

On the 11th there was no battle and but little firing; none except by Mott who made a reconnoissance to ascertain if there was a weak point in the enemy's line.

I wrote the following letter to General Halleck:

NEAR SPOTTSYLVANIA C. H.,
May 11, 1864—8.30 A.M.

MAJOR-GENERAL HALLECK, Chief of Staff of the Army,
Washington, D. C.

We have now ended the 6th day of very hard fighting. The result
up to this time is much in our favor. But our losses have been heavy
as well as those of the enemy. We have lost to this time eleven general
officers killed, wounded and missing, and probably twenty thousand
men.[4] I think the loss of the enemy must be greater—we having taken
over four thousand prisoners in battle, whilst he has taken from us
but few except a few stragglers. I am now sending back to Belle Plain

---

4. The laconic nature of Grant's discussion of the wounded differs markedly from two of
the most common registers: the sensational and the sentimental. Philip Kearny's account
of his service with the Chasseurs d'Afrique, which contains some vivid depictions of
battle and terrain, explores the ways in which his own response to the wounded was
shaped by time and place:

> When in the heat of action, the fated ball finds its mark, it adds but to the
> excitement of the scene, for the whistling of the balls tells you that there
> are more, and self prompts you to be proud and thankful to your own
> preserving star; and one's feelings are aroused with the spirit of immediate
> revenge. . . . The report of the musketry, the smoke wreathing up around
> you, the uniforms of the French, the wild costume of the Arabs all conjure
> up such a scene of excitement as none in this life realize, but the gambler
> and engaged soldier. How different when the heat of combat is over, and
> accident throws the line of your march alongside of the hospital train, or as
> you casually ride by them, and behold the long line of sick and wounded;
> and every now and then witness a litter halted from out the line, whilst the
> surgeon is administering, with a look of soldierly solicitude, to the wants of
> some poor man, whose wan and ghastly cheeks mark him so shortly to be
> death's own. You then reflect that this very day he was in the pride of his
> strength and courage, performing a soldier's duty with a soldier's gallantry.
> You see how altered he looks now and find it is impossible to regard it with
> altogether a stoic's eye. The frequency of the scene, and one's own contin-
> ual risk, prevents a thing of this kind long weighing on one's mind; but
> few can pass such a sight without an involuntary sigh. . . . These reflections
> may appear to have been out of place and indeed it is probable in a war of
> my own country or under any other circumstances, they would never have
> occurred; but here I was a traveller militant on the soil of Africa.

Service with the French Troops in Africa (New York, 1844), 42–43.

all my wagons for a fresh supply of provisions and ammunition, and purpose to fight it out on this line if it takes all summer.

The arrival of reinforcements here will be very encouraging to the men, and I hope they will be sent as fast as possible, and in as great numbers. My object in having them sent to Belle Plain was to use them as an escort to our supply trains. If it is more convenient to send them out by train to march from the railroad to Belle Plain or Fredericksburg, send them so.

I am satisfied the enemy are very shaky, and are only kept up to the mark by the greatest exertions on the part of their officers, and by keeping them intrenched in every position they take.

Up to this time there is no indication of any portion of Lee's army being detached for the defence of Richmond.

U. S. GRANT,
Lieut.-General.

And also, I received information, through the War Department, from General Butler that his cavalry under Kautz had cut the railroad south of Petersburg, separating Beauregard from Richmond, and had whipped [Daniel H.] Hill, killing, wounding and capturing many. Also that he was intrenched, and could maintain himself. On this same day came news from Sheridan to the effect that he had destroyed ten miles of the railroad and telegraph between Lee and Richmond, one and a half million rations, and most of the medical stores for his army.

On the 8th I had directed Sheridan verbally to cut loose from the Army of the Potomac and pass around the left of Lee's army and attack his cavalry and communications, which was successfully executed in the manner I have already described.

Confederate cemetery, Spotsylvania Courthouse, Virginia. *Photograph by Elizabeth D. Samet.*

Hancock's Assault—Losses of the Confederates—Promotions Recommended—Discomfiture of the Enemy—Ewell's Attack—Reducing the Artillery

In the reconnoissance made by Mott on the 11th, a salient was discovered at the right centre. I determined that an assault should be made at that point.[1] Accordingly in the afternoon Hancock was ordered to move his command by the rear of Warren and Wright, under cover of night, to Wright's left, and there form it for an assault at four o'clock the next morning. The night was dark, it rained heavily, and the road was difficult, so that it was midnight when he reached the point where he was to halt. It took most of the night to get the men in position for their advance in the morning. The men got but little rest. Burnside was ordered to attack[2] on the left of the salient at the same hour. I sent two of my staff officers to impress upon him the importance of pushing forward vigorously. Hancock was notified of this. Warren and Wright were ordered to hold themselves in readiness to join in the assault if circumstances made it advisable. I occupied a central position most convenient for receiving information from all points. Hancock put Barlow on his left, in double column, and Birney to his right. Mott followed Birney, and Gibbon was held in reserve.

The morning of the 12th opened foggy, delaying the start more than half an hour.

---

1. For the correspondence included in a note to the first edition, see Appendix 1, chapter 53, note 1.

2. For the correspondence included in a note to the first edition, see Appendix 1, chapter 53, note 2.

The ground over which Hancock had to pass to reach the enemy, was ascending and heavily wooded to within two or three hundred yards of the enemy's intrenchments. In front of Birney there was also a marsh to cross. But, notwithstanding all these difficulties, the troops pushed on in quick time without firing a gun, and when within four or five hundred yards of the enemy's line broke out in loud cheers, and with a rush went up to and over the breastworks. Barlow and Birney entered almost simultaneously. Here a desperate hand-to-hand conflict took place. The men of the two sides were too close together to fire, but used their guns as clubs. The hand conflict was soon over. Hancock's corps captured some four thousand prisoners—among them a division and a brigade commander—twenty or more guns with their horses, caissons, and ammunition, several thousand stand of arms, and many colors. Hancock, as soon as the hand-to-hand conflict was over, turned the guns of the enemy against him and advanced inside the rebel lines. About six o'clock I ordered Warren's corps to the support of Hancock's. Burnside, on the left, had advanced up east of the salient to the very parapet of the enemy. [Robert B.] Potter, commanding one of his divisions, got over but was not able to remain there. However, he inflicted a heavy loss upon the enemy; but not without loss in return.

This victory was important, and one that Lee could not afford to leave us in full possession of. He made the most strenuous efforts to regain the position he had lost. Troops were brought up from his left and attacked Hancock furiously. Hancock was forced to fall back: but he did so slowly, with his face to the enemy, inflicting on him heavy loss, until behind the breastworks he had captured. These he turned, facing them the other way, and continued to hold. Wright was ordered up to reinforce Hancock, and arrived by six o'clock. He was wounded soon after coming up but did not relinquish the command of his corps, although the fighting lasted until one o'clock the next morning. At eight o'clock Warren was ordered up again, but was so slow in making his dispositions that his orders were frequently repeated, and with emphasis. At eleven o'clock I gave Meade written orders to relieve Warren from his command if he failed to move promptly. Hancock placed batteries on high ground in his rear, which he used against the enemy, firing over the heads of his own troops.

Burnside accomplished but little on our left of a positive nature, but negatively a great deal. He kept Lee from reinforcing his centre from that quarter. If the 5th corps, or rather if Warren, had been as prompt as Wright was with the 6th corps, better results might have been obtained.

Lee massed heavily from his left flank on the broken point of his line.

Wounded trees: photograph showing the effects of musket fire on woods, Culp's Hill, Gettysburg, Pennsylvania, 1863. Mathew Brady. *Library of Congress, Prints and Photographs Division, Civil War Photographs, LC-DIG-cwpb-01634.*

Five times during the day he assaulted furiously, but without dislodging our troops from their new position. His losses must have been fearful. Sometimes the belligerents would be separated by but a few feet. In one place a tree, eighteen inches in diameter, was cut entirely down by musket balls. All the trees between the lines were very much cut to pieces by artillery and musketry. It was three o'clock next morning before the fighting ceased. Some of our troops had then been twenty hours under fire. In this engagement we did not lose a single organization, not even a company. The enemy lost one division with its commander, one brigade and one regiment, with heavy losses elsewhere.[3] Our losses were heavy, but, as stated, no whole company was captured. At night Lee took a position in rear of his former one, and by the following morning he was strongly intrenched in it.

Warren's corps was now temporarily broken up, Cutler's division sent to Wright, and [Charles] Griffin's to Hancock. Meade ordered his chief of staff, General [Andrew A.] Humphreys, to remain with Warren and the remaining division, and authorized him to give it orders in his name.

During the day I was passing along the line from wing to wing continuously.[4] About the centre stood a house which proved to be occupied by

3. For the correspondence included in a note to the first edition, see Appendix 1, chapter 53, note 3.

4. John Keegan explains the challenge expanding battlefronts presented to nineteenth-century commanders: "Wellington at Waterloo, admittedly a small though not unusually small battlefield for the period, had about a mile of ground to cover." Grant's fronts ranged from three miles at Donelson to twelve at Five Forks. "These extensions marked

an old lady and her daughter. She showed such unmistakable signs of being strongly Union that I stopped. She said she had not seen a Union flag for so long a time that it did her heart good to look upon it again. She said her husband and son, being Union men, had had to leave early in the war, and were now somewhere in the Union army, if alive. She was without food or nearly so, so I ordered rations issued to her, and promised to find out if I could where the husband and son were.

There was no fighting on the 13th, further than a little skirmishing between Mott's division and the enemy. I was afraid that Lee might be moving out, and I did not want him to go without my knowing it. The indications were that he was moving, but it was found that he was only taking his new position back from the salient that had been captured. Our dead were buried this day. Mott's division was reduced to a brigade, and assigned to Birney's division.

During this day I wrote to Washington recommending Sherman and Meade[5] for promotion to the grade of Major-General in the regular army; Hancock for Brigadier-General; Wright, Gibbon and Humphreys to be Major-Generals of Volunteers; and Upton and Carroll to be Brigadiers. Upton had already been named as such, but the appointment had to be confirmed by the Senate on the nomination of the President.

The night of the 13th Warren and Wright were moved by the rear to the left of Burnside. The night was very dark and it rained heavily, the roads were so bad that the troops had to cut trees and corduroy the road a part of the way, to get through. It was midnight before they got to the point where they were to halt, and daylight before the troops could be organized to advance to their position in line. They gained their position in line, however, without any fighting, except a little in Wright's front. Here Upton had to contend for an elevation which we wanted and which the enemy was not disposed to yield. Upton first drove the enemy, and was then repulsed in turn. Ayres coming to his support with his brigade (of Griffin's division, Warren's corps), the position was secured and fortified. There was no more battle during the 14th. This brought our line east of the Court House and running north and south and facing west.

---

an irreversible trend. . . . But in 1861–5 it was still just possible for a general with the will to do so to ride about his line while his army was in action. Grant had the will." *Mask of Command*, 221.

5. For the correspondence included in a note to the first edition, see Appendix 1, chapter 53, note 4.

During the night of the 14th–15th Lee moved to cover this new front. This left Hancock without an enemy confronting him. He was brought to the rear of our new centre, ready to be moved in any direction he might be wanted.

On the 15th news came from Butler and Averill. The former reported the capture of the outer works at Drury's Bluff, on the James River, and that his cavalry had cut the railroad and telegraph south of Richmond on the Danville road: and the latter, the destruction of a depot of supplies at Dublin, West Virginia, and the breaking of New River Bridge on the Virginia and Tennessee Railroad. The next day news came from Sherman and Sheridan. Sherman had forced Johnston out of Dalton, Georgia, and was following him south. The report from Sheridan embraced his operations up to his passing the outer defences of Richmond. The prospect must now have been dismal in Richmond. The road and telegraph were cut between the capital and Lee. The roads and wires were cut in every direction from the rebel capital. Temporarily that city was cut off from all communication with the outside except by courier. This condition of affairs, however, was of but short duration.

I wrote Halleck:

> NEAR SPOTTSYLVANIA C. H.,
> *May* 16, 1864, 8 A.M.
>
> MAJOR-GENERAL HALLECK,
> Washington, D. C.:
>
> We have had five days almost constant rain without any prospect yet of it clearing up. The roads have now become so impassable that ambulances with wounded men can no longer run between here and Fredericksburg. All offensive operations necessarily cease until we can have twenty-four hours of dry weather. The army is in the best of spirits, and feel the greatest confidence of ultimate success.
>
> ★　★　★　★　★　★　★
>
> You can assure the President and Secretary of War that the elements alone have suspended hostilities, and that it is in no manner due to weakness or exhaustion on our part.
>
> U. S. GRANT,
> Lieut.-General.

The condition of the roads was such that nothing was done on the 17th. But that night Hancock and Wright were to make a night march back to their old positions, and to make an assault at four o'clock in the morning. Lee got troops back in time to protect his old line, so the assault was unsuccessful. On this day (18th) the news was almost as discouraging to us as it had been two days before in the rebel capital. As stated above, Hancock's and Wright's corps had made an unsuccessful assault. News came that Sigel had been defeated at New Market, badly, and was retreating down the valley. Not two hours before, I had sent the inquiry to Halleck whether Sigel could not get to Staunton to stop supplies coming from there to Lee. I asked at once that Sigel might be relieved, and some one else put in his place. Hunter's name was suggested, and I heartily approved. Further news from Butler reported him driven from Drury's Bluff, but still in possession of the Petersburg road. Banks had been defeated in Louisiana, relieved, and Canby put in his place. This change of commander was not on my suggestion. All this news was very discouraging. All of it must have been known by the enemy before it was by me. In fact, the good news (for the enemy) must have been known to him at the moment I thought he was in despair, and his anguish had been already relieved when we were enjoying his supposed discomfiture, But this was no time for repining. I immediately gave orders for a movement by the left flank, on towards Richmond, to commence on the night of the 19th. I also asked Halleck to secure the co-operation of the navy in changing our base of supplies from Fredericksburg to Port Royal, on the Rappahannock.

Up to this time I had received no reinforcements, except six thousand raw troops under Brigadier General Robert O. Tyler, just arrived. They had not yet joined their command, Hancock's corps, but were on our right. This corps had been brought to the rear of the centre, ready to move in any direction. Lee, probably suspecting some move on my part, and seeing our right entirely abandoned, moved Ewell's corps about five o'clock in the afternoon, with Early's as a reserve, to attack us in that quarter. Tyler had come up from Fredericksburg, and had been halted on the road to the right of our line, near Kitching's brigade of Warren's corps. Tyler received the attack with his raw troops, and they maintained their position, until reinforced, in a manner worthy of veterans.

Hancock was in a position to reinforce speedily, and was the soldier to do it without waiting to make dispositions. Birney was thrown to Tyler's right and Crawford to his left, with Gibbon as a reserve; and Ewell was whirled back speedily and with heavy loss.

Warren had been ordered to get on Ewell's flank and in his rear, to cut him off from his intrenchments. But his efforts were so feeble that under the cover of night Ewell got back with only the loss of a few hundred prisoners, besides his killed and wounded. The army being engaged until after dark, I rescinded the order for the march by our left flank that night.

As soon as it was discovered that the enemy were coming out to attack, I naturally supposed they would detach a force to destroy our trains. The withdrawal of Hancock from the right uncovered one road from Spottsylvania to Fredericksburg over which trains drew our supplies. This was guarded by a division of colored troops, commanded by General [Edward] Ferrero, belonging to Burnside's corps. Ferrero was therefore promptly notified, and ordered to throw his cavalry pickets out to the south and be prepared to meet the enemy if he should come; if he had to retreat to do so towards Fredericksburg. The enemy did detach as expected, and captured twenty-five or thirty wagons which, however, were soon retaken.

In consequence of the disasters that had befallen us in the past few days, Lee could be reinforced largely, and I had no doubt he would be. Beauregard had come up from the south with troops to guard the Confederate capital when it was in danger. Butler being driven back, most of the troops could be sent to Lee. [Robert F.] Hoke was no longer needed in North Carolina; and Sigel's troops having gone back to Cedar Creek, whipped, many troops could be spared from the valley.

The Wilderness and Spottsylvania battles convinced me that we had more artillery than could ever be brought into action at any one time. It occupied much of the road in marching, and taxed the trains in bringing up forage. Artillery is very useful when it can be brought into action, but it is a very burdensome luxury where it cannot be used.[6] Before leaving Spottsyl-

---

6. Here again, Grant departs radically from contemporaries such as McClellan, who had a Napoleonic faith in artillery and therefore employed a large Artillery Reserve. Thus encumbered with equipment, McClellan reduced the maneuverability of his army. "Some time ago it was reported that McClellan considered this war had become a duel of artillery," Count Adam Gurowski, who in the context of his work as a translator for the State Department encountered the general in Washington, confided to his diary. "Fools wondered and applauded. I then protested against putting such an absurdity in McClellan's mouth; now I must believe it. . . . No position can be taken by cannonading alone, and shells alone do not always force an enemy to abandon a position. Napoleon, an artillerist *par excellence*, considered campaigns and battles to be something more than duels of artillery." October 6, 1861, *Diary* (Boston: Lee and Shepard, 1862), 1:107.

For example, the monumental Union artillery bombardment of Fredericksburg, Virginia, in December 1862—Burnside had replaced McClellan in command by this time—terrified the population and reduced the town to rubble, but it did not produce a victory in the end. See George C. Rable, *Fredericksburg! Fredericksburg!* (Chapel Hill: University of North Carolina Press, 2002).

vania, therefore, I sent back to the defences of Washington over one hundred pieces of artillery, with the horses and caissons. This relieved the roads over which we were to march of more than two hundred six-horse teams, and still left us more artillery than could be advantageously used. In fact, before reaching the James River I again reduced the artillery with the army largely.

I believed that, if one corps of the army was exposed on the road to Richmond, and at a distance from the main army, Lee would endeavor to attack the exposed corps before reinforcements could come up; in which case the main army could follow Lee up and attack him before he had time to intrench. So I issued the following orders:

NEAR SPOTTSYLVANIA C. H., VA.,

May 18, 1864.

MAJOR-GENERAL MEADE,
Commanding Army of the Potomac.

Before daylight to-morrow morning I propose to draw Hancock and Burnside from the position they now hold, and put Burnside to the left of Wright. Wright and Burnside should then force their way up as close to the enemy as they can get without a general engagement, or with a general engagement if the enemy will come

A scene from the Crimean War, a war McClellan had observd: Sebastopol from Cathcart's Hill, 1855. Photograph by Roger Fenton. *Metropolitan Museum of Art, Gilman Collection, Purchase, Mrs. Walter Annenberg and The Annenberg Foundation Gift, 2005.*

out of their works to fight, and intrench. Hancock should march and take up a position as if in support of the two left corps. To-morrow night, at twelve or one o'clock, he will be moved south-east with all his force and as much cavalry as can be given to him, to get as far towards Richmond on the line of the Fredericksburg Railroad as he can make, fighting the enemy in whatever force he can find him. If the enemy make a general move to meet this, they will be followed by the other three corps of the army, and attacked, if possible, before time is given to intrench.

Suitable directions will at once be given for all trains and surplus artillery to conform to this movement.

U. S. GRANT.

On the 20th, Lee showing no signs of coming out of his lines, orders were renewed for a left-flank movement, to commence after night.

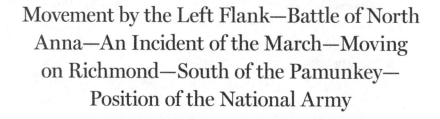

Movement by the Left Flank—Battle of North Anna—An Incident of the March—Moving on Richmond—South of the Pamunkey— Position of the National Army

We were now to operate in a different country from any we had before seen in Virginia. The roads were wide and good, and the country well cultivated. No men were seen except those bearing arms, even the black man having been sent away.[1] The country, however, was new to us, and we had neither guides nor maps to tell us where the roads were, or where they led to. Engineer and staff officers were put to the dangerous duty of supplying the place of both maps and guides. By reconnoitring they were enabled

---

1. In her 1997 novel *Beloved* Toni Morrison explores through the story of Paul D some of the wartime and postwar dangers confronting African Americans:

> After a few months on the battlefields of Alabama, he was impressed to a foundry in Selma along with three hundred captured, lent or taken coloredmen. That's where the War's end found him, and leaving Alabama when he had been declared free should have been a snap. He should have been able to walk from the foundry in Selma straight to Philadelphia, taking the main roads, a train if he wanted to, or passage on a boat. But it wasn't like that. When he and two colored soldiers . . . walked from Selma to Mobile, they saw twelve dead blacks in the first eighteen miles. Two were women, four were little boys. He thought this, for sure, would be the walk of his life. . . .
>
> By the time he got to Mobile, he had seen more dead people than living ones, but when he got to Trenton the crowds of alive people, neither hunting nor hunted, gave him a measure of free life so tasty he never forgot it.

Beloved (New York: Vintage, 2004), 316–17.

to locate the roads in the vicinity of each army corps. Our course was south, and we took all roads leading in that direction which would not separate the army too widely.

Hancock who had the lead had marched easterly to Guiney's Station, on the Fredericksburg Railroad, thence southerly to Bowling Green and Milford. He was at Milford by the night of the 21st. Here he met a detachment of Pickett's division coming from Richmond to reinforce Lee. They were speedily driven away, and several hundred captured. Warren followed on the morning of the 21st, and reached Guiney's Station that night without molestation. Burnside and Wright were retained at Spottsylvania to keep up the appearance of an intended assault, and to hold Lee, if possible, while Hancock and Warren should get start enough to interpose between him and Richmond.

Lee had now a superb opportunity to take the initiative either by attacking Wright and Burnside alone, or by following by the Telegraph Road and striking Hancock's and Warren's corps, or even Hancock's alone, before reinforcements could come up. But he did not avail himself of either opportunity. He seemed really to be misled as to my designs; but moved by his interior line—the Telegraph Road—to make sure of keeping between his capital and the Army of the Potomac. He never again had such an opportunity of dealing a heavy blow.

The evening of the 21st Burnside, 9th corps, moved out followed by Wright, 6th corps. Burnside was to take the Telegraph Road; but finding Stanard's Ford, over the Po, fortified and guarded, he turned east to the road taken by Hancock and Warren without an attempt to dislodge the enemy. The night of the 21st I had my headquarters near the 6th corps, at Guiney's Station, and the enemy's cavalry was between us and Hancock. There was a slight attack on Burnside's and Wright's corps as they moved out of their lines; but it was easily repulsed. The object probably was only to make sure that we were not leaving a force to follow upon the rear of the Confederates.

By the morning of the 22d Burnside and Wright were at Guiney's Station. Hancock's corps had now been marching and fighting continuously for several days, not having had rest even at night much of the time. They were, therefore, permitted to rest during the 22d. But Warren was pushed to Harris's Store, directly west of Milford, and connected with it by a good road, and Burnside was sent to New Bethel Church. Wright's corps was still back at Guiney's Station.

I issued the following order for the movement of the troops the next day:

NEW BETHEL, VA.,
May 22, 1864.

MAJOR-GENERAL MEADE,
Commanding Army of the Potomac.

Direct corps commanders to hold their troops in readiness to march at five A.M. to-morrow. At that hour each command will send out cavalry and infantry on all roads to their front leading south, and ascertain, if possible, where the enemy is. If beyond the South Anna, the 5th and 6th corps will march to the forks of the road, where one branch leads to Beaver Dam Station, the other to Jericho Bridge, then south by roads reaching the Anna, as near to and east of Hawkins Creek as they can be found.

The 2d corps will move to Chesterfield Ford. The 9th corps will be directed to move at the same time to Jericho Bridge. The map only shows two roads for the four corps to march upon, but, no doubt, by the use of plantation roads, and pressing in guides, others can be found, to give one for each corps.

The troops will follow their respective reconnoitring parties. The trains will be moved at the same time to Milford Station.

Headquarters will follow the 9th corps.

U. S. GRANT,
Lieut.-General.

Warren's corps was moved from Harris's Store to Jericho Ford, Wright's following. Warren arrived at the ford early in the afternoon, and by five o'clock effected a crossing under the protection of sharpshooters. The men had to wade in water up to their waists. As soon as enough troops were over to guard the ford, pontoons were laid and the artillery and the rest of the troops crossed. The line formed was almost perpendicular to the course of the river—Crawford on the left, next to the river, Griffin in the centre, and Cutler on the right. Lee was found intrenched along the front of their line. The whole of Hill's corps was sent against Warren's right before it had got in position. A brigade of Cutler's division was driven back, the enemy following, but assistance coming up, the enemy was in turn driven back into his trenches with heavy loss in killed and wounded, with about five hundred prisoners left in our hands. By night Wright's corps was up ready to reinforce Warren.

On the 23d Hancock's corps was moved to the wooden bridge which spans the North Anna River just west of where the Fredericksburg Railroad crosses. It was near night when the troops arrived. They found the bridge guarded, with troops intrenched, on the north side. Hancock sent two brigades, Egan's and Pierce's, to the right and left, and when properly disposed they charged simultaneously. The bridge was carried quickly, the enemy retreating over it so hastily that many were shoved into the river, and some of them were drowned. Several hundred prisoners were captured. The hour was so late that Hancock did not cross until next morning.

Burnside's corps was moved by a middle road running between those described above, and which strikes the North Anna at Ox Ford, midway between Telegraph Road and Jericho Ford. The hour of its arrival was too late to cross that night.

On the 24th Hancock's corps crossed to the south side of the river without opposition, and formed line facing nearly west. The railroad in rear was taken possession of and destroyed as far as possible. Wright's corps crossed at Jericho early the same day, and took position to the right of Warren's corps, extending south of the Virginia Central Railroad. This road was torn up for a considerable distance to the rear (west), the ties burned, and the rails bent and twisted by heating them over the burning ties. It was found, however, that Burnside's corps could not cross at Ox Ford. Lee had taken a position with his centre on the river at this point, with the two wings thrown back, his line making an acute angle where it overlooked the river.

Before the exact position of the whole of Lee's line was accurately known, I directed Hancock and Warren each to send a brigade to Ox Ford by the south side of the river. They found the enemy too strong to justify a serious attack. A third ford was found between Ox Ford and Jericho. Burnside was directed to cross a division over this ford, and to send one division to Hancock. Crittenden was crossed by this newly-discovered ford, and formed up the river to connect with Crawford's left. Potter joined Hancock by way of the wooden bridge. Crittenden had a severe engagement with some of Hill's corps on his crossing the river, and lost heavily. When joined to Warren's corps he was no further molested. Burnside still guarded Ox Ford from the north side.

Lee now had his entire army south of the North Anna. Our lines covered his front, with the six miles separating the two wings guarded by but a single division. To get from one wing to the other the river would have to be crossed twice. Lee could reinforce any part of his line from all points of it in a very short march; or could concentrate the whole of it wherever he might choose to assault. We were, for the time, practically two armies besieging.

Lee had been reinforced, and was being reinforced, largely. About this

Worker straightening twisted rails, sometimes called "Sherman's neckties." Photograph by Andrew J. Russell. *Library of Congress, Prints and Photographs Division, LC-DIG-ppmsca-10413.*

time the very troops whose coming I had predicted, had arrived or were coming in. Pickett with a full division from Richmond was up; Hoke from North Carolina had come with a brigade; and Breckinridge was there: in all probably not less than fifteen thousand men. But he did not attempt to drive us from the field.

On the 22d or 23d I received dispatches from Washington saying that Sherman had taken Kingston, crossed the Etowah River and was advancing into Georgia.[2]

I was seated at the time on the porch of a fine plantation house waiting for Burnside's corps to pass. Meade and his staff, besides my own staff, were with me. The lady of the house, a Mrs. Tyler, and an elderly lady, were present. Burnside seeing us, came up on the porch, his big spurs and saber rattling as he walked. He touched his hat politely to the ladies, and remarked that he supposed they had never seen so many "live Yankees" before in their lives. The elderly lady spoke up promptly saying, "Oh yes, I

2. Sallust recounts a turning point in Rome's second-century war against the Numidian king Jugurtha when the Roman general Metellus, understanding that a victory cost him more than a defeat did the Numidians, decided to avoid pitched battles in favor of destroying his enemy's country: "Accordingly he marched into the richest part of Numidia, laid waste the countryside, and captured and burnt a number of strongholds and towns that were ill fortified or ungarrisoned, massacring the men of military age and letting his soldiers take the rest of the inhabitants and their possessions as plunder. This terrorization of the population had its effect. . . . These operations frightened Jugurtha much more than any defeat could have done. For the only policy which offered him any hope of success was to retreat, and now he was forced to go after the Romans." *The Jugurthine War, The Jugurthine War/The Conspiracy of Catiline*, trans. S. A. Handford (New York: Penguin Classics, 1963), 91.

have; many more." "Where?" said Burnside. "In Richmond." Prisoners, of course, was understood.[3]

---

3. Historians estimate a total of 195,000 Union and 215,000 Confederate prisoners of war—approximately 15.5 percent of the former and 12 percent of the latter—died. The U.S. Sanitary Commission collected testimony about Confederate prisons. While the suffering of Northern prisoners is better documented, conditions were often inadequate in the North as well, especially at Elmira in Upstate New York, where almost three thousand Confederates died largely as a result of exposure, deprivation, and poor sanitation. The Sanitary Commission's 1864 report documents "famine" at Libby Prison in the Confederate capital:

> It was about the middle of last autumn that this process of slow starvation became intolerable, injurious, and cruel. . . . The corn bread began to be of the roughest and coarsest description. Portions of the cob and husk were often found ground in with the meal. The crust was so thick and hard that the prisoners called it iron-clad. To render the bread eatable, they grated it, and made mush out of it, but the crust they could not grate.
>
> Now and then, after long intervals, often of many weeks, a little meat was given them, perhaps two or three mouthfuls. At a later period, they received a pint of black peas, with some vinegar, every week. The peas were often full of worms, or maggots in a chrysalis state, which, when they made soup, floated on the surface.
>
> Those who were entirely dependent on the prison fare, and who had no friends at the North to send them boxes of food, began to suffer the horrible agony of craving food, and feeling themselves day by day losing strength. Dreams and delusions began to distract their minds. . . .
>
> Surgeon Ferguson, who was confined there at that time gives a most painful picture of what he saw.
>
> "No one can appreciate, without experience, the condition of the officers in the prison during the twelve days of my stay; their faces were pinched with hunger. I have seen an officer, standing by the window, gnawing a bone like a dog. I asked him, 'What do you do it for?' His reply was, 'It will help fill up.'
>
> "They were constantly complaining of hunger; there was a sad, and insatiable expression of face impossible to describe."
>
> There is no suffering that can be mentioned greater than that of the slow and lingering pains of famine, except it be perhaps the agonies of absolute death from hunger—but of this no Libby evidence was collected. . . .
>
> But the inhumanity was not confined to the living. It extended even to the disposal of the dead. The bodies were placed in the cellar, to which the animals of the street had access, and very often were partly devoured by hogs, dogs and rats. The officers had the curiosity to mark the coffins in which they were carried off, to find out whether they were buried in them. But they proved to be only vehicles for bearing them away, returning a score of times for others.

Libby Prison, Richmond, Virginia. *From the New York Public Library, https://digitalcollections. nypl.org/items/510d47e1–bc7a–a3d9– e040–e00a18064a99.*

I read my dispatch aloud, when it was received. This threw the younger lady into tears. I found the information she had received (and I suppose it was the information generally in circulation through the South) was that Lee was driving us from the State in the most demoralized condition, and that in the South-west our troops were but little better than prisoners of war. Seeing our troops moving south was ocular proof that a part of her information was incorrect, and she asked me if my news from Sherman was true.[4] I assured her that there was no doubt about it. I left a guard to protect the house from intrusion until the troops should have all passed, and assured her that if her husband was in hiding she could bring him in and he should be protected also. But I presume he was in the Confederate army.

On the 25th I gave orders, through Halleck, to Hunter, who had relieved Sigel, to move up the Valley of Virginia, cross over the Blue Ridge to Charlottesville and go as far as Lynchburg if possible, living upon the country and

Commission of Inquiry, U.S. Sanitary Commission, *Narrative of Privations and Sufferings of United States Officers and Soldiers while Prisoners of War in the Hands of the Rebel Authorities* (Philadelphia: King & Baird, 1864), 37–38, 40–42.

4. Shakespeare's Othello demands "ocular proof" from Iago of Desdemona's infidelity with Cassio in *Othello* (3.3.360). The circumstantial evidence Iago produces—a handkerchief embroidered with strawberries, which Othello had once given his wife—is in fact proof of nothing, but it is sufficiently damning to set Othello on his murderous course. Perhaps in making the allusion, Grant recalled his brief run as Desdemona in the amateur theatricals at Corpus Christi before the Mexican War.

cutting the railroads and canal as he went. After doing this he could find his way back to his base, or join me.

On the same day news was received that Lee was falling back on Richmond. This proved not to be true. But we could do nothing where we were unless Lee would assume the offensive. I determined, therefore, to draw out of our present position and make one more effort to get between him and Richmond. I had no expectation now, however, of succeeding in this; but I did expect to hold him far enough west to enable me to reach the James River high up. Sheridan was now again with the Army of the Potomac.

On the 26th I informed the government at Washington of the position of the two armies; of the reinforcements the enemy had received; of the move I proposed to make;[5] and directed that our base of supplies should be shifted to White House, on the Pamunkey. The wagon train and guards moved directly from Port Royal to White House. Supplies moved around by water, guarded by the navy. Orders had previously been sent, through Halleck, for Butler to send Smith's corps to White House. This order was repeated on the 25th, with directions that they should be landed on the north side of the Pamunkey, and marched until they joined the Army of the Potomac.

The actor Edwin Booth (1833–1893) as Iago in
Shakespeare's *Othello. Library of Congress,
Prints and Photographs Division, LC-USZ62-40345.*

5. For the correspondence included in a note to the first edition, see Appendix 1, chapter 54, note 1.

It was a delicate move to get the right wing of the Army of the Potomac from its position south of the North Anna in the presence of the enemy. To accomplish it, I issued the following order:

QUARLES' MILLS, VA.,
May 25, 1864.

MAJOR GENERAL MEADE,
Commanding A. P.

Direct Generals Warren and Wright to withdraw all their teams and artillery, not in position, to the north side of the river to-morrow. Send that belonging to General Wright's corps as far on the road to Hanover Town as it can go, without attracting attention to the fact. Send with it Wright's best division or division under his ablest commander. Have their places filled up in the line so if possible the enemy will not notice their withdrawal. Send the cavalry to-morrow afternoon, or as much of it as you may deem necessary, to watch and seize, if they can, Littlepage's Bridge and Taylor's Ford, and to remain on one or other side of the river at these points until the infantry and artillery all pass. As soon as it is dark to-morrow night start the division which you withdraw first from Wright's corps to make a forced march to Hanover Town, taking with them no teams to impede their march. At the same time this division starts commence withdrawing all of the 5th and 6th corps from the south side of the river, and march them for the same place. The two divisions of the 9th corps not now with Hancock, may be moved down the north bank of the river where they will be handy to support Hancock if necessary, or will be that much on their road to follow the 5th and 6th corps. Hancock should hold his command in readiness to follow as soon as the way is clear for him. To-morrow it will leave nothing for him to do, but as soon as he can he should get all his teams and spare artillery on the road or roads which he will have to take. As soon as the troops reach Hanover Town they should get possession of all the crossings they can in that neighborhood. I think it would be well to make a heavy cavalry demonstration on the enemy's left, to-morrow afternoon, also.

U. S. GRANT,
Lieut.-General.

Wilson's division of cavalry was brought up from the left and moved by our right south to Little River. Here he manœuvred to give the impression that we were going to attack the left flank of Lee's army.

Under cover of night our right wing was withdrawn to the north side of the river, Lee being completely deceived by Wilson's feint. On the afternoon of the 26th Sheridan moved, sending Gregg's and Torbert's cavalry to Taylor's and Littlepage's fords towards Hanover. As soon as it was dark both divisions moved quietly to Hanover Ferry, leaving small guards behind to keep up the impression that crossings were to be attempted in the morning. Sheridan was followed by a division of infantry under General Russell. On the morning of the 27th the crossing was effected with but little loss, the enemy losing thirty or forty, taken prisoners. Thus a position was secured south of the Pamunkey.

Russell stopped at the crossing while the cavalry pushed on to Hanover Town. Here Barringer's, formerly Gordon's, brigade of rebel cavalry was encountered, but it was speedily driven away.

Warren's and Wright's corps were moved by the rear of Burnside's and Hancock's corps. When out of the way these latter corps followed, leaving pickets confronting the enemy. Wilson's cavalry followed last, watching all the fords until everything had recrossed; then taking up the pontoons and destroying other bridges, became the rear-guard.

Two roads were traversed by the troops in this move. The one nearest to and north of the North Anna and Pamunkey was taken by Wright, followed by Hancock. Warren, followed by Burnside, moved by a road farther north, and longer. The trains moved by a road still farther north, and had to travel a still greater distance. All the troops that had crossed the Pamunkey on the morning of the 27th remained quiet during the rest of the day, while the troops north of that stream marched to reach the crossing that had been secured for them.

Lee had evidently been deceived by our movement from North Anna; for on the morning of the 27th he telegraphed to Richmond: "Enemy crossed to north side, and cavalry and infantry crossed at Hanover Town."[6] The troops that had then crossed left his front the night of the 25th.

---

6. During this period, while Lee and Grant were trying to outfox each other along the North Anna, the relationship between the latter and Meade continued to develop. Attempting "to handle Meade gingerly," Brooks Simpson observes, Grant "had flattered Meade's performance in dispatches and defended his performance to others. Yet

The country we were now in was a difficult one to move troops over. The streams were numerous, deep and sluggish, sometimes spreading out into swamps grown up with impenetrable growths of trees and underbrush. The banks were generally low and marshy, making the streams difficult to approach except where there were roads and bridges.

Hanover Town is about twenty miles from Richmond. There are two roads leading there; the most direct and shortest one crossing the Chickahominy at Meadow Bridge, near the Virginia Central Railroad, the second going by New and Old Cold Harbor. A few miles out from Hanover Town there is a third road by way of Mechanicsville to Richmond. New Cold Harbor was important to us because while there we both covered the roads back to White House (where our supplies came from), and the roads southeast over which we would have to pass to get to the James River below the Richmond defences.

On the morning of the 28th the army made an early start, and by noon all had crossed except Burnside's corps. This was left on the north side temporarily to guard the large wagon train. A line was at once formed extending south from the river, Wright's corps on the right, Hancock's in the centre, and Warren's on the left, ready to meet the enemy if he should come.

At the same time Sheridan was directed to reconnoitre towards Mechanicsville to find Lee's position. At Hawes' Shop, just where the middle road leaves the direct road to Richmond, he encountered the Confederate cavalry dismounted and partially intrenched. Gregg attacked with his division, but was unable to move the enemy. In the evening Custer came up with a brigade. The attack was now renewed, the cavalry dismounting and charging as infantry. This time the assault was successful, both sides losing a considerable number of men. But our troops had to bury the dead, and found that more Confederate than Union soldiers had been killed.[7] The position was easily held, because our infantry was near.

---

it was also evident that he was intervening more directly in the operations of the army than he had originally intended." At this point Grant decided to change course: "Now he pulled back in significant ways. First, he ended Burnside's career as an independent corps commander, placing him under Meade—a step long overdue. Between the collapse of Sigel's campaign in the Valley and growing concern about Butler and the Army of the James, Grant simply could not take the time to direct Burnside; doing so absorbed too much energy and was at best marginally effective. Second, he decided to let Meade manage his own army." *Triumph over Adversity*, 317.

7. In "A Natural History of the Dead" Ernest Hemingway catalogues the many strange and unglamorous ways to die in war:

On the 29th a reconnoissance was made in force, to find the position of Lee. Wright's corps pushed to Hanover Court House. Hancock's corps pushed toward Totopotomoy Creek; Warren's corps to the left on the Shady Grove Church Road, while Burnside was held in reserve. Our advance was pushed forward three miles on the left with but little fighting. There was now an appearance of a movement past our left flank, and Sheridan was sent to meet it.

On the 30th Hancock moved to the Totopotomoy, where he found the enemy strongly fortified. Wright was moved to the right of Hancock's corps, and Burnside was brought forward and crossed, taking position to the left of Hancock. Warren moved up near Huntley Corners on the Shady Grove Church Road. There was some skirmishing along the centre, and in the evening Early attacked Warren with some vigor, driving him back at first, and threatening to turn our left flank. As the best means of reinforcing the left, Hancock was ordered to attack in his front. He carried and held the rifle-pits. While this was going on Warren got his men up, repulsed Early, and drove him more than a mile.

On this day I wrote to Halleck ordering all the pontoons in Washington to be sent to City Point. In the evening news was received of the arrival of Smith with his corps at White House. I notified Meade, in writing, as follows:

NEAR HAWES' SHOP, VA.,
6.40 P.M., *May* 30, 1864.

MAJOR-GENERAL MEADE,
Commanding A. P.

General Smith will debark his force at the White House tonight and start up the south bank of the Pamunkey at an early hour, probably at 3 A.M. in the morning. It is not improbable that the

---

The first thing that you found about the dead was that, hit badly enough, they died like animals. Some quickly from a little wound you would not think would kill a rabbit. They died from little wounds as rabbits die sometimes from three or four small grains of shot that hardly seem to break the skin. Others would die like cats; a skull broken in and iron in the brain, they lie alive two days like cats that crawl into the coal bin with a bullet in the brain and will not die until you cut their heads off. Maybe cats do not die then, they say they have nine lives, I do not know, but most men die like animals, not men. I'd never seen a natural death, so called, and so I blamed it on the war.

Hemingway on War, ed. Seán Hemingway (New York: Scribner, 2003), 46.

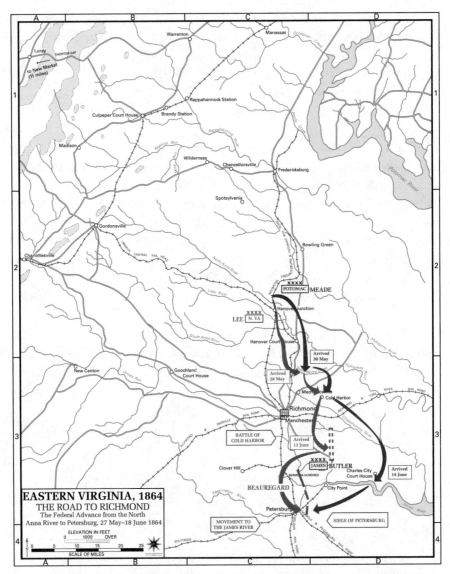

Federal advance from the North Anna to Petersburg. May 27–June 18, 1864. *West Point Atlas of the Civil War. Courtesy of Department of History, USMA.*

enemy, being aware of Smith's movement, will be feeling to get on our left flank for the purpose of cutting him off, or by a dash to crush him and get back before we are aware of it. Sheridan ought to be notified to watch the enemy's movements well out towards Cold Harbor, and also on the Mechanicsville road. Wright should be got well massed on Hancock's right, so that, if it becomes necessary, he can take the place of the latter readily whilst troops are being thrown east of the Totopotomoy if necessary.

I want Sheridan to send a cavalry force of at least half a brigade, if not a whole brigade, at 5 a.m. in the morning, to communicate with Smith and to return with him. I will send orders for Smith by the messenger you send to Sheridan with his orders.

U. S. GRANT.

I also notified Smith of his danger, and the precautions that would be taken to protect him.

The night of the 30th Lee's position was substantially from Atlee's Station on the Virginia Central Railroad south and east to the vicinity of Cold Harbor. Ours was: The left of Warren's corps was on the Shady Grove Road, extending to the Mechanicsville Road and about three miles south of the Totopotomoy. Burnside to his right, then Hancock, and Wright on the extreme right, extending towards Hanover Court House, six miles southeast of it. Sheridan with two divisions of cavalry was watching our left front towards Cold Harbor. Wilson with his division on our right was sent to get on the Virginia Central Railroad and destroy it as far back as possible. He got possession of Hanover Court House the next day after a skirmish with Young's cavalry brigade. The enemy attacked Sheridan's pickets, but reinforcements were sent up and the attack was speedily repulsed and the enemy followed some distance towards Cold Harbor.

Pontoon bridge across the North Anna River below Taylor's Bridge, Virginia, May 1864. *Library of Congress, Prints and Photographs Division, Civil War Photographs, LC-DIG-cwpb-01379.*

55

Advance on Cold Harbor—An Anecdote of the War—Battle of Cold Harbor— Correspondence with Lee—Retrospective

On the 31st Sheridan advanced to near Old Cold Harbor. He found it intrenched and occupied by cavalry and infantry. A hard fight ensued but the place was carried. The enemy well knew the importance of Cold Harbor to us, and seemed determined that we should not hold it. He returned with such a large force that Sheridan was about withdrawing without making any effort to hold it against such odds; but about the time he commenced the evacuation he received orders to hold the place at all hazards, until reinforcements could be sent to him. He speedily turned the rebel works to face against them and placed his men in position for defence. Night came on before the enemy was ready for assault.

Wright's corps was ordered early in the evening to march directly to Cold Harbor passing by the rear of the army. It was expected to arrive by daylight or before; but the night was dark and the distance great, so that it was nine o'clock the 1st of June before it reached its destination. Before the arrival of Wright the enemy had made two assaults on Sheridan, both of which were repulsed with heavy loss to the enemy. Wright's corps coming up, there was no further assault on Cold Harbor.

Smith, who was coming up from White House, was also directed to march directly to Cold Harbor, and was expected early on the morning of the 1st of June; but by some blunder the order which reached Smith directed him to Newcastle instead of Cold Harbor. Through this blunder Smith did not reach his destination until three o'clock in the afternoon, and then with tired and worn-out men from their long and dusty march. He landed twelve thousand five hundred men from Butler's command, but a division was left at White House temporarily and many men had fallen out of ranks in their long march.

Before the removal of Wright's corps from our right, after dark on the 31st, the two lines, Federal and Confederate, were so close together at that point that either side could detect directly any movement made by the other. Finding at daylight that Wright had left his front, Lee evidently divined that he had gone to our left. At all events, soon after light on the 1st of June Anderson, who commanded the corps on Lee's left, was seen moving along Warren's front. Warren was ordered to attack him vigorously in flank, while Wright was directed to move out and get on his front. Warren fired his artillery at the enemy; but lost so much time in making ready that the enemy got by, and at three o'clock he reported the enemy was strongly intrenched in his front, and besides his lines were so long that he had no mass of troops to move with. He seemed to have forgotten that lines in rear of an army hold themselves while their defenders are fighting in their front. Wright reconnoitred some distance to his front: but the enemy finding Old Cold Harbor already taken had halted and fortified some distance west.

By six o'clock in the afternoon Wright and Smith were ready to make an assault. In front of both the ground was clear for several hundred yards, and then became wooded. Both charged across this open space and into the wood, capturing and holding the first line of rifle-pits of the enemy, and also capturing seven or eight hundred prisoners.

While this was going on, the enemy charged Warren three separate times with vigor, but were repulsed each time with loss. There was no officer more capable, nor one more prompt in acting, than Warren when the enemy forced him to it. There was also an attack upon Hancock's and Burnside's corps at the same time; but it was feeble and probably only intended to relieve Anderson who was being pressed by Wright and Smith.

During the night the enemy made frequent attacks with the view of dispossessing us of the important position we had gained, but without effecting their object.

Hancock was moved from his place in line during the night and ordered to the left of Wright. I expected to take the offensive on the morning of the 2d, but the night was so dark, the heat and dust so excessive and the roads so intricate and hard to keep, that the head of column only reached Old Cold Harbor at six o'clock, but was in position at 7.30 A.M. Preparations were made for an attack in the afternoon, but did not take place until the next morning. Warren's corps was moved to the left to connect with Smith: Hancock's corps was got into position to the left of Wright's, and Burnside was moved to Bethesda Church in reserve. While Warren and Burnside were making these changes the enemy came out several times and attacked them, capturing several hundred prisoners. The attacks were repulsed, but not followed up as they should have been. I was so annoyed at this that I directed Meade to instruct his corps commanders that they should seize all such opportunities when they occurred, and not wait for orders, all of our manœuvres being made for the very purpose of getting the enemy out of his cover.

On this day Wilson returned from his raid upon the Virginia Central Railroad, having damaged it considerably. But, like ourselves, the rebels had become experts in repairing such damage. Sherman, in his memoirs, relates an anecdote of his campaign to Atlanta that well illustrates this point. The rebel cavalry lurking in his rear to burn bridges and obstruct his communications had become so disgusted at hearing trains go whistling by within a few hours after a bridge had been burned, that they proposed to try blowing up some of the tunnels. One of them said, "No use, boys, Old Sherman carries duplicate tunnels with him, and will replace them as fast as you can blow them up; better save your powder."

Sheridan was engaged reconnoitring the banks of the Chickahominy, to find crossings and the condition of the roads. He reported favorably.

During the night Lee moved his left up to make his line correspond to ours. His lines extended now from the Totopotomoy to New Cold Harbor. Mine from Bethesda Church by Old Cold Harbor to the Chickahominy, with a division of cavalry guarding our right. An assault was ordered for the 3d, to be made mainly by the corps of Hancock, Wright and Smith; but Warren and Burnside were to support it by threatening Lee's left, and to attack with great earnestness if he should either reinforce more threatened points by drawing from that quarter or if a favorable opportunity should present itself.[1]

---

1. Horace Porter makes clear how the soldiers reckoned the odds at Cold Harbor:

> As I came near one of the regiments which was making preparations for the next morning's assault, I noticed that many of the soldiers had taken off their coats, and seemed to be engaged in sewing up rents in them. This exhibition of tailoring seemed rather peculiar at such a moment, but upon closer examination it was found that the men were calmly writing their names and home addresses on slips of paper, and pinning them on the backs of their coats, so that their dead bodies might be recognized upon the field, and their fate made known to their families at home.

Porter, *Campaigning*, 174–75.

Grant at Headquarters, Cold Harbor, Virginia, 1864. *Library of Congress, Prints and Photographs Division, Civil War Photographs, LC-DIG-cwpb-01694.*

The corps commanders were to select the points in their respective fronts where they would make their assaults. The move was to commence at half-past four in the morning. Hancock sent Barlow and Gibbon forward at the appointed hour, with Birney as a reserve. Barlow pushed forward with great vigor, under a heavy fire of both artillery and musketry, through thickets and swamps. Notwithstanding all the resistance of the enemy and the natural obstructions to overcome, he carried a position occupied by the enemy outside their main line where the road makes a deep cut through a bank affording as good a shelter for troops as if it had been made for that purpose. Three pieces of artillery had been captured here, and several hundred prisoners. The guns were immediately turned against the men who had just been using them. No assistance coming to him, he (Barlow) intrenched under fire and continued to hold his place. Gibbon was not so fortunate in his front. He found the ground over which he had to pass cut up with deep ravines, and a morass difficult to cross. But his men struggled on until some of them got up to the very parapet covering the enemy. Gibbon gained ground much nearer the enemy than that which he left, and here he intrenched and held fast.[2]

Wright's corps moving in two lines captured the outer rifle-pits in their front, but accomplished nothing more. Smith's corps also gained the outer rifle-pits in its front. The ground over which this corps (18th) had to move was the most exposed of any over which charges were made. An open plain

2. For the correspondence included in a note to the first edition, see Appendix 1, chapter 55, note 1.

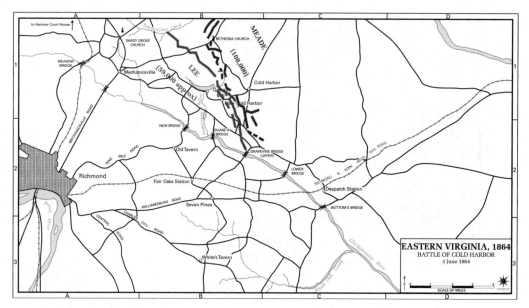

Battle of Cold Harbor, June 3, 1864. *West Point Atlas of the Civil War. Courtesy of Department of History, USMA.*

intervened between the contending forces at this point, which was exposed both to a direct and a cross fire. Smith, however, finding a ravine running towards his front, sufficiently deep to protect men in it from cross fire, and somewhat from a direct fire, put Martindale's division in it, and with Brooks supporting him on the left and Devens on the right succeeded in gaining the outer—probably picket—rifle-pits. Warren and Burnside also advanced and gained ground—which brought the whole army on one line.

This assault cost us heavily and probably without benefit to compensate: but the enemy was not cheered by the occurrence sufficiently to induce him to take the offensive. In fact, nowhere after the battle of the Wilderness did Lee show any disposition to leave his defences far behind him.

Fighting was substantially over by half-past seven in the morning. At eleven o'clock I started to visit all the corps commanders to see for myself the different positions gained and to get their opinion of the practicability of doing anything more in their respective fronts.

Hancock gave the opinion that in his front the enemy was too strong to make any further assault promise success. Wright thought he could gain the lines of the enemy, but it would require the co-operation of Hancock's and Smith's corps. Smith thought a lodgment possible, but was not sanguine: Burnside thought something could be done in his front, but Warren differed.

I concluded, therefore to make no more assaults, and a little after twelve directed in the following letter that all offensive action should cease.[3]

---

3. Perhaps more than any other engagement, the assault at Cold Harbor gave Grant a reputation as a butcher. The correspondent William Swinton argues that Grant's "conduct in this campaign ranks him with that class of generals who have been named Thor-strikers" and whose sole military principle is to hammer the enemy. Cold Harbor—and Spotsylvania before it—Swinton continues, "presents the *reductio ad absurdum* of the theory of 'hammering.' And besides, General Grant's best successes were accomplished only when, departing from his own principle, he manœuvred as well as attacked." *Campaigns*, 494.

The modern historian Brooks Simpson offers a more complex picture in which several factors contributed to the failure: Grant's underestimation of the Army of Northern Virginia's will to fight on, Meade's failure to prepare adequately (including a lack of reconnaissance) after the postponement of the assault originally planned for June 2 until the next morning, obliviousness to the fact that Confederates would also make use of the delay, the utter lack of coordination between Meade and his corps commanders, and those commanders' unwillingness to cooperate with each other. See *Grant: Triumph*, 324–31.

Defending Grant against the charge of butchery, Charles Dana compiled a table illustrating that "Grant in eleven months secured the prize with less loss than his predecessors suffered in failing to win it during a struggle of three years." At the end of the war, the difference in aggregate losses between Grant's and those of his predecessors combined was, Dana calculated, a grisly 19,535. See *Recollections*, 210–11.

In the following description of attacking the formidable Confederate breastworks at Cold Harbor, Adams, the Massachusetts officer, gives a human dimension to the numbers:

> We stood in line three hours, waiting for the order to advance, and when it came the rebels were ready and waiting for us, yet over the field we went. Men were mowed down by hundreds. . . .
>
> We changed brigade commanders several times that forenoon; first one colonel would fall, then another, until at last a lieutenant-colonel commanded. We reached a ravine within a few yards of the rebel works and lay down. By forming line to the rear, the men lying flat on the ground, we were able during the night to get a few rails and before morning had quite a good breastwork. . . .
>
> We were in a peculiar position,—so near the rebel works that we could throw a stone over, and no man on either side could show his head without getting a shot. Rations could not be brought to us until we dug a trench over the hill to the rear, which we did the second night. The second day we were in this place we saw a pile of dirt in our front, on a little knoll, and once in a while a shot would be fired, followed by a yell. Mark Kimball, Gus Bridges, Frank Osborne and Milt Ellsworth dug out and found Alonzo W. Bartlett of Andrews, Mass., sharpshooter. Bart. had come out after the body of the colonel of the 8th New York, who fell at the foot of the rebel works. He had managed to get a rope around the body, but the rebels made it so hot that he was forced to intrench, which he did with his dipper, and was fighting the war on his own hook. His face was cut and bleeding from

Assistant Secretary of War Charles A. Dana, Cold Harbor, Virginia, 1864. *Library of Congress, Prints and Photographs Division, Civil War Photographs, LC-DIG-cwpb-01697.*

COLD HARBOR,
June 3, 1864.—12.30 P.M.

MAJOR-GENERAL MEADE,
Commanding A. P.

The opinion of corps commanders not being sanguine of success in case an assault is ordered, you may direct a suspension of farther advance for the present. Hold our most advanced positions and strengthen them. Whilst on the defensive our line may be contracted from the right if practicable. Reconnoissances should be made in front of every corps and advances made to advantageous positions by regular approaches. To aid the expedition under General Hunter it is necessary that we should detain all the army now with Lee until the former gets well on his way to Lynchburg. To do this effectually it will be better to keep the enemy out of the intrenchments of Richmond than to have them go back there.

---

gravel stones which had struck him, but he had held his own, and having a good rifle with plenty of ammunition thought he could hold out as long as they. . . .

From the 9th to the 12th the firing was constant day and night; men were killed every hour in the day. Captain Hincks was severely wounded while lying in rear of the works. The duty was very hard. One-half the men must be on guard during the night, and all in line at three A.M. The officer in charge was obliged to go from right to left, as the men would drop to sleep as soon as they were posted, being exhausted from long hours of duty. The mental strain was unspeakable.

Adams, *Reminiscences*, 98–101.

Wright and Hancock should be ready to assault in case the enemy should break through General Smith's lines, and all should be ready to resist an assault.

U. S. GRANT,
Lieutenant-General.

The remainder of the day was spent in strengthening the line we now held. By night we were as strong against Lee as he was against us.

During the night the enemy quitted our right front, abandoning some of their wounded, and without burying their dead. These we were able to care for. But there were many dead and wounded men between the lines of the contending forces, which were now close together, who could not be cared for without a cessation of hostilities.[4]

---

4. Colonel Beckwith describes the grotesque aftermath of the assault, when the wounded were stranded in between the lines:

> On the 4th of June we made an effort, and got all we could of the poor fellows, who had been lying wounded between the lines, since the previous day's battles. But many were left, it being impossible to get them on account of the fire of the sharpshooters. The poorly interred corpses of our men within our line, and the dead lying between the lines had now become decomposed and putrid, and made an awful stench. The water was very poor and a long way off, and many of the men complained of being sick. On the 7th of June under a flag of truce we gathered the wounded between the lines that were still alive and buried the putrid bodies of the dead that threatened a pestilence to the living. The wounded were in a horrible condition. One officer of the 106th New York I think, had a wound in the thigh that was infested with maggots. All the wounded yet alive could have survived but a little time longer. They had exhausted their water supply, and sucked their moist clothing to get the rain and dew from it. They had scooped out holes in the ground to shelter themselves, and put moist clay in their mouths to prolong life. Imagine, if you can, their horrible predicament, lying on a bullet-swept field, without ability to crawl, their wounds infested with maggots, and existing five days or more before being succored, and you can get some idea of the horrors of war.

Quoted in Best, *History of the 121st*, 158–59.

Beckwith did not know that maggots are a natural disinfectant and debriding agent. What he took to be the "horrible condition" of maggot infestation in fact increased a soldier's chances of surviving. In 1829, Baron Dominique Jean Larrey, a surgeon in Napoleon's army, observed their possible implications for soldier mortality in Syria, where the larvae of the indigenous blue fly had infested most of the wounds, a circumstance that horrified the soldiers but clearly aided the healing process. Larrey thus took advantage of an accident of climate. The Confederate surgeon John Forney Zacharias claims to have deliberately introduced maggots into gangrenous wounds during the Civil War. A history of the Frederick County, Maryland, Medical Society, of which Zacharias was a member, quotes his description of his methods: "During my service in the hospital at Danville, Va., I first used maggots to remove the decayed tissue in Hospital gangrene, and with eminent satisfaction. In a single day they would clean a wound much better than any agents we had at our command. I used them afterwards at various places. I am sure I saved many lives by their use, escaped septicaemia, and had rapid recoveries." T. J. C. Williams and Folger McKinsey, *History of Frederick County Maryland*, 2 vols. (N.p.: Titsworth, 1910), 1: 596. See also Baron D. J. Larrey, *Observations on Wounds, and Their Complications by Erysipelas, Gangrene and Tetanus*, trans. E. F. Rivinus (Philadelphia: Key, Mielke & Biddle, 1832), 34.

These earlier discoveries about the effectiveness of maggots in aiding the healing of wounds did not gain widespread acceptance in the medical community. In the twentieth century, William S. Baer pioneered the study and use of maggot therapy in civilian medicine at Johns Hopkins after observing the otherwise inexplicable improvement of soldiers whose wounds had been infested as a result of their having been abandoned for several days in the woods during World War I. See William S. Baer, "The Treatment of Chronic Osteomyelitis with the Maggot (Larva of the Blow Fly)," *Journal of Bone and Joint Surgery* 13 (1931): 438–75, and Yamni Nigam et al., "Maggot Therapy: The Science and Implication for CAM Part I—History and Bacterial Resistance," *Evidence Based Complementary and Alternative Medicine* 3, no. 2 (June 2006): 223–27.

Alexander Cavalié Mercer, a British artillery officer at Waterloo, records an encounter with a wounded French soldier left on the field overnight after the battle:

> I had satisfied my curiosity at Hougoumont, and was retracing my steps
> up the hill, when my attention was called to a group of wounded French-
> men by the calm, dignified, and soldierlike oration addressed by one of
> them to the rest. I cannot, like Livy, compose a fine harangue for my hero,
> and, of course, I could not retain the precise words, but the import of them
> was to exhort them to bear their sufferings with fortitude; not to repine,
> like women or children, at what every soldier should have made up his
> mind to suffer as the fortune of war, but, above all, to remember that they
> were surrounded by Englishmen, before whom they ought to be doubly
> careful not to disgrace themselves by displaying such an unsoldierlike want
> of fortitude. The speaker was sitting on the ground, with his lance stuck
> upright beside him—an old veteran, with a thick bushy grizzly beard, coun-
> tenance like a lion—a lancer of the Old Guard, and no doubt had fought
> in many a field. One hand was flourished in the air as he spoke, the other,
> severed at the wrist, lay on the earth beside him; one ball (case-shot, prob-
> ably) had entered his body, another had broken his leg. His suffering, after
> a night of exposure so mangled, must have been great: yet he betrayed it
> not. His bearing was that of a Roman, or perhaps of an Indian warrior. . . .
> I could not but feel the highest veneration for this brave man, and told him
> so, at the same time offering him the only consolation in my power—a
> drink of cold water, and assurances that the waggons would soon be sent
> round to collect the wounded. He thanked me with a grace peculiar to

So I wrote the following:

COLD HARBOR, VA.,
June 5, 1864.

GENERAL R. E. LEE,
Commanding Confederate Army.

It is reported to me that there are wounded men, probably of
both armies, now lying exposed and suffering between the lines
occupied respectively by the two armies. Humanity would dictate that
some provision should be made to provide against such hardships.[5]
I would propose, therefore, that hereafter, when no battle is raging,
either party be authorized to send to any point between the pickets
or skirmish lines, unarmed men bearing litters to pick up their dead
or wounded, without being fired upon by the other party. Any other
method, equally fair to both parties, you may propose for meeting the
end desired will be accepted by me.

U. S. GRANT,
Lieut.-General.

> Frenchmen, and eagerly inquired the fate of their army. On this head I
> could tell him nothing consolatory, so merely answered that it had retired
> last night. . . . After a very interesting conversation, I begged his lance as a
> keepsake, observing that it never could be of further use to him. The old
> man's eyes kindled as I spoke, and he emphatically assured me that it would
> delight him to see it in the hands of a brave soldier, instead of being torn
> from him, as he had feared, by those vile peasants. So I took my leave, and
> walked away with the lance in my hand.

General Cavalié Mercer, *Journal of the Waterloo Campaign*, 2 vols. (Edinburgh: William
Blackwood and Sons, 1870), 1:350–52.

5. The novelist Hans Herbert Grimm describes what it was like to watch and listen to a
comrade caught between the lines on the Western Front:

> One of them, a really young fellow, became stuck in the barbed wire and
> couldn't go forwards or backwards. He got shot in the stomach and his guts
> started pouring out. Grabbing them with his hand, he pressed them to his
> body and howled in pain like an animal. The Tommies were firing like
> crazy and the poor young man had to stay where he was. No one could
> come and get him. With his glassy eyes he stared at the trench, occasionally
> screaming "Mother! Mother!"

Schlump, 128.

Lee replied that he feared such an arrangement would lead to misunderstanding, and proposed that in future, when either party wished to remove their dead and wounded, a flag of truce be sent. I answered this immediately by saying:

COLD HARBOR, VA.,
June 6, 1864.

GENERAL R. E. LEE,
Commanding Army of N. Va.

Your communication of yesterday's date is received. I will send immediately, as you propose, to collect the dead and wounded between the lines of the two armies, and will also instruct that you be allowed to do the same. I propose that the time for doing this be between the hours of 12 M. and 3 P.M. to-day. I will direct all parties going out to bear a white flag, and not to attempt to go beyond where we have dead or wounded, and not beyond or on ground occupied by your troops.

U. S. GRANT,
Lieut.-General.

Lee's response was that he could not consent to the burial of the dead and removal of the wounded in the way I proposed, but when either party desired such permission it should be asked for by flag of truce; and he had directed that any parties I may have sent out, as mentioned in my letter, to be turned back. I answered:

COLD HARBOR, VA.,
June 6, 1864.

GENERAL R. E. LEE,
Commanding Army, N. Va.

The knowledge that wounded men are now suffering from want of attention, between the two armies, compels me to ask a suspension of hostilities for sufficient time to collect them in, say two hours. Permit me to say that the hours you may fix upon for this will be agreeable to me, and the same privilege will be extended to such parties as you may wish to send out on the same duty without further application.

U. S. GRANT,
Lieut.-General.

Lee acceded to this; but delays in transmitting the correspondence brought it to the 7th of June—forty-eight hours after it commenced—before parties were got out to collect the men left upon the field. In the meantime all but two of the wounded had died. And I wrote to Lee:

> COLD HARBOR, VA.,
> *June* 7, 1864.
> 10.30 A.M.

GEN. R. E. LEE,
Commanding Army of N. Va.

I regret that your note of seven P.M. yesterday should have been received at the nearest corps headquarters, to where it was delivered, after the hour which had been given for the removal of the dead and wounded had expired; 10.45 P.M. was the hour at which it was received at corps headquarters, and between eleven and twelve it reached my headquarters. As a consequence, it was not understood by the troops of this army that there was a cessation of hostilities for the purpose of collecting the dead and wounded, and none were collected. Two officers and six men of the 8th and 25th North Carolina Regts., who were out in search of the bodies of officers of their respective regiments, were captured and brought into our lines, owing to this want of understanding. I regret this, but will state that as soon as I learned the fact, I directed that they should not be held as prisoners, but must be returned to their commands. These officers and men having been carelessly brought through our lines to the rear, I have not determined whether they will be sent back the way they came, or whether they will be sent by some other route.

Regretting that all my efforts for alleviating the sufferings of wounded men left upon the battle-field have been rendered nugatory, I remain, &c.,

> U. S. GRANT,
> Lieutenant-General.[6]

---

6. About this bizarre exchange of messages, Simpson notes, "Lee had turned a muddled discussion over how best to recover the dead and wounded into an exercise in military protocol. Most of the dead and wounded belonged to Grant's command, and his initial proposal was inadequate. But to prolong the suffering between the lines in the name of propriety was a bit much—what harm could it have done to accede to

I have always regretted that the last assault at Cold Harbor was ever made. I might say the same thing of the assault of the 22d of May, 1863, at Vicksburg. At Cold Harbor no advantage whatever was gained to compensate for the heavy loss we sustained. Indeed, the advantages other than those of relative losses, were on the Confederate side. Before that, the Army of Northern Virginia seemed to have acquired a wholesome regard for the courage, endurance, and soldierly qualities generally of the Army of the Potomac. They no longer wanted to fight them "one Confederate to five Yanks." Indeed, they seemed to have given up any idea of gaining any

---

Grant's second proposal? More than anything else, Lee wanted the acknowledgment of defeat that accompanied a flag of truce." *Triumph over Adversity*, 328–29.

Antiquity offers an analogue in the 425 BCE Battle of Solgyia between Athens and Corinth. After defeating the Corinthians, the Athenians had buried their dead and boarded their ships. As they were about to embark, however, word was brought to the Athenian commander Nicias that the burial party had inadvertently left two bodies unburied on the field. As enemy reinforcements had by this time already arrived, Nicias sent word to the Corinthians for permission to retrieve the two soldiers, thereby technically forfeiting his victory:

> There it happened that two of his men were left by an oversight, when they carried off the dead, which when he understood, he stopped the fleet, and sent a herald to the enemy for leave to carry off the dead; though by law and custom, he that by a truce craved leave to carry off the dead, was hereby supposed to give up all claim to the victory. Nor was it lawful for him that did this to erect a trophy, for his is the victory who is master of the field, and he is not master who asks leave, as wanting power to take. But he chose rather to renounce his victory and his glory, than to let two citizens lie unburied.

Nicias, Plutarch's Lives, 3:297.

Despite forfeiting an ostensible victory, Nicias's decision to honor the dead demonstrates a cohesive, successfully functioning Athenian community. Pamela Vaughn suggests that this episode emphasizes at once Nicias's personal "piety" and "the strategic importance of recovering bodies" for the Greeks. She posits some of the underlying psychological and political reasons for this dedication to the identification process: the retrieval of bodies for funerary rites not only satisfied "obligations" among hoplites, who would be reassured of similar attention in the event of their own deaths, but also connected the soldier to the polis "by reaffirming the basic belief in the sanctity of the dead." "The Identification and Retrieval of the Hoplite Battle-Dead," *Hoplites: The Classical Greek Battle Experience*, ed. Victor Davis Hanson (London: Routledge, 1993), 50, 40.

For a nuanced exploration of the challenges of honoring Northern war dead buried in the South, see Constance Fenimore Woolson's short story "Rodman the Keeper," *Atlantic Monthly* 39, no. 233 (March 1877): 261–77

advantage of their antagonist in the open field. They had come to much prefer breastworks in their front to the Army of the Potomac. This charge seemed to revive their hopes temporarily; but it was of short duration. The effect upon the Army of the Potomac was the reverse.[7] When we reached the James River, however, all effects of the battle of Cold Harbor seemed to have disappeared.

There was more justification for the assault at Vicksburg. We were in a Southern climate, at the beginning of the hot season. The Army of the Tennessee had won five successive victories over the garrison of Vicksburg in the three preceding weeks. They had driven a portion of that army from Port Gibson with considerable loss, after having flanked them out of their stronghold at Grand Gulf. They had attacked another portion of the same army at Raymond, more than fifty miles farther in the interior of the State, and driven them back into Jackson with great loss in killed, wounded, captured and missing, besides loss of large and small arms: they had captured the capital of the State of Mississippi, with a large amount of materials of war and manufactures. Only a few days before, they had beaten the enemy then penned up in the town first at Champion's Hill, next at Big Black River Bridge, inflicting upon him a loss of fifteen thousand or more men (including those cut off from returning) besides large losses in arms and ammuni-

---

7. Mary Lincoln's confidante Elizabeth Keckley reports that the First Lady was no fan of Grant's methods:

> Mrs. Lincoln could not tolerate General Grant. "He is a butcher," she would often say, "and is not fit to be at the head of an army."
>
> "But he has been very successful in the field," argued the President.
>
> "Yes, he generally manages to claim a victory, but such a victory! He loses two men to the enemy's one. He has no management, no regard for life. If the war should continue four years longer, and he should remain in power, he would depopulate the North. I could fight an army as well myself. According to his tactics, there is nothing under the heavens to do but to march a new line of men up in front of the rebel breastworks to be shot down as fast as they take their position, and keep marching until the enemy grows tired of the slaughter. Grant, I repeat is an obstinate fool and a butcher."
>
> "Well, mother, supposing that we give you command of the army. No doubt you would do much better than any general that has tried." There was a twinkle in the eyes, and a ring of irony in his voice.

Behind the Scenes, Or, Thirty Years a Slave, and Four Years in the White House, ed. William L. Andrews (New York: Penguin Classics, 2005), 59–60.

tion. The Army of the Tennessee had come to believe that they could beat their antagonist under any circumstances. There was no telling how long a regular siege might last. As I have stated, it was the beginning of the hot season in a Southern climate. There was no telling what the casualties might be among Northern troops working and living in trenches, drinking surface water filtered through rich vegetation, under a tropical sun. If Vicksburg could have been carried in May, it would not only have saved the army the risk it ran of a greater danger than from the bullets of the enemy, but it would have given us a splendid army, well equipped and officered, to operate elsewhere with. These are reasons justifying the assault. The only benefit we gained—and it was a slight one for so great a sacrifice—was that the men worked cheerfully in the trenches after that, being satisfied with digging the enemy out. Had the assault not been made, I have no doubt that the majority of those engaged in the siege of Vicksburg would have believed that had we assaulted it would have proven successful, and would have saved life, health and comfort.[8]

---

8. For an evocative chronicle of life in a city under siege—of the devastation as well as of the ways in which ordinary life stubbornly endures—see Leo Tolstoy's *Sevastopol Stories.*

Left Flank Movement across the Chickahominy and James—General Lee—Visit to Butler—The Movement on Petersburg—The Investment of Petersburg

Lee's position was now so near Richmond, and the intervening swamps of the Chickahominy so great an obstacle to the movement of troops in the face of an enemy, that I determined to make my next left flank move carry the Army of the Potomac south of the James River.[1] Preparations for this were promptly commenced. The move was a hazardous one to make: the Chickahominy River, with its marshy and heavily timbered approaches, had to be crossed; all the bridges over it east of Lee were destroyed; the enemy had a shorter line and better roads to travel on to confront me in crossing; more than fifty miles intervened between me and Butler, by the roads I should have to travel, with both the James and the Chickahominy unbridged to cross; and last, the Army of the Potomac had to be got out of a position but a few hundred yards from the enemy at the widest place. Lee, if he did not choose to follow me, might, with his shorter distance to travel and his bridges over the Chickahominy and the James, move rapidly on Butler and crush him before the army with me could come to his relief. Then too he might spare troops enough to send against Hunter who was approaching Lynchburg, living upon the country he passed through, and without ammunition further than what he carried with him.

But the move had to be made, and I relied upon Lee's not seeing my danger as I saw it. Besides we had armies on both sides of the James River

---

1. For the correspondence included in a note to the first edition, see Appendix 1, chapter 56, note 1.

and not far from the Confederate capital. I knew that its safety would be a matter of the first consideration with the executive, legislative and judicial branches of the so-called Confederate government, if it was not with the military commanders. But I took all the precaution I knew of to guard against all dangers.[2]

Sheridan was sent with two divisions, to communicate with Hunter and to break up the Virginia Central Railroad and the James River Canal, on the 7th of June, taking instructions to Hunter to come back with him.[3] Hunter was also informed by way of Washington and the Valley that Sheridan was

---

2. Grant's recognition of the fact that there were no entirely safe options and that a necessarily imperfect decision had to be made is the quality that carried him to victory in the West and that differentiated him from his dilatory predecessors in the East. The crossing of the James was a complex feat of logistics. Rebel general Edward Porter Alexander reflected that in "risking but escaping another great disaster, & gaining a strategic position of controlling value," Grant engendered "the last crisis of the war." *Fighting for the Confederacy: The Personal Recollections of General Edward Porter Alexander*, ed. Gary W. Gallagher (Chapel Hill: University of North Carolina Press, 1989), 415.

In effectively sealing his victory, Grant's crossing of the James is in a sense the symbolic inverse of Caesar's crossing of the Rubicon, an action that brought his army onto Italian soil and thereby launched a civil war. The latter event was commemorated by the Roman poet Lucan in the first book of his epic *Pharsalia*:

> The cavalry first form across the stream
> To break the torrent's force; the rest with ease
> Beneath their shelter gain the further bank.
> When Cæsar crossed and trod beneath his feet
> The soil of Italy's forbidden fields,
> "Here," spake he, "peace, here broken laws be left;
> Farewell to treaties. Fortune, lead me on;
> War is our judge, and in the fates our trust."
> Then in the shades of night he leads the troops
> Swifter than Balearic sling or shaft
> Winged by retreating Parthian, to the walls
> Of threatened Rimini, while fled the stars,
> Save Lucifer, before the coming sun,
> Whose fires were veiled in clouds, by south wind driven,
> Or else at heaven's command: and thus drew on
> The grey first morning of the civil war.

The Pharsalia of Lucan, trans. Edward Ridley, vol. 1 (London: Arthur L. Humphreys, 1919), ll. 251–66.

3. For the correspondence included in a note to the first edition, see Appendix 1, chapter 56, note 2.

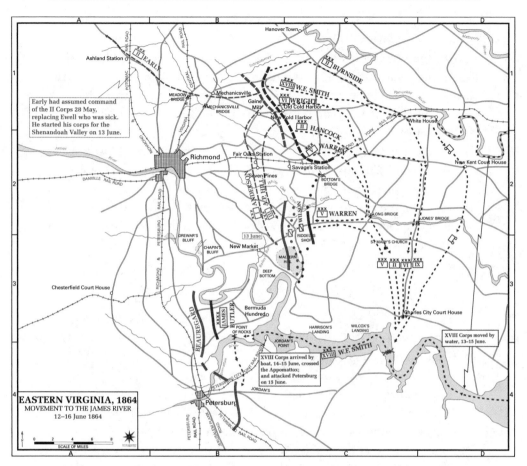

Movement to the James River, June 12–16, 1864. *West Point Atlas of the Civil War.*
Courtesy of Department of History, USMA.

on the way to meet him. The canal and Central Road, and the regions
penetrated by them, were of vast importance to the enemy, furnishing and
carrying a large per cent. of all the supplies for the Army of Northern Virginia and the people of Richmond. Before Sheridan got off on the 7th news
was received from Hunter reporting his advance to Staunton and successful engagement with the enemy near that place on the 5th, in which the
Confederate commander, W. S. Jones, was killed. On the 4th of June the
enemy having withdrawn his left corps, Burnside on our right was moved up
between Warren and Smith. On the 5th Birney returned to Hancock, which
extended his left now to the Chickahominy, and Warren was withdrawn to
Cold Harbor. Wright was directed to send two divisions to the left to extend

down the banks of that stream to Bottom's Bridge. The cavalry extended still farther east to Jones's Bridge.

On the 7th [John J.] Abercrombie—who was in command at White House, and who had been in command at our base of supplies in all the changes made from the start—was ordered to take up the iron from the York River Railroad and put it on boats, and to be in readiness to move by water to City Point.

On the 8th Meade was directed to fortify a line down the bank overlooking the Chickahominy, under cover of which the army could move.

On the 9th Abercrombie was directed to send all organized troops arriving at White House, without debarking from their transports, to report to Butler. Halleck was at this time instructed to send all reinforcements to City Point.

On the 11th I wrote:

COLD HARBOR, VA.,
June 11, 1864.

MAJOR-GEN. B. F. BUTLER,
Commanding Department of Va. and N. C.

The movement to transfer this army to the south side of the James River will commence after dark to-morrow night. Col. Comstock, of my staff, was sent specially to ascertain what was necessary to make your position secure in the interval during which the enemy might use most of his force against you, and also, to ascertain what point on the river we should reach to effect a crossing if it should not be practicable to reach this side of the river at Bermuda Hundred. Colonel Comstock has not yet returned, so that I cannot make instructions as definite as I would wish, but the time between this and Sunday night being so short in which to get word to you, I must do the best I can. Colonel Dent goes to make arrangements for gunboats and transportation to send up the Chickahominy to take to you the 18th corps. The corps will leave its position in the trenches as early in the evening, tomorrow, as possible, and make a forced march to Cole's Landing or Ferry, where it should reach by ten A.M. the following morning. This corps numbers now 15,300 men. They take with them neither wagons nor artillery; these latter marching with the balance of the army to the James River. The remainder of the army will cross the Chickahominy at Long Bridge and at Jones's, and strike the river at the most practicable crossing below City Point.

I directed several days ago that all reinforcements for the army should be sent to you. I am not advised of the number that may have gone, but suppose you have received from six to ten thousand. General Smith will also reach you as soon as the enemy could, going by the way of Richmond.

The balance of the force will not be more than one day behind, unless detained by the whole of Lee's army, in which case you will be strong enough.

I wish you would direct the proper staff officers, your chief-engineer and your chief-quartermaster, to commence at once the collection of all the means in their reach for crossing the army on its arrival. If there is a point below City Point where a pontoon bridge can be thrown, have it laid.

Expecting the arrival of the 18th corps by Monday night, if you deem it practicable from the force you have to seize and hold Petersburg, you may prepare to start, on the arrival of troops to hold your present lines. I do not want Petersburg visited, however, unless it is held, nor an attempt to take it, unless you feel a reasonable degree of confidence of success. If you should go there, I think troops should take nothing with them except what they can carry, depending upon supplies being sent after the place is secured. If Colonel Dent should not succeed in securing the requisite amount of transportation for the 18th corps before reaching you, please have the balance supplied.

U. S. GRANT,
Lieut.-General.

P. S.—On reflection I will send the 18th corps by way of White House. The distance which they will have to march will be enough shorter to enable them to reach you about the same time, and the uncertainty of navigation on the Chickahominy will be avoided.

U. S. GRANT.

COLD HARBOR, VA.,
June 11, 1864.

MAJOR-GENERAL G. G. MEADE,
Commanding Army of the Potomac.

Colonel Comstock, who visited the James River for the purpose of ascertaining the best point below Bermuda Hundred to which to march the army has not yet returned. It is now getting so late, however, that all preparations may be made for the move to-morrow night without waiting longer.

The movement will be made as heretofore agreed upon, that is, the 18th corps make a rapid march with the infantry alone, their wagons and artillery accompanying the balance of the army to Cole's Landing or Ferry, and there embark for City Point, losing no time for rest until they reach the latter point.

The 5th corps will seize Long Bridge and move out on the Long Bridge Road to its junction with Quaker Road, or until stopped by the enemy.

The other three corps will follow in such order as you may direct, one of them crossing at Long Bridge, and two at Jones's Bridge. After the crossing is effected, the most practicable roads will be taken to reach about Fort Powhattan. Of course, this is supposing the enemy makes no opposition to our advance. The 5th corps, after securing the passage of the balance of the army, will join or follow in rear of the corps which crosses the same bridge with themselves. The wagon trains should be kept well east of the troops, and if a crossing can be found, or made lower down than Jones's they should take it.

U. S. GRANT,

Lieut.-General.

P. S.—In view of the long march to reach Cole's Landing, and the uncertainty of being able to embark a large number of men there, the direction of the 18th corps may be changed to White House. They should be directed to load up transports, and start them as fast as loaded without waiting for the whole corps or even whole divisions to go together.

U. S. GRANT.

About this time word was received (through the Richmond papers of the 11th) that Crook and Averell had united and were moving east. This, with the news of Hunter's successful engagement near Staunton, was no doubt known to Lee before it was to me.[4] Then Sheridan leaving with two divi-

---

4. Hunter's raid on the Shenandoah Valley (May 26–June 18, 1864) met with initial success. After defeating Confederate troops under William "Grumble" Jones at Piedmont on June 5, Hunter destroyed supplies and transportation at Staunton, where George Crook's command joined him. On June 11, Hunter proceeded to Lexington, where he

sions of cavalry, looked indeed threatening, both to Lee's communications and supplies. Much of his cavalry was sent after Sheridan, and Early with Ewell's entire corps was sent to the Valley. Supplies were growing scarce in Richmond, and the sources from which to draw them were in our hands. People from outside began to pour into Richmond to help eat up the little on hand. Consternation reigned there.

On the 12th Smith was ordered to move at night to White House, not to stop until he reached there, and to take boats at once for City Point, leaving his trains and artillery to move by land.

Soon after dark some of the cavalry at Long Bridge effected a crossing by wading and floundering through the water and mud, leaving their horses behind, and drove away the cavalry pickets. A pontoon bridge was speedily thrown across, over which the remainder of the army soon passed and pushed out for a mile or two to watch and detain any advance that might be made from the other side. Warren followed the cavalry, and by the morning

---

burned the Virginia Military Institute and raided the town. Crook claims that he did all that he could "to dissuade" Hunter from this course of action. See Crook, *Autobiography*, 117.

At Lynchburg, on June 17, Hunter tangled with Confederate troops under Breckinridge. Aware that Jubal Early was on the way from Cold Harbor, he retreated to the safety of West Virginia leaving Early free to menace Washington, D.C. Grant relieved Hunter and replaced him with Sheridan on August 6. Crook describes the retreat as one of the most difficult experiences of the war: "We were worn out by constant marching, and no sleep at nights. It was almost a constant fight since we left Lynchburg. We had little or nothing to eat. One ear of corn was all that I had. I felt the whole responsibility on my shoulders. I had no confidence in those in front. I was so worn out that it was only with the greatest exertions I could keep awake." *Autobiography*, 119.

Jubal Early later wrote of the operation as a decided success:

> When I was detached from General Lee's army, Hunter was advancing on Lynchburg, 170 miles south of Winchester, with a very considerable force, and threatening all of General Lee's communications with a very serious danger.
>
> By a rapid movement, my force had been thrown to Lynchburg, just in time to arrest Hunter's march into that place, and he had been driven back and forced to escape into the mountains of Western Virginia, with a loss of ten pieces of artillery and subsequent terrible suffering to his troops. Maryland and Pennsylvania had been invaded, Washington threatened and thrown into a state of frantic alarm, and Grant had been compelled to detach two corps of infantry and two divisions of cavalry from his army.

Autobiographical Sketch and Narrative of the War between the States, ed. R. H. Early (Philadelphia: J. B. Lippincott, 1912), 455.

of the 13th had his whole corps over. Hancock followed Warren. Burnside took the road to Jones's Bridge, followed by Wright. Ferrero's division, with the wagon train, moved farther east, by Window [or Windsor] Shades and Cole's Ferry, our rear being covered by cavalry.

It was known that the enemy had some gunboats at Richmond. These might run down at night and inflict great damage upon us before they could be sunk or captured by our navy. General Butler had, in advance, loaded some vessels with stone ready to be sunk so as to obstruct the channel in an emergency. On the 13th I sent orders to have these sunk as high up the river as we could guard them, and prevent their removal by the enemy.

As soon as Warren's corps was over the Chickahominy it marched out and joined the cavalry in holding the roads from Richmond while the army passed. No attempt was made by the enemy to impede our march, however, but Warren and Wilson reported the enemy strongly fortified in their front. By the evening of the 13th Hancock's corps was at Charles City Court House on the James River. Burnside's and Wright's corps were on the Chickahominy, and crossed during the night, Warren's corps and the cavalry still covering the army. The material for a pontoon bridge was already at hand and the work of laying it was commenced immediately, under the superintendence of Brigadier-General Benham, commanding the engineer brigade. On the evening of the 14th the crossing commenced, Hancock in advance, using both the bridge and boats.

When the Wilderness campaign commenced the Army of the Potomac, including Burnside's corps—which was a separate command until the 24th of May when it was incorporated with the main army—numbered about 116,000 men. During the progress of the campaign about 40,000 reinforcements were received. At the crossing of the James River June 14th–15th the army numbered about 115,000. Besides the ordinary losses incident to a campaign of six weeks' nearly constant fighting or skirmishing, about one-half of the artillery was sent back to Washington, and many men were discharged by reason of the expiration of their term of service.[5] In estimating our strength every enlisted man and every commissioned officer present is included, no matter how employed; in bands, sick in field hospitals, hospital attendants, company cooks and all. Operating in an enemy's country, and being supplied always from a distant base, large detachments had at all times to be sent from the front, not only to guard the base of supplies and the roads

---

5. For the casualty list included in a note to the first edition, see Appendix 1, chapter 56, note 3.

to it, but all the roads leading to our flanks and rear. We were also operating in a country unknown to us, and without competent guides or maps showing the roads accurately.

The manner of estimating numbers in the two armies differs materially. In the Confederate army often only bayonets are taken into account, never, I believe, do they estimate more than are handling the guns of the artillery and armed with muskets or carbines. Generally the latter are far enough away to be excluded from the count in any one field. Officers and details of enlisted men are not included. In the Northern armies the estimate is most liberal, taking in all connected with the army and drawing pay.

Estimated in the same manner as ours, Lee had not less than 80,000 men at the start. His reinforcements were about equal to ours during the campaign, deducting the discharged men and those sent back. He was on the defensive, and in a country in which every stream, every road, every obstacle to the movement of troops and every natural defence was familiar to him and his army. The citizens were all friendly to him and his cause, and could and did furnish him with accurate reports of our every move. Rear guards were not necessary for him, and having always a railroad at his back, large wagon trains were not required. All circumstances considered we did not have any advantage in numbers.

General Lee, who had led the Army of Northern Virginia in all these contests, was a very highly estimated man in the Confederate army and States, and filled also a very high place in the estimation of the people and press of the Northern States. His praise was sounded throughout the entire North after every action he was engaged in: the number of his forces was always lowered and that of the National forces exaggerated. He was a large, austere man, and I judge difficult of approach to his subordinates. To be extolled by the entire press of the South after every engagement, and by a portion of the press North with equal vehemence, was calculated to give him the entire confidence of his troops and to make him feared by his antagonists. It was not an uncommon thing for my staff-officers to hear from Eastern officers, "Well, Grant has never met Bobby Lee yet."[6] There were good

---

6. Lee continues to exert a sentimental fascination for many Americans to whom he is the epitome of a chivalric warrior. John Keegan called him "the only cult general in the English-speaking world . . . the paladin" of the Confederacy. See *The Face of Battle: A Study of Agincourt, Waterloo and the Somme* (New York: Penguin, 1978), 54.

To celebrate Lee as a hero is to sever him from the cause for which he fought: not, as enthusiasts would have it, for some totemic investment in the soil of Virginia, but rather for the preservation of the state right that trumped all others, the right to own

and true officers who believe now that the Army of Northern Virginia was superior to the Army of the Potomac man to man. I do not believe so, except as the advantages spoken of above made them so. Before the end I believe the difference was the other way. The Army of Northern Virginia became despondent and saw the end. It did not please them. The National army saw the same thing, and were encouraged by it.

The advance of the Army of the Potomac reached the James on the 14th of June. Preparations were at once commenced for laying the pontoon bridges and crossing the river. As already stated, I had previously ordered General Butler to have two vessels loaded with stone and carried up the river to a point above that occupied by our gunboats, where the channel was narrow, and sunk there so as to obstruct the passage and prevent Confederate gunboats from coming down the river. Butler had had these boats filled and put in position, but had not had them sunk before my arrival. I ordered this done, and also directed that he should turn over all material and boats not then in use in the river to be used in ferrying the troops across.

I then, on the 14th, took a steamer and ran up to Bermuda Hundred to see General Butler for the purpose of directing a movement against Petersburg, while our troops of the Army of the Potomac were crossing.

I had sent General W. F. Smith back from Cold Harbor by the way of White House, thence on steamers to City Point for the purpose of giving General Butler more troops with which to accomplish this result. General Butler was ordered to send Smith with his troops reinforced, as far as that could be conveniently done, from other parts of the Army of the James. He gave Smith about six thousand reinforcements, including some twenty-five hundred cavalry under Kautz, and about thirty-five hundred colored infantry under Hinks.

The distance which Smith had to move to reach the enemy's lines was about six miles, and the Confederate advance line of works was but two miles outside of Petersburg. Smith was to move under cover of night, up close to the enemy's works, and assault as soon as he could after daylight. I believed then, and still believe, that Petersburg could have been easily captured at that time. It only had about 2,500 men in the defences besides some

---

other human beings. There is no finer account of Lee's appeal than W. E. B. Du Bois's brief, searing essay on the annual attempt to canonize the Confederate general: "It is the punishment of the South that its Robert Lees," Du Bois argued, "will always be tall, handsome and well-born. That their courage will be physical and not moral." "Robert E. Lee," *Crisis* 35 (March 1928): 97.

irregular troops, consisting of citizens and employees in the city who took up arms in case of emergency. Smith started as proposed, but his advance encountered a rebel force intrenched between City Point and their lines outside of Petersburg. This position he carried, with some loss to the enemy; but there was so much delay that it was daylight before his troops really got off from there. While there I informed General Butler that Hancock's corps would cross the river and move to Petersburg to support Smith in case the latter was successful, and that I could reinforce there more rapidly than Lee could reinforce from his position.[7]

I returned down the river to where the troops of the Army of the Potomac now were, communicated to General Meade, in writing, the directions I had given to General Butler and directed him (Meade) to cross Hancock's corps over under cover of night, and push them forward in the morning to Petersburg; halting them, however, at a designated point until they could hear from Smith. I also informed General Meade that I had ordered rations from Bermuda Hundred for Hancock's corps, and desired him to issue them speedily, and to lose no more time than was absolutely necessary. The rations did not reach him, however, and Hancock, while he got all his corps over during the night, remained until half-past ten in the hope of receiving them. He then moved without them, and on the road received a note from General W. F. Smith, asking him to come on. This seems to be the first information that General Hancock had received of the fact that he was to go to Petersburg, or that anything particular was expected of him. Otherwise he would have been there by four o'clock in the afternoon.

Smith arrived in front of the enemy's lines early in the forenoon of the 15th, and spent the day until after seven o'clock in the evening in reconnoitering what appeared to be empty works. The enemy's line consisted of redans occupying commanding positions, with rifle-pits connecting them. To the east side of Petersburg, from the Appomattox back, there were thirteen of these redans extending a distance of several miles, probably three. If they had been properly manned they could have held out against any force that could have attacked them, at least until reinforcements could have got up from the north of Richmond.

Smith assaulted with the colored troops, and with success. By nine o'clock at night he was in possession of five of these redans and, of course, of

7. W. F. Smith was slow and ineffective, just as he had been before Cold Harbor. His failures in the field, coupled with a penchant for intrigue, would eventually lead to his removal.

the connecting lines of rifle-pits. All of them contained artillery, which fell into our hands. Hancock came up and proposed to take any part assigned to him; and Smith asked him to relieve his men who were in the trenches.

Next morning, the 16th, Hancock himself was in command, and captured another redan. Meade came up in the afternoon and succeeded Hancock, who had to be relieved, temporarily, from the command of his corps on account of the breaking out afresh of the wound he had received at Gettysburg. During the day Meade assaulted and carried one more redan to his right and two to his left. In all this we lost very heavily. The works were not strongly manned, but they all had guns in them which fell into our hands, together with the men who were handling them in the effort to repel these assaults.

Up to this time Beauregard, who had commanded south of Richmond, had received no reinforcements, except Hoke's division from Drury's Bluff,[8] which had arrived on the morning of the 16th; though he had urged the authorities very strongly to send them, believing, as he did, that Petersburg would be a valuable prize which we might seek.

During the 17th the fighting was very severe and the losses heavy; and at night our troops occupied about the same position they had occupied in the morning, except that they held a redan which had been captured by Potter during the day. During the night, however, Beauregard fell back to the line which had been already selected, and commenced fortifying it. Our troops advanced on the 18th to the line which he had abandoned, and found that the Confederate loss had been very severe, many of the enemy's dead still remaining in the ditches and in front of them.

Colonel J. L. Chamberlain, of the 20th Maine, was wounded on the 18th.[9] He was gallantly leading his brigade at the time, as he had been in the habit of doing in all the engagements in which he had previously been

---

8. For the correspondence included in a note to the first edition, see Appendix 1, chapter 56, note 4.

9. Joshua Lawrence Chamberlain, colonel of the 20th Maine Regiment, was a professor at Maine's Bowdoin College before the war. He led the heroic defense of Little Round Top at Gettysburg, an episode celebrated in Michael Shaara's novel *The Killer Angels*. Chamberlain's wound at Petersburg was grievous. The damage done by a bullet in the hip would plague him for the rest of his life. Yet he recuperated sufficiently to manage the formal surrender at Appomattox. After the war, he served as the governor of Maine and then as the president of Bowdoin. In the latter capacity, he instituted military drill, which was deeply unpopular with the students, who rebelled against the practice in 1874.

engaged. He had several times been recommended for a brigadier-generalcy for gallant and meritorious conduct. On this occasion, however, I promoted him on the spot, and forwarded a copy of my order to the War Department, asking that my act might be confirmed and Chamberlain's name sent to the Senate for confirmation without any delay. This was done, and at last a gallant and meritorious officer received partial justice at the hands of his government, which he had served so faithfully and so well.

If General Hancock's orders of the 15th had been communicated to him, that officer, with his usual promptness, would undoubtedly have been upon the ground around Petersburg as early as four o'clock in the afternoon of the 15th. The days were long and it would have given him considerable time before night. I do not think there is any doubt that Petersburg itself could have been carried without much loss; or, at least, if protected by inner detached works, that a line could have been established very much in rear of the one then occupied by the enemy. This would have given us control of both the Weldon and South Side railroads. This would also have saved an immense amount of hard fighting which had to be done from the 15th to the 18th, and would have given us greatly the advantage in the long siege which ensued.

I now ordered the troops to be put under cover and allowed some of the rest which they had so long needed. They remained quiet, except that there was more or less firing every day, until the 22d, when General Meade ordered an advance towards the Weldon Railroad. We were very anxious to get to that road, and even round to the South Side Railroad if possible.

Meade moved Hancock's corps, now commanded by Birney, to the left, with a view to at least force the enemy to stay within the limits of his own line. General Wright, with the 6th corps, was ordered by a road farther south, to march directly for the Weldon road. The enemy passed in between these two corps and attacked vigorously, and with very serious results to the National troops, who were then withdrawn from their advanced position.

The Army of the Potomac was given the investment of Petersburg, while the Army of the James held Bermuda Hundred and all the ground we possessed north of the James River. The 9th corps, Burnside's, was placed upon the right at Petersburg; the 5th, Warren's, next; the 2d, Birney's, next; then the 6th, Wright's, broken off to the left and south. Thus began the siege of Petersburg.[10]

---

10. In his account of the 1899–1900 siege of Mafeking, South Africa, then held by British forces under Colonel Robert Baden-Powell, during the Boer War, Arthur Conan

Doyle documents the way in which the besieged garrison succeeded in enraging the Boer commander by their insouciant behavior:

> Vigilant and indomitable, throwing away no possible point in the game which he was playing, the new year found him [Baden-Powell] and his hardy garrison sternly determined to keep the flag flying. . . .
>
> . . . On Sunday a truce was usually observed, and the snipers who had exchanged rifle-shots all the week met occasionally on that day with good-humoured chaff. Snyman, the Boer General, showed none of that chivalry at Mafeking which distinguished the gallant old Joubert at Lady-smith. Not only was there no neutral camp for women or sick, but it is beyond all doubt or question that the Boer guns were deliberately turned upon the women's quarters inside Mafeking in order to bring pressure upon the inhabitants. Many women and children were sacrificed to this brutal policy. . . .
>
> The garrison, in the face of increasing losses and decreasing food, lost none of the high spirits which it reflected from its commander. The pro-gramme of a single day of jubilee—Heaven only knows what they had to hold jubilee over—shows a cricket match in the morning, sports in the afternoon, a concert in the evening, and a dance, given by the bachelor officers, to wind up. Baden-Powell himself seems to have descended from the eyrie from which, like a captain on the bridge, he rang bells and tele-phoned orders, to bring the house down with a comic song and a humor-ous recitation. The ball went admirably, save that there was an interval to repel an attack which disarranged the programme. Sports were zealously cultivated, and the grimy inhabitants of casemates and trenches were pitted against each other at cricket or football.* The monotony was broken by the occasional visits of a postman, who appeared or vanished from the vast barren lands to the west of the town, which could not all be guarded by the besiegers. Sometimes a few words from home came to cheer the hearts of the exiles, and could be returned by the same uncertain and expensive means. The documents which found their way up were not always of an essential or even of a welcome character. At least one man received an unpaid bill from an angry tailor.

> *Sunday cricket so shocked Snyman that he threatened to fire upon it if it were continued.

The Great Boer War (London: Smith, Elder, 1900), 411–12.

A similar instance of British bravado can be found in the actions of Captain W. P. Nevill, 8th East Surreys, who led an infantry advance by kicking a football across No Man's Land on the first day of the Battle of the Somme, July 1, 1916. Nevill was killed in the attack. He had purchased a football for each of his four platoons and offered a prize to the one that could "kick its football up to the German trenches" first. One platoon had inscribed on their ball:

The Great European Cup
The Final
East Surreys v Bavarians
Kick Off at Zero

See Martin Middlebrook, *The First Day on the Somme: 1 July 1916*, rev. ed. (Barnsley, UK: Pen & Sword Books, 2016), 86–87, 124.

Winslow Homer, "Holiday in camp—soldiers playing 'foot-ball,'" *Harper's Weekly*, July 15, 1865. *Metropolitan Museum of Art, Harris Brisbane Dick Fund, 1936.*

Raid on the Virginia Central Railroad—Raid
on the Weldon Railroad—Early's Movement
upon Washington—Mining the Works before
Petersburg—Explosion of the Mine before
Petersburg—Campaign in the Shenandoah
Valley—Capture of the Weldon Railroad

On the 7th of June, while at Cold Harbor, I had as already indicated sent
Sheridan with two divisions of cavalry to destroy as much as he could
of the Virginia Central Railroad. General Hunter had been operating up the
Shenandoah Valley with some success, having fought a battle near Staunton
where he captured a great many prisoners, besides killing and wounding
a good many men. After the battle he formed a junction at Staunton with
Averell and Crook, who had come up from the Kanawha, or Gauley River.
It was supposed, therefore, that General Hunter would be about Charlottesville, Virginia, by the time Sheridan could get there, doing on the way the
damage that he was sent to do.

I gave Sheridan instructions to have Hunter, in case he should meet
him about Charlottesville, join and return with him to the Army of the
Potomac. Lee, hearing of Hunter's success in the valley, started Breckinridge out for its defence at once. Learning later of Sheridan's going with
two divisions, he also sent Hampton with two divisions of cavalry, his own
and Fitz-Hugh Lee's.

Sheridan moved to the north side of the North Anna to get out west, and
learned of the movement of these troops to the south side of the same stream

almost as soon as they had started. He pushed on to get to Trevilian Station to commence his destruction at that point. On the night of the 10th he bivouacked some six or seven miles east of Trevilian, while Fitz-Hugh Lee was the same night at Trevilian Station and Hampton but a few miles away.

During the night Hampton ordered an advance on Sheridan, hoping, no doubt, to surprise and very badly cripple him. Sheridan, however, by a counter move sent Custer on a rapid march to get between the two divisions of the enemy and into their rear. This he did successfully, so that at daylight, when the assault was made, the enemy found himself at the same time resisted in front and attacked in rear, and broke in some confusion. The losses were probably very light on both sides in killed and wounded, but Sheridan got away with some five hundred prisoners and sent them to City Point.

During that day, the 11th, Sheridan moved into Trevilian Station, and the following day proceeded to tear up the road east and west. There was considerable fighting during the whole of the day, but the work of destruction went on. In the meantime, at night, the enemy had taken possession of the crossing which Sheridan had proposed to take to go north when he left Trevilian. Sheridan learned, however, from some of the prisoners he had captured here, that General Hunter was about Lynchburg, and therefore that there was no use of his going on to Charlottesville with a view to meet him.

Sheridan started back during the night of the 12th, and made his way north and farther east, coming around by the north side of White House, and arriving there on the 21st. Here he found an abundance of forage for his animals, food for his men, and security while resting. He had been obliged to leave about ninety of his own men in the field-hospital which he had established near Trevilian, and these necessarily fell into the hands of the enemy.

White House up to this time had been a depot; but now that our troops were all on the James River, it was no longer wanted as a store of supplies. Sheridan was, therefore, directed to break it up; which he did on the 22d of June, bringing the garrison and an immense wagon train with him. All these were over the James River by the 26th of the month, and Sheridan ready to follow.

In the meantime Meade had sent Wilson's division on a raid to destroy the Weldon and South Side roads. Now that Sheridan was safe and Hampton free to return to Richmond with his cavalry, Wilson's position became precarious. Meade therefore, on the 27th, ordered Sheridan over the river to make a demonstration in favor of Wilson. Wilson got back, though not without severe loss, having struck both roads, but the damage done was soon repaired.[1]

After these events comparative quiet reigned about Petersburg until late in July. The time, however, was spent in strengthening the intrenchments and making our position generally more secure against a sudden attack. In the meantime I had to look after other portions of my command, where things had not been going on so favorably, always, as I could have wished.

General Hunter, who had been appointed to succeed Sigel in the Shenandoah Valley, immediately took up the offensive. He met the enemy on the 5th of June at Piedmont, and defeated him. On the 8th he formed a junction with Crook and Averell at Staunton, from which place he moved direct on Lynchburg, via Lexington, which he reached and invested on the 16th. Up to this time he was very successful; and but for the difficulty of taking with him sufficient ordnance stores over so long a march, through a hostile country, he would, no doubt, have captured Lynchburg. The destruction of the enemy's supplies and manufactories had been very great.[2] To meet this movement under General Hunter, General Lee sent

1. Wilson's expedition to destroy the Weldon Railroad, on which Grant does not dwell, to say nothing of the coordinated offensive at Petersburg of which it formed a part, was an almost total failure. Wilson later blamed a general lack of Union vigilance, "divided command and responsibility" between Grant and Meade, and Sheridan's failure to connect with Hunter or to return to the Army of the Potomac. The Confederate commander Wade Hampton took advantage of all of these failings, and the two met at Reams Station. As for Kautz, according to Wilson, he "simply lay down and quit." *Under the Old Flag*, 1:493, 510.

Luman Harris Tenney, a second lieutenant in the 2nd Ohio Cavalry, confided in his diary about the engagement at Reams Station: "Moved on to the 2nd Corps inside of the entrenchments. 6th Corps moved out too late yesterday to relieve us. Tore up several miles of the Welden R. R. We are satisfied with our work. Several miles on the south side R. R. and 25 or 30 miles of the Danville R. R. Sorry that we could not get out without so much loss. Blame Wilson. No grain and no day's rations." *War Diary of Luman Harris Tenney, 1861–1865* (Cleveland, OH: Evangelical, 1914), 123.

Meanwhile, back at Petersburg, Stephen Weld Minot of the Massachusetts 56th wrote to his sister on June 19, "Things begin to look like a siege now. I doubt if much more charging is done. We shall rely on our heavy guns and shovels a great deal. Such a course is absolutely necessary, I think. Grant has wasted a great many of his men in useless charges, and a few days must be given to recuperate and reorganize." *War Diary and Letters of Stephen Minot Weld, 1861–1865* (Boston: Riverside Press, 1912), 315.

2. The threatened destruction of civilian property has sometimes been used as a negotiating tool, as it was by the medieval Frankish king Clovis during the siege of Vienna. He received some sage counsel from his envoy Aridius:

Early with his corps, a part of which reached Lynchburg before Hunter. After some skirmishing on the 17th and 18th, General Hunter, owing to a want of ammunition to give battle, retired from before the place. Unfortunately, this want of ammunition left him no choice of route for his return but by the way of the Gauley and Kanawha rivers, thence up the Ohio River, returning to Harper's Ferry by way of the Baltimore and Ohio Railroad. A long time was consumed in making this movement. Meantime the valley was left open to Early's troops, and others in that quarter; and Washington also was uncovered. Early took advantage of this condition of affairs and moved on Washington.[3]

In the absence of Hunter, General Lew Wallace, with headquarters at Baltimore, commanded the department in which the Shenandoah lay. His surplus of troops with which to move against the enemy was small in number. Most of these were raw and, consequently, very much inferior to our veterans and to the veterans which Early had with him; but the situation of Washington was precarious, and Wallace moved with commendable promptitude to meet the enemy at the Monocacy. He could hardly have expected to defeat him badly, but he hoped to cripple and delay him until

Clovis remained encamped with his entire army round the city walls. "If you who are a king with absolute power would deign to accept a little advice from me who am no one," said Aridius to him, "this is the loyal proposition which I should like to put to you. . . . What is the point of keeping all these troops under arms when your enemy is safe in a stronghold which is too well fortified for you to capture? You are destroying the fields, spoiling the meadows, cutting up the vineyards, ruining the olivegroves and ravaging the whole countryside, which is a very fruitful one. In doing this you are causing no harm whatsoever to Gundobad. Why don't you send an ultimatum to him to say that he must pay whatever annual tribute you care to exact? In that way the region will be saved and he will have to submit to you and pay tribute to you for ever. If he doesn't accept this, you can do whatever you wish."

Clovis took this advice, sent envoys to his adversary, and demanded an annual tribute in exchange for lifting the siege. His terms were accepted. Gregory of Tours, *The History of the Franks*, trans. Lewis Thorpe (New York: Penguin Classics, 1974), 146–47.

3. John Esten Cooke, who seemed able to discover virtues in the most inept Confederate commander, found something to celebrate even in Early's generalship: "everything about General Early was bold, straightforward, masculine, and incisive. Combativeness was one of his great traits," Cooke wrote. "There were many persons in and out of the army who doubted the soundness of his judgment; there were none who ever called in question the tough fibre of his courage." *Wearing of the Gray*, 111.

Washington could be put into a state of preparation for his reception. I had previously ordered General Meade to send a division to Baltimore for the purpose of adding to the defences of Washington, and he had sent [James B.] Ricketts's division of the 6th corps (Wright's), which arrived in Baltimore on the 8th of July. Finding that Wallace had gone to the front with his command, Ricketts immediately took the cars and followed him to the Monocacy with his entire division. They met the enemy and, as might have been expected, were defeated; but they succeeded in stopping him for the day on which the battle took place. The next morning Early started on his march to the capital of the Nation, arriving before it on the 11th.

Learning of the gravity of the situation I had directed General Meade to also order Wright with the rest of his corps directly to Washington for the relief of that place, and the latter reached there the very day that Early arrived before it.[4] The 19th corps, which had been stationed in Louisiana,

4. Dana, who set out for Washington "to keep Grant informed," arrived to discover "panic" at the capital, including the Confederates' burning of Postmaster General Montgomery Blair's house:

> With the troops coming from Grant, there was force enough to save the capital; but I soon saw that nothing could possibly be done toward pursuing or cutting off the enemy for want of a commander. . . . [T]here was no head to the whole. General Halleck would not give orders, except as he received them from Grant; the President would give none; and, until Grant directed positively and explicitly what was to be done, everything was practically at a standstill. Things, I saw, would go on in the deplorable and fatal way in which they had been going for a week. Of course, this want of a head was causing a great deal of sharp comment on all sides. Postmaster-General Blair was particularly incensed, and, indeed, with real cause, for he had lost his house at Silver Springs.

Recollections, 229–31.

When Halleck got wind of Blair's complaints, he somehow found the time, amid all the confusion, to write the following letter to Stanton on July 13:

> I deem it my duty to bring to your notice the following facts: I am informed by an officer of rank and standing in the military service that the Hon. M. Blair, Postmaster General, in speaking of the burning of his house in Maryland, this morning, said, in effect, that "the officers in command about Washington are poltroons; that there were not more than 500 rebels on the Silver Spring road, and we had 1,000,000 of men in arms; that it was a disgrace; that General Wallace was in comparison with them far better, as he would at least fight." As there have been for the last few days a large number of officers on duty in and about Washington who have

having been ordered up to reinforce the armies about Richmond, had about
this time arrived at Fortress Monroe, on their way to join us. I diverted them
from that point to Washington, which place they reached, almost simultaneously with Wright, on the 11th. The 19th corps was commanded by
Major-General [William H.] Emory.

Early made his reconnoissance with a view of attacking on the following morning, the 12th; but the next morning he found our intrenchments,
which were very strong, fully manned. He at once commenced to retreat,
Wright following. There is no telling how much this result was contributed
to by General Lew Wallace's leading what might well be considered almost a
forlorn hope. If Early had been but one day earlier he might have entered the
capital before the arrival of the reinforcements I had sent. Whether the delay
caused by the battle amounted to a day or not, General Wallace contributed
on this occasion, by the defeat of the troops under him a greater benefit to

---

devoted their time and energies, night and day, and have periled their lives
in the support of the Government, it is due to them, as well as to the War
Department, that it should be known whether such wholesale denounce-
ment and accusation by a member of the Cabinet receives the sanction and
approbation of the President of the United States. If so, the names of the
officers accused should be stricken from the rolls of the Army; if not it is
due to the honor of the accused that the slanderer should be dismissed from
the Cabinet.

OR, ser. 1, vol. 37, pt. 2, 260–61.

For a lively twentieth-century account of the confusion in Washington—and Halleck's incapacity during the crisis—see Leech, *Reveille in Washington*, chapter 16.

**Ruins of Postmaster General Blair's
house, Silver Spring, Maryland.**
*Library of Congress, Prints and
Photographs Division, LC-DIG-stereo-
1s02990.*

the cause than often falls to the lot of a commander of an equal force to render by means of a victory.

Farther west also the troubles were threatening. Some time before, Forrest had met [Samuel D.] Sturgis in command of some of our cavalry in Mississippi and handled him very roughly, gaining a very great victory over him.[5] This left Forrest free to go almost where he pleased, and to cut the roads in rear of Sherman who was then advancing. Sherman was abundantly able to look after the army that he was immediately with, and all of his military division so long as he could communicate with it; but it was my place to see that he had the means with which to hold his rear. Two divisions under A. J. Smith had been sent to Banks in Louisiana some months before. Sherman ordered these back, with directions to attack Forrest. Smith met and defeated him very badly. I then directed that Smith should hang to Forrest and not let him go; and to prevent by all means his getting upon the Memphis and Nashville Railroad. Sherman had anticipated me in this matter, and given the same orders in substance; but receiving my directions for this order to Smith, he repeated it.

On the 25th of June General Burnside had commenced running a mine from about the centre of his front under the Confederate works confronting him. He was induced to do this by Colonel [Henry] Pleasants, of the Pennsylvania Volunteers, whose regiment was mostly composed of miners, and who was himself a practical miner. Burnside had submitted the scheme to Meade and myself, and we both approved of it, as a means of keeping the men occupied. His position was very favorable for carrying on this work,

---

5. With Forrest to the rear of his army, threatening garrisons and supply lines alike, Sherman had ordered an expedition out of Memphis to attack the Confederate cavalryman. On June 10, Forrest, vastly outnumbered, defeated Samuel Sturgis at Brices Cross Roads. On July 14, Forrest, again outnumbered, attacked Union forces at Tupelo and failed. He was wounded in the encounter. After receiving word of Sturgis's disaster, Sherman telegraphed Stanton:

> I cannot but believe he had troops enough. I know I would have been willing to attempt the same task with that force; but Forrest is the very devil, and I think he has got some of our troops under cower. I have two officers at Memphis that will fight all the time—A. J. Smith and Mower. The latter is a young brigadier of fine promise, and I commend him to your notice. I will order them to make up a force and go out and follow Forrest to the death, if it cost 10,000 lives and breaks the Treasury. There never will be peace in Tennessee till Forrest is dead.

Letter to E. M. Stanton, June 15, 1864, *OR*, ser. 1, vol. 39, pt. 2, 121.

but not so favorable for the operations to follow its completion. The position of the two lines at that point were only about a hundred yards apart with a comparatively deep ravine intervening. In the bottom of this ravine the work commenced. The position was unfavorable in this particular: that the enemy's line at that point was re-entering, so that its front was commanded by their own lines both to the right and left. Then, too, the ground was sloping upward back of the Confederate line for a considerable distance, and it was presumable that the enemy had, at least, a detached work on this highest point. The work progressed, and on the 23d of July the mine was finished ready for charging; but I had this work of charging deferred until we were ready for it.

On the 17th of July several deserters came in and said that there was great consternation in Richmond, and that Lee was coming out to make an attack upon us—the object being to put us on the defensive so that he might detach troops to go to Georgia where the army Sherman was operating against was said to be in great trouble. I put the army commanders, Meade and Butler, on the lookout, but the attack was not made.

I concluded, then, a few days later, to do something in the way of offensive movement myself, having in view something of the same object that Lee had had. Wright's and Emory's corps were in Washington, and with this reduction of my force Lee might very readily have spared some troops from the defences to send West. I had other objects in view, however, besides keeping Lee where he was. The mine was constructed and ready to be exploded, and I wanted to take that occasion to carry Petersburg if I could. It was the object, therefore, to get as many of Lee's troops away from the south side of the James River as possible. Accordingly, on the 26th, we commenced a movement with Hancock's corps and Sheridan's cavalry to the north side by the way of Deep Bottom, where Butler had a pontoon bridge laid. The plan, in the main, was to let the cavalry cut loose and, joining with Kautz's cavalry of the Army of the James, get by Lee's lines and destroy as much as they could of the Virginia Central Railroad, while, in the mean time, the infantry was to move out so as to protect their rear and cover their retreat back when they should have got through with their work. We were successful in drawing the enemy's troops to the north side of the James as I expected. The mine was ordered to be charged, and the morning of the 30th of July was the time fixed for its explosion. I gave Meade minute orders[6]

6. For Grant's orders to Meade, included in a note to the first edition, see Appendix 1, chapter 57, note 1.

on the 24th directing how I wanted the assault conducted, which orders he amplified into general instructions for the guidance of the troops that were to be engaged.

Meade's instructions, which I, of course, approved most heartily, were all that I can see now was necessary. The only further precaution which he could have taken, and which he could not foresee, would have been to have different men to execute them.

The gallery to the mine was over five hundred feet long from where it entered the ground to the point where it was under the enemy's works, and with a cross gallery of something over eighty feet running under their lines. Eight chambers had been left, requiring a ton of powder each to charge them. All was ready by the time I had prescribed; and on the 29th Hancock and Sheridan were brought back near the James River with their troops. Under cover of night they started to recross the bridge at Deep Bottom, and to march directly for that part of our lines in front of the mine.

Warren was to hold his line of intrenchments with a sufficient number of men and concentrate the balance on the right next to Burnside's corps, while Ord, now commanding the 18th corps, temporarily under Meade, was to form in the rear of Burnside to support him when he went in. All were to clear off the parapets and the *abatis* in their front so as to leave the space as open as possible, and be able to charge the moment the mine had been sprung and Burnside had taken possession. Burnside's corps was not to stop in the crater at all but push on to the top of the hill, supported on the right and left by Ord's and Warren's corps.

Warren and Ord fulfilled their instructions perfectly so far as making ready was concerned. Burnside seemed to have paid no attention whatever to the instructions, and left all the obstruction in his own front for his troops to get over in the best way they could. The four divisions of his corps were commanded by Generals Potter, Willcox, [James H.] Ledlie and Ferrero. The last was a colored division; and Burnside selected it to make the assault. Meade interfered with this. Burnside then took Ledlie's division—a worse selection than the first could have been.[7] In fact, Potter and Willcox were

7. The debacle at the Crater is one of the most notorious episodes in the war. One can still see contours of the Confederate earthworks and the Crater itself at Petersburg today. Grant alludes to a few of the contributing causes for the inept execution of the attack: Meade's late-hour veto of the plan to put the African American division in the vanguard; the failure to clear a path through the Union defenses for the advancing columns; and the cowardice of Ledlie, the drunken division commander. He does not mention the insuperable friction between Burnside and Meade, of which he was well

the only division commanders Burnside had who were equal to the occasion. Ledlie besides being otherwise inefficient, proved also to possess disqualification less common among soldiers.

There was some delay about the explosion of the mine so that it did not go off until about five o'clock in the morning. When it did explode it was very successful, making a crater twenty feet deep and something like a hundred feet in length. Instantly one hundred and ten cannon and fifty mortars, which had been placed in the most commanding positions covering the ground to the right and left of where the troops were to enter the enemy's lines, commenced playing. Ledlie's division marched into the crater immediately on the explosion, but most of the men stopped there in the absence of any one to give directions; their commander having found some safe retreat

---

aware, or his own culpability in not seizing control of the operation. Grant's failure to see the Pennsylvania miners' scheme through is one of the things for which the customarily laudatory Fuller refuses to excuse him: "The Petersburg mine operation was, in my opinion, one of the most disgraceful episodes of the war, and Grant cannot be exonerated from blame; for when a novel means of attack is decided upon, it is the duty of a general-in-chief to take a personal interest in it." *Generalship*, 300.

Ledlie's reprehensible behavior finds a fictional analogue in that of Lieutenant Roget in Humphrey Cobb's *Paths of Glory*, later made into a movie directed by Stanley Kubrick and starring Kirk Douglas. Selected to lead a patrol, Roget, having first fortified himself with cognac, kills one of his men with a grenade and then abandons the other. Roget returns to the trenches and is in the process of writing up his report when he is surprised by the return of Didier, one of the soldiers he had left to die:

> "Well?" said Roget at last, without looking up.
> "Well?" said Didier.
> Roget gave a start at the sound of the voice, then looked up. The expression on his face was one of unpleasant, almost angry surprise.
> "Well, I'll be . . . I thought you were killed. In fact I reported here in the . . ."
> "But you didn't wait to make sure, did you, Roget?"
> "Now look here . . . What d'you mean, anyway?"
> "When you ran away. After killing Lejeune. . . ."
> "I've had enough of this!"
> "I don't doubt it. You've gotten yourself into a bit of a mess, Roget. . . . Drunk on duty. Endangering the lives of your men through drunken recklessness. Refusal to take counsel. Wanton murder of one of your men. Gross incompetence in general and finally, Roget, cowardice in the face of the enemy. Don't forget you ran away. How did you explain that in your report."

Paths of Glory (New York: Penguin Classics, 2010), 60–61.

to get into before they started. There was some delay on the left and right in advancing, but some of the troops did get in and turn to the right and left, carrying the rifle-pits as I expected they would do.[8]

There had been great consternation in Petersburg, as we were well aware, about a rumored mine that we were going to explode. They knew we were mining, and they had failed to cut our mine off by countermining, though Beauregard had taken the precaution to run up a line of intrenchments to the rear of that part of their line fronting where they could see that our men were at work. We had learned through deserters who had come in that the people had very wild rumors about what was going on on our side.[9]

---

8. On July 8, several weeks before the attack on the Crater, Stephen Weld wrote to his father with his hope that the mine might end the stalemate and that African American troops were to lead the way into the Crater: "In front of our division we can certainly do nothing. If we attempt to charge, we shall be cut to pieces. Our only hope lies in General Potter's front. He is mining under a battery of the enemy, and as soon as the mine is completed, 10,000 pounds of powder are to be placed in it. As soon as it is exploded, the negro division is to charge. Our brigade is to be the next in order, followed by a brigade from Willcox's division and then Potter's division." For weeks, he had found it difficult to get much "accurate information" and "began to think that they were merely the usual camp rumors," but on July 26, Weld reported the mine complete. As late as July 28, he did not know whether his brigade would "be in the scrimmage or not," but the next day he was summoned to headquarters, where he learned, "the mine was to be sprung, and our division was to lead in the charge." *War Diary*, 333, 348–49, 351.

9. Rumor is a perennial problem in war; it is only the technology of transmission that changes. In this passage Caesar explains the psychology of rumor in the camp of one of his commanders: "in Curio's camp they all began to be very frightened, and their fear grew rapidly as they talked amongst themselves. Each one of them gave his imagination play and added something of his own fright to what he had heard from someone else. When this had spread from its original author to a larger group," Caesar continues, "and they had passed it from one to another, there seemed to be a wide authority for it. . . . Some details too were invented by those who wished to seem better informed." *Civil War*, 66.

In *The Red Badge of Courage* Stephen Crane illustrates rumor's pernicious effects on the battlefield:

> The youth wished to launch a joke—a quotation from newspapers. He desired to say, "All quiet on the Rappahannock," but the guns refused to permit even a comment upon their uproar. He never successfully concluded the sentence. But at last the guns stopped, and among the men in the rifle pits rumors again flew, like birds, but they were now for the most part black creatures who flapped their wings drearily near to the ground and refused to rise on any wings of hope. The men's faces grew doleful from the interpreting of omens. Tales of hesitation and uncertainty on the part of those high in

They said that we had undermined the whole of Petersburg; that they were resting upon a slumbering volcano and did not know at what moment they might expect an eruption. I somewhat based my calculations upon this state of feeling, and expected that when the mine was exploded the troops to the right and left would flee in all directions, and that our troops, if they moved promptly, could get in and strengthen themselves before the enemy had come to a realization of the true situation. It was just as I expected it would be. We could see the men running without any apparent object except to get away. It was half an hour before musketry firing, to amount to anything, was opened upon our men in the crater. It was an hour before the enemy got artillery up to play upon them; and it was nine o'clock before Lee got up reinforcements from his right to join in expelling our troops.

The effort was a stupendous failure. It cost us about four thousand men, mostly, however, captured; and all due to inefficiency on the part of the corps commander and the incompetency of the division commander who was sent to lead the assault.[10]

---

place and responsibility came to their ears. Stories of disaster were borne into their minds with many proofs. This din of musketry on the right, growing like a released genie of sound, expressed and emphasized the army's plight.

The men were disheartened and began to mutter. They made gestures expressive of the sentence: "Ah, what more can we do?" And it could always be seen that they were bewildered by the alleged news and could not fully comprehend a defeat.

Red Badge of Courage, 155–56.

10. On July 30, the troops formed up forty-five minutes before the explosion of the mine, and Stephen Weld's "feelings were anything but pleasant," especially because his brigade "had no confidence in Ledlie," who had already failed them on more than one occasion. Here he narrates the horrific events that followed:

At 4.30 A.M. the mine was blown up. It was just early dawn, light enough to distinguish a person a few yards off. The explosion was the grandest spectacle I ever saw. The first I knew of it, was feeling the earth shaking. I looked up and saw a huge mass of earth and flame rising some 50 or 60 feet in the air, almost slowly and majestically, as if a volcano had just opened, followed by an immense volume of smoke rolling out in every direction. The noise was very slight indeed, considering that there were nine tons of powder exploded. The men of the division were stampeded at first, but were soon rallied. We charged, having to go by the flank, as we could only get over in one or two places, and entered the enemy's pits under a moderately heavy fire. We found an immense hole here, formed by the explosion, some 30 feet deep by 100 long and 40 wide. We were ordered to go to the right

The Mine, Petersburg, 1864. Photograph by Timothy O'Sullivan. *Metropolitan Museum of Art, Harris Brisbane Dick Fund, 1933.*

of the crater, and here I endeavored to re-form my regiments. The scene inside was horrible. Men were found half buried; some dead, some alive, some with their legs kicking in the air, some with the arms only exposed, and some with every bone in their bodies apparently broken. We held the enemy's line about three or four hours, capturing some 500 prisoners. When we had been there about four hours, the negro troops charged over, filling our pits and crowding us so that our men could not use their muskets. They made a charge on the enemy in our front, which was repulsed and followed by a countercharge, driving the negroes head over heels on to us trampling down every one, and adding still more to the confusion.

Weld was captured, but he concealed his diary in his boot to prevent its confiscation. Fifty years later, the events had lost none of their vividness or clarity. In particular, he remembered Ledlie's conspicuous absence: "There was no head. Our division commander was off on the other side and did not come over with us." He recalled the "perfect pandemonium" of being "packed" in the crater together with the 29th U.S. Colored Regiment, which had joined the assault-in-progress, "like sardines in a box. I literally could not raise my arms from my side." Weld also witnessed the murder of a black soldier who had surrendered with him:

> I got cut off and took refuge in a bomb-proof, as I could not run away, being surrounded on all sides. Pretty soon the rebels yelled, "Come out of there, you Yanks." I walked out, and the negro who had gone in there with me, and Captain Fay came out also. The negro was touching my side. The rebels were about eight feet from me. They yelled out, "Shoot the nigger, but don't kill the white man"; and the negro was promptly shot down by my side. . . . I got over the embankment all right, and was walking to the rear, when I saw a negro soldier ahead of me. Three rebels rushed up to him in succession and shot him through the body. He dropped dead finally at the third shot. It was altogether the most miserable and meanest experience I ever had in my life. You could not fight, you could not give an order, you

After being fully assured of the failure of the mine, and finding that most of that part of Lee's army which had been drawn north of the James River were still there, I gave Meade directions to send a corps of infantry and the cavalry next morning, before Lee could get his forces back, to destroy fifteen or twenty miles of the Weldon Railroad. But misfortunes never come singly. I learned during that same afternoon that Wright's pursuit of Early was feeble because of the constant and contrary orders he had been receiving from Washington, while I was cut off from immediate communication by reason of our cable across Chesapeake Bay being broken. Early, however, was not aware of the fact that Wright was not pursuing until he had reached Strasburg. Finding that he was not pursued he turned back to Winchester, where Crook was stationed with a small force, and drove him out. He then pushed north until he had reached the Potomac, then he sent McCausland across to Chambersburg, Pa., to destroy that town. Chambersburg was a purely defenceless town with no garrison whatever, and no fortifications; yet McCausland, under Early's orders, burned the place and left about three hundred families houseless. This occurred on the 30th of July. I rescinded my orders for the troops to go out to destroy the Weldon Railroad, and directed them to embark for Washington City. After burning Chambersburg McCausland retreated, pursued by our cavalry, towards Cumberland. They were met and defeated by General Kelley and driven into Virginia.

The Shenandoah Valley was very important to the Confederates, because it was the principal storehouse they now had for feeding their armies about Richmond. It was well known that they would make a desperate struggle to maintain it. It had been the source of a great deal of trouble to us heretofore to guard that outlet to the north, partly because of the incompetency of some of the commanders, but chiefly because of interference from Washington. It seemed to be the policy of General Halleck and Secretary Stanton to keep any force sent there, in pursuit of the invading army, moving right and left so as to keep between the enemy and our capital; and, generally speaking, they

could not get anything done. Out of the nine regiments in my brigade I was the only regimental commander left alive.

War Diary, 353–57.

On the subsequent scapegoating of Ferrero's African American division, see Kevin M. Levin, "The Devil Himself Could Not Have Checked Them: Fighting with Black Soldiers at the Crater," *Cold Harbor to the Crater: The End of the Overland Campaign*, ed. Gary W. Gallagher and Caroline E. Janney (Chapel Hill: University of North Carolina Press, 2015), 264–82.

pursued this policy until all knowledge of the whereabouts of the enemy was lost. They were left, therefore, free to supply themselves with horses, beef cattle, and such provisions as they could carry away from Western Maryland and Pennsylvania. I determined to put a stop to this. I started Sheridan at once for that field of operation, and on the following day sent another division of his cavalry.

I had previously asked to have Sheridan assigned to that command, but Mr. Stanton objected, on the ground that he was too young for so important a command. On the 1st of August when I sent reinforcements for the protection of Washington, I sent the following orders:

> CITY POINT, VA.,
> *August* 1, 1864, 11.30 A.M.
>
> MAJOR-GENERAL HALLECK,
> Washington D. C.
>
> I am sending General Sheridan for temporary duty whilst the enemy is being expelled from the border. Unless General Hunter is in the field in person, I want Sheridan put in command of all the troops in the field, with instructions to put himself south of the enemy and follow him to the death. Wherever the enemy goes let our troops go also. Once started up the valley they ought to be followed until we get possession of the Virginia Central Railroad. If General Hunter is in the field, give Sheridan direct command of the 6th corps and cavalry division. All the cavalry, I presume, will reach Washington in the course of to-morrow.
>
> U. S. GRANT,
> Lieutenant-General.

The President in some way or other got to see this dispatch of mine directing certain instructions to be given to the commanders in the field, operating against Early, and sent me the following very characteristic dispatch:

> OFFICE U. S. MILITARY TELEGRAPH,
> WAR DEPARTMENT,
> WASHINGTON, D. C., August 3, 1864.
>
> Cypher. 6 P.M.,
> LT.-GENERAL GRANT,
> City Point, Va.
>
> I have seen your despatch in which you say, "I want Sheridan put in command of all the troops in the field, with instructions to put

himself south of the enemy, and follow him to the death. Wherever the enemy goes, let our troops go also." This, I think, is exactly right, as to how our forces should move. But please look over the despatches you may have received from here, even since you made that order, and discover, if you can, that there is any idea in the head of any one here, of "putting our army *south* of the enemy," or of "following him to the *death*" in any direction. I repeat to you it will neither be done nor attempted unless you watch it every day, and hour, and force it.

A. LINCOLN.

I replied to this that "I would start in two hours for Washington," and soon got off, going directly to the Monocacy without stopping at Washington on my way. I found General Hunter's army encamped there, scattered over the fields along the banks of the Monocacy, with many hundreds of cars and locomotives, belonging to the Baltimore and Ohio Railroad, which he had taken the precaution to bring back and collect at that point. I asked the general where the enemy was. He replied that he did not know. He said the fact was, that he was so embarrassed with orders from Washington moving him first to the right and then to the left that he had lost all trace of the enemy.

I then told the general that I would find out where the enemy was, and at once ordered steam got up and trains made up, giving directions to push for Halltown, some four miles above Harper's Ferry, in the Shenandoah

Locomotive on the Baltimore and Ohio, near Oakland, Maryland, ca. 1860. *Metropolitan Museum of Art, Purchase, The Horace W. Goldsmith Foundation Gift, through Joyce and Robert Menschel, 1991.*

Valley. The cavalry and the wagon trains were to march, but all the troops that could be transported by the cars were to go in that way. I knew that the valley was of such importance to the enemy that, no matter how much he was scattered at that time, he would in a very short time be found in front of our troops moving south.

I then wrote out General Hunter's instructions.[11] I told him that Sheridan was in Washington, and still another division was on its way; and suggested that he establish the headquarters of the department at any point that would suit him best, Cumberland, Baltimore, or elsewhere, and give Sheridan command of the troops in the field. The general replied to this, that he thought he had better be relieved entirely. He said that General Halleck seemed so much to distrust his fitness for the position he was in that he thought somebody else ought to be there. He did not want, in any way, to embarrass the cause; thus showing a patriotism that was none too common in the army. There were not many major-generals who would voluntarily have asked to have the command of a department taken from them on the supposition that for some particular reason, or for any reason, the service would be better performed. I told him, "very well then," and telegraphed at once for Sheridan to come to the Monocacy, and suggested that I would wait and meet him there.

Sheridan came at once by special train, but reached there after the troops were all off. I went to the station and remained there until he arrived. Myself and one or two of my staff were about all the Union people, except General Hunter and his staff, who were left at the Monocacy when Sheridan arrived. I hastily told Sheridan what had been done and what I wanted him to do, giving him, at the same time, the written instructions which had been prepared for General Hunter and directed to that officer.

Sheridan now had about 30,000 men to move with, 8,000 of them being cavalry. Early had about the same number, but the superior ability of the National commander over the Confederate commander was so great that all the latter's advantage of being on the defensive was more than counterbalanced by this circumstance. As I had predicted, Early was soon found in front of Sheridan in the valley, and Pennsylvania and Maryland were speedily freed from the invaders. The importance of the valley was so great to the Confederates that Lee reinforced Early, but not to the extent that we thought and feared he would.

---

11. A note to the first edition directs readers to consult the August 5 letter to Hunter included in Grant's official report. See Appendix 2.

To prevent as much as possible these reinforcements from being sent out from Richmond, I had to do something to compel Lee to retain his forces about his capital. I therefore gave orders for another move to the north side of the James River, to threaten Richmond. Hancock's corps, part of the 10th corps under Birney, and Gregg's division of cavalry were crossed to the north side of the James during the night of the 13th–14th of August.[12] A threatening position was maintained for a number of days, with more or less skirmishing, and some tolerably hard fighting; although it was my object and my instructions that anything like a battle should be avoided, unless opportunities should present themselves which would insure great success. General Meade was left in command of the few troops around Petersburg, strongly intrenched; and was instructed to keep a close watch upon the enemy in that quarter, and himself to take advantage of any weakening that might occur through an effort on the part of the enemy to reinforce the north side. There was no particular victory gained on either side; but during that time no more reinforcements were sent to the valley.

I informed Sheridan of what had been done to prevent reinforcements

12. Grant does not mention that on August 9, after he had returned to his headquarters at City Point, a barge loaded with ordnance and an adjacent warehouse exploded there. Thomas Morris Chester, a *Philadelphia Press* war correspondent on assignment with the 3rd Division, United States Colored Troops, at Petersburg, revealed that it was the African American stevedores who suffered most:

> [M]y attention was attracted by a huge volume of smoke, through the center of which like flames from the center of a volcano, a terrible blaze suddenly ascended, intermingled with dark objects which were thrown in every conceivable direction. Then followed a tremendous report and a spherical body of smoke. . . . The dust now rose in darkening confusion, and literally obscured everything within a half mile of the scene. . . . The million of property destroyed was but little thought of in the midst of the immense loss of life. Fragments of humanity were scattered around in the immediate vicinity of the tragedy in frightful profusion. Sorrow was depicted in every countenance that gazed on the ruins, but those loudest in their grief were the contrabands who mourned their relatives and comrades. Being employed in great numbers where the accident occurred, more of them were killed and wounded than any other class of individuals.

August 14, 1864, *Thomas Morris Chester, Black Civil War Correspondent: His Dispatches from the Virginia Front*, ed. R. J. M. Blackett (New York: Da Capo, 1991), 95–96.

It was subsequently discovered that a Confederate spy named John Maxwell had caused the explosion by planting a timed device—or "horological torpedo"—onboard a barge.

being sent from Richmond against him, and also that the efforts we had made had proven that one of the divisions which we supposed had gone to the valley was still at Richmond, because we had captured six or seven hundred prisoners from that division, each of its four brigades having contributed to our list of captures. I also informed him that but one division had gone, and it was possible that I should be able to prevent the going of any more.

To add to my embarrassment at this time Sherman, who was now near Atlanta, wanted reinforcements. He was perfectly willing to take the raw troops then being raised in the North-west, saying that he could teach them more soldiering in one day among his troops than they would learn in a week in a camp of instruction. I therefore asked that all troops in camps of instruction in the North-west be sent to him. Sherman also wanted to be assured that no Eastern troops were moving out against him. I informed him of what I had done and assured him that I would hold all the troops there that it was possible for me to hold, and that up to that time none had gone. I also informed him that his real danger was from Kirby Smith, who commanded the trans–Mississippi Department. If Smith should escape Steele, and get across the Mississippi River, he might move against him. I had, therefore, asked to have an expedition ready to move from New Orleans against Mobile in case Kirby Smith should get across. This would have a tendency to draw him to the defence of that place, instead of going against Sherman.

Right in the midst of all these embarrassments Halleck informed me that there was an organized scheme on foot in the North to resist the draft, and suggested that it might become necessary to draw troops from the field to put it down. He also advised taking in sail, and not going too fast.

The troops were withdrawn from the north side of the James River on the night of the 20th. Before they were withdrawn, however, and while most of Lee's force was on that side of the river, Warren had been sent with most of the 5th corps to capture the Weldon Railroad. He took up his line of march well back to the rear, south of the enemy, while the troops remaining in the trenches extended so as to cover that part of the line which he had vacated by moving out. From our left, near the old line, it was about three miles to the Weldon Railroad. A division was ordered from the right of the Petersburg line to reinforce Warren, while a division was brought back from the north side of the James River to take its place.

This road was very important to the enemy. The limits from which his supplies had been drawn were already very much contracted, and I knew that he must fight desperately to protect it. Warren carried the road, though with heavy loss on both sides. He fortified his new position, and our trenches were then extended from the left of our main line to connect with his new one. Lee made repeated attempts to dislodge Warren's corps, but without success, and with heavy loss.

As soon as Warren was fortified and reinforcements reached him, troops were sent south to destroy the bridges on the Weldon Railroad; and with such success that the enemy had to draw in wagons, for a distance of about thirty miles, all the supplies they got thereafter from that source. It was on the 21st that Lee seemed to have given up the Weldon Railroad as having been lost to him; but along about the 24th or 25th he made renewed attempts to recapture it; again he failed and with very heavy losses to him as compared with ours.

On the night of the 20th our troops on the north side of the James were withdrawn, and Hancock and Gregg were sent south to destroy the Weldon Railroad. They were attacked on the 25th at Reams's Station, and after desperate fighting a part of our line gave way, losing five pieces of artillery. But the Weldon Railroad never went out of our possession from the 18th of August to the close of the war.

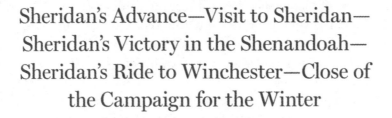

58

Sheridan's Advance—Visit to Sheridan—
Sheridan's Victory in the Shenandoah—
Sheridan's Ride to Winchester—Close of
the Campaign for the Winter

We had our troops on the Weldon Railroad contending against a large force that regarded this road of so much importance that they could afford to expend many lives in retaking it; Sherman just getting through to Atlanta with great losses of men from casualties, discharges and detachments left along as guards to occupy and hold the road in rear of him; Washington threatened but a short time before, and now Early being strengthened in the valley so as, probably, to renew that attempt. It kept me pretty active in looking after all these points.

On the 10th of August Sheridan had advanced on Early up the Shenandoah Valley, Early falling back to Strasburg. On the 12th I learned that Lee had sent twenty pieces of artillery, two divisions of infantry and a considerable cavalry force to strengthen Early. It was important that Sheridan should be informed of this, so I sent the information to Washington by telegraph, and directed a courier to be sent from there to get the message to Sheridan at all hazards, giving him the information. The messenger, an officer of the army, pushed through with great energy and reached Sheridan just in time. The officer went through by way of Snicker's Gap, escorted by some cavalry. He found Sheridan just making his preparations to attack Early in his chosen position. Now, however, he was thrown back on the defensive.

On the 15th of September I started to visit General Sheridan in the Shenandoah Valley. My purpose was to have him attack Early, or drive him out of the valley and destroy that source of supplies for Lee's army. I knew it was impossible for me to get orders through Washington to Sheridan to make a move, because they would be stopped there and such orders as Halleck's caution (and that of the Secretary of War) would suggest would be given instead, and would, no doubt, be contradictory to mine. I therefore, without stopping at Washington, went directly through to Charlestown, some ten miles above Harper's Ferry, and waited there to see General Sheridan, having sent a courier in advance to inform him where to meet me.[1]

When Sheridan arrived I asked him if he had a map showing the positions of his army and that of the enemy. He at once drew one out of his side pocket, showing all roads and streams, and the camps of the two armies. He said that if he had permission he would move so and so (pointing out how) against the Confederates, and that he could "whip them." Before starting I had drawn up a plan of campaign for Sheridan, which I had brought with me; but, seeing that he was so clear and so positive in his views and so confident of success, I said nothing about this and did not take it out of my pocket.[2]

Sheridan's wagon trains were kept at Harper's Ferry, where all of his stores were. By keeping the teams at that place, their forage did not have to

1. Grant was mindful of Lincoln's warning, which he quotes in the previous chapter, about what happened to orders when they went through Halleck: "But please look over the despatches you may have received from here," Lincoln had telegraphed to him on August 3, "even since you made that order, and discover, if you can, that there is any idea in the head of any one here, of 'putting our army south of the enemy,' or of 'following him to the death' in any direction. I repeat to you it will neither be done nor attempted unless you watch it every day and hour and force it." *OR*, ser. 1, vol. 37, pt. 2, 582.

Charles H. Lynch, 18th Connecticut Volunteers, mentions in his diary the excitement caused by Grant's visit to Sheridan: "Pleasant morning. Detailed for picket duty. Located northeast of town, between the Harper's Ferry Pike and the Shenandoah River, on the ground where old John Brown was hung in 1859. About noontime saw a company of cavalrymen come flying down the pike from Harper's Ferry. Wondered what it meant. Later we learned that General Grant and General Sheridan were in town. Caused much excitement and comment as they held a conference at a large house just southeast of town. The company I saw from our picket post was General Grant and his escort. All is quiet tonight." September 17, 1864, *The Civil War Diary, 1862–1865* (Hartford, CT: Lockwood & Brainard, 1915), 125.

2. Sheridan writes, "In our resulting interview at Charlestown, I went over the situation very thoroughly, and pointed out with so much confidence the chances of a complete victory should I throw my army across the Valley pike near Newtown that he fell in with the plan at once, authorized me to resume the offensive, and to attack Early as soon as I deemed it most propitious to do so; and although before leaving City Point he had outlined certain operations for my army, yet he neither discussed nor disclosed his plans, my knowledge of the situation striking him as being so much more accurate than his own." *Personal Memoirs*, 2:9.

be hauled to them. As supplies of ammunition, provisions and rations for the men were wanted, trains would be made up to deliver the stores to the commissaries and quartermasters encamped at Winchester. Knowing that he, in making preparations to move at a given day, would have to bring up wagon trains from Harper's Ferry, I asked him if he could be ready to get off by the following Tuesday. This was on Friday. "O yes," he said, he "could be off before daylight on Monday." I told him then to make the attack at that time and according to his own plan; and I immediately started to return to the army about Richmond. After visiting Baltimore and Burlington, New Jersey, I arrived at City Point on the 19th.[3]

On the way out to Harper's Ferry I had met Mr. Robert Garrett, President of the Baltimore and Ohio Railroad. He seemed very anxious to know when workmen might be put upon the road again so as to make repairs and put it in shape for running. It was a large piece of property to have standing idle. I told him I could not answer then positively but would try and inform him before a great while. On my return Mr. Garrett met me again with the same question and I told him I thought that by the following Wednesday he might send his workmen out on his road. I gave him no further information however, and he had no suspicion of how I expected to have the road cleared for his workmen.[4]

---

3. Grant's family was living in Burlington. Dodge visited City Point in October and observed the strain on Grant:

> While I was at City Point was evidently the most anxious days for Grant, although he had no doubt that his next campaign would end the war. The troops coming to him were drafted men. I was told that desertions were very heavy; that as high as 1,400 had left in a week. Hancock and other officers were becoming discouraged. Some commanders were on leave of absence, and it was so blue around there that one evening I suggested to Rawlins that it looked to me like the rats deserting a sinking ship. I could not appreciate the feeling, for the Army of the Potomac was the finest, best equipped and best appointed army I had ever seen. General Ingall's single sample depot at City Point would have been a supply to one of our Western Corps.

Personal Recollections, 79–80.

4. John W. Garrett was the president of the Baltimore and Ohio Railroad. Sheridan would complain about the undue influence of the railroad interest at this crucial time: "it was difficult to resist the persistent pressure of those whose judgment, warped by their interests in the Baltimore and Ohio railroad, was often confused and misled by stories of scouts (sent out from Washington), averring that Kershaw and Fitzhugh Lee had

Map showing the extent of the Baltimore and Ohio Railroad in 1860.
Library of Congress, Geography and Map Division.

Sheridan moved at the time he had fixed upon. He met Early at the crossing of Opequon Creek, and won a most decisive victory—one which electrified the country. Early had invited this attack himself by his bad generalship and made the victory easy.[5] He had sent G. T. Anderson's division

---

returned to Petersburg, Breckenridge [John C. Breckinridge] to southwestern Virginia, and at one time even maintaining that Early's whole army was east of the Blue Ridge, and its commander himself at Gordonsville." *Personal Memoirs*, 2:6–8.

5. Opequon, also known as the Third Battle of Winchester, was a costly victory. There were more than 5,000 Union casualties, 9,000 altogether. After the battle, Sheridan had the opportunity to meet a woman who had furnished him with vital intelligence. It was in her house that he wrote his dispatch to Grant: "I expressed a desire to find some place where I could write a telegram to General Grant informing him of the result of the battle, and General Crook conducted me to the home of Miss Wright, where I met for the first time the woman who had contributed so much to our success, and on a desk in her school-room wrote the despatch announcing that we had sent Early's army whirling up the valley." *Personal Memoirs*, 2:28–29.

Sheridan's connection with Rebecca Wright arose from his attempt to revamp the "defective" intelligence service in the Valley:

east of the Blue Ridge before I went to Harper's Ferry; and about the time I arrived there he started with two other divisions (leaving but two in their camps) to march to Martinsburg for the purpose of destroying the Baltimore and Ohio Railroad at that point. Early here learned that I had been with Sheridan and, supposing there was some movement on foot, started back as soon as he got the information. But his forces were separated and, as I have said, he was very badly defeated. He fell back to Fisher's Hill, Sheridan following.[6]

> I therefore began to organize my scouts on a system which I hoped would give better results than had the method hitherto pursued in the department, which was to employ on this service doubtful citizens and Confederate deserters. If these should turn out untrustworthy, the mischief they might do us gave me grave apprehension, and I finally concluded that those of our own soldiers who should volunteer for the delicate and hazardous duty would be the most valuable material, and decided that they should have a battalion organization and be commanded by an officer, Major H. K. Young, of the First Rhode Island Infantry. These men were disguised in Confederate uniforms whenever necessary, were paid from the Secret-Service Fund in proportion to the value of the intelligence they furnished, which often stood us in good stead in checking the forays of Gilmore, Mosby, and other irregulars.

On Crook's recommendation, Sheridan enlisted the services of Wright, who lived in Winchester. Although "under constant surveillance," Wright provided invaluable information on rebel troop movements. Sheridan communicated with her through an African American man who lived nearby and carried Sheridan's message, wrapped in a tin-foil pellet, in his mouth:

> On reading my communication Miss Wright was much startled by the perils it involved, and hesitatingly consulted her mother, but her devoted loyalty soon silenced every other consideration, and the brave girl resolved to comply with my request, notwithstanding it might jeopardize her life.

Wright's information about the departure of Kershaw's division, which had left the Valley to join Lee, led Sheridan to engage Early at Opequon. See *Personal Memoirs*, 2: 2:28–29, 1–5.

6. Union forces under Crook outflanked Early, who was forced to retreat seventy miles, leaving the valley open to Sheridan, who proceeded to destroy anything that could be of use to the Confederates. The locals would come to refer to the ensuing period as "The Burning" or "Red October." When it was over, Sheridan reportedly boasted, "A crow would have to carry its rations if it flew across the valley." Quoted in W. A. Smith, *The Anson Guards: Company C, Fourteenth Regiment North Carolina Volunteers, 1861–1865* (Charlotte, North Carolina: Stone, 1914), 271.

The valley is narrow at that point, and Early made another stand there, behind works which extended across. But Sheridan turned both his flanks and again sent him speeding up the valley, following in hot pursuit. The pursuit was continued up the valley to Mount Jackson and New Market. Sheridan captured about eleven hundred prisoners and sixteen guns. The houses which he passed all along the route were found to be filled with Early's wounded, and the country swarmed with his deserters. Finally, on the 25th, Early turned from the valley eastward, leaving Sheridan at Harrisonburg in undisputed possession.

Now one of the main objects of the expedition began to be accomplished. Sheridan went to work with his command, gathering in the crops, cattle, and everything in the upper part of the valley required by our troops; and especially taking what might be of use to the enemy. What he could not take away he destroyed, so that the enemy would not be invited to come back there. I congratulated Sheridan upon his recent great victory and had a salute of a hundred guns fired in honor of it, the guns being aimed at the enemy around Petersburg. I also notified the other commanders throughout the country, who also fired salutes in honor of his victory.

I had reason to believe that the administration was a little afraid to have a decisive battle fought at that time, for fear it might go against us and have a bad effect on the November elections. The convention which had met and made its nomination of the Democratic candidate for the presidency had declared the war a failure. Treason was talked as boldly in Chicago at that convention as ever it had been in Charleston. It was a question whether the government would then have had the power to make arrests and punish

---

Most accounts of Sheridan's operations in the Shenandoah and Sherman's on the march through Georgia and the Carolinas understandably focus on all they took away. Nevertheless, as Gloria Emerson's description of the invasion of Laos in 1971 suggests, armies also deposit a tremendous amount of garbage in their wake:

> Now there is only the garbage of war. Empty C-ration cans of fruit cocktail and turkey loaf, an empty Pall Mall cigarette package, a single khaki sock and two mounds of sandbags are strewn about at the border crossing into Laos on Route 9.
>
> A week ago it was here that thousands of South Vietnamese troops, supported by American planes and artillery, marched into Laos, leaving the litter behind.

"At Border Crossing into Laos, the Litter of Troops and History," *New York Times*, February 18, 1971, p. 12.

those who thus talked treason. But this decisive victory was the most effective campaign argument made in the canvass.

Sheridan, in his pursuit, got beyond where they could hear from him in Washington, and the President became very much frightened about him. He was afraid that the hot pursuit had been a little like that of General [Lewis] Cass was said to have been, in one of our Indian wars, when he was an officer of the army. Cass was pursuing the Indians so closely that the first thing he knew he found himself in their front, and the Indians pursuing him.[7] The President was afraid that Sheridan had got on the other side of Early and that Early was in behind him. He was afraid that Sheridan was getting so far away that reinforcements would be sent out from Richmond to enable Early to beat him. I replied to the President that I had taken steps to prevent Lee from sending reinforcements to Early, by attacking the former where he was.

On the 28th of September, to retain Lee in his position, I sent Ord with the 18th corps and Birney with the 10th corps to make an advance on Richmond, to threaten it. Ord moved with the left wing up to Chaffin's Bluff; Birney with the 10th corps took a road farther north; while Kautz with the cavalry took the Darby road, still farther to the north. They got across the river by the next morning, and made an effort to surprise the enemy. In that, however, they were unsuccessful.

The enemy's lines were very strong and very intricate. Stannard's division of the 18th corps with General Burnham's brigade leading, tried an assault against Fort Harrison and captured it with sixteen guns and a good many prisoners. Burnham was killed in the assault. Colonel Stevens who succeeded him was badly wounded; and his successor also fell in the same way. Some works to the right and left were also carried with the guns in them—six in number—and a few more prisoners. Birney's troops to the right captured the enemy's intrenched picket-lines, but were unsuccessful in their efforts upon the main line.

Our troops fortified their new position, bringing Fort Harrison into the new line and extending it to the river. This brought us pretty close to the enemy on the north side of the James, and the two opposing lines maintained their relative positions to the close of the siege.

In the afternoon a further attempt was made to advance, but it failed. Ord fell badly wounded, and had to be relieved; the command devolved

---

7. Lewis Cass was a veteran of the War of 1812. As Andrew Jackson's Secretary of War, Cass vigorously prosecuted the administration's Indian Removal Policy.

upon General Heckman, and later General Weitzel was assigned to the command of the 18th corps. During the night Lee reinforced his troops about Fort Gilmer, which was at the right of Fort Harrison, by transferring eight additional brigades from Petersburg, and attempted to retake the works which we had captured by concentrating ten brigades against them. All their efforts failed, their attacks being all repulsed with very heavy loss. In one of these assaults upon us General Stannard, a gallant officer who was defending Fort Harrison, lost an arm. Our casualties during these operations amounted to 394 killed, 1,554 wounded and 324 missing.

Whilst this was going on General Meade was instructed to keep up an appearance of moving troops to our extreme left. Parke and Warren were kept with two divisions, each under arms, ready to move, leaving their enclosed batteries manned, with a scattering line on the other intrenchments. The object of this was to prevent reinforcements from going to the north side of the river. Meade was instructed to watch the enemy closely and, if Lee weakened his lines, to make an attack.

On the 30th these troops moved out, under Warren, and captured an advanced intrenched camp at Peeble's farm, driving the enemy back to the main line. Our troops followed and made an attack in the hope of carrying the enemy's main line; but in this they were unsuccessful and lost a large number of men, mostly captured. The number of killed and wounded was not large. The next day our troops advanced again and established themselves, intrenching a new line about a mile in front of the enemy. This advanced Warren's position on the Weldon Railroad very considerably.

Sheridan having driven the enemy out of the valley, and taken the productions of the valley so that instead of going there for supplies the enemy would have to bring his provisions with him if he again entered it, recommended a reduction of his own force, the surplus to be sent where it could be of more use. I approved of his suggestion, and ordered him to send Wright's corps back to the James River. I further directed him to repair the railroad up the Shenandoah Valley towards the advanced position which we would hold with a small force. The troops were to be sent to Washington by the way of Culpeper, in order to watch the east side of the Blue Ridge, and prevent the enemy from getting into the rear of Sheridan while he was still doing his work of destruction.[8]

---

8. Joshua Chamberlain caught a glimpse of Sheridan in the final days before Appomattox and was struck by the general's ferocity:

The valley was so very important, however, to the Confederate army that, contrary to our expectations, they determined to make one more strike, and save it if possible before the supplies should be all destroyed. Reinforcements were sent therefore to Early, and this before any of our troops had been withdrawn. Early prepared to strike Sheridan at Harrisonburg; but the latter had not remained there.

On the 6th of October Sheridan commenced retiring down the valley, taking or destroying all the food and forage and driving the cattle before him, Early following. At Fisher's Hill Sheridan turned his cavalry back on that of Early, which, under the lead of Rosser, was pursuing closely, and routed it most completely, capturing eleven guns and a large number of prisoners. Sheridan lost only about sixty men. His cavalry pursued the enemy back some twenty-five miles. On the 10th of October the march down the valley was again resumed, Early again following.[9]

I now ordered Sheridan to halt, and to improve the opportunity if afforded by the enemy's having been sufficiently weakened, to move back

---

Sharp work now. Pushing through the woods at cavalry speed, we come out right upon Sheridan's battle flag gleaming amidst the smoke of his batteries in the edge of the open field. Weird-looking flag it is: fork-tailed, red and white, the two bands that composed it each charged with a star of the contrasting color; two eyes sternly glaring through the cannon-cloud. Beneath it, that stormcenter spirit, that form of condensed energies, mounted on the grim charger, Rienzi, that turned the battle of the Shenandoah,—both, rider and steed, of an unearthly shade of darkness, terrible to look upon, as if masking some unknown powers.

The Passing of the Armies (New York: G. P. Putnam's Sons, 1915), 233–34.

9. De Forest provides the stark details of Sheridan's destruction of the Valley:

On the 6th of October we commenced moving north, the Eighth Corps leading, then the Sixth, then the Nineteenth. Behind came the cavalry, in a broad line from mountain to mountain, burning the mills and barns and driving off the cattle and sheep. Between Mt. Crawford and Woodstock over seventy mills and two thousand barns, crammed with flour, wheat, corn and hay, were destroyed. The inhabitants were left so stripped of food that I cannot imagine how they escaped starvation. The valley was thus desolated, partly as a punishment for the frequent bushwhacking of our trains and stragglers, but mainly to prevent Early from subsisting his army in it and marching once more to the Potomac. It was a woful sight for civilized eyes; but as a warlike measure it was very effective.

A Volunteer's Adventures, 197.

again and cut the James River Canal and Virginia Central Railroad. But this order had to go through Washington where it was intercepted; and when Sheridan received what purported to be a statement of what I wanted him to do it was something entirely different. Halleck informed Sheridan that it was my wish for him to hold a forward position as a base from which to act against Charlottesville and Gordonsville; that he should fortify this position and provision it.

Sheridan objected to this most decidedly; and I was impelled to telegraph him, on the 14th, as follows:

CITY POINT, VA.,
October 14, 1864.—12.30 P.M.

MAJOR-GENERAL SHERIDAN,
Cedar Creek, Va.

What I want is for you to threaten the Virginia Central Railroad and canal in the manner your judgment tells you is best, holding yourself ready to advance, if the enemy draw off their forces. If you make the enemy hold a force equal to your own for the protection of those thoroughfares, it will accomplish nearly as much as their destruction. If you cannot do this, then the next best thing to do is to send here all the force you can. I deem a good cavalry force necessary for your offensive, as well as defensive operations. You need not therefore send here more than one division of cavalry.

U. S. GRANT,
Lieutenant-General.

Sheridan having been summoned to Washington City, started on the 15th leaving Wright in command. His army was then at Cedar Creek, some twenty miles south of Winchester. The next morning while at Front Royal, Sheridan received a dispatch from Wright, saying that a dispatch from Longstreet to Early had been intercepted. It directed the latter to be ready to move and to crush Sheridan as soon as he, Longstreet, arrived. On the receipt of this news Sheridan ordered the cavalry up the valley to join Wright.

On the 18th of October Early was ready to move, and during the night succeeded in getting his troops in the rear of our left flank, which fled precipitately and in great confusion down the valley, losing eighteen pieces of artillery and a thousand or more prisoners. The right under General Getty maintained a firm and steady front, falling back to Middletown where it took a position and made a stand. The cavalry went to the rear, seized the

James E. Taylor,
"Confederate Attack on
Union Headquarters,
Belle Grove, Middletown,
Virginia." *Library of
Congress, HABS VA-259.*

roads leading to Winchester and held them for the use of our troops in falling
back, General Wright having ordered a retreat back to that place.

Sheridan having left Washington on the 18th, reached Winchester that
night. The following morning he started to join his command. He had
scarcely got out of town, when he met his men returning in panic from the
front and also heard heavy firing to the south. He immediately ordered the
cavalry at Winchester to be deployed across the valley to stop the stragglers.
Leaving members of his staff to take care of Winchester and the public property there, he set out with a small escort directly for the scene of battle.[10] As
he met the fugitives he ordered them to turn back, reminding them that they

10. Sheridan's ride from Winchester on his horse Rienzi would become the stuff of
legend through Thomas Buchanan Read's wildly popular yet emphatically mediocre
poem, "Sheridan's Ride," the concluding stanza of which gives a sense of the style:

Hurrah! hurrah for Sheridan!
Hurrah! hurrah for horse and man!
And when their statues are placed on high,
Under the dome of the Union sky,
The American soldier's Temple of Fame;
There with the glorious general's name,
Be it said, in letters both bold and bright,
    "Here is the steed that saved the day,
By carrying Sheridan into the fight,
    From Winchester, twenty miles away!"

Yale Book of American Verse, ed. Thomas R. Lounsbury (New Haven, CT: Yale University Press, 1912), 341.

were going the wrong way. His presence soon restored confidence.[11] Finding themselves worse frightened than hurt the men did halt and turn back. Many

11. Like the death of Albert Sidney Johnston at Shiloh, the appearance of Sheridan at Cedar Creek is often pointed to as a moment when the actions of an individual determined the outcome of a battle. George Crook believed that he and his division had never received proper credit for their role in this victory. He was infuriated by the version of the battle—decades later Crook called Sheridan's circulation of "fiction . . . contemptible"—that had been handed down by Sheridan and his partisans: "Sitting around the campfires that night, Gen. Sheridan was feeling very good. He said, 'Crook, I am going to get much more credit for this than I deserve, for, had I been here in the morning the same thing would have taken place, and had I not returned today, the same thing would have taken place.' This saying was full of meat, but it made little impression at the time." *Autobiography*, 134.

Lieutenant George Crook, Cadet Philip Sheridan, and Lieutenant John Nugen, 1852 or 1853. *Special Collections, United States Military Academy Library.*

Increasingly, historians have argued for the influence of a more complex concatenation of factors on the battlefield; nevertheless, the idea that one leader can change a battle's course still exerts a powerful hold on the popular imagination. Moreover, it has a long, rich history. In a classic example, Ammianus Marcellinus recounts the moment when the Roman emperor Julian arrived at the Battle of Strasbourg in 357:

> The Caesar, seeing from a distance his cavalry turning to flight, put spurs to his horse and threw himself in their path. He was recognized by the purple dragon attached to the tip of a long lance and streaming on the wind like the cast skin of a snake, and the tribune of the squadron stopped and turned back, pale and trembling, to renew the fight. The Caesar took the course usual in moments of crisis, and addressed the men in terms of mild reproach: "Where are we off to, my brave fellows? Don't you know that flight never saved anyone? It is simply a proof of the folly of a vain enterprise. Let us return to our comrades, and at least have a share in their glory, even though we have thoughtlessly abandoned them in their fight for our country." This tactful speech brought them all back to their duty.

The Later Roman Empire, trans. Walter Hamilton (New York: Penguin Classics, 2004), 111.

of those who had run ten miles got back in time to redeem their reputation as gallant soldiers before night.

When Sheridan got to the front he found Getty and Custer still holding their ground firmly between the Confederates and our retreating troops. Everything in the rear was now ordered up. Sheridan at once proceeded to intrench his position; and he awaited an assault from the enemy. This was made with vigor, and was directed principally against Emory's corps, which had sustained the principal loss in the first attack. By one o'clock the attack was repulsed. Early was so badly damaged that he seemed disinclined to make another attack, but went to work to intrench himself with a view to holding the position he had already gained. He thought, no doubt, that Sheridan would be glad enough to leave him unmolested; but in this he was mistaken.

About the middle of the afternoon Sheridan advanced. He sent his cavalry by both flanks, and they penetrated to the enemy's rear. The contest was close for a time, but at length the left of the enemy broke, and disintegration along the whole line soon followed. Early tried to rally his men, but they were followed so closely that they had to give way very quickly every time they attempted to make a stand. Our cavalry, having pushed on and got in the rear of the Confederates, captured twenty-four pieces of artillery, besides retaking what had been lost in the morning. This victory pretty much closed the campaigning in the Valley of Virginia. All the Confederate troops were sent back to Richmond with the exception of one division of infantry and a little cavalry. Wright's corps was ordered back to the Army of the Potomac, and two other divisions were withdrawn from the valley. Early had lost more men in killed, wounded and captured in the valley than Sheridan had commanded from first to last.[12]

---

12. Early's attack at Cedar Creek was a masterpiece of stealth aided by early morning fog and Union complacency. Stephen Ramseur was in command of the lead element. "A skilful and energetic commander of the enemy's forces would have crushed Ramseur before any assistance could have reached him, and thus ensured the destruction of my whole force," Early opined, "and later in the day, when the battle had turned against us, with the immense superiority in cavalry which Sheridan had, and the advantage of the open country, would have destroyed my whole force and captured everything I had." Continuing in this vein, Early proposes that his enemy's incompetence proved his salvation:

> As it was, considering the immense disparity in numbers and equipment, the enemy had very little to boast of. I had lost a few pieces of artillery and

some very valuable officers and men, but the main part of my force and all my trains had been saved, and the enemy's loss in killed and wounded was far greater than mine. When I look back to this battle, I can but attribute my escape from utter annihilation to the incapacity of my opponent.

Autobiographical Sketch, 427–28.

The Confederates were certainly outnumbered. There was, moreover, a loss of momentum in the Confederate advance after Ramseur's initial successes. The likely reason was that many of Early's troops stopped "to plunder" the Union tents, as they had reportedly done at Shiloh. Early certainly thought this was the case and expressed as much in his report to Lee. See *OR*, ser. 1, vol. 43, pt. 1, 562.

John H. Worsham, who was wounded at Opequon but whose company fought at Cedar Creek, suggested that the soldiers stopped because they were ragged, barefoot, and starving. "The world will never know the extreme poverty of the Confederate soldier at that time!" Worsham wrote years later:

> Hundreds of the men who were in the charge and captured the enemy's works were barefooted, every one of them was ragged, many had nothing but what they had on, and *none* had eaten a square meal for weeks! In passing through Sheridan's camp they had great temptation thrown in their way; many of the tents were open, and in plain sight were rations, shoes, overcoats and blankets! The fighting continued farther and farther, and some of the men stopped, secured well-filled haversacks, and as they investigated their contents, the temptation to stop and eat was too great, as they had had nothing since the evening before, and they yielded.

One of Jackson's Foot Cavalry: His Experience and What He Saw during the War 1861–1865 (New York: Neale, 1912), 276.

John B. Gordon was eager to exonerate the soldiers from the charge of plundering. Instead, he heaped blame on Early for calling a "fatal halt":

> When the battle began in the morning my command was on the Confederate right; but at the end of the morning's fight, when the fatal halt was called, my immediate division was on the Confederate left. General Early in his report, now published, states that I had gotten on the left with my division. He did not seem to understand how we reached the left, when we were on the right at the opening of the morning fight. Had General Early been there when our ringing rifles were sounding a reveille to Sheridan's sleeping braves, had he seen Evans and Kershaw as I saw them, sweeping with the scattering fury of a whirlwind down the Union intrenchments, and following the flying Federals far beyond our extreme left, he would have known exactly how we got there. From the Confederate right to the Confederate left we had passed in swift pursuit of the routed enemy. Across the whole length of the Confederate front these divisions had swept, trying to catch Sheridan's panic-stricken men, and they did catch a great many of them.

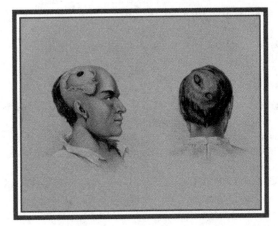

Examples of gunshot fractures to the cranium, *The Medical and Surgical History of the War of the Rebellion. Courtesy of NIH U.S. National Library of Medicine.*

On more than one occasion in these engagements General R. B. Hayes, who succeeded me as President of the United States, bore a very honorable part.[13] His conduct on the field was marked by conspicuous gallantry as well as the display of qualities of a higher order than that of mere personal daring. This might well have been expected of one who could write at the

Analyzing Early's "great mistake" in depth, Gordon exonerates the "chivalrous and self-sacrificing" soldiers of the charge of plundering. See *Reminiscences of the Civil War* (New York: Scribner's, 1904), 346–47, 352, 364.

13. Future president Rutherford B. Hayes (1822–1893) rose to command the 23rd Ohio Volunteer Infantry. He fought at Antietam, joined the pursuit of Morgan through Ohio, and fought in all of the major engagements of Sheridan's 1864 Shenandoah Valley campaign. After the Battle of Cedar Creek, Hayes wrote to his wife: "As usual with me I had some narrow escapes. While galloping rapidly, my fine large black horse was killed instantly, tumbling heels over head and dashing me on the ground violently. Strange to say I was only a little bruised and was able to keep the saddle all day. . . . I was also hit fairly in the head by a ball which had lost its force in getting (I suppose) through somebody else! It gave me only a slight shock.—I think serious fighting on this line is now over." October 21, 1864, *The Diary and Letters of Rutherford B. Hayes*, ed. Charles Richard Williams (Columbus: Ohio State Archaeological and Historical Society, 1922), 2:528.

Another future president, James A. Garfield (1831–1881), who organized and commanded the 42nd Ohio Volunteer Infantry, was decidedly less ebullient about war in his letters home: "The horrible sights we have witnessed on this field I can never describe," he wrote his wife from the field at Shiloh. "No blaze of glory that flashes around the magnificent triumphs of war can ever atone for the unwritten and unutterable horrors of the scene of carnage." Letter to Lucretia Garfield, April 21, 1862, *Crete and James: Personal Letters of Lucretia and James Garfield*, ed. John Shaw (East Lansing: Michigan State University Press, 1994), 136.

time he is said to have done so: "Any officer fit for duty who at this crisis would abandon his post to electioneer for a seat in Congress, ought to be scalped." Having entered the army as a Major of Volunteers at the beginning of the war, General Hayes attained by meritorious service the rank of Brevet Major-General before its close.

On the north side of the James River the enemy attacked Kautz's cavalry on the 7th of October, and drove it back with heavy loss in killed, wounded and prisoners, and the loss of all the artillery. This was followed up by an attack on our intrenched infantry line, but was repulsed with severe slaughter. On the 13th a reconnoissance was sent out by General Butler, with a view to drive the enemy from some new works he was constructing, which resulted in heavy loss to us.

On the 24th I ordered General Meade to attempt to get possession of the South Side Railroad, and for that purpose to advance on the 27th. The attempt proved a failure, however, the most advanced of our troops not getting nearer than within six miles of the point aimed for. Seeing the impossibility of its accomplishment I ordered the troops to withdraw, and they were all back in their former positions the next day.

Butler, by my directions, also made a demonstration on the north side of the James River in order to support this move, by detaining there the Confederate troops who were on that side. He succeeded in this, but failed of further results by not marching past the enemy's left before turning in on the Darby road and by reason of simply coming up against their lines in place.

This closed active operations around Richmond for the winter. Of course there was frequent skirmishing between pickets, but no serious battle was fought near either Petersburg or Richmond. It would prolong this work to give a detailed account of all that took place from day to day around Petersburg and at other parts of my command, and it would not interest the general reader if given. All these details can be found by the military student in a series of books published by the Scribners, Badeau's history of my campaigns, and also in the publications of the War Department, including both the National and Confederate reports.[14]

---

14. The contrast between most of the novels Grant read in formative cadet days and the way in which he depicted battles could not be sharper. In Charles Lever's often comic novel *Charles O'Malley, the Irish Dragoon*, however, Grant would have encountered a

In the latter part of November General Hancock was relieved from the command of the 2d corps by the Secretary of War and ordered to Washing-

---

more ambivalent treatment of combat, an initially romantic account of the Battle of Porto, fought during the Peninsular War, followed by its apparent deflation:

> "Forward—close up—charge!"
>
> The word was scarcely spoken, when the loud cheer answered the welcome sound, and the same instant the long line of shining helmets passed with the speed of a whirlwind; the pace increased at every stride, the ranks grew closer, and, like the dread force of some mighty engine, we fell upon the foe. I have felt all the glorious enthusiasm of a fox-hunt, when the loud cry of the hounds, answered by the cheers of the joyous huntsman, stirred the very heart within, but never till now did I know how far higher the excitement reaches, when, man to man, sabre to sabre, arm to arm, we ride forward to the battlefield. On we went, the loud shout of "Forward!" still ringing in our ears. One broken, irregular discharge from the French guns shook the head of our advancing column, but stayed us not as we galloped madly on.
>
> I remember no more. The din, the smoke, the crash—the cry for quarter, mingled with the shout of victory—the flying enemy—the agonizing shrieks of the wounded—all are commingled in my mind, but leave no trace of clearness or connexion between them; and it was only when the column wheeled to re-form, behind the advancing squadrons, that I awoke from my trance of maddening excitement, and perceived that we had carried the position, and cut off the guns of the enemy. . . .
>
> I turned my head towards the scene of our late encounter. Some dismounted guns and broken waggons alone marked the spot; while, far in the distance, the dust of the retreating columns showed the beaten enemy, as they hurried towards the frontiers of Spain. . . .
>
> There are few sadder things in life than the day after a battle. The high-beating hope, the bounding spirits, have passed away; and in their stead comes the depressing reaction by which every overwrought ex[c]itement is followed. With far different eyes do we look upon the compact ranks and glistening files,—
>
> > "With helm arrayed.
> > And lance and blade,
> > And plume in the gay wind dancing!"
>
> and upon the cold and barren heath, whose only memory of the past is the blood-stained turf, a mangled corpse, the broken gun, the shattered wall, the well-trodden earth where columns stood, the cut-up ground where cavalry had charged—these are the sad relics of all the chivalry of yesterday.

Charles O'Malley, the Irish Dragoon (London: Routledge, 1872), 1:348, 350–53.

ton, to organize and command a corps of veteran troops to be designated the 1st corps. It was expected that this would give him a large command to co-operate with in the spring. It was my expectation, at the time, that in the final operations Hancock should move either up the valley, or else east of the Blue Ridge to Lynchburg; the idea being to make the spring campaign the close of the war. I expected, with Sherman coming up from the South, Meade south of Petersburg and around Richmond, and Thomas's command in Tennessee with depots of supplies established in the eastern part of that State, to move from the direction of Washington or the valley towards Lynchburg. We would then have Lee so surrounded that his supplies would be cut off entirely, making it impossible for him to support his army.

General Humphreys, chief-of-staff of the Army of the Potomac, was assigned to the command of the 2d corps, to succeed Hancock.

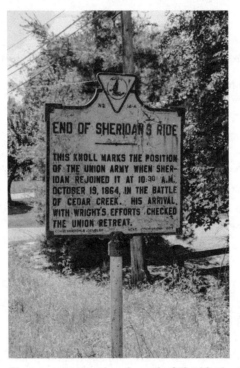

Sign commemorating the end of Sheridan's ride, Middletown, Virginia. *Photograph by Elizabeth D. Samet.*

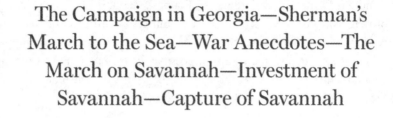

The Campaign in Georgia—Sherman's March to the Sea—War Anecdotes—The March on Savannah—Investment of Savannah—Capture of Savannah

Let us now return to the operations in the military division of the Mississippi, and accompany Sherman in his march to the sea.

The possession of Atlanta by us narrowed the territory of the enemy very materially and cut off one of his two remaining lines of roads from east to west.

A short time after the fall of Atlanta Mr. Davis visited Palmetto and Macon and made speeches at each place. He spoke at Palmetto on the 20th of September, and at Macon on the 22d. Inasmuch as he had relieved Johnston and appointed Hood, and Hood had immediately taken the initiative, it is natural to suppose that Mr. Davis was disappointed with General Johnston's policy. My own judgment is that Johnston acted very wisely: he husbanded his men and saved as much of his territory as he could, without fighting decisive battles in which all might be lost. As Sherman advanced, as I have shown, his army became spread out, until, if this had been continued, it would have been easy to destroy it in detail. I know that both Sherman and I were rejoiced when we heard of the change. Hood was unquestionably a brave, gallant soldier and not destitute of ability; but unfortunately his policy was to fight the enemy wherever he saw him, without thinking much of the consequences of defeat.

In his speeches Mr. Davis denounced Governor Brown, of Georgia, and General Johnston in unmeasured terms, even insinuating that their loyalty to the Southern cause was doubtful. So far as General Johnston is concerned, I think Davis did him a great injustice in this particular. I had known the

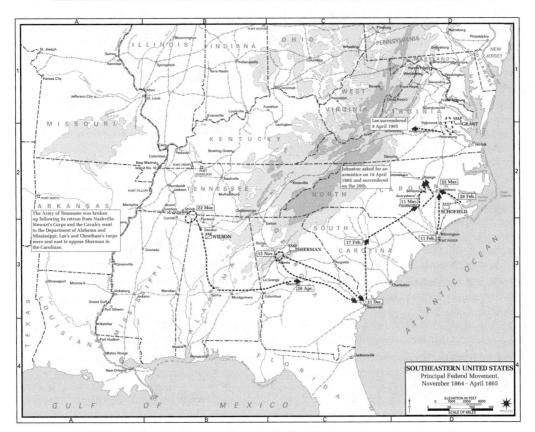

Map of major federal movements, including Sherman's marches through
Georgia and the Carolinas, from November 1864–April 1865. *West Point
Atlas of the Civil War. Courtesy of Department of History, USMA.*

general before the war and strongly believed it would be impossible for him
to accept a high commission for the purpose of betraying the cause he had
espoused. Then, as I have said, I think that his policy was the best one that
could have been pursued by the whole South—protract the war, which was all
that was necessary to enable them to gain recognition in the end. The North
was already growing weary, as the South evidently was also, but with this difference. In the North the people governed, and could stop hostilities whenever they chose to stop supplies. The South was a military camp, controlled
absolutely by the government with soldiers to back it, and the war could have
been protracted, no matter to what extent the discontent reached, up to the
point of open mutiny of the soldiers themselves. Mr. Davis's speeches were
frank appeals to the people of Georgia and that portion of the South to come
to their relief. He tried to assure his frightened hearers that the Yankees were

rapidly digging their own graves; that measures were already being taken to cut them off from supplies from the North; and that with a force in front, and cut off from the rear, they must soon starve in the midst of a hostile people. Papers containing reports of these speeches immediately reached the Northern States, and they were republished. Of course, that caused no alarm so long as telegraphic communication was kept up with Sherman.

When Hood was forced to retreat from Atlanta he moved to the southwest and was followed by a portion of Sherman's army. He soon appeared upon the railroad in Sherman's rear, and with his whole army began destroying the road. At the same time also the work was begun in Tennessee and Kentucky which Mr. Davis had assured his hearers at Palmetto and Macon would take place. He ordered Forrest (about the ablest cavalry general in the South) north for this purpose; and Forrest and Wheeler carried out their orders with more or less destruction, occasionally picking up a garrison. Forrest indeed performed the very remarkable feat of capturing, with cavalry, two gunboats and a number of transports, something the accomplishment of which is very hard to account for.[1] Hood's army had been weakened by Governor Brown's withdrawing the Georgia State troops for the purpose of gathering in the season's crops for the use of the people and for the use of the army. This not only depleted Hood's forces but it served a most excellent purpose in gathering in supplies of food and forage for the use of our army

1. In late October 1864, under orders from Forrest, Abraham Buford concealed batteries close to the mouth of the Big Sandy River, near the old Confederate Fort Heiman, on the opposite shore from Fort Henry, an area Grant knew well from his battles there in 1862. First, Thomas Jordan and J. P. Pryor explain in their 1868 history of Forrest's campaigns, Buford captured the unsuspecting transport *Mazeppa*, "heavily freighted with hard bread, blankets, shoes, clothing, axes, and other military stores" of value to the Confederates. The next day, October 29, Buford disabled another transport, *J. W. Cheeseman*, and forced a third transport, *Venus*, and a federal tin-clad gunboat, *Undine*, to withdraw beyond the bend of the river. Thus protected, the *Undine* began to shell Fort Heiman and attempted to make repairs, while the Confederates moved their artillery and eventually shelled the transport into submission. The surviving crew of the *Undine* abandoned ship, and it fell into Confederate hands: "Crews and officers were detailed from the command for the Undine and Venus," Jordan and Pryor write, "upon both of which the Confederate flag was now floating, to the great delight of the men, none of whom had seen that flag upon an armed vessel since the Confederate gunboats went down to Memphis in 1862." Within a few days, the *Venus*—laden with the stores from the *Mazeppa*—had been retaken, while *Undine* survived a few skirmishes on the Tennessee River before "the short-lived operations of Forrest's Cavalry afloat" came to an end. See Thomas Jordan and J. P. Pryor, *The Campaigns of Lieut.-Gen. N. B. Forrest and the Forrest Cavalry* (New Orleans, LA: Blelock, 1868), 592–99.

in its subsequent march. Sherman was obliged to push on with his force and go himself with portions of it hither and thither, until it was clearly demonstrated to him that with the army he then had it would be impossible to hold the line from Atlanta back and leave him any force whatever with which to take the offensive. Had that plan been adhered to, very large reinforcements would have been necessary; and Mr. Davis's prediction of the destruction of the army would have been realized, or else Sherman would have been obliged to make a successful retreat, which Mr. Davis said in his speeches would prove more disastrous than Napoleon's retreat from Moscow.[2]

---

2. In a speech at Macon on September 23, 1864, Davis tried to rally Georgians: "Our cavalry and our people will harass and destroy his army as did the Cossacks that of Napoleon, and the Yankee General, like him will escape with only a body guard." Speech at Macon, September 23, 1864, transcribed from Macon *Telegraph*, September 24, 1864, *The Papers of Jefferson Davis*, ed. Lynda Lasswell Crist (Baton Rouge: Louisiana State University Press, 2003), 11:61.

None of this came to pass, of course, but Eliza Andrews does record a story heard from a local near Sparta who claimed to be "a rebel soldier" about what might have happened to those of Sherman's bummers (undisciplined parties of foragers) who strayed too far from the main body of troops:

> He told awful tales about the things Sherman's robbers had done; it made my blood boil to hear them, and when the captain asked him if some of the rascals didn't get caught themselves sometimes—stragglers and the like—he answered with a wink that said more than words:
> "Yes; our folks took lots of prisoners; more'n'll ever be heard of agin."
> "What became of them?" asked the lieutenant.
> "Sent 'em to Macon, double quick," was the laconic reply. "Got 'em thar in less'n half an hour."
> "How did they manage it?" continued the lieutenant, in a tone that showed he understood Sam's metaphor.
> "Just took 'em out in the woods and *lost* 'em," he replied, in his jerky, laconic way. "Ever heerd o' *losin'* men, lady?" he added, turning to me, with an air of grim waggery that made my flesh creep—for after all, even Yankees are human beings, though they don't always behave like it.
> "Yes," I said, "I had heard of it, but thought it a horrible thing. . . ."
> I said he ought to be ashamed to tell it; even a Yankee was entitled to protection when a prisoner of war.
> "But these fellows wasn't regular prisoners of war, lady," said the sick soldier; "they were thieves and houseburners,"—and I couldn't but feel there was something in that view of it.

War-Time Diary, 29–31.

One of the most popular, widely translated nineteenth-century accounts of the French retreat from Russia was that of Philippe-Paul de Ségur, aide-de-camp to Napo-

These speeches of Mr. Davis were not long in reaching Sherman. He took advantage of the information they gave, and made all the preparation possible for him to make to meet what now became expected, attempts to break his communications. Something else had to be done: and to Sherman's sensible and soldierly mind the idea was not long in dawning upon him, not only that something else had to be done, but what that something else should be.

On September 10th I telegraphed Sherman as follows:

> CITY POINT, VA.,
> *Sept.* 10, 1864.
>
> MAJOR-GENERAL SHERMAN,
> Atlanta, Georgia.
>
> So soon as your men are sufficiently rested, and preparations can be made, it is desirable that another campaign should be commenced. We want to keep the enemy constantly pressed to the end of the war. If we give him no peace whilst the war lasts, the end cannot be distant. Now that we have all of Mobile Bay that is valuable, I do not know but it will be the best move to transfer Canby's troops to act

---

leon. Here Ségur records the horrors of the first snowstorm and what happened to those soldiers who could not keep pace with the retreating army:

> Most of the stragglers, tempted by the sight of side roads, scattered over the fields in the hope of finding food and shelter from the coming night. But when they had passed that way before, they had left a swath of desolation from fifteen to twenty miles wide. Now they met only armed civilians or Cossacks who fell upon them with ferocious laughter, wounded them, stripped them of everything they had, and left them to perish naked in the snow. These guerrillas, incited by Alexander and Kutuzov, who did not then know how to avenge nobly the country they had been unable to defend, kept abreast of the army on both sides of the road, under cover of the trees. They threw back on the deadly highway the soldiers whom they did not finish off with their spears and axes.
>
> Night came on—a night sixteen hours long! But on this waste of snow where were we to stop, where sit down or rest, where find some root to gnaw on, or dry wood for our fires?

Defeat: Napoleon's Russian Campaign, trans. J. David Townsend (New York: New York Review Books Classics, 2008), 171.

upon Savannah, whilst you move on Augusta. I should like to hear from you, however, in this matter.

U. S. GRANT,
Lieutenant-General.

Sherman replied promptly:

"If I could be sure of finding provisions and ammunition at Augusta, or Columbus, Georgia, I can march to Milledgeville, and compel Hood to give up Augusta or Macon, and then turn on the other. ★ ★ ★ If you can manage to take the Savannah River as high up as Augusta, or the Chattahoochee as far up as Columbus, I can sweep the whole State of Georgia."

On the 12th I sent a special messenger, one of my own staff, with a letter inviting Sherman's views about the next campaign.

CITY POINT, VA.,
Sept. 12, 1864.

MAJOR-GENERAL W. T. SHERMAN,
Commanding Mil. Division of the Mississippi.

I send Lieutenant-Colonel Porter, of my staff, with this. Colonel Porter will explain to you the exact condition of affairs here better than I can do in the limits of a letter.[3] Although I feel myself strong

---

3. Horace Porter, who had never met Sherman, "the famous soldier of the West," was intensely curious:

> As I approached I saw the captor of Atlanta on the porch, sitting tilted back in a large arm-chair, reading a newspaper. His coat was unbuttoned, his black felt hat slouched over his brow, and on his feet were a pair of slippers very much down at the heels. He was in the prime of life and in the perfection of physical health. He was just forty-four years of age, and almost at the summit of his military fame. With his large frame, tall, gaunt form, restless hazel eyes, aquiline nose, bronzed face, and crisp beard, he looked the picture of "grim-visaged war." . . .
>
> . . . He exhibited a strong individuality in every movement, and there was a peculiar energy of manner in uttering the crisp words and epigrammatic phrases which fell from his lips as rapidly as shots from a magazine-gun. I soon realized that he was one of the most dramatic and picturesque characters of the war. . . . He said: "I knew Grant would make the fur fly when he started down through Virginia. Wherever he is the enemy will never find any trouble about getting up a fight. He has all the tenacity of a Scotch terrier. . . . When Grant cried 'Forward!' after

enough for offensive operations, I am holding on quietly to get advantage of recruits and convalescents, who are coming forward very rapidly. My lines are necessarily very long, extending from Deep Bottom north of the James across the peninsula formed by the Appomattox and the James, and south of the Appomattox to the Weldon Road. This line is very strongly fortified, and can be held with comparatively few men, but from its great length takes many in the aggregate. I propose, when I do move, to extend my left so as to control what is known as the South Side, or Lynchburg and Petersburg Road, then if possible to keep the Danville Road cut. At the same time this move is made, I want to send a force of from six to ten thousand men against Wilmington.

The way I propose to do this is to land the men north of Fort Fisher, and hold that point. At the same time a large naval fleet will be assembled there, and the iron-clads will run the batteries as they did at Mobile. This will give us the same control of the harbor of Wilmington that we now have of the harbor of Mobile. What you are to do with the forces at your command, I do not see. The difficulties of supplying your army, except when you are constantly moving, beyond where you are, I plainly see. If it had not been for Price's movements Canby would have sent twelve thousand more men to Mobile. From your command on the Mississippi an equal number could have been taken. With these forces my idea would have been to divide them, sending one half to Mobile and the other half to Savannah. You could then move as proposed in your telegram, so as to threaten Macon and Augusta equally. Whichever was abandoned by the enemy you could take and open up a new base of supplies. My object now in sending a staff officer is not so much to suggest operations for you, as to get your views and have plans matured by the time everything can be got ready. It will probably be the 5th of October before any of the plans herein indicated will be executed.

---

the battle of the Wilderness, I said: 'This is the grandest act of his life; now I feel that the rebellion will be crushed.' I wrote him, saying it was a bold order to give, and full of significance; that it showed the mettle of which he was made, and if Wellington could have heard it he would have jumped out of his boots."

Porter, *Campaigning*, 289–91.

If you have any promotions to recommend, send the names forward and I will approve them. ★ ★ ★

U. S. GRANT,
Lieutenant-General.

This reached Sherman on September 20th.

On the 25th of September Sherman reported to Washington that Hood's troops were in his rear. He had provided against this by sending a division to Chattanooga and a division to Rome, Georgia, which was in the rear of Hood, supposing that Hood would fall back in the direction from which he had come to reach the railroad. At the same time Sherman and Hood kept up a correspondence relative to the exchange of prisoners, the treatment of citizens, and other matters suitable to be arranged between hostile commanders in the field. On the 27th of September I telegraphed Sherman as follows:

CITY POINT, VA.,
September 27, 1864—10.30 A.M.

MAJOR-GENERAL SHERMAN:

I have directed all recruits and new troops from the Western States to be sent to Nashville, to receive their further orders from you. ★ ★ ★

U. S. GRANT,
Lieutenant-General.

On the 29th Sherman sent Thomas back to Chattanooga, and afterwards to Nashville, with another division (Morgan's) of the advanced army. Sherman then suggested that, when he was prepared, his movements should take place against Milledgeville and then to Savannah. His expectation at that time was, to make this movement as soon as he could get up his supplies. Hood was moving in his own country, and was moving light so that he could make two miles to Sherman's one. He depended upon the country to gather his supplies, and so was not affected by delays.

As I have said, until this unexpected state of affairs happened, Mobile had been looked upon as the objective point of Sherman's army. It had been a favorite move of mine from 1862, when I first suggested to the then commander-in-chief that the troops in Louisiana, instead of frittering away their time in the trans-Mississippi, should move against Mobile. I recommended this from time to time until I came into command of the army, the last of March 1864. Having the power in my own hands, I now ordered the concentration of supplies, stores and troops, in the department of the

Gulf about New Orleans, with a view to a move against Mobile, in support of, and in conjunction with, the other armies operating in the field.
Before I came into command, these troops had been scattered over the
trans-Mississippi department in such a way that they could not be, or were
not, gotten back in time to take any part in the original movement; hence
the consideration, which had caused Mobile to be selected as the objective
point for Sherman's army to find his next base of supplies after having cut
loose from Atlanta, no longer existed.[4]

General G. M. Dodge, an exceedingly efficient officer, having been
badly wounded, had to leave the army about the first of October. He was
in command of two divisions of the 16th corps, consolidated into one.
Sherman then divided his army into the right and left wings—the right
commanded by General O. O. Howard and the left by General Slocum.
General Dodge's two divisions were assigned, one to each of these wings.
Howard's command embraced the 15th and 17th corps, and Slocum's the
14th and 20th corps, commanded by Generals Jeff. C. Davis and A. S. Williams. Generals Logan and Blair commanded the two corps composing the

---

4. Farragut had fought the Battle of Mobile Bay that summer. It is the victory with
which he is chiefly identified. There is no evidence that in the heat of the battle he
actually exclaimed: "Damn the torpedoes. Full speed ahead!" Nevertheless, the legend
proved irresistible to the navy, which used it a half-century later for a World War I
recruiting poster.

World War I recruiting poster featuring
Farragut's heroics at the Battle of
Mobile Bay. *Library of Congress, Prints and
Photographs Division, WWI Posters, LC-
USZC4-8136.*

right wing. About this time they left to take part in the presidential election, which took place that year, leaving their corps to Osterhaus and Ransom.[5] I have no doubt that their leaving was at the earnest solicitation of the War Department. General Blair got back in time to resume his command and to proceed with it throughout the march to the sea and back to the grand review at Washington. General Logan did not return to his command until after it reached Savannah.

Logan felt very much aggrieved at the transfer of General Howard from that portion of the Army of the Potomac which was then with the Western Army, to the command of the Army of the Tennessee, with which army General Logan had served from the battle of Belmont to the fall of Atlanta—having passed successively through all grades from colonel commanding a regiment to general commanding a brigade, division and army corps, until upon the death of McPherson the command of the entire Army of the Tennessee devolved upon him in the midst of a hotly contested battle. He conceived that he had done his full duty as commander in that engagement; and I can bear testimony, from personal observation, that he had proved himself fully equal to all the lower positions which he had occupied as a soldier. I will not pretend to question the motive which actuated Sherman in taking an officer from another army to supersede General Logan. I have no doubt, whatever, that he did this for what he considered would be to the good of the service, which was more important than that the personal feelings of any individual should not be aggrieved; though I doubt whether he had an officer with him who could have filled the place as Logan would have done. Differences of opinion must exist between the best of friends as to policies in war, and of judgment as to men's fitness. The officer who has the command, however, should be allowed to judge of the fitness of the officers under him, unless he is very manifestly wrong.

Sherman's army, after all the depletions, numbered about sixty thousand effective men. All weak men had been left to hold the rear, and those remaining were not only well men, but strong and hardy, so that he had sixty thousand as good soldiers as ever trod the earth; better than any European soldiers, because they not only worked like a machine but the machine thought. European armies know very little what they are fighting for, and care less.[6] Included in these sixty thousand troops, there were two small

5. Political generals were essential recruiters of voters as well as soldiers.

6. This is a prime example of Grant's esteem for American soldiers in contrast to the conscripts of European armies. More sinister versions of Grant's metaphor of a "think-

divisions of cavalry, numbering altogether about four thousand men. Hood had about thirty-five to forty thousand men, independent of Forrest, whose forces were operating in Tennessee and Kentucky, as Mr. Davis had promised they should. This part of Mr. Davis's military plan was admirable, and promised the best results of anything he could have done, according to my judgment. I say this because I have criticised his military judgment in the removal of Johnston, and also in the appointment of Hood. I am aware, however, that there was high feeling existing at that time between Davis and his subordinate, whom I regarded as one of his ablest lieutenants.

On the 5th of October the railroad back from Atlanta was again very badly broken, Hood having got on the track with his army. Sherman saw after night, from a high point, the road burning for miles. The defence of the railroad by our troops was very gallant, but they could not hold points between their intrenched positions against Hood's whole army; in fact they made no attempt to do so; but generally the intrenched positions were held, as well as important bridges, and stores located at them. Allatoona, for instance, was defended by a small force of men under the command of General Corse, one of the very able and efficient volunteer officers produced by the war. He, with a small force, was cut off from the remainder of the National army and was attacked with great vigor by many times his own number. Sherman from his high position could see the battle raging, with the Confederate troops between him and his subordinate. He sent men, of course, to raise the temporary siege, but the time that would be necessarily consumed in reaching Corse, would be so great that all occupying the intrenchments might be dead. Corse was a man who would never surrender. From a high position some of Sherman's signal corps discovered a signal flag waving from a hole in the block house at Allatoona. It was from Corse. He had been shot through the face, but he signalled to his chief a message which left no doubt of his determination to hold his post at all hazards. It was at this point probably, that Sherman first realized that with the forces at his disposal,

---

ing machine" can be found in contemporary writers like Melville and Thoreau as well as in the novelist E. L. Doctorow's 2005 novel *The March*, in which he created a haunting vision of Sherman's army as a "floating world" sufficient unto itself. "Imagine a great segmented body moving in contractions and dilations at a rate of twelve or fifteen miles a day," explains a Union surgeon in Doctorow's novel, "a creature of a hundred thousand feet. It is tubular in its being and tentacled to the roads and bridges over which it travels. It sends out as antennae its men on horses. It consumes everything in its path. It is an immense organism, this army, with a small brain. That would be General Sherman, whom I have never seen." *The March* (New York: Random House, 2005), 61–62.

the keeping open of his line of communications with the North would be impossible if he expected to retain any force with which to operate offensively beyond Atlanta. He proposed, therefore, to destroy the roads back to Chattanooga, when all ready to move, and leave the latter place garrisoned. Yet, before abandoning the railroad, it was necessary that he should repair damages already done, and hold the road until he could get forward such supplies, ordnance stores and small rations, as he wanted to carry with him on his proposed march, and to return to the north his surplus artillery; his object being to move light and to have no more artillery than could be used to advantage on the field.[7]

Sherman thought Hood would follow him, though he proposed to prepare for the contingency of the latter moving the other way while he was moving south, by making Thomas strong enough to hold Tennessee and Kentucky. I, myself, was thoroughly satisfied that Hood would go north, as he did. On the 2d of November I telegraphed Sherman authorizing him definitely to move according to the plan he had proposed: that is, cutting loose from his base, giving up Atlanta and the railroad back to Chattanooga. To strengthen Thomas he sent Stanley (4th corps) back, and also ordered Schofield, commanding the Army of the Ohio, twelve thousand strong, to report to him. In addition to this, A. J. Smith, who, with two divisions of Sherman's army, was in Missouri aiding Rosecrans in driving the enemy from that State, was under orders to return to Thomas and, under the most unfavorable circumstances, might be expected to arrive there long before Hood could reach Nashville.

In addition to this, the new levies of troops that were being raised in the North-west went to Thomas as rapidly as enrolled and equipped. Thomas, without any of these additions spoken of, had a garrison at Chattanooga—which had been strengthened by one division—and garrisons at Bridgeport, Stevenson, Decatur, Murfreesboro, and Florence. There were already with him in Nashville ten thousand soldiers in round numbers, and many thousands of employees in the quartermaster's and other departments who could be put in the intrenchments in front of Nashville, for its defence. Also, Wilson was there with ten thousand dismounted cavalrymen, who were

---

7. Sherman telegraphed Grant from Allatoona on the evening of October 9: "Until we can repopulate Georgia, it is useless to occupy it, but the utter destruction of its roads, houses, and people will cripple their military resources. By attempting to hold the roads we will lose a thousand men monthly, and will gain no result. I can make the march, and make Georgia howl." *OR*, ser. 1, vol. 39, pt. 3, 162.

being equipped for the field. Thomas had at this time about forty-five thousand men without any of the reinforcements here above enumerated. These reinforcements gave him altogether about seventy thousand men, without counting what might be added by the new levies already spoken of.

About this time Beauregard arrived upon the field, not to supersede Hood in command, but to take general charge over the entire district in which Hood and Sherman were, or might be, operating. He made the most frantic appeals to the citizens for assistance to be rendered in every way: by sending reinforcements, by destroying supplies on the line of march of the invaders, by destroying the bridges over which they would have to cross, and by, in every way, obstructing the roads to their front. But it was hard to convince the people of the propriety of destroying supplies which were so much needed by themselves, and each one hoped that his own possessions might escape.

Hood soon started north, and went into camp near Decatur, Alabama, where he remained until the 29th of October, but without making an attack on the garrison of that place.

The Tennessee River was patrolled by gunboats, from Muscle Shoals east; and, also, below the second shoals out to the Ohio River. These, with the troops that might be concentrated from the garrisons along the river at any point where Hood might choose to attempt to cross, made it impossible for him to cross the Tennessee at any place where it was navigable. But Muscle Shoals is not navigable, and below them again is another shoal which also obstructs navigation.[8] Hood therefore moved down to a point nearly opposite Florence, Alabama, crossed over and remained there for some time, collecting supplies of food, forage and ammunition. All of these had to come from a considerable distance south, because the region in which he was then situated was mountainous, with small valleys which produced but little, and what they had produced had long since been exhausted. On the 1st of November I suggested to Sherman, and also asked his views thereon, the propriety of destroying Hood before he started on his campaign.

---

8. Today Muscle Shoals is better known for its role in the history of popular music than for its wartime significance on the Tennessee River. During the 1960s and 1970s, artists came to various studios in the area and created what came to be called the Muscle Shoals sound. Songs recorded there include Wilson Pickett's "Land of 1,000 Dances," Percy Sledge's "When a Man Loves a Woman," Etta James's "Tell Mama," Aretha Franklin's "I Never Loved a Man (The Way I Love You)," the Rolling Stones' "Wild Horses," the Staples Singers' "I'll Take You There," Paul Simon's "Kodachrome," and Lynyrd Skynyrd's "What's Your Name."

On the 2d of November, as stated, I approved definitely his making his proposed campaign through Georgia, leaving Hood behind to the tender mercy of Thomas and the troops in his command. Sherman fixed the 10th of November as the day of starting.

Sherman started on that day to get back to Atlanta, and on the 15th the real march to the sea commenced. The right wing, under Howard, and the cavalry went to Jonesboro, Milledgeville, then the capital of Georgia, being Sherman's objective or stopping place on the way to Savannah.[9] The left

---

9. The *New York Times* published a celebratory dispatch about Sherman's march to the coast declaring, "his tired but triumphant army may, after an anabasis shorter but more wonderful than that led by XENOPHON, begin like those old Greeks, to shout, 'The Sea! the Sea!'" "The Great March," *New York Times*, December 3, 1864, p. 4.

In 401–399 BCE Xenophon led an army of ten thousand Greek mercenaries on an arduous, fighting march—the anabasis ("expedition up from")—across hostile Persian territory and ultimately to the Black Sea, the sight of which they greeted with the cry alluded to in the *Times* dispatch:

> They came to the mountains on the fifth day. . . . When the men in front reached the summit and caught sight of the sea there was great shouting. Xenophon and the rearguard heard it and thought that there were some more enemies attacking in the front. . . . However, when the shouting got louder and drew nearer . . . it looked then as though this was something of considerable importance. So Xenophon mounted his horse and, taking Lycus and the cavalry with him, rode forward to give support, and, quite soon, they heard the soldiers shouting out "The sea! The sea!" and passing the word down the column.

Xenophon, *The Persian Expedition*, trans. Rex Warner, ed. George Cawkwell (New York: Penguin Classics, 1972), 210–11.

Jaroslav Hašek used the conceit of the anabasis to comic effect in his novel of World War I, *The Good Soldier Švejk*. The clueless protagonist, having been left behind by his regiment, is ordered to rejoin it at a town called České Budějovice:

> And God knows how it happened, but the good soldier Švejk instead of going south to Budějovice went on marching straight to the west.
>
> He trudged through the snow along the road in the frost wrapped up in his military greatcoat, like the last of Napoleon's old guard returning from the Moscow campaign, with the only difference that he sang merrily to himself. . . .
>
> Xenophon . . . travelled through the whole of Asia Minor and got to God knows where without any maps at all. . . . Marching forward all the time is what is called an anabasis: penetrating into unknown regions: being cut off by enemies who are waiting for the first convenient opportunity to wring your neck. . . .

wing moved to Stone Mountain, along roads much farther east than those taken by the right wing. Slocum was in command, and threatened Augusta as the point to which he was moving, but he was to turn off and meet the right wing at Milledgeville.

Atlanta was destroyed so far as to render it worthless for military purposes before starting, Sherman himself remaining over a day to superintend the work, and see that it was well done. Sherman's orders for this campaign were perfect. Before starting, he had sent back all sick, disabled and weak men, retaining nothing but the hardy, well-inured soldiers to accompany him on his long march in prospect. His artillery was reduced to sixty-five guns. The ammunition carried with them was two hundred rounds for musket and gun. Small rations were taken in a small wagon train, which was loaded to its capacity for rapid movement. The army was expected to live on the country, and to always keep the wagons full of forage and provisions against a possible delay of a few days.

The troops, both of the right and left wings, made most of their advance along the line of railroads, which they destroyed. The method adopted to perform this work, was to burn and destroy all the bridges and culverts, and for a long distance, at places, to tear up the track and bend the rails. Soldiers to do this rapidly would form a line along one side of the road with crowbars and poles, place these under the rails and, hoisting all at once, turn over many rods of road at one time. The ties would then be placed in piles, and the rails, as they were loosened, would be carried and put across these log heaps. When a sufficient number of rails were placed upon a pile of ties it would be set on fire. This would heat the rails very much more in the middle, that being over the main part of the fire, than at the ends, so that they would naturally bend of their own weight; but the soldiers, to increase the damage, would take tongs and, one or two men at each end of the rail, carry it with force against the nearest tree and twist it around, thus leaving rails forming bands to ornament the forest trees of Georgia. All this work was going on

---

Caesar's Roman legions . . . had no maps either. Once they said they would march back to Rome again by another route so that they could get more out of it. And they got there too. And it is obviously from that time that people say that all roads lead to Rome.

And all roads lead to České Budějovice too. The good soldier Švejk was fully convinced.

The Good Soldier Švejk and His Fortunes in the World War, trans. Cecil Parrott (London: Penguin, 1974), 239–41.

at the same time, there being a sufficient number of men detailed for that purpose. Some piled the logs and built the fire; some put the rails upon the fire; while others would bend those that were sufficiently heated: so that, by the time the last bit of road was torn up, that it was designed to destroy at a certain place, the rails previously taken up were already destroyed.

The organization for supplying the army was very complete. Each brigade furnished a company to gather supplies of forage and provisions for the command to which they belonged. Strict injunctions were issued against pillaging, or otherwise unnecessarily annoying the people; but everything in shape of food for man and forage for beast was taken. The supplies were turned over to the brigade commissary and quartermaster, and were issued by them to their respective commands precisely the same as if they had been purchased. The captures consisted largely of cattle, sheep, poultry, some bacon, cornmeal, often molasses, and occasionally coffee or other small rations.[10]

The skill of these men, called by themselves and the army "bummers," in collecting their loads and getting back to their respective commands,

---

10. The Georgia diarist Dolly Sumner Lunt accused Sherman's bummers of "wantonly" destroying her home. Her journal contains essential elements of the plantation myth that would come to dominate postwar memory, including the docile, childlike devotion of slaves to their masters, the superiority of the old plantation ways, and the unremitting savagery of Union soldiers:

> Alas! little did I think while trying to save my house from plunder and fire that they were forcing my boys from home at the point of the bayonet.
> . . .
> . . . I had not believed they would force from their homes the poor, doomed negroes, but such has been the fact here, cursing them and saying that "Jeff Davis wanted to put them in his army, but that they should not fight for him, but for the Union." No! Indeed no! They are not friends to the slave. We have never made the poor, cowardly negro fight, and it is strange, passing strange, that the all-powerful Yankee nation with the whole world to back them, their ports open, their armies filled with soldiers from all nations, should at last take the poor negro to help them out against this little Confederacy which was to have been brought back into the Union in sixty days' time!
> My poor boys! My poor boys! What unknown trials are before you! How you have clung to your mistress and assisted her in every way you knew.

A Woman's Wartime Journal, ed. Julian Street (New York: Century, 1918), 24–26.

Adolph Metzner, Chicken thieves being disciplined by General
Alexander McDowell McCook, Camp Nevin, Kentucky,
November 1861. Grant's celebration of the bummers' exploits
shows how much the war had evolved since the early days when
the same actions would have been matter for punishment. *Library
of Congress, Prints and Photographs, LC-DIG-ppmsca-51208.*

was marvellous.[11] When they started out in the morning, they were always
on foot; but scarcely one of them returned in the evening without being
mounted on a horse or mule. These would be turned in for the general use of
the army, and the next day these men would start out afoot and return again
in the evening mounted.

Many of the exploits of these men would fall under the head of romance;
indeed, I am afraid that in telling some of their experiences, the romance
got the better of the truth upon which the story was founded, and that, in
the way many of these anecdotes are told, very little of the foundation is left.

---

11. In *The March* Doctorow imagines the activities of the bummers from the perspective
of a Union officer:

> The men now took it upon themselves to explore the house and see what they
> could find for their amusement. Impatient as he was to get moving, Clarke
> knew better than not to go along. . . . In the great mass of men that was an
> army, strange currents of willfulness and self-expression flowed within the
> structure of military discipline. The best officers knew when to look aside.
> Even the generals issued orders for the sake of the record only. . . . His bum-
> mers liked their independence. They liked to benefit themselves, and they
> could do so with impunity, because their takings were crucial to the success
> of an army designed by General Sherman to live, unencumbered, off the land.

The March, 11–12.

I suspect that most of them consist chiefly of the fiction added to make the stories better.[12] In one instance it was reported that a few men of Sherman's army passed a house where they discovered some chickens under the dwelling. They immediately proceeded to capture them, to add to the army's supplies. The lady of the house, who happened to be at home, made piteous appeals to have these spared, saying they were a few she had put away to save by permission of other parties who had preceded and who had taken all the others that she had. The soldiers seemed moved at her appeal; but looking at the chickens again they were tempted and one of them replied: "The rebellion must be suppressed if it takes the last chicken in the Confederacy," and proceeded to appropriate the last one.

Another anecdote characteristic of these times has been told. The South,

---

12. Grant's relentless demythologizing seems to belong less to the nineteenth than to the twentieth century. It finds many echoes in post–World War I writing. Joseph Roth's 1932 novel *The Radetsky March* opens with a vignette that emblematizes the period's disillusion. Captain Trotta, who has become a convenient exemplar of military heroism in the Austro-Hungarian Empire for saving the Emperor's life at the Battle of Solferino, happens to read of his exploits in his young son's elementary school reading primer only to discover that his actions have been "grossly misrepresented," embellished, and fictionalized. When he complains to an acquaintance, he is told, "you're taking it too seriously. Remember, it's for children. . . . Children need examples which they can understand, which impress them. They can learn later what actually occurred." In his quest for the truth, Trotta takes his case first to the Minister of Culture and Education, who protests, "It is the heartfelt aim of . . . our education authorities to set before the pupils of the Monarchy deeds of value of all arms in such a fashion as may seem adaptable to the child's character and imagination . . . ; yet at the same time eschewing a bare, dry style of narrative, devoid of imaginative stimulus or lacking incentive to patriotic feelings." Undeterred, the captain then takes his case all the way to the Emperor:

> "Look here, my dear Trotta," said the Emperor, "it's a bit awkward, but you know, neither of us shows up too badly in the story. Forget it."
> "Your Majesty," replied the Captain, "it's a lie."
> "A great many lies are told," agreed the Emperor.
> I can't forget it, Your Majesty," gulped out the Captain.
> The Emperor moved closer to him. He was not much taller than Trotta. Their eyes met.
> "My ministers," said Francis Joseph, "know what they're doing, and I am obliged to rely on them. Do you understand, my dear Captain Trotta?" then, after a silence, "We'll do something about it, you'll see."

The lesson is subsequently deleted from the schoolbooks, and Trotta's story is thereafter confined to the regimental records. See *The Radetsky March*, trans. Eva Tucker (Woodstock, NY: Overlook Press, 1974), 8–10.

prior to the rebellion, kept bloodhounds to pursue runaway slaves who took refuge in the neighboring swamps, and also to hunt convicts. Orders were issued to kill all these animals as they were met with. On one occasion a soldier picked up a poodle, the favorite pet of its mistress, and was carrying it off to execution when the lady made a strong appeal to him to spare it. The soldier replied, "Madam, our orders are to kill every bloodhound." "But this is not a bloodhound," said the lady. "Well, madam, we cannot tell what it will grow into if we leave it behind," said the soldier as he went off with it.

Notwithstanding these anecdotes, and the necessary hardship they would seem to imply, I do not believe there was much unwarrantable pillaging considering that we were in the enemy's territory and without any supplies except such as the country afforded.

On the 23d Sherman, with the left wing, reached Milledgeville. The right wing was not far off: but proceeded on its way towards Savannah destroying the road as it went. The troops at Milledgeville remained over a day to destroy factories, buildings used for military purposes, etc., before resuming its march.

The governor, who had been almost defying Mr. Davis before this, now fled precipitately, as did the legislature of the State and all the State officers. The governor, Sherman says, was careful to carry away even his garden vegetables, while he left the archives of the State to fall into our hands. The only military force that was opposed to Sherman's forward march was the Georgia militia, a division under the command of General G. W. Smith, and a battalion under Harry Wayne. Neither the quality of the forces nor their numbers was sufficient to even retard the progress of Sherman's army.

The people at the South became so frantic at this time at the successful invasion of Georgia that they took the cadets from the military college and added them to the ranks of the militia. They even liberated the State convicts under promise from them that they would serve in the army. I have but little doubt that the worst acts that were attributed to Sherman's army were committed by these convicts, and by other Southern people who ought to have been under sentence—such people as could be found in every community, North and South—who took advantage of their country being invaded to commit crime. They were in but little danger of detection, or of arrest even if detected.

The Southern papers in commenting upon Sherman's movements pictured him as in the most deplorable condition: stating that his men were starving, that they were demoralized and wandering about almost without object, aiming only to reach the sea coast and get under the protection of our navy. These papers got to the North and had more or less effect upon the minds of the people, causing much distress to all loyal persons—particularly to those who had husbands, sons or brothers with Sherman. Mr. Lincoln seeing these accounts, had a letter written asking me if I could give him anything that he could say to the loyal people that would comfort them. I told him there was not the slightest occasion for alarm; that with 60,000 such men as Sherman had with him, such a commanding officer as he was could not be cut off in the open country. He might possibly be prevented from reaching the point he had started out to reach, but he would get through somewhere and would finally get to his chosen destination: and even if worst came to worst he could return North. I heard afterwards of Mr. Lincoln's saying, to those who would inquire of him as to what he thought about the safety of Sherman's army, that Sherman was all right: "Grant says they are safe with such a general, and that if they cannot get out where they want to, they can crawl back by the hole they went in at."

While at Milledgeville the soldiers met at the State House, organized a legislature, and proceeded to business precisely as if they were the legislative body belonging to the State of Georgia. The debates were exciting, and were upon the subject of the situation the South was in at that time, particularly the State of Georgia. They went so far as to repeal, after a spirited and acrimonious debate, the ordinance of secession.[13]

The next day (24th) Sherman continued his march, going by the way of Waynesboro and Louisville, Millen being the next objective and where the two columns (the right and left wings) were to meet. The left wing moved to the left of the direct road, and the cavalry still farther off so as to make it look as though Augusta was the point they were aiming for. They moved on all the roads they could find leading in that direction. The cavalry was sent to make a rapid march in hope of surprising Millen before the Union prisoners could be carried away; but they failed in this.

The distance from Milledgeville to Millen was about one hundred miles. At this point Wheeler, who had been ordered from Tennessee, arrived and swelled the numbers and efficiency of the troops confronting Sherman. Hardee, a native of Georgia, also came, but brought no troops with him. It

13. Sherman learned from the citizens of Milledgeville that the governor and legislature had "ignominiously fled, in the utmost disorder and confusion." He made his headquarters in the abandoned governor's mansion, which, according to Sherman, the previous resident "had hastily stripped . . . of carpets, curtains, and furniture of all sorts . . . even the cabbages and vegetables from his kitchen and cellar—leaving behind muskets, ammunition, and the public archives." *Memoirs*, 2:188.

was intended that he should raise as large an army as possible with which to intercept Sherman's march. He did succeed in raising some troops, and with these and those under the command of Wheeler and Wayne, had an army sufficient to cause some annoyance but no great detention. Our cavalry and Wheeler's had a pretty severe engagement, in which Wheeler was driven towards Augusta, thus giving the idea that Sherman was probably making for that point.

Millen was reached on the 3d of December, and the march was resumed the following day for Savannah, the final objective. Bragg had now been sent to Augusta with some troops. Wade Hampton was there also trying to raise cavalry sufficient to destroy Sherman's army. If he ever raised a force it was too late to do the work expected of it. Hardee's whole force probably numbered less than ten thousand men.

From Millen to Savannah the country is sandy and poor, and affords but very little forage other than rice straw, which was then growing. This answered a very good purpose as forage, and the rice grain was an addition to the soldier's rations. No further resistance worthy of note was met with, until within a few miles of Savannah. This place was found to be intrenched and garrisoned. Sherman proceeded at once on his arrival to invest the place, and found that the enemy had placed torpedoes in the ground, which were to explode when stepped on by man or beast. One of these exploded under an officer's horse, blowing the animal to pieces and tearing one of the legs of the officer so badly that it had to be amputated.[14] Sherman at once ordered his

---

14. Landmines in Georgia, trench warfare in Virginia, death on an unprecedented scale—none of this was easy to reconcile with inherited understandings of heroic warfare, which would be dealt a further blow in the mechanized slaughter of the Western Front early in the next century. Jean Renoir, who chronicled the collision between the chivalric commitments of aristocratic army officers and the realities of the World War I battlefield in his masterful film *Grand Illusion* (1937), begins his biography of his father, the painter Auguste Renoir, with the story of his own homecoming after a sniper does him "the favor" of shooting him in the leg. Renoir the elder, having no truck with heroic ideals, enjoyed his son's more "absurd" war stories. One story which "particularly amused" Renoir *père* concerned a cavalry patrol:

> From the top of a hill we caught sight of half a dozen or so Uhlans, also patrolling. We deployed in battle formation, each man taking his stand at twenty yards' distance from the next and bracing his lance, while the Uhlans on the opposite hill did the same. . . . We felt as though we were back in the time of François I, at the Battle of Marignan. The space between us narrowed. We could make out the expressions on the drawn faces of our adversaries under their chapskas, just as they could ours,

under our helmets. In a few seconds the affair was over. In spite of our spurring them on and jerking the bridles, our horses showed little desire to be run through, and veered away, taking us out of range of the opposing lances. The two patrols rushed past each other at a furious pace, treating a few grazing sheep to a brilliant if harmless display of horsemanship. Somewhat crestfallen we returned to our lines, and the Germans went back to theirs.

Jean Renoir, *Renoir, My Father*, trans. Randolph and Dorothy Weaver (1962; New York: New York Review Books, 2001), 3–5.

World War I–era fighter planes. *Library of Congress, Prints and Photographs, LC-DIG-ppmsca-40045.*

Only in aerial combat, as Renoir suggests in *Grand Illusion*, did the old codes— the sense of war as high-stakes sport—persist. *New York World* reporter Herbert Bayard Swope discerned the code in an encounter between a downed English pilot and the German ace Oswald Boelcke. The piece is tellingly titled "Boelcke, Knight of the Air":

> Boelcke outguessed, outmanœvered, and outshot the Englishman, who dropped safely to the ground after having a wing broken. Boelcke landed near him, and in surrendering, the Englishman asked the name of his captor.
>
> "Boelcke," replied the German.
>
> The chagrin and humiliation of defeat and capture were forgotten for a moment as the Englishman put out his hand and, as Boelcke shook it, said:
>
> "If I had to be shot down, I am glad it was by so good a man."
>
> Wilson was sent back to Cambrai. The next day Boelcke invited him to lunch with the officers at the flying park, where the captured flier expressed appreciation of the exceptional treatment he had received and told of the high regard in which the English held the German fliers. That night he was sent to a German prison camp.

Inside the German Empire, in the Third Year of the War (London: Constable, 1917), 186–87.

prisoners to the front, moving them in a compact body in advance, to either explode the torpedoes or dig them up. No further explosion took place.[15]

On the 10th of December the siege of Savannah commenced. Sherman then, before proceeding any further with operations for the capture of the place, started with some troops to open communication with our fleet, which he expected to find in the lower harbor or as near by as the forts of the enemy would permit. In marching to the coast he encountered Fort McAllister, which it was necessary to reduce before the supplies he might find on shipboard could be made available. Fort McAllister was soon captured by an assault made by General Hazen's division. Communication was

---

15. In his *Memoirs* Sherman revealed both his rage and its consequences:

> On the 8th, as I rode along, I found the column turned out of the main road, marching through the fields. Close by, in the corner of a fence, was a group of men standing around a handsome young officer, whose foot had been blown to pieces by a torpedo planted in the road. He was waiting for a surgeon to amputate his leg, and told me that he was riding along with the rest of his brigade-staff of the Seventeenth Corps, when a torpedo trodden on by his horse had exploded, killing the horse and literally blowing off all the flesh from one of his legs. I saw the terrible wound, and made full inquiry into the facts. There had been no resistance at that point, nothing to give warning of danger, and the rebels had planted eight-inch shells in the road, with friction-matches to explode them by being trodden on. This was not war, but murder, and it made me very angry. I immediately ordered a lot of rebel prisoners to be brought from the provost-guard, armed with picks and spades, and made them march in close order along the road, so as to explode their own torpedoes, or to discover and dig them up. They begged hard, but I reiterated the order, and could hardly help laughing at their stepping so gingerly along the road, where it was supposed sunken torpedoes might explode at each step, but they found no other torpedoes till near Fort McAllister.

Memoirs, 2:194.

Both sides made use of human shields. The South used prisoners of war—especially black prisoners—in this way. Sherman and Hood exposed civilians freely to the hazards of war. See Harry S. Stout, *Upon the Altar of the Nation: A Moral History of the Civil War* (New York: Penguin, 2006).

Rule 97 of the Geneva Convention prohibits the use of human shields: the Third Convention of 1929 prohibited the use of prisoners of war in this way, while the Fourth Convention of 1949 added civilians to the prohibition. The practice is punishable as a war crime by the International Criminal Court. For a powerful cinematic representation of the Nazis' use of French civilians as hostages and shields and of the practice of killing in reprisal for sabotage, see *The Train* (1964), directed by John Frankenheimer and starring Burt Lancaster and Paul Scofield.

then established with the fleet. The capture of Savannah then only occupied a few days, and involved no great loss of life. The garrison, however, as we shall see, was enabled to escape by crossing the river and moving eastward.

When Sherman had opened communication with the fleet he found there a steamer, which I had forwarded to him, carrying the accumulated mails for his army, also supplies which I supposed he would be in need of. General J. G. Foster, who commanded all the troops south of North Carolina on the Atlantic sea-board, visited General Sherman before he had opened communication with the fleet, with the view of ascertaining what assistance he could be to him. Foster returned immediately to his own head-quarters at Hilton Head, for the purpose of sending Sherman siege guns, and also if he should find he had them to spare, supplies of clothing, hard bread, etc., thinking that these articles might not be found outside. The mail on the steamer which I sent down, had been collected by Colonel A. H. Markland of the Post Office Department, who went in charge of it. On this same vessel I sent an officer of my staff (Lieutenant Dunn) with the following letter to General Sherman:

CITY POINT, VA.,
Dec. 3, 1864.

MAJOR-GENERAL W. T. SHERMAN,
Commanding Armies near Savannah, Ga.

The little information gleaned from the Southern press, indicating no great obstacle to your progress, I have directed your mails (which had been previously collected at Baltimore by Colonel Markland, Special Agent of the Post Office Department) to be sent as far as the blockading squadron off Savannah, to be forwarded to you as soon as heard from on the coast.

Not liking to rejoice before the victory is assured, I abstain from congratulating you and those under your command, until bottom has been struck. I have never had a fear, however, for the result.

Since you left Atlanta, no very great progress has been made here. The enemy has been closely watched though, and prevented from detaching against you. I think not one man has gone from here, except some twelve or fifteen hundred dismounted cavalry. Bragg has gone from Wilmington. I am trying to take advantage of his absence to get possession of that place. Owing to some preparations Admiral Porter and General Butler are making to blow up Fort Fisher (which, while hoping for the best, I do not believe a particle in), there is a delay in getting this expedition off. I hope they will be ready to start by the 7th, and that Bragg will not have started back by that time.

In this letter I do not intend to give you anything like directions for future action, but will state a general idea I have, and will get your views after you have established yourself on the sea-coast. With your veteran army I hope to get control of the only two through routes from east to west possessed by the enemy before the fall of Atlanta. The condition will be filled by holding Savannah and Augusta, or by holding any other port to the east of Savannah and Branchville. If Wilmington falls, a force from there can co-operate with you.

Thomas has got back into the defences of Nashville, with Hood close upon him. Decatur has been abandoned, and so have all the roads except the main one leading to Chattanooga. Part of this falling back was undoubtedly necessary and all of it may have been. It did not look so, however, to me. In my opinion, Thomas far outnumbers Hood in infantry. In cavalry, Hood has the advantage in *morale* and numbers. I hope yet that Hood will be badly crippled if not destroyed. The general news you will learn from the papers better than I could give it.

After all becomes quiet, and roads become so bad up here that there is likely to be a week or two when nothing can be done, I will run down the coast to see you. If you desire it, I will ask Mrs. Sherman to go with me.

> Yours truly,
> U. S. GRANT,
> Lieutenant-General.

I quote this letter because it gives the reader a full knowledge of the events of that period.

Sherman now (the 15th) returned to Savannah to complete its investment and insure the surrender of the garrison. The country about Savannah is low and marshy, and the city was well intrenched from the river above to the river below; and assaults could not be made except along a comparatively narrow causeway. For this reason assaults must have resulted in serious destruction of life to the Union troops, with the chance of failing altogether. Sherman therefore decided upon a complete investment of the place. When he believed this investment completed, he summoned the garrison to surrender. General Hardee, who was in command, replied in substance that the condition of affairs was not such as Sherman had described. He said he was in full communication with his department and was receiving supplies constantly.

Hardee, however, was cut off entirely from all communication with the west side of the river, and by the river itself to the north and south. On the South Carolina side the country was all rice fields, through which it would have been impossible to bring supplies—so that Hardee had no possible communication with the outside world except by a dilapidated plank road starting from the west bank of the river. Sherman, receiving this reply, proceeded in person to a point on the coast, where General Foster had troops stationed under General Hatch, for the purpose of making arrangements with the latter officer to go through by one of the numerous channels running inland along that part of the coast of South Carolina, to the plank road which General Hardee still possessed, and thus to cut him off from the last means he had of getting supplies, if not of communication.

While arranging for this movement, and before the attempt to execute the plan had been commenced, Sherman received information through one of his staff officers that the enemy had evacuated Savannah the night before. This was the night of the 21st of December. Before evacuating the place Hardee had blown up the navy yard. Some iron-clads had been destroyed, as well as other property that might have been valuable to us; but he left an immense amount of stores untouched, consisting of cotton, railroad cars, workshops, numerous pieces of artillery, and several thousand stands of small arms.

A little incident occurred, soon after the fall of Savannah, which Sherman relates in his Memoirs, and which is worthy of repetition. Savannah was one of the points where blockade runners entered. Shortly after the city fell into our possession, a blockade runner came sailing up serenely, not doubting but the Confederates were still in possession. It was not molested, and the captain did not find out his mistake until he had tied up and gone to the Custom House, where he found a new occupant of the building, and made a less profitable disposition of his vessel and cargo than he had expected.[16]

---

16. Here is Sherman's account of the episode:

> The Savannah River was found to be badly obstructed by torpedoes, and by log piers stretched across the channel below the city, which piers were filled with the cobble stones that formerly paved the streets. Admiral Dahlgren was extremely active, visited me repeatedly in the city, while his fleet still watched Charleston, and all the avenues, for the blockade-runners

As there was some discussion as to the authorship of Sherman's march to the sea, by critics of his book when it appeared before the public, I want to state here that no question upon that subject was ever raised between General Sherman and myself. Circumstances made the plan on which Sherman expected to act impracticable, and as commander of the forces he necessarily had to devise a new one which would give more promise of success: consequently he recommended the destruction of the railroad back to Chattanooga, and that he should be authorized then to move, as he did, from Atlanta forward. His suggestions were finally approved, although they did not immediately find favor in Washington. Even when it came to the time of starting, the greatest apprehension, as to the propriety of the campaign he was about to commence, filled the mind of the President, induced no doubt by his advisers. This went so far as to move the President to ask me to suspend Sherman's march for a day or two until I could think the matter over. My recollection is, though I find no record to show it, that out of deference to the President's wish I did send a dispatch to Sherman asking him to wait a day or two, or else the connections between us were already cut so that I could not do so. However this may be, the question of who devised the plan of march from Atlanta to Savannah is easily answered: it was clearly Sherman, and to him also belongs the credit of its brilliant execution. It was hardly possible that any one else than those on the spot could have devised a new plan of campaign to supersede one that did not promise success.[17]

I was in favor of Sherman's plan from the time it was first submitted to me. My chief of staff, however, was very bitterly opposed to it and, as I learned subsequently, finding that he could not move me, he appealed to the authorities at Washington to stop it.

---

that infested the coast, which were notoriously owned and managed by Englishmen, who used the island of New Providence (Nassau) as a sort of entrepot. One of these small blockade-runners came into Savannah after we were in full possession, and the master did not discover his mistake till he came ashore to visit the custom-house. Of course his vessel fell a prize to the navy. A heavy force was at once set to work to remove the torpedoes and obstructions in the main channel of the river, and, from that time forth, Savannah became the great depot of supply for the troops operating in that quarter.

Memoirs, 2:218–19.

17. A note in the first edition directs readers to consult the October 11 letters included in Grant's official report. See Appendix 2.

The Battle of Franklin—The Battle of Nashville

As we have seen, Hood succeeded in crossing the Tennessee River between Muscle Shoals and the lower shoals at the end of October, 1864. Thomas sent Schofield with the 4th and 23d corps, together with three brigades of Wilson's cavalry to Pulaski to watch him. On the 17th of November Hood started and moved in such a manner as to avoid Schofield, thereby turning his position. Hood had with him three infantry corps, commanded respectively by Stephen D. Lee, [Alexander P.] Stewart and [Benjamin Franklin] Cheatham. These, with his cavalry, numbered about forty-five thousand men. Schofield had, of all arms, about thirty thousand. Thomas's orders were, therefore, for Schofield to watch the movements of the enemy, but not to fight a battle if he could avoid it; but to fall back in case of an advance on Nashville, and to fight the enemy, as he fell back, so as to retard the enemy's movements until he could be reinforced by Thomas himself. As soon as Schofield saw this movement of Hood's, he sent his trains to the rear, but did not fall back himself until the 21st, and then only to Columbia. At Columbia there was a slight skirmish but no battle. From this place Schofield then retreated to Franklin. He had sent his wagons in advance, and Stanley had gone with them with two divisions to protect them. Cheatham's corps of Hood's army pursued the wagon train and went into camp at Spring Hill, for the night of the 29th.

Schofield retreating from Columbia on the 29th, passed Spring Hill, where Cheatham was bivouacked, during the night without molestation,

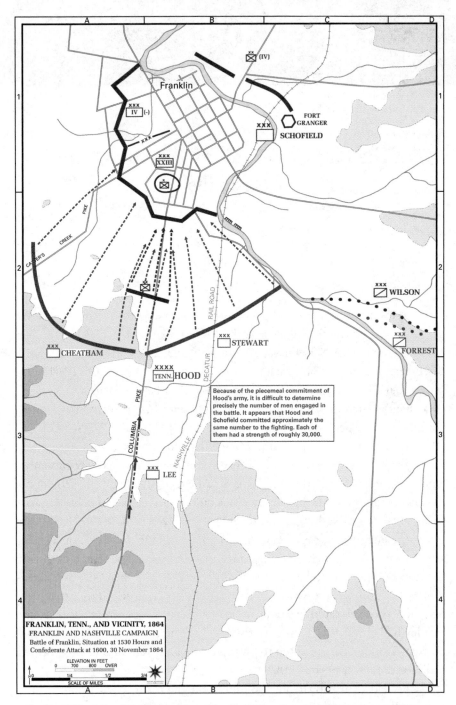

Battle of Franklin. *West Point Atlas of the Civil War. Courtesy of Department of History, USMA.*

though within half a mile of where the Confederates were encamped. On the morning of the 30th he had arrived at Franklin.

Hood followed closely and reached Franklin in time to make an attack the same day.[1] The fight was very desperate and sanguinary. The Confederate generals led their men in the repeated charges, and the loss among them was of unusual proportions. This fighting continued with great severity until long after the night closed in, when the Confederates drew off. General Stanley, who commanded two divisions of the Union troops, and whose troops bore the brunt of the battle, was wounded in the fight, but maintained his position.

The enemy's loss at Franklin, according to Thomas's report, was 1,750 buried upon the field by our troops, 3,800 in the hospital, and 702 prisoners besides. Schofield's loss, as officially reported, was 189 killed, 1,033 wounded, and 1,104 captured and missing.[2]

---

1. For an account of the battle by a member of Schofield's army, see Ambrose Bierce, "What Occurred at Franklin."

2. The Battle of Franklin was the first major engagement of Hood's ill-fated invasion of Tennessee, which was designed to force Sherman to give up on Georgia and return to Tennessee. Hood attempted to get in between Thomas's forces at Nashville and Schofield's at Pulaski, but Schofield was able to pull back and thus to avoid being encircled by Forrest's cavalry at Spring Hill. Then Schofield pulled back again to Franklin, about fifteen miles south of Nashville, where he entrenched and gathered artillery support. On November 30, Hood ordered a frontal assault on the Union position. As James McPherson points out, Hood lost more soldiers on this one afternoon than Grant had lost at Cold Harbor or McClellan during the Battle of the Seven Days: "Having proved even to Hood's satisfaction that they would assault breastworks, the Army of Tennessee had shattered itself beyond the possibility of ever doing so again." *Battle Cry*, 812–13.

Samuel T. Foster, a captain in the 24th Texas Cavalry, excoriated Hood in his diary:

> And the wails and cries of widows and orphans made at Franklin Tenn Nov 30th 1864 will heat up the fires of the bottomless pit to burn the soul of Gen J B Hood for Murdering their husbands and fathers at that place that day. It can't be called anything else but cold blooded Murder.
>
> He sacrificed those men to make the name of Hood famous; when if the History of it is ever written it will make him *infamous*.

One of Cleburne's Command: The Civil War Reminiscences and Diary of Captain Samuel T. Foster, Granbury's Texas Brigade, CSA, ed. Norman D. Brown (Austin: University of Texas Press, 1980), 151.

In his own apologia Hood ungenerously calls attention to the insubordination of his officers and to his army's lack of fighting spirit. A "revolution in feeling" and morale having taken place on the morning of the battle, however, he gave "orders to drive the enemy from his position into the river *at all hazards*." Only nightfall, he would later

Battle of Franklin, November 30, 1864. *Library of Congress, Prints and Photographs Division, Popular Graphic Arts, LC-DIG-pga-01852.*

Thomas made no effort to reinforce Schofield at Franklin, as it seemed to me at the time he should have done, and fight out the battle there. He simply ordered Schofield to continue his retreat to Nashville, which the latter did during that night and the next day.

Thomas, in the meantime, was making his preparations to receive Hood. The road to Chattanooga was still well guarded with strong garrisons at Murfreesboro, Stevenson, Bridgeport and Chattanooga. Thomas had previously given up Decatur and had been reinforced by A. J. Smith's two divisions just returned from Missouri. He also had Steedman's division and R. S. Granger's, which he had drawn from the front. His quartermaster's men, about ten thousand in number, had been organized and armed under the command of the chief quartermaster, General J. L. Donaldson, and placed in the fortifications under the general supervision of General Z. B. Tower, of the United States Engineers.

Hood was allowed to move upon Nashville, and to invest that place almost without interference. Thomas was strongly fortified in his position, so that he would have been safe against the attack of Hood. He had troops enough even to annihilate him in the open field. To me his delay was unaccountable—sitting there and permitting himself to be invested, so that, in the end, to raise the siege he would have to fight the enemy strongly posted behind fortifications.[3]

---

insist, had "saved Schofield's Army from destruction," *Advance and Retreat*, 297, 293, 295.

Schofield withdrew overnight and joined Thomas at Nashville.

3. Grant and Stanton were equally frustrated by Thomas's methodical preparations. James McPherson suggests that they imagined Hood's army to be a much greater threat than it actually was in its depleted and demoralized state. When Thomas finally did strike on

It is true the weather was very bad. The rain was falling and freezing as it fell, so that the ground was covered with a sheet of ice, that made it very difficult to move. But I was afraid that the enemy would find means of moving, elude Thomas and manage to get north of the Cumberland River. If he did this, I apprehended most serious results from the campaign in the North, and was afraid we might even have to send troops from the East to head him off if he got there, General Thomas's movements being always so deliberate and so slow, though effective in defence.[4]

I consequently urged Thomas in frequent dispatches sent from City Point[5] to make the attack at once. The country was alarmed, the administration was alarmed, and I was alarmed lest the very thing would take place which I have just described—that is, Hood would get north. It was all without avail further than to elicit dispatches from Thomas saying that he was getting ready to move as soon as he could, that he was making preparations, etc. At last I had to say to General Thomas that I should be obliged to remove him unless he acted promptly. He replied that he was very sorry, but he would move as soon as he could.

General Logan happening to visit City Point about that time, and knowing him as a prompt, gallant and efficient officer, I gave him an order to proceed to Nashville to relieve Thomas. I directed him, however, not to deliver the order or publish it until he reached there, and if Thomas had moved, then

---

December 15, he dismantled Hood's army in two days. McPherson likens the result to that of the second Joe Louis–Max Schmeling fight. See *Battle Cry*, 813. Schmeling had knocked Louis down in their first fight. But this 124-second bout at Yankee Stadium on June 22, 1938, ended with Schmeling on the canvas after having thrown only two punches in response to Louis's devastating combinations. "It was a shocking thing," journalist Bob Considine reported: "short, sharp, merciless, complete. . . . Schmeling was . . . a man caught and mangled in the whirring claws of a mad and feverish machine." "Louis Knocks Out Schmeling," June 22, 1938, *International News Service*.

4. Dodge writes,

> Thomas, while a great soldier, was of an entirely different disposition from Grant, Sherman and Sheridan, whose great effort was to always be the attacking party. Grant held that this gave an advantage of twenty-five per cent. Thomas preferred to wait until he was certain, or to receive an attack on his own chosen ground, and in that way destroy the enemy. He was rightly named the "Rock of Chicamauga."

Personal Recollections, 85.

5. For the dispatches to Thomas included in a note to the first edition, see Appendix 1, chapter 60, note 1.

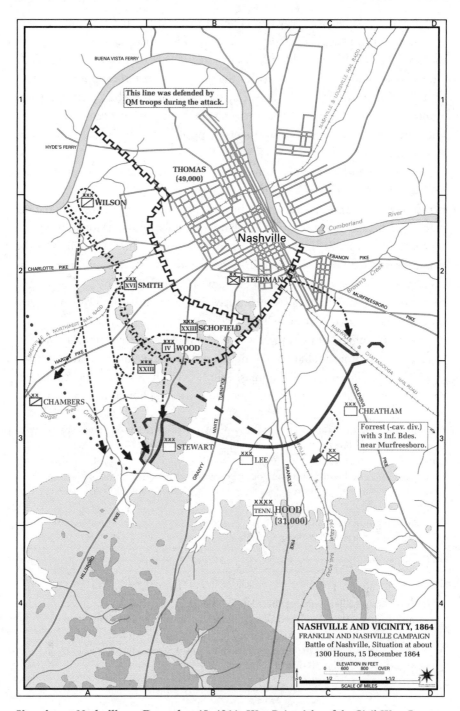

Situation at Nashville on December 15, 1864. *West Point Atlas of the Civil War. Courtesy of Department of History, USMA.*

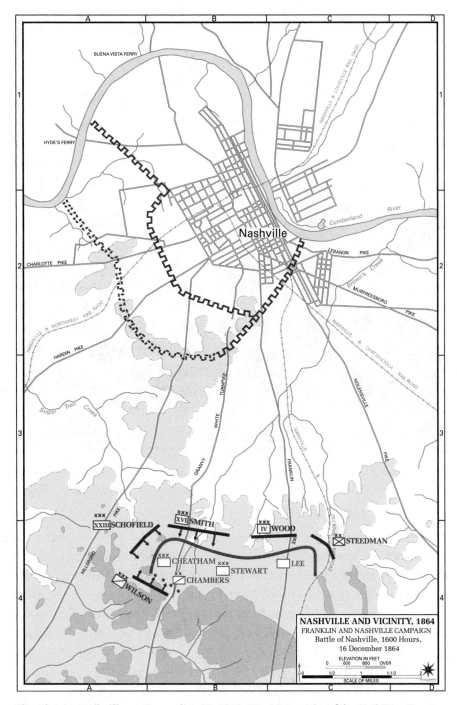

Situation at Nashville on December 16, 1864. *West Point Atlas of the Civil War. Courtesy of Department of History, USMA.*

Federal Outer Line, Battle of Nashville. Photograph by Jacob F. Coonley. *Library of Congress, Prints and Photographs Division, Civil War Photographs, LC-DIG-cwpb-02089.*

not to deliver it at all, but communicate with me by telegraph. After Logan started, in thinking over the situation, I became restless, and concluded to go myself. I went as far as Washington City, when a dispatch was received from General Thomas announcing his readiness at last to move, and designating the time of his movement. I concluded to wait until that time. He did move, and was successful from the start. This was on the 15th of December. General Logan was at Louisville at the time this movement was made, and telegraphed the fact to Washington, and proceeded no farther himself.

The battle during the 15th was severe, but favorable to the Union troops, and continued until night closed in upon the combat. The next day the battle was renewed. After a successful assault upon Hood's men in their intrenchments the enemy fled in disorder, routed and broken, leaving

Cannon commemorating Union victory at Nashville, Battle Monument, West Point, New York. *Photograph by Elizabeth D. Samet.*

their dead, their artillery and small arms in great numbers on the field, besides the wounded that were captured. Our cavalry had fought on foot as infantry, and had not their horses with them; so that they were not ready to join in the pursuit the moment the enemy retreated. They sent back, however, for their horses, and endeavored to get to Franklin ahead of Hood's broken army by the Granny White Road, but too much time was consumed in getting started. They had got but a few miles beyond the scene of the battle when they found the enemy's cavalry dismounted and behind intrenchments covering the road on which they were advancing. Here another battle ensued, our men dismounting and fighting on foot, in which the Confederates were again routed and driven in great disorder. Our cavalry then went into bivouac, and renewed the pursuit on the following morning. They were too late. The enemy already had possession of Franklin, and was beyond them. It now became a chase in which the Confederates had the lead.

Our troops continued the pursuit to within a few miles of Columbia, where they found the rebels had destroyed the railroad bridge as well as all other bridges over Duck River. The heavy rains of a few days before had swelled the stream into a mad torrent, impassable except on bridges. Unfortunately, either through a mistake in the wording of the order or otherwise, the pontoon bridge which was to have been sent by rail out to Franklin, to be taken thence with the pursuing column, had gone toward Chattanooga. There was, consequently, a delay of some four days in building bridges out of the remains of the old railroad bridge. Of course Hood got such a start in this time that farther pursuit was useless, although it was continued for some distance, but without coming upon him again.[6]

---

6. Hood ended up in Tupelo, Mississippi, having lost half his army. Within a month, he had resigned his command. Years later he attempted to refute the reputation of "rashness" he had earned among commentators North and South in the extraordinary concluding chapter to his memoirs, a disquisition on the Roman defeat of Hannibal that ends in a riot of analogies:

> Since General Johnston failed to practice the art of war in accordance with the principles either of Fabius Maximus or of Scipio Africanus, and since he fought not a single *general* battle during the entire war of Secession, what just claim has he to generalship? A man may be learned in anatomy, and perfect in the theory of surgery; he may be able to thoroughly describe the manner in which the most difficult operation should be performed, but may never have possessed sufficient nerve to undertake even one operation in which serious risk was involved, and thus give life to his theories by practical work. Who would employ a surgeon who had never used the knife? Furthermore, who could, under the circumstances, declare him with reason an eminent man in his profession? Ruskin can, probably, better describe a painting than any artist of ancient or modern times. His gorgeous descriptions attracted the attention of the world to the wonderful genius of Turner; but who would venture to assert that he himself was a great painter, when he has perhaps never used the brush? Thus it is as it should be: no man is justly entitled to be considered a great General, unless he has won his spurs. Had General Johnston possessed the requisite spirit and boldness to seize the various chances for victory, which were offered him, he never would have allowed General Sherman to push him back one hundred miles in sixty-six days, from one mountain stronghold to another, down into the very heart of the Confederacy.

Advance and Retreat, 316.

61

Expedition against Fort Fisher—Attack on the Fort—Failure of the Expedition— Second Expedition against the Fort— Capture of Fort Fisher

U p to January, 1865, the enemy occupied Fort Fisher, at the mouth of Cape Fear River and below the City of Wilmington. This port was of immense importance to the Confederates, because it formed their principal inlet for blockade runners by means of which they brought in from abroad such supplies and munitions of war as they could not produce at home. It was equally important to us to get possession of it, not only because it was desirable to cut off their supplies so as to insure a speedy termination of the war, but also because foreign governments, particularly the British Government, were constantly threatening that unless ours could maintain the blockade of that coast they should cease to recognize any blockade. For these reasons I determined, with the concurrence of the Navy Department, in December, to send an expedition against Fort Fisher for the purpose of capturing it.[1]

To show the difficulty experienced in maintaining the blockade, I will mention a circumstance that took place at Fort Fisher after its fall. Two English blockade runners came in at night. Their commanders, not supposing the fort had fallen, worked their way through all our fleet and got into the river unobserved. They then signalled the fort, announcing their arrival.

---

1. Once Fisher fell, the last major supply route to Lee's Army of Northern Virginia was cut off. The formidable fort guarded the approach to Wilmington, North Carolina. Blockade-runners were a major source of supply for Lee's Army of Northern Virginia, and although the navy had been agitating for an attack since 1862, Halleck claimed he did not have enough troops for an expedition. See McPherson, *War on the Waters*, 213.

There was a colored man in the fort who had been there before and who understood these signals. He informed General Terry what reply he should make to have them come in, and Terry did as he advised. The vessels came in, their officers entirely unconscious that they were falling into the hands of the Union forces. Even after they were brought in to the fort they were entertained in conversation for some little time before suspecting that the Union troops were occupying the fort. They were finally informed that their vessels and cargoes were prizes.[2]

I selected General Weitzel, of the Army of the James, to go with the expedition, but gave instructions through General Butler. He commanded the department within whose geographical limits Fort Fisher was situated, as well as Beaufort and other points on that coast held by our troops; he was, therefore, entitled to the right of fitting out the expedition against Fort Fisher.

General Butler conceived the idea that if a steamer loaded heavily with powder could be run up to near the shore under the fort and exploded, it would create great havoc and make the capture an easy matter. Admiral Porter, who was to command the naval squadron, seemed to fall in with the idea, and it was not disapproved of in Washington; the navy was therefore given the task of preparing the steamer for this purpose. I had no confidence in the success of the scheme, and so expressed myself; but as no serious harm could come of the experiment, and the authorities at Washington seemed desirous to have it tried, I permitted it. The steamer was sent to Beaufort, North Carolina, and was there loaded with powder and prepared for the part she was to play in the reduction of Fort Fisher.

General Butler chose to go in command of the expedition himself, and was all ready to sail by the 9th of December (1864). Very heavy storms prevailed, however, at that time along that part of the sea-coast, and prevented

---

2. Admiral Porter reported his amusement at this trap to Assistant Secretary of the Navy Gustavus Fox: "Cushing has charge of the trap. He does it up in style. He makes all kind of unintelligible signals and the Runners seem to think it is all right." Letter to Gustavus Fox, January 21, 1865, quoted in James M. Merrill, "The Fort Fisher and Wilmington Campaign: Letters from Rear Admiral David D. Porter," *The North Carolina Historical Review* 35, no. 4 (October 1958): 472.

Porter recognized the improvements in shipbuilding that had made the blockade-runners more effective in the latter days of the war: "Towards the last the English commenced building these vessels of steel—long, narrow and shallow—which were capable of great speed, and could cross the bar of Cape Fear River at all times day or night, for at night range-lights were kept burning. Once under the guns of Fort Fisher they were safe. The gun-boats generally drew too much water to follow the blockade-runners over the bar, where the depth never exceeded ten feet." *Naval History*, 685.

him from getting off until the 13th or 14th. His advance arrived off Fort
Fisher on the 15th. The naval force had been already assembled, or was
assembling, but they were obliged to run into Beaufort for munitions, coal,
etc.; then, too, the powder-boat was not yet fully prepared. The fleet was
ready to proceed on the 18th; but Butler, who had remained outside from
the 15th up to that time, now found himself out of coal, fresh water, etc.,
and had to put into Beaufort to replenish. Another storm overtook him, and
several days more were lost before the army and navy were both ready at the
same time to co-operate.

On the night of the 23d the powder-boat was towed in by a gunboat
as near to the fort as it was safe to run. She was then propelled by her own
machinery to within about five hundred yards of the shore. There the clock-
work, which was to explode her within a certain length of time, was set and
she was abandoned. Everybody left, and even the vessels put out to sea to prevent the effect of the explosion upon them. At two o'clock in the morning the
explosion took place—and produced no more effect on the fort, or anything
else on land, than the bursting of a boiler anywhere on the Atlantic Ocean
would have done. Indeed when the troops in Fort Fisher heard the explosion
they supposed it was the bursting of a boiler in one of the Yankee gunboats.

Fort Fisher was situated upon a low, flat peninsula north of Cape Fear
River. The soil is sandy. Back a little the peninsula is very heavily wooded,
and covered with fresh-water swamps. The fort ran across this peninsula,
about five hundred yards in width, and extended along the sea coast about
thirteen hundred yards. The fort had an armament of 21 guns and 3 mortars on the land side, and 24 guns on the sea front. At that time it was only
garrisoned by four companies of infantry, one light battery and the gunners
at the heavy guns—less than seven hundred men—with a reserve of less
than a thousand men five miles up the peninsula. General Whiting of the
Confederate army was in command, and General Bragg was in command
of the force at Wilmington. Both commenced calling for reinforcements
the moment they saw our troops landing. The Governor of North Carolina
called for everybody who could stand behind a parapet and shoot a gun, to
join them. In this way they got two or three hundred additional men into
Fort Fisher; and Hoke's division, five or six thousand strong, was sent down
from Richmond. A few of these troops arrived the very day that Butler was
ready to advance.

On the 24th the fleet formed for an attack in arcs of concentric circles,
their heavy iron-clads going in very close range, being nearest the shore, and
leaving intervals or spaces so that the outer vessels could fire between them.

Porter was thus enabled to throw one hundred and fifteen shells per minute. The damage done to the fort by these shells was very slight, only two or three cannon being disabled in the fort. But the firing silenced all the guns by making it too hot for the men to maintain their positions about them and compelling them to seek shelter in the bomb-proofs.

On the next day part of Butler's troops under General Adelbert Ames effected a landing out of range of the fort without difficulty. This was accomplished under the protection of gunboats sent for the purpose, and under cover of a renewed attack upon the fort by the fleet. They formed a line across the peninsula and advanced, part going north and part toward the fort, covering themselves as they did so. Curtis pushed forward and came near to Fort Fisher, capturing the small garrison at what was called the Flag Pond Battery. Weitzel accompanied him to within a half a mile of the works. Here he saw that the fort had not been injured, and so reported to Butler, advising against an assault. Ames, who had gone north in his advance, captured 228 of the reserves. These prisoners reported to Butler that sixteen hundred of Hoke's division of six thousand from Richmond had already arrived and the rest would soon be in his rear.

Upon these reports Butler determined to withdraw his troops from the peninsula and return to the fleet.[3] At that time there had not been a man on our side injured except by one of the shells from the fleet. Curtis had got within a few yards of the works. Some of his men had snatched a flag from the parapet of the fort, and others had taken a horse from the inside of the stockade. At night Butler informed Porter of his withdrawal, giving the reasons above stated, and announced his purpose as soon as his men could embark to start for Hampton Roads. Porter represented to him that he had sent to Beaufort for more ammunition. He could fire much faster than he had been doing, and would keep the enemy from showing himself until our men were within twenty yards of the fort, and he begged that Butler would leave some brave fellows like those who had snatched the flag from the parapet and taken the horse from the fort.

---

3. Secretary of the Navy Gideon Welles confided his misgivings about Butler and his scheme to his diary on December 28: "The powder-boat was blown up about three hundred yards from Fort Fisher. No mention is made of results. I apprehend nothing serious. Have had no faith in this experiment at any time. I fear Porter relied too much upon it, and should not be surprised if the expedition would have done better without than with it. The troops are said to have disembarked above Fort Fisher, to have taken some earthworks and prisoners, and then to have reëmbarked. This reads of and like Butler." *Diary of Gideon Welles* (Boston: Houghton Mifflin, 1911), 2:210–11.

Butler was unchangeable. He got all his troops aboard, except Curtis's brigade, and started back. In doing this, Butler made a fearful mistake. My instructions to him, or to the officer who went in command of the expedition, were explicit in the statement that to effect a landing would be of itself a great victory, and if one should be effected, the foothold must not be relinquished; on the contrary, a regular siege of the fort must be commenced and, to guard against interference by reason of storms, supplies of provisions must be laid in as soon as they could be got on shore. But General Butler seems to have lost sight of this part of his instructions, and was back at Fort Monroe on the 28th.

I telegraphed to the President as follows:

> CITY POINT, VA.,
> *Dec.* 28, 1864.—8.30 P.M.
>
> The Wilmington expedition has proven a gross and culpable failure. Many of the troops are back here. Delays and free talk of the object of the expedition enabled the enemy to move troops to Wilmington to defeat it. After the expedition sailed from Fort Monroe, three days of fine weather were squandered, during which the enemy was without a force to protect himself. Who is to blame will, I hope, be known.
>
> U. S. GRANT,
> Lieutenant-General.

Porter sent dispatches to the Navy Department in which he complained bitterly of having been abandoned by the army just when the fort was nearly in our possession, and begged that our troops might be sent back again to co-operate, but with a different commander.[4] As soon as I heard this I sent a messenger to Porter with a letter asking him to hold on.[5] I assured him that

4. Porter, writing of himself in the third person, remembered, "The next thing was to select a General to command, who would act in harmony with the Navy. . . . Admiral Porter merely suggested one thing—namely, that General Butler should not go in command." *Naval History*, 684.

Welles noted, "I do not think Grant entirely exempt from blame in having permitted such a man as Butler to have command of such an expedition." *Diary*, 2:216.

5. After the first expedition, Porter was in steady contact with Assistant Secretary of the Navy Fox. As late as January 7, he expressed doubt about the troops Grant promised. In the process, he also revealed his odious thoughts about black soldiers: "I don't believe in Grant's troops coming—he says to me—'hold on Dear Admiral, I will be back with

General Alfred Terry. *Library of Congress, Prints and Photographs Division, Brady-Handy Collection, LC-DIG-cwpbh-00101.*

I fully sympathized with him in his disappointment, and that I would send the same troops back with a different commander, with some reinforcements to offset those which the enemy had received. I told him it would take some little time to get transportation for the additional troops; but as soon as it could be had the men should be on their way to him, and there would be no delay on my part. I selected A. H. Terry to command.

It was the 6th of January before the transports could be got ready and the troops aboard. They sailed from Fortress Monroe on that day. The object and destination of the second expedition were at the time kept a secret to all except a few in the Navy Department and in the army to whom it was necessary to impart the information. General Terry had not the slightest idea of where he was going or what he was to do. He simply knew that he was going to sea and that he had his orders with him, which were to be opened when out at sea.

He was instructed to communicate freely with Porter and have entire harmony between army and navy, because the work before them would require the best efforts of both arms of service.[6] They arrived off Beaufort

more troops soon, and with another commander'—that says a good deal but no troops are yet in sight—we want white men here—not niggers—I don't believe in them." In the same letter Porter claimed with bravado that his "web-footers" could do the job alone. See Letter to Gustavus Fox, January 7, 1865, "Fort Fisher and Wilmington Campaign," 468, 467.

6. The second amphibious operation of January 13, 1865, was better planned and executed than the first had been. Terry was a significant improvement over Butler, and

on the 8th. A heavy storm, however, prevented a landing at Fort Fisher until the 13th. The navy prepared itself for attack about as before, and the same time assisted the army in landing, this time five miles away. Only iron-clads fired at first; the object being to draw the fire of the enemy's guns so as to ascertain their positions. This object being accomplished, they then let in their shots thick and fast. Very soon the guns were all silenced, and the fort showed evident signs of being much injured.

Terry deployed his men across the peninsula as had been done before, and at two o'clock on the following morning was up within two miles of the fort with a respectable *abatis* in front of his line. His artillery was all landed on that day, the 14th. Again Curtis's brigade of Ames's division had the lead. By noon they had carried an unfinished work less than a half mile from the fort, and turned it so as to face the other way.

Terry now saw Porter and arranged for an assault on the following day. The two commanders arranged their signals so that they could communicate with each other from time to time as they might have occasion. At day light the fleet commenced its firing. The time agreed upon for the assault was the middle of the afternoon, and Ames who commanded the assaulting column moved at 3.30. Porter landed a force of sailors and marines to move against the sea-front in co-operation with Ames's assault. They were under Commander Breese of the navy. These sailors and marines had worked their way up to within a couple of hundred yards of the fort before the assault. The signal was given and the assault was made; but the poor sailors and marines were repulsed and very badly handled by the enemy, losing 280 killed and wounded out of their number.

Curtis's brigade charged successfully though met by a heavy fire, some of the men having to wade through the swamp up to their waists to reach the fort. Many were wounded, of course, and some killed; but they soon reached the palisades. These they cut away, and pushed on through. The other troops then came up, Pennypacker's following Curtis, and Bell, who commanded the 3d brigade of Ames's division, following Pennypacker. But the fort was not yet captured though the parapet was gained.

The works were very extensive. The large parapet around the work

---

the naval bombardment—a total of fifty-nine federal vessels were involved—was more precise. Porter wrote approvingly of his new counterpart: "Terry had no staff, wore no spurs, and we do not think he owned a sword. He had a well-formed head, full of sense, which served him in lieu of feathers, sword, boots, spurs and staff—of which a General can have too many." *Naval History*, 711.

Capture of Fort Fisher, January 15, 1865. **Painting by John W. Grattan, ensign on Porter's staff.** *NH 50469-KN. Courtesy of the Naval History and Heritage Command.*

would have been but very little protection to those inside except when they were close up under it. Traverses had, therefore, been run until really the work was a succession of small forts enclosed by a large one. The rebels made a desperate effort to hold the fort, and had to be driven from these traverses one by one. The fight continued till long after night. Our troops gained first one traverse and then another, and by 10 o'clock at night the place was carried. During this engagement the sailors, who had been repulsed in their assault on the bastion, rendered the best service they could by reinforcing Terry's northern line—thus enabling him to send a detachment to the assistance of Ames. The fleet kept up a continuous fire upon that part of the fort which was still occupied by the enemy. By means of signals they could be informed where to direct their shots.

During the succeeding nights the enemy blew up Fort Caswell on the opposite side of Cape Fear River, and abandoned two extensive works on Smith's Island in the river.

Our captures in all amounted to 169 guns, besides small-arms, with full supplies of ammunition, and 2,083 prisoners. In addition to these, there were about 700 dead and wounded left there. We had lost 110 killed and 536 wounded.[7]

In this assault on Fort Fisher, Bell, one of the brigade commanders, was killed, and two, Curtis and Pennypacker, were badly wounded.

Secretary Stanton, who was on his way back from Savannah, arrived off Fort Fisher soon after it fell. When he heard the good news he promoted all the officers of any considerable rank for their conspicuous gallantry. Terry had been nominated for major-general, but had not been confirmed. This confirmed him; and soon after I recommended him for a brigadier-generalcy in the regular army, and it was given to him for this victory.

---

7. The waters off the North Carolina coast are littered with wrecks. Researchers with the Underwater Archaeology Branch of the North Carolina Office of State Archaeology estimate that there are more than thirty of them. North Carolina's first heritage dive site is the *Condor*, a steamer built in Scotland for the purpose of blockade running that ran aground on its maiden voyage. Drowned in this incident was the Confederate spy Rose Greenhow. For more information on the site, see https://archaeology.ncdcr.gov/underwater-archaeology-branch/heritage-dive-site.

62

Sherman's March North—Sheridan Ordered to Lynchburg—Canby Ordered to Move against Mobile—Movements of Schofield and Thomas—Capture of Columbia, South Carolina—Sherman in the Carolinas

When news of Sherman being in possession of Savannah reached the North, distinguished statesmen and visitors began to pour in to see him.[1] Among others who went was the Secretary of War, who seemed much pleased at the result of his campaign. Mr. Draper, the collector of customs of New York, who was with Mr. Stanton's party, was put in charge of the public property that had been abandoned and captured. Savannah was then turned over to General Foster's command to hold, so that Sherman might have his own entire army free to operate as might be decided upon in the future. I sent the chief engineer of the Army of the Potomac (General Barnard) with letters to General Sherman. He remained some time with the general, and when he returned brought back letters, one of which contained suggestions from Sherman as to what ought to be done in co-operation with him, when he should have started upon his march northward.

I must not neglect to state here the fact that I had no idea originally of having Sherman march from Savannah to Richmond, or even to North

---

1. It was in Savannah that Sherman issued Special Field Orders No. 15, which distributed 400,000 acres of coastal lands (encompassing parts of South Carolina and Georgia, including the Sea Islands, abandoned by plantation owners who had fled) to freed slaves in forty-acre parcels. This order was later rescinded by President Andrew Johnson.

Carolina. The season was bad, the roads impassable for anything except such an army as he had, and I should not have thought of ordering such a move. I had, therefore, made preparations to collect transports to carry Sherman and his army around to the James River by water, and so informed him. On receiving this letter he went to work immediately to prepare for the move, but seeing that it would require a long time to collect the transports, he suggested the idea then of marching up north through the Carolinas.[2] I was only too happy to approve this; for if successful, it promised every advantage. His march through Georgia had thoroughly destroyed all lines of transportation in that State, and had completely cut the enemy off from all sources of supply to the west of it. If North and South Carolina were rendered helpless so far as capacity for feeding Lee's army was concerned, the Confederate garrison at Richmond would be reduced in territory, from which to draw supplies, to very narrow limits in the State of Virginia; and,

---

2. The final phase of Sherman's march brought his army in two columns up from Savannah through Columbia, South Carolina, to Raleigh, North Carolina, where Joseph Johnston eventually surrendered. In February, Mary Chesnut, then in Lincolnton, North Carolina, lamented, "my heart wanders and my mind strays back to South Carolina. Oh, vandal Sherman! what are you at there, hard-hearted wretch that you are!" February 26, 1865, *Diary*, 355.

Melville devoted two of his *Battle-Pieces* to Sherman's progress: "The March to the Sea" and "The Frenzy in the Wake." Almost a century later, in 1940, the war correspondent Virginia Cowles evocatively described the misery of evacuation, this time complicated by mechanization, as Parisians streamed south before the German advance:

> We saw terrible sights. All along the way cars that had run out of petrol or broken down, were pushed into the fields. Old people, too tired or ill to walk any farther, were lying on the ground under the merciless glare of the sun. . . . One car ran out of petrol halfway up a hill. It was a bakery van, driven by a woman. Everyone shouted and honked their horns, while she stood in the middle of the road with her four children around her begging someone to give her some petrol. No one had any to spare. Finally, three men climbed out of a truck and in spite of her agonized protests, shoved the car into the ditch. . . . She screamed out a frenzy of abuse, then flung herself on the ground and sobbed. Once again the procession moved on.
>
> In that world of terror, panic and confusion, it was difficult to believe that these were the citizens of Paris, citizens whose forefathers had fought for their freedom like tigers and stormed the Bastille with their bare hands. For the first time, I began to understand what had happened to France.

Looking for Trouble, 6th ed. (New York: Harper & Brothers, 1941), 375–76.

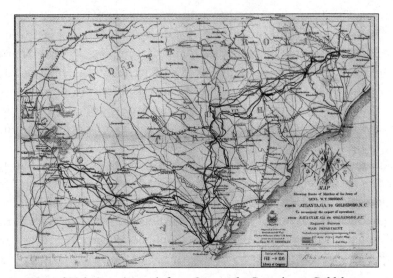

Map of 20th Corps' march from Savannah, Georgia, to Goldsboro,
North Carolina. *Library of Congress, Geography and Map Division.*

although that section of the country was fertile, it was already well exhausted
of both forage and food. I approved Sherman's suggestion therefore at once.

The work of preparation was tedious, because supplies, to load the
wagons for the march, had to be brought from a long distance. Sherman
would now have to march through a country furnishing fewer provisions
than that he had previously been operating in during his march to the sea.
Besides, he was confronting, or marching toward, a force of the enemy vastly
superior to any his troops had encountered on their previous march; and the
territory through which he had to pass had now become of such vast importance to the very existence of the Confederate army, that the most desperate
efforts were to be expected in order to save it.

Sherman, therefore, while collecting the necessary supplies to start with,
made arrangements with Admiral [John A. B.] Dahlgren, who commanded
that part of the navy on the South Carolina and Georgia coast, and General
Foster, commanding the troops, to take positions, and hold a few points
on the sea coast, which he (Sherman) designated, in the neighborhood of
Charleston.

This provision was made to enable him to fall back upon the sea coast,
in case he should encounter a force sufficient to stop his onward progress.
He also wrote me a letter, making suggestions as to what he would like to
have done in support of his movement farther north. This letter was brought
to City Point by General Barnard at a time when I happened to be going to

Washington City, where I arrived on the 21st of January. I cannot tell the provision I had already made to co-operate with Sherman, in anticipation of his expected movement, better than by giving my reply to this letter.

> HEADQUARTERS ARMIES OF THE UNITED STATES,
> Washington, D. C., *Jan.* 21, 1865.
>
> MAJOR-GENERAL W. T. SHERMAN,
> Commanding Mil. Div. of the Mississippi.
>
> GENERAL:—Your letters brought by General Barnard were received at City Point, and read with interest. Not having them with me, however, I cannot say that in this I will be able to satisfy you on all points of recommendation. As I arrived here at one P.M., and must leave at six P.M., having in the meantime spent over three hours with the Secretary and General Halleck, I must be brief. Before your last request to have Thomas make a campaign into the heart of Alabama, I had ordered Schofield to Annapolis, Md., with his corps. The advance (six thousand) will reach the seaboard by the 23d, the remainder following as rapidly as railroad transportation can be procured from Cincinnati. The corps numbers over twenty-one thousand men. I was induced to do this because I did not believe Thomas could possibly be got off before spring. His pursuit of Hood indicated a sluggishness that satisfied me that he would never do to conduct one of your campaigns. The command of the advance of the pursuit was left to subordinates, whilst Thomas followed far behind. When Hood had crossed the Tennessee, and those in pursuit had reached it, Thomas had not much more than half crossed the State, from whence he returned to Nashville to take steamer for Eastport. He is possessed of excellent judgment, great coolness and honesty, but he is not good on a pursuit. He also reported his troops fagged, and that it was necessary to equip up. This report and a determination to give the enemy no rest determined me to use his surplus troops elsewhere.
>
> Thomas is still left with a sufficient force surplus to go to Selma under an energetic leader. He has been telegraphed to, to know whether he could go, and, if so, which of the several routes he would select. No reply is yet received. Canby has been ordered to act offensively from the sea-coast to the interior, towards Montgomery and Selma. Thomas's forces will move from the north at an early day, or some of his troops will be sent to Canby. Without further

Major General Edward R. S. Canby. *Library of Congress, Prints and Photographs Division, Civil War Photographs, LC-DIG-cwpb-07417.*

reinforcements Canby will have a moving column of twenty thousand men.

Fort Fisher, you are aware, has been captured. We have a force there of eight thousand effective. At New Bern about half the number. It is rumored, through deserters, that Wilmington also has fallen. I am inclined to believe the rumor, because on the 17th we knew the enemy were blowing up their works about Fort Caswell, and that on the 18th Terry moved on Wilmington.

If Wilmington is captured, Schofield will go there. If not, he will be sent to New Bern. In either event, all the surplus forces at the two points will move to the interior toward Goldsboro in co-operation with your movements. From either point, railroad communications can be run out, there being here abundance of rolling-stock suited to the gauge of those roads.

There have been about sixteen thousand men sent from Lee's army south. Of these, you will have fourteen thousand against you, if Wilmington is not held by the enemy, casualties at Fort Fisher having overtaken about two thousand.

All these troops are subject to your orders as you come in communication with them. They will be so instructed. From about Richmond I will watch Lee closely, and if he detaches much more, or attempts to evacuate, will pitch in. In the meantime, should you be brought to a halt anywhere, I can send two corps of thirty thousand effective men to your support, from the troops about Richmond.

To resume: Canby is ordered to operate to the interior from the Gulf. A. J. Smith may go from the north, but I think it doubtful. A force of twenty-eight or thirty thousand will co-operate with you from New Bern or Wilmington, or both. You can call for reinforcements.

This will be handed you by Captain Hudson, of my staff, who will return with any message you may have for me. If there is anything I can do for you in the way of having supplies on ship-board, at any point on the sea-coast, ready for you, let me know it.

Yours truly,

U. S. GRANT,

Lieut.-General.

I had written on the 18th of January to General Sherman, giving him the news of the battle of Nashville. He was much pleased at the result, although, like myself, he had been very much disappointed at Thomas for permitting Hood to cross the Tennessee River and nearly the whole State of Tennessee, and come to Nashville to be attacked there. He, however, as I had done, sent Thomas a warm congratulatory letter.

On the 10th of January, 1865, the resolutions of thanks to Sherman and his army passed by Congress were approved.

Sherman, after the capture, at once had the *débris* in Savannah cleared up, commencing the work by removing the piling and torpedoes from the river, and taking up all other obstructions. He had then intrenched the city, so that it could be held by a small garrison. By the middle of January all his work was done, except the accumulation of supplies to commence his movements with.

He proposed to move in two columns, one from Savannah, going along by the river of the same name, and the other by roads farther east, threatening Charleston. He commenced the advance by moving his right wing to Beaufort, South Carolina, then to Pocotaligo by water. This column, in moving north, threatened Charleston, and, indeed, it was not determined at first that they would not have a force visit Charleston. South Carolina had done so much to prepare the public mind of the South for secession, and had been so active in precipitating the decision of the question before the South was fully prepared to meet it, that there was, at that time, a feeling throughout the North and also largely entertained by people of the South, that the State of South Carolina, and Charleston, the hot-bed of secession in particular, ought to have a heavy hand laid upon them. In fact, nothing but the decisive results that followed, deterred the radical portion of the people from condemning the movement, because Charleston had been left out. To pass into the interior would, however, be to insure the evacuation of the city, and its possession by the navy and Foster's troops. It is so situated between two formidable rivers that a small garrison could have held it against all odds as long as their supplies would hold out. Sherman therefore passed it by.[3]

By the first of February all preparations were completed for the final march, Columbia, South Carolina, being the first objective; Fayetteville, North Carolina, the second; and Goldsboro, or neighborhood, the final one, unless something further should be determined upon. The right wing went from Pocotaligo, and the left from about Hardeeville on the Savannah River, both columns taking a pretty direct route for Columbia. The cavalry, however, were to threaten Charleston on the right, and Augusta on the left.

On the 15th of January Fort Fisher had fallen, news of which Sherman had received before starting out on his march. We already had New Bern and had soon Wilmington, whose fall followed that of Fort Fisher; as did other points on the sea coast, where the National troops were now in readiness to co-operate with Sherman's advance when he had passed Fayetteville.

On the 18th of January I ordered Canby, in command at New Orleans, to move against Mobile, Montgomery and Selma, Alabama, for the purpose of destroying roads, machine shops, etc.[4] On the 8th of February I ordered

---

3. Trying to predict Sherman's path caused great anxiety among South Carolinians. As Sherman's troops continued their march through the state, Chesnut wrote from the town of Chester,

> Then Mrs. Prioleau Hamilton, *née* Levy, came with the story of family progress, not a royal one, from Columbia here: "Before we left home," said she, "Major Hamilton spread a map of the United States on the table, and showed me with his finger where Sherman was likely to go. Womanlike, I demurred. 'But, suppose he does not choose to go that way?' 'Pooh, pooh! what do you know of war?' So we set out, my husband, myself, and two children, all in one small buggy. The 14th of February we took up our line of march, and straight before Sherman's men for five weeks we fled together. By incessant hurrying and scurrying from pillar to post, we succeeded in acting as a sort of *avant-courier* of the Yankee army. Without rest and with much haste, we got here last Wednesday, and here we mean to stay and defy Sherman and his legions. Much the worse for wear were we."

March 27, 1865, *Diary*, 370.

4. E. R. S. Canby (1817–1873) graduated from West Point in 1839. He served in Florida in the Indian Wars (1839–42), and was subsequently involved in the transfer of Native Americans to Arkansas. He fought in the Mexican War from the siege of Veracruz to the capture of Mexico City. Over the next several years he had a variety of assignments, largely in the south and southwest. He began the Civil War in command of the Department of New Mexico and then went east to take charge of a draft intake center

Sheridan, who was in the Valley of Virginia, to push forward as soon as the weather would permit and strike the canal west of Richmond at or about Lynchburg; and on the 20th I made the order to go to Lynchburg as soon as the roads would permit, saying: "As soon as it is possible to travel, I think you will have no difficulty about reaching Lynchburg with a cavalry force alone. From there you could destroy the railroad and canal in every direction, so as to be of no further use to the rebellion. ★ ★ ★ This additional raid, with one starting from East Tennessee under [George] Stoneman, numbering about four or five thousand cavalry; one from Eastport, Mississippi, ten thousand cavalry; Canby, from Mobile Bay, with about eighteen thousand mixed troops—these three latter pushing for Tuscaloosa, Selma and Montgomery; and Sherman with a large army eating out the vitals of South Carolina—is all that will be wanted to leave nothing for the rebellion to stand upon. I would advise you to overcome great obstacles to accomplish this. Charleston was evacuated on Tuesday last."

On the 27th of February, more than a month after Canby had received his orders, I again wrote to him, saying that I was extremely anxious to hear of his being in Alabama. I notified him, also, that I had sent Grierson to take command of his cavalry, he being a very efficient officer. I further suggested that Forrest was probably in Mississippi, and if he was there, he would find him an officer of great courage and capacity whom it would be difficult to get by. I still further informed him that Thomas had been ordered to start a cavalry force into Mississippi on the 20th of February, or as soon as possible thereafter. This force did not get off however.

All these movements were designed to be in support of Sherman's march, the object being to keep the Confederate troops in the West from leaving there. But neither Canby nor Thomas could be got off in time. I had some time before depleted Thomas's army to reinforce Canby, for the reason that Thomas had failed to start an expedition which he had been ordered to send out, and to have the troops where they might do something. Canby seemed to be equally deliberate in all of his movements. I ordered him to go in person; but he prepared to send a detachment under another officer. General

in Pittsburgh, to assume special duty at the War Department, Washington, D.C., and then to supervise the suppression of the Draft Riots in New York City in the summer of 1863. Canby returned to the command of the Division of West Mississippi in 1864, and he spent the rest of the war in the South. He accepted the surrenders of Richard Taylor and Edward Kirby Smith in May 1865.

Granger had got down to New Orleans, in some way or other, and I wrote Canby that he must not put him in command of troops. In spite of this he asked the War Department to assign Granger to the command of a corps.

Almost in despair of having adequate service rendered to the cause in that quarter, I said to Canby: "I am in receipt of a dispatch ★ ★ ★ informing me that you have made requisitions for a construction corps and material to build seventy miles of railroad. I have directed that none be sent. Thomas's army has been depleted to send a force to you that they might be where they could act in winter, and at least detain the force the enemy had in the West. If there had been any idea of repairing railroads, it could have been done much better from the North, where we already had the troops. I expected your movements to be co-operative with Sherman's last. This has now entirely failed. I wrote to you long ago, urging you to push promptly and to live upon the country, and destroy railroads, machine shops, etc., not to build them. Take Mobile and hold it, and push your forces to the interior—to Montgomery and to Selma. Destroy railroads, rolling stock, and everything useful for carrying on war, and, when you have done this, take such positions as can be supplied by water. By this means alone you can occupy positions from which the enemy's roads in the interior can be kept broken."

Most of these expeditions got off finally, but too late to render any service in the direction for which they were designed.

The enemy, ready to intercept his advance, consisted of Hardee's troops and Wheeler's cavalry, perhaps less than fifteen thousand men in all; but frantic efforts were being made in Richmond, as I was sure would be the case, to retard Sherman's movements. Everything possible was being done to raise troops in the South. Lee dispatched against Sherman the troops which had been sent to relieve Fort Fisher, which, including those of the other defences of the harbor and its neighborhood, amounted, after deducting the two thousand killed, wounded and captured, to fourteen thousand men. After Thomas's victory at Nashville what remained of Hood's army were gathered together and forwarded as rapidly as possible to the east to co-operate with these forces; and, finally, General Joseph E. Johnston, one of the ablest commanders of the South though not in favor with the administration (or at least with Mr. Davis), was put in command of all the troops in North and South Carolina.

Schofield arrived at Annapolis in the latter part of January, but before sending his troops to North Carolina I went with him down the coast to see the situation of affairs, as I could give fuller directions after being on the ground than I could very well have given without. We soon returned, and the troops were sent by sea to Cape Fear River. Both New Bern and Wilmington are connected with Raleigh by railroads which unite at Goldsboro. Schofield was to land troops at Smithville, near the mouth of the Cape Fear River on the west side, and move up to secure the Wilmington and Charlottesville Railroad. This column took their pontoon bridges with them, to enable them to cross over to the island south of the city of Wilmington. A large body was sent by the north side to co-operate with them. They succeeded in taking the city on the 22d of February. I took the precaution to provide for Sherman's army, in case he should be forced to turn in toward the sea coast before reaching North Carolina, by forwarding supplies to every place where he was liable to have to make such a deflection from his projected march. I also sent railroad rolling stock, of which we had a great abundance, now that we were not operating the roads in Virginia. The gauge of the North Carolina railroads [not] being the same as the Virginia railroads had been altered too; these cars and locomotives were ready for use there without any change.

On the 31st of January I countermanded the orders given to Thomas to move south to Alabama and Georgia. (I had previously reduced his force by sending a portion of it to Terry.) I directed in lieu of this movement, that he should send Stoneman through East Tennessee, and push him well down toward Columbia, South Carolina, in support of Sherman. Thomas did not get Stoneman off in time, but, on the contrary, when I had supposed he was on his march in support of Sherman I heard of his being in Louisville, Kentucky. I immediately changed the order, and directed Thomas to send him toward Lynchburg. Finally, however, on the 12th of March, he did push down through the north-western end of South Carolina, creating some consternation. I also ordered Thomas to send the 4th corps (Stanley's) to Bull Gap and to destroy no more roads east of that. I also directed him to concentrate supplies at Knoxville, with a view to a probable movement of his army through that way toward Lynchburg.

Goldsboro is four hundred and twenty-five miles from Savannah. Sherman's march was without much incident until he entered Columbia, on the 17th of February. He was detained in his progress by having to repair and corduroy the roads, and rebuild the bridges. There was constant skirmishing and fighting between the cavalry of the two armies, but this did not retard the advance of the infantry. Four days, also, were lost in making complete the destruction of the most important railroads south of Columbia; there was

William Waud, Sherman's army crossing the North Edisto, February 12–13, 1865. *Library of Congress, Prints and Photographs Division, LC-DIG-ppmsca-17671.*

also some delay caused by the high water, and the destruction of the bridges on the line of the road. A formidable river had to be crossed near Columbia, and that in the face of a small garrison under General Wade Hampton. There was but little delay, however, further than that caused by high water in the stream. Hampton left as Sherman approached, and the city was found to be on fire.

There has since been a great deal of acrimony displayed in discussions of the question as to who set Columbia on fire.[5] Sherman denies it on the part

5. The burning of Columbia has long been one of the great controversies of Sherman's march. Although Sherman and other soldiers attempted to put out the fires, they were inevitably blamed for the conflagration. Mary Chesnut records the rumors in Columbia about how the fire started and expresses her personal conviction that Sherman's army was the culprit: "They meant to make a clean sweep. They were howling round the fires like demons, these Yankees in their joy and triumph at our destruction. Well, we have given them a big scare and kept them miserable for four years—the little handful of us." March 8, 1865, *Diary*, 362.

The eleventh-century Arab courtier and soldier Usma ibn Munqidh once sagely counseled the vizier 'Abbas ibn Abi al-Futuh not to burn a rebel stronghold in Cairo after he regained control of the city: "He also ordered the quarter of Barqiya to be razed, because it was where many of the soldiers' houses were located. But I managed to calm him down about that and said, 'My lord, if you set a fire, you will burn both what you want burned and what you don't want burned, and you won't know how to put it out.' In this way, I changed his mind about it." *The Book of Contemplation: Islam and the Crusades*, trans. and ed. Paul M. Cobb (New York: Penguin Classics, 2008), 31.

of his troops, and Hampton denies it on the part of the Confederates. One thing is certain: as soon as our troops took possession, they at once proceeded to extinguish the flames to the best of their ability with the limited means at hand. In any case, the example set by the Confederates in burning the village of Chambersburg, Pa., a town which was not garrisoned, would seem to make a defence of the act of firing the seat of government of the State most responsible for the conflict then raging, not imperative.

The Confederate troops having vacated the city, the mayor took possession, and sallied forth to meet the commander of the National forces for the purpose of surrendering the town, making terms for the protection of property, etc. Sherman paid no attention at all to the overture, but pushed forward and took the town without making any conditions whatever with its citizens. He then, however, co-operated with the mayor in extinguishing the flames and providing for the people who were rendered destitute by this destruction of their homes. When he left there he even gave the mayor five hundred head of cattle to be distributed among the citizens, to tide them over until some arrangement could be made for their future supplies. He remained in Columbia until the roads, public buildings, workshops and everything that could be useful to the enemy were destroyed. While at Columbia, Sherman learned for the first time that what remained of Hood's army was confronting him, under the command of General Beauregard.

Charleston was evacuated on the 18th of February, and Foster garrisoned the place. Wilmington was captured on the 22d. Columbia and Cheraw farther north, were regarded as so secure from invasion that the wealthy people of Charleston and Augusta had sent much of their valuable property to these two points to be stored. Among the goods sent there were valuable carpets, tons of old Madeira, silverware, and furniture. I am afraid much of these goods fell into the hands of our troops. There was found at Columbia a large amount of powder, some artillery, small-arms and fixed ammunition. These, of course were among the articles destroyed. While here, Sherman also learned of Johnston's restoration to command. The latter was given, as already stated, all troops in North and South Carolina. After the completion of the destruction of public property about Columbia, Sherman proceeded on his march and reached Cheraw without any special opposition and without incident to relate. The railroads, of course, were thoroughly destroyed on the way. Sherman remained a day or two at Cheraw; and, finally, on the 6th of March crossed his troops over the Pedee and advanced straight for Fayetteville. Hardee and Hampton were there, and barely escaped. Sherman reached Fayetteville on the 11th of March. He had dispatched scouts from Cheraw with letters to General Terry, at Wilmington, asking him to send a steamer with some supplies of bread, clothing and other articles which he enumerated. The scouts got through successfully, and a boat was sent with the mail and such articles for which Sherman had asked as were in store at Wilmington; unfortunately, however, those stores did not contain clothing.

Four days later, on the 15th, Sherman left Fayetteville for Goldsboro. The march, now, had to be made with great caution, for he was approaching Lee's army and nearing the country that still remained open to the enemy. Besides, he was confronting all that he had had to confront in his previous march up to that point, reinforced by the garrisons along the road and by what remained of Hood's army. Frantic appeals were made to the people to come in voluntarily and swell the ranks of our foe. I presume, however, that Johnston did not have in all over 35,000 or 40,000 men. The people had grown tired of the war, and desertions from the Confederate army were much more numerous than the voluntary accessions.

There was some fighting at Averysboro on the 16th between Johnston's troops and Sherman's, with some loss; and at Bentonville on the 19th and 21st of March, but Johnston withdrew from the contest before the morning of the 22d. Sherman's loss in these last engagements in killed, wounded, and missing, was about sixteen hundred. Sherman's troops at last reached Goldsboro on the 23d of the month and went into bivouac; and there his men were destined to have a long rest. Schofield was there to meet him with the troops which had been sent to Wilmington.

Sherman was no longer in danger.[6] He had Johnston confronting him;

---

6. Sherman's Southern odyssey, culminating in the march through the Carolinas, became, as he predicted, the subject of Southern outrage for years to come—the ultimate expression of Yankee cruelty. By the twentieth century, Lillian Hellman could use the march's place in Southern mythology as a kind of joke in *The Little Foxes*, her masterful indictment of the postbellum South as a society still predicated on the effective exploitation of black labor. Addie, the Giddens family's savvy maid, attempts to describe the level of excitement in the town at the prospect of a new cotton mill: "There ain't been so much talk around here since Sherman's army didn't come near." *The Little Foxes, Six Plays* (New York: Vintage, 1979), 202.

The star of the first production of Hellman's play in New York was Tallulah Bankhead. Her grandfather, John H. Bankhead, had served in Company K of the 16th Alabama Infantry, which fought at Shiloh, Murfreesboro, Chickamauga, Chattanooga, and other major engagements in the Western Theater of the war. John Bankhead eventually became a United States senator from Alabama, and he was the last Confederate veteran to serve in that capacity when he died in 1920. Senator Bankhead was heavily involved in the post-Reconstruction drive toward reconciliation that spurred a major rewriting of Civil War history.

In 1918, on the occasion of the annual reunion of the Confederate Veterans in Washington, D.C., Bankhead remarkably wore his old C.S.A. uniform to address his colleagues in the Senate chamber. He also marched in the parade with a former enemy: "Senator Bankhead and Senator Knute Nelson, of Minnesota, a veteran of the Union Army, wearing the blue marched down Pennsylvania Avenue side by side, denoting to the cheering throngs the established fact of a reunited country," according to his fellow Alabaman Senator Oscar W. Underwood. Bankhead continued to fight for the recognition of Confederate soldiers, the restitution of lost Southern property, and the return of Confederate flags and banners then held by the United States government. In his remarks on Bankhead's death, Underwood called him "a great American, loyal to his reunited country, but he never forgot the hardships and the suffering of his comrades with whom he fought so valiantly for the flag that only lives in history." Today that flag has gained a new lease on life, as it did during the Civil Rights era, but the fetishizing of Confederate artifacts entered perhaps its most significant phase in the late nineteenth century and first part of the twentieth century, when reunion was the order of the day, and all the peculiar paradoxes of simultaneously proclaiming unity and idolizing the Lost Cause took shape. In his 1920 memorial address for Bankhead, Senator Henry Cabot Lodge of Massachusetts, the state of Radical Republican Charles Sumner, emphasized unity above all:

> Two years before his death there was held here in Washington the twenty-seventh annual reunion of the Confederate Veterans, and Senator BANKHEAD made on this floor a motion that the Senate adjourn over the day of their parade. I imagine that all who were present must recall the scene when Senator BANKHEAD, dressed in a uniform of Confederate gray, simple, as always, without notice and without parade, arose and addressed the Senate in support of his motion. It was an occasion far more memorable than most of those which . . . have in this Chamber drawn crowds of sight-seers and arrested public attention; the more memorable because it was a most significant expression of the union of a great people.

Lodge explained that he could not conclude his remarks without reading from Bankhead's own 1918 address to the Senate:

> To-day the shattered remnants of the armies of Lee and Jackson, Johnston and Bragg, and of the navies of the Confederacy, who are physically and financially able, are in Washington and on Thursday will march with their sons down Pennsylvania Avenue in review before the President of the United States. Think, Senators, of the significance of a spectacle like this! A little more than half a century ago these same men in arms were hammering at the gates of Washington in an effort to sever their relations with the National Government. Thursday, marching with broken body and faltering step on a mission of peace and love, not of hatred and bloodshed, but in a spirit of resolute reconciliation and absolute loyalty to

but with an army much inferior to his own, both in numbers and morale. He had Lee to the north of him with a force largely superior; but I was holding Lee with a still greater force, and had he made his escape and gotten down to reinforce Johnston, Sherman, with the reinforcements he now had from Schofield and Terry, would have been able to hold the Confederates at bay for an indefinite period. He was near the sea-shore with his back to it, and our navy occupied the harbors. He had a railroad to both Wilmington and New Bern, and his flanks were thoroughly protected by streams, which intersect that part of the country and deepen as they approach the sea. Then, too, Sherman knew that if Lee should escape me I would be on his heels, and he and Johnston together would be crushed in one blow if they attempted to make a stand. With the loss of their capital, it is doubtful whether Lee's

---

our flag, they will voice in vibrant tones to all the world an indissoluble Union of the United States. I am grateful that God has spared me to see this day, when my old comrades in arms of the Confederacy are here in the Capital of that Nation which for four years they struggled desperately to destroy, but which none in all this great Republic are now more anxious to preserve.

For five years I marched and fought under the Stars and Bars. Five immediate members of my family are now enlisted under the Stars and Stripes—a son, two grandsons, and two nephews. They will even up our records.

John Hollis Bankhead: Memorial Addresses Delivered in the Senate and the House of Representatives of the United States, 66th Congress, 2nd Session (Washington, D.C.: Government Printing Office, 1921), 10–11, 29–30.

Senator John Hollis Bankhead and his granddaughters at the annual Confederate reunion, Washington, D.C., 1917. *Library of Congress, Prints and Photographs Division, photograph by Harris & Ewing, LC-DIG-hec-08878.*

army would have amounted to much as an army when it reached North Carolina. Johnston's army was demoralized by constant defeat and would hardly have made an offensive movement, even if they could have been induced to remain on duty.[7] The men of both Lee's and Johnston's armies were, like their brethren of the North, as brave as men can be; but no man is so brave that he may not meet such defeats and disasters as to discourage him and dampen his ardor for any cause, no matter how just he deems it.

---

7. In his epic novel of World War II Vasily Grossman provides insight into the moment of demoralization in battle:

> The intuition of a deafened and isolated soldier often turns out to be nearer the truth than judgements delivered by staff officers as they study the map.
>
> An extraordinary change takes place at the turning-point in a battle: a soldier looks round, after apparently gaining his objective, and suddenly finds he has lost sight of his comrades; while the enemy, who had seemed so weak, scattered and stupid, is now united and therefore invincible. A deep change in perception takes place at this mysterious turning-point: a gallant, intelligent "We" becomes a frail, timid "I," while the enemy changes from a hunted, isolated prey to a terrible, threatening "Them".

Grossman, *Life and Fate*, trans. Robert Chandler (New York: New York Review Books, 2006), 47–48.

63

Arrival of the Peace Commissioners—Lincoln and the Peace Commissioners—An Anecdote of Lincoln—The Winter before Petersburg—Sheridan Destroys the Railroad—Gordon Carries the Picket Line—Parke Recaptures the Line—The Battle of White Oak Road

On the last of January, 1865, peace commissioners from the so-called Confederate States presented themselves on our lines around Petersburg, and were immediately conducted to my headquarters at City Point. They proved to be Alexander H. Stephens, Vice-President of the Confederacy, Judge [John A.] Campbell, Assistant-Secretary of War, and R. M. T. Hunter, formerly United States Senator and then a member of the Confederate Senate.[1]

---

1. Alexander H. Stephens had once been Lincoln's colleague in the United States Congress. Stephens was perhaps best known for what came to be called the Corner-stone Speech, delivered on March 21, 1861, after he was elected Vice President of the Confederacy. In it, he argued that slavery *"was the immediate cause of the late rupture and present revolution."* The foundations of the Confederacy, he proclaimed, "are laid, its corner-stone rests upon, the great truth that the negro is not equal to the white man; that slavery, subordination to the superior race, is his natural and moral condition. This, our new Government, is the first, in the history of the world, based upon this great physical, philosophical, and moral truth." *Great Debates in American History*, ed. Marion Mills Miller (New York: Current Literature, 1913), 5:288–90.

After the war, in his 1868 *Constitutional View of the Late War between the States*, Stephens conveniently revised his earlier view: "It is a postulate, with many writers of

It was about dark when they reached my headquarters, and I at once conducted them to the steamer *Mary Martin,* a Hudson River boat which was very comfortably fitted up for the use of passengers. I at once communicated by telegraph with Washington and informed the Secretary of War and the President of the arrival of these commissioners and that their object was to negotiate terms of peace between the United States and, as they termed it,

---

this day, that the late War was the result of two opposing ideas, or principles, upon the subject of African Slavery. . . . Those who assume this postulate, and so theorize upon it, are but superficial observers. . . . It was a strife between the principles of Federation, on the one side, and Centralism, or Consolidation, on the other." Within his new framework of a states' rights argument, slavery, "so called, was but *the question* on which these antagonistic principles, which had been in conflict, from the beginning, on diverse *other questions,* were finally brought into actual and active collision with each other on the field of battle." Alexander H. Stephens, *A Constitutional View of the Late War between the States* (Philadelphia: National Publishing, 1868), 1:9–10.

Stephens was imprisoned at Fort Warren, on Boston Harbor's Georges Island, for several months in 1865. There, he launched a new war, this time against vermin:

> Night once more upon the earth, and I am alone in these quarters which constitute my present home. Unless the little mouse is eyeing me from his hole, I have no other companion. . . . In speaking of companions, however, I ought not to omit the flies. I should do them as great injustice by such omission as they do me by their annoyance. I have much more of their company than I like. Perhaps I ought not to omit companions of another sort; whose nature is to stick to you closer than a brother and to keep you awake all night. Since my row with them the other day, I have not seen or heard anything more from them. If they have made any attack, it has been a sly one in small force. I have little doubt that some are about, for the fort is well stocked with them. Of course, I mean bedbugs.
>
> Alone! Did I say? Oh I am far from ever being alone. Right by my window the sentry or guard is ever walking; by night and day, in rain or shine, his step sounds on the hard stone. Like the ticking of a clock at all hours of the night that step is heard if I chance to be awake. . . .
>
> Had another row with bedbugs. I searched the coats I use as pillows, and the corners and edges of the shuck mattress; discovered a good many, though small. To none did I give quarter. . . . It may be a low calling and a rather mean business in the eyes of one of my guards—this of a man pursuing and slaying bedbugs—but no one knows what he will come to. I hold nothing low or mean for a man to do which is necessary to health and comfort, when he has no one else to do it for him. . . . Prison life is a horrible misfortune.

Recollections of Alexander H. Stephens, ed. Myrta Lockett Avary (New York: Doubleday, Page, 1910), 405–6, 409–10.

the Confederate Government. I was instructed to retain them at City Point, until the President, or some one whom he would designate, should come to meet them. They remained several days as guests on board the boat. I saw them quite frequently, though I have no recollection of having had any conversation whatever with them on the subject of their mission. It was something I had nothing to do with, and I therefore did not wish to express any views on the subject. For my own part I never had admitted, and never was ready to admit, that they were the representatives of a *government*. There had been too great a waste of blood and treasure to concede anything of the kind. As long as they remained there, however, our relations were pleasant and I found them all very agreeable gentlemen. I directed the captain to furnish them with the best the boat afforded, and to administer to their comfort in every way possible. No guard was placed over them and no restriction was put upon their movements; nor was there any pledge asked that they would not abuse the privileges extended to them. They were permitted to leave the boat when they felt like it, and did so, coming up on the bank and visiting me at my headquarters.

I had never met either of these gentlemen before the war, but knew them well by reputation and through their public services, and I had been a particular admirer of Mr. Stephens. I had always supposed that he was a very small man, but when I saw him in the dusk of the evening I was very much surprised to find so large a man as he seemed to be. When he got down on to the boat I found that he was wearing a coarse gray woollen overcoat, a manufacture that had been introduced into the South during the rebellion. The cloth was thicker than anything of the kind I had ever seen, even in Canada. The overcoat extended nearly to his feet, and was so large that it gave him the appearance of being an average-sized man. He took this off when he reached the cabin of the boat, and I was struck with the apparent change in size, in the coat and out of it.

After a few days, about the 2d of February, I received a dispatch from Washington, directing me to send the commissioners to Hampton Roads to meet the President and a member of the cabinet. Mr. Lincoln met them there and had an interview of short duration. It was not a great while after they met that the President visited me at City Point. He spoke of his having met the commissioners, and said he had told them that there would be no use in entering into any negotiations unless they would recognize, first: that the Union as a whole must be forever preserved, and second: that slavery must be abolished. If they were willing to concede these two points, then he was ready to enter into negotiations and was almost willing to hand them a blank sheet of paper with his signature attached for them to fill in the terms upon which they were willing to live with us in the Union and be one people. He always showed a generous and kindly spirit toward the Southern people, and I never heard him abuse an enemy. Some of the cruel things said about President Lincoln, particularly in the North, used to pierce him to the heart; but never in my presence did he evince a revengeful disposition—and I saw a great deal of him at City Point, for he seemed glad to get away from the cares and anxieties of the capital.

Right here I might relate an anecdote of Mr. Lincoln. It was on the occasion of his visit to me just after he had talked with the peace commissioners at Hampton Roads. After a little conversation, he asked me if I had seen that overcoat of Stephens's. I replied that I had. "Well," said he, "did you see him take it off?" I said yes. "Well," said he, "didn't you think it was the biggest shuck and the littlest ear that ever you did see?" Long afterwards I told this story to the Confederate General J. B. Gordon, at the time a member of the Senate. He repeated it to Stephens, and, as I heard afterwards, Stephens laughed immoderately at the simile of Mr. Lincoln.

The rest of the winter, after the departure of the peace commissioners, passed off quietly and uneventfully, except for two or three little incidents. On one occasion during this period, while I was visiting Washington City for the purpose of conferring with the administration, the enemy's cavalry under General Wade Hampton, passing our extreme left and then going to the south, got in east of us. Before their presence was known, they had driven off a large number of beef cattle that were grazing in that section. It was a fair capture, and they were sufficiently needed by the Confederates.[2] It was

---

2. In September 1864, Wade Hampton (J. E. B. Stuart's successor in command of the Cavalry Corps of the Army of Northern Virginia) led troops on a remarkable cattle raid—it came to be called the Beefsteak Raid—behind Union lines. The three thousand raiders stole approximately the same number of cattle from pens at Coggins Point, Virginia. Just over a hundred years later, Hollywood made a fictionalized version of the raid, *Alvarez Kelly* (1966), starring William Holden and Richard Widmark. One Confederate soldier described the raiding party's triumphant return: "General Lee came into the fight before it was over, and I well remember how his dismounted men, as they advanced to a mill-pond through the bushes, called to the Yankees to come over and get their bulls, and bellowed at them in derision. We had some little fighting—not half as much as we anticipated—and before 9 o'clock we had left our enemy far in the rear and crossed the water by a dam, and were trotting toward our own lines." D. Cardwell, "A Brilliant Coup: How Wade Hampton Captured Grant's Entire Beef Supply," Charleston *News and Courier*, October 10, 1894, rpt. *Southern Historical Society Papers* 22 (1894): 153.

only retaliating for what we had done, sometimes for many weeks at a time, when out of supplies—taking what the Confederate army otherwise would have gotten. As appears in this book, on one single occasion we captured five thousand head of cattle which were crossing the Mississippi River near Port Hudson on their way from Texas to supply the Confederate army in the East.

One of the most anxious periods of my experience during the rebellion was the last few weeks before Petersburg. I felt that the situation of the Confederate army was such that they would try to make an escape at the earliest practicable moment, and I was afraid, every morning, that I would awake from my sleep to hear that Lee had gone, and that nothing was left but a picket line. He had his railroad by the way of Danville south, and I was afraid that he was running off his men and all stores and ordnance except such as it would be necessary to carry with him for his immediate defence. I knew he could move much more lightly and more rapidly than I, and that, if he got

Alfred R. Waud, "Wade Hampton's Cattle Raid." *Library of Congress, Prints and Photographs Division, LC-DIG-ppmsca-22447.*

Harper's Weekly artist Alfred R. Waud sketching on the battlefield, Gettysburg, Pennsylvania, July 1863. Photograph by Timothy H. O'Sullivan. *Library of Congress, Prints and Photographs Division, Civil War Photographs, LC-DIG-cwpb-00074 .*

Horace Porter recalled that soon after the raid a visitor to City Point asked Grant when he planned "to starve out Lee and capture Richmond?" "Never," Grant replied, "if our armies continue to supply him with beef-cattle." Porter, *Campaigning,* 299.

the start, he would leave me behind so that we would have the same army to fight again farther south—and the war might be prolonged another year.

I was led to this fear by the fact that I could not see how it was possible for the Confederates to hold out much longer where they were. There is no doubt that Richmond would have been evacuated much sooner than it was, if it had not been that it was the capital of the so-called Confederacy, and the fact of evacuating the capital would, of course, have had a very demoralizing effect upon the Confederate army. When it was evacuated (as we shall see further on), the Confederacy at once began to crumble and fade away. Then, too, desertions were taking place, not only among those who were with General Lee in the neighborhood of their capital, but throughout the whole Confederacy. I remember that in a conversation with me on one occasion long prior to this, General Butler remarked that the Confederates would find great difficulty in getting more men for their army; possibly adding, though I am not certain as to this, "unless they should arm the slave."[3]

The South, as we all knew, were conscripting every able-bodied man between the ages of eighteen and forty-five; and now they had passed a law for the further conscription of boys from fourteen to eighteen, calling them the junior reserves, and men from forty-five to sixty to be called the senior reserves. The latter were to hold the necessary points not in immediate danger, and especially those in the rear. General Butler, in alluding to this conscription, remarked that they were thus "robbing both the cradle and the grave," an expression which I afterwards used in writing a letter to Mr. Washburne.

It was my belief that while the enemy could get no more recruits they were losing at least a regiment a day, taking it throughout the entire army, by desertions alone. Then by casualties of war, sickness, and other natural causes, their losses were much heavier. It was a mere question of arithmetic to calculate how long they could hold out while that rate of depletion was going on. Of course long before their army would be thus reduced to nothing the army which we had in the field would have been able to capture theirs. Then too I knew from the great number of desertions, that the men who had fought so bravely, so gallantly and so long for the cause which they believed in—and

---

3. Late in the war, General Patrick Cleburne made a formal proposal for enlisting the slaves and granting them freedom in exchange. Severe Confederate manpower shortages notwithstanding, the plan met with resistance, as had several similar schemes. After the evacuation of Richmond, the Confederate Congress did approve the enlistment of as many as 300,000 black soldiers, but the measure came to nothing because Lee's surrender followed so soon thereafter.

as earnestly, I take it, as our men believed in the cause for which they were fighting—had lost hope and become despondent. Many of them were making application to be sent North where they might get employment until the war was over, when they could return to their Southern homes.

For these and other reasons I was naturally very impatient for the time to come when I could commence the spring campaign, which I thoroughly believed would close the war.

There were two considerations I had to observe, however, and which detained me. One was the fact that the winter had been one of heavy rains, and the roads were impassable for artillery and teams. It was necessary to wait until they had dried sufficiently to enable us to move the wagon trains and artillery necessary to the efficiency of an army operating in the enemy's country. The other consideration was that General Sheridan with the cavalry of the Army of the Potomac was operating on the north side of the James River, having come down from the Shenandoah. It was necessary that I should have his cavalry with me, and I was therefore obliged to wait until he could join me south of the James River.

Let us now take account of what he was doing.

On the 5th of March I had heard from Sheridan. He had met Early between Staunton and Charlottesville and defeated him, capturing nearly his entire command. Early and some of his officers escaped by finding refuge in the neighboring houses or in the woods.[4]

On the 12th I heard from him again. He had turned east, to come to White House. He could not go to Lynchburg as ordered, because the rains had been so very heavy and the streams were so very much swollen. He had a pontoon train with him, but it would not reach half way across some of the streams, at their then stage of water, which he would have to get over in going south as first ordered.

---

4. This was the Battle of Waynesboro, in which Custer decisively scattered Early's command. Early, ever ready with an excuse, later wrote: "The only solution of this affair which I can give is that my men did not fight as I had expected them to do. Had they done so, I am satisfied that the enemy could have been repulsed; and I was and am still of opinion that the attack at Waynesboro was a mere demonstration, to cover a movement to the south towards Lynchburg. Yet some excuse is to be made for my men, as they knew that they were weak and the enemy very strong." *Autobiographical Sketch*, 464.

Sheridan went on to inflict further damage on the Virginia Central Railroad and the James River canal, while Early escaped across the Blue Ridge. After the Confederate surrender, he fled in disguise to Mexico.

I had supplies sent around to White House for him, and kept the depot there open until he arrived. We had intended to abandon it because the James River had now become our base of supplies.

Sheridan had about ten thousand cavalry with him, divided into two divisions commanded respectively by Custer and Devin. General Merritt was acting as chief of cavalry. Sheridan moved very light, carrying only four days' provisions with him, with a larger supply of coffee, salt and other small rations, and a very little else besides ammunition. They stopped at Charlottesville and commenced tearing up the railroad back toward Lynchburg. He also sent a division along the James River Canal to destroy locks, culverts etc. All mills and factories along the lines of march of his troops were destroyed also.

Sheridan had in this way consumed so much time that his making a march to White House was now somewhat hazardous. He determined therefore to fight his way along the railroad and canal till he was as near to Richmond as it was possible to get, or until attacked. He did this, destroying the canal as far as Goochland, and the railroad to a point as near Richmond as he could get. On the 10th he was at Columbia. Negroes had joined his column to the number of two thousand or more, and they assisted considerably in the work of destroying the railroads and the canal. His cavalry was in as fine a condition as when he started, because he had been able to find plenty of forage. He had captured most of Early's horses and picked up a good many others on the road. When he reached Ashland he was assailed by the enemy in force. He resisted their assault with part of his command, moved quickly across the South and North Anna, going north, and reached White House safely on the 19th.

The time for Sherman to move had to be fixed with reference to the time he could get away from Goldsboro where he then was. Supplies had to be got up to him which would last him through a long march, as there would probably not be much to be obtained in the country through which he would pass. I had to arrange, therefore, that he should start from where he was, in the neighborhood of Goldsboro on the 18th of April, the earliest day at which he supposed he could be ready.

Sherman was anxious that I should wait where I was until he could come up, and make a sure thing of it; but I had determined to move as soon as the roads and weather would admit of my doing so. I had been tied down somewhat in the matter of fixing any time at my pleasure for starting, until Sheridan, who was on his way from the Shenandoah Valley to join me,

THE ANNOTATED MEMOIRS OF ULYSSES S. GRANT

should arrive, as both his presence and that of his cavalry were necessary to the execution of the plans which I had in mind. However, having arrived at White House on the 19th of March, I was enabled to make my plans.

Prompted by my anxiety lest Lee should get away some night before I was aware of it, and having the lead of me, push into North Carolina to join with Johnston in attempting to crush out Sherman, I had, as early as the 1st of the month of March, given instructions to the troops around Petersburg to keep a sharp lookout to see that such a movement should not escape their notice, and to be ready to strike at once if it was undertaken.

It is now known that early in the month of March Mr. Davis and General Lee had a consultation about the situation of affairs in and about Richmond and Petersburg, and they both agreed that these places were no longer tenable for them, and that they must get away as soon as possible. They, too, were waiting for dry roads, or a condition of the roads which would make it possible to move.

General Lee, in aid of his plan of escape, and to secure a wider opening to enable them to reach the Danville Road with greater security than he would have in the way the two armies were situated, determined upon an assault upon the right of our lines around Petersburg. The night of the 24th of March was fixed upon for this assault, and General Gordon was assigned to the execution of the plan. The point between Fort Stedman and Battery No. 10, where our lines were closest together, was selected as the point of his attack. The attack was to be made at night, and the troops were to get possession of the higher ground in the rear where they supposed we had intrenchments, then sweep to the right and left, create a panic in the lines of our army, and force me to contract my lines. Lee hoped this would detain me a few days longer and give him an opportunity of escape. The plan was well conceived and the execution of it very well done indeed, up to the point of carrying a portion of our line.

Gordon assembled his troops under the cover of night, at the point at which they were to make their charge, and got possession of our picket-line, entirely without the knowledge of the troops inside of our main line of intrenchments; this reduced the distance he would have to charge over to not much more than fifty yards. For some time before, the deserters had been coming in with great frequency, often bringing their arms with them, and this the Confederate general knew. Taking advantage of this knowledge he sent his pickets, with their arms, creeping through to ours as if to desert. When they got to our lines they at once took possession and sent

One of the sights at City Point: soldiers' graves near General Hospital. *Library of Congress, Prints and Photographs Division, Civil War Photographs, LC-DIG-cwpb-01872.*

our pickets to the rear as prisoners. In the main line our men were sleeping serenely, as if in great security. This plan was to have been executed and much damage done before daylight; but the troops that were to reinforce Gordon had to be brought from the north side of the James River and, by some accident on the railroad on their way over, they were detained for a considerable time; so that it got to be nearly daylight before they were ready to make the charge.

The charge, however, was successful and almost without loss, the enemy passing through our lines between Fort Stedman and Battery No. 10. Then turning to the right and left they captured the fort and the battery, with all the arms and troops in them. Continuing the charge, they also carried batteries Eleven and Twelve to our left, which they turned toward City Point.

Meade happened to be at City Point that night, and this break in his line cut him off from all communication with his headquarters. Parke, however, commanding the 9th corps when this breach took place, telegraphed the facts to Meade's headquarters, and learning that the general was away, assumed command himself and with commendable promptitude made all preparations to drive the enemy back. General Tidball gathered a large number of pieces of artillery and planted them in rear of the captured works so as to sweep the narrow space of ground between the lines very thoroughly. Hartranft was soon out with his division, as also was Willcox. Hartranft to the right of the breach headed the rebels off in that direction and rapidly drove them back into Fort Stedman. On the other side they were driven back into the intrenchments which they had captured, and batteries eleven and twelve were retaken by Willcox early in the morning.

Parke then threw a line around outside of the captured fort and batteries, and communication was once more established. The artillery fire was kept up so continuously that it was impossible for the Confederates to retreat, and equally impossible for reinforcements to join them. They all, therefore, fell captives into our hands. This effort of Lee's cost him about four thousand men, and resulted in their killing, wounding and capturing about two thousand of ours.

After the recapture of the batteries taken by the Confederates, our troops made a charge and carried the enemy's intrenched picket line, which they strengthened and held. This, in turn, gave us but a short distance to charge over when our attack came to be made a few days later.

The day that Gordon was making dispositions for this attack (24th of March) I issued my orders for the movement to commence on the 29th. Ord, with three divisions of infantry and Mackenzie's cavalry, was to move in advance on the night of the 27th, from the north side of the James River and take his place on our extreme left, thirty miles away. He left Weitzel with the rest of the Army of the James to hold Bermuda Hundred and the north of the James River. The engineer brigade was to be left at City Point, and Parke's corps in the lines about Petersburg.[5]

Ord was at his place promptly. Humphreys and Warren were then on our extreme left with the 2d and 5th corps. They were directed on the arrival of Ord, and on his getting into position in their places, to cross Hatcher's Run and extend out west toward Five Forks, the object being to get into a position from which we could strike the South Side Railroad and ultimately the Danville Railroad. There was considerable fighting in taking up these new positions for the 2d and 5th corps, in which the Army of the James had also to participate somewhat, and the losses were quite severe.

This was what was known as the Battle of White Oak Road.[6]

---

5. A note to the first edition directs readers to consult the March 24 orders to Major-Generals Meade, Ord, and Sheridan included in Grant's official report. See Appendix 2.

6. This engagement was the prelude to the conclusive Battle of Five Forks, which took place on April 1.

64

Interview with Sheridan—Grand Movement of the Army of the Potomac—Sheridan's Advance on Five Forks—Battle of Five Forks—Parke and Wright Storm the Enemy's Line—Battles before Petersburg

Sheridan reached City Point on the 26th day of March. His horses, of course, were jaded and many of them had lost their shoes. A few days of rest were necessary to recuperate the animals and also to have them shod and put in condition for moving.[1] Immediately on General Sheridan's arrival

---

1. One solution to the problem of maintaining horses was the bicycle, a mode of military transportation embraced as early as the 1870s by Italian units of infantry and *bersaglieri* (marksmen). The U.S. Army first experimented with bicyclists as couriers in 1892, under the direction of General Nelson Miles. See Henry H. Whitney, "The Adaptation of the Bicycle to Military Uses," *Journal of the Military Service Institution* 17 (November 1895): 542–63.

In California during the 1890s, "the Signal Corps constantly sought more efficient methods to perform line repair and maintenance. In keeping with the bicycle craze then rolling across the nation, the Corps found its own uses for the velocipede, as it was then called," writes Signal Corps historian Rebecca Robbins Raines. "Bicycles provided a faster and more economical means for making repairs. In the time it took to secure a horse and wagon, a linesman could jump on his bicycle, repair the line, and return to his station. The Corps also began adapting the bicycle to lay and take up wire." *Getting the Message Through: A Branch History of the U.S. Army Signal Corps* (Washington, D.C.: Center of Military History, U.S. Army, 1999), 83.

In several late nineteenth- and twentieth-century conflicts, including the Boer, Spanish-American, and Russo-Japanese Wars, World War I, and World War II, the bicycle was used for scouting, signal, ambulance, and other service. Meanwhile, the last U.S. cavalry charge did not take place until 1942, when the 26th Cavalry Regiment

at City Point I prepared his instructions for the move which I had decided upon. The movement was to commence on the 29th of the month.

After reading the instructions I had given him, Sheridan walked out of my tent, and I followed to have some conversation with him by himself—not in the presence of anybody else, even of a member of my staff. In preparing his instructions I contemplated just what took place; that is to say, capturing Five Forks, driving the enemy from Petersburg and Richmond and terminating the contest before separating from the enemy. But the Nation had already become restless and discouraged at the prolongation of the war, and many believed that it would never terminate except by compromise. Knowing that unless my plan proved an entire success it would be interpreted as a disastrous defeat, I provided in these instructions that in a certain event he was to cut loose from the Army of the Potomac and his base of supplies, and living upon the country proceed south by the way of the Danville Railroad, or near it, across the Roanoke, get in the rear of Johnston, who was guarding that road, and co-operate with Sherman in destroying Johnston; then with these combined forces to help carry out the instructions which Sherman already had received, to act in co-operation with the armies around Petersburg and Richmond.

I saw that after Sheridan had read his instructions he seemed somewhat disappointed at the idea, possibly, of having to cut loose again from the Army of the Potomac, and place himself between the two main armies of the enemy. I said to him: "General, this portion of your instructions I have put in merely as a blind;" and gave him the reason for doing so, heretofore described. I told him that, as a matter of fact, I intended to close the war right here, with this movement, and that he should go no farther. His face at once

---

attacked Japanese soldiers in the Philippines. The romance of the cavalry dies hard; it remains today a community steeped in tradition.

French Army cyclists in World War I. *Library of Congress, Prints and Photographs Division, LC-DIG-ggbain-17027.*

brightened up, and slapping his hand on his leg he said: "I am glad to hear it, and we can do it."[2]

Sheridan was not however to make his movement against Five Forks until he got further instructions from me.

One day, after the movement I am about to describe had commenced, and when his cavalry was on our extreme left and far to the rear, south, Sheridan rode up to where my headquarters were then established, at Dabney's Mills. He met some of my staff officers outside, and was highly jubilant over the prospects of success, giving reasons why he believed this would prove the final and successful effort. Although my chief-of-staff had urged very strongly that we return to our position about City Point and in the lines around Petersburg, he asked Sheridan to come in to see me and say to me what he had been saying to them. Sheridan felt a little modest about giving his advice where it had not been asked; so one of my staff came in and told me that Sheridan had what they considered important news, and suggested that I send for him. I did so, and was glad to see the spirit of confidence with which he was imbued. Knowing as I did from experience, of what great value that feeling of confidence by a commander was, I determined to make a movement at once, although on account of the rains which had fallen after I had started out the roads were still very heavy. Orders were given accordingly.

Finally the 29th of March came, and fortunately there having been a few days free from rain, the surface of the ground was dry, giving indications that the time had come when we could move. On that date I moved out with all the army available after leaving sufficient force to hold the line about Petersburg. It soon set in raining again however, and in a very short time the roads became practically impassable for teams, and almost so for cavalry. Sometimes a horse or mule would be standing apparently on firm ground, when all at once one foot would sink, and as he commenced scrambling to catch himself all his feet would sink and he would have to be drawn by hand out of the quicksands so common in that part of Virginia and other southern States.[3] It became necessary therefore to build corduroy

2. Sheridan notes that Sherman appealed to him personally the following day: "Very early the next morning, while I was still in bed, General Sherman came to me and renewed the subject of my joining him, but when he saw that I was unalterably opposed to it the conversation turned into other channels, and after we had chatted awhile he withdrew." *Memoirs*, 2:133.

3. Excerpts from a report by Charles W. Howell, a brevet captain of engineers, make clear the challenges of operating in such terrain:

roads every foot of the way as we advanced, to move our artillery upon. The army had become so accustomed to this kind of work, and were so well prepared for it, that it was done very rapidly. The next day, March 30th, we had made sufficient progress to the south-west to warrant me in starting Sheridan with his cavalry over by Dinwiddie with instructions to then come up by the road leading north-west to Five Forks, thus menacing the right of Lee's line.

This movement was made for the purpose of extending our lines to the west as far as practicable towards the enemy's extreme right, or Five Forks. The column moving detached from the army still in the trenches was, excluding the cavalry, very small. The forces in the trenches were themselves extending to the left flank. Warren was on the extreme left when the extension began, but Humphreys was marched around later and thrown into line between him and Five Forks.

My hope was that Sheridan would be able to carry Five Forks, get on the enemy's right flank and rear, and force them to weaken their centre to protect their right so that an assault in the centre might be successfully made. General Wright's corps had been designated to make this assault, which I intended to order as soon as information reached me of Sheridan's success. He was to move under cover as close to the enemy as he could get.

It is natural to suppose that Lee would understand my design to be to get up to the South Side and ultimately to the Danville Railroad, as soon as he had heard of the movement commenced on the 29th. These roads were so important to his very existence while he remained in Richmond and

---

On the 30th I was again sent to the Second Corps, but was soon after ordered to find roads to communicate with the different divisions of the corps and to put them in good condition. I found the roads, but, owing to the heavy rains in the morning, found it impossible to get them more than barely passable by corduroying the worst places. . . . I was afterward sent from Sutherland's Station with orders . . . to examine the country from that to Bevill's Bridge. . . . I found the roads, after the passage of artillery and a few heavy wagons, in very bad condition, the country hilly, the soil a sandy clay, and in the bottom land disposed to quicksand. The road had been much cut up by the passage of the rebel army with its trains, and our movements were, in consequence, rendered more difficult and laborious.

April 19, 1865, *OR*, ser. 1, vol. 46, pt. 1, 655–56.

Sheridan and Warren both echo Howell's assessment of the poor conditions. See, respectively, *Memoirs*, 2:137–38, and Report, February 21, 1865 [1866], *OR*, ser. 1, vol. 46, pt. 1, 797.

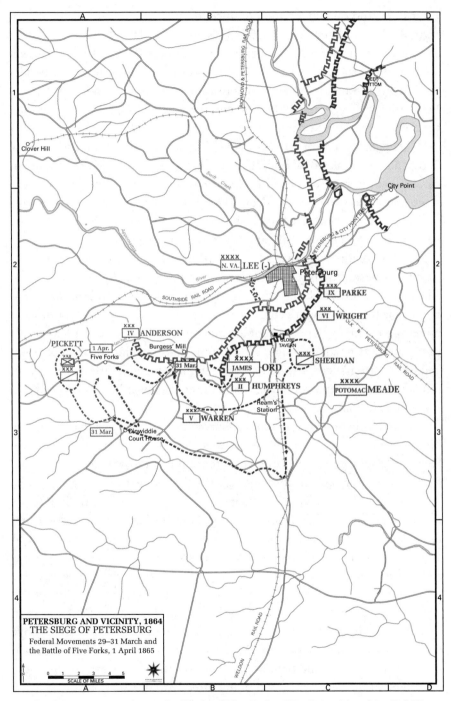

Federal movements prior to the Battle of Five Forks. *West Point Atlas of the Civil War.*
Courtesy of Department of History, USMA.

Petersburg, and of such vital importance to him even in case of retreat, that naturally he would make most strenuous efforts to defend them. He did on the 30th send Pickett with five brigades to reinforce Five Forks. He also sent around to the right of his army some two or three other divisions, besides directing that other troops be held in readiness on the north side of the James River to come over on call. He came over himself to superintend in person the defence of his right flank.

Sheridan moved back to Dinwiddie Court-House on the night of the 30th, and then took a road leading north-west to Five Forks. He had only his cavalry with him. Soon encountering the rebel cavalry he met with a very stout resistance. He gradually drove them back however until in the neighborhood of Five Forks. Here he had to encounter other troops besides those he had been contending with, and was forced to give way.

In this condition of affairs he notified me of what had taken place and stated that he was falling back toward Dinwiddie gradually and slowly, and asked me to send Wright's corps to his assistance. I replied to him that it was impossible to send Wright's corps because that corps was already in line close up to the enemy, where we should want to assault when the proper time came, and was besides a long distance from him; but the 2d (Humphreys's) and 5th (Warren's) corps were on our extreme left and a little to the rear of it in a position to threaten the left flank of the enemy at Five Forks, and that I would send Warren.

Accordingly orders were sent to Warren to move at once that night (the 31st) to Dinwiddie Court-House and put himself in communication with Sheridan as soon as possible, and report to him. He was very slow in moving, some of his troops not starting until after 5 o'clock next morning. When he did move it was done very deliberately, and on arriving at Gravelly Run he found the stream swollen from the recent rains so that he regarded it as not fordable. Sheridan of course knew of his coming, and being impatient to get the troops up as soon as possible, sent orders to him to hasten. He was also hastened or at least ordered to move up rapidly by General Meade. He now felt that he could not cross that creek without bridges, and his orders were changed to move so as to strike the pursuing enemy in flank or get in their rear; but he was so late in getting up that Sheridan determined to move forward without him. However, Ayres's division of Warren's corps reached him in time to be in the fight all day, most of the time separated from the remainder of the 5th corps and fighting directly under Sheridan.

Warren reported to Sheridan about 11 o'clock on the 1st, but the whole of his troops were not up so as to be much engaged until late in the afternoon.

Statue of Gouverneur Kemble
Warren, Grand Army Plaza,
Brooklyn, New York. *Photograph by
Elizabeth D. Samet.*

Griffin's division in backing to get out of the way of a severe cross fire of the enemy was found marching away from the fighting. This did not continue long, however; the division was brought back and with Ayres's division did most excellent service during the day. Crawford's division of the same corps had backed still farther off, and although orders were sent repeatedly to bring it up, it was late before it finally got to where it could be of material assistance. Once there it did very excellent service.

Sheridan succeeded by the middle of the afternoon or a little later, in advancing up to the point from which to make his designed assault upon Five Forks itself. He was very impatient to make the assault and have it all over before night, because the ground he occupied would be untenable for him in bivouac during the night. Unless the assault was made and was successful, he would be obliged to return to Dinwiddie Court-House, or even further than that for the night.

It was at this junction of affairs that Sheridan wanted to get Crawford's division in hand, and he also wanted Warren. He sent staff officer after staff officer in search of Warren, directing that general to report to him, but they were unable to find him. At all events Sheridan was unable to get that officer to him. Finally he went himself. He issued an order relieving Warren and assigning Griffin to the command of the 5th corps. The troops were then brought up and the assault successfully made.[4]

I was so much dissatisfied with Warren's dilatory movements in the battle of White Oak Road and in his failure to reach Sheridan in time, that I was very much afraid that at the last moment he would fail Sheridan. He was a man of fine intelligence, great earnestness, quick perception, and could

4. The result was disastrous for the Confederates, and the Battle of Five Forks came to be called the Confederate Waterloo. Sheridan's resounding victory set the end in motion: a Union assault broke through the next day, Petersburg fell, and Richmond was soon evacuated.

make his dispositions as quickly as any officer, under difficulties where he was forced to act. But I had before discovered a defect which was beyond his control, that was very prejudicial to his usefulness in emergencies like the one just before us. He could see every danger at a glance before he had encountered it. He would not only make preparations to meet the danger which might occur, but he would inform his commanding officer what others should do while he was executing his move.

I had sent a staff officer to General Sheridan to call his attention to these defects, and to say that as much as I liked General Warren, now was not a time when we could let our personal feelings for any one stand in the way of success; and if his removal was necessary to success, not to hesitate. It was upon that authorization that Sheridan removed Warren. I was very sorry that it had been done, and regretted still more that I had not long before taken occasion to assign him to another field of duty.[5]

---

5. The controversy over Warren's relief lingered on, and the general's campaign to vindicate his reputation consumed him for the rest of his life. A court of inquiry ultimately upheld Sheridan's decision. Sheridan reports that despite the fact that Warren "seemed to understand" him "clearly," he did not move his column up promptly. Instead, Sheridan found him "sitting under a tree making a rough sketch of the ground. I was disappointed that more of the corps was not already up, and as the precious minutes went by without any apparent effort to hurry the troops on to the field, this disappointment grew into disgust." Sheridan continues: "Warren did not seem to me to be at all solicitous; his manner exhibited decided apathy, and he remarked with indifference that 'Bobby Lee was always getting people into trouble.' With unconcern such as this, it is no wonder that fully three hours' time was consumed in marching his corps . . . but two miles." *Memoirs*, 2:160–61.

Full of sympathy for Warren, George Cullum's biographical sketch quotes liberally from the testimony of Warren's allies, one of whom claims that Warren died "of a broken heart." Another, General Henry L. Abbot, lavishly describes Warren's heroism in the moments before his relief:

Here a pause occurred, and personal magnetism seemed called for to lead on the troops, who for a moment had lost their organizations in the confusion. Warren, having discharged the more pressing duty of directing the whole force of his Corps upon the enemy, now found time to yield to his natural impulse. He seized his headquarters flag, rode into the opening, and, calling on the color-bearers to advance, led the charge. His horse fell dead under him close to the enemy's lines, an orderly by his side was killed, and his own life was probably saved by the gallant act of Colonel Richardson, 7th Wisconsin, who sprung between him and the enemy, receiving a severe wound. This charge put an end to all resistance. Surrounded by his captures and flushed with victory, Warren sent back a staff officer to report to General Sheridan and ask for further orders.

It was dusk when our troops under Sheridan went over the parapets of the enemy. The two armies were mingled together there for a time in such manner that it was almost a question which one was going to demand the surrender of the other. Soon, however, the enemy broke and ran in every direction; some six thousand prisoners, besides artillery and small-arms in large quantities, falling into our hands. The flying troops were pursued in different directions, the cavalry and 5th corps under Sheridan pursuing the larger body which moved north-west.

This pursuit continued until about nine o'clock at night, when Sheridan halted his troops, and knowing the importance to him of the part of the enemy's line which had been captured, returned, sending the 5th corps across Hatcher's Run to just south-west of Petersburg, and facing them toward it. Merritt, with the cavalry, stopped and bivouacked west of Five Forks.

This was the condition which affairs were in on the night of the 1st of April. I then issued orders for an assault by Wright and Parke at four o'clock on the morning of the 2d. I also ordered the 2d corps, General Humphreys, and General Ord with the Army of the James, on the left, to hold themselves in readiness to take any advantage that could be taken from weakening in their front.

I notified Mr. Lincoln at City Point of the success of the day; in fact I had reported to him during the day and evening as I got news, because he was so much interested in the movements taking place that I wanted to relieve his mind as much as I could. I notified Weitzel on the north side of the James River, directing him, also, to keep close up to the enemy, and take

These orders came in writing. They relieved him from the command of his Corps, and ordered him to report to General Grant.

If the bullet which killed his horse had pierced the heart of the rider, Warren, like Wolfe dying upon the Heights of Abraham, would have gone down in history the hero of the battle. This order, more cruel than the bullet, doubtless caused his death after seventeen years of suffering which intimate friends who understood his sensitive organization can alone appreciate. It is pitiful that one of his last requests was to be laid in the grave without the usual military ceremonial, without soldierly emblems on his coffin or uniform upon his body. The iron had entered his soul.

Biographical Register, vol. 2, s.v. "Warren, Gouverneur K."

Joshua Chamberlain's reflections on the battle can be found in *Five Forks: A Paper Read before the Military Order of the Loyal Legion, Commandery of Maine*, May 2, 1901 (Portland, ME: Lefavor-Tower, 1902).

advantage of the withdrawal of troops from there to promptly enter the city of Richmond.

I was afraid that Lee would regard the possession of Five Forks as of so much importance that he would make a last desperate effort to retake it, risking everything upon the cast of a single die. It was for this reason that I had ordered the assault to take place at once, as soon as I had received the news of the capture of Five Forks. The corps commanders, however, reported that it was so dark that the men could not see to move, and it would be impossible to make the assault then. But we kept up a continuous artillery fire upon the enemy around the whole line including that north of the James River, until it was light enough to move, which was about a quarter to five in the morning.

At that hour Parke's and Wright's corps moved out as directed, brushed the *abatis* from their front as they advanced under a heavy fire of musketry and artillery, and went without flinching directly on till they mounted the parapets and threw themselves inside of the enemy's line. Parke, who was on the right, swept down to the right and captured a very considerable length of line in that direction, but at that point the outer was so near the inner line which closely enveloped the city of Petersburg that he could make no advance forward and, in fact, had a very serious task to turn the lines which he had captured to the defence of his own troops and to hold them; but he succeeded in this.

Wright swung around to his left and moved to Hatcher's Run, sweeping everything before him. The enemy had traverses in rear of his captured line, under cover of which he made something of a stand, from one to another, as Wright moved on; but the latter met no serious obstacle. As you proceed to the left the outer line becomes gradually much farther from the inner one, and along about Hatcher's Run they must be nearly two miles apart. Both Parke and Wright captured a considerable amount of artillery and some prisoners—Wright about three thousand of them.

In the meantime Ord and Humphreys, in obedience to the instructions they had received, had succeeded by daylight, or very early in the morning, in capturing the intrenched picket-lines in their front; and before Wright got up to that point, Ord had also succeeded in getting inside of the enemy's intrenchments. The second corps soon followed; and the outer works of Petersburg were in the hands of the National troops, never to be wrenched from them again. When Wright reached Hatcher's Run, he sent a regiment to destroy the South Side Railroad just outside of the city.

My headquarters were still at Dabney's saw-mills. As soon as I received the news of Wright's success, I sent dispatches announcing the fact to all points around the line, including the troops at Bermuda Hundred and those on the north side of the James, and to the President at City Point. Further dispatches kept coming in, and as they did I sent the additional news to these points. Finding at length that they were all in, I mounted my horse to join the troops who were inside the works. When I arrived there I rode my horse over the parapet just as Wright's three thousand prisoners were coming out. I was soon joined inside by General Meade and his staff.

Lee made frantic efforts to recover at least part of the lost ground. Parke on our right was repeatedly assaulted, but repulsed every effort. Before noon Longstreet was ordered up from the north side of the James River thus bringing the bulk of Lee's army around to the support of his extreme right. As soon as I learned this I notified Weitzel and directed him to keep up close to the enemy and to have Hartsuff, commanding the Bermuda Hundred front, to do the same thing, and if they found any break to go in; Hartsuff especially should do so, for this would separate Richmond and Petersburg.

Sheridan, after he had returned to Five Forks, swept down to Petersburg, coming in on our left. This gave us a continuous line from the Appomattox River below the city to the same river above. At eleven o'clock, not having heard from Sheridan, I reinforced Parke with two brigades from City Point. With this additional force he completed his captured works for better defence, and built back from his right, so as to protect his flank. He also carried in and made an *abatis* between himself and the enemy. Lee brought additional troops and artillery against Parke even after this was done, and made several assaults with very heavy losses.[6]

---

6. While Union forces were enveloping the Confederates at Five Forks, their commanders, George Pickett and Fitzhugh Lee, could not be found. They were enjoying a shad bake two miles behind the line, on the north side of Hatcher's Run, at the invitation of General Thomas L. Rosser. And when notified of the federal advance and preparation for attack, they stayed on. In an unpublished sketch of the battle Confederate General Thomas Munford subsequently explained what happened when he became aware that pickets on his left had been engaged:

> I instantly dispatched to General Fitz Lee and to General Pickett, giving them this information and ordered my division to move to that point as quickly as they could come through the woods over a very narrow road. I sent Capt. Henry Lee of my staff . . . to bring up my men and to tell Gen. Pickett and Gen. Fitz Lee what he personally had seen. He rode the whole of the line of battle hoping to meet Gen. Pickett—not being able to find

The enemy had in addition to their intrenched line close up to Petersburg, two enclosed works outside of it, Fort Gregg and Fort Whitworth. We thought it had now become necessary to carry them by assault. About one o'clock in the day, Fort Gregg was assaulted by Foster's division of the

General Pickett, he notified his staff officers. Meanwhile I dispatched several other couriers, repeating this information and urging General Pickett and General Fitzhugh Lee to come in person to the front, but unfortunately the two Generals had gone to Rosser's headquarters, two miles off.

The host himself, Rosser, published his own version of events thirty years later, on April 5, 1895, in a letter to the Philadelphia *Weekly Times*:

I had brought some excellent fresh shad from the Nottoway River with me, and I invited General Pickett to go back and lunch with me—he promised to be with me in an hour. He and Fitz Lee came back to me. While we were at lunch, Couriers came back . . . reporting the advance of the enemy. Some time was spent over the lunch, during which no firing was heard. . . . And we concluded that the enemy was not in much of a hurry to find us at Five Forks. A courier sent to the Five Forks from us, was fired at over the creek and came galloping back—reporting the enemy were in the road in front of us and in rear of our position at Five Forks. General Pickett made an effort to join his command. He came riding back in a great hurry and called for the Dinwiddie Troops as guide and rode off with them, but I think his troops were routed before he reached them. The battle of Five Forks was of short duration, but quite used up that portion of the Army engaged. It seems to have been a surprise to General Pickett. One would have supposed that he would have been on the alert in the presence of the enemy he had been so recently fighting.

This incident provides yet another example of the mutual recrimination that textures postwar writing on both sides: Pickett omitted the shad bake entirely from his reports, while Fitzhugh Lee blamed General Richard Anderson for not coming to the aid of the Confederates. Anderson's biographer, Irvin C. Walker, sought to vindicate his subject by including abundant testimony from participants north and south. Walker bitterly observes: "Fitzhugh Lee knew nothing, from his own experience, of the battle, being engaged in the enjoyment of the luscious 'Shad Bake.' He was guarding his throat from the feathery shad bones, and not guarding the great Lee against the disaster which the failure at Five Forks brought upon the Army of Northern Virginia." All testimony above about the notorious shad bake comes from C. Irvine Walker, *The Life of Lieutenant General Richard Heron Anderson of the Confederate States Army* (Charleston, SC: Art Publishing, 1917), 227, 229–30, 225.

John Mosby later recounted a secondhand version of what happened when Pickett passed Lee during the retreat after Five Forks: "General Lee said, with deep feeling: 'Is that man still with this army?'" "Picture Pickett as Enemy of Lee," Richmond *Times Dispatch*, March 21, 1911, p. 10.

24th corps (Gibbon's), supported by two brigades from Ord's command. The battle was desperate and the National troops were repulsed several times; but it was finally carried, and immediately the troops in Fort Whitworth evacuated the place. The guns of Fort Gregg were turned upon the retreating enemy, and the commanding officer with some sixty of the men of Fort Whitworth surrendered.

I had ordered Miles in the morning to report to Sheridan. In moving to execute this order he came upon the enemy at the intersection of the White Oak Road and the Claiborne Road. The enemy fell back to Sutherland Station on the South Side Road and were followed by Miles. This position, naturally a strong and defensible one, was also strongly intrenched. Sheridan now came up and Miles asked permission from him to make the assault, which Sheridan gave. By this time Humphreys had got through the outer works in his front, and came up also and assumed command over Miles, who commanded a division in his corps. I had sent an order to Humphreys to turn to his right and move towards Petersburg. This order he now got, and started off, thus leaving Miles alone. The latter made two assaults, both of which failed, and he had to fall back a few hundred yards.

Hearing that Miles had been left in this position, I directed Humphreys to send a division back to his relief. He went himself.

Sheridan before starting to sweep down to Petersburg had sent Merritt with his cavalry to the west to attack some Confederate cavalry that had assembled there. Merritt drove them north to the Appomattox River. Sheridan then took the enemy at Sutherland Station on the reverse side from where Miles was, and the two together captured the place, with a large number of prisoners and some pieces of artillery, and put the remainder, portions of three Confederate corps, to flight. Sheridan followed, and drove them until night, when further pursuit was stopped. Miles bivouacked for the night on the ground which he with Sheridan had carried so handsomely by assault. I cannot explain the situation here better than by giving my dispatch to City Point that evening:

BOYDTON ROAD, NEAR PETERSBURG,
April 2, 1865.—4.40 P.M.

COLONEL T. S. BOWERS,
City Point.

We are now up and have a continuous line of troops, and in a few hours will be intrenched from the Appomattox below Petersburg to the river above. Heth's and Wilcox's divisions, such part of them as were not captured, were cut off from town, either designedly on their part or because they could not help it. Sheridan with the cavalry and 5th corps is above them. Miles's division, 2d corps, was sent from the White Oak Road to Sutherland Station on the South Side Railroad, where he met them, and at last accounts was engaged with them. Not knowing whether Sheridan would get up in time, General Humphreys was sent with another division from here. The whole captures since the army started out gunning will amount to not less than twelve thousand men, and probably fifty pieces of artillery. I do not know the number of men and guns accurately however. ★ ★ ★ I think the President might come out and pay us a visit tomorrow.

U. S. GRANT,
Lieutenant-General.

During the night of April 2d our line was intrenched from the river above to the river below. I ordered a bombardment to be commenced the next morning at five A.M., to be followed by an assault at six o'clock; but the enemy evacuated Petersburg early in the morning.

65

The Capture of Petersburg—Meeting President Lincoln in Petersburg—The Capture of Richmond—Pursuing the Enemy—Visit to Sheridan and Meade

General Meade and I entered Petersburg on the morning of the 3d and took a position under cover of a house which protected us from the enemy's musketry which was flying thick and fast there.[1] As we would occasionally look around the corner we could see the streets and the Appomattox bottom, presumably near the bridge, packed with the Confederate army. I did not have artillery brought up, because I was sure Lee was trying to make his escape, and I wanted to push immediately in pursuit.[2]

Statue of George G. Meade, flanked by Loyalty and Chivalry, Washington, D.C. *Photograph by Elizabeth D. Samet.*

1. Philadelphia *Press* correspondent Thomas Morris Chester proudly reported that the 7th and 8th United States Colored Troops formed part of the vanguard: "It must be a source of great gratification to the friends of this element of Union strength to be assured that the first organizations to enter these strongholds of the rebellion, Richmond and Petersburg, were colored troops." *Civil War Correspondent*, 313.

2. Of Grant's decision essentially to bypass Petersburg, Longstreet writes: "Again, in our own war, when the Union army carried the Confederate works west of Petersburg on the 2d of April, 1865, General Meade got his army together and

At all events I had not the heart to turn the artillery upon such a mass of defeated and fleeing men, and I hoped to capture them soon.

Soon after the enemy had entirely evacuated Petersburg, a man came in who represented himself to be an engineer of the Army of Northern Virginia. He said that Lee had for some time been at work preparing a strong enclosed intrenchment, into which he would throw himself when forced out of Petersburg, and fight his final battle there; that he was actually at that time drawing his troops from Richmond, and falling back into this prepared work. This statement was made to General Meade and myself when we were together. I had already given orders for the movement up the south side of the Appomattox for the purpose of heading off Lee; but Meade was so much impressed by this man's story that he thought we ought to cross the Appomattox there at once and move against Lee in his new position. I knew that Lee was no fool, as he would have been to have put himself and his army between two formidable streams like the James and Appomattox rivers, and between two such armies as those of the Potomac and the James. Then these streams coming together as they did to the east of him, it would be only necessary to close up in the west to have him thoroughly cut off from all supplies or possibility of reinforcement. It would only have been a question of days, and not many of them, if he had taken the position assigned to him by the so-called engineer, when he would have been obliged to surrender his army. Such is one of the ruses resorted to in war to deceive your antagonist.[3]

---

was about to march east to finish his work by the capture of Petersburg. General Grant objected,—that the Confederates would retreat during the night; at Petersburg he would be behind them; in his then position he would be alongside of them, and have an even start, with better prospect to strike across their march and force them to general battle or surrender; and he ordered arrangements for the march west at daylight." *Manassas to Appomattox*, 405.

3. One of the most literary ruses in the annals of war is one reportedly used by England's Henry IV against rebels at the Battle of Shrewsbury in 1403, where several knights appeared on the field wearing the king's colors. According to the Tudor chronicler Raphael Holinshed, the Earl of Douglas "slue sir Walter Blunt, and three other, apparelled in the kings sute and clothing, saieng: I marvell to see so many kings thus suddenlie rise one in the necke of an other." *Holinshed's Chronicles of England, Scotland, and Ireland* (London, 1808), 3:26.

Seizing on the poetic potential of this stratagem, Shakespeare depicts one of the rebels, the Earl of Douglas, encountering the king himself after having already met several impostors:

DOUGLAS. Another king! they grow like Hydra's heads:
I am the Douglas, fatal to all those

My judgment was that Lee would necessarily have to evacuate Richmond, and that the only course for him to pursue would be to follow the Danville Road. Accordingly my object was to secure a point on that road south of Lee, and I told Meade this. He suggested that if Lee was going that way we would follow him. My reply was that we did not want to follow him; we wanted to get ahead of him and cut him off, and if he would only stay in the position he (Meade) believed him to be in at that time, I wanted nothing better; that when we got in possession of the Danville Railroad, at its crossing of the Appomattox River, if we still found him between the two rivers, all we had to do was to move eastward and close him up. That we would then have all the advantage we could possibly have by moving directly against him from Petersburg, even if he remained in the position assigned him by the engineer officer.

I had held most of the command aloof from the intrenchments, so as to start them out on the Danville Road early in the morning, supposing that Lee would be gone during the night. During the night I strengthened Sheridan by sending him Humphreys's corps.

Lee, as we now know, had advised the authorities at Richmond, during the day, of the condition of affairs, and told them it would be impossible for him to hold out longer than night, if he could hold out that long. Davis was at church when he received Lee's dispatch. The congregation was dismissed with the notice that there would be no evening service. The rebel government left Richmond about two o'clock in the afternoon of the 2d.

At night Lee ordered his troops to assemble at Amelia Court House, his object being to get away, join Johnston if possible, and to try to crush Sherman before I could get there. As soon as I was sure of this I notified Sheridan

---

      That wear those colours on them: what art thou,
      That counterfeit'st the person of a king?

KING. The King himself; who, Douglas, grieves at heart
      So many of his shadows thou hast met
      And not the very King. I have two boys
      Seek Percy and thyself about the field:
      But, seeing thou fall'st on me so luckily,
      I will assay thee: so, defend thyself.

DOUGLAS. I fear thou art another counterfeit;
      And yet, in faith, thou bear'st thee like a king:
      But mine I am sure thou art, whoe'er thou be,
      And thus I win thee.

1 Henry IV 5.4.25–38.

and directed him to move out on the Danville Railroad to the south side of the Appomattox River as speedily as possible. He replied that he already had some of his command nine miles out. I then ordered the rest of the Army of the Potomac under Meade to follow the same road in the morning. Parke's corps followed by the same road, and the Army of the James was directed to follow the road which ran alongside of the South Side Railroad to Burke's Station, and to repair the railroad and telegraph as they proceeded. That road was a 5 feet gauge, while our rolling stock was all of the 4 feet 8½ inches gauge; consequently the rail on one side of the track had to be taken up throughout the whole length and relaid so as to conform to the gauge of our cars and locomotives.

Mr. Lincoln was at City Point at the time, and had been for some days. I would have let him know what I contemplated doing, only while I felt a strong conviction that the move was going to be successful, yet it might not prove so; and then I would have only added another to the many disappointments he had been suffering for the past three years. But when we started out he saw that we were moving for a purpose, and bidding us Godspeed, remained there to hear the result.

The next morning after the capture of Petersburg, I telegraphed Mr. Lincoln asking him to ride out there and see me, while I would await his arrival. I had started all the troops out early in the morning, so that after the National army left Petersburg there was not a soul to be seen, not even an animal in the streets. There was absolutely no one there, except my staff officers and, possibly, a small escort of cavalry. We had selected the piazza of a deserted house, and occupied it until the President arrived.

About the first thing that Mr. Lincoln said to me, after warm congratulations for the victory, and thanks both to myself and to the army which had accomplished it, was: "Do you know, general, that I have had a sort of a sneaking idea for some days that you intended to do something like this." Our movements having been successful up to this point, I no longer had any object in concealing from the President all my movements, and the objects I had in view. He remained for some days near City Point, and I communicated with him frequently and fully by telegraph.[4]

4. "Grant's strategy of attacking the enemy wherever he found them also carried out Lincoln's strategy of trying to cripple the enemy army as far from Richmond (or any other base) as possible rather than maneuver to occupy or capture *places*," James McPherson writes. "Clearly, the conquest and occupation of places would not win the war so long as enemy armies remained capable of reconquering them." "A. Lincoln, Commander in

Mr. Lincoln knew that it had been arranged for Sherman to join me at a fixed time, to co-operate in the destruction of Lee's army. I told him that I had been very anxious to have the Eastern armies vanquish their old enemy who had so long resisted all their repeated and gallant attempts to subdue them or drive them from their capital. The Western armies had been in the main successful until they had conquered all the territory from the Mississippi River to the State of North Carolina, and were now almost ready to knock at the back door of Richmond, asking admittance. I said to him that if the Western armies should be even upon the field, operating against Richmond and Lee, the credit would be given to them for the capture, by politicians and non-combatants from the section of country which those troops hailed from. It might lead to disagreeable bickerings between members of Congress of the

---

Chief," *Our Lincoln: New Perspectives on Lincoln and his World*, ed. Eric Foner (New York: Norton, 2008), 32.

James Rusling relates a conversation between General Sickles, on whose staff Rusling was serving, and Lincoln, which although heavily embroidered, is nonetheless suggestive of the sympathy between the president and Grant. Rusling also ends up making Lincoln sound just a bit like Gertrude Stein:

> "Well, Mr. President, what are you thinking about Vicksburg, nowadays? How are things getting along down there?"
>
> "O," answered Mr. Lincoln, very gravely, "I don't quite know. Grant is still pegging away down there. As we used to say out in Illinois, I think he 'will make a spoon or spoil a horn' before he gets through. Some of our folks think him slow and want me to remove him. But, to tell the truth, I kind of like U. S. Grant. He doesn't worry and bother me. He isn't shrieking for reinforcements all the time. He takes what troops we can safely give him, considering our big job all around—and we have a pretty big job in this war—and does the best he can with what he has got, and doesn't grumble and scold all the while. Yes, I confess, I like General Grant—U. S. Grant—'Uncle Sam Grant!' . . . There is a great deal to him, first and last. . . .
>
> . . . I have done the very best I could to help General Grant along, and all the rest of our generals, though some of them don't think so, and now it is kind of borne in on me that somehow or other we are going to win at Vicksburg too. I can't tell how soon. But I believe we will. For this will save the Mississippi and bisect the Confederacy; and be in line with God's laws besides. And if Grant only does this thing down there—I don't care much how, so he does it *right*—why, Grant is my man and I am his the rest of this war!"

James Fowler Rusling, *Men and Things I Saw in Civil War Days* (New York: Methodist Book Concern, 1914), 16–17.

East and those of the West in some of their debates. Western members might be throwing it up to the members of the East that in the suppression of the rebellion they were not able to capture an army, or to accomplish much in the way of contributing toward that end, but had to wait until the Western armies had conquered all the territory south and west of them, and then come on to help them capture the only army they had been engaged with.

Mr. Lincoln said he saw that now, but had never thought of it before, because his anxiety was so great that he did not care where the aid came from so the work was done.

The Army of the Potomac has every reason to be proud of its four years' record in the suppression of the rebellion. The army it had to fight was the protection to the capital of a people which was attempting to found a nation upon the territory of the United States. Its loss would be the loss of the cause. Every energy, therefore, was put forth by the Confederacy to protect and maintain their capital. Everything else would go if it went. Lee's army had to be strengthened to enable it to maintain its position, no matter what territory was wrested from the South in another quarter.

I never expected any such bickering as I have indicated, between the soldiers of the two sections; and, fortunately, there has been none between the politicians. Possibly I am the only one who thought of the liability of such a state of things in advance.

When our conversation was at an end Mr. Lincoln mounted his horse and started on his return to City Point, while I and my staff started to join the army, now a good many miles in advance. Up to this time I had not received the report of the capture of Richmond.

Soon after I left President Lincoln I received a dispatch from General Weitzel which notified me that he had taken possession of Richmond at about 8.15 o'clock in the morning of that day, the 3d, and that he had found the city on fire in two places. The city was in the most utter confusion. The authorities had taken the precaution to empty all the liquor into the gutter, and to throw out the provisions which the Confederate government had left, for the people to gather up. The city had been deserted by the authorities, civil and military, without any notice whatever that they were about to leave. In fact, up to the very hour of the evacuation the people had been led to believe that Lee had gained an important victory somewhere around Petersburg.

Weitzel's command found evidence of great demoralization in Lee's army, there being still a great many men and even officers in the town. The city was on fire. Our troops were directed to extinguish the flames, which they finally succeeded in doing. The fire had been started by some one connected with the retreating army. All authorities deny that it was authorized, and I presume it was the work of excited men who were leaving what they regarded as their capital and may have felt that it was better to destroy it than have it fall into the hands of their enemy. Be that as it may, the National troops found the city in flames, and used every effort to extinguish them.

The troops that had formed Lee's right, a great many of them, were cut off from getting back into Petersburg, and were pursued by our cavalry so hotly and closely that they threw away caissons, ammunition, clothing, and almost everything to lighten their loads, and pushed along up the Appomattox River until finally they took water and crossed over.

I left Mr. Lincoln and started, as I have already said, to join the command, which halted at Sutherland Station, about nine miles out. We had still time to march as much farther, and time was an object; but the roads were bad and the trains belonging to the advance corps had blocked up the road so that it was impossible to get on. Then, again, our cavalry had struck some of the enemy and were pursuing them; and the orders were that the roads should be given up to the cavalry whenever they appeared. This caused further delay.

General Wright, who was in command of one of the corps which were left back, thought to gain time by letting his men go into bivouac and trying to get up some rations for them, and clearing out the road, so that when they did start they would be uninterrupted. Humphreys, who was far ahead, was also out of rations. They did not succeed in getting them up through the night; but the Army of the Potomac, officers and men, were so elated by the reflection that at last they were following up a victory to its end, that they preferred marching without rations to running a possible risk of letting the enemy elude them. So the march was resumed at three o'clock in the morning.

Merritt's cavalry had struck the enemy at Deep Creek, and driven them north to the Appomattox, where, I presume, most of them were forced to cross.

On the morning of the 4th I learned that Lee had ordered rations up from Danville for his famishing army, and that they were to meet him at Farmville. This showed that Lee had already abandoned the idea of following the railroad down to Danville, but had determined to go farther west, by the way of Farmville. I notified Sheridan of this and directed him to get possession of the road before the supplies could reach Lee. He responded that he had already sent Crook's division to get upon the road between Burkesville and Jetersville, then to face north and march along the road upon the latter place; and he thought Crook must be there now. The bulk of the army moved directly for Jetersville by two roads.

After I had received the dispatch from Sheridan saying that Crook was on the Danville Road, I immediately ordered Meade to make a forced march with the Army of the Potomac, and to send Parke's corps across from the road they were on to the South Side Railroad, to fall in the rear of the Army of the James and to protect the railroad which that army was repairing as it went along.

Our troops took possession of Jetersville and in the telegraph office, they found a dispatch from Lee, ordering two hundred thousand rations from Danville. The dispatch had not been sent, but Sheridan sent a special messenger with it to Burkesville and had it forwarded from there. In the meantime, however, dispatches from other sources had reached Danville, and they knew there that our army was on the line of the road; so that they sent no further supplies from that quarter.

At this time Merritt and Mackenzie, with the cavalry, were off between the road which the Army of the Potomac was marching on and the Appomattox River, and were attacking the enemy in flank. They picked up a great many prisoners and forced the abandonment of some property.

Lee intrenched himself at Amelia Court House, and also his advance north of Jetersville, and sent his troops out to collect forage. The country was very poor and afforded but very little. His foragers scattered a great deal; many of them were picked up by our men, and many others never returned to the Army of Northern Virginia.

Griffin's corps was intrenched across the railroad south of Jetersville, and Sheridan notified me of the situation. I again ordered Meade up with all dispatch, Sheridan having but the one corps of infantry with a little cavalry confronting Lee's entire army. Meade, always prompt in obeying orders, now pushed forward with great energy, although he was himself sick and hardly able to be out of bed. Humphreys moved at two, and Wright at three o'clock in the morning, without rations, as I have said, the wagons being far in the rear.

I stayed that night at Wilson's Station on the South Side Railroad. On the morning of the 5th I sent word to Sheridan of the progress Meade was making, and suggested that he might now attack Lee. We had now no other objective than the Confederate armies, and I was anxious to close the thing up at once.

On the 5th I marched again with Ord's command until within about ten miles of Burkesville, where I stopped to let his army pass. I then received from Sheridan the following dispatch:

"The whole of Lee's army is at or near Amelia Court House, and on this side of it. General Davies, whom I sent out to Painesville on their right flank, has just captured six pieces of artillery and some wagons. We can capture the Army of Northern Virginia if force enough can be thrown to this point, and then advance upon it. My cavalry was at Burkesville yesterday, and six miles beyond, on the Danville Road, last night. General Lee is at Amelia Court House in person. They are out of rations, or nearly so. They were advancing up the railroad towards Burkesville yesterday, when we intercepted them at this point."

It now became a life and death struggle with Lee to get south to his provisions.

Sheridan, thinking the enemy might turn off immediately towards Farmville, moved Davies's brigade of cavalry out to watch him. Davies found the movement had already commenced. He attacked and drove away their cavalry which was escorting wagons to the west, capturing and burning 180 wagons. He also captured five pieces of artillery. The Confederate infantry then moved against him and probably would have handled him very roughly, but Sheridan had sent two more brigades of cavalry to follow Davies, and they came to his relief in time. A sharp engagement took place between these three brigades of cavalry and the enemy's infantry, but the latter was repulsed.

Meade himself reached Jetersville about two o'clock in the afternoon, but in advance of all his troops. The head of Humphreys's corps followed in about an hour afterwards. Sheridan stationed the troops as they came up, at Meade's request, the latter still being very sick. He extended two divisions of this corps off to the west of the road to the left of Griffin's corps, and one division to the right. The cavalry by this time had also come up, and they were put still farther off to the left, Sheridan feeling certain that there lay the route by which the enemy intended to escape. He wanted to attack, feeling that if time was given, the enemy would get away; but Meade prevented this, preferring to wait till his troops were all up.

At this juncture Sheridan sent me a letter which had been handed to him by a colored man, with a note from himself saying that he wished I was there myself. The letter was dated Amelia Court House, April 5th, and signed by Colonel Taylor. It was to his mother, and showed the demoralization of the Confederate army. Sheridan's note also gave me the information as here related of the movements of that day. I received a second message from Sheridan on the 5th, in which he urged more emphatically the importance of my presence. This was brought to me by a scout in gray uniform. It was written on tissue paper, and wrapped up in tin-foil such as chewing tobacco is folded in. This was a precaution taken so that if the scout should be captured he could take this tin-foil out of his pocket and putting it into his mouth, chew it. It would cause no surprise at all to see a Confederate soldier chewing tobacco.[5] It was nearly night when this letter was received. I gave Ord direc-

5. J. A. Campbell, Sheridan's intrepid young scout, has two dramatic cameos in Horace Porter's memoir. "Campbell was only nineteen years of age," Porter notes. "Sheridan always addressed him as 'Boy,' and the history of his many hairbreadth escapes that year would fill a volume. Campbell has always remained a scout and is still in the employ of the government in that capacity at Fort Custer." In the first episode, Campbell rides into Grant's headquarters at City Point after Sheridan's defeat of Early at Waynesboro; later, he reappears with another message from Sheridan, carried in a tin-foil pellet in his mouth. Within the pellet was "a sheet of tissue-paper, on which was written the famous despatch, so widely published at the time, in which Sheridan described the situation at Jetersville, and added, 'I wish you were here yourself.'" When Grant decides to go to Sheridan, with Campbell as his escort, the ride, as Porter narrates it, is full of drama. Despite his subsequent enthusiasm for Campbell, Porter was suspicious of him at this stage:

The general said he would go at once to Sheridan, and dismounted from his black pony "Jeff Davis," which he had been riding, and called for his horse "Cincinnati." He stood in the road for a few minutes, and wrote a despatch to Ord, using the pony's back for a desk, and then, mounting the fresh horse, told Campbell to lead the way. It was found that we would have to skirt pretty closely to the enemy's lines, and it was thought that it would be prudent to take some cavalry with us; but there was none near at hand, and the general said he would risk it with our mounted escort of fourteen men. Calling upon me and three other officers to accompany him, he started off. I had in the mean while questioned the scout about the trip, and found that we would have to follow some cross-roads through a wooded country and travel nearly twenty miles. It was now dark, but there was enough moonlight to enable us to see the way without difficulty. After riding for nearly two hours, the enemy's camp-fires were seen in the distance, and it was noticed that the fence-rails were thrown down in a number of places, indicating that cavalry had been moving across this part of the country, though we were certain our cavalry had not been there. Knowing that scouts are seldom trustworthy, and are often in the employ of both sides, and feeling that the general's safety was now entirely in the power of a comparatively unknown man, I, for one, began to grow suspicious. Just then Campbell fell back several paces and suddenly turned his horse into a piece of woods which we were skirting, and seemed to be acting in a manner that indicated either confusion or treachery. I cocked

tions to continue his march to Burkesville and there intrench himself for the night, and in the morning to move west to cut off all the roads between there and Farmville.

I then started with a few of my staff and a very small escort of cavalry, going directly through the woods, to join Meade's army. The distance was about sixteen miles; but the night being dark our progress was slow through the woods in the absence of direct roads. However, we got to the outposts about ten o'clock in the evening, and after some little parley convinced the sentinels of our identity and were conducted in to where Sheridan was bivouacked. We talked over the situation for some little time, Sheridan explaining to me what he thought Lee was trying to do, and that Meade's orders, if carried out, moving to the right flank, would give him the coveted opportunity of escaping us and putting us in rear of him.

We then together visited Meade, reaching his headquarters about midnight. I explained to Meade that we did not want to follow the enemy; we wanted to get ahead of him, and that his orders would allow the enemy to escape, and besides that, I had no doubt that Lee was moving right then. Meade changed his orders at once. They were now given for an advance on Amelia Court House, at an early hour in the morning, as the army then lay; that is, the infantry being across the railroad, most of it to the west of the road, with the cavalry swung out still farther to the left.[6]

---

my pistol, and rode close behind him, thinking his feelings would stand that much in the way of precaution anyhow, and determined that if he was caught giving any suspicious signals I would at once arrest him. The scout, however, was thoroughly loyal, and one of Sheridan's most trusted men; no thought of treachery had crossed his mind; he was only looking for a short cut through the woods.

Porter, *Campaigning*, 399–400, 454–56.

6. Grant trusted Sheridan's aggressiveness as he did Sherman's, but the relationship between Sheridan and Meade was fraught almost from the beginning. Meade's staff officer Theodore Lyman surmised in his journal that the origins of Sheridan's animosity toward Meade and Warren may have begun in May 1864: "Sheridan now came to Headquarters—we were at dinner. Meade told him sharply that his cavalry was in the way, though he had sent him orders to leave the road clear. S. replied that he never got the order. Meade then apologized, but Sheridan was plainly full of suppressed anger, and Meade too was in ill temper. S. went on to say that he could see nothing to oppose the advance of the 5th Corps; that the behavior of the infantry was disgraceful, etc., etc. Maybe this was the beginning of his dislike of Warren and ill-feeling against Meade." *Meade's Headquarters*, 105–6, n. 1.

66

Battle of Sailor's Creek—Engagement at Farmville—Correspondence with General Lee—Sheridan Intercepts the Enemy

The Appomattox, going westward, takes a long sweep to the southwest from the neighborhood of the Richmond and Danville Railroad bridge, and then trends north-westerly. Sailor's Creek, an insignificant stream, running northward, empties into the Appomattox between the High Bridge and Jetersville. Near the High Bridge the stage road from Petersburg to Lynchburg crosses the Appomattox River, also on a bridge. The railroad runs on the north side of the river to Farmville, a few miles west, and from there, recrossing, continues on the south side of it. The roads coming up from the south-east to Farmville cross the Appomattox River there on a bridge and run on the north side, leaving the Lynchburg and Petersburg Railroad well to the left.

Lee, in pushing out from Amelia Court House, availed himself of all the roads between the Danville Road and Appomattox River to move upon, and never permitted the head of his columns to stop because of any fighting that might be going on in his rear. In this way he came very near succeeding in getting to his provision trains and eluding us with at least part of his army.

As expected, Lee's troops had moved during the night before, and our army in moving upon Amelia Court House soon encountered them. There was a good deal of fighting before Sailor's Creek was reached. Our cavalry charged in upon a body of theirs which was escorting a wagon train in order to get it past our left. A severe engagement ensued, in which we captured many prisoners, and many men also were killed and wounded. There was as much gallantry displayed by some of the Confederates in these little engage-

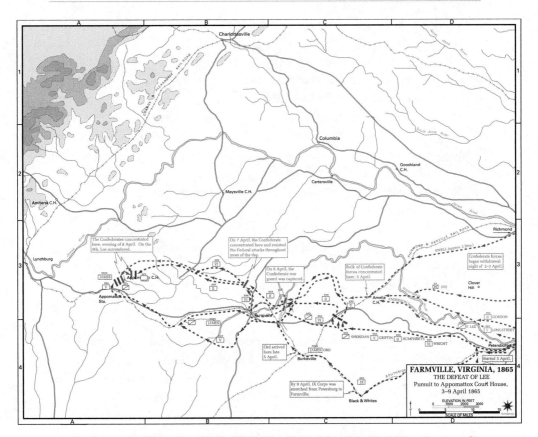

Final pursuit of Lee, April 3–9, 1865. *West Point Atlas of the Civil War. Courtesy of Department of History, USMA.*

ments as was displayed at any time during the war, notwithstanding the sad defeats of the past week.

The armies finally met on Sailor's Creek, when a heavy engagement took place, in which infantry, artillery and cavalry were all brought into action. Our men on the right, as they were brought in against the enemy, came in on higher ground, and upon his flank, giving us every advantage to be derived from the lay of the country. Our firing was also very much more rapid, because the enemy commenced his retreat westward and in firing as he retreated had to turn around every time he fired. The enemy's loss was very heavy, as well in killed and wounded as in captures. Some six general officers fell into our hands in this engagement, and seven thousand men were made prisoners. This engagement was commenced in the middle of the afternoon of the 6th, and the retreat and pursuit were continued until nightfall, when the armies bivouacked upon the ground where the night had overtaken them.

When the move towards Amelia Court House had commenced that morning, I ordered Wright's corps, which was on the extreme right, to be moved to the left past the whole army, to take the place of Griffin's, and ordered the latter at the same time to move by and place itself on the right. The object of this movement was to get the 6th corps, Wright's, next to the cavalry, with which they had formerly served so harmoniously and so efficiently in the valley of Virginia.

The 6th corps now remained with the cavalry and under Sheridan's direct command until after the surrender.

Ord had been directed to take possession of all the roads southward between Burkesville and the High Bridge. On the morning of the 6th he sent Colonel Washburn with two infantry regiments with instructions to destroy High Bridge and to return rapidly to Burkesville Station; and he prepared himself to resist the enemy there. Soon after Washburn had started Ord became a little alarmed as to his safety and sent Colonel Read, of his staff, with about eighty cavalrymen, to overtake him and bring him back. Very shortly after this he heard that the head of Lee's column had got up to the road between him and where Washburn now was, and attempted to send reinforcements, but the reinforcements could not get through. Read, however, had got through ahead of the enemy. He rode on to Farmville and was on his way back again when he found his return cut off, and Washburn confronting apparently the advance of Lee's army. Read drew his men up into line of battle, his force now consisting of less than six hundred men, infantry and cavalry, and rode along their front, making a speech to his men to inspire them with the same enthusiasm that he himself felt. He then gave the order to charge. This little band made several charges, of course unsuccessful ones, but inflicted a loss upon the enemy more than equal to their own entire number. Colonel Read fell mortally wounded, and then Washburn; and at the close of the conflict nearly every officer of the command and most of the rank and file had been either killed or wounded. The remainder then surrendered. The Confederates took this to be only the advance of a larger column which had headed them off, and so stopped to intrench; so that this gallant band of six hundred had checked the progress of a strong detachment of the Confederate army.

This stoppage of Lee's column no doubt saved to us the trains following. Lee himself pushed on and crossed the wagon road bridge near the High Bridge, and attempted to destroy it. He did set fire to it, but the flames had

High Bridge, Appomattox, Virginia. Photograph by Timothy L. O'Sullivan. *Library of Congress, Prints and Photographs Division, Civil War Photographs, LC-DIG-ppmsca-33390.*

made but little headway when Humphreys came up with his corps and drove away the rear-guard which had been left to protect it while it was being burned up.[1] Humphreys forced his way across with some loss, and followed

---

1. Racing Lee to his likeliest resupply points, Sheridan engaged the Confederate rear at the Battle of Sailor's—or Sayler's—Creek. He captured six thousand of the enemy and, in the words of James Longstreet, "the Confederate rear was crushed to fragments." Longstreet quotes the report of William Mahone, who held on until 11:00 p.m., retreated, and attempted to burn a bridge behind him:

> On reaching the south crest of the high ground at the crossing of the river road overlooking Sailor's Creek, the disaster which had overtaken our army was in full view, and the scene beggars description,—hurrying teamsters with their teams and dangling traces (no wagons), retreating infantry without guns, many without hats, a harmless mob, with the massive columns of the enemy moving orderly on. At this spectacle General Lee straightened himself in his saddle, and, looking more the soldier than ever, exclaimed, as if talking to himself, "My God! has the army dissolved?" As quickly as I could control my own voice I replied, "No, general, here are troops ready to do their duty;" when, in a mellowed voice, he replied, "Yes, general, there are some true men left. Will you please keep those people back?" As I was placing my division in position to "keep those people back," the retiring herd just referred to had crowded around General Lee while he sat on his horse with a Confederate battle flag in his hand. I rode up and requested him to give me the flag, which he did.
>
> . . . I wanted to know what should be done with the bridge after crossing it. He said, "Set fire to it," and I replied that the destruction of a span would as well retard the enemy as the destruction of the whole half mile of bridge, and asked him to call up Colonel Talcott, of the Engineers' Regiment, and personally direct him in the matter, which he did.

Manassas to Appomattox, 614–15.

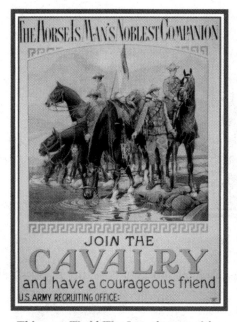

THE HORSE IS MAN'S NOBLEST COMPANION

JOIN THE
CAVALRY
and have a courageous friend
U.S. ARMY RECRUITING OFFICE:

This post–World War I cavalry recruiting poster appealed to nostalgia for an earlier age. *Library of Congress Prints and Photographs Division, World War I Posters, LC-USZC4-1350.*

Lee to the intersection of the road crossing at Farmville with the one from Petersburg. Here Lee held a position which was very strong, naturally, besides being intrenched. Humphreys was alone, confronting him all through the day, and in a very hazardous position. He put on a bold face, however, and assaulted with some loss, but was not assaulted in return.

Our cavalry had gone farther south by the way of Prince Edward's Court House, along with the 5th corps (Griffin's), Ord falling in between Griffin and the Appomattox. Crook's division of cavalry and Wright's corps pushed on west of Farmville. When the cavalry reached Farmville they found that some of the Confederates were in ahead of them, and had already got their trains of provisions back to that point; but our troops were in time to prevent them from securing anything to eat, although they succeeded in again running the trains off, so that we did not get them for some time. These troops retreated to the north side of the Appomattox to join Lee, and succeeded in destroying the bridge after them. Considerable fighting ensued there between Wright's corps and a portion of our cavalry and the Confederates, but finally the cavalry forded the stream and drove them away. Wright built a foot-bridge for his men to march over on and then marched out to the junction of the roads to relieve Humphreys, arriving there that night. I had stopped the night before at Burkesville Junction. Our troops were then pretty much all out of the place, but we had a field hospital there, and Ord's command was extended from that point towards Farmville.

Here I met Dr. Smith, a Virginian and an officer of the regular army, who

---

The Confederates successfully destroyed the bridges at Farmville, but the High Bridge survived: Confederates managed to burn four spans of the railroad bridge, but the wagon bridge below remained intact.

"Gunshot fracture of the right acetabulum and the head of the femur: Case of Colonel James C. Strong, 38th New York," *The Medical and Surgical History of the War of the Rebellion. Courtesy of NIH U.S. National Library of Medicine.*

told me that in a conversation with General Ewell, one of the prisoners and a relative of his, Ewell had said that when we had got across the James River he knew their cause was lost, and it was the duty of their authorities to make the best terms they could while they still had a right to claim concessions. The authorities thought differently, however. Now the cause was lost and they had no right to claim anything. He said further, that for every man that was killed after this in the war somebody is responsible, and it would be but very little better than murder. He was not sure that Lee would consent to surrender his army without being able to consult with the President, but he hoped he would.[2]

I rode in to Farmville on the 7th, arriving there early in the day. Sheridan and Ord were pushing through, away to the south. Meade was back towards the High Bridge, and Humphreys confronting Lee as before stated. After having gone into bivouac at Prince Edward's Court House, Sheridan learned that seven trains of provisions and forage were at Appomattox, and determined to start at once and capture them; and a forced march was necessary in order to get there

2. "Indeed," the Confederate general Edward Porter Alexander asserts, "no man who looked at our situation on a map, or who understood the geography of the country, could fail to see that Gen. Grant now had us completely in a trap. He had stood upon the hills at Farmville that morning & watched the last of our column go in. We were now in a sort of jug shaped peninsula between the James River & the Appomattox, & there was but one outlet, the neck of the jug at Appomattox C.H., and to that Grant had the shortest road!" *Fighting for the Confederacy*, 527.

before Lee's army could secure them. He wrote me a note telling me this. This fact, together with the incident related the night before by Dr. Smith, gave me the idea of opening correspondence with General Lee on the subject of the surrender of his army. I therefore wrote to him on this day, as follows:

HEADQUARTERS ARMIES OF THE U. S.,
5 P.M., *April 7, 1865.*

GENERAL R. E. LEE,
Commanding C. S. A.

The results of the last week must convince you of the hopelessness of further resistance on the part of the Army of Northern Virginia in this struggle. I feel that it is so, and regard it as my duty to shift from myself the responsibility of any further effusion of blood, by asking of you the surrender of that portion of the Confederate States army known as the Army of Northern Virginia.

U. S. GRANT,
Lieut.-General.

Lee replied on the evening of the same day as follows:

April 7, 1865.

GENERAL: I have received your note of this day. Though not entertaining the opinion you express on the hopelessness of further resistance on the part of the Army of Northern Virginia, I reciprocate your desire to avoid useless effusion of blood, and therefore before considering your proposition, ask the terms you will offer on condition of its surrender.

R. E. LEE,
General.

LIEUT.-GENERAL U. S. GRANT,
Commanding Armies of the U. S.

This was not satisfactory, but I regarded it as deserving another letter and wrote him as follows:

April 8, 1865.

GENERAL R. E. LEE,
Commanding C. S. A.

Your note of last evening in reply to mine of same date, asking the condition on which I will accept the surrender of the Army of Northern Virginia is just received. In reply I would say that, peace being my great desire, there is but one condition I would insist upon, namely: that the men and officers surrendered shall be disqualified for taking up arms again against the Government of the United States until properly exchanged. I will meet you, or will designate officers to meet any officers you may name for the same purpose, at any point agreeable to you, for the purpose of arranging definitely the terms upon which the surrender of the Army of Northern Virginia will be received.

U. S. GRANT,
Lieut.-General.

Lee's army was rapidly crumbling. Many of his soldiers had enlisted from that part of the State where they now were, and were continually dropping out of the ranks and going to their homes. I know that I occupied a hotel almost destitute of furniture at Farmville, which had probably been used as a Confederate hospital. The next morning when I came out I found a Confederate colonel there, who reported to me and said that he was the proprietor of that house, and that he was a colonel of a regiment that had been raised in that neighborhood. He said that when he came along past home, he found that he was the only man of the regiment remaining with Lee's army, so he just dropped out, and now wanted to surrender himself. I told him to stay there and he would not be molested. That was one regiment which had been eliminated from Lee's force by this crumbling process.

Although Sheridan had been marching all day, his troops moved with alacrity and without any straggling. They began to see the end of what they had been fighting four years for. Nothing seemed to fatigue them. They were ready to move without rations and travel without rest until the end. Straggling had entirely ceased, and every man was now a rival for the front. The infantry marched about as rapidly as the cavalry could.

Sheridan sent Custer with his division to move south of Appomattox Station, which is about five miles south-west of the Court House, to get west of the trains and destroy the roads to the rear. They got there the night of the 8th, and succeeded partially; but some of the train men had just discovered the movement of our troops and succeeded in running off three of the trains. The other four were held by Custer.

The head of Lee's column came marching up there on the morning of the 9th, not dreaming, I suppose, that there were any Union soldiers near. The Confederates were surprised to find our cavalry had possession of the trains. However, they were desperate and at once assaulted, hoping to recover them. In the melée that ensued they succeeded in burning one of the trains, but not in getting anything from it. Custer then ordered the other trains run back on the road towards Farmville, and the fight continued.

So far, only our cavalry and the advance of Lee's army were engaged. Soon, however, Lee's men were brought up from the rear, no doubt expecting they had nothing to meet but our cavalry. But our infantry had pushed forward so rapidly that by the time the enemy got up they found Griffin's corps and the Army of the James confronting them. A sharp engagement ensued, but Lee quickly set up a white flag.

Negotiations at Appomattox—Interview with Lee at McLean's House—The Terms of Surrender—Lee's Surrender—Interview with Lee after the Surrender

On the 8th I had followed the Army of the Potomac in rear of Lee. I was suffering very severely with a sick headache, and stopped at a farmhouse on the road some distance in rear of the main body of the army. I spent the night in bathing my feet in hot water and mustard, and putting mustard plasters on my wrists and the back part of my neck, hoping to be cured by morning.[1] During the night I received Lee's answer to my letter of the 8th, inviting an interview between the lines on the following morning.[2] But it was for a different purpose from that of surrendering his army, and I answered him as follows:

HEADQUARTERS ARMIES OF THE U. S.,
April 9, 1865.

GENERAL R. E. LEE,
Commanding C. S. A.

Your note of yesterday is received. As I have no authority to treat on the subject of peace, the meeting proposed for ten A.M. to-day could lead to no good. I will state, however, General, that I

---

1. Jean Edward Smith suggests that Grant's headache was an instance of the psychosomatic illnesses he sometimes suffered "in the hours leading up to major events." *Grant*, 401.

2. A note to the first edition directs readers to consult the copy of Lee's letter included in Grant's official report. See Appendix 2.

am equally anxious for peace with yourself, and the whole North entertains the same feeling. The terms upon which peace can be had are well understood. By the South laying down their arms they will hasten that most desirable event, save thousands of human lives and hundreds of millions of property not yet destroyed. Sincerely hoping that all our difficulties may be settled without the loss of another life, I subscribe myself, etc.,

U. S. GRANT,
Lieutenant-General.

I proceeded at an early hour in the morning, still suffering with the headache, to get to the head of the column. I was not more than two or three miles from Appomattox Court House at the time, but to go direct I would have to pass through Lee's army, or a portion of it. I had therefore to move south in order to get upon a road coming up from another direction.[3]

When the white flag was put out by Lee, as already described, I was

---

3. Chamberlain describes the end, which echoed in its confusion an event near the beginning, the Union retreat from Bull Run:

> In the hollow is the Appomattox,—which we had made the dead-line for our baffled foe, for its whole length, a hundred miles; here but a rivulet that might almost be stepped over dry-shod, and at the road crossing not thought worth while to bridge. Around its edges, now trodden to mire, swarms an indescribable crowd: worn-out soldier struggling to the front; demoralized citizen and denizen, white, black, and all shades between,—following Lee's army, or flying before these suddenly confronted terrible Yankees pictured to them as demon-shaped and bent; animals, too, of all forms and grades; vehicles of every description and nondescription,—public and domestic, four-wheeled, or two, or one,—heading and moving in every direction, a swarming mass of chaotic confusion. . . .
>
> I was doubtful of my duty. The flag of truce was in, but I had no right to act upon it without orders. . . . But I did not press things quite so hard. Just then a last cannon-shot from the edge of the town plunges through the breast of a gallant and dear young officer in my front line,—Lieutenant Clark, of the 185th New York,—the last man killed in the Army of the Potomac, if not the last in the Appomattox lines. Not a strange thing for war,—this swift stroke of the mortal; but coming after the truce was in, it seemed a cruel fate for one so deserving to share his country's joy, and a sad peace-offering for us all.

Passing of the Armies, 237–38, 241–42.

in this way moving towards Appomattox Court House, and consequently could not be communicated with immediately, and be informed of what Lee had done. Lee, therefore, sent a flag to the rear to advise Meade and one to the front to Sheridan, saying that he had sent a message to me for the purpose of having a meeting to consult about the surrender of his army, and asked for a suspension of hostilities until I could be communicated with. As they had heard nothing of this until the fighting had got to be severe and all going against Lee, both of these commanders hesitated very considerably about suspending hostilities at all. They were afraid it was not in good faith, and we had the Army of Northern Virginia where it could not escape except by some deception. They, however, finally consented to a suspension of hostilities for two hours to give an opportunity of communicating with me in that time, if possible. It was found that, from the route I had taken, they would probably not be able to communicate with me and get an answer back within the time fixed unless the messenger should pass through the rebel lines.

Lee, therefore, sent an escort with the officer bearing this message through his lines to me.

April 9, 1865.

GENERAL: I received your note of this morning on the picket-line whither I had come to meet you and ascertain definitely what terms were embraced in your proposal of yesterday with reference to the surrender of this army. I now request an interview in accordance with the offer contained in your letter of yesterday for that purpose.

R. E. LEE, General.[4]

LIEUTENANT-GENERAL U. S. GRANT,
Commanding U. S. Armies.

---

4. Edward Porter Alexander reports with disdain that while Lee was awaiting Grant's answer, Custer independently demanded a surrender from Longstreet: "Longstreet explained that Lee was in communication with Gen. Grant upon that matter. Custer said, 'Well, Sheridan & I are independent here today, & unless you surrender immediately we are going to pitch in.' Longstreet answered, 'Pitch as much as you like,' & turning to one of his staff said, 'Take this gentleman & conduct him back to his lines, & he may consider himself lucky to get back safely after his impertinent errand.' Custer went back apparently crest fallen, & the episode seems to have been very little known for years after." *Fighting for the Confederacy*, 537.

When the officer reached me I was still suffering with the sick headache; but the instant I saw the contents of the note I was cured. I wrote the following note in reply and hastened on:

April 9, 1865.

GENERAL R. E. LEE,
Commanding C. S. Armies.

Your note of this date is but this moment (11.50 A.M.) received, in consequence of my having passed from the Richmond and Lynchburg road to the Farmville and Lynchburg road. I am at this writing about four miles west of Walker's Church and will push forward to the front for the purpose of meeting you. Notice sent to me on this road where you wish the interview to take place will meet me.

U. S. GRANT,
Lieutenant-General.

I was conducted at once to where Sheridan was located with his troops drawn up in line of battle facing the Confederate army near by. They were very much excited, and expressed their view that this was all a ruse employed to enable the Confederates to get away. They said they believed that Johnston was marching up from North Carolina now, and Lee was moving to join him; and they would whip the rebels where they now were in five minutes if I would only let them go in. But I had no doubt about the good faith of Lee, and pretty soon was conducted to where he was. I found him at the house of a Mr. McLean, at Appomattox Court House, with Colonel Marshall, one of his staff officers, awaiting my arrival. The head of his column was occupying a hill, on a portion of which was an apple orchard, beyond a little valley which separated it from that on the crest of which Sheridan's forces were drawn up in line of battle to the south.

Before stating what took place between General Lee and myself, I will give all there is of the story of the famous apple tree.

Wars produce many stories of fiction, some of which are told until they are believed to be true. The war of the rebellion was no exception to this rule, and the story of the apple tree is one of those fictions based on a slight foundation of fact. As I have said, there was an apple orchard on the side of the hill occupied by the Confederate forces. Running diagonally up the hill was a wagon road, which, at one point, ran very near one of the trees, so that the wheels of vehicles had, on that side, cut off the roots of this tree, leaving a little embankment. General Babcock, of my staff, reported to me that when he first met General Lee he was sitting upon this embankment with his feet in the road below and his back resting against the tree. The story had no other foundation than that. Like many other stories, it would be very good if it was only true.[5]

I had known General Lee in the old army, and had served with him in the Mexican War; but did not suppose, owing to the difference in our age and rank, that he would remember me; while I would more naturally remember him distinctly, because he was the chief of staff [chief engineer] of General Scott in the Mexican War.

When I had left camp that morning I had not expected so soon the result that was then taking place, and consequently was in rough garb. I was without a sword, as I usually was when on horseback on the field, and wore a soldier's blouse for a coat, with the shoulder straps of my rank to indicate to the army who I was. When I went into the house I found General Lee. We greeted each other, and after shaking hands took our seats. I had my staff with me, a good portion of whom were in the room during the whole of the interview.[6]

---

5. Throughout this chapter, Grant clearly relishes dispelling all of the myths that had grown up around the surrender. As he had done on other occasions, most notably in his account of Pemberton's surrender at Vicksburg, Grant surgically dissects the "romance" of Appomattox. For an entirely different account of the surrender, see James Thurber's spoof on a series of counterfactual pieces, the first of which was "If Booth Had Missed Lincoln," that began appearing in *Scribner's Magazine* in 1930: "If Grant Had Been Drinking at Appomattox," *The New Yorker*, December 6, 1930.

6. The contents of McLean's house became prized relics—like the tree at Vicksburg—and McLean profited by them: "Union soldiers' awareness of the epochal importance of the surrender translated not only into eloquent reflections on the moment but also into a seemingly more down-to-earth impulse: a mania for relics," notes historian Elizabeth R. Varon:

> General Ord procured the marble-topped table at which Lee had sat, while Sheridan claimed the table on which Grant drafted the surrender terms; he then offered it as a gift to Libbie Custer, in tribute to her "gallant husband." George Sharpe seized the candlesticks, while an aide-de-camp of Sheridan's . . . took home a rag doll belonging to McLean's daughter Lulu—and dubbed it "Silent Witness." While the evidence suggests that Sheridan and Ord bought the tables from McLean, it is unclear whether the other relics were purchased or purloined. In some accounts, McLean eagerly sold the items, but this claim was disputed by his family. Some relics were discreetly tucked away.

Appomattox: Victory, Defeat, and Freedom at the End of the Civil War (New York: Oxford University Press, 2014), 89.

What General Lee's feelings were I do not know. As he was a man of much dignity, with an impassible face, it was impossible to say whether he felt inwardly glad that the end had finally come, or felt sad over the result, and was too manly to show it. Whatever his feelings, they were entirely concealed from my observation; but my own feelings, which had been quite jubilant on the receipt of his letter, were sad and depressed. I felt like anything rather than rejoicing at the downfall of a foe who had fought so long and valiantly, and had suffered so much for a cause, though that cause was, I believe, one of the worst for which a people ever fought, and one for which there was the least excuse. I do not question, however, the sincerity of the great mass of those who were opposed to us.[7]

7. Grant is very precise here in suggesting at once the "sincerity" with which the rebels fought and the unjustness of their cause. In his description of Lee, there is cool respect but little enthusiasm or suggestion of common ground. That they were vastly different men is obvious, and Grant in this important description of a pivotal moment resists the temptations of vindictiveness on the one hand and sentimentality on the other. In this civil war, in which there were so many similarities between enemies, Grant preserves a crucial distance.

One might contrast the British writer Patrick Leigh Fermor's description of a moment of fellow-feeling with a German general. As a commando during World War II, Fermor participated in the April 1944 kidnapping of General Kreipe, the German commander on Crete. Awaiting the arrival of a British submarine to take them off the island, the prisoner and his captors spent several nights together in a cave—often sharing the same blanket to keep warm—to elude German troops combing the island for the missing general. Leigh Fermor recalled one early morning episode:

> We woke up among the rocks, just as a brilliant dawn was breaking over the crest of Mount Ida which we had been struggling across for two days. We were all three lying smoking in silence, when the General, half to himself, slowly said:
>
> "Vides ut alta stet nive candidum
> Soracte . . ."

I was in luck. It is the opening line of one of the few odes of Horace I know by heart (*Ad Thaliarchum*, I.ix). I went on reciting where he had broken off:

> ". . . Nec iam sustineant onus
> Silvae laborantes, geluque
> Flumina constiterint acuto"

and so on, through the remaining five stanzas to the end.
The General's blue eyes swivelled away from the mountain-top to mine—and when I'd finished, after a long silence, he said: "Ach so, Herr

General Lee was dressed in a full uniform which was entirely new, and was wearing a sword of considerable value, very likely the sword which had been presented by the State of Virginia; at all events, it was an entirely different sword from the one that would ordinarily be worn in the field. In my rough traveling suit, the uniform of a private with the straps of a lieutenant-general, I must have contrasted very strangely with a man so handsomely dressed, six feet high and of faultless form. But this was not a matter that I thought of until afterwards.[8]

We soon fell into a conversation about old army times. He remarked that he remembered me very well in the old army; and I told him that as a matter of course I remembered him perfectly, but from the difference in our rank and years (there being about sixteen years' difference in our ages), I had thought it very likely that I had not attracted his attention sufficiently to be remembered by him after such a long interval. Our conversation grew so pleasant that I almost forgot the object of our meeting. After the conversation had run on in this style for some time, General Lee called my attention to the object of our meeting, and said that he had asked for this interview for the purpose of getting from me the terms I proposed to give his army. I said that I meant merely that his army should lay down their arms, not to take them up again during the continuance of the war unless duly and properly exchanged. He said that he had so understood my letter.

Then we gradually fell off again into conversation about matters foreign to the subject which had brought us together. This continued for some little

---

Major!" It was very strange. "Ja, Herr General." As though, for a long moment, the war had ceased to exist. We had both drunk at the same fountains long before; and things were different between us for the rest of our time together.

Words of Mercury, ed. Artemis Cooper (London: John Murray, 2004), 95–96.

Noting its "blokeish tone," the classicist Mary Beard refers to this exchange as "the upmarket equivalent of singing 'Silent Night' across the trenches" during the Christmas truce of 1914. See "Don't forget your pith helmet," *London Review of Books* (August 18, 2005): 5. With its smoky fraternity and rosy-fingered vista, Leigh Fermor's recollection of the recitation has a cinematic quality. (A film, *Ill Met by Moonlight*, starring Dirk Bogarde as Leigh Fermor, was in fact made about the abduction in 1957.) The episode also advances the deeply romantic proposition that a few lines of Horace can momentarily transcend hostilities and silence the guns.

8. Grant was certainly modest by nature, his distaste for pomp genuine, but he clearly recognized the advantage of the reputation he had cultivated, and this chapter is artfully drawn in every respect.

General Ely S. Parker. *National Archives photo no. 111-B-4121 (Brady Collection).*

time, when General Lee again interrupted the course of the conversation by suggesting that the terms I proposed to give his army ought to be written out. I called to General Parker,[9] secretary on my staff, for writing materials, and commenced writing out the following terms:

APPOMATTOX C. H., VA.,

Ap'l 19th, 1865.

GEN. R. E. LEE,
Comd'g C. S. A.

GEN: In accordance with the substance of my letter to you of the 8th inst., I propose to receive the surrender of the Army of N. Va. on the following terms, to wit: Rolls of all the officers and men to be made in duplicate. One copy to be given to an officer designated by me, the other to be retained by such officer or officers as you may designate. The officers to give their individual

---

9. Ely S. Parker (1828–1895) was a Native American of the Seneca tribe. He and Grant became acquainted when Parker moved to Galena, and he joined Grant's staff in 1863. During Grant's presidency Parker served as Commissioner of Indian Affairs. His tenure was brief owing to false accusations of impropriety. Cleared of all charges, he nevertheless resigned. Parker reportedly referred to himself as "a savage Jack Falstaff of 200 weight." William H. Armstrong, *Warrior in Two Camps: Ely S. Parker, Union General and Seneca Chief* (Syracuse, NY: Syracuse University Press, 1989), 84.

paroles not to take up arms against the Government of the United States until properly exchanged, and each company or regimental commander sign a like parole for the men of their commands. The arms, artillery and public property to be parked and stacked, and turned over to the officer appointed by me to receive them. This will not embrace the side-arms of the officers, nor their private horses or baggage. This done, each officer and man will be allowed to return to their homes, not to be disturbed by United States authority so long as they observe their paroles and the laws in force where they may reside.

Very respectfully,

U. S. GRANT,

Lt. Gen.

When I put my pen to the paper I did not know the first word that I should make use of in writing the terms. I only knew what was in my mind, and I wished to express it clearly, so that there could be no mistaking it.[10] As I wrote on, the thought occurred to me that the officers had their own private horses and effects, which were important to them, but of no value to us; also that it would be an unnecessary humiliation to call upon them to deliver their side arms.

No conversation, not one word, passed between General Lee and myself, either about private property, side arms, or kindred subjects. He appeared to have no objections to the terms first proposed; or if he had a point to make against them he wished to wait until they were in writing to make it. When he read over that part of the terms about side arms, horses and private property of the officers, he remarked, with some feeling, I thought, that this would have a happy effect upon his army.

Then, after a little further conversation, General Lee remarked to me again that their army was organized a little differently from the army of the United States (still maintaining by implication that we were two countries); that in their army the cavalrymen and artillerists owned their own horses; and he asked if he was to understand that the men who so owned their horses were to be permitted to retain them. I told him that as the terms were written they would not; that only the officers were permitted to take their private

10. Grant here repeats verbatim the phrase he had used in chapter 10 to describe the prose style of Zachary Taylor.

property. He then, after reading over the terms a second time, remarked that that was clear.

I then said to him that I thought this would be about the last battle of the war—I sincerely hoped so; and I said further I took it that most of the men in the ranks were small farmers. The whole country had been so raided by the two armies that it was doubtful whether they would be able to put in a crop to carry themselves and their families through the next winter without the aid of the horses they were then riding. The United States did not want them and I would, therefore, instruct the officers I left behind to receive the paroles of his troops to let every man of the Confederate army who claimed to own a horse or mule take the animal to his home. Lee remarked again that this would have a happy effect.

He then sat down and wrote out the following letter:

> HEADQUARTERS ARMY OF NORTHERN VIRGINIA,
> *April* 9, 1865.
> GENERAL:—I received your letter of this date containing the terms of the surrender of the Army of Northern Virginia as proposed by you. As they are substantially the same as those expressed in your letter of the 8th inst., they are accepted. I will proceed to designate the proper officers to carry the stipulations into effect.
> R. E. LEE, General.
> LIEUT.-GENERAL U. S. GRANT.

While duplicates of the two letters were being made, the Union generals present were severally presented to General Lee.

The much talked of surrendering of Lee's sword and my handing it back, this and much more that has been said about it is the purest romance.[11] The

---

11. Southern newspapers circulated, and diarists repeated, the story of the surrender of Lee's ceremonial sword: "Gen. Lee tendered his sword to Grant in token of surrender," a South Carolina paper reported. "That officer, however, with a courtesy for which we must accord him due respect declined to receive it, or, receiving, declined to retain it, and accompanied its return with substantially the following remark: 'General Lee keep that sword. You have won it by your gallantry. You have not been whipped, but overpowered, and I cannot receive it as a token of surrender from so brave a man.'" "From Virginia!" *Yorkville Enquirer*, April 26, 1865, p. 1.

For a detailed account of the myth's creation and perpetuation, see Varon, *Appomattox.* Lee would deny the story as vehemently as did Grant, but it proved too appealing to die. Lee's sword was eventually returned to Appomattox, together with the scabbard

word sword or side arms was not mentioned by either of us until I wrote it in the terms. There was no premeditation, and it did not occur to me until the moment I wrote it down. If I had happened to omit it, and General Lee had called my attention to it, I should have put it in the terms precisely as I acceded to the provision about the soldiers retaining their horses.

General Lee, after all was completed and before taking his leave, remarked that his army was in a very bad condition for want of food, and that they were without forage; that his men had been living for some days on parched corn exclusively, and that he would have to ask me for rations and forage. I told him "certainly," and asked for how many men he wanted rations. His answer was "about twenty-five thousand:" and I authorized him to send his own commissary and quartermaster to Appomattox Station, two or three miles away, where he could have, out of the trains we had stopped, all the provisions wanted. As for forage, we had ourselves depended almost entirely upon the country for that.

Generals Gibbon, Griffin and Merritt were designated by me to carry into effect the paroling of Lee's troops before they should start for their homes—General Lee leaving Generals Longstreet, Gordon and Pendleton for them to confer with in order to facilitate this work. Lee and I then separated as cordially as we had met, he returning to his own lines, and all went into bivouac for the night at Appomattox.

Soon after Lee's departure I telegraphed to Washington as follows:

HEADQUARTERS APPOMATTOX C. H., VA.,
April 9th, 1865, 4.30 P.M.
HON. E. M. STANTON, Secretary of War,
Washington.
General Lee surrendered the Army of Northern Virginia this afternoon on terms proposed by myself. The accompanying additional correspondence will show the conditions fully.
U. S. GRANT,
Lieut.-General.

When news of the surrender first reached our lines our men commenced firing a salute of a hundred guns in honor of the victory. I at once sent word,

and Lee's uniform, where it became a featured item in the collection of the Museum of the Confederacy.

however, to have it stopped. The Confederates were now our prisoners, and we did not want to exult over their downfall.

I determined to return to Washington at once, with a view to putting a stop to the purchase of supplies, and what I now deemed other useless outlay of money. Before leaving, however, I thought I would like to see General Lee again; so next morning I rode out beyond our lines towards his headquarters, preceded by a bugler and a staff-officer carrying a white flag.[12]

Lee soon mounted his horse, seeing who it was, and met me. We had there between the lines, sitting on horseback, a very pleasant conversation of over half an hour, in the course of which Lee said to me that the South was a big country and that we might have to march over it three or four times before the war entirely ended, but that we would now be able to do it as they could no longer resist us. He expressed it as his earnest hope, however, that we would not be called upon to cause more loss and sacrifice of life; but he could not foretell the result. I then suggested to General Lee that there was not a man in the Confederacy whose influence with the soldiery and the whole people was as great as his, and that if he would now advise the surrender of all the armies I had no doubt his advice would be followed with alacrity. But Lee said, that he could not do that without consulting the President first. I knew there was no use to urge him to do anything against his ideas of what was right.

I was accompanied by my staff and other officers, some of whom seemed to have a great desire to go inside the Confederate lines. They finally asked permission of Lee to do so for the purpose of seeing some of their old army friends, and the permission was granted. They went over, had a very pleasant time with their old friends, and brought some of them back with them when they returned.

When Lee and I separated he went back to his lines and I returned to the house of Mr. McLean. Here the officers of both armies came in great numbers, and seemed to enjoy the meeting as much as though they had been friends separated for a long time while fighting battles under the same flag. For the time being it looked very much as if all thought of the war had escaped their minds. After an hour pleasantly passed in this way I set out on

---

12. For the original publishers' note regarding a facsimile of the surrender document included in the first edition, see Appendix 1, chapter 67, note 1.

horseback, accompanied by my staff and a small escort, for Burkesville Junction, up to which point the railroad had by this time been repaired.[13]

---

13. In a diplomatic gesture, Grant did not stay to watch the surrender. Joshua Chamberlain was selected to supervise it, and he notes that Grant's orders were to keep "the ceremony . . . as simple as possible," with "nothing . . . done to humiliate the manhood of the Southern soldiers." Chamberlain claims that he took it on his own authority to salute (in what amounted to an echo of Fort Sumter) the passing Confederate columns. See *Passing of the Armies*, 249, 260. Stephen Cushman proposes that Chamberlain's account is probably a fiction that has come by dint of repetition to assume the status of fact. See *Belligerent Muse*, chapter 5.

Setting aside the question of its veracity, Chamberlain's account is radically different from Grant's in both detail and tone: "On they come, with the old-swinging route step and swaying battleflags. In the van, the proud Confederate ensign—the great field of white with canton of star-strewn cross of blue on a field of red, the regimental battle-flags with the same escutcheon following on, crowded so thick, by thinning out of men, that the whole column seemed crowned with red." Chamberlain proceeds to enumerate the Confederate regiments in a description that evokes Homer's catalogue of ships:

> Here comes Cobb's Georgia Legion, which held the stone wall on Marye's Heights at Fredericksburg. . . .
> Here too come Gordon's Georgians and Hoke's North Carolinians. . . .
> Here are the men of McGowan, Hunton, and Scales. . . .
> Now comes Anderson's Fourth Corps. . . .
> Here passes the proud remnant of Ransom's North Carolinians. . . .
> Now makes its last front A. P. Hill's old Corps. . . .
> What is this but the remnant of Mahone's Division, last seen by us at the North Anna? . . .
> Now the sad great pageant—Longstreet and his men! . . .
> Now comes the sinewy remnant of fierce Hood's Division, which at Gettysburg we saw pouring through the Devil's Den, and the Plum Run gorge. . . .
> Ah, is this Pickett's Division?—this little group left of those who on the lurid last day of Gettysburg breasted level cross-fire and thunderbolts of storm, to be strewn back drifting wrecks, where after that awful, futile, pitiful charge we buried them in graves a furlong wide, with names unknown! . . .
> Thus, all day long, division after division comes and goes.

Passing of the Armies, 259–65.

68

Morale of the Two Armies—Relative
Conditions of the North and South—
President Lincoln Visits Richmond—
Arrival at Washington—President Lincoln's
Assassination—President Johnson's Policy

After the fall of Petersburg, and when the armies of the Potomac and the James were in motion to head off Lee's army, the *morale* of the National troops had greatly improved. There was no more straggling, no more rear guards. The men who in former times had been falling back, were now, as I have already stated, striving to get to the front. For the first time in four weary years they felt that they were now nearing the time when they could return to their homes with their country saved. On the other hand, the Confederates were more than correspondingly depressed. Their despondency increased with each returning day, and especially after the battle of Sailor's Creek. They threw away their arms in constantly increasing numbers, dropping out of the ranks and betaking themselves to the woods in the hope of reaching their homes.[1] I have already instanced the case of the entire

1. When Confederate soldiers did reach their homes, the economic devastation they found there prompted many to head west. In 1862, Lincoln had approved the Homestead Act, which offered 160 acres of land west of the Mississippi for $10 and a promise to cultivate the land. The flood of homesteaders, veterans prominent among them, grew sharply after the war. In 1867, Confederate veterans were eligible as long as they signed an oath of allegiance, and in 1872, veterans were authorized to put their military service toward the total time necessary (five years) to validate a claim. See Greg Bradsher, "How the West Was Settled," *Prologue: Quarterly of the National Archives and Records Administration* 44, no. 4 (Winter 2012): 27–35.

disintegration of a regiment whose colonel I met at Farmville. As a result of these and other influences, when Lee finally surrendered at Appomattox, there were only 28,356 officers and men left to be paroled, and many of these were without arms. It was probably this latter fact which gave rise to the statement sometimes made, North and South, that Lee surrendered a smaller number of men than what the official figures show. As a matter of official record, and in addition to the number paroled as given above, we captured between March 29th and the date of surrender 19,132 Confederates, to say nothing of Lee's other losses, killed, wounded and missing, during the series of desperate conflicts which marked his headlong and determined flight. The same record shows the number of cannon, including those at Appomattox, to have been 689 between the dates named.

There has always been a great conflict of opinion as to the number of troops engaged in every battle, or all important battles, fought between the sections, the South magnifying the number of Union troops engaged and belittling their own. Northern writers have fallen, in many instances, into the same error. I have often heard gentlemen, who were thoroughly loyal to the Union, speak of what a splendid fight the South had made and successfully continued for four years before yielding, with their twelve million of people against our twenty, and of the twelve four being colored slaves, non-combatants. I will add to their argument. We had many regiments of brave and loyal men who volunteered under great difficulty from the twelve million belonging to the South.

But the South had rebelled against the National government. It was not bound by any constitutional restrictions. The whole South was a military camp. The occupation of the colored people was to furnish supplies for the army. Conscription was resorted to early, and embraced every male from the age of eighteen to forty-five, excluding only those physically unfit to serve in the field, and the necessary number of civil officers of State and intended National government. The old and physically disabled furnished a good por-

---

Meanwhile, the Pacific Railway Act of 1862 subsidized the building of the transcontinental railroad, which veterans from both sides of the conflict helped to build. The figure of the displaced veteran—in particular the aggrieved Confederate—became an elemental part of the mythology of the West. Veterans are ubiquitous in Western films, in which they often serve as agents of violence and civilization both together: men who have grown used to fighting yet also long for stability. In some of these films, Union and Confederate veterans join together to fight Native Americans or, in another nod to the popular view of Reconstruction, to avenge the depredations of unscrupulous carpetbaggers and profiteers.

Arts of Peace: "Fauchers, Somme," 1890–98. Photograph by Eugène Atget. *Metropolitan Museum of Art, David Hunter McAlpin Fund, 1956.*

Arts of War: "The wood called Des Fermes in the Somme," World War I. *Library of Congress, Prints and Photographs Division, LC-DIG-ggbain-24107.*

tion of these. The slaves, the non-combatants, one-third of the whole, were required to work in the field without regard to sex, and almost without regard to age. Children from the age of eight years could and did handle the hoe; they were not much older when they began to hold the plough. The four million of colored non-combatants were equal to more than three times their number in the North, age for age and sex for sex, in supplying food from the soil to support armies. Women did not work in the fields in the North, and children attended school.[2]

2. In the 1890s, Frederick Douglass praised Grant and suggested that he had transcended both his West Point training and his erstwhile political allegiances (to the Democrats and Know-Nothings):

> My confidence in Gen. Grant was not entirely due to his brilliant military successes, but there was a moral as well as military basis for my faith in him. He had shown his single-mindedness and superiority to popular prejudice by his prompt coöperation with President Lincoln in his policy of employing colored troops and by his order commanding his soldiers to treat such troops with due respect. In this way he proved himself to be not only a wise general, but a great man—one who could adjust himself to new conditions, and adopt the lessons taught by the events of the hour. This quality in General Grant was and is made all the more conspicuous and striking in

The arts of peace were carried on in the North.[3] Towns and cities grew during the war. Inventions were made in all kinds of machinery to increase the products of a day's labor in the shop, and in the field. In the South no opposition was allowed to the government which had been set up and which would have become real and respected if the rebellion had been successful. No rear had to be protected. All the troops in service could be brought to the front to contest every inch of ground threatened with invasion. The press of the South, like the people who remained at home, were loyal to the Southern cause.

In the North, the country, the towns and the cities presented about the same appearance they do in time of peace. The furnace was in blast, the shops were filled with workmen, the fields were cultivated, not only to supply the population of the North and the troops invading the South, but to ship abroad to pay a part of the expense of the war. In the North the press was free up to the point of open treason. The citizen could entertain his views and express them. Troops were necessary in the Northern States to prevent prisoners from the Southern army being released by outside force, armed and set at large to destroy by fire our Northern cities. Plans were formed by Northern and Southern citizens to burn our cities, to poison the water supplying them, to spread infection by importing clothing from infected regions, to blow up our river and lake steamers—regardless of the destruction of innocent lives. The copperhead disreputable portion of the press magnified rebel successes, and belittled those of the Union army. It was, with a large following, an auxiliary to the Confederate army. The North would have been much stronger with a hundred thousand of these men in the Confederate ranks and the rest of their kind thoroughly subdued, as the Union sentiment was in the South, than we were as the battle was fought.

As I have said, the whole South was a military camp. The colored people, four million in number, were submissive, and worked in the field and took

contrast with his West Point education and his former political associations; for neither West Point nor the Democratic party have been good schools in which to learn justice and fair play to the negro.

The Life and Times of Frederick Douglass, rev. ed. (Boston: De Wolfe & Fisk, 1892), 434.

3. Grant's juxtaposition of the South's armed camp with the "arts of peace" practiced in the North is reminiscent of the shield of Achilles in Homer's *Iliad*, which depicts "Two cities radiant . . . / The image one of peace, and one of war." *Homer*, trans. Pope, bk. 18, ll. 567–68.

care of the families while the able-bodied white men were at the front fighting for a cause destined to defeat. The cause was popular, and was enthu-
siastically supported by the young men. The conscription took all of them.
Before the war was over, further conscriptions took those between fourteen
and eighteen years of age as junior reserves, and those between forty-five
and sixty as senior reserves. It would have been an offence, directly after the
war, and perhaps it would be now, to ask any able-bodied man in the South,
who was between the ages of fourteen and sixty at any time during the war,
whether he had been in the Confederate army. He would assert that he had,
or account for his absence from the ranks. Under such circumstances it is
hard to conceive how the North showed such a superiority of force in every
battle fought. I know they did not.

During 1862 and '3, John H. Morgan, a partisan officer, of no military
education, but possessed of courage and endurance, operated in the rear
of the Army of the Ohio in Kentucky and Tennessee. He had no base of
supplies to protect, but was at home wherever he went. The army operating against the South, on the contrary, had to protect its lines of communication with the North, from which all supplies had to come to the
front. Every foot of road had to be guarded by troops stationed at convenient distances apart. These guards could not render assistance beyond the
points where stationed. Morgan was foot-loose and could operate where his
information—always correct—led him to believe he could do the greatest
damage. During the time he was operating in this way he killed, wounded
and captured several times the number he ever had under his command at
any one time. He destroyed many millions of property in addition. Places
he did not attack had to be guarded as if threatened by him. Forrest, an
abler soldier, operated farther west, and held from the National front quite
as many men as could be spared for offensive operations. It is safe to say that
more than half the National army was engaged in guarding lines of supplies,
or were on leave, sick in hospital or on detail which prevented their bearing
arms. Then, again, large forces were employed where no Confederate army
confronted them. I deem it safe to say that there were no large engagements
where the National numbers compensated for the advantage of position and
intrenchment occupied by the enemy.[4]

---

4. Grant discusses Morgan and Forrest to illustrate some of the logistical advantages of
the South. But the effective guerrilla tactics of both commanders, as well as those of
partisan outlaw groups like the Missouri-Kansas border raiders, had larger implications
for the postwar period. After the war, both Sherman and Sheridan would apply the

While I was in pursuit of General Lee, the President went to Richmond in company with Admiral Porter, and on board his flagship. He found the people of that city in great consternation. The leading citizens among the people who had remained at home surrounded him, anxious that something should be done to relieve them from suspense. General Weitzel was not then in the city, having taken offices in one of the neighboring villages after his troops had succeeded in subduing the conflagration which they had found in progress on entering the Confederate capital. The President sent for him, and, on his arrival, a short interview was had on board the vessel, Admiral Porter and a leading citizen of Virginia being also present. After this interview the President wrote an order in about these words, which I quote from memory: "General Weitzel is authorized to permit the body calling itself the Legislature of Virginia to meet for the purpose of recalling the Virginia troops from the Confederate armies."

Immediately some of the gentlemen composing that body wrote out a call for a meeting and had it published in their papers. This call, however, went very much further than Mr. Lincoln had contemplated, as he did not say the "Legislature of Virginia" but "the body which called itself the Legislature of Virginia." Mr. Stanton saw the call as published in the Northern

concepts they practiced in the South and in the Shenandoah Valley respectively to their management of the wars against the Plains Indians. "'Regular' wars can be won by the use of 'irregular' tactics and Indian wars can be won by applying lessons learned in regular warfare," argues Richard Slotkin in his landmark study of the American frontier myth. "The war was 'totalized' through systematic attacks on civilian economic targets. After Appomattox, Sherman and Sheridan systematically applied these same methods to the subjugation of the Plains Indians." *Gunfighter Nation: The Myth of the Frontier in Twentieth-Century America* (Norman: University of Oklahoma Press, 1998), 456.

General Nelson Miles, Buffalo Bill Cody, and others observing a Lakota Sioux camp near Deadwood, South Dakota, during the time of the last Sioux resistance, the Ghost Dance War, which ended at the Massacre of Wounded Knee. Photograph by John C. H. Grabill. *Library of Congress, Prints and Photographs Division, John C.H. Grabill Collection, LC-DIG-ppmsc-02555.*

papers the very next issue and took the liberty of countermanding the order authorizing any meeting of the Legislature, or any other body, and this notwithstanding the fact that the President was nearer the spot than he was.

This was characteristic of Mr. Stanton. He was a man who never questioned his own authority, and who always did in war time what he wanted to do. He was an able constitutional lawyer and jurist; but the Constitution was not an impediment to him while the war lasted. In this latter particular I entirely agree with the view he evidently held. The Constitution was not framed with a view to any such rebellion as that of 1861–5. While it did not authorize rebellion it made no provision against it. Yet the right to resist or suppress rebellion is as inherent as the right of self-defence, and as natural as the right of an individual to preserve his life when in jeopardy. The Constitution was therefore in abeyance for the time being, so far as it in any way affected the progress and termination of the war.[5]

Those in rebellion against the government of the United States were not restricted by constitutional provisions, or any other, except the acts of their Congress, which was loyal and devoted to the cause for which the South was then fighting. It would be a hard case when one-third of a nation, united in rebellion against the national authority, is entirely untrammeled, that the other two-thirds, in their efforts to maintain the Union intact, should be restrained by a Constitution prepared by our ancestors for the express purpose of insuring the permanency of the confederation of the States.

After I left General Lee at Appomattox Station, I went with my staff and a few others directly to Burkesville Station on my way to Washington. The road from Burkesville back having been newly repaired and the ground being soft, the train got off the track frequently, and, as a result, it was after midnight of the second day when I reached City Point. As soon as possible I took a dispatch-boat thence to Washington City.

While in Washington I was very busy for a time in preparing the necessary orders for the new state of affairs; communicating with my different commanders of separate departments, bodies of troops, etc. But by the 14th I was pretty well through with this work, so as to be able to visit my children, who were then in Burlington, New Jersey, attending school. Mrs. Grant was with me in Washington at the time, and we were invited by President and

5. Constitutional rights were abridged during the Civil War, just as they have been in almost every other American war. Lincoln defended his suspension of the writ of habeas corpus as a necessary wartime measure. James Madison is conspicuous among U.S. presidents for resisting pressure to circumscribe civil liberties during wartime.

Mrs. Lincoln to accompany them to the theatre on the evening of that day. I replied to the President's verbal invitation to the effect, that if we were in the city we would take great pleasure in accompanying them; but that I was very anxious to get away and visit my children, and if I could get through my work during the day I should do so. I did get through and started by the evening train on the 14th, sending Mr. Lincoln word, of course, that I would not be at the theatre.[6]

At that time the railroad to New York entered Philadelphia on Broad Street; passengers were conveyed in ambulances to the Delaware River, and then ferried to Camden, at which point they took the cars again. When I reached the ferry, on the east side of the City of Philadelphia, I found people

---

6. John Russell Young reported Ulysses and Julia Grant's recollection of the day of the assassination:

"The darkest day of my life," said the General, "was the day I heard of Lincoln's assassination. I did not know what it meant. Here was the rebellion put down in the field, and starting up in the gutters; we had fought it as war, now we had to fight it as assassination. . . . I arrived in Washington on the 13th. I was busy sending out orders to stop recruiting, the purchase of supplies, and to muster out the army. Lincoln had promised to go to the theater, and wanted me to go with him. While I was with the President, a note came from Mrs. Grant saying she must leave Washington that night. She wanted to go to Burlington to see our children. . . . I was glad to have the note, as I did not want to go to the theater. So I made my excuse to Lincoln, and at the proper hour we started for the train. As we were driving along Pennsylvania Avenue, a horseman drove past us on a gallop, and back again around our carriage, looking into it. Mrs. Grant said, 'There is the man who sat near us at lunch to-day, with some other men, and tried to overhear our conversation. He was so rude that we left the dining-room. Here he is now riding after us.' I thought it was only curiosity, but learned afterward that the horseman was Booth. It seems I was to have been attacked, and Mrs. Grant's sudden resolve to leave deranged the plan. A few days later I received an anonymous letter from a man, saying he had been detailed to kill me, that he rode on my train as far as Havre de Grace, and as my car was locked he could not get in. He thanked God he had failed. I remember the conductor locked our car, but how true the letter was I cannot say. I learned of the assassination as I was passing through Philadelphia. I turned around, took a special train, and came on to Washington. It was the gloomiest day of my life."

Around the World with General Grant, 2:355–56.

For a detailed account of Lincoln's habitual imperviousness to threats against his life, of the assassination plot, and of all that followed, see Leech, *Reveille in Washington*.

Reward poster for Lincoln's murderer.
*Library of Congress, Prints and Photographs
Division, photograph by Carol M. Highsmith,
LC-DIG-highsm-04756.*

awaiting my arrival there; and also dispatches informing me of the assassination of the President and Mr. Seward, and of the probable assassination of the Vice President, Mr. Johnson, and requesting my immediate return.

It would be impossible for me to describe the feeling that overcame me at the news of these assassinations, more especially the assassination of the President. I knew his goodness of heart, his generosity, his yielding disposition, his desire to have everybody happy, and above all his desire to see all the people of the United States enter again upon the full privileges of citizenship with equality among all. I knew also the feeling that Mr. Johnson had expressed in speeches and conversation against the Southern people, and I feared that his course towards them would be such as to repel, and make them unwilling citizens; and if they became such they would remain so for a long while. I felt that reconstruction had been set back, no telling how far.

I immediately arranged for getting a train to take me back to Washington City; but Mrs. Grant was with me; it was after midnight and Burlington was but an hour away. Finding that I could accompany her to our house and return about as soon as they would be ready to take me from the Philadelphia station, I went up with her and returned immediately by the same special train. The joy that I had witnessed among the people in the street and in public places in Washington when I left there, had been turned to grief; the city was in reality a city of mourning. I have stated what I believed then the effect of this would be, and my judgment now is that I was right. I believe the South would have been saved from very much of the hardness of feeling that was engendered by Mr. Johnson's course towards them during the first few months of his administration. Be this as it may, Mr. Lincoln's assassination was particularly unfortunate for the entire nation.

Mr. Johnson's course towards the South did engender bitterness of feeling. His denunciations of treason and his ever-ready remark, "Treason is a crime and must be made odious," was repeated to all those men of the South who came to him to get some assurances of safety so that they might go to work at something with the feeling that what they obtained would be secure to them. He uttered his denunciations with great vehemence, and as they were accompanied with no assurances of safety, many Southerners were driven to a point almost beyond endurance.[7]

The President of the United States is, in a large degree, or ought to be, a representative of the feeling, wishes and judgment of those over whom he presides; and the Southerners who read the denunciations of themselves and

7. Grant recommended amnesty for Lee because he realized the powerful influence his opponent had on Southern behavior and thought it would be the best way to ensure the peace. With the notable exceptions of James Longstreet and John S. Mosby, former rebel commanders, including Lee, did little to further the postwar settlement. In many cases, they worked to undermine the government's policies, especially with regard to African Americans. The terror campaigns of the Ku Klux Klan and other organizations amounted to a guerrilla insurgency of the type Grant had hoped to avoid through amnesty.

Grant's letter to Halleck recommending amnesty for Lee, May 6, 1865. *Special Collections, United States Military Academy.*

their people must have come to the conclusion that he uttered the sentiments of the Northern people; whereas, as a matter of fact, but for the assassination of Mr. Lincoln, I believe the great majority of the Northern people, and the soldiers unanimously, would have been in favor of a speedy reconstruction on terms that would be the least humiliating to the people who had rebelled against their government. They believed, I have no doubt, as I did, that besides being the mildest, it was also the wisest, policy.

The people who had been in rebellion must necessarily come back into the Union, and be incorporated as an integral part of the nation. Naturally the nearer they were placed to an equality with the people who had not rebelled, the more reconciled they would feel with their old antagonists, and the better citizens they would be from the beginning. They surely would not make good citizens if they felt that they had a yoke around their necks.

I do not believe that the majority of the Northern people at that time were in favor of negro suffrage. They supposed that it would naturally follow the freedom of the negro, but that there would be a time of probation, in which the ex-slaves could prepare themselves for the privileges of citizenship before the full right would be conferred; but Mr. Johnson, after a complete revolution of sentiment, seemed to regard the South not only as an oppressed people, but as the people best entitled to consideration of any of our citizens. This was more than the people who had secured to us the perpetuation of the Union were prepared for, and they became more radical in their views. The Southerners had the most power in the executive branch, Mr. Johnson having gone to their side; and with a compact South, and such sympathy and support as they could get from the North, they felt that they would be able to control the nation at once, and already many of them acted as if they thought they were entitled to do so.

Thus Mr. Johnson, fighting Congress on the one hand, and receiving the support of the South on the other, drove Congress, which was over-whelmingly republican, to the passing of first one measure and then another to restrict his power. There being a solid South on one side that was in accord with the political party in the North which had sympathized with the rebellion, it finally, in the judgment of Congress and of the majority of the legislatures of the States, became necessary to enfranchise the negro, in all his ignorance. In this work, I shall not discuss the question of how far the policy of Congress in this particular proved a wise one. It became an absolute necessity, however, because of the foolhardiness of the President and the blindness of the Southern people to their own interest. As to myself, while strongly favoring the course that would be the least humiliating to the people who had been in rebellion, I gradually worked up to the point where, with the majority of the people, I favored immediate enfranchisement.[8]

---

8. Amid the turmoil of the Johnson administration and the ascendance of the Radical Republicans, the figure of Lincoln found in death a place in some strains of Southern mythology. The idea that had Lincoln only lived absolution would have been the order of the day took root. See, for example, D. W. Griffith's film *The Birth of a Nation*, in which Lincoln's death extinguishes the last best hope for a blighted South. Confederate general John B. Gordon expresses a similar sentiment in his memoir:

> The magnanimity exhibited at Appomattox justifies me in recording here my conviction that, had it been possible for General Grant and his soldiers to foresee the bloody sweat which through ten successive years was wrung from Southern brows, the whole Union army would then and there have resolved to combat all unfriendly legislation. Or, later, if Booth's bullet had not terminated the life filled with "charity to all and malice toward none," President Lincoln's benign purposes, seconded by the great-hearted among our Northern countrymen, would have saved the South from those caricatures of government which cursed and crushed her.
>
> In looking back now over that valley of death—the period of recon-struction,—its waste and its woe, it is hard to realize that the worn and impoverished Confederates were able to go through it. The risen South of to-day is a memorial of the same patience, endurance, and valor which immortalized the four years' struggle for Southern independence.

Reminiscences, 457.

69

Sherman and Johnston—Johnston's Surrender to Sherman—Capture of Mobile— Wilson's Expedition—Capture of Jefferson Davis—General Thomas's Qualities— Estimate of General Canby

When I left Appomattox I ordered General Meade to proceed leisurely back to Burkesville Station with the Army of the Potomac and the Army of the James, and to go into camp there until further orders from me. General Johnston, as has been stated before, was in North Carolina confronting General Sherman. It could not be known positively, of course, whether Johnston would surrender on the news of Lee's surrender, though I supposed he would; and if he did not, Burkesville Station was the natural point from which to move to attack him. The army which I could have sent against him was superior to his, and that with which Sherman confronted him was also superior; and between the two he would necessarily have been crushed, or driven away. With the loss of their capital and the Army of Northern Virginia it was doubtful whether Johnston's men would have the spirit to stand. My belief was that he would make no such attempt; but I adopted this course as a precaution against what might happen, however improbable.[1]

---

1. Jubal Early boasted that he remained at war even after Johnston's surrender:

> I was not embraced in the terms of General Lee's surrender or that of General Johnston, and, as the order relieving me from command had also relieved me from all embarrassment as to the troops which had been under me, as soon as I was in a condition to travel, I started on horseback for the Trans-Mississippi Department to join the army of General Kirby

Augustus Saint-Gaudens, Statue of William T. Sherman, Grand Army Plaza, New York, New York. *Photograph by Elizabeth D. Samet.*

Simultaneously with my starting from City Point, I sent a messenger to North Carolina by boat with dispatches to General Sherman, informing him of the surrender of Lee and his army; also of the terms which I had given him; and I authorized Sherman to give the same terms to Johnston if the latter chose to accept them. The country is familiar with the terms that Sherman agreed to *conditionally,* because they embraced a political question as well as a military one and he would therefore have to confer with the government before agreeing to them definitely.

General Sherman had met Mr. Lincoln at City Point while visiting there to confer with me about our final movement, and knew what Mr. Lincoln had said to the peace commissioners when he met them at Hampton Roads, viz.: that before he could enter into negotiations with them they would have

Smith, should it hold out; with the hope of at least meeting an honorable death while fighting under the flag of my country. Before I reached that Department, Smith's army had also been surrendered, and, without giving a parole, after a long, weary and dangerous ride from Virginia, through the states of North Carolina, South Carolina, Georgia, Alabama, Mississippi, Arkansas, and Texas, I finally succeeded in leaving the country.

Autobiographical Sketch, 468.

to agree to two points: one being that the Union should be preserved, and the other that slavery should be abolished; and if they were ready to concede these two points he was almost ready to sign his name to a blank piece of paper and permit them to fill out the balance of the terms upon which we would live together. He had also seen notices in the newspapers of Mr. Lincoln's visit to Richmond, and had read in the same papers that while there he had authorized the convening of the Legislature of Virginia.

Sherman thought, no doubt, in adding to the terms that I had made with General Lee, that he was but carrying out the wishes of the President of the United States. But seeing that he was going beyond his authority, he made it a point that the terms were only conditional. They signed them with this understanding, and agreed to a truce until the terms could be sent to Washington for approval; if approved by the proper authorities there, they would then be final; if not approved, then he would give due notice, before resuming hostilities. As the world knows, Sherman, from being one of the most popular generals of the land (Congress having even gone so far as to propose a bill providing for a second lieutenant-general for the purpose of advancing him to that grade), was denounced by the President and Secretary of War in very bitter terms. Some people went so far as to denounce him as a traitor—a most preposterous term to apply to a man who had rendered so much service as he had, even supposing he had made a mistake in granting such terms as he did to Johnston and his army. If Sherman had taken authority to send Johnston with his army home, with their arms to be put in the arsenals of their own States, without submitting the question to the authorities at Washington, the suspicions against him might have some foundation. But the feeling against Sherman died out very rapidly, and it was not many weeks before he was restored to the fullest confidence of the American people.[2]

---

2. Sherman never forgave Stanton. In his *Memoirs* he writes that when the two met earlier in Savannah, the secretary had authorized him "to control all matters, *civil and military*" and that Stanton had perpetrated an "outrage" by publishing a bulletin announcing the disapproval of Sherman's terms and suggesting that the general had overstepped his authority: "he gave warrant to the impression . . . that I might be bribed by banker's gold to permit Davis to escape," Sherman seethed. Regarding his treatment "as a personal and official insult," the general recollected that, in a gesture "universally noticed," he "publicly" refused Stanton's proffered hand on the reviewing stand during the parade of the armies through the capital in May. See *Memoirs*, 2:364–65, 377.

Grant repeats the same story in chapter 70, but Charles Dana offers a slightly different version of what happened:

When, some days after my return to Washington, President Johnson and the Secretary of War received the terms which General Sherman had forwarded for approval, a cabinet meeting was immediately called and I was sent for. There seemed to be the greatest consternation, lest Sherman would commit the government to terms which they were not willing to accede to and which he had no right to grant. A message went out directing the troops in the South not to obey General Sherman. I was ordered to proceed at once to North Carolina and take charge of matters there myself. Of course I started without delay, and reached there as soon as possible. I repaired to Raleigh, where Sherman was, as quietly as possible, hoping to see him without even his army learning of my presence.

When I arrived I went to Sherman's headquarters, and we were at once closeted together. I showed him the instruction and orders under which I visited him. I told him that I wanted him to notify General Johnston that the terms which they had conditionally agreed upon had not been approved in Washington, and that he was authorized to offer the same terms I had given General Lee. I sent Sherman to do this himself. I did not wish the knowledge of my presence to be known to the army generally; so I left it to Sherman to negotiate the terms of the surrender solely by himself, and without the enemy knowing that I was anywhere near the field. As soon as possible I started to get away, to leave Sherman quite free and untrammelled.

At Goldsboro, on my way back, I met a mail, containing the last newspapers, and I found in them indications of great excitement in the North over the terms Sherman had given Johnston; and harsh orders that had been promulgated by the President and Secretary of War. I knew that Sherman must see these papers, and I fully realized what great indignation they would cause him, though I do not think his feelings could have been more excited than were my own. But like the true and loyal soldier that he was, he carried out

---

I was, of course, curious to see what General Sherman would do in passing before Mr. Stanton to take his place on the stand. The general says in his Memoirs that, as he passed, Stanton offered his hand and he refused to take it. He is entirely mistaken. I was watching narrowly. The Secretary made no motion to offer his hand, or to exchange salutations in any manner. As the general passed, Mr. Stanton gave him merely a slight forward motion of his head, equivalent, perhaps, to a quarter of a bow.

Recollections, 290.

the instructions I had given him, obtained the surrender of Johnston's army, and settled down in his camp about Raleigh, to await final orders.

There were still a few expeditions out in the South that could not be communicated with, and had to be left to act according to the judgment of their respective commanders. With these it was impossible to tell how the news of the surrender of Lee and Johnston, of which they must have heard, might affect their judgment as to what was best to do.

The three expeditions which I had tried so hard to get off from the commands of Thomas and Canby did finally get off: one under Canby himself, against Mobile, late in March; that under Stoneman from East Tennessee on the 20th; and the one under Wilson, starting from Eastport, Mississippi, on the 22d of March. They were all eminently successful, but without any good result. Indeed much valuable property was destroyed and many lives lost at a time when we would have liked to spare them. The war was practically over before their victories were gained. They were so late in commencing operations, that they did not hold any troops away that otherwise would have been operating against the armies which were gradually forcing the Confederate armies to a surrender. The only possible good that we may have experienced from these raids was by Stoneman's getting near Lynchburg about the time the armies of the Potomac and the James were closing in on Lee at Appomattox.

Stoneman entered North Carolina and then pushed north to strike the Virginia and Tennessee Railroad. He got upon that road, destroyed its bridges at different places and rendered the road useless to the enemy up to within a few miles of Lynchburg. His approach caused the evacuation of that city about the time we were at Appomattox, and was the cause of a commotion we heard of there. He then pushed south, and was operating in the rear of Johnston's army about the time the negotiations were going on between Sherman and Johnston for the latter's surrender. In this raid Stoneman captured and destroyed a large amount of stores, while fourteen guns and nearly two thousand prisoners were the trophies of his success.

Canby appeared before Mobile on the 27th of March. The city of Mobile was protected by two forts, besides other intrenchments—Spanish Fort, on the east side of the bay, and Fort Blakely, north of the city. These forts were invested. On the night of the 8th of April, the National troops having carried the enemy's works at one point, Spanish Fort was evacuated; and on the 9th, the very day of Lee's surrender, Blakely was carried by assault, with a considerable loss to us. On the 11th the city was evacuated.

I had tried for more than two years to have an expedition sent against

Mobile when its possession by us would have been of great advantage. It finally cost lives to take it when its possession was of no importance, and when, if left alone, it would within a few days have fallen into our hands without any bloodshed whatever.

Wilson moved out with full 12,000 men, well equipped and well armed. He was an energetic officer and accomplished his work rapidly. Forrest was in his front, but with neither his old-time army nor his old-time prestige. He now had principally conscripts. His conscripts were generally old men and boys. He had a few thousand regular cavalry left, but not enough to even retard materially the progress of Wilson's cavalry. Selma fell on the 2d of April, with a large number of prisoners and a large quantity of war material, machine shops, etc., to be disposed of by the victors. Tuscaloosa, Montgomery and West Point fell in quick succession. These were all important points to the enemy by reason of their railroad connections, as depots of supplies, and because of their manufactories of war material. They were fortified or intrenched, and there was considerable fighting before they were captured. Macon surrendered on the 21st of April. Here news was received of the negotiations for the surrender of Johnston's army. Wilson belonged to the military division commanded by Sherman, and of course was bound by his terms. This stopped all fighting.

General Richard Taylor had now become the senior Confederate officer still at liberty east of the Mississippi River, and on the 4th of May he surrendered everything within the limits of this extensive command. General E. Kirby Smith surrendered the trans-Mississippi department on the 26th of May, leaving no other Confederate army at liberty to continue the war.

Wilson's raid resulted in the capture of the fugitive president of the defunct confederacy before he got out of the country. This occurred at Irwinsville, Georgia, on the 11th of May. For myself, and I believe Mr. Lincoln shared the feeling, I would have been very glad to have seen Mr. Davis succeed in escaping, but for one reason: I feared that if not captured, he might get into the trans-Mississippi region and there set up a more contracted confederacy. The young men now out of homes and out of employment might have rallied under his standard and protracted the war yet another year. The Northern people were tired of the war, they were tired of piling up a debt which would be a further mortgage upon their homes.[3]

---

3. Harrison's raid through Alabama in order to destroy munitions factories, ironworks, coalmines, and other industries in the spring of 1865 was the largest cavalry raid of the war. Having received a tip that Davis was hiding in Georgia, Harrison, not wanting

Richard Taylor, C.S.A., son of Zachary Taylor.
Library of Congress, Prints and Photographs Division,
Civil War Photographs, LC-DIG-cwpb-06290.

Mr. Lincoln, I believe, wanted Mr. Davis to escape, because he did not wish to deal with the matter of his punishment. He knew there would be people clamoring for the punishment of the ex-Confederate president, for high treason. He thought blood enough had already been spilled to atone for our wickedness as a nation. At all events he did not wish to be the judge to decide whether more should be shed or not. But his own life was sacrificed at the hands of an assassin before the ex-president of the Confederacy was a prisoner in the hands of the government which he had lent all his talent and all his energies to destroy.

All things are said to be wisely directed, and for the best interest of all concerned. This reflection does not, however, abate in the slightest our sense of bereavement in the untimely loss of so good and great a man as Abraham Lincoln.

He would have proven the best friend the South could have had, and saved much of the wrangling and bitterness of feeling brought out by reconstruction under a President who at first wished to revenge himself upon Southern men of better social standing than himself, but who still sought their recognition, and in a short time conceived the idea and advanced the proposition to become their Moses to lead them triumphantly out of all their difficulties.

The story of the legislation enacted during the reconstruction period to stay the hands of the President is too fresh in the minds of the people to be

to risk sending even a "cipher message" to Sherman, proceeded on his own initiative. Harrison provides no details about the capture itself. He merely suggests that subsequent stories have been "ridiculously exaggerated" and refers readers to Davis's own account for the "essential particulars." *Under the Old Flag,* 2:305–6.

"Jeff's Last Shift," cartoon depicting Jefferson Davis being captured while wearing women's clothing. *Library of Congress, Prints and Photographs Division, LC-DIG-pga-04901.*

told now. Much of it, no doubt, was unconstitutional; but it was hoped that the laws enacted would serve their purpose before the question of constitutionality could be submitted to the judiciary and a decision obtained. These laws did serve their purpose, and now remain "a dead letter" upon the statute books of the United States, no one taking interest enough in them to give them a passing thought.

Much was said at the time about the garb Mr. Davis was wearing when he was captured. I cannot settle this question from personal knowledge of the facts; but I have been under the belief, from information given to me by General Wilson shortly after the event, that when Mr. Davis learned that he was surrounded by our cavalry he was in his tent dressed in a gentleman's dressing gown. Naturally enough, Mr. Davis wanted to escape, and would not reflect much how this should be accomplished provided it might be done successfully. If captured, he would be no ordinary prisoner. He represented all there was of that hostility to the government which had caused four years of the bloodiest war—and the most costly in other respects of which history makes any record. Every one supposed he would be tried for treason if captured, and that he would be executed. Had he succeeded in making his escape in any disguise it would have been adjudged a good thing afterwards by his admirers.[4]

4. Grant characteristically tries to dispel yet another rumor and to save Davis, who was still alive in 1885, further embarrassment. It was the "delighted" Secretary Stanton himself who encouraged the rumor that Davis had escaped wearing women's clothing. See Marvel, *Lincoln's Autocrat*, 388.

The story was naturally seized on by the Northern newspapers, which published gleeful cartoons. Mary Chesnut recorded an acquaintance's suggestion that the story

As my official letters on file in the War Department, as well as my remarks in this book, reflect upon General Thomas by dwelling somewhat upon his tardiness, it is due to myself, as well as to him, that I give my estimate of him as a soldier. The same remark will apply also in the case of General Canby. I had been at West Point with Thomas one year, and had known him later in the old army. He was a man of commanding appearance, slow and deliberate in speech and action; sensible, honest and brave. He possessed valuable soldierly qualities in an eminent degree. He gained the confidence of all who served under him, and almost their love. This implies a very valuable quality. It is a quality which calls out the most efficient services of the troops serving under the commander possessing it.

Thomas's dispositions were deliberately made, and always good. He could not be driven from a point he was given to hold. He was not as good, however, in pursuit as he was in action. I do not believe that he could ever have conducted Sherman's army from Chattanooga to Atlanta against the defences and the commander guarding that line in 1864. On the other hand, if it had been given him to hold the line which Johnston tried to hold, neither that general nor Sherman, nor any other officer could have done it better.

Thomas was a valuable officer, who richly deserved, as he has received, the plaudits of his countrymen for the part he played in the great tragedy of 1861–5.

---

was conceived in the North as retribution for the mockery made of Lincoln's 1861 ride through Baltimore:

> "Look here: taken in woman's clothes?" asked Mr. Trapier. "Rubbish, stuff, and nonsense. If Jeff Davis has not the pluck of a true man, then there is no courage left on earth. If he does not die game, I give it up. Something, you see, was due to Lincoln and the Scotch cap that he hid his ugly face with, in that express car, when he rushed through Baltimore in the night. It is that escapade of their man Lincoln that set them on making up the woman's clothes story about Jeff Davis."

May 21, 1865, *Diary*, 395.

Davis eventually offered his own version of the story: "As it was quite dark in the tent, I picked up what was supposed to be my 'raglan'—a water-proof light overcoat without sleeves; it was subsequently found to be my wife's, so very like my own as to be mistaken for it; as I started, my wife thoughtfully threw over my head and shoulders a shawl." Accompanying this text is a dignified illustration clearly showing Davis dressed in men's clothing and with a hat rather than a shawl. See *A Short History of the Confederate States of America* (New York: Belford, 1890), 495.

General Canby was an officer of great merit. He was naturally studious, and inclined to the law. There have been in the army but very few, if any, officers who took as much interest in reading and digesting every act of Congress and every regulation for the government of the army as he. His knowledge gained in this way made him a most valuable staff officer, a capacity in which almost all his army services were rendered up to the time of his being assigned to the Military Division of the Gulf. He was an exceedingly modest officer, though of great talent and learning. I presume his feelings when first called upon to command a large army against a fortified city, were somewhat like my own when marching a regiment against General Thomas Harris in Missouri in 1861. Neither of us would have felt the slightest trepidation in going into battle with some one else commanding. Had Canby been in other engagements afterwards, he would, I have no doubt, have advanced without any fear arising from a sense of the responsibility. He was afterwards killed in the lava beds of Southern Oregon, while in pursuit of the hostile Modoc Indians. His character was as pure as his talent and learning were great. His services were valuable during the war, but principally as a bureau officer. I have no idea that it was from choice that his services were rendered in an office, but because of his superior efficiency there.[5]

5. Canby was commanding the Department of the Pacific on April 11, 1873, when he was murdered together with another peace commissioner near Lava Beds, Oregon, while attempting to negotiate with a small band of Modocs who had left their reservation and returned to their home, to the consternation of white settlers in the area. Another commissioner, Alfred B. Meacham, survived the attack and subsequently gave his eyewitness account of Canby's death at the hands of a Modoc called Captain Jack:

> Quick, general, quick! He is too late. Another instant, and a shot is passing through his head. He does not fall, but turns and flees. Jack and "Ellen's Man" pursue him until he falls on the rocks. They close on him. Captain Jack holds him by the shoulder, while the other cuts him across the neck. In the fall his chin struck on the rocks and shattered his lower jaw. The monsters strip him of every article of clothing, while he is struggling in the agonies of death. Barncho comes up now, and "Ellen's Man" snatches a rifle from his hands, and, pointing at the general, discharges it, and another ball passes entirely through his head. They turn him on his face, and leave him in the last agony of a horrible death, while, with his uniform on their arms, they go back to the council tent.

Wigwam and War-Path; or the Royal Chief in Chains (Boston: John P. Dale, 1875), 492.

Many white Americans, Sherman conspicuous among them, clamored for vengeance against the Modocs. He telegraphed to Schofield on April 13, 1873: "I hope to hear that they have met the doom they so richly have earned by their insolence and perfidy." The government eventually hanged four Modocs for the killing, and the so-called war was effectively ended. Grant's Indian peace policy had been dealt a keen blow, and widespread unrest in the ensuing years, including Custer's debacle at Little Big Horn, effectively emptied it of its promise. For a detailed account of the ways in which subsequent representations of the event served the interests of white settlers, see Boyd Cothran, *Remembering the Modoc War: Redemptive Violence and the Making of American Innocence* (Chapel Hill: University of North Carolina Press, 2014).

The episode demonstrated several aspects of the Civil War's legacy: the postwar influx of white settlers onto the frontier as well as the brutality of Sherman and Sheridan. In the end, these influences thwarted the attempted accommodations of Grant's policy and its would-be implementers, such as O. O. Howard. Letters written by private citizens to Grant and Columbus Delano, the secretary of the interior, suggest that at least some white Americans resisted the pull of manifest destiny that had reasserted itself after the war. "Why must one thousand rifles in cold blood range themselves, urged on by greed and covetousness, against forty to sixty who are not to blame in this matter?" Bronson Murray of New York City demanded in a letter to Grant: "Destiny? Can you not stand guard between the two? Can you not leave the Modocs at rest?" The American Indian Aid Association published an announcement in the newspapers railing against the invocation of "manifest destiny" to justify "the extinction of the Indian race." Outraged at Sherman's publicized wish to punish the Modocs, Mary L. Benham, from Fort Ross, Sonoma County, sent a letter to Delano in which she characterized the episode as the inevitable result of entrusting peacekeeping to an army:

> Mr. Secretary, I do not feel that I am intruding, although I am personally unknown to you. You have not ordered the extermination of the Modocs. It is General Sherman who, under the authority of President Grant, commanded their "utter extermination," and sent large military forces to effect it. . . .
>
> The only moving things that are ordered for extermination are "rats;" and now General Sherman can exterminate all the Modocs, from the aged squaws to the infants at their mothers' breasts.

Executive Document No. 22, 43rd Congress, 1st Session 77, 274, 317, 291 (1874).

70

The End of the War—The March
to Washington—One of Lincoln's
Anecdotes—Grand Review at
Washington—Characteristics of Lincoln
and Stanton—Estimate of the Different
Corps Commanders

Things began to quiet down, and as the certainty that there would be no
more armed resistance became clearer, the troops in North Carolina
and Virginia were ordered to march immediately to the capital, and go into
camp there until mustered out. Suitable garrisons were left at the prominent
places throughout the South to insure obedience to the laws that might be
enacted for the government of the several States, and to insure security to
the lives and property of all classes. I do not know how far this was necessary, but I deemed it necessary, at that time, that such a course should be
pursued. I think now that these garrisons were continued after they ceased
to be absolutely required; but it is not to be expected that such a rebellion as
was fought between the sections from 1861 to 1865 could terminate without
leaving many serious apprehensions in the mind of the people as to what
should be done.[1]

---

1. By the twentieth century, the tyranny of military rule in the South had become
enshrined in histories of the Reconstruction era such as Woodrow Wilson's *A History
of the American People*, which explains the origins of the Ku Klux Klan as a justified
response to a social revolution. Wilson also proposes that the Klan provided a diversion to veterans longing to recapture the thrill of battle. Here he weaves a benign

Sherman marched his troops from Goldsboro, up to Manchester, on the south side of the James River, opposite Richmond, and there put them in camp, while he went back to Savannah to see what the situation was there.

It was during this trip that the last outrage was committed upon him. Halleck had been sent to Richmond to command Virginia, and had issued orders prohibiting even Sherman's own troops from obeying his, Sherman's, orders. Sherman met the papers on his return, containing this order of Halleck, and very justly felt indignant at the outrage. On his arrival at Fortress Monroe returning from Savannah, Sherman received an invitation from Halleck to come to Richmond and be his guest. This he indignantly refused, and informed Halleck, furthermore, that he had seen his order. He also stated that he was coming up to take command of his troops, and as he marched through it would probably be as well for Halleck not to show himself, because he (Sherman) would not be responsible for what some rash person might do through indignation for the treatment he had received. Very soon after that, Sherman received orders from me to proceed to Washington City, and to go into camp on the south side of the city pending the mustering-out of the troops.

There was no incident worth noting in the march northward from Goldsboro, to Richmond, or in that from Richmond to Washington City. The army, however, commanded by Sherman, which had been engaged in all the battles of the West and had marched from the Mississippi through the Southern States to the sea, from there to Goldsboro, and thence to Washington City, had passed over many of the battle-fields of the Army of the Potomac, thus having seen, to a greater extent than any other body of troops, the entire theatre of the four years' war for the preservation of the Union.

The march of Sherman's army from Atlanta to the sea and north to Goldsboro, while it was not accompanied with the danger that was antic-

origin story: "In May, 1866, a little group of young men in the Tennessee village of Pulaski, finding time hang heavy on their hands after the excitements of the field, so lately abandoned, formed a secret club for the mere pleasure of association, for private amusement,—for anything that might promise to break the monotony of the too quiet place, as their wits might work upon the matter, and one of their number suggested that they call themselves the *Kuklos*, the Circle. Secrecy and mystery were at the heart of the pranks they planned." *A History of the American People* (New York: Harper & Brothers, 1902), 5:59.

For the definitive history of reconstruction, see Eric Foner, *Reconstruction: America's Unfinished Revolution, 1863–1877* (New York: Harper & Row, 1988). See also David W. Blight, *Race and Reunion: The Civil War in American Memory* (Cambridge, MA: Harvard, Belknap, 2002).

ipated, yet was magnificent in its results, and equally magnificent in the way it was conducted. It had an important bearing, in various ways, upon the great object we had in view, that of closing the war. All the States east of the Mississippi River up to the State of Georgia, had felt the hardships of the war. Georgia, and South Carolina, and almost all of North Carolina, up to this time, had been exempt from invasion by the Northern armies, except upon their immediate sea-coasts. Their newspapers had given such an account of Confederate success, that the people who remained at home had been convinced that the Yankees had been whipped from first to last, and driven from pillar to post, and that now they could hardly be holding out for any other purpose than to find a way out of the war with honor to themselves.

Even during this march of Sherman's the newspapers in his front were proclaiming daily that his army was nothing better than a mob of men who were frightened out of their wits and hastening, panic-stricken, to try to get under the cover of our navy for protection against the Southern people. As the army was seen marching on triumphantly, however, the minds of the people became disabused and they saw the true state of affairs. In turn they became disheartened, and would have been glad to submit without compromise.

Another great advantage resulting from this march, and which was calculated to hasten the end, was the fact that the great storehouse of Georgia was entirely cut off from the Confederate armies. As the troops advanced north from Savannah, the destruction of the railroads in South Carolina and the southern part of North Carolina, further cut off their resources and left the armies still in Virginia and North Carolina dependent for supplies upon a very small area of country, already very much exhausted of food and forage.

In due time the two armies, one from Burkesville Junction and the other from the neighborhood of Raleigh, North Carolina, arrived and went into camp near the Capital, as directed. The troops were hardy, being inured to fatigue, and they appeared in their respective camps as ready and fit for duty as they had ever been in their lives. I doubt whether an equal body of men of any nation, take them man for man, officer for officer, was ever gotten together that would have proved their equal in a great battle.

The armies of Europe are machines; the men are brave and the officers capable; but the majority of the soldiers in most of the nations of Europe are taken from a class of people who are not very intelligent and who have very little interest in the contest in which they are called upon to take part. Our armies were composed of men who were able to read, men who knew what they were fighting for, and could not be induced to serve as soldiers, except in an emergency when the safety of the nation was involved, and so necessarily must have been more than equal to men who fought merely because they were brave and because they were thoroughly drilled and inured to hardships.[2]

There was nothing of particular importance occurred during the time these troops were in camp before starting North.

I remember one little incident which I will relate as an anecdote characteristic of Mr. Lincoln. It occurred a day after I reached Washington, and about the time General Meade reached Burkesville with the army. Governor Smith of Virginia had left Richmond with the Confederate States government, and had gone to Danville. Supposing I was necessarily with the army at Burkesville, he addressed a letter to me there informing me that, as governor of the Commonwealth of the State of Virginia, he had temporarily removed the State capital from Richmond to Danville, and asking if he would be permitted to perform the functions of his office there without molestation by the Federal authorities. I give this letter only in substance. He also inquired of me whether in case he was not allowed to perform the duties of his office, he with a few others might not be permitted to leave the country and go abroad without interference. General Meade being informed that a flag of truce was outside his pickets with a letter to me, at once sent out and had the letter brought in without informing the officer who brought it that I was not present. He read the letter and telegraphed me its contents. Meeting Mr. Lincoln shortly after receiving this dispatch, I repeated its contents to him. Mr. Lincoln, supposing I was asking for instructions, said, in reply to that part of Governor Smith's letter which inquired whether he with a few friends would be permitted to leave the country unmolested, that his position was like that of a certain Irishman (giving the name) he knew in Springfield who was very popular with the people, a man of considerable promise, and very much liked. Unfortunately he had acquired the habit of drinking, and his friends could see that the habit was growing on him. These friends determined to make an effort to save him, and to do this they drew up a pledge to abstain from all alcoholic drinks. They asked Pat to join them in signing the pledge, and he consented. He had been so long out of the habit of using plain water as a beverage that he resorted to soda-water as a substi-

---

2. This is Grant's final hymn to the volunteers, and it anticipates the celebration of the citizen-soldier that would reach its apogee during World War II.

tute. After a few days this began to grow distasteful to him. So holding the glass behind him, he said: "Doctor, couldn't you drop a bit of brandy in that unbeknownst to myself."

I do not remember what the instructions were the President gave me, but I know that Governor Smith was not permitted to perform the duties of his office. I also know that if Mr. Lincoln had been spared, there would have been no efforts made to prevent any one from leaving the country who desired to do so. He would have been equally willing to permit the return of the same expatriated citizens after they had time to repent of their choice.[3]

On the 18th of May orders were issued by the adjutant-general for a grand review by the President and his cabinet of Sherman's and Meade's armies. The review commenced on the 23d and lasted two days.[4] Meade's

---

3. Grant's unnecessary inclusion of a final example of Lincoln's canny folksiness is a testament to his fondness for the man. In dwelling on Lincoln's potential for post-war flexibility, it offers an implicit condemnation of Andrew Johnson. It also puts the modern reader in mind of the Grant administration's uneven handling of Reconstruction's challenges. We will never know the extent to which Lincoln's management of the postbellum dispensation would have borne out the faith—cherished by North and South alike—in his ability to do so.

4. Bret Harte responded to the two-day event in his long poem "A Second Review of the Grand Army," in which he envisions a ghostly parade of the dead:

> And I saw a phantom army come,
> With never a sound of fife or drum,
> But keeping time to a throbbing hum
>   Of wailing and lamentation:
> The martyred heroes of Malvern Hill,
> Of Gettysburg and Chancellorsville,
> The men whose wasted figures fill
>   The patriot graves of the nation.
> . . . .
> So all night long swept the strange array,
> So all night long, till the morning gray
> I watch'd for one who had passed away;
>   With a reverent awe and wonder,—
> Till a blue cap waved in the length'ning line,
> And I knew that one who was kin of mine
> Had come; and I spake—and lo! that sign
>   Awakened me from my slumber.

Poems and Two Men of Sandy Bar, a Drama, vol. 12 of *The Writings of Bret Harte* (Boston: Houghton Mifflin, 1910), 18–19.

army occupied over six hours of the first day in passing the grand stand which had been erected in front of the President's house. Sherman witnessed this review from the grand stand which was occupied by the President and his cabinet. Here he showed his resentment for the cruel and harsh treatment that had unnecessarily been inflicted upon him by the Secretary of War, by refusing to take his extended hand.

Sherman's troops had been in camp on the south side of the Potomac. During the night of the 23d he crossed over and bivouacked not far from the Capitol. Promptly at ten o'clock on the morning of the 24th, his troops commenced to pass in review. Sherman's army made a different appearance from that of the Army of the Potomac. The latter had been operating where they received directly from the North full supplies of food and clothing regularly: the review of this army therefore was the review of a body of 65,000 well-drilled, well-disciplined and orderly soldiers inured to hardship and fit for any duty, but without the experience of gathering their own food and supplies in an enemy's country, and of being ever on the watch. Sherman's army was not so well-dressed as the Army of the Potomac, but their marching could not be excelled; they gave the appearance of men who had been thoroughly drilled to endure hardships, either by long and continuous marches or through exposure to any climate, without the ordinary shelter of a camp. They exhibited also some of the order of march through Georgia where the "sweet potatoes sprung up from the ground" as Sherman's army went marching through. In the rear of a company there would be a captured horse or mule loaded with small cooking utensils, captured chickens and other food picked up for the use of the men. Negro families who had followed the army would sometimes come along in the rear of a company, with three or four children packed upon a single mule, and the mother leading it.[5]

----

5. As Grant notes, the army of the West cut a rather different figure than did the more polished Army of the Potomac. Joshua Chamberlain, a member of the latter, expressed his enthusiasm for Sherman's more idiosyncratic troops:

> We were told that General Sherman witnessing our review had told his leading commanders that our military appearance and even marching could not be surpassed or even equalled by their own men, and it was resolved that they would not make the attempt to rival us in this regard but would appear as nearly as possible as they looked while "marching through Georgia." But they did both. As was to be expected, their marching was superb, both steady and free, not as if forced for the occasion, but by habit

The sight was varied and grand: nearly all day for two successive days, from the Capitol to the Treasury Building, could be seen a mass of orderly soldiers marching in columns of companies. The National flag was flying from almost every house and store; the windows were filled with spectators; the door-steps and side-walks were crowded with colored people and poor whites who did not succeed in securing better quarters from which to get a view of the grand armies. The city was about as full of strangers who had come to see the sights as it usually is on inauguration day when a new President takes his seat.

It may not be out of place to again allude to President Lincoln and the Secretary of War, Mr. Stanton, who were the great conspicuous figures in the executive branch of the government. There is no great difference of opinion now, in the public mind, as to the characteristics of the President. With Mr. Stanton the case is different. They were the very opposite of each other in almost every particular, except that each possessed great ability. Mr. Lincoln gained influence over men by making them feel that it was a pleasure to serve him. He preferred yielding his own wish to gratify others, rather than to insist upon having his own way. It distressed him to disappoint others. In matters of public duty, however, he had what he wished, but in the least offensive way. Mr. Stanton never questioned his own authority to command, unless resisted. He cared nothing for the feeling of others. In fact

---

or second nature: distances maintained; lines perfectly "dressed" on the "guide left"; eyes steady to the front.

Passing of the Armies, 366.

The differences between the armies reached deeper than appearances. Thomas Wentworth Higginson, a thoroughgoing New Englander, once described a fellow officer as "a wild slap-dash free & easy Westerner from Grant's Army." *The Complete Civil War Journal and Selected Letters of Thomas Wentworth Higginson*, ed. Christopher Looby (Chicago: University of Chicago Press, 2000), 212.

As for "Marching Through Georgia," the song by Henry Clay Work to which the armies advanced, Sherman reportedly did not like it. This is its chorus:

> "Hurrah! Hurrah! We bring the Jubilee!
> Hurrah! Hurrah! The flag that makes you free!"
> So we sang the chorus from Atlanta to the sea,
> While we were marching through Georgia.

Historic Sheet Music Collection, 898, Connecticut College, http://digitalcommons.conn coll.edu/sheetmusic/898.

Grand Review of the Army, Sherman's 20th Corps. *Library of Congress, Prints and Photographs Division, Civil War Photographs, LC-DIG-cwpb-02949.*

it seemed to be pleasanter to him to disappoint than to gratify. He felt no hesitation in assuming the functions of the executive, or in acting without advising with him. If his act was not sustained, he would change it—if he saw the matter would be followed up until he did so.

It was generally supposed that these two officials formed the complement of each other. The Secretary was required to prevent the President's being imposed upon. The President was required in the more responsible place of seeing that injustice was not done to others. I do not know that this view of these two men is still entertained by the majority of the people. It is not a correct view, however, in my estimation. Mr. Lincoln did not require a guardian to aid him in the fulfilment of a public trust.

Mr. Lincoln was not timid, and he was willing to trust his generals in making and executing their plans. The Secretary was very timid, and it was impossible for him to avoid interfering with the armies covering the capital when it was sought to defend it by an offensive movement against the army guarding the Confederate capital. He could see our weakness, but he could not see that the enemy was in danger. The enemy would not have been in danger if Mr. Stanton had been in the field. These characteristics of the two officials were clearly shown shortly after Early came so near getting into the capital.[6]

6. This double-portrait of Lincoln and Stanton can be seen as a companion piece to Grant's diptych of Scott and Taylor in chapter 10. These concluding appraisals of various commanders reveal Grant's ability to parse with precision and equanimity others' strengths and weaknesses—and never to let the latter prevent his acknowledgment of the former. The son of one president and the grandson of another, Charles Francis Adams, who served at the Army of the Potomac headquarters, curated a portrait gallery of a decidedly different style in his autobiography:

> At Headquarters . . . I did not ingratiate myself to the degree that would have been easily possible with one differently constituted. At the same time I must confess that even now, looking back, the men I saw handling large

Among the army and corps commanders who served with me during the war between the States, and who attracted much public attention, but of whose ability as soldiers I have not yet given any estimate, are Meade, Hancock, Sedgwick, Burnside, Terry and Hooker. There were others of great merit, such as Griffin, Humphreys, Wright and Mackenzie. Of those first named, Burnside at one time had command of the Army of the Potomac, and later of the Army of the Ohio. Hooker also commanded the Army of the Potomac for a short time.

General Meade was an officer of great merit, with drawbacks to his usefulness that were beyond his control. He had been an officer of the engineer corps before the war, and consequently had never served with troops until he was over forty-six years of age. He never had, I believe, a command of less than a brigade. He saw clearly and distinctly the position of the enemy, and the topography of the country in front of his own position. His first idea was to take advantage of the lay of the ground, sometimes without reference to the direction we wanted to move afterwards. He was subordinate to his

affairs in those military operations do not seem to me to have been as a rule imposing. . . . General Meade was a gentleman and man of high character; but he was irritable, petulant and dyspeptic. He did not give the idea of calm, reserved force. Grant did; but Grant was a man of coarse fibre, and did not impress with a sense of character. Hancock was a dashing field-marshal; a handsome, superb commander of a corps. Warren left on me a sense of lightness. Humphreys and Sedgwick were the only two generals I ever met who inspired me with an adequate sense of force and reliability. Officers, they were also quiet, unassuming gentlemen. About them there was no pretence, no posing for effect, no stage tricks. I felt for them a profound respect; and, could I have been a staff officer on the corps commanded by either, I should have found my proper army position. Sheridan I never saw until long after the war was over, and then only casually. He was essentially an Irish adventurer—a species of brilliant Charles O'Malley; with a well-developed natural aptitude for military life, he was not conspicuous for character. Thomas, I never laid eyes on; but I imagine he was a man of the Sedgwick type—solid and full of character. Sherman, I only saw after the war was over; but he then impressed me much, more than any of those I have named, not even excepting Humphreys. He bore the stamp of true genius. Curiously natural, very fond of talking, there was about him nothing of the *poseur*. He was a delightful dinner-table companion, humorous, easy, striking, full of reminiscence. He and Humphreys, very different, but each great, were my two army ideals; under either, it would have been a delight and glory to serve.

An Autobiography (Boston: Houghton Mifflin, 1916), 157–58.

Generals of the Army of the Potomac: *(l. to r.)* Gouverneur K. Warren, William H. French, George G. Meade, Henry J. Hunt, Andrew A. Humphreys, George Sykes, Culpeper, Virginia, 1863. *Library of Congress, Prints and Photographs Division, Civil War Photographs, LC-DIG-cwpb-03981.*

superiors in rank to the extent that he could execute an order which changed his own plans with the same zeal he would have displayed if the plan had been his own. He was brave and conscientious, and commanded the respect of all who knew him. He was unfortunately of a temper that would get beyond his control, at times, and make him speak to officers of high rank in the most offensive manner. No one saw this fault more plainly than he himself, and no one regretted it more. This made it unpleasant at times, even in battle, for those around him to approach him even with information. In spite of this defect he was a most valuable officer and deserves a high place in the annals of his country.

General Burnside was an officer who was generally liked and respected. He was not, however, fitted to command an army. No one knew this better than himself. He always admitted his blunders, and extenuated those of officers under him beyond what they were entitled to. It was hardly his fault that he was ever assigned to a separate command.

Of Hooker I saw but little during the war. I had known him very well before, however. Where I did see him, at Chattanooga, his achievement in bringing his command around the point of Lookout Mountain and into Chattanooga Valley was brilliant. I nevertheless regarded him as a dangerous man. He was not subordinate to his superiors. He was ambitious to the extent of caring nothing for the rights of others. His disposition was, when engaged in battle, to get detached from the main body of the army and exercise a separate command, gathering to his standard all he could of his juniors.

Hancock stands the most conspicuous figure of all the general officers who did not exercise a separate command.[7] He commanded a corps longer than any other one, and his name was never mentioned as having committed in battle a blunder for which he was responsible. He was a man of very conspicuous personal appearance. Tall, well-formed and, at the time of which I now write, young and fresh-looking, he presented an appearance that would attract the attention of an army as he passed. His genial disposition made him friends, and his personal courage and his presence with his command in the thickest of the fight won for him the confidence of troops serving under him. No matter how hard the fight, the 2d corps always felt that their commander was looking after them.

Sedgwick was killed at Spottsylvania before I had an opportunity of forming an estimate of his qualifications as a soldier from personal observation. I had known him in Mexico when both of us were lieutenants, and when our service gave no indication that either of us would ever be equal to the command of a brigade. He stood very high in the army, however, as an officer and a man. He was brave and conscientious. His ambition was not great, and he seemed to dread responsibility. He was willing to do any amount of battling, but always wanted some one else to direct. He declined the command of the Army of the Potomac once, if not oftener.

General Alfred H. Terry came into the army as a volunteer without a military education. His way was won without political influence up to an important separate command—the expedition against Fort Fisher, in Janu-

7. Winfield Scott Hancock (1824–1886) graduated from West Point as a second lieutenant of infantry in 1844, a year behind Grant. He served on frontier duty in Oklahoma and in the Mexican War, and he was involved in actions in Bleeding Kansas. He served in all of the major Civil War campaigns in the east, from McClellan's Peninsular Campaign of 1862 to Grant's Overland Campaign of 1864–65. Seriously wounded at Gettysburg, Hancock sometimes found it necessary to travel by ambulance.

ary, 1865. His success there was most brilliant, and won for him the rank of brigadier-general in the regular army and of major-general of volunteers. He is a man who makes friends of those under him by his consideration of their wants and their dues. As a commander, he won their confidence by his coolness in action and by his clearness of perception in taking in the situation under which he was placed at any given time.[8]

---

8. After the war, Alfred Terry, a lawyer by training, served on the frontier and in Georgia, where he battled the emerging Ku Klux Klan. Terry was in command of the Department of Dakota when Custer was routed at the Battle of Little Big Horn.

One of the most complicated figures to participate in the campaigns against the Native Americans during this period was George Crook. On July 10, 1876, encamped with his troops along Goose Creek, in the northwest corner of what is today Wyoming, Crook received word that Custer's 7th Cavalry—and with it a lot of assumptions about what it meant to fight on the frontier—had been destroyed on June 25, at the hands of Crazy Horse and a combined force of Lakota, Cheyenne, and Arapaho along the Little Big Horn River, about a hundred miles north, in the Montana Territory.

Crook and Custer were both part of the Big Horn and Yellowstone Expedition, which had been organized in the wake of the failure of a government commission led by Iowa senator William Allison to buy the gold-rich Black Hills from the Sioux. As the HBO series *Deadwood* dramatized in such vivid detail several years ago, the hordes of miners, seized by gold-fever, were disinclined to wait for anyone's permission before invading the Black Hills, which were sacred to the Plains Indians. On June 17, Crook had fought his own engagement against Crazy Horse along the Rosebud River. As Thomas Powers notes, many of Crook's troops, trained largely in the "mass battles" of the Civil War, were for the first time "probed and assaulted by a fluid and shifting enemy in a manner that astounded them all." There was to be no victory in such a contest, although Crook claimed one, and his elusive enemy moved easily toward its confrontation with Custer at the Little Big Horn while Crook's column retreated south to regroup and await reinforcements. See *The Killing of Crazy Horse* (New York: Vintage, 2011), 185–86.

Crook stayed put until August, when he decided to increase his mobility by cutting loose from his supply train. After a rendezvous with Terry at the Yellowstone, he decided to strike out on what his staff officer and biographer John Gregory Bourke called "a hot trail" in miserable weather with insufficient rations. "There is one thing certain about a hot trail," Bourke explains, "you'll find Indians on it if you go far enough, and you'll find them nowhere else." *On the Border with Crook*, 2nd ed. (New York: Scribner's, 1892), 365.

This advance came to be known as the "Horse-Meat March" or the "Starvation March." By the beginning of September, reported the journalist John F. Finerty, who accompanied Crook, "nothing remained . . . but to eat one another or our animals." *War-Path and Bivouac, or The Conquest of the Sioux* (Chicago: Donohue & Henneberry, 1890), 248.

When Crook's command did meet up with elements of the enemy force at Slim Buttes, they were so exhausted that they could not pursue the skirmish to a conclusion.

Griffin, Humphreys, and Mackenzie were good corps commanders, but came into that position so near to the close of the war as not to attract public attention. All three served as such, in the last campaign of the armies of the Potomac and the James, which culminated at Appomattox Court House, on the 9th of April, 1865. The sudden collapse of the rebellion monopolized

---

The failure of the expedition continued to haunt Crook. Over the years, thanks in large part to Bourke's hagiography but also to his own careful management, Crook acquired a reputation as, in Bourke's words, the "ablest" of the Indian fighters but also as a man whose word the Indians believed "as they believed in the stars." *Biographical Register*, vol. 2, s.v. "Crook, George."

Crook had been fighting Indians since his days as a new second lieutenant in the Pacific Northwest, where he found himself, not for the last time, ambivalent about his mission. Crook himself was quick to note the depredations the Indians suffered at the hands of white settlers, against whom they were powerless to obtain justice. "Then when they were pushed beyond endurance [and went] on the war path," he wrote, "we had to fight when our sympathies were with the Indians." *Autobiography*, 16.

But fight them he did, and his experience in the 1850s later proved invaluable during the Civil War, when he found himself fighting Confederate bushwhackers, most notably Mosby's Rangers. Crook continued to pursue irregular warfare—what we today call counterinsurgency campaigns—against various Oregon and California tribes, the Apaches in Arizona, and the Plains Indians.

Crook was a man of contradictions: There were times when he seemed as much a friend to the Indians as he was a sworn enemy. He died of a heart attack in a Chicago hotel in 1890, after having lobbied unsuccessfully on behalf of Apaches—including those who had served as Army scouts—who had been deceived and permanently relocated to the East after surrendering in Arizona. He served in a morally and militarily ambiguous environment lacking clear lines of battle, decisive victories and losses, and transparent codes of conduct.

At West Point, Crook had been an indifferent student. However, as the archives reveal, he was a regular reader whose tastes, in an age in which the campaigns of Napoleon were all the rage among his contemporaries, was more catholic: Goldsmith's *History of Rome*, Kendall's *Narrative of the Texan Santa Fe Expedition*, Thiers's *The History of the French Revolution*, Humboldt's *Travels*, and a *Life of Mahomet*. In 1884, Crook paid a visit to his alma mater to address the graduating class just as veterans of the counterinsurgency campaigns in Iraq and Afghanistan do today. "Make them no promises which you can not fulfill; make no statements you can not verify," Crook instructed the new lieutenants. "Let the Indian see that you administer one law to both the white-skinned and the red-skinned, and that you do this without regard to blame or censure, and you will gain his confidence, because you have shown yourself worthy of it." *Harper's Weekly* 28 (July 5, 1884): 427.

As Powers reminds us, however, it was Crook's breaking of his promise of a buffalo hunt to the Sioux that created an irrevocable rift with Crazy Horse, one that ultimately led to the chief's murder. Nevertheless, it is his message about faithful promises with which Crook has long been identified—even by his enemies.

attention to the exclusion of almost everything else. I regarded Mackenzie
as the most promising young officer in the army. Graduating at West Point,
as he did, during the second year of the war, he had won his way up to the
command of a corps before its close. This he did upon his own merit and
without influence.[9]

9. As is so often the case, the private Civil War soldier's postwar experience for the most
part lacked the glamour of the general's postwar celebrity. Grant offers little insight—
either in this final chapter or in the conclusion—into the lives of the rank and file after
the war, especially during the so-called Gilded Age of his two-term presidency. For a
detailed account of the complex and often very difficult veteran experience, see James
Marten, *Sing Not War: The Lives of Union & Confederate Veterans in Gilded Age America*
(Chapel Hill: University of North Carolina Press, 2011).

Thomas Waterman Wood, *A Bit of War History:
The Veteran*, 1866. The third in a series of
paintings—the other two are *The Contraband*
and *The Recruit*—chronicling the experience
of the African American soldier. *Metropolitan
Museum of Art, Gift of Charles Stewart Smith, 1884.*

"I gave my eyes," World War I veteran,
1932 or 1933. *Library of Congress, Prints and
Photographs, LC-DIG-hec-36930.*

Conclusion

The cause of the great War of the Rebellion against the United States will have to be attributed to slavery.[1] For some years before the war began it was a trite saying among some politicians that "A state half slave and half free cannot exist." All must become slave or all free, or the state will go down. I took no part myself in any such view of the case at the time, but since the war is over, reviewing the whole question, I have come to the conclusion that the saying is quite true.

Slavery was an institution that required unusual guarantees for its security wherever it existed; and in a country like ours where the larger portion of it was free territory inhabited by an intelligent and well-to-do population, the people would naturally have but little sympathy with demands upon them for its protection. Hence the people of the South were dependent upon keeping control of the general government to secure the perpetuation of their favorite institution. They were enabled to maintain this control long after the States where slavery existed had ceased to have the controlling power, through the assistance they received from odd men here and there throughout the Northern States. They saw their power waning, and this led

---

1. As the several state documents specifying slavery as the cause of their secession indicate, this was the states' right for which Americans proved willing to die. Southern states had no complaints about federal power when it was used to enforce the Fugitive Slave Law. On Americans' wartime political engagement, see Mark E. Neely Jr., *The Boundaries of American Political Culture in the Civil War Era* (Chapel Hill: University of North Carolina Press, 2005).

"Effects of the Fugitive-Slave Law." Antebellum depiction of the law's horrific consequences accompanied by quotations from the Bible and the Declaration of Independence, 1850. *Library of Congress, Prints and Photographs Division, LC-USZ62-1286.*

them to encroach upon the prerogatives and independence of the Northern States by enacting such laws as the Fugitive Slave Law. By this law every Northern man was obliged, when properly summoned, to turn out and help apprehend the runaway slave of a Southern man. Northern marshals became slave-catchers, and Northern courts had to contribute to the support and protection of the institution.

This was a degradation which the North would not permit any longer than until they could get the power to expunge such laws from the statute books. Prior to the time of these encroachments the great majority of the people of the North had no particular quarrel with slavery, so long as they were not forced to have it themselves. But they were not willing to play the role of police for the South in the protection of this particular institution.

In the early days of the country, before we had railroads, telegraphs and steamboats—in a word, rapid transit of any sort—the States were each almost a separate nationality. At that time the subject of slavery caused but little or no disturbance to the public mind. But the country grew, rapid transit was established, and trade and commerce between the States got to be so much greater than before, that the power of the National government became more felt and recognized and, therefore, had to be enlisted in the cause of this institution.

It is probably well that we had the war when we did. We are better off now than we would have been without it, and have made more rapid progress than we otherwise should have made.[2] The civilized nations of

2. For a provocative reappraisal of the war's legacy in various spheres of American life—from labor practices to proslavery theology to Indian Policy—see the essays in

Europe have been stimulated into unusual activity, so that commerce, trade, travel, and thorough acquaintance among people of different nationalities, has become common; whereas, before, it was but the few who had ever had the privilege of going beyond the limits of their own country or who knew anything about other people. Then, too, our republican institutions were regarded as experiments up to the breaking out of the rebellion, and monarchical Europe generally believed that our republic was a rope of sand that would part the moment the slightest strain was brought upon it. Now it has shown itself capable of dealing with one of the greatest wars that was ever made, and our people have proven themselves to be the most formidable in war of any nationality.

But this war was a fearful lesson, and should teach us the necessity of avoiding wars in the future.[3]

The conduct of some of the European states during our troubles shows the lack of conscience of communities where the responsibility does not come upon a single individual. Seeing a nation that extended from ocean to ocean, embracing the better part of a continent, growing as we were growing in population, wealth and intelligence, the European nations thought it would be well to give us a check. We might, possibly, after a while threaten their peace, or, at least, the perpetuity of their institutions. Hence, England was constantly finding fault with the administration at Washington because we were not able to keep up an effective blockade. She also joined, at first, with France and Spain in setting up an Austrian prince upon the throne in

---

The World the Civil War Made, ed. Gregory P. Downs and Kate Masur (Chapel Hill: University of North Carolina Press, 2015).

3. Henry James's secretary Theodora Bosanquet records her expatriate employer's opinion that the Civil War marked in a sense the end of history in the United States:

> There is a pleasant account in *The Middle Years* of his blankness when he was asked at a London breakfast-table for "distinctness about General Grant's first cabinet, upon the formation of which the light of the newspaper happened then to beat." The question was embarrassing. "There were, it appeared, things of interest taking place in America, and I had had, in this absurd manner, to come to England to learn it: I had had over there on the ground itself no conception of any such matter—nothing of the smallest interest, by any perception of mine, as I suppose I should still blush to recall, had taken place in America since the War."

"Henry James at Work," *The Hogarth Essays* (Richmond UK: Hogarth Press, 1924), 270–71.

Mexico, totally disregarding any rights or claims that Mexico had of being treated as an independent power. It is true they trumped up grievances as a pretext, but they were only pretexts which can always be found when wanted.

Mexico, in her various revolutions, had been unable to give that protection to the subjects of foreign nations which she would have liked to give, and some of her revolutionary leaders had forced loans from them. Under pretence of protecting their citizens, these nations seized upon Mexico as a foothold for establishing a European monarchy upon our continent, thus threatening our peace at home. I, myself, regarded this as a direct act of war against the United States by the powers engaged, and supposed as a matter of course that the United States would treat it as such when their hands were free to strike. I often spoke of the matter to Mr. Lincoln and the Secretary of War, but never heard any special views from them to enable me to judge what they thought or felt about it. I inferred that they felt a good deal as I did, but were unwilling to commit themselves while we had our own troubles upon our hands.

All of the powers except France very soon withdrew from the armed intervention for the establishment of an Austrian prince upon the throne of Mexico; but the governing people of these countries continued to the close of the war to throw obstacles in our way. After the surrender of Lee, therefore, entertaining the opinion here expressed, I sent Sheridan with a corps to the Rio Grande to have him where he might aid Juarez in expelling the French from Mexico. These troops got off before they could be stopped; and went to the Rio Grande, where Sheridan distributed them up and down the river, much to the consternation of the troops in the quarter of Mexico bordering on that stream. This soon led to a request from France that we should withdraw our troops from the Rio Grande and to negotiations for the withdrawal of theirs. Finally Bazaine was withdrawn from Mexico by order of the French Government. From that day the empire began to totter. Mexico was then able to maintain her independence without aid from us.

France is the traditional ally and friend of the United States. I did not blame France for her part in the scheme to erect a monarchy upon the ruins of the Mexican Republic. That was the scheme of one man, an imitator without genius or merit. He had succeeded in stealing the government of his country, and made a change in its form against the wishes and instincts of his people. He tried to play the part of the first Napoleon, without the ability to sustain that role. He sought by new conquests to add to his empire and his glory; but the signal failure of his scheme of conquest was the precursor of his own overthrow.

Like our own war between the States, the Franco-Prussian war was an expensive one; but it was worth to France all it cost her people. It was the completion of the downfall of Napoleon III. The beginning was when he landed troops on this continent. Failing here, the prestige of his name—all the prestige he ever had—was gone. He must achieve a success or fall. He tried to strike down his neighbor, Prussia—and fell.[4]

I never admired the character of the first Napoleon; but I recognize his great genius. His work, too, has left its impress for good on the face of Europe. The third Napoleon could have no claim to having done a good or just act.

To maintain peace in the future it is necessary to be prepared for war. There can scarcely be a possible chance of a conflict, such as the last one, occurring among our own people again; but, growing as we are, in population, wealth and military power, we may become the envy of nations which led us in all these particulars only a few years ago; and unless we are prepared for it we may be in danger of a combined movement being some day made to crush us out. Now, scarcely twenty years after the war, we seem to have forgotten the lessons it taught, and are going on as if in the greatest security, without the power to resist an invasion by the fleets of fourth-rate European powers for a time until we could prepare for them.

We should have a good navy, and our sea-coast defences should be put in the finest possible condition. Neither of these cost much when it is considered where the money goes, and what we get in return. Money expended in a fine navy, not only adds to our security and tends to prevent war in the future, but is very material aid to our commerce with foreign nations in the meantime. Money spent upon sea-coast defences is spent among our own people, and all goes back again among the people. The work accomplished, too, like that of the navy, gives us a feeling of security.

England's course towards the United States during the rebellion exasperated the people of this country very much against the mother country. I regretted it. England and the United States are natural allies, and should be the best of friends. They speak one language, and are related by blood and

---

4. Some American officers, Sheridan among them, went to observe the Franco-Prussian War. Sheridan includes an extensive account of his European travels in his *Personal Memoirs*.

Grant's "good navy," realized by Theodore Roosevelt: The Great White Fleet of 1907 Illuminated. *Library of Congress, Prints and Photographs Division, Detroit Publishing Company Collection, LC-DIG-det-4a15935.*

other ties. We together, or even either separately, are better qualified than any other people to establish commerce between all the nationalities of the world.

England governs her own colonies, and particularly those embracing the people of different races from her own, better than any other nation. She is just to the conquered, but rigid. She makes them self-supporting, but gives the benefit of labor to the laborer. She does not seem to look upon the colonies as outside possessions which she is at liberty to work for the support and aggrandizement of the home government.

The hostility of England to the United States during our rebellion was not so much real as it was apparent. It was the hostility of the leaders of one political party. I am told that there was no time during the civil war when they were able to get up in England a demonstration in favor of secession, while these were constantly being gotten up in favor of the Union, or, as they called it, in favor of the North. Even in Manchester, which suffered so fearfully by having the cotton cut off from her mills, they had a monster demonstration in favor of the North at the very time when their workmen were almost famishing.[5]

5. Grant included Manchester on his world tour. John Russell Young recorded Grant's remarks in response to his enthusiastic welcome:

> I am, and have been for many years, fully aware of the great amount of manufactures of Manchester, many of which find a market in my own country. I was very well aware, during the war, of the sentiments of the great mass of the people of Manchester toward the country to which I have the honor to belong, and also of the sentiments with regard to the struggle

It is possible that the question of a conflict between races may come up in the future, as did that between freedom and slavery before. The condition of the colored man within our borders may become a source of anxiety, to say the least. But he was brought to our shores by compulsion, and he now should be considered as having as good a right to remain here as any other class of our citizens. It was looking to a settlement of this question that led me to urge the annexation of Santo Domingo during the time I was President of the United States.

Santo Domingo was freely offered to us, not only by the administration, but by all the people, almost without price. The island is upon our shores, is very fertile, and is capable of supporting fifteen millions of people. The products of the soil are so valuable that labor in her fields would be so compensated as to enable those who wished to go there to quickly repay the cost of their passage. I took it that the colored people would go there in great numbers, so as to have independent states governed by their own race. They would still be States of the Union, and under the protection of the General Government; but the citizens would be almost wholly colored.

By the war with Mexico, we had acquired, as we have seen, territory almost equal in extent to that we already possessed. It was seen that the volunteers of the Mexican war largely composed the pioneers to settle up the Pacific coast country. Their numbers, however, were scarcely sufficient to be a nucleus for the population of the important points of the territory acquired by that war. After our rebellion, when so many young men were at liberty to return to their homes, they found they were not satisfied with the farm, the store, or the work-shop of the villages, but wanted larger fields. The mines of the mountains first attracted them; but afterwards they found that rich valleys and productive grazing and farming lands were there. This territory, the geography of which was not known to us at the close of the rebellion, is now as well mapped as any portion of our country. Railroads traverse it in every direction, north, south, east, and west. The mines are worked. The high lands are used for grazing purposes, and rich agricultural lands are found in many of the valleys. This is the work of the volunteer. It is probable that the Indians would have had control of these lands for a century yet but for the

in which it fell to my lot to take a humble part. It was a great trial for us. For your expressions of sympathy at that time there exists a feeling of friendship toward Manchester distinct and separate from that which my countrymen also feel, and I trust always will feel, toward every part of England.

Around the World with Grant, 1:15–16.

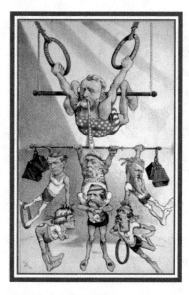

J. Keppler, cartoon depicting the Grant administration's legacy of scandal and corruption, published in response to reports that he might run for a third term, *Puck*, February 4, 1880. *Library of Congress, Prints and Photographs Division, LC-USZC4-5606.*

war. We must conclude, therefore, that wars are not always evils unmixed with some good.[6]

Prior to the rebellion the great mass of the people were satisfied to remain near the scenes of their birth. In fact an immense majority of the whole people did not feel secure against coming to want should they move among entire strangers. So much was the country divided into small communities that localized idioms had grown up, so that you could almost tell what section a person was from by hearing him speak. Before, new territories were settled by a "class"; people who shunned contact with others; people who, when the country began to settle up around them, would push out farther from civilization. Their guns furnished meat, and the cultivation of a very limited amount of the soil, their bread and vegetables. All the streams abounded with fish. Trapping would furnish pelts to be brought into the States once a year, to pay for necessary articles which they could not raise—powder, lead, whiskey, tobacco and some store goods. Occasionally some little articles of luxury would enter into these purchases—a quarter of a pound of tea, two or three pounds of coffee, more of sugar, some playing cards, and if anything was left over of the proceeds of the sale, more whiskey.

---

6. Grant's sweeping political pronouncements here are rarely as trenchant as his military commentary; sometimes, as is the case here, they resolve themselves into platitudes. Moreover, the rather offhand dismissal of Native Americans does not accord fully with Grant's more progressive, if ultimately failed, presidential policies.

**Buffalo soldiers of the 25th Infantry, Fort Keogh, Montana, 1890.
Photograph by Christian Barthelmess.** *Library of Congress, Prints and
Photographs Division, LC–DIG–ppmsca–11406.*

Little was known of the topography of the country beyond the settlements of these frontiersmen. This is all changed now. The war begot a spirit
of independence and enterprise. The feeling now is, that a youth must cut
loose from his old surroundings to enable him to get up in the world. There
is now such a commingling of the people that particular idioms and pronun-
ciation are no longer localized to any great extent; the country has filled up
"from the centre all around to the sea"; railroads connect the two oceans and
all parts of the interior; maps, nearly perfect, of every part of the country are
now furnished the student of geography.[7]

The war has made us a nation of great power and intelligence. We have
but little to do to preserve peace, happiness and prosperity at home, and the
respect of other nations. Our experience ought to teach us the necessity of
the first; our power secures the latter.

---

7. Since the expansionist stirrings of Manifest Destiny in the antebellum period, we
have grown accustomed to associating the West with American promise. Joan Didion,
writing about post–World War II America, offers a counterpoint that suggests the ways
in which the Civil War's legacy in the South might complicate this vision: "I had only
some dim and unformed sense, a sense which struck me now and then, and which I
could not explain coherently, that for some years the South and particularly the Gulf
Coast had been for America what people were still saying California was, and what
California seemed to me not to be: the future, the secret source of malevolent and
benevolent energy, the psychic center. I did not much want to talk about this." *South
and West: From a Notebook* (New York: Knopf, 2017), 14.

I feel that we are on the eve of a new era, when there is to be great harmony between the Federal and Confederate.[8] I cannot stay to be a living witness to the correctness of this prophecy; but I feel it within me that it is to be so. The universally kind feeling expressed for me at a time when it was supposed that each day would prove my last, seemed to me the beginning of the answer to "Let us have peace."

The expression of these kindly feelings were not restricted to a section of the country, nor to a division of the people. They came from individual citizens of all nationalities; from all denominations—the Protestant, the Catholic, and the Jew; and from the various societies of the land—scientific, educational, religious or otherwise. Politics did not enter into the matter at all.

I am not egotist enough to suppose all this significance should be given because I was the object of it. But the war between the States was a very bloody and a very costly war. One side or the other had to yield principles they deemed dearer than life before it could be brought to an end. I commanded the whole of the mighty host engaged on the victorious side. I was,

---

8. Grant does not note here that any harmony existing in the 1880s had occurred at the expense of African Americans. His experience as general-in-chief and later president enforcing Reconstruction as well as battling the Ku Klux Klan had nevertheless revealed to him the depths of Southern resentment and the degree to which the precondition of amity was federal withdrawal from Southern affairs. In the decades following his death, the hold of Jim Crow would grow only tighter, while nostalgia for the Old South flourished.

If particular racial, social, and cultural factors shaped the rhetoric of reconciliation in the United States, however, there was also a universal phenomenon at work: the veteran's disillusion, resentment—and sometimes hatred. "They had been abandoned," wrote the novelist Jean Larteguy of the veterans of France's war in Indochina, who returned home to find a France utterly changed in their absence:

> Cut off from their own country, they had re-created an artificial motherland for themselves in the friendship of the Vietnamese and in the arms of their slant-eyed women.
>
> They were almost horrified to realize that they now had more in common with the Vietminh whom they had hated, with the Voice and his mysterious smile, with the oafish bo-dois, than with these people who were waiting for them on the quayside with a wretched little military band and a detachment of soldiers sloppily presenting arms. . . .
>
> Even the morning air smelled alien to them.

The Centurions, trans. Xan Fielding (New York: Penguin Classics, 2015), 206–7.

no matter whether deservedly so or not, a representative of that side of the controversy. It is a significant and gratifying fact that Confederates should have joined heartily in this spontaneous move. I hope the good feeling inaugurated may continue to the end.[9]

End of Volume II

9. At his death Grant became a prime focus for the energies of reconciliation. The composition of pallbearers—Sherman, Johnston, Sheridan, and Buckner—was itself a measure of the desire to erase former antagonisms. For a comprehensive and thoughtful account of the symbol Grant became, see Joan Waugh, *U. S. Grant: American Hero, American Myth* (Chapel Hill: University of North Carolina Press, 2009).

The poet and Civil War nurse Walt Whitman found in Grant "nothing heroic . . . and yet the greatest hero." On the occasion of the general's return from his world tour in 1879, Whitman reflected in *Specimen Days*:

> Cynical critics are wondering "what the people can see in Grant" to make such a hubbub about. They aver (and it is no doubt true) that he has hardly the average of our day's literary and scholastic culture, and absolutely no pronounc'd genius or conventional eminence of any sort. Correct: but he proves how an average western farmer, mechanic, boatman, carried by tides of circumstances, perhaps caprices, into a position of incredible military or civic responsibilities, . . . may steer his way fitly and steadily through them all, carrying the country and himself with credit year after year . . . and then, retiring, quietly (with a cigar in his mouth) make the promenade of the whole world . . . as phlegmatically as he ever walk'd the portico of a Missouri hotel after dinner. I say all this is what people like—and I am sure I like it. . . . A mere plain man—no art, no poetry—only practical sense, ability to do, or try his best to do, what devolv'd upon him. A common trader, money-maker, tanner, farmer of Illinois—general for the republic, in its terrific struggle with itself, in the war of attempted secession—President following, (a task of peace, more difficult than war itself)—nothing heroic, as the authorities put it—and yet the greatest hero.

Complete Prose Works (New York: D. Appleton, 1910), 146–47.

Grant with Cincinnati. *Library of Congress,*
Prints and Photographs Division, LC–DIG–stereo–1s02872.

The cottage where Grant finished his book,
Mount McGregor, New York. *Photograph by*
Elizabeth D. Samet.

Appendix 1: Notes to the First Edition

Chapter 24, note 1

Since writing this chapter I have received from Mrs. W. H. L. Wallace, widow of the gallant general who was killed in the first day's fight on the field of Shiloh, a letter from General Lew. Wallace to him dated the morning of the 5th. At the date of this letter it was well known that the Confederates had troops out along the Mobile & Ohio railroad west of Crump's landing and Pittsburg landing, and were also collecting near Shiloh. This letter shows that at that time General Lew. Wallace was making preparations for the emergency that might happen for the passing of reinforcements between Shiloh and his position, extending from Crump's landing westward, and he sends it over the road running from Adamsville to the Pittsburg landing and Purdy road. These two roads intersect nearly a mile west of the crossing of the latter over Owl Creek, where our right rested. In this letter General Lew. Wallace advises General W. H. L. Wallace that he will send "to-morrow" (and his letter also says "April 5th," which is the same day the letter was dated and which, therefore, must have been written on the 4th) some cavalry to report to him at his headquarters, and suggesting the propriety of General W. H. L. Wallace's sending a company back with them for the purpose of having the cavalry at the two landings familiarize themselves with the road so that they could "act promptly in case of emergency as guides to and from the different camps."

This modifies very materially what I have said, and what has been said by others, of the conduct of General Lew. Wallace at the battle of Shiloh. It shows that he naturally, with no more experience than he had at the time in the profession of arms, would take the particular road that he did start upon in the absence of orders to move by a different road.

The mistake he made, and which probably caused his apparent dilatoriness, was that of advancing some distance after he found that the firing, which would be at first directly to his front and then off to the left, had fallen back until it had got very much in rear of the position of his advance. This falling back had taken place before I sent General Wallace orders to move up to Pittsburg landing and, naturally, my order was to follow the road nearest the river. But my order was verbal, and to a staff officer who was to deliver it to General Wallace, so that I am not competent to say just what order the General actually received.

General Wallace's division was stationed, the First brigade at Crump's landing, the Second out two miles, and the Third two and a half miles out. Hearing the sounds of battle General Wallace early ordered his First and Third brigades to concentrate on the Second. If the position of our front had not changed, the road which Wallace took would have been somewhat shorter to our right than the River road.

U. S. GRANT.

MOUNT MACGREGOR, NEW YORK, *June* 21, 1885

Chapter 37, note 1

When General Sherman first learned of the move I proposed to make, he called to see me about it. I recollect that I had transferred my headquarters from a boat in the river to a house a short distance back from the levee. I was seated on the piazza engaged in conversation with my staff when Sherman came up. After a few moments' conversation he said that he would like to see me alone. We passed into the house together and shut the door after us. Sherman then expressed his alarm at the move I had ordered, saying that I was putting myself in a position voluntarily which an enemy would be glad to manœuvre a year—or a long time—to get me in. I was going into the enemy's country, with a large river behind me and the enemy holding points strongly fortified above and below. He said that it was an axiom in war that when any great body of troops moved against an enemy they should do so from a base of supplies, which they would guard as they would the apple of the eye, etc. He pointed out all the difficulties that might be encountered in the campaign proposed, and stated in turn what would be the true campaign to make. This was, in substance, to go back until high ground could be reached on the east bank of the river; fortify there and establish a depot of supplies, and move from there, being always prepared to fall back upon it in case of disaster. I said this would take us back to Memphis. Sherman then said that was the very place he would go to, and would move by railroad from Memphis to Grenada, repairing the road as we advanced. To this I replied, the country is already disheartened over the lack of success on the part of our armies; the last election went against the vigorous prosecution of the war, voluntary enlistments had ceased throughout most of the North and conscription was already resorted to, and if we went back so far as Memphis it would discourage the people so much that bases of supplies would be of no use: neither men to hold them nor supplies to put in them would be furnished. The problem for us was to move forward to a decisive victory, or our cause was lost. No progress was being made in any other field, and we had to go on.

Sherman wrote to my adjutant general, Colonel J. A. Rawlins, embodying his views of the campaign that should be made, and asking him to advise me to at least get the views of my generals upon the subject. Colonel Rawlins showed me the letter, but I did not see any reason for changing my plans. The letter was not answered and the subject was not subsequently mentioned between Sherman and myself to the end of the war, that I remember of. I did not regard the letter as official, and consequently did not preserve it. General Sherman furnished a copy himself to General Badeau, who printed it in his history of my campaigns. I did not regard either the conversation between us or the letter to my adjutant-general as protests, but simply friendly advice which the relations between us fully justified. Sherman gave the same energy to make the campaign a success that he would or could have done if it had been ordered by himself. I make this statement here to correct an impression which was circulated at the close of the war to Sherman's prejudice, and for which there was no fair foundation.

Chapter 42, note 1

CHATTANOOGA,
November 18, 1863.

MAJOR-GENERAL W. T. SHERMAN:

Enclosed herewith I send you copy of instructions to Major-General Thomas. You having been over the ground in person, and having heard the whole matter discussed, further instructions will not be necessary for you. It is particularly desirable that a force should be got through to the railroad between Cleveland and Dalton, and Longstreet thus cut off from communication with the South; but being confronted by a large force here, strongly located, it is not easy to tell how this is to be effected until the result of our first effort is known.

I will add, however, what is not shown in my instructions to Thomas, that a brigade of cavalry has been ordered here which, if it arrives in time, will be thrown across the Tennessee above Chickamauga, and may be able to make the trip to Cleveland or thereabouts.

U. S. GRANT,
Maj.-Gen'l.

CHATTANOOGA,
November 18, 1863.

MAJOR-GENERAL GEO. H. THOMAS,
Chattanooga:

All preparations should be made for attacking the enemy's position on Missionary Ridge by Saturday at daylight. Not being provided with a map giving names of roads, spurs of the mountains, and other places, such definite instructions cannot be given as might be desirable. However, the general plan, you understand, is for Sherman, with the force brought with him strengthened by a division from your command, to effect a crossing of the Tennessee River just below the mouth of Chickamauga; his crossing to be protected by artillery from the heights on the north bank of the river (to be located by your chief of artillery), and to secure the heights on the northern extremity to about the railroad tunnel before the enemy can concentrate against him. You will co-operate with Sherman. The troops in Chattanooga Valley should be well concentrated on your left flank, leaving only the necessary force to defend fortifications on the right and centre, and a movable column of one division in readiness to move wherever ordered. This division should show itself as threateningly as possible on the most practicable line for making an attack up the valley. Your effort then will be to form a junction with Sherman, making your advance well towards the northern end of Missionary Ridge, and moving as near simultaneously with him as possible. The junction once formed and the ridge carried, communications will be at once established between the two armies by roads on the south bank of the river. Further movements will then depend on those of the enemy. Lookout Valley, I think, will be easily held by Geary's division and what troops you may still have there belonging to the old Army of the Cumberland. Howard's corps can then be held in readiness to act either with you at Chattanooga or with Sherman. It should be marched on Friday night to a position on the north side of the river, not lower down than the first pontoon-bridge, and there held in readiness for such orders as may become necessary. All these troops will be provided with two days' cooked rations in haversacks, and one hundred rounds of ammunition on the person of each infantry soldier. Special care should be taken by all officers to see that ammunition is not wasted or unnecessarily fired away. You will call on the engineer department for such preparations as you may deem necessary for carrying your infantry and artillery over the creek.

U. S. GRANT,
Major-General.

Chapter 44, note 1

CHATTANOOGA,
November 24, 1863.

MAJOR-GENERAL. GEO. H. THOMAS,
Chattanooga:

General Sherman carried Missionary Ridge as far as the tunnel with only slight skirmishing. His right now rests at the tunnel and on top of the hill, his left at Chickamauga Creek. I have instructed General Sherman to advance as soon as it is light in the morning, and your attack, which will be simultaneous, will be in co-operation. Your command will either carry the rifle-pits and ridge directly in front of them, or move to the left, as the presence of the enemy may require. If Hooker's position on the mountain [cannot be maintained] with a small force, and it is found impracticable to carry the top from where he is, it would be advisable for him to move up the valley with all the force he can spare, and ascend by the first practicable road.

U. S. GRANT,
Major-General.

Chapter 45, note 1

WASHINGTON, D. C.,
December 8, 1863, 10.2 A.M.

MAJ.-GENERAL U. S. GRANT:

Understanding that your lodgment at Knoxville and at Chattanooga is now secure, I wish to tender you, and all under your command, my more than thanks, my profoundest gratitude for the skill, courage, and perseverance with which you and they, over so great difficulties, have effected that important object. God bless you all.

A. LINCOLN,
President U. S.

Chapter 46, note 1

WASHINGTON, D. C.,
December 29, 1863.

MAJ.-GENERAL U. S. GRANT:

General Foster has asked to be relieved from his command on account of disability from old wounds. Should his request be granted, who would you like as his successor? It is possible that Schofield will be sent to your command.

H. W. HALLECK,
General-in-Chief.

(*Official.*)

[*Private and Confidential.*]

HEADQUARTERS ARMIES OF THE UNITED STATES,

WASHINGTON, D. C., *April* 4, 1864.

MAJOR-GENERAL W. T. SHERMAN,

Commanding Military Division of the Mississippi.

General:—It is my design, if the enemy keep quiet and allow me to take the initiative in the spring campaign, to work all parts of the army together, and somewhat towards a common centre. For your information I now write you my programme, as at present determined upon.

I have sent orders to Banks, by private messenger, to finish up his present expedition against Shreveport with all dispatch; to turn over the defence of Red River to General Steele and the navy, and to return your troops to you and his own to New Orleans; to abandon all of Texas, except the Rio Grande, and to hold that with not to exceed four thousand men; to reduce the number of troops on the Mississippi to the lowest number necessary to hold it, and to collect from his command not less than twenty-five thousand men. To this I will add five thousand men from Missouri. With this force he is to commence operations against Mobile as soon as he can. It will be impossible for him to commence too early.

Gillmore joins Butler with ten thousand men, and the two operate against Richmond from the south side of the James River. This will give Butler thirty-three thousand men to operate with, W. F. Smith commanding the right wing of his forces and Gillmore the left wing. I will stay with the Army of the Potomac, increased by Burnside's corps of not less than twenty-five thousand effective men, and operate directly against Lee's army, wherever it may be found.

Sigel collects all his available force in two columns, one, under Ord and Averell, to start from Beverly, Virginia, and the other, under Crook, to start from Charleston on the Kanawha, to move against the Virginia and Tennessee Railroad.

Crook will have all cavalry, and will endeavor to get in about Saltville, and move east from there to join Ord. His force will be all cavalry, while Ord will have from ten to twelve thousand men of all arms.

You I propose to move against Johnston's army, to break it up and to get into the interior of the enemy's country as far as you can, inflicting all the damage you can against their war resources.

I do not propose to lay down for you a plan of campaign, but simply lay down the work it is desirable to have done and leave you free to execute it in your own way. Submit to me, however, as early as you can, your plan of operations.

As stated, Banks is ordered to commence operations as soon as he can.

Gillmore is ordered to report at Fortress Monroe by the 18th inst., or as soon thereafter as practicable. Sigel is concentrating now. None will move from their places of rendezvous until I direct, except Banks. I want to be ready to move by the 25th inst., if possible. But all I can now direct is that you get ready as soon as possible. I know you will have difficulties to encounter in getting through the mountains to where supplies are abundant, but I believe you will accomplish it.

From the expedition from the Department of West Virginia I do not calculate on very great results; but it is the only way I can take troops from there. With the long line of railroad Sigel has to protect, he can spare no troops except to move directly to his front. In this way he must get through to inflict great damage on the enemy, or the enemy must detach from one of his armies a large force to prevent it. In other words, if Sigel can't skin himself he can hold a leg while some one else skins.

I am, general, very respectfully, your obedient servant,

U. S. GRANT,
Lieutenant-General.

Chapter 47, note 2

IN FIELD, CULPEPER C. H., VA.,
April 9, 1864.

MAJ.-GENERAL GEO. G. MEADE,
Com'd'g Army of the Potomac.

For information and as instruction to govern your preparations for the coming campaign, the following is communicated confidentially for your own perusal alone.

So far as practicable all the armies are to move together, and towards one common centre. Banks has been instructed to turn over the guarding of the Red River to General Steele and the navy, to abandon Texas with the exception of the Rio Grande, and to concentrate all the force he can, not less than 25,000 men, to move on Mobile. This he is to do without reference to other movements. From the scattered condition of his command, however, he cannot possibly get it together to leave New Orleans before the 1st of May, if so soon. Sherman will move at the same time you do, or two or three days in advance, Jo. Johnston's army being his objective point, and the heart of Georgia his ultimate aim. If successful he will secure the line from Chattanooga to Mobile with the aid of Banks.

Sigel cannot spare troops from his army to reinforce either of the great armies, but he can aid them by moving directly to his front. This he has been directed to do, and is now making preparations for it. Two columns of his command will make south at the same time with the general move; one from Beverly, from ten to twelve thousand strong, under Major-General Ord; the other from Charleston, Va., principally cavalry, under Brig.-General Crook. The former of these will endeavor to reach the Tennessee and Virginia Railroad, about south of Covington, and if found practicable will work eastward to Lynchburg and return to its base by way of the Shenandoah Valley, or join you. The other will strike at Saltville, Va., and come eastward to join Ord. The cavalry from Ord's command will try to force a passage southward, if they are successful in reaching the Virginia and Tennessee Railroad, to cut the main lines of the road connecting Richmond with all the South and South-west.

Gillmore will join Butler with about 10,000 men from South Carolina. Butler can reduce his garrison so as to take 23,000 men into the field directly to his front. The force will be commanded by Maj.-General W. F. Smith. With Smith and Gillmore, Butler will seize City Point, and operate against Richmond from the south side of the river. His movement will be simultaneous with yours.

Lee's army will be your objective point. Wherever Lee goes, there you will go also. The only point upon which I am now in doubt is, whether it will be better to cross the Rapidan above or below him. Each plan presents great advantages over the other with corresponding objections. By crossing above, Lee is cut off from all chance of ignoring Richmond and going north on a raid. But if we take this route, all we do must be done whilst the rations we start with hold out. We separate from Butler so that he cannot be directed how to co-operate. By the other route Brandy Station can be used as a base of supplies until another is secured on the York or James rivers.

These advantages and objections I will talk over with you more fully than I can write them.

Burnside with a force of probably 25,000 men will reinforce you. Immediately upon his arrival, which will be shortly after the 20th inst., I will give him the defence of the road from Bull Run as far south as we wish to hold it. This will enable you to collect all your strength about Brandy Station and to the front.

There will be naval co-operation on the James River, and transports and ferries will be provided so that should Lee fall back into his intrenchments at Richmond, Butler's force and yours will be a unit, or at least can be made to act as such. What I would direct then, is that you commence at once reducing baggage to the very lowest possible standard. Two wagons to a regiment of five hundred men is the greatest number that should be allowed, for all baggage, exclusive of subsistence stores and ordnance stores. One wagon to brigade and one to division headquarters is sufficient and about two to corps headquarters.

Should by Lee's right flank be our route, you will want to make arrangements for having supplies of all sorts promptly forwarded to White House on the Pamunkey. Your estimates for this contingency should be made at once. If not wanted there, there is every probability they will be wanted on the James River or elsewhere.

If Lee's left is turned, large provision will have to be made for ordnance stores. I would say not much short of five hundred rounds of infantry ammunition would do. By the other, half the amount would be sufficient.

U. S. GRANT,
Lieutenant-General.

Chapter 50, note 1

UNION ARMY ON THE RAPIDAN, MAY 5, 1864.
[COMPILED.]

LIEUTENANT-GENERAL U. S. GRANT, Commander-in-Chief.
MAJOR-GENERAL GEORGE G. MEADE, Commanding Army of the Potomac.

MAJ.-GEN. W. S. HANCOCK, commanding Second Army Corps.

First Division, Brig.-Gen. Francis C. Barlow.
    First Brigade, Col. Nelson A. Miles.
    Second Brigade, Col. Thomas A. Smyth.
    Third Brigade, Col. Paul Frank.
    Fourth Brigade, Col. John R. Brooke.

Second Division, Brig.-Gen. John Gibbon.
    First Brigade, Brig.-Gen. Alex. S. Webb.
    Second Brigade, Brig.-Gen. Joshua T. Owen.
    Third Brigade, Col. Samuel S. Carroll.

Third Division, Maj.-Gen. David B. Birney.
    First Brigade, Brig.-Gen. J. H. H. Ward.
    Second Brigade, Brig.-Gen. Alexander Hays.

Fourth Division, Brig.-Gen. Gershom Mott.
    First Brigade, Col. Robert McAllister.
    Second Brigade, Col. Wm. R. Brewster.

    Artillery Brigade, Col. John C. Tidball.

MAJ.-GEN. G. K. WARREN, commanding Fifth Army Corps.

First Division, Brig.-Gen. Charles Griffin.
    First Brigade, Brig.-Gen. Romeyn B. Ayres.

Second Brigade, Col. Jacob B. Sweitzer.
Third Brigade, Brig.-Gen. J. J. Bartlett.

Second Division, Brig.-Gen. John C. Robinson.
First Brigade, Col. Samuel H. Leonard.
Second Brigade, Brig.-Gen. Henry Baxter.
Third Brigade, Col. Andrew W. Denison.

Third Division, Brig.-Gen. Samuel W. Crawford.
First Brigade, Col. Wm. McCandless.
Third Brigade, Col. Joseph W. Fisher.

Fourth Division, Brig.-Gen. James S. Wadsworth.
First Brigade, Brig.-Gen. Lysander Cutler.
Second Brigade, Brig.-Gen. James C. Rice.
Third Brigade, Col. Roy Stone.

Artillery Brigade, Col. S. S. Wainwright.

MAJ.-GEN. JOHN SEDGWICK, commanding Sixth Army Corps.

First Division, Brig.-Gen. H. G. Wright.
First Brigade, Col. Henry W. Brown.
Second Brigade, Col. Emory Upton.
Third Brigade, Brig.-Gen. D. A. Russell.
Fourth Brigade, Brig.-Gen. Alexander Shaler.

Second Division, Brig.-Gen. George W. Getty.
First Brigade, Brig.-Gen. Frank Wheaton.
Second Brigade, Col. Lewis A. Grant.
Third Brigade, Brig.-Gen. Thos. H. Neill.
Fourth Brigade, Brig.-Gen. Henry L. Eustis.

Third Division, Brig.-Gen. James Ricketts.
First Brigade, Brig.-Gen. Wm. H. Morris.
Second Brigade, Brig.-Gen. T. Seymour.

Artillery Brigade, Col. C. H. Tompkins.

MAJ.-GEN. P. H. SHERIDAN, commanding Cavalry Corps.

First Division, Brig.-Gen. A. T. A. Torbert.
First Brigade, Brig.-Gen. G. A. Custer.
Second Brigade, Col. Thos. C. Devin.
Reserve Brigade, Brig.-Gen. Wesley Merritt.

Second Division, Brig.-Gen. D. McM. Gregg.
  First Brigade, Brig.-Gen. Henry E. Davies, Jr.
  Second Brigade, Col. J. Irvin Gregg.

Third Division, Brig.-Gen. J. H. Wilson.
  First Brigade, Col. T. M. Bryan, Jr.
  Second Brigade, Col. Geo. H. Chapman.

MAJ.-GEN. A. E. BURNSIDE, commanding Ninth Army Corps.

First Division, Brig.-Gen. T. G. Stevenson.
  First Brigade, Col. Sumner Carruth.
  Second Brigade, Col. Daniel Leasure.

Second Division, Brig.-Gen. Robert B. Potter.
  First Brigade, Col. Zenas R. Bliss.
  Second Brigade, Col. Simon G. Griffin.

Third Division, Brig.-Gen. Orlando B. Willcox.
  First Brigade, Col. John F. Hartranft.
  Second Brigade, Col. Benj. C. Christ.

Fourth Division, Brig.-Gen. Edward Ferrero.
  First Brigade, Col. Joshua K. Sigfried.
  Second Brigade, Col. Henry G. Thomas.

  Provisional Brigade, Col. Elisha G. Marshall.

BRIG.-GEN. HENRY J. HUNT, commanding Artillery.

Reserve, Col. H. S. Burton.
  First Brigade, Col. J. H. Kitching.
  Second Brigade, Maj. J. A. Tompkins.
  First Brig. Horse Art., Capt. J. M. Robertson.
  Second Brigade, Horse Art., Capt. D. R. Ransom.
  Third Brigade, Maj. R. H. Fitzhugh.

GENERAL HEADQUARTERS.

  Provost Guard, Brig.-Gen. M. R. Patrick.
  Volunteer Engineers, Brig.-Gen. H. W. Benham.

CONFEDERATE ARMY.

Organization of the Army of Northern Virginia, Commanded by GENERAL ROBERT E. LEE, August 31st, 1864.

First Army Corps: LIEUT.-GEN. R. H. ANDERSON, Commanding.

MAJ.-GEN. GEO. E. PICKETT'S DIVISION.

Brig.-Gen. Seth M. Barton's Brigade. (*a*)
    "   M. D. Corse's   "
    "   Eppa Hunton's   "
    "   Wm. R. Terry's   "

MAJ.-GEN. C. W. FIELD'S DIVISION. (*b*)

Brig.-Gen. G. T. Anderson's Brigade
    "   E. M. Law's (*c*)   "
    "   John Bratton's   "

MAJ.-GEN. J. B. KERSHAW'S DIVISION. (*d*)

Brig.-Gen. W. T. Wofford's Brigade
    "   B. G. Humphreys' "
    "   Goode Bryan's   "
    "   Kershaw's (Old) "

Second Army Corps: MAJOR-GENERAL JUBAL A. EARLY, Commanding

MAJ.-GEN. JOHN B. GORDON'S DIVISION.

Brig.-Gen. H. T. Hays' Brigade. (*e*)
    "   John Pegram's " (*f*)
    "   Gordon's   " (*g*)
Brig.-Gen. R. F. Hoke's "

MAJ.-GEN. EDWARD JOHNSON'S DIVISION.

Stonewall Brig. (Brig.-Gen. J. A. Walker). (*h*)
Brig.-Gen. J. M. Jones' Brigade. (*h*)
    "   Geo. H. Stewart's " (*h*)
    "   L. A. Stafford's   " (*e*)

MAJ.-GEN. R. E. RODES' DIVISION.

Brig.-Gen. J. Daniel's Brigade. (*i*)
"   Geo. Dole's   " (*k*)
"   S. D. Ramseur's Brigade.
"   C. A. Battle's   "
"   R. D. Johnston's   " (*f*)

Third Army Corps: LIEUT.-GEN. A. P. HILL, Commanding.

MAJ.-GEN. WM. MAHONE'S DIVISION. (l)

Brig.-Gen. J. C. C. Sanders' Brigade.
"   Mahone's   "
Brig.-Gen. N. H. Harris's   " (*m*)
"   A. R. Wright's   "
"   Joseph Finegan's   "

MAJ.-GEN. C. M. WILCOX'S DIVISION.

Brig.-Gen. E. L. Thomas's Brigade (*n*)
"   James H. Lane's   "
"   Sam'l McGowan's   "
"   Alfred M. Scale's   "

MAJ.-GEN. H. HETH'S DIVISION. (o)

Brig.-Gen. J. R. Davis's Brigade.
"   John R. Cooke's   "
"   D. McRae's   "
"   J. J. Archer's   "
"   H. H. Walker's   "

Unattached: 5th Alabama Battalion.

Cavalry Corps: LIEUTENANT-GENERAL WADE HAMPTON, Commanding. (*p*)

MAJ.-GEN. FITZHUGH LEE'S DIVISION

Brig.-Gen. W. C. Wickham's Brigade
"   L. L. Lomax's   "

MAJ.-GEN. M. C. BUTLER'S DIVISION.

Brig.-Gen. John Dunovant's Brigade.
"   P. M. B. Young's   "
"   Thomas L. Rosser's "

MAJ.-GEN. W. H. F. LEE'S DIVISION.

Brig.-Gen. Rufus Barringer's Brigade.
"   J. R. Chambliss's   "

Artillery Reserve: BRIG.-GEN. W. N. PENDLETON, Commanding.

BRIG.-GEN. E. P. ALEXANDER'S DIVISION.★

Cabell's Battalion.
    Manly's Battery.
    1st Co. Richmond Howitzers.
    Carleton's Battery.
    Calloway's Battery.

Haskell's Battalion.
    Branch's Battery.
    Nelson's   "
    Garden's   "
    Rowan   "

Huger's Battalion.
    Smith's Battery.
    Moody   "
    Woolfolk   "
    Parker's   "
    Taylor's   "
    Fickling's   "
    Martin's   "

Gibb's Battalion.
    Davidson's Battery.
    Dickenson's   "
    Otey's   "

BRIG.-GEN. A. L. LONG'S DIVISION.

Braxton's Battalion.
    Lee Battery.
    1st Md. Artillery.
    Stafford   "
    Alleghany   "

Cutshaw's Battalion.
    Charlotteville Artillery.
    Staunton   "
    Courtney   "

Carter's Battalion.
    Morris Artillery.
    Orange   "
    King William Artillery.
    Jeff Davis   "

Nelson's Battalion.
    Amherst Artillery.
    Milledge   "
    Fluvauna   "

Brown's Battalion.
    Powhatan Artillery.
    2d Richmond Howitzers.
    3d   "   "
    Rockbridge Artillery.
    Salem Flying Artillery.

COL R. L. WALKER'S DIVISION.

Cutt's Battalion.
    Ross's Battery.
    Patterson's Battery.
    Irwin Artillery.

Richardson's Battalion.
    Lewis Artillery.
    Donaldsonville Artillery.
    Norfolk Light   "
    Huger   "

McIntosh's Battalion.
    Johnson's Battery.
    Hardaway Artillery.
    Danville   "
    2d Rockbridge Artillery.

Pegram's Battalion.
    Peedee Artillery.
    Fredericksburg Artillery.
    Letcher   "
    Purcell Battery.
    Crenshaw's Battery.

Poague's Battalion.
    Madison Artillery.
    Albemarle   "
    Brooke   "
    Charlotte   "

NOTE.

(a) COL. W. R. Aylett was in command Aug. 29th, and probably at above date.

(b) Inspection report of this division shows that it also contained Benning's and Gregg's Brigades.

(c) Commanded by Colonel P. D. Bowles.

(d) Only two brigadier-generals reported for duty; names not indicated.

Notes e-k constitute Organization of the Army of the Valley District.

(e) Constituting York's Brigade.

(f) In Ramseur's Division.

(g) Evan's Brigade, Colonel E. N. Atkinson commanding, and containing 12th Georgia Battalion.

(h) The Virginia regiments constituted Terry's Brigade, Gordon's Division.

(i) Grimes' Brigade.

(k) Cook's   "

(l) Returns report but one general officer present for duty; name not indicated.

(m) Colonel Joseph M. Jayne, commanding.

(n) Colonel Thomas J. Simmons, commanding.

(o) Four brigadier-generals reported present for duty; names not indicated.

(p) On face of returns appears to have consisted of Hampton's, Fitz-Lee's, and W. H. F. Lee's Division, and Dearing's Brigade.

★ But one general officer reported present for duty in the artillery, and Alexander's name not on the original.

Chapter 53, note 1

HEADQUARTERS ARMIES U. S.,
May 11, 1864.—3 P.M.

MAJOR-GENERAL MEADE,
Commanding Army of the Potomac.

Move three divisions of the 2d corps by the rear of the 5th and 6th corps, under cover of night, so as to join the 9th corps in a vigorous assault on the enemy at four o'clock A.M. to-morrow. I will send one or two staff officers over to-night to stay with Burnside, and impress him with the importance of a prompt and vigorous attack. Warren and Wright should hold their corps as close to the enemy as possible, to take advantage of any diversion caused by this attack, and to push in if any opportunity presents itself. There is but little doubt in my mind that the assault last evening would have proved entirely successful if it had commenced one hour earlier and had been heartily entered into by Mott's division and the 9th corps.

U. S. GRANT,
Lieut.-General.

Chapter 53, note 2

HEADQUARTERS, ARMIES U. S.,
May 11, 1864.—4 P.M.

MAJOR-GENERAL A. E. BURNSIDE,
Commanding 9th Army Corps.

Major-General Hancock has been ordered to move his corps under cover of night to join you in a vigorous attack against the enemy at 4 o'clock A.M. to-morrow. You will move against the enemy with your entire force promptly and with all possible vigor at precisely 4 o'clock A.M. to-morrow the 12th inst. Let your preparations for this attack be conducted with the utmost secrecy and veiled entirely from the enemy.

I send two of my staff officers, Colonels Comstock and Babcock, in whom I have great confidence and who are acquainted with the direction the attack is to be made from here, to remain with you and General Hancock with instructions to render you every assistance in their power. Generals Warren and Wright will hold their corps as close to the enemy as possible, to take advantage of any diversion caused by yours and Hancock's attack, and will push in their whole force if any opportunity presents itself.

U. S. GRANT,
Lieut.-General.

Chapter 53, note 3

HEADQUARTERS ARMIES U. S.,
May 12, 1864, 6.30 P.M.

MAJOR-GENERAL HALLECK,
Washington, D. C.

The eighth day of the battle closes, leaving between three and four thousand prisoners in our hands for the day's work, including two general officers, and over thirty pieces of artillery. The enemy are obstinate, and seem to have found the last ditch. We have lost no organizations, not even that of a company, whilst we have destroyed and captured one division (Johnson's), one brigade (Doles'), and one regiment entire from the enemy.

U. S. GRANT,
Lieut.-General.

Chapter 53, note 4

SPOTTSYLVANIA C. H.,
May 13, 1864.

HON. E. M. STANTON, SECRETARY OF WAR,
Washington, D. C.

I beg leave to recommend the following promotions be made for gallant and distinguished services in the last eight days' battles, to wit: Brigadier-General H. G. Wright and Brigadier-General John Gibbon to be Major-Generals; Colonel S. S. Carroll, 8th Ohio Volunteers; Colonel E. Upton, 121st New York Volunteers; Colonel William McCandless, 2d Pennsylvania Reserves, to be Brigadier-Generals. I would also recommend Major-General W. S. Hancock for Brigadier-General in the regular army. His services and qualifications are eminently deserving of this recognition. In making these recommendations I do not wish the claims of General G. M. Dodge for promotion forgotten, but recommend his name to be sent in at the same time. I would also ask to have General Wright assigned to the command of the Sixth Army Corps. I would further ask the confirmation of General Humphreys to the rank of Major-General.

General Meade has more than met my most sanguine expectations. He and Sherman are the fittest officers for large commands I have come in contact with. If their services can be rewarded by promotion to the rank of Major-Generals in the regular army the honor would be worthily bestowed, and I would feel personally gratified. I would not like to see one of these promotions at this time without seeing both.

U. S. GRANT,
Lieut.-General.

Chapter 54, note 1

QUARLES' MILLS, VA.,
May 26, 1864.

MAJOR-GENERAL HALLECK,
Washington, D. C.

The relative position of the two armies is now as follows: Lee's right rests on
a swamp east of the Richmond and Fredericksburg road and south of the North
Anna, his centre on the river at Ox Ford, and his left at Little River with the
crossings of Little River guarded as far up as we have gone. Hancock with his
corps and one division of the 9th corps crossed at Chesterfield Ford and covers
the right wing of Lee's army. One division of the 9th corps is on the north bank
of the Anna at Ox Ford, with bridges above and below at points nearest to it
where both banks are held by us, so that it could reinforce either wing of our
army with equal facility. The 5th and 6th corps with one division of the 9th
corps run from the south bank of the Anna from a short distance above Ox Ford
to Little River, and parallel with and near to the enemy.

To make a direct attack from either wing would cause a slaughter of our men
that even success would not justify. To turn the enemy by his right, between the
two Annas, is impossible on account of the swamp upon which his right rests.
To turn him by the left leaves Little River, New Found River and South Anna
River, all of them streams presenting considerable obstacles to the movement of
our army, to be crossed. I have determined therefore to turn the enemy's right
by crossing at or near Hanover Town. This crosses all three streams at once, and
leaves us still where we can draw supplies.

During the last night the teams and artillery not in position, belonging to the
right wing of our army, and one division of that wing were quietly withdrawn
to the north bank of the river and moved down to the rear of the left. As soon as
it is dark this division with most of the cavalry will commence a forced march
for Hanover Town to seize and hold the crossings. The balance of the right wing
will withdraw at the same hour, and follow as rapidly as possible. The left wing
will also withdraw from the south bank of the river to-night and follow in rear
of the right wing.

Lee's army is really whipped. The prisoners we now take show it, and
the action of his army shows it unmistakably. A battle with them outside of
intrenchments cannot be had. Our men feel that they have gained the *morale*
over the enemy, and attack him with confidence. I may be mistaken, but I
feel that our success over Lee's army is already assured. The promptness and
rapidity with which you have forwarded reinforcements has contributed largely
to the feeling of confidence inspired in our men, and to break down that of the
enemy.

We are destroying all the rails we can on the Central and Fredericksburg roads. I want to leave a gap on the roads north of Richmond so big that to get a single track they will have to import rail from elsewhere.

Even if a crossing is not effected at Hanover Town it will probably be necessary for us to move on down the Pamunkey until a crossing is effected. I think it advisable therefore to change our base of supplies from Port Royal to the White House. I wish you would direct this change at once, and also direct Smith to put the railroad bridge there in condition for crossing troops and artillery and leave men to hold it.

U. S. GRANT,
Lieut.-General.

Chapter 55, note 1

NEAR COLD HARBOR,
June 3, 1864, 7 A.M.

MAJOR-GENERAL MEADE,
Commanding A. P.

The moment it becomes certain that an assault cannot succeed, suspend the offensive; but when one does succeed, push it vigorously and if necessary pile in troops at the successful point from wherever they can be taken. I shall go to where you are in the course of an hour.

U. S. GRANT,
Lieut.-General.

Chapter 56, note 1

COLD HARBOR,
June 5, 1864.

MAJOR-GENERAL HALLECK, Chief of Staff of the Army,
Washington, D. C.

A full survey of all the ground satisfies me that it would be impracticable to hold a line north-east of Richmond that would protect the Fredericksburg Railroad to enable us to use that road for supplying the army. To do so would give us a long vulnerable line of road to protect, exhausting much of our strength to guard it, and would leave open to the enemy all of his lines of communication on the south side of the James. My idea from the start has been to beat Lee's army if possible north of Richmond; then after destroying his lines of communication on the north side of the James River to transfer the army to the south side and besiege Lee in Richmond, or follow him south if he should retreat.

I now find, after over thirty days of trial, the enemy deems it of the first importance to run no risks with the armies they now have. They act purely on the defensive behind breastworks, or feebly on the offensive immediately in front of them, and where in case of repulse they can instantly retire behind them. Without a greater sacrifice of human life than I am willing to make all cannot be accomplished that I had designed outside of the city. I have therefore resolved upon the following plan:

I will continue to hold substantially the ground now occupied by the Army of the Potomac, taking advantage of any favorable circumstance that may present itself until the cavalry can be sent west to destroy the Virginia Central Railroad from about Beaver Dam for some twenty-five or thirty miles west. When this is effected I will move the army to the south side of the James River, either by crossing the Chickahominy and marching near to City Point, or by going to the mouth of the Chickahominy on north side and crossing there. To provide for this last and most possible contingency, several ferry-boats of the largest class ought to be immediately provided.

Once on the south side of the James River, I can cut off all sources of supply to the enemy except what is furnished by the canal. If Hunter succeeds in reaching Lynchburg, that will be lost to him also. Should Hunter not succeed, I will still make the effort to destroy the canal by sending cavalry up the south side of the river with a pontoon train to cross wherever they can.

The feeling of the two armies now seems to be that the rebels can protect themselves only by strong intrenchments, whilst our army is not only confident of protecting itself without intrenchments, but that it can beat and drive the enemy wherever and whenever he can be found without this protection.

U. S. GRANT,
Lieutenant-General.

Chapter 56, note 2

COLD HARBOR, VA.,
June 6, 1864.

MAJOR-GENERAL D. HUNTER
Commanding Dept. W. Va.

General Sheridan leaves here to-morrow morning, with instructions to proceed to Charlottesville, Va., and to commence there the destruction of the Va. Cen. R. R., destroying this way as much as possible. The complete destruction of this road and of the canal on James River is of great importance to us. According to the instructions I sent to General Halleck for your guidance, you were to proceed to Lynchburg and commence there. It would be of great value to us to get possession of Lynchburg for a single day. But that point is of so much importance to the enemy, that in attempting to get it such resistance may be met as to defeat your getting onto the road or canal at all. I see, in looking over the letter to General Halleck on the subject of your instructions, that it rather indicates that your route should be from Staunton via Charlottesville. If you have so understood it, you will be doing just what I want. The direction I would now give is, that if this letter reaches you in the valley between Staunton and Lynchburg, you immediately turn east by the most practicable road. From thence move eastward along the line of the road, destroying it completely and thoroughly, until you join General Sheridan. After the work laid out for General Sheridan and yourself is thoroughly done, proceed to join the Army of the Potomac by the route laid out in General Sheridan's instructions.

If any portion of your force, especially your cavalry, is needed back in your Department, you are authorized to send it back.

If on receipt of this you should be near to Lynchburg and deem it practicable to reach that point, you will exercise your judgment about going there.

If you should be on the railroad between Charlottesville and Lynchburg, it may be practicable to detach a cavalry force to destroy the canal. Lose no opportunity to destroy the canal.

U. S. GRANT,
Lieut.-General.

Chapter 56, note 3

FROM A STATEMENT OF LOSSES COMPILED IN THE ADJUTANT GENERAL'S OFFICE.

FIELD OF ACTION AND DATE.	KILLED.	WOUNDED.	MISSING.	AGGREGATE.
Wilderness, May 5th to 7th	2,261	8,785	2,902	13,948
Spottsylvania, May 8th to 21st	2,271	9,360	1,970	13,601
North Anna, May 23d to 27th	186	792	165	1,143
Totopotomoy, May 27th to 31st	99	358	52	509
Cold Harbor, May 31st to June 12th	1,769	6,752	1,537	10,058
Total	6,586	26,047	6,626	39,259

Chapter 56, note 4

CITY POINT, VA.,
June 17, 1864. 11 A.M.

MAJOR-GEN. HALLECK,
Washington, D. C.

    ★ ★ ★ ★ ★ ★ ★

The enemy in their endeavor to reinforce Petersburg abandoned their
intrenchments in front of Bermuda Hundred. They no doubt expected troops
from north of the James River to take their place before we discovered it.
General Butler took advantage of this and moved a force at once upon the
railroad and plank road between Richmond and Petersburg, which I hope to
retain possession of. Too much credit cannot be given to the troops and their
commanders for the energy and fortitude displayed during the last five days. Day
and night has been all the same, no delays being allowed on any account.

U. S. GRANT,
Lieut.-General.

Chapter 57, note 1

CITY POINT, VA.,
July 24, 1864.

MAJOR-GENERAL MEADE,
Commanding, etc.

The engineer officers who made a survey of the front from Bermuda Hundred
report against the probability of success from an attack there. The chances they
think will be better on Burnside's front. If this is attempted it will be necessary
to concentrate all the force possible at the point in the enemy's line we expect
to penetrate. All officers should be fully impressed with the absolute necessity
of pushing entirely beyond the enemy's present line, if they should succeed in
penetrating it, and of getting back to their present line promptly if they should
not succeed in breaking through.

To the right and left of the point of assault all the artillery possible should be
brought to play upon the enemy in front during the assault. Their lines would
be sufficient for the support of the artillery, and all the reserves could be brought
on the flanks of their commands nearest to the point of assault, ready to follow
in if successful. The field artillery and infantry held in the lines during the first
assault should be in readiness to move at a moment's notice either to their front
or to follow the main assault, as they should receive orders. One thing, however,

should be impressed on corps commanders. If they see the enemy giving away on their front or moving from it to reinforce a heavily assaulted portion of their line, they should take advantage of such knowledge and act promptly without waiting for orders from army commanders. General Ord can co-operate with his corps in this movement, and about five thousand troops from Bermuda Hundred can be sent to reinforce you or can be used to threaten an assault between the Appomattox and James rivers, as may be deemed best.

This should be done by Tuesday morning, if done at all. If not attempted, we will then start at the date indicated to destroy the railroad as far as Hicksford at least, and to Weldon if possible.

★   ★   ★   ★   ★   ★   ★

Whether we send an expedition on the road or assault at Petersburg, Burnside's mine will be blown up. . . .

U. S. GRANT,
Lieutenant-General.

Chapter 60, note 1

CITY POINT, VA.,
December 2, 1864.

MAJOR-GENERAL THOMAS,
Nashville, Tenn.

If Hood is permitted to remain quietly about Nashville, you will lose all the road back to Chattanooga and possibly have to abandon the line of the Tennessee. Should he attack you it is all well, but if he does not you should attack him before he fortifies. Arm and put in the trenches your quartermaster employees, citizens, etc.

U. S. GRANT,
Lieutenant-General.

CITY POINT, VA.,
December 2, 1864.—1.30 P.M.

MAJOR-GENERAL THOMAS,
Nashville, Tenn.

With your citizen employees armed, you can move out of Nashville with all your army and force the enemy to retire or fight upon ground of your own choosing. After the repulse of Hood at Franklin, it looks to me that instead of falling back to Nashville we should have taken the offensive against the enemy where he was. At this distance, however, I may err as to the best method of dealing with the enemy. You will now suffer incalculable injury upon your railroads if Hood is not speedily disposed of. Put forth therefore every possible exertion to attain this end. Should you get him to retreating give him no peace.

U. S. GRANT,
Lieutenant-General.

CITY POINT, VA.,
December 5, 1864.

MAJOR-GENERAL THOMAS,
Nashville, Tenn.

Is there not danger of Forrest moving down the Cumberland to where he can cross it? It seems to me whilst you should be getting up your cavalry as rapidly as possible to look after Forrest, Hood should be attacked where he is. Time strengthens him in all possibility as much as it does you.

U. S. GRANT,
Lieutenant-General.

CITY POINT, VA.,
December 6, 1864—4 P.M.

MAJOR-GENERAL THOMAS,
Nashville, Tenn.

Attack Hood at once and wait no longer for a remnant of your cavalry. There is great danger of delay resulting in a campaign back to the Ohio River.

U. S. GRANT,
Lieutenant-General.

CITY POINT, VA.,
December 8, 1864.—8.30 P.M.

MAJOR-GENERAL THOMAS,
Nashville, Tenn.

Your dispatch of yesterday received. It looks to me evident the enemy are trying to cross the Cumberland River, and are scattered. Why not attack at once? By all means avoid the contingency of a foot race to see which, you or Hood, can beat to the Ohio. If you think necessary call on the governors of States to send a force into Louisville to meet the enemy if he should cross the river. You clearly never should cross except in rear of the enemy. Now is one of the finest opportunities ever presented of destroying one of the three armies of the enemy.

If destroyed he never can replace it. Use the means at your command, and you can do this and cause a rejoicing that will resound from one end of the land to the other.

U. S. GRANT,
Lieutenant-General.

CITY POINT, VA.,
December 11, 1864.—4 P.M.

MAJOR-GENERAL THOMAS,
Nashville, Tenn.

If you delay attack longer the mortifying spectacle will be witnessed of a rebel army moving for the Ohio River, and you will be forced to act, accepting such weather as you find. Let there be no further delay. Hood cannot even stand a drawn battle so far from his supplies of ordnance stores. If he retreats and you follow, he must lose his material and much of his army. I am in hopes of receiving a dispatch from you to-day announcing that you have moved. Delay no longer for weather or reinforcements.

U. S. GRANT,
Lieutenant-General.

WASHINGTON, D. C.,
December 15, 1864.

MAJOR-GENERAL THOMAS,
Nashville, Tenn.

I was just on my way to Nashville, but receiving a dispatch from Van Duzer detailing your splendid success of to-day, I shall go no further. Push the enemy now and give him no rest until he is entirely destroyed. Your army will cheerfully suffer many privations to break up Hood's army and render it useless for future operations. Do not stop for trains or supplies, but take them from the country as the enemy have done. Much is now expected.

U. S. GRANT,
Lieutenant-General.

Chapter 67, note 1

NOTE.—The fac-simile of the terms of Lee's surrender inserted at this place, was copied from the original document furnished the publishers through the courtesy of General Ely S. Parker, Military Secretary on General Grant's staff at the time of the surrender.

Three pages of paper were prepared in General Grant's manifold order book on which he wrote the terms, and the interlineations and erasures were added by General Parker at the suggestion of General Grant. After such alteration it was handed to General Lee, who put on his glasses, read it, and handed it back to General Grant. The original was then transcribed by General Parker upon official headed paper and a copy furnished General Lee.

The fac-simile herewith shows the color of the paper of the original document and all interlineations and erasures.

There is a popular error to the effect that Generals Grant and Lee each signed the articles of surrender. The document in the form of a letter was signed only by General Grant, in the parlor of McLean's house while General Lee was sitting in the room, and General Lee immediately wrote a letter accepting the terms and handed it to General Grant.

PUBLISHERS.

Artillery group, Grant Memorial, Washington, D.C. *Photograph by Elizabeth D. Samet.*

Appendix 2: Report of Lieutenant-General U. S. Grant, of the United States Armies—1864–'65

HEADQUARTERS ARMIES OF THE UNITED STATES,
WASHINGTON, D. C., *July* 22, 1865.

HON. E. M. STANTON, Secretary of War.

SIR:—I have the honor to submit the following report of the operations of the Armies of the United States from the date of my appointment to command the same.

From an early period in the rebellion I had been impressed with the idea that active and continuous operations of all the troops that could be brought into the field, regardless of season and weather, were necessary to a speedy termination of the war. The resources of the enemy and his numerical strength were far inferior to ours; but as an offset to this, we had a vast territory, with a population hostile to the government, to garrison, and long lines of river and railroad communications to protect, to enable us to supply the operating armies.

The armies in the East and West acted independently and without concert, like a balky team, no two ever pulling together, enabling the enemy to use to great advantage his interior lines of communication for transporting troops from East to West, reinforcing the army most vigorously pressed, and to furlough large numbers, during seasons of inactivity on our part, to go to their homes and do the work of producing, for the support of their armies. It was a question whether our numerical strength and resources were not more than balanced by these disadvantages and the enemy's superior position.

From the first, I was firm in the conviction that no peace could be had that would be stable and conducive to the happiness of the people, both North and South, until the military power of the rebellion was entirely broken.

I therefore determined, first, to use the greatest number of troops practicable against the armed force of the enemy; preventing him from using the same force at different seasons against first one and then another of our armies, and the possibility of repose for refitting and producing necessary supplies for carrying on resistance. Second, to hammer continuously against the armed force of the enemy and his resources, until by mere attrition, if in no other way, there should be nothing left to him but an equal submission with the loyal section of our common country to the constitution and laws of the land.

These views have been kept constantly in mind, and orders given and campaigns made to carry them out. Whether they might have been better in conception and execution is for the people, who mourn the loss of friends fallen, and who have to pay the pecuniary cost, to say. All I can say is, that what I have done has been done conscientiously, to the best of my ability, and in what I conceived to be for the best interests of the whole country.

At the date when this report begins, the situation of the contending forces was about as follows: The Mississippi River was strongly garrisoned by Federal troops, from St. Louis, Missouri, to its mouth. The line of the Arkansas was also held, thus giving us armed possession of all west of the Mississippi, north of that stream. A few points in Southern Louisiana, not remote from the river, were held by us, together with a small garrison at and near the mouth of the Rio Grande. All the balance of the vast territory of Arkansas, Louisiana, and Texas was in the almost undisputed possession of the enemy, with an army of probably not less than eighty thousand effective men, that could have been brought into the field had there been sufficient opposition to have brought them out. The let-alone policy had demoralized this force so that probably but little more than one-half of it was ever present in garrison at any one time. But the one-half, or forty thousand men, with the bands of guerillas scattered through Missouri, Arkansas, and along the Mississippi River, and the disloyal character of much of the population, compelled the use of a large number of troops to keep navigation open on the river, and to protect the loyal people to the west of it. To the east of the Mississippi we held substantially with the line of the Tennessee and Holston rivers, running eastward to include nearly all of the State of Tennessee. South of Chattanooga, a small foothold had been obtained in Georgia, sufficient to protect East Tennessee from incursions from the enemy's force at Dalton, Georgia. West Virginia was substantially within our lines. Virginia, with the exception of the northern border, the Potomac River, a small area about the mouth of James River, covered by the troops at Norfolk and Fort Monroe, and the territory covered by the Army of the Potomac lying along the Rapidan, was in the possession of the enemy. Along the sea-coast footholds had been obtained at Plymouth, Washington, and New Bern, in North Carolina; Beaufort, Folly and Morris Islands, Hilton Head, Fort Pulaski, and Port Royal, in South Carolina; Fernandina and St. Augustine, in Florida. Key West and Pensacola were also in our possession, while all the important ports were blockaded by the navy. The accompanying map, a copy of which was sent to General Sherman and other commanders in March, 1864, shows by red lines the territory occupied by us at the beginning of the rebellion, and at the opening of the campaign of 1864, while those in blue are the lines which it was proposed to occupy.[1]

---

1. The map to which Grant refers was not included in the first edition.

Behind the Union lines there were many bands of guerillas and a large population disloyal to the government, making it necessary to guard every foot of road or river used in
supplying our armies. In the South, a reign of military despotism prevailed, which made
every man and boy capable of bearing arms a soldier; and those who could not bear arms
in the field acted as provosts for collecting deserters and returning them. This enabled the
enemy to bring almost his entire strength into the field.

The enemy had concentrated the bulk of his forces east of the Mississippi into two armies,
commanded by Generals R. E. Lee and J. E. Johnston, his ablest and best generals. The army
commanded by Lee occupied the south bank of the Rapidan, extending from Mine Run
westward, strongly intrenched, covering and defending Richmond, the rebel capital, against
the Army of the Potomac. The army under Johnston occupied a strongly intrenched position
at Dalton, Georgia, covering and defending Atlanta, Georgia, a place of great importance
as a railroad centre, against the armies under Major-General W. T. Sherman. In addition to
these armies he had a large cavalry force under Forrest, in North-east Mississippi; a considerable force, of all arms, in the Shenandoah Valley, and in the western part of Virginia and
extreme eastern part of Tennessee; and also confronting our sea-coast garrisons, and holding
blockaded ports where we had no foothold upon land.

These two armies, and the cities covered and defended by them, were the main objective
points of the campaign.

Major-General W. T. Sherman, who was appointed to the command of the Military
Division of the Mississippi, embracing all the armies and territory east of the Mississippi
River to the Alleghanies and the Department of Arkansas, west of the Mississippi, had the
immediate command of the armies operating against Johnston.

Major-General George G. Meade had the immediate command of the Army of the Potomac, from where I exercised general supervision of the movements of all our armies.

General Sherman was instructed to move against Johnston's army, to break it up, and to
go into the interior of the enemy's country as far as he could, inflicting all the damage he
could upon their war resources. If the enemy in his front showed signs of joining Lee, to
follow him up to the full extent of his ability, while I would prevent the concentration of
Lee upon him, if it was in the power of the Army of the Potomac to do so. More specific
written instructions were not given, for the reason that I had talked over with him the plans
of the campaign, and was satisfied that he understood them and would execute them to the
fullest extent possible.

Major-General N. P. Banks, then on an expedition up Red River against Shreveport,
Louisiana (which had been organized previous to my appointment to command), was
notified by me on the 15th of March, of the importance it was that Shreveport should be
taken at the earliest possible day, and that if he found that the taking of it would occupy
from ten to fifteen days' more time than General Sherman had given his troops to be absent
from their command, he would send them back at the time specified by General Sherman,
even if it led to the abandonment of the main object of the Red River expedition, for
this force was necessary to movements east of the Mississippi; that should his expedition

prove successful, he would hold Shreveport and the Red River with such force as he might deem necessary, and return the balance of his troops to the neighborhood of New Orleans, commencing no move for the further acquisition of territory, unless it was to make that then held by him more easily held; that it might be a part of the spring campaign to move against Mobile; that it certainly would be, if troops enough could be obtained to make it without embarrassing other movements; that New Orleans would be the point of departure for such an expedition; also, that I had directed General Steele to make a real move from Arkansas, as suggested by him (General Banks), instead of a demonstration, as Steele thought advisable.

On the 31st of March, in addition to the foregoing notification and directions, he was instructed as follows:

> 1st. If successful in your expedition against Shreveport, that you turn over the defence of the Red River to General Steele and the navy.
>
> 2d. That you abandon Texas entirely, with the exception of your hold upon the Rio Grande. This can be held with four thousand men, if they will turn their attention immediately to fortifying their positions. At least one-half of the force required for this service might be taken from the colored troops.
>
> 3d. By properly fortifying on the Mississippi River, the force to guard it from Port Hudson to New Orleans can be reduced to ten thousand men, if not to a less number. Six thousand more would then hold all the rest of the territory necessary to hold until active operations can again be resumed west of the river. According to your last return, this would give you a force of over thirty thousand effective men with which to move against Mobile. To this I expect to add five thousand men from Missouri. If however, you think the force here stated too small to hold the territory regarded as necessary to hold possession of, I would say concentrate at least twenty-five thousand men of your present command for operations against Mobile. With these and such additions as I can give you from elsewhere, lose no time in making a demonstration, to be followed by an attack upon Mobile. Two or more iron-clads will be ordered to report to Admiral Farragut. This gives him a strong naval fleet with which to co-operate. You can make your own arrangements with the admiral for his co-operation, and select your own line of approach. My own idea of the matter is that Pascagoula should be your base; but, from your long service in the Gulf Department, you will know best about the matter. It is intended that your movements shall be co-operative with movements elsewhere, and you cannot now start too soon. All I would now add is, that you commence the concentration of your forces at once. Preserve a profound secrecy of what you intend doing, and start at the earliest possible moment.
>
> U. S. GRANT, Lieutenant-General.

MAJOR-GENERAL N. P. BANKS.

Major-General Meade was instructed that Lee's army would be his objective point; that wherever Lee went he would go also. For his movement two plans presented themselves: One to cross the Rapidan below Lee, moving by his right flank; the other above, moving by his left. Each presented advantages over the other, with corresponding objections. By crossing above, Lee would be cut off from all chance of ignoring Richmond or going north on a raid. But if we took this route, all we did would have to be done whilst the rations we started with held out; besides, it separated us from Butler, so that he could not be directed how to co-operate. If we took the other route, Brandy Station could be used as a base of supplies until another was secured on the York or James rivers. Of these, however, it was decided to take the lower route.

The following letter of instruction was addressed to Major-General B. F. Butler:

FORT MONROE, VIRGINIA, *April* 2, 1864.

GENERAL:—In the spring campaign, which it is desirable shall commence at as early a day as practicable, it is proposed to have co-operative action of all the armies in the field, as far as this object can be accomplished.

It will not be possible to unite our armies into two or three large ones to act as so many units, owing to the absolute necessity of holding on to the territory already taken from the enemy. But, generally speaking, concentration can be practically effected by armies moving to the interior of the enemy's country from the territory they have to guard. By such movement, they interpose themselves between the enemy and the country to be guarded, thereby reducing the number necessary to guard important points, or at least occupy the attention of a part of the enemy's force, if no greater object is gained. Lee's army and Richmond being the greater objects towards which our attention must be directed in the next campaign, it is desirable to unite all the force we can against them. The necessity of covering Washington with the Army of the Potomac, and of covering your department with your army, makes it impossible to unite these forces at the beginning of any move. I propose, therefore, what comes nearest this of anything that seems practicable: The Army of the Potomac will act from its present base, Lee's army being the objective point. You will collect all the forces from your command that can be spared from garrison duty—I should say not less than twenty thousand effective men—to operate on the south side of James River, Richmond being your objective point. To the force you already have will be added about ten thousand men from South Carolina, under Major-General Gillmore, who will command them in person. Major-General W. F. Smith is ordered to report to you, to command the troops sent into the field from your own department.

General Gillmore will be ordered to report to you at Fortress Monroe, with all the troops on transports, by the 18th instant, or as soon thereafter as practicable. Should you not receive notice by that time to move, you will make such disposition of them and your other forces as you may deem best calculated to deceive the enemy as to the real move to be made.

When you are notified to move, take City Point with as much force as possible. Fortify, or rather intrench, at once, and concentrate all your troops for the field there as rapidly as you can. From City Point directions cannot be given at this time for your further movements.

The fact that has already been stated—that is, that Richmond is to be your objective point, and that there is to be co-operation between your force and the Army of the Potomac—must be your guide. This indicates the necessity of your holding close to the south bank of the James River as you advance. Then, should the enemy be forced into his intrenchments in Richmond, the Army of the Potomac would follow, and by means of transports the two armies would become a unit.

All the minor details of your advance are left entirely to your direction. If, however, you think it practicable to use your cavalry south of you, so as to cut the railroad about Hicksford, about the time of the general advance, it would be of immense advantage.

You will please forward for my information, at the earliest practicable day, all orders, details, and instructions you may give for the execution of this order.

U. S. GRANT, Lieutenant-General.

MAJOR-GENERAL B. F. BUTLER.

On the 16th these instructions were substantially reiterated. On the 19th, in order to secure full co-operation between his army and that of General Meade, he was informed that I expected him to move from Fort Monroe the same day that General Meade moved from Culpeper. The exact time I was to telegraph him as soon as it was fixed, and that it would not be earlier than the 27th of April; that it was my intention to fight Lee between Culpeper and Richmond, if he would stand. Should he, however, fall back into Richmond, I would follow up and make a junction with his (General Butler's) army on the James River; that, could I be certain he would be able to invest Richmond on the south side, so as to have his left resting on the James, above the city, I would form the junction there; that circumstances might make this course advisable anyhow; that he should use every exertion to secure footing as far up the south side of the river as he could, and as soon as possible after the receipt of orders to move; that if he could not carry the city, he should at least detain as large a force there as possible.

In co-operation with the main movements against Lee and Johnston, I was desirous of using all other troops necessarily kept in departments remote from the fields of immediate operations, and also those kept in the background for the protection of our extended lines between the loyal States and the armies operating against them.

A very considerable force, under command of Major-General Sigel, was so held for the protection of West Virginia, and the frontiers of Maryland and Pennsylvania. Whilst these troops could not be withdrawn to distant fields without exposing the North to invasion by comparatively small bodies of the enemy, they could act directly to their front, and give better protection than if lying idle in garrison. By such a movement they would either compel the enemy to detach largely for the protection of his supplies and lines of communication, or he would lose them. General Sigel was therefore directed to organize all his available force into two expeditions, to move from Beverly and Charleston, under command of Generals Ord and Crook, against the East Tennessee and Virginia Railroad. Subsequently, General Ord having been relieved at his own request, General Sigel was instructed at his own suggestion, to give up the expedition by Beverly, and to form two columns, one under General Crook, on the Kanawha, numbering about ten thousand men, and one on the Shenandoah, numbering about seven thousand men. The one on the Shenandoah to assemble between Cumberland and the Shenandoah, and the infantry and artillery advanced to Cedar Creek with such cavalry as could be made available at the moment, to threaten the enemy in the Shenandoah Valley, and advance as far as possible; while General Crook would take possession of Lewisburg with part of his force and move down the Tennessee Railroad, doing as much damage as he could, destroying the New River Bridge and the salt-works, at Saltville, Va.

Owing to the weather and bad condition of the roads, operations were delayed until the 1st of May, when, everything being in readiness and the roads favorable, orders were given for a general movement of all the armies not later than the 4th of May.

My first object being to break the military power of the rebellion, and capture the enemy's important strongholds, made me desirous that General Butler should succeed in his movement against Richmond, as that would tend more than anything else, unless it were the capture of Lee's army, to accomplish this desired result in the East. If he failed, it was my determination, by hard fighting, either to compel Lee to retreat, or to so cripple him that he could not detach a large force to go north, and still retain enough for the defence of Richmond. It was well understood, by both Generals Butler and Meade, before starting on the campaign, that it was my intention to put both their armies south of the James River, in case of failure to destroy Lee without it.

Before giving General Butler his instructions, I visited him at Fort Monroe, and in conversation pointed out the apparent importance of getting possession of Petersburg, and destroying railroad communication as far south as possible. Believing, however, in the practicability of capturing Richmond unless it was reinforced, I made that the objective point of his operations. As the Army of the Potomac was to move simultaneously with him, Lee could not detach from his army with safety, and the enemy did not have troops elsewhere to bring to the defence of the city in time to meet a rapid movement from the north of James River.

I may here state that, commanding all the armies as I did, I tried, as far as possible, to leave General Meade in independent command of the Army of the Potomac. My instructions for that army were all through him, and were general in their nature, leaving all the details and the execution to him. The campaigns that followed proved him to be the right man in the right place. His commanding always in the presence of an officer superior to him in rank, has drawn from him much of that public attention that his zeal and ability entitle him to, and which he would otherwise have received.

The movement of the Army of the Potomac commenced early on the morning of the 4th of May, under the immediate direction and orders of Major-General Meade, pursuant to instructions. Before night, the whole army was across the Rapidan (the fifth and sixth corps crossing at Germania Ford, and the second corps at Ely's Ford, the cavalry, under Major-General Sheridan, moving in advance,) with the greater part of its trains, numbering about four thousand wagons, meeting with but slight opposition. The average distance travelled by the troops that day was about twelve miles. This I regarded as a great success, and it removed from my mind the most serious apprehensions I had entertained, that of crossing the river in the face of an active, large, well-appointed, and ably commanded army, and how so large a train was to be carried through a hostile country, and protected. Early on the 5th, the advance corps (the fifth, Major-General G. K. Warren commanding,) met and engaged the enemy outside his intrenchments near Mine Run. The battle raged furiously all day, the whole army being brought into the fight as fast as the corps could be got upon the field, which, considering the density of the forest and narrowness of the roads, was done with commendable promptness.

General Burnside, with the ninth corps, was, at the time the Army of the Potomac moved, left with the bulk of his corps at the crossing of the Rappahannock River and Alexandria Railroad, holding the road back to Bull Run, with instructions not to move until he received notice that a crossing of the Rapidan was secured, but to move promptly as soon as such notice was received. This crossing he was apprised of on the afternoon of the 4th. By six o'clock of the morning of the 6th he was leading his corps into action near the Wilderness Tavern, some of his troops having marched a distance of over thirty miles, crossing both the Rappahannock and Rapidan rivers. Considering that a large proportion, probably two-thirds of his command, was composed of new troops, unaccustomed to marches, and carrying the accoutrements of a soldier, this was a remarkable march.

The battle of the Wilderness was renewed by us at five o'clock on the morning of the 6th, and continued with unabated fury until darkness set in, each army holding substantially the same position that they had on the evening of the 5th. After dark, the enemy made a feeble attempt to turn our right flank, capturing several hundred prisoners and creating considerable confusion. But the promptness of General Sedgwick, who was personally present and commanded that part of our line, soon reformed it and restored order. On the morning of the 7th, reconnoissances showed that the enemy had fallen behind his intrenched lines, with pickets to the front, covering a part of the battle-field. From this it was evident to my mind that the two days' fighting had satisfied him of his inability to further maintain the contest in the open field, notwithstanding his advantage of position, and that he would wait an attack behind his works. I therefore determined to push on and put my whole force between him and Richmond; and orders were at once issued for a movement by his right flank. On the night of the 7th, the march was commenced towards Spottsylvania Court House, the fifth corps moving on the most direct road. But the enemy having become apprised of our movement, and having the shorter line, was enabled to reach there first. On the 8th, General Warren met a force of the enemy, which had been sent out to oppose and delay his advance, to gain time to fortify the line taken up at Spottsylvania. This force was steadily driven back on the main force, within the recently constructed works, after considerable fighting, resulting in severe loss to both sides. On the morning of the 9th, General Sheridan started on a raid against the enemy's lines of communication with Richmond. The 9th, 10th, and 11th were spent in manœuvring and fighting, without decisive results. Among the killed on the 9th was that able and distinguished soldier Major-General John Sedgwick, commanding the sixth army corps. Major-General H. G. Wright succeeded him in command. Early on the morning of the 12th a general attack was made on the enemy in position. The second corps, Major-General Hancock commanding, carried a salient of his line, capturing most of Johnson's division of Ewell's corps and twenty pieces of artillery. But the resistance was so obstinate that the advantage gained did not prove decisive. The 13th, 14th, 15th, 16th, 17th, and 18th, were consumed in manœuvring and awaiting the arrival of reinforcements from Washington. Deeming it impracticable to make any further attack upon the enemy at Spottsylvania Court House, orders were issued on the 18th with a view to a movement to the North Anna, to commence at twelve o'clock on the night of the 19th. Late in the afternoon of the 19th, Ewell's corps came out of its works on our extreme right flank; but the attack was promptly repulsed, with heavy loss. This delayed the movement to the North Anna until the night of the 21st, when it was commenced. But the enemy again, having the shorter line, and being in possession of the main roads, was enabled to reach the North Anna in advance of us, and took position behind it. The fifth corps reached the North Anna on the afternoon of the 23d, closely followed by the sixth corps. The second and ninth corps got up about the same time, the second holding the railroad bridge, and the ninth lying between that and Jericho Ford. General Warren effected a crossing the same afternoon, and got a position without much opposition. Soon after getting into position he was violently attacked, but repulsed the enemy with great slaughter. On the 25th, General Sheridan rejoined the Army of the Potomac from the raid on which he started from Spottsylvania, having destroyed the depots at Beaver Dam and Ashland stations, four trains of cars, large supplies of rations, and many miles of railroad-track; recaptured about four hundred of our men on their way to Richmond as prisoners of war; met and defeated the enemy's cavalry at Yellow Tavern; carried the first line of works around Richmond (but finding the second line too strong to be carried by assault), recrossed to the north bank of the Chickahominy at Meadow Bridge under heavy fire, and moved by a detour to Haxall's Landing, on the James River, where he communicated with General Butler. This raid had the effect of drawing off the whole of the enemy's cavalry force, making it comparatively easy to guard our trains.

General Butler moved his main force up the James River, in pursuance of instructions, on the 4th of May, General Gillmore having joined him with the tenth corps. At the same time he sent a force of one thousand eight hundred cavalry, by way of West Point, to form a junction with him wherever he might get a foothold, and a force of three thousand cavalry, under General Kautz, from Suffolk, to operate against the road south of Petersburg and Richmond. On the 5th, he occupied, without opposition, both City Point and Bermuda Hundred, his movement being a complete surprise. On the 6th, he was in position with his main army, and commenced intrenching. On the 7th he made a reconnoissance against the Petersburg and Richmond Railroad, destroying a portion of it after some fighting. On the 9th he telegraphed as follows:

HEADQUARTERS, NEAR BERMUDA LANDING,
May 9, 1864.

HON. E. M. STANTON, Secretary of War.

Our operations may be summed up in a few words. With one thousand seven hundred cavalry we have advanced up the Peninsula, forced the Chickahominy, and have safely, brought them to their present position. These were colored cavalry, and are now holding our advance pickets towards Richmond.

General Kautz, with three thousand cavalry from Suffolk, on the same day with our movement up James River, forced the Black Water, burned the railroad bridge at Stony Creek, below Petersburg, cutting into Beauregard's force at that point.

We have landed here, intrenched ourselves, destroyed many miles of railroad, and got a position which, with proper supplies, we can hold out against the whole of Lee's army. I have ordered up the supplies.

Beauregard, with a large portion of his force, was left south by the cutting of the railroads by Kautz. That portion which reached Petersburg under Hill I have whipped to-day, killing and wounding many, and taking many prisoners, after a severe and well-contested fight.

General Grant will not be troubled with any further reinforcements to Lee from Beauregard's force.

BENJ. F. BUTLER, Major-General.

On the evening of the 13th and morning of the 14th he carried a portion of the enemy's first line of defences at Drury's Bluff, or Fort Darling, with small loss. The time thus consumed from the 6th lost to us the benefit of the surprise and capture of Richmond and Petersburg, enabling, as it did, Beauregard to collect his loose forces in North and South Carolina, and bring them to the defence of those places. On the 16th, the enemy attacked General Butler in his position in front of Drury's Bluff. He was forced back, or drew back, into his intrenchments between the forks of the James and Appomattox rivers, the enemy intrenching strongly in his front, thus covering his railroads, the city, and all that was valuable to him. His army, therefore, though in a position of great security, was as completely shut off from further operations directly against Richmond as if it had been in a bottle strongly corked. It required but a comparatively small force of the enemy to hold it there.

On the 12th, General Kautz, with his cavalry, was started on a raid against the Danville Railroad, which he struck at Coalfield, Powhatan, and Chula Stations, destroying them, the railroad-track, two freight trains, and one locomotive, together with large quantities of commissary and other stores; thence, crossing to the South Side Road, struck it at Wilson's,

Wellsville, and Black's and White's Stations, destroying the road and station-houses; thence he proceeded to City Point, which he reached on the 18th.

On the 19th of April, and prior to the movement of General Butler, the enemy, with a land force under General Hoke and an iron-clad ram, attacked Plymouth, N.C., commanded by General H. W. Wessells, and our gunboats there, and, after severe fighting, the place was carried by assault, and the entire garrison and armament captured. The gunboat *Smithfield* was sunk, and the *Miami* disabled.

The army sent to operate against Richmond having hermetically sealed itself up at Bermuda Hundred, the enemy was enabled to bring the most, if not all, the reinforcements brought from the south by Beauregard against the Army of the Potomac. In addition to this reinforcement, a very considerable one, probably not less than fifteen thousand men, was obtained by calling in the scattered troops under Breckinridge from the western part of Virginia.

The position of Bermuda Hundred was as easy to defend as it was difficult to operate from against the enemy. I determined, therefore, to bring from it all available forces, leaving enough only to secure what had been gained; and accordingly, on the 22d, I directed that they be sent forward, under command of Major-General W. F. Smith, to join the Army of the Potomac.

On the 24th of May, the 9th army corps, commanded by Major-General A. E. Burnside, was assigned to the Army of the Potomac, and from this time forward constituted a portion of Major-General Meade's command.

Finding the enemy's position on the North Anna stronger than either of his previous ones, I withdrew on the night of the 26th to the north bank of the North Anna, and moved *via* Hanover Town to turn the enemy's position by his right.

Generals Torbert's and Merritt's divisions of cavalry, under Sheridan, and the 6th corps, led the advance; crossed the Pamunkey River at Hanover Town, after considerable fighting, and on the 28th the two divisions of cavalry had a severe, but successful engagement with the enemy at Hawes's Shop. On the 29th and 30th we advanced, with heavy skirmishing, to the Hanover Court House and Cold Harbor Road, and developed the enemy's position north of the Chickahominy. Late on the evening of the last day the enemy came out and attacked our left, but was repulsed with very considerable loss. An attack was immediately ordered by General Meade, along his whole line, which resulted in driving the enemy from a part of his intrenched skirmish line.

On the 31st, General Wilson's division of cavalry destroyed the railroad bridges over the South Anna River, after defeating the enemy's cavalry. General Sheridan, on the same day, reached Cold Harbor, and held it until relieved by the 6th corps and General Smith's command, which had just arrived, *via* White House, from General Butler's army.

On the 1st day of June an attack was made at five P.M. by the 6th corps and the troops under General Smith, the other corps being held in readiness to advance on the receipt of orders. This resulted in our carrying and holding the enemy's first line of works in front of the right of the 6th corps, and in front of General Smith. During the attack the enemy made repeated assaults on each of the corps not engaged in the main attack, but was repulsed with heavy loss in every instance. That night he made several assaults to regain what he had lost in the day, but failed. The 2d was spent in getting troops into position for an attack on the 3d. On the 3d of June we again assaulted the enemy's works, in the hope of driving him from his position. In this attempt our loss was heavy, while that of the enemy, I have reason to believe, was comparatively light. It was the only general attack made from the Rapidan to the James which did not inflict upon the enemy losses to compensate for our own losses. I would not be understood as saying that all previous attacks resulted in victories to our arms, or accomplished as much as I had hoped from them; but they inflicted upon the enemy severe losses, which tended, in the end, to the complete overthrow of the rebellion.

From the proximity of the enemy to his defences around Richmond, it was impossible, by any flank movement, to interpose between him and the city. I was still in a condition to either move by his left flank, and invest Richmond from the north side, or continue my move by his right flank to the south side of the James. While the former might have been better as a covering for Washington, yet a full survey of all the ground satisfied me that it would be impracticable to hold a line north and east of Richmond that would protect the Fredericksburg Railroad, a long, vulnerable line, which would exhaust much of our strength to guard, and that would have to be protected to supply the army, and would leave open to the enemy all his lines of communication on the south side of the James. My idea, from the start, had been to beat Lee's army north of Richmond, if possible. Then, after destroying his lines of communication north of the James River, to transfer the army to the south side, and besiege Lee in Richmond, or follow him south if he should retreat. After the battle of the Wilderness, it was evident that the enemy deemed it of the first importance to run no risks with the army he then had. He acted purely on the defensive, behind breastworks, or feebly on the offensive immediately in front of them, and where, in case of repulse, he could easily retire behind them. Without a greater sacrifice of life than I was willing to make, all could not be accomplished that I had designed north of Richmond. I therefore determined to continue to hold substantially the ground we then occupied, taking advantage of any favorable circumstances that might present themselves, until the cavalry could be sent to Charlottesville and Gordonsville to effectually break up the railroad connection between Richmond and the Shenandoah Valley and Lynchburg; and when the cavalry got well off, to move the army to the south side of the James River, by the enemy's right flank, where I felt I could cut off all his sources of supply, except by the canal.

On the 7th, two divisions of cavalry, under General Sheridan, got off on the expedition against the Virginia Central Railroad, with instructions to Hunter, whom I hoped he would meet near Charlottesville, to join his forces to Sheridan's, and after the work laid out for them was thoroughly done, to join the Army of the Potomac by the route laid down in Sheridan's instructions.

On the 10th of June, General Butler sent a force of infantry, under General Gillmore, and of cavalry under General Kautz, to capture Petersburg, if possible, and destroy the railroad and common bridges across the Appomattox. The cavalry carried the works on the south side, and penetrated well in towards the town, but were forced to retire. General Gillmore, finding the works which he approached very strong, and deeming an assault impracticable, returned to Bermuda Hundred without attempting one.

Attaching great importance to the possession of Petersburg, I sent back to Bermuda Hundred and City Point, General Smith's command by water, *via* the White House, to reach there in advance of the Army of the Potomac. This was for the express purpose of securing Petersburg before the enemy, becoming aware of our intention, could reinforce the place.

The movement from Cold Harbor commenced after dark on the evening of the 12th. One division of cavalry, under General Wilson, and the 5th corps, crossed the Chickahominy at Long Bridge, and moved out to White Oak Swamp, to cover the crossings of the other corps. The advance corps reached James River, at Wilcox's Landing and Charles City Court House, on the night of the 13th.

During three long years the Armies of the Potomac and Northern Virginia had been confronting each other. In that time they had fought more desperate battles than it probably ever before fell to the lot of two armies to fight, without materially changing the vantage ground of either. The Southern press and people, with more shrewdness than was displayed in the North, finding that they had failed to capture Washington and march on to New York, as they had boasted they would do, assumed that they only defended their Capital and Southern territory. Hence, Antietam, Gettysburg, and all the other battles that had been fought, were by them set down as failures on our part, and victories for them. Their army believed this. It produced a morale which could only be overcome by desperate and continuous hard fighting. The battles of the Wilderness, Spottsylvania, North Anna and Cold Harbor, bloody and terrible as they were on our side, were even more damaging to the enemy, and so crippled him as to make him wary ever after of taking the offensive. His losses in men were probably not so great, owing to the fact that we were, save in the Wilderness, almost invariably the attacking party; and when he did attack, it was in the open field. The details of these battles, which for endurance and bravery on the part of the soldiery, have rarely been surpassed, are given in the report of Major-General Meade, and the subordinate reports accompanying it.

During the campaign of forty-three days, from the Rapidan to the James River, the army had to be supplied from an ever-shifting base, by wagons, over narrow roads, through a densely wooded country, with a lack of wharves at each new base from which to conveniently discharge vessels. Too much credit cannot, therefore, be awarded to the quartermaster and commissary departments for the zeal and efficiency displayed by them. Under the general supervision of the chief quartermaster, Brigadier-General R. Ingalls, the trains were made to occupy all the available roads between the army and our water-base, and but little difficulty was experienced in protecting them.

The movement in the Kanawha and Shenandoah valleys, under General Sigel, commenced on the 1st of May. General Crook, who had the immediate command of the Kanawha expedition, divided his forces into two columns, giving one, composed of cavalry, to General Averell. They crossed the mountains by separate routes. Averell struck the Tennessee and Virginia Railroad, near Wytheville, on the 10th, and proceeding to New River and Christiansburg, destroyed the road, several important bridges and depots, including New River Bridge, forming a junction with Crook at Union on the 15th. General Sigel moved up the Shenandoah Valley, met the enemy at New Market on the 15th, and, after a severe engagement, was defeated with heavy loss, and retired behind Cedar Creek. Not regarding the operations of General Sigel as satisfactory, I asked his removal from command, and Major-General Hunter was appointed to supersede him. His instructions were embraced in the following dispatches to Major-General H. W. Halleck, chief of staff of the army:

NEAR SPOTTSYLVANIA COURT HOUSE, VA., *May* 20, 1864.

★   ★   ★   ★   ★   ★   ★

The enemy are evidently relying for supplies greatly on such as are brought over the branch road running through Staunton. On the whole, therefore, I think it would be better for General Hunter to move in that direction; reach Staunton and Gordonsville or Charlottesville, if he does not meet too much opposition. If he can hold at bay a force equal to his own, he will be doing good service. ★ ★ ★

U. S. GRANT, Lieutenant-General.

MAJOR-GENERAL H. W. HALLECK.

JERICHO FORD, VA., *May* 25, 1864.

If Hunter can possibly get to Charlottesville and Lynchburg, he should do so, living on the country. The railroads and canal should be destroyed beyond possibility of repairs for weeks. Completing this, he could find his way back to his original base, or from about Gordonsville join this army.

U. S. GRANT, Lieutenant-General.

MAJOR-GENERAL H. W. HALLECK.

General Hunter immediately took up the offensive, and, moving up the Shenandoah Valley, met the enemy on the 5th of June at Piedmont, and, after a battle of ten hours, routed and defeated him, capturing on the field of battle one thousand five hundred men, three pieces of artillery, and three hundred stand of small arms. On the 8th of the same month he formed a junction with Crook and Averell at Staunton, from which place he moved direct on Lynchburg, *via* Lexington, which place he reached and invested on the 16th day of June. Up to this time he was very successful; and but for the difficulty of taking with him sufficient ordnance stores over so long a march, through a hostile country, he would, no doubt, have captured that, to the enemy important, point. The destruction of the enemy's supplies and manufactories was very great. To meet this movement under General Hunter, General Lee sent a force, perhaps equal to a corps, a part of which reached Lynchburg a short time before Hunter. After some skirmishing on the 17th and 18th, General Hunter, owing to a want of ammunition to give battle, retired from before the place. Unfortunately, this want of ammunition left him no choice of route for his return but by way of Kanawha. This lost to us the use of his troops for several weeks from the defence of the North.

Had General Hunter moved by way of Charlottesville, instead of Lexington, as his instructions contemplated, he would have been in a position to have covered the Shenandoah Valley against the enemy, should the force he met have seemed to endanger it. If it did not, he would have been within easy distance of the James River Canal, on the main line of communication between Lynchburg and the force sent for its defence. I have never taken exception to the operations of General Hunter, and am not now disposed to find fault with him, for I have no doubt he acted within what he conceived to be the spirit of his instructions and the interests of the service. The promptitude of his movements and his gallantry should entitle him to the commendation of his country.

To return to the Army of the Potomac: The 2d corps commenced crossing the James River on the morning of the 14th by ferry-boats at Wilcox's Landing. The laying of the pontoon-bridge was completed about midnight of the 14th, and the crossing of the balance of the army was rapidly pushed forward by both bridge and ferry.

After the crossing had commenced, I proceeded by steamer to Bermuda Hundred to give the necessary orders for the immediate capture of Petersburg.

The instructions to General Butler were verbal, and were for him to send General Smith immediately, that night, with all the troops he could give him without sacrificing the position he then held. I told him that I would return at once to the Army of the Potomac, hasten its crossing and throw it forward to Petersburg by divisions as rapidly as it could be done; that we could reinforce our armies more rapidly there than the enemy could bring troops against us. General Smith got off as directed, and confronted the enemy's pickets near Petersburg before daylight next morning, but for some reason that I have never been able to satisfactorily understand, did not get ready to assault his main lines until near sundown. Then, with a part of his command only, he made the assault, and carried the lines north-east of Petersburg from the Appomattox River, for a distance of over two and a half miles, capturing fifteen pieces of artillery and three hundred prisoners. This was about seven P.M. Between the line thus captured and Petersburg there were no other works, and there was no evidence that the enemy had reinforced Petersburg with a single brigade from any source. The night was clear—the moon shining brightly—and favorable to further operations. General Hancock, with two divisions of the 2d corps, reached General Smith just after dark, and offered the service of these troops as he (Smith) might wish, waiving rank to the named commander, who he naturally supposed knew best the position of affairs, and what to do with the troops. But instead of taking these troops and pushing at once into Petersburg, he requested General Hancock to relieve a part of his line in the captured works, which was done before midnight.

By the time I arrived the next morning the enemy was in force. An attack was ordered to be made at six o'clock that evening by the troops under Smith and the 2d and 9th corps. It required until that time for the 9th corps to get up and into position. The attack was made as ordered, and the fighting continued with but little intermission until six o'clock the next morning, and resulted in our carrying the advance and some of the main works of the enemy to the right (our left) of those previously captured by General Smith, several pieces of artillery, and over four hundred prisoners.

The 5th corps having got up, the attacks were renewed and persisted in with great vigor on the 17th and 18th, but only resulted in forcing the enemy into an interior line, from which he could not be dislodged. The advantages of position gained by us were very great. The army then proceeded to envelop Petersburg towards the South Side Railroad, as far as possible without attacking fortifications.

On the 16th the enemy, to reinforce Petersburg, withdrew from a part of his intrenchment in front of Bermuda Hundred, expecting, no doubt, to get troops from north of the James to take the place of those withdrawn before we could discover it. General Butler, taking advantage of this, at once moved a force on the railroad between Petersburg and Richmond. As soon as I was apprised of the advantage thus gained, to retain it I ordered two divisions of the 6th corps, General Wright commanding, that were embarking at Wilcox's Landing, under orders for City Point, to report to General Butler at Bermuda Hundred, of which General Butler was notified, and the importance of holding a position in advance of his present line urged upon him.

About two o'clock in the afternoon General Butler was forced back to the line the enemy had withdrawn from in the morning. General Wright, with his two divisions, joined General Butler on the forenoon of the 17th, the latter still holding with a strong picket-line the enemy's works. But instead of putting these divisions into the enemy's works to hold them, he permitted them to halt and rest some distance in the rear of his own line. Between four and five o'clock in the afternoon the enemy attacked and drove in his pickets and re-occupied his old line.

On the night of the 20th and morning of the 21st a lodgment was effected by General Butler, with one brigade of infantry, on the north bank of the James, at Deep Bottom, and connected by pontoon-bridge with Bermuda Hundred.

On the 19th, General Sheridan, on his return from his expedition against the Virginia Central Railroad, arrived at the White House just as the enemy's cavalry was about to attack it, and compelled it to retire. The result of this expedition was, that General Sheridan met the enemy's cavalry near Trevilian Station, on the morning of the 11th of June, whom he attacked, and after an obstinate contest drove from the field in complete rout. He left his dead and nearly all his wounded in our hands, and about four hundred prisoners and several hundred horses. On the 12th he destroyed the railroad from Trevilian Station to Louisa Court House. This occupied until three o'clock P.M., when he advanced in the direction of Gordonsville. He found the enemy reinforced by infantry, behind well-constructed rifle-pits, about five miles from the latter place and too strong to successfully assault. On the extreme right, however, his reserve brigade carried the enemy's works twice, and was twice driven therefrom by infantry. Night closed the contest. Not having sufficient ammunition to continue the engagement, and his animals being without forage (the country furnishing but inferior grazing), and hearing nothing from General Hunter, he withdrew his command to the north side of the North Anna, and commenced his return march, reaching White House at the time before stated. After breaking up the depot at that place, he moved to the James River, which he reached safely after heavy fighting. He commenced crossing on the 25th, near Fort Powhatan, without further molestation, and rejoined the Army of the Potomac.

On the 22d, General Wilson, with his own division of cavalry of the Army of the Potomac, and General Kautz's division of cavalry of the Army of the James, moved against the enemy's railroads south of Richmond. Striking the Weldon Railroad at Reams's Station, destroying the depot and several miles of the road, and the South Side road about fifteen miles from Petersburg, to near Nottoway Station, where he met and defeated a force of the enemy's cavalry. He reached Burkesville Station on the afternoon of the 23d, and from there destroyed the Danville Railroad to Roanoke Bridge, a distance of twenty-five miles, where he found the enemy in force, and in a position from which he could not dislodge him. He then commenced his return march, and on the 28th met the enemy's cavalry in force at the Weldon Railroad crossing of Stony Creek, where he had a severe but not decisive engagement. Thence he made a detour from his left with a view of reaching Reams's Station (supposing it to be in our possession). At this place he was met by the enemy's cavalry, supported by infantry, and forced to retire, with the loss of his artillery and trains. In this last encounter, General Kautz, with a part of his command, became separated, and made his way into our lines. General Wilson, with the remainder of his force, succeeded in crossing the Nottoway River and coming in safely on our left and rear. The damage to the enemy in this expedition more than compensated for the losses we sustained. It severed all connection by railroad with Richmond for several weeks.

With a view of cutting the enemy's railroad from near Richmond to the Anna rivers, and making him wary of the situation of his army in the Shenandoah, and, in the event of failure in this, to take advantage of his necessary withdrawal of troops from Petersburg, to explode a mine that had been prepared in front of the 9th corps and assault the enemy's lines at that place, on the night of the 26th of July the 2d corps and two divisions of the cavalry corps and Kautz's cavalry were crossed to the north bank of the James River and joined the force General Butler had there. On the 27th the enemy was driven from his intrenched position, with the loss of four pieces of artillery. On the 28th our lines were extended from Deep Bottom to New Market Road, but in getting this position were attacked by the enemy in heavy force. The fighting lasted for several hours, resulting in considerable loss to both sides. The first object of this move having failed, by reason of the very large force thrown there by the enemy, I determined to take advantage of the diversion made, by assaulting Petersburg before he could get his force back there. One division of the 2d corps was withdrawn on the night of the 28th, and moved during the night to the rear of the 18th corps, to relieve that corps in the line, that it might be foot-loose in the assault to be made. The other two divisions of the 2d corps and Sheridan's cavalry were crossed over on the night of the 29th and moved in front of Petersburg. On the morning of the 30th, between four and five o'clock, the mine was sprung, blowing up a battery and most of a regiment, and the advance of the assaulting column, formed of the 9th corps, immediately took possession of the crater made by the explosion, and the line for some distance to the right and left of it, and a detached line in front of it, but for some cause failed to advance promptly to the ridge beyond. Had they done this, I have every reason to believe that Petersburg would have fallen. Other troops were immediately pushed forward, but the time consumed in getting them up enabled the enemy to rally from his surprise (which had been complete), and get forces to this point for its defence. The captured line thus held being untenable, and of no advantage to us, the troops were withdrawn, but not without heavy loss. Thus terminated in disaster what promised to be the most successful assault of the campaign.

Immediately upon the enemy's ascertaining that General Hunter was retreating from Lynchburg by way of the Kanawha River, thus laying the Shenandoah Valley open for raids into Maryland and Pennsylvania, he returned northward and moved down that valley. As soon as this movement of the enemy was ascertained, General Hunter, who had reached the Kanawha River, was directed to move his troops without delay, by river and railroad, to Harper's Ferry; but owing to the difficulty of navigation by reason of low water and breaks in the railroad, great delay was experienced in getting there. It became necessary, therefore, to find other troops to check this movement of the enemy. For this purpose the 6th corps was taken from the armies operating against Richmond, to which was added the 19th corps, then fortunately beginning to arrive in Hampton Roads from the Gulf Department, under orders issued immediately after the ascertainment of the result of the Red River expedition. The garrisons of Baltimore and Washington were at this time made up of heavy-artillery regiments, hundred days' men, and detachments from the invalid corps. One division under command of General Ricketts, of the 6th corps, was sent to Baltimore, and the remaining two divisions of the 6th corps, under General Wright, were subsequently sent to Washington. On the 3d of July the enemy approached Martinsburg. General Sigel, who was in command of our forces there, retreated across the Potomac at Shepherdstown; and General Weber, commanding at Harper's Ferry, crossed the river and occupied Maryland Heights. On the 6th the enemy occupied Hagerstown, moving a strong column towards Frederick City. General Wallace, with Ricketts's division and his own command, the latter mostly new and undisciplined troops, pushed out from Baltimore with great promptness, and met the enemy in force on the Monocacy, near the crossing of the railroad bridge. His force was not sufficient to insure success, but he fought the enemy nevertheless, and although it resulted in a defeat to our arms, yet it detained the enemy, and thereby served to enable General Wright to reach Washington with two divisions of the 6th corps, and the advance of the 19th corps, before him. From Monocacy the enemy moved on Washington, his cavalry advance reaching Rockville on the evening of the 10th. On the 12th a reconnoissance was thrown out in front of Fort Stevens, to ascertain the enemy's position and force. A severe skirmish ensued, in which we lost about two hundred and eighty in killed and wounded. The enemy's loss was probably greater. He commenced retreating during the night. Learning the exact condition of affairs at Washington, I requested by telegraph, at forty-five minutes past eleven P.M., on the 12th, the assignment of Major-General H. G.

Wright to the command of all the troops that could be made available to operate in the field against the enemy, and directed that he should get outside of the trenches with all the force he could, and push Early to the last moment. General Wright commenced the pursuit on the 13th; on the 18th the enemy was overtaken at Snicker's Ferry, on the Shenandoah, when a sharp skirmish occurred; and on the 20th, General Averell encountered and defeated a portion of the rebel army at Winchester, capturing four pieces of artillery and several hundred prisoners.

Learning that Early was retreating south towards Lynchburg or Richmond, I directed that the 6th and 19th corps be got back to the armies operating against Richmond, so that they might be used in a movement against Lee before the return of the troops sent by him into the valley; and that Hunter should remain in the Shenandoah Valley, keeping between any force of the enemy and Washington, acting on the defensive as much as possible. I felt that if the enemy had any notion of returning, the fact would be developed before the 6th and 19th corps could leave Washington. Subsequently, the 19th corps was excepted from the order to return to the James.

About the 25th it became evident that the enemy was again advancing upon Maryland and Pennsylvania, and the 6th corps, then at Washington, was ordered back to the vicinity of Harper's Ferry. The rebel force moved down the valley, and sent a raiding party into Pennsylvania which on the 30th burned Chambersburg, and then retreated, pursued by our cavalry, towards Cumberland. They were met and defeated by General Kelley, and with diminished numbers escaped into the mountains of West Virginia. From the time of the first raid the telegraph wires were frequently down between Washington and City Point, making it necessary to transmit messages a part of the way by boat. It took from twenty-four to thirty-six hours to get dispatches through and return answers back; so that often orders would be given, and then information would be received showing a different state of facts from those on which they were based, causing a confusion and apparent contradiction of orders that must have considerably embarrassed those who had to execute them, and rendered operations against the enemy less effective than they otherwise would have been. To remedy this evil, it was evident to my mind that some person should have the supreme command of all the forces in the Departments of West Virginia, Washington, Susquehanna, and the Middle Department, and I so recommended.

On the 2d of August, I ordered General Sheridan to report in person to Major-General Halleck, chief of staff, at Washington, with a view to his assignment to the command of all the forces against Early. At this time the enemy was concentrated in the neighborhood of Winchester, while our forces, under General Hunter, were concentrated on the Monocacy, at the crossing of the Baltimore and Ohio Railroad, leaving open to the enemy Western Maryland and Southern Pennsylvania. From where I was, I hesitated to give positive orders for the movement of our forces at Monocacy, lest by so doing I should expose Washington. Therefore, on the 4th, I left City Point to visit Hunter's command, and determine for myself what was best to be done. On arrival there, and after consultation with General Hunter, I issued to him the following instructions:

MONOCACY BRIDGE, MARYLAND,

August 5, 1864—8 P.M.

GENERAL:—Concentrate all your available force without delay in the vicinity of Harper's Ferry, leaving only such railroad guards and garrisons for public property as may be necessary. Use, in this concentrating, the railroad, if by so doing time can be saved. From Harper's Ferry, if it is found that the enemy has moved north of the Potomac in large force, push north, following him and attacking him wherever found; follow him, if driven south of the Potomac, as long as it is safe to do so. If it is ascertained that the enemy has but a small force north of the Potomac, then push south with the main force, detaching under a competent commander, a sufficient force to look after the raiders, and drive them to their homes. In detaching such a force, the brigade of the cavalry now *en route* from Washington *via* Rockville may be taken into account.

There are now on their way to join you three other brigades of the best cavalry, numbering at least five thousand men and horses. These will be instructed, in the absence of further orders, to join you by the south side of the Potomac. One brigade will probably start to-morrow. In pushing up the Shenandoah Valley, where it is expected you will have to go first or last, it is desirable that nothing should be left to invite the enemy to return. Take all provisions, forage, and stock wanted for the use of your command; such as cannot be consumed, destroy. It is not desirable that the buildings should be destroyed—they should rather be protected; but the people should be informed that, so long as an army can subsist among them, recurrences of these raids must be expected, and we are determined to stop them at all hazards.

Bear in mind, the object is to drive the enemy south; and to do this you want to keep him always in sight. Be guided in your course by the course he takes.

Make your own arrangements for supplies of all kinds, giving regular vouchers for such as may be taken from loyal citizens in the country through which you march.

U. S. GRANT, Lieutenant-General.

MAJOR-GENERAL D. HUNTER.

The troops were immediately put in motion, and the advance reached Halltown that night.

General Hunter having, in our conversation, expressed a willingness to be relieved from command, I telegraphed to have General Sheridan, then at Washington, sent to Harper's Ferry by the morning train, with orders to take general command of all the troops in the field, and to call on General Hunter at Monocacy, who would turn over to him my letter of instructions. I remained at Monocacy until General Sheridan arrived, on the morning of the 6th, and, after a conference with him in relation to military affairs in that vicinity, I returned to City Point by way of Washington.

On the 7th of August, the Middle Department, and the Departments of West Virginia, Washington, and Susquehanna, were constituted into the "Middle Military Division," and Major-General Sheridan was assigned to temporary command of the same.

Two divisions of cavalry, commanded by Generals Torbert and Wilson, were sent to Sheridan from the Army of the Potomac. The first reached him at Harper's Ferry about the 11th of August.

His operations during the month of August and the fore part of September were both of an offensive and defensive character, resulting in many severe skirmishes, principally by the cavalry, in which we were generally successful, but no general engagement took place. The two armies lay in such a position—the enemy on the west bank of the Opequon Creek covering Winchester, and our forces in front of Berryville—that either could bring on a battle at any time. Defeat to us would lay open to the enemy the States of Maryland and Pennsylvania for long distances before another army could be interposed to check him. Under these circumstances I hesitated about allowing the initiative to be taken. Finally, the use of the Baltimore and Ohio Railroad, and the Chesapeake and Ohio Canal, which were both obstructed by the enemy, became so indispensably necessary to us, and the importance of relieving Pennsylvania and Maryland from continuously threatened invasion so great, that I determined the risk should be taken. But fearing to telegraph the order for an attack without knowing more than I did of General Sheridan's feelings as to what would be the probable result, I left City Point on the 15th of September to visit him at his headquarters, to decide, after conference with him, what should be done. I met him at Charlestown, and he pointed out so distinctly how each army lay; what he could do the moment he was authorized, and expressed such confidence of success, that I saw there were but two words of instructions necessary—Go in! For the conveniences of forage, the teams for supplying the army were kept at Harper's Ferry. I asked him if he could get out his teams and supplies in time to make an attack on the ensuing Tuesday morning. His reply was, that he could before daylight on Monday. He was off promptly to time, and I may here add, that the result was such that I have never since deemed it necessary to visit General Sheridan before giving him orders.

Early on the morning of the 19th, General Sheridan attacked General Early at the crossing on the Opequon Creek, and after a most sanguinary and bloody battle, lasting until five o'clock in the evening, defeated him with heavy loss, carrying his entire position from Opequon Creek to Winchester, capturing several thousand prisoners and five pieces of artillery. The enemy rallied, and made a stand in a strong position at Fisher's Hill, where he was attacked, and again defeated with heavy loss on the 20th [22d]. Sheridan pursued him with great energy through Harrisonburg, Staunton, and the gaps of the Blue Ridge. After stripping the upper valley of most of the supplies and provisions for the rebel army, he returned to Strasburg, and took position on the north side of Cedar Creek.

Having received considerable reinforcements, General Early again returned to the valley, and, on the 9th of October, his cavalry encountered ours near Strasburg, where the rebels were defeated, with the loss of eleven pieces of artillery and three hundred and fifty prisoners. On the night of the 18th, the enemy crossed the mountains which separate the branches of the Shenandoah, forded the North Fork, and early on the morning of the 19th, under cover of the darkness and the fog, surprised and turned our left flank, and captured the batteries which enfiladed our whole line. Our troops fell back with heavy loss and in much confusion, but were finally rallied between Middletown and Newtown. At this juncture, General Sheridan, who was at Winchester when the battle commenced, arrived on the field, arranged his lines just in time to repulse a heavy attack of the enemy, and immediately assuming the offensive, he attacked in turn with great vigor. The enemy was defeated with great slaughter, and the loss of most of his artillery and trains, and the trophies he had captured in the morning. The wreck of his army escaped during the night, and fled in the direction of Staunton and Lynchburg. Pursuit was made to Mount Jackson. Thus ended this, the enemy's last attempt to invade the North *via* the Shenandoah Valley. I was now enabled to return the 6th corps to the Army of the Potomac, and to send one division from Sheridan's army to the Army of the James, and another to Savannah, Georgia, to hold Sherman's new acquisitions on the sea-coast, and thus enable him to move without detaching from his force for that purpose.

Reports from various sources led me to believe that the enemy had detached three divisions from Petersburg to reinforce Early in the Shenandoah Valley. I therefore sent the 2d corps and Gregg's division of cavalry, of the Army of the Potomac, and a force of General Butler's army, on the night of the 13th of August, to threaten Richmond from the north side of the James, to prevent him from sending troops away, and, if possible, to draw back those sent. In this move we captured six pieces of artillery and several hundred prisoners, detained troops that were under marching orders, and ascertained that but one division (Kershaw's), of the three reputed detached, had gone.

The enemy having withdrawn heavily from Petersburg to resist this movement, the 5th corps, General Warren commanding, was moved out on the 18th, and took possession of the Weldon Railroad. During the day he had considerable fighting. To regain possession of the road, the enemy made repeated and desperate assaults, but was each time repulsed with great loss. On the night of the 20th, the troops on the north side of the James were withdrawn, and Hancock and Gregg returned to the front at Petersburg. On the 25th, the 2d corps and Gregg's division of cavalry, while at Reams's Station destroying the railroad, were attacked, and after desperate fighting, a part of our line gave way, and five pieces of artillery fell into the hands of the enemy.

By the 12th of September, a branch railroad was completed from the City Point and Petersburg Railroad to the Weldon Railroad, enabling us to supply, without difficulty, in all weather, the army in front of Petersburg.

The extension of our lines across the Weldon Railroad compelled the enemy to so extend his, that it seemed he could have but few troops north of the James for the defence of Richmond. On the night of the 28th, the 10th corps, Major-General Birney, and the 18th corps, Major-General Ord commanding, of General Butler's army, were crossed to the north side of the James, and advanced on the morning of the 29th, carrying the very strong fortifications and intrenchments below Chaffin's Farm, known as Fort Harrison, capturing fifteen pieces of artillery, and the New Market Road and intrenchments. This success was followed up by a gallant assault upon Fort Gilmer, immediately in front of the Chaffin Farm fortifications, in which we were repulsed with heavy loss. Kautz's cavalry was pushed forward on the road to the right of this, supported by infantry, and reached the enemy's inner line, but was unable to get further. The position captured from the enemy was so threatening to Richmond, that I determined to hold it. The enemy made several desperate attempts to dislodge us, all of which were unsuccessful, and for which he paid dearly. On the morning of the 30th, General Meade sent out a reconnoissance with a view to attacking the enemy's line, if it was found sufficiently weakened by withdrawal of troops to the north side. In this reconnoissance we captured and held the enemy's works near Poplar Spring Church. In the afternoon, troops moving to get to the left of the point gained were attacked by the enemy in heavy force, and compelled to fall back until supported by the forces holding the captured works. Our cavalry under Gregg was also attacked, but repulsed the enemy with great loss.

On the 7th of October, the enemy attacked Kautz's cavalry north of the James, and drove it back with heavy loss in killed, wounded, and prisoners, and the loss of all the artillery— eight or nine pieces. This he followed up by an attack on our intrenched infantry line, but was repulsed with severe slaughter. On the 13th, a reconnoissance was sent out by General Butler, with a view to drive the enemy from some new works he was constructing, which resulted in very heavy loss to us.

On the 27th, the Army of the Potomac, leaving only sufficient men to hold its fortified line, moved by the enemy's right flank. The 2d corps, followed by two divisions of the 5th corps, with the cavalry in advance and covering our left flank, forced a passage of Hatcher's Run, and moved up the south side of it towards the South Side Railroad, until the 2d corps and part of the cavalry reached the Boydton Plank Road where it crosses Hatcher's Run. At this point we were six miles distant from the South Side Railroad, which I had hoped by this movement to reach and hold. But finding that we had not reached the end of the enemy's fortifications, and no place presenting itself for a successful assault by which he might be doubled up and shortened, I determined to withdraw to within our fortified line. Orders were given accordingly. Immediately upon receiving a report that General Warren had connected with General Hancock, I returned to my headquarters. Soon after I left[,] the enemy moved out across Hatcher's Run, in the gap between Generals Hancock and Warren, which was not closed as reported, and made a desperate attack on General Hancock's right and rear. General Hancock immediately faced his corps to meet it, and after a bloody combat drove the enemy within his works, and withdrew that night to his old position.

In support of this movement, General Butler made a demonstration on the north side of the James, and attacked the enemy on the Williamsburg Road, and also on the York River Railroad. In the former he was unsuccessful; in the latter he succeeded in carrying a work which was afterwards abandoned, and his forces withdrawn to their former positions.

From this time forward the operations in front of Petersburg and Richmond, until the spring campaign of 1865, were confined to the defence and extension of our lines, and to offensive movements for crippling the enemy's lines of communication, and to prevent his detaching any considerable force to send south. By the 7th of February, our lines were extended to Hatcher's Run, and the Weldon Railroad had been destroyed to Hicksford.

General Sherman moved from Chattanooga on the 6th of May, with the Armies of the Cumberland, Tennessee, and Ohio, commanded, respectively, by Generals Thomas, McPherson, and Schofield, upon Johnston's army at Dalton; but finding the enemy's position at Buzzard's Roost, covering Dalton, too strong to be assaulted, General McPherson was sent through Snake Gap to turn it, while Generals Thomas and Schofield threatened it in front and on the north. This movement was successful. Johnston, finding his retreat likely to be cut off, fell back to his fortified position at Resaca, where he was attacked on the afternoon of May 15th. A heavy battle ensued. During the night the enemy retreated south. Late on the 17th, his rear-guard was overtaken near Adairsville, and heavy skirmishing followed. The next morning, however, he had again disappeared. He was vigorously pursued, and was overtaken at Cassville on the 19th, but during the ensuing night retreated across the Etowah. While these operations were going on, General Jefferson C. Davis's division of Thomas's army was sent to Rome, capturing it with its forts and artillery, and its valuable mills and foundries. General Sherman, having given his army a few days' rest at this point, again put it in motion on the 23d, for Dallas, with a view of turning the difficult pass at Allatoona. On the afternoon of the 25th, the advance, under General Hooker, had a severe battle with the enemy, driving him back to New Hope Church, near Dallas. Several sharp encounters occurred at this point. The most important was on the 28th, when the enemy assaulted General McPherson at Dallas, but received a terrible and bloody repulse.

On the 4th of June, Johnston abandoned his intrenched position at New Hope Church, and retreated to the strong positions of Kenesaw, Pine, and Lost mountains. He was forced to yield the two last-named places, and concentrate his army on Kenesaw, where, on the 27th, Generals Thomas and McPherson made a determined but unsuccessful assault. On the night of the 2d of July, Sherman commenced moving his army by the right flank, and on the morning of the 3d, found that the enemy, in consequence of this movement, had abandoned Kenesaw and retreated across the Chattahoochee.

General Sherman remained on the Chattahoochee to give his men rest and get up stores until the 17th of July, when he resumed his operations, crossed the Chattahoochee, destroyed a large portion of the railroad to Augusta, and drove the enemy back to Atlanta. At this place General Hood succeeded General Johnston in command of the rebel army, and assuming the offensive-defensive policy, made several severe attacks upon Sherman in the vicinity of Atlanta, the most desperate and determined of which was on the 22d of July. About one P.M. of this day the brave, accomplished, and noble-hearted McPherson was killed. General Logan succeeded him, and commanded the Army of the Tennessee through this desperate battle, and until he was superseded by Major-General Howard, on the 26th, with the same success and ability that had characterized him in the command of a corps or division.

In all these attacks the enemy was repulsed with great loss. Finding it impossible to entirely invest the place, General Sherman, after securing his line of communications across the Chattahoochee, moved his main force round by the enemy's left flank upon the Montgomery and Macon roads, to draw the enemy from his fortifications. In this he succeeded, and after defeating the enemy near Rough-and-Ready, Jonesboro, and Lovejoy's, forcing him to retreat to the south, on the 2d of September occupied Atlanta, the objective point of his campaign.

About the time of this move, the rebel cavalry, under Wheeler, attempted to cut his communications in the rear, but was repulsed at Dalton, and driven into East Tennessee, whence it proceeded west to McMinnville, Murfreesboro, and Franklin, and was finally driven south of the Tennessee. The damage done by this raid was repaired in a few days.

During the partial investment of Atlanta, General Rousseau joined General Sherman with a force of cavalry from Decatur, having made a successful raid upon the Atlanta and Montgomery Railroad, and its branches near Opelika. Cavalry raids were also made by Generals McCook, Garrard, and Stoneman, to cut the remaining Railroad communication with Atlanta. The first two were successful—the latter, disastrous.

General Sherman's movement from Chattanooga to Atlanta was prompt, skilful, and brilliant. The history of his flank movements and battles during that memorable campaign will ever be read with an interest unsurpassed by anything in history.

His own report, and those of his subordinate commanders, accompanying it, give the details of that most successful campaign.

He was dependent for the supply of his armies upon a single-track railroad from Nashville to the point where he was operating. This passed the entire distance through a hostile country, and every foot of it had to be protected by troops. The cavalry force of the enemy under Forrest, in Northern Mississippi, was evidently waiting for Sherman to advance far enough into the mountains of Georgia, to make a retreat disastrous, to get upon this line and destroy it beyond the possibility of further use. To guard against this danger, Sherman left what he supposed to be a sufficient force to operate against Forrest in West Tennessee. He directed General Washburn, who commanded there, to send Brigadier-General S. D. Sturgis in command of this force to attack him. On the morning of the 10th of June, General Sturgis met the enemy near Guntown, Mississippi, was badly beaten, and driven back in utter rout and confusion to Memphis, a distance of about one hundred miles, hotly pursued by the enemy. By this, however, the enemy was defeated in his designs upon Sherman's line of communications. The persistency with which he followed up this success exhausted him, and made a season for rest and repairs necessary. In the meantime, Major-General A. J. Smith, with the troops of the Army of the Tennessee that had been sent by General Sherman to General Banks, arrived at Memphis on their return from Red River, where they had done most excellent service. He was directed by General Sherman to immediately take the offensive against Forrest. This he did with the promptness and effect which has characterized his whole military career. On the 14th of July, he met the enemy at Tupelo, Mississippi, and whipped him badly. The fighting continued through three days. Our loss was small compared with that of the enemy. Having accomplished the object of his expedition, General Smith returned to Memphis.

During the months of March and April this same force under Forrest annoyed us considerably. On the 24th of March it captured Union City, Kentucky, and its garrison, and on the 24th attacked Paducah, commanded by Colonel S. G. Hicks, 40th Illinois Volunteers. Colonel H., having but a small force, withdrew to the forts near the river, from where he repulsed the enemy and drove him from the place.

On the 13th of April, part of this force, under the rebel General Buford, summoned the garrison of Columbus, Kentucky, to surrender, but received for reply from Colonel Lawrence, 34th New Jersey Volunteers, that being placed there by his Government with adequate force to hold his post and repel all enemies from it, surrender was out of the question.

On the morning of the same day Forrest attacked Fort Pillow, Tennessee, garrisoned by a detachment of Tennessee cavalry and the 1st Regiment Alabama colored troops, commanded by Major Booth. The garrison fought bravely until about three o'clock in the afternoon, when the enemy carried the works by assault; and, after our men threw down their arms, proceeded to an inhuman and merciless massacre of the garrison.

On the 14th, General Buford, having failed at Columbus, appeared before Paducah, but was again driven off.

Guerillas and raiders, seemingly emboldened by Forrest's operations, were also very active in Kentucky. The most noted of these was Morgan. With a force of from two to three thousand cavalry, he entered the State through Pound Gap in the latter part of May. On the 11th of June they attacked and captured Cynthiana, with its entire garrison. On the 12th he was overtaken by General Burbridge, and completely routed with heavy loss, and was finally driven out of the State. This notorious guerilla was afterwards surprised and killed near Greenville, Tennessee, and his command captured and dispersed by General Gillem.

In the absence of official reports of the commencement of the Red River expedition, except so far as relates to the movements of the troops sent by General Sherman under General A. J. Smith, I am unable to give the date of its starting. The troops under General Smith, comprising two divisions of the 16th and a detachment of the 17th army corps, left Vicksburg on the 10th of March, and reached the designated point on Red River one day earlier than that appointed by General Banks. The rebel forces at Fort de Russy, thinking to defeat him, left the fort on the 14th to give him battle in the open field; but, while occupying the enemy with skirmishing and demonstrations, Smith pushed forward to Fort de Russy, which had been left with a weak garrison, and captured it with its garrison—about three hundred and fifty men, eleven pieces of artillery, and many small-arms. Our loss was but slight. On the 15th he pushed forward to Alexandria, which place he reached on the 18th. On the 21st he had an engagement with the enemy at Henderson's Hill, in which he defeated him, capturing two hundred and ten prisoners and four pieces of artillery.

On the 28th, he again attacked and defeated the enemy under the rebel General Taylor, at Cane River. By the 26th, General Banks had assembled his whole army at Alexandria, and pushed forward to Grand Ecore. On the morning of April 6th he moved from Grand Ecore. On the afternoon of the 7th, he advanced and met the enemy near Pleasant Hill, and drove him from the field. On the same afternoon the enemy made a stand eight miles beyond Pleasant Hill, but was again compelled to retreat. On the 8th, at Sabine Cross Roads and Peach Hill, the enemy attacked and defeated his advance, capturing nineteen pieces of artillery and an immense amount of transportation and stores. During the night, General Banks fell back to Pleasant Hill, where another battle was fought on the 9th, and the enemy repulsed with great loss. During the night, General Banks continued his retrograde movement to Grand Ecore, and thence to Alexandria, which he reached on the 27th of April. Here a serious difficulty arose in getting Admiral Porter's fleet which accompanied the expedition, over the rapids, the water having fallen so much since they passed up as to prevent their return. At the suggestion of Colonel (now Brigadier-General) Bailey, and under his superintendence, wing-dams were constructed, by which the channel was contracted so that the fleet passed down the rapids in safety.

The army evacuated Alexandria on the 14th of May, after considerable skirmishing with the enemy's advance, and reached Morganzia and Point Coupée near the end of the month. The disastrous termination of this expedition, and the lateness of the season, rendered impracticable the carrying out of my plans of a movement in force sufficient to insure the capture of Mobile.

On the 23d of March, Major-General Steele left Little Rock with the 7th army corps, to co-operate with General Banks's expedition on the Red River, and reached Arkadelphia on the 28th. On the 16th of April, after driving the enemy before him, he was joined, near Elkin's Ferry, in Washita County, by General Thayer, who had marched from Fort Smith. After several severe skirmishes, in which the enemy was defeated, General Steele reached Camden, which he occupied about the middle of April.

On learning the defeat and consequent retreat of General Banks on Red River, and the loss of one of his own trains at Mark's Mill, in Dallas County, General Steele determined to fall back to the Arkansas River. He left Camden on the 26th of April, and reached Little Rock on the 2d of May. On the 30th of April, the enemy attacked him while crossing Saline River at Jenkins's Ferry, but was repulsed with considerable loss. Our loss was about six hundred in killed, wounded and prisoners.

Major-General Canby, who had been assigned to the command of the "Military Division of the West Mississippi," was therefore directed to send the 19th army corps to join the armies operating against Richmond, and to limit the remainder of his command to such operations as might be necessary to hold the positions and lines of communications he then occupied.

Before starting General A. J. Smith's troops back to Sherman, General Canby sent a part of it to disperse a force of the enemy that was collecting near the Mississippi River. General Smith met and defeated this force near Lake Chicot on the 5th of June. Our loss was about forty killed and seventy wounded.

In the latter part of July, General Canby sent Major-General Gordon Granger, with such forces as he could collect, to co-operate with Admiral Farragut against the defences of Mobile Bay. On the 8th of August, Fort Gaines surrendered to the combined naval and land forces. Fort Powell was blown up and abandoned.

On the 9th, Fort Morgan was invested, and, after a severe bombardment, surrendered on the 23d. The total captures amounted to one thousand four hundred and sixty-four prisoners, and one hundred and four pieces of artillery.

About the last of August, it being reported that the rebel General Price, with a force of about ten thousand men, had reached Jacksonport, on his way to invade Missouri, General A. J. Smith's command, then *en route* from Memphis to join Sherman, was ordered to Missouri. A cavalry force was also, at the same time, sent from Memphis, under command of Colonel Winslow. This made General Rosecrans's forces superior to those of Price, and no doubt was entertained he would be able to check Price and drive him back; while the forces under General Steele, in Arkansas, would cut off his retreat. On the 26th day of September, Price attacked Pilot Knob and forced the garrison to retreat, and thence moved north to the Missouri River, and continued up that river towards Kansas. General Curtis, commanding Department of Kansas, immediately collected such forces as he could to repel the invasion of Kansas, while General Rosecrans's cavalry was operating in his rear.

The enemy was brought to battle on the Big Blue and defeated, with the loss of nearly all his artillery and trains and a large number of prisoners. He made a precipitate retreat to Northern Arkansas. The impunity with which Price was enabled to roam over the State of Missouri for a long time, and the incalculable mischief done by him, shows to how little purpose a superior force may be used. There is no reason why General Rosecrans should not have concentrated his forces, and beaten and driven Price before the latter reached Pilot Knob.

September 20th, the enemy's cavalry, under Forrest, crossed the Tennessee near Waterloo, Alabama, and on the 23d attacked the garrison at Athens, consisting of six hundred men, which capitulated on the 24th. Soon after the surrender two regiments of reinforcements arrived, and after a severe fight were compelled to surrender. Forrest destroyed the railroad westward, captured the garrison at Sulphur Branch trestle, skirmished with the garrison at Pulaski on the 27th, and on the same day cut the Nashville and Chattanooga Railroad near Tullahoma and Dechard. On the morning of the 30th, one column of Forrest's command, under Buford, appeared before Huntsville, and summoned the surrender of the garrison. Receiving an answer in the negative, he remained in the vicinity of the place until next morning, when he again summoned its surrender, and received the same reply as on the night before. He withdrew in the direction of Athens, which place had been regarrisoned, and attacked it on the afternoon of the 1st of October, but without success. On the morning of the 2d he renewed his attack, but was handsomely repulsed.

Another column under Forrest appeared before Columbia on the morning of the 1st, but did not make an attack. On the morning of the 3d he moved towards Mount Pleasant. While these operations were going on, every exertion was made by General Thomas to destroy the forces under Forrest before he could recross the Tennessee, but was unable to prevent his escape to Corinth, Mississippi.

In September, an expedition under General Burbridge was sent to destroy the salt-works at Saltville, Virginia. He met the enemy on the 2d of October, about three miles and a half from Saltville, and drove him into his strongly intrenched position around the salt-works, from which he was unable to dislodge him. During the night he withdrew his command and returned to Kentucky.

General Sherman, immediately after the fall of Atlanta, put his armies in camp in and about the place, and made all preparations for refitting and supplying them for future service. The great length of road from Atlanta to the Cumberland River, however, which had to be guarded, allowed the troops but little rest.

During this time Jefferson Davis made a speech in Macon, Georgia, which was reported in the papers of the South, and soon became known to the whole country, disclosing the plans of the enemy, thus enabling General Sherman to fully meet them. He exhibited the weakness of supposing that an army that had been beaten and fearfully decimated in a vain attempt at the defensive, could successfully undertake the offensive against the army that had so often defeated it.

In execution of this plan, Hood, with this army, was soon reported to the south-west of Atlanta. Moving far to Sherman's right, he succeeded in reaching the railroad about Big Shanty, and moved north on it.

General Sherman, leaving a force to hold Atlanta, with the remainder of his army fell upon him and drove him to Gadsden, Alabama. Seeing the constant annoyance he would have with the roads to his rear if he attempted to hold Atlanta, General Sherman proposed the abandonment and destruction of that place, with all the railroads leading to it, and telegraphed me as follows:

> CENTREVILLE, GEORGIA,
>
> *October* 10—noon.
>
> Dispatch about Wilson just received. Hood is now crossing Coosa River, twelve miles below Rome, bound west. If he passes over the Mobile and Ohio road, had I not better execute the plan of my letter sent by Colonel Porter, and leave General Thomas with the troops now in Tennessee to defend the State? He will have an ample force when the reinforcements ordered reach Nashville.
>
> W. T. SHERMAN, Major-General.

LIEUTENANT-GENERAL GRANT.

For a full understanding of the plan referred to in this dispatch, I quote from the letter sent by Colonel Porter: "I will therefore give my opinion, that your army and Canby's should be reinforced to the maximum; that after you get Wilmington, you strike for Savannah and the river; that Canby be instructed to hold the Mississippi River, and send a force to get Columbus, Georgia, either by the way of the Alabama or the Appalachicola, and that I keep Hood employed and put my army in final order for a march on Augusta, Columbia, and Charleston, to be ready as soon as Wilmington is sealed as to commerce and the city of Savannah is in our possession." This was in reply to a letter of mine of date September 12th, in answer to a dispatch of his containing substantially the same proposition, and in which I informed him of a proposed movement against Wilmington, and of the situation in Virginia, etc.

CITY POINT, VIRGINIA,

October 11, 1864—11 A.M.

Your dispatch of October 10th received. Does it not look as if Hood was going to attempt the invasion of Middle Tennessee, using the Mobile and Ohio and Memphis and Charleston roads to supply his base on the Tennessee River, about Florence or Decatur? If he does this, he ought to be met and prevented from getting north of the Tennessee River. If you were to cut loose, I do not believe you would meet Hood's army, but would be bushwhacked by all the old men and little boys, and such railroad guards as are still left at home. Hood would probably strike for Nashville, thinking that by going north he could inflict greater damage upon us than we could upon the rebels by going south. If there is any way of getting at Hood's army, I would prefer that, but I must trust to your own judgment. I find I shall not be able to send a force from here to act with you on Savannah. Your movements, therefore, will be independent of mine; at least until the fall of Richmond takes place. I am afraid Thomas, with such lines of road as he has to protect, could not prevent Hood from going north. With Wilson turned loose, with all your cavalry, you will find the rebels put much more on the defensive than heretofore.

U. S. GRANT, Lieutenant-General.

MAJOR-GENERAL W. T. SHERMAN.

KINGSTON, GEORGIA,

October 11—11 A.M.

Hood moved his army from Palmetto Station across by Dallas and Cedartown, and is now on the Coosa River, south of Rome. He threw one corps on my road at Acworth, and I was forced to follow. I hold Atlanta with the 20th corps, and have strong detachments along my line. This reduces my active force to a comparatively small army. We cannot remain here on the defensive. With the twenty-five thousand men, and the bold cavalry he has, he can constantly break my roads. I would infinitely prefer to make a wreck of the road, and of the country from Chattanooga to Atlanta including the latter city—send back all my wounded and worthless, and with my effective army, move through Georgia, smashing things, to the sea. Hood may turn into Tennessee and Kentucky, but I believe he will be forced to follow me. Instead of my being on the defensive, I would be on the offensive; instead of guessing at what he means to do, he would have to guess at my plans. The difference in war is full twenty-five per cent. I can make Savannah, Charleston, or the mouth of the Chattahoochee.

Answer quick, as I know we will not have the telegraph long.

W. T. SHERMAN, Major-General.

LIEUTENANT-GENERAL GRANT.

CITY POINT, VIRGINIA,

October 11, 1864—11.30 P.M.

Your dispatch of to-day received. If you are satisfied the trip to the sea-coast can be made, holding the line of the Tennessee River firmly, you may make it, destroying all the railroad south of Dalton or Chattanooga, as you think best.

U. S. GRANT, Lieutenant-General.

MAJOR-GENERAL W. T. SHERMAN.

It was the original design to hold Atlanta, and by getting through to the coast, with a garrison left on the southern railroads, leading east and west, through Georgia, to effectually sever the east from the west. In other words, cut the would-be Confederacy in two again, as it had been cut once by our gaining possession of the Mississippi River. General Sherman's plan virtually effected this object.

General Sherman commenced at once his preparations for his proposed movement, keeping his army in position in the meantime to watch Hood. Becoming satisfied that Hood had moved westward from Gadsden across Sand Mountain, General Sherman sent the 4th corps, Major-General Stanley commanding, and the 23d corps, Major-General Schofield commanding, back to Chattanooga to report to Major-General Thomas, at Nashville, whom he had placed in command of all the troops of his military division, save the four army corps and cavalry division he designed to move with through Georgia. With the troops thus left at his disposal, there was little doubt that General Thomas could hold the line of the Tennessee, or, in the event Hood should force it, would be able to concentrate and beat him in battle. It was therefore readily consented to that Sherman should start for the sea-coast.

Having concentrated his troops at Atlanta by the 14th of November, he commenced his march, threatening both Augusta and Macon. His coming-out point could not be definitely fixed. Having to gather his subsistence as he marched through the country, it was not impossible that a force inferior to his own might compel him to head for such point as he could reach, instead of such as he might prefer. The blindness of the enemy, however, in ignoring his movement, and sending Hood's army, the only considerable force he had west of Richmond and east of the Mississippi River, northward on an offensive campaign, left the whole country open, and Sherman's route to his own choice.

How that campaign was conducted, how little opposition was met with, the condition of the country through which the armies passed, the capture of Fort McAllister, on the Savannah River, and the occupation of Savannah on the 21st of December, are all clearly set forth in General Sherman's admirable report.

Soon after General Sherman commenced his march from Atlanta, two expeditions, one from Baton Rouge, Louisiana, and one from Vicksburg, Mississippi, were started by General Canby to cut the enemy's lines of communication with Mobile and detain troops in that field. General Foster, commanding Department of the South, also sent an expedition, *via* Broad River, to destroy the railroad between Charleston and Savannah. The expedition from Vicksburg, under command of Brevet Brigadier-General E. D. Osband (colonel 3d

United States colored cavalry), captured, on the 27th of November, and destroyed the Mississippi Central Railroad bridge and trestle-work over Big Black River, near Canton, thirty miles of the road, and two locomotives, besides large amounts of stores. The expedition from Baton Rouge was without favorable results. The expedition from the Department of the South, under the immediate command of Brigadier-General John P. Hatch, consisting of about five thousand men of all arms, including a brigade from the navy, proceeded up Broad River and debarked at Boyd's Neck on the 29th of November, from where it moved to strike the railroad at Grahamsville. At Honey Hill, about three miles from Grahamsville, the enemy was found and attacked in a strongly fortified position, which resulted, after severe fighting, in our repulse with a loss of seven hundred and forty-six in killed, wounded, and missing. During the night General Hatch withdrew. On the 6th of December General Foster obtained a position covering the Charleston and Savannah Railroad, between the Coosawhatchie and Tulifinny rivers.

Hood, instead of following Sherman, continued his move northward, which seemed to me to be leading to his certain doom. At all events, had I had the power to command both armies, I should not have changed the orders under which he seemed to be acting. On the 26th of October, the advance of Hood's army attacked the garrison at Decatur, Alabama, but failing to carry the place, withdrew towards Courtland, and succeeded, in the face of our cavalry, in effecting a lodgment on the north side of the Tennessee River, near Florence. On the 28th, Forrest reached the Tennessee, at Fort Heiman, and captured a gunboat and three transports. On the 2d of November he planted batteries above and below Johnsonville, on the opposite side of the river, isolating three gunboats and eight transports. On the 4th the enemy opened his batteries upon the place, and was replied to from the gunboats and the garrison. The gunboats becoming disabled were set on fire, as also were the transports, to prevent their falling into the hands of the enemy. About a million and a half dollars' worth of stores and property on the levee and in storehouses was consumed by fire. On the 5th the enemy disappeared and crossed to the north side of the Tennessee River, above Johnsonville, moving towards Clifton, and subsequently joined Hood. On the night of the 5th, General Schofield, with the advance of the 23d corps, reached Johnsonville, but finding the enemy gone, was ordered to Pulaski, and put in command of all the troopers there, with instruction to watch the movements of Hood and retard his advance, but not to risk a general engagement until the arrival of General A. J. Smith's command from Missouri, and until General Wilson could get his cavalry remounted.

On the 19th, General Hood continued his advance. General Thomas, retarding him as much as possible, fell back towards Nashville for the purpose of concentrating his command and gaining time for the arrival of reinforcements. The enemy coming up with our main force, commanded by General Schofield, at Franklin, on the 30th, assaulted our works repeatedly during the afternoon until late at night, but were in every instance repulsed. His loss in this battle was one thousand seven hundred and fifty killed, seven hundred and two prisoners, and three thousand eight hundred wounded. Among his losses were six general officers killed, six wounded, and one captured. Our entire loss was two thousand three hundred. This was the first serious opposition the enemy met with, and I am satisfied was the fatal blow to all his expectations. During the night, General Schofield fell back towards Nashville. This left the field to the enemy—not lost by battle, but voluntarily abandoned—so that General Thomas's whole force might be brought together. The enemy followed up and commenced the establishment of his line in front of Nashville on the 2d of December.

As soon as it was ascertained that Hood was crossing the Tennessee River, and that Price was going out of Missouri, General Rosecrans was ordered to send to General Thomas the troops of General A. J. Smith's command, and such other troops as he could spare. The advance of this reinforcement reached Nashville on the 30th of November.

On the morning of the 15th December, General Thomas attacked Hood in position, and, in a battle lasting two days, defeated and drove him from the field in the utmost confusion, leaving in our hand most of his artillery and many thousand prisoners, including four general officers.

Before the battle of Nashville I grew very impatient over, as it appeared to me, the unnecessary delay. This impatience was increased upon learning that the enemy had sent a force of cavalry across the Cumberland into Kentucky. I feared Hood would cross his whole army and give us great trouble there. After urging upon General Thomas the necessity of immediately assuming the offensive, I started West to superintend matters there in person. Reaching Washington City, I received General Thomas's dispatch announcing his attack upon the enemy, and the result as far as the battle had progressed. I was delighted. All fears and apprehensions were dispelled. I am not yet satisfied but that General Thomas, immediately upon the appearance of Hood before Nashville, and before he had time to fortify, should have moved out with his whole force and given him battle, instead of waiting to remount his cavalry, which delayed him until the inclemency of the weather made it impracticable to attack earlier than he did. But his final defeat of Hood was so complete, that it will be accepted as a vindication of that distinguished officer's judgment.

After Hood's defeat at Nashville he retreated, closely pursued by cavalry and infantry, to the Tennessee River, being forced to abandon many pieces of artillery and most of his transportation. On the 28th of December our advanced forces ascertained that he had made good his escape to the south side of the river.

About this time, the rains having set in heavily in Tennessee and North Alabama, making it difficult to move army transportation and artillery, General Thomas stopped the pursuit by his main force at the Tennessee River. A small force of cavalry, under Colonel W. J. Palmer, 15th Pennsylvania Volunteers, continued to follow Hood for some distance, capturing considerable transportation and the enemy's pontoon-bridge. The details of these operations will be found clearly set forth in General Thomas's report.

A cavalry expedition, under Brevet Major-General Grierson, started from Memphis on the 21st of December. On the 25th he surprised and captured Forrest's dismounted camp at Verona, Mississippi, on the Mobile and Ohio Railroad, destroyed the railroad, sixteen cars loaded with wagons and pontoons for Hood's army, four thousand new English carbines, and large amounts of public stores. On the morning of the 28th he attacked and captured a force of the enemy at Egypt, and destroyed a train of fourteen cars; thence turning to the south-west, he struck the Mississippi Central Railroad at Winona, destroyed the factories and large amounts of stores at Bankston, and the machine-shops and public property at Grenada, arriving at Vicksburg January 5th.

During the operations in Middle Tennessee, the enemy, with a force under General Breckinridge, entered East Tennessee. On the 13th of November he attacked General Gillem, near Morristown, capturing his artillery and several hundred prisoners. Gillem, with what was left of his command, retreated to Knoxville. Following up his success, Breckinridge moved to near Knoxville, but withdrew on the 18th, followed by General Ammen. Under the directions of General Thomas, General Stoneman concentrated the commands of Generals Burbridge and Gillem near Bean's Station, to operate against Breckinridge, and destroy or drive him into Virginia—destroy the salt-works at Saltville, and the railroad into Virginia as far as he could go without endangering his command. On the 12th of December he commenced his movement, capturing and dispersing the enemy's forces wherever he met them. On the 16th he struck the enemy, under Vaughn, at Marion, completely routing and pursuing him to Wytheville, capturing all his artillery, trains, and one hundred and ninety-eight prisoners; and destroyed Wytheville, with its stores and supplies, and the extensive lead-works near there. Returning to Marion, he met a force under Breckinridge, consisting, among other troops, of the garrison of Saltville, that had started in pursuit. He at once made arrangements to attack it the next morning; but morning found Breckinridge gone. He then moved directly to Saltville, and destroyed the extensive salt-works at that place, a large amount of stores, and captured eight pieces of artillery. Having thus successfully executed his instructions, he returned General Burbridge to Lexington and General Gillem to Knoxville.

Wilmington, North Carolina, was the most important sea-coast port left to the enemy through which to get supplies from abroad, and send cotton and other products out by blockade-runners, besides being a place of great strategic value. The navy had been making strenuous exertions to seal the harbor of Wilmington, but with only partial effect. The nature of the outlet of Cape Fear River was such, that it required watching for so great a distance that, without possession of the land north of New Inlet, or Fort Fisher, it was impossible for the navy to entirely close the harbor against the entrance of blockade-runners.

To secure the possession of this land required the co-operation of a land force, which I agreed to furnish. Immediately commenced the assemblage in Hampton Roads, under Admiral D. D. Porter, of the most formidable armada ever collected for concentration upon one given point. This necessarily attracted the attention of the enemy, as well as that of the loyal North; and through the imprudence of the public press, and very likely of officers of both branches of service, the exact object of the expedition became a subject of common discussion in the newspapers both North and South. The enemy, thus warned, prepared to meet it. This caused a postponement of the expedition until the later part of November, when, being again called upon by Hon. G. V. Fox, Assistant Secretary of the Navy, I agreed to furnish the men required at once, and went myself, in company with Major-General Butler, to Hampton Roads, where we had a conference with Admiral Porter as to the force required and the time of starting. A force of six thousand five hundred men was regarded as sufficient.

The time of starting was not definitely arranged, but it was thought all would be ready by the 6th of December, if not before. Learning, on the 30th of November, that Bragg had gone to Georgia, taking with him most of the forces about Wilmington, I deemed it of the utmost importance that the expedition should reach its destination before the return of Bragg, and directed General Butler to make all arrangements for the departure of Major-General Weitzel, who had been designated to command the land forces, so that the navy might not be detained one moment.

On the 6th of December, the following instructions were given:

CITY POINT, VIRGINIA, *December 6, 1864.*

GENERAL:—The first object of the expedition under General Weitzel is to close to the enemy the port of Wilmington. If successful in this, the second will be to capture Wilmington itself. There are reasonable grounds to hope for success, if advantage can be taken of the absence of the greater part of the enemy's forces now looking after Sherman in Georgia. The directions you have given for the numbers and equipment of the expedition are all right, except in the unimportant matter of where they embark and the amount of intrenching tools to be taken. The object of the expedition will be gained by effecting a landing on the main land between Cape Fear River and the Atlantic, north of the north entrance to the river. Should such landing be effected while the enemy still holds Fort Fisher and the batteries guarding the entrance to the river, then the troops should intrench themselves, and, by co-operating with the navy, effect the reduction and capture of those places. These in our hands, the navy could enter the harbor, and the port of Wilmington would be sealed. Should Fort Fisher and the point of land on which it is built fall into the hands of our troops immediately on landing, then it will be worth the attempt to capture Wilmington by a forced march and surprise. If time is consumed in gaining the first object of the expedition, the second will become a matter of after consideration.

The details for execution are intrusted to you and the officer immediately in command of the troops.

Should the troops under General Weitzel fail to effect a landing at or near Fort Fisher, they will be returned to the armies operating against Richmond without delay.

U. S. GRANT, Lieutenant-General.

MAJOR-GENERAL B. F. BUTLER.

General Butler commanding the army from which the troops were taken for this enterprise, and the territory within which they were to operate, military courtesy required that all orders and instructions should go through him. They were so sent; but General Weitzel has since officially informed me that he never received the foregoing instructions, nor was he aware of their existence, until he read General Butler's published official report of the Fort Fisher failure, with my indorsement and papers accompanying it. I had no idea of General Butler's accompanying the expedition until the evening before it got off from Bermuda Hundred, and then did not dream but that General Weitzel had received all the instructions, and would be in command. I rather formed the idea that General Butler was actuated by a desire to witness the effect of the explosion of the powder-boat. The expedition was detained several days at Hampton Roads, awaiting the loading of the powder-boat.

The importance of getting the Wilmington expedition off without any delay, with or without the powder-boat, had been urged upon General Butler, and he advised to so notify Admiral Porter.

The expedition finally got off on the 13th of December, and arrived at the place of rendezvous, off New Inlet, near Fort Fisher, on the evening of the 15th. Admiral Porter arrived on the evening of the 18th, having put in at Beaufort to get ammunition for the monitors. The sea becoming rough, making it difficult to land troops, and the supply of water and coal being about exhausted, the transport fleet put back to Beaufort to replenish; this, with the state of the weather, delayed the return to the place of rendezvous until the 24th. The powder-boat was exploded on the morning of the 24th, before the return of General Butler from Beaufort; but it would seem, from the notice taken of it in the Southern newspapers, that the enemy were never enlightened as to the object of the explosion until they were informed by the Northern press.

On the 25th a landing was effected without opposition, and a reconnoissance, under Brevet Brigadier-General Curtis, pushed up towards the fort. But before receiving a full report of the result of this reconnoissance, General Butler, in direct violation of the instructions given, ordered the re-embarkation of the troops and the return of the expedition. The re-embarkation was accomplished by the morning of the 27th.

On the return of the expedition officers and men—among them Brevet Major-General (then Brevet Brigadier-General) N. M. Curtis, First Lieutenant G. W. Ross, 117th Regiment New York Volunteers, First Lieutenant William H. Walling, and Second Lieutenant George Simpson, 142d New York Volunteers—voluntarily reported to me that when recalled they were nearly into the fort, and, in their opinion, it could have been taken without much loss.

Soon after the return of the expedition, I received a dispatch from the Secretary of the Navy, and a letter from Admiral Porter, informing me that the fleet was still off Fort Fisher, and expressing the conviction that, under a proper leader, the place could be taken. The natural supposition with me was, that when the troops abandoned the expedition, the navy would do so also. Finding it had not, however, I answered on the 30th of December, advising Admiral Porter to hold on, and that I would send a force and make another attempt to take the place. This time I selected Brevet Major-General (now Major-General) A. H. Terry to command the expedition. The troops composing it consisted of the same that composed the former, with the addition of a small brigade, numbering about one thousand five hundred, and a small siege train. The latter it was never found necessary to land. I communicated direct to the commander of the expedition the following instructions:

CITY POINT, VIRGINIA, *January* 3, 1865.

GENERAL: The expedition intrusted to your command has been fitted out to renew the attempt to capture Fort Fisher, N. C., and Wilmington ultimately, if the fort falls. You will then proceed with as little delay as possible to the naval fleet lying off Cape Fear River, and report the arrival of yourself and command to Admiral D. D. Porter, commanding North Atlantic Blockading Squadron.

It is exceedingly desirable that the most complete understanding should exist between yourself and the naval commander. I suggest, therefore, that you consult with Admiral Porter freely, and get from him the part to be performed by each branch of the public service, so that there may be unity of action. It would be well to have the whole programme laid down in writing. I have served with Admiral Porter, and know that you can rely on his judgment and his nerve to undertake what he proposes. I would, therefore, defer to him as much as is consistent with your own responsibilities. The first object to be attained is to get a firm position on the spit of land on which Fort Fisher is built, from which you can operate against that fort. You want to look to the practicability of receiving your supplies, and to defending yourself against superior forces sent against you by any of the avenues left open to the enemy. If such a position can be obtained, the siege of Fort Fisher will not be abandoned until its reduction is accomplished, or another plan of campaign is ordered from these headquarters.

My own views are, that if you effect a landing, the navy ought to run a portion of their fleet into Cape Fear River, while the balance of it operates on the outside. Land forces cannot invest Fort Fisher, or cut it off from supplies or reinforcements, while the river is in possession of the enemy.

A siege-train will be loaded on vessels and sent to Fort Monroe, in readiness to be sent to you if required. All other supplies can be drawn from Beaufort as you need them.

Keep the fleet of vessels with you until your position is assured. When you find they can be spared, order them back, or such of them as you can spare, to Fort Monroe, to report for orders.

In case of failure to effect a landing, bring your command back to Beaufort, and report to these headquarters for further instructions. You will not debark at Beaufort until so directed.

General Sheridan has been ordered to send a division of troops to Baltimore and place them on sea-going vessels. These troops will be brought to Fort Monroe and kept there on the vessels until you are heard from. Should you require them, they will be sent to you.

U. S. GRANT, Lieutenant-General.

BREVET MAJOR-GENERAL A. H. TERRY.

Lieutenant-Colonel C. B. Comstock, aide-de-camp (now brevet brigadier-general), who accompanied the former expedition, was assigned, in orders, as chief-engineer to this.

It will be seen that these instructions did not differ materially from those given for the first expedition; and that in neither instance was there an order to assault Fort Fisher. This was a matter left entirely to the discretion of the commanding officer.

The expedition sailed from Fort Monroe on the morning of the 6th, arriving at the rendezvous, off Beaufort, on the 8th, where, owing to the difficulties of the weather, it lay until the morning of the 12th, when it got under way and reached its destination that evening. Under cover of the fleet, the disembarkation of the troops commenced on the morning of the 13th, and by three o'clock P.M. was completed without loss. On the 14th a reconnoissance was pushed to within five hundred yards of Fort Fisher, and a small advance work taken possession of and turned into a defensive line against any attempt that might be made from the fort. This reconnoissance disclosed the fact that the front of the work had been seriously injured by the navy fire. In the afternoon of the 15th the fort was assaulted, and after most desperate fighting was captured, with its entire garrison and armament. Thus was secured, by the combined efforts of the navy and army, one of the most important successes of the war. Our loss was: killed, one hundred and ten; wounded, five hundred and thirty-six. On the 16th and the 17th the enemy abandoned and blew up Fort Caswell and the works on Smith's Island, which were immediately occupied by us. This gave us entire control of the mouth of the Cape Fear River.

At my request, Major-General B. F. Butler was relieved, and Major-General E. O. C. Ord assigned to the Department of Virginia and North Carolina.

The defence of the line of the Tennessee no longer requiring the force which had beaten and nearly destroyed the only army now threatening it, I determined to find other fields of operation for General Thomas's surplus troops—fields from which they would co-operate with other movements. General Thomas was therefore directed to collect all troops, not essential to hold his communications at Eastport, in readiness for orders. On the 7th of January, General Thomas was directed, if he was assured of the departure of Hood south from Corinth, to send General Schofield with his corps east with as little delay as possible. This direction was promptly complied with, and the advance of the corps reached Washington on the 23d of the same month, whence it was sent to Fort Fisher and New Bern. On the 26th he was directed to send General A. J. Smith's command and a division of cavalry to report to General Canby. By the 7th of February the whole force was *en route* for its destination.

The State of North Carolina was constituted into a military department, and General Schofield assigned to command, and placed under the orders of Major-General Sherman. The following instructions were given him:

CITY POINT, VA., *January* 31, 1865.

GENERAL:— ★ ★ ★ Your movements are intended as co-operative with Sherman's through the States of South and North Carolina. The first point to be attained is to secure Wilmington. Goldsboro will then be your objective point, moving either from Wilmington or New Bern, or both, as you deem best. Should you not be able to reach Goldsboro, you will advance on the line or lines of railway connecting that place with the sea-coast—as near to it as you can, building the road behind you. The enterprise under you has two objects: the first is to give General Sherman material aid, if needed, in his march north; the second, to open a base of supplies for him on his line of march. As soon, therefore, as you can determine which of the two points, Wilmington or New Bern, you can best use for throwing supplies from, to the interior, you will commence the accumulation of twenty days' rations and forage for sixty thousand men and twenty thousand animals. You will get of these as many as you can house and protect to such point in the interior as you may be able to occupy. I believe General Palmer has received some instructions direct from General Sherman on the subject of securing supplies for his army. You will learn what steps he has taken, and be governed in your requisitions accordingly. A supply of ordnance stores will also be necessary.

Make all requisitions upon the chiefs of their respective departments in the field with me at City Point. Communicate with me by every opportunity, and should you deem it necessary at any time, send a special boat to Fortress Monroe, from which point you can communicate by telegraph.

The supplies referred to in these instructions are exclusive of those required for your own command.

The movements of the enemy may justify, or even make it your imperative duty, to cut loose from your base, and strike for the interior to aid Sherman. In such case you will act on your own judgment without waiting for instructions. You will report, however, what you purpose doing. The details for carrying out these instructions are necessarily left to you. I would urge, however, if I did not know that you are already fully alive to the importance of it, prompt action. Sherman may be looked for in the neighborhood of Goldsboro any time from the 22d to the 28th of February; this limits your time very materially.

If rolling-stock is not secured in the capture of Wilmington, it can be supplied from Washington. A large force of railroad men have already been sent to Beaufort, and other mechanics will go to Fort Fisher in a day or two. On this point I have informed you by telegraph.

U. S. GRANT, Lieutenant-General.

MAJOR-GENERAL J. M. SCHOFIELD.

Previous to giving these instructions I had visited Fort Fisher, accompanied by General Schofield, for the purpose of seeing for myself the condition of things, and personally conferring with General Terry and Admiral Porter as to what was best to be done.

Anticipating the arrival of General Sherman at Savannah—his army entirely foot-loose, Hood being then before Nashville, Tennessee, the Southern railroads destroyed, so that it would take several months to re-establish a through line from west to east, and regarding the capture of Lee's army as the most important operation towards closing the rebellion—I sent orders to General Sherman on the 6th of December, that after establishing a base on the sea-coast, with necessary garrison, to include all his artillery and cavalry, to come by water to City Point with the balance of his command.

On the 18th of December, having received information of the defeat and utter rout of Hood's army by General Thomas, and that, owing to the great difficulty of procuring ocean transportation, it would take over two months to transport Sherman's army, and doubting whether he might not contribute as much towards the desired result by operating from where he was, I wrote to him to that effect, and asked him for his views as to what would be best to do. A few days after this I received a communication from General Sherman, of date 16th December, acknowledging the receipt of my order of the 6th, and informing me of his preparations to carry it into effect as soon as he could get transportation. Also that he had expected, upon reducing Savannah, instantly to march to Columbia, South Carolina, thence to Raleigh, and thence to report to me; but that this would consume about six weeks' time after the fall of Savannah, whereas by sea he could probably reach me by the middle of January. The confidence he manifested in this letter of being able to march up and join me pleased me, and, without waiting for a reply to my letter of the 18th, I directed him, on the 28th of December, to make preparations to start, as he proposed, without delay, to break up the railroads in North and South Carolina, and join the armies operating against Richmond as soon as he could.

On the 21st of January I informed General Sherman that I had ordered the 23d corps, Major-General Schofield commanding, east; that it numbered about twenty-one thousand men; that we had at Fort Fisher, about eight thousand men; at New Bern, about four thousand; that if Wilmington was captured, General Schofield would go there; if not, he would be sent to New Bern; that, in either event, all the surplus force at both points would move to the interior towards Goldsboro, in co-operation with his movement; that from either point railroad communication could be run out; and that all these troops would be subject to his orders as he came into communication with them.

In obedience to his instructions, General Schofield proceeded to reduce Wilmington, North Carolina, in co-operation with the navy under Admiral Porter, moving his forces up both sides of the Cape Fear River. Fort Anderson, the enemy's main defence on the west bank of the river, was occupied on the morning of the 19th, the enemy having evacuated it after our appearance before it.

After fighting on 20th and 21st, our troops entered Wilmington on the morning of the 22d, the enemy having retreated towards Goldsboro during the night. Preparations were at once made for a movement on Goldsboro in two columns—one from Wilmington, and the other from New Bern—and to repair the railroad leading there from each place, as well as to supply General Sherman by Cape Fear River, towards Fayetteville, if it became necessary. The column from New Bern was attacked on the 8th of March, at Wise's Forks, and driven back with the loss of several hundred prisoners. On the 11th the enemy renewed his attack upon our intrenched position, but was repulsed with severe loss, and fell back during the night. On the 14th the Neuse River was crossed and Kinston occupied, and on the 21st

Goldsboro was entered. The column from Wilmington reached Cox's Bridge, on the Neuse River, ten miles above Goldsboro, on the 22d.

By the 1st of February, General Sherman's whole army was in motion from Savannah. He captured Columbia, South Carolina, on the 17th; thence moved on Goldsboro, North Carolina, *via* Fayetteville, reaching the latter place on the 12th of March, opening up communication with General Schofield by way of Cape Fear River. On the 15th he resumed his march on Goldsboro. He met a force of the enemy at Averysboro, and after a severe fight defeated and compelled it to retreat. Our loss in this engagement was about six hundred. The enemy's loss was much greater. On the 18th the combined forces of the enemy, under Joe Johnston, attacked his advance at Bentonville, capturing three guns and driving it back upon the main body. General Slocum, who was in the advance, ascertaining that the whole of Johnston's army was in the front, arranged his troops on the defensive, intrenched himself and awaited reinforcements, which were pushed forward. On the night of the 21st the enemy retreated to Smithfield, leaving his dead and wounded in our hands. From there Sherman continued to Goldsboro, which place had been occupied by General Schofield on the 21st (crossing the Neuse River ten miles above there, at Cox's Bridge, where General Terry had got possession and thrown a pontoon-bridge on the 22d), thus forming a junction with the columns from New Bern and Wilmington.

Among the important fruits of this campaign was the fall of Charleston, South Carolina. It was evacuated by the enemy on the night of the 17th of February, and occupied by our forces on the 18th.

On the morning of the 31st of January, General Thomas was directed to send a cavalry expedition, under General Stoneman, from East Tennessee, to penetrate South Carolina well down towards Columbia, to destroy the railroads and military resources of the country, and return, if he was able, to East Tennessee by way of Salisbury, North Carolina, releasing our prisoners there, if possible. Of the feasibility of this latter, however, General Stoneman was to judge. Sherman's movements, I had no doubt, would attract the attention of all the force the enemy could collect, and facilitate the execution of this. General Stoneman was so late in making his start on this expedition (and Sherman having passed out of the State of South Carolina), on the 27th of February I directed General Thomas to change his course, and order him to repeat his raid of last fall, destroying the railroad towards Lynchburg as far as he could. This would keep him between our garrisons in East Tennessee and the enemy. I regarded it not impossible that in the event of the enemy being driven from Richmond, he might fall back to Lynchburg and attempt a raid north through East Tennessee. On the 14th of February the following communication was sent to General Thomas:

CITY POINT, VA., *February* 14, 1865.

General Canby is preparing a movement from Mobile Bay against Mobile and the interior of Alabama. His force will consist of about twenty thousand men, besides A. J. Smith's command. The cavalry you have sent to Canby will be debarked at Vicksburg. It, with the available cavalry already in that section, will move from there eastward, in co-operation. Hood's army has been terribly reduced by the severe punishment you gave it in Tennessee, by desertion consequent upon their defeat, and now by the withdrawal of many of them to oppose Sherman. (I take it a large portion of the infantry has been so withdrawn. It is so asserted in the Richmond papers, and a member of the rebel Congress said a few days since in a speech, that one-half of it had been brought to South Carolina to oppose Sherman.) This being true, or even if it is not true, Canby's movement will attract all the attention of the enemy, and leave the advance from your standpoint easy. I think it advisable, therefore, that you prepare as much of a cavalry force as you can spare, and hold it in readiness to go south. The object would be threefold: first, to attract as much of the enemy's force as possible, to insure success to Canby; second, to destroy the enemy's line of communications and military resources; third, to destroy or capture their forces brought into the field. Tuscaloosa and Selma would probably be the points to direct the expedition against. This, however, would not be so important as the mere fact of penetrating deep into Alabama. Discretion should be left to the officer commanding the expedition to go where, according to the information he may receive, he will best secure the objects named above.

Now that your force has been so much depleted, I do not know what number of men you can put into the field. If not more than five thousand men, however, all cavalry, I think it will be sufficient. It is not desirable that you should start this expedition until the one leaving Vicksburg has been three or four days out, or even a week. I do not know when it will start, but will inform you by telegraph as soon as I learn. If you should hear through other sources before hearing from me, you can act on the information received.

To insure success your cavalry should go with as little wagon-train as possible, relying upon the country for supplies. I would also reduce the number of guns to a battery, or the number of batteries, and put the extra teams to the guns taken. No guns or caissons should be taken with less than eight horses.

Please inform me by telegraph, on receipt of this, what force you think you will be able to send under these directions.

U. S. GRANT, Lieutenant-General.
MAJOR-GENERAL G. H. THOMAS.

On the 15th, he was directed to start the expedition as soon after the 20th as he could get it off.

I deemed it of the utmost importance, before a general movement of the armies operating against Richmond, that all communications with the city, north of James River, should be cut off. The enemy having withdrawn the bulk of his force from the Shenandoah Valley and sent it south, or replaced troops sent from Richmond, and desiring to reinforce Sherman, if practicable, whose cavalry was greatly inferior in numbers to that of the enemy, I determined to make a move from the Shenandoah, which, if successful, would accomplish the first at least, and possibly the latter of these objects. I therefore telegraphed General Sheridan as follows:

CITY POINT, VA., *February* 20, 1865—1 P.M.

GENERAL:—As soon as it is possible to travel, I think you will have no difficulty about reaching Lynchburg with a cavalry force alone. From there you could destroy the railroad and canal in every direction, so as to be of no further use to the rebellion. Sufficient cavalry should be left behind to look after Mosby's gang. From Lynchburg, if information you might get there would justify it, you will strike south, heading the streams in Virginia to the westward of Danville, and push on and join General Sherman. This additional raid, with one now about starting from East Tennessee under Stoneman, numbering four or five thousand cavalry, one from Vicksburg, numbering seven or eight thousand cavalry, one from Eastport, Mississippi, ten thousand cavalry, Canby from Mobile Bay, with about thirty-eight thousand mixed troops, these three latter pushing for Tuscaloosa, Selma, and Montgomery, and Sherman with a large army eating out the vitals of South Carolina, is all that will be wanted to leave nothing for the rebellion to stand upon. I would advise you to overcome great obstacles to accomplish this. Charleston was evacuated on Tuesday last.

U. S. GRANT, Lieutenant-General.

MAJOR-GENERAL P. H. SHERIDAN.

On the 25th I received a dispatch from General Sheridan, inquiring where Sherman was aiming for, and if I could give him definite information as to the points he might be expected to move on, this side of Charlotte, North Carolina. In answer, the following telegram was sent him:

CITY POINT, VA., *February* 25, 1865.

GENERAL:—Sherman's movements will depend on the amount of opposition he meets with from the enemy. If strongly opposed, he may possibly have to fall back to Georgetown, S. C., and fit out for a new start. I think, however, all danger for the necessity of going to that point has passed. I believe he has passed Charlotte. He may take Fayetteville on his way to Goldsboro. If you reach Lynchburg, you will have to be guided in your after movements by the information you obtain. Before you could possibly reach Sherman, I think you would find him moving from Goldsboro towards Raleigh, or engaging the enemy strongly posted at one or the other of these places, with railroad communications opened from his army to Wilmington or New Bern.

U. S. GRANT, Lieutenant-General.

MAJOR-GENERAL P. H. SHERIDAN.

General Sheridan moved from Winchester on the 27th of February, with two divisions of cavalry, numbering about five thousand each. On the 1st of March he secured the bridge, which the enemy attempted to destroy, across the middle fork of the Shenandoah, at Mount Crawford, and entered Staunton on the 2d, the enemy having retreated to Waynesboro. Thence he pushed on to Waynesboro, where he found the enemy in force in an intrenched position, under General Early. Without stopping to make a reconnoissance, an immediate attack was made, the position was carried, and sixteen hundred prisoners, eleven pieces of artillery, with horses and caissons complete, two hundred wagons and teams loaded with subsistence, and seventeen battle-flags, were captured. The prisoners, under an escort of fifteen hundred men, were sent back to Winchester. Thence he marched on Charlottesville, destroying effectually the railroad and bridges as he went, which place he reached on the 3d. Here he remained two days, destroying the railroad towards Richmond and Lynchburg, including the large iron bridges over the north and south forks of the Rivanna River and awaited the arrival of his trains. This necessary delay caused him to abandon the idea of capturing Lynchburg. On the morning of the 6th, dividing his force into two columns, he sent one to Scottsville, whence it marched up the James River Canal to New Market, destroying every lock, and in many places the bank of the canal. From here a force was pushed out from this column to Duiguidsville, to obtain possession of the bridge across the James River at that place, but failed. The enemy burned it on our approach. The enemy also burned the bridge across the river at Hardwicksville. The other column moved down the railroad towards Lynchburg, destroying it as far as Amherst Court House, sixteen miles from Lynchburg; thence across the country, uniting with the column at New Market. The river being very high, his pontoons would not reach across it; and the enemy having destroyed the bridges by which he had hoped to cross the river and get on the South Side Railroad about Farmville, and destroy it to Appomattox Court House, the only thing left for him was to return to Winchester or strike a base at the White House. Fortunately, he chose the latter. From New Market he took up his line of march, following the canal towards Richmond, destroying every lock upon it and cutting the banks wherever practicable, to a point eight miles east of Goochland, concentrating the whole force at Columbia on the 10th. Here he rested one day, and sent through by scouts information of his whereabouts and purposes, and a request for supplies to meet him at White House, which reached me on the night of the 12th. An infantry force was immediately sent to get possession of White House, and supplies were forwarded. Moving from Columbia in a direction to threaten Richmond, to near Ashland Station, he crossed the Annas, and after having destroyed all the bridges and many miles of the railroad, proceeded down the north bank of the Pamunkey to White House, which place he reached on the 19th.

Previous to this the following communication was sent to General Thomas:

CITY POINT, VIRGINIA,
March 7, 1865—9.30 A.M.

GENERAL:—I think it will be advisable now for you to repair the railroad in East Tennessee, and throw a good force up to Bull's Gap and fortify there.

Supplies at Knoxville could always be got forward as required. With Bull's Gap fortified, you can occupy as outposts about all of East Tennessee, and be prepared, if it should be required of you in the spring, to make a campaign towards Lynchburg, or into North Carolina. I do not think Stoneman should break the road until he gets into Virginia, unless it should be to cut off rolling-stock that may be caught west of that.

U. S. GRANT, Lieutenant-General.
MAJOR-GENERAL G. H. THOMAS.

Thus it will be seen that in March, 1865, General Canby was moving an adequate force against Mobile and the army defending it under General Dick Taylor; Thomas was push-ing out two large and well-appointed cavalry expeditions—one from Middle Tennessee under Brevet Major-General Wilson against the enemy's vital points in Alabama, the other from East Tennessee, under Major-General Stoneman, towards Lynchburg—and assem-bling the remainder of his available forces, preparatory to commence offensive operations from East Tennessee; General Sheridan's cavalry was at White House; the armies of the Potomac and James were confronting the enemy, under Lee, in his defences of Richmond and Petersburg; General Sherman with his armies, reinforced by that of General Schofield, was at Goldsboro; General Pope was making preparations for a spring campaign against the enemy under Kirby Smith and Price, west of the Mississippi; and General Hancock was concentrating a force in the vicinity of Winchester, Virginia, to guard against invasion or to operate offensively, as might prove necessary.

After the long march by General Sheridan's cavalry over winter roads, it was necessary to rest and refit at White House. At this time the greatest source of uneasiness to me was the fear that the enemy would leave his strong lines about Petersburg and Richmond for the purpose of uniting with Johnston, and before he was driven from them by battle, or I was prepared to make an effectual pursuit. On the 24th of March, General Sheridan moved from White House, crossed the James River at Jones's Landing, and formed a junction with the Army of the Potomac in front of Petersburg on the 27th. During this move, General Ord sent forces to cover the crossings of the Chickahominy.

On the 24th of March the following instructions for a general movement of the armies operating against Richmond were issued:

CITY POINT, VIRGINIA,
March 24, 1865.

GENERAL: On the 29th instant the armies operating against Richmond will be moved by our left, for the double purpose of turning the enemy out of his present position around Petersburg, and to insure the success of the cavalry under General Sheridan, which will start at the same time, in its efforts to reach and destroy the South Side and Danville railroads. Two corps of the Army of the Potomac will be moved at first in two columns, taking the two roads crossing Hatcher's Run, nearest where the present line held by us strikes that stream, both moving towards Dinwiddie Court House.

The cavalry under General Sheridan, joined by the division now under General Davies, will move at the same time by the Weldon Road and the Jerusalem Plank Road, turning west from the latter before crossing the Nottoway, and west with the whole column before reaching Stony Creek. General Sheridan will then move independently, under other instructions which will be given him. All dismounted cavalry belonging to the Army of the Potomac, and the dismounted cavalry from the Middle Military Division not required for guarding property belonging to their arm of service, will report to Brigadier-General Benham, to be added to the defences of City Point. Major-General Parke will be left in command of all the army left for holding the lines about Petersburg and City Point, subject of course to orders from the commander of the Army of the Potomac. The 9th army corps will be left intact, to hold the present line of works so long as the whole line now occupied by us is held. If, however, the troops to the left of the 9th corps are withdrawn, then the left of the corps may be thrown back so as to occupy the position held by the army prior to the capture of the Weldon Road. All troops to the left of the 9th corps will be held in readiness to move at the shortest notice by such route as may be designated when the order is given.

General Ord will detach three divisions, two white and one colored, or so much of them as he can, and hold his present lines, and march for the present left of the Army of the Potomac. In the absence of further orders, or until further orders are given, the white divisions will follow the left column of the Army of the Potomac, and the colored division the right column. During the movement Major-General Weitzel will be left in command of all the forces remaining behind from the Army of the James.

The movement of troops from the Army of the James will commence on the night of the 27th instant. General Ord will leave behind the minimum number of cavalry necessary for picket duty, in the absence of the main army. A cavalry expedition, from General Ord's command, will also be started from Suffolk, to leave there on Saturday, the 1st of April, under Colonel Sumner, for the purpose of cutting the railroad about Hicksford. This, if accomplished, will have to be a surprise, and therefore from three to five hundred men will be sufficient. They should, however, be supported by all the infantry that can be spared from Norfolk and Portsmouth, as far out as to where the cavalry crosses the Blackwater. The crossing should probably be at Uniten. Should Colonel Sumner succeed in reaching the Weldon Road, he will be instructed to do all the damage possible to the triangle of roads between Hicksford, Weldon, and Gaston. The railroad bridge at Weldon being fitted up for the passage of carriages, it might be practicable to destroy any accumulation of supplies the enemy may have collected south of the Roanoke. All the troops will move with four days' rations in haversacks and eight days' in wagons. To avoid as much hauling as possible, and to give the Army of the James the same number of days' supplies with the Army of the Potomac, General Ord will direct his commissary and quartermaster to have sufficient supplies delivered at the terminus of the road to fill up in passing. Sixty rounds of ammunition per man will be taken in wagons, and as much grain as the transportation on hand will carry, after taking the specified amount of other supplies. The densely wooded country in which the army has to operate making the use of much artillery impracticable, the amount taken with the army will be reduced to six or eight guns to each division, at the option of the army commanders.

All necessary preparations for carrying these directions into operation may be commenced at once. The reserves of the 9th corps should be massed as much as possible. While I would not now order an unconditional attack on the enemy's line by them, they should be ready and should make the attack if the enemy weakens his line in their front, without waiting for orders. In case they carry the line, then the whole of the 9th corps could follow up so as to join or co-operate with the balance of the army. To prepare for this, the 9th corps will have rations issued to them, same as the balance of the army. General Weitzel will keep vigilant watch upon his front, and if found at all practicable to break through at any point, he will do so. A success north of the James should be followed up with great promptness. An attack will not be feasible unless it is found that the enemy has detached largely. In that case it may be regarded as evident that the enemy are relying upon their local reserves principally for the defence of Richmond. Preparations may be made for abandoning all the line north of the James, except inclosed works—only to be abandoned, however, after a break is made in the lines of the enemy.

By these instructions a large part of the armies operating against Richmond is left behind. The enemy, knowing this, may, as an only chance, strip their lines to the merest skeleton, in the hope of advantage not being taken of it, while they hurl everything against the moving column, and return. It cannot be impressed too strongly upon commanders of troops left in the trenches not to allow this to occur without taking advantage of it. The very fact of the enemy coming out to attack, if he does so, might be regarded as almost conclusive evidence of such a weakening of his lines. I would have it particularly enjoined upon corps commanders that, in case of an attack from the enemy, those not attacked are not to wait for orders from the commanding officer of the army to which they belong, but that they will move promptly, and notify the commander of their action. I would also enjoin the same action on the part of division commanders when other parts of their corps are engaged. In like manner, I would urge the importance of following up a repulse of the enemy.

U. S. GRANT, Lieutenant-General.

MAJOR-GENERALS MEADE, ORD, and SHERIDAN.

Early on the morning of the 25th the enemy assaulted our lines in front of the 9th corps (which held from the Appomattox River towards our left), and carried Fort Stedman, and a part of the line to the right and left of it, established themselves and turned the guns of the fort against us; but our troops on either flank held their ground until the reserves were brought up, when the enemy was driven back with a heavy loss in killed and wounded, and one thousand nine hundred prisoners. Our loss was sixty-eight killed, three hundred and thirty-seven wounded, and five hundred and six missing. General Meade at once ordered the other corps to advance and feel the enemy in their respective fronts. Pushing forward, they captured and held the enemy's strongly intrenched picket-line in front of the 2d and 6th corps, and eight hundred and thirty-four prisoners. The enemy made desperate attempts to retake this line, but without success. Our loss in front of these was fifty-two killed, eight hundred and sixty-four wounded, and two hundred and seven missing. The enemy's loss in killed and wounded was far greater.

General Sherman having got his troops all quietly in camp about Goldsboro, and his preparations for furnishing supplies to them perfected, visited me at City Point on the 27th of March, and stated that he would be ready to move, as he had previously written me, by the 10th of April, fully equipped and rationed for twenty days, if it should become necessary to bring his command to bear against Lee's army, in co-operation with our forces in front of Richmond and Petersburg. General Sherman proposed in this movement to threaten Raleigh, and then, by turning suddenly to the right, reach the Roanoke at Gaston or there-abouts, whence he could move on to the Richmond and Danville Railroad, striking it in the vicinity of Burkesville, or join the armies operating against Richmond, as might be deemed best. This plan he was directed to carry into execution, if he received no further directions in the meantime. I explained to him the movement I had ordered to commence on the 29th of March. That if it should not prove as entirely successful as I hoped, I would cut the cavalry loose to destroy the Danville and South Side railroads, and thus deprive the enemy of further supplies, and also to prevent the rapid concentration of Lee's and Johnston's armies.

I had spent days of anxiety lest each morning should bring the report that the enemy had retreated the night before. I was firmly convinced that Sherman's crossing the Roanoke would be the signal for Lee to leave. With Johnston and him combined, a long, tedious, and expensive campaign, consuming most of the summer, might become necessary. By moving out I would put the army in better condition for pursuit, and would at least, by the destruc-tion of the Danville Road, retard the concentration of the two armies of Lee and Johnston, and cause the enemy to abandon much material that he might otherwise save. I therefore determined not to delay the movement ordered.

On the night of the 27th, Major-General Ord, with two divisions of the 24th corps, Major-General Gibbon commanding, and one division of the 25th corps, Brigadier-General Birney commanding, and Mackenzie's cavalry, took up his line of march in pursuance of the foregoing instructions, and reached the position assigned him near Hatcher's Run on the morning of the 29th. On the 28th the following instructions were given to General Sheridan:

CITY POINT, VA., *March* 28, 1865.

GENERAL:—The 5th army corps will move by the Vaughn Road at three A.M. to-morrow morning. The 2d moves at about nine A.M., having but about three miles to march to reach the point designated for it to take on the right of the 5th corps, after the latter reaching Dinwiddie Court House. Move your cavalry at as early an hour as you can, and without being confined to any particular road or roads. You may go out by the nearest roads in rear of the 5th corps, pass by its left, and passing near to or through Dinwiddie, reach the right and rear of the enemy as soon as you can. It is not the intention to attack the enemy in his intrenched position, but to force him out, if possible. Should he come out and attack us, or get himself where he can be attacked, move in with your entire force in your own way, and with the full reliance that the army will engage or follow, as circumstances will dictate. I shall be on the field, and will probably be able to communicate with you. Should I not do so, and you find that the enemy keeps within his main intrenched line, you may cut loose and push for the Danville Road. If you find it practicable, I would like you to cross the South Side Road, between Petersburg and Burkesville, and destroy it to some extent. I would not advise much detention, however, until you reach the Danville Road, which I would like you to strike as near to the Appomattox as possible. Make your destruction on that road as complete as possible. You can then pass on to the South Side Road, west of Burkesville, and destroy that in like manner.

After having accomplished the destruction of the two railroads, which are now the only avenues of supply to Lee's army, you may return to this army, selecting your road further south, or you may go on into North Carolina and join General Sherman. Should you select the latter course, get the information to me as early as possible, so that I may send orders to meet you at Goldsboro.

U. S. GRANT, Lieutenant-General.

MAJOR-GENERAL P. H. SHERIDAN.

On the morning of the 29th the movement commenced. At night the cavalry was at Dinwiddie Court House, and the left of our infantry line extended to the Quaker Road, near its intersection with the Boydton Plank Road. The position of the troops from left to right was as follows: Sheridan, Warren, Humphreys, Ord, Wright, Parke.

Everything looked favorable to the defeat of the enemy and the capture of Petersburg and Richmond, if the proper effort was made. I therefore addressed the following communication to General Sheridan, having previously informed him verbally not to cut loose for the raid contemplated in his orders until he received notice from me to do so:

GRAVELLY CREEK, *March* 29, 1865.

GENERAL:—Our line is now unbroken from the Appomattox to Dinwiddie. We are all ready, however, to give up all, from the Jerusalem Plank

Road to Hatcher's Run, whenever the forces can be used advantageously. After getting into line south of Hatcher's, we pushed forward to find the enemy's position. General Griffin was attacked near where the Quaker Road intersects the Boydton Road, but repulsed it easily, capturing about one hundred men. Humphreys reached Dabney's Mill, and was pushing on when last heard from.

I now feel like ending the matter, if it is possible to do so, before going back. I do not want you, therefore, to cut loose and go after the enemy's roads at present. In the morning push around the enemy, if you can, and get on to his right rear. The movements of the enemy's cavalry may, of course, modify your action. We will act all together as one army here, until it is seen what can be done with the enemy. The signal-officer at Cobb's Hill reported, at half-past eleven A.M., that a cavalry column had passed that point from Richmond towards Petersburg, taking forty minutes to pass.

U. S. GRANT, Lieutenant-General.

MAJOR-GENERAL P. H. SHERIDAN.

From the night of the 29th to the morning of the 31st the rain fell in such torrents as to make it impossible to move a wheeled vehicle, except as corduroy roads were laid in front of them. During the 30th, Sheridan advanced from Dinwiddie Court House towards Five Forks, where he found the enemy in full force. General Warren advanced and extended his line across the Boydton Plank Road to near the White Oak Road, with a view of getting across the latter; but, finding the enemy strong in his front and extending beyond his left, was directed to hold on where he was, and fortify. General Humphreys drove the enemy from his front into his main line on the Hatcher, near Burgess's Mills. Generals Ord, Wright, and Parke made examinations in their fronts to determine the feasibility of an assault on the enemy's lines. The two latter reported favorably. The enemy confronting us as he did, at every point from Richmond to our extreme left, I conceived his lines must be weakly held, and could be penetrated if my estimate of his forces was correct. I determined, therefore, to extend our line no farther, but to reinforce General Sheridan with a corps of infantry, and thus enable him to cut loose and turn the enemy's right flank, and with the other corps assault the enemy's lines. The result of the offensive effort of the enemy the week before, when he assaulted Fort Stedman, particularly favored this. The enemy's intrenched picket-line captured by us at that time threw the lines occupied by the belligerents so close together at some points that it was but a moment's run from one to the other. Preparations were at once made to relieve General Humphreys's corps, to report to General Sheridan; but the condition of the roads prevented immediate movement. On the morning of the 31st, General Warren reported favorably to getting possession of the White Oak Road, and was directed to do so. To accomplish this, he moved with one division, instead of his whole corps, which was attacked by the enemy in superior force and driven back on the 2d division before it had time to form, and it, in turn, forced back upon the 3d division, when the enemy was checked. A division of the 2d corps was immediately sent to his support, the enemy driven back with heavy loss, and possession of the White Oak Road gained. Sheridan advanced, and with a portion of his cavalry got possession of the Five Forks; but the enemy, after the affair with the 5th corps, reinforced the rebel cavalry, defending that point with infantry, and forced him back towards Dinwiddie Court House. Here General Sheridan displayed great generalship. Instead of retreating with his whole command on the main army, to tell the story of superior forces encountered, he deployed his cavalry on foot, leaving only mounted men enough to take charge of the horses. This compelled the enemy to deploy over a vast extent of wooded and broken country, and made his progress slow. At this juncture he dispatched to me what had taken place, and that he was dropping back slowly on Dinwiddie Court House. General Mackenzie's cavalry and one division of the 5th corps were immediately ordered to his assistance. Soon after receiving a report from General Meade that Humphreys could hold our position on the Boydton Road, and that the other two divisions of the 5th corps could go to Sheridan, they were so ordered at once. Thus the operations of the day necessitated the sending of Warren, because of his accessibility, instead of Humphreys, as was intended, and precipitated intended movements. On the morning of the 1st of April, General Sheridan, reinforced by General Warren, drove the enemy back on Five Forks, where, late in the evening, he assaulted and carried his strongly fortified position, capturing all his artillery and between five and six thousand prisoners.

About the close of this battle, Brevet Major-General Charles Griffin relieved Major-General Warren in command of the 5th corps. The report of this reached me after nightfall. Some apprehensions filled my mind lest the enemy might desert his lines during the night, and by falling upon General Sheridan before assistance could reach him, drive him from his position and open the way for retreat. To guard against this, General Miles's division of Humphreys's corps was sent to reinforce him, and a bombardment was commenced and kept up until four o'clock in the morning (April 2), when an assault was ordered on the enemy's lines. General Wright penetrated the lines with his whole corps, sweeping everything before him, and to his left towards Hatcher's Run, capturing many guns and several thousand prisoners. He was closely followed by two divisions of General Ord's command, until he met the other division of General Ord's that had succeeded in forcing the enemy's lines near Hatcher's Run. Generals Wright and Ord immediately swung to the right, and closed all of the enemy on that side of them in Petersburg, while General Humphreys pushed forward with two divisions and joined General Wright on the left. General Parke succeeded in carrying the enemy's main line, capturing guns and prisoners, but was unable to carry his inner line. General Sheridan being advised of the condition of affairs, returned General Miles to his proper command. On reaching the enemy's lines immediately surrounding Petersburg, a portion of General Gibbon's corps, by a most gallant charge, captured two strong inclosed works—the most salient and commanding south of Petersburg—thus materially shortening the line of investment necessary for taking in the city. The enemy south of Hatcher's Run retreated westward to Sutherland's Station, where they were overtaken by Miles's division. A severe engagement ensued, and lasted until both his right and left flanks were threatened by the approach of General Sheridan, who was moving from Ford's Station towards Petersburg, and a division sent by General Meade from the front of Petersburg, when he broke in the utmost confusion, leaving in our hands his guns and many prisoners. This force retreated by the main road along the Appomattox River. During the night of the 2d the enemy evacuated Petersburg and Richmond, and retreated towards Danville. On the morning of the 3d pursuit was commenced. General Sheridan pushed for the Danville Road, keeping near the Appomattox, followed by General Meade with the 2d and 6th corps, while General Ord moved for Burkesville, along the South Side Road; the 9th corps stretched along that road behind him. On the 4th, General Sheridan struck the Danville Road near Jetersville, where he learned that Lee was at Amelia Court House. He immediately intrenched himself and awaited the arrival of General Meade, who reached there the next day. General Ord reached Burkesville on the evening of the 5th.

On the morning of the 5th, I addressed Major-General Sherman the following communication:

> WILSON'S STATION, *April* 5, 1865.
>
> GENERAL: All indications now are that Lee will attempt to reach Danville with the remnant of his force. Sheridan, who was up with him last night, reports all that is left, horse, foot, and dragoons, at twenty thousand, much demoralized. We hope to reduce this number one-half. I shall push on to Burkesville, and if a stand is made at Danville, will in a very few days go there. If you can possibly do so, push on from where you are, and let us see if we cannot finish the job with Lee's and Johnston's armies. Whether it will be better for you to strike for Greensboro, or nearer to Danville, you will be better able to judge when you receive this. Rebel armies now are the only strategic points to strike at.
>
> U. S. GRANT, Lieutenant-General.
>
> MAJOR-GENERAL W. T. SHERMAN.

On the morning of the 6th, it was found that General Lee was moving west of Jetersville, towards Danville. General Sheridan moved with his cavalry (the 5th corps having been returned to General Meade on his reaching Jetersville) to strike his flank, followed by the 6th corps, while the 2d and 5th corps pressed hard after, forcing him to abandon several hundred wagons and several pieces of artillery. General Ord advanced from Burkesville towards Farmville, sending two regiments of infantry and a squadron of cavalry, under Brevet Brigadier-General Theodore Read, to reach and destroy the bridges. This advance met the head of Lee's column near Farmville, which it heroically attacked and detained until General Read was killed and his small force overpowered. This caused a delay in the enemy's movements, and enabled General Ord to get well up with the remainder of his force, on meeting which, the enemy immediately intrenched himself. In the afternoon, General Sheridan struck the enemy south of Sailors' Creek, captured sixteen pieces of artillery and about four hundred wagons, and detained him until the 6th corps got up, when a general attack of infantry and cavalry was made, which resulted in the capture of six or seven thousand prisoners, among whom were many general officers. The movements of the 2d corps and General Ord's command contributed greatly to the day's success.

On the morning of the 7th the pursuit was renewed, the cavalry, except one division, and the 5th corps moving by Prince Edward's Court House; the 6th corps, General Ord's command, and one division of cavalry, on Farmville; and the 2d corps by the High Bridge Road. It was soon found that the enemy had crossed to the north side of the Appomattox; but so close was the pursuit, that the 2d corps got possession of the common bridge at High Bridge before the enemy could destroy it, and immediately crossed over. The 6th corps and a division of cavalry crossed at Farmville to its support.

Feeling now that General Lee's chance of escape was utterly hopeless, I addressed him the following communication from Farmville:

April 7, 1865.

GENERAL:—The result of the last week must convince you of the hopelessness of further resistance on the part of the Army of Northern Virginia in this struggle. I feel that it is so, and regard it as my duty to shift from myself the responsibility of any further effusion of blood, by asking of you the surrender of that portion of the Confederate States army known as the Army of Northern Virginia.

U. S. GRANT, Lieutenant-General.

GENERAL R. E. LEE.

Early on the morning of the 8th, before leaving, I received at Farmville the following:

April 7, 1865.

GENERAL:—I have received your note of this date. Though not entertaining the opinion you express on the hopelessness of further resistance on the part of the Army of Northern Virginia, I reciprocate your desire to avoid useless effusion of blood, and therefore, before considering your proposition, ask the terms you will offer on condition of its surrender.

R. E. LEE, General.

LIEUTENANT-GENERAL U. S. GRANT.

To this I immediately replied:

April 8, 1865.

GENERAL:—Your note of last evening, in reply to mine of same date, asking the condition on which I will accept the surrender of the Army of Northern Virginia, is just received. In reply, I would say, that *peace* being my great desire, there is but one condition I would insist upon—namely, That the men and officers surrendered shall be disqualified for taking up arms again against the Government of the United States until properly exchanged. I will meet you, or will designate officers to meet any officers you may name for the same purpose, at any point agreeable to you, for the purpose of arranging definitely the terms upon which the surrender of the Army of Northern Virginia will be received.

U. S. GRANT, Lieutenant-General.

GENERAL R. E. LEE.

Early on the morning of the 8th the pursuit was resumed. General Meade followed north of the Appomattox, and General Sheridan, with all the cavalry, pushed straight for Appomattox Station, followed by General Ord's command and the 5th corps. During the day General Meade's advance had considerable fighting with the enemy's rear-guard, but was unable to bring on a general engagement. Late in the evening General Sheridan struck the railroad at Appomattox Station, drove the enemy from there, and captured twenty-five pieces of artillery, a hospital-train, and four trains of cars loaded with supplies for Lee's army. During this day I accompanied General Meade's column, and about midnight received the following communication from General Lee:

April 8, 1865.

GENERAL:—I received, at a late hour, your note of to-day. In mine of yesterday I did not intend to propose the surrender of the Army of Northern Virginia, but to ask the terms of your proposition. To be frank, I do not think the emergency has arisen to call for the surrender of this army; but as the restoration of peace should be the sole object of all, I desired to know whether your proposals would lead to that end. I cannot, therefore, meet you with a view to the surrender of the Army of Northern Virginia; but as far as your proposal may affect the Confederate States forces under my command, and tend to the restoration of peace, I should be pleased to meet you at ten A.M. to-morrow on the old stage-road to Richmond, between the picket-lines of the two armies.

R. E. LEE, General.

LIEUTENANT-GENERAL U. S. GRANT.

Early on the morning of the 9th I returned him an answer as follows, and immediately started to join the column south of the Appomattox:

April 9, 1865.

GENERAL:—Your note of yesterday is received. I have no authority to treat on the subject of peace; the meeting proposed for ten A.M. to-day could lead to no good. I will state, however, general, that I am equally anxious for peace with yourself, and the whole North entertains the same feeling. The terms upon which peace can be had are well understood. By the South laying down their arms they will hasten that most desirable event, save thousands of human lives, and hundreds of millions of property not yet destroyed. Seriously hoping that all our difficulties may be settled without the loss of another life, I subscribe myself, etc.

U. S. GRANT, Lieutenant-General.

GENERAL R. E. LEE.

On the morning of the 9th, General Ord's command and the 5th corps reached Appomattox Station just as the enemy was making a desperate effort to break through our cavalry. The infantry was at once thrown in. Soon after a white flag was received, requesting a suspension of hostilities pending negotiations for a surrender.

Before reaching General Sheridan's headquarters, I received the following from General Lee:

April 9, 1865.

GENERAL:—I received your note of this morning on the picket-line, whither I had come to meet you, and ascertain definitely what terms were embraced in your proposal of yesterday with reference to the surrender of this army. I now ask an interview, in accordance with the offer contained in your letter of yesterday, for that purpose.

R. E. LEE, General.

LIEUTENANT-GENERAL U. S. GRANT.

The interview was held at Appomattox Court-House, the result of which is set forth in the following correspondence:

APPOMATTOX COURT-HOUSE, Virginia, *April* 9, 1865.

GENERAL:—In accordance with the substance of my letter to you of the 8th instant, I propose to receive the surrender of the Army of Northern Virginia on the following terms, to wit: Rolls of all the officers and men to be made in duplicate, one copy to be given to an officer to be designated by me, the other to be retained by such officer or officers as you may designate. The officers to give their individual paroles not to take up arms against the Government of the United States until properly exchanged; and each company or regimental commander sign a like parole for the men of their commands. The arms, artillery, and public property to be parked and stacked, and turned over to the officers appointed by me to receive them. This will not embrace the side-arms of the officers, nor their private horses or baggage. This done, each officer and man will be allowed to return to his home, not to be disturbed by United States authority so long as they observe their paroles and the laws in force where they may reside.

U. S. GRANT, Lieutenant-General.

GENERAL R. E. LEE.

HEADQUARTERS ARMY OF NORTHERN VIRGINIA, *April* 9, 1865.

GENERAL:—I have received your letter of this date containing the terms of surrender of the Army of Northern Virginia as proposed by you. As they are substantially the same as those expressed in your letter of the 8th instant, they are accepted. I will proceed to designate the proper officers to carry the stipulations into effect.

R. E. LEE, General.

LIEUTENANT-GENERAL U. S. GRANT.

The command of Major-General Gibbon, the 5th army corps under Griffin, and Mackenzie's cavalry, were designated to remain at Appomattox Court-House until the paroling of the surrendered army was completed, and to take charge of the public property. The remainder of the army immediately returned to the vicinity of Burkesville.

General Lee's great influence throughout the whole South caused his example to be followed, and to-day the result is that the armies lately under his leadership are at their homes, desiring peace and quiet, and their arms are in the hands of our ordnance officers.

On the receipt of my letter of the 5th, General Sherman moved directly against Joe Johnston, who retreated rapidly on and through Raleigh, which place General Sherman occupied on the morning of the 13th. The day preceding, news of the surrender of General Lee reached him at Smithfield.

On the 14th a correspondence was opened between General Sherman and General Johnston, which resulted on the 18th in an agreement for a suspension of hostilities, and a memorandum or basis for peace, subject to the approval of the President. This agreement was disapproved by the President on the 21st, which disapproval, together with your instructions, was communicated to General Sherman by me in person on the morning of the 24th, at Raleigh, North Carolina, in obedience to your orders. Notice was at once given by him to General Johnston for the termination of the truce that had been entered into. On the 25th another meeting between them was agreed upon, to take place on the 26th, which terminated in the surrender and disbandment of Johnston's army upon substantially the same terms as were given to General Lee.

The expedition under General Stoneman from East Tennessee got off on the 20th of March, moving by way of Boone, North Carolina, and struck the railroad at Wytheville, Chambersburg, and Big Lick. The force striking it at Big Lick pushed on to within a few miles of Lynchburg, destroying the important bridges, while with the main force he effectually destroyed it between New River and Big Lick, and then turned for Greensboro, on the North Carolina Railroad; struck that road and destroyed the bridges between Danville and Greensboro, and between Greensboro and the Yadkin, together with the depots of supplies along it, and captured four hundred prisoners. At Salisbury he attacked and defeated a force of the enemy under General Gardiner, capturing fourteen pieces of artillery and one thousand three hundred and sixty-four prisoners, and destroyed large amounts of army stores. At this place he destroyed fifteen miles of railroad and the bridges towards Charlotte. Thence he moved to Slatersville.

General Canby, who had been directed in January to make preparations for a movement from Mobile Bay against Mobile and the interior of Alabama, commenced his movement on the 20th of March. The 16th corps, Major-General A. J. Smith commanding, moved from Fort Gaines by water to Fish River; the 13th corps, under Major-General Gordon Granger, moved from Fort Morgan and joined the 16th corps on Fish River, both moving thence on Spanish Fort and investing it on the 27th; while Major-General Steele's command moved from Pensacola, cut the railroad leading from Tensas to Montgomery, effected a junction with them, and partially invested Fort Blakely. After a severe bombardment of Spanish Fort, a part of its line was carried on the 8th of April. During the night the enemy evacuated the fort. Fort Blakely was carried by assault on the 9th, and many prisoners captured; our loss was considerable. These successes practically opened to us the Alabama River, and enabled us to approach Mobile from the north. On the night of the 11th the city was evacuated, and was taken possession of by our forces on the morning of the 12th.

The expedition under command of Brevet Major-General Wilson, consisting of twelve thousand five hundred mounted men, was delayed by rains until March 22d, when it moved from Chickasaw, Alabama. On the 1st of April, General Wilson encountered the enemy in force under Forrest near Ebenezer Church, drove him in confusion, captured three hundred prisoners and three guns, and destroyed the central bridge over the Cahawba River. On the 2d he attacked and captured the fortified city of Selma, defended by Forrest, with seven thousand men and thirty-two guns, destroyed the arsenal, armory, naval foundry, machine-shops, vast quantities of stores, and captured three thousand prisoners. On the 4th he captured and destroyed Tuscaloosa. On the 10th he crossed the Alabama River, and after sending information of his operations to General Canby, marched on Montgomery, which place he occupied on the 14th, the enemy having abandoned it. At this place many stores and five steamboats fell into our hands. Thence a force marched direct on Columbus, and another on West Point, both of which places were assaulted and captured on the 16th. At the former place we got one thousand five hundred prisoners and fifty-two field-guns, destroyed two gunboats, the navy yard, foundries, arsenal, many factories, and much other public property. At the latter place we got three hundred prisoners, four guns, and destroyed nineteen locomotives and three hundred cars. On the 20th he took possession of Macon, Georgia, with sixty field-guns, one thousand two hundred militia, and five generals, surrendered by General Howell Cobb. General Wilson, hearing that Jeff. Davis was trying to make his escape, sent forces in pursuit and succeeded in capturing him on the morning of May 11th.

On the 4th day of May, General Dick Taylor surrendered to General Canby all the remaining rebel forces east of the Mississippi.

A force sufficient to insure an easy triumph over the enemy under Kirby Smith, west of the Mississippi, was immediately put in motion for Texas, and Major-General Sheridan designated for its immediate command; but on the 26th day of May, and before they reached their destination, General Kirby Smith surrendered his entire command to Major-General Canby. This surrender did not take place, however, until after the capture of the rebel President and Vice-President; and the bad faith was exhibited of first disbanding most of his army and permitting an indiscriminate plunder of public property.

Owing to the report that many of those lately in arms against the government had taken refuge upon the soil of Mexico, carrying with them arms rightfully belonging to the United States, which had been surrendered to us by agreement—among them some of the leaders who had surrendered in person—and the disturbed condition of affairs on the Rio Grande, the orders for troops to proceed to Texas were not changed.

There have been severe combats, raids, expeditions, and movements to defeat the designs and purposes of the enemy, most of them reflecting great credit on our arms, and which contributed greatly to our final triumph, that I have not mentioned. Many of these will be found clearly set forth in the reports herewith submitted; some in the telegrams and brief dispatches announcing them, and others, I regret to say, have not as yet been officially reported.

For information touching our Indian difficulties, I would respectfully refer to the reports of the commanders of departments in which they have occurred.

It has been my fortune to see the armies of both the West and the East fight battles, and from what I have seen I know there is no difference in their fighting qualities. All that it was possible for men to do in battle they have done. The Western armies commenced their battles in the Mississippi Valley, and received the final surrender of the remnant of the principal army opposed to them in North Carolina. The armies of the East commenced their battles on the river from which the Army of the Potomac derived its name, and received the final surrender of their old antagonists at Appomattox Court House, Virginia. The splendid achievements of each have nationalized our victories, removed all sectional jealousies (of which we have unfortunately experienced too much), and the cause of crimination and recrimination that might have followed had either section failed in its duty. All have a proud record, and all sections can well congratulate themselves and each other for having done their full share in restoring the supremacy of law over every foot of territory belonging to the United States. Let them hope for perpetual peace and harmony with that enemy, whose manhood, however mistaken the cause, drew forth such herculean deeds of valor.

I have the honor to be,
Very respectfully, your obedient servant,
U. S. GRANT,
Lieutenant-General.

Grant's Tomb, New York, New York. *Photograph by Elizabeth D. Samet.*

Editor's Afterword:
A Closer Look at Grant's Tomb

The hero of Frank Capra's 1936 film *Mr. Deeds Goes to Town* really wants to see Grant's Tomb. Longfellow Deeds, played by Gary Cooper, is a happy, tuba-playing poet from Mandrake Falls, Vermont, who must travel to New York City to secure the twenty million dollars he has unexpectedly inherited. The idea of going to the city makes him "nervous," and Deeds seems excited less about the money than about the prospect of visiting the tomb. In what is meant to signal his eccentricity, Deeds voices this wish on three separate occasions until finally, in the company of an undercover journalist named Babe Bennett (Jean Arthur), who has been assigned to get the goods on this apparent innocent, Deeds gets his chance. Babe worries that Deeds might be disillusioned: "To most people," she tells him as they stand before the monument, "it's an awful letdown . . . a washout." To an awestruck Deeds, however, it is a "wonderful" sight. When Babe asks him just what he sees in it, he replies:

> Oh, I see a small Ohio farm boy becoming a great soldier. I see thousands of marching men. I see General Lee with a broken heart, surrendering, and I can see the beginning of a new nation, like Abraham Lincoln said. And I can see that Ohio boy being inaugurated as President—

(dreamily)

Things like that can only happen in a country like America.[1]

It is a clue to the vicissitudes of Civil War memory in America that while Deeds dreams of visiting Grant's Tomb, what he sees once he gets there is Robert E. Lee.

Longfellow Deeds is typical of Capra's Depression-era heroes. Mocked by a host of cynical, greedy city slickers who hope to victimize him—they try to have Deeds declared insane when he announces his intention of giving the inheritance away to those in need—he eventually triumphs. The homespun Vermonter, a kind of hick savant, is meant to serve as the embodiment of American values. Nevertheless, as the film historian David Thomson notes, Capra's naïve idealists often seem more threatening to democracy than do their worldlier opponents: "[T]he films," Thomson proposes, "are a kind of fascistic inspirationalism in which the true daily, tedious difficulty of being American is exposed in the proposed rediscovery of simple goodness."[2] And what does Deeds's virtuous political philosophy amount to? It is perhaps best expressed in his lament to Bennett: "What puzzles me is why people seem to get so much pleasure out of hurting each other. Why don't they try liking each other once in a while?"[3] This commentary is of a piece with the brainless sentimentality that prompts Deeds while standing in front of Grant's Tomb to include Lee with his broken heart at the center of his vision of the birth of a new nation.

In Cooper, Capra found an exquisite vessel for his message. James Baldwin called the actor's screen persona one of "the most grotesque appeals to innocence the world has ever seen." Baldwin believed that Cooper's onscreen yokels constituted a rebuke to the deep complexity and complicity of American history. To him, Cooper, the hero of a white American fable, represented one of "two levels" of American "experience" that exist in parallel. The other level, Baldwin explains, remains "subterranean, indispensible, and denied." He perceived it "in the tone and in the face" of the musician Ray Charles.[4]

---

1. Robert Riskin, *Mr. Deeds Goes to Town*, *Six by Riskin: Six Screenplays by Robert Riskin*, ed. Pat McGilligan (Berkeley: University of California Press, 1997), 346, 355, 380, 391.

2. David Thomson, *The New Biographical Dictionary of Film* (New York: Knopf, 2003), s.v. "Frank Capra." For a different reading of this scene, see Joan Waugh's superb *U. S. Grant: American Hero, American Myth*, 305–6.

3. Riskin, *Mr. Deeds*, 394.

4. James Baldwin, "The White Problem," *The Cross of Redemption: Uncollected Writings*, ed. Randall Kenan (New York: Vintage, 2010), 96.

This underground current of American experience lurked, according to Baldwin, as a kind of national unconscious, both elemental and repressed.

The dangerously innocent Deeds visits Grant's Tomb at night. Had there been daylight, he might have read out in rapturous tones the inscription on its façade, high above the entrance: "Let us have peace." It is another symptom of the rewriting of Civil War memory that this sentence—from the letter Grant wrote accepting the Republican nomination for the presidency in 1868—should grace the memorial. It was a "famous phrase," Henry Adams admitted, "echoed" by everyone but in reality a commonplace: one of "a score of such reversible sentences generally to be gauged by their sententiousness."[5] As is the case with perhaps too many of Grant's political pronouncements—as distinguished from the rich observations on character and circumstance to be found in the memoirs and in his correspondence—this one, whatever its popular appeal, is an empty piety, a hopeful exhortation. What it communicated in 1897, the year of the tomb's dedication, was the exhaustion of a country's moral will twenty years earlier in the Compromise of 1877, which marked the end of Grant's presidency and of Reconstruction.

Grant himself invokes this maxim in the final pages of *Personal Memoirs*, where he suggests that the country is "on the eve of a new era"—although it is as yet a "prophecy" unrealized—"when there is to be great harmony between the Federal and Confederate." Grant wrote gratefully of the national outpouring in response to his illness and saw in it an optimistic sign: "The universally kind feeling expressed for me at a time when it was supposed that each day would prove my last, seemed to me the beginning of the answer to 'Let us have peace.'" Here the phrase that had seemed to be a declaration in 1868—*Let us have peace*—becomes something of an open question, as Grant proceeds to offer the valedictory wish that "the good feeling inaugurated" by his sickness, "may continue to the end." This hardly amounts to a political philosophy, yet it does hint at the unfinished nature of the nation's work and the imperfection of the peace, over eight years of which Grant presided, that followed "a very bloody and a very costly war." The historian Joan Waugh notes how often Grant's closing sentiments have been quoted. Indeed, it occurs in the part of his book that fits most neatly within a narrative of reconciliation. Grant "promoted reconciliation," Waugh points out, "but on Northern terms."[6]

---

5. Adams, *Education*, 260, 265. David Blight calls it a "splendidly ambiguous slogan." *Race and Reunion*, 99.

6. Joan Waugh, "U. S. Grant, Historian," *The Memory of the Civil War in American Culture*, ed. Fahs and Waugh, 30. Edmund Wilson argues that Grant offers here an "almost utopian" vision of the future: "Grant had, without being aware of it, quite walked out of Lincoln's vision, and he was living in a different world. The murder of Lincoln had ended this vision." *Patriotic Gore*, 159.

A superstitious dread of dying words should not conceal from us that "Let us have peace" is a far cry from "unconditional surrender." By the time the monument was completed, the new curators of Civil War memory had been unleashed, and Grant, together with a martyred Lincoln, was made to serve a post-Reconstruction narrative of the war. That manipulation began at his death in 1885, when his very body was turned into a symbol of forgiveness. Erstwhile enemies joined together as his pallbearers: Sherman and Johnston, Sheridan and Buckner. Such unity was a measure of the nation's eagerness to erase former antagonisms; to bury causes; and, as an inevitable result, to condemn African Americans in the South to the rule of Jim Crow and in the North to a less overt yet no less real segregationist agenda.

Grant began the conclusion to his *Personal Memoirs* unequivocally: "The cause of the great War of the Rebellion against the United States will have to be attributed to slavery." In this claim, which is less often quoted than is his rhetoric about harmonious feelings, he was simply echoing wartime beliefs in the North and South, including the tenets of several state secession documents and the philosophy of Alexander H. Stephens, the vice president of the Confederacy. Slavery, Stephens declared in a March 21, 1861, speech in Savannah, Georgia, "was the immediate cause of the late rupture and present revolution." He insisted that founders such as Thomas Jefferson who believed "that the enslavement of the African was in violation of the laws of nature; that it was wrong in *principle*, socially, morally, and politically, . . . were fundamentally wrong." Far from being an "evil," Stephens contended, slavery was a positive good on which the new Confederate Republic was founded: "its corner-stone rests upon the great truth, that the negro is not equal to the white man; that slavery—subordination to the superior race—is his natural and normal condition." The Confederacy, he proclaimed, "is the first, in the history of the world, based upon this great physical, philosophical, and moral truth."[7]

Historical fact notwithstanding, the consensus that slavery lay at the root of the contest had already dissolved to a greater degree than Grant's confident statement might suggest. A new version of events replaced the original narrative almost as soon as the war ended, and the campaign to revise its history continued to gather momentum in the period after Grant's death. One of the prime examples of the rebel volte-face was Stephens himself, whose postwar change of tune can be discerned in *A Constitutional View of the Late*

7. *Alexander H. Stephens, in Public and Private*, ed. Henry Cleveland (Philadelphia: National Publishing, 1866), 721.

War between the States, in which he demoted slavery to the proximate "*minor question*" that brought "opposing principles" about the relationship of federal and state power, "into active collision with each other."[8] As Grant was writing his memoirs in the 1880s, and certainly by the end of the century, slavery and emancipation were being expertly edited out of the story of the war in order to facilitate a narrative of reconciliation between white North and South.

The decline of Grant's reputation was but one consequence of the wholesale revision of Civil War memory. Grant was a global celebrity at the time of his death. As he made his way across the country in 1879, after returning from the world tour that followed his two-term presidency, massive crowds lined the streets from San Francisco to Philadelphia. And when he died, more than a million and a half people thronged the streets of Manhattan to watch his funeral procession. His memorial remained New York City's most popular monument, attracting half a million visitors each year, until 1916.[9] Thereafter Grant's reputation languished, a victim of the very movement of which his death had served as such a potent symbol. Even during his lifetime, politics certainly complicated matters; he became, for some, synonymous with the Gilded Age excesses over which he presided. While the incendiary Sherman proved a more sensational villain in the South, Grant always had his detractors. And the scandals that wracked his administration inevitably tarnished his image as the savior of the Union even for some in the North.

Grant's own contributions to Reconstruction were significant. Passage of the Ku Klux Klan bill of 1871 strengthened the hand of his attorney general, Amos T. Akerman, who brought thousands of indictments and several hundred convictions of Klansmen. As the biographer Jean Edward Smith notes, Grant "paid dearly" for his commitment to Reconstruction and his willingness to use federal force to suppress insurrection: "White supremacist historians . . . savaged his efforts to protect the freedmen, just as many in the West ridiculed his peace policy toward Native Americans."[10] The end of Reconstruction in the Compromise of 1877, which secured the presidency

---

8. Alexander H. Stephens, *A Constitutional View of the Late War between the States*, 2 vols. (Philadelphia: National Publishing, 1868), 1:12.

9. See Joan Waugh's illuminating account of Grant's nineteenth-century fame, *U. S. Grant: American Hero, American Myth*. See also the photographs in *Seven Mile Funeral Cortège of Genl. Grant in New York, August 8, 1885* (Boston: Instantaneous Photographic Co., 1886). On Grant's contributions to American foreign policy throughout his world tour, see Edwina S. Campbell, *Citizen of a Wider Commonwealth: Ulysses S. Grant's Postpresidential Diplomacy* (Carbondale: Southern Illinois University Press, 2016).

10. Smith, *Grant*, 568.

to Republican Rutherford B. Hayes, another Union veteran, in exchange for the withdrawal of federal troops from Southern states, gave new impetus to the custodians of the Lost Cause. It took some time, but Grant's fame diminished until it reached a low point in the 1930s, by which point the war's losers had decisively won the battle for its memory. Southern memorial engines had started up almost before the war ended. Through the labors of Stephens, Jefferson Davis, Jubal Early, and other rebel leaders; the United Daughters of the Confederacy (UDC); and the various authors who contributed to the *Southern Historical Society Papers* and to *Confederate Veteran*, the role of slavery was effaced. States' rights were fetishized and Grant vilified together with the Southern generals James Longstreet and John Mosby, both of whom had participated in postwar Reconstruction efforts, while other rebel commanders were canonized. These rebel saints are the generals whom ten U.S. Army installations, including some of the largest and most important posts, honor today: Beauregard, Benning, Bragg, Gordon, Hill, Hood, Lee, Pickett, Polk, and Rucker.

To the reminiscences of veterans were added collections of poetry, song, adult fiction, and children's literature, most of it unabashedly infused with the doctrine of white supremacy. The influence of the UDC was felt in many spheres, from the Confederate soldier monuments that began appearing in many Southern towns at the turn of the century to the textbooks adopted by public schools.[11] Those popular accounts were buttressed at the turn of the twentieth century by the work of professional historians. By World War II, the Lost Cause was ascendant while Grant had become a byword for drunkenness and butchery, and the advancement of black civil rights that took place during Reconstruction had been eclipsed by Jim Crow. There is no finer encapsulation of the oblivion to which Grant was consigned than the joke Groucho Marx made a staple of his 1950s television show *You Bet Your Life*: "Who's buried in Grant's Tomb?"

Grant was only one casualty of the successful drive toward reconciliation Frederick Douglass referred to in 1875 as "peace among the whites" in a speech ominous with allusions to Shakespearean tragedy:

---

11. On various ways in which history was rewritten, see the excellent essays in *The Memory of the Civil War in American Culture*, ed. Fahs and Waugh. On textbooks in particular, see James M. McPherson's "Long-Legged Yankee Lies: The Southern Textbook Crusade," 64–78. Waugh notes in her contribution to the volume that Grant's definitive statement on the cause of the war was a challenge to "the idea, just beginning to take hold in the 1880s, that the Northern and Southern causes were equivalent." "U. S. Grant, Historian," 6. See also Blight, *Race and Reunion*.

Frederick Douglass, ca. 1880. Photograph by Mathew B. Brady. *Metropolitan Museum of Art, Gilman Collection, Museum Purchase, 2005.*

Now when this mighty quarrel has ceased, when all the asperities and resentments have gone as they are sure to go, when all the clouds that a few years ago lowered about our national house, shall be in the deep bosom of the ocean buried, when this great white race has renewed its vows of patriotism and flowed back into its accustomed channels, the question for us is: in what position will this stupendous reconciliation leave the colored people? What tendencies will spring out of it, and how will they affect us? If war among the whites brought peace and liberty to the blacks, what will peace among the whites bring?[12]

The peace among the whites Douglass foretold reached its sentimental acme on the fiftieth anniversary of Gettysburg in 1913, when former adversaries met on the battlefield in a "Great Reunion" presided over by Woodrow Wilson, the first Southern president since the antebellum period. Before he became a politician, Wilson was a historian, and his multivolume *History of the American People* is steeped in Lost Cause mythology. Its depiction of Reconstruction portrays black Americans as helpless children victimized by Yankee carpetbaggers and explains the first Ku Klux Klan as a necessary

12. Frederick Douglass, "The Color Question: An Address Delivered in Washington, D.C.," July 5, 1875, *Frederick Douglass Papers*, ser. 1, vol. 4, ed. John W. Blassingame and John R. McKivigan (New Haven, CT: Yale University Press, 1991), 417.

Erstwhile adversaries meet on the field at Gettysburg during the "Great Reunion," July 1913. *Library of Congress, Prints and Photographs Division, photograph by Harris & Ewing, LC-DIG-hec-02902.*

instrument of law and order. As the recent debate over the name of Princeton's Woodrow Wilson School of Public and International Affairs suggests, for many years we successfully divorced Wilson's forward-looking utopian vision of international fraternity from his conception of domestic history, especially that of nineteenth-century race relations. His *History* provides a sinister counterpoint to the rhetoric for which he is celebrated. It was Wilson, after all, who brought segregation to Washington, D.C.

Wilson voiced the spirit of his age on matters of race. As Eric Foner has noted, the popular interpretation of Reconstruction "was accorded scholarly legitimacy—to its everlasting shame—by the nation's fraternity of professional historians." Chief among them were John W. Burgess and William A. Dunning, who taught a generation of disciples at Columbia University at the turn of the twentieth century. Their new historiography successfully elided the story of slavery and emancipation from the narrative just as Jim Crow began to take a firm grip on the South.[13] In 1901, five years after *Plessy v. Ferguson* decreed a "separate but equal" social and political existence for African Americans, Dunning wrote in the *Atlantic* that by the end of the Reconstruction period the North had finally seen the truth the South had known all along, "that the ultimate root of the trouble in the South had been, not the institution of slavery, but the coexistence in one society of two races so distinct in characteristics as to render coalescence impossible." Slavery, he insisted, "had been a *modus vivendi* through which social life was possible; and that, after its disappearance, its place must be taken by some set of conditions

---

13. Foner, *Reconstruction*, 609.

President Wilson at the "Great Reunion." *Library of Congress, Prints and Photographs Division, LC-DIG-ggbain-13859.*

which, if more humane and beneficent in accidents, must in essence express the same fact of racial inequality."[14] As these words make plain, the Dunning school's historiography was underwritten by a faith in racial inequality.[15] Even when such overt racism had become an embarrassment, however, replaced by euphemism and coded language, the cultic figure of Lee and his broken heart continued to endure in popular culture as the perfect symbol of a bygone chivalry. He was the leading figure in a narrative that sanitized the war by ignoring its true cause and sentimentalized warriors by emphasizing their elemental white fraternity, while evoking nostalgia for the antebellum South. This reworking also demanded unfounded claims that Lee was personally opposed to slavery.[16]

---

14. William A. Dunning, "The Undoing of Reconstruction," *Atlantic Monthly* 88, no. 528 (October 1901): 449.

15. For a detailed account of the historiography, consult Clarence L. Mohr's bibliographical essay, "Southern Blacks in the Civil War: A Century of Historiography," *Journal of Negro History* 59, no. 2 (1974): 177–95.

16. In her pathbreaking biography of Lee, the diplomat and biographer Elizabeth Pryor drew on a trove of documentary evidence found in an Alexandria, Virginia, bank vault in 2002 to debunk the sanitized view of the general:

> The tradition that Robert E. Lee was opposed to slavery has become part of the mythology that surrounds him. . . .
> In fact, Lee's political views are remarkably consistent. He thought slavery was an unfortunate historical legacy, an inherited problem for which he was not responsible, and one that could only be resolved over time and probably only by God. As for any injustice to the slaves, he defended a "Christian" logic of at least temporary black bondage. . . .

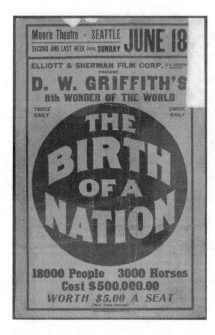

Klansmen in *Birth of a Nation*, dir. D. W. Griffith. *David W. Griffith Corp. and Epoch Producing Corporation, 1915.*

Poster announcing *The Birth of a Nation* as "D. W. Griffith's 8th Wonder of the World," 1915. *Library of Congress, Prints and Photographs Division, LC-DIG-ppmsc-03661.*

In *Forever Free*, a history of emancipation and reconstruction, Foner reminds us that the "most popular manifestation" of the Lost Cause in American culture during this period "was the romantic resurrection of the Ku Klux Klan" appearing in various media, including Thomas Dixon's popular novel *The Clansman: An Historical Romance of the Ku Klux Klan* (1905), which became the foundation for D. W. Griffith's film *The Birth of a Nation* (1915).[17] Perhaps no work of art until David O. Selznick's *Gone with the Wind* contributed more to the tectonic shift in national memory than did Griffith's epic. It cost $100,000 to produce and, despite a protest mounted by the NAACP, it went on to earn millions in the theaters. Indeed, *Birth* set a box office record not eclipsed until Selznick's film in 1939. Quotations from Wilson's *History of the American People* appear on several of *Birth's* title cards to lend it further authority. "Adventurers swarmed out of the North," reads one, "as much the enemies of the one race as of the other, to cozen, beguile, and use the negroes. . . . In the villages the negroes were the

---

Lee may have hated slavery, but it was not because of any ethical dilemma. What Lee disliked about slavery was its inefficiency, the messiness of its relationships, the responsibility it entailed, and the taint of it.

Reading the Man, 144–45.

17. Eric Foner, *Forever Free: The Story of Emancipation and Reconstruction* (New York: Vintage, 2005), 217.

office holders, men who knew none of the uses of authority, except its inso-
lences."[18] A triumph of pernicious mythmaking, the film enacted Wilson's
claim that while some blacks "stayed very quietly by their old masters and
gave no trouble, . . . most yielded," like children, "to the novel impulse and
excitement of freedom" without ever really understanding its significance.[19]

At a special premiere at the White House in 1915, on the fiftieth anniversary of the end of the war, Wilson saw his vision of the Reconstruction
South realized on screen as the hooded knights of the Ku Klux Klan gallantly
ride to the rescue of a South made to suffer, as one title card phrases it, "the
anarchy of black rule." The postwar South's political and legal machinery is
completely dominated in the film by newly emancipated black men, who are
themselves the dupes of unscrupulous carpetbaggers and Union League agi-
tators. *Birth* depicts a polarized black community in which loyal mammies
and faithful servants resent ambitious "mulattoes" and lawless black soldiers;
it closes with a new alliance of Northern and Southern whites united against
the threat of black violence and hypersexuality.[20]

One of the most significant casualties of Griffith's film is the African
American soldier, in whom the various ills visited on the postbellum South
are all embodied. "Once let the black man get upon his person the brass letters U. S.; let him get an eagle on his button, and a musket on his shoulder
and bullets in his pocket," Frederick Douglass had declared in 1863, "and
there is no power on the earth or under the earth which can deny that he
has earned the right to citizenship in the United States." Fellow abolitionist William Wells Brown likewise invested the uniform with a talismanic
significance. "Are these men who have been regenerated by wearing the
United-States uniform . . . to be, can they ever again be, handed over to the
taskmaster?" Brown demanded in 1867.[21] For Northern proponents of black
enlistment, the Union uniform represented the metamorphosis of slave into

---

18. *The Birth of a Nation*, dir. D. W. Griffith, David W. Griffith Corp. and Epoch Producing Corporation, 1915. The card recombines language found in *A History of the American People*, 5:46, 50, 49.

19. *A History of the American People*, 5:18–19.

20. See Michael Rogin, "'The Sword Became a Flashing Vision': D. W. Griffith's *The Birth of a Nation*,"
in *The New American Studies: Essays from Representations*, ed. Philip Fisher (Berkeley: University of
California Press, 1991), 383, 348. On the historical replacement of sectional with racial conflict in the
American South, see Walter Benn Michaels, *Our America: Nativism, Modernism, and Pluralism* (Durham,
NC: Duke University Press, 1995), 17–18, 23, 32–33.

21. "Address for the Promotion of Colored Enlistments," July 6, 1863, in *The Life and Writings of
Frederick Douglass*, ed. Philip S. Foner (New York: International Publishers, 1952), 3:365; William
Wells Brown, *The Negro in the American Rebellion: His Heroism and His Fidelity* (Boston: Lee & Shepard,
1867), 191.

"Men of Color, to Arms! Now or Never!" Civil War recruiting broadside, 1863. *Library of Congress, Rare Book and Special Collections Division, Alfred Whital Stern Collection of Lincolniana.*

citizen. Precisely because it reduced difference and implied equality, however, the prospect of black men in blue uniforms, notes James McPherson, also "carried disturbing implications" for those white soldiers as yet unprepared to accept blacks as fellow men and citizens.[22] Griffith's film altogether transforms the story of black soldiers' participation in the Civil War from a tale of heroism and humanity to one of savagery.[23] Black soldiers are a ubiquitous threat in Griffith's depiction of the Reconstruction South despite the fact that the federal government ultimately removed many black regiments

---

22. James McPherson, *For Cause and Comrades: Why Men Fought in the Civil War* (New York: Oxford University Press, 1997), 126.

23. Everett Carter suggests that Griffith's black Union soldier "is a monster of ingratitude, a renegade from the feudal code, and only evil can be expected of him." "Cultural History Written with Lightning: The Significance of *The Birth of a Nation* (1915)," *Hollywood as Historian: American Film in a Cultural Context*, ed. Peter C. Rollins, rev. ed. (Lexington: University Press of Kentucky, 1998), 14.

to the Western frontier in response to Southern protests.[24] In fact, black militia units were the victims of massacres at Colfax, Louisiana, and Hamburg, South Carolina, perpetrated by members of the Klan and the Knights of the White Camelia, in 1873.

Griffith unfolded Dixon's story on the screen by means of an arsenal of cinematic tools, ranging from the culturally crude (actors in blackface) to the technically sophisticated (suspenseful parallel editing). Perhaps apocryphal, Wilson's reported response to the film—"It's like writing history with lightning. My only regret is that it is all so terribly true"—resonates with Griffith's own assessment of the tale he was telling. In an interview with the actor Walter Huston conducted on the occasion of the film's rerelease in 1930, Griffith offered some key insights into the forces that shaped his film. When Huston asked him whether his film were "true," Griffith replied with a grossly sentimental memory of watching his mother sew robes for the Klan late into the night and listening to his father telling war stories about eating nothing but "parched corn." He declared that the Klan "served a purpose" during that period as the defender of an elemental innocence symbolized by his image of young girls wearing cotton and young boys dying on the battlefield.[25] In Griffith's vision, the beautiful act of sacrifice transcends the purpose for which it was made. Griffith's sense of the ease and naturalness of the story—of the way it "tells itself "—was vital to the political project of domesticating and normalizing white rule as a necessary response to black savagery.

In the century since Griffith's film, the revisionist narrative has exchanged naked racism for euphemism. But today's apparently defanged narrative of reconciliation still conceals that "other, subterranean, indispensible, and denied" level of American history on which James Baldwin insisted. That other level can be discerned in the educator J. Saunders Redding's 1942 meditation on African American attitudes toward military heroism. In an essay

---

24. Reading Grant's readiness to withdraw black troops in response to Southern complaints as a nod toward reconciliation, Brooks Simpson proposes that Grant "seemed less sensitive to protecting blacks from whites than to protecting whites from themselves." Brooks D. Simpson, *Let Us Have Peace: Ulysses S. Grant and the Politics of War and Reconstruction, 1861–1868* (Chapel Hill: University of North Carolina Press, 1991), 114.

25. *D. W. Griffith: Interviews*, ed. Anthony Slide (Jackson: University of Mississippi Press, 2012), 187–88. On the authenticity of Wilson's oft-quoted reaction, see Mark E. Benbow, "Birth of a Quotation: Woodrow Wilson and 'Like Writing History with Lightning,'" *The Journal of the Gilded Age and Progressive Era* 8.4 (October 2010): 509–33. For another account of the Civil War as a contest between ardent boys, see Willa Cather's short story "The Namesake," *McClure's Magazine* (March 1907).

published in the *American Mercury*, Redding recorded the story Dixon and Griffith so studiously ignored. He declared that as a black American he grew up without heroic traditions. Wars belonged to "white folks." His parents fought instead "a fierce, bitter, soul-searing war of spiritual and economic attrition." Redding traced their cynicism about white people's war back to his grandmother, a former slave who used to tell her grandchildren a Civil War story about her master's son: "An' he done som'pin big an' brave away down dere to Chickymorgy an' dey made a iron image of him 'cause he got his head blowed off an' his stomick blowed out fightin' to keep his slaves."[26] This "iron image" cast of one particular man who died "to keep his slaves" stands in for the thousands of statues and plaques throughout the country that perpetuate an ingenious and seductive lie North and South were together complicit in crafting: namely, that the war, which in fact tested the country's founding premise, amounted to a battle between honorable brothers.

The moral equivalency of North and South is assumed by many Americans as established fact, an eventuality anticipated not only by Frederick Douglass but also by the Union officer Grenville Dodge, who reports in his memoirs that the editors of the *Century* magazine, for whom Grant had begun writing a series of articles on Civil War battles before Twain signed him up to write the memoirs, wanted, in the service of a reconciliationist impulse, to soften the general's language. Grant's son Fred told Dodge: "[H]is father had been having considerable trouble with the publishers or editors of the magazine who were to publish the war articles—Shiloh, Vicksburg, Wilderness and Appomattox—that they had made his father very angry—they wanted him to change the word 'Rebel' in his article to 'Confederate' and the word 'Union' to 'Federal.'" Fred Grant explained that his father "wrote a short letter, demanding that his articles be published as written." Dodge reported this exchange to William Sherman:

> Sherman said:
> This trying to soften treason by expunging the words of the General was wrong, and that if it kept on, pretty soon the sons of Southern soldiers would consider it as much of an honor that their fathers fought under Lee, as the sons of Union soldiers, that their fathers fought under Grant; that the Line of Union and Rebel, of loyalty and treason, should be kept always distinct.

---

26. J. Saunders Redding, "A Negro Looks at This War," *American Mercury*, November 1942, rpt. in *Reporting World War II*, vol. 1, ed. Samuel Hynes et al. (New York: Library of America, 1995), 426–27.

I answered:

As long as our veterans live it will be; but the tendency all the time is, to wipe out history, to forget it, forgive, excuse and soften, and when all the soldiers pass from this age it will be easy to slip into the idea, that one side was as good as the other.

Sherman said:

It was a conspiracy until Sumpter [*sic*] was fired upon; after that, a Rebellion.[27]

Dodge was prescient, and the softened version of history he describes continues to hold sway among many Americans. Witness White House chief of staff and retired marine general John Kelly's insistence in the fall of 2017, not long after deadly violence erupted after a white nationalist rally in Charlottesville, Virginia, to protest the planned removal of a Confederate monument, that the Civil War resulted from a failure to compromise and that fighting for one's state constituted a principled, honorable choice. Kelly argued in effect what Dodge predicted he would: "one side was as good as the other." The legacy of revisionist history is all around us: in the sophistry with which the Civil War is discussed, in the honoring of rebel commanders through statuary and the naming of everything from local schools to federal property, in the defense of the Confederate flag as a symbol of heritage, and in the Texas state guidelines for teaching history in the public school system.[28]

Gilded with words such as *honor, bravery, suffering,* and *sacrifice,* this perverse mythology helped to sustain the postwar nostalgia for antebellum days. It is a myth that has refused to surrender its death grip on the American mind. The persistent project of unconditional reconciliation likewise requires us to remember only a single phrase from the end of Lincoln's Second Inaugural:

---

27. Grenville Mellen Dodge, *Personal Recollections of President Abraham Lincoln, General Ulysses S. Grant and General William T. Sherman* (Council Bluffs, Iowa: Monarch, 1914), 110–11.

On Americans' political engagement throughout the period, see Mark E. Neely Jr., *The Boundaries of American Political Culture in the Civil War Era* (Chapel Hill: University of North Carolina Press, 2005).

28. See "John Kelly calls Robert E. Lee an 'honorable man' and says 'lack of compromise' caused the Civil War," *Washington Post,* October 31, 2017, https://www.washingtonpost.com/news/morning-mix/wp/2017/10/31/john-kelly-calls-robert-e-lee-an-honorable-man-and-says-lack-of-compromise-caused-the-civil-war/?utm_term=.4b660e2ab91a.

The Texas guidelines relegate slavery to the last of several causes. Middle school students, for example, are expected to be able to "explain the causes of the Civil War, including sectionalism, states' rights, and slavery." Texas Education Agency, Essential Knowledge and Skills for Social Studies, chapter 113, http://ritter.tea.state.tx.us/rules/tac/chapter113/index.html.

"With malice toward none; with charity for all." In order for the vision to be sustained, we must simultaneously forget the grim warning that precedes it:

> Fondly do we hope—fervently do we pray—that this mighty scourge of war may speedily pass away. Yet, if God will that it continue, until all the wealth piled by the bond-man's two hundred and fifty years of unrequited toil shall be sunk, and until every drop of blood drawn with the lash, shall be paid by another drawn with the sword, as was said three thousand years ago, so still it must be said, "the judgments of the Lord, are true and righteous altogether."

Lincoln's strict accounting makes clear not only the centrality of slavery to the conflict but also the mandate for justice rather than for the forgiveness that promotes forgetfulness. Grant, like Lincoln, was not confused about what was at stake in the Civil War. As, in a welcome development, Grant's reputation trends upward at the beginning of the twenty-first century, it is well to remember the clarity with which he understood the war he did so much to win. Rather than making Grant conform to the reconciliationist narrative to which we continue to cling so assiduously, we would do well to remember the precision of his assessment of his enemy's cause: "[O]ne of the worst for which a people ever fought, and one for which there was the least excuse." If therefore when we visit Grant's Tomb, we remember Lee and his broken heart, we end up forgetting that what actually broke it—and what Grant's victory secured—was the emancipation of four million people.

Eagle with flags in front of Grant's Tomb. *Photograph by Elizabeth D. Samet.*

Selected Bibliography

Full publication information is given for all sources in the notes. However, I thought it would be useful for readers to have a separate bibliography of key sources. In addition to many of the works that have informed this edition, I have included texts that might help to illuminate the people, events, and ideas about which Grant writes. In the case of works in languages others than English, I have whenever feasible used translations that would have been available to Grant and his contemporaries.

Manuscripts and Photographic Archives

Library of Congress, Manuscripts Division, Washington, D.C.
Library of Congress, Prints and Photographs Division, Washington, D.C.
Metropolitan Museum of Art, New York, NY
Naval History and Heritage Command, Washington, D.C.
New York Public Library, New York, NY
Ulysses S. Grant Presidential Library, Mississippi State University, Starkville, MS
United States Military Academy Library, Archives and Special Collections, West Point, NY
    Simon Bolivar Buckner Papers
    George W. Cullum Papers
    William Dutton Papers
    Ulysses S. Grant Papers
    Oliver Otis Howard Papers
    John C. Pemberton Papers
    John Pitman Papers

John Pope Papers
Philip H. Sheridan Papers
William T. Sherman Papers
Charles F. Smith Papers
George H. Thomas Papers
West Point Museum, West Point, NY

Official Government Records and Histories

Atlas to Accompany the Official Records of the Union and Confederate Armies. 2 vols. Washington, D.C.: Government Printing Office, 1891.

The Negro in the Military Service of the United States, 1639–1886. 7 vols. Washington, D.C.: Adjutant General's Office, 1888.

Official Army Register. Washington, D.C.: Adjutant General's Office, 1861.

Official Army Register of Volunteer Force of U.S. Army for Years 1861–1865. 8 parts. Washington, D.C.: Government Printing Office, 1865.

Official Records of the Union and Confederate Navies in the War of the Rebellion. 30 vols. Washington, D.C.: Government Printing Office, 1894–1922.

Sanderson, James M. *Camp Fires and Camp Cooking.* Washington, D.C.: Government Printing Office, 1862. Rpt. in Surgeon-General's Office, *A Report on the Hygiene of the United States Army.* Circular No. 8. Washington, D.C.: Government Printing Office, 1875.

Surgeon-General's Office. *The Medical and Surgical History of the War of the Rebellion.* 6 vols. Washington, D.C.: Government Printing Office, 1870–1888.

The War of the Rebellion: A Compilation of the Official Records of the Union and Confederate Armies. 128 vols. Washington, D.C.: Government Printing Office, 1880–1901.

Nineteenth-Century Newspapers and Periodicals

The Army and Navy Journal, New York, NY
The Atlantic Monthly, Boston, MA
The Century Magazine, New York, NY
Confederate Veteran, Nashville, TN
Frank Leslie's Illustrated Newspaper, New York, NY
The Galaxy, New York, NY
Harper's Monthly Magazine, New York, NY
Harper's Weekly, New York, NY
Littel's Living Age, New York, NY
The New York Times
The New York Tribune
The North American Review, Cedar Falls, IA
The North Star, Rochester, NY

Overland Monthly, San Francisco, CA

Papers of the Southern Historical Society, Richmond, VA

Putnam's Monthly, New York, NY

Richmond Times, Richmond, VA

Scribner's Magazine, New York, NY

Scribner's Monthly, New York, NY

Southern Literary Messenger, Richmond, VA

Southern Quarterly Review, Columbia, SC

United States Democratic Review, New York, NY

Documentary Histories and Other Reference Works

American Civil War: The Definitive Encyclopedia and Document Collection. Edited by Spencer C. Tucker. 6 vols. Santa Barbara: ABC-Clio, 2013.

Battles and Leaders of the Civil War. 4 vols. Edited by Robert Underwood Johnson and Clarence Clough Buel. New York: Century, 1887–1888.

Battles and Leaders of the Civil War. Vols. 5–6. Edited by Peter Cozzens. Urbana: University of Illinois Press, 2004.

Bibliographic Register of the Officers and Graduates of the U.S. Military Academy at West Point, N.Y. Edited by George W. Cullum. 3rd ed. Boston: Houghton Mifflin, 1891.

Encyclopedia of the Confederacy. Edited by Richard N. Current. 4 vols. New York: Simon & Schuster, 1993.

The Encyclopedia of the Mexican-American War. Edited by Spencer C. Tucker. 2 vols. Santa Barbara: ABC-Clio, 2012.

Freedom: A Documentary History of Emancipation, 1861–1867. Series 1. Edited by Ira Berlin et al. 3 vols. Cambridge, UK: Cambridge University Press, 1985–1990; Series 2. The Black Military Experience. Edited by Ira Berlin et al. Cambridge, UK: Cambridge University Press, 1982; Series 3. Edited by Leslie S. Rowland et al. 2 vols. Chapel Hill: University of North Carolina Press, 2008–2013.

Nineteenth- and Early Twentieth-Century American Memoirs and Histories

Adams, Charles Francis. *An Autobiography*. Boston: Houghton Mifflin, 1916.

Adams, Henry. *The Education of Henry Adams*. Boston: Houghton Mifflin, 1918.

Adams, John G. B. *Reminiscences of the Nineteenth Massachusetts Regiment*. Boston: Wright & Potter, 1899.

Alcott, Louisa May. *Hospital Sketches*. Boston: James Redpath, 1863.

Alexander, Edward Porter. *Fighting for the Confederacy: The Personal Recollections of General Edward Porter Alexander*. Edited by Gary W. Gallagher. Chapel Hill: University of North Carolina Press, 1989.

———. *Military Memoirs of a Confederate: A Critical Narrative.* New York: Scribner's, 1907.

Andrews, Eliza. *The War-Time Journal of a Georgia Girl, 1864–1865.* New York: D. Appleton, 1908.

Badeau, Adam. *Grant in Peace: From Appomattox to Mount McGregor; A Personal Memoir.* New York: D. Appleton, 1887.

———. *Military History of Ulysses S. Grant, from April, 1861, to April, 1865.* 3 vols. New York: D. Appleton, 1868–81.

Barnum, P. T. *Life of P. T. Barnum.* Buffalo: Courier, 1888.

Bates, David Homer. *Lincoln in the Telegraph Office.* New York: Century, 1907.

Beatty, John. *The Citizen-Soldier; or, Memoirs of a Volunteer.* Cincinnati, OH: Wilstach, Baldwin, 1879.

Beers, Fannie A. *Memories: A Record of Personal Experience and Adventure during Four Years of War.* Philadelphia: J. B. Lippincott, 1891.

Best, Isaac O. *History of the 121st New York State Infantry.* Chicago: Privately printed, 1921.

Bierce, Ambrose. *The Collected Works of Ambrose Bierce.* 12 vols. New York: Neale, 1909.

Blackett, R. J. M., ed. *Thomas Morris Chester, Black Civil War Correspondent: His Dispatches from the Virginia Front.* New York: Da Capo, 1991.

Blair, Francis P. *The Life and Public Services of Gen. William O. Butler.* Baltimore, MD: N. Hickman, 1848.

Bourke, John Gregory. *On the Border with Crook.* 2nd ed. New York: Scribner's, 1892.

Boynton, H. V. *Sherman's Historical Raid: The Memoirs in the Light of the Record.* Cincinnati, OH: Wilstach, Baldwin, 1875.

Brinton, John H. *Personal Memoirs of John H. Brinton, Major and Surgeon U.S.V. 1861–1865.* New York: Neale, 1914.

Britton, Wiley. *Memoirs of the Rebellion on the Border, 1863.* Chicago: Cushing, Thomas, 1882.

Brown, Alonzo L. *History of the Fourth Regiment of Minnesota Infantry Volunteers during the Great Rebellion 1861–1865.* St. Paul: Pioneer Press, 1892.

Brown, William Wells. *The Negro in the American Rebellion: His Heroism and His Fidelity.* Edited by William Edward Farrison. Boston: Lee & Shepard, 1867.

Buck, Irving A. *Cleburne and His Command.* New York: Neale, 1908.

Buckner, Simon Bolivar. "A Visit to Popocatepetl." *Putnam's Monthly Magazine* 1 (April 1853): 408–16.

Burlingame, Michael, ed. *Lincoln Observed: Civil War Dispatches of Noah Brooks.* Baltimore, MD: Johns Hopkins University Press, 1998.

Burlingame, Michael, and John R. Turner Ettlinger, eds. *Inside Lincoln's White House: The Complete Civil War Diary of John Hay.* Carbondale: Southern Illinois University Press, 1997.

Burnett, Alf. *Incidents of the War: Humorous, Pathetic, and Descriptive.* Cincinnati, OH: Rickey & Carroll, 1863.

Butler, Benjamin F. *Butler's Book: Autobiography and Personal Reminiscences of Major-General Benjamin F. Butler.* Boston: A. M. Thayer, 1892.

Cadwallader, Sylvanus. *Three Years with Grant*. Edited by Benjamin P. Thomas. Lincoln: University of Nebraska Press, 1996.

Catlin, George. *Letters and Notes on the Manners, Customs and Condition of the North American Indians*. 2 vols. New York: Wiley and Putnam, 1842.

Chamberlain, Joshua Lawrence. *The Passing of the Armies*. New York: G. P. Putnam's Sons, 1915.

Chesnut, Mary. *A Diary from Dixie*. Edited by Isabella D. Martin and Myrta Lockett Avary. New York: D. Appleton, 1906.

Church, William Conant. *Ulysses S. Grant*. New York: G. P. Putnam's Sons, 1897.

Clap, Roger. *Memoirs of Roger Clap, 1630. Collections of the Dorchester Antiquarian and Historical Society* 1. 2nd ed. Boston, 1854.

Clinton, Catherine, ed. *Fanny Kemble's Journals*. Cambridge, MA: Harvard University Press, 2000.

Commission of Inquiry, U.S. Sanitary Commission. *Narrative of Privations and Sufferings of United States Officers and Soldiers while Prisoners of War in the Hands of the Rebel Authorities*. Philadelphia: King & Baird, 1864.

Comstock, Cyrus B. *The Diary of Cyrus B. Comstock*. Edited by Merlin E. Sumner. Dayton, OH: Morningside, 1987.

Cooke, John Esten. *Wearing of the Gray: Being Personal Portraits, Scenes, and Adventures of War*. New York: E. B. Treat, 1867.

Crook, George. *General George Crook: His Autobiography*. Edited by Martin F. Schmitt. Norman: University of Oklahoma Press, 1946.

Dana, Charles A. *Recollections*. New York: D. Appleton and Company, 1902.

Davis, Jefferson. *The Papers of Jefferson Davis*. Edited by Lynda Lasswell Crist. Baton Rouge: Louisiana State University Press, 2003.

———. *A Short History of the Confederate States of America*. New York: Belford, 1890.

Davis, Varina. *Jefferson Davis, Ex-President of the Confederate States of America: A Memoir by his Wife*. New York: Belford, 1890.

De Forest, John William. *A Union Officer in the Reconstruction*. Edited by James H. Croushore and David Morris Potter. New Haven, CT: Yale University Press, 1976.

———. *A Volunteer's Adventures: A Union Captain's Record of the Civil War*. Edited by James H. Croushore. Baton Rouge: Louisiana State University Press, 1996.

De Peyster, John Watts. *Personal and Military History of Philip Kearny*. Elizabeth, NJ: Palmer, 1870.

Dodge, Grenville Mellen. *Personal Recollections of President Abraham Lincoln, General Ulysses S. Grant and General William T. Sherman*. Council Bluffs, IA: Monarch, 1914.

Dorchester Antiquarian and Historical Society. *History of the Town of Dorchester, Massachusetts*. Boston, 1859.

Douglass, Frederick. *The Frederick Douglass Papers*. Edited by John W. Blassingame and John R. McKivigan. New Haven, CT: Yale University Press, 1991–.

———. *The Life and Times of Frederick Douglass*. Boston: De Wolfe & Fisk, 1892.

————. *My Bondage and My Freedom.* New York: Miller, Orton & Mulligan, 1855.

————. *Narrative of the Life of Frederick Douglass, an American Slave.* Boston: Anti-Slavery Office, 1845.

Doyle, A. Conan. *The Great Boer War.* London: Smith, Elder, 1900.

Dozier, Graham T., ed. *A Gunner in Lee's Army: The Civil War Letters of Thomas Henry Carter.* Chapel Hill: University of North Carolina Press, 2014.

Dunning, William A. "The Undoing of Reconstruction." *The Atlantic Monthly* (October 1901): 437–48.

Dyer, J. Franklin. *The Journal of a Civil War Surgeon.* Edited by Michael B. Chesson. Lincoln: University of Nebraska Press, 2003.

Early, Jubal Anderson. *Autobiographical Sketch and Narrative of the War between the States.* Philadelphia: J. B. Lippincott, 1912.

Emilio, Luis F. *A Brave Black Regiment.* New York: Da Capo, 1995.

Evans, Clement Anselm, ed. *Confederate Military History: A Library of Confederate States History.* 12 vols. Atlanta: Confederate Publishing, 1899.

Evans, Elwood. *History of the Pacific Northwest: Oregon and Washington.* Portland: North Pacific History Company, 1889.

Exercises at the Dedication of the Monument of Colonel Robert Gould Shaw and the Fifty-Fourth Regiment of Massachusetts Infantry. May 31, 1897. Boston Municipal Printing Office, 1897.

Fehrenbacher, Don E., and Virginia Fehrenbacher, eds. *Recollected Words of Abraham Lincoln.* Stanford, CA: Stanford University Press, 1996.

Finerty, John F. *War-Path and Bivouac, or The Conquest of the Sioux.* Chicago: Donohue & Henneberry, 1890.

Fitzhugh, George. *Cannibals All! or, Slaves without Masters.* Richmond, VA: A. Morris, 1857.

Flower, Frank Abial. *Edwin McMasters Stanton.* Akron, OH: Saalfield Publishing, 1905.

Folsom, George, trans. and ed. *The Despatches of Hernando Cortés.* New York: Wiley and Putnam, 1843.

Forbes, S. A. "Grierson's Cavalry Raid." *Transactions of the Illinois State Historical Society for the Year 1907* 12 (1908): 102–3.

Foster, Samuel T. *One of Cleburne's Command: The Civil War Reminiscences and Diary of Captain Samuel T. Foster, Granbury's Texas Brigade, CSA.* Edited by Norman D. Brown. Austin: University of Texas Press, 1980.

Frémont, John Charles. *Memoirs of My Life.* Chicago: Belford, Clarke, 1886.

Fry, James B. *Military Miscellanies.* New York: Brentano's, 1889.

Garland, Hamlin. *Ulysses S. Grant: His Life and Character.* New York: Doubleday & McClure, 1898.

Gooding, James. *On the Altar of Freedom: A Black Soldier's Civil War Letters from the Front.* Edited by Virginia Matzke Adams. Amherst: University of Massachusetts Press, 1991.

Gordon, John Brown. *Reminiscences of the Civil War.* New York: Scribner's, 1904.

Grant, Julia Dent. *The Personal Memoirs of Julia Dent Grant (Mrs. Ulysses S. Grant).* Edited by John Y. Simon. New York: Putnam, 1975.

Grant, Ulysses S. *The Papers of Ulysses S. Grant*. 32 vols. Edited by John Y. Simon and John F. Marszalek, et al. Carbondale: Southern Illinois University Press, 1967–2012.

Gurowski, Adam. *Diary*. Boston: Lee and Shepard, 1862.

Halleck, H. Wager. *Elements of Military Art and Science*. 2nd ed. New York: D. Appleton, 1860.

Hawthorne, Nathaniel. "Chiefly about War-Matters, by a Peaceable Man." *Atlantic Monthly* 10 (July 1862): 43–61.

Herndon, William H., and Jesse William Weik. *Herndon's Lincoln: The True Story of a Great Life*. 2 vols. Springfield, IL: Herndon's Lincoln Publishing, 1921.

Higginson, Thomas Wentworth. *Army Life in a Black Regiment*. Boston: Lee & Shepard, 1890.

Hitchcock, Ethan Allen. *Fifty Years in Camp and Field*. Edited by W. A. Croffut. New York: G. P. Putnam's Sons, 1909.

Hood, J. B. *Advance and Retreat: Personal Experiences in the United States and Confederate Armies*. New Orleans, LA: G. T. Beauregard, Hood Orphan Memorial Fund, 1880.

Howard, Oliver O. *Autobiography of Oliver Otis Howard*. 2 vols. New York: Baker & Taylor, 1907.

Howe, Julia Ward. *Reminiscences: 1819–1899*. Boston: Houghton Mifflin, 1899.

Howe, M. A. DeWolfe, ed. *Home Letters of General Sherman*. New York: Scribner's, 1909.

Hunter, David A. *Report of the Military Services of Gen. David Hunter, U.S.A., during the War of the Rebellion, Made to the U.S. War Department*. New York: D. Van Nostrand, 1873.

Jacobs, Harriet. *Incidents in the Life of a Slave Girl*. Edited by Lydia Maria Child. Boston, 1860.

James, Henry. *Autobiographies*. Edited by Philip Horne. New York: Library of America, 2016.
———. *A Small Boy and Others*. New York: Scribner's, 1914.

Johns, Jane Martin. *Personal Recollections of Early Decatur, Abraham Lincoln, Richard J. Oglesby and The Civil War*. Decatur [Illinois] Chapter, Daughters of the American Revolution, 1912.

Johnson, R. W. *A Soldier's Reminiscences in Peace and War*. Philadelphia: J. B. Lippincott, 1886.

Johnston, Joseph E. *Narrative of Military Operations, Directed, during the Late War between the States*. New York: D. Appleton, 1874.

Johnston, William Preston. *The Life of Gen. Albert Sidney Johnston*. New York: D. Appleton, 1878.

Jordan, Thomas, and J. P. Pryor. *The Campaigns of Lieut.-Gen. N. B. Forrest and the Forrest Cavalry*. New Orleans, LA: Blelock, 1868.

Kautz, August V. *Customs of the Service for Officers of the Army*. Philadelphia: Lippincott, 1866.

Kearny, Philip. *Service with the French Troops in Africa*. New York, 1844.

Keckley, Elizabeth. *Behind the Scenes, Or, Thirty Years a Slave, and Four Years in the White House*. New York: Penguin Classics, 2005.

Kemble, Frances Anne. *Journal of a Residence on a Georgian Plantation in 1838–1839.* Athens: University of Georgia Press, 1984.

Kephart, Horace. *Our Southern Highlanders.* New York: Macmillan, 1913.

Lincoln, Abraham. *The Collected Works of Abraham Lincoln.* 8 vols. Edited by Roy P. Basler. New Brunswick, NJ: Rutgers University Press, 1953.

Lincoln, Abraham, and Stephen A. Douglas. *Political Debates between Hon. Abraham Lincoln and Hon. Stephen A. Douglas.* Columbus: Follett, Foster, 1860.

Longstreet, James. *From Manassas to Appomattox: Memoirs of the Civil War in America.* Philadelphia: Lippincott, 1896.

Looby, Christopher, ed. *Complete Civil War Journal and Selected Letters of Thomas Wentworth Higginson.* Chicago: University of Chicago Press, 2000.

Loughborough, Mary Ann. *My Cave Life in Vicksburg.* New York: D. Appleton, 1864.

Lunt, Dolly Sumner. *A Woman's Wartime Journal.* Edited by Julian Street. New York: Century, 1918.

Lyman, Theodore. *Meade's Headquarters 1863–1865: Letters of Colonel Theodore Lyman.* Edited by George R. Agassiz. Boston: Atlantic Monthly Press, 1922.

Lynch, Charles H. *The Civil War Diary, 1862–1865.* Hartford, CT: privately printed, 1915.

Mahan, Dennis Hart. "The Cadet Life of Grant and Sherman." *Army and Navy Journal* 3, no. 32 (March 31, 1866): 507.

Mann, T. H. "A Yankee in Andersonville." *The Century Illustrated Monthly Magazine* 40, new ser. 18 (1890): 447–61, 606–22.

Martin, Thomas. *The Circle of the Mechanical Arts.* 2nd ed. London: Richard Rees, 1815.

Maury, Dabney Herndon. *Recollections of a Virginian in the Mexican, Indian, and Civil Wars.* New York: Scribner's, 1894.

McClure, Alexander K. *Abraham Lincoln and Men of War-Times: Some Personal Recollections of War and Politics during the Lincoln Administration.* Philadelphia: Times Publishing, 1892.

———, ed. *The Annals of the War, Written by Leading Participants North and South.* Philadelphia: Times Publishing, 1879.

McCord, Louisa S. "Uncle Tom's Cabin." *Southern Quarterly Review* 7, no. 13 (January 7, 1853): 81–120.

McKinley, Emilie. *From the Pen of a She-Rebel: The Civil War Diary of Emilie Riley McKinley.* Edited by Gordon A. Cotton. Columbia: University of South Carolina Press, 2001.

Meacham, A. B. *Wigwam and War-Path; or the Royal Chief in Chains.* Boston: John P. Dale, 1875.

Meade, George Gordon. *The Life and Letters of George Gordon Meade.* 2 vols. New York: Scribner's, 1913.

Miller, Francis Trevelyan, ed. *The Photographic History of the Civil War.* 10 vols. New York: Review of Reviews, 1911.

Minot, Stephen Weld. *War Diary and Letters of Stephen Minot Weld, 1861–1865.* Boston: Riverside Press, 1912.

Mitchell, Silas Weir. *In War Time*. New York: Century, 1915.

The Modern Pocket Hoyle. New York: Dick & Fitzgerald, 1868.

Mosby, John S. *The Memoirs of Colonel John S. Mosby*. Edited by Charles Wells Russell. Boston: Little, Brown, 1917.

———. *Mosby's War Reminiscences and Stuart's Cavalry Campaigns*. New York: Dodd, Mead, 1898.

Nicolay, Helen. *Lincoln's Secretary: A Biography of John G. Nicolay*. New York: Longmans, Green, 1949.

Olmsted, Frederick Law. *Writings on Landscape, Culture, and Society*. Edited by Charles E. Beveridge. New York: Library of America, 2015.

O'Sullivan, John L. "Annexation." *The United States Magazine and Democratic Review* 17, no. 1 (July–August 1845): 5–10.

———. "The Great Nation of Futurity." *The United States Magazine and Democratic Review* 6, no. 23 (November 1839): 426–30.

Parkman, Francis. *Montcalm and Wolfe*. Vol. 2. *France and England in North America*. Pt. 7. Boston: Little, Brown, 1888.

Pinkerton, Allan. *The Spy of the Rebellion*. New York: G. W. Carleton, 1886.

Plum, William R. *The Military Telegraph during the Civil War in the United States*. Chicago: Jansen, McClurg, 1882.

Pollard, Edward A. *The Lost Cause: A New Southern History of the War of the Confederates*. New York: E. B. Treat, 1866.

Porter, David D. *The Naval History of the Civil War*. New York: Sherman, 1886.

Porter, Horace. *Campaigning with Grant*. New York: Century, 1906.

Preliminary Report touching the Condition and Management of Emancipated Refugees; made to the Secretary of War by the American Freedmen's Inquiry Commission, June 30, 1863. New York: John F. Trow, 1863.

Prescott, William H. *History of the Conquest of Mexico*. New York: Harper & Brothers, 1843.

Reed, William Howell. *Hospital Life in the Army of the Potomac*. Boston: William V. Spencer, 1866.

Reid, Mayne. "A Dashing Dragoon: The Murat of the American Army." Rpt. in *Service with the French Troops in Africa*. 1846. New York, ca. 1889.

Richardson, Albert D. *A Personal History of Ulysses S. Grant*. Hartford, CT: American Publishing, 1868.

Rood, Hosea W., compiler. *Wisconsin at Vicksburg*. Madison: Wisconsin-Vicksburg Monument Commission, 1914.

Roosevelt, Theodore. *The Rough Riders*. New York: P. F. Collier & Son, 1899.

———. *The Strenuous Life: Essays and Addresses*. New York: Century, 1902.

Rose, Victor M. *Ross' Texas Brigade*. Louisville: Courier-Journal, 1881.

Rusling, James Fowler. *Men and Things I Saw in Civil War Days*. New York: Methodist Book Concern, 1914.

Russell, William Howard. *My Diary North and South*. Boston: T. O. H. P. Burnham, 1863.

Schaff, Morris. *The Spirit of Old West Point, 1858–1862*. Boston: Houghton Mifflin, 1907.

Schofield, John M. *Forty-Six Years in the Army*. New York: Century, 1897.

Scott, Winfield. *Memoirs*. New York: Sheldon & Company, 1864.

Semmes, Raphael. *Memoirs of Service Afloat, during the War between the States*. Baltimore, MD: Kelly, Piet, 1869.

———. *Service Afloat and Ashore during the Mexican War*. Cincinnati, OH: Wm. H. Moore & Co., 1851.

Seward, William H., and Frederick W. Seward. *Autobiography of William H. Seward, from 1801–1834, with a Memoir of His Life, and Selections from His Letters from 1831–1846*. New York: D. Appleton and Company, 1877.

Shaw, John, ed. *Crete and James: Personal Letters of Lucretia and James Garfield*. East Lansing: Michigan State University Press, 1994.

Sheridan, Philip H. *Personal Memoirs of P. H. Sheridan*. 2 vols. New York: Charles L. Webster, 1888.

Sherman, William T. *Memoirs of General William T. Sherman*. 2 vols. New York: D. Appleton, 1875.

Smith, Richard Penn. *Davy Crockett's Exploits and Adventures in Texas . . . Written by Himself*. New York: Wm. H. Graham, 1848.

Smith, W. A. *The Anson Guards: Company C, Fourteenth Regiment North Carolina Volunteers, 1861–1865*. Charlotte, NC: Stone, 1914.

Smith, Walter George, ed. *Life and Letters of Thomas Kilby Smith*. New York: G. P. Putnam's Sons, 1898.

Stanley, Henry Morton. *The Autobiography*. Edited by Dorothy Stanley. Boston: Houghton Mifflin, 1909.

Stephens, Alexander H. *A Constitutional View of the Late War between the States*. Philadelphia: National, 1868.

———. *Recollections of Alexander H. Stephens*. Edited by Myrta Lockett Avary. New York: Doubleday, Page, 1910.

Stillwell, Leander. *The Story of a Common Soldier of Army Life in the Civil War 1861–1865*. 2nd ed. Kansas City, MO: Franklin Hudson, 1920.

Swinton, William. *Campaigns of the Army of the Potomac*. New York: Scribner's, 1882.

Taylor, Richard. *Destruction and Reconstruction: Personal Experiences of the Late War*. New York: Appleton, 1879.

Tenney, Luman Harris. *War Diary of Luman Harris Tenney*. Cleveland, OH: Evangelical, 1914.

Thoreau, Henry David. *The Writings of Henry David Thoreau*. Boston: Houghton Mifflin, 1895.

Tripler, Eunice. *Some Notes of Personal Recollections*. New York: Grafton Press, 1910.

Twain, Mark. *Life on the Mississippi*. New York: Harper & Brothers, 1901.

The United States Sanitary Commission: A Sketch of Its Purposes and Its Work. Boston: Little, Brown, 1863.

Walke, Henry. *Naval Scenes and Reminiscences of the Civil War in the United States.* New York: F. R. Reed, 1877.

Walker, C. Irvine. *The Life of Lieutenant General Richard Heron Anderson of the Confederate States Army.* Charleston, SC: Art Publishing, 1917.

Wallace, Lew. *Autobiography.* 2 vols. New York: Harper & Brothers, 1906.

Washington, Booker T. *Up from Slavery: An Autobiography.* Garden City, NY: Doubleday, 1901.

Watkins, Sam R. *"Co. Aytch," Maury Grays, First Tennessee Regiment; or, A Side Show of the Big War.* Chattanooga, TN: Times, 1900.

Weems, M. L. *The Life of Washington.* Philadelphia, 1853.

Welles, Gideon. *Diary of Gideon Welles.* Boston: Houghton Mifflin, 1911.

Weston, David. *Among the Wounded: Experiences of a Delegate, U.S. Christian Commission.* Philadelphia: Jas. B. Rodgers, 1864.

Whitman, Walt. *Complete Prose Works.* New York: D. Appleton, 1910.

Williams, Charles Richard, ed. *The Diary and Letters of Rutherford B. Hayes.* Columbus: Ohio State Archaeological and Historical Society, 1922.

Williams, George Washington. *A History of the Negro Troops in the War of the Rebellion 1861–1865.* New York: Harper & Brothers, 1888.

Williams, Richard Brady, ed. *Stonewall's Prussian Mapmaker: The Journals of Captain Oscar Hinrichs.* Chapel Hill: University of North Carolina Press, 2014.

Wilson, James Grant. *General Grant.* New York: D. Appleton, 1897.

Wilson, James Harrison. *Life and Campaigns of General Grant.* New York: De Witt, 1868.

———. *The Life of John A. Rawlins.* New York: J. J. Little & Ives, 1916.

———. *Under the Old Flag.* New York: D. Appleton, 1912.

Wilson, Joseph T. *The Black Phalanx: A History of the Negro Soldiers of the United States in the Wars of 1773–1812, 1861–'65.* Hartford, CT: American Publishing, 1888.

Wilson, Rufus Rockwell, ed. *Intimate Memories of Lincoln.* Elmira, NY: Primavera Press, 1945.

Wilson, Woodrow. *A History of the American People.* 5 vols. New York: Harper & Brothers, 1902.

Winkler, Mrs. C. M. *The Life and Character of Gen. John B. Hood.* Austin: Draughton & Lambert, 1885.

Wister, Owen. *Ulysses S. Grant.* Boston: Small, Maynard, 1900.

Woodward, C. Vann, ed. *Mary Chesnut's Civil War.* New Haven, CT: Yale University Press, 1981.

Worsham, John H. *One of Jackson's Foot Cavalry: His Experience and What He Saw during the War 1861–1865.* New York: Neale, 1912.

Young, John Russell. *Around the World with General Grant.* 2 vols. New York: American News, 1879.

Twentieth- and Twenty-First-Century Sources on the Mexican War, the Civil War, and Related Subjects

Aaron, Daniel. *The Unwritten War: American Writers and the Civil War.* Madison: University of Wisconsin Press, 1987.

Adams, Michael C. C. *Living Hell: The Dark Side of the Civil War.* Baltimore, MD: Johns Hopkins University Press, 2005.

Ambrose, Stephen E. *Halleck: Lincoln's Chief of Staff.* Baton Rouge: Louisiana State University Press, 1998.

Anderson, Fred. *Crucible of War: The Seven Years' War and the Fate of British North America, 1754–1766.* New York: Vintage, 2001.

Beckert, Sven. *Empire of Cotton: A Global History.* New York: Vintage, 2014.

Berlin, Ira, et al., *Slaves No More: Three Essays on Emancipation and the Civil War.* Cambridge, UK: Cambridge University Press, 1992.

Blanton, DeAnne, and Lauren M. Cook. *They Fought Like Demons: Women Soldiers in the Civil War.* Baton Rouge: Louisiana State University Press, 2002.

Blight, David W. *Race and Reunion: The Civil War in American Memory.* Cambridge, MA: Harvard University Press, 2001.

Boardman, Andrea. "The U.S.-Mexican War and the Beginnings of American Tourism in Mexico." *Holiday in Mexico: Critical Reflections on Tourism and Tourist Encounters.* Edited by Diane Berger and Andrew Grant Wood. Durham, NC: Duke University Press, 2010.

Brands, H. W. *The Man Who Saved the Union: Ulysses S. Grant in War and Peace.* New York: Random House, 2012.

Buinicki, Martin T., and David M. Owens. "The Last Campaign of *John Brown's Body*: West Point and America's Forgotten Civil War Epic." *War, Literature & the Arts* 27 (2015): 1–25.

Campbell, Edwina S. *Citizen of a Wider Commonwealth: Ulysses S. Grant's Postpresidential Diplomacy.* Carbondale: Southern Illinois University Press, 2016.

Carter, Everett. "Cultural History Written with Lightning: The Significance of *The Birth of a Nation* (1915)." *Hollywood as Historian: American Film in a Cultural Context.* Edited by Peter C. Rollins. Rev. ed. Lexington: University Press of Kentucky, 1998.

Castel, Albert. *General Sterling Price and the Civil War in the West.* Baton Rouge: Louisiana State University Press, 1968.

Catton, Bruce. *Grant Moves South.* Boston, Little, Brown, 1960.

———. *Grant Takes Command.* Boston: Little, Brown, 1969.

———. *A Stillness at Appomattox.* Garden City, NY: Doubleday, 1953.

———. *U. S. Grant and the American Military Tradition.* Edited by Oscar Handlin. Boston: Little, Brown, 1954.

Chaffin, Tom. *Pathfinder: John C. Frémont and the Path of American Empire.* Norman: University of Oklahoma Press, 2002.

Chernow, Ron. *Grant.* New York: Penguin, 2017.

Cimprich, John, and Robert C. Mainfort Jr. "Fort Pillow Revisited: New Evidence about an Old Controversy," *Civil War History* 28, no. 4 (December 1982): 297–99.

Connelly, Thomas Lawrence. *Army of the Heartland: The Army of Tennessee, 1861–1862.* Baton Rouge: Louisiana State University Press, 1967.

Cothran, Boyd. *Remembering the Modoc War: Redemptive Violence and the Making of American Innocence.* Chapel Hill: University of North Carolina Press, 2014.

Cozzens, Peter. *The Darkest Days of the War: The Battles of Iuka & Corinth.* Chapel Hill: University of North Carolina, 1997.

———. *The Shipwreck of Their Hopes: The Battles for Chattanooga.* Urbana: University of Illinois Press, 1998.

Cushman, Stephen. *Belligerent Muse: Five Northern Writers and How They Shaped Our Understanding of the Civil War.* Chapel Hill: University of North Carolina Press, 2014.

Dawes, James. *The Language of War: Literature and Culture in the U.S. from the Civil War through World War II.* Cambridge, MA: Harvard University Press, 2002.

Devine, Shauna. *Learning from the Wounded: The Civil War and the Rise of American Medical Science.* Chapel Hill: University of North Carolina Press, 2014.

DeVoto, Bernard. *The Year of Decision: 1846.* 1942. New York: St. Martin's, 2000.

Dinges, Bruce J., and Shirley A. Leckie. *A Just and Righteous Cause: Benjamin H. Grierson's Civil War Memoir.* Carbondale: University of Southern Illinois Press, 2008.

Donald, David Herbert. *Lincoln.* London: Jonathan Cape, 1995.

Downs, Gregory P., and Kate Masur, eds. *The World the Civil War Made.* Chapel Hill: University of North Carolina Press, 2015.

Du Bois, W. E. B. *Writings.* New York: Library of America, 1986.

Eisenhower, John S. D. *So Far from God: The U.S. War with Mexico 1846–1848.* New York: Random House, 1989.

Fahs, Alice, and Joan Waugh. *The Memory of the Civil War in American Culture.* Chapel Hill: University of North Carolina Press, 2004.

Faust, Drew Gilpin. "Equine Relics of the Civil War." *Southern Cultures* 6 (Spring 2000): 23–49.

———. *Mothers of Invention: Women of the Slaveholding South in the American Civil War.* Chapel Hill: University of North Carolina Press, 1996.

———. *This Republic of Suffering: Death and the American Civil War.* New York: Vintage, 2008.

———, ed. *The Ideology of Slavery: Proslavery Thought in the Antebellum South, 1830–1860.* Baton Rouge: Louisiana State University Press, 1981.

Fellman, Michael. *Citizen Sherman: A Life of William Tecumseh Sherman.* New York: Random House, 1995.

Flood, Charles Bracelen. *Grant and Sherman: The Friendship That Won the Civil War.* New York: Farrar, Straus & Giroux, 2005.

Foner, Eric. *Reconstruction: America's Unfinished Revolution, 1863–1877.* New York: Harper & Row, 1988.

———, ed. *Our Lincoln: New Perspectives on Lincoln and his World.* New York: Norton, 2008.

Foote, Shelby. *The Civil War: A Narrative.* 3 vols. New York: Random House, 1958–1974.

Freeman, Douglas Southall. *Lee's Lieutenants: A Study in Command.* 3 vols. New York: Scribner's, 1942–44.

———. *R. E. Lee: A Biography.* 4 vols. New York: Scribner's, 1934–1935.

Fuller, J. F. C. *The Generalship of Ulysses S. Grant.* New York: Da Capo, 1991.

Fuller, Randall. *From Battlefields Rising: How the Civil War Transformed American Literature.* New York: Oxford University Press, 2011.

Gallagher, Gary W. *The Shenandoah Valley Campaign of 1864.* Chapel Hill: University of North Carolina Press, 2006.

Gallagher, Gary W., and Caroline E. Janney, eds. *Cold Harbor to the Crater: The End of the Overland Campaign.* Chapel Hill: University of North Carolina Press, 2015.

Greenberg, Amy C. *A Wicked War: Clay, Lincoln, and the 1846 U.S. Invasion of Mexico.* New York: Knopf, 2012.

Griffin, Martin. *Ashes of the Mind: War and Memory in Northern Literature, 1865–1900.* Amherst: University of Massachusetts Press, 2009.

Hesseltine, William B. *Ulysses S. Grant, Politician.* New York: Dodd, Mead & Co., 1935.

Hollandsworth, James G. Jr. *The Louisiana Native Guards: The Black Military Experience during the Civil War.* Baton Rouge: Louisiana State University Press, 1995.

Hughes, Nathaniel Cheairs Jr. *The Battle of Belmont: Grant Strikes South.* Chapel Hill: University of North Carolina Press, 2008.

Hurst, Jack. *Nathan Bedford Forrest: A Biography.* New York: Vintage, 1994.

John Hollis Bankhead: Memorial Addresses Delivered in the Senate and the House of Representatives of the United States, 66th Congress, 2nd Session. Washington, D.C.: Government Printing Office, 1921.

Leech, Margaret. *Reveille in Washington.* Garden City, NY: Garden City Publishing, 1941.

Lewis, Berkeley R. *Small Arms and Ammunition in the United States Service.* Smithsonian Miscellaneous Collections 129. Washington, D.C.: Smithsonian Institution, 1956.

Lewis, Lloyd. *Captain Sam Grant.* Boston: Little, Brown, 1950.

———. *Sherman: Fighting Prophet.* New York: Harcourt, Brace, 1932.

Limon, John. *Writing after War: American War Fiction from Realism to Postmodernism.* New York: Oxford University Press, 1994.

Marszalek, John F. *Sherman: A Soldier's Passion for Order.* New York: Free Press, 2003.

Marten, James. *Sing Not War: The Lives of Union & Confederate Veterans in Gilded Age America.* Chapel Hill: University of North Carolina Press, 2011.

Marvel, William. *Lincoln's Autocrat: The Life of Edwin Stanton.* Chapel Hill: University of North Carolina Press, 2015.

McCullough, David. *The Battle between the Seas: The Creation of the Panama Canal.* New York: Simon & Schuster, 1978.

McDonough, James Lee. *William Tecumseh Sherman: In the Service of My Country, A Life.* New York: Norton, 2016.

McFeely, William S. *Grant: A Biography.* New York: Norton, 1981.

McPherson, James M. *Battle Cry of Freedom*. New York: Oxford University Press, 1988.

———. *For Cause and Comrades*. New York: Oxford University Press, 1998.

———. *War on the Waters: The Union & Confederate Navies, 1861–1865*. Chapel Hill: University of North Carolina Press, 2012.

McPherson, James M., and William J. Cooper Jr., eds. *Writing the Civil War: The Quest to Understand*. Columbia: University of South Carolina Press, 2000.

Mohr, Clarence L. "Southern Blacks in the Civil War: A Century of Historiography." *Journal of Negro History* 59, no. 2 (1974): 177–95.

Morsberger, Robert E., and Katharine M. Morsberger. *Lew Wallace: Militant Romantic*. New York: McGraw Hill, 1980.

Moten, Matthew. *The Delafield Commission and the American Military Profession*. College Station: Texas A&M University Press, 2000.

Neely, Mark E. Jr. *The Boundaries of American Political Culture in the Civil War Era*. Chapel Hill: University of North Carolina Press, 2005.

Ochs, Stephen J. *A Black Patriot and a White Priest: Andre Cailloux and Claude Paschal Maistre in Civil War New Orleans*. Baton Rouge: Louisiana State University Press, 2002.

Patterson, Orlando. *Slavery and Social Death: A Comparative Study*. Cambridge, MA: Harvard University Press, 1982.

Perret, Geoffrey. *Ulysses S. Grant: Soldier and President*. New York: Modern Library, 1998.

Perry, Mark. *Grant and Twain: The Story of a Friendship that Changed America*. New York: Random House, 2004.

Pitkin, Thomas M. *The Captain Departs: Ulysses S. Grant's Last Campaign*. Carbondale: Southern Illinois University Press, 1973.

Powers, Thomas. *The Killing of Crazy Horse*. New York: Vintage, 2011.

Pryor, Elizabeth. *Reading the Man: A Portrait of Robert E. Lee through His Private Letters*. New York: Penguin, 2007.

Quarles, Benjamin. *The Negro in the Civil War*. Boston: Little, Brown, 1953.

Rable, George C. *Fredericksburg! Fredericksburg!* Chapel Hill: University of North Carolina Press, 2002.

Raines, Rebecca Robbins. *Getting the Message Through: A Branch History of the U.S. Army Signal Corps*. Washington, D.C.: Center of Military History, U.S. Army, 1999.

Rogin, Michael. "'The Sword Became a Flashing Vision': D. W. Griffith's *The Birth of a Nation*." *The New American Studies: Essays from Representations*. Edited by Philip Fisher. Berkeley: University of California Press, 1991.

Royster, Charles. *The Destructive War: William Tecumseh Sherman, Stonewall Jackson, and the Americans*. New York: Knopf, 1991.

Sarna, Jonathan D. *When General Grant Expelled the Jews*. New York: Nextbook/Schocken, 2012.

Schultz, Jane E. *Women at the Front: Hospital Works in Civil War America*. Chapel Hill: University of North Carolina Press, 2004.

Sears, Stephen W. "The Ordeal of General Stone." *Controversies and Commanders: Dispatches from the Army of the Potomac*. Boston: Houghton Mifflin, 1999.

———. *To the Gates of Richmond: The Peninsula Campaign*. Boston: Houghton Mifflin, 1992.

Showalter, Elaine. *The Civil Wars of Julia Ward Howe: A Biography*. New York: Simon & Schuster, 2016.

Simpson, Brooks D. *Let Us Have Peace: Ulysses S. Grant and the Politics of War and Reconstruction, 1861–1868*. Chapel Hill: University of North Carolina Press, 1991.

———. *Ulysses S. Grant: Triumph over Adversity, 1822–1865*. Boston: Houghton Mifflin, 2000.

Simpson, Brooks D., and Jean V. Berlin, eds. *Sherman's Civil War: Selected Correspondence of William T. Sherman, 1860–1865*. Chapel Hill: University of North Carolina Press, 1999.

Smith, Jean Edward. *Grant*. New York: Simon & Schuster, 2001.

Stout, Harry S. *Upon the Altar of the Nation: A Moral History of the Civil War*. New York: Penguin, 2006.

Taylor, Paul. *Orlando M. Poe: Civil War General and Great Lakes Engineer*. Kent, OH: Kent State University Press, 2009.

Thomas, Benjamin P., and Harold M. Hyman. *Stanton: The Life and Times of Lincoln's Secretary of War*. New York: Knopf, 2013.

Varon, Elizabeth R. *Appomattox: Victory, Defeat, and Freedom at the End of the Civil War*. New York: Oxford University Press, 2014.

Wachtell, Cynthia. *War No More: The Antiwar Impulse in American Literature, 1861–1914*. Baton Rouge: Louisiana State University Press, 2010.

Ward, Geoffrey C. *A Disposition to Be Rich: Ferdinand Ward, the Greatest Swindler of the Gilded Age*. New York: Vintage, 2013.

Waugh, Joan. *U.S. Grant: American Hero, American Myth*. Chapel Hill: University of North Carolina Press, 2009.

Welsh, Peter C. *Tanning in the United States to 1850: A Brief History*. Washington, D.C.: Smithsonian Institution, 1964.

Wert, Jeffry D. *General James Longstreet: The Confederacy's Most Controversial Soldier*. New York: Simon & Schuster, 1993.

White, Ronald C. *American Ulysses: A Life of Ulysses S. Grant*. New York: Random House, 2016.

Wilson, Edmund. *Patriotic Gore*. 1962. New York: Norton, 1994.

Winders, Richard Bruce. *Mr. Polk's Army: The American Experience in the Mexican War*. College Station: Texas A&M University Press, 1997.

Wolmar, Christian. *The Great Railroad Revolution*. New York: PublicAffairs, 2013.

Yetman, Norman R., ed. *Voices from Slavery: 100 Authentic Slave Narratives*. Mineola, NY: Dover, 2000.

Nonfiction Accounts of Other Conflicts and Studies of American Culture

Ammianus Marcellinus. *The Later Roman Empire*. Translated by Walter Hamilton. New York: Penguin Classics, 2004.

Appian. *The Civil War*. Translated by John Carter. New York: Penguin Classics, 1996.

Babur. *The Baburnama: Memoirs of Babur, Prince and Emperor*. Translated by Wheeler M. Thackston. New York: Modern Library, 2002.

Baldwin, James. *Collected Essays*. Edited by Toni Morrison. New York: Library of America, 1998.

———. *The Cross of Redemption: Uncollected Writings*. Edited by Randall Kenan. New York: Vintage, 2011.

Blunden, Edmund. *Undertones of War*. Chicago: University of Chicago Press, 2007.

Brown, Malcolm, ed. *The Imperial War Museum Book of the Western Front*. London: Pan Macmillan, 2001.

Caesar. *The Civil War*. Translated by John Carter. Oxford World's Classics. New York: Oxford University Press, 2008.

Carr, E. H. *What Is History?* New York: Vintage, 1961.

Clausewitz, Carl von. *On War*. Edited and translated by Michael Howard and Peter Paret. Princeton, NJ: Princeton University Press, 1984.

Didion, Joan. *South and West: From a Notebook*. New York: Knopf, 2017.

Eakin, Paul John, ed. *American Autobiography: Retrospect and Prospect*. Madison: University of Wisconsin Press, 1991.

Fermor, Patrick Leigh. *Words of Mercury*. Edited by Artemis Cooper. London: John Murray, 2004.

Filkins, Dexter. *The Forever War*. New York: Random House, 2008.

Finkel, David. *The Good Soldiers*. New York: Farrar, Straus and Giroux, 2009.

Flavius Vegetius Renatus *The Military Institutions of the Romans*. Translated by John Clark. Edited by Thomas R. Phillips. 1944; Westport, CT: Greenwood Press, 1985.

Fussell, Paul. *Uniforms: Why We Are What We Wear*. New York: Mariner, 2003.

———. *Wartime: Understanding Behavior in the Second World War*. New York: Oxford University Press, 1989.

Graves, Robert. *Good-bye to All That*. New York: Anchor-Doubleday, 1985.

Gregory of Tours. *The History of the Franks*. Translated by Lewis Thorpe. New York: Penguin Classics, 1974.

Haag, Pamela. *The Gunning of America: Business and the Making of American Gun Culture*. New York: Basic Books, 2016.

Hemingway, Ernest. *Hemingway on War*. Edited by Seán Hemingway. New York: Scribner's, 2003.

Holinshed, Raphael. *Holinshed's Chronicles of England, Scotland, and Ireland*. London, 1808.

Hughes, Daniel, ed. *Moltke on the Art of War: Selected Writings*. New York: Random House, Presidio, 1995.

ibn Munqidh, Usama. *The Book of Contemplation: Islam and the Crusades*. Translated by Paul M. Cobb. New York: Penguin Classics, 2008.

Imbarrato, Susan Clair. *Declarations of Independence in Eighteenth-Century Autobiography*. Knoxville: University of Tennessee Press, 1998.

Jomini, Antoine-Henri. *Summary of the Art of War*. Translated by O. F. Winship and E. E. McLean. New York: G. P. Putnam, 1854.

Josephus. *The Jewish War of Flavius Josephus*. Translated by Robert Traill. London: Houlston and Stoneman, 1851.

Jünger, Ernst. *Storm of Steel*. New York: Penguin, 2004.

Kahn, Coppélia. "Forbidden Mixtures: Shakespeare in Blackface Minstrelsy, 1844." *Shakespeare and the Cultures of Performance*. Edited by Paul Yachnin and Patricia Badir. Aldershot, UK: Ashgate, 2008.

Keegan, John. *Face of Battle: A Study of Agincourt, Waterloo and the Somme*. New York: Penguin, 1978.

———. *The Mask of Command*. New York: Penguin, 1987.

Knightley, Phillip. *The First Casualty: The War Correspondent as Hero and Myth-Maker from the Crimea to Iraq*. Baltimore, MD: Johns Hopkins University Press, 2004.

Lamore, Eric D., ed. *Reading African American Autobiography*. Madison: University of Wisconsin Press, 2017.

Las Casas, Bartolomé de. *A Short Account of the Destruction of the Indies*. Edited and translated by Nigel Griffin. New York: Penguin Classics, 2004.

Leibowitz, Herbert. *Fabricating Lives: Explorations in American Autobiography*. 1975; New York: New Directions, 1989.

Liebling, A. J. *World War II Writings*. Edited by Pete Hamill. New York: Library of America, 2008.

Livy. *The War with Hannibal*. Books XXI–XXX of *The History of Rome from Its Foundation*. Translated by Aubrey de Sélincourt. Edited by Betty Radice. New York: Penguin Classics, 1972.

Mercer, General [Alexander] Cavalié. *Journal of the Waterloo Campaign*. 2 vols. Edinburgh: William Blackwood and Sons, 1870.

Michaels, Walter Benn. *Our America: Nativism, Modernism, and Pluralism*. Durham, NC: Duke University Press, 1995.

Middlebrook, Martin. *The First Day on the Somme: 1 July 1916*. Barnsley, South Yorkshire: Pen & Sword Books, 2006.

Montague, Mary Wortley. *The Letters and Works of Lady Mary Wortley Montague*. Ed. Lord Wharncliffe. 3 vols. London: Richard Bentley, 1837.

O'Brien, Tim. *If I Die in a Combat Zone: Box Me Up and Ship Me Home*. New York: Broadway Books, 1999.

Orwell, George. *Essays*. Edited by John Carey. New York: Everyman's Library, 2002.

Packer, George. *The Assassins' Gate: America in Iraq.* New York: Farrar, Straus and Giroux, 2005.

Parini, Jay, ed. *The Norton Book of American Autobiography.* New York: Norton, 1999.

Plutarch's Lives: The Translation Called Dryden's. 2 vols. Revised by Arthur Hugh Clough. Boston: Little, Brown, 1895.

Pyle, Ernie. *Ernie's War: The Best of Ernie Pyle's World War II Dispatches.* Edited by David Nichols. New York: Simon & Schuster, 1987.

Renoir, Jean. *Renoir, My Father.* Translated by Randolph and Dorothy Weaver. 1962; New York: New York Review Books, 2001.

Saint-Exupéry, Antoine de. *Wind, Sand and Stars.* Translated by Lewis Galantiére. (New York: Harcourt, Harvest, 2002).

Sallust. *The Jugurthine War/The Conspiracy of Catiline.* Translated by S. A. Handford. New York: Penguin Classics, 1963.

Ségur, Philippe-Paul de. *Defeat: Napoleon's Russian Campaign.* Translated by J. David Townsend. New York: New York Review Books, 2008.

Shea, Daniel B. Jr. *Spiritual Autobiography in Early America.* Princeton, NJ: Princeton University Press, 1968.

Sledge, E. B. *With the Old Breed at Peleliu and Okinawa.* New York: Ballantine, Presidio, 2010.

Slide, Anthony, ed. *D. W. Griffith: Interviews.* Jackson: University of Mississippi Press, 2012.

Slotkin, Richard. *Gunfighter Nation: The Myth of the Frontier in Twentieth-Century America.* Norman: University of Oklahoma Press, 1998.

Solnit, Rebecca. *River of Shadows: Eadweard Muybridge and the Technological Wild West.* New York: Penguin, 2004.

Stein, Gertrude. *Four in America.* New Haven, CT: Yale University Press, 1947.

Steinbeck, John. *Once There Was a War.* 1943; New York: Penguin Classics, 2007.

Stone, Albert E. *Autobiographical Occasions and Original Acts.* Philadelphia: University of Pennsylvania Press, 1982.

Tuchman, Barbara W. *A Distant Mirror: The Calamitous 14th Century.* New York: Ballantine, 1979.

Weber, Eugen. "The Ups and Downs of Honor." *The American Scholar* 68, no. 1 (Winter 1999): 79–92.

Weil, Simone. "The Iliad, or the Poem of Force." *War and the Iliad.* Translated by Mary McCarthy. New York: New York Review Books, 2005.

Woolf, Virginia. *Moments of Being.* 2nd ed. Edited by Jeanne Schulkind. Orlando: Harcourt Brace, 1985.

Xenophon. *Education of Cyrus.* Translated and edited by Wayne Ambler. Ithaca, NY: Cornell University Press, 2001.

———. *The Persian Expedition.* Translated by Rex Warner. New York: Penguin Classics, 1972.

Yagoda, Ben. *Memoir: A History.* New York: Riverhead, 2010.

Anthologies and Sourcebooks of Nonfiction War Writing

The American Revolution: Writings from the War of Independence 1775–1783. Edited by John Rhodehamel. New York: Library of America, 2001.

The Art of War in World History: From Antiquity to the Nuclear Age. Edited by Gérard Chaliand. Berkeley: University of California Press, 1994.

The Blue and the Gray. 2 vols. Edited by Henry Steele Commager. New York: Plume, 1994.

The Book of War: 25 Centuries of Great War Writing. Edited by John Keegan. New York: Viking, 1999.

The Civil War: Told by Those Who Lived It. 4 vols. Edited by Brooks D. Simpson et al. New York: Library of America, 2011–2014.

The Lincoln Anthology: Great Writings on His Life and Legacy from 1860 to Now. Edited by Harold Holzer. New York: Library of America, 2008.

The Norton Book of Modern War. Edited by Paul Fussell. New York: Norton, 1991.

The Oxford Book of Military Anecdotes. Edited by Max Hastings. New York: Oxford, 1985.

President Lincoln Assassinated!! The Firsthand Story of the Murder, Manhunt, Trial, and Mourning. Edited by Harold Holzer. New York: Library of America, 2015.

Reporting Vietnam. 2 vols. Edited by Milton J. Bates et al. New York: Library of America, 1998.

Reporting World War II. 2 vols. Edited by Samuel Hynes et al. New York: Library of America, 1995.

War No More: Three Centuries of American Antiwar and Peace Writing. Edited by Lawrence Rosenwald. New York: Library of America, 2016.

The War of 1812: Writings from America's Second War of Independence. Edited by Donald R. Hickey. New York: Library of America, 2013.

World War I and America. Edited by A. Scott Berg. New York: Library of America, 2017.

Fiction, Poetry, and Song

American War Poetry: An Anthology. Edited by Lorrie Goldensohn. New York: Columbia University Press, 2006.

Ariosto. *Orlando Furioso.* Translated by Barbara Reynolds. New York: Penguin Classics, 1975.

Banks, Russell. *Cloudsplitter.* New York: HarperPerennial, 1999.

Barbusse, Henry. *Under Fire.* Translated by Robin Buss. New York: Penguin Classics, 2004.

Bierce, Ambrose. *Tales of Soldiers and Civilians.* San Francisco: E. L. G. Steele, 1891.

Brooks, Geraldine. *March.* New York: Penguin, 2006.

Chevallier, Gabriel. *Fear.* Translated by Malcolm Imrie. New York: New York Review Books, 2011.

Churchill, Winston. *The Crisis.* New York: Macmillan, 1901.

Cobb, Humphrey. *Paths of Glory*. New York: Penguin Classics, 2010.

The Columbia Book of Civil War Poetry: From Whitman to Walcott. Edited by Richard Marius and Keith Frome. New York: Columbia University Press, 1994.

Cooper, James Fenimore. *The Last of the Mohicans, Or, A Narrative of 1757*. Cambridge, MA: Houghton, Mifflin, 1876.

Crane, Stephen. *The Red Badge of Courage: An Episode of the American Civil War*. New York: D. Appleton, 1896.

De Forest, John W. *Miss Ravenel's Conversion from Secession to Loyalty*. New York: Harper & Brothers, 1867.

Dickens, Charles. *Great Expectations*. 3 vols. London: Chapman and Hall, 1861.

Dixon, Thomas Jr. *The Clansman: An Historical Romance of the Ku Klux Klan*. New York: Grosset & Dunlap, 1905.

Doctorow, E. L. *The March*. New York: Random House, 2005.

Dryden, John, trans. *Virgil's Æneid*. Vol. 13 of *The Harvard Classics*. Edited by Charles W. Eliot. New York: P. F. Collier & Son, 1909.

Dunbar, Paul Laurence. *The Complete Poems of Paul Laurence Dunbar*. New York: Dodd, Mead, 1922.

Ferdowsi, Abolqasem. *Shahnameh*. Translated by Dick Davis. New York: Penguin Classics, 2006.

Foote, Shelby. *Shiloh*. New York: Vintage, 1991.

Frazier, Charles. *Cold Mountain*. New York: Grove, 2006.

Grimm, Hans Herbert. *Schlump*. Translated by Jamie Bulloch. New York: New York Review Books, 2015.

Grossman, Vasily. *Life and Fate*. Translated by Robert Chandler. New York: New York Review Books, 2006.

Gurganus, Allan. *Oldest Living Confederate Widow Tells All*. New York: Ballantine, 1996.

Harper, Frances Ellen Watkins. *Iola Leroy*. New York: Penguin Classics, 2010.

Harte, Bret. *Poems and Two Men of Sandy Bar, a Drama*. Vol. 12 of *The Writings of Bret Harte*. Boston: Houghton Mifflin, 1910.

Hašek, Jaroslav. *The Good Soldier Švejk and His Fortunes in the World War*. Translated by Cecil Parrott. London: Penguin, 1974.

Heller, Joseph. *Catch-22*. New York: Simon & Schuster, 2011.

Hellman, Lillian. *The Little Foxes, Six Plays*. New York: Vintage, 1979.

Hicks, Robert. *The Widow of the South*. New York: Time Warner, 2005.

Homer. Translated by Alexander Pope. 3 vols. New York: Harper & Brothers, 1836.

Jones, James. *The Thin Red Line*. New York: Dell, 1998.

Lartéguy, Jean. *The Centurions*. Translated by Xan Fielding. New York: Penguin Classics, 2015.

Ledig, Gert. *The Stalin Front*. Translated by Michael Hofmann. New York: New York Review Books, 2004.

Lever, Charles. *Charles O'Malley, the Irish Dragoon*. London: Routledge, 1872.

Library of Southern Literature. 16 vols. Edited by Edwin Anderson Alderman and Joel Chandler Harris. Atlanta, GA: Martin & Hoyt, 1910.

Lomax, John A., and Alan Lomax, compilers. *American Ballads and Folksongs*. New York: Macmillan, 1934.

Marryat, Frederick. *Mr. Midshipman Easy*. London: Macmillan, Saunders and Otley, 1836.

Melville, Herman. *Battle-Pieces and Aspects of the War*. New York: Harper & Brothers, 1866.

Mitchell, Margaret. *Gone with the Wind*. 1936; New York: Pocket, 2008.

Morrison, Toni. *Beloved*. New York: Vintage, 1987.

Norris, Frank. *McTeague: A Story of San Francisco*. New York: Doubleday, 1899.

The New Oxford Book of War Poetry. 2nd ed. Edited by Jon Stallworthy. New York: Oxford University Press, 2016.

The Penguin Book of First World War Poetry. Edited by George Walter. New York: Penguin, 2007.

The Penguin Book of First World War Stories. Edited by Barbara Korte. New York: Penguin, 2007.

Poems of the Civil War. Edited by J. D. McClatchy. New York: Library of America, 2005.

Poetry of the First World War: An Anthology. Edited by Tim Kendall. New York: Oxford University Press, 2014.

Poets of World War II. Edited by Harvey M. Shapiro. New York: Library of America, 2003.

Pound, Ezra. *Cathay, Lustra*. London: Elkin Mathews, 1916.

Pushkin, Alexander. "The Queen of Spades." In *Novels, Tales, Journeys: The Complete Prose of Alexander Pushkin*. Translated by Richard Pevear and Larissa Volokhonsky. New York: Knopf, 2016.

Remarque, Erich Maria. *All Quiet on the Western Front*. Translated by A. W. Wheen. New York: Ballantine, 1982.

Ridley, Edward, trans. *The Pharsalia of Lucan*. London: Arthur L. Humphreys, 1919.

Riskin, Robert. *Mr. Deeds Goes to Town, Six by Riskin: Six Screenplays by Robert Riskin*. Edited by Pat McGilligan. Berkeley: University of California Press, 1997.

Roth, Joseph. *The Radetsky March*. Translated by Eva Tucker. Woodstock, NY: Overlook Press, 1974.

Ruiz de Burton, María Amparo. *Who Would Have Thought It?* 1872; New York: Penguin Classics, 2009.

Sassoon, Siegfried. *Memoirs of a Fox-Hunting Man*. New York: Penguin Classics, 2013.

———. *Memoirs of an Infantry Officer*. New York: Penguin Classics, 2013.

———. *Sherston's Progress*. New York: Penguin Classics, 2013.

Scott, Walter. *Waverley Novels*. Edinburgh: Adam and Charles Black, 1860.

Service, Robert W. *Songs of a Sourdough*. Toronto: William Briggs, 1907.

Shaara, Michael. *The Killer Angels*. New York: Ballantine, 1987.

Sherwood, Kate Brownlee. *Camp-Fire, Memorial-Day, and Other Poems*. Chicago: Jansen, McClurg, 1885.

Smith, John D., trans. *The Mahābhārata*. Abridged ed. New York: Penguin Classics, 2009.

Stendhal. *The Charterhouse of Parma*. Translated by Richard Howard. New York: Modern Library, 2000.

Stowe, Harriet Beecher. *Uncle Tom's Cabin; or, Life among the Lowly*. Boston: John P. Jewett, 1853.

Styron, William. *The Suicide Run: Five Tales of the Marine Corps*. New York: Random House, 2009.

Tale of the Heike. Translated by Royall Tyler. New York: Penguin, 2014.

Tennyson, Alfred Lord. *The Poetical Works of Alfred Tennyson*. Chicago: National Library Association, 1887.

Thomas, Edward. *Poems*. New York: Holt, 1917.

Tolstoy, Leo. *The Cossacks and Other Tales of the Caucasus*. Translated by Louise and Aylmer Maude. London: Oxford University Press, 1916.

———. *Sevastopol and Other Military Tales*. Translated by Louise and Aylmer Maude. New York: Funk & Wagnalls, 1903.

———. *War and Peace*. Translated by Constance Garnett. New York: John Lane, 1911.

Troyes, Chrétien de. *Arthurian Romances*. Translated by William W. Kibler. New York: Penguin Classics, 2004.

Waley, Arthur. *A Hundred and Seventy Chinese Poems*. Translated by Arthur Waley. New York: Knopf, 1919.

Wallace, Lew. *Ben-Hur: A Tale of the Christ*. 1880; New York: Harper & Brothers, 1908.

Wharton, H. M. *War Songs and Poems of the Southern Confederacy, 1861–1865*. Philadelphia: John C. Winston, 1904.

White, Richard Grant, ed. *Mr. William Shakespeare's Comedies, Histories, Tragedies and Poems*. 1857–1866. Reprinted as *The Riverside Shakespeare*, 6 vols. Boston: Houghton, Mifflin, 1883.

Whitman, Walt. *Drum-Taps*. New York, 1865.

Acknowledgments

Many people have been extraordinarily giving of time and counsel over the course of this project. John Marszalek, executive director and managing editor of the Ulysses S. Grant Association, gave me free run of the Grant Presidential Library at Mississippi State University and permission to quote from the remarkable *Papers of Ulysses S. Grant*. At the library, Louis Gallo, David Nolen, and Ryan Semmes cheerfully shared their insights with me. I would also like to thank John and Jeanne Marszalek for their personal kindness during my visit to Starkville.

Suzanne Christoff and the entire staff of the United States Military Academy's Special Collections and Archives have been wonderful partners in so many endeavors over the years; I especially appreciate the expertise, resourcefulness, and good humor of Susan Lintelmann and Casey Madrick. I am grateful to the West Point Museum and to the Military Academy's Department of History for consultation and access to works of art and maps. Michelle Krowl at the Library of Congress's Manuscript Division guided me through Grant's papers and other material. Michelle is deeply knowledgeable and wonderfully generous with what she knows. I also thank the Library's Elizabeth Brown; Lisa Crunk for her assistance in navigating the rich photo archive at the U.S. Naval History & Heritage Command; and my friend Andrew Ziebell, formerly of the U.S. Army Center of Military History.

Kind and loyal friends have accompanied me on battlefield tours in the last several years: Jonathan Lewis and Matthew Boethin campaigned in Tennessee and Mississippi; Suzanne Nielsen followed the Army of the Potomac's several lines of march back and forth through Maryland and Virginia. Anne Taranto helped me inventory Civil War statuary in Washington, D.C., and explore the Shenandoah Valley. Anne and her family—Frank, Ava, Philip, and Stella Rotondo—gamely trekked across battlefields and cemeteries searching for, among other things, Stonewall Jackson's arm. And they were, as usual, terrific hosts during my numerous trips to Washington.

David Barnes, David Bromwich, Andrew Delbanco, Martin Dempsey, Drew Faust, Stephen Greenblatt, Ryan Gunderman, David Harper, Seth Herbst, Suzanne Keen, Adam Keller, Steven Johnson, Elizabeth Lazzari, Christopher Looby, Robert Norwood, Andrew Scott, Gordon Sullivan, and Rosanna Warren have all contributed to my understanding of Grant and a constellation of related subjects. Ongoing conversations with, and encouragement from, Nicholas Utzig and Karin Roffman have been invaluable. I remain especially grateful for Karin's enduring friendship and impeccable judgment. I could not have completed this project without the assistance of the tireless Kate, who was never at a loss for words. My parents were always at the ready to help me find an out-of-the-way abolitionist monument or to spend an hour on the phone discussing a footnote.

I am very glad to have been able to share aspects of this project with audiences at Brandeis University; the Harvard University English Department's Early Modern Colloquium; MIT's Sloan School of Management; Yale University's Public Humanities Program; the AUSA Institute of Land Warfare; the Vermont Humanities Council; and White Haven, the Ulysses S. Grant National Historic Site in St. Louis, Missouri. A portion of the introduction appeared, in different form, in an essay in *Portland Magazine* (Spring 2015), and it is reprinted by permission. I am deeply thankful that the late Brian Doyle, a lovely and thoughtful editor, invited me to write it in the first place.

As always, I am grateful for my agent, the dynamic David Kuhn, at Aevitas Creative Management, and to the efficient and encouraging Nate Muscato. It has been a pleasure to work with the many wonderful professionals at W. W. Norton/Liveright. Marie Pantojan was unfailingly helpful. Julia Reidhead and Robert Weil surprised me with a fabulous gift: the opportunity to work on a project of extraordinary personal significance. And Bob graciously gave me the freedom to do it in my own way. I am in their debt for the faith they have placed in me.

About Ulysses S. Grant

The man we know today as Ulysses Simpson Grant was born Hiram Ulysses Grant on April 27, 1822, in the village of Point Pleasant, Ohio, to Hannah Simpson Grant and Jesse Root Grant. His name was incorrectly entered into the West Point records. It was an error to which military bureaucracy proved indifferent but one that yielded a new, more resonant name suited to celebrity: U. S. Grant. His fellow cadets immediately seized on the nickname "Uncle Sam," which they shortened to "Sam." In his name and in certain other respects, Grant was almost accidentally prepared for his future. He grew up in Georgetown, Ohio, where his father owned a tannery. It was a trade that physically repulsed the young Grant, yet he did not dream of soldiering as an escape. Instead, he spent much of his time with horses, traveling long distances from an early age and thereby acquiring a comfort with unfamiliar terrain that would later prove invaluable in war. West Point was his ambitious father's idea. Once at the Military Academy, Grant hoped Congress would close it. He was an average student who excelled in horsemanship and spent his free time reading novels, "but not," he would later insist, "those of a trashy sort." It was an activity that helped to hone a facility with language he would later need.

After graduating from West Point in 1843, Second Lieutenant Grant reported to the 4th Infantry Regiment at Jefferson Barracks in St. Louis, Missouri, where he met his future wife Julia Dent, the sister of his former roommate. Service in the Mexican War (1846–1848) was followed by several peacetime assignments culminating in two lonely and miserable years at remote posts in the Pacific Northwest, where he resigned his commission under somewhat mysterious circumstances in 1854. For the next several years Grant eked out a living as a farmer and on the periphery of various business enterprises in St. Louis. The outbreak of the Civil War in 1861 found him in Galena, Illinois, working in his father's leather-goods store. After initial successes as the colonel of a volunteer regiment, Grant went on to command Union forces in the West. In 1864, as a result of his victories at Shiloh, Vicksburg, and Chattanooga, he was promoted to lieutenant general, a rank that had last been held by George Washington, with command over the entire Union Army. In this capacity, Grant coordinated the final campaigns of the war. He accepted Robert E. Lee's surrender on April 9, 1865.

In 1868, Grant the war hero was elected president without ever having made a campaign speech. Grant's own personal integrity notwithstanding, his two-term administration was compromised by scandal and corruption. After his status as a global celebrity was cemented by a post-presidential world tour, Grant settled in New York City, where he ultimately entered into a disastrous banking partnership with the swindler Ferdinand Ward. Once again, events took him unawares, and it was this late-life crisis that turned him into an autobiographer. Bankrupt and diagnosed with terminal cancer by the fall of 1884, Grant signed a contract with the publishing house of Charles L. Webster, in which Mark Twain was a partner, for 70 percent of the profits realized on the book. He completed the manuscript of *Personal Memoirs of U. S. Grant* about a week before his death on July 23, 1885, at a cottage in the Adirondacks. Grant's tomb on Manhattan's Upper West Side may be the largest physical monument to the man, but his book—that unexpected harvest of a final emergency—is the artifact that does justice to his achievement as the leader of an army that preserved a nation and emancipated four million people.

About the Editor

Elizabeth D. Samet is the author of *No Man's Land: Preparing for War and Peace in Post-9/11 America*; *Soldier's Heart: Reading Literature Through Peace and War at West Point*, for which she won a *Los Angeles Times* Book Prize; and *Willing Obedience: Citizens, Soldiers, and the Progress of Consent in America, 1776–1898*. Samet is also the editor of the Norton anthology *Leadership: Essential Writings by Our Greatest Thinkers*. She is a past recipient of the Hiett Prize in the Humanities and of a Guggenheim Fellowship. Her essays and reviews have appeared in the *New York Times*, the *Washington Post*, and the *New Republic*. Samet is professor of English at the United States Military Academy, where she has directed the first-year literature program and teaches courses in literature, writing, and film. Samet speaks often to civilian and military audiences about the importance of literature and language to the formation of future military officers. She has also written and lectured widely about the intellectual lives of Ulysses S. Grant and his contemporaries. She lives in New York City.

Winslow Homer, *The Veteran in a New Field*, 1865. *Metropolitan Museum of Art, Bequest of Miss Adelaide Milton de Groot (1876–1967), 1967.*